ALFRED A. KNOPF

1915 · 100 YEARS · 2015

JAMES MERRILL
LIFE AND ART

JAMES MERRILL

LIFE AND ART

LANGDON HAMMER

ALFRED A. KNOPF | NEW YORK | 2015

THIS IS A BORZOI BOOK
PUBLISHED BY ALFRED A. KNOPF

Copyright © 2015 by Langdon Hammer
All rights reserved. Published in the United States by Alfred A. Knopf,
a division of Penguin Random House LLC, New York,
and distributed in Canada by Random House of Canada,
a division of Penguin Random House, Ltd., Toronto.
www.aaknopf.com

Knopf, Borzoi Books, and the colophon are registered trademarks
of Penguin Random House LLC.

Library of Congress Cataloging-in-Publication Data
Hammer, Langdon, [date]
James Merrill : life and art / Langdon Hammer. — First edition.
pages cm
ISBN 978-0-375-41333-9 (hardback) — ISBN 978-0-385-35308-3 (eBook)
1. Merrill, James, 1926–1995 2. Poets, American—20th century—Biography. 3. Gay
authors—United States—Biography. 4. Gay men—United States—Biography. I. Title.
PS3525.E6645Z674 2015
811'.54—dc23
2014029325

Front-of-jacket photograph: James Merrill at Rhodes, May 1950, by Kimon Friar.
Courtesy of The American College of Greece, Attica Tradition Educational Foundation.
Jacket design by Chip Kidd

Manufactured in the United States of America
First Edition

For Uta

Diese Tage

CONTENTS

FOREWORD

"*I* merely live to work." That's James Merrill replying to David Kalstone. Merrill had been needling him about how slow a writer he was, and Kalstone, a professor of literature, defended himself: "Some of us have to work for a living"—referring to how little time he had left over after teaching.

Typical of Merrill to turn a cliché on its head. Typical of him to pack a serious statement into a quip. As his friend pointed out, he had no need to work: the wealth he was born to ensured that. But rather than freeing him from work, his money allowed him to devote himself to the work he wanted to do. It was a kind of work—the writing of poetry—that drew on and shaped the rest of his life, giving meaning and design, a tone and a style, to everything he did. "Poetry made me who I am," he commented on another occasion, slyly reversing the usual relation between maker and made.

Merrill sounds in these remarks like Oscar Wilde, the subversive master of antithesis, for whom the self was not a natural fact but material to be fashioned, like a work of art. He also sounds like his father, Charles Merrill, who made his fortune working very hard on Wall Street. Indeed, strange to say, Merrill resembled both of these self-made men. He created a version of Wilde's aesthetic lifestyle, updating the artist-dandy's role for late-twentieth-century America, and he brought to the project an intensity of industry his father would have understood.

The teenage Merrill wanted to be like Wilde; it was only a phase, though a phase he would build on more than outgrow. He was energized by a sense of artistic vocation and, almost as if they were the same thing, the secret recognition that he was homosexual. He didn't expect his father to be pleased on either count—not that he was about to say anything to anyone, even to himself in the privacy of his diary, about the homosexual part. He was still freshly wounded from his parents' divorce, after which he'd sided with his injured mother, Hellen Ingram, who had been the muse of his poetry in childhood. After the divorce, the boy had been packed off to boarding school. His home was "broken"; it was lost. Poetry and love both seemed like ways to create a more beautiful and durable one.

Why do we read poets' lives? To better understand their poetry, yes, although that's not at all the only reason. Samuel Johnson's *Lives of the English Poets*, which essentially invented this kind of book, were commissioned as prefaces to editions of poetry by Milton, Pope, and others. But Johnson's *Lives* soon cut loose from the poems they introduced, and circulated as best sellers in their own right. In effect, the poet had become a new type of person: a hero of the interior life, as exemplary in his domain as the soldier, scientist, politician, and saint were in theirs. His charge was to discover and unfold, through artful words and long labor, what was within him, and within anyone and everyone in potential.

That was the idea, the ideology or myth, behind the life Merrill was choosing; by definition he would have to live it in his own way. "He approached life as an experiment," the novelist Allan Gurganus, a friend, says about him. "It was a possibility, not just an entitlement." Poetry was about possibility: it enabled—and required—him to make his own meanings. After college, there would be no office to go to, no definite rules for how to become a poet or how to behave like one. The years lay open before him, a book of fresh, blank pages.

In his twenties, he considered plausible options. Like many poets of his era, when English Departments were expanding and creative writing became a staple of the American college curriculum, he tried teaching, but only briefly. In the early 1950s, he played the part of a Jamesian expatriate in postwar Europe, roaming galleries, gardens, and opera houses; he went into psychoanalytic treatment in Rome. When he returned to New York, he made friends with poets and painters in the downtown avant-garde, and flirted with a career writing for the theater. Eventually he found his way by moving with David Jackson, an aspiring novelist, into a third-floor apartment in a commercial building in Stonington, a town on the Connecticut coast. Tiny Stonington offered not much more than the essentials: a chance to write poetry every day and live with his lover largely unobserved.

Right and even inevitable as it seems in retrospect, the choice was unlikely at the time. But perhaps any choice of life a gay man made was going to seem unlikely. "Society will not condone it," his mother had warned him about his homosexuality early on, as if that should be reason enough to change his ways. Yet Hellen had a point: to be queer in the 1940s and 1950s in America, even if you happened to be white and wealthy, made you vulnerable to scorn, social exclusion, blackmail, political suspicion, arrest, bullying, or worse brutality. Increasingly American society would, in some contexts, "condone it," but his mother never did. Even as he achieved the public success she craved for him, which he must have hoped would legitimate his whole life in her eyes, her son could never forget that his mother hated the fact that he was gay.

Of course, being gay (not a term Merrill used until the 1970s) never meant just one thing. He lived his experiment against the shifting backdrops of the closet, gay liberation, and AIDS, the vocabulary, options, and conditions for leading a queer life changing with the times and with the locales in which he found himself. In the 1950s, in Stonington, hidden in plain sight in the center of town, he and Jackson created a miniature pleasure palace filled with curios, paintings by friends, and souvenirs from their travels. Local types and "summer people" orbited around them. The atmosphere mixed Jane Austen and E. F. Benson (the author of classic camp novels about characters named Lucia and Mapp)—the comedy, intrigues, and epiphanies of daily life set down in Merrill's chatty, fluent letters, and sometimes worked into poems.

At the same time, something else was going on. Using a Ouija board, he and Jackson were learning how to converse with the dead. Neither of them was an obvious candidate for dabbling in the occult—Merrill with his shrewd, ironic wit, Jackson with his down-to-earth good nature. Beginning as lighthearted fun and moving, intermittently, into the region of obsession, the Ouija board would be a part of Merrill's life for more than forty years. Already readers of this book will be wondering, "Did he really . . . ?" He took different attitudes toward the board at different times. Suffice it to say for now that the spirits came when he and Jackson called.

It was a condition of his experimental life that Merrill could dwell in no world for long (not his Stonington apartment, not the Other World of the spirits). In the late 1950s, he and Jackson began going to Greece, not for the monuments or beaches, but "the Sex Cure." With the Greeks they met in the tavernas and parks, they discovered a new sexual freedom. Merrill bought a house in Athens; a mixed Greek-American circle (part clique and part open, ongoing party) sprang up around them; and they each fell in love with someone else. Merrill's Strato, a young Greek enlisted man, was his fiercest love affair, and the most improbable. In time, their romance would run its course, no less poignant for being predictable, even if Merrill didn't see the end coming. He was too busy writing some of the best love poetry of his career.

The Other World and Greece were parallel intoxications to which Merrill gave himself freely, even while he managed to keep his head and pull back from the perils of complete immersion in either the spirit or the flesh.

That the point was to turn his life into writing (and not just live it) helped. Yet "living to work" led him to take considerable emotional, psychological, and artistic risks, trusting in his power to transform almost any experience into poetry.

In the 1970s, his work won major awards, and the audience for it was growing. Riding this success, he published a ninety-two-page poem about his and Jackson's encounters on the Ouija board called *The Book of Ephraim*. Now they began taking dictation from a bizarre new class of spirits who demanded that Merrill write "POEMS OF SCIENCE." For more than two years, for hours a day in some periods, he and Jackson sat at the board and took down the spirits' messages. He knew it looked like madness, this activity, but it felt like inspiration, too, and he couldn't stop until the spirits released him. At that point, the board had supplied the materials for a mythological work unlike anything he'd written before. He produced at a dazzling pace two more long poems, each one longer than the last—another sort of madness, perhaps.

By the time these Ouija poems were brought together and published as a single volume called *The Changing Light at Sandover* in 1982, Merrill had become a famous poet. His work was the focus of academic panels, articles, and books. Giving poetry readings across the country, sitting on prize juries, and helping young poets to start their careers, he led a life now more official than experimental. Jackson had begun a new phase by buying a house in Key West; Merrill joined him in the winter there—Athens was over for them. But in contrast to Merrill, Jackson was depressed, diminished, and aging fast.

Feeling Jackson slip away, and pushing him away too, although he would never quite give him up, Merrill fell in love for the last time. Peter Hooten, a young movie actor, made sure that Merrill wouldn't go gently into his old age. Hooten and Jackson chafed each other, and Merrill's friends blamed Hooten for taking Jackson's place. Tall and handsome, he brought romance back in Merrill's life, and a faith in love that Merrill hadn't felt since his first days with Strato.* He and Merrill would collaborate by putting an abridged version of *Sandover* onstage and adapting it for film. And if all of that wasn't energizing enough, Hooten turned out to have an explosive temper.

Meanwhile, AIDS was sweeping America. "The Plague" arrived in the 1980s with a surge of wild rumor and homophobic hatred, tabloid head-

---

* When they first declared their feelings for each other in 1984, Merrill told Hooten that he hadn't been in love for eighteen years—that is, since 1966, when he was in love with Mouflouzélis.

lines, press conferences, experimental treatments, memorial services, and protesters shouting in the streets. Some of Merrill's cherished friends would die of it, although that makes it sound too easy: they would have to go through agonies first. And Merrill also was infected. Now it was clear, more or less, how he would die. Clear also that he still had something to write about.

Merrill had been widely known as a gifted lyric poet at least since his *Nights and Days* won the National Book Award in 1967. Yet it wasn't until his posthumous *Collected Poems* was published in 2001 that the enormous scale and variety of his achievement in the lyric—or it would be more accurate to say simply "shorter poem"—could be fully appreciated. The book gathered eleven volumes of poetry, assorted translations, and uncollected poems. It didn't include occasional or uncompleted poems; even so, it came to 885 pages. A reviewer in the *Los Angeles Times* nicely describes the book's abundance: "Reading the collected works of certain poets can feel enervating or claustrophobic; one feels trapped in a mind that lacked range or variety of response. But here, there's more than enough—in humor and sorrow, in tones of voice, in diction, in subjects—to keep one engaged for days, for years, for life."

That review compared Merrill to Marvell, Keats, and Dickinson; other commentators mentioned Pope, Tennyson, Byron, Auden, Frost, Yeats, Stevens, and Bishop. With their all-star lists, reviewers were groping to classify the huge collection, but they weren't being hyperbolic: remarkably, Merrill bears comparison with some of the great poets in English. And not only in English: we could add Mallarmé, Valéry, Rilke, Montale, Ponge, and Cavafy, all of whom he loved and learned from. His *Collected Poems* reveals on every page some fresh fusion of language, thought, and feeling.

In contrast to the mighty moderns who dominated English-language poetry when he began writing, Merrill's shorter poems resist absolutes and abstractions, and bring poetry down to the scale of the personal and contingent, taking his life for a subject. That was typical enough of American poetry of his era. Yet unlike the Beats or Confessional poets (or the claims once made for them), the "I" in his lyrics is never naked; it's an elegant performance, and usually a funny one.

The poetry's consistent theatricality and rhetorical self-consciousness are underlined by Merrill's surpassing skill with rhyme and meter: traditional techniques to which he remained devoted, even while free verse was winning the field all around him. "William Carlos Williams talks about

breaking the back of the pentameter," he told an interviewer. "The pentameter has been a good friend to me; you'd think I'd have noticed a little
thing like a broken back."*

One of the clever moves Merrill's poetry makes is to remind us that we
aren't overhearing someone speaking: of course, the man is writing at
his desk, weighing rhymes and choosing words in a painstaking process
of revision. The emphasis is on discovering what he has to say. His most
distinctive poems—a hybrid combination of lyric and autobiographical
narrative—stretch the boundaries of the well-made poem into something
unpredictable, introducing characters from "real life," interpolations,
excursus, and even footnotes, switching up focus, diction, tone, and verse
form, and registering the passage of time in a way rare in anyone's shorter
poems.

Merrill wrote a great deal more than that big book of poems, however.
He wrote thousands of letters. Even his most trivial postcard is meant to
amuse and challenge the writer and correspondent both. He kept a journal
and wrote in it wherever he happened to be (an airport lounge, a café, a
friend's house, a museum). Open to uses and impulses of all sorts, containing drafts of letters, shopping lists, overheard speech, quotations from his
reading, epigrams, meditations, calendars, anagrams, and jokes, as well
as the soul searching and record keeping we expect from a diary, Merrill's
journal is the place where his poems typically began.

Although he disliked writing criticism, he produced a considerable
amount of it in miscellaneous forms: book reviews, school talks, tributes,
introductions, and interviews, which he usually conducted by mail. He also
wrote three plays and two novels. The plays and novels, though impressive on many levels, matter today primarily for the ways he used them to
understand his life, and as laboratories in which he broached topics and
developed techniques he would return to in poetry. His last prose work, *A
Different Person*, recalls his expatriate years in Europe, but it reaches backward and forward in time to convey a sense of his life as a whole. Composed
in the face of illness and approaching death, *A Different Person* is a comic,
prismatic autobiography in miniature and a neglected classic of recent
life-writing.

Then there is *The Changing Light at Sandover*, the epic-length history in
verse of Merrill's and Jackson's conversations with the spirits of the Other

---

* JM, "An Interview with Donald Sheehan," *Prose*, 50. It wasn't Williams, but Ezra Pound, who
declared "To break the pentameter, that was the first heave" (*Canto* 81). Merrill's misquotation probably wasn't intentional and suggests how loosely he knew Williams's work. Pound's
Cantos he didn't read seriously until the 1970s.

World. The poem records a host of weird voices speaking in the capital letters of the Ouija board. The mediums' dead friends, great writers, the familiar spirit Ephraim, God Biology, and Mother Nature—these and many other speakers have their turn. "Speakers" should be in scare quotes, however, because the spirits were always "mute spellers out"—their voices being constructed out of the twenty-six letters of the alphabet on the board, chosen by the careening teacup the mediums used as a pointer.

Merrill alludes in *Sandover* to Dante and Milton, Blake, Hugo, and Yeats, Mme. Blavatsky, Tolkien, and *Star Trek*, but these sources and analogs are of little help: *Sandover* is a poem without useful precedent, and it requires more than the usual suspension of disbelief. Some critics and—privately at least—not a few of Merrill's friends were unwilling to grant him that big grain of salt. They regarded *Sandover* as a folly, a betrayal of his lyric gift and skeptical intelligence. Yes, *Sandover* won prizes—its skill, scale, and audacity all but demanded them. In contrast, however, to Merrill's generally pleasing, reader-friendly lyrics, *Sandover* dares to offend, confound, and even bore its readers.

This book approaches Merrill's Ouija board and the poetry he made out of it as an exploit. Rather than assess *Sandover*'s credentials as a masterpiece, we will focus on the mechanics of the board and the process of poetic composition Merrill based on it. With his Ouija board and Jackson's willing hand to help, Merrill renewed poetry's ancient task of soliciting speech from the gods. He activated a source of inspiration existing in language itself, inviting us into that basic mystery by which voice and presence ("human or otherwise," as he puts it) emerge from the letters on a page—not only in *Sandover*, but in almost any literary text.

Viewed in this way, Merrill's fascination with the Ouija board puts his shorter poems (which have little to do with it) in a fresh light. He is usually seen as a poet of the self, occupied with love and loss. *Sandover* encourages us to see him as a poet of the not-self—a poet of the impersonal and supra-personal, whose commitment is less to self-expression than to coaxing forth, through magic tricks of verse technique and wordplay, what he called "the hidden wish of words."

Sandover's cosmic perspective and apocalyptic themes also ought to make us rethink his reputation as a private poet. He was, I will suggest, not a mandarin, private sensibility, but a worldly writer who grasped how the self is involved in history and myth, language and culture. The question *Sandover* poses—how can the world (not just the human world) survive the threats of nuclear war and environmental destruction?—is present in Merrill's lyrics too, especially but not only in his late, post-*Sandover* poems, where the march of global capital, consumerism, climate change, species extinction, and AIDS are desperately urgent subjects.

It is hard to recognize this dimension of Merrill's work because he so disliked political and moral editorializing. He was reluctant to take any position, apart from the aesthete's studied refusal to take positions. He had little interest in philosophy, and he often makes a convincing show in his poetry of preferring sound over sense. Indeed, he professed not to have any "ideas" at all. But the ideas that pour forth from the Ouija board in *Sandover*, loopy as they are, suggest otherwise. In fact, Merrill was always thinking hard. His shorter poems, letters, interviews, and journal provide more evidence of that. One goal of this book, drawing on the full range of his writing, is to bring out the richness and continuing relevance of his thought about such basic human matters as love, friendship, identity, time, memory, language, myth, divinity, disease, death, and, of course, poetry.*

Doubleness is a key to it all. "I've tried, Lord knows," he says in "To a Butterfly," "To keep from seeing double." But that's not true. Seeing double: seeing two sides of every conflict, seeing one thing as another—he knew this was a gift and a skill to be cultivated, and he was proud of it. On one level, it was the privilege and punishment of a homosexual whose cherished desires were despised by the people who taught him how to love—his parents—as well as by the public at large. (That last point explains a lot about his dislike of public poetry and public position taking by poets.) On another level, doubleness was the attitude of a postmodern metaphysician who believed in keeping "MEANING SPINNING LIKE A COIN." It was the discovery of an occultist who communicated with another world existing side by side with this one. And it was a piece of practical, this-worldly wis-

---

* In 1988 *Life* asked a few dozen prominent people to "ponder why we are here" in a feature called "The Meaning of Life." On a page with contributions by Richard Nixon, Norman Vincent Peale, and Kareem Adbul-Jabbar, JM made this statement: " 'I am that I am,' said the God of Abraham. Only some such divine tautology would seem to do justice to us all: the old woman who sees ultimate meaning in her grandchild, the mathematician who sees it in a formula, the tribesman who sees it in a crocodile. The meaning of life is that it should mean.

"At everyday levels surely meaning is one with nourishment. Clean air, uncontaminated food and water for the body, ideas that exercise the mind and spirit—without these what on earth is meaningful? In our time meaning is threatened at every turn. Nuclear waste, deforestation, greed, plague. God accordingly may be said (by those who still 'believe') to have exchanged the mask of creator and judge for that of the firefighter and the paramedic. I put 'believe' in quotes because our beautiful human feelings aren't to be trusted. As a poet I know how words, even those words brought together under laboratory conditions, breed meanings not intended by the author. The resulting surprise needn't always be a nasty one. The planet blackened by us as never before may of its own accord break into leaf tomorrow. But this is a mere literary man's daydream, and under no circumstances are the world's lawmakers and corporate heads entitled to share it." *Life*, vol. 11, no. 14 (December 1988), p. 90.

dom, gained by observation of his and other people's vanities and ruses in the course of a highly social life.

In "At a Texas Wishing Well," a slight, jokey poem that, like many of Merrill's slight, jokey poems, is also profound and disturbing, he describes peering into a wishing well, obedient to instructions: "*Stranger, look down [. . .] & you / Will see the face of one who loves you true.*" Beneath the face looking back at him, he sees shining coins: "a ground of hard cold cash— // Pennies aglint from either eye, / Silver in hair, teeth, value everywhere!" Often other people saw him that way. Friends and acquaintances expected him to pick up the bill. Reviewers, some of them, more or less openly resented his wealth. Merrill himself occasionally wondered whether he was, despite his best intentions, merely a mouthpiece for the moneyed class. Because poetry doesn't make any money in America, the poet with money—especially one with a lot of money—is a suspicious anomaly, sometimes even in his own eyes.

Just how much money did he have? It's hard to say since he didn't keep careful financial records. He paid little attention to how much money there was in the bank. He depended on his brother-in-law, Robert Magowan, and his nephew, Merrill Magowan, to invest his capital, and he received their quarterly reports without thanks (probably without reading them). He lived quite modestly on the whole. He traveled when and where he wanted; he had good seats at the opera; when he was in Paris, he enjoyed eating at a restaurant like Tour d'Argent. But he didn't buy expensive cars or extravagant real estate. Normally, he gave away more money then he spent on himself. He did this informally through gifts to friends, or to friends of friends known to be in need; and he did it systematically through grants to artists and writers made by the Ingram Merrill Foundation, the private charity he created in the late 1950s, which awarded money annually until his death in 1995. At that time, his income from investments was about $300,000 per year, and the trusts of which he was the beneficiary had a net worth of about $20 million, the equivalent of about $31 million today. Not a major pile of money by the standards of the new 1 percent. But he could have chosen a very different life from the one he led.

He displayed a certain Yankee parsimony. "Now see," he snapped at one houseguest who was helping out with the dishes, "you've thrown out a perfectly good pot of coffee! I could heat that up tomorrow morning"—when he would be back in his study very early. His painful struggle to learn how to live with his money—which in his mind was not his but his father's—is the subject of his bitter, aggressive novel *The Seraglio*. He knew that the wealthy people among whom he grew up didn't understand or respect what he did. "Where is the money in writing poetry?" his brother-in-law, Bobby Magowan, grumbled. In his work, Merrill achieved a power over language capable of putting such opinions in their place. Yet year after year in the back of his notebooks, as if to prove he was worth something by other people's standards, he carefully tallied the sums he was paid for his poems and readings.

Besides a joke about being rich, "At a Texas Wishing Well" is a joke about narcissism and the stereotype of gays as men who are in love with themselves. The wish Merrill ends up making—"Let me love myself until I die"—is tinged with defiance: he will go on being who he is, whatever anyone may think. But it's also the sincere and troubled wish of a man who didn't find it easy to love himself or feel he was worthy of being loved. One sign of that self-doubt is his persistent effort to charm, both in person and on the page. He felt that his money and sexuality (also, his writing of poetry) set him apart from other people, making him less than fully human. Over and over in his poetry, he struggles toward a self-acceptance that was always in need of being reaffirmed. Once he dreamed he was a fish, pleading for the attention of a man beyond the aquarium's glass: *Look! I'm not what I seem, I'm a man like you!* " Unconvinced, the stranger laughs at this fish claiming to be a man.

Winning over the course of his career every major prize an American poet could win, Merrill didn't lack for praise. But he also received reviews that react to his writing with a sharp distaste, in which class resentment and homophobia mingle. Even some of the celebratory reviews of his *Collected Poems* in 2001 represented him as an uncanny alien intelligence, a visitor from another planet.* There is something right about that image: his irony, his technical virtuosity, and his traffic with spirits together give off a supernatural glow.

But that image misses his warmth and humanity, and those qualities matter all the more because he had to strive for them. He feared in himself a coldness of heart, an inability to feel what others feel—a fear that friends who met him later in life can hardly understand. In a draft page eventually cut from *A Different Person*, he describes his life story as a long process of "becoming human." He didn't think of this as a special task, but as what

---

* For example, see David Gates, "Jimmy of the Spirits," *Newsweek* (March 5, 2001), and Daniel Mendelsohn, "A Poet of Love and Loss," *NYT* (March 4, 2001), who, in an admiring and penetrating review, describes Merrill's work as "extraterrestrial," "uncanny," and "supernatural."

everyone must do: give up the particular wounds and distinctions that we think make us who we are in order to claim our share of the common lot. This is what Merrill's late poems accomplish, where the poet has to accept his disease and the decaying body that links him to so many others suffering in the same position. There's nothing otherworldly about the life he led and the poems he wrote in the midst of the AIDS epidemic.

In his sixties, Merrill accompanied his mother to a funeral parlor to discuss her final arrangements. She let him know that she had bought enough space in the cemetery to accommodate him and even David Jackson: wouldn't he like to lie beside her in eternity? He tactfully kept silent. Then, on their way out the door, her mind occupied with a "green" option for disposal of her body, Hellen stopped short: "One last thing. Did I make it clear that I want to be buried in a *biographical* container?"

There was no need to insist. Merrill knew that he (and, with him, his family and friends) would eventually repose in the pages of a biography. He began preparing for that day in 1964 when he agreed to give his papers to the Olin Library at Washington University in St. Louis. Over the decades, he contributed a mass of documents to the library, including correspondence, detailed calendars, guest books, chronologies, poetry worksheets, Ouija board transcripts, and fifty years of notebooks, diaries, and journals no one but he had ever read. He urged his friends and former lovers to donate his letters to Washington University; he arranged for some of them to be paid for doing so. His zeal for building the collection expressed his interest in his writing process, and his sense that revision was crucial to it. But clearly he felt that much more was relevant than his drafts: he wanted to give other people access to the life that his work grew out of. The Merrill Papers fulfilled one of his deepest wishes: to waste nothing, to turn his whole life to account.

He did little to edit the person on view in his papers. Not many writers have left a comparably large archive, and he put few restrictions on its use. He didn't expect those who looked into it to find him virtuous or endlessly interesting (though, on balance, I find him both). The point was to leave a more or less complete record, without censorship. To be sure, Merrill could keep a secret. It's only in his journal that he ever explicitly stated, in writing, that he was infected with HIV. But he gave that journal to the library for others to read. It had been a wounding experience for him as a young man when his mother destroyed letters from his lovers and friends, fearing lest evidence of his homosexuality fall into the wrong hands, or so she said in her defense. The Merrill Papers made sure that wouldn't happen again: a history of his romantic and sexual life would be on file in a university library.

Quoting frequently from Merrill's letters and journal, I relate that history in his own words. I reconstruct both his nights and days, aiming for the right proportion between these parts of his life. Some readers may feel we peer too long over Merrill's shoulder as the drafts of a poem take shape, while others may object that we pay too much attention to his love affairs and promiscuity. But his poetry demands a central place here because it was at the center of his life. As to the space it shares with love and sex: love is of paramount importance to a love poet, and, for Merrill, sex wasn't very far behind.

Where love and sex were concerned, the moral codes in effect were as experimental as other aspects of his life. He barely bothered to hide the fact that he went to bed with the father of the immigrant family living in his home in Stonington, and this while he was serving as godfather to the man's baby daughter. Readers may be baffled or offended by this behavior; it's difficult to be merely amused. Merrill often makes light of his romantic entanglements and sexual escapades; sufficient *sprezzatura*, he seemed to feel, can carry almost anything off. But his fizzy tone mustn't be taken at face value. It was hard for him to make up the rules he lived by. Taking everything as lightly, as merrily as possible gave him cover. The attitude allowed him to do as he liked, and defended him against pain, guilt, depression, and shame, which even so, at times, he couldn't escape feeling.

In 1990, he began a poem, never completed, with the title "To a Poet's Biographer":

> The deepest nastiness comes—don't you wish!—
> Closest to truth, as if the ocean floor
> Of eyeless ____ + worms with fangs had somehow more
> To teach than porpoises and flying fish.

This biography takes pleasure in "porpoises and flying fish," but it doesn't shrink from the depths either. In *Sandover*, the fate of the cosmos depends on a contest between the forces of life and death, creation and destruction, sunlight and terrible black holes. Merrill understood both on the basis of his own nature. For all of the "light" in his poetry (it's a word he uses again and again), there are dire shadows. The affirmations his poems make are willed, and they emerge from a background of negation and despair. He regretted little that he did, but he knew he had made choices that were destructive for him and (still harder for him to abide) those closest to him.

His journal gives us a look into his solitude. Even in company, he often lived in his head. But he enjoyed people, and he needed lots of them. His friends were arrayed around him like an opera cast: the principals, supporting singers, fabled stars with cameos, comic relief, an ingénue or two, and the full chorus behind. He was the most important person in the lives of many people even in the back row. For all of them, his charisma was complex. It was made of money and talent. But it had more to do with how he attended to their lives and shared his. He had a capacity to see people in a vivid light, and to recognize their interest and promise. (Some grumbled that he had merely invented this or that person's interest and promise.) It made him an influential mentor and a magnetic friend. And he rarely dropped or lost track of someone. So his life grew increasingly crowded and burdened by obligations, though he never lost his appetite for the social round. In the weeks just before his death, he was making new friends.

This book is as full of people therefore as one of the triple-decker nineteenth-century novels Merrill relished. I reconstruct the multiple social worlds he moved in, now lost to time, that were populated by well-known writers and artists, but more often by obscure people, eccentric and ordinary both, in places all over the map: not only Stonington, Athens, and Key West, but in Alexandria, Isfahan, Istanbul, Venice, Munich, Tokyo, Santa Fe, St. Louis, and little Pawlet, Vermont. In our era, when even literary criticism (even literary criticism!) looks to Big Data for light and truth, biography pushes back, patient and long-winded, laying claim to that single, slowly unfolding datum, a life. Yet many lives, many histories, are wrapped up in this one.

David Jackson is a central character in this story. How many writers are there, like Merrill, whose life *and work* are so intertwined with a domestic partner? The Brownings, the Woolfs, Plath and Hughes—but these examples all involve two writers of stature, and all were man and wife.

Of course, Jackson was not Merrill's only important love relationship. Kimon Friar, Merrill's first lover, influenced him in fundamental ways; he kept turning up despite Merrill's concerted efforts to forget him. Claude Fredericks spent less than two years as his lover and more than forty as his trusted friend. Strato Mouflouzélis and David McIntosh were very different sources of inspiration for Merrill in the 1960s and 1970s. In the 1980s and 1990s, Merrill's life revolved around Peter Hooten; and it was Hooten he wanted with him at the end. This book is also a portrait of these men.

A word about names. What a biography calls its subject defines a point of view and tone. There are problems with any choice. Initials—WBY, LBJ—are concise but turn the subject into a corporation. Use the last name and it sounds formal and remote, but use the first and it cloys, implying a familiarity that soon feels banal or presumptuous. Use any name over and over, and no one will want to hear it again. For that matter, it's falsifying to choose any one name, since people have many names, expressing diverse facets of a self and its history.

Take James Ingram Merrill. Letters from his youth are composed on stationery monogrammed "JIM." Many who knew him as a young man or only distantly called him "Jim." The bullies at prep school taunted him as "Toots." (It was a good thing they didn't know his mother's pet name for him, "Bimby," which is how he pronounced his name as a toddler.) Alice B. Toklas called him "Jamie." He liked that: "it lent me the winsome air of a lover in a ballad." Claude Fredericks and then David Jackson picked it up as a lover's private nickname. "James"—he liked that too since "it makes me sound in control of my life." It was used by senior writers like John Hollander and Mona Van Duyn, but also, in Merrill's later years, by younger people, including some of those closest to him: Stephen Yenser, David McIntosh, and Peter Hooten. "Still others," he notes in *A Different Person*, "who've known me first from reading *The Changing Light at Sandover* feel easier with the semifictional 'JM,' " which is what the spirits called him. In Greece, he was "Jimaki" or "Tzimi" to Strato and "Enfant" to Maria Mitsotáki. In his previous life, he had been "Rufus Farmetton." In his novels, he called the characters based on him "Francis" and "Sandy." To most people most of the time, however, he was "Jimmy." I refer to him as "Merrill" to keep the public figure in view. But I also use "Jimmy" to bring him closer to us, as well as other names to remind us of the multiple ways he was known.

I myself called him "Mr. Merrill." Over the years of writing this book, I've often been asked if I knew him. The answer is: slightly. In 1979, I was a Yale English major. I'd recently attended a reading he gave at the university. That evening had been half theater and half séance: with his face spookily lit up by the lectern lamp, the spirit voices of Auden, Maria, and the bat-peacock Mirabell took turns speaking. The overflow crowd was rapt. Professor Harold Bloom, a portly man, lay on his back on the floor, eyes closed, long fingers folded on his chest. Now Merrill was scheduled to read in honor of Wallace Stevens's centenary at the University of Connecticut, and Sandy McClatchy, another Yale professor, asked if I could drive the poet there: apparently he didn't like to make even short trips alone.

At the appointed hour I climbed the stairs of his home in Stonington and knocked on a canary-yellow door. My host, small and lithe, opened it. He was more than thirty years older than I, but he seemed buoyant and youthful as he ushered me into a home I half knew from his poetry and could hardly take in at a glance. I sat down at the round white table where Merrill and David Jackson ate their meals and chatted with the dead. He poured me a cup of tea. The walls, painted a shade of reddish pink, pulsed. Gauze curtains—a flash of the sea beyond them. Then we were outside, and I settled in behind the wheel of his small red Ford. The license plate read "POET."

On the road, Merrill's voice took over: suave, modulated, surprisingly low and deep, vaguely southern or "mid-Atlantic," like a movie actor's from the 1940s. He asked me about my poems (he'd heard that I wrote poems), and we talked about poets. He spoke oddly as if we were equals, or as if we were both involved in a pursuit (poetry, or it might have just been life) that was much larger and more important than either of us. He said he'd been going back over his early poems for a selected volume. To demonstrate how well I knew his work, I praised *The Country of a Thousand Years of Peace*, his second book, and mentioned titles I hoped he would include. A shadow of vexation crossed his face: he hadn't asked me for advice.

When he spoke about *Sandover*, he referred to the spirits with a nonchalance that implied that they were no less real for me than they were for him—or, confusingly, that they were no *more* real for him than they were for me. To reassure him that I wasn't put off by the Ouija board (although he hadn't asked for reassurance), I told him my mother was interested in Jung, the Tarot, meditation. This topic—my mother, not her "mysticism"—*he* was interested in. I explained that I was her only child. Was she, he asked, very important to me? He took it for granted that I was important to her. Did she accept my independence? "She's philosophical," I said. "So you say," he said, arching an eyebrow meant to recall her mystical side.

The UConn event was a type of evening familiar to Merrill from many years of giving readings. It began with a dinner. Holly Stevens, the poet's daughter, was there; so were the poet and translator Robert Fitzgerald and his wife, Penelope Laurans, friends of Merrill's. I sat at the far end of the table beside Marilyn Nelson, a young poet whom Merrill liked (he told me later) and the only African American in the room. Executives from Stevens's Hartford insurance company filled out the table. One woman asked how I liked being Mr. Merrill's escort, which sounded friendly until I caught her smirking implication.

In the packed auditorium, Merrill rose, shedding the rest of us. He spoke of how much Stevens had meant to him as a young poet and then read his own poems. A party followed at a house in the woods. Tipsy poetry lovers lined up to schmooze. Hugs, handshakes, kisses; names, addresses; wine in plastic cups. As we drove off, Merrill was too spent to talk much. Still, when he invited me upstairs for a nightcap, I accepted. Now, sunken in his black leather Eames chair, backed by a man-sized, gilt-framed mirror, he was no longer buoyant and youthful. He seemed to have gone somewhere far away. Soon, to dispatch me, he located a copy of *The Country of a Thousand Years of Peace* and signed it.

I sent him some of my poems, and a letter came back with comments. He scolded me gently for my poetry's excessive "music" and weighty symbols. He liked best the shortest and simplest, a poem about the objects in a room. *Things*, he said, were what he missed in the other poems. Encouraged, I went back to work. A year later, I sent him a new batch of poems, these clumsily imitative of his. A longer letter came back this time, coaching me about poetic borrowings. But the letter was heartening, if only for the time he'd taken with it: blue felt-tip notes decorated every onionskin page I'd sent. (Later I would learn that he replied with the same seriousness and sympathy to countless beginning poets.) He signed off with a cheerful, nonspecific invitation to drop by on Water Street. I never did. It wasn't that I didn't want to get to know him better. I just assumed, as young people do, that there would be time for that later, and there never was.

Yet my one evening with James Merrill had been memorable. I'd been a guest in his home. I'd observed his silky way of moving through a room; heard his subtle voice inquiring, musing, teasing, confiding; noticed how quickly he found out everything we had in common and, no doubt, everything we didn't. I'd seen him onstage in a hushed auditorium and caught up in a swirling, giddy party. I'd left him at midnight, tired and alone, shutting the door to an apartment that, however enchanted it had seemed to me that afternoon, and will always seem in the pages of his poems, was now as dim and dark as anyone's.

PART I

LOVE AND MONEY

1926–52

THE ORCHARD

1

THE BROKEN HOME

1926–38

Light strikes the little boy. Shining, backlit, his brown hair is a halo. He leans at ease into the lap of his father, the tycoon, who is fully playing the part, barrel-chested and rakish, leaning on his left arm to support them both, in the corner of his mouth a cigarette, the breeze stirring his whitening hair. They gaze to one side across the pool they sit beside with matching grins. Dressed all in white, they seem made of one sunny substance. Jimmy is just three: short pants, ankle socks. Someone has supplied a cushion to keep his backside clean. He is as feminine and delicate as the Old Man is bluff and hearty, but they are equally assured.

The photo was taken around Christmas 1929. Black Tuesday, October 29, when the Dow Jones lost 13 percent of its value, is very recent history; soon the Great Depression will grip the nation. Here, by the reflecting pool behind Charles Merrill's house on Brazilian Avenue in Palm Beach, the bank panics and breadlines to come, like the winter cold, are very far away. Charlie had the insight to foresee the stock market crash that brought the Roaring Twenties to a bitter, sudden close. He had restructured the brokerage firm he cofounded in 1915, Merrill Lynch, to focus on investment bank-

ILLUSTRATION The Orchard, aerial view, with a caption by young JM, placed first in his childhood photo album, c. 1930

ing rather than the retail sale of stock, and he urged his clients to get out of the market. He put his own money in Safeway supermarkets, the chain of grocery stores he created through a massive merger in 1926. He closed the deal himself in one heroic, headlong session of accounting. The company took off before the Crash and survived it with considerable momentum. By 1932, when its growth finally leveled out, Charlie would be the de facto boss of some 3,400 stores, making Safeway America's second-largest grocery chain, after the Great Atlantic & Pacific Tea Co., and the largest west of the Mississippi River. Relaxing with his son in Florida in 1929, both of them in spotless whites, he has the easy swagger of an unchallenged ruler, slightly overweight. For the moment, he has nothing to prove.

It wasn't always so. Charlie was a born competitor. He insisted on playing bridge for money, if only for small stakes, just to make it interesting. After college, he spent a summer as a hustling semipro baseball player—Class D, but the team was the best entertainment in that corner of Mississippi, and he was paid for playing. When he read books, they were mainly military history. He volunteered to fight in World War I and became a test pilot and flight instructor. At thirty-one, "Pop Merrill" was the oldest man in his company, and he was never sent overseas to fight. Even so, his service would remain a source of pride for the rest of his life. Having asked to be buried in his military uniform, he entered heaven dressed for battle.

It had been his basic attitude in life. A short man, he joked about his charter membership in the "Everybody Over Five-Feet-Six is a Sonuvabitch Club." When, on one of his regular returns to his alma mater, Amherst College, after drinks, dinner, and more drinks, he rose to speak as the national president of the Chi Psi Fraternity—an office as important to him as any he ever held—his fraternity brothers, knowing how to get under his skin, would roar, "Come on, Charlie, get up off your knees!" Jimmy's childhood photo album shows his father hoisting the infant onto a pony. In other photos, he lifts his son onto a barrel. Evidently the first lesson to be learned was how to get on top and ride; it mattered less on what.

Drawing puzzled looks or smirks, James Merrill liked to say he was glad he was born to "poor parents," by which he meant people whose values were formed before they had money. True: although he was never "poor," except by the standards of the rich, the fact that Charlie had grown up without much money, and lived among people who had less, deeply shaped him. It meant that—what Jimmy had in mind—Charlie valued common people, commonsense frugality, and practical industry. But it meant much more than that: not having money, the kind of money the rich relied on, was a wound and a stain, a parlous state that mingled with his memories of growing up in the defeated South.

Charles Edward Merrill was born in 1885 in Green Cove Springs, Florida, the county seat and a resort town with a year-round population of 350 situated up the St. John's River about thirty miles south of Jacksonville in the northeast corner of the state. He was the first child and only son of Octavia Wilson and Charles Morton Merrill; sister Edith followed in 1892, Mary in 1902. His father was a doctor and a pharmacist who tended not only to his neighbors in Green Cove Springs but also—it was why he located there in 1882—to wealthy winter visitors from the North. Along with citrus farming, the town depended on those tourists, who came for the mineral springs and mild weather, swelling the population from January through February, and giving the Merrills a glimpse of how rich people lived. In the 1880s and early 1890s, with paddle-wheelers steaming on the broad river and travelers arriving from as far away as Europe, Green Cove Springs was no mean backwater but, in Charlie's words, "an up-and-coming potential Carlsbad of America." But its heyday was brief. Severe, back-to-back freezes hit in 1894 and 1895; the citrus crop failed; and tourists began to explore points further south, beckoned by the expanding railroad system.

"Economic conditions in the south had been so bad for years," Charlie said, "that most Southerners just took it for granted that the 'going was rough.' So far as I knew, the going had always been rough." Two stories he told about his childhood suggest how those conditions affected him. The first came from when he was a small boy. His mother brought him out onto the porch to show him the full moon. Charlie pointed, shouted, "I want it! I want it!," and threw a tantrum when he couldn't get it. "Thereafter," as Robin Magowan, his grandson, relates, "Octavia had him believing that anything he wanted—even the moon—could be his, if he wanted it badly enough. Over and over, as he saw her despairing over some unpayable bill, he would promise, 'Don't worry, Mama, when I grow up I'll buy you rubies and diamonds.' "

Charlie recounts the second story in a letter to his son Charles in 1940. Attempting to impress a "sense of responsibility" on the young man, who was twenty, Charlie recalls events of 1906, when he himself was coming of age:

My mother and father and Edith were living in West Palm Beach Florida; it was a sad year for us all for in January my sister Mary died [of diphtheria at the age of three]. Had the family been living then in Jacksonville my father could have saved her life, but there was no hospital then in West Palm Beach, and he did not have available the proper tools of his trade. The fact that my father knew how to save his daughter's life, and yet, because of limited finances, did not possess the equipment, crushed him. Money, [of] course, is not everything, but, my friend, emergency after emergency comes up in this world of ours in which for a few brief moments, at least, and maybe longer, money is the equivalent of everything.

Mary's death was the last and worst in a line of calamities that began in 1898 when the Merrills left Green Cove Springs. They moved to Knoxville, Tennessee, a boom town; but the doctor set up shop in a working-class area, and business was slower than expected. So he moved his family back to Florida, this time to a comfortable address in Jacksonville, the largest city in the state, but there was more rough going ahead. In 1901 Jacksonville was devastated by fire. The business district burned, and a third of the city's 25,000 residents were left homeless. Although the Merrills' home survived, the city schools were damaged, and Charlie was sent to Stetson, a boarding school one hundred miles away. Then, in 1902, shortly before Mary was born, Dr. Merrill was robbed, severely beaten, and left on the street in a coma. His recovery was slow and only partial; for a time, he was confined to a wheelchair. When he recovered enough to return to work, he moved to West Palm Beach in 1903 and tried to rebuild his practice where the tourists had gone. He opened another pharmacy; now Octavia not only worked behind the counter, but opened two boardinghouses, while caring for a small child. In short, Charles Morton Merrill was wounded—economically and physically—even before Mary died. It was not so unreasonable for his son to decide that money was the "equivalent of everything."

Charlie's future lay in the North. When he got the news of Mary's death, he was enrolled in Worcester Academy in Massachusetts. From there he progressed—an uninspired but passing student—to Amherst for two years and then the University of Michigan for a year, before he broke off his studies without completing a degree. That his parents would send their only boy away first to boarding school in Florida, then in distant Massachusetts, in the midst of a family financial crisis, indicates how much they staked on his education, and specifically his education in the North, which they expected to equip him for a professional life.

Dr. Merrill's family had roots in the North. His parents, carpetbaggers, came to Jacksonsville from Ohio in 1870; he trained as a medical student at the University of Michigan and served as a surgical intern in Bellevue Hospital in New York City, where he took his medical degree. He'd met Octavia Wilson, a Mississippi girl, when they were both students at Maryville College in Tennessee. Their fathers had fought on opposite sides in the Battle of Vicksburg. It was unusual for a young woman to be sent to college, even, as in this case, for a year. Octavia's father taught her Latin and the classics; she read Shakespeare and poetry; and her mother was a reader: Miss Emily, as she was known, introduced her grandson to books of history and to J. M. Barrie's novel *Sentimental Tommy*—a work of literature, one of the few, that Charlie swore by in later life. Miss Emily was the force behind his enrollment at Michigan. Feeling he was destined to be a lawyer, for which Michigan was top-notch preparation, she raised money from her hard-pressed Wilson relatives to pay his tuition.

His two years at Amherst had a much greater effect. Amherst was known as a conservative, small-town alternative to Harvard, safe from the free thinking of the university and loose living of the big city. He arrived on campus with savings from a summer job and a $300 scholarship from the college. For Charlie, Amherst would be a way into the moneyed Northeast society from which the college drew most of its students. Like all of the best schools, Amherst was an elite WASP institution. There were few Catholics, only "non-practicing" Jews, and no blacks; women were enrolled at nearby Smith and Mount Holyoke. Charlie came to campus with, he joked, "four strikes" against him: he was short and small, he was from the South, he had no money, and he had his mother with him. For Octavia hovered while he got settled, because he'd had a tough time of it at Worcester Academy, where he had been ridiculed for his southern drawl and inferior academic preparation, and assigned to live in cramped quarters shared with an "octoroon"—which he took as a deliberate insult.

He quickly found his place at Amherst by joining the Chi Psi Fraternity. Fraternity boys were sworn brothers. Indifferent to their studies, they played sports, acted in plays, and partied hard, aware that their fortunes depended less on their grades than on the friendships they were forming with each other and on the possibility that one of their dates might turn into a favorable marriage. Charlie was the consummate fraternity man. "I never studied," he said, "because I was a damn conceited cuss and knew I could cram in a few days before exams and thus 'get by.' " In Chi Psi, he flashed what was already being called his "million-dollar smile." He ingratiated himself with his brothers while making money by arranging for the fraternity's food and drink at a local rooming house and selling fine clothes to collegians on commission from a Springfield tailor, who, to advertise his wares, kept Charlie himself dressed in the latest styles, so that he didn't look like a poor boy.*

---

* Charles Merrill, Charlie's son, distinguishing between his father's college stories and the reality of his experience, puts these commercial successes in a different light: "My father

He was off and running. His time at Michigan proved only that he had no gift for the law. Business was less prestigious, but there was money in it, and he had a job waiting for him in New York as a credit manager for Robert Sjostrom, a textile manufacturer and the father of a Smith girl to whom Charlie was engaged for several years before she broke it off and he left her father's firm. In the meantime, he'd learned accounting, and become an expert in buying and selling credit. He went to work next for Burr & Co., a small bond house dealing in low-grade investments. He opened his own office with a staff of one (a secretary whom he kept on for decades, longer than any of his wives) and started out as a securities broker and investment banker. He added as a partner the hard-nosed Eddie Lynch, who was good at negotiations and at reading the fine print. They were a strong team at work and sidekicks after hours. Pinching pennies, they headed out late once a week to posh watering holes where they relieved elderly gents of their escorts, who were well fed by that hour and ready to "stay out the balance of the night with a couple of young blades who were fun and who could dance." By horning in on Wall Street's securities business, they were playing another trick on the old guard. Merrill, Lynch (there was a comma between the names at first) broke the code of silence that made the stock market an insider's club, pulling back the veil on investment by experimenting with direct-mail advertising and detailed prospectuses and earnings reports to show their clients what they were buying.

These techniques, novel in the 1910s, were essential tools when Charlie directed an aggressive expansion of the firm in the 1940s—without his partner Lynch, who died suddenly at the age of fifty-two in 1938. Working, during the war years and after, to reestablish the discredited reputation of Wall Street, Merrill Lynch put in place many policies new to the industry: no service fees, expanded advertising, an emphasis on research, profit sharing and training for employees, and salary rather than commissions for account executives. With such strategies encouraging public trust in financial services and promoting personal, small-scale investment for the expanding middle class, the firm emerged as the nation's leading retail broker during the postwar decade. By the end of his career, when the number of individual stock-market investors reached more than 7.5 million across the United States, Charlie had transformed how Americans think

---

was not proud of his position as business manager for a boarding house, and when he sold secondhand clothes he felt that friends bought them because they felt sorry for him." CM, *The Checkbook: The Politics and Ethics of Foundation Philanthropy* (Oegleschlager, Gunn & Hain, 1986), 6.

of finance. He had brought "Wall Street to Main Street."* He was "We, the People's Boss."

Preoccupied in his final years with his own myth, he commissioned official biographies of himself, but none came to fruition—not surprisingly perhaps, since his story was fascinating, but not easy to sum up. In business, Charlie rode—often he was out in front of—the waves of commerce transforming daily life for millions. He'd seen that chain stores, with centralized purchasing and warehousing and national advertising, would displace the independent retail store, and that shoppers would follow en masse—above all women shoppers, for Charlie's knack for pleasing women in his private life was part of what he did at work as well. Before Safeway, he was the underwriter who helped build McCrory's, the five-and-dime store chain, and Kresge's, ancestor of Kmart. He and Lynch went into the movie business when they bought Pathé films, the future RKO Pictures, which they sold at a profit to Joe Kennedy, a Democrat with dynastic ambitions of his own, whom Charlie came to despise. In all that he did, he was aware of the figure he cut. He was the banker as Jazz Age celebrity in plus fours or a double-breasted Van Sickle suit, a confessed hedonist and the hardest worker going. He was an innovator in business, always ready to try out a new idea, who loved the Old South and English aristocracy. A southern gentleman and a Yankee entrepreneur, he stepped on toes and took pride in his handsome apologies. Bent on making money, he gave it away freely to friends, family, and institutions; though he never graduated from the college, he became one of Amherst's leading donors. He traversed the nation restlessly, looking in on his several homes and multiplying interests, kindling old flames and sparking new ones, a ladies' man and a devoted family member. He was a defender of the underdog and an outspoken anti-Semite. He believed in the American Dream, and he filled his house with a staff of black servants. He was a charmer at work who was feared for his rages at home. A loyal friend, he divorced three wives. "I am," he said, "a mixture of Santa Claus, Lady Bountiful, the Good Samaritan, Baron Richtofen, J. P. Morgan, [and] Casanova[.] I am tender as a woman, brave as a lion, and can fight like a cat."

Jimmy always called him Daddy. The ordinary intimacy (or the longing for it) expressed in that name is touching, given the stiff, self-conscious quality of their relations as demonstrated on both sides of their correspon-

---

* The slogan "Wall Street to Main Street," used by Edwin J. Perkins as the title of his biography of CEM, was "one of the firm's major strategic themes in the early 1940s." Perkins, *Wall Street to Main Street: Charles Merrill and Middle-Class Investors* (Cambridge University Press, 1999), 11.

dence over the years. It would be hard to invent a father and son apparently more unlike each other than Charles and James Merrill. "The Broken Home," Merrill's poem about his parents' marriage and divorce, includes a portrait of his father that counters the man's blunt drive and reckless appetite with spinning puns and precise rhymes, his hot temper and soppy sentiments with his son's rhetorical and emotional cool. Writing after his father's death, Merrill gets the last word, but he takes little pleasure in it:

> My father, who had flown in World War I,
> Might have continued to invest his life
> In cloud banks well above Wall Street and wife.
> But the race was run below, and the point was to win.
>
> Too late now, I make out in his blue gaze
> (Through the smoked glass of being thirty-six)
> The soul eclipsed by twin black pupils, sex
> And business; time was money in those days.
>
> Each thirteenth year he married. When he died
> There were already several chilled wives
> In sable orbit—rings, cars, permanent waves.
> We'd felt him warming up for a green bride.
>
> He could afford it. He was "in his prime"
> At three score ten. But money was not time.

For the son, the father posed a nice problem. On the one hand, Daddy was permanently and massively in the way: Jimmy would feel compelled to journey far and wide in order to establish his own credit, beyond the reach of his father's reputation. On the other hand, his father was never very present to him. Charlie saw the boy little even before he divorced his mother, as Charlie himself realized with regret near the end of his life. And for his part, if Jimmy needed to get away from his father, he was in search of him too, to judge from the qualities of the Old Man (his masculinity, his drinking, his adventurousness, his storytelling, his grandiosity, his temper) that Jimmy found in varying quantities in his lovers.

But in fact he had only to look in the mirror. For Jimmy was no less of a competitor than his father and no less hungry for public recognition. And his poetic career was not a repudiation, so much as a subtle transposition, of his father's career in finance. Charlie could have used for his motto Wallace Stevens's adage, "Money is a kind of poetry"—it was that magical, that plastic in his hands. Jimmy turned that proposition around, substituting the transformative powers of language for his father's faith in capital: through metaphor, he would discover equivalents for everything, including money. The money that came from his father, meanwhile, he would use in the service of art, both his own and, through the grants administered by his personal foundation, many other people's creativity. And even as he worked very hard every day, sweating to make his verbal magic, James Merrill would live a libertine's life of the senses that rivaled his father's—the sultan's queer heir inventing his own seraglio.

The photo of them lounging together in the Florida sun in 1929 tells the truth. They shine and flow into each other. In just a moment, however, the man will stand and take a call from New York. His valet has mixed a daiquiri for him to enjoy before lunch. The boy will be sent away to play, or delivered into the arms of his mother.

At eighty-nine, after a third drink, Hellen Ingram Plummer launched on "one of her tragic, passionate scenes" with her son as audience. The topic was the articles about Jimmy and his work that she saved in scrapbooks. The problem was that they mentioned his father and his business exploits, never her and her stint in journalism. "It's as if your father borned you by himself, like the holy ghost! I don't exist! . . . You have no mother, as far as the world is concerned." Jimmy, as if it were his fault, explained why his father got that attention, what he himself had done to correct the record, and why she shouldn't care anyway; all to no avail until, sobered up by bedtime, she was ready to let it go: "Forget what I said—just ego talking."

The fact is, it's easier to bring James Merrill's father into focus than his mother. It's not simply that Charles Merrill was a colorful, well-documented public man. He is easier because he stands at a relaxed distance from his son's poetry—a bemused benefactor who was secure in his own achievements and therefore had no great stake in his son's, much as it gratified him to see Jimmy succeed in his chosen field. Whereas with his mother, Jimmy was so closely, so privately, and so ambivalently identified, it is hard—it was hard for the two of them—to say where the boundaries were, where one began and the other ended. "[O]f course she's here / Throughout," Merrill says of his mother in *The Book of Ephraim*, the first book of his Ouija board trilogy, in which she is otherwise unmentioned. He means that her presence, her pulse, can be felt everywhere in his poetry—in "the breath drawn after every line, / Essential to its making as to mine[.]" It's a poignant acknowledgment of a debt as fundamental as life itself, beside which his father's money was easier to calculate.

It's not clear, however, whether he really believed that, or whether he merely felt the need to cover for his mother's absence in the poem, lest it prompt one of "her passionate, tragic scenes." The mention of his mother in *The Book of Ephraim* needs to be placed in the context of certain other references to their relationship. At sixty, for instance, he recorded two dreams in his journal: "Dream A: Arms round my old mother (my young father roaming in the background) I tell her I love her. It is hard as pulling a tooth to do so. B: I am fighting to get free of her—biting, scratching, anything. She has locked us in. I wake trying to pry the key from her." Feeling his mother's presence in "the breath drawn at the end of every line" must have made it hard for him, at times, to breathe. Then he had to bite and scratch to get free.

His mother is the subject of a poem he wrote at the age of six, probably his first. The date of composition was October 29, 1932.

LOOKING AT MUMMY

One day when she was sleeping
    I don't know who
But it was a pretty lady
    That knows me and you.

So, one day when she was sleeping
    I took "Mike" a-peeping
The "do-not-disturb" was on the door.
    And I looked around the room and floor

Then I looked to the bed
    Where that pretty head lay
And the hair was more beautiful
    Than I could say.

The poem feels like a fragment from a fairy tale or myth. The boy follows Mike (his father's red setter, Michael) to an upstairs bedroom. A "do-not-disturb" sign on the door protects the lady of the house while she sleeps off a late night. The boy enters anyway, transgressing. There, after some flirtatious suspense, he is granted a vision. It's "Mummy" he is looking at, but only the title lets on: the boy, like Oedipus, doesn't seem to know to whom he's drawn. She is mysterious specifically because she's sleeping: motionless and unaware of being looked at, she might be a goddess in repose—or Sleeping Beauty, and her son the prince come to kiss her awake. She's unguarded, alone; the place beside her is free. Here the story pulls up short, leaving the boy simply, safely admiring. Meanwhile, Jimmy has made something for which *he* will be admired—a poem in rhyme and a loose ballad meter, like one of the children's poems he was already memorizing. The poem's technique and the will to charm that it serves heighten the coy, theatrical quality of his innocence—an effect that, very much refined, of course, would become a trademark tone of the mature poet. It seems that, though only six years old, and absurd as it sounds to say so, Jimmy Merrill has found his voice.

But is that his voice? Although the poem is signed "Jimmy Merrill" across from the date, he hasn't signed it: the writing is in Hellen's hand. She has made a copy of the poem, dated it, and signed her son's name to it. Well tutored, Jimmy's handwriting was legible at six; Hellen must have wished to preserve the poem and felt it needed to be tidied up. She wanted to "publish" it by sharing it with family and friends, and printed the words, with the date and author's name, in a way that makes it look like a poem on the page of a book or magazine. Showing Jimmy's compositions around, something she would do for the rest of her life, was a way for Hellen to show off, inviting praise for her son's cleverness and indirectly her own (and for her beauty, in this case). Besides copying the poem, moreover, she may have helped compose it. Did she suggest rhymes, correct grammar? Whose idea was it to write a poem in the first place, and a poem on this theme? Whose wish does it express? The son's or the mother's?

In "The Broken Home," Merrill returned to and rewrote "Looking at Mummy":

> One afternoon, red, satyr-thighed
> Michael, the Irish setter, head
> Passionately lowered, led
> The child I was to a shut door. Inside,
>
> Blinds beat sun from the bed.
> The green-gold room throbbed like a bruise.
> Under a sheet, clad in taboos,
> Lay whom we sought, her hair undone, outspread,
>
> And of a blackness found, if ever now, in old
> Engravings where the acid bit.
> I must have needed to touch it

Or the whiteness—was she dead?
Her eyes flew open, startled strange and cold.
The dog slumped to the floor. She reached for me. I fled.

Composed thirty-two years later, these lines turn the early poem into a
Gothic daydream, playing variations on Freud's Oedipal plot. Michael,
Charlie's red setter, is again the chaperone, a guide to instinct showing the
boy where he wants to go, or where from a normative developmental perspective he is supposed to go (that is, precisely where he's not supposed to
go, toward a woman "clad in taboos"). The parental bed, where again the
woman is alone, becomes a sadomasochistic scene. While "Blinds beat sun
from the bed" (a weird sentence whose implications it would take a long
time to tease out), the room "throbs" like a hangover or a battered woman's body. Mummy, objectified, eerily inanimate in the childhood poem,
is deathly here: a mummy? When she opens her eyes ("strange and cold")
and reaches for the boy, there is no longer any lingering wondering at the
inexpressible beauty of her "undone, outspread" hair. He realizes he'd better get out of there.

This woman so admired and feared by her son was born in Jacksonville
on August 14, 1898, to Annie Beloved Hill and James Willmot Ingram. Mis'
Annie, as Mrs. Ingram was known in the family, had grown up in Fer-
nandina, a beach town north of Jacksonville. Her father having died when
she was small, Mis' Annie was especially close to her mother, establishing a pattern that would be repeated in Hellen's relationship to her and
in Jimmy's relationship to Hellen. James Ingram, a Tennessean by birth,
had come to Jacksonville as a young boy, completed high school there, and
then worked in a bank and as a bookkeeper. After the Jacksonville fire, he
and his brother formed the Electric Supply & Construction Company and
made a profit when the city converted to electrical lighting. Later, he was
the primary owner of the memorably named R. I. P. Sprinkler Company.
A Mason and an Elk, twice called to serve as "Exalted Ruler of the Lodge,"
Mr. Ingram was, by the time of Hellen's birth, a pillar of local society. The
Ingrams were a churchgoing family who lived on "Holy Hill" behind the
Episcopal church that would later become St. John's Cathedral.

Hellen was named after her father's mother, Hellen Kasson Willmot,
whom Hellen spoke of proudly as a woman of distinction. Though unable
because of her sex to pursue a career as a doctor, Hellen's namesake "interested herself in medical subjects" and was perhaps "the first woman ever to
address the American Association for the Advancement of Science" when
in 1877 she delivered a scientific paper on "Atmospheric Concussion as a

Means of Disinfection"—her proposal being to kill mosquitoes by exploding gunpowder. Genealogical papers that Hellen copied and preserved note that her grandmother, though born in New York State, was "an earnest and ardent advocate of the Confederate cause," who was arrested for smuggling quinine across the border to aid wounded Southern soldiers. She became a teacher with "a national reputation" and "literary ability," which she demonstrated as an editorial writer and society editor of Jacksonville's *Florida Times-Union*. Hellen would emulate her grandmother, whom she never met, in specific ways.

Her parents doted on their only child. Mis' Annie called her daughter "Baby" throughout her life. Recognized as a beauty very early on, Hellen was the six-year-old maid of honor at a Tom Thumb wedding held by the Jacksonville Women's Club in 1905: a stunning junior ingénue, dark eyes, a model's open mouth, curled hair tied up on top, a bouquet of roses, and a two-foot train of white ruffled silk. A popular teenager known among her friends as "Pink," Hellen was the maid of honor at the Twenty-fourth General Reunion of the United Confederate Veterans in Jacksonville in 1914. She attended Jacksonville schools, including Charlie's high school, Duval, where she was chosen to be Mascot of the class of 1916, and, fifty years later, Mistress of Ceremonies at the class reunion.

Directly after graduation, on the strength of her English teacher's recommendation, she was invited to become "society editor" of the *Metropolis*, Jacksonville's evening newspaper. When she expressed doubts about her ability—she didn't even know how to type—the editor told her to rent a typewriter and teach herself: "besides, you know everyone in town." Hellen was a quick study, and in her role as society journalist, she became a local fixture. By 1922, she was confident enough to strike out on her own in the *Silhouette*, a weekly social chronicle published through the winter, twenty-six times a year, and so named because, to cut costs, the paper substituted silhouettes for photos of the notables whose balls and marriages it reported. Hellen was a one-woman newsroom and journalistic entrepreneur: "I sold ads, wrote the copy, corrected proof, pasted up the 'dummy,' rolled the magazines for mailing, and carted them to the P.O. to send them on their way to subscribers, taking leftovers to local news stands for sale." In 1924, she brought the *Silhouette* to Miami, the newest tourist mecca. Growing in size from eight to thirty-two pages, the paper was distributed in the hotels lining Miami Beach, and spunky Hellen was hailed as "the youngest Owner-Editor-Publisher in the U.S.A." Shrewdly, she arranged to stay for free at the Flamingo in exchange for advertising in the *Silhouette*. Over the summers, when the hum of social life subsided in South Florida, she put her paper on hold and enrolled in journalism and fiction-writing classes at Columbia University. In New York, she made friends with one of her teachers, Condé Nast, publisher of *Vanity Fair* and *Vogue*. At his Manhattan parties, she mixed with a glamorous, altogether new level of society.

Hellen and Charlie had met when she interviewed him for her paper. Having learned from a mutual friend that he was separated from his wife, Hellen took a chance and called him when she came north in 1924. Soon Charlie was courting her. Over that fall and winter, after she headed back to Miami, he discovered business reasons to be in Florida. They had a great deal in common, beginning with the mores and manners of middle-class white Jacksonville. She had ambition and ingenuity to rival his, in potential. She knew business; why, she was a businesswoman herself. And Charlie knew something about journalism, he fancied, on the strength of having delivered newspapers as a boy (he liked to tell stories about the route, which took him into Jacksonville's red-light district), and later on having worked in a Florida newsroom over the summer during college.

As a society reporter, Hellen had had an opportunity to survey the marriage market from Miami to New York. She would have seen Charlie as a catch, a bona fide big fish: gallant and rich, this one had come a long way and meant to go farther, just as she did. True, he was divorcing and had two small children, but he lived in a hotel, and his family was not in evidence. An adopted "aunt" of Hellen's advised her to be wary: Charlie "was older than any suitor I had ever had and he was a 'bad risk,' having one matrimonial failure chalked up against him." Charlie knew exactly how to deal with the situation. "When 'Aunt' Babe was up north for a fall visit," Hellen remembered, "the matter finally was clinched when an orange tree, heavy with fruit, was delivered to her hotel room. She later said no Southern woman could resist an orange tree in New York."

With her Cupid's-bow lips and cool, fashion-model poses, her hair pulled back tight in the helmeted style of a flapper, Hellen was pretty and proud. It appealed to Charlie that she smoked and drove a car: she was a Florida girl, but a modern woman too. Fourteen years his junior, she was youthful enough to flatter him, as a trophy wife should, but she was also experienced and independent, in no way shy, with a warm, conspiratorial, seductive charm that, as she leaned forward, placing her hand on a companion's arm and squeezing for emphasis, made her a hit at parties. She and Charlie both liked to be the center of attention. They both liked to drink and dine and entertain. She took an interest in a class of people—musicians, actors—whom he didn't know much about and perhaps thought he should. With a girlfriend she had already made a tour of must-see sights in Europe. So she promised to increase the level of culture in his life. But their chemistry was not a matter of calculation. Hellen spoke of the "rapture" she felt with Charlie, and he must have felt something similar with her. She had a force of personality, an animal vitality that everyone who knew her remarks on, and that would last uncannily the rest of a very long life. Here, Charlie must have sensed, was a woman who could stand up to him. In fact, in heels, she was slightly taller.

Pressed by her suitor, Hellen agreed to marry him immediately after his divorce was decreed. The wedding ceremony was performed by a Congregational minister in the Ingrams' Jacksonville home on February 19, 1925. It was a small gathering: Charlie's sister Edith and two of Hellen's girlfriends attended; Eddie Lynch served as the best man. For a honeymoon, Charlie took his bride to Paris—"to study merchandising methods abroad," as the purpose of the trip was announced in *The New York Times* (Charlie didn't want his clients and competitors to think he was taking a vacation). The newlyweds returned to set up their home in a brick, four-story nineteenth-century town house at 18 West Eleventh Street, a quiet, tree-lined street not so far away from Wall Street and a short walk to Washington Square. The elegant house was snug in the middle of old New York, Henry James country; but the people in it were shiny and new, like the Veneerings in Dickens's *Our Mutual Friend*.

The *Silhouette* published its last number in March. Hellen had left the ranks of society journalists to become a society news item herself; henceforth reporters would be keeping tabs on Mrs. C. E. Merrill. Charlie gave her $50,000 to furnish their home (a huge sum for that purpose) as well as a free hand to select styles, fabrics, colors, and furniture, instructing her only "NOT to leave a single room half-decorated." They hired a butler, a cook, and a maid, all of them black, as Hellen wished it. They joined the Church of the Ascension, an Episcopal congregation with a history of charity, housed in a splendid Gothic Revival building around the corner on Fifth Avenue, where Charlie served on the vestry and passed the offering plate. By the middle of the summer, the Merrills had climbed to a high perch in New York society, and Hellen was pregnant.

James Ingram Merrill was born on March 3, 1926, at a private hospital on New York City's Upper East Side. His mother's influence in the marriage and her large stake in her son's future were reflected in the choice of Hellen's father's name for his first and middle names. Dr. Warren Hildreth ("one of the doctors to bring one's babies into this world") was the delivering physician. Charlie, Mis' Annie, and Old Jane Reed, Hellen's African American nurse from childhood, summoned from Jacksonville, attended.

Dr. Hildreth announced, "You have a fine baby boy, weighing 5 lbs. 10 oz." Hellen gasped, then pleaded with the man: "Please, please, this is embarrassing. Can't you say 6 lbs.?" She was not impressed with her son's looks, either, he being "so teeny, rather shriveled." "I exclaimed to my nurse, 'He's not very good looking,' " to which Jane replied, "Maybe not, Mrs Merrill, but he has personality!" Jimmy came home three weeks later on March 25. It was a long hospital stay by today's standards, but not so unusual at the time; Hellen and Jimmy stayed as long as they did because of his size and because the Merrills could pay for the custom care. His weight picked up (Hellen recorded it weekly through December), and he began to look as his mother had expected when he was born. Still, she would remain anxious about his weight for years to come. In her eyes, Jimmy would be undersized throughout childhood and different from his peers because of it. Already his birth introduced a question about whether or not he was meeting her expectations and how his appearance reflected on her. These would be important, permanent themes.

In *A Different Person*, his memoir published in 1993, Merrill describes discovering, in his sixties, the "little book bound in pink quilted moiré" in which his mother noted his week-by-week weight gain and other facts from his earliest days. What struck him was the list of gifts he received at birth. "The 'five shares of stock' from my father's partner, the inevitable silver spoons (nine of them), the six pairs of 'silver military brushes' and the upright masculine life these recommended, were lost in an avalanche of dainty apparel and accessories—lace and net pillows; monogrammed carriage robes; embroidered dresses; a 'pink crêpe de chine coat'; a 'silk shawl and sacque'; caps of organdy or lace; gold diaper pins, blue pins, pink-and-pearl pins; rattles and bootees and yet more dresses. I counted over a hundred such items"—chosen by the givers to please his mother, "Pink." Those gloriously frivolous goods say a lot about the social world into which this newborn was gently placed. The environment of 18 West Eleventh Street was silky and soft, clean and cozy, insulated, very expensive, and decidedly feminine. His first nurse, who took over when Old Jane went home, was British and (Hellen noted) "royally-trained"; she and Jimmy occupied the fourth floor of the house. Pampered—it hardly describes the cooing over his crib, surrounded by all that fluffy, monogrammed tribute. Implied too by that list of gifts was a dense web of entitlements and obligations, including the more than one hundred thank-you notes that Hellen used her list to produce that spring.

CEM had little part in these goings-on. No man of his era was likely to involve himself in child rearing, and Charlie was no different—unless he was away from home even more than most. "During the week," Hellen wrote in 1953, remembering their marriage without explicit resentment, "the urgency to make money was all that mattered. Charlie never let anything interfere with business. He was working on his first important deal, [. . .] when his mother telephoned him to come at once because his sister [Edith] was critically ill. He replied, 'I can't come, Mama. If I leave this deal now, we won't even be able to pay for the doctor.' " In 1926, Charlie was occupied with the Safeway acquisition, his biggest deal ever, which took him to the West Coast for long stretches. The new company's stock went on offer in November.

He was also busy with the purchase of the Orchard, which would become the Merrill family's showpiece summer and weekend home and at times their primary residence. He bought the property on Hill Street in the Long Island town of Southampton for $350,000 in October 1926, when Jimmy was seven months old. It was characteristic, Hellen noted, that once Charlie had decided to buy the place, "he could not wait until business hours to close the deal. Papers were brought to a Broadway theater, where he signed the contract between acts." He used an entity called Merchard Inc., merging "Merrill" and "Orchard" in the name, to buy it for cash. He must have written the purchase off his taxes as a business expense; he put the property in his name when the portmanteau company, Merchard Inc., sold it to him for a dollar in 1935.

Situated on the grounds of an old farmhouse and apple orchard, the house had been built for James L. Breese. Breese was a stockbroker, born in 1854 and thus one of the Wall Street old guard, though not of the usual kind. The idea of owning Breese's house in particular must have excited Charlie, who flirted with the man's daughter, an actress, after he bought Breese's home. Besides being very rich, Breese was a prizewinning photographer, a race car driver, and a collector of the finest automobiles. He'd been the host of a bohemian salon known for its bacchanals. "The Carbonites," as they called themselves, referring to a process for developing photographs, included the painter John Singer Sargent, the chorus girl and artist's model Evelyn Nesbit, and her lover, Stanford White, the eminent architect and Breese's best friend. It was the Beaux-Arts firm of McKim, Mead & White that collaborated with Breese on the design of the Orchard. White had charge of the interiors and the ornamental touches in the gardens—until he was shot dead at Madison Square Garden Theater by Nesbit's millionaire husband. In 1907, the "Trial of the Century" was front-page news as the final touches were being applied to the Orchard's music room.

The grace and scale of this scandal-scented home were intoxicating. A short drive led to the house from a white picket fence on Hill Street, the main thoroughfare from New York City to Montauk. Broad lawns unrolled on either side of the drive, with huge squat boxwood hedges for sentinels and wistful, champagne-glass-shaped elms shading the gravel circle at the front door, which faced south. "One might not have been surprised to have looked in upon it through some old Virginia hedge," observed *House & Garden* in a feature on the Orchard. Modeled on George Washington's estate at Mount Vernon, the house's two-story columned portico nodded to colonial-era plantation homes. The wood construction, slim columns, and white paint gave the building delicacy despite its enormity. Symmetrical wings fanned out, and wings off of those wings. Inside were more than twenty bedrooms, a dining room, a blue-tiled conservatory, a billiard room, a studio, and a library.

If the exterior was Old South, the interior was Old Europe: chandeliers, seventeenth-century oil paintings, Flemish tapestries, and Magna Carta shields on the leaded casements and bay windows. The music room featured a giant Milanese fireplace, wood-paneled walls, a coffered, twenty-foot-high ceiling, four gilt, spiraling wood pillars in the corners, and an organ whose pipes filled the upper half of one wall. "Stanford White put his *heart* into that room," one Southampton socialite remarked of the late, valedictory commission. Breese had added decorations of his own: the heads and hides of bison, deer, antelope, and a lion, all of which he'd shot; Hellen, modernizing, donated them to a local social club in the mid-1930s. Behind the house were a formal garden with herringbone-patterned brick paths, flanking Doric pergolas, statuary, a burbling fountain, and an abundant rose garden. Trellised walkways and tree-lined avenues led to a small village of outbuildings and then acres of open fields beyond. In charge of the plants were a Scotsman, who had toiled for royalty at Balmoral, and the eight gardeners under him. A hedge surrounded the whole of the sixteen-acre estate.

On the first page of James Merrill's childhood photo album are pictures not of himself, nor of his parents, but of the Orchard. One is of the big house as seen from the drive. The other is of the entire property taken from an airplane. It is an exalted, breathtaking view: the house and gardens are extravagant in extent, exactly ordered, and crowded by no neighbor. This was the formative setting of Merrill's childhood. The Orchard taught the boy the power of interior space and the pleasures of ornament. It showed him that a house could be a self-enclosed world, expressive of its owner. It left him both attracted to and resistant to everything that was grand. It tended to shrink even the outsized figures of his parents, whose marriage would come to stand for in his imagination. It was the home he thought of when he spoke of "The Broken Home."

It was also the setting where, over the summers that they spent together, Jimmy came to know Doris and Charles, the children from his father's first family. For before there was Hellen, there was Eliza Church, and her daughter and son, his half-siblings, were an important part of his life from the first. Charlie had married Eliza in 1912. Doris was born in 1914, and Charles in 1920—so they were twelve and six years older than Jimmy. The Church family had made its money in Pennsylvania railroads and the steel industry. Eliza's father, Samuel Harden Church, the author of a biography of Oliver Cromwell, plays, and a novel, was the long-serving president of the Carnegie Institute Board of Trustees. He was also a powerful Republican and an advocate of the pseudoscience of eugenics, which called for enforced sterilization of blacks and other minorities. Charlie, although not a eugenicist, was a Republican with convictions, and, marrying Eliza, he must have felt he had arrived among people with the right ideas and the right genes.

But they were ill-matched. Eliza might have been a fitting choice had he aspired to be "a Montclair banker," as his son Charles puts it, referring to the rented home in suburban New Jersey where he and Doris lived when they were small. Eliza, whose mother had left the family when she was nine, was a modest woman, a homebody who was "sensitive to criticism" and unhappy in the Manhattan parties and Long Island tennis weekends to which Charlie was soon bringing her. She was also a serious, convent-educated, Irish Roman Catholic. When her daughter was ten, Eliza arranged for Doris to receive her first communion as a Catholic—while Charlie was away on business (as he often was), since he wouldn't have approved. Once he found out, he was outraged, not only by the communion, but by the fact that Eliza had gone around his back to accomplish it. The argument escalated. When he didn't relent, Eliza declared, "I want a divorce. I can't stand these horrible rages of yours." Charlie must have been waiting for the opportunity, because he took advantage of it and vowed to divorce her. When Doris saw her mother that day, she looked "absolutely awful, [. . .] as if her life had ended. Which in truth it had."

Jimmy met Eliza Church only once. She moved every few years from one apartment to another in New York City, sustained by Charlie's alimony checks and by contributions from her children once they came of age (she had agreed to use Charlie's lawyer during the divorce and the settlement was unfavorable to her). The breakup had been well prepared for by the mismatch in temperaments and by Charlie's infidelities on the road. But for Doris and Charles, who continued to live with their mother, it came as a baffling, violent blow. The results for Doris, the fought-over, were ambiguous, since she'd kept her father's regard—he made that clear—just when her mother hadn't: Eliza's defeat was, in this limited sense, Doris's triumph. But it was also a warning about what might happen to her if she opposed her father's will. She settled into the position of the favored first child of a powerful father with whom it was best not to misbehave. For Charles, the matter was different. He was the second child from a rejected bed, who had less to lose of his father's regard because he'd started with less. Even in his childhood and adolescence, the fact that he was named after CEM underlined their differences, rather than the opposite. He never adopted the "Jr."

Charles remembered meeting his stepmother and baby brother for the first time when he visited West Eleventh Street more than a year after his father married Hellen, and he found her nursing her son in bed. "I had never witnessed that procedure before," he explained, "and was even more disconcerted to be informed that the baby was my brother." "He'll look up to you," Hellen told him. "You can teach him all sorts of things, like how to play baseball." But Charles was no more of a baseball player than Jimmy would turn out to be. He was shy and brooding; he tended to look down or away rather than meet other people's eyes. In the nursing princeling on West Eleventh Street, his father's new son, there was plenty for him to resent, and it took a long time, decades even, for the two brothers to become good friends. Hellen, by contrast, was easy for Charles to warm to. "Pretty," "interesting," and barely old enough to be his mother, she treated "Carlos," as she called him, as if he were older than he was—"like an adult." In fact, "Hellen was the first rational adult I'd met," he recalled. When he threw his father's newspaper into the fire (it was something he would keep doing, symbolically, for much of his life), Hellen calmly reasoned with him, as his father never would have. He went home and asked his mother, "Why don't you like Hellen?"

Doris might have seen Hellen as a rival. Hellen had already taken her mother's place, and she meant to be loyal to her mother: "I will always be nice to Hellen," she wrote in her diary, "yet she must not win me over." Hellen won her over soon enough, however. Doris was six years closer in age to their stepmother than Charles was, and Hellen approached her as a mentor, inviting a girlish, big-sister intimacy. Hellen wrote to Doris, not to Doris and Charles, to confide that she was pregnant and to assure Doris that she wouldn't be replaced by the new baby: Doris was her father's "beloved first-born daughter and he cherishes you more than you can imagine," Hellen wrote. On her twelfth birthday, three days after Jimmy's birth, Doris visited the baby in the hospital. Skinny and knock-kneed, but prepared to learn the social game, "Dorrie," as Hellen called her, could model herself on her stepmother in her approach to this infant brother.* She was big enough to hold him on her lap with a smile ("he was so sweet and his fingers were so small") while waving for the camera; she went home carrying a bouquet of flowers "from him." In photos of Doris and little Jimmy, pride and gentle amusement show on her face, whereas when Charles is required to pose with his brother, it's wariness and discomfort that we see.

Doris and Charles visited the baby and his parents rarely during the school year. The two of them appeared on West Eleventh Street one Sunday per month for lunch and then a matinée at the music hall or the movies. It was at the Orchard over the summer months that these three children and their father and Hellen lived together as one family. The *Southampton Press* indicated Mr. C. E. Merrill among those in residence in its annual summer "Cottage List" for the first time in 1927 (the great homes owned by the town's wealthy summer visitors, even the Orchard, were called "cottages"). By New Year's 1928, Doris's diary listed both her mother's address and the Orchard as home.

While a new family formed around Jimmy's birth, Charlie, no doubt encouraged by Hellen, delved into his roots. Records traced the Merrill family genealogy to the *Mayflower* and beyond that to a Suffolk village in the sixteenth century. The name was said to have come into England "at the time of the Conquest" and to derive from *merle*, the French for "blackbird." On the basis of his direct descent from Mead Merrill, a private who saw duty in 1777, Charlie would enroll in the Empire State Society of the Sons of the American Revolution. Hellen joined the National Society of the Colonial Dames of America. The Ingrams had a family coat of arms, and the Merrills adopted one too: the head of a peacock (perhaps in witty tribute to Charlie, the clotheshorse?) above a gray shield ribbed with lavender and a scroll, also lavender, bearing a motto. The Latin was a trifle self-pitying: "Vincit Qui Patitur"—he who suffers patiently, triumphs. Or, as Charlie liked to translate it, "He who takes his lumps, comes out on top."

There was more than mere class snobbery in these invented insignia and the family identity they expressed. In 1951, Jimmy held a cocktail party

---

* Jimmy's baby book was a gift from Doris and included a dedicatory poem composed by Doris, which plays on "the rhyme" between the baby's and mother's initials: "And with these names / I can write this rhime / Of how J.I.M. and H.I.M. / Must stay like two pins" (WUSTL).

for his mother at which he introduced her to some of his friends, including an African American couple; afterward he found her in a funk, bent over her needlepoint. Hellen was stitching the Merrill and Ingram crests, which she planned to give her son to remind him "of the kind of people you come from." "Do you know," she went on, explaining her angry, suddenly urgent project, "that this is the first time in my entire life that I've had to meet coloured people socially?" She was sure her son would never subject his father to the same indignity. Jimmy challenged her with the memory of her own nurse: "Didn't you ever sit down in the kitchen with Old Jane?" Hellen replied, "We're not *talking* about *servants*, son. I loved Old Jane more than anyone in the whole world. [. . .] But never, never would you have seen me shake her hand."

The white clothes Charlie favored and that Hellen dressed her son in, fashionable in the 1920s and 1930s, conveyed a message about class: they were summer garb whose wearers could afford to keep them clean and had the leisure for a contrasting tan, even in winter. Like the big white house in Southampton, however, the style also conveyed a message about racial identity, reinforced by the discreet presence of those black servants, whose job it was to keep the Merrills well fed, on time, and clean and white. The help included Jackson, a reserved head butler, aware of his importance; kind, imposingly handsome James, the chauffeur, who handled the fireworks on the Fourth of July; Irving, another driver, his legs wounded by shrapnel taken during World War I, when he served in a black regiment; William, a flamboyant cook who served fried chicken, black-eyed peas, okra, corn, and other southern dishes; and the head maid, Emma Davis. The family referred to their servants only by first names. Their relation to these people beside whom they lived was like Hellen's to Old Jane: intimate but remote, mutually dependent but securely hierarchical, with the family in command and their employees careful to remain in the shadows. Charlie's valet, Louis LeRoy, who had served Eddie Lynch in the same role, became a Leporello to the aging Don in the 1940s. Crossing the Atlantic by ship, Charlie introduced the brown-skinned man as a banker from Cairo so that they could travel together first class, sharing the same cabin while enjoying bourbon and smokes in the saloon. Yet the tactful servant resumed his post in private, and he made a point of never using his master's toilet.

Charlie's and Hellen's attitudes toward race were formed in the Jim Crow South of their youth, where whites and blacks lived in closer proximity, with more interaction and familiarity, but also with more potential for violence, than was common in the North. Racial segregation became the law across the South when the "separate but equal" doctrine was elaborated in 1890.

A phase of savage white reaction took hold in reply to the economic and political gains won by blacks during Reconstruction. The lynching of African Americans escalated, especially in the Cotton Belt states from Georgia to Texas, but also in Florida. As a boy in Green Cove Springs, Charlie attended the "the first legal hanging [of a black man] in Clay County." His family's relationship with "Negroes" or "coloreds" was complex. The men who robbed Dr. Merrill and left him for dead in 1902 were dark-skinned; so was the Good Samaritan who discovered him and saved his life. While he recovered, one of the rooming houses that Octavia managed was for whites, the other for blacks. Dr. Merrill always treated patients without regard to race or whether they could pay (he had treated the unfortunate man whom little Charlie saw hanged). The family took pride in the charitable work of his parents, northern-born Abigail and Riley Merrill, who taught both black and poor white children to read and write.

Charlie's family also took pride, however, in his mother's Mississippi heritage. Octavia Wilson had grown up on Round Hill Plantation, a prosperous cotton farm whose total property, comprised of 350 acres and five black slaves, was valued at $17,000 in 1860, the end of the boom years that led up to the Civil War. In the decade after the war, with abolition and the collapse of local land values, those assets were reduced by a full three-quarters when Octavia's father died at the age of forty-two, leaving her mother, Miss Emily, in charge of the farm and her eleven children. The Wilsons managed, although their reduced circumstances fed anger at the outcome of the war and a feeling of deprivation both actual and symbolic. It also promoted a nostalgic, "moonlight and roses" vision of the Old South, which Charlie, born twenty years after the end of the war, absorbed not only from his mother but from the rest of her family during the summer visits he made to Mississippi as a child. Slavery was the foundation of the lost society he learned to dream about, and there were signs of the South's "peculiar institution" all around. He met the freedmen who worked the farm under the mocking names given to them as slaves, probably by Octavia's father, the Latinist: Caesar, Scipio, Cicero, Hannibal. A hunchback named Sherman, in allusion to the Union's hated general, carried Charlie around on his hump. Green Cove Springs and Jacksonville were influenced in the 1890s by commerce with the North. In Mississippi, Charlie was in the Deep South, and it made a deep impression on him.

Buying the Orchard entailed for him a return in fantasy to Round Hill Plantation. But he wasn't done with the idea. In October 1927, just a year after purchasing Breese's house, Charlie paid $500,000 for the real thing, a plantation called Wildwood in the Mississippi Delta. "Wildwood," *The New*

York Times reported, no doubt alerted to the story by Charlie himself, "has for three-quarters of a century been a famous landing place for steamboats. It is one of the few ante-bellum plantations left intact. The big Colonial house facing the river is a fine specimen of Southern architecture. There are 4,690 acres in the tract. The new owner, it is said, intends to restore Wildwood to its former grandeur." The plantation was close to Round Hill, Charlie had visited it as a boy, and, to complete the family connection, he installed a Wilson relative to manage his cotton fields. The address of the post office—it was actually called Money, Mississippi—must have been irresistible. He planned to make it a winter retreat from New York, but the first visit that he and Hellen made was "a fiasco," she recalled. The place so little resembled what Charlie remembered, and he and Hellen had so little experience of bragging roosters and 6 a.m. calls to work, that they were glad to leave it, and "we never went back." Even so, Charlie held on to the place for a decade. He sent his sons there, on their own, for an unhappy vacation in 1936. He gave up and sold it for a sharp loss in 1938.

Charlie and Hellen preferred Palm Beach, where a smart café society with hotels and clubs had transformed the quasi-sanatorium air of the place during Charlie's youth. In 1933, he replaced his modest winter home on Brazilian Avenue with a second remarkable estate. Called "Merrill's Landing," the property stretched from Lake Worth to the Atlantic Ocean. The house and grounds designed by Howard Major featured a second-floor library with a sunset view over the lake (this, like the library at the Orchard, was a room for cocktails, not reading), curved verandas and louvered doors for cool air, a garden under tall palm trees, a strong-smelling but reputedly healthy sulfur spring that flowed into a long swimming pool, cabanas on the beach for family and guests, and a boathouse with a yacht for deep-sea fishing. In contrast to the Orchard, Merrill's Landing was modern and chic in an Art Deco style. This and the big house in Southampton would have to do for Charlie's dreams of owning a plantation.

Houses, grand houses north and south. The Merrills moved between them seasonally while trying out still other locales: Hellen and Jimmy spent a winter in Tryon, North Carolina, and another—1931—in Tucson, Arizona. Back in New York, Charlie sold the house on West Eleventh Street in 1930 and moved his family into a penthouse—it was simpler to maintain—in the Carlyle Hotel on East Seventy-sixth Street. Before it was "broken," Jimmy's home was in motion. That was one reason that the Orchard, where he spent more time than any other place, mattered so much to him. For most of his adult life, he would have two or even three addresses, and, even when he was settled in one of them for a period of time, he continued to travel almost constantly to see friends, attend opera and plays, and give poetry readings. The pattern was set in childhood.

His early schooling was unsettled, therefore. He went to first grade at St. Bernard's School in New York, then to the Palm Beach Day School, then to the Southampton Day School, and back to Palm Beach, private schools all of them. He spent two winters, 1936 and 1937, at the Arizona Desert School in Tucson, while returning to St. Bernard's for the rest of those school years, when he was ten and eleven. He stayed on an extra year at St. Bernard's, not because his grades were poor—they were good—but, his mother felt, "because he was small for his age + would be outsized physically" when he moved to boarding school in grade nine.

As that comment suggests, Hellen continued to worry about her son's size and physical strength. When she took him to Tucson in 1931, it was "on the advice of doctors" because "he suffered from ear problems + bad head colds." Once a doctor camped in the room next to Jimmy's for three days because of "the threat of a mastoid infection," which, it was feared, might damage his brain. Jimmy's health required close monitoring by his mother and the attention of the best doctors, although there was no obvious basis for ongoing concern. This too was a pattern set for the future: once Jimmy was an adult, both his letters and his mother's comment on his health and hers and exchange tips on treatments for one or another health concern. Even on his visits to her as a middle-aged man, he was regularly treated by doctors his mother recommended.

Contributing to the sense of Jimmy's delicacy was poor eyesight. When drawing, his favorite early activity, he had no difficulty. But it was hard for him to focus on an object in a shopwindow, and, Hellen noted, "Charlie, never known for an excess of patience, would simply tell Jimmy that he wasn't paying attention and not <u>trying</u> to see what Daddy was calling attention to." It was his first-grade teacher at St. Bernard's who grasped the problem and moved the boy to the front of the schoolroom so he could see the blackboard. Thick dark-framed glasses followed; these were "more of a distress to me," Hellen recalled, "than to Jimmy, who felt a tad more intellectual wearing the ugly things." The glasses meant that he was, as his mother put it, "seriously handicapped athletically." He struggled to keep them on when he ran, or he took them off and became muddled. One reason he loved to swim (the only sport he ever tolerated) was that he didn't have to keep his eye on a ball.

Jimmy hardly knew his grandfathers: Charles Morton Merrill died in

1929 at seventy-two and James Ingram in 1931 at sixty-two. Hellen's father's death was sudden and a shock, and Jimmy absorbed his mother's distress as translated into her worry about him: it was during the "scary time" of her father's death when she feared a mastoid infection might carry her son away too. Death—or, rather, the afterlife—would be a major preoccupation of his life and poetry, and there are signs of his brooding on mortality already as a young child. "Transfigured Bird," a poem from college, recalls an incident from childhood when he found a robin's egg with a dead bird's claw protruding from it. The boy took it as a sign that "there should be nothing cleanly for years to come, / Nor godly, nor reasons found, nor prayers spoken": it was a brute worldly fact giving the lie to the sweet consolations offered up in Sunday school. (The incident also figures in one of Jimmy's adolescent stories and in a play he wrote in college; he spoke about it with his friend Frederick Buechner, who was sufficiently struck by the anecdote to put a version of it in his second novel.) A story that Hellen told about her son, though cute and comic, shows the little boy working through the same idea. Jimmy came to his mother one day to ask her what the word "ephemeral" meant. "Living a very short time—there are even insects that are born and die in one day," she told him. Jimmy thought about that definition overnight and was relieved when he woke up and found himself still alive. He rushed into her bedroom the next morning, exclaiming, "Oh Mama! I'm so glad I'm not ephemeral!"

Octavia, Charlie's mother, who was in her sixties when Jimmy was born, saw him only on his winter visits to Palm Beach. Mis' Annie, however, from his birth forward, was a familiar presence in her grandson's life. The Merrills visited her in Jacksonville on their way to and from Palm Beach, where she was sometimes a guest, as she was at the Orchard. After her husband's death, she moved to New York City, where she bought an apartment at 164 East Seventy-second Street. This modest flat in a dowdy brick building on a busy street became a basic reference point for Jimmy and, in the 1980s, his primary address. (He never stopped marveling at how little his grandmother had paid for it: just $3,000.) Mis' Annie was devoted to him, as his mother was, but without Hellen's worrying and insistent, overbearing identification. Small, with a smiling, dried-apple face, long fingernails painted red, and a blue-tinged pompadour, Mis' Annie was funny, feisty, and opinionated, and not very intellectual or cultured, although she was glad to dress up for a fine dinner or an evening at the opera. As Jimmy grew into a teenager, his grandmother would be his dependable date at the Metropolitan Opera.

One of Jimmy's first letters is a thank-you note to Mis' Annie (addressed as "Dan Dan," his name for her when he was small), written just after his seventh birthday. He thanks his grandmother for her presents, a "lovly book" and a jigsaw puzzle, and reports that he's been taken to see "Alice" (a Broadway adaptation of *Alice in Wonderland*, directed by Eva Le Gallienne) and an Italian marionette performance of "Japanease operaetta" (probably a version of Gilbert and Sullivan's *Mikado*). Already his interests lie in art and intellectual things, rather than in sports or another clearly masculine pursuit. Already he is attending theater, and the musical theater in particular; already he has a taste for the miniature, the lighthearted, and the foreign.

The letter contains a sketch of the marionettes. Jimmy drew a box around them as if to say: a work of art requires a frame, a formal border. Mount Fuji is in the background; in the foreground are figures in kimonos, a costume to which he would be attracted for the rest of his life (and dressed in after death, in contrast to his father in his military uniform). Jimmy concentrates on the puppets' costumes and the strings that control them, which fill the picture. Another child might have been annoyed by the visible artifice, or failed to notice it, whereas this one focuses on it. As an adult, Merrill would take as his aesthetic ideal what he called "transparently sustained illusion," suggesting that technique and the acknowledgment of it were necessary to both the magic and the truth in art. Also noteworthy: one of the figures manipulated by strings from unseen hands above, like gods, is a small, dark-haired boy.

Any child might feel like a puppet in the grasp of his or her parents, but how much more so this boy who was subject to the commanding, frequently unseen parents he had. Puppets always fascinated Merrill; they were a ready metaphor for the human condition, since all of us are motivated, he came to feel, by forces beyond our power to recognize or understand. He played with marionettes as a child, and he created his own puppet theater at the Orchard. An elegantly printed program announced the public performance in August 1937 of Dickens's children's story *The Magic Fish-bone* by "The Jimmy Merrill Marionettes," given on behalf of the Southampton Fresh Air Home. *The Magic Fish-bone* was an ambitious production: six scenes, eight characters. A crowd of rapt children and their minders pressed close to the small proscenium, intent on the action. The eleven-year-old Jimmy took charge of "Script direction" and manipulated and gave voice to the puppets King Watkins I, the Queen, and Jerry the Announcer. Other people helped, including "Madame 'Zelly,' the famous couturier," who was credited with the costumes.

Zelly was Lilla Howard, or "Mademoiselle," as Jimmy was at first not quite able to address his governess. Over the summer, on weekends and after school, or while living with the family in Southampton and Palm Beach, Mrs. Howard was the boy's playmate and first confidante. Because of the many interruptions in his early schooling, she was his most important early teacher. She was hired in 1933 and dismissed in 1938, but they stayed in touch until she died in 1977. "I worshipped this kind, sad woman," Merrill wrote in 1982: "her sensible clothes, her carrot hair and watery eyes, the sunburnt triangle at her throat, the lavender wen on her wrist." Zelly gave him his first book of foreign postage stamps, and fussed over his ever-expanding collection with its scent of faraway places. In a curling, womanly cursive, she copied prayers and poems for him to read and memorize. She stitched costumes for his marionettes, told him stories, and helped him to make up his own.

He puzzled over her origins; she was the first of several older women whose obscure European backgrounds stimulated his fantasies and speculation. Despite the "Mademoiselle," she wasn't a spinster but a widow whose teenage daughter, Stella Maris Howard, was often in evidence (Stella managed one of the puppets in *The Magic Fish-bone*). "Neither was she French," Merrill recalled, "or even, as she led us to believe, Belgian, but part English and part, to her undying shame, Prussian." She taught Jimmy bits and pieces of both French and German. She helped him to write to "Lieber heiliger Nikolaus" with his Christmas wish list (he wanted a set of watercolors) and to Mis' Annie to wish her "une joyeuse fête de Thanksgiving." She taught him to say the Lord's Prayer in French and to sing the words to Carmen's "Habanera." She tucked him into bed bilingually: "Schlaf wohl, chéri."

This early introduction to French and German had an effect on the child. Learning to move between one language and another made language itself feel foreign, uncertain and tricky, but also intriguing, mysterious, and available for play. There were consequences even for his experience of English:

> By the time I was eight I had learned from her enough French and German to understand that English was merely one of many ways to express things. A single everyday object could be called *assiette* or *Teller* as well as *plate*—or were plates themselves subtly different in France and Germany? Mademoiselle's French and Latin prayers seemed to invoke absolutes beyond the ken of our Sunday school pageants. At the same time, I was discovering how the everyday sounds of English could mislead you by having more than one meaning. One

afternoon at home I opened a random book and read: "Where is your husband Alice?" "In the library, sampling the port." If samples were little squares of wallpaper or chintz, and ports were where ships dropped anchor, this hardly clarified the behavior of Alice's husband. Long after Mademoiselle's exegesis, the phrase haunted me. Words weren't what they seemed. The mother tongue could inspire both fascination and distrust.

Puns, anagrams, and wordplay of all kinds are a key to the imaginative play of his poetry, and Zelly put it in his hand.

Jimmy's brother Charles recalls her as "a mix of intellectual seriousness and kindness, which Jimmy wasn't getting from Hellen," who was more exacting, less well read, not at all international, and not, like Zelly, always at the boy's disposal. Even when she wasn't attending to him, however, Hellen at her desk was an image of dutiful application that influenced her son's conscientious habits as a writer. (That was one of Doris's lasting memories of her stepmother: Hellen sitting down every day to compose her thank-yous, send out invitations, answer letters, and pay bills.) And she contributed to her son's creativity in other ways. For example, like Charlie, in whom the oral culture of the South was deep, she knew how to tell a story to effect, and she could dramatize a situation in such a way as to recruit a listener to her side. Hellen was also a rhymer who wrote doggerel to please family and friends throughout her life, and she played rhyming games with her son when he was small.

Jimmy early on acquired, and as a mature poet he never gave up, the notion that a poem was writing in rhyme and meter meant to impress and entertain. In adult life, with the ease and sophistication of a Cole Porter, he wrote his own version of his mother's occasional poetry: clever rhymes for birthday cards, invitations, and inscriptions accompanying gifts. In the serious poems he collected in his books, light verse remained a resource and touchstone used to moderate his seriousness and to remind his readers of the origins of art (or at any rate his art) in children's play.

Of course, in Merrill's poetry, rhyme and meter are essential techniques that amount to much more than light verse. The mature poet's unparalleled virtuosity was the result of long training and labor. But there's an uncanny, instinctive quality to his facility that was evident from the beginning, as "Looking at Mummy" suggests. A grasp of rhythm and an ability to listen for complicated structures of sound show in the child's appreciation of classical music. That was encouraged by Zelly and by Jimmy's piano lessons, which taught him the discipline of practice and performance.

Another gift, his memory for poetic language, was developed by St. Bernard's. The Upper East Side school for boys offered a superior education, dignified and Episcopalian, with British-born masters steeped in English literature, and the memorization of poetry was a hallmark of the curriculum, starting early. For getting by heart one hundred lines of Sir Walter Scott's "Lay of the Last Minstrel," Jimmy and the rest of his first-grade glass each received an apple. He later worked up for school recitation long swaths of Longfellow's *Evangeline*, choice bits from *As You Like It*, and "The Chambered Nautilus." The pinnacle of a student's career at St. Bernard's came in the eighth grade, when it was customary for the graduating class to mount a Shakespeare play, suitably abridged.

These assignments in reading, memorization, and recitation taught students to recognize and articulate the unfolding of sense across lines of verse, modulated by meter and underlined by rhyme. The theatrical potential in reciting someone else's words excited the young Jimmy, who responded so sympathetically to puppets. In "The School Play," a poem that he wrote decades later about his eighth grade's *Henry IV, Part 2* (Jimmy was "the First Herald, 'a small part,' " but "I was small too"), Merrill describes the transformation he and his classmates underwent. These "skinny nobodies" emerged onstage "[v]ivid with character" because they'd done as they were told and learned to speak the deathless verse, putting themselves "into the masters' hands"—"the masters" being both their teachers and the poets they'd memorized.

Jimmy also wrote poems of his own. Two sentences, arranged as a rhyming quatrain, were printed in *Junior Home Magazine* when he was eight. This first published poem went: "Pushing slowly every day / Autumn finally makes its way. / Now when the days are cool, / We children go to school." Like "Looking at Mummy," this is a strikingly precocious poem from the point of view of technique and diction. That last phrase in particular, ending the poem in bland affirmation of what is customary, in which young Jimmy sees himself from a distance as part of a general category ("We children . . ."), is hardly an idiom typical of a child. Along with the poem, he submitted a sketch of a schoolhouse. The windows were perfectly straight: he'd used a ruler to make sure. When it appeared in print and the boy saw that the magazine's editors had "corrected" his effort by inserting crooked lines in place of his neat ones, "as befitted a child's drawing," he was dismayed. The lesson, Merrill remembered, "sank in: one must act one's age and give people what they expect."

The poetry he was reading, in 1935, included "The Wreck of the Hesperus," Lord Tennyson's "Lady Clare," and Scottish ballads such as "Sir

Patrick Spence" and "Lord Randal." Frances Hodgson Burnett's novel *Little Lord Fauntleroy* is the first book noted in a catalog he made in the same year of "Books that Belong in My Library." These are mainly the sort of thing we'd expect to find on a boy's bookshelf: *20,000 Leagues Under the Sea*, *The Wind in the Willows*, *Kidnapped*, *The Deerslayer*, *The Travels of Marco Polo*, *Tom Sawyer* and (one of his father's favorites) *Huckleberry Finn*, *Robinson Crusoe* (a gift from his mother that he gave to Allan Gurganus at the end of his life), and a couple of dozen more titles in handsome illustrated editions. They are notable only for being almost exclusively adventure books. In his school notebooks, we find synopses of the Siegfried legend, *The Song of Roland*, *The Cid*, *Don Quixote*, *Rip Van Winkle*, *Lohengrin*, "An Indian Legend," and John Ruskin's popular Victorian fable "The King of the Golden River." All his life he quoted fairy tales.

The curious can scan these for clues to his literary or psychological development. The main point is generic: the boy was immersed in romance and legend—the dream side of the self—to which his father, schooled in "moonlight and roses" and J. M. Barrie by his mother and grandmother, also was drawn. Charlie was perhaps ready to see his son indulge the imagination on his behalf, at least up to a point. His sponsoring influence shows itself in a typewriter given at Christmas 1934, when Jimmy was eight. But it's Hellen to whom the boy dedicates his compositions. His school notebook in English for the year 1935–36 bears a mock-formal title page: "Adventures in Writing / Illustrated by the author / Volume I / Dedicated to my best friend, my Mother / by Jimmy Merrill." Volume II is dedicated again to "the best Mother / in the world / by"—more formal this time—"James Merrill." Already, if only in a spirit of play (but what other spirit does he know?), Jimmy is thinking of himself as a writer. He sees the act of writing as an adventure, a romance, and the romance is with his mother.

As a child, Jimmy was always attended by someone: if not Hellen or Mis' Annie, then nurses, maids, Zelly, or a swimming or tennis instructor. He obviously enjoyed the company of other children: in one photo he hugs and kisses a pint-sized cashmere-coated playmate; he plays a board game with Vernon Lynch, daughter of his father's partner, in another. Birthdays came with considerable fanfare: sons of stockbrokers turned out in neckties; a pony for cheering children to ride.

So it's striking that, as an adult, he remembered his childhood as painfully lonely. That feeling may have developed after his parents' divorce. Or it may have been present already—the loneliness of a young mind engaged with private thoughts of mortality, puppets, and romantic legends. With older half-siblings who lived elsewhere most of the year, Jimmy was essentially an only child. It's also true that his family's traveling discouraged him from forming close attachments. The playdates and parties that punctuated his weekends and school vacations, which required planning in advance and deportment when they came, were compulsory ceremonies. His precocity made him expert in interests hard to share with other children. Moreover, most of the people who cared for him were paid to do so, which he must have noticed even when he was small.

His parents were leading hectic social lives. In Manhattan, there were frequent formal dinners as well as grander occasions—for instance, the dinner dance and bridge tournament hosted by the Merrills at the Plaza Hotel in honor of Mrs. Edmund Lynch, which was a party for one hundred. It was the Gatsby era, and a very heady time. Looking back on it, Hellen would recall moments of sheer exhilaration: the pleasure of standing naked in the rain on a hotel room balcony that overlooked Central Park, or the excitement of racing to a nightclub in a chauffeured car through late, deserted city streets. Part of the thrill was the experience of privilege itself, especially after the stock market crash brought so many even of the wealthy low. "I know I shouldn't be saying this," she remarked, "but if you had the money, New York could be lots of fun."

The Orchard was the center of the Merrill family's entertaining. Charlie preferred hosting to being hosted, and Hellen made all the arrangements. A note in the Southampton press gave her high marks:

> One of the most gracious women in all of Southampton is Mrs. Charles Merrill [. . .]. Pretty and chic, and with a delightful Southern manner and Southern drawl, Mrs. Merrill is a prime favorite in the younger married set, and is to be noted wherever the more notable younger matrons are foregathered. "The Orchards" is beautifully adapted to the giving of entertainments, and Mrs. Merrill makes a charming hostess.

That "delightful Southern manner and Southern drawl" were exotic in Southampton, a farming and whaling town made over in the later nineteenth century as a blue-blooded resort on the crashing Atlantic, where the Orchard, though the most central and spectacular, was only one of many grand homes. The cool summer and mild autumn of the Long Island climate and the fact that Southampton was less than three hours by train from Manhattan made it the preferred retreat for the Wall Street–connected families of bankers and lawyers who came on Friday night and left by Monday (this in contrast to the older money and greater gentility of a more distant resort like Newport, Rhode Island, where husbands might settle in for a period).

Southampton was founded in 1640 as the first English colony in what became New York State, a fact that fed into the place's snobbery as a rich WASP enclave. Jews, with whom Southampton's wealthy did business from Monday through Friday in Manhattan, were few in town, since they were excluded from membership in the local social institutions: the Beach Club, the Meadow Club for tennis, the Riding and Hunt Club, and two prestigious golf clubs, the National and Shinnecock Hills (where Charlie became a "founder member" in 1928). With her middle-class Jacksonville origins, Hellen might have been looked down upon by her northern neighbors, but she used her southernness to advantage. She hosted gatherings around the barbecue pit and became known for her southern storytelling. Some of these tales were sentimental, like her account of the gospel harmonies that surged up spontaneously from the grateful black former pupils at the funeral for Charlie's grandmother Abigail. She also had a repertoire of "black jokes," some of them quite naughty. To deliver them, she slipped into dialect as if donning blackface, no doubt titillating "the more notable younger matrons."

On summer weekends, Hellen brought in Broadway: the songwriter Hoagy Carmichael, for instance, or the actresses Helen Hayes and Gloria Swanson (the latter became Hellen's good friend). In the music room one morning, she listened while Gertrude Lawrence and George Gershwin (for Jews were welcome as guests and entertainers) worked up the hit song "Oh, Kay!" Charlie's invitations went to business partners, prospective clients, Amherst men, and old friends from the South. Harry Evans was the editor of *Family Circle*, a magazine that Charlie created to be distributed free of charge in Safeway stores; he was a regular at the house, a lively bachelor Hellen had known as a sportswriter in her Jacksonsville journalism days, perhaps gay, who was good for pairing up with the unaccompanied female. One weekend, little Jimmy shook hands with Melvin Purvis, the FBI agent who captured John Dillinger, the scariest of Depression-era bank robbers (Jimmy wrote a theme about it for school). Charlie had other prominent associates, such as John M. Woolsey, the judge who ruled in 1933 that James Joyce's *Ulysses* was not obscene and thus could be imported and sold in the U.S. In his landmark decision, Woolsey referred to two unnamed men of the world to whom he'd shown the book to test its effect on them. One of them was Charlie, who evidently gave *Ulysses* the thumbs-up.

For Jimmy, Charles, and Doris, the summer meant a round of lessons. There were lessons for everything: golf, tennis, languages, music, horseback riding (which Doris particularly loved), and boxing for the boys—when Charles would take the opportunity to punch his kid brother freely. In the afternoon, Jimmy and Charles splashed in the surf, the single activity in which there was no question about whether they were doing the thing correctly. More often, though, when he was not in a lesson or playing with Zelly, Jimmy was left to his own devices. He read and wrote, or wandered the grounds of the Orchard, where he was separated from the nearest neighbors by a busy street and acres of lawn, with the blank-eyed stone gods in the garden for company.

"Dad," Charles remembered, "arrived at the Orchard on Friday with the weekend guests, and immediately life became more interesting and a bit more dangerous." Typically Jimmy saw his father briefly when he appeared washed and scrubbed to be introduced in the library where Charlie and Hellen and their guests gathered for drinks. The little boy took most meals either with Zelly or by himself in his room. But he was present for lunch with the family on Saturday and for, as Charles experienced them, "those large deadly Sunday lunches" following church on Sunday. The table talk meandered among bridge parties and golf scores, invective about the New Deal, Civil War battles, old Mississippi personalities, and the newest fashions. Mention of anyone's illness, accident, or misfortune was forbidden. Though lulled by this sort of conversation, the children had to remain on their toes, for they might have to tell a story or make an account of themselves in front of the assembled.

Or they might be taken to task. "Charlie," Hellen observed, "was never able to reprimand his children in private," but only "before an audience." Sunday lunches were suited to this. There had been a late night on Saturday; Monday and the workweek approached; tension was building. Mostly Charlie's blowups were trivial. Jimmy carried enough uneaten spinach to his room "to astound even Popeye." (He would let the green stuff slide off his plate out the window, or flush it down the toilet. For a while he stuffed it behind the radiator, until it began to stink.) There was always a risk of Charlie's temper getting out of hand, however. His father had once whipped him when he was caught smoking in the barn; Charlie's own reprimands were verbal, and he was soft-spoken, not a shouter. But the exchange could be cutting.

Sunday lunches were preceded by highballs, accompanied by new wines with each course, and polished off with cordials—all on top of whatever had been tossed down the night before and would be consumed in the evening to come. Charlie led the way in this demanding regimen, but Hellen held her own. The pace of drinking was not unusual in an era credited with the invention of the cocktail party, and nobody was falling down drunk. But there was always a good deal of alcohol in the house, even during Prohibition (Charlie's favorite bootleg scotch was known as "Heart's Blood"); and during the meals and cocktail hours when Jimmy most often saw his father, the man was often slightly, or more than slightly, lit.

Drinking partly explains why life for the children was "more dangerous" with the Old Man around. The drinks fed his unpredictable alterations of mood: now merry, now combustible, now maudlin. In his mid-sixties, Merrill recalled his father approaching him "with tears in his eyes" to warn the nine-year-old boy against "the glass in his hand." Jimmy heeded Daddy's advice, insofar as he learned to drink in moderation. But he was attracted to people who drank heavily. He'd had training in how to deal with them. To bear up as a child living in range of his parents' liquored emotions, he had learned to keep cool and swallow his own strong feelings, if they ever arose. The strategy worked, and, as he got good at it, he learned to appreciate exciting, volatile behavior, to the point of seeking it, or at any rate tolerating it, in people close to him, including several of his lovers, but also good friends such as Chester Kallman and Elizabeth Bishop.

Doris responded to the same pressure in a related way, trying, as best she could, to be a perfect daughter. Perfectionism of one kind or another was encouraged by the environment. All those lessons were one symptom. Another was the premium placed on presentation. Charlie and Hellen and the children were used to posing with an appropriate expression for portraits by photographers and painters; a sculptor named Lazlo made a bronze head of the six-year-old Jimmy. On their twelfth birthdays, the children all received increased allowances, which rose to $100 per month at fifteen. From these funds they were expected to choose and buy their own clothes (evening clothes and coats came as Christmas and birthday gifts). Style, cleanliness, and good repair were expected from them. So was the right garment for the hour and activity. Charlie held that being well outfitted had been a key to his success in society, and he passed the idea on to his children. Over the course of a day at the Orchard, the children, like the adults, might change clothes several times, subject to Father's approval.

He was particularly strict with Doris. A chauffeur and a maid chaperoned her at parties, and Charlie inspected her himself before she went out. If a dress was wrinkled or judged wrong for the occasion, Doris went back upstairs to change. Her son Robin writes, "Charlie Merrill did not spend his lifetime courting an array of luscious women without also seeking to turn his daughter into one [. . .]. It was a control all the more insidious in that he was so good at it. He knew exactly what fabrics, colors and styles looked best on her and bought her the most stunning outfits himself. [. . .] She had it in her to be the Miss It he desired: pretty, popular, successful, and a good girl. But at the key moment her nerves invariably failed her and the pretense of being Charlie's Doris showed its insecure face. She took bad pictures not because her nose was slightly too large or her bottom teeth overcrowded, but because she had too much at stake."

Doris attended the Spence School on East Ninety-first Street and Ethel Walker, a girls' boarding school in Connecticut. She made lifelong friends wherever she went, but her grades were weak, especially in math, and school was a struggle. Charlie consoled her in a way that laid out the path ahead: "I feel confident your future husband is not going to want to see your report card when he proposes matrimony." In 1932, at the bottom of the Depression, her father gave her a coming-out party for approximately one thousand guests under tents on the lawn of the Orchard. At seventeen, she was sent to a finishing school in Florence. She returned from this happy phase to work for the Junior League and study silver connoisseurship at the Metropolitan Museum of Art. She was already an exceptionally graceful, gracious young woman, a fine dancer, with brown hair, pert chin, long neck, and blue eyes like her father's. At a dinner dance in March 1934, which Charlie hosted at the Everglades Club in Palm Beach to celebrate her twentieth birthday, Doris met the man whom she would marry.

Robert Magowan was not part of Southampton society. He was born in the mill town of Chester, Pennsylvania, in 1903. He came from modest means; his father, a descendant of Scots immigrants, was the stationmaster in town. He used a postgraduate year at the Kent School to get himself into Harvard. (A neighbor paid for that year at Kent, and Robert emulated the favor in later life by helping to fund the education of his employees.) In college, he helped support his ailing father, mother, and younger brother by taking odd jobs; he went into journalism as a stringer for the *Boston Globe*, announced Harvard football games on the radio, and became an editor of the *Crimson*, Harvard's student newspaper. He got a job after college at Macy's in New York through a college classmate, and then became the store's foreign buyer based in Paris. When he didn't get the raise he wanted, he went into advertising. The man Doris met in Palm Beach was thirty-two years old, and had already amassed personal wealth of about a quarter of a million dollars.

The wedding took place in Southampton in June 1935. The ceremony was performed at St. Andrew's Dune Church on the beach, a fanciful wooden house of worship with Tiffany windows, perfect for a fairy-tale wedding. The church was so close to the Beach Club, you could hear the cocktails tinkle when you emerged from a service. Beneath a photo of the bride, *The New York Times* devoted a paragraph to Doris's tulle and satin gown and (all was white that day) her gardenia and lily of the valley bouquet. Charlie and Hellen greeted more than six hundred guests in the music room of the Orchard, while an orchestra played on the east porch for dancing. Hellen, who had been married in her parents' parlor with a handful of guests, pitched in with enthusiasm to help Doris plan the grand occasion and make the necessary decisions, acting in place of Doris's mother. In fact, Hellen pointedly didn't invite Eliza Church to the reception. "What would Southampton think of me?" she asked, as if the town might disapprove and that somehow mattered more than what Doris thought and felt. Jimmy, nine years old that June, presented the wedding couple with a ballad. The poem, his most polished effort from childhood, ended in a spirit of cheerful, inane redundancy: "When they were married, they were glad, / And very glad were they. / I am sure they will always remember, / Their joyful wedding day."

Some marriages remove the bride from her family. This one brought the groom into the bride's. In Robert Magowan, Doris gave her father a son prepared to serve the Old Man in ways his own sons would never be. (Jimmy and Charles might have resented him for taking their place at Charlie's side, but in the long run they would be grateful to him.) He was known in the family as "Bobby." His monogram was RAM. He had a sharp, thin nose and a square, determined face, with blue eyes like Charlie's. He was taller than Charlie, but not by much. When he served in tennis at the Meadow Club, he made a comic impression by jumping with both feet off the ground, turning red in the face, and grunting. He was brisk in everything he did. He expected those around him to be as decisive, speedy, and efficient as he was, whether at home or the office, and he barked when they weren't. He was honest, direct, prudent, and just as hard a worker as Charlie, without Charlie's penchant for playing the rake or the rascal. Like Charlie, he believed that business was the business of America, and it was a virtuous thing to turn a profit. Like Charlie, Bobby made anti-Semitic remarks, and he would fight long and hard against unionized labor when he had to. He was made to be Charles Merrill's lieutenant.

Bobby joined Merrill Lynch after his honeymoon in Cuba. He and Charlie bonded on trips to distant branches of the firm; they shared hotel rooms out of companionship more than convenience, and sent jointly signed letters back to New York. Then Charlie set the newlyweds up in a home high atop Nob Hill in San Francisco; Bobby was sent across the bay to Oakland to work for Safeway—where, ultimately, after returning to Merrill Lynch for a long period as a senior partner, he would become the grocery chain's CEO. Robin, who was born to Bobby and Doris in 1936, sums up the merger that had taken place: "One can see those two men, with their not dissimilar backgrounds, conspiring while the heiress was sold, or rather transferred from one ledger to another." It was so, except that the heiress had had a hand in the deal. For the marriage served her purposes as well as theirs. By marrying Bobby, Doris not only pleased Charlie. She had chosen a man who would help her and her father remain as close as possible.

At nine in "My Autobiography," a theme composed for school, Jimmy wrote that he liked Southampton "better than any place I have been, because my Irish Setters, Bahne and Michael, are kept there." He was well stocked with pets (tropical fish, a turtle, a pony), but the setters were the most important. He pasted into his schoolbook a photo of Bahne and Michael cavorting with him. The sleek dogs were kenneled below his bedroom window. They liked to leap on him, paws on his shoulders, licking his face, jostling his heavy glasses. Fiery, impulsive barkers, dashing off when they had a chance to, they were associated in his mind with his father. They raced up and down the long hallways of the house, whining for Charlie—who loved his red setters inordinately, especially Mike. When Mike was hit by a car and killed, "Charlie sobbed like a child and for weeks was inconsolable," Hellen recalled. The result was a portrait in oil of Michael placed just inside the front door, the first thing to be noticed on entering the Orchard.

Jimmy's delight in the dogs' loud, unruly, free-flowing affection hints at how much pressure he felt to be on good behavior, and how restrained the adults around him normally were. The servants, leading their lives out back or just down the hall, made for an intriguing contrast with his family. Looking for food and attention, Jimmy liked to wander into the kitchen where they congregated. These people were as familiar to him, and as trusted, as anyone in his young life. Emma often took care of him; he would remember her strong arms, her dark skin, and the steaming soups she carried to his room when he was sick. In a sad, rather stiff poem from the 1980s called "The Help," Merrill recalls being "the white / Small boy" on her lap: rich with "common scents. Starch, sweat, snuff, they excite / Me still." Other sensations were impressed on him in the garage when he saw good-natured James, the chauffeur, return from a fistfight with his shirt off and blood streaming down his broad back.

While Zelly introduced Jimmy to foreign languages, the servants made him conscious of his race and class and curious about theirs. Allowed backstage, he watched them arrange themselves in a tableau of purposeful activity whenever their employers appeared, showing that they "Knew Their Place." He could sense if not explain the power of the "Gods they lived by"—for instance, "the Numbers Man" standing "Supremely dapper in the porchlight" as he waited to collect their bets. These people weren't particularly mysterious, however. In fact, the opposite: cooking and cleaning or driving a car were practical activities a boy noticed and appreciated, as opposed to Daddy buying and selling at the office, or Mama writing place cards at her desk. And the servants always made time for him. They were "physically warm, instinctive, *real*."

Not that Jimmy felt more at home in their quarters than he did in the rest of the house, or that he ever came to know the inner lives of Emma, James, and the rest. But the experience of growing up on terms with them made him aware of parallel societies and the clashing perspectives produced by class, each with its claim to the truth. It prepared him for the high/low, upstairs/downstairs comedies to which he would be attracted in Mozart, Shakespeare, and even some aspects of the Ouija board—and which he would create his own version of in his household arrangements in Stonington and Athens. It equipped him for the "double life" he would lead as an adult who, without ever giving up the social position he was born into, often sought warmth, acceptance, and companionship, indeed love, from people of a lower social class.

The household that his parents had constructed gave him an intimate view of social inequality and racism. He never shared his parents' strong racial prejudice. Yet he never challenged it in his own choices except in so mild a way as to make a few African American friends over the course of his life. This was in contrast to his brother Charles, who made racial justice a major theme of his life's work, and in contrast to Jimmy's partner David Jackson, for whom racial equality was a deeply felt political concern. Still, it was not an accident that the psychiatrist Merrill relied on in the turbulent last decade of his life, Jeanette Aycock, was black and a woman.

Contrary to popular belief, the rich don't always sleep easy. That class difference carried creeping danger with it was brought home to Jimmy as a young boy after the kidnapping of the infant son of Charles Lindbergh, "Lucky Lindy," the national hero who made the first solo flight across the Atlantic. The child was snatched from his crib in New Jersey in March 1932 (two days before Jimmy's sixth birthday) and found nearby, murdered and dismembered, two months later. The case obsessed the nation and New York in particular. Reports about real and fake ransom notes and the search for the kidnappers unfolded in the newspapers as a terrible public melodrama. There was thought to be a kidnapping ring at work in the New York region, and they, or copycats inspired by them, might strike again with another prominent family as their target.

The case especially affected the Merrills because Charlie and Hellen were friends with Dwight Morrow, a J. P. Morgan banker, diplomat, and Amherst man, and his daughter Anne, who was Mrs. Lindbergh. The privileged isolation of the Orchard, which might have made the family feel safe, made them feel vulnerable instead, and they took precautions against kidnappers. The groundskeeper carried a revolver. Charles and Jimmy slept in the same room, although twenty others were available, and neither boy was allowed to go out alone. For a time, Charles attended the Arizona Desert School in Tucson, where he was sent for a taste of outdoor life, with saddles to polish and a cowboy hat and chaps to wear. Jimmy was sent there too, the idea being to put him somewhere safe for the winter, far from the shadowy agents plotting to steal the boy and force Daddy to pay—that is, if Daddy really loved him.

What his parents taught him to fear, Jimmy learned to desire. Or so Merrill himself decided, looking back on the way that the Lindbergh kidnapping fanned the flames of his youthful fantasy life and the adult eroticism that grew out of it. "Days of 1935," written in 1970, is a long, canny, comic exercise in self-analysis. It recalls how as a boy Jimmy dreamed of being plucked from his home and held for ransom by a gangster and his moll. Like the servants, Floyd and Jean gratify him simply by paying attention to him. (Floyd has an easy time grabbing the child because his parents are "out partying.") It's not hard for him to be a prisoner: he's used to taking orders and sitting quietly. He listens in fascination to the kidnappers' 1930s, working-class, cops-and-robbers slang:

> "Gimme—Wait—Hey, watch that gun—
> Why don't these dumb matches work—
> See you later—Yeah, have fun—
> Wise guy—Floozie—Jerk—"

A fresh, vital way of being emanates from this rough-edged talk, which was forbidden to the boy Merrill had been (busy learning his French and German) but was nonetheless familiar to him from the radio, the movies, and New York City streets. As expressed in their speech, Floyd and Jean have a no-nonsense approach to everything they do, which is limited to the basics: sleeping, eating, and sex. The boy, lying awake on the floor beside the crooks' bed, overhears this last in arousing detail.

Jean is considerate of him, and likes to listen to his stories. But "Lean, sallow, lantern-jawed" Floyd is the prime object of his interest—rough and powerful, with masculinity to spare, as represented by his pistol and cartridge belt, by the "prone tango" he performs on top of Jean, and by the bruise he leaves on her cheek after a slap to the face. One night, while Jean snoozes, Floyd lies down next to the boy, cuddles up to him, and masturbates. Before the situation can get any worse (that is, any more exciting), the hoodlums are caught, put up for trial, and, when he sits down in the witness box, betrayed by the boy who had fallen in love with them: "You I adored I now accuse . . ."

It's unlikely that all of this ran through Jimmy's head at nine, but bits and pieces of it must have, and Merrill used them much later to explain the direction his adult desires took. The poem suggests that, even as Jimmy was drawn to his mother with the sort of submerged sexual excitement we see in "Looking at Mummy," the depth of his identification with her left him feeling a lack in another department, a deficit in masculinity that was expressed in his attraction to Floyd, who is both the coarse, working-class opposite of Charlie and merely Charlie in disguise. The poem reminds us too that Jimmy grew up with a problem that he would always have: his wish to be loved was bound up with the question of what he was worth. The fantasy kidnappers were hardly the only ones to put the question in terms of cash. Plenty of friends, throughout his life, would eye him in the same way.

Merrill sets the poem in 1935 rather than closer to the time of the Lindbergh kidnapping. The case had dragged on for two years by the time that a culprit, Bruno Richard Hauptmann, stood trial for murder in 1935; when his appeals failed in 1936, Hauptmann was electrocuted. So the crime remained in the news throughout the middle 1930s, which is reason enough for Merrill to have set the poem in 1935. But the year was significant for the Merrill family, as the time of Doris's wedding. The buildup to that event preoccupied the household for months, and Doris was Jimmy's adored older sister. In school at the time, he was learning about the ballad—the verse form he used when he wrote his wedding poem presented to Bobby and Doris, "the prince and princess." Merrill returns to the ballad form in "Days of 1935," making it a revision of that well-behaved childhood effort; it focuses on the themes of love and money, power and desire, that were kept out of sight in the grand white wedding, and yet underlay it. "Days of 1935" also suggests that, when he fit himself into the heterosexual, fairy-tale scenario that his sister and her fiancé were extravagantly playing out, Jimmy didn't imagine himself as the shining knight, but as the damsel in distress. In "Days of 1935," Floyd gags the little captive with his hand, and carries him off "Trailing bedclothes like a bride."

In "Days of 1935," the kidnapped boy sees photos of his parents in the newspaper: his mother is armored behind her fashionable accessories ("gloved, / Hatted, bepearled, chin deep in fur") and Daddy is "glowering." Speaking for his young self, Merrill asks about his father, "was it true he loved / Others beside her?" It's hard to say exactly when the question first came up for Jimmy. In the early 1930s, Charlie carried on a dalliance with Dottie Stafford, Hellen's best friend in Southampton, who was widowed when her husband killed himself after the Crash. Hellen discovered her husband in bed with Mrs. Stafford when Mike led her to the room, just as the red setter had led Jimmy to hers. Whether or not there were other infidelities, Hellen lived with the threat of them. "Women friends were a necessity to Charlie Merrill," she wrote in her 1953 memoir. "He always had more women friends than men friends. He was naturally attractive to them, and when it came to 'courtin',' he was unsurpassed." Charlie was never one to keep a secret in this or any other department of life, and he bragged about his catnip-like charm—for example, to his son Charles: "Women go wild, simply wild over me."

There were other tensions at work in the marriage. In "The Broken Home," Merrill imagines overhearing his parents talking after a party on the gravel drive outside the Orchard. "They love each other still":

> She: Charlie, I can't stand the pace.
> He: Come on, honey—why, you'll bury us all!

It's a conversation between two runners in a killer race. Probably their life together felt like that, and appeared that way to their son. Charlie and Hellen were both competitors—a quality that drew them together; but they couldn't help competing with each other too. After dinner at the Orchard with nothing else planned, Charlie would tell Hellen to stir up company, and, after a few telephone calls, the Merrills and whoever was free at the last minute would play bridge far into the night. They played cards as partners in Southampton bridge tournaments and often brought home a "silver matchbox," the first-place trophy. But Hellen, who was more experienced and had more time to hone her skill, was a better player than Charlie, which she didn't try to conceal. Low-level rivalry also showed at the dinner table. When Charlie was telling a story, Hellen would interrupt him—"No, you're telling it wrong"—and then show their company how to tell it right.

Doris learned her taste in interior design from Hellen; Hellen might have learned from Doris that it was wise not to contradict Charlie. Hellen was no suffragette, but she was too proud to be at ease in the subordinate role of an important man's wife; and even as he was attracted to her modern ways, Charlie was irritated by them too. They'd always kept a certain distance from each other. In his notebooks at nine and ten, Jimmy drew up plans for houses, ones he lived in and others he dreamed up; his parents each have their own bedroom, which is what he was used to. In one of his architectural sketches, Daddy gets a "sleeping porch" next to Mama's bedroom. Did that arrangement represent for Charlie a greater-than-usual intimacy with his wife, or did it mean the doghouse? In any case, their adjacency is the point. In Jimmy's childhood photo album, there are very few pictures of his parents together.

After their marriage had fallen apart, Hellen wrote to Charlie regretting "how miserably unhappy you must have been the last 6 yrs. we were together." She didn't say how she felt during the same period, or why he might have been so miserable. For his part, Charlie complained about Hellen's "shell." Probably he meant the regal front seen in her formal portraits; she must have retreated behind that practiced pose, mustering all her dignity, after her discovery of his affair with Dottie Stafford. In any case, by the mid-1930s, there was serious trouble in the house. "A marriage on the rocks," Merrill calls it in "The Broken Home," inviting us to picture his parents clutching their highballs, as the ship foundered. Charlie and Hellen both had a theatrical side, and there were scenes. During their divorce proceedings, they argued over why Charlie had once locked Hellen in a closet, not whether he had.

They were on the way to repeating the fate of Charlie's first marriage, only this time in a more florid, gossip-worthy form. In 1936, Hellen found a perfumed note on her husband's dresser. It had come from a petite brunette named Kinta Des Mares. Kinta was a belle from New Orleans, just Hellen's age, as sultry as Charlie now found Hellen cold, and he fell violently in love with her. During May and June of that year, Miss Des Mares took a room in the New Weston Hotel in Midtown Manhattan, where Charlie visited her daily between three and four in the afternoon; he would return to the hotel in the evening, and they would go out to a nightclub. These and other details of their routine came to light when Josephine Skraback, the day maid on the nineteenth floor of the New Weston, was deposed by Hellen's lawyers. "I really regarded KINTA DESMARE and MR. MERRILL as an extremely happy couple," Mrs. Skraback explained.

As usual, the Merrills decamped from Manhattan to Southampton in June 1936. In August, Charlie and Hellen traveled to San Francisco to be present for the birth of Doris and Bobby's first child, Robert Anderson Magowan Jr., who would be known as Robin (and who, like his uncle Charles, never adopted the "Jr."). For a while it seemed that the trip, which they made without Charles and Jimmy (this was the unhappy summer the boys were sent to Wildwood to discover the pleasures of plantation life), might patch things up. As a much older woman, Hellen told Jimmy about a romantic dinner that she and Charlie had at the "21" club in Manhattan around this time. Over champagne, Charlie declared that he was going to give up his mistress and turn over a new leaf with Hellen. "As always," Merrill writes, retelling the story, "my father believes his words. So does my mother." But as they held hands in the car home, resolved now to be "closer than ever," Charlie mused, as if to himself, "But God, I sure do love that little girl." It was too much for Hellen. "My heart simply turned to ice," she said. "When we got home I collapsed, I fell to the floor. He had to call a doctor." Before the game was over, Kinta had more cards to play. The false pregnancy and threatened suicide that ensued were time-worn ploys but winners that sufficed to bind Charlie to her. He moved into the Ritz when Kinta was in town that spring, so as to be "considerate" of Hellen. By June 1937, when Charlie wrote a brief letter informing Hellen that he was about to sail to Europe with Kinta, their marriage was effectively over, and a long, rancorous divorce process was about to begin.

Hellen summoned her eleven-year-old son into her bedroom to show him his father's letter. Having already been to the theater enough to suppose he knew how to act in such a situation, Jimmy read it, then let the page float from his fingers to the floor. "Oh, don't be dramatic," Hellen scolded, who had her own ideas about how to act. As recounted by Merrill decades later, the scene is more comic than tragic. But no one was smiling at the time. In their shared desertion, Hellen and Jimmy were left to face each other in her bedroom, abandoned to a charged, stagy intimacy.

Of course, however precocious an actor he may have been, Jimmy was still a tender child who didn't wholly grasp the situation. He wondered why his father had left him without saying goodbye and "why he cried and acted so strangely." "Mummy," he asked, "does Daddy like someone better than he does you?" Hellen had been "tortured and tormented for so long" over the state of her marriage that she could hardly answer. As angry and aggrieved at Charlie as she was and had every right to be, she tried to keep those feelings in check for the sake of her son and for her stepchildren and the future of her relationships with them. She wrote to Doris,

> Your father has not meant to hurt me and he is truly sorry
> for all that has happened these past several years. And I would
> be willing to take not only my share, but all of the blame if by
> so doing, he could be happy. I loved Charlie so completely for

twelve years and never caused him the slightest embarrassment where another man was concerned, but fidelity is old-fashioned and doesn't seem to count any more.

You both [Doris and Bobby] have been close to my heart for a long time now and I want you to remain there. And God spare you from such a tragedy as this.

Relaxing on board ship, Charlie addressed his son:

At Sea, July 2, 1937

Dear Jim:

Here on this big boat, lying in the sun near a swimming pool I have had plenty of time to think and rest and remember.

And among my most pleasant memories are those of our breakfasts together at Palm Beach when all the gang had fled.

I like to think of the strides forward you have made this year and I wish that you could have been spared the strain of watching hearts break.

But, as I told you, it is your duty to play a man's part even though you are only a little boy in some respects.

Boys, no older than you have carried messages in times of war and at a great peril of their lives.

You can do anything and be all that is fine and brave and good if you set your mind to it. This is the time for you to show the stuff you are made of.

So please be of good courage and especially loving and kind to your mother.

And keep an open mind about your daddy for that is only fair. My mistakes have been errors of judgment, not of the heart. Surely you can understand that.

I hope you will have a nice summer and I know you will love inspecting your nephew, seeing Doris and Bobby and having fun with them.

My love to Zellie and a great big hug and kiss to you.

Your loving Daddy

Although he usually called him "Jimmy," Charlie chose the more grown-up "Jim" here. Requiring a premature heroism from the boy and telling him to soldier on was a way not to deal with him emotionally and allow that he might have a legitimate complaint. Charlie later thought sufficiently well of this composition to send a copy to Jimmy (who hadn't kept the original) to be placed in the scrapbook that Charlie expected him to keep. How could a child react to such a message, except to conclude that he was more alone in the world than he had thought?

Summer 1937: Jimmy was busy preparing for his marionette performance of *The Magic Fish-bone*, which must have kept him from thinking too much about anything else. But it wasn't merely a distraction: Dickens's fairy tale suggested a fantasy resolution to the Merrill family's problems. Manipulating King Watkins, who is out of money and unable to feed his family, and the Queen, who is ill and must be cared for by her eldest child, Jimmy pulled strings for a husband and wife fallen on hard times. The story turns on a magic fish bone good for granting wishes in an emergency and then the arrival of a kindly godmother (Mis' Annie? Zelly?) who sets everything right. It was meant to cheer up handicapped children in Southampton belonging to a charity in which Hellen was active, but her son needed consolation too. He was powerless to keep his family from falling apart, but he could write a script for his puppets, and make them do what he wished. "Art. It cures affliction," Merrill wrote in the late lyric "Farewell Performance." Already, at eleven, he was testing that cure.

That same summer, Jimmy was introduced to the art form that, besides poetry, would mean the most to him. In the music room at the Orchard one morning, a new friend of Hellen's, Carol Longone, sat him on the bench beside her at a grand piano (one of two in the room) and played through the score of Leoncavallo's *verismo* opera *Pagliacci*, while making comments on the music, the drama, the staging, and the interaction of these elements. It was his first taste of grand opera, and it captivated him. The story concerns a troupe of comic actors. In the prologue, to a melody that Merrill would always find "unspeakably beautiful," the clown Tonio addresses the audience. Although he and his fellow players perform stock roles, he warns the operagoer not to think their tears artificial: "We have human hearts, beating with passion!" As the opera proceeds, sexual desire and jealousy erupt when the actors put on a comic play about adultery (a foolish husband, a young rival for the wife's affection), the real takes over, and one of the clowns murders his wife and her lover. *Pagliacci* involved comic types Jimmy knew from the puppet theater, but it was closer to the drama his parents were living than to *The Magic Fish-bone*.

Jimmy had a high-level guide in Carol Longone. A Floridian by birth, she had an intriguing, operatic story of her own, having been married to an impresario and "Lived Abroad." She was a skilled pianist who had been on tour as an accompanist with premier artists like the soprano Rosa Raisa and the tenor Beniamino Gigli. She was best known for her "capsule concentrate" versions of grand operas called "Operalogues." Presented in hotels and clubs from New York City to the hinterlands, these events were a "fitting prelude to the literature of opera, an enticement to those who would learn of opera without travail," the *Toledo Blade* wrote. "Mrs. Longone explains and plays, cues in her singers"—the mostly young but expert singers she collaborated with—"and calls upon the imaginations of her audience to engender the scenes she describes." This is what she did with Jimmy, who began weekly piano lessons with her that fall. Longone meanwhile became a friend to Hellen and Jimmy both. After the death of Charlie's sister Edith, who had been Jimmy's godmother, she took on that role.

When the fall season of the Metropolitan Opera opened, Jimmy had a seat for every production. Looking back on his youthful fandom, Merrill wrote, "[O]pera was from the start an education less musical than sentimental. [. . .] Why else had we paid (or our mothers paid for us) to hear Violetta suffer, Wotan turn upon his wife, and Gilda disobey her father?" The sentiments he was experiencing were vivid, even wildly passionate, but expressed through stylized roles, long rehearsed, and performed with poise and discipline before an audience for applause. As in the case of *Pagliacci*, opera made him aware of art's potential to give voice to the most powerful feelings—and aware of the rhetorical, performed nature of any expression of such feeling. It was a way to study, within the safe frame of the proscenium, the passions and intrigues that his parents had set before him at home. Opera's people were prey to primitive, dreamlike violence, but always as an effect of visible artistic choices (stage business, lighting, props), and their characters were safely caricatures—larger than life, just as his puppets were smaller.

With Carol at the keyboard and Hellen or Mis' Annie as his escorts at the Metropolitan, opera was for Jimmy a woman's world, and he was drawn to the strongest women on the stage. In Wagner's *Ring* cycle, he was fascinated not by the sword-wielding Siegfried, but by Brünnhilde, whom Siegfried awakens from the circle of fire in which she sleeps (the Sleeping Beauty story again). Jimmy heard a twenty-five-year-old Erich Leinsdorf conduct *Die Walküre* at the Met in 1938. Kirsten Flagstad sang the heroine's role. According to the *Herald Tribune*, the Norwegian blonde was "the greatest singer in the world." She immediately became Jimmy's favorite, and merged in his mind with this role. Brünnhilde is the Valkyrie who gives up immortality for human love, which she perceives as her father Wotan's will, though he opposes her, and her actions will bring about his downfall. In *A Different Person*, Merrill looks back on his early infatuation with this woman warrior: "Her love threw a wrench into the entire celestial machinery; when the flames died down and the Rhine subsided"—at the end of the cycle in *Götterdämmerung*—"nothing was left but the elemental powers that prevailed long before the gods (narrow-minded nouveaux riches, like the people we knew in Southampton) sprang up to embody them."

As that remark about Southampton nouveaux riches suggests, there were analogies for young Jimmy to draw, if only subliminally at this point, between Wagner's people and his own family, who were blessed and cursed by their gold. Flagstad's Brünnhilde was an ambiguous figure for the boy to identify with—a rebel who would burn down her father's house (Valhalla), but redeem it too, singing all the while. To admire her as fiercely as Jimmy did was a not-so-covert gender rebellion. "Next to the powers of such a woman," he continues in *A Different Person*, "all male activity—Siegfried's dragon slaying, Einstein's theorizing, the arcana of password and sweat lodge—seemed tame and puerile. I longed throughout adolescence to lead my own predestined hero, whose face changed every month, into music's radiant abyss."

That cautiously homosexual fantasy lay somewhat in the future. Just barely advancing on puberty, Jimmy tried on various identities, like any eleven- or twelve-year-old. On the Upper East Side after school on Tuesday and Friday, he wore the uniform of the Knickerbocker Grays, the society cadet corps in which he learned to march in step with other boys of good families. At the Arizona Desert School over the winter, he donned a cowboy hat and spats and rode among saguaro cactus. In Florida over spring break, he went deep-sea fishing—a thrill for him—and he displayed his impressive catch, a little Hemingway.

All that year he'd seen his father only once, for a lunch in New York. He wrote to CEM in Florida after his twelfth birthday:

Dear Daddy:

How are you? I hope you are having a good time with Doris + Bobby + Charles. Caught any more sailfish?? It's a pity Robin could not come. He would love it.

This Saturday I am going to "Carmen" at last. It will be my 18th opera. That ends the winter season at the Metropolitan. Then I'll have to go to the Hippodrome. My first there are "Cavalleria Rusticana" + "Pagliacci."

I got some swell stamps with the 12 dollars.

School is getting along O.K. I shot a bulls eye at shooting class.

Sunday I am going to an Operatic Program in commemoration of Martinelli's 25th year with the Met. (I think I told you that before.)

Much love to you, Doris, Bobby, Charles.

Jimmy

Despite the bull's-eye, Charlie wasn't pleased by his son's progress. In reply he enumerated for Jimmy the many small jobs he'd held by the time he was twelve. "There never was a time when I did not have my own money, in my own pocket. By my own money, I mean money that I worked for, and earned by my own efforts." Jimmy showed no interest in making money or in any number of other activities his father felt a boy ought to like. Charlie wrote to Ed Wilson, a Mississippi relative living in New York, asking him to spend time with Jimmy. "I'm particularly anxious to have someone develop Jimmy's interest in things that most boys like—hockey, football, boxing, sight-seeing, visits to Museums, the Aquarium"—Charlie gathered momentum as he thought about it—"the Statue of Liberty, Grant's Tomb, and the many wonderful and interesting things there are to see and learn in and around New York City. Jimmy has plenty of people who can take him to the Opera, and encourage the development of his aesthetic side, but he has no one who will kick him around, and make a man out of him."

While wanting to make a man out of Jimmy through this proxy, Charlie worried that his son had somehow gotten "the fool idea that I don't love him." In preparation for the boy's summer visit to the Orchard in 1937, which would be reduced to a month this year, Charlie wrote to Charles, "[P]lease keep in mind that this particular summer Jimmy Merrill is the family's problem child. I am very hopeful that between all of us"—the Merrills and the Magowans—"we can handle this boy without him ever knowing it, to the end that he will have had a grand four weeks visit on the one hand, and will have been set on the right path on the other." This didn't mean he wanted "to have Jimmy love his mother less," only that "I want him to be at ease with me, and to be on affectionate and good-natured terms with all the other members of the family." Whether or not Jimmy loved his father was involved now with the question of his interests, and Charlie came back to it: "I am glad that Jimmy likes music, books, painting, the opera, etc., but I think his routine is bad because it is not well balanced. [. . .] I think a balanced regime, for a normal boy of twelve, should be about one part for the aesthetic side [. . .] and three parts outdoors bumming with other boys."

Behind Charlie's anxiety about his son's gender identity, and the confusion Jimmy himself must have felt about his alliances with his parents, was the tug-of-war of a raging divorce. In fall 1937, when she and Jimmy left the Orchard for the Carlyle Hotel, his mother arranged for furniture and other items to be trucked from Southampton to the city; when Charlie's lawyers challenged her about this action, she itemized her haul and justified each entry. Next, she served Charlie with papers suing for a separation on grounds of his "cruelty and habitual intemperance"—the first step toward divorce. Charlie responded with a notice in a New York newspaper saying he would no longer be responsible for his wife's bills. Then, trying to turn the tables on Hellen, he enlisted the help of the FBI man Mel Purvis and had his wife spied on, with notation made when she met with a man. This research, leaked to the newspapers, produced public speculation about her relations with one Henri di Sabour and "an unnamed Brazilian diplomat." Meanwhile, Emma had gone with Hellen to serve her and Jimmy. But Emma was in Charlie's pay and reported to him on Hellen's mail and her comings and goings; when Hellen caught her at it, she fired her. Emma would later confess all in a tearful scene witnessed by Jimmy.

In the midst of these maneuverings, Charlie asked Hellen to permit Jimmy to visit him at Merrill's Landing in spring 1938. Jimmy was being used by Hellen, though she denied it, as a bargaining point. She replied to Charlie,

> It is no more my desire now than it has ever been to keep you and Jimmy apart. The fact of the past eight months would indicate that you have no particular wish to see Jimmy since you have only requested to see him once despite your frequent visits to New York at which times you have not even telephoned him.
>
> Now that you request to have him visit you in Palm Beach during his Easter vacation, I feel that it is only natural for me to prefer to keep him with me. You told him in a recent communication that he was now "the head of the family." I regard him in this light. I find myself more completely alone than I have ever been in my life and am reluctant to part with him. However, I would not be so unwilling if you and I could come to some understanding, exclusive of legal advice, as to where this sordid mess is to end.

Hellen was willing to let Charlie see Jimmy in New York, but not to send him "1000 miles away from me to visit you and whomever you might have staying with you at the time." She continued, "Since I have assumed practically all of the financial responsibility of Jimmy since you deserted me in June [. . .] and ALL of the moral responsibility of his upbringing, I feel that I am justified in keeping him with me."

Charlie filed his countersuit for divorce with its flimsy charges of infidelity in May 1938. Around this time Eddie Lynch died of a sudden heart attack in London, and Charlie, deeply grieving, lost his appetite for a battle he knew he wasn't going to win. He started communicating with Hellen, she changed her tone, and eventually their lawyers drafted child custody and financial arrangements agreeable to all parties. Doris quietly intervened to assure that Hellen's settlement was better than Eliza's had been. Hellen and Jimmy appeared in a photo—she smiling, he openmouthed as if dazed—in the *Daily Mirror* on February 23, 1939, under the headline "Awarded Custody of Her Son" in a story misleadingly titled "Friendly Divorce Parts the Merrills." In the *New York Journal-American*, the society pundit "Cholly Knickerbocker" wrote,

> Now that the final curtain has been rung down, in the Florida courts, on the Charles Merrill domestic drama, you can expect "Charlie" Merrill to select another wife, while Helen [*sic*] Merrill, who won her divorce decree—and complete vindication—will devote her time to the Merrill son, whose custody she has. The Merrill divorce was, indeed, a tragic happening. Here were two people who came up from the ranks to achieve a pleasant position in the Southampton set, only to spoil everything when the green-eyed monster reared its ugly head. The charges and counter-charges in the Merrill case scandalized all those who had welcomed the Merrills into the social ranks. And wrecked everything the Merrills had struggled to obtain.

Charlie was indeed ready to "take another plunge into the matrimonial seas." He wedded Kinta almost as soon after his divorce from Hellen as he'd married Hellen after his divorce from Eliza.* Jimmy was not invited to the ceremony. Sounding, at thirteen, immensely older than the boy who'd written about the opera season and his bull's-eye a year before, he congrat-

---

* The Merrills' divorce was granted on February 22 in Jacksonville, where Charlie had divorced Eliza Church. See "Divorces Charles Merrill," *NYT* (February 23, 1939). Charlie married Kinta Des Mares on March 8. See "Society Notes," *Southampton Press* (March 3, 1939), 8.

ulated his father in a frank but forgiving letter. Charlie could have dictated it, and Hellen probably did:

> Daddy, I do wish you happiness, because I have always felt that you have never gotten your full share of it. And now, you are taking a third try at life and I hope you will be successful.
>
> You refer to me taking this like Doris in 1925. In 1925 there were totally different proceedings, but now that the battle has worn off, I have no hard feelings toward you. I can only wish that you will at last, be happy and that you will not regret anything.

Hellen emerged from her ordeal smiling for the newspapers but with her social capital much diminished. When she visited her son in Southampton in the midst of her divorce proceedings in July 1938, it merited a notice in the *New York World-Telegram*: "Mrs. Charles E. Merrill is arriving here today to be the guest of Mrs. Goodhue Livingston. Society interprets this bit of news as a great personal triumph for Mrs. Merrill. Mrs. Livingston is acknowledged the social arbiter of Southampton." Even so, society didn't rally around Hellen. She discovered that for twelve years she'd been hosting at the Orchard not her friends but her husband's, or people who now hoped to remain his friends: she could do nothing for them but give them a chance to prove their loyalty to him by snubbing her. Her "black jokes" and barbecue pit were things of the past.

In September, Hellen drove up the gravel to the Orchard to collect her son. If there was a moment when James Merrill's childhood ended, this was it. They drove back to New York—Hellen herself took the wheel these days—through increasingly furious rain, the windshield wipers flailing, the two of them anxiously peering ahead, alone together in the car. Only the next day did they learn that they'd driven through the 1938 hurricane. The most devastating storm ever to strike the region, with twenty-foot waves and winds gusting over 150 miles per hour, the hurricane drove water and sand through the walls of the Beach Club and St. Andrew's Dune Church, sweeping away organ and pews, destroying the sanctuary where Doris and Bobby had been married. The property damage and loss of life across eastern Long Island and the New England coast were terrible and historic. Yet, before long, with the money to manage it, the Beach Club and St. Andrew's would be beautifully repaired.

2

COSTUMES AND MASKS

1939–49

O ur son has suffered more than you have any idea," Hellen wrote to Charlie, bitterly, in 1938. Jimmy had indeed suffered, and it was probably true that his father had no idea how much, preoccupied as he was with his son's growing interest in the "aesthetic side" of life. Probably Jimmy himself didn't know what he felt. Suddenly called on by both parents to stand up as "head of the family," whatever that meant, he had simply thrown himself headlong into the Metropolitan Opera season. His beloved Zelly, who might have found a way to sound his feelings and assure him that not everything had changed, was let go that June: Hellen couldn't pay to keep her any longer, and Charlie wouldn't. Apparently it was time to grow up.

Compared to other forms of suffering and deprivation, the breakup of a wealthy child's home may not count for very much. But for James Merrill, it opened a rift in the world that would never be repaired. Divorce, far less common at the time than it is today, was stigmatizing for children as well as their parents; to be the child of a "broken home" amounted to a diagnosis. The boy's distress was manifest in lower than normal marks at St. Bernard's and a notable weight gain. Around this time, Jimmy begins to look away from the camera, blank and distracted, whereas, when he was smaller, he'd smiled and mugged for it, the happy center of attention. His glasses had become a shield. His upper lip, by nature lifted, revealed a chipmunk's front teeth and gave his face a slight, involuntary sneer (or, when he managed to close his lips tight, a grimace). He had little practice in making friends his own age, and no idea of how people with less money than the Merrills lived. And who, at this point, were the Merrills, who was part of his family and who was not, now that his mother was no longer welcome in his father's house? The thirteen-year-old boy exuded a combination of raw woundedness and plump entitlement that promised to make him permanently defensive, awkward, passive, and resentful: a first-class prig.

And yet a decade later he would bravely set out to live in Europe with another young man, his lover. By that time he'd made a circle of warm friends, and he wanted to enlarge it; he wanted to learn more about the world—and about himself. No idle rich boy, he would be preparing a volume of poetry for publication, his first commercial book but the third collection with his name on its title page. The difference between the young man he would become and the adolescent he had been shouldn't be exaggerated: the dedicated, industrious poet and the adventurous lover were present in potential in the pudgy thirteen-year-old, just waiting to burn through the fat. And something of his preteen self would cling to him in later life: even as a wise old man of letters, known for his generosity and kindness, he could revert to an injured, snobbish teenager, and turn cutting or peevish. Still, over the 1940s, important changes took place.

It began at the Lawrenceville School in New Jersey, located near Princeton, where Jimmy entered the ninth grade in 1939. Deerfield, the Massachusetts boarding school that Jimmy's brother Charles attended, would have better pleased his father (Charlie was a good friend of the headmaster, an Amherst graduate and a famous educator, Frank Boyden). Lawrenceville was Hellen's choice: about an hour by train from Penn Station, it would keep Jimmy close to home and in the company of boys from wealthy families from the New York City area. The school's reputation was colored by the "Lawrenceville Stories" of Owen Johnson, an alumnus whose popular novels followed the progress of their preppie hero Dink Stover through boarding school to his arrival at Yale. With red and black colors, proud nineteenth-century bricks and mortar, and rolling green sports fields, Lawrenceville looked like a boy's book come to life.

The education offered was demanding and innovative. Most Lawrenceville masters had Ivy League degrees. Rather than lecture, they led seminar discussions around oval wooden tables recently introduced for that purpose. The new style of teaching promoted engaged attention, debate, and independent thinking. Students worked hard and the competition was stiff: the yearbook shows them propping their eyes open over textbooks late at night. The school used number grades and posted them, so everyone knew just how well or poorly everyone else was doing. Jimmy took English, Latin, mathematics, French, and music his first year. He kept a close eye on his and his classmates' marks. When he took a test, he underlined his name with a ruler—not the usual practice. At the end of the fall term 1939, along with athletic "Letter" winners from the season just ended, the student newspaper, the *Recorder*, announced that "Merrill led the second form"—as the ninth grade was called—"with an average of 89.304." He did well in every subject, but he excelled in languages and literature. His teacher Thomas Johnson, who edited an important edition of Emily Dickinson's poems a few years later, put into words what was evident to all: "Jim has a flair for English, and a very real talent."

Residential life at Lawrenceville was organized on the house system used in British boarding schools: students were assigned to particular houses supervised by live-in masters, who provided coffee after dinner and an occasional excursion to the movies or theater. In addition to doing their schoolwork, boys were expected to take part in house activities, make house friends, play sports for the house or the school in the afternoon, and attend games between Lawrenceville and other schools on the weekend. Jimmy failed to bond in these regulation ways. Perhaps because he had just gotten braces on his teeth, he was excused from sports in fall 1939. In his report, his housemaster regretted that Jimmy had been "hampered in mingling with other boys" by having missed out on athletics, and hoped he would soon "develop the ability to mix more readily." The report announced a theme. Over the next two years, his housemasters would become worried, not to say indignant, over his lack of interest in his housemates. In March 1941, one wrote, "Jim still does not mingle with most of the boys in the house. We feel that he should learn to get along with others whether he approves of them or not, even though this would require an effort on his part which he apparently does not choose to make."

The case was not so simple as a boy who thought himself too fine to mix with his fellows. There was pride in it, but Jimmy's aloofness evolved as a defense against the sometimes hostile culture of a boys' school. Boys in the first and second years lived in the Lower School dorms. They were each assigned to "cubes," not rooms but cubicles with thin plaster walls and pull curtains for doors. The arrangement left each student on his own yet without much privacy and vulnerable to bullying. A certain amount of hazing was school custom. "Rhines," as ninth graders were called, were expected to wear red and black Lawrenceville caps and memorize school songs or be subject to punishments by the older boys. Boys gave each other nicknames that pointed up some embarrassing physical feature or weakness: "The Tub," "Chesty," "Baby-legs," "Shorty," "Muscle." The names Jimmy was called—"Toots," "Jelly-fish," and "Gypsy Babe"—played on his flab and effeminacy. This much might sound like good-natured abuse. When the lights went out, however, a gang would invade someone's cube, and serious bullying would begin.

"The Lower School was a searing experience," says Pete Forcey, a class-mate and friend of Jimmy's who recalls the bullying vividly. The young Forcey was alarmed by it, went to his housemaster asking, "Why do you do nothing about this?," and got no answer from him. Bullying was hardly official school policy, but stopping it wasn't either. What did it consist of? A boy might be taunted, pushed down on the ground, or, as happened to one freshman, hauled outside and tossed in the lake. The primary threat was being "depantsed": this meant stripping a boy naked, then rubbing his penis and anus with stinging peppermint oil. "What it involved was forc-ibly jerking people off," Forcey remembers. "It was a nightmare."

Rich, shy, used to being fussed over by maids at home, and having already staked his place on the honor roll at school, Jimmy was a prime target for the bullies. His nemesis was David Mixsell, a small boy with, in Forcey's words, "a congenitally mean face and a streak of genius for knowing how to torture someone." He was James Merrill's first "True hate," as he explains in "Days of 1941 and '44," a poem from the 1980s. Merrill and Mixsell stood side by side when the ninth graders lined up alphabetically, and their cubes faced each other, establishing the two boys as opposites. In contrast to his tor-mentor's Spartan walls, Jimmy's were cushioned, hung with posters, and supplied by Hellen with cotton in case of nosebleeds. Mixsell would enter when Jimmy was out and read his diary or steal his candy. He whistled when Jimmy crossed the campus with the swishy, hips-first walk the boy was developing. He grabbed Jimmy's towel in the showers, waved it just out of reach, and jeered, leering at his crotch. Once Mixsell and his posse chased Jimmy into the furnace room. Cornered, Jimmy avoided being "depantsed" by starting to take his trousers off himself—the "old strip tease gag." They said "it wasn't any fun if I didn't put up a fight + left."

Even during his first year at Lawrenceville, Jimmy was not without friends. There were Southampton boys like Palmer Loenig and Orson Munn who had played with him at the Orchard when they were small, but their interests did not much overlap with his. Jimmy gave away the entirety of his large and expensive collection of lead toy soldiers, a gift from his father, to Orson. ("He was writing poetry and I was playing with toy sol-diers," Munn comments.) So he would have been quite alone emotionally if he hadn't gotten to know Tony Harwood, another ninth grader.

Tony was Jewish; his surname had been Anglicized. Jimmy was so unfamiliar with the type that he assumed this tall, dark-complexioned boy with the long face and black eyes was "South American." The Harwoods weren't wealthy, but Tony was an aesthete in the making, who'd learned, like Jimmy, to appreciate "good things—paintings, furniture, etc." "He likes himself very much," Jimmy commented, "and thinks he is (he may be—I don't know) very very chi-chi." It would have been more accurate to say Tony was affected. He wore pink and mauve cashmere sweaters; his manner was droll and languid; he spoke with an imitation upper-crust drawl *and* a lisp. He was vulnerable to the bullies, too, and Jimmy took a protective attitude toward him. Jimmy was not above making a Jewish joke at Tony's expense, though he was pained when Tony suffered an anti-Semitic snub. Most afternoons the two of them could be found at the Jigger, the school's snacks and supplies shop, where they "STUFFED" themselves with milk shakes, bacon sandwiches, and sweets. They played gin rummy, backgammon, and Monopoly, went to the movies, met each other's mothers, and squabbled and made up every week like a pair of old ladies.

Jimmy's effeminacy showed in ways besides his walk. His new weight, without the muscle to match, made his body soft, his bottom padded. Even as he vowed to diet, he kept munching the candy and cake sent from home; "woe is me, I'm getting fatter," he complained with no intention of holding back. Besides the Met's sopranos, he sighed over screen actresses like Joan Fontaine in *Rebecca*, Vivien Leigh in *Romeo and Juliet*, and Katharine Hepburn in *Holiday*, which he saw four times. (He was thrilled in summer 1941 to sit beside a tennis court in Connecticut, watching Kate play. At one point the actress asked the boy to fetch an errant ball—a highlight of that year.) In his diary he doodled images of beautiful women. A sketch of a female statue, breasts exposed and head and arms cut off, he titled "Venus de Merrill." He drew a woman's back with a strapless gown, a woman with hearts for breasts and buttocks, and many versions of the same female face: chic, pouty, cool.

These imaginary women embodied a metropolitan sophistication that Jimmy aspired to as an antidote to the masculine styles offered in his New Jersey boys' school. Perhaps they were also fantasy images of his mother. In her son's eyes, Hellen had emerged from her divorce as she wished to be seen—not as a helpless victim, but as an independent woman who had faced her husband's "cruelty" with composure, her head held high, and her character, like her beauty, unblemished. Naturally her sensitivity to his suffering made Jimmy sensitive to hers, whether or not she complained to him.

After a winter weekend at home in the city, he wrote, "Mama looked very bad—she's been working on a job where she has to address about 50,000 envelopes to socially prominent people for Steuben Glass. She has lost 7 pounds." Jimmy chipped in and addressed two hundred envelopes himself.

Though she fared better in her divorce settlement than Eliza Church had in hers, Hellen didn't come away with the millions gossip imputed to her. She had to take a job if she was going to get the best seats in the house for her and Jimmy to hear *Das Rheingold*, as she did on that weekend which they otherwise spent addressing envelopes. It wasn't easy for a divorced woman, forty years old, to find work. Enterprising as ever, Hellen put to use the education in design and manners which she'd gotten during her marriage by going into business with a girlfriend. The duo managed elaborate parties, decorated interiors for society clients, and provided custom services to retailers like Steuben Glass. The commissions could be challenging. Hellen might be asked to deliver a white grand piano for a cocktail party later the same day. For one of Carol Longone's Operalogues, she hustled up an organ grinder and a monkey.

If Hellen was working for Jimmy, he was working for her, in his own way, when he competed with his classmates for top honors. His letters home report on his academic progress—not without resentment, reflecting the pressure of her expectations, as when he failed to test into an upper-level math class and wrote to her, "But you should appreciate the fact that I was selected (with another boy) out of the whole class to try to get in the higher one." Jimmy had his own demands, material ones, to make on his mother. He wanted a Victrola with a good tone and a sapphire needle. And despite his feminine sense of style, he rejected the fabric that Hellen sent for his bedspread: "how could [she pick] PINK flannel with green sequins for a boy's room at school"? The bossy tone he takes in his letters home poorly masks his dependency on her.

Hellen was too wounded and too proud to begin to date, and, on weekends and vacations, Jimmy was more than ever her close companion. They went to the theater and cried at the movies together ("which was very unfortunate," he wrote, "as we only had one Kleenex between us"). Over spring break 1940, they visited Mis' Annie in her house on the beach in Ponte Vedra near Jacksonville, a winter visit that was a routine, annual event. "If only boys in school would treat me half as nice as folks down here do," Jimmy sniffled. On this trip Hellen took him to Silver Springs to meet Ross Allen, a showman and naturalist dressed like Tarzan in an animal skin who wrestled alligators and handled snakes. Jimmy posed in his Poindexter glasses beside the half-naked hero; in another photo he posed with a snake, looking clumsy but determined as he tried to get a grip on the wriggling phallic symbol. On the same trip, his mother introduced him to Marjorie Kinnan Rawlings, a Floridian whose novel *The Yearling* won the Pulitzer Prize for 1939. Jimmy came away with her autograph for Tony and himself. But the highlight of the trip had come on his visit to Silver Springs. "The water," he wrote in his diary, "is as clear as crystal and in the glass-bottomed boats you can see everything. There are heavenly colors and swell fish."

"Heavenly colors and swell fish": Merrill cringed when he came upon that conjunction of clichés in his diary forty years later. Yet he could see that the touchingly innocent bad writing pointed to "the issue most crucial to this boy not quite fourteen," his parents' divorce and his wish somehow to reunite them. "What is that phrase," he asks in "Acoustical Chambers," an essay from 1982, "but an attempt to bring my parents together, to remarry on the page their characteristic inflections—ladylike gush and regular guy terseness?" The point holds whether or not Hellen and Charlie ever spoke quite like that. The phrase expresses the uncertainty of a boy caught between his mother and his father—and the feminine and masculine stereotypes he associates with them—as he tries to learn to speak for himself in his diary. He is trying to stay connected to both parents, and keep them connected, in his prose.

Writing a diary had been his father's idea. Though Charlie feared that his son was turning into a sissy with an overdeveloped "aesthetic side," he never opposed Jimmy's wish to become a writer; in fact he encouraged it. With a future-oriented financial metaphor typical of his thinking, Charlie advised him, "I think it would pay you enormous dividends, in years to come, if you would keep a Private Diary, entering into it not merely the events of the day, but your thoughts and dreams; by dreams, I don't mean necessarily those when asleep, but rather your ambitions, hopes and fears. A diary in detail of your life at school and college would equip you to write many interesting books later on." Charlie was treating the boy as a writer with potentially a long future ahead of him, which he could build toward day by day like a Merrill Lynch investor. He was also pointing out that a writer could take his own life for his subject and live in such a way as to have something to write about. Jimmy rose to the idea. He wrote to Hellen, "Daddy wants me to start a diary, so I'll get one. Mis' A's is only a line-a-day so that won't do!" That letter is dated January 10, 1940. He began his diary the next week, and he would keep it in one form or another for the rest of his life. His diary was the pivot between life and writing, where the one began to turn into the other. His rediscovery of "Heavenly colors and swell fish" is just one example of how he used it. When, in his fifties, he saw the phrase in his diary from 1940 (he worked it into his poem about Mixsell, "Days of 1941 and '44"), he was a poet of memory, reaping the dividends his father had predicted.

Despite his influential suggestion, Charlie rarely appears in Jimmy's diary. He kept missing Lawrenceville's annual father's day.* When he did pay a visit, Jimmy complained that Daddy made "an exhibition" of himself: "I never was so embarrassed." One summer evening he took the boy to dinner and then to—"(horrors)"—a "NIGHT BASEBALL GAME of all the dull things, and they even played an extra inning!" Jimmy's tone works hard here to hide how much he missed his father, and it's doubtful the boy risked seeming bored in Charlie's company. After he visited Lawrenceville in 1940, Charlie told Doris that Jimmy was "extasized" to show him around the school. Charlie had brought a friend—he usually came with a buddy in tow—"and we all had a top afternoon." "Toward evening we left, and I hated to leave him there. Really Jimmy is a sweet fine boy and I know you are all going to be proud of him. He has one of the most direct—strong—honest and lovely characters I have ever seen." Charlie, who was direct and honest too, must have expressed these feelings to his son.

Jimmy didn't meet Kinta until more than two years after her marriage to his father. Charlie made no effort to bring his third wife into the lives of his children: her role in the family would be less like a stepmother than a mistress with the legitimizing credential of a marriage license. Kinta preferred the South to the North and made Merrill's Landing her headquarters. Her southern voice was shrill and strident, and she usually had a point to make. She stuck out as willful and extravagant even beside a husband known for his will and extravagance. She ordered the gardener to pull up the splendid variety of roses at the Orchard and replace them entirely with white ones. She wore tight white sweaters and avoided tanning. Proud of her sexiness and loath to lose it, she bathed her breasts in ice water to "preserve their freshness." After her divorce from Charlie in 1953, she married twice more; these husbands were men of advanced age who didn't live long after the exchange of vows. (Doris: "That Kinta has the worst luck.") Jimmy eventually settled into polite relations with "Mrs. Merrill," as he called her until, at twenty-one, he received permission to address her by her first name. On the subject of Kinta, tactful Doris held her peace, while Charles grumbled. "Why be difficult, if you can be impossible?" he snorted, summing the woman up.

---

* "All the fathers are here except mine—Thank God." JM, journal, November 2, 1940, Jnl 57; also October 25, 1941, Jnl57 (WUSTL).

Jimmy's long summers in Southampton were over. In 1940, he and his mother came to stay with Mrs. Livingston before he visited his father briefly at the Orchard. Then he was off to Camp Duncan in Vermont, where he did what boys are supposed to do at camp: swim, hike, get sunburned and "eaten alive" by mosquitoes while playing capture the flag, baseball, and soccer ("I made 3 goals!"). It was his third go at summer camp; after being severely homesick the first time, during the summer his parents were divorcing, he'd started to enjoy himself, especially when he could be onstage. He acted in *Julius Caesar* (the production stank, and "[e]veryone died laughing"), took a female part in a skit, danced "a ballet," and sang and danced in a revue. One photo from camp, probably taken the prior summer, shows him in the role of Puck, with cape and cap, a bow in one hand, his other hand sailing off to the side in a flourish, and his thick thighs exposed as he bends on the ball of his foot like a dancer. He couldn't be more pretty or more poised.

Back at Lawrenceville, he put on more costumes. He played a maid in a comedy: in his bright red wig, everyone said that he looked "just like Judy Garland." Dressed in a sheet with a lamp shade on his head and rolled-up socks for breasts, he took first place in a beauty contest. He was so known for his cross-dressing that one master turned him away at a tryout: "Jimmy, I don't want you to play a girl's part." He saw plays in Manhattan, bought works by Eugene O'Neill, Lillian Hellman, and Noël Coward, and tried his hand at writing drama himself. His increasing interest in theater and female impersonation in particular indicate a teenager gaining the confidence to pursue his inclinations. Buoyed by the laughter and applause of his peers, Jimmy saw he could flaunt the sissy qualities for which he was mocked, as he'd done in the face of Mixsell and his cronies by breaking into a striptease.

His parents were aware of the trend and tried to counteract it. Hellen now lived in a small town house on East Fifty-seventh Street. In fall 1940, Charlie paid for her to buy a second house in New Canaan, a quaint Connecticut town fast becoming a bedroom community for Manhattan executives and their families; the idea was to provide Jimmy with a wholesome environment during the summers, when he would be expected to play sports. He began a course of injections meant to promote his growth and get rid of those extra pounds. He would eventually grow to a modest, respectable height—five feet eight, which made him a few inches taller than his father. Meanwhile, he became habituated to needles. For the rest of his life, like his mother, who took B12 shots, he regularly had injections of vitamins and hormones given by doctors or often by himself. As an adult, he would pop a needle in his leg through his trousers to show friends how easily it was done.

In his diary from 1940–41 appear the first frail wisps of same-sex romance. At camp he made a great friend in Bruce ("He's really the nicest boy I ever knew"). When Bruce visited him at school, Jimmy broke into Carmen's "Habanera" in his diary ("L'amour est enfant de boheme . . ."). Not much more came of this, though Jimmy fixed his attention fast enough on other boys. One was S. J. Wright, whom Jimmy met at Lawrenceville in tenth grade. Jimmy mentions assignations—"Jigger with S. J."—that may not have been so notable to S.J. But his housemaster took note. "Dr. Diehl gave me a big talking-to about me + S. J. He said we were together too much for our own good, and made some deep insinuations; I was really very embarrassed, and I didn't possibly see how he could construe anything like that." That's Jimmy in his diary, sounding thrilled. Another entry: "Rumour has it that SJ has measles—if so I'll get them," which Jimmy punctuates with a smiling female face.*

Crushes like these didn't involve any holding of hands, let alone a kiss. But the idea of having sex—specifically sex with boys—must have been on Jimmy's mind. The poet Daryl Hine remembers Merrill telling him that as a Lawrenceville student he used to take the train into New York City and cruise Times Square in the hopes of finding a stranger for sex. Probably this was nothing more than the sort of adventure Jimmy described in his diary in December 1940: "went to get Fantasia tickets. Had the most nasty experience. A young man walked by me asking all sorts of questions, and wanted me to go to the Roxy with him." We can imagine how briskly he declined the invitation, swiveling where he stood. But the boy was aware—from plays, from books, from New York City streets—that there was a world inside the world where men made love to other men. It was in prospect an answer, or at the least an alternative, to his parents' broken home, and perhaps he wanted to be part of it.

Jimmy's life was changed for the better by the arrival at Lawrenceville of a new tenth grader, Frederick Buechner. Though Tony was Jimmy's first friend, Freddy quickly became his best and would remain a prime influence on Jimmy for the next decade and more. He was assigned to the cube next to Jimmy's, but they had more in common than that. Freddy was an enthu-

---

* Jimmy did come down with the measles, and his worried mother, to help him recover, supplied him with a transfusion of her own blood.

siastic reader and a talented writer, with a confident, energetic mind that reveled in words and stories. His young life was already marked by a terrible event. Around the time Jimmy seemed to be losing his father through divorce, Freddy lost his to suicide. Mr. Buechner had gone into the garage one Sunday morning, turned on the car, and gassed himself to death—with his wife and two sons in the house. Somehow the boy survived that morning with his spirit intact. It left Freddy, like Jimmy, closely attached to his mother and his grandmother. His pain was expressed indirectly if at all in the determined quality of his charm. Tallish and very good-looking, with healthy square shoulders, a long face, dreamy green eyes, and a warm, expressive, sentimental nature, he stood out among his schoolmates as both sensitive and a regular guy.

Freddy gave Jimmy a layer of insulation from the bullies, while some of Jimmy's wealth and luster rubbed off on him. With Freddy, Jimmy learned how to open up to a friend, revealing not only his depth of soul but a penchant for goofiness. He made Freddy laugh by belching out the opening bars of "The Bells of St. Mary's"; once Freddy made Jimmy laugh so hard that applesauce shot out his nose. They called themselves "the Uglies" after characters in E. Nesbit's fantasy novel *The Enchanted Castle*. "The Uglies," Buechner explains in a memoir, "were people who much of the time felt beleaguered and out of step, who didn't usually laugh or cry at the same kinds of things that other people did, and who both rejoiced in not being like everybody else and of course longed to be. [. . .] We decided that as far as we knew, there were only two Uglies in existence, and we were they." The Uglies teamed up one Saturday afternoon at the Jigger when a boy who was eating a hamburger splashed Freddy with his ketchup, "whereupon Jimmy handed me a great spoonful of butterscotch sauce from the sundae he had just ordered, and I smeared it lavishly down first one of my assailant's red cheeks and then the other with spectacular effect. Singly we could neither of us ever have pulled it off. Together we were a match for the world."

And a lively match for each other. "We were rivals in so many things," Buechner comments, illustrating the point with a memory of the teenage Jimmy waving his croquet mallet in front of Buechner's as the latter attempted to strike the ball. Their rivalry was productive rather than bitter or desperate because each boy was sufficiently assured in his talent (and encouraged by the other's esteem and ideas) to use the provocation of his pal's successes to try something new or learn to do something better. Where it counted most for Jimmy was in poetry. He had been rhyming, of course, since childhood. But Buechner led the way into print with a poem in the Lawrenceville *Lit*. Stylistically, Freddy's effort was in "a delectable pre-WWI mode"—lush, soulful, decadent. "It was," Merrill remembered, "like a sibylline, aesthetic maiden aunt" in contrast to "those red-blooded lyrics by Housman or Rupert Brooke" that made the British masters at St. Bernard's "blow their noses after reading them aloud."

Soon Jimmy was publishing the same sort of stuff. Besides Freddy's poems, he read the Pre-Raphaelites, the Parnassians, and Baudelaire, whom he translated. "If I had lived a thousand years, I could / Not have more memories," his supremely world-weary "Spleen" begins. His version of "Le Serpent qui Danse" winds up:

> Beneath the load of your indolence,
> Your childish head and face,
> Are balanced with the nonchalance
> Of a young elephant's grace.

The poets to whom Jimmy responded were women, homosexuals, French, or some combination thereof, although he didn't select them with those labels in mind. Among the moderns he was reading in anthologies, he had no time for the heroic male innovators—Eliot, Williams, Pound; instead he dwelled on old-school lyric poets like Edna St. Vincent Millay or, more important, Elinor Wylie. The work of these women poets he approached as he would a performance of French songs by the soprano Maggie Teyte, whom he idolized: he was attracted not to the text, so to speak, but to the force of a passionate, artful female voice and the lush score supporting it.

Wylie was a sonneteer of precise rhymes and smooth meter. Hugely popular in the 1920s and 1930s and since then more or less unread, she was Jimmy's favorite. Her sensuous imagery, fluent formal technique, and love-lorn, proto-confessional allure, augmented by her scandal-ridden personal life, influenced his poetry in a lingering way. His most extended early piece of literary criticism is an essay about her poetry, "Angel or Earthly Creature." The essay demonstrates his thorough knowledge of her poetry, novels, and life, and comments on her links to Shelley and Donne. Wylie was obsessed with Shelley: she believed she was a reincarnation of him, and that their spirits were in communication. Donne, Jimmy argued, was an intellectual influence who helped her to see the metaphysical side of her love affairs. The two sides of Wylie, the mystic and the intellectual love poet, point to the two directions in which Merrill's own poetry would develop.

Freddy's major contribution to his taste was Oscar Wilde. He recommended *The Picture of Dorian Gray* and, at Jimmy's request, Hellen produced for his fifteenth birthday a second edition of the novel; for his sixteenth birthday, in 1942, Jimmy bought himself a first edition. By then he had collected a great deal more Wilde. His diary record of these purchases, which involved expeditions to bookstores and rare book dealers in Manhattan, rose to a fever pitch in 1941, at the end of his second year at Lawrenceville, when he bought thirteen or more books by or about Wilde.* He also bought fine editions by other authors (Baudelaire, Paul Verlaine, Pierre Louÿs, Thomas Mann, Aldous Huxley, Virginia Woolf, and Dante), but Wilde he coveted. The Wilde he wanted so much of wasn't the author of drawing room comedies, though he liked these well enough; he was buying the hedonistic, homoerotic, censored Wilde of *Dorian Gray, Salome,* and *The Portrait of Mr. W. H.*—a short story that identifies "Mr. W. H.," the dedicatee of Shakespeare's sonnets, as a boy in the bard's company who played the heroine's roles. Wilde's trial for "gross indecency," his imprisonment, and the end of his life in France made him a figure of dark glamour for young queer men who saw him as a hero; Jimmy approached him in that spirit. The list of his purchases culminates in "A Ballad of Reading Gaol": a first edition of Wilde's prison poem, costing $45, signed by the author. "I'm a bad boy," this adolescent aesthete writes, clearly titillated by, and half guilty about, more than his spending spree.

Freddy shared this infatuation with Wilde. He and Jimmy expressed their alliance with him and each other by wearing matching overcoats with fur lapels, which they chose in imitation of one of Oscar's. In one letter to Freddy, Jimmy signed himself "Bosie," Wilde's pet name for Lord Alfred Douglas, his perfidious lover. We might infer from all this dress-up and role playing that Jimmy was in love with Freddy. In a Platonic sense, that was certainly true. But only in a Platonic sense: Jimmy saw that Freddy was interested romantically in girls, not boys, and it was part of what he liked in his friend. It meant that, with Freddy's friendship to guard him, Jimmy had the cover he needed to dress up like Wilde and immerse himself freely in his story without risking too much, above all in the eyes of his mother, who approved of Freddy and welcomed him in her home. For his part, Buechner

---

* On April 10 he bought *Poems and Fairy Tales of Oscar Wilde*; on May 24, a "1st edition of O.W.'s 'Sebastian Melmoth,'" "O.W.'s poems" with "lovely binding," and *Salome* illustrated by Aubrey Beardsley; on June 20, *Portrait of Mr. W. H.,* " 'Oscar Wilde' the play and the poem," *Salome* in French, and a limited edition of *Portrait of Mr. W. H.* as a gift for Freddy; on June 30, "O. W.'s 'Children in Prison' "; and on July 12, Frank Harris's *Life of Oscar Wilde*, Alan Devoe's *Portrait of Mr. O. W.,* and a stage adaptation of *Dorian Gray*. During his lecture tour of the United States in 1882, Wilde lived for a time at 48 West Eleventh Street, a few doors down from Jimmy's early childhood home. Jimmy never mentions the coincidence, but he probably knew about it.

saw in his and Jimmy's craze for Wilde simply a wish "to be famous and colorful and sought after and witty like him and to go our own ways as he went his." The two boys didn't talk about Wilde's homosexuality. If it entered Buechner's mind, it was only as further evidence of the author's "exoticness, his 'ugly-ness,' his independence and general dazzle."

Freddy was more interested in Jesus Christ. He enrolled in a confirmation class at school, and Jimmy joined him in it, ready to follow Freddy wherever he might lead. The boys were both confirmed in May 1941 in the Lawrenceville chapel by "the florid, Medieval-looking" Episcopal bishop of New Jersey, as Buechner remembers him. This spiritual training was a preliminary step for Freddy toward realizing his vocation as a Christian minister, although he was still more than a decade away from entering a seminary. For Jimmy, it meant something else. Confirmation class seems to have made no more impression on him than Sunday school in Southampton; what was being confirmed was his friendship with Freddy. "Fred + I are related by marriage," he wrote in his diary the day after the ceremony. These two young friends had both felt the fragility of human bonds in their families, and each, in his own way, wanted to be part of something permanent.

Around the time that Jimmy's mania for Wilde was peaking, Japanese planes bombed Pearl Harbor. War had been in the news since Nazi tanks rolled across Poland during Jimmy's early days on the Lawrenceville campus, but it was a remote thing to begin with. Students hoisted a flag that read "Heil Heely!"—Allen Heely was the headmaster—and they couldn't get it down: as far as Jimmy noticed, that was the impact on campus in 1939. Then, in spring 1940, when the Nazis invaded Scandinavia, Jimmy feared for the fate of Zelly's sister in Copenhagen, and war took on a troubling reality even for him.

The American mobilization drew Lawrenceville staff into the armed service. The boys had to make their own beds and pitch in with work on campus. Students crowded around the crackling radio voice of Lowell Thomas to hear what had happened in Europe or Asia that day; and athletics now included army-style physical fitness exercises. When Jimmy graduated in 1943, Headmaster Heely would remark, "Everything [. . .] has been done in the daily consciousness of war and in the atmosphere with which war has surrounded us." Not that the atmosphere was always solemn. During one of their fitness drills, Jimmy and "Bucky" Buchsbaum, a chubby kid who later became a vice president at Merrill Lynch, got hung up on the bars they were climbing, their legs waving. Enemy marksmen would have made short work of them, and their mates dropped on the ground laughing.

But war was no joke, and Jimmy was frightened. "If they draft us at eighteen think what will happen," he wrote to Freddy at sixteen. "It's too ghastly. I don't want to be in the service and get killed." Killed, like handsome, cheerful Mr. Candy, a history teacher who was in charge of Dawes House when Jimmy lived there during sophomore year, a popular bachelor master who drove a convertible and played Liberty Recordings of Ethel Merman on his Magnavox for boys like Jimmy who visited his rooms for conversation in the evening. Soon after he had his hero's send-off in winter 1942, the boys learned he was dead.

The war affected Jimmy through his family, starting with the arrival at the Orchard of three British children, two sisters and their brother, whom CEM took in as guests in Southampton and Palm Beach for the duration of the war. Charlie was moved by the heroism of the British, affected in particular by a friend's death at Dunkirk, and eager to do something for the war effort. Jean, Anne, and Alistair Elliot were the children of a Scottish doctor in Liverpool whom Charlie knew indirectly; he welcomed them as foster children, seeing not only to their safety but to their upbringing and education by hiring an English governess for them, a Miss Love. The children were accepted by Kinta, and became an instant family for Charlie during this third marriage. "Mr. Merrill," the little Elliots called him to his face, "Father Christmas" and "Bonnie Prince Charlie" behind his back, tickling him no end.

Alistair, being six years younger than Jimmy, gave Charlie another crack at raising a boy as he thought best. Elliot recalls his benefactor tearing up after taking him and his sisters to see Disney's *Snow White*. Another day, Charlie took the boy to a boxing match in West Palm Beach. This event featured a "Battle Royal" of the type Ralph Ellison describes in his novel *Invisible Man*: black boys no older than Alistair climbed into the ring and scrambled to pick up coins—with their gloves on—while trying to knock each other unconscious, which shocked Alistair. Charlie arranged for him to have his own boxing lessons, in order to prepare him for the bullies back in England who would challenge him, Charlie anticipated, for having spent the war years in America. Looking back, Elliot recognized that Mr. Merrill was "trying his best to show me something of the masculine world." "I really gave you more time than I ever had available to give to my own sons," Charlie wrote to him in 1951, having been "hurt" by the pacifist views that the by then nineteen-year-old young man had expressed to him. Charlie's paternal influence worked just as well on a boy with no genetic inheritance from him, for Alistair would turn out to share much with Charlie's two sons. Like Jimmy, he would become a poet; like Charles, he would become a liberal who argued with Charlie about politics and society.

Charles's contention with his father, which had gone on noisily for years, came to a head with the U.S. entry into the war. CEM's efforts to steer Charles's course in life kept producing the opposite of the intended result. As a teenager, Charles poured drinks for Dad and his cronies at the Orchard; although proud of his role as "family bartender," he came away with no interest in Merrill Lynch, small talk, or bourbon. When he and Jimmy were sent to Wildwood Plantation, Charles was struck by scenes of racial and economic injustice; these, rather than Charlie's happy dream of the Old South, stayed with him. At the Arizona Desert School and then at Deerfield, his teachers, rather than toughen him up, developed the boy's interest in books and ideas. Charlie had taken Charles to Amherst College reunions for years; when the time came for him to choose a college, the young man decided on Harvard. In principle, Charlie accepted his son's choice of college, though he put up a fight in a long letter extolling Amherst alumni and vigorously complaining about his son's "intolerance" and "aloofness from reality."

"At Harvard," Charles notes, drawing the contrast with the more conservative environment of Amherst, "you could believe anything." He used his education there to become, in his words, "a Jew and a left-wing intellectual." He took a class in fascism and communism and read Russian and Polish Jewish writers. He saw a parallel between the poverty and anti-Semitism he'd witnessed in Europe in summer 1939, when he traveled to Warsaw on the verge of the Nazi invasion, and the poverty and racism he'd encountered on Wildwood Plantation. After graduating from Harvard in 1941, he returned to Mississippi to work as a clerk in the store on a Christian-Socialist farm, selling pigs' feet, snuff, and rifles to the poor for ten cents an hour. His fiancée, Mary Klohr, educated at Pembroke College, was a like-minded young woman; she was also—troubling to CEM—an adopted child, from Chicago, whose biological father was Jewish. After Pearl Harbor was attacked, Charles and Mary decided to marry at once; then Charles would enlist, but in the Canadian, not the U.S., army.

The Christian-Socialist farm, Mary Klohr, and now the Canadian army: that was the last straw as far as Charlie was concerned. He blew off steam in a seven-page letter to Doris. "One infraction of orders"—he wrote of his older son as if he were an insubordinate soldier—"one break in the very lax discipline led to another, and I foresaw and predicted the ultimate result," which seemed to him now "nothing less than tragic." To Doris, who urged her father to be patient with Charles, Mary was pleasingly "friendly and sincere." Charlie saw only a young woman lacking in the qualities he most valued in her sex: "beauty, vivacity, wit, charm, chic, figure, and all the subtle things that set one apart from the crowd. [. . .] And she looks Jewish! Oh! me, oh my! The whole situation, I think, is awful." Why Charles had joined the Canadians, Charlie had no idea, but that—to mystify his father—must have been half the point.

"Charles and I had quite different ways of coping with the paternal menace," Merrill wrote about his brother in *A Different Person*. "He had actually taken a course in military strategy at college. Thus, while I sought to postpone or altogether avoid confrontation, my brother's breathtaking repertoire of shock tactics, diversionary movements, positions secured by verbal barbed wire, and so forth, kept the old man on the defensive and the rest of the family on the edge of our chairs." Jimmy may have been fascinated to watch his brother at work, but Charles's influence operated on him negatively by taking options off the table. To stand up to CEM and establish his own ideals and identity, he wouldn't go the political route: when it came to espousing liberal ideas like racial uplift in the U.S. or the struggle for sovereignty in eastern Europe, Charles was already there, his flag firmly planted. It wasn't the content of Charles's beliefs so much as his earnestness, his tone, for which Jimmy would seek his own alternatives. Merrill's mature attitudes toward history and politics, his studied irony about their claim to first importance, were rooted in his adolescent reaction to his father's and brother's priorities.

Then there was Bobby Magowan. Shortly after Pearl Harbor, he came to Merrill's Landing to discuss with Daddy, man to man, his sense of duty and the impact on the family and the firm if he were to serve. With Charlie's blessing, Bobby enlisted in the U.S. Navy and deployed on an Air Force carrier in the Pacific, although he was a man in his forties, a senior executive at Merrill Lynch, and a father of three boys: Robin, Merrill, and baby Peter, born in 1942. Long, eloquent, typed letters came home, chronicles of bravery and bonhomie, daring sea rescues and raucous shore leaves, that circulated among Doris and her sons, Charlie, Jimmy, and other family members. "For Father," Robin wrote, "the war was the epitome of everything heroic. Danger, adventure, and people—pilots young enough to be his sons, Americans from all walks of life—were present to him as they never would be again." Bobby as usual behaved like Charlie's good son.

Yet Charlie might have seen himself in Charles's dream of flying into battle in the brilliant British-style uniform of the Royal Canadian Air Force. That dream didn't exactly work out: Charles found himself ("a bit surprised") assigned to the artillery. He applied for officer training and was turned down. Next he worked a transfer to the U.S. Army and was dispatched to North Africa, then Italy, where, like any foot soldier, he dug holes and read letters from home—for Mary, pregnant with their daughter Catherine, was writing every day. Charles survived heavy mortar fire in Italy, and he was ready to fight, but before his regiment joined the assault on Monte Cassino (a pivotal battle that left many thousands of Americans dead), he was removed to a desk job at headquarters. That was his father's doing: satisfied at this point by Charles's patriotism, Charlie wanted to see his son come home alive, and he pulled strings to make sure he did.

Photos of Charles at Merrill's Landing after his discharge show a young man, never before at ease in his father's house, suddenly smiling in a loose white shirt, sporting a thin, well-trimmed, rather dashing mustache. Charles and Charlie would never be on the same side politically. But by locking horns with the Old Man, Charles was drawing closer to him. In fact, he was well on his way to proving to his father—and discovering for himself—how much they had in common. For all their differences, they shared a belief in American ideals, a respect for common people, and a basic moral seriousness. Charles returned to the U.S. to take up a career in teaching. Charlie was overjoyed at the news, and revealed that he sometimes wished he himself had become a teacher. Even Mary, who was invited to the Orchard with infant Catherine in Charles's absence, CEM had come to approve of, appreciating in her the warmth and sincerity that Doris had recognized first and that would endear her to Jimmy too. CEM made no complaint when Charles moved his family to St. Louis, where he and a friend founded Thomas Jefferson, a boys' boarding school based on the educational ideals of Plato's *Republic*. Charles and Mary had more children over their eight years in Missouri—Amy, Bruce, and David, followed later by Paul. In 1957, Charles would go on to found another educational institution: the Commonwealth School in Boston, a private high school for girls and boys based on progressive social principles. He would serve as an inspired, colorful headmaster there for the next twenty-five years.

Charles came home from Europe in 1945 having befriended a thirteen-year-old boy who had been a prisoner at Auschwitz. Bernat Rosner, who grew up in Hungary, was the only member of his Orthodox Jewish family to survive the Holocaust. Charles arranged for the teenager to immigrate to the United States, brought him into his family, and paid for his education all the way through Harvard Law School. Charles was following the example of his father, who had brought the little Elliots into his home; at the same time, by rescuing a Jew and treating him as his own, he was rebuking Charlie for his anti-Semitism. The twist in the story is this: Rosner used the opportunity Charles had given him to take up the business side of CEM's patrimony, which Charles himself had rejected. Over the years, Rosner would become closer to the Magowans than to the Merrills, rising in Safeway to the position of general counsel. It was hard to predict what direction a son or protégé might take.

Even as Charles began his career as an educator, he hoped to make himself a writer. He would eventually become the self-published and (in his words) "easily overlooked" author of numerous works of privately printed history and memoir. His younger brother had always been formidable competition as a writer, even as a Lawrenceville student. To their father's delight, the teenage Jimmy staked out literature as decisively as Charles would claim education and politics. Jimmy shared his school compositions with CEM, who shared them with Charles and the rest of the family, proud of the writer's accomplishment and his teachers' ringing praise. Surreptitiously, Charlie gathered copies of the boy's Lawrenceville poems and prose, most of which had appeared in the *Lit*, ordered these by chronology, and had them printed on thick stock in a hardbound limited edition of two hundred copies, which Charlie titled *Jim's Book*.

The book was a surprise timed for Christmas 1942. Hellen wrote to Charlie in gratitude: "Now is the time for you to retire from all gift giving—you reached the apex when you had *Jim's Book* published—I've never seen such rapture—Jimmy is in a complete daze." She went on to relate her conversation about it with Jimmy. He told her, "You know mama, I decided to sign my full name because autographed editions are more valuable. For instance [E. A.] Robinson's privately printed poems brought $650.00 a volume!" This was said "with a perfectly straight face." Fishing for more, Hellen had asked him whether he thought *Jim's Book* too might be valuable one day. "Well sometimes I have my doubts!" he replied, but the book gave him new confidence. There were seventy-two pages, and his efforts looked "so much more important" here than they had in the *Lit*. "I've dreamed for years of publishing my first book. How could Daddy have known?" "Jim," Hellen prodded, "you seem to be much happier over your book than over the enormous check Daddy gave you." When he'd shown her the check (what the sum was, Hellen's letter doesn't mention), Jimmy said only that he was "overwhelmed" by it. Yet, he explained, "My book is far more important than anything else could be."

Jim's Book, Merrill commented forty years later, "thrilled me for days, then mortified me for a quarter century." He doesn't say what was mortifying, to have so much of his juvenilia between covers, or to know that his first book, privately printed, testified to his father's largesse, not his own merit. In that sense, the book—the handsome, unexpected, material fact of it—was as much Charlie's production as Jim's. "I wouldn't put it past my father," Merrill mused in 1982, "to have foreseen the furthest consequences of his brilliant, unsettling gesture, which, like the pat on a sleepwalker's back, looked like approbation but was aimed at waking me up." The message of *Jim's Book* was that Jimmy really could be a writer; why, he was one already—it was no "dream"; and he had better get on with it if he was going to publish his own books without Daddy's assistance.

Yet *Jim's Book* is imporessive as the work of a fifteen- and sixteen-year-old author. It includes twenty-six titles, beginning with a sketch about an eccentric elderly woman ("Miss Georgina Tinker") that Jimmy wrote in sophomore English in October 1940, and ending with his assured translation of Baudelaire's "Spleen," composed in July 1942. The book impresses not because anything in it is marvelous, but because the writing is so various and stylistically controlled in a range of forms (prose sketch, short story, dialogue, fairy tale, sonnets, quatrains, critical essay, poetic translation). Merrill was already keenly aware of literary conventions, approaching anything he wrote as an example of a genre with expectations he could absorb and manipulate.

That doesn't mean he had nothing to write about. The social milieu of his stories is the wealthy one that he knew firsthand, and he probes it. One sketch features two women on a bus talking about a black servant who is treated with dehumanizing insensitivity. A story called "Madonna" sympathetically explores the plight of a European governess forced by her WASP employers to keep her Catholicism hidden from the children she cares for. Charlie and Hellen didn't impose this condition on Zelly, a Roman Catholic, but his governess's religion, with its Latin prayers and sacred images, had for Jimmy the quality of a charged secret, glowing with strangeness. It was part of the allure of her private life and her veiled hints of past suffering. "Madonna" is a story about her.

The war, a frequent topic in Lawrenceville student publications, appears just once in *Jim's Book* in a story called "Ambition's Debt Is Paid!" written in October 1941. Set in Berlin, the story concerns a German violinist who has been exempted from military service so that he can continue to perform his music. But his wife is ashamed that he isn't fighting, and she goads him into enlisting, although he is ill suited to be a soldier. After Anton is wounded in battle, the story ends when his wife learns that he has lost an arm and will never play the violin again. How Germany, the home of so much music he loved, could have thrown the world into war was a problem for Jimmy: surely its musicians were not to blame? (He didn't yet know, but he may have intuited, that Zelly was German by origin.) He was trying to sketch a position for himself from which it was honorable as well as prudent to stand on the sidelines, occupied with art, when other able men were putting on uniforms and going to war.

These stories typically end with a neat narrative twist and someone in tears. Their artfulness and emotion are at odds with each other; the strong feelings they involve—grief, moral outrage—are put out of reach by the conspicuous skill that evokes them. This was a problem Merrill would always face as a writer, to some degree. The tension can be felt in "Mozart," where Jimmy's metaphors for Mozart's music neatly characterize his own juvenilia:

> With suavely polished joy, restrained exuberance,
> The violin sings its bland Rococo harmonies,
> Smoothly fashioned phrases soaring to the skies
> In sinuous silver trills of sham insouciance.
>
> Music free from passion, passionately played,
> Plumed with cool perfection, powdered with despair!
> Each delicious flourish daintily debonair,
> Purity on paper, brilliance on brocade!

These lines, smooth and suave as Anton's violin music, were produced in winter 1941–42 when America had entered the war and Jimmy's brother and his brother-in-law both decided to enlist.

At Lawrenceville, Buechner recalls, Jimmy wanted to be a musician and a composer. "He had a little Mozart act. He would roll up his pants to make knickers"—another of the budding poet's teenage costumes. The "little Mozart act" was very much a fantasy: Jimmy never composed his own music, and his report cards make it clear that, although he was a skilled pianist, he read sheet music slowly and his fingering needed work. Mozart was a metaphor for the sort of artist he dreamed of becoming: working on both large and small scales, writing for the theater, for performance, and virtuosic in all he would do, aiming to amuse and move his audience at the same time. The Rococo Mozart's decorative, insistent lightness appealed strongly to him, but even as an adolescent he knew that the music was "powdered with despair," and if it was "free from passion," it must be "passionately played." Merrill would retain and realize a version of this aesthetic ideal over his poetic career. It became a commonplace for critics to describe his poetry as "Mozartian." The comparison is only plausible if we are thinking of the Romantic as well as the Rococo Mozart, a composer melancholy and metaphysical even when "daintily debonair," whose sunlight deepens the shadows. Much later in life, Merrill's favorite work of literary criticism, frequently recommended to friends, was Donald Sutherland's eccentric, impressionistic study *On, Romanticism* (1971), which has a chapter on Mozart. Sutherland mentions that, as Merrill had surely noticed, Mozart's name "contains the terminal letters of the alphabet (*ZA*) surrounded by the word *MORT.* Plainly," the impish critic deduces, "the name means music from *A* to *Z* or from *Z* to *A* (reversible like *WM*), all music, surrounded by death."

The Marriage of Figaro, Così Fan Tutte, The Magic Flute, and *Don Giovanni* were among the operas Merrill loved the best and heard most often. But the opera he was most affected by, beginning when he was a teenage regular at the Met and Lotte Lehmann appeared year after year in the role of the Marschallin, was Richard Strauss's Mozart-inspired *Der Rosenkavalier.* This work, Merrill later declared, "all but made me who I was." What influenced him in particular was the attitude of tender, ironic resignation embodied by the Marschallin, the wife of a never-seen field marshal, who at the climax of the opera, in a sublime, soaring trio, accepts her age and gives up her considerably younger lover Octavian so that he can follow his heart and join hands with the equally young and innocent Sophie. Strauss and his librettist Hugo von Hofmannsthal set the opera in eighteenth-century Vienna and deployed aspects of farce from Mozart's comic operas. These included the choice to have Octavian, like Cherubino in *The Marriage of Figaro*, sung by a mezzo-soprano in a cross-dressed role, which puts two women at the center of this love story. For young Jimmy, the work constituted "a bittersweet, faintly homosexual, wholly survivable alternative to my dreams of immolation and all-consuming love," which had been stoked in him by Wagner's apocalyptic *Ring.*

Over time, Merrill applied the moral lessons of *Der Rosenkavalier*'s plot to new life situations as they arose. But when he came to it as a teenager, the opera resonated with his family drama. The Marschallin's grand home was easy to transpose onto the Orchard. He could see his father in the absent field marshal, or less charitably in the boorish, lascivious Baron Ochs, the Marschallin's cousin, while the Marschallin herself was crossed with his image of his mother, who had behaved beautifully in her time of trial. On some level, Jimmy must have hoped that Hellen would one day let *him* leave and love someone else, just as elegantly—and peaceably—as the Marschallin gives up Octavian.

While the plot entered Jimmy's moral imagination, Strauss's score set a standard that his poetic music could aspire to. Neoclassical pastiche and

Mozartian gaiety, a full, thick, Wagnerian orchestral palette, and an array of atonal effects—vertiginous leaps, turbulent eddies—play off each other in *Der Rosenkavalier*, constantly shifting the opera's manner and mood, and keeping it, despite all the retro decor, from settling on one side of the contest between new and old, modernism and tradition. That mobile, multiform musical texture was an influence on the poet that Merrill eventually became. But it would take years before he could begin to catch up as an artist with this and the other operatic masterpieces that he listened to in adolescence.

Shortly after the appearance of *Jim's Book*, he got his first bad review. Wendell Frederici, a Lawrenceville master, singled out Jimmy's work for comment in a review of the most recent issue of the *Lit*, published in a student newspaper. He praised a short story and a poem by Jimmy, then wrote,

> I have only one adverse criticism to make of Merrill's writing. I don't know Merrill from Adam but I imagine he has an almost feminine fineness of appreciation of color, of flowers, of curious and precious objects d'art—and alas, some of the feminine gush about them. He sometimes drags in color by the ears, seems like a finical interior decorator fussing over the right shade of topaz, vermillion, or mauve.
>
> One is reminded of that famous wit and poseur Oscar Wilde affecting velvet knee breeches and having a lily in his hand. We all have our literary fads and phases. Let's hope Merrill gets over this one quickly. We wallow in sensuous delights like the early Keats, strike cynical, world-weary Byronic poses, grow hair on our chests and brutalize with Hemingway. Some of Hemingway's hairy-chested terse reality wouldn't be a bad antidote for too many red roses and white lilies.

Mr. Frederici's comment anticipates the specifics and tone of almost every negative review that Merrill would receive over his long career, a line on his work that is best exemplified by Mary Karr's biting polemical essay "Against Decoration," published forty-three years later. It is not so different either from the housemaster reports that Jimmy received at Lawrenceville, scolding him for not mixing with the other boys. An evident limitation in his prep-school-era writing—its distance from the real, the corollary of its delicacy, polish, and idealism—elicits a visceral aversion to "interior decoration," smacking as it does of Wildean chic and effeminacy. Like Mary Karr and other future critics, Mr. Frederici is reacting to more than Merrill's poetry. No wonder this writer grew up hating Hemingway.

"Merrill, in my opinion," Mr. Frederici stated, "is the outstanding writer of the issue," although "Buechner, one vaguely feels, is the finest potential poet in the school." The two boys laughed off this publicity, yet they were sensitive to each other's feelings, and the comparison must have made them uneasy. Jimmy waited to give Freddy his copy of *Jim's Book* for fear of spoiling his Christmas holiday. He presented it in January with an inscription: "There are so many things I could say that I don't believe I shall say any of them except that you are the closest and dearest friend I ever hope to have."

They had together established themselves as the school's top writers. (But not the only ones with talent: destined to be famous for his plays was a slightly younger, shadowy boy of their acquaintance, not long after expelled, named Edward Albee.) They belonged to the school's literary organizations: the Reading Club, the Bibliophiles, Pipe and Quill. They had faculty friends and supporters, including Thomas Johnson and Charles ("Pa") Raymond, head of the English Department, whom Merrill treats satirically in "Days of 1941 and '44":

> In vain old Mr. Raymond's sky-blue stare
> Paled with revulsion when I spoke to him
> About my final paper. "Jim,"
> He quavered, "don't, *don't* write on Baudelaire."

Most important was modest Gerrish Thurber, who took their poems as seriously as any adult productions and gave them considered critiques. Thurber was the school librarian and adviser to the *Lit*. Jimmy and Freddy served the magazine as editors; Pete Forcey was editor in chief. Their senior year, with Buechner and Merrill filling its pages, the *Lit* won first prize in Columbia University's national contest for prep-school literary magazines.

One of Jimmy's many senior-year publications was an essay about Virginia Woolf. Woolf was a significant new influence for him. Reading like a reply to Mr. Frederici, his essay is an elegy for a writer (Woolf had died in 1941) who made refined perception her subject. The essay praises her simultaneous attention to sense perception and to abstract "design"—perspectives that might seem opposed to each other, but that Jimmy sees as complementary and united in symbols like a lighthouse at sea or the death of a moth. "Let us never inquire too deeply about her meaning; let us, like her, be content with symbols and surfaces," he writes, defending an aesthetic approach to which he is already committed, and which Woolf is helping him to understand. His new poems were patently decadent, as a title like "Nero Dines in the Gardens of the Golden House" suggests. Most intriguing, although awkward and stagy in the extreme, is a poem called

"Death Masks," published in the *Lit.* This is a dramatic monologue (a form Merrill rarely ever wrote in) spoken by a man who sells death masks made from the faces of artists such as Flaubert and Sarah Bernhardt. Creepiest is the mask he makes of himself. In the process of making it, he lost the ability to smile, so that his own face has become frozen and masklike—a grotesque symbol of art overcoming life.

Lawrenceville celebrated commencement exercises for the Class of 1943 on Monday morning, June 7. It was the middle of World War II, eighteen months after Pearl Harbor and a year before D-Day. Merrill and Buechner wore their hair in the current style: parted in the middle, slicked down with Vitalis. Their starched shirts were clammy under new suits. In his class's mock elections, Jimmy had been named "Best Athlete," "Hungriest," and "Queen of the Showers." At commencement, he garnered the senior prizes in Creative Prose, Poetry, Research, Advanced French, and Greek. But he came in second, behind Freddy, for the Best Private Library, despite (or because of?) all those volumes of Oscar Wilde. And it was Freddy who was selected to write and deliver the Class Poem. Most of the seniors were off to college, the largest number to nearby Princeton, where Freddy was headed. Some, like David Mixsell, planned to enlist and face the war. The sky was hazy, and the campus smelled of cut grass.

Jimmy had decided to attend Amherst. After *Jim's Book*, he must have thought, How can I deny Daddy this? His college choice in one stroke satisfied Charlie and gave him an advantage over brother Charles in Daddy's eyes. He arrived on the graceful hilltop campus, with its stirring view of the Holyoke Range to the south, in June, soon after his graduation from Lawrenceville, because wartime Amherst operated all year. He can't have known yet how good a choice the college was for a young man interested in literature, or how much his education there would count for his future as a writer.

During freshman year, Jimmy took two classes on Renaissance poetry with George Roy Elliott, a sixty-year-old specialist in Shakespeare, English prose, and romantic and modern poetry. In spring 1944, he enrolled in the composition course that was the foundation of the English curriculum. The course was the creation of Theodore Baird, who, breaking with standard procedures for teaching grammar and argument, treated writing as a tool for intellectual exploration and experiment: the aim was to find out what and how one thinks by writing. But before students could use composition for self-knowledge, they needed to be shown how conventional were their notions of the world and how little they really knew about it. Baird might enter the classroom by climbing through a window and ask his students whether it should not be called a door. Such theatrics were distantly indebted to the philosophy of William James. But the course communicated its guiding ideas only indirectly through passages from modern autobiographers such as Henry Adams. Writing prompts were meant to puzzle students and force them to use self-reflection to find a way out of their bafflement.

The two-term course was required of every student. In 1944 it was team-taught by Baird, Reuben Brower, and G. Armour Craig. Craig was in charge of Jimmy's section. He was writing a dissertation about Renaissance Platonism. Craig was an Amherst graduate and a protégé of Baird's who went on to teach at Amherst for forty-five years and serve briefly as college president. But in 1944, he was new on the job, and the eighteen-year-old Merrill liked to lean back in his chair and test his teacher with questions about fashionable contemporaries like Jean-Paul Sartre or Albert Camus. Students would laugh about Jimmy's impudence and imitate his drawling questions after class.

He took the second half of composition in his final term, fall 1946, when his teacher was Walker ("Bill") Gibson, a young, gentle-voiced poet from Jacksonville, then a graduate student at Harvard, with whom Jimmy became lasting friends. "Freshman composition dominated all our lives," Gibson recalls, referring to how Baird's course defined the values and mind-set of teachers and students, through which it left a mark on Merrill. Jimmy was already resistant not only to the brawny real things that Mr. Friderici had found missing in his work, but to Meaning with a capital M. This stance would develop into the militantly casual diffidence about ideas that can make Merrill seem anti-intellectual in his mature approach to poetry. But he had an intellectual, in fact an academic, justification for his attitude in his education at Amherst. The dandified French aesthete he was growing into was being influenced by American pragmatism as embodied in Amherst English and its composition program in particular. Merrill liked to say that he wrote in order to find out what he thought, and he never knew what he wanted to say in a poem until he finished it. Baird would have approved.

Merrill took two classes with Baird: Shakespeare (spring 1945) and Science and Literature in the Nineteenth Century (fall 1945). But the teacher who affected him most deeply was Brower. Brower was a learned, genial, quietly charismatic professor of Greek and English—an unusual double appointment. He'd risen from a boyhood in rural New York State to study at Amherst; at Cambridge, where he encountered the English wing of the New

Criticism in F. R. Leavis, I. A. Richards, and William Empson; and at Harvard. His training in philology and New Critical close reading combined with a stress on the sound of literature that was particular to Amherst.

Brower, like Baird, had encountered Robert Frost at Amherst, and he assimilated Frost's insistence on the dramatic nature of poetic language and the role of voice in creating meaning. It was a piece of local lore at Amherst that the young Ben Brower had volunteered in Frost's class to read aloud an obscure Elizabethan poem, after which the white-haired poet declared before the class, "I give you an A for life." The story captures the approach to literature that Brower developed out of Frost's poetics. "Literature of the first order," he said of his method as a teacher, "calls for lively reading; we must almost act it out as if we were taking parts in a play." Oral performance of a text, a nuanced reading that entered into and communicated the tone of a poem, voicing meaning rather than decoding it, was itself an act of interpretation; and poetry was the quintessential literary form because of its verbal density and reliance on voice. But Brower brought the same focus on "the sound of sense" (Frost's phrase) to the novel, and he helped to develop Merrill's appreciation of fiction too. Jimmy read Jane Austen in tutorial with him, and Proust would be the subject of his senior essay under Brower's supervision in 1946.

Merrill had first encountered Proust in freshman composition, where he was one of the autobiographers Baird featured in that course (indeed Proust was the source of more examples than any other author assigned). He at once became a transformative passion for Merrill, sweeping away Baudelaire, Wilde, and Wylie like schoolboy crushes. Asked by an interviewer years later why Proust meant so much to him, Merrill pointed first to the scale of Proust's seven-volume novel, its "wonderful size." But *À la recherche du temps perdu* was not *War and Peace* or *Bleak House* (big books Merrill came to love later): its setting was Belle Époque French society as seen through the prism of Proust's life; its monumentality contrasted with the subjective focus epitomized in the stand-alone, quasi-lyric passages picked out by Baird (such as the pages about the madeleine, the steeple of Saint-Hilaire, and Marcel's obsession with the actress Berma). The novel's material was the life of a writer rather like Jimmy, an exquisitely self-conscious young man at ease in wealthy society, preoccupied with music, art, drama, and books, whose tale begins with a boy alone in his room, desperate for his mother's goodnight kiss.

Reading *À la recherche*, Merrill was captivated in particular by a voice—Brower's theme, however far Proust might seem from Frost. In the voice of his narrator, Proust's youth as a habitué of salon society was turned to artistic aims, which Proust managed without rejecting, but by building on,

his good manners. "The real triumph of manners in Proust," Merrill told
an interviewer in 1968,

> is the extreme courtesy toward the reader, the voice explaining at
> once formally and intimately. Though it can be heard, of course, as
> megalomania, there is something wonderful in the reasonableness,
> the long-windedness of that voice, in its desire to be understood, in
> its treatment of *every* phenomenon (whether the way someone pro-
> nounces a word, or the article of clothing worn, or the color of a flower)
> as having ultimate importance. Proust says to us in effect, "I will not
> patronize you by treating these delicate matters with less than total,
> patient, sparkling seriousness."

In 1944, defending his newfound hero against charges of narcissism,
Jimmy ruminated, "And how is it possible to say that Proust gives us only
his own happiness, his own love? If he does so, it is only because his symbols are smaller, more particular, than Woolf's, than Lawrence's. We can,
nonetheless, substitute names, find our own painter to be, for us, Elstir,
our own Vinteuil, our own Albertine." The point was to live in such a way to
be able to turn one's life into writing. It was the ambition Merrill's father
had planted when he urged him to keep a diary, and Proust had realized it
on a grand scale in his circular book.

Merrill's obsession with memory dates from this time. With Proust as
tutor, he began to remember "so much of my own life"—he was just eighteen when he wrote this—"that said life is beginning to appear immensely
richer than it really was, or perhaps it really was + I never knew it." In his
"disjointed memories," he told Freddy, "Southampton figures very largely,"
including the wallpaper pattern in his bedroom, his father's setters, and
the jigsaw puzzles he pored over "until Mama became convinced I was
going blind doing them. All of these [memories] make up a puzzle so much
greater + more blinding." These are the metaphors he would explore in
"Lost in Translation," his Proustian memory poem in which "Southampton
figures very largely," written thirty years later. "Everything will remind me
of something now," he concluded, as you might speak of an affliction or gift.

Naturally Proust's homosexuality and the homosexual themes of the
novel were a crucial part of Jimmy's identification with him. In contrast to Wilde, Proust was a homosexual writer whose story did not end in
ignominy and martyrdom: why, he was being read in freshman courses.
Merrill argued with a friend who objected to Proust's changing of the sex
of the people on whom certain of his characters were based, as in the nar-

rator's love for Albertine, who was modeled on Proust's lover Alfred Agostinelli. To this Jimmy replied forcefully, "[S]ince the tremendous thing in the book itself is the revelation of a philosophy, of a mode of perception, rather than a catalogue of louche adventures, it actually, I insist, does not matter how faithfully Proust's physical society corresponds to the one in his imagination." To be faithful to one's "mode of perception" was the criterion. Sexuality implied a sensibility, and that mattered more than fidelity to any "physical society."

About the direction of his own desires, Jimmy was entirely clear. Back in 1942, he'd written a letter to his mother justifying his refusal to attend society dances in New York. "You have to understand this: it is more than just disliking dances." He simply could not bring himself to act like "one of the fellows." "I have accepted this feeling," he said, "and I believe there is nothing you or I can do." The pressure that mother and son both felt about this issue expresses a mutual awareness that much more was at stake than whether he would show up to a Junior League ball.

At Amherst Jimmy found a social situation rather different from Lawrenceville. Soldiers, either preparing to become officers or, after 1944, returning from duty to study on the GI Bill, dominated the campus. The number of regularly admitted students had been drastically reduced to young men who were either too young to serve at sixteen and seventeen or classified 4F, unfit for military service. The dorms were occupied by military men, and students like Jimmy were scattered among fraternities. As one student who entered Amherst in 1943 puts it, "[W]e were all on the fringe." At the same time, despite the reduced size of the student body, there were more students at Amherst interested in literature and drama than there had been at Lawrenceville; and Jimmy—or Jim, as his teachers and classmates called him—was ready to make friends.

He was known to everyone as Charles Merrill's son. Merrill Lynch, in the midst of major reorganization and a national marketing campaign, was a prominent national brand, and the cofounder of the firm arrived at his alma mater like a potentate, chauffeur-driven onto the gridiron to cheer the purple-clad Amherst football team. Even if he refused to join Charlie's fraternity, which caused CEM real distress,* Jimmy was no longer so intent on shrinking from association with his father and the fact of his own wealth. He was learning to be generous with money, rather, and to express

---

* CEM to JM, excerpt from a letter, October 13, 1946 (Amh). In a letter to the author, December 16, 2001, Paul Leahy, who was deputed to invite JM to join Chi Psi, explained that the fraternity made the invitation in order to please his father: JM "was polite about my quest, but not a little 'superior,' and in any event gave me a firm 'No.' "

his ideas and taste freely, all of which had an effect. "He was smarter, richer, and maybe better than the rest of us, and we wanted to get as much of him as we could," remembers Bob Wilson, a freshman from Michigan. Without prep-school housemasters to supervise students, drinking created camaraderie. French 75s (champagne, gin, and a sugar cube) were favored by the sophisticates in Jimmy's circle.

He had the good fortune to draw as his freshman roommate Horton Grant, a bespectacled, sweet-natured boy from Los Angeles and the nephew of the film actor Edward Everett Horton. Horton, like his uncle, was a comedian, and he and Jimmy were active in Amherst's theater scene, which included a role for Jimmy as the butler in P. G. Wodehouse's *The Play's the Thing* in fall 1943. Curtis Canfield, the director of the theater program at Amherst, put on exceptional undergraduate productions of Shakespeare as well as risky modern and contemporary plays for which Amherst faculty wives and their families filled out casts and helped to create costumes and sets. Jimmy joined the Masquers, which grew into the Kirby Theater Guild. The group made a respectable alternative to weekend excitement at the football field. More than a couple of the young men Merrill befriended in the theater turned out after college to be homosexual. But there were no confidences exchanged; same-sex desires were wrestled with silently, not talked about openly. "These students," Bill Gibson says about the theater crowd, "weren't 'gay'; they were 'talented.' "

An exception to that rule was tall, broad-chested, raffish Tom Howkins. Howkins was "an acknowledged queer." He had a booming voice, imperial manner, smart style, and devil-may-care love of fun. His family roots were in the South, but he'd grown up in the town of Amherst. He spent weekends in New York going to jazz clubs and—being queer didn't preclude this—picking up girls for the night. Merrill would meet him in Greenwich Village at the San Remo, a mob-owned bar that catered to artists, writers, and hipsters like Allen Ginsberg, who was then a student at Columbia. Howkins was Merrill's introduction to a bohemian New York that this New York native knew nothing of. He was also Merrill's first more or less openly gay friend. Together they developed an idiom laced with catty remarks, cozy endearments, and coy exclamations—a first draft of the camp style Jimmy used when it suited him for the rest of his life.

As slight and soft-spoken as Howkins was loud and flamboyant, Rosemary Sprague was the other intimate friend Merrill made during his first year at Amherst. They met on the set of the Wodehouse play while she was still in high school and not yet a Smith College student. Like Howkins, Rosemary was a local product, being the only child of Atherton Sprague, an Amherst mathematics professor, and his wife Mary. The Spragues welcomed Merrill into their home, gratified by his interest in their daughter. Gangly, with straight brown hair, and an idiosyncratic sense of fashion, Rosie appealed to Jimmy as an intelligent wallflower who was as unhappy as he when obliged to attend a local dance. He could point to their friendship when he wanted to allay his mother's anxieties about his manhood. But he wasn't merely using her. He understood her discomfort living up to the gender expectations of her mother, one of Amherst's leading matrons. Rosemary's health was delicate—she was sent more than once to a sanatorium to be treated for tuberculosis—and he admired how she carried on. She loved books and art. Her closest companions were a large collection of stuffed animals. Like an Austen heroine, she was sincere, unpresuming, and kept in reserve a peppery wit Jimmy admired too.

Hanging over Merrill's first three terms at Amherst was the knowledge that he would be called by the Army after his eighteenth birthday. His father urged him to prepare by getting himself in top shape, but all he managed were a few wistful walks in the hills. In May, interrupting his studies in the middle of his sophomore year, he entered the Army Enlisted Reserve. Reporting for duty on June 14, 1944, at Fort Dix, New Jersey, he buttoned up a private's uniform. A month later he was sent to Camp Croft in South Carolina, where he learned to march, clean a gun, dig a foxhole, wear a gas mask, and crawl under barbed wire while explosions roared overhead. In his loneliness and boredom, he depended on the companionship of a pal from Amherst, Robert Brown, and correspondence with his mother, Rosemary, Howkins, and Freddy, who'd been called up by the Army too. Somehow he had time to read a lot: this "Marcelomaniac" was consuming quantities of Proust, poetry by Rilke, Yeats, and Valéry, and novels by Stendhal and Henry James. His mind drifted to Isabel Archer and the "Archaic Torso of Apollo" while he was making notes about the range and caliber of ordnance.

"I am in this dreadful affair," he wrote about the war to Coley Newman, another friend from Amherst. "I have a very good chance of being killed or emotionally sterilized." He was afraid of "losing time" "cleaning the latrines," not to mention the prospect of dying on the battlefield. "I have such a huge desire to live [. . .]. I want to write so much and so well[.]" That letter was written shortly before he learned that David Mixsell, his Lawrenceville nemesis, had died from combat wounds in France. It was hard for Jimmy to know what to feel. "Elegy for an Enemy," a poem he wrote in response to the news, begins,

> Death was by far too good for him, we said.
> The small, pale eyes, the soul of blunted lead,

The snake-swift smile tracing the shape of dread.
Can he be dead?

Not long after that came a shocking report from Amherst: Horton Grant
had died in a car crash one Saturday night, along with a buddy and their two
dates. It wasn't necessary for a young man to go to war to die an arbitrary,
violent death.

Jimmy also had his father's health to think about. Decades of hard living
and the strain of his recent work for Merrill Lynch had left Charlie's arteries blocked and his heart vulnerable. In April 1944, he suffered a major
heart attack, followed by another in July. He spent more than four months
in a New York hospital, where doctors had no treatment to offer but rest.
Suddenly and severely restricted in his activities, this man who lived for
sex and business couldn't engage in either. Bobby Magowan was released
in a hurry from the Navy and returned to New York to help run the firm.
Charlie's care fell to Kinta, who, with a nurse and doctors' approval, kept
a close watch on him, managing his constant angina pain with nitroglyc-
erin and limiting visitors. Jimmy blamed "la belle Nouvelle Orléanaise" for
"solicitously nagging him to distraction. [She] will not leave his side (she
knows it is buttered)."

With his father's life threatened, and his memory stimulated by Proust,
the eighteen-year-old soldier longed to return to childhood. A letter from
his nephew Merrill Magowan, Doris and Bobby's second son, released a
flood of feeling in him. The little boy described being left alone in a rowboat and drifting "all the way over to the swans" before he was rescued.
"That phrase," Jimmy wrote to his mother from Camp Croft, "somehow
makes me so homesick for not Southampton but for being a child again,
being in a position to experience the fear and magical delight of the little
boy caught among the big white, beautifully evil birds, to utter the squeaks
and gasps he must have uttered. I envy him more than I can say for that."
Barely having come of age himself, Jimmy looked into his past and found a
character who would soon appear in his poetry: a child magnetically drawn
to the "beautifully evil" swans.

Before entering the service, Jimmy and Hellen had visited Charlie in the
hospital. His advice to his son had to do not with courage or survival but
sex: "Never let another man put his hand on you," he counseled. "I begged
him not to worry," Merrill writes, recounting the incident in *A Different
Person*, and explaining that the exchange was followed by his "prompt surrender to an opera buff with chevrons." His diary from 1944 suggests that
that was not quite the case, although he did meet a soldier who liked opera

and had even read Proust; and Jimmy's temperature rose when the man was around. He wrote a trembling poem about wanting to reach out and touch his sleeping head. But he settled for giving the man a recording of *Pelléas* and a copy of Rilke.

In late 1944, he took an Army physical exam, for which he prepared by popping Benzedrine, hoping to push his heart rate up to an alarming level. But that was unnecessary: his eyesight was found to be poor, and he was designated for "limited service" only, which meant that he wouldn't be sent overseas; he was assigned to the typing pool. Then, in January 1945, with Allied troops advancing on the Rhine, he was abruptly discharged. He was exhilarated, but he'd done nothing to be proud of; he had merely escaped.* When victory in Europe and then Asia came later that year, Jimmy wouldn't share in the national euphoria, and it would be some time before he made any reference to the horrors of 1945—the revelation of the Holocaust, the Allied bombing of civilians in Germany and Japan, and the detonation of the atom bomb on Hiroshima and Nagasaki. He fled from the war like a bad dream he wanted not to remember.

There was no one to come home to. His father was convalescing in Florida. His mother was in the Pacific: she'd volunteered to serve in the Red Cross, had been sent as administrative support to American nurses on Guam and in Hawaii, and wouldn't return home for good until October. Jimmy tried to transfer to Princeton, where Freddy would return when he was discharged; but that plan failed and he had to "squeeze" himself back into Amherst in time to resume classes in February.

Aware of having been spared in the war, and feeling a mounting pressure to make himself a writer, Jimmy brooded on aesthetics in his diary. In April, he was summoned to an audience with a distinguished campus visitor: Robert Frost. The poet was seventy. He wore old-style black shoes laced to the ankles. Rheumy and tired, yet "with brilliant blue eyes and an enchanting smile," Frost read and reacted to Merrill's poems. He warned the young man away from "vague words," while praising him for phrases that forced readers to "say things in a new way." He said, "When you're young you can be sensuous or—damn it—sensual, yet it is still fine. When you're older it becomes coarse, gross, and is rather dreadful."

Semester to semester, the war shuffled students in and out of Amherst, and Merrill made new friends, including an attractively quiet, olive-

---

* Did CEM intervene on his younger son's behalf, as he had in his older son's timely discharge from the service? It's possible. But if so, and Jimmy knew or even suspected it, he always kept the thought to himself.

skinned young man named Seldon James. Seldon was the son of an American businessman and British-Argentine mother; an Amherst professor
who'd met his father in Argentina had arranged for him to come north to
study, though the Spanish-speaking Seldon couldn't read English well at
the time. He was an uprooted teenager who carried three passports. His
manners were elegant and formal. He couldn't play sports and preferred a
walk in the woods to the usual collegiate socializing.

During the summer term, Jimmy and Seldon shared a room, but the
arrangement was short-lived, because Seldon enlisted in the Navy that July.
There was a backstory to this development: the boy had been admitted to
Amherst without his academic record, which seemed to have been lost en
route from Argentina; when it finally turned up, and his preparation was
judged inadequate, a school official advised him to withdraw, enlist, and
then ask to return since "We'll have to take you back" under the GI Bill. To
Jimmy, who knew nothing about all this, Seldon's decision to enlist was a
tragic mystery. In his diary, in ludicrously purple prose, he recorded his
agony minute by minute as Seldon's leaving approached—until, Jimmy
having said "forever farewell" and done his crying, Seldon walked back
through the door, not yet obliged to spend the night in the Navy.

Merrill wasn't in love, but he wanted to be, and he was practicing what it
would feel like. He was practicing also what it would be like to write about
being in love, both in his diary and in poems where Seldon James served as
muse. Feeling the will to write, he was aware of needing a theme, "something so magnificently worth writing that I can spend a lot of time on it."
For that, he would need to fall in love for real.

Merrill met Kimon Friar over lunch in Amherst's suitably named Valentine Hall on September 9, 1945. Friar was a temporary instructor in the
college's program for veterans and the director of the Poetry Center at the
92nd Street YMHA. Short, wiry, and dark, he was a high-minded, charismatic man of letters and an unabashed self-promoter. He was born on an
island under Ottoman rule in the Sea of Marmara to Greek parents who
immigrated to Chicago when he was a child; his surname was an English
translation of the Greek Kalogeropoulos. He planned to travel to Greece, the
homeland he'd never seen, at the end of the spring term. At thirty-three, he
was fourteen years older than Merrill. A blurry photo taken in his rooms at
Amherst one evening that fall shows the two of them looking into a mirror,
the bouncing locks of the one and receding crown of the other, the camera
flash in both their eyes.

Friar had sat down for lunch with the students, rather than his faculty colleagues, saying, "I'm tired of polite conversation." Merrill introduced himself: "Mr. Brower thought I should meet you, we might have kindred interests." Friar "groaned inwardly" when Merrill asked to show him his poems. He hardly expected what he found:

> Several days later, when I glanced at the poems, I was thunderstruck. I'd never seen such quality and dexterity since I'd played the role of mentor to John Malcolm Brinnin in Detroit and John was eighteen and I was twenty-three. I called in Merrill and said: "You're already a superb poet. I cannot, of course, make anyone a poet who isn't one initially; I can only teach you all the techniques I know during the remaining time I have here. [. . .] You must be willing, in this short period of eight months or so, to give yourself over to my dictatorial direction in a purely professional manner. I shall set you exercises in all forms of poetic techniques and, at the same time, commission you to write for me about three poems a week embodying the lessons. I'll set the themes, the stanza forms, the meters, the rhymes schemes, the orchestration, everything. [. . .] What do you say?" "Try me!" Merrill replied.

"Something of enormous, unthinkable importance has happened to me," Jimmy wrote in his diary, "which <u>will</u> be important because he (Kimon Friar his name) and I both wish it to be. I shall write, be brilliant, be great. Oh but I am tired, and a fool, and must, as fools must, sleep." He had become Friar's poetry student, not a student in his classroom but "my *private* student" whose education would go on in the evening in Friar's rooms and on weekends in New York. And it wasn't only poetry, but love, that Friar was teaching him. A diary entry dated "29 October midnight" announced it: "We are in love, Kimon and I, tenderly, passionately, completely." Friar was Merrill's first lover and an older man with experience—including experience with a younger poet; indeed, he had been lover as well as mentor to poet John Malcolm Brinnin (who would much later become a good friend of Merrill's). Jimmy's joy was exalted, operatic. "I have been taught to love," he wrote on November 12, "and it is a thing so incredible and so <u>moving</u> that I can say nothing, even to myself, except 'I love you.' "

Then, in December, everything changed. "Mama opened a letter I sent him, having been suspicious, she said, all along," Jimmy reported in his diary. Hellen was outraged by her discovery. At first she wanted to separate her son and Friar forcibly. "Either he or I must leave Amherst." Jimmy protested: "All of this I feel is <u>wrong</u>. . . . It is <u>wrong</u> when love is broken into; it is <u>wrong</u> for the first fullness, the first joy, the first loving of my life to be paralyzed." There were bitter displays, as when, upright in his dressing gown in his mother's bedroom, he insisted that he loved Kimon and always would. But he was deeply attached to his mother; only recently, while she was in the Pacific, he'd missed her "intensely."* He'd been careful to conceal his homosexuality from her, and yet he seems not to have foreseen that, when the push came, she would actually oppose his happiness. Worse yet, the situation restaged the broken home, with Jimmy in his father's role, being pulled away from his mother by his love for someone else.

Whatever Hellen herself may have felt about Jimmy's affair, she was concerned about other people's perceptions of him, and indirectly their view of her and the job she had done raising him. Appearances mattered. That winter, Freddy found himself alone with Hellen in a car idling by the curb outside her East Fifty-seventh Street house. As a rule, Buechner remembers, "Hellen's face was wonderfully made-up"; strong emotions never broke the smiling surface. But this time she raised her voice to threaten him: if he ever told anyone that Jimmy was homosexual, he would never again be welcome in her house. She was strong-arming an ally: in addition to Jimmy and Kimon's letters, she had opened a letter from Freddy to Jimmy and learned that he disapproved of the affair. Still, Freddy was put off by her pressure. "Why is it so shameful? Little boys do it," he reasoned. "Don't think that little girls don't," she shot back, possibly referring to some experience of her own? No implication was filled in. But the upshot was clear: the horror had to do not so much with what Jimmy did in bed than with the threat that it might be made public.

Hellen threatened Jimmy by insisting that it would kill his father—literally: it would bring about a fatal final heart attack—if Charlie ever learned of the affair. Hellen wasn't telling the whole story, however. For without Jimmy's knowing, she herself had already told Charlie about it. A war council had been convened (Hellen, Charlie, Bobby Magowan, and the lawyer Larry Condon were in on the discussion), and grotesque proposals were bruited about. Could a mobster be hired to have Friar "rubbed out"? It would be easier to pressure President Cole to dismiss Friar, although that course of action had the makings of a scandal. Or a more seemly alternative: there was a woman of loose reputation in Southampton, with an interest in the arts, who might be paid to introduce Jimmy to the pleasures of

---

* "The other day I saw a boy on the street in Amherst laughing with his mother; I could have wept; I miss her suddenly, miss her intensely." JM, journal, March 12, 1947, Jnl 1 (WUSTL).

female flesh, then disappear. In the end, hiring neither hit man nor whore, Charlie simply said nothing to his son, and Hellen settled for discretion and the fig leaf of a promise. She called Friar to New York, and made the lovers swear they wouldn't go on seeing each other. Soon they were back in each other's arms.

In December, in the midst of his Christmas crisis, desperate that his love affair might be over, Merrill told his diary how it began in Friar's "wonderful rooms." These were not the large immaculate rooms he'd known as a child, with their chintz curtains, George III chairs, and French clocks, but another sort of luxury, expressing a style of life unfamiliar and fascinating to him. As if to preserve them, Jimmy catalogued Friar's talismanic possessions: flowering narcissus and amaryllis, books, little magazines, a "littered" desk, late Beethoven and Hindemith recordings, reproductions of Picasso, Mondrian, and de Chirico, a fur cloak on the couch, a Mexican blanket over the door, grass rugs, *Jim's Book* in the drawer of the nightstand, and, by the bed, a recent photo of Jimmy in Army uniform, across which he'd written in block letters, *S'AGAPO*—"I love you" in modern Greek. He continued,

> and I do, I love him so that I feel dead now. And how he would sit and read my poems and more often than not like them, kiss me[:] "Jimmy, I love you most of all when you're a good poet." And he himself, the lean square face with black rimmed glasses, black hair, very soft brown eyes, tender strong hands, the face of love, the face of all kind and beautiful things. I don't want to write this. I am driven to it for fear these things may move from me, disappear altogether.

Friar's Greek heritage was part of what attracted Merrill to him. With Merrill, Friar assumed the ancient Greek role of the *eromenos*, the mentor and lover who helps the *erastes*, a beautiful youth, to discover the passion for knowledge through their erotic relationship. Only those classical roles were being updated with inspiration from the same-sex love poems of C. P. Cavafy, the modern poet from Alexandria whom Friar introduced to Merrill through his own translations. Jimmy knew ancient Greek well; he'd studied Homer, the lyric poets, and Plato at Amherst. Now Friar was teaching him the demotic.

Besides language, the lovers played with props and symbols. In his Christmas Eve catalog of the objects in Friar's rooms, the most significant items Merrill mentions are a plaster head of Hermes ("the messenger of the gods, and therefore the medium between poets and the infinities," Friar wrote) and Friar's own life mask, which he had made at twenty-two in imitation of Keats's life mask made at the same age.

Friar had a complex fantasy relationship with Keats. It began in high school, in Chicago, where Friar read "Ode on a Grecian Urn." The poem connected Greek art and the language of Friar's new country, and "[s]uddenly I realized how beautiful English was." Friar "fell madly in love with John Keats as a person, as a man." He read Keats's poetry and letters in coordination with his own growth, "so that when I was, let's say, seventeen years old, two months, and three days, I would read that poem or letter which Keats wrote" when he was that age. He would pretend that Keats had sent him "Ode to a Nightingale," and write a letter in reply as Keats's beloved Fanny Brawne, say, or one of his friends. In the process, Friar was studying English meter and diction, and learning how to respond to poetry as a teacher and critic.

Now, encouraging Merrill to fall in love with him, Friar drew the young man into the sort of erotic literary apprenticeship he had had in fantasy with Keats. A series of photos taken by Merrill and Friar in Friar's rooms at Amherst capture their role playing as the lovers (now one, now the other) pose with the Hermes head, Friar's mask, and a copy of Keats's life mask. In one photo, Merrill's face appears between the Hermes head and Keats's mask, as if he were trying out how it might feel to be a god or a great poet, under Friar's direction. Friar poses with Keats's mask too, placing it over his face in one photo and holding it to one side while he turns away in another, so that the face and mask, both in profile, are twinned. Another photo shows Merrill with Keats's mask placed over his face. The mask magnifies his identity ("I shall write, be brilliant, be great") but also erases it: no one would know that this is a photo of James Merrill. And that may have felt liberating. Wearing Keats's mask, Jimmy was no longer his foolish nineteen-year-old self, with his money and broken home defining him. Yet it must have been hard to breathe or speak with that mask in place.

At the Poetry Center in New York, Friar hosted a reading series that included, among many other poets, W. H. Auden, to whom he introduced Merrill. Friar was teaching at the Poetry Center, too. He gave lecture courses in the fall and spring and led a poetry workshop throughout the year, both of which Jimmy attended.* In his workshop, Friar focused on the interplay of technique and imagination with Chard Powers Smith's *Pattern*

---

* A syllabus of Friar's from the 1950s that merges the matter of both of these courses includes a bibliography of the heterogeneous texts from which he created his aesthetics, including Carl Jung's *Psychological Types*, Henry Adams's *Education*, Oswald Spengler's *Decline of the West*, J. W. N. Sullivan's biography of Beethoven, Julien Levy's *Surrealism*, and a number of works in poetics (KF Papers, American College of Greece).

and Variation in Poetry (1932) as his bible, but as a lecturer, he was concerned with cultural and spiritual issues. In the fall, in a course on "duality," he lectured on Keats, Milton, Dante, and Shakespeare, the idea of love in psychoanalysis and Plato's *Symposium*, "The Swan in Literature and Painting," and the Electra story. In the spring, his topic was "The Modern Poet and the Lack of a Myth." Readings included *The Waste Land, Four Quartets, The Bridge*, and *The Cantos*; five classes, the most for any author, were devoted to Yeats's late poetry and his occult treatise, *A Vision*, which Friar had written about in his master's thesis at the University of Michigan. For Friar, these works were examples of "the modern poet's search for a mythology [. . .] which might offer him some concrete body of belief for metaphor and metaphysic" to replace Christianity.

Friar himself was obsessed with the myth of Medusa. In "Medusa-Mask," an essay that appeared in *Poetry* in 1940, he presents the myth as a fable of "artistic purpose" in which Perseus is a model for young poets. Born from Zeus's rape of Danaë, Perseus is banished with his mother by his grandfather, who fears a prophecy that Danaë's child will kill him. Mother and son are taken in by King Seriphus, who falls in love with Danaë. To get her son out of the way, Seriphus challenges Perseus to cut off the head of Medusa—an impossible task, which heroes before him have died trying to perform. Medusa, Friar writes, was "a maiden of Hellenic proportion [. . .] whose serpentine locks and hypnotic glance gave her that portion of Evil before which every artist shudders in temptation." In Friar's allegory, Medusa represents the temptation in all artistic beauty: "pattern devoid of subject," "the final reach of form." Since, if Perseus gazes into the Gorgon's eyes, he will be fatally paralyzed, he "must seek Medusa obliquely, and guided by her reflected image in the bright shield he bears, must slay her by subtle indirection."

It was easy for Jimmy to locate himself in the story. His first diary entry about Friar is headed "Perseus." Like Perseus, Jimmy was born of an Olympian father whose financial power and sexual appetite were suggested by the golden shower with which Zeus rapes Danaë. But CEM was also an older man, distant in relation to his son; with his weakened heart, he was less like Zeus than like a grandfather, and Jimmy's preference was to confront him blandly, not in open contest and hate. Like Perseus, Jimmy had been banished with his mother; Danaë and Medusa were masks for Hellen, whom he both served and battled, and who "paralyzed" him, he felt, when she opposed his love for Friar. He would have noticed his mother's first name in Friar's reference to the Gorgon as "a maiden of Hellenic proportion." The myth must have seemed made to describe his struggles with his parents.

And with his art. Merrill was a precocious formal poet, and already the question was whether he could ever be anything more. Petrification in the Medusa story described the fate of a poet hypnotized by the allure of form without content, or impressions without ideas, to which Jimmy was certainly vulnerable. Friar, helping him to name the threat, taught Merrill not to reject poetic "form," but to use it as a weapon, as Perseus uses the mirror of his shield.

Merrill responded to this education with a rush of activity. Even while attending Friar's classes in New York and writing poems to his lover's specifications, he flourished in his courses at Amherst, which that year included two terms of elementary Italian. (Hungry for languages, he'd already taken three terms of German and two of advanced French, in addition to ancient Greek and Friar's informal tutorial in modern Greek.) In December 1945, he took the title role in a student production of Jean Cocteau's play *Orphée*—Orpheus, another mask of the poet. In spring 1946, his essay "The Transformation of Rilke" came out in the *Yale Poetry Review*; the issue also printed poetry by Wallace Stevens and William Carlos Williams.

And in March, four of his poems, placed first, were published in *Poetry*. This marked his national debut as a poet and the beginning of a lifelong association with the Chicago-based magazine. His father, who relied on expert opinion whenever possible, "had *Poetry* investigated to see if it was a reputable publication." After having published some of the great modernist poems of the 1910s and 1920s, the magazine had "gone down a little," Merrill admitted, "but is still watched by critics and writers to the extent that Archibald MacLeish has asked me to submit a manuscript to the Yale Younger Poets series"—which he didn't do. He wound up the school year by winning the Glascock Poetry Prize given by Mount Holyoke College, a prestigious student competition that Buechner would win the following year and Sylvia Plath not long after that. Then he joined Muriel Rukeyser and two poets from Friar's workshop on the stage of the Poetry Center for his first reading in New York.

Over the same school year, he met through Friar a number of intriguing New York artists and intellectuals. They included Frances Steloff, founder of the Gotham Book Mart and a champion of the banned moderns James Joyce, D. H. Lawrence, and Henry Miller; the Jungian mythologist and scholar of comparative religion, Joseph Campbell, and his wife Jean Erdman, the modern dancer and choreographer; a patrician young editor, writing his first novel, named Gore Vidal; Anaïs Nin, better known today for her love affair with Henry Miller and her posthumously published erotica than for the novels she wrote in the 1940s; and the dancer and experimental filmmaker Maya Deren. Friar shared ideas with Campbell and Erdman, whose dance *The Transformations of Medusa* (1942) explored his myth. Vidal went to Friar's lectures at the Poetry Center in fall 1945, as did Nin and Deren, where Merrill made friends easily with the seductive, confessional Nin. She came to Amherst in spring 1946 to read from a novel, and he praised her writing in a letter she copied into her diary. They traded visits over the next year, and Merrill bought gloomy, surrealist artworks by her husband Hugh Parker Guiler, but they soon drifted apart.

Deren, by contrast, grew in interest and importance for him. He encountered her first in a picture hanging in Friar's Amherst rooms: a still from her film *Meshes of the Afternoon* (1943) in which her face floats behind a window like a gorgeous, placid mask; she signed it on the back for Friar "Maya (Medusa)." Later, he would attend her parties and screenings, and she took a series of arresting portrait photos of him. Born in Kiev in 1917, Deren had come to the U.S. as a child when her family left Russia to escape the anti-Jewish pogroms of the 1920s. After writing a master's thesis on French Symbolism and modern poetry, she became active in progressive politics and avant-garde cinema and dance. She was physically compact and strong, with a cloud of frizzy red hair, thick, sensuous lips, and bright green eyes. Playing with masks and mirrors in her films, she explored the dynamics of female self-portraiture. She chose for herself the name "Maya," meaning "illusion" in Sanskrit. Most important for Merrill, she was a student of Haitian Vodoun and its ritual trances, which she filmed and participated in as an initiate. Deren introduced Merrill to spirit possession not as a metaphor, but as a relation to the divine that an artist could directly experience.

In May 1946, Friar departed for Greece. Hellen had her son home for the summer in New Canaan, and she made an appointment for him with a psychoanalyst. Jimmy distrusted this doctor his mother had produced to treat his sexual "abnormality," and he got little out of the therapy, though he kept at it for some time. Meanwhile he rented a post office box so he could correspond in secret with his lover. The long-distance affair was hard to manage under Hellen's watchful eye. Each man worried that the other would give the game away. When Friar sent him a fez at his mother's address, Merrill fretted: it would be "stored up" for his "next 'talk' " with her. When Jimmy admitted to her that they had been writing to each other, Friar feared that it would "tear down what we have so laboriously, like moles underground, like towers underground, built."

By "towers underground," Friar meant their secret plans for a future together in Greece. "Life is something entirely other on this side of the world," he wrote to Jimmy. "Dream about it my dear, and dream of me." And a few days later: "Here in Greece I have found another world, another planet, one which you also will recognize as your spiritual home. It is here for our colonizing." For the time being, he instructed his young lover to "wait with me, in the serene confidence of our love for one another, until you are twenty-one"—as Jimmy would be on his next birthday, at which point he could not "be touched either in person or property. This, my dear, is a wily Greek's advice."

Merrill's cramped letters to Friar suggest that he felt torn between his lover and his mother and guilty toward them both. By contrast, he was writing expansive, eloquent letters to William Burford, his Amherst classmate. Merrill and Burford were involved that summer in editing a magazine called the *Medusa*, a showcase for Friar's ideas and influence that reprinted "Medusa-Mask" from *Poetry*, along with an essay by Deren on cinema, a short story by Nin, offerings from Amherst faculty and students, four Merrill poems, and a poem by Friar. Burford was a wealthy young man from a Texas oil family and a poet. He was the friend of Merrill's who objected to Proust disguising men as women in his novel. Their argument about Proust implied, for Merrill, attitudes about money and class: Jimmy didn't want to be isolated by his sexual choices or his wealth. What he longed for, he told Burford, were "the inconceivable joys of 'the blond and blue-eyed' "—he was quoting Mann's story "Tonio Kröger"—and "the bliss of the commonplace, which is so violently uncommon." Another letter to Burford expands on the idea and sets an agenda:

> It is not inconceivable that one day we shall find in ourselves that all the contradictions and desires and angers have through their quarreling created a way of life, a way of thought, an element as lucid, revealing as many wonders as we had always imagined existing outside ourselves. We will have created our own commonplace, and whether we drown from love of it like Narcissus or find that it is an atmosphere accessible to the entire world it will be the achievement, of all others, that is most perfect, personal, and liberating.
>
> That (in case I die in a plane crash) is what I believe, what I honestly believe I believe; it explains, now, what I must do with my poem and with all poems.

Merrill wrote that letter on the eve of traveling to Mexico City—it would be his first trip outside the U.S.—in the company of his brother Charles and sister-in-law Mary. They visited colonial-era churches and Mayan ruins, and saw murals by Diego Rivera and paintings by Frida Kahlo. Charles arranged for them to meet Gustav Regler, a German author, socialist, veteran of the Spanish Civil War, and friend to Hemingway. Jimmy respected Regler, but didn't like him, representative as he was of his brother's political side. Regler at one point observed in private to Charles that his brother was obviously a homosexual: it was the first time Charles and Mary had considered the idea.

Besides the *Medusa*, Friar and Merrill had another publication in the works. Friar took with him to Greece copies of twelve poems that Merrill had written over the past year, including the four in the *Medusa*, and ordered these in a thirty-page chapbook called *The Black Swan*; it was printed in Athens in October 1946 in an edition of one hundred copies "not for sale." "Since I was positive that Merrill would one day be acknowledged one of America's foremost poets," Friar explained many years later, "I deliberately published the book privately (for $100) in a limited edition [. . .] knowing that one day it would be a rare item." Icaros, the small house that printed the book, also published Cavafy, George Seferis, and other eminent Greek poets. The cover design was a black swan and its reflection by the Greek painter and stage set designer Ghika.

The Black Swan was a collection similar in kind to *Jim's Book*: a private edition of Merrill's college poems, titled this time by Friar rather than his father. Yet the best of these poems were startlingly accomplished; and, unlike *Jim's Book*, *The Black Swan* was not a miscellany: it had a coherent, intimately personal story to tell, albeit obliquely. From the title poem, which Merrill produced for one of Friar's assignments in fall 1945, to the leave-taking "Embarkation Sonnets," which he wrote in spring 1946 in a verse form Friar had prescribed, *The Black Swan* traced the intertwined course of Merrill's poetic tutorial with Friar and their love affair, being the product of both. Merrill dedicated the book to Friar. Beneath the dedication was an untitled poem about the dying Keats, an acrostic. The first letters of its two five-line stanzas spelled "KIMON FRIAR."

The black swan in the title poem alludes to the black-haired Friar, as Friar liked to point out. On this level, the poem reads like the young poet's declaration of love for his teacher. Here is the first stanza, then the fifth and final one:

> Black on flat water past the jonquil lawns
> Riding, the black swan draws
> A private chaos warbling in its wake,

Assuming, like a fourth dimension, splendor
That calls the child with white ideas of swans
  Nearer to that green lake
Where every paradox means wonder.

[· · ·]

Always the black swan moves on the lake, always
  The blond child stands to gaze
As the tall emblem pivots and rides out
To the opposite side, always. The child upon
The bank, hands full of difficult marvels, stays
  Forever to cry aloud
In anguish: I love the black swan.

Friar initiated Merrill into an enchanted, inverted world, where white was black and black white. Or more accurately, since Merrill's ideas of love and beauty were not "white" to begin with (in the sense of innocent and conventional), Friar gave Merrill symbols and stories, masks and myths, by means of which he could understand the inverted world in which he already lived, a psychological space—a "fourth dimension"—of double meanings and divided feelings where boys love what is "beautifully evil" and every paradox means "wonder."

The lake where the swan circles "always" is an idealized realm, like the work of art as Merrill defined it in his diary ("Art [. . .] is to life, as the pond, perfectly round, is to the river"). The poems in *The Black Swan* long for permanence and timelessness, which they try to embody in their smooth, "perfectly round" verse forms. Yet these are also poems of personal "anguish" that acknowledge and even welcome the disruptive violence of love. The tension between strong feeling and technical refinement in *Jim's Book* reemerges, only the feelings are much stronger and the technique much more refined. So the message is mixed. In "The Broken Bowl," Merrill values "fragments" and "splinters" over wholeness, broken glass over the intact vessel, even while his intricate stanzas and winding syntax (the result of all that Proust and Henry James) create a wadded, insulated effect. There's nothing to cut one's hands on in a stanza like this:

To say it once held daisies and bluebells
  Ignores, if nothing else,
Its diehard brilliance where, crashed on the floor,

> The wide bowl lies that seemed to cup the sun,
> Its green leaves curled, its constant blaze undone,
> Spilled all its glass integrity everywhere;
>   Spectrums, released, will speak
> Of colder flowerings where cold crystal broke.

"The Broken Bowl" was a symbol for Merrill's shattering confrontation with his mother and the collapse of the "glass integrity" of their relations—which, the poem implies, he hoped to repair or redeem. "Of course, I am terribly afraid of breaking with her," Merrill confided to Burford, and afraid in particular "of her mind, of her unimpeachable morality which she has somehow in her own thoughts projected around me." That spellbound condition is the theme of "Medusa." The poem comes to something short of a climax:

> The blank eyes gaze past suns of no return
> On vast irrelevancies that form deforms,
> The maladies of dream
> Where the stone face revolves like a sick eye
> Beneath its lid: so we
> Watch through the crumbling surfaces and noons
> The single mask of stone
> And the dry serpent horror
> Of days reflected in a doubtful mirror
> With all their guileful melody, until
> We raise our quivering swords and think to kill.

Medusa is clearly a mask for Hellen Merrill, who stares down "suns of no return," daring her boy to make a move against her. Which he doesn't. The poem leaves those ambiguously "quivering swords" up in the air; it is about Merrill wanting to break with his mother and being unable to. But his mother is not the only problem: there is a quality of self-disgust in these lines that makes the poet seem sick of himself and his symbols.

Perhaps he was also sick of writing poetry under Friar's supervision. He must have recognized that, while Friar promised to free him from his parents' control, he would have to free himself from Friar's, too. When Friar published *The Black Swan*, Merrill had completed his private course of study. But it would take a long time before he asserted his intellectual independence from Friar to his own satisfaction. It was much easier to give up Kimon as a lover. "Kimon is back but, oh, with a difference," Jimmy wrote in his diary on January 4, 1947. He was afraid of turning cold, of forgetting how to feel, but he was also afraid of Friar and wanted "calm": it had cost too much to fight with his mother. So he told Friar he "couldn't cope" with their relationship any longer. The rupture left him "numb, confused, guilty." Though wounded, Friar took the high road. Didactic and grandiose but eloquent as well, he wrote to Merrill on the twenty-first birthday they had once looked forward to together:

> Love, like the idea of God, is for each of us an ideal of the best possible life we may create and live, an image of ourselves as we would like to be. Like poetry, it is a dedication to something we know is ultimately beyond our reach, but in the pursuit of which our lives take meaning and joy. It is unabashedly grand and godlike, and it brings with it an almost unbearable realization of what we actually are, of our pettiness and limitations. It is like death, for as we know that we can never die for someone else, we also know that we can never really love anyone but our ideal of our inmost self. The lover, the one we love, is like the material we make into poetry: the love he brings may pass over the threshold of the other's solitude, but not he. Love and the lover gaze at each other like Narcissus in the water. [. . .] You have been for me incentive and material for such reflection, and I have the calm assurance that I have been this for you also. [. . .] For the proof is that we have not written a bad poem, you and I together.

Friar and Merrill were in one way a perfect match. Friar's creativity was notably vicarious: as a translator and lecturer, he spoke through other writers as through a series of masks. And Merrill was peculiarly open to this vicariousness. "Try me!" he had chirped when Friar challenged him to submit to his "dictatorial direction." Far from dreading influence, Merrill welcomed it; that was one of the reasons he'd always been such a good student. Buechner was thinking of this quality—of his friend's assimilative nature and talent for mimicry—when he named a pet monkey in one of his stories "Jimmy." Much later Merrill himself called the young man he'd been a "[y]oung chameleon."

A chameleon is a changeable creature, and Merrill maintained his autonomy by drawing from many influences. One reason he had the strength to break with Friar in 1947 was the friend that he made in Hans Lodeizen. A student from the Netherlands doing graduate-level work in biology, Lodeizen was a poet and the son of a Dutch shipping magnate who found in America an escape from a conservative Dutch society and his powerful father. Two years older than Merrill, he had blue eyes and thick brown hair. He made a quick, quaint bow upon meeting or taking his leave—an Old World touch, Jimmy supposed. He invited Hans home to New York and introduced him to his mother, knowing she would view him as an improvement over Friar. Lodeizen, familiar with the Dutch version of such a woman, depicts her rather wickedly in these lines from "Meeting the Merrills," as translated from the Dutch:

> Madame arrives back home outside
> it's cold the show was *marvelous*
>
> are the guests no the guests haven't
> arrived yet here's the newspaper
>
> they wait for the afternoon to end
> the afternoon itself would rather be evening
> here are the guests take off your coats
> kiss on the cheek, *darling.*
> Oh good, the cocktails are ready.

Lodeizen and Merrill had lofty conversations about Plato, Chamfort, Nietzsche, and the French Existentialists. Their relations were conducted on this plane, but distance was no bar to idealization, and a few personal gestures were sufficient to live in memory for Merrill. He didn't see the melancholy and alienation for which the poet would shortly become known to readers in his own country; he saw instead a young man gifted with a natural grace and dignity of spirit that he envied. One afternoon when Merrill was ill, Lodeizen gave him the scarf from around his own neck, opened a bottle of sherry, played a record of Beethoven's "Spring" Sonata, and recounted an episode from Casanova's *Memoirs*.

As with other young men who made an impression on him, Merrill was smitten by Lodeizen. But the scarf and the "Spring" Sonata were the apex of their intimacy that year. It had been that way with Seldon James. Seldon was back in college, but Jimmy hardly noticed until he realized that Seldon and Hans were friends. Observing them seated together at a Maggie Teyte recital on campus, he suffered from pangs "reserved exclusively for the gay": "I was jealous of both parties at once." As it happened, Seldon became a muse for Hans, whose infatuation with him went unrequited, just as Jimmy's had.

During this, his last term in college, fall 1946, Merrill was working hard on his senior essay on Proust, "*À la recherche du temps perdu*: Impressionism in Literature." The essay, at 106 pages, is by far Merrill's longest work of literary criticism and his most scholarly production. He begins it by discussing French Impressionist painting, but his real subject is Proust's complex use of metaphor. The power of metaphor, he explains, is that "it permits discovery. What is unknown may be known through analogy, as Einstein is said to have taught a blind man what 'white' is by letting him feel the neck of a swan." The essay is throughout a controlled academic performance. Yet there are glimmers of the personal where more is at stake.

While discussing the opening of *Sodome et Gomorrhe*, where Baron de Charlus and the tailor Jupien meet and then disappear to make love, Merrill has this to say: "The homosexual, [Proust] tells us, is [. . .] a member of a race that must live by falsehood and perjury, obliged like a Christian on the day of judgment to renounce his strongest desires. He is a son who must betray his mother, a friend who cannot accept friendship, pardoned only as the Jew is pardoned for treason because of the destiny of his race." But there is nothing so eccentric, Merrill insists, about the homosexual: "Such a man is shunned not so much for his difference from other men, but because these others recognize in him certain fleeting aspects of their own natures." A few pages further, describing the "protecting surface of metaphor" in Proust, Merrill perhaps describes some of his own motives for writing: "It is as though we were skating upon a sheet of ice that had formed above a black torrent; we may skate with an assurance of safety, but the ice does not make the water beneath us less terrible."

The essay was a smashing success with the English Department. One Amherst alumnus remembers Brower walking into his class and announcing "in the most reverent, even awestruck manner that Merrill had turned in his Senior Thesis on Proust, that it was brilliant, and that we were all privileged to be students at the same time and in the same place as Jim Merrill, who was destined for some sort of greatness. I had never heard a student praised in this manner, and it made quite an impression." Other eminent professors, C. L. Barber and George Whicher, had similar things to say, and the faculty voted to award Merrill's diploma summa cum laude. President Cole wrote to Charlie Merrill to convey the good news.

Having finished his senior-year classes and submitted his thesis in February, Jimmy had time on his hands before commencement. He was living in his own apartment on Tyler Place, close by Emily Dickinson's house. (He claimed that he broke in one night with a couple of friends, each making off with an item—he with a sherry glass, in tribute to the color of the poet's eyes—but it's unlikely that took place.) He passed his twenty-first birthday quietly with the Spragues; Rosemary's mother baked a cake.

He spent inordinate time on plans for a spring costume party. It was to be the "Paris Party," and printed invitations went out telling the guests whom they were to come dressed as. An empty house near campus was rented for the occasion. When the evening came, Japanese lanterns glowed on the lawn; a small band played. Howkins came as Diaghilev and Burford as Nijinsky; the Browers as Mallarmé and Berthe Morisot. Nancy Gibson, Bill's wife, was Manet's barmaid at the Folies Bergère; Rosemary was Maupassant's innocent Yvette, who chooses death rather than follow in the steps of her courtesan mother. Cast as Apollinaire, Hans leaned on a cane with a ketchup-stained bandage on his head, alluding to the World War I wound that the poet never recovered from. Hans's roommate, Ray Daum, equipped with a camera and asked to document the occasion, impersonated Man Ray. Merrill was Proust. Daubed with a greasepaint mustache, he leapt in his tux on a table and declaimed from memory the zany tango "Pasodoble" from Edith Sitwell and William Walton's *Façade*. The party ended in mayhem soon after that. As Daum recalls, a fraternity had heard "that a bunch of queers were putting on a party," football players crashed the fête, "and we all had to run for our lives."

Merrill inherited his love of parties from his parents. But he was also influenced by the soirées that punctuate Proust's novel, and parties show up at important points in his own writing. Parties satisfied his faith in frivolity as a balm and his pleasure in drama and ritual, costumes and masks. These elements were combined in his one-act play *The Birthday*. Written during summer 1946, it was produced by the Dramatic Arts Class at Amherst in May 1947. The play concerns a birthday party for an ordinary young man named Raymond. The sly, distinguished host is Charles (who was played by Howkins); the guests are Max, a painter, the society matron Mrs. Crane, and Mr. Knight, "a wizard" (played by Burford). The name "Charles" came from Merrill's father and brother—he would use it several more times in his work to create a comic alter ego. The play has the setting and clever dialogue of drawing room comedy, but it veers at once toward the mystical, since it isn't in fact Raymond's birthday: the occasion being celebrated is purely symbolic. Raymond thinks he knows none of the others, and yet each of them represents some aspect of the person he will become or a dimension of himself he has yet to learn about.

Merrill was ready to see his life as an adventure, as Raymond is encouraged to; and at twenty-one he hoped the adventure was beginning. When the question of what he would do after college came up at commencement, he replied mildly, "Oh, nothing," smiling to himself about how much he intended to accomplish (in life, in art) without going to work like other graduates, while aware of how much work that might turn out to be. Raymond runs away from his birthday party. He fails to grasp the sort of drama he's been thrust into; or maybe he understands perfectly well, and shies away from the task of self-creation before him, unsure how to begin.

Merrill must have been unsure too. He started his post-college career by moving into East Fifty-seventh Street behind the lemon-yellow door where his mother lived. When he had a coughing fit at night, Hellen rushed in to help. Even so, there was room in the house for friends, and Freddy, William Meredith, and Charles Shoup stayed there off and on that summer. Merrill mooned over both Shoup and Meredith at one time or another.* Just graduated from Yale, Shoup was a painter of still life and society portraits with an acidic wit and brassy ways who, being of middle-class origins himself, liked living the high life with the son of Charles Merrill. "Jimmy," he judged, "didn't know how to enjoy his money," with the implication that it was wasted on him. By winter Shoup would push on to Paris and more glamorous company.

Merrill had met Meredith on visits to Freddy at Princeton, where Meredith taught creative writing. At the cocktail parties Meredith hosted in his rooms, Merrill encountered Princeton literati, among them the erudite, excitable John Berryman (whose antic work Merrill would always admire), the poet-critic R. P. Blackmur, and a soft-spoken undergraduate poet named W. S. Merwin. Bill Meredith himself was seven years older than Jimmy, a Princeton graduate, and a winner of the Yale Younger Poets Prize for 1944, who until recently had served as a Navy pilot in the Pacific. Merrill approached this square-jawed, serious man with deference. Meredith was a well-born New Yorker and avid operagoer (Jimmy got him into the Metropolitan Opera Club) who had a discrete romantic interest in men. Merrill grew "tremendously fond of him," but the intensity of feeling faded, despite the fact that, for decades, they would live only a few miles from each other in Connecticut. To Bill's sister Kay, whom he met around the same time, Jimmy was more warmly devoted.

In New York, where everyone was busy and ambitious, it was easy not to get much done. When Jimmy's day was over at the desk, there were too

---

* "It was hard to know who was sleeping with whom or why or even if" (FB to the author, letter, December 7, 2001). JM refers to Shoup in *ADP* as "Barney Crop" (e.g., *ADP*, 496).

many options: the opera, the San Remo, a vernissage, book parties, and more parties, which made it hard to get to the desk the next morning. He had friends from every period of his life in the city, and he made friends with their friends. The fun was certifiably decadent. At a New Year's Eve party hosted by Suzel Parker, "we all wore masks and danced, pretending not to recognize anybody." Suzel appeared in "emerald green satin, a Flemish coiffure, with a glistering mask like mica, from which black lace hung to cover her mouth and flutter when she spoke." Jimmy sipped champagne from her slipper.

Charlie Merrill noted these developments from a distance. He had long been realistic enough not to expect his son to join Merrill Lynch, and he approved of Jimmy's choice of literature as a profession, especially after he collected his laurels at Amherst. Still, there was cause for concern, and he wrote to his son in December 1947:

> You were just a child when I first became conscious of the fact that you had the promise in you of doing great things. I think it is historically correct to say that many poets have shown flashes of genius in their early years. I think it is also historically correct to say that many of them were, in some respects, too mature and, in other respects, too immature. Perhaps, it is because I feel that in some respects you are still too immature is one of the reasons [sic] for my desire to have you undertake a definite job—the tougher the better, and carry it to completion.

After that letter from Daddy, Jimmy resolved "to teach next year—English or French or both in a small unfashionable prep school or college," he wrote to Friar in Greece. "I want to make myself be alone, and this is the only way I can see it can be done." He didn't hesitate therefore when Theodore Weiss, a poet teaching at Bard College and editor of the *Quarterly Review*, who'd been impressed by poems Jimmy had submitted, encouraged him to apply for a temporary opening in his department. The temporariness of it was attractive. So was the proximity to Manhattan of this small liberal arts college on the Hudson River. Jimmy met the Bard faculty, gave a poetry reading, and (it was the only time he interviewed for a job, ever!) got the position.

Before he took up his duties in September 1948, he and the recently graduated Freddy rented a summer cottage on Georgetown Island on the coast of Maine. Buechner was finishing a novel he'd been at work on since Lawrenceville. Merrill was testing what it was like to write without the distractions of New York. He opened his diary every day and copied yesterday's stanzas again, growing his poems by increments, establishing the laborious process of daily revision that would be his mature writing practice.

Even in the wilds of Maine, they acquired a social life. Georgetown had long been popular with Greenwich Village artists like the sculptor Gaston Lachaise. Gaston was gone, but Belle, or Madame Lachaise, as she was known, the wide-hipped model for his massive nudes, remained. Other sculptors lived there too: William Zorach, a veteran of the heroic Armory Show of 1913, who displayed the first audiotape recorder that Freddy and Jimmy had ever seen (and used it to record a half hour of vapid party chatter); and Morris Levine, who that summer produced a bronze head of Jimmy, which Jimmy brought back for his mother. Charles and Jo Shain, a Princeton English professor and his wife, taught them how to dig for clams and heat canned spaghetti over a fire on the beach. The house Buechner and Merrill had rented had no plumbing, only a pump across the road and a latrine in the barn. For baths, they floated on the tidal river that rushed out to sea twice a day; or they turned to their neighbors, a pair of spinsters who raised angora rabbits and offered a tub of hot water for barter when the two young writers agreed to shear the ladies' small, pulsing creatures.

Merrill and Buechner would never be so close again. They took turns jumping up from their compositions to change the 78 rpm recordings of Mozart, Stravinsky, and Satie that they'd brought as inspiration. They shared a typewriter. When it broke down, they brought it to a local repairman named Mr. Merrill. Sensing deep pockets, he charged a fee so much higher than the estimate that, rather than pay it, they consulted a lawyer. His best advice was to get the machine back, somehow, and send a check for the agreed-upon price. The Uglies warmed to the challenge. They occupied the repairman with fast talk, snatched their property from under his nose, and made a getaway spitting gravel.

That fall, while Buechner took a job teaching at Lawrenceville, Merrill settled in at Bard. On the second floor of the faculty house where he lived was a youngish English Department couple: Joseph Summers, a specialist in Renaissance poetry, and his wife U. T., who was working at Houghton Mifflin and pregnant with their first child. The Summerses were the first of many families to which he would attach himself. He made another friend on the Bard faculty in Irma Brandeis, an Italian-language teacher and Dante scholar (her book *The Ladder of Vision: A Study of Dante's Comedy* appeared in 1962). Twenty-one years older than he, Brandeis was an assured, enigmatic single woman. She had some of the moral authority Merrill imputed to his mother and a veiled past of the sort he'd found intriguing in Zelly. Eventually he would learn that she had been the lover of Eugenio Montale and inspiration for his poems in the 1930s. Montale had called her his "Jewish-American Beatrice." Merrill liked to think of her surrounded by her books, playing the flute, her cat for company, self-possessed in a way he had never felt.

Bard, known for progressive education and its focus on the arts, was rapidly expanding in size and had recently admitted women students. At twenty-two, Merrill was barely older than his students; Mis' Annie shook with laughter when her grandson told her that they called him "Sir." One of those students was Louise Fitzhugh, a pert tomboy from Memphis. She took a tutorial with him on metrics that led one night late in the year to her undressing him in his rooms, before she thought better of it and ran off. Marveling at this sudden "cure" for homosexuality, Jimmy "hoped to have fallen in love." But Fitzhugh didn't reply to his notes, and soon, as he tells it in *A Different Person*, she had "changed her major from contemporary literature to child psychology, and moved in with the lesbian head of that department. So much for heterosexuality." The attraction had been real and mutual, however. "We even went to bed one sunny, tipsy dusk," Merrill writes about a reunion some time later, "but were by then so set in our ways that nothing came of it. Instead we made do with a lifelong friendship." Fitzhugh, having a career ahead of her in contemporary literature and child psychology both, would become the author of *Harriet the Spy* and other children's books.

Some weeks into her tutorial, she flopped into her teacher's chair and asked in frustration, "Why meter?" The question had never come up for Merrill, but it was in the air. That November, Bard held a poetry conference in which meter and free verse, pro and con, were debated by invited poets, among them William Carlos Williams, Louise Bogan, Richard Eberhart, Jean Garrigue, Robert Lowell, Richard Wilbur, Elizabeth Bishop, and, as Bishop described him in a letter, "a wild man from California in a bright red shirt and yellow braces named [Kenneth] Rexroth, who did his best to start a fight with everyone and considered us all effete and snobbish Easterners. He never quite succeeded and had to prove his mettle [. . .] by taking three of the prettiest undergraduates off for an evening in the cemetery." It was an early skirmish in the battle between the East Coast and the West that would agitate American poetry for much of Merrill's career.

He discovered in Bishop a crucial, flexible model. He first encountered her work when Joe and U. T. Summers, who were friends with Bishop, gave him a copy of her first book, *North & South*, published in 1946. Shortly after the Bard conference, he met her at a reception at the Gotham Book Mart for Edith and Osbert Sitwell. More than a dozen authors posed for a group photograph, among them Marianne Moore, Bishop (Moore's proté-gée) standing beside her like a glum, puffy-faced niece, and W. H. Auden atop a ladder, towering over everyone. Jimmy had been shunted to another room with writers deemed less notable. Over the next year, with care but determination too, he approached Bishop, who was fifteen years older and by nature quite reserved. He had been so "bowled over" by her "Over 2,000 Illustrations and a Complete Concordance" when it appeared in *Partisan Review* that he had typed out the seventy-four-line poem in a letter to Friar, to share the revelation. He invited her to lunch expecting to spend it prais-ing the poem, but he discovered that the topic was exhausted in a minute or two: Bishop had little to say about her work. If they were going to be friends, it would have to be on other grounds.

In addition to Bishop, he was reading Stevens and Auden. Stevens he'd come to at Amherst when he read *Notes Toward a Supreme Fiction* (1942)—it was one of the long poems Friar lectured on—and Stevens's wartime essay "The Noble Rider and the Sound of Words." The latter, in which Stevens speaks of imagination pressing back against the brute "pressure of reality," became a touchstone text for Jimmy, providing a way to understand poetry's relation to history and politics. The Auden he was reading was not the left-ist political poet of the 1930s, nor yet the Christian moralist Auden would become, but the author of *The Sea and the Mirror: A Commentary on Shake-speare's "The Tempest"* (1944), in which the characters in Shakespeare's romance, each with his or her own poetic form, speak in turn, producing a combination of music hall revue and verse opera.

Merrill ended his year at Bard by organizing a student performance, with music, of *The Waste Land*. He also gave a formal lecture on *The Wings of the Dove*, Henry James's late novel. He and Buechner had read that book aloud to each other in Maine. This time he went at it with a fine-tooth comb, making exhaustive notes.* He was concerned with the fate of James's hero-ine, Milly Theale, a young, fabulously wealthy heiress who is terminally ill but bent on living fully. How will she spend her time and money? It was a question Jimmy asked himself. He understood how her wealth placed Milly in the eyes of the world. As her friends Kate Croy and the impecunious Merton Densher work their way into her heart, plotting to their own pur-pose, Milly can never know whether they love her or her fortune. But it was hard to tell the two apart. As James puts it,

---

* JM, journal, May 1949, Jnl 2. "Many books are greater + more profound than *The Wings of the Dove* . . . but none is more earnest, none is more lyrical, none is more pure." His lecture title was "Basic Living and Alchemy in *The Wings of the Dove*."

She couldn't dress it away, nor walk it away, nor read it away, nor think it away; she could neither smile it away in any dreamy absence nor blow it away in any softened sigh. She couldn't lose it if she had tried—that was what it was to be really rich. It had to be *the* thing you were.

Milly's task is to convert her money into spiritual value, a personal transformation Merrill described as "alchemy." It was a metaphor he would return to again and again in his poetry, where it suggests the magic he hoped his poetry would work on his fortune, making himself something more than his money.

His wealth weighed on him in a new way. He'd always been rich, yet now he was richer, and free to do what he wished with his funds. When he turned twenty-one, he gained access to the trust that his father had established for him (as Charlie had done for Doris and Charles). Jimmy lived on the income, and only a portion of that. Jimmy depended on Larry Condon to handle his taxes and make the legal arrangements necessary for the "loans" he'd begun dispensing. He tried to respond ("intensely," as he put it) to the financial needs of his friends, whether it meant meeting an emergency or making a dream come true. He gave Buechner a stipend until Freddy had a salary, at which point payments were transferred to his mother. Tony Harwood was writing poetry in Paris with his old friend's support, and his mother too received help. Howkins set up a small bookstore in New York, thanks to Jimmy. When Suzel Parker found herself divorced with a small child, Jimmy stepped in. He paid for Kay Meredith's husband to see a psychiatrist. He helped Maya Deren pay for her films. He supported Friar's life as a translator in Greece. He wrote checks to Friar's father and brother as well. He gave ungrudgingly, but requests kept coming, he didn't have "enough control over my hoard to arrange [to give money] without red tape," he disliked seeing friends turn supplicants, and he feared they "will all end by hating me."

Slowly he had come closer to his father. Charlie's pride in his writing gratified Jimmy, and illness made the old man touchingly vulnerable. He joked that his heart treatments had left him with two navels and one nipple, and he pulled open his shirt to show Jimmy it was so. Still, they approached each other across a considerable distance. For Christmas 1949, Jimmy sent his father a suite of poems dedicated to him, "Variations and Elegy: White Stag, Black Bear." He presented the poems almost as if he were addressing a patron: "[I]t is with the greatest pleasure and gratitude that I offer them to you with this formal dedication. Above and beyond this, there is the deep personal dedication acknowledging the extent to which you have made not only these, but all my poems, and the life from which they come, possible and real."

Merrill had prepared his poems in a book manuscript. He sent it to Harcourt, where it was turned down, and then to Houghton Mifflin, where he hoped to appear in the same list as Bishop, but again it was refused. After Bard, he moved into an apartment on East Thirty-fifth Street. He acquired a boyfriend: a tall, red-haired young man with whom for once he was not besotted. Wayne Kerwood was about Jimmy's age and had just landed a job working as a personal assistant to Blanche Knopf, cofounder with her husband Alfred of the publishing house. Kerwood brought Merrill's book to the office, where it was read enthusiastically by Herbert Weinstock, an influential editor, and Mrs. Knopf herself. A letter came from *Poetry* reinforcing his case: the editors had awarded him the Levinson Prize for poems that appeared in the magazine in 1949. (The magazine had given him a prize in 1947 as well.) Still, Knopf delayed: the slighter poems in the manuscript needed to be replaced by strong new work before a contract could be issued.

Jimmy, already stationed at his desk, planned to do just as advised: he would deliver a publishable manuscript to Knopf as soon as possible. And then what? He had a novel in mind—and Europe. He'd scouted out the territory over the winter break from Bard on a trip to Paris, when he crossed the Atlantic for the first time to see Shoup and Harwood, wander the Louvre, and visit scenes from Proust's life and fiction. Though the notion was indistinct in his mind, he felt he might write the next chapter of his story there.

3

ROME

1950–52

A Different Person, Merrill's memoir of the years 1950–52, published in 1993, uses this part of his life to stand for the whole. It was a period when, by gaining distance on his parents and their struggles, he resolved to become a "different person." He would have to face the difference that his talent, wealth, and sexuality made, and the isolation that came with that difference. The question was not so much who he was as who he might become: "I felt that I alone in this or that circle of friends could see no way into the next phase," he writes in his memoir. He had to imagine a future for himself that wouldn't be defined by his ascent on a company ladder or a college faculty, nor by the familiar, familial narrative that marriage and children supplied—normative models for identity that were insistent in postwar America. He wanted to love and write with greater freedom and generosity. The goal was to turn his sense of difference into a basis for connection with other people. That transformation wasn't complete by 1952; not even by 1993 perhaps. But he had begun it.

In January 1950, Merrill attended a party hosted by Blanche Knopf to celebrate the publication of Buechner's novel, *A Long Day's Dying*, the book Freddy had been writing on Georgetown Island in 1948. This first novel's "ecstatic reception" (it was praised in *Newsweek* and the *Saturday Review*) made Buechner "the wonder of that winter of 1950." Jimmy took pleasure in his friend's success, and, eager to match it, he started work on a novel of his own. He thought of Freddy as his "dearest" friend, but he felt the friendship's limitations: "there is a kind of constraint between Freddy + me," he wrote in a letter, "due in part to [. . .] the curious horror he has of homosexuality, whereby I am kept from talking deeply about myself to him [. . .]. We are very close, and I hope shall always be. But I suspect that our closeness is historical."

Merrill had just met, or so he supposed, "the love of my life." Claude Fredericks, whom Friar had introduced him to a few years ago, was present at Buechner's publication party too. "Because Kimon was my first lover and Freddy my best friend," Merrill explains in *A Different Person*, "I could pretend [. . .] that Claude was perfectly at home in my life, and I greeted him with a warmth that must have taken him aback." Indeed he swept the young man off his feet. Fredericks described their meeting: "I saw him across the room, talking to some girls, [. . .] and then a little later, to my surprise, I looked up and there he was wending his way through the people, to me, taking my hand, smiling, and saying, Hello, Claude, in that voice that was the first instrument of bewitching." They chatted about Merrill's poetry and T. S. Eliot's play *The Cocktail Party*, which was then onstage in New York. Fredericks continues: "something took place in my body while we spoke that was organic and chemical—I was not drunk, I think, at all, or drunk only enough to recognise truly what I was feeling most deeply inside myself."

Whose hand had Merrill grasped? Born in Springfield, Missouri, in the Ozark hills about two hundred miles from St. Louis, Fredericks was, like Merrill, the only child of divorced parents. His father, a member of the Elks Club and the manager of a local oil company, hunted and fished, drank and gambled ("we weren't close enough even to have a rupture," Fredericks once recalled), while his mother encouraged her son in his precocious intellectual life. As a boy, he listened to weekly radio broadcasts of the Metropolitan Opera and the NBC Orchestra conducted by Arturo Toscanini. He read all of Proust and much of Freud in volumes ordered from the Kansas City public library. From early on, he had recognized and accepted his homosexuality. He began keeping a journal in 1932 at the age of eight and continued religiously; typing, often many pages at a sitting, he set down the events of daily life, while trying to grasp and analyze his shifting moods. Over time the journal would become a unique archival record and a massive literary work in its own right—a project of intimate self-knowledge tirelessly pursued. It was purchased by the Getty Research Center in 1988, at which point it consisted of more than thirty million words.

The first in his family to attend college, Fredericks studied Asian art and classics at Harvard. But he was frustrated by the institutional requirements of college life, and he ended his formal studies after two years and moved to New York. In 1946, with his lover Milton Saul, Fredericks created the Banyan Press, which printed handsome hand-set editions of works by Wallace Stevens, André Gide, Gertrude Stein, John Berryman, Robert Duncan, and other important twentieth-century writers. Seeking solitude and a life he could afford on the budget allowed by the modest support he received from his mother, Fredericks bought a nineteenth-century farmhouse on 150 acres in Pawlet, a small town in western Vermont, several hours from New York—and as safe as possible, he felt, in a world where the atomic bomb now threatened great cities. He installed the press—a man-sized iron machine, painted red—and went to work making fine books. He continued to write his journal and poetry and plays (one of which, *The Idiot King*, would later be performed by the Living Theatre in New York).

It was a simple, Thoreauvian life. By 1950, however, Fredericks was discouraged as a writer and unhappy in his relationship with Saul. He had been reading Dante. Three days after he met Merrill, he typed at the top of a fresh page of his diary, "Here commences the Vita Nuova of C. F." The entry was written by a man rapturously in love. "My life is indeed cracked open," he wrote; "but that is what I wanted. I said anything was possible, and now suddenly what I said I can act upon; for I believe anything is possible, and I feel reckless enough to cast up anything for anything and recognise there are a hundred ways I can choose to live."

Jimmy was just as captivated. He was ready, in principle, to "cast up anything" too: "I want this to cost me everything—my gaining you," he wrote, stirred by the fantasies of total sacrifice and absolute possession. Fredericks had the reverence for great art that Merrill had admired in Friar, but his ambitions were less worldly and more inward than Friar's. His face was round and honest; he had brown hair; he was gentle-voiced and idealistic; his manner could be solemn, sentimental, or elfin. Jimmy was flattered by the vision of himself he saw reflected in this new lover's smitten gaze. "The wide-eyed, open quality I was drawn to," Fredericks recalled, "not the elegant young man. I found him handsome, which he wasn't used to, and I trusted my feelings, whereas he did not."

They went to a song recital by Elisabeth Schumann, Bach's *St. John's Passion*, and *Die Meistersinger* at the Met. They took long walks through city streets at night and talked in the bar atop the Art Deco Beekman Towers while snow swirled on the East River below. Their sudden love protected them like a pact, giving them strength to face a threatening society. "It felt daring to take Jimmy's arm in Times Square," Fredericks noted many years later. They had reason to be careful: shame and even prosecution were not imaginary dangers; Fredericks's lover, Saul, had been arrested for solicitation in the city. Surely it would be better to live somewhere else? Fredericks was dreaming of Europe. Merrill had his own plans to travel there: he intended to make his long-contemplated visit to Friar in Greece in April; then he would spend a month in Rome with his father, who had arranged this chance to get to know his son better and get away from his deteriorating marriage to Kinta. Claude and Jimmy could meet in Europe once Mr. Merrill had gone home. After that, they could go anywhere they wished. By late February, pledging their love to each other, Claude and Jimmy had exchanged rings.

But they were not quite ready to ride off into the sunset. For instance, there was still the matter of Wayne Kerwood. Only slowly did it dawn on Fredericks that this boy who came and went in Jimmy's apartment had a key of his own. Kerwood reacted to the appearance of this rival by threatening to kill himself. Merrill told Fredericks he loved Kerwood, and he found it possible to love more than one person at once. (He'd been reading *The Tale of Genji* and was charmed by the prince's passionate wooing of many women at once.) Meanwhile, Fredericks kept his feelings about Merrill a secret from Saul.

Fredericks went home to Vermont—and to Saul—to prepare an edition of Gertrude Stein's novel, *Q.E.D.*, which the Banyan Press published in collaboration with Alice B. Toklas as *Things as They Are* (Stein had left this early work with a lesbian theme unpublished during her lifetime); and Merrill flew south to Florida to visit his father. On March 3, Jimmy's twenty-fourth birthday, Claude wrote to him about their present separation: "this can be a period of purging, fasting, purifying, sanctifying oneself in order to enter the temple." "I love you," Jimmy reassured him, launching into a lyrical display. "I shall never stop, I know, these movements of love that rise + fall in one like waves, it can only be a perpetual ecstasy: there is no other."

But it was hard for Jimmy to keep up with Claude's love letters, let alone purge and fast, while a guest at Merrill's Landing. "Such a party last night," he sighed. "Champagne. 12 people on the terrace with an accordion + guitar combine playing those inevitable gems from South Pacific. . . . I 'had' an unusually charming debutante from St. Louis, named Moony—+ because she was very young + I was very drunk we talked about love, which delighted me, to be, as it were, talking about you under that name." Fredericks was not delighted by such a report, but he told himself, "These are all things he has no part in really, that he hates, that his upbringing and the camouflage of heterosexuality with his parents have forced him into—he detests them."

They reunited briefly late in March. Fredericks met Merrill in Williamstown, Massachusetts, then drove north with him to Vermont into the idyllic valley in which Pawlet is set, the road playing a game with the river, appearing first on one side of it, then on the other. Merrill had to marvel at Fredericks's house. With walls of simple white clapboard and right angles everywhere, the structure was dignified and upright, like a New England farmer. A white pine, even older than the house, towered out front. Inside was austere refinement; as Fredericks had advertised, there was "little furniture," and "little means one object in each room"—in vivid contrast to the crowded, cozy spaces of the poet's Thirty-fifth Street apartment. On the shelves in the press room, Merrill found, were books "of a breathtaking high-mindedness: Greek philosophers and Latin poets in scholarly editions, Aquinas and Dante, Gibbon and Donne, scores of the Bach Passions and the Beethoven Quartets." The windows had no curtains or shades. In dawn light, Merrill hopped naked to his clothes, then shivered while the fire caught. He told Fredericks, nonetheless, that he "could be very happy" living there. They played piano four hands, drank scotch, ate caviar, walked by the brook, and had a revelatory conversation, which Fredericks put down in his journal. Noticing his lover's clothes and style of life, he had assumed he must have money.

> But I fancied it was an allowance a little more than mine—perhaps $300 or $400 a month. . . . I began [. . .]: Are you willing to live simply? And that brought forth from him then evidently what he had been wishing to say. He somehow assumed that I knew more than I did. He said, Yes, that is the way I want to live . . . exactly. And he went ahead to say he indeed did not know how much money he did have though he knew it was a great deal—and a great deal more than he spent. He said he didn't want to know. He never used it all. . . . and he didn't want to know how much he could indeed use. He said he used to be troubled by it in a way, embarrassed—but he said he thought that an ingratitude to his father and now decided he must live with it.

The talk was "healthy," but it stirred Claude's doubts. "I am indeed sometimes terrified that he is in love with my love, with my virtue, not with ME." He recognized how he would be seen at the side of James Merrill: "Everyone will THINK I am supported by him whether I am or not."

A few days before, Knopf had approved Merrill's revised poetry manuscript for publication. He stayed in Pawlet only one night before poetry drew him and Fredericks to Amherst. Reuben Brower had arranged a reading by recent graduates of the college—Merrill and Richard Wilbur—in support of the promotion of Bill Gibson, who read alongside them. It was a challenging occasion for Jimmy. His teachers were in the audience, and Wilbur, five years his senior, was already celebrated for his first book, *The Beautiful Changes*. Merrill saw Wilbur's performance as "a master class in resonance and poise." In Claude's eyes, Jimmy "read with clarity and without affectation: but with feeling." But the poet himself was unconvinced. He sounded to himself "nasal, educated, world-weary as only those without any experience of the world can be"; he felt "how much I would like this sound to change; or failing that, what a relief it would be"—he was looking ahead to Europe—"to live among Frenchmen or Italians, who wouldn't automatically 'place' me each time I opened my mouth."

He returned to New York for packing and appointments before he sailed for France with Tony Harwood on March 30. Where exactly was he going? How long would he be gone? Nothing was certain beyond his meeting with Fredericks, and there was no sense yet when and where that would be. His vagueness expressed the open-ended nature of the adventure; it also disguised a course of action his mother would be likely to protest. "I don't know how long I'll be away—I don't want to know," he wrote to her. "I expect to have a beautiful and enriching trip, and it only saddens me we are not sailing together"—although putting an ocean between her and him must have been one of his prime motives. He assured his mother that, while he planned to visit Friar, their relations were now strictly literary and "impersonal." He didn't mention Claude to her until May, when he introduced his lover as a chum it was convenient to travel with.

He took his manuscript to his father's secretary to prepare carbon copies and went to the Knopf offices to sign a contract. He wrote to Claude, "Weinstock suggested that a better title than POEMS would be FIRST POEMS—and that is how it stands now; I'm pleased [. . .]. To call it FIRST poems gives a flavor of youthfulness that I don't mind at all, especially as I am making sure my photograph does not appear in any connection with the book." It was not, of course, his first book of poems; there'd been *The Black Swan*, and *Jim's Book* behind that. But those were private editions, sponsored by his father and Kimon. He could claim this one wholly as his own, and he was backed by a major publisher. The title's modesty and naïveté were only apparent. It confidently declared that there were more books to come. Jimmy had embarked on a literary career.

The idea for the book's plain title had come from Rilke's *Neue Gedichte*. Having just read Rilke's *Sonnets to Orpheus* in March, Jimmy finished *The Notebooks of Malte Laurids Brigge*, Rilke's autobiographical novel about a young poet, while he crossed the Atlantic, shivering in a deck chair under a blanket provided by his mother. He had "said what amounts to a final farewell to many people who are dear to me." He hoped that "to travel is to change." He pictured himself as Orpheus at the moment when—he'd just seen the film version of Cocteau's *Orphée* (1949)—the poet "penetrates the Mirror, fearfully, his feet dragging, to find the land where everything is clear." He landed with eight bags, a suitcase, a briefcase, a box of books, and a typewriter. He stayed in Paris long enough to store his luggage, take the measure of Charlie Shoup, who was now established as a society painter in France, and touch base with the Magowans and their thirteen-year-old Robin, who was enrolled in school in Switzerland. Then he flew to Rome, and from there to Greece.

The days that followed introduced him to scenes and sensations he would want to experience again and again. He arrived in Athens in its legendary "purple dusk." Friar met his plane and took him at once to visit the Acropolis by moonlight. They ate that night in a taverna lit by dim bare bulbs. Merrill drank *retsina*—pine-resin-flavored wine—out of tin cans, listened to the piercing laments and stirring rhythms rung out on the bouzouki, watched as sailors in crisp white uniforms rose to dance, and pantomimed his part in the conversations Friar struck up with the men around them. The National Museum was still closed due to damage caused by the recent civil war. But Friar knew a curator who opened a warehouse to show them some of its treasures. Jimmy marveled at the bronze *Charioteer of Delphi*—a young man holding the reins of horses that have escaped him (the statue became the subject of a Merrill poem about passions that have gotten out of hand)—and the Zeus or Poseidon (experts disagree on which he is) that was recovered from the sea, his great muscled arms extended, ready to hurl a missing lightning bolt or trident.

From Athens, they boarded a ship that "wound through islands over the ancient water, clouds resting upon the water, curled in the hills," on the way to Poros, a small island in the Saronic Gulf, separated by a narrow passage from the northern coast of the Peloponnese, a few hours by boat from Athens. The harbor town of Poros was a striking destination. Its "flat-faced houses, pink and white and blue," climbed quickly from the quai to a high bell tower, while, to the west, a system of overlapping mountains took on the unmistakable shape of a massive female figure in repose, a configuration known as the Sleeping Woman. The sight took Merrill's breath away: a majestic, myth-sized Gaia, the archaic Greek goddess, archetype of Mother Earth, her lips ready to be kissed awake, like the sleeping mother in Jimmy's first poem. (Two decades later, a photo of the Sleeping Woman, a gift from Stephen Yenser, would hang above his desk in Connecticut.)

Mitso, a young Greek, met the Americans on the quai and rowed them for a mile through azure water to the house where Friar lived as the guest of Mina Diamantipoulous. Friar had moved into a cottage on the property following the death of Christo, Friar's friend and Mina's husband, in 1949. Friar was at work translating Nikos Kazantzakis's *Odyssey*, a long poem over which he would labor for a decade and ultimately dedicate to Merrill. Mina, with literary interests of her own, was translating Lao-Tzu into Greek. Kimon was devoted to her as to a doting patron: she'd given him the use of a cottage in an olive grove on a radiant Greek island—unimaginable luxury for an immigrant Greek intellectual who had grown up in a Chicago slum. But she was in love with him, he was not in love with her, and it had required patient negotiations before they could put her passion to rest and become, as Merrill perceived them, "the dear good friends life meant them to be." Meanwhile, Friar had started up an affair with Mitso, who also lived on the property with his wife, two children, and a sister-in-law. The two men met as lovers when they were both in "Athens on one pretext or another. Mitso's wife could then rest easy: the abstemious Professor would keep her young husband from the fleshpots." The cast was rounded out by little Dimitri, Diamantopoulous's six-year-old grandson, whom Friar photographed in faunlike poses, rising from a lily pond, or blowing on a conch.

Friar's two-room cottage looked out on Love Bay, so named because of the heart-shaped island in the center of it. Above the door to the cottage, which he called "The Medusa," was a mask of the Gorgon, a sculpture made out of "tiles and shells, bones and metal fixtures in all colors" by Ghika, the artist who had created the cover illustration for *The Black Swan*. There was a flower garden around the cottage with, Merrill noted, "poppies and cacti, daisies and laurel," all in "seductive dishabille." The main house and other buildings, including a waterside chapel, had been built by Christo in 1912. The materials had to be brought by boat, since there was no road to the house, isolated on its rocky headland. Water accumulated in cisterns; there was no electricity. In the foyer were a chessboard floor and a wooden staircase that wound up to second-floor bedrooms. Ten-foot-high windows faced west with a view of the Sleeping Woman.

Merrill was fascinated by this house and its odd ménage. He saw the latter as "a benign revision of my own family romance: a father who read Yeats, a mother without prejudice—parents whose primary interests were cultural and whose mutual attraction, bewildering to a youngster, had burned off like fog in morning sunlight." Despite all that fantasied harmony, he tended to view these surrogate parents as opposites, and, as with his actual parents, he instinctively took the woman's side. Born in 1892, Mina was the well-to-do daughter of a shipbuilding family on the island of Hydra, and Merrill identified with her as if they were cousin aristocrats: "Comfort and privilege, ours from birth, had left us with a lightness of tone that worked like a charm in the right company but could quickly frustrate whoever wanted, as Kimon often did, to get to the bottom of things. His was the tragic view of life; the affirmation added inches to his slight frame. Mina's view and mine [. . .] counted on its being seemlier to shrug and smile."

Even forty-two years later, when he wrote that in *A Different Person*, Merrill evidently needed to cut Friar down to size—a sign of how large he must have loomed in 1950. Though no longer lovers, Friar and Merrill had hardly broken with each other. In their frequent letters, Jimmy had done his best to define their relationship as a collegial exchange between fellow poets, and his financial support of Kimon had given him, to some extent, the upper hand. But he still felt beholden to his former teacher, and Friar remained a domineering personality who treated Jimmy as his protégé.

Snapshots from these days on Poros illustrate the point. One taken by Friar shows Jimmy in a romantic pose, blond tassels of grain set against his dark sweater, a straw hat on his head and a flower in his ear. The photo is sexy, stagy, and constrained, like the mask photos in Amherst. In another, Friar, wearing a Greek fisherman's cap, pulls Jimmy close, locking him tight with a cane behind his back. The young man peers at the camera warily, his glasses off. How tense he felt beside Kimon that day is made clear by a third photo in which he poses with Mina. Here is the lighthearted, jaunty Jimmy, relaxed, arm around his hostess, smiling and shrugging.

One afternoon the group crossed the channel to a festival at a monastery in a pine wooded ravine. Merrill, by now dressed in Greek clothes, fed candies to "at least thirty children," drank *retsina* for hours, and watched as Friar and Mitso locked arms and danced. The group walked home singing—a grand outing. But Jimmy was sick the next day, and sicker the day after that. With intestinal cramps and fever, he set up as an invalid in the Medusa. Soon his condition became an emergency. A British party, who had moored their sailboat below the house, took the patient back to Athens. For the next five days, Merrill ate grated apples, sipped tea, and submitted to injections and tests in a hospital in Athens. He had contracted an intestinal microbe. But, as he began to recover, it struck him "that it was because of Kimon that I was ill. [. . .] In a way I am frightened of him, in a way horrified. To set it in its worst light, I feel a greed, a vanity, a coarseness in him—of which I had perhaps always been somewhat aware. [. . .] What I sensed about my illness was that I had created it, or at least prolonged it, in order not to have to talk to him."

Merrill was released then into the sensory revelation that was Greece. For the first time, he heard nightingales sing and peacocks cry. He strolled in Athens's "extraordinarily lovely" gardens: "Lemon and bitter orange flowering, the air filled with their odors—a sense of wafting that I have never before known." Friar gave him a primer, *Greek Made Easy*,* and introduced him to Greek notables: George Katsimbalis, the hero of Henry Miller's *The Colossus of Maroussi*; the artist Ghika; the national poet Angelos Sikelianos; and Yannis Tsarouchis, "a kind of Matisse of the underworld, whose paintings I don't really like," Merrill remarked of a man who would come to be known as Greece's greatest modern artist. The paintings Merrill saw with Friar were small oils portraying young Greek men in military uniforms or naked in frank sexual poses. "Why don't you buy one?" Kimon prodded him when they saw Tsarouchis's "vast and squalid bedroom-studio," reeking of the chamber pot his young models used. Jimmy blushed: "What, and hang it in the back of my closet?"

Friar took him to Rhodes. There they had a long talk about Jimmy's poems, which Friar criticized sharply. Merrill was disturbed by vivid dreams: in one, "T. S. Eliot was trying to kill me, and wryly offering me weapons against himself, none of which I could use—the knives were rubber, the pistols would not fire"; in another, "I had a long talk with my father, who was very drunk, yet talked determinedly of returning to live with my mother, unaware that she would never have him back." With Friar, he returned to Poros—where his intestinal symptoms returned, and with them the suspicion that Friar was making him sick. His relationship with Kimon was deteriorating. Yet Greece had made a deep impression. He left "fired" with a longing for "adventure" and impatient "to start writing seriously and steadily."

In Naples, he took up his place in his father's movable court. The party included Doris's brother-in-law Ned Magowan, a natty, hale fellow recruited as company for the financier; Miss MacHattie, an Irish nurse; and a travel planner paid to ease their way through customs and on to the island of Capri. There they explored Tiberius's villa, the Blue Grotto, and other storied sites. Daddy, his son thought, did "not look at all well." Elegant as ever, but weak, CEM traveled now with oxygen tanks and submitted to a regimen of injections. As usual, father and son seldom saw eye-to-eye. While one read about Alger Hiss and Whittaker Chambers in the *New York Herald Tribune*, the other gazed out to sea.

---

* George C. Divry, *Greek Made Easy* (New York: Divry, 1948). It is inscribed: "For Jimmy / Young dog, do thou give tongue! / Kimon / Athens, April 25, 1950" (Yale). It was the grammar book the poet used to learn the language in the 1960s.

Yet they both knew that the purpose of the trip was to spend it together, and there were moments of unprecedented intimacy. Jimmy was struck by alterations in his father's personality. "His spiritual change in the past six years, or seven, since he fell ill, has been extraordinary," he wrote to Claude. CEM demonstrated a new "patience and understanding and growing responsibility towards his own acts." With tears welling up, he spoke "of the loneliness that brought us together, and of his intuition, somewhat belated, he knew, that, of his three children, it was I who had most needed him as a child."

Taking in this affection, as sweet and bland as the crème brûlée that the Old Man ordered twice a day against his doctor's orders, Jimmy drowsed in a state of "almost limitless boredom." His docility may have had to do with the need to suppress certain feelings. While his father shared memories of "a business deal, an old mistress, family stories and boyhood exploits," the son could only sit and nod, gratified by these confidences but unable to reciprocate. It was hard to explain, for example, the letters from Fredericks that came in a big, conspicuous bundle when the Merrills returned to their hotel in Rome. Claude had arrived in Paris at this point; he was visiting Alice B. Toklas and sightseeing (this was his first trip abroad), but he was impatient to meet Jimmy, and he was writing to him faithfully.

Young Robin joined the party in Rome. Toasting his grandson's arrival with a dinner at Alfredo's, where the proprietor twirled his fabled fettuccine with a golden spoon at their table, the patriarch suddenly turned red, coughed, and threw his dental bridge into the pasta. Jimmy called a taxi. Back at the hotel, he assured his frightened nephew that his grandfather merely needed rest. As it happened, Jimmy was carrying the novel that he'd started in New York. In this roman à clef he had imagined just such a scene as they had observed, in effect depicting his father's crisis before the fact. He handed the novel in progress to Robin, as if to say that no scene is ever unscripted or beyond imaginative control. Yet the episode must have disturbed him too.

His own health nagged him. Those intestinal symptoms persisted, and he had developed a painful hemorrhoid, which resisted Miss MacHattie's remedies. So Jimmy consulted the physician attending his father in Rome, Dr. Albert Simeons. A British-born endocrinologist with high-society clients, Simeons was, Jimmy found, "a very charming man." For the hemorrhoid, Simeons recommended surgery. Jimmy consented, though he was nervous about the operation. Under Claude's influence, he'd been reading the *Purgatorio*, and he viewed the operation as a spiritual trial—which it would turn into before he left the hospital.

As they chatted prior to surgery, Simeons soothed his young patient, playing Virgil to this impressionable Dante by dispensing consoling wisdom. Simeons, Jimmy explained to Claude, was the author of "a book on psychosomatic medicine"—the book was eventually published in 1960 as *Man's Presumptuous Brain: An Evolutionary Interpretation of Psychosomatic Disease*—"+ [he] is giving a series of 25 lectures on it in Rome: he tells me there is not a single physician in the audience. They refuse to accept his approach as valid." To Jimmy, that approach—Simeons's view that "every physical symptom is to some degree psychological"—seemed "beautifully natural."

While Jimmy recovered from the procedure, Simeons ordered psychological tests for him. In the abstract ink blots of the Rorschach test, the poet discerned "Victorian gentlemen, kangaroos, and Oriental idols," which Simeons judged "very interesting." He prescribed pain medication and kept the patient overnight. He returned the following morning with a young colleague, a Hungarian named Thomas Detre. Detre administered another test, the Szondi, in which "the patient is asked to evaluate a rogues' mad gallery of crones and elderly murderers."

What followed next shook Merrill. With the test results in hand, Detre "talked for over an hour, while he described my life + personality to me. We touched on many things—childhood, poetry, sex—he seemed, in a fantastic way, to know me intimately: I could talk with him," Merrill wrote to Fredericks. "I was afraid almost to refuse." Merrill told him

about the past months—Kimon, my father, you— . . . and, with many admissions as to the rigidity of these tests, he drew several tentative conclusions. He said my sickness was expressive of great tension, that I was a very nervous person, of sufficient intelligence to know myself intellectually, but expending all my energy upon existing, holding myself in check, with the result that I had hardly any energy left for my work or a joyous participation in life; that I am a person of considerable creative imagination, but that it does not operate freely; that I have a mild tendency towards self-destruction; that, in terms of sex, I was not naturally homosexual, that my greatest happiness would come from a woman; that I feel guilt as a result of my family life + my sexual expression: + finally, that none of this was very urgent, . . . but that I needed, at one point or another, some kind of treatment.

When Detre finished, Jimmy felt "crushed"—then relieved, energized, even uplifted. "Claude, my dearest," he wrote, "I am forced in all honesty to take this man seriously. [. . .] [H]e speaks of a life of total acceptance + activity: it is that to which he recommends me—he does not say that my own is anything but less than, granted my gifts, it might be." The letter continues, swelling with devotion: "I have never loved before this moment. I give myself to you as I had never dreamed possible. [. . .] Claude, I love you, I am completely, eternally in love. I am certain that"—Jimmy was quoting from Shakespeare's sonnet "Let me not to the marriage of true minds"—"if what I am saying is not true, then no man ever loved." By the next morning, however, when he added still another page to the letter, Merrill was sober, even depressed: "The doctor speaks of, as something in the distance, the ultimate death of feeling in 'cases' such as mine."

Painkillers probably played a part in those dramatic fluctuations of mood. But Merrill was also responding to the magnetism of this young doctor. He referred to Detre as "a prophet" suddenly "most dear to me"; though "quiet" and "gentle," he "disarms" and "disturbs me," Jimmy told Claude during his second day in the hospital. Detre mentioned that he and Simeons had talked to CEM for "a few hours" the previous day. Mr. Merrill was "very much concerned—not altogether for me, but for himself in relation to me: he accepts the difference between us, but wants now very much to bridge that difference, do something together with me. The Dr. says he considers himself the basis of my life, he broods about his failure to introduce me to life as he conceives it, and is concerned that I be, in worldly terms, successful." In the next breath, Detre told Jimmy "that the only patients he ever cared to treat were those he felt drawn to in a human way, those whom he understood, who were not hysterical but who suffered deeply, and went on to say he felt drawn to me in this way." Plainly this was an invitation. Merrill didn't take Detre up on it, but he wouldn't forget about it either.

Discharged from his second hospital stay in a month, Jimmy reunited with his father to attend Leoncavallo's rare *verismo* opera *Zazà*—"a lusty, pathetic tale of a married man's affair with an actress," a story of anguish and heartbreak, after which CEM "remarked that the greater part of it was something more than familiar to him." Before they went their separate ways, the Merrills appeared for an audience with long-reigning Pope Pius XII. Jimmy described the protocol in a letter: "[W]e stood around the walls, knelt suddenly at a signal, and in he sailed. We were the first to be greeted, accidentally, among much genuflection, and the Holy Hand placed graciously at our disposal; I missed the ring, felt only his soft elderly skin upon my lips." In *A Different Person*, what Merrill recalled from that day long ago was the "snowy, double-breasted swank" that his father had ordered from a Roman tailor for the occasion, and the gold dollar-bill-sign clip that he used to hold his silk tie in place. (Ned Magowan cracked, "Hey, Charlie, great! [. . .] His Holiness'll kiss *your* hand when he sees that.") This meeting between the "waxen, white-robed ascetic" and the cofounder of Merrill Lynch—"two men who had 'reached the top' in their respective fields of godliness and finance"—suggested "some long-awaited conjunction of Jupiter and Pluto."

Jimmy's letters to Claude had toyed with one plan after another for their long-awaited rendezvous, trying to get the setting right. They settled on Les Roches Blanches, a hotel with a spectacular view dominated by the cape at Cassis, where Merrill pulled up in a black Citroën after a fifteen-hour drive, thrilled, exhausted, and expectant. "Claude himself, closing his Herbert or Traherne, rising so abruptly that his chair fell over, for a long moment answered fully to the ardent phantom he'd become during our separation." The blissful moment lasted two weeks while the lovers got to know each other again, phantoms no more, free from the eyes of family and friends in a fragrant foreign land.

From Cassis, they intended to drive across northern Italy to Salzburg, where they would spend the summer. But a detour intervened. Ray Daum from Amherst days had written to Jimmy from Lausanne to say that Hans Lodeizen was in a clinic there, suffering in the advanced stages of leukemia. So Merrill and Fredericks drove north to see him. "The large, lived-in room, full of books and records, overlooked the lake. Hans lay cranked up in bed, a picture of health thanks to his daily transfusion" and the misleadingly ruddy cheeks it gave him. They talked of Hans's hoped-for convalescence in Italy and the prospect of reuniting there in the fall. Lodeizen presented Merrill with his book of poems, *Het Innerlijk Behang* (*The Wallpaper Within*), published in 1949, and, in impromptu English translation, read aloud the poem about visiting Jimmy at his mother's called "Meeting the Merrills," another poem that began with a line by Merrill, and two poems dedicated to Merrill. One of these was a challenge to the healthy, industrious writer standing beside Lodeizen's deathbed:

> Jim I would like to know
> what makes it worthwhile
> for you to keep on writing
> letters, essays, and poems
> in which you recommend the world
> and weigh her like an expert merchant.

How come you never
tire and shut your eyes and
think I wish they'd all go
to hell with their idle
gossip and keep on writing
letters, essays, and poems
from which I recognize you and
through which I meet you laughing
and telling me to keep faith
for I am very tired and as
I speak hope flows out of me.
Jim what makes it worthwhile
for you to keep on writing
letters, essays, and poems . . . etc.

The other poem dedicated to Merrill, a lyric fragment just four lines long, Merrill later translated this way:

the stars & the incurable
moment of the two crossed beams.
Orion discovered & in his hand
o fate in his hand the sword.

On his way out the door, Jimmy saw a "brilliant stripe of late sun" fall across Hans's face. "Why didn't he shift, or squint?" The answer: a blood vessel had burst in his left eye, and he was blind on that side.

From Salzburg, Merrill wrote to Hans about the city's preparations for the start of the music festival that had drawn him and Fredericks there. Although he knew better than to expect it, Merrill hoped that

you are steadily recovering your strength. It was such a great pleasure to see you and to recognize even during such an illness, how constantly resourceful and lively you are in spirit. Thank you again + again, too, for your book of poems: I am so often moved to receive poems from friends, in letters, or in little books: it seems such an act of faith, a kind of gentle love, that has nothing to do with the poems themselves, but only that they should first have been written, then given. In time, of course, I shall learn Dutch! It touched me also, as you know, to hear from you of whatever part I played in some of the poems—to know that

for you as well the strange energy we elicited from one another,
always recognized, never articulated, had found an expression,
in its own way.

Hans died before he received the letter. Jimmy took the news inside
himself. Writing to his mother, he waited to mention it until the third
paragraph:

> I don't quite know how to tell you that Hans died last week. I feel
> a tremendous sense of loss, and that the world as well has lost so
> much. I can't think of any of my friends who to such a degree is
> free of the traces of that interior death by which a man can truly
> perish. He was free of it, entirely, and it's a terrible thing to
> think of him as gone. I learned so much from him, about music,
> the world, and myself.

On the back of the letter, Jimmy typed a draft of an elegy for his friend:

> Here they all come to die,
> Fluent in death since childhood.
> But being a young man, never of their race,
> It was madness he should lie
>
> Blind in one eye, and fed
> By the blood of a scrubbed face:
> It was madness to look down
> On the toy city where
>
> The glittering neutrality
> Of clocks and chocolate and lake and cloud
> Made every morning somewhat
> Less than he could bear,
>
> And makes me cry aloud
> At the old masters of disease
> Who dangled close above him on a hair
> The name of Switzerland,
>
> The sword that, never falling, kills.
> There is a countryside his shut eye sees

No man shall travel to until
He takes the sword into his own hands.

Merrill made refinements over several years before "The Country of a Thousand Years of Peace," dedicated to Lodeizen with the dates of his life (1924–50), was at last finished. The closing conceit grew more intricate, powerful but hard to parse, and weighted with poetic allusion:

> And makes me cry aloud
> At the old masters of disease
> Who dangling high above you on a hair
> The sword that, never falling, kills
>
> Would coax you still back from that starry land
> Under the world, which no one sees
> Without a death, its finish and sharp weight
> Flashing in his own hand.

The "old masters of disease" call to mind the masters of Flemish painting Auden refers to in "Musée des Beaux Arts":

> About suffering, they were never wrong,
> The Old Masters; how well they understood
> Its human position; how it takes place
> While someone else is eating or opening a window or just walking
>   dully along

Merrill's poem is a variation on the same theme. Lodeizen might be Icarus, his bare legs plunging into the sea while a ploughman looks down and turns his field, in the painting traditionally attributed to Peter Brueghel the Elder. Just so, it was "madness" that this young man should be dying in a land of placid, ordinary, orderly life, a picturesque landscape indifferent to his suffering, and in that respect an image of "that interior death by which a man can truly perish." The "glittering neutrality" of everyday life is "somewhat / Less than he," the poem's poet-hero, "could bear," who is made for—and who finally seizes—greater things. Going forward into his death, Lodeizen appears in Merrill's poem as an intrepid traveler, no mere expatriate, like Jimmy, but a poetic quester seeking, like Orpheus, knowledge of that "starry land / Under the world"—which Merrill had glimpsed, perhaps, in the quatrain Lodeizen read to him in Lausanne. Mixed into Merrill's thinking, if not his precise choice of words, are motifs from Hamlet's soliloquy describing death as "the undiscover'd country from whose bourn / No traveller returns." Unafraid and affirming his fate, Lodeizen disarms death by taking it, like a "flashing" sword, "in his own hand."

In its imagining of a world "under the world," the poem announced a major theme in Merrill's work. Access to that other world comes with "a death." Merrill's use of the indefinite article is pregnant. It implies that death is not a singular, final event; because it is not "his" exclusively, it makes Hans's death something that Merrill can share in, that permits him too to see the country Hans looked on with his "shut eye." Learning from his friend, identifying with him, and feeling his loss, Merrill himself suffered "a death," the first important one in his life. And his reward is the poem itself, which has the crafted "finish and sharp weight" of a sword. That sword, a figure for poetic power, improves on the poor "quivering" weapon raised by the thwarted poet-son at the end of "Medusa." It is the weapon Merrill felt the lack of when on Rhodes he dreamed of doing battle with T. S. Eliot, the old master who was "trying to kill" him. The poem's echoes of Auden and Shakespeare are not incidental: they show a young poet taking literary tradition in his own hands and using it to his purpose. Merrill knew very well that he was writing here in one of the oldest and most elevated of genres, a pastoral elegy composed by one young poet for another, a poem like Milton's "Lycidas." Jimmy and Hans had elicited from each other a "strange energy." Merrill gave poems to Lodeizen; now Hans had given one to him. It was the first poem by Merrill that openly declares its basis in his life: the type of lived experience from which his mature work would spring.

When he wrote to her about Hans's death, Jimmy's mother had important news of her own: Hellen was planning to remarry. She had known General William Plummer when they were both young people in Jacksonville. In the spring of 1950, they met again; Bill proposed marriage, and Hellen wrote to Jimmy with the question. He struggled at once to advise her and to disclaim any authority for doing so: "I feel with genuine pleasure that I have no responsibility in this matter, except the responsibility [. . .] to encourage you in whatever impulse you may feel toward happiness or love or life." Solemnly, with some confusion, he summed things up: "I'm 'for' it, very much so; but, more, I'm 'for' you. You have gone splendidly far on your own, I cannot imagine you will lack the courage to accept him. Or the courage to refuse him—[. . .]."

He was writing at that point on stationery from Les Roches Blanches, where he and Claude were in the midst of their rapturous reunion. He told his mother, "Claude comes tomorrow," but they'd been together and in each other's arms for five days. Now, in Salzburg, he continued to lie about their relationship: "Claude has a room down the next street; we usually meet in the late afternoon to explore part of the city and have dinner." Perhaps, were Hellen to marry again, Jimmy would have the freedom he needed to develop his relationship with this lover.

Bill and Hellen soon married in Atlanta, Bill's home, where they would live. Two years older than she, and twice widowed, the general had one daughter. Beatrice, known as Betty, was a senior at Duke, and she quickly made friends with her father's intended. Charles Merrill would be a hard act to follow. But Bill was a southern gentleman, well placed in business after his discharge from the Air Force as a war hero. He had been in command of Orly Field in Paris in 1944: on the wall in Atlanta hung a photo of him standing beside Field Marshal Montgomery. He rose to brigadier general, and was decorated with a Bronze Star, the Army Commendation Ribbon, the Croix de Guerre, and the palm of a Chevalier in the Legion of Honor. In a poem written twenty years later, Merrill calls Bill "the gentle General she married / Late, for both an old way out of harm's." If Jimmy had mixed feelings about this romance that sprang up directly after he left for Europe, he shared with friends only his relief. He told Meredith, "[F]or the first time since I can remember, she has written me really glowing, radiant letters, intimate not in respect to me, but to her own life [. . .]; and I am tremendously touched by so much that seems implicit in her decision." All that was at stake for him was made amusingly apparent by the announcement of the Plummers' wedding in *The New York Times*, which identified Hellen's former husband as James Ingram Merrill.

The general, writing to Jimmy to introduce himself, explained the military situation in North Korea and predicted a draft. American ground troops had engaged with North Korean forces in early July, while in Europe the Soviet Union and the U.S. faced off with atomic bombs in both arsenals. World War III seemed entirely thinkable, and the mood was feverish. Their mothers urged Jimmy and Claude to come home before the communists poured over the border. "[B]ut it seems questionable that the U.S. is any safer than Paris, or Paris than Vienna," Merrill reflected. He and Fredericks thought "seriously of going to Africa"—to the symbolically named Liberia—"if only to escape this tension." Meanwhile, they carried on as tourists at the Salzburg Music Festival, ignoring the rumors of Nazi collaboration that clung to Maestro Wilhelm Furtwängler and Merrill's idol

Kirsten Flagstad, and applauding the "noble plea for brotherly love" made by Sarastro, the high priest in *The Magic Flute*, as if Mozart's solemn basso might solve the global crisis if only given the chance.

In August, they drove to see Tony Harwood in Venice. Merrill found the city ravishing: with its "peeling paint, rubbed gold, [and] stone consumed by water," it was like "a vast theatre abandoned after a pageant of Venice; or the estate of an 18th century eccentric whom, even while he was alive, none of his guests ever saw." Harwood was in the company of a princess, Nina Mdivani Conan Doyle, and her husband, the son of the creator of Sherlock Holmes. The princess was one of five siblings of Georgian nobility, known as the "Marrying Mdivanis," who fled Russia in 1917 and married into spectacular wealth and celebrity (with equally spectacular divorces and, in two cases, grim fatal accidents). When Denis Conan Doyle died in 1955, Harwood married Nina. Drawn together by the study of theosophy, they would travel the world in search of occult knowledge. Merrill found his old friend from the Jigger costumed "like a figure from a 1907 picnic, in white flannel trousers, evening-pumps, shirtsleeves, tie and straw hat." Tony presented a slim chapbook of his poems that he had had printed by monks. Finding in these trembling poems a promise no one else did when he sent out copies of the book, Merrill improbably saw in Harwood the makings of "an American Mallarmé."

In Italy, they were joined by Claude's mother. The threat of war hadn't kept her from making her first trip to Europe. Merrill found Vira a "tough cookie, bossy and independent," a female type he liked; where her son and his lover were concerned, she tactfully left unsaid, Merrill noted, "a number of things whose saying all but severed the lines of communication between my mother and me." She set off by herself for Capri, while the young men drove south through Florence, Padua, Siena, Perugia, and Assisi in an orgy of sightseeing (it was "not I, who was insatiable, but the places themselves, shouting out to be seen," Merrill quipped). In Rome, they took rooms in the Hotel Eden near the Borghese Gardens, overlooking a convent courtyard where chickens clucked by day and nightingales sang at night. Taking a page from Hellen Plummer's book, Mrs. Fredericks returned from Capri with a beau from Texas who wasted no time before proposing to her. In one of the many fibs and contrivances that make *A Different Person* unreliable as a record of facts, the memoirist turned this suitor into a Saudi Arabian businessman who promised to take Vira to his "grand villa with servants" on the Persian Gulf. Yet the real romance turned out just as the invented one does. The night before the wedding back home in Missouri, Vira's fiancé jilted her.

Correspondence from Knopf caught up with Merrill in September, asking for help with publicity for *First Poems*. Merrill wanted the proofs to go to "Stevens, Ransom, Eliot, Marianne Moore, Blackmur, Tate, Elizabeth Bishop, Louise Bogan," and, he suggested "less forcefully," Robert Lowell, Richard Eberhart, and John Berryman. "Perhaps William Empson" and Edith Sitwell. "Although I don't particularly care whom you ask for opinion," he added, writing to Herbert Weinstock, "I hope you will let me see the quotes, if not a proof of the jacket [. . .] before it is too late to alter it."

The book's designer also wrote to him. Harry Ford, a southerner seven years older than Merrill, would become a trusted friend and lifelong collaborator. Ford was soon promoted to editor at Knopf; after 1959, he moved to Atheneum, where he continued to publish Merrill's poetry in the simple, serious, plain-style design that became Ford's trademark. Ford described to Merrill his choices of type and layout for *First Poems*: the jacket "is, according to your request, extremely simple, bold, and I think you will find it sufficiently Faberish"—referring to the British publisher Faber and Faber, which published Eliot and Auden, and which apparently set the industry standard for both Ford and Merrill.

In early October, with Mrs. Fredericks still in tow, Merrill and Fredericks sailed to the island of Mallorca, a beautiful place not as distant as their fantasized Liberia but remote enough to feel far from the rest of the world. They settled into the Hotel Maricel, a short tram ride away from Palma, with each member of the party in a room of his or her own, Jimmy's and Claude's adjoining. Prices were low—a haircut cost ten cents—and distractions were modest: they made excursions to the island's two hundred caves, its ancient olive groves (which became the subject of a Merrill poem), windy beaches, and "the little white convent where Chopin and George Sand spent their unhappy months, thought to be demons by the natives." Jimmy and Claude read and wrote in the morning; a picnic lunch and a walk or excursion followed; then more reading and writing. Later they played recorders, working through tunes by Haydn or Bach, before drinks and dinner. They began to live the quiet creative life they had dreamed of.

Up to now, Fredericks wrote in his journal, he and Merrill had experienced together mainly "a certain failure and unhappiness." Competition was part of their problem. Fredericks had qualities that Merrill believed he lacked and wanted: independence, earnestness, knowledge of the classics, and a taste for the honest and unadorned. But more often than not, the difference in their temperaments prodded Merrill to defend his own. When they discussed their aesthetic aims, Claude "had to realise Jimmy does not truly have sympathy for what I am seeking to do. [. . .] I perhaps feel dissatisfied he should admire the effete & useless little sheaf of T[ony]. H[arwood]." Although he was a fledgling author, Merrill was awaiting proofs of his first book from Knopf: he had already gained a level of recognition Fredericks hadn't. What's more, as he watched the life he was living with Jimmy being turned into poetry, Claude felt subtly betrayed: "How difficult for two writers to love each other, [. . .] or even when only one is; the thoughts, the experiences, the feelings, that should be the sole property of the other is apportioned out, saved, thought about, in other ways; and with all artists the desire for fame, or the fear of the other's at least, enters in."

The topic of "fame" had come up back in Salzburg when they were "seized" by "fantastic horror," fearing that the world would end soon in atomic war. Their panic, Fredericks recalled, led to a conversation in which Merrill spoke

> about his conception of himself as poet. I said, You know you lead me to believe [. . .] that you write for the sake of immortality: I mean that you use your poetry as a weapon against your mortality. He admitted that that was indeed so, that one of the most vivid and particular horrors of his anxiety ("Forgive me," he said, "if I sound frivolous, for I am not") was that such a war could mean the end of an American literature, the very destruction of the language, or at least of the book, as Rilke in Germany, and thereby the smothering of all his hopes. He has a particular anxiety for the safety of his book . . . I had just objected that it was a paltry immortality, such a book, and he must regard its achievement and its need on a different level. He conceded that. He does however keep faith that merely having "a book" is a great safety . . . and he desires, like a near Eastern potentate, to have his NAME inscribed somewhere so that men cannot forget it.

War fears followed them to Mallorca. Jimmy had visions of "America conquered, of all people such as himself and his family, even all poets, lined up and shot." And Claude, equally frightened and fanciful, disturbed by nightmares, wondered whether the winter fog enveloping the island was "gas or the aftermath of a great bomb." When they talked about fame and ambition again, Jimmy told Claude that "he is rarely 'moved' to a poem. He takes up his pen because he wishes to write a poem ('I have slept long enough') that will bear his name." In fact Hans's death and the Korean crisis made personal mortality and historical catastrophe seem like entirely present threats. Thinking of his book as a safeguard against them, Merrill resembles poets of the past like Milton (who said, "A good book is the pre-

cious lifeblood of a master spirit, embalmed and treasured up on purpose
to a life beyond life") and Wordsworth (in whose "dream of the Arab" the
fate of civilization rests on the survival of books).

When *First Poems* arrived at the Hotel Maricel, the physical object
pleased its author enormously. To Mrs. Knopf, he wrote to say "how thoroughly delighted I am by every aspect of the book—it is all, and more than I
could have hoped for; and how deeply I appreciate your faith in me." Buechner, who was in Europe for a *Wanderjahr* of his own, visited Mallorca in late
November, where he took the place of Mrs. Fredericks. Merrill rushed to
show Freddy *First Poems*, which was dedicated to him. Freddy was at work on
The Seasons' Difference, a novel based on his friendship with Merrill; Jimmy
was working on his own novel. Fredericks admired their exchanges: "F. is
not afraid to take all J. gives him for his esthetic growth, nor is J. afraid to
give. Likewise J. accepted freely from Kimon, from Tony, from me.—they
dare give & take—," which, Claude recognized, he found impossible to do.

Merrill and Fredericks celebrated Christmas Eve in the cathedral. They
watched a boy in red surplice flanked by candle bearers march down the
aisle, ascend to the pulpit, raise a sword, and chant in Mallorquín the
Cumean Sibyl's prophecy of the Apocalypse. The next morning, around
the crèche assembled in Jimmy's room, the lovers exchanged stockings
stuffed with presents. Merrill had composed a shape-poem for Fredericks:

O
see
my love:
than every
returned kiss
which you for me
upon the green boughs of
our mutual heart bestow
(and I for you, assuredly)
no fairer gift, us to content,
shines anywhere, nor ornament.
This
Be
Our only tree.

In his workroom, Claude unveiled a special gift: a pair of finches,
"gray-brown, the male with a scarlet ascot." Jimmy called them Ivy and
Ralph.

As winter wore on, they made friends with the hotel's staff and guests; Hans's parents appeared unexpectedly for a holiday. But it was a lonely winter, and Merrill sounded homesick in letters to his friends. "I miss much in America," he told Meredith, "+ most of all a place I can call home, but whether it's worth leaving for, particularly in view of the spiritual changes in the country, due to politics; and moreover all that remains to see + do here, I haven't decided. If I come back it will be on the spur of the moment, because I shall have begun to be unhappy, but that is not yet the case."

Or was it the case? Looking back on this period, Merrill admitted, "I hadn't learned how to love. [. . .] I had counted on 'being a lover' with no credentials beyond a certain expectant footlit intensity." Which "wasn't up to Claude's. [. . .] Claude's love, like his taste in music or art, abashed me. Where I was content to 'find myself' in a Fauré song or a Degas interior, he identified manfully with a Zen scroll or the *St John Passion*. We weren't of course competing, yet how not to feel superficial next to him?" What might have meant satisfaction for another man meant the opposite for him: since May, Jimmy had gone from 130 pounds to 154.

Complaining of his weight, his laziness, and lack of passion, he increased the hours at his desk. Pages of the novel accumulated. So did new poems, some of which were quite strong. "Orfeo," titled like Monteverdi's opera about Orpheus and Eurydice, is a sonnet-length sentence whose gradual unfolding feels like an extended baroque vocal flourish; it introduces a metaphor—Hell as an opera house—that Merrill would return to in other works. "The Octopus," written after a visit to the aquarium in Naples, is cleverly ordered in paired lines of different lengths in which the penultimate syllable of the first line is rhymed with the last syllable of the shorter one that follows, a rhyme scheme of Merrill's invention. "There are many monsters that a glassen surface / Restrains," it begins, hinting at "monsters" behind the "glassen surface" of the poet's own perfect manners.

Fredericks was watching closely: "He works, without stopping, for hours, writing hundreds of phrases in his notebook, reading the dictionary hour after hour, dragging each word out of his unconscious—finally, assembling the parts, he puts the poem together." Merrill was reading too: Gaston Bachelard's *Psychoanalysis of Fire* and Henri Mondor's massive biography of Mallarmé. One afternoon he and Fredericks paid a visit to Robert Graves, the English poet who lived on Mallorca. Graves appeared with a "green hat smashed on his uncombed, unwashed curly gray locks, a ragged tan coat wrapped around his great hulking body." It happened that William Merwin, Merrill's acquaintance from Princeton, was there as Graves's secretary and a tutor to his children. Graves held forth, maintaining the view, as Fredericks summarized it, that Yeats's poetry "was all showmanship, manipulation, fraud"; "poetry depends entirely on inspiration: one writes poetry only when the muse speaks within." Merrill, though silent, was disturbed by this demand for inspired speech. Later Fredericks remarked that Graves "couldn't defend his statements about Yeats. 'Really?' Jimmy said, 'that is so good to know. Sitting there I assumed it was all <u>true</u> and that Yeats <u>was</u> a fraud and I, not writing from inspiration, had never written a poem.' "

They began to feel trapped in their island retreat. Merrill liked to release the finches in his room and watch them flutter against the mirror. One day he opened the cage—and Ralph darted out an open window and perched in a tree. Merrill carried the weeping Ivy outside in the cage, but Ralph wasn't coming back: "His cries, as evening fell, came from farther and farther away." The birds' miniature melodrama hardly needed to be interpreted. The next day Merrill insisted that they shop for a new friend for Ivy; it "shocked" Fredericks that "one could so easily substitute a loss, particularly in the symbolic way I saw the departure, [as though] love [were] a cage." They didn't bother to name the substitute and soon gave both birds away.

The lovers themselves bickered and pecked. JM: "You make me feel everything I do is ugly and wicked." CF: "You make me feel I am worthless." As if relocation were the solution, they made plans to leave for France. Merrill's feelings of homesickness, disorientation, and alienation from his lover and himself coalesced in "Hôtel de l'Univers et Portugal," a poem that describes lovers tossing and turning in a "strange" bed in a hotel, "whose recurrent dream we are." The life the hotel offers is an ascetic, almost monastic one: here "the ambitious dreaming head" tosses "the world away" and dwells "In the pillow's dense white dark" while the lovers' speech peels from the wall like so many drafts of a poem. "Bare room," Merrill apostrophizes,

> bleak problem set for space,
> Fold us ever and over in less identity
> Than six walls hold, the oval mirror face
> Showing us vacantly how to become only
> Bare room, mere air, no hour and no place,
>
> Lodging of chance, and bleak as all beginning.

Commenting on the poem to Friar, Merrill reflected, "[O]ne travels in order <u>not</u> to want, to possess, in order to lose what one has acquired, to become one's small empty self at last, which may turn out to be total emptiness."

Fredericks didn't like the poem; he felt it took "a sharp and cynical attitude towards what concerns us both," and he said so. When, a year ago in New York, they first speculated about where to travel, and Portugal seemed like a delightfully unlikely choice, the name became a private code word signifying "every delirious possibility of love"; now it had appeared in a poem about "bleak" anonymity and the improvised, temporary character of their life together. Merrill saw the justice of the complaint: he "had betrayed our lovers' code for the sake of mere art." But it was more than a poem that was causing them pain. Jimmy put it to Claude simply and sharply: "We don't really, after all, seem to get along, do we?"

France wasn't a solution. As they toured Toulouse, the Cathedral town of Albi, the fortress at Carcassonne, and the cave paintings at Lascaux, Merrill quarreled with officials, hotel staff, and waiters—and then with Fredericks when he objected to these scenes. It rained. The hotels were empty. Merrill coughed through the night, suffering asthma-like symptoms, straining to breathe. He read Flaubert's *L'Éducation sentimentale*, and mocked his own novel in progress ("it is hideously boring and for the most part bad"). Paris had somewhat more to offer. Fredericks took Merrill to the rue Christine to meet Alice B. Toklas, who "couldn't be more charming," Merrill felt, "tiny and bent and mustached with great gleaming eyes and the assurance of having known Everybody." Toklas started calling Jimmy "Jamie," and Claude adopted the name too. In the evenings, they took in serious music: Flagstad's farewell to Paris in *Götterdämmerung, Phèdre* at the Comédie Française, and Abby Solomon playing Beethoven's final piano sonata, op. 111.

But Merrill's mind was on Rome. He flew there to meet the Magowans, who had arrived for Robin's school holiday. Jimmy convinced Doris to consult Simeons about the severe headaches she suffered, and he went with her to his office. The doctor "was almost positive the headaches came from a nervous source," and he offered to treat her, but she declined. In a letter to his father, Merrill implied his own diagnosis of Doris's condition in a description of his brother-in-law: Bobby was "as usual, terribly nervous" and "irritable. [. . .] They took [. . .] great pains to be kind and loving towards one another, not always successfully; but I've observed that such charity is often in proportion to a sense of failure and misunderstanding."

Jimmy took the opportunity to consult Simeons too, which must have been his idea all along. On the surface, his complaint was not the emotional one that Detre had diagnosed, but his "hopeless, fluctuating fatness." Since his early Lawrenceville days, when he was indeed plump, he had maintained a normal weight, but the idea that he was fat and soft had worked its way into his mind. Doctors whom he consulted about it over the years had dismissed his concern outright. Now Simeons not only agreed that he was heavy, but knew what to do about it: the extra pounds, he explained, were the result of a deficiency in the pituitary gland and could be rectified by injections of a hormone, hCG, "extracted from the urine of pregnant women." The injections would "absorb and redistribute" weight and "dissipate the listlessness" that Merrill felt prey to. Jimmy had felt for years "that my body is not normal, that the fatness is unnatural, that I feel a bit smothered in it, never able to feel myself <u>move</u>." So the promise of a physical transformation thrilled him. He agreed on the spot to live in Rome while Simeons treated him. Jimmy's weight always signified for him idleness and effeminacy. Now he would overcome that stigma by means of a regimen created for rich Italian ladies.

He might have been more cautious. The treatment, which Simeons eventually marketed in the U.S., was bound in 1976 by federal regulation requiring the Simeons Management Corporation to state that hCG was not proven to promote weight loss. It is commonly viewed today as a diet fraud; surely a less credulous patient than Merrill would have seen it as pure quackery.

It helped that his father knew Simeons. Merrill described the proposed treatment to him and to his mother; from most of his friends and family he kept his reason for moving to Rome a secret. Encouraging his father to approve of him, Jimmy made it clear that he approved of his father. CEM was again the subject of gossip: the Old Man had begun an affair with a married woman in Southampton, Lilian Coe, and his marriage to Kinta was falling apart. Privately Jimmy found this funny: he thought that Mrs. Coe played "a splendid 'fire' to Kinta's 'frying pan.' " But to his father he wrote, "[A]ll I see is <u>you</u>, making after so many disappointments, another fine effort to take what you must from life, not to turn your back to it; and surely that is what we're put on earth for, simply to live—for others at times, to be sure, but for ourselves first and foremost, because nobody else can do it for us."

His routine in Rome was simple: once a day he showed up at the hospital, where Dr. Simeons gave him a shot in the buttocks. His first reaction to the hormone was highly positive. "I have never within my memory felt better—continuously, exuberantly so," he told Howkins. "I had always imagined that neurosis curtailed my energies; and these past ten days, for the first time in my life, I have the experience of energy—[. . .] a disposition of the mind to work and of the conscience to accomplish." The peeling away of the past imagined in "Hôtel de l'Univers et Portugal" was being realized each morning as he stepped on the scale. "In seven days of dieting," he reported to his father, "I've lost seven pounds, and all around the waist and backside. The point is to get all the fat off, then build me up again[.]"

Fredericks came to Rome with Merrill, and, getting into the act, he approached Simeons for help with his anxiety. Simeons passed him on to Detre, who interviewed him under the influence of sodium pentothal, a barbiturate, and on the basis of this conversation prescribed ten months of psychoanalysis. Fredericks was wary because Detre was no orthodox analyst. As a Jew during the war, he had been unable to attend medical school in his native Budapest; he had learned to do counseling and administer psychological tests like the Szondi, but he had never been analyzed, and he had no analytic training. In Rome after the war, he enrolled in medical school, and became affiliated with Salvator Mundi International Hospital, where Simeons practiced. Fredericks commented: : "He is 'stateless' it seems and cannot use a bank; he has his patients part of the day in his apartment"—a "shabby" one in suburban Parioli. "I get the feeling of that undercover quality, consulting an abortionist [. . .]. It doesn't seem on the up-and-up." But Simeons had "complete faith in him," and Fredericks started therapy anyway.

Merrill's novel in draft, which centered on his father, languished "half-done" (the typescript stalled at 208 pages), and that was a source of frustration. But he had written ten new poems over the past year, and in these he felt "a certain freedom" and "a loosening of rhythm." Having a first book published and "out of the way" was "a great release." Still, reviews of the book were less than celebratory. In the *Nation*, Rolfe Humphries admired Merrill's technique, but noted "a dearth of ardor in the temperament." The point was put more harshly in *The New Yorker* by Louise Bogan, a critic Merrill respected, who was writing in a venue where her comments were sure to be widely noticed. Bogan classified Merrill as one of the "neo-Formalists" who reduce poetry to "a well organized set of rules." This new poetry, obeying T. S. Eliot's dictum that "emotion must be concealed," was "directly derived from literature, without so much as a side glance at life." Merrill's poems, she wrote, "are impeccably written, but everything about them smells of the lamp; they are frigid and dry as diagrams." This was the most cutting criticism he'd ever received. "Really, I think she is unnecessarily cruel," he wrote to Freddy; yet he agreed that "this and nothing else is my problem in writing at present: to discover warmth, find the feeling. Consequently no other criticism can touch me, and touch me it does." To his mother, he wrote about Bogan's review, "I don't mind as much for myself, as I do for, say, Daddy, who could so easily feel it's all a waste of time, what I'm doing." Whether or not the review was responsible, Merrill would write no poems for more than a year and a half after he read it.

"To discover warmth, to find the feeling": Merrill confronted the same challenge in his relationship with Fredericks, and he hardly knew how to meet it. That spring Wayne Kerwood had turned up in Rome with an office job in the Food and Agricultural Organization of the United Nations; he and Merrill went to dinner, to the beach, and—secretly—to bed. Meanwhile, Jimmy and Claude tried taking separate vacations: Claude left alone to see the celebrated Byzantine mosaics in Ravenna, and Jimmy went off on his own to Positano, a resort south of Naples. He came back from that weekend having made a new friend. Guitou Knoop was a Dutch sculptor, born in Russia in 1902, who'd been a student of Brancusi. Used to living by her wits, she was tough and talkative and had a big, braying laugh. They met when she emerged from the sea he was idly contemplating and splashed him with a spray of words: "Aren't you coming in? What's the matter, can't you swim? The water's divine even if the fishermen do make ka-ka in it. Twenty years ago I had a hygiene complex, but my analyst got rid of that."

By the end of June, Jimmy was ready to follow Knoop's example and dive in: admitting that the transformation he wanted might involve more than weight loss, he was ready to have "another go at analysis." He spoke to Simeons, and it was decided that, since Fredericks was Detre's patient and treating both partners in a couple made for a conflict of interest, Merrill's analyst would be Simeons, although he had even less analytic training than Detre.

Up to this point, Jimmy and Claude's relationship, conducted entirely in hotel rooms, had had the quality of an affair. In June, they moved together into an apartment on Via Gregoriana. Their rooms were "all tiled, cool, a bit dim and empty, with the blessing of a stair leading down to the large kitchen where daily a woman comes to make our lunch and wash our shirts." Merrill took his typewriter outside to a courtyard when the seamstress's shop on the ground floor was closed (her name amused him: Miss Camp). The handsome stucco house was set on a quiet street at the top of the Spanish Steps. They descended that marble cascade daily, passing the narrow room in which Keats died, to retrieve their mail at the American Express office in the piazza. Merrill did not at first include the address in letters home. In July, he told his mother that he planned to look for an apartment soon, without saying that he would be living in it with Claude. Probably no one had mentioned Fredericks, or for that matter Merrill's sexual orientation, to Bill Plummer.

Merrill had reason to feel his mother wanted his sexual life hidden. Kerwood, before he came to Rome, had been living in Jimmy's New York apartment, and that winter it was broken into. No valuables were taken. This aroused Hellen's suspicions when she heard about it. Worried that her son was vulnerable to blackmail, she went to the apartment and destroyed the letters she found from Friar, Fredericks, and Buechner.* The deed, meant to protect her son, instead hurt him badly. "In the context of Claude's and my deteriorating love, her actions struck a crippling blow. It left me with little evidence of having been loved by anyone, except her"—which perhaps was her deeper aim.

The arrival in Rome of Betty Plummer, making a postcollege tour of Europe, posed a serious problem to finesse. It was important that Merrill make friends with this "new sister" and that she have a good time, but she could not be taken to the apartment on Via Gregoriana. "Although by July Claude was sleeping no longer in the bedroom but on an austere couch in the *salone*, the big incriminating bed spoke for itself." Jimmy took her for a starlit carriage ride from the Forum to the Colosseum, and they visited the Tivoli Gardens and the Villa d'Este with some girls from her tour. Boyish Jimmy was snapped by one of their cameras standing aloof, notably thin from his diet, with a wary look behind his glasses, in an unlikely pair of lederhosen, suspenders, and knee socks (a costume he'd acquired in Salzburg). Betty was hard for him not to like. Sweet, pretty, blond, smart, and wondering at the Old World laid at her feet, she made Jimmy think of "a young version of women I'd known since babyhood," Hellen's Jacksonville friends, or indeed a young Hellen herself.

By Betty's third and final night in Rome, Jimmy was ready to present Claude, who had all that was needed—"intellectual dignity, plus a new mustache, which lent him the air of a young Flaubert"—in order "to impersonate exactly the friend he was, for that matter, on his way to becoming: sober, reliable, a Good Influence, as Betty might say when questioned." Betty invited the most "grown up" of her train, one Grace Van Nest, to make it

---

* JM to William Meredith, letter, July 7, 1951 (WUSTL). In *A Different Person*, Merrill says that, when his mother was preparing to move from New York to Atlanta after her wedding, she asked permission to destroy letters addressed to him that were stored in her home; he cabled back agreeing, since he thought that the letters to which she referred were of no value, and he believed that his important letters (including correspondence from Buechner, Friar, and Fredericks) were safe in his own apartment. She replied that "she knew I would be relieved to hear that *all* letters had been destroyed—those under her roof and those under mine" (537). This account, which attributes his mother's action partially to miscommunication, is probably an invention meant to put the best face on the event. Hellen had married and moved to Atlanta in fall 1950; she destroyed the letters in his apartment on a visit to New York in late spring 1951.

a foursome. They set off for drinks and dinner and a trip to a casino. Late in their meal, woozy with wine, Betty asked her stepbrother about the ring he was wearing: "Rings have to have a story, I always think." Jimmy didn't tell the story of his and pretended he couldn't take the ring off when she asked him to—prompting Betty's friend to ask to inspect Claude's, who, ever forthright, produced the gold ring Jimmy had given him in February 1950: it was decorated with the Merrill crest, and JIM's and HIM's initials were inscribed on the interior band. When, too late, Claude awkwardly withdrew it, Grace "snarled a little drunkenly, 'You don't think I can read, do you? Well, I can.' "

The encounter couldn't be brushed away. In his journal, Claude wrote, "Jimmy and I both suffered from anxiety over the ring (damn the mother, damn the mother, what if Grace DOES tell Betty who tells her father who tells Hellen—what indeed? do we live controlled by such nonsensical and stupid little ghosts?)." The answer was yes. The ring on Fredericks's hand was a symbol not only of his bond with Merrill, but of Merrill's bond with his mother, and the idea that word would get back to her that he had given it to Claude was unbearable to Jimmy.

Fredericks responded by becoming infatuated with a young American recently arrived in Rome, Robert Isaacson. In fact, in late July, Claude told Jimmy he had fallen in love with Robert. Jimmy wasn't jealous, he claimed at first. To prove the point, he accompanied Claude and Robert for a picnic and swim at Lake Nemi, a circular volcanic pool known as "Diana's Mirror." Friends from Bard were visiting that day, including Irma Brandeis, who'd come to Rome for a week, encouraged by Jimmy, her "darling boy," who paid for her travel. While the serious-minded Fredericks and Brandeis "kept drawing Virgil and Caligula and *The Golden Bough* up from the depths of the reputedly bottomless lake," Isaacson and Merrill tittered, discovering their shared pleasure in the shimmering surfaces of camp wit.

A few days later, Jimmy backtracked and told Claude, "I simply cannot see Robert, [. . .] it is a torture and a pain I cannot, cannot endure." Fredericks replied by making love to Isaacson and announcing to Jimmy, "We have failed in all we hoped for, and however we relate to each other in the future, it will be in a different way." They went on living together until they had to give up their rooms on Via Gregoriana in October. Yet the first, passionate phase of their relationship was over.

In early August 1951, a few weeks into his analysis with Simeons, Merrill wrote letters describing his newest treatment to his parents and siblings.

Jimmy sounded in control: his condition was "serious" but "not grave"; if this course of action seemed "self-indulgent," it was less so than the way he had led his life so far; he was in good hands with Simeons, "the Family Doctor Abroad," who was "quick and efficient" and promised a treatment of not more than a year. The problem was that for the "past four or five years" many things had caused him "unnatural difficulty and anxiety." He gave his mother the fullest account. He said that "the sexual difficulty" was not the "primary" one—there were "others equally severe, though less apparent to people outside myself"; and there was no cause for "secrecy": he wanted to shake off the feeling he had had with the analyst in 1947 "that I was engaged in some dark and shameful cure." In actuality, he was more discouraged and less the master of his destiny than these letters suggested. He was silent about the failure of his relationship with Fredericks, except by implication, in a letter to Meredith: "I have been dangling, again, from only one or two strings and, unlike the spider, have reached the end of them. [. . .] I am left with what I imagine I had always seen coming, an utter failure of all feeling, ability to feel, respond, work, think."

But his treatment by Simeons was a failure. After just a month of work together, the doctor decided that they "knew one another too well, were too real for one another, liked one another too much ever to have a proper relation for analysis." This didn't mean the end of treatment, however. When Simeons took himself off the case, Detre took Merrill on; the prospect that Fredericks and Merrill would separate had cleared the way, he felt, for both men to be his patients. Five days per week now, Claude and Jimmy would each take the long bus ride to Parioli and back for a fifty-minute analytic session, lying on the same couch at different hours of the day.

Kimon and Mina passed through Rome in late August on their way to New York, where they would live in Merrill's vacant apartment. As a parting gift, they gave him an amber cigarette holder that had belonged to Mina's Christo. Merrill carried it into his first session with Detre; and, as he gestured with it, it slipped from his hand and shattered on the floor. That seemed to answer Detre's question: "Why are you consulting me?" "Wasn't it enough," Merrill reasoned silently, "to be disturbed, or 'shattered,' even, like my piece of amber?" The problem was a sense of incapacity that had advanced so far as to undermine his ability to write poetry: "I didn't know how to love, I didn't know how to live, but I did know how to write a poem. Did once and didn't now [. . .]. That was my reason for seeking help. I wrote, therefore I was; if I couldn't write, I was nobody."

Merrill and Detre sat facing each other in Detre's rented parlor that day. This only slightly older man—Detre was born in 1924—was "soberly dressed and gave out an air of sallow, almost funereal gravity." He held for Merrill the mystery of an Eastern European refugee, small and dark, who was somehow able to see into Merrill's life from behind thick black-rimmed glasses that mirrored the poet's own. His verbal style counted too. Detre was capable not only of producing penetrating insights, but of putting them into concise, disarming formulations in English. If he was a "seer," as Merrill called him when they first met in 1950, he was a mordant comedian, too, with a sense of timing and tone, whose best lines remained in the poet's ear for decades—to judge from the exchanges recounted in *A Different Person*, which, Detre says, are an accurate record of what passed between them.

Detre's given name was Tamas Feldmeier. After his parents and other family members died in Auschwitz, he took a new surname from the French *d'être*, "to be." In time, the will, vitality, and cleverness expressed in that self-naming spurred him on to a distinguished medical career in the U.S. at Mount Sinai Hospital in New York, where he trained in psychiatry; the Yale Medical School, where he became psychiatrist in chief at Yale New Haven Hospital and established himself as an early proponent of psychopharmacology; and finally the University of Pittsburgh, where he led the university's health science schools for thirty years, working aggressively to integrate research, teaching, and patient care, and build the international reputation of Pittsburgh medicine. In every position he held, Detre would be commanding, controversial, and effective.

And so he was, though still a medical student and untrained psychoanalyst, in 1951. In Merrill's therapy, Detre recalled, "I was strongly engaged, not someone nodding in the background. I believe that what psychotherapy can accomplish is very limited. If the matchmaking is good, then you can learn something about intimacy and how you screw it up." The therapist imparts this knowledge, according to Detre, "simply by holding up a mirror and saying, Look, this is what you are doing." Merrill lay on the couch and free-associated while Detre sat to one side behind him, an invisible auditor. Detre used the analyst's couch—which doubled as his living room settee—merely because "people want that." In general, he discounted the "impact" of his patients' early experiences on their adult behavior. "If they wanted to talk about the past, I didn't mind," but his focus was "on how people related to me."

Merrill early on told Detre about a dream in which he found himself trapped in the body of a fish in an aquarium, pleading with a man outside the tank to recognize that he was a man too. "The message got across, but with the wrong results," Merrill said. "The stout man broke into smiles and pointed me out to his neighbors—*voyez donc*, a fish who imagined he was

human, what next!" Detre made no attempt to analyze this dream expressing Merrill's discomfort in his body and his wish to be accepted as a man
like others. About his lack of interest, as a therapist, in dreams, Detre later
remarked, "Freud called dreams the rocky road to the unconscious. It's
so rocky that it can't be traveled." Freud called dreams "the royal road" to
the unconscious. Detre's misquotation, whether it was a mistake or intentional, shows how little of a Freudian he was.

One of the first "sore points" Jimmy had to address was "the whole business of money," including the money he would pay his analyst. Detre set his
fee in proportion to the patient's income, believing that it should be "large
enough to give the patient a sense of the importance, the symbolic 'cost' of
the treatment." In this instance, he charged $30 per hour, for a monthly
cost of $660. Since Merrill received $750 per month from his trust fund, he
had to ask Bobby Magowan to raise his monthly allowance to $1,050. This
budget would force him to reduce his monthly expenses. He also chose to
limit his gifts to friends. He recognized that he was reluctant to spend his
money—"because I think of it as my father's"; yet he had an "exhaustive
need to be loved, thought well of—and this has kept me using the money, for
myself and for others." He wrote to Harwood to say that he would no longer
support him, once he'd fulfilled Tony's expectation of $10,000. He told Dora
Cook, a composer he had been funding, that he wouldn't do so any longer.
And he told his mother that he would stop paying her $300 per month; the
monthly sum had been intended to help with the upkeep of her house in
New Canaan, which she'd sold after her remarriage.

In September, Merrill traveled with Fredericks to Venice for a performance that he had looked forward to for months and would remember for
decades. It was the premiere of *The Rake's Progress*, Igor Stravinsky's opera
based on William Hogarth's moral tableaux of the same title, with a libretto
by Auden and his lover Chester Kallman. The theater La Fenice hosted the
premiere. "The most beautiful theater in the world," it was a five-tiered
glittering horseshoe, at once grand and intimate, with a gilt phoenix and
a great clock above the proscenium. Works by Rossini, Bellini, and Verdi
were first performed on its stage.

In sweltering heat, the audience approached through a maze of canals
and stone streets, the splendid arriving by gondola and motorboat. Inside,
Merrill picked out Cecil Beaton "in a flowing Bohemian tie"; he watched
Auden fan himself in his box with a sheaf of roses. Elsewhere in the audience he might have caught sight of Isaacson and Kerwood, who, introduced to each other by Jimmy, had come to Venice together. The "sublime
Schwarzkopf" sang the part of the heroine, Anne Trulove; Jennie Tourel put

on a beard to play Baba the Turk; and the diminutive Stravinsky conducted. Borrowing from Pergolesi, Mozart, Donizetti, and a host of other models, his score showed how a composer could, as he put it, "re-use the past and at the same time move in a forward direction." Receiving his ovation in a blaze of flashbulbs, Stravinsky was joined onstage by the librettists. Suggesting the two faces of the Rake, Auden "looked wonderfully well, tan and strong and nice," while Kallman was "a vision of Sin, puffy and purpled and scarred."

The opera lodged in Merrill's imagination because of his acquaintance (eventually his friendships) with Auden and Kallman, and because the Rake's career offered a fable about the perils of the life he was choosing. The story begins with Tom Rakewell betrothed to Anne Trulove, whose father has arranged for Tom to work in a counting house, the Merrill Lynch of its day. When Tom wishes for money of his own, Nick Shadow, his Mephistophelian servant and counselor, suddenly provides an inheritance. Tom at once leaves Anne to take up a life of pleasure in London under Shadow's tutelage. In Mother Goose's brothel, Nick quizzes Tom, who answers with the wit of a Wildean aesthete:

SHADOW
What is thy duty to thyself?

RAKEWELL
To shut my ears to prude and preacher
And follow Nature as my teacher.

When Shadow prods him to define Love in cynical terms, Tom draws back, however. Soliloquizing, wracked with guilt, he sings,

Love, too frequently betrayed
For some plausible desire
Or the world's enchanted fire,
Still thy traitor in his sleep
Renews the vow he did not keep,
Weeping, weeping,
He kneels before thy wounded shade.

Nick persuades Tom to marry and set up house with a Bearded Lady, Baba the Turk—a joke by Auden and Kallman about two men living together? But Tom never quite gives up on Anne and the ideal love she represents. In act 3, when Shadow brings him to the graveyard and demands that he pay for Shadow's services with his soul, Tom begs to try his luck one last time and wager his soul in a game of cards. Nick agrees, draws a card, and challenges him to guess which one it is. Tom, thinking of Anne, picks correctly: the Queen of Hearts. Through sheer luck he guesses correctly on his second try. Determined to win, Shadow cheats on the final round by drawing the Queen of Hearts again. Against all reason, but urged on by Anne singing offstage, Tom calls on Love once more: "Love, first and last, assume eternal reign: / Renew my life, O Queen of Hearts, again." Foiled, Shadow sinks into the grave with a curse: "To reason blind shall be your mind. / Henceforth be you insane!" The final scene takes place in Bedlam, where Tom, an inmate now, believes he is Adonis and Anne is Venus.

Merrill, like Tom, would call on "Love, first and last," again and again, to renew his life, hoping his luck would hold. He didn't care for the opera's final scene with its madhouse and broken hearts. He preferred the set-piece epilogue, where the characters come forward, the men without wigs, to address the audience directly, each with a limerick for moral. Baba, sans beard, imparts a lesson Merrill was learning in Italy:

> Let Baba warn the ladies:
> You will find out soon or later
> That, good or bad,
> All men are mad;
> All they say or do is theater.

Together Merrill and Fredericks went to look for apartments they would live in separately. They found a good one on the top floor, five flights up, of a stately nineteenth-century building on Via Quattro Novembre, owned by a Count Bracci. "One of us was to have it but which?" Fredericks wrote. "It was hard to decide. If I didn't want it, Jimmy didn't—it worked that way." Finally Merrill took it. It wasn't Fredericks's farmhouse, but he could practice simplicity there. With skylights but no windows, there was plenty of light but no view.

Fredericks eventually found rooms on the Piazza di Spagna. He and Merrill would share Quinta, a maid who went from one apartment to the other to cook meals and iron the bachelors' shirts. For the first time, Merrill set to work painting a desk, table, and shelves. He added chairs, a sofa, an upright piano; "100 great books, 3 modern lamps, and 2 rag rugs that take me back to my childhood almost as effectively as my analyst."

Via Quattro Novembre was a busy street, lacking in charm, set on the edge of ancient Rome. Had Merrill been able to look out, his gaze would have fallen on Trajan's market, the Forum of Augustus, and, a hundred yards beyond that, the sunbaked splendor of the Forum. For Freud, Rome was an image of the psyche's overlay of past and present in which "all the earliest stages of development continue to exist alongside the latest one." But Merrill didn't care about the classical past, even as a metaphor. He settled into this high, secluded space to contemplate the state of his own soul.

Not surprisingly, homosexuality was a central issue in his analysis. Merrill, Detre remarks, lived as "part of a despised minority." With reason, Merrill feared that his parents despised him for it, or would if the fact were spoken of: his mother had told him it would kill his father if he learned the facts of his son's "life." On hearing this, Detre interceded. He explained that, while Jimmy was recovering from surgery in the hospital in 1950, Detre had discussed his homosexuality with his father. This came as a revelation and a relief to Merrill.* CEM's silence on the subject suddenly seemed respectful, even generous, to Jimmy: "Tenderness and gratitude flooded me. He loved me intelligently, without wanting to change me into somebody I wasn't."

Regarding his consultation with the poet's father, Detre observes, "I told him the truth—that these choices have nothing to do with will power. Charles Merrill was a very bright man, and he accepted it. The impulse of psychotherapy was to deposit anything that went wrong at the doorstep of the parents, and my explanation absolved him of that." Charlie replied to Detre cheerfully, "I'm finally talking to someone who is making sense to me, not like those god-damned Jewish psychiatrists in New York." Detre replied, "Mr. Merrill, I'm afraid I'm one of those god-damned Jewish psychiatrists." The tycoon apologized for the comment, if not for his views, in a letter Detre prized: "I'm an old fool, and I should have known better," he wrote to the young doctor. The father's anti-Semitism, Detre adds, was not passed on to his son: "There was never a trace of it in James or any other prejudice—not in therapy or the many years after during which I knew him, when it could have come out, and it is something that comes out if it's there—it doesn't require special conditions or watchfulness."

That fall Merrill was increasingly interested in another Jewish man. Robert Isaacson, at twenty-five, was a very romantic figure. Heavy-lidded,

---

* Detre remembers that he spoke to Charles Merrill about his son's homosexuality "with James's permission." The letters Merrill wrote to Fredericks from the hospital on June 7 and 8, 1950, don't mention giving the doctor approval to talk to his father about any topic.

dark-haired, and olive-skinned, with a slight frame, quick, expressive gestures, and round lips, he could be puckish or sultry. He came from a well-to-do family in St. Louis, an only child who grew up in the house of his divorced mother. He was an accomplished musician and played the harpsichord with a relaxed nonchalance. Jimmy found in Robert a kindred spirit. Indeed, his bow ties, pale cotton suits, and fluttering manners gave Jimmy the uncanny sensation of being in the presence of his double.

Claude's affair with Robert hadn't progressed. Instead, Isaacson had gone to bed with Kerwood on their trip to Venice, and now Kerwood was infatuated with him. Merrill heard about this development from Wayne once they had both returned to Rome; with Anne Trulove's voice still in his ear, Jimmy urged Wayne to find Isaacson, who had stayed behind in Venice, and tell him he was in love. But when Kerwood did so, Robert rejected him.

The dance steps of this *pas à quatre* became more intricate, as Jimmy, for a time, went back to Wayne, and Claude pursued Robert. One night in November, Claude invited Robert to a restaurant. Jimmy, who just happened to be sitting by himself in the same establishment, was invited to join them. As at Lake Nemi, camp conversation ricocheted between Isaacson and Merrill, and Fredericks sat "slumped and silent." Finally Jimmy announced that he was going for cigarettes. Robert jumped up with him, leaving Claude alone at the table. Outside in the night air, the two men sat down on the Spanish Steps. Suddenly intimate, Merrill asked Isaacson if he was in love with him. In *A Different Person*, he turns what happened next into a sparkling comic vignette:

> Robert gave a murmur of protest, as if he'd been seized too roughly. Had I spoiled everything as usual? Then, *"Cosa fate qui?"* new, official voices were demanding. We blinked up into eyes inscrutable beneath visors: a pair of *carabinieri*. As we set about stringing together some few lame words, *"Stranieri* [foreigners]," said the second policeman, in a contemptuous undertone. (Was no Italian capable of the iniquities he had in mind?) His partner, the bright one, put out a restraining hand. *"Somigliano,"* he observed, *"guarda. Sembrano fratelli."* And to us, indicating our upturned faces, our matching summer jackets and bow-ties: "You a-re brothers, no? *Gemelli*—touins?" Yes, yes! we excessively nodded, still trembling but relieved; amused, too, by his acumen. Or was he slyly letting us off the hook? *"Adesso a casa,"* he smiled. *"Dormire, hanno capito?"* We understood, and thanked them. The splendid figures saluted in unison—maybe *they* were twins too—and marched briskly down the steps.

Following orders, the American twins went home to Merrill's rooms on Via Quattro Novembre. The next day, when Merrill picked up the phone, it was Claude on the line: "I despise you with all of my heart for what you did last night." Jimmy murmured, "Thank you," and hung up. Fredericks and Merrill had long been competing—for recognition and attention, for Simeons and Detre. Now, Merrill had won Isaacson. His analyst put the victory in perspective:

"You have been wanting to establish your independence of Claude for several months now," said Dr Detre. "This move was long overdue."

"But *thanking* him? Thanking him for what?"

"Well, since you are as yet incapable of breaking with someone you once loved—something the rest of the world does every three weeks—you took your time and found a sure way to make him do it for you. Do not forget, you were raised in a house full of servants."

In a book of names, Merrill discovered that "my very name, James, meant 'the supplanter.' " The romantic competition he'd fallen into with Fredericks resonated with the complex history of supplantings that was his family romance. His father had replaced his first wife with Hellen, and Hellen with Kinta. In his youthful affections, Zelly had taken his mother's place, and one boy after another had taken Zelly's. His solution was to buy a substitute when Ralph, the finch, deserted Ivy. He was always ready to protect himself by investing in a new relationship. And yet he was reluctant to let go of anyone he had loved. For evidence, he could look at the way he remained entangled with Friar and kept Kerwood on a string.

Or he could reflect on his relationship with his mother. In Italy, he was testing the limits of their bond. He hadn't seen her in a year and a half. That fall Hellen decided that enough was enough: if her son wouldn't come to her, she would come to him. When she wrote suggesting a visit, his response was polite and equivocal in the extreme, wiggling this way and that. "Dear Mama," he began,

Your letter came this morning with its lovely proposal of a visit to me. I've been trying, the past six hours, to find the proper response. Offhand, without being quite prepared, I was genuinely delighted at the thought; and I believe I still am. I miss you—one says it so weakly, but I do; and I have been lonely, and shall be. The questions that come to mind are of the sort that cannot be answered except by your coming [. . .]. But, all things being equal—I'm trying to say it dispassionately—I believe that I should enjoy tremendously having you with me for a little while.

When she arrived in late November, he was delighted; they drank and communed, laughed and cried—and the next day he was desperately sick to his stomach. He went to Simeons and Detre. "Both of my doctors agree that my symptoms are caused by no more than my reaction to her presence; by the strides I have made towards facing squarely the truth of my relation to her," he told Freddy. As Simeons noted, the reaction was entirely common: "one out of every five Italians had trouble stomaching family life."

Recovered, Merrill introduced his mother to Isaacson (without, of course, explaining their relationship) and to Marilyn Aronberg. Aronberg was a friend of Isaacson's from St. Louis, an art historian on a Fulbright fellowship in Italy. A small, attractive woman, intelligent and direct, she was deputed to help host Mrs. Merrill. She later described Hellen Plummer as "a seriously vulgar woman" with evident prejudices. "Someone mentioned an actor who was a homosexual, and Hellen said, 'You know, he's just not quite right.' " For a cocktail party in Hellen's honor, Merrill invited Isaacson and Aronberg, Dr. and Mrs. Simeons, and Ben Johnson, an Italianist and fellow expatriate with whom Merrill was collaborating on translations of poems by Eugenio Montale. Johnson and his wife were African American. It was after this party that Hellen expressed her outrage at being obliged to meet black people socially.

Another day, in a rented car outside Hadrian's Villa, Merrill confronted his mother with the news from Detre: his father knew he was homosexual and, despite her fears, "the knowledge hasn't killed him." Unimpressed, she said that she herself had first informed Daddy of the awful truth—back in December 1945, when she discovered Jimmy's affair with Kimon and Charlie reacted by proposing to hire a hit man to kill Friar. According to Hellen, she calmed him down. "I thought he was going to have another heart attack that day. That's why I said it would be the death of Daddy if he had to go on hearing things about you. Before you judge me too harshly, please remember, son," she ended, teary-eyed, "that I saved Kimon's life." Somehow emerging as the heroine of this story, Hellen put Jimmy in a position to admire her conduct rather than protest it.

While mother and son reunited, General Plummer waited offstage. Jimmy and Hellen joined him in Paris at the Ritz Hotel, where, after the Allied liberation, Bill had been in charge of accommodations for top-ranking officers. "This slight, barrel-chested man with thin blond hair and ice-blue eyes radiated dependability." Those adjectives ("slight," "thin," "ice-blue") imply that he also radiated chilliness, with a lack of stature in the eyes of his new stepson. Jimmy was certain that his mother's feeling for Bill, however dependable, would never replace those that made her memories of Charlie shine.

Back in Rome, he had more family on his hands. Charles and Mary Merrill, in Austria while Charles was on a Fulbright fellowship, came for Christmas week with their three small children. Fourteen-year-old Merrill Magowan was present too. Joining them in Jimmy's rooms on Christmas morning were Dr. Simeons, his wife, and their three sons, Marilyn Aronberg, and the trio of lovers: Isaacson, Fredericks, and Kerwood. "Bizarre," Fredericks marveled, "that Wayne and Robert and I should be in the same room [. . .] after all of these feverish promiscuities on our parts." Jimmy had so arranged the day that the four of them were required to shake hands and exchange gifts in the glow of his tree.

As a romantic choice, Isaacson made a dramatic contrast with Fredericks. While Claude and Jimmy had played recorders together, making simple, dignified music, Isaacson and Merrill took turns reading *The Way of the World* aloud in public, delighting to play Congreve's clever fops. In Fredericks, Merrill fell in love with an image of a "better" self, more serious and earnest, more capable of open, frank response, less wayward and superficial, than he felt himself to be. The adventure Merrill set out on when he came to Europe in 1950 had required Claude as a steadying companion. In Isaacson, he found a lover with manners that felt natural to him. Rather than reject his arch, theatrical, "feminine" side, Merrill had fallen in love with it. "You have been creating a duplicate self out of Robert," Detre observed. Merrill represents the exchange this way in his memoir:

> "Is that bad?"
> "Put yourself in his place. How would you feel?"
> "If someone did that to me? Oh dear. Misunderstood, ignored . . . But if he is 'me,' then by loving him I could be learning to love myself. At least that's to the good?"
> "No doubt. But there is only so much to be gained by paying court to the mirror."

In their early, passionate letters, Merrill and Fredericks allowed love to lead the way; lust was implied, but delicately. Isaacson's entrance into Merrill's life brought out sexual desire and encouraged experiment despite the fact that they were living as a couple. Rome was a fitting place for a lover trained at the opera: it was a city of stage sets to be explored at night among shadows and spotlights, permitting, even calling for, displays of temperament and male preening. Kerwood had quickly figured it out and blazed a promiscuous path across the city, impressing Jimmy. Tentatively, venturing out on his own, Jimmy tried to imitate the sexual adventures with strangers of which Wayne boasted. He investigated the spots Wayne recommended. This meant evenings spent studying the eyes of other men reflected in shopwindows and cruising in the parks where the matches of anonymous smokers glowed like fireflies around a rusty pissoir.

At the same time, he was developing family feeling. "I think," he told his father after his brother's Christmas visit, "that this is the first time in my life that I've felt really close to Charles." That week was the most time they'd spent together in years, and Jimmy found that he and Charles "had more in common than I'd ever expected." He didn't explain to CEM that finding their way around *him* was what they had in common. They now both enjoyed the freedom to "live far from home in poorly furnished apartments, wear suits of burnt-orange Turkish wool tailored in Prague"—Charles's style—"or cheap puce velvet too tight to sit down in"—Jimmy's—and "entertain left-wing ideas or moot young men—it hardly mattered which." Christmas had been such a success that Jimmy visited Charles and Mary in Austria for Easter, 1952. His nieces and nephew, "Cathy and Amy in their dirndls, little Bruce in his lederhosen," climbed about him "like vines." "Would they have happy lives? Would I be a father myself one day?" Apparently the question was still open.

While Claude completed his analysis with Detre that spring, Jimmy pressed on with his treatment. An exchange represented in *A Different Person*, too artful to be wholly accurate and yet too vivid to be wholly invented, indicates how Detre viewed Jimmy's homosexuality:

> "Sex between men is by its character frustrating," Dr. Detre said. "The anus is full of shit; the mouth is a well of flattery and untruth. The honest penis is left with no reliable place to go."
>
> Embarrassed, I studied the ceiling.
>
> "It might be worth considering," he went on, "that this masculine self you crave is available within you, only you have not accepted the power to harm that goes with it."
>
> "Must one do harm in order to be a man?"
>
> "You seem to have received that impression."
>
> "From . . . ?"

"A woman who, hurt and rejected, turned to you."

A woman whom I [. . .] kept echoing in spite of myself. "Are you saying it is time I went out and hurt someone?"

"Not necessarily. Is there someone you wish to hurt?"

"No, but . . ." I couldn't shake the idea. "Supposing there were, though, and that I did. Would I inflict the man's kind of harm or the woman's?"

It seemed to be the ultimate question until Dr. Detre took it a step further: "Or the child's?"

Deep in his analysis, Merrill all but stopped writing letters to family and friends. He made an exception for Kimon, but only in order to say that he didn't wish to see him when he passed through Italy on his way to Greece from New York. In Rome, Merrill's isolation from the people he loved had been "intensely fortunate"; it had given him the freedom to feel anger and not inflict it ("I have done them great violence in my heart"), and he didn't want to force the issue with Friar. But Friar pushed him, asking for another of his "loans." "I will not deny, now or ever, how much you have given me, or how much I am grateful," Merrill wrote to him. "Surely you have been as significant in my life as any person I have ever known, probably more so." It didn't follow, however, "that we shall be close together for the rest of our lives," and it was time now "to call a halt." Jimmy tried to shut the door firmly ("I honestly don't want to see you, and don't want to hear from you"), but couldn't help leaving it slightly ajar, allowing that his current feeling might someday be "charmed into its opposite."

In June, Isaacson's ex-lover, a German photographer named Rolf Tietgens, appeared in Rome. There were echoes in Robert's relation to Rolf of Jimmy's relation to Kimon: the German was willful, "manly," European, and fifteen years older than Robert. Very soon Tietgens and Merrill tumbled into bed—which they didn't bother to hide from Robert, and it left him depressed, making self-destructive jokes and gestures (as when he stubbed a cigarette out on his leg). "This trick," Detre scolded Merrill, "of stealing from your lovers someone to whom they are or once were attracted, you and Robert have already played on Claude. Try not to get into a rut." Detre proposed that, by seducing Tietgens, Merrill was punishing Isaacson. Merrill admitted this was the case, but couldn't see why he was doing it. Was he punishing Isaacson "for loving me? For being like me himself?" With "his flair for the last word," Detre answered, "[T]o punish both yourself and him for being homosexual."

Of course, Jimmy had a model for his promiscuity in his father, whose turbulent love life was still sparking gossip. Mrs. Coe was out of the picture, but Charlie's divorce from Kinta was going forward anyway. To keep the Orchard out of her clutches, Mr. Merrill had given the house to Amherst College, and yet, "Lear-like," he still wanted to live in it. His son was far enough removed from the action to appreciate its comedy. The newspaper accounts of his parents' divorce had hurt him; the stories of his father's current predicament just made him laugh. CEM was said to have accused Kinta "of having ordered twelve steaks to be thrown in the garbage, expressed a wish that Merrill's Landing might burn down, called his children little brats, bought a thousand dollar dress and never wore it—all of which, given a chance," Jimmy noted, "I feel myself perfectly capable of."

Comic detachment from his parents came with what Merrill called "understanding" in a birthday letter to his mother that reflected on his gains in analysis. He assured her that she had been in his thoughts all year, "not as a merely cordial image, but ever sharpening into a focus I wouldn't have imagined possible." He had the sense of knowing her "absolutely as you are; this will have come, I suppose, through knowing myself." Self-knowledge might open the way to loving other people. He put the idea in a Christian idiom Hellen would appreciate:

> Only now does the absolute truth of the words break on me, about loving one's neighbor as oneself. If one doesn't love oneself, one can love nothing and nobody. Everything starts from that, and it isn't to be confused with vanity, or even self-respect. It is simply the seeing of one's life, the unhoped-for good and the trivial and the irremediable bad, that there is nothing to be made of the past, that it is all right, that it can't be helped, that there is nothing to be made of it but the best.

He had felt "bitterness" toward her, "but I think it is gone for ever now"—though he'd learned too much from analysis to expect that. He ended with a deep-seated wish to bring his parents back together:

> Just now, I feel that something is missing in this letter, and I know what it is. I want to be writing to you and Daddy together. Would it seem a curious request, my asking you to send it on to him? It's so much for you both, and for nobody else; and after all, I am the child you made and raised between you, and I love you both very much—

It might even be possible to make peace with Friar. In August, while Detre went on vacation, Merrill returned to Greece with Isaacson. They ran into Kimon in Syntagma Square; Merrill and his mentor reconciled for a night of café hopping; then he and Robert paid a visit to Poros. Merrill and Isaacson returned to Rome via Istanbul, and Jimmy was enchanted by the city: it was "a new country, a new continent." In the Grand Bazaar, they bought rings for themselves, rather than for each other; Merrill's was a child's ring, gold, with a bunch of grapes in relief—a Dionysian emblem and a pledge of future visits to Turkey and Greece. "To Kimon, I suppose, I am reconciled," he conceded; "the effort at rupture was valuable, but he is another cross to bear, and who am I not to bear it, who indeed?" Friar had told Merrill that he and Mina planned to marry in the fall. The marriage was meant to give Mina U.S. citizenship, but it was also a source of pride for Friar, satisfying, Merrill noted, the "homosexual's desire for a conventional life." He had to ask himself, "If Kimon of all people was taking a wife, what hopes had I of resisting the undertow of generations?"

Did he want to resist? When he began his analysis with Detre, Merrill had had a "curious feeling that when once again, I fall deeply in love it will be with a woman, and that I shall want to marry her." But it's likely that that "curious feeling" was merely a wish to please the friend to whom he was writing, Freddy, or for that matter his psychiatrist. If Detre was tolerant of Merrill's homosexuality, and thereby gave him permission to express it, he also suggested that Merrill's chances for "intimacy" ultimately depended, as Merrill put it, "on my adjustment to women." Now the end of his analysis was approaching, Detre told him, when he returned to Parioli in September 1952. Treatment would end that fall, though Detre "wants to see me again at the end of 6 months" for a checkup—in New York, where Detre planned to relocate. Claude was back in Vermont by this point, and Robert would be going home soon too. He and Jimmy agreed that they would not live together back in New York. The prospect was "sad, but for the time being, for the best." Isaacson suffered from the same social pressures that weighed on Merrill, and he was ready to make that adjustment to women. Two years later, like Friar, he would marry "a delightful woman older than himself," Jane Zabrisky. He went into business with Zabrisky as a New York art dealer, and embarked on an influential career championing Bouguereau and other French salon painters, becoming a postmodernist *avant la lettre*. Jimmy, in his fashion, would establish friendly relations with them both.

If there was ever a woman Merrill considered marrying, it was Marilyn Aronberg. "When we saw each other every day in Rome," she commented later, "we could read each other's minds." Aronberg was in love, however, with Irving Lavin, who was, exactly like her, from St. Louis and a graduate student in art history. Having no romantic interest in other men, she spent her days with Isaacson and Merrill, "and we saw each other all day." In the afternoon, with Guitou Knoop, they drank Negronis in the Flora Hotel. With Marilyn, Jimmy could be confiding, gallant, even flirtatious. A couple of years later, he gave her a paper fan on which he inscribed these lines in imitation of Mallarmé, who wrote poems both about and *on* women's fans:

> One summer evening, pausing in
> The cloister of a lemon grove,
> Unfold me in your hand and prove
> No wind so chaste but will not sin
> On the soft throat of Marilyn.

In *The Seraglio*, Merrill's roman à clef from 1957, Aronberg is the model for Jane, Francis's friend and daily companion in Rome. Francis casually jokes about wanting to marry her, but the joking is uneasy. The story comes to a crisis when he takes Jane to dinner with his father. That scene in *The Seraglio* was based on an actual meal hosted by Charles Merrill at the Ritz-Carlton Hotel in Boston in August 1953. The party consisted of Mr. Merrill, his companion, Lady Saint, Jimmy, and Marilyn, who had married Irving Lavin by that time. The drinking was major league: cocktails, new wines with each course, then liqueurs. When Jimmy had left the table, Charlie turned to Lady Saint and said, "Why didn't he bring her along sooner. She'd make a perfect wife." Marilyn protested, "Why, Mr. Merrill, I'm married!" "Why didn't you wait!" he shot back.

According to Lavin, "Jimmy wasn't very visual." When they looked at art together, searching out obscure Renaissance altarpieces for her work on the iconography of St. John the Baptist, "he always waited for me to say something first." Despite his love of ornament, Merrill was not a connoisseur or Gilbert Osmond–style aesthete. He was impatient to translate images into other terms, to discover the stories in objects—a disposition that made for a bond with both of the Lavins. "Jimmy was what we call an iconographer," noted Irving, who became an authority on Bernini and the Italian Baroque. "He saw significance in things. That's what he wanted to talk about: the meaning of pictures, not just how beautiful they are." It was the same impulse that prompted him to write verse in the voice of a paper fan, inscribed on the object itself.

During his time in Rome, Merrill formed an enduring friendship with Count Umberto Morra, who had a flat in the same building as Jimmy's. Morra had served as director of the Italian Cultural Institute in London when it was founded in 1949. He was a man of integrity whom Jimmy idealized. He had a short left leg, the trace of childhood tuberculosis, which "he managed with the suavity of a latter-day Byron." He became an anti-Fascist hero in 1943 when he traveled alone and on foot for days to make a liaison for the Italian resistance with American troops. Eloquent in English, he told stories about his mentor, Bernard Berenson, and Berenson's friend Edith Wharton. He had been a contributor to *Rivoluzione Liberale* and a friend of its editor, Piero Gobetti, a supporter of Montale's poetry. "His face, at once goatish and austere under a high brow from which sparse reddish hair had been slicked straight back, hardly moved as he talked; his hands, however, were restless as a satyr's. I caught myself trying to see how far up his cuffs the glinting red-gold wrist-hair went," Merrill confesses in *A Different Person*. "Part of me longed to seduce him, part of me despaired of ever living up to him."

The attraction of Morra's character was inseparable from his family seat in Cortona, called the Villa Morra—a house to which, like Fredericks's home in Pawlet, Merrill would keep returning, year after year. Approached through a green alley and surrounded by gardens and olive groves on a slope rising steeply behind it, it was a three-story stucco building from the eighteenth century, shuttered, and as reticent as Morra himself. Inside the rooms were as idiosyncratic and fanciful as Joseph Cornell boxes. The foyer was decorated by murals of classical ruins, sunny vistas, a sphinx, and an eighteenth-century couple counting flower petals, like young lovers in a Mozart opera. On the walls of the library was a trompe l'oeil mural representing the red interior of a sultan's tent. A third room was, as Merrill describes it, "hideous beyond description. Heavy, turn-of-the-century furniture that looked machine-made, dried grasses, glassed cabinets jammed with medals and bibelots, surrounded a full-length portrait of a man in uniform. A tapestried stool in front of it invited the guest to kneel" before this image of Umberto I, the last king of Italy. Facing it was a large portrait of Morra's mother, a medallion of carved ivory. Adjacent to the house, a small family chapel memorialized Morra's mother's two husbands. It was her second husband, Roberto di Lavriano, Morra's father, who had inherited the house.

It took Merrill years to put together the puzzle these rooms constituted. By inference, Merrill concluded that Morra was not only named for the king; he was the king's son by the wife of the king's friend—which explained why their images were placed so as to behold each other, with no sign of Morra's father in the same room. The story thrilled Merrill. Morra was a cultured role model of whom he wanted to be worthy. But there was a Gothic side to this bachelor. Indeed, the Villa Morra could have served as the setting for a ghost story by Henry James. Here Merrill probed the made world of an aristocratic life full of enigmatic characters and sexual secrets.

Merrill's time in Rome was nearly over. Hubbell Pierce, a suave southerner whom Merrill had met in New York, was in town that fall, and Jimmy often went to hear him play the piano and sing Cole Porter songs in the blue and gold bar at the Orso restaurant. The music evoked for Jimmy "a Byronic elite of fox-trotters classy enough to crack jokes while their hearts were breaking." Perhaps Cole Porter had as much to teach as Freud? In fact Merrill was unsure what his analysis added up to. He feared "that nothing much" had been accomplished. The problem, he felt, was his father: "I simply cannot do anything that he has done—be it seduce a woman, or interest myself in public affairs," and the realization left him feeling "hopeless." "But Detre smiles and is confident," he wrote to Claude, "so I might as well be." If nothing else, Jimmy had achieved a reconciled view of Claude and the romance they brought to Europe almost three years before: "Detre remarked the other day [. . .] that lovers didn't become friends, that they had exhausted one another [. . .]. I think though, in our own case, that we were somehow [. . .] spared that experience. I mean I don't think we exhausted each other, we only exhausted ourselves, I myself, you yourself, in the effort [to] live up to what we were dreaming of; which might even be to say that the years were more beautiful than we knew."

Merrill was at work on a play called *The Bait*, his first composition of any kind since he began analysis in summer 1951. The play, set in both a fishing boat in the Gulf Stream and a café in Venice, would be put on in New York in May. In the central scene, a husband and wife and her brother are deep-sea fishing. Charles (Merrill kept using the name) is so wounded by his wife's "taunts" that he accepts a dare from his brother-in-law: he will go into the water while the other man "plays" him on a fishing line—to show that he can survive the open ocean and its monsters. And he does, but the victory leaves him at a loss, lonely and disoriented.

Hearing Merrill explain the play in these terms, Detre offered an interpretation that made the play seem an apt conclusion to analysis and even to these years in Europe:

> "It will have occurred to you," he said when I finished, "that your hero's adventure is made possible by a line attached to himself. The word 'line' suggests something besides fishing, no?"
> I had to think for a moment. "You mean, like a line of poetry?" Never before had Dr. Detre acknowledged my—could I say?—calling. For him to so do after all these months thrilled and silenced me.

"If I am not mistaken," he presently went on, "in one of our first meetings you related a dream in which you were a fish trying to become human. That has now come to pass. In your scenario it is a healthy and goodhearted man who is hauled from the sea by those he loves."

My heart leapt, my eyes stung. "But they don't love *him* any longer," I pointed out.

"Perhaps," said Dr. Detre, "they loved a different person."

"The person he no longer is . . ."

"Exactly. The person who, by the way, is now free to decide whether he still loves *them*."

Merrill's last hour with Detre came, followed by "martinis + chit-chat, after which one could only say goodbye + thank you + feel that strange sweet weepy fear on the stairs." He left for fog-shrouded London in the company of Hubbell Pierce. En route, he read *The Europeans* and "The Reverberator" by Henry James and a new book of criticism, *The Complex Fate: Hawthorne, Henry James, and Some Other American Writers* by Marius Bewley. He praised Bewley for revealing "<u>what</u> is there, or could be," in American literature. He docked in Manhattan before Christmas.

A Different Person ends with a scene that is pure commedia dell'arte: Merrill leaves his apartment for the last time only to realize that he has forgotten his wallet or his passport; when he goes back up the stairs, he finds his maid and the owner of the house fighting with each other to claim a down pillow he had left behind, producing a "white blizzard" of feathers. He has "walked in on two people my parents' age struggling to contain the damage"—which he leaves them to do as he slips away unnoticed from the ridiculous fray, having found whatever it was he came for. Quinta and Count Bracci were not only his parents' age; they might as well have been his parents, battling over nothing, as people do. The scene requires no further caption: the Broken Home has become a pillow fight, as seen from the wry, relieved perspective on his own life that he had achieved in Rome (which was what he "came for," whether he knew it or not when he left for Europe). This is an inspired ending to the memoir—and a wholly invented one. Count Bracci had died in August; he was not fighting over any pillows in December. The lesson of Merrill's time in Europe would not be arranged in this safely artificial tableau for another forty years. But he wasn't writing his memoirs yet. To the contrary, he was ready to have a future.

PART II

WATER STREET

1953–61

4

DAVID JACKSON

1953–55

Merrill would make that future with David Jackson. They met on May 18, 1953, outside the tiny Comedy Club off Lexington Avenue after the first performance of *The Bait*. Jimmy was intrigued by this "slender blond man with a voice that didn't sound at all like New York, a perfectly convincing wedding ring on his finger, and the friendliest smile." But he had to wait to learn his name until they ran into each other a short time later in the San Remo bar. The first mention of Jackson in Merrill's papers comes in a postcard addressed to "Old Dave" on June 10. A week later, Merrill wrote to Fredericks, "I have met someone I'm very fond of." When he and Claude saw each other that summer, David would have to be included: "to be sure there is David now." It was true: David was there in Jimmy's life for good.

How did their relationship take hold so fast and so firmly? Merrill was determined not to become what he had every reason to be—an effete aesthete, a brittle snob; he must have sensed that Jackson would help him avoid that fate by drawing him out of himself. They quickly became passionate lovers. Over time they became world travelers, "the Rover Boys," ready for hijinks and fun wherever they went. They would travel to the Other World

ILLUSTRATION JM and DJ at home on Water Street in front of a painting by Larry Rivers, 1957. Photo by Rollie McKenna too, the realm of spirits, which they discovered together with their hands joined above the Ouija board. But David's domesticity, at a moment when Jimmy was ready to make a home for himself, was just as important as his adventurousness. Their shared life would be centered in the homes they created together over successive decades in Stonington, Athens, and Key West. They spent long stretches of time apart, and they took other lovers, but they remained attached to each other and to those homes. Twenty-five years after they met, Merrill wrote to Jackson about "the absolute <u>trust</u> I felt in you even from the beginning. Trust in your goodness and honesty, trust in your feeling for me. I don't believe I could have understood at the time how few people there would be, in a whole lifetime, that I could say as much for." They are buried side by side in the Stonington cemetery. David's stone is inscribed with his dates, 1922–2001, and Jimmy's loving tribute: "Dearest hand and heart."

When he arrived back in New York from Rome that winter, before he met Jackson, Merrill moved into a garden apartment on West Tenth Street, a spacious duplex near his childhood home on West Eleventh. His New York didn't look that different from his Rome: Wayne Kerwood, Robert Isaacson, and Guitou Knoop were living in the city, and he continued to meet with Detre from time to time, once the doctor had received a visa and moved to the United States. Merrill feared that, despite Rome, despite psychoanalysis, nothing in his life had really changed. He brooded on "my failure with my mother, my half-failure with Freddy"—meaning that he continued to keep his romantic and sexual life hidden from his mother and, to an extent, Buechner.

He visited his father in Barbados and the Plummers in Atlanta, where he was presented to Georgia society at a private club as, rather misleadingly, "an internationally known poet and novelist" (he'd lived abroad, but he was hardly "internationally known," and he hadn't finished the novel he'd brought to Europe). He returned to New York to find a copy of Hans's second book of poems waiting in the mail, a gift from the Lodeizens, and he burst into tears. "He is so alive for me, <u>in</u> me," Merrill wrote about his lost friend, "I cannot distinguish his presence in my heart from a positive virtue, almost a physical characteristic that I have assumed." He wrote a short, exquisite poem about this continuing connection, "A Dedication."

> Hans, there are moments when the whole mind
> Resolves into a pair of brimming eyes, or lips
> Parting to drink from the deep spring of a death
> That freshness they do not yet need to understand.

> These are the moments, if ever, an angel steps
> Into the mind, as kings into the dress
> Of a poor goatherd, for their acts of charity.
> There are moments when speech is but a mouth pressed
> Lightly and humbly against the angel's hand.

Yet he remained emotionally cramped and sexually closeted, apprehensive, burdened by "fear and paralysis." "I want to hold on to myself," he admitted to Claude, as if it would be dangerous to let go.

That self-isolating impulse was the emotional problem he had confronted in psychoanalysis, and it was a theme in *The Bait*. The theme was embodied not in the play's earnest Charles who undergoes his trial at sea, but in Julie, his wife, and in her brother, Gilbert, who "plays" Charles at the end of his fishing line. Chilly and capricious to the point of being cruel, Julie and Gilbert expressed, Merrill saw, "aspects of myself I shrank from facing directly." The play, performed by the Artists' Theatre, was produced by John Myers and directed by Herbert Machiz on a bill with two other one-act plays by young New York poets, Barbara Guest and John Ashbery. The play's climax comes when Charles recounts his ordeal, a soliloquy Merrill cast in the fanciest pattern possible: a sestina. While Charles spoke his lines, a stir ran through the audience: heads swiveled as "Arthur Miller and Dylan Thomas, whom Kimon had brought to see the play, stumbled out," passing judgment on *The Bait* with their feet. "Years later," Merrill relates in *A Different Person*, "I learned what Mr. Miller, with uncanny insight, had whispered in Dylan's ear shortly after the curtain rose: 'You know, this guy's got a secret, and he's gonna keep it.' "

It was just then, at intermission, as if conjured by his need to move beyond the emotional limitations of his play, that Jimmy met David. The voice "that didn't sound at all like New York" came from the American West. David Noyes Jackson was born in Lead, South Dakota. His parents were George L. Jackson and Mary Fogelsong, native South Dakotans both; George Jr., or Jojo, an older brother whom David always liked, was his only sibling. George Sr. worked in the collection office of the Lead *Daily Call* and Deadwood *Pioneer-Times* and later as a Chevrolet salesman in Lead. Like many midwesterners in the 1930s, he moved his family to Southern California, where they lived on the unfashionable end of Muirfield Road in Los Angeles; when that neighborhood declined after the war, the Jacksons moved to a new ranch house in Tarzana, a suburb of Los Angeles, on the edge of the San Fernando Valley. George held a job in an ice cream company; at one point he sold Philip Morris cigarettes from his car. In this series of dreary occupations and fresh starts, we see a man struggling to support his family on the shifting tide line of middle-class white respectability. George Jackson was an irascible husband and father who grew meaner, even brutish in old age. David's forbearing mother was funny, sweet, sociable, and a heavy drinker. "The queen of the story-tellers," with a slow, down-home, Great Plains voice, she read novels and wrote sentimental poems of her own.

When World War II began, Jackson was a student at UCLA, with artistic and literary leanings but no definite direction, and he enlisted in the Army. In basic training, he met Bob Grimes, who became a close friend for the rest of his life. Jackson went to Europe as an infantryman, and served as an MP in Berlin. He returned to UCLA after the war, joined a fraternity, reunited with Grimes—and met a student at a women's college named Doris Sewell, nicknamed "Sewelly." With a thick head of close-cropped blond hair, her build was short and compact. She was matter-of-fact and just as fun-loving as David. They set up their easels and painted outdoors, then drank late in Hollywood bars. One night, David asked her to marry him. Sewelly told him she couldn't because she "might be queer." They married anyway in 1947: David's charm and daring had won out. "I wanted to be doing things that no one else had done," she remembered, and so did David: he was "a dear, risk-taking rascal." They bought a castoff Army jeep—Grimes painted the horn red—and drove it across the country. Walking by the offices of *The New Yorker* in Manhattan, David told Sewelly to wait while he went in and changed the address on his subscription; he came back a half hour later having talked his way into temporary jobs for them both, which they used to pay for their fares in steerage to France. They spent the next three years living on the cheap in Marshall Plan Europe. While Sewelly painted, David read fiction and started to write a novel.

Sewelly had been right about being queer. In Europe, she was drawn to same-sex relationships, while her husband found that he was too. Uncertainty about the direction of their sexual preferences may have been part of their attraction to each other to begin with. "David was a very sexual man," Sewelly reflected. "He adored sex. He liked to talk about sex, and he exaggerated little flirtations. If someone made a pass at him, he was very open to it—it didn't matter whether it was a man or a woman." Yet they loved each other ("David was my beloved!"), and these new experiences were hard for them to assimilate. Grimes, who made the same discovery about himself around this time, later noted that homosexuality did not necessarily have or need a label: "We didn't think of ourselves as gay; we just did certain things." Sewelly and David came back to California in 1949, and he enrolled in courses at Stanford. Soon they moved to Colorado, where David studied briefly at Colorado College. In 1951, after Sewelly suffered a failed pregnancy, they separated: she returned to Los Angeles, and David went back to New York, then Europe. By 1952, they were facing the end not of their marriage—they never divorced—but of the conventional expectations they had brought to it. "We felt heartsick, devastated," Sewelly remembered, "but also ready to begin life a little more realistically."

When he met Merrill in May 1953, Jackson had recently returned to New York. He had the manuscript of a novel and the pages of his journal in his suitcase, a loan to repay, and no job. In a draft of a letter he may not have sent, he asked his father for help: "I am still living on meager savings and meagerer hopes." The novel was called *Sebastian*. (Jackson titled this and later novels after the main character in them and referred to them familiarly, as if the manuscripts were his alter egos or children.) His journal shows him pushing himself to remain upbeat amid mounting self-doubts. It records his self-education in literature: he makes notes on his reading, drafts book reviews (none of which was published), and lists the titles of books, mostly serious novels, to be read. His style is nervous, his syntax confusing. Modifiers pile up. Names are misspelled and words misused. One feels the writer's strain and lack of confidence.

The impression Jackson made in person was very different. Open and funny, he put people at their ease and encouraged their trust. His friends agree that he was, as a young man, extremely good-looking. He had light brown hair (Merrill calls him "blond") and blue eyes that peered up moodily—a Hollywood touch—from his lowered brow. A level forehead gave his face a square, proud look. He was not a big man, but he was bigger than Jimmy, taller and broad-chested; he had long, loose arms and wide, strong hands. In photographs he usually has a cigarette. Sewelly was drawn to "something effeminate" in his manner, while Jimmy liked it that he seemed straight: David's "perfectly convincing wedding ring" was sexy. Indeed, as a gay man watching his friends (and even his former lover) marry, Merrill may have thought it was time to find a husband of his own. This was the role David slipped into when friends came to dinner: while Jimmy cooked, he mixed cocktails and made conversation. On another level, the wedding ring was just that—"perfectly convincing"—and thus convenient. When they needed an alibi to explain their relationship to their families or neighbors, David's ring turned the question aside.

Lies, or at least fibs, came easily to Jackson. "David was a *terrible* fibber," Sewelly commented later. These fibs usually made him appear more accomplished, glamorous, or wealthy than he was. He bragged that he had won the Purple Heart, that his uncle owned *Popular Mechanics*, and that his father had founded Braniff Airlines. "You would have felt like a cad," Grimes explained, charitably, "if you said, 'Your Daddy doesn't own Braniff Airlines!' " These implausible lies were that childlike. Later, with Merrill as an accomplice, Jackson composed a life story appropriate to the companion of a sophisticated, wealthy poet. Their friends, even those who prided themselves on skepticism and worldliness, were ready to believe it. The novelist Alison Lurie, who became friends with Jackson and Merrill in 1955, is typical. In her memoir about her friendship with them, she maintains that David lived on "$40,000 per year" from his successful businessman father, and that "at UCLA he studied music composition with Hindemith and Schoenberg." Jackson owed money to his father, who was never a success in business. David learned to play the piano, and he took a course in music composition at UCLA; but he was a novice composer, he did not train as a concert pianist, and he did not study with Schoenberg (or Hindemith, who taught at Yale).

David's fibbing also took the form of improvised fantasies meant to entertain friends. These might involve speculation about the love lives of a couple at a nearby café table, or a racy, hilarious anecdote about his past: David drove a car and pimped for a whorehouse in South Dakota; he was the first boy to kiss his neighbor in Los Angeles, Shirley Temple. Or the fantasy might be sustained and collaborative. During basic training, he and Grimes invented a primitive religion in which they both had important roles. "We were precious metal, the leaders of a cult. It was like Oz," Grimes remembered. "David was not the son of a cigarette vendor, he was the head priest of a Central American sun god." When Grimes was sent to fight in the Pacific and Jackson left for Europe, they kept the fantasy going in letters. "We poured everything into that realm of dreams," Grimes said. "With David it was OK to be non-literal. He entered your fantasy and transformed it. You gave him an idea, and he picked it right up. There was a split second—and suddenly he would become one with you. It felt like total sympathy."

Merrill discovered that capacity for "total sympathy" when he and David experimented with the Ouija board, the popular device for communicating with spirits that would preoccupy the two of them, on and off, for forty years. How it works is very simple: with the board placed between them, two people sitting side by side or face to face each place one or both hands on a pointer or planchette, which moves to indicate letters of the alphabet displayed on the board, spelling words that respond to the inquiries from the two partners. With analogs in the spirit-spelling and symbol-divining arts of ancient cultures, the Ouija board is a legacy of Victorian spiritualism and its table turning, automatic writing, and spirit materialization. The first commercial board was manufactured in 1890. William Fuld and the Baltimore Talking Board Company began making a hugely popular model in 1898. Fuld's success spawned competitors who played on the board's Eastern aura by introducing pictures of crystal balls, flying carpets, and turbaned swamis, and vaguely "Arabic" lettering. By the 1950s, the Ouija board had developed a mass following as a parlor game.

Merrill's first board came as a birthday gift from Buechner in 1953, gift-wrapped with a message: "You know you've always wanted one." Freddy had seen the game in a toy store and thought, "Yes, that's just the kind of thing he would like!" It was cheap, unpretentious—in fact, a piece of kitsch. It spoke to Jimmy's pleasure in games and word games in particular; and for Freddy, who was about to enter a Presbyterian seminary, it was a half-joking appeal to his friend's spiritual side. Merrill and Buechner sat down there and then to try it. They successfully contacted a young engineer "from Cologne" who died—as if by the logic of alliteration—from "cholera in Cairo." The poor soul had "KNOWN / NO HAPPINESS," but he'd had a brush with greatness: he'd met Goethe, who told him to "PERSEVERE."* It wasn't much, but Merrill had made a start, and he was intrigued. Soon he tried the board with Jackson.

There is no record of Jimmy's response to their first séance. But David refers to it in a letter to Sewelly on June 29, 1953, which is also the first mention of Jimmy in David's papers: apparently they fell in love and discovered the Other World at exactly the same time. He describes "a delightful week-end of parties, cool perspiration, three hours with an ouija board, working over the 50–52 revisions of SEB"—Jackson's novel-in-progress, *Sebastian*—"in James Merrill's Village garden," where "Maryln and Irv Lavin [*sic*]" paid a visit. The Ouija board appears in this list as nothing out of the ordinary, as if it were just one more activity among others in a round of parties, literary work, and relaxed domesticity—and to that extent, nothing out of the ordinary, a game. David moves on to other subjects, but he returns to the Ouija board in a series of urgent postscripts. He asks Sewelly to tell his mother ("PLEASE") that he and Jimmy have used the board to speak to Jack King (a deceased friend or relative), who confessed to a murder and told them that another friend or relative had "become queer." The sensational content of this long ("three hours") Ouija board session is striking. So is the mood in which Jackson reports it. He seems absorbed by the story as he relates it for his mother's benefit, who, he assumes, will not

---

* JM, "Voices from the Other World," *CP*, 112. Merrill incorporated the results of that session with Buechner, in 1953, in this poem written in fall 1955. JM, "An Interview with J. D. McClatchy," *Prose*, 108.

be astonished to receive this intelligence from beyond the grave. He also mentions a message addressed to him personally: "J. K. warned me that I lied and treated life, generally, too light-heartedly." Merrill would say the same things to him many times over the years.

How precisely the Ouija board worked and what Merrill and Jackson felt they were doing with it will take time for us to explore, just as it took time for the two of them to discover the board's potential. They went back to it six months after that first experience. This time they reached a spirit called "Kabel Barns." (This is the first séance Merrill transcribed and preserved.) Barns, "A DAMN GOOD FARMER" in colonial America, had no lurid family gossip to relate à la Jack King. Instead, he suggested the literary possibilities of the Ouija board. Whitman was "there" with him, he explained. Walt told Jimmy and David, "DO NOT O DO NOT CHILDREN BELIEVE IN SHAME." Then Whitman gave way to Sappho, another poet of unashamed same-sex desire. "Is she there?" Merrill asked, surprised by the ease with which his interlocutor seemed to change identity. "WE THAT SING ARE ONE," declared the strange, composite voice. Merrill wondered whether spirit-singers like Whitman and Sappho read "what's written now." They didn't need to, since "WE KNOW THAT BEFORE IT IS WRITTEN." Could they "convey those thoughts?" Merrill asked; clearly, he hoped to tap their literary foreknowledge and establish a creative shortcut for himself. "WE ARE ARE ARE THOSE THOUGHTS," the answer came back. Merrill tried again, more explicit this time: "Do you help writers living now?" "THERE IS A CHANNEL TO EACH." Merrill's curiosity was high. He asked versions of the same question over and over: "Have you any messages for us? . . . Will you ever have messages for us?" No answers came. But when the séance ended, Kabel Barns left the line open: "May we call any time? IF IN EARNEST."

The first letter Jimmy wrote to David, in June 1953, conveys the quality of their early days together. The tone is lighthearted and loving, with some lies and lewdness thrown in. Addressed in a pretend-child's-script with comic misspellings to "Dear Uncle David" from his "affectio loving nephew Jamie," it was written after Merrill had spent the Fourth of July with Jackson on Fire Island, after which he visited his father in Southampton. Merrill missed the train and decided—for the first time in his life—to hitchhike. The letter narrates this minor adventure as a series of narrow escapes from the clutches of "cruising" drivers ("an old man wanted me to get into his car, but I saw the ½ empty wisky bottle on the seat next to him and remembered what you had said about Old Men and, as he wasnt going very far anyhow I thanked him politely and said I would try to get a beter ride"). But it is not just a joke. Protected by this mock innocence, Merrill was able to write with something approaching real innocence: "The sea is very loud out the window. It is cold too and I am sorry you aren't here with me we could keep each other warm and happy. I didn't get mutch of a chance to tell you how I did enjoy the weekend with you dear Unc. David. I love you very mutch and hope you recipprocate." The next morning he added a postscript in his adult hand: "I love you David. These have been strange and wonderful days. [. . .] I love you!"

Merrill wrote that letter from a guest room in his father's Beach House on Gin Lane in Southampton. Pressed up against the dunes, with a long manicured lawn, enclosed swimming pool, patio sheltered from the wind, steep tiled roof, and Spanish-style bar, this timbered playhouse had briefly belonged to Charlie's partner, Eddie Lynch. Grand by most standards but modest by comparison to the Orchard in the center of town, the house announced Mr. Merrill's dignified retreat after his divorce from Kinta. In a pun that poked fun at both his father's Anglophilia and his three failed marriages, Jimmy proposed that the property be called "Dunweddin."

Furnished with "the spoils of Poynton" and staffed by loyal Leroy, Emma, and Josephinc, thc Beach House supplied a new stage for the Merrill family drama. Or, perhaps fiction was a better metaphor for the goings-on Jimmy noted during his visits to the Beach House that summer: he had walked in on, he left, "the opening of the 3rd volume of a great family novel." The family was growing. The Magowans lived in a summerhouse nearby, and Doris was pregnant with her fifth child; Mary and Charles Merrill in St. Louis were expecting as well. In lieu of a baby, Jimmy produced Guitou Knoop—"in the same spirit," Robin Magowan observes, "that an earlier generation might have returned [from Europe] with a marble Venus or an Adam-designed rococo salon." Jimmy commissioned Guitou to make a bronze bust of his father. Then, while Knoop lived in a bungalow on the Beach House property, CEM commissioned her to make a bust of Doris's third son, Peter, and one of Jimmy himself.

Charlie had suffered another heart attack in November and a serious stroke in December, after which his eyesight only slowly returned. ("For two months I could not read, write, or play bridge.") He recovered in Barbados in the care of Lady Constance Saint and her husband, a British businessman living in the Caribbean. Jimmy's visit to him in Barbados had been the highlight of his father's winter. Mr. Merrill told an old friend,

> He was there for about two weeks, every minute of which I enjoyed and most of them I think he enjoyed. We were very congenial and I find Jimmy one of the most understanding, com-

panionable, pleasant, interested and interesting young men
that I have almost ever met. Of course I love him because he is
my son but, in addition to that, I admire him for his kindness,
his generosity, his patience and his complete absence of any
kind of demands for himself.

"Besides all this," he added, boasting of his son's career prospects, "he is a
very brilliant and promising writer. I think he's going to go far in his profession."

Rather than merely passive in his father's company, Jimmy was busy
making mental notes. He had gone back to the novel he'd carried with him
to Europe—which he would recast on the basis of his visits to Barbados and
the Beach House in 1953. He had a title: *The Seraglio*. At the center of the story
would be Benjamin Tanning, an aging financier surrounded by female
admirers, like a sultan and his harem, with his intellectual son, Francis,
and his daughter Enid and her family, the Buchanans, filling out the company. Much of the book would be drawn very close to life. It is easy to imagine James and Charles Merrill interacting just as Francis and Benjamin
do. When Francis returns from three years in Rome, he reunites with his
father. Mr. Tanning is napping when he arrives: "In the full light of afternoon his father lay, a black mask shielding his eyes, one hand on his heart.
The big fourposter had been replaced years ago by a narrow hospital bed
whose cranks and hinges kept the old man in a half-sitting position, like
invalids in opera." Roused by his Irish nurse, he purses his lips to invite
her to kiss him; Francis looks on "delighted" and laughs out loud. "Is that
my stalwart son?" he asks. "Welcome to the seraglio." The young man bends
to kiss his cheek. While Mrs. McBride oils his feet, restoring circulation,

> Francis looked on spellbound. There was an atmosphere of helpless
> old age in the room, of impotent wrath, slumbers, tears, things he had
> never so vividly connected with his father. He had of course known
> him old and sick, but not to this degree. Perhaps the "mild stroke"
> hadn't been mild at all—yet wouldn't the old man, in that event, have
> been removed to a hospital? Was it simply a matter of his having aged
> three years since Francis's last sight of him?

As Mr. Tanning rises, his son sees him in another light:

> Getting out of bed, ringing for Louis to help him dress, pouring and
> downing a shot of whisky from a decanter on the bureau, he slowly

dispelled, or at least complicated, Francis's early impression. Helpless old age, by countless small touches, was transformed into something approaching a parody of itself. The slumped shoulder, the wisp of white hair disarrayed had to be reconciled to the roguish rolling of eyes, a stagger and groan that smacked of the footlights, as he leaned on his valet's arm. Mr. Tanning had furthermore a face that would have made the fortune of any actor. Frank, earnest, noble in repose, it was kept from plain tiresome fineness by being always on the verge of some unlikely humor, mischief or doltishness or greed; and would fall at times into a subjectivity so stricken, so elegiac, that you [. . .] wondered, as before each new aspect, if you hadn't finally hit upon the man's real face.

At last the old actor turns to his son and says, "quietly, 'I've missed you more than I can say.' " The statement is disarmingly frank and subtly dramatic; Francis takes it in as if from a seat in the theater. If he missed Ben while he was away, he doesn't mention it.

In actuality, Charlie's illness was quite real. He was in the habit of counting "heart pains": he noted "only 26" in the first week of May, but "127" in the last week of June. Without recourse to the bypass surgery and pacemakers in use today, the sixty-seven-year-old tycoon had volunteered to become a patient of Dr. Samuel Levine of Harvard Medical School, who was conducting an experimental heart treatment: a potion of radioactive iodine, obtained from "Oak Ridge, Tennessee where the atom bombs are made," was repeatedly administered to CEM in a lead-shielded hospital room in Boston. "The transforming effect of Doctor Levine's radioactive cocktail was like an episode from The Amazing Hulk," recalls Robin Magowan. "I remember Grandfather pointing in awe to the two-inch increase in his neck size." There were other side effects: "along with the fuller neck came a return to sexual potency."

CEM could again play "Good-Time Charlie." His Beach House harem was crowded with former and prospective lovers: the bohemian Guitou, raging Kinta, lubricious Lilian Coe, old flame Dotty Stafford, and dignified Lady Saint (who are referred to in The Seraglio as Xenia, Fern, Mrs. Cheek, Natalie Bigelow, and Lady Good, respectively). "Jimmy met Lady Saint on Barbados, and, with his penchant for mother figures, was quite charmed by her," Robin noted. "But not everyone was. Charlie's servant, Josephine, was heard remarking, 'That lady's no saint,' a much-repeated verdict in my family." Seeing "only harpies out for his money" and dismayed by the threat of fresh scandal, not to mention the example he was setting for his grandchildren, Doris and Bobby tried to keep the pater familias out of the clutches of these women; one of them, it seems likely, punished Doris for interfering. That summer, gossip focused on an oil portrait of her that hung in the Beach House. The work of Gerald L. Brockhurst, a fashionable English artist who painted portraits of Marlene Dietrich and the Duchess of Windsor, it showed Doris wearing a Chinese brocade bed coat that Mrs. Coe had given to her father. Doris herself had found her smiling portrait "slashed 'to ribbons,' " stabbed in a manic series of Xs. Who would dare to strike at Mr. Merrill's daughter in this vicious, vicarious way? Fingers pointed, tongues wagged: in Jimmy's words, "Daddy suspects Kinta; Doris suspects Mrs. Coe; Mrs. Coe (like Toad, giggling feebly) suspects one of the workmen and there is a $1000 reward for information leading to the apprehension" of the vandal. The mystery was never solved, but the nasty slashes were sewn up and the portrait expertly restored.

After the relative solitude of his years in Europe, Merrill was meeting "a lot of people all at once, poets and painters." These introductions were mostly courtesy of John Bernard Myers. Born in Buffalo in 1920, Myers had come to New York City in 1944 as a puppeteer and stand-up comedian. Friar introduced Merrill to him in 1945; their shared love of puppets cemented a friendship that lasted until Myers's death in 1988. Merrill called him "an ageless, hulking Irishman with the self-image of a pixie." "One had to cut a figure or be ignored in New York City," remarked Myers, who fancied himself "a latter-day Ambroise Vollard or Diaghilev." With Tibor de Nagy, he founded the Tibor de Nagy Gallery, which sponsored the first single-artist New York shows of Larry Rivers, Helen Frankenthaler, Fairfield Porter, Jane Freilicher, and Grace Hartigan in the generation of New York painters who succeeded the Abstract Expressionists of the 1940s. Through the gallery, in editions illustrated by his painters, Myers printed the first books of poetry by Frank O'Hara, John Ashbery, James Schuyler, and Kenneth Koch, whom he branded the New York School of poets. He published a mimeographed magazine called *Semi-Colon*, in which work by both Merrill and Jackson appeared. At Merrill's behest, he printed David's mother's homemade verse in a chapbook, making *The Poems of Mary Jackson* an unlikely addition to Tibor de Nagy Editions.

The Artists' Theatre brought this collaboration between painters and poets to the stage. Myers created the theater with the director Herbert Machiz after Machiz had returned from Paris, where he'd seen the drama of Jean Cocteau and Jean-Louis Barrault. "The curtain," Machiz recalled, describing his theatergoing in France, "often rose on stage decoration whose boldness of invention, both in the use of perspective and color, created an immediate atmosphere of magic. Audiences were thus subtly prepared to experience plays which were often at variance with the naturalistic language and conventions then prevalent in America." The Artists' Theatre aimed to bring these qualities to New York with Machiz as director and Myers as producer. It opened in February 1953 with one-act plays by Tennessee Williams, O'Hara, Schuyler, and Koch, and sets designed by painters associated with the Tibor de Nagy Gallery. When *The Bait* appeared in the theater's first season, Merrill didn't like the production. "The set"—designed by Arthur Kresch—"[. . .] looked messy and abstract expressionist rather than spare and ambivalent. The leading lady had a German accent." For his part, Merrill had not even tried to write "speakable verse"; his script was less a play than "a kind of closet opera," featuring "arias, duets, trios, and the odd prose recitative"—a formal tour de force that had more life on the page than on the stage.

Yet Merrill was drawn into the world of the theater, as he had been at Lawrenceville and Amherst. That summer, he took classes in Machiz's school for actors; he played the part of John in a workshop performance of O'Hara's *Try! Try!* Myers and Machiz meanwhile were hosting the "best" parties that Merrill "ever went to." Among the assembled, he especially liked Ashbery. He soon felt the influence of the slightly younger, Harvard-educated poet's work on his own poems, which made him uneasy, and he was shy in Ashbery's presence. They would remain friends and admirers of each other's poetry for the rest of their lives, with a subtle undercurrent of rivalry.

Larry Rivers was easier to befriend, although, or perhaps because, Merrill had much less in common with this ebullient saxophonist from an immigrant Jewish family. In 1954, Merrill bought a big landscape by Rivers, painted in Water Mill, near Southampton. Robin Magowan described it as a picture of "cows, grass and clouds rendered with the freshness of an ex-jazz musician from the Bronx discovering the countryside for the first time." In 1955, Rivers made oil portraits of both Jackson and Merrill; in his, Jimmy looks like a junior Merrill Lynch executive in his glasses, button-down shirt, and striped tie. Robin, who met Rivers through his uncle in 1956, noted that "Jimmy then longed to write the way Larry painted": loosely and casually, with confident self-display and "colloquial exuberance." The big Water Mill landscape was a kind of aesthetic challenge to Merrill, daring him to loosen up. But he was too proud, and too skeptical about claims for artistic innovation, ever to enroll in the New York School. About the parties packed into Myers and Machiz's one-room apartment, he joked snidely and defensively, "A bomb falling on one of these gatherings would have set the arts in America back six weeks."

Around this time, Merrill began to contribute money specifically to encourage artists, writers, and musicians in their work. In 1953, he gave Rivers $2,500 that enabled him to buy a house in Southampton, where the painter set up a studio. Among other personal gifts, he sent a check to Harold Norse that helped the poet to get by in Rome. New York Pro Musica Antiqua, a pioneering early music ensemble founded by Noah Greenberg, performed at parties Merrill hosted; and he made gifts to Greenberg in 1953 and 1954 totaling $10,000, which enabled the group to survive. In response to the civic philanthropy of his father, Doris, and Charles, Jimmy formulated a philosophy of giving that he articulated in a letter to the lawyer Larry Condon in 1955: "It seems to me more important to be of considerable help to five or six people, than of little help to 5 or 6 thousand." The people he wished to support were artists and, at this point, humanitarians (Henry James and Albert Schweitzer were his examples) who "work alone" and who might "give the rest of us an inkling of where the course lies" in the "spiritual" direction that their era had to travel. "Personally," Merrill explained, "I want to give to groups or individuals whom nobody else is as yet willing to risk helping. That seems to me far more valuable than swelling by a fraction of 1 per cent the annual revenue of the Metropolitan Opera (much as I love it) or the United Hospital Fund (worthy though it be), or Amherst College." This was the vision behind Jimmy's establishment of the Ingram Merrill Foundation, which gained tax-exempt status in 1955. The name "Ingram Merrill," by suppressing "James," distanced him from it slightly, while honoring his parents equally, remarrying them in the name of the good deeds that the foundation would do.

Merrill's letter to Condon proposed to give "40 or 50 thousand" to the Artists' Theatre. By that time, he had already given more than $12,000 to Myers and Machiz in the form of loans that, it was understood, need not be repaid. These were made through a limited partnership that Merrill created with the Artists' Theatre to fund the production of his new play, *The Immortal Husband*. He began "seriously thinking" about the play in September 1953, and he called it "more or less finished" in December, although he went on making revisions through much of 1954.

Like *The Heroes*, the one-act play by Ashbery that had been "the hit of the evening" when *The Bait* was first performed, *The Immortal Husband* updates classical myth,* in this case the story of Aurora and Tithonus, the goddess of dawn and her mortal lover. A more ambitious play than the one-act *Bait*, *The Immortal Husband* has a complex three-act structure. Act 1 is set in 1854 in England, implicitly invoking Tennyson and his dramatic monologue, "Tithonus." When we meet him, Tithonus is a young man whose mother has just died. He refuses to accept her death, while those around him—a housekeeper named Mrs. Mallow, the maid and gardener who are lovers, and his father, the stuffy, former military man Laomedon—insist that he give up mourning and go on with his life. He is revolted by Mrs. Mallow and Laomedon, whose insensitivity to his mother's death makes them seem "dry inside, dry and old." Then Aurora enters. She announces that the father of the gods has granted her wish to make her lover immortal. But there's a catch, of course: Aurora has requested eternal life, not eternal youth, for Tithonus. He realizes with horror that he has been saved from death, but not from what he fears even more—the process of aging and its consequences.

The rest of the play follows Tithonus as he grows older. Act 2 is set in Russia in 1894. Tithonus is now a sixty-year-old dilettante, traveling the world with his eternally youthful wife. The maid and the gardener of act 3 have been replaced by a pair of young lovers, Fanya and Konstantin, while the older generation is represented by their chaperone, Olga. The party discovers Tithonus on a hilltop, where he is painting en plein air. He soon finds himself sparring in conversation with the headstrong young man; the scene repeats the generational conflict he had with his father, only Tithonus is no longer on the side of youth. He feels an instinctive sympathy with Olga. She is mortally ill, as even the self-involved Tithonus can see, and her proximity to death stirs him. Reviewing the forty years that he has spent with the goddess of dawn, he remembers only "[s]unlight in cities, brilliance of theaters, [. . .] nothing but light, light, light! It is not to be borne." He cries out for Olga to "break the spell!" and he proposes himself as her lover, but she refuses him. The act ends with the arrival of Aurora, who is pregnant with Tithonus's child.

Act 3 is set in America in 1954. The giddy goddess has become a bored suburban wife bound by duty to a helpless husband she no longer loves. She

---

* Ashbery's *The Heroes* puts heroes from Homeric epic onstage for a weekend of witty philosophical conversation in a country house by the sea. It belongs to a subgenre of postwar playwriting in which classical stories are reworked in contemporary language and settings. Other examples by playwrights associated with the Artists' Theatre include John Latouche's *The Golden Apple*, V. R. Lang's *Fire Exit*, and Lionel Abel's *The Death of Odysseus*. Behind these works is Cocteau's *Orpheus*.

has a lover, the handsome young Mark, whose wife, Enid, spends her time sitting with Tithonus. It is Tithonus's 120th birthday, and Memnon, his and Aurora's son, arrives for the occasion. Memnon, a "pompous" former military man like his grandfather Laomedon, is in the curious position of being older than his mother and sixty years younger than his father. "[W]e never had too much to say to each other, Dad and I," he opines; on this occasion he settles for the gratuitous cliché, "Many happy returns, Dad!" Tithonus himself is reduced to incoherent memories and stale bromides of the type his father favored (when Enid cries at the end of the play, "He'll never die!" Tithonus delivers his last words: "A watched pot never boils"). So it is no wonder Aurora gives up her ambition to be faithful to her husband and instead runs off with the dashing Mark.

Merrill reduced the play's message to a few maxims: " 'One cannot live if one cannot die,' 'Whoever fears death fears life,' or (thinking of Aurora [. . .]) 'Some people have no capacity for sorrow or guilt; these people often injure others.' " But "the 'theme' of the play, the content of it—these things were always secondary to me," by comparison to a "curiosity about a new form." Action was so little important to this experiment in Symbolist theater that the hero becomes progressively more immobile until he is swaddled in blankets in a chair, his face barely visible, in the third act. The supporting characters in each act are versions of one another—which Merrill underlined by requiring actors to play two or three parts in a total cast of six. Aurora is a foil for Tithonus. By act 3, she has tasted Moxie and Fig Newtons and learned about ordinary boredom and grief ("I wanted to go through what *people* go through"), but she never essentially changes. *The Immortal Husband* is a full-length play about physical decay, emotional paralysis, and rote behavior: character and plot development, like the life course it concerns, are weirdly distorted. No recipe for popular success, its eccentric design provoked Brooks Atkinson, theater critic of *The New York Times*, to wonder, when at last the work was staged, "whether Aurora has not included the play in her gift of endless time, permitting the audience to grow aged as the acts drag on toward the last curtain."

The theatrical strategies that strained Atkinson's attention had personal as well as artistic motivations for Merrill. Sympathetic to Tithonus's wish to put off change, and more ready to parody conventional plots than to take any of them seriously, *The Immortal Husband* reflects the playwright's uncertainty, in 1953, about how to shape the life before him. Tithonus does not want to die: "I'm too young! So much is expected of me. I've done nothing yet to make my name endure, to give me immortality." It is easy to hear in this speech the anxieties of a young man burdened by the expectation that he make his name "endure," shaken by the premature death of a talented friend, and frightened by the prospect of aging—a fear intensified for Merrill by American culture's (as well as gay male culture's) idealization of youth.

And the older generation responds to Tithonus with advice Merrill's parents might have given him. Laomedon's hearty practicality, expressed in mottoes like "Time is money," links him to Charles Merrill; then, as he lives on and on, Tithonus himself starts to suggest CEM, sustained in his sixties by Dr. Levine's magical "radioactive cocktail." Dull-witted Memnon involves a caricature of Bill Plummer: both are ex-generals turned businessmen. Hellen Plummer has no obvious surrogate, since Tithonus's mother dies before the action begins. But Mrs. Plummer speaks through Mrs. Mallow when the housekeeper urges Tithonus to stop his unmanly crying: "What can a mother ask of her child, but that he grow strong and virtuous? By doing that, a son shows his love. Not by tears, but by living the way she has taught him to live."

Tithonus's love for Aurora defends him against these pragmatic and moralizing alternatives. Rather than grow up and behave as a young man of his station is supposed to, he chooses youth, light, and pleasure—principles marked as feminine here—and rejects masculine sobriety, maturity, and compromise. Aurora embodies that preference so fully she cannot pronounce the word "death." Her sensibility—combining gaiety and otherworldliness with a cruelty that comes of her lack of common feeling—represents a complex of attitudes that Merrill feared in himself. Her gift of immortality seems at first to save Tithonus from the trials that mortals endure, like Tom Rakewell's fortune, or, for that matter, Merrill's. Tithonus reacts to Aurora's news with the same breathless enthusiasm that Merrill felt, and even some of the phrases he used, when he submitted to Dr. Simeons miracle diet cure: "How glorious the world is! [. . .] I feel such excitement, a tingling in me, as if I were never again to be tired or bored, an energy that will never exhaust itself!" But he learns that there is no rescue from time. Mrs. Mallow summarizes the play's moral wisdom when she says, "Tithonus, what you have feared is not so much death as—," and Aurora brightly, wickedly adds the missing word: "Life!" Merrill's moral, meant for himself above all, is clear. Youth, privilege, and talent save no one. The point in facing up to mortality is to live as fully as possible.

Yet *The Immortal Husband* offers no vision of what a full life might be like. The life choice it focuses on is marriage. Merrill traces a sad trajectory in the three supporting couples: the play moves from the sexual teasing of the maid and gardener to the naive confidence of the affianced Fanya and

Konstantin to the dull estrangement and disappointment of the married couple, Enid and Mark. The play amounts to a bitter critique of heterosexual romance and the institution of marriage. But it also makes a prophetic comment on Merrill's developing relationship to David Jackson. In the end, Aurora keeps faith only with the demands of her own nature as she turns away from her diminished, dependent husband in favor of a handsome young man. Jimmy and David would act out a version of that script three decades later.

Stonington: neither Merrill nor Jackson had heard of the seaside Connecticut town until January 1954, when they paid a visit to Guitou Knoop, who was living there with a boyfriend. Jimmy and David were so charmed by the town that they began looking for a place of their own at once. They found one with five rooms and a view of the harbor on the third floor of a creaking, three-story, turn-of-the-century building on Water Street, the village's commercial street. In February, Jimmy went to see his father in Barbados, while David began setting up the new apartment, "talking to the by-the-hour workers, secondhand shops, plumbers, the fire chief, etc." By April, he and Merrill had moved in, renting their handful of small rooms for $25 per month. They liked it so well that they stayed on, that first year, all the way into December.

They had discovered a place of great natural beauty. Set in the far southeastern corner of the state, the town is built on a point about a mile long and less than half a mile wide. Fringed with wharves and moorings, it tapers to a finger of land reaching into Fishers Island Sound. At the end of it are a small beach and a rocky shore. To the west is Stonington Harbor, sheltered by a breakwater. To the east is Little Narragansett Bay and Sandy Point, an island formed by the mighty 1938 hurricane; on the other side of the bay are the resort town of Watch Hill, Rhode Island, and the dunes of Napatree Point. Rather than open sea, the view to the south is of Latimer Light and Fishers Island, New York, making this a three-state view. The sea surrounds the town, and the long low shapes of land on the horizon ring the sea, creating a natural theater. The scene is lit by the sun as it rises behind Watch Hill, climbs over the town, and drops beyond the harbor at dusk. Blue, gray, green, tan, violet, pink—the colors of the land and sea keep shifting. Behind the sound track of church clock, seabirds, bell buoy, and foghorn, there is intense quiet. At night, the sky fills with stars.

The town plan is very simple. The principal streets, Water and Main, run north and south in tandem, linking Wadawanuck Park, where the Stonington Free Library stands, and Cannon Square, where the iron guns that repelled a British naval attack during the War of 1812 are preserved. Crossing these are small streets named Diving, Harmony, Union, Grand, Pearl, Church, and Wall. Alpha Avenue crosses the railroad tracks that separate Stonington Borough, as the point is called, from the rest of the town, which extends inland. Trains bound for Boston and New York rumble and whistle as they shoot past without stopping. Bordering the old Stonington Harbor Light and ending at the sea is little Omega Street.

Stonington felt to Merrill, pleasingly, like a miniature Manhattan. Having never had room to expand, the town is densely packed with eighteenth- and nineteenth-century houses. Some of these, decorated with cupolas and Greek Revival columns, were built as stately homes for the local worthies who captained whaling ships, traded Arctic seal furs, and sailed into Stonington Harbor with wealth and curios from Java, Shanghai, and Macao. Others were the snug homes built by the Portuguese sailors who came from the Azores to man those ships. Their children and grandchildren formed the town's fishing fleet, or went to work in its factories, the velvet mill on the other side of the train tracks, and the hulking plastics plant on Water Street.

From their new address at 107 Water Street, in the center of town, Jimmy and David had the necessaries close at hand: a post office, a used bookstore, a liquor store, a drugstore, and, on the first floor of their building, an A&P market. There was no movie theater, and they never joined the yacht club. A walk to the point and back took about twenty minutes. Even the town's historic names seemed pocket-sized: Edmund Fanning, for whom the Pacific reefs and atolls called the Fanning Islands were named; Nathaniel Palmer, who discovered Antarctica in 1820 as the twenty-one-year-old commander of the *Hero;* the painter James McNeill Whistler, who lived in Stonington briefly as a child; and the poet Stephen Vincent Benét, who had sent the teenage Jimmy an encouraging letter about his poetry, and whose widow was still a resident when Jimmy and David came to town. There were interesting characters to meet, mainly "summer people" or retirees who had led mildly glamorous lives elsewhere—for instance, John Mason Brown, a theater critic, or elderly George Copeland, a pianist who had met Debussy and performed with Isadora Duncan and Maggie Teyte. But the town was not an exciting cultural center, a Provincetown or Taos. "Ston.," David quipped, "is chuck full of celebrities of an order which makes it seem like a 5 cent chocolate bar studded with peanuts (as opposed to the 10 cent bar with almonds)."

"I love this town," Merrill declared. On the road to New York, he and

Jackson stopped in a New Canaan coffee shop, familiar from the days when he and his mother lived there. "What a difference," he reflected, "to live in a small town where one's family doesn't live!" In its far corner of Connecticut, more than three hours by car from Manhattan, Stonington felt safely remote from the world he came from, but not so cut off that he couldn't get to the city quickly. In their new apartment, three floors above the street, they could do as they liked. Decades later in *Sandover*, Merrill describes the freedom they felt: "Now, strangers to the village, did we even / Have a telephone? Who needed one! / We had each other for communication / And all the rest." "And all the rest" is an offhand reference to their lovemaking, their afternoons spent swimming naked or wandering the shore on Sandy Point, and the deepening intimacy that came with those hours alone together. "How pleasant these days have been," Merrill exclaimed in his journal, "+ what a joy D. is!"

Perhaps every pair of lovers creates a private world. But Merrill and Jackson had reasons to feel they needed to hide. For gays and lesbians in America, this was the era of the closet. In 1953, newly elected President Eisenhower signed an executive order that authorized the firing of any federal employee determined to be homosexual. The order was a product of the Cold War culture of surveillance epitomized by Senator Joseph McCarthy's investigation of subversives, which focused on communists and homosexuals as threats to national security. Jimmy and David moved into 107 Water Street while America was transfixed by the Army-McCarthy hearings. Televised between March and June 1954 (Merrill and Jackson, "fascinated," listened to them on the radio), these hearings brought four years of red baiting by McCarthy's Senate subcommittee to a climax by turning official scrutiny on the subcommittee's chief counsel, Roy Cohn, and McCarthy himself. That the hearings ended by shaming McCarthy did not so much free the nation from the power he had wielded as demonstrate that McCarthy too could be investigated. Merrill was thinking about the spectacle in late April when he drafted a cynical political poem, never completed, called "The Hearings." Later that summer, the demon appeared in the flesh when Jackson spotted (or so he claimed) the big-bellied senator in his swimsuit on the sidewalk in Watch Hill.

The oppressive political climate did not constrain their style at home. The apartment's five small rooms were whimsical. From the sitting room, Jimmy and David gazed out at the harbor through colored panes—purple, two blues, a yellow. Just adjacent was the "tower" room, where they ate their meals. Built into a tower on the corner of the building crowned by a witch's pointy cap in days gone by, the room was round beneath a pressed-tin dome.

David painted the room an outrageous "watermelon red." Their wicker couch he made a lavish, "orchid" purple. Jimmy tipped his head back and painted the dome white "around peeling ornamental motifs" of fleur-de-lis. Around the "milk glass" tabletop, they placed four high-back cane chairs, painted lavender and pink. For the floor of the little bedroom, they chose Granny Smith—apple green, and for the bedroom walls, robin's-egg blue. Jimmy liked the "fringed 1905 lampshade, black with brown and yellow butterflies," that David found in an antiques store, along with a shining brass bed. If the 1950s were the age of the closet, and *The Man in the Gray Flannel Suit* (the title of Sloan Wilson's 1955 novel) symbolized middle-class America's anxious conformism, the third-floor apartment on Water Street was a vibrant protest.

In this charmed space, Merrill and Jackson went to work as writers. Merrill set up shop at a small table in the dining room. Jackson sat at a desk in the kitchen, or typed on Merrill's new Olivetti on the dining table next to where Merrill sat. The freedom to devote himself entirely to his writing was a new experience for David. A year before, shortly after he met Merrill, he'd taken a job in the offices of Junior Achievement in Brooklyn. He worked at that job until fall 1953, when he left to devote himself full time to fiction writing. In November, with a loan from Merrill, he bought and furnished a railroad-style, walk-up apartment at 950 First Avenue, near Fifty-second Street and the East River, in a building where a friend, Bernie Winebaum, was living. While he was in Stonington, Jackson rented 950 First Avenue to Bill Meredith; it was his only source of income. He talked about renovating the other half of the third floor of 107 Water Street and subletting those rooms for more money. Meanwhile, debts to Merrill piled up. Carefully recorded by Jackson in his journal, the loans from "Jamey" mounted to $1,859.50 by October 1954.

Jackson's fiction had not yet brought in any cash. The manuscript of his novel *Sebastian* had been rejected by Harcourt, Doubleday, and Knopf, despite Merrill's effort to open doors at these publishers; Scribner's and Viking, where again Merrill had friends, would turn him down that summer. He had begun work on a new novel, entitled *Amy*, and he exhorted himself in his journal ("I have been idle too long"). At the same time, Merrill pushed himself forward in his diary: "I must finish a book. Either the novel, or a new book of poems must appear next year!" The Artists' Theatre staging of *The Immortal Husband*, initially scheduled for spring 1954, had been postponed while Myers and Machiz looked around for wealthy backers. "Tennessee W. loves the play, for what that's worth," Merrill told Friar, both bragging and uneasy about this step toward the commercial theater.

"It's all a very curious experience, involving so many personal contacts, ingratiations, even appearances at Sardi's." He made plans with Claude to publish a chapbook of new poems called *Short Stories* with the Banyan Press.

Cramped at the bottom of the page, David added a postscript to a letter from Jimmy to Claude that discusses their plans for the chapbook and includes two poems. The note shows Jackson acutely aware of Merrill's talent and ambition. Already he was imagining that, to posterity, his life would look like a mere adjunct to his brilliant companion's biography: "I wonder what biographers would do with this [. . .]: 'An interesting and irritating feature of one of the Merrill-Fredericks [letters] (26 May, 1954, Stonington-Pawlet), in which Merrill proposes [to] incl[ude] two poems [. . .]; it is with some regret one finds only a small postscript signed, 'David,' [. . .] (Assuming JIM's poems become separated)." Jackson was not Merrill's equal, they both recognized. Yet Merrill expected Jackson to be equal to his critical judgment. It was only what Jimmy himself expected when, at the end of the workday, over drinks, they shared the day's results, saying, "David, I would much prefer some hard words about my writing, which I (God Knows) know very well as not so thoroughly beyond reproach as you'd each day make it out, page by page, to be." Merrill's own "hard words" could be overwhelming to Jackson. This journal entry by Jackson describes one of their exchanges in detail:

> Well, taking [a story] into JM—even with a certain indifference, as he had seen it, now, three times—I was, in a profound way, panicked to hear his criticisms. These occurred within, approximately, every four lines: "too many 'The's', I believe"; "Why do you use 'how'—it's absolutely ungrammatical?" [. . .] "You are too obscure, you choose words with obscure intent [. . .]. The entire paragraph, like others, disintegrates into a search for meaning. Your story breaks down for a reader, therefore." Until, because I so completely trust his taste and his training, I felt without support, a groundswell lifting me off my firm sandbar and floating me away—to sea, again. Back, again, to that pointless drifting I've always endured when I believed not at all in the direction, technical skill, possibility of articulation in my writing.

Jackson felt "refreshed" when the talk ended and ready to return to work, but the feeling was hard to sustain. He lost his wallet, and Jimmy complained about "how careless, beau monde, dandy I am about money +

speech." David felt that he needed a job. It would be "a way <u>out</u> [. . .] beyond morning recriminations and flurries of energy. [. . .] I am living too much on JM's graces, his come and go flashes of approval. This will be increasingly impossible."

He developed that thought further when Robert Arner, a painter who had been Merrill's student at Bard, came to Stonington to visit:

> Bob told a strange little story about JM at a Bard picnic when all of them were quite drunk on Rhein wine, JM + all went swimming in a waterfall, BA lost his footing and could not grab hold of the pebbles and felt himself pushed toward the edge of the fall; looking up, panic[k]ed, he saw JM, standing within reach, but just watching, watching the panic. Until BA got himself upright. I found myself considering if, perhaps, this wasn't an accurate parable of JM's cruelty [. . .]. Haven't I underestimated it; isn't it actually existent? Such a persistent experience of wealth, jabbed with emotional insecurities, with all of it, couldn't he be, simpl[y] curious + cold (despite <u>my</u> denying to himself, several times now)?

If Jackson was in danger of being carried out to sea or pulled over the falls, Merrill was not standing idly by. Although he was twenty-eight to Jackson's thirty-two, he responded to his lover's creative struggles with doses of motherly care and paternal discipline, shining a light on the seedlings of David's creativity. Jimmy's attention was heartening, yet it aroused David's guilt and sense of insufficiency. He wrote in his journal on August 1,

> Now, guilty, hearing JM's chair scrape back in the tower room, I wince at having written here, indulged myself, when I have taken so much of his time talking about "getting started on Amy." I have spent—perhaps—the happiest of my life's separate months with him, lolling in his sympathy, feeding on his comfort, relying on his belief. [. . .] Last night, when the late sun filled the tower room, falling across him—There, thoughtfully tapping that chapt. of Sebastian I intend to abstract as a story he said "I hope you do <u>not</u> type 10 pages of the novel a day. This is a critical point in your life. You must justify setting out in it by readying that and <u>extending</u> yourself."—unsmilingly, refusing <u>to</u> smile even when, suffering by my own self-consciousness, I

put my hand on his leg and tried to laugh us away from it. I felt, then, pulled up. Not, really, totally aware of a tradition of work in art, of a ceremony of labor; but knowing <u>what</u> he was underlining. I know he would like to see me accepted, published, recognized.

Fredericks sent copies of *Short Stories* to 107 Water Street in August. The small book, hand-sewn in a jacket of marbleized paper, contained nine poems in what Merrill called "my new 'talkative' manner";* they displayed his emerging interest in storytelling and speech (which he was exploring at the same time in other genres by writing *The Immortal Husband* and *The Seraglio*). Merrill dedicated the book to Jackson, who thought it a "beautiful" gift. It also stirred his jealousy: "What <u>would</u> a novel in print, stories out, others sold do to me? Now, I am nervous and strained at everything. Excessively jealous—which state is working such havoc on my feeling <u>for</u> JM, not to mention, I know, his for me." Jackson pressed on with *Amy*. He finished the novel at last in a "flood of tears," but he wasn't proud of the results: "It limps, [. . .], shuffles off into corners, crawls around twisting and flopping and trying to do tricks, mimics and laments, and is—in short—a very dog of a book."

Yet, when he looked back on the summer, he was happy: "Hasn't it all been, I ask myself, the very best summer of my life? Surely, thinking soberly, one of the best I <u>shall</u> have, best in moral and physical and emotional comfort, best in working conditions and (because of reading and talking such good things) mentally the best."

The summer ended with a terrific storm. Hurricane Carol passed over Stonington on August 31, flooding the town. "Ships + trees + multicolored plastic beads from the factory all over," Merrill noted. He and Jackson had sat out the hurricane in the home of "old George Copeland, who, driven by sheer terror, played Albeniz + Mompou + Debussy with a relentless, adolescent virtuosity." On Labor Day weekend, Merrill and Jackson went to Southampton for the christening of the fifth of Doris and Bobby Magowan's sons, Mark. Jimmy was glad to see the eighteen-year-old Robin

---

* JM to KF, letter, May 15, 1954 (WUSTL). The nine poems printed in *Short Stories* were "Gothic Novel," "A View of the Burning," "The Octopus," "The Cruise," "The Wintering Weeds," "The Greenhouse," "About the Phoenix," "A Narrow Escape," and "Midas Among Goldenrod"; all but "Gothic Novel" were included in *The Country of a Thousand Years of Peace*. Fredericks printed 250 copies; 60 were for sale.

showing signs of rising "in Full Revolt against the community [. . .]. One had waited many years for that." Jackson viewed the scene as "staggeringly de-luxe, a champagned-ridden [sic] series of parties and people. One is most impressed at the accuracy with which JM has tacked it all down in Seraglio." *The Seraglio*, still in progress, was taking shape as Jimmy's own "Full Revolt": the story of Francis Tanning's struggle to free himself from the business world of his father not only describes a filial rebellion; it *was* one, and would be received as such by his family.

Later that fall, he was called on to demonstrate his familial loyalty, with Guitou as the occasion. She had kept returning to the Beach House, as her work on Mr. Merrill's bust went on and on. They quarreled, and the tycoon sent her away for good. Doris joined forces with her father in blaming the sculptress for the falling out, but Jimmy did not. Instead, he wrote angry letters to both Doris and his father, the tone of which can be inferred from the further correspondence that survives. Stopping short of an apology for his words to her, he acknowledged to his sister "the sense of a fire fanned by feelings that have no intrinsic connection with the situation."

> One of these feelings, I believe, is an inexperience, on my part, of family life. I have often looked enviously upon those very intimate households of parents and children, brothers and sisters, who live so close together for so many years that, sooner or later (it seems) everything is said, all emotions, kind or unkind, expressed; loyalties put daily to the test—all of which would amount to a total ease and freedom, although any single incident might appear mean or meanly motivated. [. . .]
>
> You may say that it is my own adult choice that I do not live more closely to my family. That is true; but it is also one's whole family (not just a mother or whatever) that teaches one how to live and what to choose. Lord knows, I don't enjoy the sense of tentativeness and even tension that comes from trying to draw near to Daddy or you or Charles; say even that I succeed in drawing near, as I do, over + over; still it's there, it imposes formalities, and discourages absolute faith. I agree with you that a failure of faith, or loyalty, shows in my letter.

Father hung fire. When he wrote to his son, he made it clear what kind of behavior was expected in the family: "I hold to the belief that it is of the utmost importance for blood kin to stick together and to fight for each other and not to be divided by anything else. There is nothing that you can say or do which would change my love and affection and respect for you. I am on your side now and forever. I hope and believe that you are on my side." But Guitou was not important enough to put his son to the test. He ended this letter—the last one from him to Jimmy that survives—with a benediction:

> You are my beloved and youngest son. I would make any sacri-
> fice within my power to protect and help you. I hope that you feel
> the same way toward me. At any rate, I take this for granted. I
> hope that God will bless, protect, and help you to find the path
> which will enable you to do the work that you are prepared to do
> with the wonderful tools with which you are equipped.

As his guide on that path, Merrill looked in particular to Wallace Stevens, whom he saw as "the best American poet, today." Stevens, the Connecticut insurance executive who walked to work every day and wrote poetry after hours, suggested how money might be placed in the service of private life and the imagination. As Merrill understood him, he was a poet for whom art—rather than business, religion, or politics—was life's "primary concern." In the mid-1940s, reading Stevens with Friar, Merrill had assimilated the older poet's aims and ideas, his tastes and his manner, including his taste for the mannered. In his commentary on Stevens in an anthology of modern poetry he edited, Friar quoted a phrase from Stevens to describe his work—"the essential gaudiness of poetry." The phrase stayed with Merrill. In Stevens, he remarked in 1968, the "inessential"—the "gaudy," the personal and reputedly frivolous—could be "suddenly felt as essential."

Stevens was on Merrill's mind in the fall of 1954. When *Short Stories* appeared, he sent copies to family and friends. (Only three poets appear on the list of people to receive books that he gave Fredericks: Richard Wilbur, Elizabeth Bishop, and T. S. Eliot, beside whose name, he wrote, "why not?") Fredericks sent a copy to Stevens, who collected fine books and published his own poems in beautiful limited editions. Stevens responded in a letter to Fredericks that Merrill copied into his notebook: "Thanks for the copy of Mr Merrill's Short Stories. His idea is a prolific one and his poems are neat as pins . . . and so is your end of the job as neat as pins. The mere existence of such things is important nowadays although they grow to be more + more like the high beaver hats of our grandfathers." Merrill met Stevens only once. The occasion was the gala luncheon hosted by Alfred Knopf in October 1954 at the Harmonie Club in New York in honor of Stevens's seventy-fifth birthday and the publication of his *Collected Poems*. Among the seventy-five guests were Auden, Marianne Moore, Conrad Aiken, Louise Bogan, Lionel Trilling, and Delmore Schwartz. Blanche Knopf seated Merrill at Stevens's table as the company's rising poet, and he made an impression on the guest of honor. Stevens mentions Merrill—and only him—in the account of the occasion he shared with Witter Bynner, another longtime Knopf poet: "There were a lot of people there whom you would have enjoyed quite as much as I did, including young James Merrill, who is about the age which you and I were when we were in New York."

The young man who identified with Stevens was the contemplative poet who lived in Connecticut. In New York, where he attended drama and opera three or four nights per week, Merrill was trying out a different literary identity. Looking back on this phase of his uncle's career, Robin comments, "[W]hat he was aiming at was clear—someone bigger than a mere poet. A Cocteau, an Oscar Wilde." Or a Yeats: Merrill was reading Yeats's letters, just published, and found them filled with "PLAYS!!!" Plans for putting on his own play were progressing. Myers and Machiz had hired the Theatre de Lys on Christopher Street in Greenwich Village for a six-week run of *The Immortal Husband*, with an option for two additional weeks. This was not the Broadway production for which Myers and Machiz had been aiming. But they had secured an experienced set designer, Richard V. Hare, and a talented cast with Scott Merrill (no relation) in the title role and Anne Meacham as Aurora. The best seats sold for $3.45, twice the price the Artists' Theatre usually charged. The hope was that the play would turn a profit, and fund another season of Myers and Machiz's work.

Machiz, Merrill felt, was a conventional director who had been drawn into avant-garde theater by Myers, and it made for a mismatch of talent and aims. But Merrill was "so excited" and "giddy" as he reviewed costume choices and attended rehearsals that he began "to think that Herbert is, after all, a genius." The play opened on Valentine's Day, and Jackson, listed as "Production Assistant" in the playbill, wrote to his family about the first performance:

> We had a bang-up Opening Night with Claude Raines, and wife, [. . .] all the major critics, Tennessee Williams, Gore Vidal, [. . .], JIM's mother, up from Florida, photographers, telegrams, + full evening dress. Then a long (to 5:00 am) party waiting for the late edition of papers, Brooks Atkinson, Kerr, etc, to give their weighty verdicts. Which, considering it was not Kismet or Fanny, or Guys and Dolls were long, grave, and, on the whole, verifying.

But Merrill described opening night as "perfectly Horrible. Cold audience of friends either nervous or unwilling to be the first to respond. Mis' Annie in a wreath of camellias and tears. Poor performance. Really the most disagreeable experience I've <u>ever</u> had."

Tennessee Williams provided a puff for the play ("James Merrill is my favorite young American poet, and he has written a play which is pure poetry plus theatre, a rare and magical combination"), and Auden rather tepidly endorsed it ("the only new play in some time which I have both enjoyed and admired"). Newspaper reviews were mixed; and Atkinson's, for which friends and family stayed up late, must have hurt the playwright. While praising the direction, acting, and sets, the review, which was entitled "Closet Drama," said that the "prolix" script of *The Immortal Husband* was an "esoteric" creation meant to be "savored by friends in the library or the studio." If the term "closet" did not imply homosexuality for Atkinson, his insinuation that the playwright had just graduated from a Browning study group did so by clearly conveying his distaste for the play's decadent inspiration.

Richard Hayes wrote in praise of the play's "wisdom and troubling beauty" in *Commonweal*.* But the review was aimed at highbrow readers who would catch its allusions to Joyce and Eliot; it did not appear until March; and too many seats stayed empty, night after night. Three weeks into the run, Myers protested the lack of an audience in an interview that he arranged to give in the *New York Herald Tribune*. The "town should be happier than it indicates over such an unusual play," he insisted; "we shouldn't be having such a struggle. In Paris or London, we would have far less difficulty than we are having." Myers's protest was pointless: New York theatergoers could not be shamed into buying tickets, and *The Immortal Husband* limped to the end of its six-week lease, with Tithonus running off to his next engagement and Aurora "sick and dissatisfied and <u>ingrate</u>." For Jimmy, it had been a long, frustrating, embarrassing, and ultimately chastening experience. He never wrote for the commercial theater again.

He had been planning his escape. When the play closed, he flew south to see both his parents. David drove to meet him, and together, in early April, they started west in a convertible Volkswagen Bug. Like Jack Kerouac's Sal Paradise, Nabokov's Humbert Humbert, and any number of vacation-

---

* Richard Hayes, "The Stage: 'The Immortal Husband,' " *Commonweal* (March 1955): 630. "It is a drama of the most faultlessly wrought texture, within the meshes of which we travel from levity to an intimate tragic truth; everywhere it speaks with the accents of authority and moral poise; everywhere, too, it suggests the presence of a talent operating under the most intense pressure, sustaining, as it were, the full weight of intellect."

ing Americans in the 1950s, they set out to see the country by automobile. The goal was a visit to David's family and Sewelly in Los Angeles. David had introduced Jimmy to bowling, delicatessens, and working-class bars. Now he would show him the American West. He wrote to his wife, coaching her: "I would like both JM and I to have a fine California-style time. He has never (accepting [sic] a trip when he was 8 or 9) been west of Chicago. It will all be new and strange to him." He was anxious about what Jimmy would think, and, for that matter, about what his parents would think of his new pal.

Their route passed through Biloxi, New Orleans, and Houston, where Vira Fredericks threw her arms around Jimmy ("something I can only wish my own mother were capable of," he told Claude). She fed him and David at the restaurant she owned, and sent them off with a pecan fudge pie. On the road, Merrill recorded local accents and idioms with the wonder of an urban innocent: "Y'all from New York?" "Y'all hurry back!" They passed through San Antonio and Santa Fe, the Petrified Forest and the Painted Desert. Cooped up in the car, bored and fatigued, they argued with each other, then smoldered in silence approaching the Grand Canyon. At last, as they stood at the edge of the chasm, David spoke first, asking, "So this is America's answer to Mount Fuji?"—and they both broke up laughing.

In Tarzana, the Jacksons appraised James Merrill. Sewelly recalled, "The important thing for George"—David's father—"was that this was the son of Charles Merrill. It had to be alright." But how much could be explained by his being rich? In order to thank his hosts properly, Jimmy offered to make dinner for the whole family—the Jacksons, David's brother's family, and Sewelly—rather than, as they would have preferred, taking everyone out. Banishing Mary from the kitchen, he stood at the stove and produced the meal while wearing lavender knee socks and shorts and a lavender striped shirt. Then, at the table, he gobbled and sucked. Sewelly remembered, "Jimmy made so much noise—no one had taught him how to eat!" David had to kick her under the table when she stared. "Everyone was fascinated and mystified."

Jimmy instantly took to David's wife. "Sewelly is heaven," he exclaimed. The three of them—David, Jimmy, and Sewelly—slipped off for a night together in Laguna Beach. They checked into a "superdelux" motel, as David put it, then "raced out into the town to find excitement" in "a damp crowded little bar where the flotsam-jetsam of that particular section of our coast giggled and twirled around in their shorts and halters and jeans and t-shirts drinking long complicated drinks." Back at the motel, they drank more, then "fell into one bed." The next day they "greeted the morning with all our old vigour, reading the funny papers on the little cliff where they served breakfast." The photos from that Sunday breakfast shine with mischief. With the Pacific crashing behind them, the sun beating down, and the comics spread out on the table, they made a lively, unlikely trio: two brand-new friends, two male lovers, and a devoted husband and wife.

Having driven to the edge of the continent, "the world's two worst drivers" (as Sewelly termed them) had to drive back. They saw the Magowans in San Francisco, then drove east to Salt Lake City and Denver. A restaurant slogan caught Jimmy's eye: "What foods these morsels be!" The western landscape thrilled him ("a road at the top of the world, and a day so brilliant!"), but the names were baffling: "Who—I keep wanting to ask—Who is Calamity Jane? Who is Buffalo Bill? Poker Alice?" They visited Jackson's relatives in South Dakota, stopped in Chicago, crossed "an ulcerous stretch of Canada," and caught their breath with Claude in Vermont before returning to New York, where they stayed just long enough to pack up more of Jimmy's possessions into the Bug and drive to Stonington. Over two months, they had drawn a wide, wandering circle across the nation and put 10,300 miles on the Volkswagen's odometer.

The summer of 1955 began inauspiciously. In June, Hellen brought her mother to New York City for a cataract operation. The surgery went badly, and another operation was needed, this one to remove Mis' Annie's left eye. The sweet old woman was left weak, looking "suspiciously about with her one eye," and showing signs of "some faint brain injury." Hellen blamed herself for having urged Mis' Annie to submit to the operation. "I think I've understood more deeply than you may know what you've been going through," Jimmy wrote to her, reflecting on "the confusion you must feel now and then of not knowing whether it's your mother or your child you're caring for." The whole situation, he declared, is "unutterably sad. The sadness seems to be that of the very <u>heart</u> of life, somehow, I don't know how else to say it."

What he meant by the "very <u>heart</u> of life" becomes slowly clear in this letter. The anger Mis' Annie directed at Hellen after these surgeries brought Merrill around to the crisis that he and his mother went through during his affair with Friar. "What I know now," he explained, "is that it takes two to bring about these crises. As far as Mis' A's eye goes, <u>deep inside</u> us, where our consciences lie, we know that the doctors' role in the situation means <u>nothing</u>; subjectively the disaster has been created by the people who matter emotionally—herself, yourself, myself." Perhaps there was a strategy in his grandmother's grief. "I wonder if at last Mis' A hasn't let herself give in, not altogether, but enough to accomplish a transition she needed to make, between relative independence and, now, relative dependence on others. Only an 'accident' could have permitted her to do this, because she has such a moral horror of it." Such "transitions" must be "nearly always violent" because they expose "the violent nature of one's inner life." He reverted to the changes that his affair with Friar had brought in his relationship with his mother: "think of the circumstances that set us apart from each other; and yet they are the real raw material of our souls and we cannot repudiate them."

The ideas that Merrill develops in this letter come down to a basic conviction about human nature: in the end, people are powerless not to do what they want, whatever the cost to others and themselves. In this view, there are no accidents; all that happens to us is meaningful, because it is motivated by our natures. "I don't know," he shrugged, "I think each of us is terribly knowing as far as his own hidden needs are concerned; even when some external disaster takes place—within a matter of hours, like the forming of a pearl, one begins to change it into the event most appropriate to his inner life; in that respect, the mind is a most marvelous thing." He ended by praising his mother not for her kindness, but for her vision: "Remember that you have chosen to be conscious of things that may hurt you, and at your very best I think you ought rightly to be proud of that. I am proud of you for it; I believe we should see as much as we possibly can."

While Merrill was absorbed in his mother's and grandmother's problems, Jackson was planning for his wife's arrival. David and Jimmy's trip west had gone so well, Sewelly was ready to return the visit. She would stay with them in the other apartment on the third floor of 107 Water Street, and then move into David's apartment at 950 First Avenue, while she tried to establish herself as a painter in New York. "It is the 'making' of the summer season, her coming," David wrote to Grimes. "All of Stonington has been wondering about me and my wedding ring and my vague stories about a west-coast bride. Well, they'll have their reward." She appeared on Water Street in July. While Jimmy pushed forward in *The Seraglio*, and David, sitting at a table in the kitchen, began a third novel, Sewelly made drawings and painted. Friends visited—Bernie Winebaum, Marilyn Lavin, John Myers, Freddy, and Robin—and they got to know more neighbors—for example, the photographer Rollie McKenna, known for her portraits of writers, who would live in Stonington for decades. But Merrill and the

Jacksons spent most days on their own. They rowed out to Sandy Point to swim. They bought lobsters at the town wharf and ate them in the tower room. After dinner, they played cards or read books.

On a Tuesday evening, August 23, the trio tried the Ouija board. By this time Jimmy and David had replaced Freddy's store-bought board with a homemade one, a piece of brown cardboard on which the letters of the alphabet were crayoned in an arc. With a breeze stirring the gauze curtains in the tower room, Jimmy and Sewelly sat down. Side by side, using a cheap willowware teacup for their planchette, they called on the spirits. The cup swung into action. They made contact with a spirit who identified himself as "Wiston" who had died of jaundice at nineteen in China. But he didn't have much more to say, and Sewelly tired of the game. So David took his wife's place.

In *The Book of Ephraim*, the first part of *Sandover*, published in 1975, Merrill leaves Sewelly and the jaundiced Wiston out of the story, and describes what happened next with an epic simile:

> Was anybody there? As when a pike
> Strikes, and the line singing writes in lakeflesh
> Highstrung runes, and reel spins and mind reels
> YES a new and urgent power YES
> Seized the cup. It swerved, clung, hesitated,
> Darted off, a devil's darning needle
> Gyroscope our fingers rode bareback
> (But stopping dead the instant one lost touch)

That "urgent," affirmative power "announced itself as Ephraim," and immediately Jimmy and David were compelled by a voice and a story. "His date [was] not quite certain, but [he had] clearly lived in the time of Christ and just after," Merrill wrote in his diary the next day. "His father 'was powerful' but 'took Christ to his bed,' " and that "drove my mother from father." Ephraim died in 36 AD on Capri, murdered by the Emperor Tiberius's guards for loving "his nephew, mad Caligula." He spoke of a book buried in the Roman Forum, which Tiberius still wanted to destroy. He talked about sex: "7 of any age, any sex, any color was—no—is the best number." And he described a system of reincarnation in which the soul, life after life, progresses from lower to higher stages of consciousness, guided by otherworldly patrons. "Kinton Ford" was Jimmy's patron, a nineteenth-century editor of Pope's poems; "John Clay," an eighteenth-century English minister, was David's. In their previous lives, Jimmy had been a Flemish countess, David "a tough in Ireland." But now "[y]ou approach full maturities," Ephraim assured them. They asked him why he was telling them these things. "We call those we know will not refute us. This science [is] a particular one. Black," he replied. "Black magic? What do you do?" they returned. "Raise the dead," he answered. "Can we raise you? 'You have.' Where are you? 'I am the cup.'"

How exactly did they respond to this uncanny voice? "Five whole minutes we were frightened stiff," Merrill says in *The Book of Ephraim*. But "The Rover Boys at thirty" were "still red-blooded / Enough not to pass up an armchair revel / And pure enough at heart to beat the devil[.]" Their interest wasn't entirely lighthearted and casual, however. That first night they spent five hours at the board. Comparably long conversations followed every night of that week. JM and DJ—Ephraim referred to them by their initials—learned that their new friend was a Greek Jew. His father, an officer in the Roman treasury, "was above all interested in gold." Ephraim told them that Jimmy had benefited from "intervention"; as a result, he was nearing the ninth and highest stage of consciousness; but David had suffered setbacks—his recent reincarnations had ended abruptly in infant deaths—and he was lower on the ladder. "U did not take to life," Ephraim explained. JM and DJ both wanted to "take to life," and they asked for exercises that might help. Ephraim obliged: "1. To see. Polish the glass of your eyes. 2. To do. Wipe rust from off your joints. 3. To feel. Cut cloths from your fingers. 4. To know. Oil parts of your mind. 5. To live. Become as children." "Love me," Ephraim added. "Wisdom is God." Sewelly, who was only an onlooker at this point, "said she didn't think God would approve of all this." "Put her hand in the candle," Ephraim instructed, as if to punish her for that remark. She did. "Does she know pain?" Ephraim asked. Yes, her hand ached. "Wisdom," he concluded, "is a candle without pain."

Through all of this, Ephraim was manifest, of course, solely in the cup's motion and the letters it indicated. "Is there anything we can do to see you?" Merrill asked. "Die," he answered, with a sense of humor it was hard to share. Or, he added, they could simply look into a mirror. "Well we tried," Jimmy wrote. "D + I held mirrors. S. used the heavy wall mirror. We twisted + turned them + laughed for a bit. Then it all grew sad. S + I became a bit seasick. Finally we returned to the board, asking what we had done wrong. He repeated our words." "Why?" they asked. "Images are echoes. I <u>saw</u> you," he replied. The next day, walking with Jackson along the silvery tide line, Merrill thought, "[H]e sees us, he knows, he loves." "Any reflective surface worked for him," *The Book of Ephraim* explains. As in Cocteau's *Orpheus*, mirrors were a door to the dead.

Not surprisingly, Merrill and Jackson "found little to confirm what E. says." Of their patrons, Ford and Clay, "Inquiry / Albeit languid" produced no trace. But they were too absorbed in the tale to doubt the teller. "This is the clearest picture I have had so far of that world," Merrill wrote in his diary. "The tone throughout so humane and largely unexcited." This was true of his own tone in the diary. But he was excited when he told Claude about this discovery of "an extraordinary voice": "We've spoken to him 3 nights in a row. There is an afterlife!!!!!" He told the whole story—or almost: he left out Ephraim's orgies—in a letter to his mother. He knew how he must appear to her:

> Well, if you think I am mad, do so. For myself, I believe it utterly, and that is an experience I've never had before in my life. In fact I have never believed in an afterlife at all—and of course, now that I do, everything on earth now seems so much more glorious and worth living for. I can feel all kinds of hatred and fear draining out of my mind—a great energy, a will not to waste myself in short, the state of mind I have kept waiting to achieve through analysis.

This ecstatic profession of belief makes it clear that, in Merrill's mind, at least at first, Ephraim was "utterly" real, and what he said pointed to "the truth," if it was not the truth itself. "I cannot calculate how much I must have suffered in my mind from the fear of absolute annihilation," Merrill said in the same letter. "Now it seems all sorts of exalted utterance, whether scripture or poetry, point to the truth." The relief he felt implies the intensity of the fear. Over the years, Merrill would turn to the Ouija board whenever death drew near. He and Jackson seemed to forget about the board for long periods, but they routinely called Ephraim when friends and family members passed on—or when the possibility of nuclear war raised the specter of "absolute annihilation." For Jimmy's fear of death was a fear not only of personal extinction, but of a meaningless universe, and of the despair that came with such a vision. Ephraim's system of reincarnation was a consolation far superior to the immortality Aurora gives Tithonus: under the dining room's pressed-tin dome, they had discovered a better stage than the New York theater. Merrill's domestic world had given way, like a trick wall, to reveal another dimension that he and Jackson could enter with a teacup and the alphabet. Ephraim spoke from a continuing life beyond life, behind appearances, through the looking glass. And the experience was thrilling.

.   .   .

It was also disturbing. In September, anxious to understand what was happening to him and David at the Ouija board, Jimmy went to Dr. Detre. To the question of who or what Ephraim was, Detre's answer was simple and predictable. "Of course," Merrill summarized, Detre "[s]aid it was my soul's voice—not that the whole experience was <u>bad</u> but I should try to 'possess my own soul.' " Detre saw Ephraim as Merrill's projection, like a ventriloquist's dummy, except that in this case the ventriloquist was not aware that he was throwing his voice. Detre's advice was "not to converse with E. any more." *The Book of Ephraim* reports the exchange in a satirical set piece. "Tom," as Merrill calls Detre here, listens to his patient's story. Then, "Exuding insight," he declares,

> "There's a phrase
> You may have heard—what you and David do
> We call folie à deux.
> Harmless; but can you find no simpler ways
>
> To sound each other's depths of spirit
> Than taking literally that epigram
> Of Wilde's I'm getting damn
> Tired of hearing my best patients parrot?"
>
> "Given a mask, you mean, we'll tell—?"
> Tom nodded. "So the truth was what we heard?"
> "*A* truth," he shrugged. "It's hard
> To speak of *the* truth. [. . .]"

Tom winds up by making sure that Jimmy has abandoned Dr. Simeons's miracle weight-loss cure: "Those thyroid / Pills—you still use them? Don't. And keep in touch."

To make his case, Detre could have pointed out how much of Ephraim's biography seemed to have been drawn from Jimmy's. Merrill had visited Tiberius's villa with his father in 1950. Like Ephraim's father, Charles Merrill was a financier, someone "interested above all in gold." Mr. Merrill also resembled the tyrannical Tiberius, insofar as he had threatened to have his son's lover killed—not by palace guards, but the near equivalent, mafia thugs—when Jimmy's affair with Kimon was first discovered. The name of Jimmy's patron—Kinton Ford—was close to Kimon Friar, the real-life patron who introduced him to Yeats's occult beliefs and practice. Merrill himself saw links between his life and Ephraim's: like Ephraim, he notes in *The Book of Ephraim*, "I too had issued from a broken home— / The first of several facts to coincide."

Merrill was not put off by Detre's rationalism, and neither was Ephraim. "We still like you," Merrill told him after the consultation. To which the ghost replied, "Ha ha. U like yourselves." That retort was clever enough to suffice. What did it matter, Merrill reasons in *The Book of Ephraim*, if Ephraim's revelations

> were a projection
> Of what already burned, at some obscure
> Level or another, in our skulls.
> We, all we knew, dreamed, felt and had forgotten,
> Flesh made word, became through him a set of
> Quasi-grammatical constructions which
> Could utter some things clearly, forcibly
> Others not. Like Tosca hadn't we
> Lived for art and love? We were not tough-
> Or literal-minded, or unduly patient
> With those who were. Hadn't—from books, from living—
> The profusion dawned on us, of "languages"
> Any one of which, to who could read it,
> Lit up the system it conceived?—bird-flight,
> Hallucinogen, chorale and horoscope:
> Each its own world, hypnotic, many-sided
> Facet of the universal gem.

Ephraim was perhaps a "language" that Merrill and Jackson were learning to speak—one of many ways to put things, or many possible orderings of experience. His account of their lives was no more or less reliable, no more or less true, than Detre's psychoanalytic one. Or, it might be that Ephraim was not "a" language, but language itself, a voice made out of the letters of the alphabet arrayed on the board, like a set of building blocks or a palette of primary colors. Merrill made the point years later: "what you have on the board are the raw materials of language—of thought itself." "Ephraim" was, in this light, simply a name for the potential of language and thought to create a world.

The name itself was significant. It was free of associations for both Jackson and Merrill, and that was part of its initial strangeness and authority. Yet the name was apt, because, as Merrill learned from *The Oxford Dictio-*

RIGHT Hellen Ingram as a maid of honor in a Tom Thumb wedding, Jacksonville, 1905

BELOW, LEFT Hellen Ingram Merrill in 1926: her "Cupid's-bow" lips

BELOW, RIGHT CEM in Air Force uniform. "My father, who had flown in World War I, / Might have continued to invest his life / In cloud banks well above Wall Street and wife. / But the race was run below, and the point was to win."

ABOVE Mother and son, Palm Beach, 1929

LEFT In the arms of Emma Davis

BELOW JM and CEM beside the reflecting pool at the Merrill's house on Brazilian Avenue, Palm Beach, around Christmas 1929

TOP The Orchard, front drive, postcard. "Everything is as it seems [. . .] / It is the house of dreams."

BOTTOM The Orchard, the music room. Model for the ballroom at Sandover. "Looking back, [. . .] I could see how much grander the room was than any of the uses we'd put it to, so maybe the ghostly presences appeared in order to make up for a thousand unrealized possibilities."

TOP Siblings Charles, Doris, and princeling JM in the rose garden of the Orchard, 1928

ABOVE JM at the beach

RIGHT JM and roadster

ABOVE JM and CEM's Irish setters. "Like fire, like fountains leaping / With love and loyalty."

ABOVE, RIGHT JM in spats at the Arizona Desert School, safe from the Lindbergh baby's kidnappers

RIGHT Kissing Mis' Annie

Matchbook souvenir from Doris and Robert Magowan's wedding in Southampton, 1935

JM in uniform of the Knickerbocker Grays

JM in Florida. Fish and fishing appear often in JM's work. He was born under Pisces. Once he dreamed he was trapped in the body of a fish.

ABOVE Jimmy's governess, Zelly
(Lilla Fanning Howard)

LEFT Carol Longone, JM's piano teacher,
who introduced him to grand opera

JM with snake on a visit to Ross Allen's Reptile
Institute, Silver Springs, Florida, 1940. The photo
appears at a decisive moment in *The Seraglio:*
"Inspired, Francis took up the photograph of
himself grappling with the snake and, removing it
from its frame, tore it lovingly into little pieces."

JM as Puck at Camp Duncan,
Vermont, 1939

ABOVE Tony Harwood and JM in their first year at Lawrenceville, 1938–39

RIGHT JM's pencil sketch of Tony, 1942

BELOW Tony around 1970—mystical, drugged, paranoid. Jimmy had seen him as a potential "American Mallarmé."

J·M

Tony Harwood
ca. 1942

TOP, LEFT Frederick Buechner at Lawrenceville School

TOP, RIGHT Freddy on the beach, the Georgetown summer, 1948

ABOVE Merrill's Landing, postcard, with a view of the sulfur-fed pool

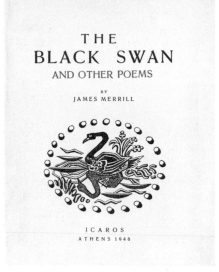

THE
BLACK SWAN
AND OTHER POEMS
BY
JAMES MERRILL

ICAROS
ATHENS 1946

ABOVE Cover of *The Black Swan* with illustration by Ghika; 1946

LEFT JM in uniform, 1945. He gave this photo, inscribed "I love you" in Greek, to Friar.

KF and JM, Amherst, 1945—a selfie, taken by Kimon in a mirror

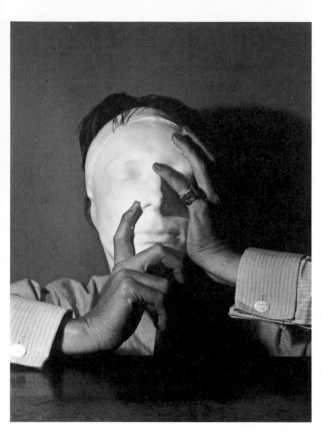

LEFT JM holding a copy of Keats's life mask over his face, in a photo taken by Friar in his rooms at Amherst, 1945–46

BELOW Maya Deren in a still from her film *Meshes of the Afternoon*. She gave a copy to Friar inscribed "Maya (Medusa)."

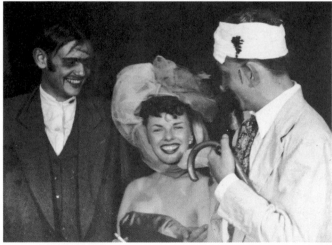

Hans Lodeizen. This photo appears in the first edition of *A Different Person*.

James, left, with a female friend and Hans Lodeizen, who is dressed as Apollinaire with a head wound from World War I, at the "Paris Party," Amherst, 1947

JM described this view of the Sleeping Woman from Poros in *The (Diblos) Notebook:* "Seen from the café, now, the Woman is more distinct: knee, belly, ribcage, breast [. . .]; mouth shut, refusal of a kiss. She gives the landscape an intense dreamlike intensity." This photo later hung above JM's desk in Stonington, a gift from Stephen Yenser.

ABOVE, LEFT KF in a Greek fisherman's cap with JM, on Poros, 1950

ABOVE, RIGHT Kimon and Mitso dancing

RIGHT A postcard of Poros seen from the mainland, c. 1950

ABOVE, LEFT Claude Fredericks's house
in Pawlet, Vermont. He called the massive
white pine "Zeus."

ABOVE, RIGHT CF in Venice, 1950

LEFT Claude, 1951. The mustache
gave him "the air of a young Flaubert."

ABOVE Dr. Detre. From
A Different Person

RIGHT Robert Isaacson and
JM at the beach, 1952

ABOVE Gerald L. Brockhurst's portrait of Doris, slashed, 1953

RIGHT CEM admiring his bust by Guitou Knoop at the Beach House, Southampton, 1954

BELOW Hellen, General William Plummer, and Mis' Annie, 1950s

TOP, LEFT David Jackson

TOP, RIGHT DJ and family (mother Mary and the Georges, father and brother) at home in Tarzana, California, 1955

MIDDLE The Jacksons, Sewelly and David, enjoying the funny papers, California, 1955. JM has gotten up from the table to take the picture.

LEFT Betty and Robin Magowan, 1958

LEFT JM and DJ with Charles and Mary Merrill in Europe, 1957

BELOW, LEFT DJ in drag

BELOW, RIGHT JM and DJ with Greek friends, early 1960s

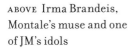

ABOVE Irma Brandeis, Montale's muse and one of JM's idols

RIGHT JM and DJ on tour, perhaps 1959. Thom Gunn, seeing the two in trenchcoats, thought, "Very American Express."

nary of English Christian Names, "Ephraim" comes from the Hebrew meaning "double fruitfulness"—which nicely describes the folie à deux in which these lovers were engaged. "Ephraim" is also an old New England name and a part of Stonington history. In the nineteenth century, Ephraim Williams owned a stately house on Water Street, and his name is first on the list of local burghers carved into the gate to the cemetery where Merrill and Jackson are also buried. Inside the gate, just to the right along the lane, "EPHRAIM" is engraved in block capitals on a tomb, meeting the eye of anyone who enters. Had Jimmy or David been out for a walk in the graveyard? If either one noticed the coincidence, neither one mentioned it.

David's journal comments little on those first Ouija sessions. He briefly mentions the second conversation with Ephraim and then remarks, "Turning from all of this back to typewriters and yellow draft sheets needs a wrench of the mind." He was discouraged by his inability to publish his novels; if he could get one in print, he thought he might give up fiction and begin to write biography or essays. "I must <u>work</u> to be able to work so that I may stop evolving bed-time stories and start work which would take hold of <u>me</u>, more. Perhaps, this morning, such is a weary rationale for not having as much fire and energy about this novel as I feel I should." What fire he had was burning through the night in those candlelit séances, to the wonder of his companion, which must have been satisfying to him. The previous summer, David and Jimmy had shared each other's writing at the end of the day, with a painful sense of the imbalance between their talents. Now they were jointly producing page after page at the Ouija board. It was a new and better idea of what being writers together could mean.

They were creating their own religion, like the one Jackson and Grimes had created in basic training, but more elaborate and compelling. For Merrill, Ephraim was a reply to the Jesus worshipped by his mother. His first letter to her about Ephraim has a defiant quality as he insists on the reality of his rival experience. Yet he also writes about Ephraim presuming her sympathy and interest. Hellen Plummer believed in an afterlife, and she wanted her son to share her belief. Nor was spiritualism utterly alien: her friend Gert Behanna was a committed spiritualist, whose ideas about the soul Jimmy referred to in his first letter about Ephraim. In his next letter to Hellen, he admitted to "certain doubts" of his own. It was crucial, he wrote,

> that these voices are essentially human—hence fallible, prejudiced, even as we. Very often they do not recall the past accurately, and are unable to predict the future except in very abstract ways. To be <u>guided</u> by it is surely dangerous. What it has

given me is simply proof of a world I had not hitherto believed in—like the proof of the existence of God. Upon such proofs one must build one's own systems, or go to priests or philosophers for guidance. Yeats quotes an ancient utterance attributed to Orpheus: "Do not open the gates of Pluto, for within is a people of dreams."

These were important qualifications. Ephraim offered "proof" of the world beyond Pluto's gates, but that proof was only available in metaphorical form. Inside the gates, if one tried to enter, was a dusty "people of dreams."

Besides his mother, Merrill was contending with the friend who'd introduced him to the Ouija board. It is not a coincidence that he discovered Ephraim while Buechner was training for his ordination as a priest. Now Merrill too had a faith to announce. For that matter, Freddy showed a knack for the board, which also was a goad to his friend's experiments with it, just as Freddy's first published poem and his first novel had been goads to Jimmy's poetry and fiction writing. Thomas Johnson, Jimmy and Freddy's former English teacher, whom Freddy got to know as a colleague when he taught at Lawrenceville, was at work on editions of Emily Dickinson's poetry and letters. Johnson supposed that there must be Dickinson letters hidden in New England attics, but, he lamented when he and Buechner talked about it, only Dickinson could tell him where to look. Then why not ask her? Buechner proposed, breezily. Johnson liked the idea, and they sat down together to a Ouija séance. Dickinson was easy to reach. She supplied plausible-sounding names and addresses, to which Johnson proceeded to write letters of inquiry—which came back marked "Return to Sender." Buechner continued to dabble with the board, and conversed with a seventeenth-century lyric poet named "William Woodman." But he gave up the game after finding that it left "a bad smell in the mind" (as G. K. Chesterton, the English man of letters, described the effect that the board had on him).

On one level, Merrill approached the Ouija board in the same spirit as Buechner—as a clever literary entertainment. And it is important that Ephraim's salon was not a hermetic society, like the Order of the Golden Dawn, of which Yeats was a member. Jimmy and David first made contact with Ephraim at home and in company. Sewelly was present for those first sessions. A week later, Maya Deren visited, and she also tried the board. Maya, the voodoo authority and avant-gardist, was wary of Ephraim's dilettantish sensualism. She had her own system of beliefs and a respect for ritual. Accompanied by "dream-drums" on tape, she spread flour and brandy in the shape of a heart—it was the emblem of Erzulie, queen of the gods or *loa*—and then lit it, burning the design into the floor of 107 Water Street.* A short time later, Merrill and Jackson did the board with Fredericks.

Over the years, they would continue to share Ephraim with friends, whose patrons and prior incarnations they duly inquired about. Those who joined their séances describe something like a party game. The hosts brought out the Ouija board after dinner with no more ceremony or solemnity than they would have reserved for a rubber of bridge. Apart from the candles, there was nothing spooky or ritualistic about the proceedings. Their guests asked questions, made comments, and took a turn at the board. Ephraim's civilized conversation was an extension of the evening's table talk.

Typically, the cup raced back and forth across the homemade board (Merrill dusted it with flour to ease the cup's movement). It moved only when two people each placed a hand on it: neither Merrill nor Jackson could make it work alone, though each of them could make it work with another partner. They had distinct roles. Jimmy was "the Scribe" and David "the Hand": while Jimmy, with his left hand on the cup, recorded letters with his right and broke them into words, reading aloud, David looked away, his left hand holding a cigarette. "Jimmy was like a boy leading another boy in a game," recalls Donald Richie, who watched them at the board in the 1950s. "He was very much in charge," Richie emphasizes, adding, "but then he was always in charge." In later years, Merrill credited Jackson as the medium to whom the spirits were drawn: "He was born with a caul—a rag of membrane pressed stiff and brown in the family Bible—and this, according to the South Dakota midwife who attended his mother, usually meant psychic powers." Jackson also told that story. In any case, because Merrill was "in charge" does not mean that Jackson was passive. When she did the board with him, Eleanor Perényi was clear about what she thought was happening: "David *pushed!*"

Who, between the two of them, was doing what? It is almost certain that neither one of them could say. "Our sense that we consciously cause what we do," argues Daniel Wegner, a research psychologist, "ebbs and flows through the day and even changes by the moment." Wegner offers a helpful approach—empirical, but not simply debunking—to the intricate play of mind and body that was set in motion when Merrill and Jackson used the Ouija board. Following David Hume in *A Treatise of Human Nature*, Wegner defines conscious will as a "feeling" that is distinct from, and by no means

---

* JM, *Sandover*, 23. Traces of it remain on the floor of the apartment today.

required by, the physical operations through which people normally act. The "feeling of will" is more or less distinct along a spectrum of actions. On one end of the spectrum are actions that are seen to be the outcome of conscious intentions, as when we think to water the houseplants and then we do it. On the other end are acts that Wegner classes as "automatisms." These are marked by "a distinct feeling that we are *not* doing" what, from a mechanical point of view, we manifestly are doing.

In the case of an "automatism" like the Ouija board, Wegner explains, the feeling of "*not* doing" is conditioned by several factors. One is "expectant attention": "the simple expectation that the automatism will happen." (Ephraim would have agreed with him. When JM and DJ asked what qualified them to receive his messages, he listed only one: "Will to hear.") Another factor is "movement confusion," which was inescapable in the type of automatism in which Merrill and Jackson were engaged. The operation of the Ouija board pointer considerably weakens, because it greatly complicates, the perception of agency. With two hands on a teacup, one person's "slight movements combine with the other person's movements," and the "co-actors" make "minute and unconscious adjustments for each other," with the result that neither partner can know "just what part of the action they personally have created." The uncertainty is amplified by the momentary delay between a thought and its realization, which is enforced by the rudimentary technology of the Ouija board, even when a teacup is moving at a great rate. So when the thought that a letter might turn out to be the first part of a specific word is gradually realized by the spelling out of that same word, the lapse of time, combined with the sense of "not doing" that comes with the force of another person's hand on the planchette, makes the initial thought feel more like an intuition than an intention. When it works, the Ouija board produces a pleasingly double sensation of surprise and inevitability, like an effective rhyme or witty remark. The partners who join hands at the Ouija board perform what Wegner calls "a mystery dance, a collective automatism that occurs when no one has conscious and specific knowledge of what self or other are doing."*

William James remarked of spiritualism, "The great *theoretic* interest

---

* Daniel M. Wegner, *The Illusion of Conscious Will* (MIT Press, 2002), 137. The aim of Wegner's analysis is not to demystify "automatisms" but to trouble the assumption that we are the agents of our actions. Most people would view the Ouija board communications of Merrill and Jackson as an exception to the rule of "conscious will," which common sense can only explain as an illusion. Wegner proposes that it is "conscious will" that is the illusion, the exception rather than the rule, and consequently that we should "turn everything around quite radically and begin to think that behavior that occurs *with* a sense of will is somehow the odd case, an add-on to a more basic underlying system" (144).

of these automatic performances, whether speech or writing, consists in the questions they awaken as to the boundaries of our individuality." The point holds for Jimmy and David's Ouija board. Merrill was a controlled type by nature, but he relinquished control, at least partially, when he gave himself over to "these automatic performances." If he had been anxious to "hold on to" himself when he returned from Rome, he let go with Jackson whenever they operated the board, with extraordinary results. Whatever or whoever he was, Ephraim was the discovery of two men. To contact him, they each had to put a hand on the cup, touching the other's hand—a subtly erotic communion. The words they produced in this fashion could not be reduced to the force or intention of only one of them. But neither were they acting with a shared plan or common intention, joining two wills in one. They acted together but not, consciously, in concert. The activity awakened questions about the boundaries between Merrill and Jackson, and between them and the spirits, beginning with Ephraim, who required their hands to speak. Self and other, the living and the dead: they were all partners in this "mystery dance."

The expansion of mind that comes with the "boundary" confusion that James describes drew many modern writers to spiritualism and the occult, from Victor Hugo and Browning in the nineteenth century to Robert Duncan (whom Merrill met in 1956 and liked) and Sylvia Plath and Ted Hughes (who discovered the Ouija board at around the same time as Merrill). But the modern spiritualist who mattered most to Merrill was Yeats. Defining poetry as "the evocation of spirits," Yeats maintained "[t]hat the borders of our mind are ever shifting, and that many minds can flow into one another, as it were, and create or reveal a single mind, a single energy." These ideas inform the spirit dictation taken by Yeats's wife, Georgie Hyde-Lees, which was the basis of Yeats's occult system in *A Vision*. Friar's work on Yeats had impressed Merrill with the importance of *A Vision* in particular.

In one of their early exchanges, Merrill asked Ephraim about the Irish poet. Ephraim said that Mrs. Yeats was "not with him" in the Other World; he also said Yeats had "simplified" in *A Vision* (a daunting thought). Over the winter, Merrill had read Yeats's selected letters. Now he picked up a new biography of the Irish poet, where he "came upon the news that Y's familiar"—his spirit guide—"was Leo Africanus. So it seems Ephraim is mine." The Other World was a source of poetic authority for Yeats, a muse that brought him, as he put it in *A Vision*, "metaphors for poetry"; and Merrill hoped that Ephraim would do the same for him. Ephraim explained that higher powers were working on JM's behalf. Jimmy asked about Lodeizen, and Ephraim replied that Hans was with him in the Other World. Having already reached the highest stage, Hans would not return to life; in fact it was he who had "intervened" on JM's behalf. "Poets are favored," Ephraim explained, as Jimmy wept.

"How is Wallace Stevens?" Jimmy asked during a séance in September. Stevens had died of stomach cancer on August 5 in Hartford. Rather than speak for him, Ephraim turned the pointer over to the poet himself. There was an initial awkwardness. "We are embarrassed," Stevens said, thinking of his and Merrill's meeting at that gala birthday luncheon the previous October, "like guests who have met too recently at one party and find themselves at another." "Are you acclimatized?" Merrill asked, as if the afterlife were merely a matter of altitude. Stevens answered, "Oh yes. Well. JM, I write poems on cloud. [I]t would seem like [a] blackboard—always being erased after each word so I have the charming experience of completely private poetry." Merrill asked to read these poems, and Stevens obliged by reciting one just composed. "Hartford 1955" begins, "Asleep above your sleep . . . ," before it drifts off into cloudy images of a mother watching her child doze. A discussion of prosody followed. Then Stevens switched topics: "E. tells me you are all quite homosexual. (Yes.) Interesting. So has been a good number of my oldest friends. . . . I was only able to experiment with 2 men. At 17 + 21," Stevens confided, but he had all but forgotten these long-ago "experiments."

That combination of topics—literary vocation and sexual identity—recurred in these séances. Like Stevens, Ephraim was curious about Jimmy's and David's sexual lives, and he related erotic experiences of his own, describing, for example, the perfumed baths at the Roman court. "Have you not had such?" he asked. JM and DJ said that they had, and told him about "a few baths in N.Y." Intrigued, he told them to set up a mirror so that he could watch them in bed, which they did that same night. The next day, they interviewed him: "(Could you see?) O yes. I am surprised u still perform the same rites as we did." Still, he felt he could add something to their sexual repertoire: "Do you not know the lovely prologue kissing of nostrils, tongue in nostril and on rims?" He described scenes of sex at court with Ethiopian slaves, dogs, oils, multiple positions and partners, and a tiger licking sweets from the genitals of the orgiasts. Perhaps he meant to excite JM and DJ; they definitely excited him. "I wd enjoy touching yr bodies," he admitted. Their conversation continues in Merrill's diary: "(It is so one-sided; we can't see or touch you.) Ah but U touch each other. (We're greedy.) Why not be greedy? (We're taught greed is <u>bad</u>)." But Ephraim was teaching them differently.

Yeats spoke of his spirit contacts as "instructors." Ephraim was a teacher too. He taught Jimmy and David how to make the most of pleasure, while encouraging them to get their work done. He was the ultimate cosmopolitan, with a long-distance historical perspective, a queer alternative to the moral voices of Senator McCarthy's America. In contrast to Merrill's mother and father, the ghost approved of, and shared in, his sexual preferences. He repeatedly validated the life that Merrill and Jackson were leading—their ambitions, friendships, appetites, humor. He slipped between subjects and moods mercurially. He was teasing and light at one moment, wistful and lyrical the next, then stern and admonitory. His voice could be prophetic, even apocalyptic. He knew that civilization had gone up in flames before:

> Nothing is new—even your bomb. (!) An explosion which I have understood from a Chinese of 3000 BC—who said a fire encircling a city was caused by the scientists of his time who used the sun's own power; and this fire,—a religion sprang up from its legend—could not be stopped. It burned even the air until they begged that it end, + it did by a disappearance of the sun behind such thick layers of smoke + cloud that for a year there was not a ray of light on the last, destroyed + blackened area which he says later became the great plain of China. . [. . .] It is our gossip that another fire chinoise must be approaching.

He also confirmed JM in his unscientific, Simeons-like belief in the psychosomatic basis of all disease:

> Cancer does not exist. It is ever according to DRs here a matter of control by the mind willfully let go in a desire 4 death + suffering. It has only been given a name of its own since the 18th cent. B4 recognized by saints and others as a will 2 die. Cells of body recognizing lack—if you like—of control in the capital rush in rebellion upon the body of the state.

During the séances narrated in the second and third parts of the *Sandover* trilogy, when JM and DJ submitted to the strange lessons of the high-ranking instructors they would speak with in the 1970s, the bats of *Mirabell* and the archangels of *Scripts for the Pageant*, they often longed to return to Ephraim's easy camp discourse. Yet the trilogy's apocalyptic question—can our world survive the threats of nuclear and environmental disaster, population explosion and epidemic?—and its claim that civilizations, like individuals, can choose life rather than death if they wish it, were present from the start of their conversations with Ephraim. They were rooted in the ideas that Merrill had tried out in embryonic form in the letter to his mother from July 1955 that speaks of "the very <u>heart</u> of life." That letter's moral perspective would be confirmed by the primary doctrine of the trilogy: there is "NO ACCIDENT"; everything is motivated; everything is meaningful. But the lessons recorded in *Mirabell* and *Scripts* lay far down the path Ephraim had shown to them. For the time being, "*He* was the revelation / (Or if we had created him, then we were)," and there was no need to choose between those alternatives.

5

THE SERAGLIO

1955–57

The Ouija board was portable, and so was Ephraim. Merrill and Jackson took him with them when they decamped from Stonington in mid-September and moved into a rambling red farmhouse, the home of Bill and Nancy Gibson, on a hilltop in Amherst. Merrill had agreed to replace Gibson in the Amherst English Department while Gibson spent the year on a sabbatical leave. The Gibsons' house, far from town with beautiful rural views, would enable Merrill and Jackson to go on living together in privacy at a distance from New York City. Jimmy's enthusiasm for it in letters indicates that staying clear of Manhattan had become important to his work. It was also important to his life with David, which, disguised by David's marriage and their separate apartments in New York, remained half hidden from Merrill's family—who could only approve of Jimmy returning to his and his father's redbrick alma mater.

Merrill was paid $5,600 to teach two courses per semester. He took a section of Advanced Composition* and a section of Introduction to Litera-

---

* Advanced Composition was a creative writing course and distinct from Composition, Theodore Baird's famous introduction to prose. William H. Pritchard describes the "truly prodigious" work the course involved: "In the course of the first semester the student wrote thirty-some times; if (as I did) an instructor taught two sections of the course (M, W, F and T, Th, S) he read thirteen hundred or so papers over the semester." Pritchard, "Amherst English," *Raritan* 16, no. 3 (1997): 150. Merrill had a lighter load.

ture, the course created by Reuben Brower, who had left Amherst for Harvard. He was not a natural in the classroom, and he didn't apologize about it. "I don't really enjoy teaching," he told Irma Brandeis. "The students aren't nearly as individual as I remember them in <u>my</u> day (does everyone remark on this?)." He complained of the generic quality of the work he got in Advanced Composition, where students could choose to write fiction or poetry: "[T]he writers write either a short version of The Old Man and the Sea which I never read, or, still worse, of Prufrock, which I wish I'd never read; the really original spirits invent dry, dead, <u>Teachable</u> little poems, in which the surface of literature is marvelously reproduced—well," he admitted, catching himself, "that is a way of learning; as long as one doesn't stay in the museum, copying . . . Many's the day I've done it myself."

He didn't let teaching stand in the way of his writing. While another writer would have been kept from the desk by his classroom duties, the opposite was true for Merrill. When Friar wrote to him skeptical about this decision to teach, he fired back, "Of course I do not need to teach; what saves me, even, is that I do not particularly like to teach." The logic, though tortured, made sense: for Friar, who threw himself into his classes, "teaching represents a pitfall," whereas for Merrill it was easy to set limits, and this gave him a freedom he didn't have in the city, with its social demands, to which he found it much harder to say no. The Amherst job afforded him "3 full days a week in which to work and get my novel done—instead of living in New York, working <u>no</u> days a week. [. . .] Surely of the last 5 or 6 years, this will be the least wasted."

Merrill made friends with Benjamin DeMott, a young professor who would become a noted critic and novelist and a force in the Amherst English Department for many years to come. But he didn't get on with most of his colleagues. All of them were men. His yellow shirt, French cuffs, and paisley ties mocked their regulation pipes and tweeds. He found them "tremendously touchy": "one has only to remark, pleasantly enough, that one dislikes the short story as a form, and from the far end of the room a colleague will rise, turn purple, reveal himself as an author of several, and with a parting thrust—once, actually, 'Well, I hate poetry!'—go off to share the incident with his coterie." Robert Frost visited the campus, and Merrill, meeting him for the second time, found him "enchanting, a kind of Job in his long-johns and dazzling drift of hair, laughing to himself and muttering under his breath, well, well, it's all been fun, it's all a lark!" Jimmy was not cowed by the master, or by the institution's reverence for him. He liked to imitate Charles Cole, the Amherst president, who introduced Frost with a lisp: "The winkles you see on Mr Fwost's bwow are not age or wowwy, but the weight of the weath!"

DeMott remembered the difference between Frost and Merrill as guests at his family's dinner table. Frost asked DeMott's young daughter to copy one of his poems by hand, which he signed and presented as a gift to her. "Jim on the other hand made zero of his poetry. He concentrated purely on the kid, and dealt with the person before him not as someone to be schooled but as someone of independent human interest." Over the years, DeMott saw that "Jimmy was very attached to *families*. He knew that 'family fun' was a crock. But his willingness to play the family game was marked." In Amherst, Jimmy and David were surrounded by married couples and young families. They visited, and hosted visits from, Joe and U. T. Summers and their three small children, who were living in Connecticut now that Joe had joined the faculty of the state university in Storrs. After one visit, David was left reeling: "what a <u>night</u>, one child or another screaming, demanding water, feet tramping up and downstairs, the baby boy screaming for his 2am, 4am, and 6am bottles, doors shutting, johns flushing, faint sobbings. <u>Boy</u> . . ." The Summers family expanded Jimmy and David's family by giving them a white kitten from their pet's litter. Thinking of Henry James, Jimmy called her Maisie—"because of what she knows"—as if the cat were the queer couple's only child, precociously sophisticated by exposure to their scandalous lives.

Another friend Merrill made during this year was Alison Lurie. Lurie was a graduate of Radcliffe and an aspiring fiction writer. She had come to Amherst with her husband Jonathan Bishop, a young instructor in the English Department and the son of the poet John Peale Bishop; they were the parents of an infant and a toddler. Merrill had met the Bishops five years before in Austria through Claude Fredericks, and the occasion had gone badly. He and Lurie faced off across a picnic blanket: he found her judgmental; she thought he was a snob; and neither one hid their reactions from the other. "After that, I hoped never to see her again," Merrill admitted. Amherst gave them a second chance, yet they might not have become friends, Lurie reflects, "if it hadn't been for David Jackson. I liked David instantly—almost everyone did, while it was common back then for people to take time to warm up to Jimmy." David, she recalls, was "wonderfully attractive: blond, tanned, strong." With a "casual, laid-back, wide-open spaces manner and slow cowboy drawl," he dressed casually in "faded khakis and corduroy jackets and white or blue shirts with the sleeves rolled up" and "old tennis shoes or loafers." He was, in short, nothing like the stereotype of an effeminate gay man. "David knew how to talk to a woman as if he were a straight man, whereas Jimmy talked to you as if between women."

Jackson recorded his first impression of the Bishops in his diary:

> J.B. strikes me as quite without compassion, [. . .] and unhap-
> pily affected in ways only sons of famous men often can be [. . .].
> Allison [*sic*], brittle, tiny-voiced, her face wrenched down by a
> paralysis of one side is often very droll—usually at the cost of
> someone [. . .]; telling indiscreet things in a faraway, innocent
> voice . . . They are not satisfied, obviously, with Amherst and,
> at the beginning of the evening, remarked that J.M. had a lucky
> position of being here one year, with detachment (money), and
> power (his father's money). Tactless, if accurate, I thought.

His feeling warmed two weeks later when he and Merrill went to the Bishops' for dinner. Encouraged that night by Lurie, who performed Tarot
readings for them that night, they made and used a Ouija board on the spot,
but had second thoughts on the way out the door:

> A Roast, with J. B. carving careful, tiny slices (one had a pic-
> ture of at least two other meals coming from it). But we began
> to feel at home. A bare, college rental, divided up house. Allison
> told our fortunes with Taro cards, at which she's splendid. Long
> white fingers, her crooked mouth and high, careful voice being
> hypnotic. JM + self got poor Ephraim on the board, how we use
> him [. . .]. Leaving, we wondered if—in front of all people—we
> should have demonstrated Ouija in front of her. She loves gos-
> sip. Ah well, would one want to slip through life unobserved?

Jackson was right: whether or not they wanted to be, he and Merrill were
being observed, and those observations would turn up in Lurie's prose.

Over the decades, they would be involved in several ways in her career
as a writer. At first, they were simply an interested, supportive audience for
her work. "I used to read my manuscripts to them," she recalls. "They were
both always flattering, and suggestions came from both of them." Jackson
liked the short novel she showed him, and commiserated when she couldn't
find a publisher. Merrill tended to have ideas about style and plot. Unlike
some poets, he knew the history of the novel, and he liked many kinds of
fiction. Lurie used to hold that "there were three writers you could use to
figure out where someone stood: Dickens, James, and Dostoevski. But that
didn't work for Jimmy," who relished all three. And of course he too was at
work on a novel. For the time being, the three friends were on equal footing
as yet-unpublished novelists.

Lurie had been involved with the Poets' Theatre in Cambridge, and Merrill and Jackson went with her to see the theater's performances of scripts by Richard Wilbur and John Ashbery. She introduced them to her friend V. R. Lang, known as Bunny, the eccentric, effervescent force behind that theater company. After Lang died of Hodgkin's disease in the summer of 1956, Lurie composed a memoir in tribute to her. "I wrote it," she explains, "because I was afraid I would forget about Bunny. People wanted copies. If Xerox had existed, the book never would have." The book was a limited edition of the eighty-page memoir with a cover illustrated by Edward Gorey—which Merrill arranged and paid for to be printed in Munich in 1959. It turned out to be Lurie's break. An editor saw it, asked if she wrote fiction, and the publication of the first of her many novels followed. "If there were no copies of the memoir" in circulation, she notes, "it is quite possible that I would never have been published."

Merrill and Jackson fueled Lurie's later work in another way by providing her with material. Her first novel, *Love and Friendship* (1962), evokes very closely the period of their friendship in Amherst a few years before. The central character is Emily Stockwell Turner, an English Department faculty wife who is alienated from her husband's struggles on the tenure ladder, burdened by motherhood, and bored by the closed society of a small-town campus. She begins an affair with Will Thomas, who, once a promising composer, "doesn't do anything now except play the piano now and then and talk." Lurie narrates the novel from Emily's point of view. But each chapter ends with a letter written by a visiting instructor in the English Department, a novelist with a camp style who describes life at Converse College ("Converse" was the name of the Amherst College Library) with bemused detachment to a painter in New York. In these epistolary codas, Lurie experiments with a voice based on Merrill's: comic, biting, weary, and detached. The novel suggests how important he and Jackson were to her in 1955 as friends who had horizons larger than the Amherst English Department. She called the letter-writing novelist "Allen Ingram" and the painter "Francis Noyes"—combining the middle names of her two friends (Ingram and Noyes) and the names of the protagonists in the novels they were writing in Amherst, "Allen" in Jackson's case, "Francis" in Merrill's. There is also more than a dash of David in the charming libertine, Will Thomas, whose languishing musical talent may have derived from Lurie's mistaken impression that Jackson had given up a potential career as a pianist and composer.

Lurie's fourth novel, *Imaginary Friends* (1967), would draw on her friendship with Merrill and Jackson again, but this time without the identification and approval expressed in *Love and Friendship*. The novel is a satirical story about two male social scientists. While researching a cult, they are bewitched by a beautiful female medium who practices automatic writing and produces block-capital messages like the kind Jimmy transcribed from Ephraim; caught up in the cult's pop-psych jargon and millennial fever, the two men succumb to the folly they came to study. Lurie was satirizing phenomena she was herself intrigued by. Jackson remarked on her talent for Tarot cards in 1955, and she cast horoscopes for her family and friends, including Jimmy and David. Yet *Imaginary Friends* reduces spiritualism to a risible mix of showmanship, vanity, and misplaced libido. She dedicated the novel to David and Jimmy in gratitude for their support of her career. But the story implied a negative judgment on their use of the Ouija board.

She made that view explicit in *Familiar Spirits: A Memoir of James Merrill and David Jackson*, which appeared in 2001, six years after Merrill's death and shortly before Jackson's. It describes their Ouija board experience as a game that got badly out of control, until they couldn't tell what was real and what was not. According to her, the board became a form of self-induced demonic possession, to which Merrill, driven by his ambition to make poetry out of spirit messages, was especially susceptible, and in which Jackson was enlisted against his will. For evidence, she quotes passages from *The Changing Light at Sandover*, as if the trilogy were a factual record of their séances rather than a poetic fiction based on them. "As I read through the last two-thirds of the book," she writes, "I sometimes had the feeling that my friend's mind"—Merrill's mind—"was intermittently being taken over by a stupid and possibly even evil intelligence."

This reaction to *Sandover* is consistent with her initial response to the Ouija board, back in Amherst in 1955. From the beginning, Lurie admits, "I didn't care for Ephraim. [. . .] He was foreign, frivolous, intermittently dishonest, selfishly sensual, and cheerfully, coldly promiscuous." In turn, Ephraim didn't care much for her. When she consulted the board with Jimmy and David, Ephraim explained that she was still at a low level of spiritual development, stage two. In her previous incarnation, she learned, "I had been a nineteenth-century English spinster missionary named Helena Pons-Toby who was sent to Africa to convert the heathen. After a while the heathen found her so annoying that they murdered her." She read the message as a not-so-veiled threat from the heathen lurking in her friends' unconscious.

When Lurie met them in Amherst, Merrill and Jackson were in the midst of the first, electrifying phase of their conversations with Ephraim, and

Jimmy was "greatly absorbed by the Ouija board." He heard more about Stevens from Ephraim ("WS is smiling a lovely smile. He speaks highly of you JM"), and Hans made an appearance too; he was "delighted" to be, as it were, back in Amherst, and he and Jim reminisced about their time together at the college. David said little in these conversations, and his reticence became a topic. "DJ I am amused at U," Ephraim prodded. "U sit there letting JM write and answer + only seem really an integral part of our little soiree when you see him, JM, respond. I am just as interested in you." David defended himself meekly: "I'm used to letting him talk when there's a 3rd person present." "DJ 4give me," Ephraim began on another occasion.

> U want expression the way a child who is too precocious wants it. A larger audience than dear JM + plates + candles. U remind me of a writer of our court who was a sec'y 2 Tibrex's astronomer [secretary to Emperor Tiberius's astronomer] who sat + sat + finally at 36 was discovered 2 have written many moving poems + a history of the senate [. . .]. Brilliant, but 4 10 years we only knew of him as the astronomer's sec'y.

If Jackson was the astronomer's secretary who "sat + sat," Merrill was the astronomer, his eyes boldly set on heaven. He asked Ephraim to send them "prophetic dreams," but the spirit brushed aside the request ("Now now—JM"). Merrill wanted to make creative use of Ephraim, but didn't yet see how to. After their first contact with Ephraim, Jimmy began a poem called "Voices from the Other World." He completed it in November, and Howard Moss took it for *The New Yorker*. It was his first, and for many years it would remain his only, treatment of the Ouija board in a poem. In "Voices from the Other World," Merrill receives a call from the Other World to which he responds hesitantly, diffidently, awaiting further instructions.

He begins by wondering whether these "mute spellers-out" should be called "voices" at all. To represent the spirits' speech, he chooses small block capital letters. These give his verse a wholly original texture and "sound." The capitals were a discovery that he made in verse: the transcripts from the Ouija board that he made in prose in the mid-1950s did not use them. Layering his voice with the spirits' voices in this poem, Merrill combined colloquial aplomb and gnomic urgency, artful syntax and the crude shouting of headlines and telegrams. The board's "voices" were an alternative to and escape from his voice as he was used to rendering it on the page, a voice that, at the same time, becomes notably more casual and colloquial, more natural and intimate in contrast to them. The first speaker is the young engineer from Cologne conjured when Merrill tried the board that first time with Buechner. He is followed by more:

> Our blind hound whined. With that, a horde
> Of voices gathered above the Ouija board,
> Some childish and, you might say, blurred
> By sleep; one little boy
> Named Will, reluctant possibly in a ruff
>
> Like a large-lidded page out of El Greco, pulled
> Back the arras for that next voice,
> Cold and portentous: ALL IS LOST.
> FLEE THIS HOUSE. OTTO VON THURN UND TAXIS.
> OBEY. YOU HAVE NO CHOICE.

Little Will seems like a joke about Merrill's reduced sense of willpower and his regression to childhood play at the Ouija board. The boy ushers in the alarming imperatives, "FLEE THIS HOUSE [. . .] OBEY. YOU HAVE NO CHOICE." The poem steadies itself, shifting focus from the Other World to this one:

> Frightened, we stopped; but tossed
> Till sunrise striped the rumpled sheets with gold.
> Each night since then, the moon waxes,
> Small insects flit round a cold torch
> We light, that sends them pattering to the porch . . .

The danger implied is that the mediums will end up like Shelleyan moths, singed by their brush with the "cold torch" of the supernatural. When they see nothing more forthcoming, however, they settle into a "nonchalant" attitude toward the spirits' demands and threats:

> But no real Sign. New voices come,
> Dictate addresses, begging us to write;
> Some warn of lives misspent, and all of doom
> In ways that so exhilarate
> We are sleeping sound of late.
>
> Last night the teacup shattered in a rage.
> Indeed, we have grown nonchalant
> Towards the other world. In the gloom here,

> Our elbows on the cleared
> Table, we talk and smoke, pleased to be stirred
>
> Rather by buzzings in the jasmine, by the drone
> Of our own voices and poor blind Rover's wheeze [. . .]

"Our lives," Merrill says, "have never seemed more full, more real." Queried by one of the scrupulous copy editors at *The New Yorker*, Merrill replied that Otto von Thurn und Taxis was a "fictitious," not a real, name. Like the old dog Rover (at one point Merrill called him "Homer"), Otto was invented for the purposes of the poem. The one "real" voice quoted in the poem had come from that séance with Buechner. As if he wanted to claim his new experience with the Ouija board for poetry and yet also keep it a secret, Merrill makes no mention of Ephraim and his teachings.

Slight as it is, "Voices from the Other World" is an important poem. Two crucial subjects—the supernatural and Merrill's domestic relationship with Jackson—enter his poetry here, and do so in tandem. Jimmy and David had discovered the Other World, but they didn't disappear into it, like Alice down the rabbit hole. Like a mirror, it showed them to themselves, and it added meaning to their daily life together. Rather than Yeatsian "metaphors for poetry," it gave them instructions for living. Merrill held the poem to a mirror so that Ephraim could read it, and he approved:

> That is what u should feel, a higher sense of the life you have. JM u are an artist. ([JM:] Help inspire us!) I do not like 2 play the parent, but I must say in the work U do, in its vision[,] U recreate in it + then (in?) urselves. U R helping urselves. The happy accident is when work + life + merit combine. [. . .] He like u who begins a work he can do + who only struggles 2 do it do more of it + better, is on his way 2 heaven. That is a law. [. . .] Have courage, revel + faith. [. . .] ([JM:] Are we too frivolous?) Never. I wd see U laughing, loving + devoting all of that + urselves 2 work. That, my earnest loves, is yr way.

Despite Ephraim's confidence in both of them, work went more easily for Merrill than for Jackson. David was proud to see his name in print that fall as the author of a note in the Amherst *Journal-Record* and of a short story in *Semi-Colon* (Merrill's poem, "Three Sketches for Europa," appeared in the same number). But other news was bad. Harcourt Brace rejected his novel; three poems (David had tried his hand at poetry) came back from the *Parti-*

san Review; and his application for support from the Saxton Foundation was turned down. "F—k 'em all," he grumbled.

Showing how it was done, Merrill pushed on in his novel. He hoped to complete it by his thirtieth birthday, but he finished six weeks sooner. Jackson was "ablaze" with admiration: "what a splendid and craftsmanlike, beautiful novel J.M. has done. I am taking careful notes on paragraphs and lines, making suggestions, but more often breaking off, rhapsodically, into praise!" (David suspected that, by means of his enthusiasm, he was trying "to get the novel out of my mind 'as an example.' Setting it too high or too distant to be a marker for my own writing.") Merrill circulated the manuscript next among friends. By July, he had finished revisions and submitted it to Knopf, which scheduled the book for publication in 1957.

The Seraglio, composed with Merrill's thirtieth birthday as a deadline, is a strange coming-of-age story. The broad lines and specific details of his own life are clearly visible in it. His parents are identifiable as Benjamin Tanning, the Wall Street tycoon, and Vinnie, Ben's second wife, whom he divorced years ago. Vinnie has a rather minor role; the action centers on the father and his son. This focus promises an Oedipal confrontation in which Francis will break with his father and his insulated, moneyed world—represented by the Buchanans, Enid and Larry, who are clearly modeled on Doris and Bobby. But the father-son conflict is curiously muted; and the violence, when it comes, is turned against Francis himself in a sensational scene of self-castration. Francis finally reconciles himself to his family and his place in it, but just what this new feeling consists in, and what it means for his future, remains mysterious.

Part of the mystery comes from the fact that *The Seraglio* is not only a coming-of-age story; it is also a coming-out story, a story of homosexual self-assertion and self-acceptance. But the homosexuality of Francis, Merrill's surrogate, can only be inferred on the basis of his refusal of the straight-male potency embodied by his father. For that reason, *The Seraglio* is a contradiction in terms: a secret coming-out story that speaks in symbols, as if in a dream. Its theme is Merrill's sexual self-censorship, his life in the closet with respect to his family and the pain that it caused him. By the end of the novel, Francis has accepted his sexual difference from his father, but that doesn't mean he is a gay man. Rather, Francis is a safely neutral, neutered presence in Benjamin's household, the "unique" in his seraglio. Francis turns himself into a child who will never have to grow up, if growing up means maturing into heterosexuality. *The Seraglio* returns to the problem of aging in *The Immortal Husband* and imagines another deviant life course.

The seraglio is Ben's Long Island beach house, called the Cottage. The novel begins with an act of generational rebellion inspired by the defacement of Doris's portrait in 1953. Francis's niece, Lily Buchanan, is the only child of Enid and Larry, who have a summerhouse nearby. Lily has been confined to her room by her mother after a morning of misbehavior, brought on by the approach of her twelfth birthday and the fact that her mother is pregnant. She escapes from her room, sneaks into her grandfather's house, and, finding an oil portrait of her mother, slashes it with a paper knife. Rushing home, she leaves the identity of the vandal a mystery.

We meet Francis in Rome, about to return home after three years abroad. When he runs into one of his father's business associates who guesses his identity, Francis denies that he is Ben's son.* He hides the fact of his trust fund from his friends Jane, an art historian based on Marilyn Lavin, and Xenia, a sculptor based on Guitou Knoop. When Xenia learns how rich he is, she protests, "How dare you allow me to pay my share all the times we've gone out!" He replies, "I loved it. I felt it was <u>me</u> you liked." Francis suffers from Merrill's self-doubt: he fears that no one will care for him apart from his name and money, both of which come from his father.

The Seraglio is a fantasia on the themes explored in Merrill's psychoanalysis with Detre in Rome. It represents paternal power by the Freudian symbol par excellence: the phallus—which Merrill introduces in a scene early in the novel. Hunting for a souvenir before he leaves Rome, Francis stops in a shop of antiquities that he and Jane had visited together. Seeing that Francis is alone this time, the shopkeeper produces a box containing "perhaps a hundred phalluses, of clay, of marble, some primitive [. . .], others monumental and detailed, evidently chipped from sculpture under whichever Pope had been responsible for fig-leaves." *"Porta fortuna!"* he croaks, promising that the "winged and erect" object catching the American's eye will bring him luck. Francis is embarrassed by the shopkeeper's intuition that he will be excited by these erotic fetishes, and, in irritation, he tries to conceal his interest. He settles for a ring that "looked Greek, of soft gold, with an owl in relief, and very small, a child's ring, found in the grave of a dead child"—like the pinkie ring Jimmy bought in the Istanbul bazaar with Robert Isaacson.

Back at home with his father in the Cottage, Francis is oppressed by a "feeling of loneliness, of being the one real person in a ghostly world."

---

* JM, *Seraglio*, 24. JM did sometimes deny that he was his father's son. Shortly after finishing *The Seraglio*, he told a fellow passenger and Merrill Lynch customer on board the *President Cleveland*, bound for Japan, who wondered if he was perhaps Charles Merrill's son, that his father owned "a small machine shop." JM, journal, September 26, 1956, Jnl 54 (WUSTL).

The grand ocean room makes him feel that he must hold still, like a child obliged to behave. "Wouldn't it help, he brooded, to leap up, cry out, smash something? But the room met his eye so trustingly; it was easier to do violence to himself." If Francis could express his anger, he might feel more adult, more independent. But Benjamin, like his house, makes protest all but impossible. Weakened by his failing heart and yet endlessly gallant, he seems too ill to withstand anyone's hostility and too charming to deserve it. He rules his house like a cheerful, gracious tyrant: "Whatever he decided to serve—whether caviar or humble pie—the victim was meant to choke it down and be grateful. Nobody had ever had a chance to refuse the brutal bounty."

But Francis tries to do just that. He drops in at his father's Wall Street firm to ask his brother-in-law Larry, an executive officer at Tanning, Burr, how to "get rid" of his money. Explaining his request, Francis describes a troubling sense of unreality:

> I don't want the power that goes with money. It's a crippling power; whoever uses it is at the mercy of it. No freedom goes with it. One's forever being watched and plotted against, or else protected from the very things that *don't* do harm! One's never in a position to find out what's real and what isn't—with the result that *nothing's* real, nothing in the whole world is real!

Larry, who wasn't born to money, reminds Francis that he can join the firm any time he likes. Or "if all you want is to have your monthly check stopped, I can arrange that in no time flat." "No," Francis quickly specifies, "I mean stopping it at its source." But that's impossible, Larry explains: the principal in their trust funds "goes to Enid's children, and to your own, after your death." Francis's own future as a father is projected in advance; Ben's money will flow through him to the next generation. "It means I'm doomed," Francis concludes, "I'm doomed never to be real."

Xenia and Jane reenter the story. Francis brings Xenia to the Cottage to make a bust of Benjamin and sets her before his father as a likely candidate for an affair. One night, however, she takes drunken Francis himself for a lover. In shame the next day, he covers his nakedness by putting on her slip: Xenia is "a vampire" who makes him feel like a little boy. Meanwhile, he ponders his feelings for Jane, who has married her sweetheart, Roger, and moved to Boston. Francis travels there with Ben, where Ben will receive an experimental heart treatment. Ben's companion is Lady Good, the wife of one of his business associates and his newest mistress. When the two of them and Francis have dinner with Jane (but not Roger, who is away), Ben is delighted by his son's companion. After dinner, Ben slips money into Francis's hand and tells him, "Paint the town red!" Ben then kisses Lady Good and winks at the young people, as if to show his son how to treat a married woman. Repelled by this display, Francis escorts Jane home. He thinks himself safe from any sexual impulse until he finds himself aroused by her; he flees, deeply embarrassed.

Back in his room, Francis is shaken and drunk. He gazes blankly at his nakedness, and draws a bath. Phrases from the Italian shopkeeper and his father echo in his mind, taunting him:

> His bath was full. He sprinkled it with a handful of pine-scented salts. Before dipping a foot in the water he unlocked the door—it had never been his wish to die—and looked about one last time. There was the mirror, the razor, the towel. He took from his finger the little gold ring with the owl, kissed it and set it upon the basin. Presently he heard—but from where?—the voice of an old man whispering *Ecco, Signore!* and the razor was placed in Francis's hand. Paint the town red! Up to his neck in warm water now, almost afloat, he used his last defense against the flesh. The blade was very sharp; something began easily to separate, then to resist, tougher than a thong of leather. The water, so dazzling clear when he began cutting, turned red instantly. *Porta fortuna!* He could no longer see what he was doing, or tell, when the severe pain overcame him, whether or not he had succeeded. He cried out once, and lost consciousness.

It's a shocking event, reported in a style as dreamlike and determined as the action described. Unable to stop his father's money "at the source," Francis has found another way to cut himself off. He survives this self-mutilation, but the doctor tells his mother when she arrives at the hospital, "It's unlikely, I'm afraid, that he'll be able to lead a normal life, in the fullest sense."

But Vinnie doesn't know the nature of his injury yet. Assuming Francis has cut his wrists, she prepares to face that fact. Keeping this scandal as private as possible is her paramount concern. At first she is relieved as she studies her son's "bare throat, his smooth wrists."

> Mercifully, the wound wouldn't be visible, wherever it was. Her gaze shifted. She froze.
> He had turned towards her a face whose open eyes, though unsee-

ing, expressed wonder and joy. It came over Vinnie that *he* knew, that nothing short of realizing what he had done could have produced the look on Francis's face.

This scene is a fantasy rewriting of the revelation of Jimmy's homosexuality in 1945. His mother had had to face then the fact that her son would not "lead a normal life, in the fullest sense," defined as becoming a father. Here, the son feels "wonder and joy" when he makes his mother confront a truth that hurts and horrifies her. Rather than castrate his father, or risk being castrated by him, he has done the job himself. While the fact is kept from his father because, his mother says, it might kill him, he has struck a blow at her, and he is satisfied.

The novel leaves to our imagination the question of precisely what part of his body Francis has wounded. Even the word "castration" was cut out of Merrill's text "so that the squeamish reader can take it as a suicide attempt, if he must." The uncertainty is consistent with a shift to indirection in Merrill's approach to his protagonist's psychology in the rest of the book. Until the castration scene, Francis is the novel's center, the consciousness through which the reader views its characters and events. When he wounds himself, he blacks out, then recedes from view. Later, after his recovery, we see him through Jane's eyes. Meeting him at his New York apartment, she finds Francis in a distracted state. She notes spilled candle wax, a shattered teacup, pages of scribbling, and a Ouija board: debris from an orgy of communication with the Other World. "You understand," Francis remarks, "I've never had the slightest interest in any of this rot. [. . .] I'd amused myself before with this," he nodded to the Ouija board, "but nothing came of it. It depends so much, you know, on who your partner is." His Ouija partner is Marcello, a suave Italian. Where Marcello has come from, and whether he is a sexual partner for Francis, Merrill doesn't say. We learn only that he and Francis have been in touch with a spirit named Meno, whose story is more or less the same as Ephraim's (except Meno is heterosexual). Francis is obsessed with arranging for the soul of Meno's representative to be born to Xenia so that Francis can take care of the child personally. For Xenia is pregnant, and Francis mistakenly believes that he's the father on the basis of their night together.

This scene was added to the novel late, drawing on Ouija board sessions from summer 1956. The scene that follows it survives from the manuscript Merrill took with him to Europe in 1950. It involves the underworld of classical mythology, rather than the Other World of the Ouija board. With Xenia, Francis and Jane attend the first performance of *Orpheus*, an opera by Tommy Utter—who has become Xenia's lover (and is actually the father of her child). Before the curtain rises, Francis leaves his seat, and we watch the performance through Jane's eyes. It is as if Francis had slipped away in order to reappear onstage as Orpheus (the role Merrill had played in Cocteau's *Orphée* at Amherst). The set, which cunningly imitates the opera house itself, is peopled by infernal doubles of the opera's audience: "Before them, beyond the glowing apron of the stage, could be distinguished the lights and boxes of a theater so like their own that a vast mirror might have been set up inside the proscenium."

The subject of the opera is apt, because Francis's story develops certain motifs from the Orpheus myth. In Ovid, after he fails to rescue Eurydice, Orpheus spurns the love of women for that of boys. So, with his razor, Francis cuts himself off not only from his father, but from women; and after this de-naturing of himself, he journeys to the land of the dead through the Ouija board. His story and Orpheus's further converge in the fact that the leading role in Monteverdi's *L'Orfeo* was written for a castrato. By linking Francis and Orpheus in these ways, Merrill invents a fable concerning his own creativity. Becoming a poet or singer, spurning women for boys, and communing with the dead, all turn out to imply each other.

The end of *The Seraglio* returns to the Cottage one year after Lily slashed her mother's portrait. On the day before her birthday, Francis finds his niece sitting in her grandfather's study, having returned to the scene of the crime. Francis happens to pick up the paper knife, and with this clue in hand, he grasps the truth. It is easy to make the deduction because he and Lily have both rebelled against their family by taking a blade in hand. When, back in the opening scene of the novel, Lily began to brush the knife against her mother's portrait, chipping the paint by accident, she had to go on: "The knife with a will of its own pierced the canvas and tore briskly down five or six inches before she succeeded in letting go." Similarly, with a dreamlike loss of agency, "the razor was placed in Francis's hand." The knife and razor, like a planchette, are impersonal tools. Lily and Francis use them to express not only anger, but also a metaphysical desire: discovering forces beyond (or deep within?) them, they cut through the resistant face of things to see what's on the other side.

The answer is mortality. When Lily frees her hand from the knife, "[s]he closed her eyes. She knew she was going to die." But mortality, as Merrill was beginning to conceive it, was far from simple. Meno teaches that death does not mean "total annihilation." "I tell you," Francis exclaims to Jane, "this other world is *real!*" Yet Merrill stops short of blindly agreeing with him. Half of his mind sides with Jane, who sees that Francis has "dumped the whole burden"—the burden of trying to speak openly and truthfully about himself—"in Meno's lap. It left him free to snap his fingers blithely at history, at human reason," as if he were above it all.

The final scene of *The Seraglio* is a fête at the Cottage. Benjamin by this time is happily wedded to Lady Good, and Francis has brought Vinnie back for a visit. In this fantasy of family repair, Benjamin gets to have a new wife while Francis's mother makes her return: Francis has put the Broken Home back together; the break, an invisible cut, is inside him. On a fantasy level, he has made the reunion possible: it is as if *his* penis had come between his parents and needed to be removed.

In this mood of reconciliation, Merrill's characters gather. The occasion is the christening of Lily's newborn brother, named Tanning Burr in honor of Benjamin's firm. At lunch, the grown-ups gobble the decorations on the cake: "a border of babies," candies with tiny pink faces and liquor inside. The real children survive this cannibalism perfectly well, and Lily's birthday party follows. Francis finds Lily and her friends playing hide-and-seek—practice for the games of secrecy the adults play. Lily invites Francis to play too, but with a condition: "Uncle Francis is It. [. . .] If he wants to play he has to be It." He agrees, counts to one hundred, and then sets out in search of the children—but they've snuck off and left him to play alone. The novel ends with these paragraphs:

> But only after coming upon the children building castles at the sea's edge, oblivious to him, did Francis stare out over the lulled water and understand. He *was* It. He tentatively said so the first time, then once more with an exquisite tremor of conviction: "I am It."
>
> The words carried with them wondrous notions of selflessness, of permanence. His father coughed behind him in the house. The children trembled against the sea. He knew the expression on his own face. The entire world was real.

Borrowing these images of children sporting on the shore from Wordsworth and the mood of hushed epiphany from Woolf, Merrill ends his book with a lyric tableau, rather than a clarifying statement or last turn of the plot. Being "It," Francis is neither "he" nor "she": he has passed beyond self and gender, the burdens of his money and his name, and found a permanent, impersonal identity, which he gained by giving something up. Now, "[t]he entire world was real." The modifier includes every possible reference, both the Other World and this one. There is a feeling of triumph and relief; Francis has nothing to fear, not even from himself.

And so, with respect to his family, Merrill seems to insist that they have no reason to fear him. *The Seraglio* imagines a position for Francis that was like the one Jimmy would occupy in life: he would come and go in Southampton when he liked, neither quite belonging to the Merrills' and Magowans' world nor wholly alien to it. He would be his nephews' and nieces' queer uncle.

What Francis gives up to achieve his neutrality is "the power to harm" symbolized by the phallus. But *The Seraglio* itself hardly renounces "the power to harm" in the case of the people who provided readily identifiable models for its characters. The point was not lost on its first readers, who saw it exactly as a betrayal, and a fearsome one at that. Lurie put it down and picked up the phone: "[S]he is shocked that JM would publish it, saying it's 'too naked,' " wrote Jackson. Others felt similarly. Irma was "upset"; she told Merrill that he had taken "a cruel way out" of his conflict with his family. "Are you Planning to Move to Another Country?" she asked. Detre, accustomed by trade to the costs of speaking freely, came to a different conclusion: "[I]t is as shocking as you warned me," but "if being shocked is the price your family and/or society must pay for great writing, it is not too much."

Merrill sought legal advice as a precaution in the event of a libel suit. At the request of his publisher, he went so far as to submit a legal release for Knoop to sign, which she did. But the real issues the novel raised were moral rather than legal ones. Merrill debated them with a friend he could trust, Ephraim. The spirit told JM to tell those friends who opposed the novel's publication that "all art is its own reality." But *The Seraglio* was too close to real life for this argument to hold water. The problem, Jimmy told him, was that the novel was "hurting people." "Life is not painless," Ephraim replied, jettisoning his argument about the special reality of art. "Books inform, not soothe." But Merrill came back to the point: "the truth hurts." If the truth had to be avoided because it hurt, Ephraim declared, it would be impossible to "read, live, or write it." *The Seraglio* was meant to prove Merrill could write the truth, even if it hurt.

Pain is at the center of the novel in the castration scene. When Jackson got off the telephone with Lurie, he laughed: "What she really wanted to know—avid as she is—is JM castrated?!?" Merrill told him what to do the next time she called: "If she asks or hints at this, I want you to draw yourself up and say, 'That I can't divulge!' " It was a funny line, but there was much more at stake than teasing Lurie. In Francis's self-castration, Merrill dramatized the pain of his sexual self-censorship in a way guaranteed to horrify and disgust his family, while showing them what they had, in effect, asked for.

When the book was published, the pain was widely distributed. Lillian Coe was portrayed as greedy, scheming Irene Cheek, whose husband Charley is a weak-kneed drunk and cuckold. Merrill, suggesting his view of the Coes and Southampton gossip, disposes of the Cheeks in two brisk sentences when they drown in a sailing accident, and their bodies are "badly mutilated by sharks." He liked Lady Constance Saint and treated her with respect and affection. But "Lady Prudence Good" is a ludicrous name, and Connie Saint must have been aghast to see her adulterous romance with Charles Merrill adapted for the plot of his son's novel and available for the public to read about in hardcover. Finally, no one whose name appeared in the *Social Register* could be proud when tipsy Boopsie Gresham corners Francis and demands, "Do you now, looking straight into my eyes, *dare* to deny the ethos of the Anglo-Saxon race?"

Enid and Larry Buchanan embody that ethos in the novel, as their models, Doris and Bobby Magowan, did in life. Larry is a war hero and a practical man of affairs whose financial savvy and common sense make Francis look foolish when he consults Larry about eliminating his trust fund. But Merrill doesn't let Bobby off the hook so easily. Habitually turning red in the face and snorting with derision, Larry is brusque and irritable with his wife and daughter, and narrowly concerned with the bottom line and the family's reputation: a dull heir to the business empire of his father-in-law. Merrill treats his sister gingerly, even tenderly, in his depiction of Enid, who has beauty, elegance, smarts, and a talent for social delicacy worthy of a character in James. But she is infantilized by her loyalty to her father: this perfect daughter uses all her energy to keep up appearances and push away pain, which she pays for with the torturous headaches Doris habitually suffered from. It's Enid who created the "swamp of chintz" that makes Benjamin's house so oppressive.

The Seraglio flagrantly breaks the code of family loyalty Doris insisted on when she and Jimmy argued about Guitou in 1953. He made partial restitution by dedicating the novel to "my nephews and nieces." Even that gesture had its subversive side, however: one of the novel's aims was to recruit allies for Jimmy from the next generation. Merrill Lynch Magowan, Doris's second son, the inspiration for Enid's "Tanning Burr," was a teenager when the book was published; he read it avidly with a mental "scorecard," keeping track of the local targets hit. His older brother Robin was in a position to identify with Francis. Having begun to think of himself as a writer and to quarrel with his parents over his sense of vocation as well as his romantic choice of Betty Rudd, a Radcliffe girl he had met at Harvard, Robin made his uncle feel "really encouraged, even at times a Prophet" as the author of *The Seraglio.* Jimmy went so far as to urge Robin to enter psychoanalysis. Like a sweet-tongued serpent, he tempted his nephew: "[Y]ou are so knowing, how can you resist knowing more?"

Merrill didn't show the novel to his father until he had sent the manuscript to his publisher and there could be no turning back. But he showed it to his mother before he made revisions. Even in the case of this novel, he wanted his writing to be something he *could* show her, which she could be proud of too, and show to others: as at every step in his career, his literary ambition was constrained by her ambitions for him. *The Seraglio* put this principle to the test. And their exchange about the book was one of the important battles they fought.

It was prepared for at a lunch in Hellen's honor hosted by David and Sewelly at 950 First Avenue in April 1956. Jimmy was in New Jersey, where he would usher at the wedding of Freddy Buechner and Judith Merck. Judy's family was prominent in drug manufacturing, and this was to be a grand occasion, a Lawrenceville reunion with champagne toasts and dancing. The plan was for the Jacksons to drive to the ceremony with Hellen, following a lunch for her when they would break out "all the disguises and subterfuge of our cozy married life," as David put it, coaching Sewelly in advance. They'd argued about this sort of deception before. Sewelly told David that she felt "cheapened by pretending to be married for easier acceptance with society. [. . .] I want to feel true and honest!" "Then," he said, "she accused me of being amoral. Which, perhaps, I am." But it would be hard to say who was fooling whom. Hellen can't have failed to grasp the nature of David's relation to her son, even if Jimmy's letters downplayed how often David had "visited" Amherst. The point for Hellen—and therefore for Jimmy, David, and, grudgingly, Sewelly—was only how plausibly they could pretend. And everyone passed. When the wedding was over and it was time to say goodbye, Hellen gave David's wife a hug that, as Sewelly experienced it, "went on and on. I thought it would never end!" They were all engaged in keeping up the social lie that *The Seraglio* protested.

David recorded his lunch conversation with Hellen in his journal. After the meal, "she finally put elbows on the table and spoke her mind, as best she could, about JM's Seraglio. She was hurt and bitter, appalled at what she thought of as his callous and deliberate insult to everyone who had 'done the best in the best way they were able' for him." David "urged her to write it to JM if she could not say it to him." He was impressed: "HP can be all charm, almost sensationally so. She misses nothing, forgets no name, catches people on little asides and remarks, and plays the comic whenever it pleases her." Her sociability was part of her toughness: "Such a mother, as Sewelly says, is almost impossible to resist and formidable to stay eye-level with. One admires JM all the more for realizing all the firmness necessary in any love for her, and however reluctantly, using what must be a family firmness in their dealings."

Hellen wrote the letter that David urged her to. She simply passed over the castration scene, treating it as unspeakable. But otherwise she didn't mince words: Jimmy's novel was "inconsiderate, disloyal, and downright callous." Her son replied in a letter displaying his "firmness." "I have had to ask myself, with every point you make, whether I have failed to communicate or whether you have failed to understand," he began, ready to prove why the failure was hers. Enid and Larry are not "ridiculous," he insisted; or if they are (and if Francis is "ridiculous" when he puts on Xenia's nightgown—a scene Hellen especially hated), that's because we see their "limitations" as well as their virtues, as we should expect in a novel, and they are "not necessarily the less lovable for it."

Hellen's objection to her portrayal as Vinnie was stronger and harder to answer, since there was a lot to object to. *The Seraglio* introduces Vinnie with a stifling monologue unbroken by comments from her son or the novel's narrator. Speaking to Francis from her bed, she begins, "Run into the next room, dearest, and bring me a little cushion [. . .]—that's a good boy." Finally, after almost three pages of cloying small talk, she breaks off: " '[I]t's,' she kissed him, '*so* wonderful to have you back. Wait! I put some lipstick on your chin. Bend down, I've a Kleenex right here.' " After which Merrill dryly concludes, "These were a few of the things Francis's mother said to him on the occasion of their first meeting in over two years."

Hellen was particularly hurt that Vinnie "bored" her son. Jimmy replied, "[W]hat I have tried to dramatize here is the failure to communicate" on both their parts since she confronted him about Kimon and expressed her "disgust" in the winter of 1946:

> Since that time, I recognize that you have made a tremendous effort to withhold judgments or questions about my life. In fact, I realize more and more that (but for this particular tact on your part) the silence is largely my own. As in the novel, it isn't that you don't let me talk [. . .]—I don't let myself talk. I would rather tax you with silence, and I know it taxes you, than with things you might not want to hear. No—that has all kinds of false impli-

cations, as if anything <u>more</u> I might tell you would be by definition dreadful. Closer to truth might be to say that, after seeing
how you were appalled <u>once</u>—or even twice, counting the matter
of the letters at 231 E 35 [when Hellen entered her son's apartment and destroyed correspondence from Friar and others]—by
something of the foremost importance in my life, I have to
admit that at these times I fear you, I fear your power to create
guilt in me to a degree that nobody or nothing else in the world
can equal. It should not be necessary to point out to you how far
from boredom such a feeling must be.

"You can perhaps see, though, how useful the mask of tedium is," Merrill
continued, discovering a new depth of feeling, "considering all that lies
beneath the surface. <u>That</u> is by no means purely fear; there is love there,
as strong as in childhood—how can you imagine one ever loses that love
for parents? Any other, yes, but not that one." He would never, could never
lose that love for his mother, which was "as strong as in childhood." But
that love, mixed with fear and guilt, brought with it a "fierce pressure" he
needed to protect himself from:

> The important thing to say is that the "mask" is kept on not by a
> whim or any cold decision; it is kept on by a fierce pressure—one
> that only a greater pressure (such as my wish now to be honest,
> preferring to hurt you rather than let you imagine I am indiffer-
> ent to your feelings [. . .]) can dislodge. There! I have a sense of
> breathing freely. I am not for a moment afraid of giving pain <u>if</u>
> I can admit not only the coldness from which that proceeds, but
> the warmth as well. I feel I am acting <u>Fairly</u>—and that this fair-
> ness lies behind the book I've written.

Commenting on the novel, Hellen made no distinction between Francis
and her son; she refers to both of them as "you." We might expect the novelist to object to this confusion of life and art, but he didn't. It was how he
himself thought of the story. *The Seraglio*, he declared, was "a symbolic unity
analogous to my own experience in the last 10 years; it has been carefully
composed and is as accurate as I can make it without its being unbearable
to myself or others," since "my experience hasn't, after all, been <u>that</u>." He
was not saying his experience had been less painful than the novel makes
out, but that he had had to take that pain, he *could* take it, and other people
should be able to take it too.

When the novel was published, Hellen wrote to Doris, commiserating with her about the picture of her father in it. At the same time, Hellen tried to justify the novel by quoting the letters Jimmy had written to her defending the book. She felt responsible for what he wrote, especially about his father. She feared that, in Doris's eyes, Jimmy had cast his mother in a bad light, and she needed to insist that his family disloyalty was not hers. When she fought with him over *The Seraglio*, she was still trying to make her son behave. Whether as a source of pride or of shame for her, her son's writing was never fully his own.

Jimmy didn't move to another country, as Irma had suggested, but he did give up his West Tenth Street apartment and moved to Stonington permanently with David. He made a bid on the property at 107 Water Street, and closed the deal in June, paying $6,000 and taking over the building's $5,000 mortgage. It gave them a home together. Yet they planned almost immediately to leave on a trip around the world in the fall. They would be gone a long time, almost nine months. It was "a daring dream" they'd been discussing for two years.

The new novelist was still a poet. He published two poems in *Poetry* in February 1956. One of them, "Upon a Second Marriage," was composed in 1950 for the Plummers' wedding* and presented "for H. I. P." (with no mention of her new husband). Its conceit is this: a life is like a tree in an apple orchard; after spring blossoms and summer fruit, "autumn reddens the whole mind"; but even for one who resists "the old persuasion," spring returns, and "the whole world grows / Fragrant and white" again. This is, the poem insists, a perfectly natural pattern of renewal in which new bonds add to prior ones without canceling them, creating a series of expanding circles, like the rhyming lines of this poem's stanzas. Thus "a tall trunk's cross-section shows / Concentric rings, those many marriages / That life on each live thing bestows"—each ring like a wedding ring that doesn't oblige one to give up the past and forsake all others. Merrill wanted to understand the history of his own heart this way. The poem was meant to reassure his mother, as if she needed it, that his love for her remained "as strong as in childhood" when they lived with his father at the Orchard.

The poem was a dutiful, ceremonial production HIP could show to Atlanta friends. Beside it, Merrill printed another sort of poem entirely,

---

* JM to HIP, letter, October 5, 1950 (WUSTL). A handwritten text of the poem was inscribed "For his mother's wedding / 7 October 1950."

"Salome." The center of it, the second of three parts, is a fable about the violence just under the surface of family life. As a child, the "I" of the poem saw a boy run out to welcome home "his runaway pet," only to be "fearfully mawled" by the chow—which the speaker's father promptly shoots dead with a pistol. The poem's sympathy is with the chow. The dog, following his natural curiosity, had disappeared "Into the brambles of a vacant lot," where he forgot the "back porch, whistle, and water bowl," and soon reverted to "his first nature, which was animal." The moral is clear. The family that wants you for a pet, and subdues you with sweet caresses, cannot tolerate your animal nature. If you give in to it, you may be shot. Even as a child, the speaker "suspected what I now know as law: / That you can have enough of human love."

In March, Merrill read his poetry at Harvard. He had been anxious about the event in advance. "I cannot promise very much by way of a 'stage presence'—have very little to say about my work," he told his inviter. He "would feel more comfortable sharing the evening with another poet," and he proposed David Ferry as a "co-star" (he and Ferry, who overlapped with him at Amherst in the 1940s, had become friends on his trips to Cambridge that year). After the reading, Merrill recorded seventeen poems for the Woodberry Poetry Room at Harvard, starting with work in *Short Stories* and winding up with "Orfeo." That tape is the earliest record of his reading voice.

He gave another reading at the Poetry Center in New York. Then, back at Amherst, he hosted a visit to campus by Marianne Moore. Before her reading, he and David served dinner for her: "roast beef, potatoes, peas, crème brûlée—an elderly Poet's menu," Jimmy wrote to Hellen (with no mention of David), "as I'd discovered last fall the day I had two dinners in honor of Frost [. . .] with exactly the same meal." For Merrill, Moore was "pure enchantment." She appeared "in a chalky faded blue ankle length dress with lace around the neck." He found her "all generosity and modesty and simplicity, and of course she is one of the half dozen poets of the century (I said so in introducing her)." At one point in her reading, Moore interjected a comment about her young introducer: "Now Mr Merrill tells me that he doesn't read the newspapers. That's hard for me to understand. Just last week I learned from the NY Times that our State Department is donating all those egret feathers confiscated by the U. S. Customs during the '20's to the Kingdom of Nepal, where they're needed. How would you find out about something like that if you didn't read the papers?"

In the evenings, Ephraim continued to give JM and DJ lessons in the workings of the Other World. He described a soul-switching system whereby a ghost enters the body of a sleeper for a single night in order to sever ties with life while the soul of the sleeper, making room below, takes the place of the revenant "Up There!" Ephraim had met Guitou this way: she'd been transported in sleep to "the Sixth Stage" where "Ephraim wooed her and made her promise to marry him!" "The funny thing is," Jimmy mused, "she has told D. and me about this wonderful dream that had left her free from all death-fears." (Merrill would later retell this story in *The Book of Ephraim*, claiming that Dante's vision of heaven was based on this sort of soul switching. But he assigns the dream there to dignified, mystical Maya Deren, rather than silly Guitou.) Eager to see Ephraim also, Jimmy and David tried hypnosis. They discovered that David was highly susceptible to suggestion. With Jimmy serving as hypnotist, David wrote his name in his child's hand, recalled certain scenes from childhood, and met a glowing angelic figure.

By summertime, the New York apartment was packed up, and Merrill and Jackson were back on Water Street, playing with the Ouija board night after night. They did the board with Irma, Stonington neighbors, and Hellen's spiritualist friend, Gert Behanna. Frederick "Boom-Boom" Beck, a friend from Amherst days, who was himself "in furious communion with the spirits," arrived in town on a mission: a literal-minded spirit had told him he could find his father reincarnated in Australia; to locate him, he needed only contact "Grandma at 32," and he wanted help from Ephraim to put through the call. Ephraim was offended by this abuse of the board: "No one is a grandma at 32," he cracked. Jimmy and David themselves were not immune to this kind of thinking, however. David, ever more desperate to get published, asked Ephraim to "infuse" the manuscript of his novel with magic powers so that Random House might accept it. Ephraim scolded him: "Now this is serious. DJ U must rely on yr work. If you are proud of it that is the compensation. [. . .] I have joshed with U about my poor powers. Yr own are more real. But DJ persistence is the greatest power of all."

If the spirits couldn't help the mediums, could the mediums help the spirits? Ephraim told them that Hans's representative was due to be reborn, and wondered whether Jimmy and David knew a suitable pregnant woman who might give birth to this hapless creature whose recent lives had all been ill-fated. (This séance worked its way into the plot of *The Seraglio*.) Jimmy volunteered Betty, his stepsister, who had married and was expecting. Ephraim noted the suggestion. But with the "hysterical" Boom-Boom as a case in point, Ephraim warned that there were limits to how the dead and living might aid each other: "No real dead suggest any involvement.

That is why I am still with U. U have not become dependent on me nor I on you. It wd be quickly ended, not by us my dears but by yr own sense. I know I am a diversion + an enlightenment at best, but I am not life and I cannot B as important as life."

Life in Stonington that summer included Truman Capote. "He is divine. Strident, earnest, hard as nails," Merrill said about the pale, squeaky-voiced Capote, who was already a best-selling writer mixing with the glamorous society that Merrill had definitively turned away from when he moved to Stonington. "He is not liking it here very much," Jimmy went on. "His boat keeps sinking. The other night he waved goodbye to friends on the street only to have a boxer dog leap from a car and sink his teeth into his little hand [. . .] . . . his writing hand." Capote didn't last long in "Creepyville." Jackson picked up the nickname for the little town and went on using it, though not out of any special affection for Truman. Perceiving what their friends preferred not to notice—the basic imbalance in Jimmy's and David's means—Capote ridiculed his neighbor as a kept boy. "Tell me, David," he poked, "how much do you get a throw?"

When Merrill completed revisions of *The Seraglio* in July, he turned to a dramatic monologue called "Mirror."* "A book, a window, another's face," Ephraim had said, "any surface concentrated upon will produce messages. Statues have spoken, and mirrors been moving dramas." "Mirror," testing the idea, is the strongest, most original poem Merrill wrote in the 1950s. His mirror suffers under the strain of being looked at by the young year after year as if for guidance:

> I grow old under an intensity
> Of questioning looks. *Nonsense,*
> I try to say, *I cannot teach you children*
> *How to live.—If not you, who will?*
> Cries one of them aloud, grasping my gilded
> Frame till the world sways. *If not you, who will?*

While inquiring faces come in and go out, the mirror stays put. It speaks with the wisdom of one who dwells in an interior world, like an old woman content to sit in her parlor, or a painter satisfied with still life:

---

* Merrill sent "Mirror" to the poet John Fandel, with whom he shared his new work in this period; he refers to it in a letter to Fandel on September 9, 1956 (Fandel).

> Between their visits the table, its arrangement
> Of Bible, fern and Paisley, all past change,
> Does very nicely.

The mirror understands that there are other ways of looking at things. It turns to the window:

> If ever I feel curious
> As to what others endure,
> Across the parlor *you* provide examples,
> Wide open, sunny, of everything I am
> Not. You embrace a world without once caring
> To set it in order. That takes thought. Out there
> Something is being picked. The red-and-white bandannas
> Go to my heart. A fine young man
> Rides by on horseback. Now the door shuts. Hester
> Confides in me her first unhappiness.
> This much, you see, would never have been fitted
> Together, but for me.

The mirror and the window stand for competing types of imagination. One is "Wide open, sunny," and transparent, while the other is lamp-lit, melancholy, reflective. The window "embraces" the world "without once caring / To set it in order." "That takes thought," the mirror observes, rather sharply. Maybe it envies the window's openness and warmth. But it expresses pride and impatience when it tells Hester's story in a few rapid sentences: "This much, you see, would never have been fitted / Together, but for me." The poem's unusual verse form is the one Merrill created in "The Octopus": the last syllable in every second line rhymes with the penultimate syllable of the previous one. This buried pattern slyly "fits together" free-verse lines of unpredictable length, just as the mirror links disparate images "Out there" in the world. The "thought" required to order experience in this way is self-conscious, reflexive: to say that we need the mirror to see the world means that we can only look out at things by also looking at (and thus through and beyond) ourselves. The mirror stands for a poetics of subtly encoded meaning and self-conscious technique, opposed to transparency. Indeed, "Mirror" is a sort of manifesto, a passionate reply to the poetry of "open form" derived from Ezra Pound and William Carlos Williams that was fast gaining adherents in the later 1950s.

On another level, "Mirror" echoes the conversation that Merrill had been having for three years with Jackson about his work. If the window's warmth and openness are David's strengths of character, its shortcomings are his weaknesses as a novelist: an inability to fit a story together, a lack of focused "thought." In June, David had found Jimmy's reaction to his most recent draft of a novel "devastating." The problem was technical: "I am episodic for want of connecting the dramatic sequences of the novel." The mirror's anger hints at Jimmy's mounting frustration with David's difficulty telling a simple tale like Hester's (Look how easily it's done! the mirror says), and his anxiety about what his companion's failure as a novelist might mean for both of them.

On still another level, "Mirror" suggests Merrill's dissatisfaction not with Jackson's novel writing, but with his own. For all of its strangeness of plot, *The Seraglio* is a relatively conventional realist novel, a window on the world; and once Merrill sent off the revised manuscript to Knopf, he abandoned that form for good. Already, in order to represent the person that Francis becomes, Merrill had had to expand the realist premises of *The Seraglio*, moving into the realm of symbol and myth with the Ouija board and the Orpheus story. He began making notes for his second novel immediately after finishing *The Seraglio*. But *The (Diblos) Notebook*, when it appeared in 1965, would be a very different kind of book—an anti-realist *nouveau roman* that self-reflexively calls attention to its own process. It is the type of novel the mirror might write.

"Mirror": Merrill was aware of how close the noun is to his name. Over time, mirrors became iconic for him, an obsessive emblem of his creativity. By speaking for the object in this poem, he spoke for aspects of his taste and temperament that were essential to his art but difficult to stand by. In the mirror, he identifies with interiority, discrimination, artifice, and a frankly superior tone; and he all but dares the reader to accuse him of narcissism, or the superficiality and selfishness, the vanity, for which gay men are derided. Its voice is the cold, hard voice of a "mask" like his mother's. But the mirror is aging and vulnerable. "Why then is it / They more and more neglect me?" it asks about those young faces as they grow older. The children prefer the window's "tall transparence" to the mirror's prismatic reflections; their "grown grandchildren" prefer it too. The mirror describes two of them gazing outside "with novels face-down on the sill." One of them exclaims airily, in a tautology both clumsy and poignant, "*How superficial / Appearances are!*"

On the final page of *The Seraglio*, Francis stands alone in an ecstatic present, fearing death no more. The mirror, by contrast, is haunted by time and mortality. The end of the poem plays with the fact that a mirror's surface

decomposes in rippling circles and black stains as it loses its silver back-
ing. The remark about the superficiality of appearances introduces Merrill's final turn of thought:

> Since then, as if a fish
> Had broken the perfect silver of my reflectiveness,
> I have lapses. I suspect
> Looks from behind, where nothing is, cool gazes
> Through the blind flaws of my mind. As days,
> As decades lengthen, this vision
> Spreads and blackens. I do not know whose it is,
> But I think it watches for my last silver
> To blister, flake, float leaf by life, each milling-
> Downward dumb conceit, to a standstill
> From which not even you strike any brilliant
> Chord in me, and to a faceless will,
> Echo of mine, I am amenable.

The black, spreading "vision" gains intensity as the rhyme sticks on "ill,"
pounding on that sound five times before the poem gives in, and the mirror
becomes "amenable." The "milling- / Downward" of each "dumb conceit"
is an image of a humbling breakdown of metaphorical "order." The mirror,
so proud of its power to fit things together and keep up appearances, comes
apart as "a faceless will" takes over, a power beyond appearances that hints
at the Other World of Ephraim, "where nothing is."

On their side of the mirror, Merrill and Jackson were busy homemakers.
That summer, 107 Water Street was wrapped in scaffolding while workmen built a terrace and a glassed-in studio on the roof, put in new gutters,
reshingled, and then painted the whole affair "a kind of chocolate-eggplant
with very dark trim and dazzling white shop-fronts." But the renovated
apartment on Water Street would stand empty until they returned from
their epic, around-the-world trip. First, Jimmy went south to pay his
respects to the Plummers and Mis' Annie. On August 5, he left a page for
David:

> While I'm away
> Please water the plants every other day,
> Not forgetting

The window-box requires a thorough wetting
In dry weather. Feed the cats
According to your own judgment, but plentifully, I beg.
One teaspoon and a quarter Vionate a day, perhaps one egg
In the time I shall be absent, and that's
That. Except for the most important part
Of all. Work on your novel. Work on your novel. Art
Outlasts the small trivialities of the daily grind.
Keep that in mind.
That and the improviser of this didac-
Tic page. He will count the days till he is back.

On the same page, DJ welcomed his partner back:

While you were away,
Plants, cats, and novels may
Have suffered some;
But none of us com-
Plained, as much as me—
See?
Now that you're back
Keeping track
Of all of us,
Cooking, suggesting, sus-
Taining—
Who's complaining?
Not me,
See.

Jimmy's visit with Mama, he told her, did him "an extraordinary amount of good"; it put the two of them "on more of an equal footing." Hellen had sent Jimmy a box of documents from the time of his parents' divorce, including letters from Charlie, sworn statements from the servants defending her honor, and once-urgent telegrams. "Even those letters—CEM's for instance—seem, if only retrospectively, woefully adept, as if he were forever saying 'What can best be <u>said</u>? I shall set about feeling <u>that</u>,' " Jimmy wrote to her. It confirmed "my description of him in the novel—that even then he should have been such a showman." Hellen must have shared with Jimmy this archive of divorce in order to produce the effect it had: this renewal of their whispering intimacy at his father's expense. But he didn't simply take his mother's side. He was interested to learn from certain letters that "Daddy and I both" had felt the strain of Hellen's "remoteness": CEM called it her "shell" while JM called it her "mask." Jimmy allowed that she'd used it for self-defense, to shield herself from Charlie. Perhaps, he told her, "your incapacity to cope with me in 1946 was nothing but a long-range effect of that disaster 10 years before." He understood from his own behavior, modeled after all on hers, that "when we suspend feeling, we get out of practice." His father was different from both of them: "He of course has never had that trouble; he is a virtuoso, a Paderewski."

Charlie's virtuosity may be one reason why Jimmy didn't take his deteriorating heart condition as seriously as he might have. In July, CEM was back in the hospital in Boston, where he sounded "dreadful" on the phone. His condition had not improved by September. Yet Jimmy went forward with his trip abroad. He noted in a letter to his mother that Lady Saint had flown from Barbados to see his father for a single day. "Strange . . . ," he trailed off. He seems not to have considered that Lady Saint had come to say farewell to a dying man. Jimmy too visited his father in late August. "I think Daddy is a bit better," he wrote to Hellen, "but still in a very sorrowful state. He has sores in his mouth + hadn't been able to eat." Jimmy sat by his bed, reading aloud from a commissioned biography of his father, who "hung on every word with the greatest interest." Doris urged Jimmy to plan to return from Asia in January to see his father, and he said he would. On September 3, back in Stonington, he told Ephraim "CEM is dying" and asked, "How long will he last?" Ephraim explained that CEM had been close to death several times, though his recent "approaches have been closer and closer." "Can one resist death?" Jimmy wondered. "O yes each morning U cd sleep on," Ephraim said. ("I could," DJ put in.) But CEM's resistance was wearing down. Ephraim put a date on the time left to him: "1 year 2 go; before another winter." "Will I really return in Jan. from Bombay to see him?" Jimmy asked. "Ah JM u will not. He will not press u. It will interrupt his grand farewell with life." "So I'll see him again though," Jimmy said, sheepishly asking for reassurance, which Ephraim supplied: "Longer than u suppose."

In New York, Merrill signed a contract for *The Seraglio* (he'd written the book without one) and made out his will. Maisie was handed off to Sewelly, like Henry James's heroine being sent to one of her stepparents. The Rover Boys had booked passage by ship from San Francisco to Yokohama. In San Francisco, they visited Doris and Bobby. With Doris running the household, she and Bobby and their bright-eyed boys in matching clothes were photographed for a magazine feature as "Togetherness Family of the Month." "No More Tilting at Windmills," read another article with a photo of Bobby, now the no-nonsense CEO of Safeway supermarkets, whose business was booming as suburban homes jumped up across California. It was a pleasant visit for all; so far the "Togetherness family" hadn't read *The Seraglio*.

The Magowans' world of fine things and high finance stood in contrast to the scene at the Poetry Center, where Jimmy had been invited by Robert Duncan to read from his plays and poetry. Allen Ginsberg had just published *Howl*, a book that included a poem about meeting Walt Whitman in—no doubt—a Safeway supermarket, and the sensational Beat poets were national news. Ruth Diamant, the Poetry Center director, fretted about audience reactions to Merrill's poetry in advance: "I hope there's no trouble . . . ," she fluttered as she escorted him to the stage. The Beats were out in force. But Jimmy's encounter with the "wild little group of Zen-hipster poets" didn't make for a historic East-West battle. After they'd heard him read, Ginsberg and Gregory Corso gave him some friendly advice. "What's the matter?" he quoted them. "Why don't you scream? That's what people out here want! Embarrass yourself! Talk about cock! We'll do anything if you just <u>scream!</u>" At the reception, Ginsberg and Corso enjoyed the spread by constructing great cold-cut sandwiches for themselves, took off their shoes, and read "<u>their</u> poems in squeaky, faint voices," showing Merrill the way. The next day, he gave away his copy of *Howl* to Kay Meredith, Bill's sister, who had come with Bob Grimes to see him and David off at the pier. Merrill fussed about the inferior cabin they had been assigned, and Jackson sweated to get them a better one. Then the ship pushed off, "the long paper streamers sank or snapped," their friends grew tiny, and they steamed under the Golden Gate Bridge into silence. Surprised by his sadness at that moment, Merrill suddenly understood "why death is spoken of to children as 'going on a trip.' "

Japan was not simply a foreign country. It was the symbol of the Foreign, a land of decadent European fantasy which Merrill knew through the *Japonisme* of French poetry and painting, Puccini, Gilbert and Sullivan, Yeats's Noh-influenced plays, and now R. H. Blyth's *Zen in English Literature and Oriental Classics* (a gift from Kay Meredith, and a book the Beats also were reading). Jimmy sent home from Japan treasures that would become part of his daily life. He also brought back attitudes and images that would be worked into poems. It was a place he would return to—one of many stage sets for the drama he was creating out of his life. But it would have special significance for him, being, as it turned out, the place where he absorbed his father's death.

Neither the *Mikado* nor R. H. Blyth prepared him and David for the

Tokyo to which Meredith Weatherby introduced them. "Tex" Weatherby,
an American expatriate and one of Guitou's many lovers, translated Yukio
Mishima's novels. (They didn't meet him on this trip, but Mishima stayed
with Merrill and Jackson once they got back to Stonington.)* They shopped
in the Ginza District; took in the scalding tubs of Tokyo Onsen, featuring a
steam bath, milk bath, mah-jongg club, and cabaret; and wandered among
the brothels of Shinjuku and the penny arcades of the old town, Asakusa,
with its bright pachinko parlors and ancient temple of Kannon, Bodhi-
sattva of Mercy. For nightlife, Weatherby took them to the Silver Dagger,
a gay bar, and Starlight Chrysanthemum Water, a working-class bar cum
strip club, for a glimpse of its star, Sada Abe. Twenty years earlier, Abe had
been convicted of a spectacular sex crime: murder by strangulation of her
lover, after which she cut off his sex and carried it away in her handbag. Her
prison term behind her, this latter-day Salome enjoyed a celebrity afterlife
as folk hero. Every night at the club, she made a grand entrance, searching
the eyes of the drinkers while they hooted and whistled, crossing their legs.

On hand those first nights was another American, a friend of Weatherby's named Donald Richie. Tex didn't stick in Jimmy's life, but Donald
did. Bighearted and sharp-eyed, equally comfortable in the memoirs of the
Duc de St. Simon and the louche bars of Athens, Richie became one of Merrill's closest friends and an intimate confidant. He was already an unusual,
self-invented man. Two years older than Jimmy, he was broad-shouldered,
assured, and quietly adventurous. He had grown up in a middle-class home
in the flatlands of western Ohio, where, like many people in Depression-era
America, he spent his free time in the movie theater. After serving in
Europe in the war, he joined the American occupation forces in Japan as a
typist. Soon he was writing "human interest" stories for *Stars and Stripes*.
He learned to speak Japanese fluently, and the language gave him access to
that culture in a period when it was still mysterious to Westerners. Having arrived less than two years after the U.S. Air Force firebombing of
Tokyo, he was in a position to watch—and interpret for English-speaking
readers—the prodigious transformation of postwar Japan. He moved on
from journalism to write short stories and fables, novels, travelogues,
and cultural notes. He studied Zen. Before he could speak Japanese, he
haunted movie houses, focusing not on the plot, but on cinematic effects
and performance styles. He became an experimental filmmaker himself,

---

* Merrill kept a letter from him, a thank-you note that Mishima sent after visiting Stonington, composed in the prim English and careful hand of a student of the foreign writing system. Yukio Mishima to JM, letter, August 13, 1957 (WUSTL).

and established himself as an authority on Japanese cinema, a friend of the directors Yasujiro Ozu and Akira Kurosawa, and their influential expositor in the West. All that lay in the future, however, when Donald took Jimmy and David to the top of Mount Tsukuba to gaze at miles of rice fields below, and mighty snow-crowned "Fuji disclosed Himself." Jimmy took the cable car down while, with Donald, David ran "singing and laughing down [the] green mountain."

On October 1, Jimmy wrote to his father about *The Seraglio*, which he had sent to him before his departure. The question was how to think about "the connection between real life and fiction." Jimmy admitted that, when they talked about the book, he himself had spoken

> as if Lillian were Irene, you Benjamin, myself Francis. This, you must realize, is a brutal oversimplification. One starts with a situation, if you will, that corresponds to something that has happened in Life; from then on the major work begins—inventing, composing, smoothing, and patching until the book is a fiction. In my treatment of Francis I project into make-believe, certain insights I have had about myself—ways I might act, things I might do, much as one does things in dreams that it perhaps never occurs to one to do in waking life. It has been the same with the other characters; the elements that I have taken from life, I have taken because they fit into the imaginative scheme of the book. This may not keep people from being hurt—It didn't keep me from painful feelings as I was writing. But I have tried to be as true to my experience as possible.

Charlie never read the novel or the letter. Telegrams from Hellen and his brother Charles reached Jimmy on October 5: his father was "very ill." He phoned Southampton and spoke with Doris as well as Charles, who had flown in from Paris where he was living that year. CEM, he learned, would "not last more than a day or two. A helpless feeling," he wrote to Alice B. Toklas, "this great distance—luckily the two other children are with him." He decided not to fly back home, even if it meant that he would miss his father's funeral. What he would miss, he told his mother, was not "the feeling of being helpful, or of seeing Daddy one last time—but the feeling of being helped, of being with Doris and Charles and with or near you, because it's to us that he has mattered most; and because by oneself, without family, there is nobody's example to get through days like these."

Merrill had of course put himself at that "great distance," which made it impossible to be close to his father and his siblings in the end, although he may very well have felt that the distance between them was his father's fault; Charlie had left first, at the time of the divorce, and now he was doing it again. Charles Merrill died on October 8, 1956. The immediate cause was "uremic poisoning," brought on by the radioactive iodine that he had been taking for his experimental heart treatments. There was a funeral for him at the Church of the Ascension on Fifth Avenue; he was buried in Palm Beach.

In the days before his father's death, Merrill chose simply to "let things work on me." He and Jackson went to the seaside town of Kamakura to visit the Daibutsu. Once housed in a temple, which was washed away by a tsunami in the fifteenth century, the massive, placid statue of Buddha sat in the open air, a monument to detachment. The Americans were getting used to the protocols of Buddhist temples and chose paper fortunes. "Mine good, D's fair," Merrill noted at one stop—the usual imbalance between their prospects. In Kyoto, they visited Ginkaku-ji, the Silver Pavilion Temple with its stark Zen garden of raked sand, and pondered the exalted view above the city at Kiyomizu-dera. They saw ancient cherry trees propped to keep them alive like venerated elders. They strolled in gardens "designed to resemble somebody's description of paradise," studying the manifold varieties of moss. "Over and over the point is reached where Art and Nature cannot be told apart," Merrill wrote, contemplating the presence of craft, design, and meaning everywhere they went. In their socks in the Shogun's rooms in Nijo Castle, they saw screen after screen that depicted, in vibrant, flat panels of color, a lonely crane, a stately peacock, gnarled pines, swirling rivers, and swirling clouds, the seasons turning as they passed from one room to the next, under the control of art.

News of Charlie's death reached Jimmy in Kyoto. Hellen wrote to her son describing how she had placed her wedding ring from Charlie among the flowers on his casket, and at last Jimmy cried. "My tears are, still, I guess, partly for myself," he replied to her, "that I wasn't there; but partly too for the terrible way in which death smoothes out all the anxieties and confusion to reveal the feelings one hadn't really been aware of feeling, they were so choked by pointless fears and awkwardnesses." The same day that Jimmy wrote to his mother, he received news from his father himself. Ephraim reported that in heaven CEM was once again "surrounded by pretty ones." Jimmy wanted to know how he looked. "O quite handsome in a green suit. 32 I would say. A beautiful smile. He asked 1st 4 his father [and] was relieved not 2 find him." Due to be reborn in two months, CEM advised his son, "Beware of the money" (he was "most sorry for that"). As to his recent change of state, he said, "Better to be in yr heart than on every-body else's shoulders." Like Jimmy, he was "bored by the eulogies." He was worried about his son Charles, and asked Jimmy if his brother had talent. Jimmy responded with some measured reassurance: "In teaching, family, maybe in writing." "He is my problem," CEM sighed. "Am I yrs?" JM asked. "U r very nearly my only claim to fame," his father said, exaggerating con-siderably. "I have felt so strangely these days," Jimmy replied, "grieving for you, as though I were you, shedding your tears . . . ." "I am the same old fool," CEM returned. "I love u Jimmy. That is enough. Now enjoy it all."

During these days in Kyoto, Merrill visited Katsura Rikyu, the Detached Palace, and, struck by the name as much as the site, he wrote a short poem, "Kyoto: At the Detached Palace," about emotional detachment and letting go. It is a silent elegy for his father, whose death the poet is too detached to mention. Also sightseeing in Kyoto was Arnold Toynbee, the British historian celebrated for his twelve-volume study of the rise and fall of civilizations. Merrill was struck by the newspaper commendation of this distinguished visitor, as rendered for him by his Japanese guide: "His magnanimity was apparent to all who met him. Never once did he show his true feelings."

From Kyoto, Merrill and Jackson traveled on a cog railway, creeping up steep green gorges, to Mount Koya, the center of Shingon Buddhism. This temple complex, founded in the ninth century, was the vision of Kobo Daishi (also known as Kukai), the sage who brought Esoteric Buddhism to Japan from China. Interred on the mountain, Kobo Daishi dwells eter-nally in a state of meditation in anticipation of the Buddha of the future. His mausoleum is the center of the largest cemetery in Japan, a vast city of the dead—which Merrill and Jackson approached down a long avenue lined by tall cedars and red maples. It was "the most magnificent place we have seen yet." They stayed in one of the monasteries and sat cross-legged for morning and evening prayers as saffron-robed priests "made weird sound effects with bells, woodblocks and their own voices." At one point, the sage of the West, Professor Toynbee, "a tall, ethereal man" who was fol-lowing the same itinerary, "drifted past in a cloud of incense and bearded priests."

At Hiroshima, Merrill and Jackson surveyed another necropolis. To visit the city, Merrill told Buechner, "is one of the most painful experiences imaginable."

Oh, some of it is built up, a big shopping section, a few buildings that either stood up under the Bomb or were purposely designed in the style of 1910 to look as if they had. But the rest—! mud streets, great empty purposeless lots full of rubble and strange stunted trees, trunks like toothpicks. [. . .] In the middle of this wilderness rise up 3 modern cement buildings, the New Hiroshima Hotel, the Peace Museum, and a special museum with a poorly-named "Grill Room" upstairs. The Peace museum is given over to displays related to the Bomb, from scientific charts and diagrams all the way to the end of a child's thumb, with nail, brown, dry, cooked, which dropped off during the five days before the little boy finally died. This is displayed with a photograph of him in school uniform, a sickly-delicate face, great big eyes, even the picture somewhat faded. Melted rock, flattened bottles, scorched clothing, photographs of horrible burns, a shot of Truman at the telephone—and beyond the plate glass, that filthy flat field with a man on crutches picking through a garbage pail. Well . . . I had never for a moment, before this, felt, what my brother would call, the national burden of guilt; but there we couldn't meet people's eyes.

If Hiroshima was what history, what the rise and fall of civilizations, looked like, it was horrifying, and Merrill wanted none of it.

By contrast, he was at ease in the theater and fascinated by the traditions of Japanese performance. In Tokyo and Kyoto, he sat for daylong programs of Kabuki, from which he found it "impossible to tear oneself away." The stage's garish colors, the actors' outsized gestures, the zany humor, sudden twists of plot, and protracted, "quavering" death scenes, carried the essential effects across the language barrier. Merrill learned the language of Kabuki's hyperconventional elements: the *hanamichi*, a narrow walkway reaching into the audience, used for exits, entrances, and exciting scenes; the *mie*, the pose that an actor strikes and holds, crying aloud, to indicate his intentions (and command applause, like a Verdi tenor with both arms raised at the end of an aria); the *kuroko*, the stagehands dressed in black and therefore "invisible," who supply a desperate hero with his weapon, or reveal the "blood-red undergarment" meant to represent a mortal wound; and the *kesho*, the white makeup and painted lines that mask the actors and indicate the vice or virtue they embody.

Part of Merrill's fascination with Kabuki had to do with gender. He and Jackson saw Nakamura Utaemon perform, a fabled actor of female parts who inherited the stage name of an eighteenth-century master of female impersonation which had been passed down over generations. In Kabuki, there are no women actors. Merrill saw their exclusion from the stage as consistent with male dominance everywhere in Japanese culture: in Japan, "[w]oman [. . .] doesn't matter much. She has less face to lose and proportionately more 'personality' than her refined husband. *He* knows that he invented her, that she is part of the Dream"—a male fantasy in which woman is costumed and scripted to act in certain ways. "At one time, the [Kabuki] actor of women's roles learned many a trick from geisha," Merrill goes on, teasing out an irony of cross-gender emulation. "But I think there must have always been geisha in the audience, white-faced, attentive, getting pointers on how to be themselves." When geishas study female impersonators in order to emulate the type of women whom the actors are imitating and audiences desire, the notion that gender is a natural human attribute, and one that will align with sexual desire predictably, simply falls away: another instance of Art and Nature confounded. But Merrill doesn't leave the thought there. Giving it another twist, this one with sardonic implications for gay men, he reflects that men themselves do not reliably impersonate the object of desire: "In the end, perhaps, even man falls short of the Dream."

Merrill also saw Noh drama and the puppet theater called Bunraku. He found the Noh simply "bewildering"; it would take a second trip to Japan, thirty years later, before he was enthralled by this ancient, hieratic mode of performance. The Bunraku puppets lent themselves more easily to appreciation and analysis. Their veiled, black-costumed manipulators "cluster, 2 or 3 to a puppet, like embodied passions," Merrill felt, noting however that the faces of "the master manipulators" are "exposed." These shadowy manifestations of impulse and convention cause "the eyebrows to move, the fans to slam shut, sending the actor onto his knees or into the air, sleeves floating, mouths wagging. [. . .] It all gives rise to a most peculiar theory of psychology, a New Meaning to the phrase 'to be moved . . .' "—an alternative to the throes of romantic passion and the Freudian unconscious both.

Merrill was exhausted by Japan. At last, he stared at what he had bought to send home to Water Street: a noble Tokugawa-era treasure chest, a deep blue cotton kimono with the pattern of a stream, more kimonos, another chest of drawers, prints depicting Kabuki actors, ladies in kimonos, and children playing, masks, tea bowls, clog shoes, fans, and "a huge Doll of a Warrior that David found in a flea market for $1.50 [. . .]—[. . .] it stares at me while I write, and gives no inkling (this goes without saying) of its true feelings."

.   .   .

Robin Magowan reflects on his uncle's lifelong wanderlust: "Jimmy wasn't a travel writer; he was a writer who traveled. He wants something new from a place. He collects objects and people. But he's not interested in the place." He did that collecting on this nine-month journey not only with his wallet, but, as usual, with his typewriter, which he unpacked at each stop. When he is typing in his bathing suit under a straw awning on the beach in Ceylon, it's hard to say whether he's in the scene or outside it, at work or at leisure, in the moment or thinking ahead to the point when he will be looking back at it. As he did in Rome, he used his correspondence as his journal: he typed letters on carbon paper and kept copies in a binder, to which he added notes, jotted on a blank page or at the bottom of a letter. He put his letters to use in "The Beaten Track," a series of travel notes written en route which appeared in *Semi-Colon* that winter. The title disclaims in advance any excitement or novelty he might offer, being painfully aware of the conventionality of the wish to see and describe exotic places. The tone of the piece follows suit: snide, taut with contained anger, and mixed with frustration, incapacity, and even something like hurt. "It *is* very lonely here, with no way of sharing in anything," Merrill says of Japan. "The language barrier is severe; that of manners, monstrous. One can endure just so long the hours spent drinking tea, or trying to get a straight answer, or holding some inscrutable ornament to the light in one's great clumsy fingers."

Hong Kong was a stopover. There was more shopping, this time for suits, shirts, and shoes. Merrill knew that the cost of the clothes said something about the quality of the lives of those making them: "It is painful to imagine people working all night long embroidering monograms at 5 cents an hour or something like that." The small children begging were still harder to contemplate. "As in Japan," he told his mother, "the cheapness of human life is a very chilling spectacle; one sees how it has helped form the glorious spiritual attainments of the East. The Chinese, I was once told, believe that man should resemble water, forever seeking the lowest level, effacing himself. But it is one thing to be effaced by oneself or by other Chinese; another thing to be effaced by Englishmen or Russians." He met a Mrs. Church, an English businesswoman who had lived in Hong Kong for forty years. "[S]triking the table and glaring about," she complained to Jimmy and David that "[t]he young people here now, [. . .] have no conception of empire-building!"

Bangkok was different. "This is the land of heart's desire," Merrill wrote to Rosie Sprague, who was confined far away in a Massachusetts sanatorium, being treated again for tuberculosis. Here people smiled at him mildly, like the antique Buddhas he admired. Gazing at the small boats heavy with shining goods, the canal-side houses on stilts, and the temple exteriors glittering with gold leaf, he compared the atmosphere to "the kind of spirit you find in Congreve, Couperin, the architect Borromini—an air of being a trifle too chic and therefore, out of sheer ennui, using dangerous, perishable mediums, ornaments that the underlying structure may or may not support; the fun is in the uncertainty." To climb to the top of a temple—the flights of interior stairs growing steeper as one square roof opened to reveal the four walls of the next platform—was to enter a secret place created for beauty and contemplation, like "the heart of a quatrain by Mallarmé."

Jimmy and David got high in another way when they spent the night in an opium den. Puffing at that "black bead" bubbling "far, far off" in the mouth of the pipe, "I tried too hard and was sick, but David had visions all night long of unknown charmers and moonlight on leaves." Robin notes that "Jimmy was really sick. He told me that his heart stopped and he thought he was going to die." That didn't stop him, however, from going back and trying a second time: Bangkok's fanciful temples, he supposed, must have been created from a vision like David's opium haze, and he wanted that experience.

During their three weeks in Thailand, Merrill was loosening up, as "The Beaten Track" suggests. After his account of Japan, he relaxes into a note on Bangkok, which concludes with two comic vignettes. The first describes a visit to the home of a new acquaintance, a friendly young man named Chew. "That fat lady is my mother," Chew says to Jimmy and David, innocent of the insult he is giving. Most of one room is taken up by a homely shrine: "twenty Buddhas on bleachers, surrounded by flowers, photographs, extinct incense." In a shrine to other gods, Chew displays snapshots of himself beside pictures of Elizabeth Taylor and James Dean: he plans to make his name in Hollywood, as they did, he explains. Then Jimmy and David put on sarongs and casually bathe with him in the river. Before they part, he signs a photo for them: "To my best American friends. I hope you will not remember me."

Merrill's touch is very light in all of this. He gives us no reason to look down on either party in this intercultural exchange; he only asks us to appreciate with him a gentle comedy of manners. The same feeling comes across when he describes himself pressed knee to knee with an American woman on the bottom of a delicate river craft paddled by a Thai prince. At the end of their jaunt to some ruins, Merrill swivels his head abruptly. He has just a moment to glimpse the prince's annoyance—a reflection of the haughty young man inside Merrill himself?—before the boat tips over, and suddenly "we were all three waist-deep in the warm exhilarating water."*

The next stop was Ceylon: "ELEPHANTS KNEELING IN MANGER," Jimmy telegrammed his mother on Christmas. He and David journeyed on from Bombay and Madras to New Delhi and Karachi. They saw the Taj Mahal and a fort in Agra, bought Moghul and Rajput miniatures, and admired brilliant saris everywhere, while doing their best to look past the extreme poverty and abject human suffering. Somewhere on high, according to Ephraim, hungry spirits "howled" to take possession of living souls. Jimmy and David had just escaped: Jainist spirit-priests struggled and failed to extract their souls one night as they slept; "they claim U r 2 earthbound and healthy[.]" Ephraim's attitude toward India was disdainful. He called Vedanta a discipline for "dullards," which he compared to "gymnastics." But then Ephraim scorned all spiritual disciplines except "that of living."

When they brought out the Ouija board in India, the mediums learned that Ephraim had followed Jimmy's advice and arranged for Hans's representative to be reborn to an Elizabeth Plummer—who was not, however, JM's stepsister, but another Betty, and not a suitable mother at all. There were consequences for all concerned: "HL [Hans Lodeizen] in his disappointment with a wretched mongolian has let me say protested and I have had many restrictions put upon me. I no longer have such interesting work 2 do, and I am often threatened with losing you. It wd be possible 4 me 2 be completely discredited by an agent." "An agent?" Jimmy replied. "How Kafka!" The spirit world was policed, it seemed, and there were rules, about which Ephraim was now explicit: "I can tell U anything but I must be sure U will not do anything abt it + U can tell me anything but we must not set up our own little system." He reported that CEM had been reborn to a Jewish haberdasher living at 3 Rogers Lane, Hampstead, in London (parents chosen, it would seem, to gratify the old clotheshorse and Anglophile—while teaching him a lesson about his anti-Semitism). Jimmy might look for the little boy's house or ask about him "at the greengrocers" but that was it: "we must not do do do anything [. . .]. Imagine the confusion!"

---

* JM, "The Beaten Track," *Prose*, 331. Merrill's published account is much more restrained than the slapstick reality recorded in a letter to Claude Fredericks: conveyed by the Prince, "a notorious pervert," with his American companion in the "itsy-bitsy boat, a mere dried peapod," Merrill was "just thinking, how far I had travelled in how many directions since, oh, Jacksonville, when suddenly I moved my head to avoid being hit by the dock and over we went, the three of us, into the warm green water. The Prince's eyes narrowed, thinking possibly: why must these Americans force democracy on us? In another boat, D. was fracturing himself laughing." JM to CF, letter, December 12, 1956 (Getty).

Merrill was deep in English fiction at the time. He read *Bleak House* in India, entranced, and went on directly to *Dombey and Son* and *Our Mutual Friend*. The colonial bureaucracy of India was positively Dickensian, it struck him, as he and David arranged to get their newest round of purchases to America and themselves to Europe. The Suez Crisis canceled their plans to sail through the Red Sea to Cairo. They flew instead to Istanbul, that "astonishingly beautiful city" where they savored the treasures of the Seraglio, before moving on to Rome, where Quinta and Dr. Simeons greeted them, as well as a crew of Americans on holiday: Bobby Isaacson and his wife Jane, the William Jay Smiths, the Browers, even Bernie Winebaum. From here on, the trip would return them to familiar places and people. In Vienna, they met up with Charles and Mary Merrill and their children. Charles was writing a historical novel, which Jimmy mildly praised. Charles had had no role in *The Seraglio*—no doubt happily, from his perspective. The choice made sense—Charles's filial rebellion had removed him from his father's retinue long before—but even so, it was pointed: a brother's presence would have compromised Francis's position as the "unique." After five days in each other's company, it was clear that CEM's death had not brought the brothers closer. As usual, his half brother struck Jimmy as "remote, perhaps unhappy, pompous, disinterested."

In Munich, German friends of David's shepherded them through the wild parties of Fasching, or Carnival, keeping them up past dawn on Mardi Gras in costume—David sporting a Chinese jacket, Jimmy a kimono and clogs. Since Rome, Merrill had been wearing, for the first time in his life, contact lenses. He marveled: these and a jet black cape produced "marked personality changes." They retired to the mountains in Switzerland, snuggled in the quaint high dairy country of Appenzell, where Jackson had begun writing his first novel in 1949. It was for him a bittersweet return to that idyllic setting. After being interested in that novel enough to ask David for revisions, C. Day Lewis at Chatto & Windus in London wrote to turn down the book. Merrill called it "a horrid disappointment." This was the closest DJ had come to commercial success. Now he proposed to friends—for example, the Lavins—that they collaborate "on a bosomy sexy Italian Novel." He was entirely serious: they could write whatever part of it they wished and simply assign him a role. He planned to publish it under the nom de plume "Hope St. Argent" ("Hope sans argent, get it?").

By now, Merrill had a copy of *The Seraglio* in hand, and it was time to face the question of what other people thought of it. He directed Knopf to send clippings to his mother. He and Hellen were still arguing over the book. She felt, after CEM's death, that it shouldn't be published, or should at least be revised. "I honestly don't see what Daddy's death does to change it," replied Jimmy, who felt he had created "a very true and lovable portrait": "Now that he is gone I'm more than ever glad to have made a kind of memorial that will offset some of the obvious garlands anybody could contrive." He also decided against Hellen's advice not to "prepare" the Magowans for the book, since that would increase their apprehension and make a "fair reading" unlikely. His mother complained that she didn't know how to answer when friends asked her what the book was about. Jimmy made two milquetoast suggestions: "old age, or: the difference between 2 generations." When it came to the reactions of friends and family, he urged her just to brazen it out, and "by showing a minimum of embarrassment," to convince everyone there was nothing to be embarrassed about. This was the approach he would take.

Jimmy himself was satisfied. *The Seraglio* seemed to him, he told Hellen, "very strong, not just as 'writing,' but as a vision of life, of a life if you will, glimpsed and expressed." If that vision was cold, as she charged, that might be "a quality of my sensibility at present, or a primarily esthetic matter: a kind of 'academic palette.' " He continued, "But as for the picture itself, and your saying I have chosen a subject unworthy, I do not even need, in order to disagree with you, to resort to the painter's tenet that all subjects are potentially worthy." For that matter, "what other subject, at this early stage, have I at my fingertips? what world comparable in complexity + richness to the formed world I have watched since infancy[?]" As to his relations with that world, he felt better now about Daddy and Doris too; and "where you are concerned," he ended, "I think you have seen how not the writing so much as the fact of the book's having been written + being the book it is has led us into a much more open relationship; simply, perhaps, a relationship, there having been precious little before." Soon after that, Hellen forwarded to him "an astonishing letter" CEM had written to Jimmy "that his sec[retar]y had kept for a year and a half[.]" In it, Charlie urged him "not to be swayed by anyone, in or out of the family, concerning the novel, and to say whatever I chose about 'Benji.' "

Still, the novel was a great deal for his family to swallow, even sympathetic Robin. "I was astounded by the anger in *The Seraglio*," he recalled. "Jimmy is saying"—to his parents, to the rest of the family, to everyone—"you wish my essence were not in existence. That rejection was devastating, and he wrote a devastating book in response. He knew that people would be angry and he didn't want to deal with it. So he went abroad." Jimmy had expected to return to America in March; in the end, he stayed in Europe all the way into summer, lying low. Doris and Bobby got their copy in March, and Bobby wrote praising it vaguely (Robin said his father never read it).

That was enough to be a relief: Jimmy had wondered "how deep in villainy I had dipped myself." Superior manners on all sides allowed him to pretend otherwise, but Doris was injured on too many counts to get over the book easily. She did not speak to her brother for two years. He'd chosen to focus his satire on her and her family for complex reasons. He was jealous of her intimacy with his father. He also understood Doris's compliant relation to the old man, and in attacking her, he was attacking part of himself. Above all, he knew his sister was a peacemaker and one day would forgive him.

Gerrish Thurber could imagine how Jimmy's family felt. Exercising the authority of a mentor, he wrote a letter forcing Merrill to admit some misgivings. The novel, Jimmy replied to him, "was written in something of a trance, there was the illusion that everything in it had to be (not altogether dispelled, that illusion), and [only] when all the work was done did I begin to perceive Consequences. I realize all too well that the link between Consequences and Motives is all too real—but I feel now that, with the book, I have reached the end of a long dark period that could not otherwise have been reached but by writing as I have, not only the novel, but a number of rather hard and cold poems," by which he probably meant "Salome" and "Mirror."

The reviews were not gratifying. Critics simply did not know what to make of Francis's story. They were put off by the novel's wealthy milieu (one quoted Fitzgerald's line to Hemingway: "The very rich are different from you and me") and baffled by Francis's sexuality; most simply avoided mention of the castration scene, and none of them used the word. The *Nation* called the novel "a Freudian diagram" and complained of its "unreality"—as if the book and Francis suffered from the same condition. The *Atlantic* described Merrill's protagonist as "an inadequate man, damaged by his background, who retreats from love and sex," and seemed to blame the author for it: the portrait of Francis, like Francis himself, was "faltering and unsatisfactory." *The New York Times* stressed the pure strangeness of the story. Its review quotes Francis's remark—"How weird"—when he learns that his father's heart treatment will not eliminate pain, only prevent him from feeling it. The review predicts that "the average reader" will say the same thing about "this excellently phrased and often witty yet somehow remote and casual novel": "How weird!"

The Seraglio is indeed a "weird" book, but the repeated charge suggests a queasy distaste on the part of reviewers in excess of the novel's peculiarities of genre and plot. It wasn't easy for Herbert Weinstock, Merrill's editor, to recruit support for the book to begin with. When he asked Richard Wilbur for a blurb, Wilbur replied with a sentence that, although just and nicely phrased, Weinstock couldn't use or even show to Merrill: "I think that James Merrill is one of the best young poets in America; the only thing that puts me off his poetry is the extent of his preoccupation with neurosis. I have, of course, the same reservations about his first novel. I am glad to say—and I hope you will find it acceptable for your purpose—that *The Sera-glio* is witty, well-shaped, finely written, and thoroughly desolating."

Wilbur's reference to Merrill's "preoccupation with neurosis" points to the homosexual subtexts in his work—for which the novel's reviewers had no more precise word than "weird." Resigned to their judgment, Merrill turned the charge of strangeness around by blandly remarking upon "how strangely other people experience things." His faded tone disguises the fact that the novel's reviews were a massive disappointment to him; he'd counted on them to defend him against opprobrium and justify the work. Detre had said that his family's pain was not "too high a price" to pay for "great writing." But no one but Detre had called this writing "great."

Jimmy and David journeyed up the Rhine. Their goal was Amsterdam, where they saw their Stonington neighbor George Copeland—"in a tail-coat (and a tizzy)"—make his return to the recital hall, to modest applause. Through April and May they zigzagged across southern England and northern France, seeing Alice B. Toklas, Tony Harwood, and Charlie Shoup in Paris, and Umberto Morra in London. Their pace was desultory, their enthusiasms mild. "Conceivably," Merrill mused, "we are far, far beyond new experiences." When the *New Amsterdam* pulled up at the pier in Chelsea at last, Claude and Sewelly met the world travelers. They put Maisie in the car and drove home to Water Street.

6

WATER STREET

1957–61

During the next four years, Merrill published two books of poems: *The Country of a Thousand Years of Peace*, in 1959, and *Water Street*, in 1962. *The Country of a Thousand Years of Peace* collected poems that were written over an eight-year period, starting in 1950. Most of the poems in *Water Street*, a shorter book, were composed rapidly between spring 1958 and fall 1960. To open *Water Street* just after closing *The Country of a Thousand Years of Peace* makes an impression. The poet speaking in "An Urban Convalescence," the first poem in the book, shows a colloquial ease and intimacy, a fluency and urgency, which are not found in the polished, poised, oddly abstract poems of the earlier book.

The development implied a new understanding of the relationship between his life and writing. The poems in *The Country of a Thousand Years of Peace* are a collection of symbols and epiphanies drawn from experience but set off from it in an ideal, timeless space, a Switzerland of the imagination. In *Water Street*, Merrill acknowledges that time is passing, and his poetry is not exempt from it. If the first title is literary and general, the second one is local and particular: it calls attention to where, and by implication how, the poet is living. The task Merrill set himself was to come to terms with his life in the process of inhabiting the world imaginatively and emotionally, day after day; and the metaphor he found for this process was the making of a house, a dwelling where he and his readers could be at home.

It was natural for Merrill to think of his poems as a kind of house, because his house was a kind of poem. In his father's homes in Southampton and Palm Beach, Kimon's rooms at Amherst and on Poros, Claude's Pawlet farmhouse, Umberto's Cortona estate, and Alice B. Toklas's flat in Paris, he had seen how rooms could collect the story of a life, and how the inner life of daydream and memory might express itself in a home, as in a work of art. He liked the fact that "stanza" was the Italian for "room": "given arrangements," whether of poetic form or interior design, were structures to be inhabited, where the self could be apprehended in a daily dialogue with spaces and objects. He pored over Gaston Bachelard's *Poetics of Space*, which describes the house as a "shell" or "nest" for poetic reverie. Yeats's Tower and Pope's Grotto intrigued him. As a student at Amherst, he'd gazed at the windows behind which Emily Dickinson wrote her poems, and brooded on his hero Proust, writing in his cork-lined bedroom.*

The apartment to which he and Jackson returned from Europe in 1957 was much changed. Up to this point, Merrill had worked on a sideboard in the dining room. Now he had a study of his own in a small, west-facing room overlooking Water Street. He turned his desk and typewriter away from the harbor view. A silhouette of Hans's profile—a gift from him—stood propped on volumes of new poetry. Jimmy lay on a small daybed to read, or sat on it cross-legged with a deck of cards, playing games of Patience between drafts of a poem. The other side of the study door was fitted with shelves; when it swung shut, the room vanished behind a wall of books. The study was Ali Baba's cave, a room hidden inside other rooms. When the house filled with guests, Jimmy disappeared behind the heavy, creaking door, maintaining his routine of morning and afternoon work at the desk. Catherine Merrill, Jimmy's niece, remembers that when she visited Water Street with her family or on her own, that room was "strictly off-limits."

A sharp turn at the study door led up a short steep flight of stairs to the attic, now remodeled as a spacious room, the biggest in the house. The north side of the room slanted under timbered eaves; windows facing south let in sun. When the contents of the West Tenth Street apartment came out of storage in June 1957, a long, stiff-backed Queen Anne couch and a shining grand piano, a Steinway Merrill had purchased in 1947, went soaring four flights above the street "in the jaws of a yellow crane," and were

---

* On the homes of Dickinson and Proust and the idea of the writer's house generally, see Diana Fuss, *The Sense of an Interior: Four Writers and the Rooms That Shaped Them* (Routledge, 2004).

safely deposited in this top-floor room with a harpsichord that Merrill had bought in Rome, a memento of his days with Bobby Isaacson. Larry Rivers's pastoral view of Water Mill covered the back of a freestanding bookshelf; his paired portraits of Jimmy and David hung downstairs. Black and white squares of linoleum made the floor a chessboard. The room was a lair, a "high retreat." Sliding glass doors gave onto a wide wooden deck where the small, interlocking rooms below opened to a view—beyond treetops, shingled roofs, chimneys, and cupolas—of sea and sky, answering to another side of Merrill's sensibility. The deck baked in the sun and glowed under the moon or stars. Seagulls sailed by at the same height, as voices drifted up from the street. Jimmy and David could lie there naked, tanning, or sit talking with friends over drinks, and yet be hidden from view: only the tower of the vacant Baptist church next door saw "eye to eye" with them.

Merrill installed a telephone in an alcove at the bottom of the stairs. He stood and talked while his right hand sketched on what paper came to hand, his squiggles turning into "sunbursts, garlands, creatures, men" (as he says in "The Doodler," a poem composed that year). Or he pulled the cord into the sitting room, reclined on a small chaise, and looked down at Water Street through colored panes. The alcove was now a tiny music room with a record player and a growing collection of classical recordings. Merrill listened to song cycles, chamber music, piano, and opera, from Mozart and bel canto to Wagner and Strauss. Bach, Mozart, Schubert, Beethoven, and Schumann dominated, but there was lots of French music, too, from Rameau to Fauré, Satie, and Ravel. Merrill's preferred performers were mid-century virtuosi like Pablo Casals and Artur Schnabel (the complete Beethoven piano sonatas in 78 and LP) and the sopranos he'd heard in the concert hall and opera house so often: Maggie Teyte, Lotte Lehmann, Elisabeth Schwarzkopf, and Kirsten Flagstad. Ralph Kirkpatrick, a Yale professor with whom Merrill became friends, performed the complete Scarlatti sonatas and Bach's *Well-Tempered Clavier* on the harpsichord. There were only a few lighter touches—such as Ruth Etting, "The Happy Singer of Sad Songs," the jazz balladeer Don Shirley doing standards like "Someone to Watch Over Me," or the Neapolitan folk singer Roberto Murolo, whose gentle strumming Merrill evokes with envy and irony in a poem written three decades later, "Self-Portrait in Tyvek™ Windbreaker."

Painting ranks below music in the hierarchy of the arts propounded in *Sandover*, but pictures covered the walls on Water Street. These included work by figures from the New York art world: Fairfield Porter, Nell Blaine, Grace Hartigan, Rivers. A tempera image of a bird in profile called *Time of Change* by the mystical Oregonian Morris Graves hung in the dining room. From Merrill's father, after his death, came a landscape by Maxfield Parrish—shadowy trees and a pale twilight sky—and a misty mother and child from the "Maternité" series, a piece of gloomy camp, by the French Symbolist Eugène Carrière. Ghika's small woodcut of a black swan, frontispiece for *The Black Swan*, moved from one room to another over the years. A pair of geisha in big Japanese prints guarded the door that led to the study and upstairs. A watercolor bouquet by Proust's friend Madeleine Lemaire, the model for his Mme. Verdurin, hung in the sitting room behind a Louis XVI chair. The stairway leading to the apartment was decorated with etchings by Philippe Jullian portraying characters from *À la recherche*.

The surfaces of the house—windowsills, bureaus, tabletops—filled up with curious objects. Some of these were toys and trinkets, talismans and totems. Others, like the pair of Empire candlesticks on the dining table, were finely crafted things. Still others were ingenious, like the Tanagra figure set in a glass lamp which came as a gift from the Lavins. Most of these objects were inexpensive; they derived their value from their place in Merrill's life and imagination. They were a lexicon he used for self-expression, even while they entered and shaped his writing, as if, in thing-poems like "Prism," "Willowware Cup," and "Radiometer," objects were using *him* to express themselves.

Mirrors symbolized that reciprocity. The apartment accumulated them, beginning with the wall mirror Jimmy and David propped upright in a chair facing them during their early séances. The surface of a decayed-looking glass in a gilt frame opened black-edged holes like the "blind flaws" in the mind of the speaker of "Mirror." Sitting in the recessed frame of another mirror, a tiny porcelain shepherd dozed among his reflections. The apartment's prize was an enormous Venetian mirror framed by a proscenium of "gilded palms and sphinxes," which Jackson brought home when the new owners of a mansion on Main Street gave it away. This unnervingly large mirror stood in the sitting room, "Exactly six feet tall like Christ our Lord," as Merrill puts it in *Sandover*. Backed by bookshelves that walled off the front door, it was revealed only when one walked fully into the room and turned to find it staring back—an uncanny surprise for the first-time visitor.

Merrill liked the sense of being looked at that his mirrors produced. He also liked how they redirected light, multiplying it. Light filled the house from morning sun to evening's lamps and candles. It was refracted by crystals and prisms, and tinted by beach glass, colored bottles, and bright stained glass salvaged from the Baptist church. It made the apartment a secular, private place of worship, a compact temple of art, setting idiosyncratic personal taste against the powers of darkness and gravity. Light: the final touch in the apartment's decor, it was also the first thing to be noticed. It suggested a metaphor for Merrill's own creative energy, which played on the house's quirky spaces and fanciful objects, bringing them to life.

Eleanor Perényi, shaking her head, called Merrill and Jackson's apartment "The Boutique." Like many, Perényi found Merrill's decision to live in those small, crowded rooms at the top of a commercial building mysterious: "Why, when he could have had any house in town . . ." Perényi lived two blocks away on Main Street with her mother, Grace Zaring Stone, in a handsome white eighteenth-century house, surrounded by a beautiful garden tended by Eleanor. Jimmy had met the Stone Women, as he liked to call them, when he and David first came to Stonington, but they did not become intimate friends until 1957, after the death of Perényi's father, Captain Ellis Stone. With Robert and Isabel Morse, also Stonington neighbors, Eleanor and Grace and Jimmy and David formed a select society, part Proustian salon, part improvised family unit. Robert christened them "the Surly Temple." The six friends had cocktails together, cooked for each other, played bridge, gossiped intensively, and convened for holiday meals in Stonington or at the Morses' house in Bedford Hills, outside New York City. The Stones and Morses were "summer people" who had other homes and traveled in the winter.

Grace Stone had lived in far-flung places with her husband, from Shanghai to Paris, where Captain Stone was stationed as the U.S. naval attaché during World War II. Not a typical navy wife, she was a novelist who combined historical drama and sentimental plots, with much popular success. *The Bitter Tea of General Yen*, the tale of a New England missionary taken captive by a Chinese warlord, who is soon captivated by her, became a film starring Barbara Stanwyck (1933). Hollywood also adapted two of the novels that she published under the pen name "Ethel Vance": *Escape* with Norma Shearer (1940) and *Winter Meeting* with Bette Davis (1948). Grace spent winters in Rome. She prized her friendships with Gore Vidal, Mary McCarthy, and other famous writers. She was determined and decisive by nature. In her seventies she fought off a mugger in New York with her umbrella. She was in her sixties when she met Merrill, and she lived to be one hundred. When her eyes began to fail, he read long works aloud to her, including the *Odyssey* and all of *The Changing Light at Sandover*. Grace was an indefatigable great lady on whom he doted, like a child. Robert Morse painted a group portrait of the Temple; it captures Jimmy leaning forward, hanging on Grace's next word. Sometimes, her daughter recalls, "he literally climbed into Mother's lap."

Eleanor was strong-willed and a match for Grace. It was no secret that they fought with each other "like an old couple." Jimmy once took Louise Fitzhugh to dinner at their house, without explaining their relationship; back on the street after dinner, she asked him, "How long have *they* been together?" Eleanor's early life was worthy of her mother's romantic fiction. In 1937, at nineteen, when she was living abroad with her parents, she fell in love with and married a Hungarian count. When the war began, Eleanor, now Baroness Perényi, came back to the U.S. to give birth to her son, Peter. Her husband, Zigismund Perényi, stayed in Europe and joined the Hungarian resistance; they divorced in 1945. She worked at *Harper's Bazaar* before becoming an editor at *Mademoiselle*. In 1946, she published a memoir of her life with the baron on his family estate, titled *More Was Lost*. *The Bright Sword*, a novel about the American Civil War, appeared in 1946. Two books followed much later: *Liszt: The Artist as Romantic Hero* (1974), a finalist for the National Book Award, and *Green Thoughts* (1981), a meditation on gardens and gardening. A classic in its genre, *Green Thoughts* consists of brief essays on topics arranged alphabetically from "annuals" to "woman's place" (the latter a reflection on "the two-thousand-odd years of women's incarceration in the flower garden"). Eleanor was brown-haired, big-featured (dark eyebrows, a strong nose), and bosomy, with a deep, gravelly voice. Merrill liked to refer to her by her initials, ESP. Both sophisticated and practical, and a staunch liberal in politics, she had a fine prose style, a sharp tongue, and utter confidence in her moral judgment and literary taste. She was a proud, independent woman, who spoke her mind without bothering to be nice.

The Morses lived in a rambling house, sections of which were built in the 1780s and 1880s, with a garden and centuries-old boxwood hedges, diagonally across the street from Grace and Eleanor. Isabel was the source of their money. The daughter of a diplomat under President Herbert Hoover and a mother from high society in New York, she was a modest woman who came from privilege and power. Small and delicate, she had broken her jaw as a child, and it was improperly set, which gave her a flat, compressed chin. She had crippling arthritis, which worsened as she aged, curling her body, and she used a cane. She didn't argue with the opinionated Stone Women, or rise to the bait of their provoking remarks. A painter who had trained as a sculptor, she made still lifes, domestic scenes, and bold, large-canvas landscapes, crosshatched with vibrant color, recording scenes from her and Robert's travels. She was an attentive mother to their only child, Daniel.

Robert was a dignified man with dark eyes and dark hair that fringed his bald head. He was born in 1906 in Toledo, Ohio. His mother had emigrated from Sweden; his father played the piano for silent films. Having grown up as the precocious youngest child in a family of girls, he was accustomed to being made much of. After he graduated from Princeton with a degree in art in 1928, he went to France to study painting. He met Isabel via her mother, whom he had befriended in New York. When they married, Isabel gave him a quarter of a million dollars (a great sum) to regard as his own fortune, relieving him of the need to make a living. Robert continued to paint, and he practiced the piano daily; he and Jimmy liked to play four-hand. There were two grand pianos in the Morses' house in Bedford Hills, where Robert and Isabel were friends with their neighbors, the composers Samuel Barber and Gian Carlo Menotti, whom Merrill made friends with too. The very type of the dilettante, Robert dabbled in poetry as well as painting and music. He published in a private edition two long narrative poems on classical themes, titled *The Two Persephones*.

But his special gift was for zany, impromptu wordplay. Verbal baubles dropped from him in conversation, spurred on by Jimmy, who gathered these witticisms in lists in his notebook. Some of the jokes were literary, as when Robert called George Eliot "a Lewes woman," playing on her scandalous liaison with George Henry Lewes. Other lines were delivered à propos de rien, such as "moist with your own moutarde." The spoonerism, a phrase in which parallel elements exchange places, was his signature form; with it, he turned clichés topsy-turvy, often to lewd and surreal effect, as in "a gritty pearl is like a titty prune." (At Jimmy's urging, Auden printed Robert's spoonerism-poem, "A Winter Eve," in his commonplace book, *A Certain World*.) He was given to Groucho Marx–style bawdy one-liners: "I'll give you just 10 minutes to take your hand off my knee!" or—replying to Grace's reference to his "expressive mouth"—"Hundreds of satisfied users!"

Despite his giggling wit, Robert was a reserved, controlled man who, in Perényi's words, "seemed slightly mysterious, as if he had some special knowledge." Morse's air of mystery was perhaps readily explained: Robert was a family man who was also a homosexual. His illustration for the jacket of *The Two Persephones*, which shows the goddess divided down the middle by light and shade, to represent her dual identity as Demeter's daughter and Hades's bride, the Queen of Hell, hints at his duality. Jimmy and David must have guessed the truth early on; usually they were too tactful even to mention it behind his back. For Robert, being gay on Main Street in Stonington meant playing madly with words and remaining "slightly mysterious."

Merrill and Jackson were almost as self-protective. For some time, even with the Morses and Grace and Eleanor, they maintained the fiction that they were friends, not lovers. David's wedding ring was the disguise. He tried to convince Eleanor that, just as he had Sewelly, Jimmy had "a mistress in Mystic," the town just west of Stonington. The ludicrous alibi registers the social pressure they lived under: both Merrill and Jackson produced amusing lies and strategic silences to defend their life together and keep other people at arm's length. They had cause to be wary of the judgment even of friends. When David taught a teenage girl in town how to drive, Eleanor reprimanded him for promoting the girl's crush on him, and told the girl to stay away from him, because he was a homosexual. Fuming, he and Jimmy spent an evening writing poison-pen letters to Eleanor. Despite the familiarity and mutual devotion that developed within the walls of the Surly Temple, there was never much openness and trust. At the end of an evening, the three odd couples retired to their separate corners, picking over what the others had just done and said.

Merrill and Jackson were at home in Stonington from June to December 1957. Jimmy went south to spend Christmas with the Plummers and Mis' Annie. David joined him, and they drove west in their Volkswagen Bug to Santa Fe, where they rented an adobe house with a patio and garden on the west slope of the Sangre de Cristo Mountains for the winter months—following in the tracks of Bill and Nancy Gibson, who'd spent their sabbatical year in the same house. They didn't abandon Maisie, who arrived after twenty-four hours of travel and a change of planes in Denver.

The chill air and elevation—Santa Fe is built at an altitude of 7,000 feet—were exhilarating. So were the desert's pinks and tans, which glistened that year after a series of heavy snows. They had just one friend in town, Mary Lou Aswell. A small woman with dark hair and a vivid smile, she was an editor from New York who lived in a house on Canyon Road with her partner, Agnes Sims, a painter. Mary Lou and Jimmy's friendship lasted twenty-five years. When she died in 1984, he felt "only pure grief." "We were alike in our love of amusement," he wrote in his journal. "Like me, she aged without maturing." She took him and David that winter to ritual dances in the nearby pueblos. She also introduced them to Witter Bynner, Wallace Stevens's friend from youth, a poet and translator from the Chinese who held court around the piñon-scented fire in his old adobe home, a short walk from where they were living. Bynner's house had begun as a "shack," to which he'd added one room after another, like railroad cars. Within were Chinese scrolls, Navajo blankets, and Hispanic santos. As he told stories and played the piano, his laugh rose "above the noise in a room like the whoop of a crane." Bynner was "a doll," Merrill thought. But he hadn't come to Santa Fe for its social life. He passed up the chance to meet the poet Robert Creeley, who lived nearby.* He wanted seclusion in order to finish the book of poems that he had been at work on, fitfully, since 1950.

It worked. "Poems drop like apples," Merrill boasted. Besides writing new poems, he was revising old ones and experimenting with the organization of the book as a whole. It was a large manuscript (he considered some fifty poems before settling on a selection of forty-one) composed over a long period during which he'd written two plays and a novel and traveled across Europe and the U.S. and around the world. His first, finicky impulse was to order poems according to strictly formal principles: "a) the earlier 'serious' poems in stanzas; b) the blank verse poems; c) lighter poems, early and late; d) later 'serious' poems in stanzas." But, stimulated by reactions to the manuscript from Barbara Deming, a poet and future political activist who was a good friend from his days at Bard, he decided to mix these groups up. The arrangement introduced "formal dissimilarity" and a "greater interchange" between one section and another, and between "serious" and "lighter" poems.

From a distance, *The Country of a Thousand Years of Peace* looks like many other books of American poetry from the 1950s. Its foreign scenes and its obsession with art and perception identify it with the "tourist" poetry being written by Americans who traveled abroad in this period with the support of newly established academic and artistic fellowships and on the strength of the postwar U.S. dollar. Its wit, elegance, personal reserve, and technical skill—everything that could be summed up as its formalism—date the poetry just as clearly. But even while it exemplified these period conventions, Merrill's poetry chafed against them. Wherever the tourist travels, he knows that what he is seeing has been seen before: his poems are only "images of images." He also knows that his expert verse forms threaten him with lifelessness or entrapment.

Merrill made that threat the theme of "Dream (Escape from the Sculpture Museum) and Waking," the longest poem in the book. The walls of the "Sculpture Museum" symbolize the conventions that set art apart from life and the artist apart from other people. The poem's chaotic flow of dream images strains against the structure of its rhymed six-line stanzas—the

---

* JM to CF, letter, February 10, 1958 (Getty). About Creeley, Merrill wrote to Fredericks, "I do rather shrink at the thought of meeting any writer; while I have liked some of his stories quite a bit I do not really get his poems and wonder if there wouldn't be, from him, the same kind of hostility that had begun to emanate from [the Beats in] San Francisco?"

unconscious pitched against controlling form. Wanting "to be more natural" than the statues, but inhibited by the self-consciousness that even his wish to be natural expresses, Merrill's speaker, trapped in the museum, is frozen in a formal "show / Of being human." Love should be a solution, a way out of the self-enclosure represented by the statues. But love is a sign of everything that's wrong here. In the closing stanzas, the speaker addresses his lover, who is asleep and as still as a statue. He recalls their conversation of the night before:

> You called me cold, I said you were a child.
> I said we must respect
> Each other's solitude. You smiled.

The poem ends with the speaker's resolve to wake his friend and communicate. His dream of "blinded" travelers on a "road in snow" suggests a pair of lovers who are isolated from other people and each other, having lost their way in life, and unable to warm themselves:

> Well, I shall wake you now,
> Smiling myself to hide my fear.
> Sun turns the stone urn's overflow
> To fire. If I had missed before
> The relevance of the road in snow,
> The little dogs, the blinded pair,
>
> I judge it now in your slow eyes
> Which meet mine, fill with things
> We do not name, then fill with the sunrise
> And close, because too much light stings,
> All the more when shed on these
> Our sleeps of stone, our wakenings.

The lovers' communion consists in shared silence. When their eyes meet, they close again, as if by agreement, because it "stings" to look at each other in the light.

Like the truth in *The Seraglio,* love hurts in *The Country of a Thousand Years of Peace.* In "Stones," a short poem probably also written during this period, the speaker hardens his heart, thinking that if he were able to be more like a stone, he would have "Neither to suffer, grow nor die." But that hard heart isolates him from his lover:

Now just the least part of you
Can be reached by love, as when
The world coming between
Causes a crescent moon.

What Merrill's speaker is trying to protect himself from is clarified in the powerfully concise "A Renewal," where love makes itself felt as a penetrating blow. This is the whole poem:

Having used every subterfuge
To shake you, lies, fatigue, or even that of passion,
Now I see no way but a clean break.
I add that I am willing to bear the guilt.

You nod assent. Autumn turns windy, huge,
A clear vase of dry leaves vibrating on and on.
We sit, watching. When I next speak
Love buries itself in me, up to the hilt.

Love involves, it seems, helpless submission to pain. The desire Merrill expresses in this passive idiom is a wish to be penetrated and to be hurt. The "hilt" of love's sword rhymes with "guilt": it punishes the lover as it wounds him, and it makes desire difficult to tell apart from the desire for punishment, or at least the need for it.

Merrill was unsure what to call the book. His draft titles show him wondering whether to stress certain symbols ("Mirrors + Stones" or "Mirrors + Journeys") or to apply a neutral label, such as "46 Poems" or "L Poems." The long, metrical title he chose—*The Country of a Thousand Years of Peace* is a line of iambic pentameter—was a significant solution. By reaching back to one of the earliest poems in the book and highlighting Hans's death, the title called attention to the drama of Merrill's creative and emotional development. He placed the two poems about his dead friend—"The Country of a Thousand Years of Peace" and "A Dedication"—first and last in the book, framing the other poems. Together, they implied that facing up to death in order to live fully, as Hans had done, was the challenge facing him in both life and art, and that Hans would show him how to do it.

Merrill finished his manuscript in February, although he made more revisions before Knopf set the book's pages for publication in January 1959. Contemplating what he had done, he noted "a kind of obsessive subject-matter which perhaps gives a curious slant to the book," foregrounding "dissolution, being consumed, evaporation, etc. But I suppose there is nothing I can do about it now, except to register the fact and see if I can't find a path into a different field under a different sky."

The Santa Fe sojourn ended in March after visits from Lurie, Fredericks, and David's parents. Before returning to Stonington, Jimmy and David spent two weeks in Mexico. Mexico City was not the "different sky" Merrill was hoping for. A journal entry shows him remembering his first visit to the city twelve years before:

> I can see, as I could not in 1946, the charm of the place. Dust + sun + pocked facades. But I am so depressed. Possibly it is one of my rare revisitations, of a place or a feeling from before that fatal year 1947, the year in which I took my first resolve not to feel. I broke it, of course, but made others and others. And now, back here in a city, in a park even, where in all good faith I sat + suffered, the geography of so much that I did not understand, it is painful to feel how these trees have grown, these faces weathered, those houses torn down and these constructed. Where is my youth and my feeling? What is this that has thickened + wrinkled, + that has turned bitter + dry?

Merrill's self-protective "resolve not to feel," like the wish expressed in "Stones" "Neither to suffer, grow nor die," was formed in the wake of his battle with his mother over Friar. Back in Mexico City, he registers the time that's passed since "that fatal year" by recalling "those houses torn down" and noting "these constructed." His resolve has made him "bitter + dry."

And where is David while Jimmy sits alone, writing in his notebook in the park? "D. is sleeping" in the hotel; "but I resist comforts today," Merrill adds, underlining the contrast between them. After a pause, he asks himself, "Am I resisting feeling or am I resisting D. today?" This journal entry's estranged lovers recall the pair of lonely, directionless travelers in "Dream [. . .] and Waking," one of whom sleeps while the other ruminates. "You called me cold. I said you were a child": surely Jimmy and David had said these words (or others very like them) to each other. Jimmy had fallen in love with David because, like Claude, he promised to open Jimmy up—to feeling, to the world. And so he did. But it was difficult to open up, and there were times when Jimmy resisted both feeling and "D." While helping him to change, David inadvertently goaded Jimmy to dig in and define himself by the differences between them. And their differences, during this, their fifth year together, were hardening.

.   .   .   .

Merrill looked back on the next nine months spent in Stonington—from April 1958 to January 1959, when he and Jackson would set out on their second long trip abroad—as a period "very aimlessly and frustratingly spent." They squabbled in court, "suing our neighbors for their share of an enormous sewer bill." Pipes leaked in their building. Friends came and went: Lurie, for a spring weekend of "Deep Dish"; the Fords, who brought Harry's cover design and the page proofs for *The Country of a Thousand Years of Peace* in July. (Merrill chose a shade of puce for the jacket: "it will be a volume that can only be looked at in our rose and violet room.") Hellen Plummer saw her son in Stonington that summer, and he visited her in Atlanta in the fall. He was taking diet pills and vitamins for energy. Weight gain and fatigue: his familiar symptoms of depression.

The period may have seemed "aimless" to him because there was, for the first time in five years, no project on his desk, no book he was burning to complete. But it may also have seemed "aimless" because, when they were not traveling, it was unclear where he and Jackson were going, as "Dream [. . .] and Waking" suggests. Their life as a couple had to be invented, partly in secret. It conformed to no obvious model or approved plot. They could not measure—and yet they could not help but measure—their passing days against the marriages and births that were milestones in the lives of their friends and family. In 1958, Robin, recently graduated from Harvard, prevailed against his parents' wishes and married Betty Rudd. The Lavins announced the birth of their first child, Amelia, and they asked Jimmy to be her godfather. John and Anne Hollander were another married couple with whom Jimmy and David became close when John took a job teaching at Connecticut College in nearby New London. John was a literary scholar and poet, Anne an art historian and authority on costume. They too were expecting their first child.

These and other young families pointed up Merrill's childlessness. It was—and would remain—a source of anxiety for him. The issue was raised by the dynastic ambition of his father, by the fruitfulness of his siblings (Doris and Charles both had five children by this time), and by the expectations of American society at large in a period known as the "Baby Boom." In *A Different Person*, Merrill recalls that "the genetic angel, as in a parody of the Annunciation, struck" during the first season that he and Jackson spent on Water Street. "What was this—nearly thirty and not yet a father!" Detre saw this feeling as Merrill's reaction to "settling down" with Jackson, and he made a few practical suggestions: "go back to teaching, don't spend so much time by yourselves."

A year later, in 1955, "the house filled up—not quite what Dr Detre had in mind—with Ephraim and Company, who were prepared, like children, to take up as much of our time as we cared to give, [. . .] and who never had to be washed or fed or driven to their school basketball games." "Ephraim and Company," who were the result of Jimmy and David's union, and offspring of a kind, put the question of reproduction in a wholly new light: reincarnation trumped reproduction as the source of human identity; and spirit-homosexuals like Ephraim were in charge of the system, or at least they knew how it worked. From the perspective of the Other World, mothers were merely the biological vessels of rebirth, and fathers hardly counted at all. Merrill may have welcomed these ideas because they relieved him from the pressure to become a father. When he proposed his pregnant stepsister as an appropriate mother for Hans's representative, he was acting as a proxy parent, a fairy godfather. He was serious enough about the project to mention it to his mother, with the implication that success in this department would be satisfying to her. Tom, as Merrill calls Detre in *The Book of Ephraim*, refers to this silliness as "insemination by psycho-roulette." Asked by the psychiatrist to explain himself, JM ventures this:

> "Somewhere a Father Figure shakes his rod

> At sons who have not sired a child?
> Through our own spirit we can both proclaim
> And shuffle off the blame
> For how we live—that good enough?"

Tom had "heard worse." But he might have asked Merrill how his mother, in addition to his mighty phallic father, entered into his feelings in this matter. Did his intimacy with her prohibit—or demand—that he procreate? Did he feel he needed to produce a baby for her in place of the other children his father never gave her?

By 1958, JM and DJ were no longer deeply absorbed by the spirit world, to judge from the few séances Merrill recorded or referred to following the fiasco of Hans's representative's rebirth. His feelings about childhood, children, and childlessness began to fuel poems on these topics, rather than Ouija board sessions. *Water Street* contains a cluster of them, including "The World and the Child," another poem about childhood loneliness called "A Vision of the Garden," the short comic variations on the Oedipal theme in "Five Old Favorites," and the rhapsody, "Childlessness." The latter poem is set on an ordinary street like the one on which Merrill lived, lined by houses like his, to whose inhabitants he compares himself and finds himself wanting. His "dream-wife," a winter storm, wakes him at night. "Ranting and raining," she has come to "Arraign" him for failing to produce what is demanded from him as a man and a citizen for "the common good": "rare growths yielding guaranteed / Gold pollen, gender of suns, large, hardy, / Enviable blooms[.]" Reproduction and financial investment are braided here as two sides of a single social imperative. The implication is that Merrill has failed to live up to a contract: only fleurs du mal grow in the barren garden of the aesthete.

"Scenes of Childhood" was the first and longest poem in this group about parents and children. Merrill began it in May 1958 after he and Jackson visited Fredericks, and Claude showed them home movies he had made at the age of twelve. Merrill dedicated the poem to him in gratitude for their friendship and in a spirit of solidarity, since they were both only sons from broken homes. Merrill was using Fredericks's childhood to explore his own. Writing in the first person, he describes a son and mother watching film from their lives "thirty years ago." He makes the son much younger than the child Fredericks was in his movie: Merrill's boy is four years old—and therefore in the throes of the Oedipus complex, according to Freud. Mother and son watch the past materialize once again. The "primal / Figures jerky and blurred / As lightning bugs / From lanterns issue." "A man's shadow mount[s]" the woman's dress. Next there appears

> A fair child, or fury—
> Myself at four, in tears.
> I raise my fist,
>
> Strike, she kneels down. The man's
> Shadow afflicts us both.
> Her voice behind me says
> It might go slower.
> I work dials, the film jams.
> Our headstrong old projector
> Glares at the scene which promptly
> Catches fire.

Those memories are still too hot to handle. The son wants to be free of them; he would like to run outside and breathe "In and out the sun / And air I am"—but even that phrase, in which he notes a homophonic pun, is enough to drag him back to his conflicted role as "son and heir."

Psychoanalysis was one frame of reference for the poem. Another was Proust's search for lost time. When he completed "Scenes of Childhood,"

Merrill turned to a poem of tribute, "For Proust,"* which he put next to "Scenes" in *Water Street*. He looked to Proust, the dilettante who became a great artist, to see how he might redeem time "very aimlessly and frustratingly spent":

> Over and over something would remain
> Unbalanced in the painful sum of things.
> Past midnight you arose, rang for your things.
> You had to go into the world again.

In order to balance the "painful sum of things," Proust must "go into the world again" in search of a friend he loved long ago. When he finds her, she seems "a child still," though "in her hair a long / White lock has made its truce with appetite." "In a voice reproachful and low / She says she understands you have been ill."

> And you, because your time is running out,
> Laugh in denial and begin to phrase
> Your questions. There had been a little phrase
> She hummed, you could not sleep tonight without
>
> Hearing again. Then, of that day she had sworn
> To come, and did not, was evasive later,
> Would she not speak the truth two decades later,
> From loving-kindness learned if not inborn?

She leaves without answering, just as she did in the past, illustrating the principle in Proust's novel that "the loved one always leaves." Merrill's vignette insists on the necessary failure not only of our desire to be loved, but even of our desire to understand why we were not.

Yet something is gained. As Merrill's syntax winds through an unusual verse form—rhymed *abba* quatrains in which the second, interior rhymes consist in the same word, repeated with subtly altered sense—he evokes a rhythmic alternation of experience and memory, life and writing. The climax comes as the writer returns home:

> Back where you came from, up the strait stair, past
> All understanding, bearing the whole past,
> Your eyes grown wide and dark, eyes of a Jew,

---

* JM sent the poem, in nearly completed form, to WM on November 17, 1958 (WUSTL).

You make for one dim room without contour
And station yourself there, beyond the pale
Of cough or of gardenia, erect, pale.
What happened is becoming literature.

Feverish in time, if you suspend the task,
An old, old woman shuffling in to draw
Curtains, will read a line or two, withdraw.
The world will have put on a thin gold mask.

Proust was on Merrill's mind as he mounted the "strait stair" of his own apartment, past those illustrations of Proust's novel on the stairs, and stationed himself in the "dim room" of his study, his brown eyes looking (when he pinned a postcard portrait of Proust to the wall beside the desk) into the novelist's own. Like Proust, he had chosen a way of life that was childless; not reproduction, but a return to his experience in writing, defended him against passing time—although there was no defense against time, he knew.

Merrill ends the poem in the future perfect tense, imagining the moment when Proust will have stopped writing. "An old, old woman," a version of the muse, will draw the curtain; and, by a sort of alchemy, the "world will have put on a thin gold mask." That mask is the aim of the writer's "task," as the rhyme emphasizes. It is an image of the world renewed by morning sun and re-created on the writer's page—stamped with the writer's face, like a death mask. This is not the gold his father worked for, nor the "Gold pollen" of a healthy garden. But Merrill could use it to settle accounts with both his parents.

Going into the world again, returning up the strait stair: that daily rhythm was writ large in the patterns of Merrill's life. As they settled into Water Street, he and Jackson continued to travel, restlessly, for long periods. In January 1959, they set out again for Europe, expecting to be gone six months, although it would be early September before they returned. They started in Paris, where Merrill bought the Pléiade edition of *À la recherche* (he reread it alongside the first volume of George D. Painter's biography of Proust, which had appeared that year). They called on Guitou Knoop, who was living in a studio on the Boulevard Raspail; as usual, she tried to sell a bronze to Merrill, purportedly at a discount ("We'll cancel part of my debt, and I'll let you have it for $2000—half what my prices are, nowadays"). They paid their respects to the "strangely youthful" Alice B. Toklas, who served them sherry in her apartment with its extraordinary collection of modern art, including still lifes by Juan Gris, early Picasso nudes, and two tiny armchairs designed for Toklas and Gertrude Stein by Picasso. Merrill had sent his new book to Alice, and she praised it. Jackson recorded their exchange in his diary: " 'Jamey, I like your new poems. [. . .] But now I want a long breath.' JM perfectly agrees that he should have new long poems. 'But first I am here to draw in a long breath,' he laughs." Toklas laughed in turn, patting his hand: "Don't draw it in, my dear. Let it out!"

Their base camp that winter was Munich, from which they took trips to Berlin, Hamburg, Lübeck, and Copenhagen. They stayed in a pension close to the vast English Gardens and the rebuilt Cuvilliés Theatre, a Rococo jewel box—"all white + gilt with 6 tiny chandeliers that go up and down"—where Mozart's *Idomeneo* had premiered. Postwar Munich, Merrill felt, "was ever so pretty, almost as good as new." Robin and Betty joined them for nine days. But Merrill had little connection to the city. David knew it from his time in Germany with Sewelly. He brought out his watercolors to sketch cityscapes and took travel notes, while he and Jimmy were caught up again in the revels of Carnival. They weathered a visit from Gregory Corso, who departed having cadged $300 from Jimmy. "He is a rather gifted poet, I'm afraid," Merrill sighed, "but terribly uneducated, and a real vampire; one is Drained after an hour with him, while he of course bursts with energy from his bloodless convives."

After Munich, they drove to Spain in a "dreadful black Mercedes," intended for delivery to Hellen Plummer when the trip was over. They liked the country, or what they saw of it from the car: "marvelous skies, granite upthrusts, tonsured hilltops, olives and oranges and corktrees and tiny cubist villages." They spent two weeks with Ben DeMott and his family in a seaside village in Portugal. Then they crossed the Straits of Gibraltar to visit Jane Bowles, the novelist and playwright who lived in Tangier near her husband, the writer and composer Paul Bowles. Though hampered by a stroke, Jane was "spry and funny." She took Jimmy and David to the Casbah and "a restaurant with real dancing boys, all wrapped up in colored stuffs and doing grinds and bumps with tea trays on their heads." They saw the Roman ruins at Volubilis—which, Merrill told Elizabeth Bishop, they went to "entirely" because of "Over 2,000 Illustrations and a Complete Concordance," her poem that mentions the archeological site. "Everything only connected by 'and' and 'and,' " Bishop laments in that poem about anxious, directionless travel. Merrill and Jackson were in the midst of such a journey.

In Madrid, they met up with Cecil Beaton, the portrait photographer, and Truman Capote. "Such a peculiar pair," Merrill reflected, "Beaton all bored and British—should he have a suit of wine red or of midnight blue velvet made? Truman terribly funny—buying capes and bullfighter's shoes and eating caviar to a ruinous degree; he showed us the beauty treatment he must go through 3 times a day in order not to change for the rest of his life." From Barcelona, they took the ferry to Genoa, making friends en route with Cesare Siepi, the basso they had recently heard sing Don Giovanni at the Met. They visited Morra ("the nicest man in the world") in Cortona, then veered north, passing through Ravenna—it was Merrill's third visit to the Byzantine mosaics—and on to Venice, where, for three weeks in May, they kept company with Chester Kallman and Alan Ansen. Ansen, crossing literary party lines, was both a friend of Auden's and an honorary Beat—in fact the model for characters in Jack Kerouac's *On the Road* (Rollo Greb) and William Burroughs's *Naked Lunch* (A.J.). Merrill tucked a sketch of him in a letter to Hollander, who was a friend of Ansen's too: "Sometimes he is wearing a bright red double-breasted suit, sometimes a white one. After midnight he is apt to be sound asleep in Ciro's bar where nothing wakes him, not even sharp prods from an umbrella." From Venice, they continued by ship, stopping in Dubrovnik (where they swam below the castle walls), Patras (a taxi ride from there to Olympia), the amusingly named port Idea (another side trip to Delphi), and at last Athens.

Charlie Shoup was their host. Shoup had moved from Paris to a large apartment with a view of the Acropolis, which he turned over to Jimmy and David for the summer. "Charles's fantasies," David noted in his diary, "revolve almost exclusively around money." In Greece, Shoup had found a place where he could live out those fantasies on a very grand scale. He gave up his society portraits and trompe-l'oeil still lifes ("I was an awful painter," he admits) and became an architect and landscape designer. Over the next forty years, he led a neoclassical movement in Greek architecture, designing extravagant private residences and elaborate gardens, with eighteenth-century ornaments, classical statues, marble obelisks, Empire furniture, and Orientalist touches. During the summer of 1959, while Jimmy and David stayed in his apartment in Athens, Shoup bought a ruined castle on the southern tip of the Peloponnese. Three years later he bought land nearby on which he built his own villa. Shoup, who had enjoyed signing Charles Merrill's name on bar bills when he visited Jimmy in Florida in 1947, used this remote patch of the Greek coast to create for himself a house grander and more fantastic than Merrill's Landing or the Orchard.

Like Tony Harwood, Shoup lived a kind of life that Merrill might have chosen and did not. They didn't remain friends much longer, but Shoup gave Merrill and Jackson a beginning in Greece. He introduced them to his circle of expatriate friends, including Tony Parigory, a Greek born in Alexandria. Shoup also introduced them to the protocols and possibilities of homosexuality in Greece. It was a world in which male beauty and gay desire were for once not forbidden subjects. The mood in Athens, Jackson marveled after a day spent watching young Greeks "swagger, crotch out," at the public swimming pool, was "so amoral and sensual, sexes seem to disappear and what looms instead is an air magnetized in all directions." Gay sex was a game played by the international "team" on one side and young Greek men on the other. For the Greeks, it was easier and safer to pursue same-sex relations with foreigners than with fellow Greeks, for whom the local culture was not the "magnetized" space of sexual freedom that it seemed to the Americans and British. The Greeks were straight, or so they presented themselves. They maintained that self-image by taking the penetrating role when they had sex with the internationals, who offered them, as Merrill liked to joke, the back door, "*l'entrée des artistes*." Thus the Greeks upheld the spirit of the masculine ideal, if not the letter of the moral law, in what was still a highly traditional, village-bound society. The arrangement appealed to a young Greek soldier or policeman for whom sex with women required wedding vows or a costly trip to the brothel. (In Greece, the police were not the threat that they were in Stonington or New York City; they were more likely to be part of the party.) Edmund White, the American novelist who became a friend of Merrill's in the 1970s, explains the codes of this gay subculture: "The old Mediterranean world operated with an almost pagan idea of homosexuality, where the older, wealthy gay man could buy the favors of the young, usually heterosexual boy, and that was fine with everyone, often even the boy's family." The older man bought the younger man's "favors," but not outright: the Greeks whom Merrill and Jackson met weren't "trade"; yet they expected gifts, "loans," or some other sort of patronage in return for sex. "After 1965," White adds, "everyone got richer, the Church declined, and teenagers started dating. But this way of doing things was well established in Greece, and it held on longer there."

From the beginning of their relationship, Merrill and Jackson had cruised for sexual partners in the parks and bathhouses of New York and other cities. "It was a truth universally acknowledged," Merrill explains in *A Different Person*, giving a twist to the first sentence of *Pride and Prejudice*,

in those innocent decades from 1950 to 1980 that a stable homosexual couple would safely welcome the occasional extramarital fling. David and I, still in our early thirties, found that a good deal of anxiety could be finessed by setting out together when we felt the itch, rather than carrying on behind each other's backs. We kept on the lookout for a threesome or a "double date" with some other couple on our wavelength. Like high-school buddies we compared notes afterwards, laughed and commiserated, took care to smooth the plumage of any third party who felt he'd been badly treated. By and large, though, we gravitated towards the kind of exploit offered by [an] unlit garden in Rome, or a New York bathhouse. For me those hours were the adolescence I'd been too shy or repressed to put into action at the time. The polymorphous abundance spilling over into our lives kept us primed and sexually alert towards each other.

In the 1950s, David was better at turning heads than Jimmy, and David went outside their relationship first, Jimmy told friends. But he followed soon enough and with an intensity all his own. Indeed, the notion that cruising simply amounted to the "adolescence" that Merrill had missed normalizes and understates an experience that absorbed him for many years. What were his motives? He was drawn to the park and bars in a spirit of competition: with Jackson, with other friends, and probably, in a way, with his father. Like Charlie, Jimmy had a great appetite for sex. He was attracted to many different men, and to men different from him in class and manners. Like a rake, he enjoyed sexual pleasure for its own sake. But he was also drawn to danger and pain (or so the erotic images in his poetry suggest). If his money put him in a position of power in Athens, he preferred sexual roles of service and submission. As a medium, he had opened himself to the will of the spirits. In his sexual adventures, he was doing something related.

A Different Person mentions nothing of the guilt and self-accusations that came with this experience. Nor does it mention the threat of betrayal, the risk of abandonment, or the anxieties of rivalry from which he and Jackson both suffered. The "polymorphous abundance" of Greece brought out those dangers. One night in Athens, Jimmy brought home a man from a bar—not a Greek but an American, breaking an unwritten rule against pairing up with a member of one's own "team"—and David, humiliated, frightened, and angry, shut the door in his rival's face. A "crisis" followed. As the days passed, David asked in his journal:

> what is meant by our living together, what is possible, what is
> the meaning of our fairly constant search for outside physical
> releases. I am not in the least embarrassed by my actions that

night; but, since, I realize I should have allowed JM to have his night and see if I was right in my fears of losing him. Neither of us will ever know, now, and, of course, the next time I cannot cry wolf and—what then? Promiscuity is the result of some kind of fear: of rejection, of death, of loss of independence. [. . .] We know we do not <u>need</u> sexual extras; but we have for a long time looked for + found them. Men <u>are</u> promiscuous, but the naturalness of that is met by the necessity of our staying together. Both conditions I accept. But each, I believe, imposes its needs: promiscuity must be experienced with truly unrelated bodies, staying together must be a constant need, expressed with the same urgency as that felt with strangers flirted with. My first reaction, and a lingering one, has been that JM is ready for a new life, but that <u>I</u> am someone he cannot bring himself to leave. My first impulse is to bring that feeling out: to offer to leave. As I did. As, of course, I've ended not doing.

This "crisis" was a chance for David to shut the door for good on third parties or to walk out himself. But he saw his and Jimmy's promiscuity as natural and inevitable, and he saw how much he depended on Jimmy. He would take other lovers in the future. And when his lover did, he wouldn't "cry wolf."

That summer, they went to Paros, Kos, Mykonos, and Delos, the Cycladic islands. They also visited Poros, close to Athens, where, in the shade of a waterfront café, with a view of the Sleeping Woman, Merrill began work on the novel that he had been thinking about off and on since he finished *The Seraglio* in 1956. While Jackson went off with his paints to capture a view, Merrill turned in memory to 1950 and the days he spent with Kimon and Mina on the island.

On their final day in Greece, Merrill climbed the Acropolis for a last look at the monuments. Then Jackson discovered that their ship to Venice left not at midnight, but at noon—which was already some time past; yet they might make it aboard if they could meet the ship at the Corinth Canal. David ran into Parigory; Parigory hailed a "pirate taxi," "a huge American car with a driver looking not unlike a pirate," who assured them that their problem was "no problem," as Parigory later told the story. They called Jimmy's name on the steps of the Parthenon; soon their pirate cab was hurtling along the "very dangerous" road to Corinth. Parigory continues, "That a customs official had to be found was again 'no problem' and as it was now siesta time, the exit-visa stamp must have been on his bedside table.

How could one get to the ship short of swimming? A tiny rowboat appeared from nowhere and was loaded with the luggage and two panting travelers. Also panting were the driver and myself watching the rather undignified boarding on a rope ladder."

Merrill and Jackson pulled into New York Harbor with "18 pieces of luggage" and a Mercedes. "Surely," Jimmy wrote to Bill Meredith from the ship in the Corinth Canal, "it is a form of lunacy, [. . .] lurching about the world, every few days asking a new person if he knows somebody somewhere else." But Greece was not merely "somewhere else," one more stop on an itinerary connected only by "and" and "and." It was a "marvelous" country and a "very strange" one. They were going to be back.

As when *The Seraglio* was published, Merrill arranged to be out of the country when reviews of *The Country of a Thousand Years of Peace* appeared. He could predict that some would be hard to swallow. James Dickey stated the negative view in the *Sewanee Review*. Soon Dickey became a friend of Merrill's and, as Merrill's work developed, he became a supporter of his poetry. But Jim Dickey was a hard-drinking southerner, a track star and a World War II fighter pilot, known for writing about experiences "of ultimate confrontation, of violence and truth"; and *The Country of a Thousand Years of Peace*, with its puce jacket, was the work of another sensibility entirely. To open the book, Dickey wrote, "is to enter a realm of connoisseurish aesthetic contemplation, where there are no things more serious than gardens (usually formal), dolls, swans, statues, works of art, operas, delightful places in Europe, the ancient gods in tasteful and thought-provoking array, more statues, many birds and public parks, and, always, 'the lovers.' " Such poetry "has enough of [Henry] James's insistence upon manners and decorum to evoke a limited admiration for the taste, wit, and eloquence that such an attitude makes possible, and also enough to drive you mad over the needless artificiality, prim finickiness, and determined inconsequence of it all."

There were sympathetic reviews by Mona Van Duyn, a young poet whom Merrill didn't know, and by Meredith and Marius Bewley, who were both his friends. Bewley's review, a copy of which Merrill kept in his study for the rest of his life, is the most discerning early appreciation of his work. Dapper, cultured, and gay, a professor of English at Rutgers, Bewley was eight years older than Merrill. He had been a protégé of F. R. Leavis at Cambridge; over the course of an evening, as drinks followed dinner in Bewley's apartment on Staten Island, his American voice became more and more British. His review described Merrill's poetic inspiration as "essentially metaphysical." "The most recurrent image in Mr. Merrill's poetry is the mirror," he wrote, "and closely related to this central symbol are images of glass panes, images of dreams that reflect hidden thoughts, of art that reflects reality, and the camera lens that reflects appearances." "The first act should be to reach toward" the real. But the poet is turned back by the glittering surfaces to which he is attracted. "Returned into himself, the person withers in loneliness, rejected by a universe of mirrors that holds him from reality." The image is tinged with a Decadent mawkishness that Merrill would not have wanted to display. But it accurately points to the pain in his early poems, and it links that pain to an epistemological condition: the problem of knowing what is real beyond one's perceptions. It also implies a course of action. "The subject that is deeply at the heart of James Merrill's poetry," Bewley ended, "is his search for integrated experience in a world of unrelated appearances. This fragmentation can be resisted, overcome, only by breaking through the prison of self, only by the discovery of others in love, only by pursuing the vision beyond the glass barrier."

Bewley's piece appeared in the *Partisan Review*, the influential magazine of the New York Intellectuals. The back cover of the same issue announced a new collection of poems by Robert Lowell: *Life Studies*. That book became a major literary event: Lowell was praised in it for shedding the rhyme, meter, and symbolism of his earlier work, for the sometimes brutal candor with which he treated his own mental breakdown and family history, and for the confidence with which he analogized his personal suffering to a state of collective, national malaise. *Life Studies* inaugurated an era in American poetry in which Confessional poetry was central, and Lowell was widely hailed as the central poet. Beside *Life Studies*, *The Country of a Thousand Years of Peace* might very well seem a work of "determined inconsequence," as Dickey put it, and Merrill took notice. Not surprisingly, he resented Lowell's dominance of the poetic landscape in the 1960s. But *Life Studies* and the general turn to autobiography in American poetry that it represented had an immediate impact on his work.

Between fall 1959 and spring 1960, Merrill completed "From a Notebook," "An Urban Convalescence," "Poem of Summer's End," "Angel," "Childlessness," "After Greece," and "A Tenancy"*—poems that, with "Scenes of Childhood" and "For Proust," make up most of *Water Street*. The

---

* JM sent "From a Notebook," "An Urban Convalescence," "For Proust," "Poem of Summer's End," "Angel," "Scenes of Childhood," and "Childlessness" to Chatto & Windus in London in March 1960 for inclusion in a potential book of selected poems, which did not eventuate. JM to Norah Smallwood, letter, March 12, 1960 (WUSTL). Merrill sent a draft of "A Tenancy," close to completion, to Irma Brandeis on April 5, 1960 (WUSTL). "After Greece" appeared in *The New Yorker* in May 1960.

key poem in this group, "An Urban Convalescence," appeared in the *Partisan Review*, where Hollander was the poetry editor. It is an ambitious poem, a stab at the "long breath" Alice B. Toklas wanted from Merrill. Though it confesses nothing very specific, it shows the influence of Confessional poetry in being a poem of stringent moral self-assessment. Its first person is not the impersonal "I" in *The Country of a Thousand Years of Peace*, but the intimate, brooding voice in Merrill's notebooks.

The poem grew out of Merrill's increasing self-consciousness about his own writing process. That self-consciousness shows in the notes he made on Poros for his novel, which would take the form of a writer's notebook, as well as in a poem like "From a Notebook." "An Urban Convalescence" was the product of many drafts, and Merrill made a careful archive of them: in addition to the notebook pages on which he began it, he preserved more than forty work sheets. These reveal him engaged in verbal self-analysis: in ink and sometimes pencil on unlined pages with a casual hand or in the margins of the typewritten text, he quibbles and doodles (making faces, lips, eyes, hands), crosses out and queries, adds new words and lines, moving on or going back, talking to himself. At times he decides to say just the opposite, or nearly the opposite, of what he began by saying.

"An Urban Convalescence" begins with the poet on a walk around his neighborhood in New York. The day is cold and inhospitable. He is recovering from an illness that has kept him "a week in bed." He watches "a huge crane / Fumble luxuriously in the filth of years" as a building is razed. "As usual in New York," he remarks, "everything is torn down / Before you have had time to care for it." The problem seems to be outside him, where money is restlessly remaking the city, erasing the past, but then he reflects that he can't remember what building used to stand on the site, although "I have lived on this same street for a decade." He falls into a reverie in which the vanished building gradually emerges as a vague presence. He can see above the lintel a "garland" of leaves and fruit carved in stone, an emblem of the former house's promise. The vision leads to another memory, this one of a "cheap engraving" of a garland he bought "for a few francs" to "stanch"—like a bandage—"dripping" branches held by a companion's "small, red-nailed hand." Her identity, like the house being torn down, has been lost to memory, "toppled under that year's fashions."

The house Merrill only half remembers "soundlessly collapses," and he is left at a loss in front of the empty lot where he began: "Wires and pipes, snapped off at the roots, quiver."

> Well, that is what life does. I stare
> A moment longer, so. And presently

> The massive volume of the world
> Closes again.

In his drafts, punning on "volume," Merrill came to a halt a few lines further:

> Upon that book I swear
> To abide by what it teaches:
> Gospels of ugliness and waste,
> Of towering voids, of soiled gusts,
> The shrieking I face into, eyes and nose
> Astream with cold as with foreknowledge of destruction.

Unsure how to continue the poem, he went on by making another inward turn, calling his rhetoric into question. This is something that goes on throughout the poem when the speaker checks himself, testing what he sees or says with questions. Now, raising an eyebrow about the source of those tears, Merrill asked at the bottom of one work sheet, "With cold?" The finished poem incorporated both that skeptical question and the answer he jotted below it:

> Gospels of ugliness and waste,
> Of towering voids, of soiled gusts,
> Of a shrieking to be faced
> Full into, eyes astream with cold—
>
> With cold?
> All right then. With self-knowledge.

He stops short of saying just what he knows about himself. It is enough to admit that the coldness bringing tears to his eyes is within him.

Merrill's effort to tell the truth in a passage like this was provoked by Confessional poetry, not only Lowell's *Life Studies*, but also W. D. Snodgrass's "Heart's Needle," which he greatly admired. Yet the form that his self-examination takes—a questioning of his own language and perceptions—derives from Bishop, for whom self-questioning was a trademark device. Her poetry was richly personal, but she shied away from Confessional poetry's bold self-dramatizations and, in Lowell's case, its claims to public authority. Her reticence was subtly adjusted to the constraints on her as a lesbian: unable or disinclined to speak of sexuality openly, the "I" in her poems assumes an intimacy with the reader like that of a friend or a lover, for whom it is unnecessary to spell everything out. Casual (at least in appearance) and exploratory, her style made what was most personal in her poetry accessible as a matter of sensibility and idiom—of how things were felt and seen, and how they were put.

Merrill learned from this strategy of Bishop's. He also took something from Bishop's sense of poetic form. Bishop approached the given form of a poem not as a fixed plan but as a provisional structure, open to modulation and revision in the course of a poem's unfolding, depending on shifts of perspective and mood. Merrill experiments with the same principle in "An Urban Convalescence." In a bolder modulation than anything in Bishop or his own work previously, he moves, after the stop arrived at in the phrase "With self-knowledge," from free verse into rhymed pentameter quatrains. Part of the power of this abrupt shift lies in the way it reverses attitudes toward poetic form prevailing in American poetry of the period. From the 1950s to the 1960s, American poets moved en masse from meter and rhyme to free verse, the new period style. *Life Studies* exemplified this development. The poems at the start of that book, like most of Lowell's earlier poems, were composed in rhyme and meter, while the poems later in the book, which included the ones about Lowell's mental illness and his family, were composed in free verse—making free verse seem like the necessary vehicle for telling personal truths.

Merrill goes in the opposite direction in "An Urban Convalescence" when he moves from free verse to quatrains. The move is correlated with the relief he expresses as the focus shifts from the public space of the street to the privacy of his home. "Indoors at last," he exhales. His manner becomes argumentative and crisp after the poem's wayward self-questioning. About "the new / buildings" going up everywhere, he writes,

> The sickness of our time requires
> That these as well be blasted in their prime.
> You would think the simple fact of having lasted
> Threatened our cities like mysterious fires.
>
> There are certain phrases which to use in a poem
> Is like rubbing silver with quicksilver. Bright
> But facile, the glamour deadens overnight.
> For instance, how "the sickness of our time"
>
> Enhances, then debases, what I feel.

To speak of "the sickness of our time" is to indulge in an inflated, cliché rhetoric, the language of Madison Avenue and *Time*, which reaches for a spurious public authority as it deflects responsibility away from the self. Merrill takes responsibility for his language, scrutinizing phrases like "with cold" or "the sickness of our time" along with his motives for using them. He insists that his desk is the scene of moral action for the writer, not the street.

"The poet is a man choosing the words he lives by," Merrill remarked in an interview in 1967. In "An Urban Convalescence," he dedicates himself to a discipline in which life and work are two aspects of a single process, for which revision, his laborious practice of composition, is both the instrument and the symbol. This idea emerges in the poem's closing lines. The poet gazes again at the city, this time from high above it:

> back into my imagination
> The city glides, like cities seen from air,
> Mere smoke and sparkle to the passenger
> Having in mind another destination
>
> Which is now not that honey-slow descent
> Of the Champs-Elysées, her hand in his,
> But the dull need to make some kind of house
> Out of the life lived, out of the love spent.

Letting go of that daydream, Merrill drops the hand of—whom exactly? The unnamed woman mentioned earlier? His mother? Or the wife she imagined for him? Without that female companion, he must make something on his own "Out of the life lived, out of the love spent." The last phrase gestures toward a profligate sexual self. Merrill's goal is to keep from wasting his life and love by making "some kind of house" out of them. That phrase, purposefully and fruitfully vague, evokes a figurative structure, a dwelling both actual and imagined. It suggests the house on Water Street where he wrote and the writing he produced there, beginning with a book of poems bearing the street's name. The making of *that* "house" would be as dull, ordinary, and repetitive as any domestic task, a matter of going over and carrying forward what he wrote the day before. The drama would come down to his daily choice of words.

The type of autobiography that Merrill learned to write in "An Urban Convalescence" drew on his experience, but not in a literal, documentary way.

The poem suggests that he wrote it while living alone in New York. Yet he had packed up his apartment on West Tenth Street in 1956, and he and Jackson had lived together in Stonington since 1954. The pain and loneliness in "An Urban Convalescence" were real, however, and probably the "illness" mentioned in the poem was real too. Merrill returned home from Europe in September 1959 with a prostate infection, which was probably sexually transmitted. Symptoms persisted over the next year with an "occasional flare-up," prompting him to fear he was becoming "impotent"—as Jackson noted in his diary. To prove to himself and Jackson that "we are complete wastrels and sensualists," Merrill would go on "to mournfully list all our past trips, sex, indigence [sic], etc." The vague tints of shame and regret coloring "An Urban Convalescence" make sense when we see Merrill trying to overcome his feeling that his and Jackson's lives had been cheapened—fallen, as David put it, to a "low rate of exchange"—due to their promiscuous sexual lives.

Perhaps, in this context, the "illness" in "An Urban Convalescence" refers less to any physical condition than to homosexuality, which American society understood as an illness, a "neurosis," from which one could be cured. Over the course of the poem, Merrill seems, if not to welcome, then to accept his illness. It's tempting, when he gives up the vision of walking hand in hand with a female companion on the Champs-Élysées, to feel that he has "come out" as a gay writer. Yet "coming out" was no more of an option for him now than it had been when he wrote The Seraglio. Merrill's concern in this poem is with "self-knowledge," with the price and the feel of it, not with self-revelation. Rather than come out, he brings his reader "indoors" with him.

"Convalescence" was a literary pose that Merrill adopted in imitation of the invalid Proust (the allusions to Paris in the poem evoke Proust too). Merrill's feeling for Proust was profound, but never pious. At least since the "Proust Party" in 1947, he approached the novelist in a spirit of winking gay identification, which he shared with friends like Howard Moss. Moss was known for his Mr. Magoo looks: bald head, nearsighted squint, and sagging, rueful expression. As the poetry editor of The New Yorker, he was an important ally for Merrill's poetry. With Moss's support, the magazine printed some of Merrill's longest, most ambitious poems in the 1960s, making him a poet whose new work many, many readers were sure to see. Moss himself was a poet, funny, sad, and elegant, and the author of a short critical study, The Magic Lantern of Marcel Proust. On a visit to Water Street in winter 1960, he and Merrill amused themselves by writing rhymes on Proustian themes which could be sung to the tune of "Colonel Bogey's March" in the popular war movie The Bridge on the River Kwai. Several other friends made contributions; Merrill collected these in what he called the "Balbec Liederbuch," after the seaside resort in Proust's novel. Moss's effort led off:

> "Wednesday," said Mme. Verdurin,
>> Ready to serve her dreadful flan.
>> Morel
>> Has had a quarrel
>> With Baron Charlus for using Man-Tan.

Merrill gleefully shared these and other rhymes in letters to friends. For Bishop, he provided a footnote for Moss's: "Man-Tan, in case you haven't heard, has covered New York. It is a colorless liquid that turns skin brown several hours after application. As it streaks and clots easily, one has no trouble telling it from a real suntan, but that hasn't kept people from using it." He had composed a ditty of his own:

> "Swann's Way," a book by Marcel Proust
>> Tells how the hero took to roust
>> Racy
>> Odette de Crécy
>> Who to his friends could not be introduced.

Lest he offend the reticent Bishop with a "smutty note," he didn't show her the most inspired entry, this one by Bernie Winebaum, in which the child Marcel addresses his nanny:

> "Francoise, why must I go to bed?
>> I'd rather play with girls instead.
>> Later
>> I'll have a waiter,
>> But only after my grandmother's dead."

Whether or not Merrill spent "a week in bed" in September when he began "An Urban Convalescence," he was flat on his back with the flu in January. He recovered slowly. As feelings of weakness and lassitude persisted, he saw a doctor in March in Atlanta on a visit to his mother and Mis' Annie. He returned north freshly supplied with vitamins and thyroid pills, and prepared for "the imminent extinction of my grandmother," who was almost blind now and rapidly failing. "The Water Hyacinth," a poem Merrill wrote that spring, ponders the ironies in the reversal of the child's relation to his grandmother:

Now all is upside down.
I sit while you babble.
I watch your sightless face
Jerked swiftly here and there,
Set in a puzzled frown.
Your face! It is no more yours
Than its reflected double
Bobbing on scummed water.
Other days, the long pure
Sobs break from a choked source
Nobody here would dare
Fathom, even if able.

Despite his physical complaints, Merrill gave a reading in New York; he was again a judge for the Glascock Poetry Prize at Mount Holyoke College; and he was writing new poems. In May, he looked back on the past months with satisfaction: "I can't think when we've worked so well."

"We" included Jackson, who had drafted a new novel and completed a short story, "The English Gardens." The story grew out of his and Merrill's encounter with Gregory Corso in Munich. It concerns three characters: Meredith Wilder, a young American poet in Munich on a fellowship; Nicolas Manas, a Beat poet freeloading his way across Europe; and a young American, Mary Jane Lerner, who comes to Munich in pursuit of Manas. The story is an amusing satire of an expatriate milieu Jackson had observed firsthand, but its comedy is very broad. Wilder is the postwar American model of the aesthete who enjoys the largesse of private foundation support without deserving it; Mary Jane is impressionable, shallow, and too well heeled to do more than toy with bohemian living; and Manas, based on Corso, is simply ridiculous. A pretender to poetry, he uses his clumsy boyish "reactions to, say, jazz, cars, and sex" to get "what he wanted: a beer, a convert, a fix (marijuana, heroin, or opium), or at least a 'connection' or money, or a place to stay—a 'pad' in the new jazz language." The tone is superior but fragile. A man on the fringes of the literary scene, David Jackson, is trying to secure a place for himself by laughing at another, Corso, whom readers of the *Partisan Review*—where the story appeared in the company of writers like Lowell and Mary McCarthy—are already prepared to find risible.

In the 1960s, Jackson continued to write fiction, but his publication in *Partisan Review*, gratifying when letters of congratulation came in, did not open publishers' doors to his novels. From the late 1950s to the early 1970s, he spent much of his time painting and drawing. Watercolors were an afternoon pastime; they didn't demand or allow for the careful revision that David found so hard to face in his prose (exasperating Jimmy, the inveterate reviser). As an artist, Jackson could render with freshness and charm a room or a view, a bouquet or a façade, or nicely catch the expression on a face. But he had no formal training, and his figures tend to be awkwardly placed; his effort and his lack of ease show in the sheer meticulousness of his work. Unlike his fiction, David's art wasn't intended for the public. He made it to please himself, and to share with friends. For better or worse, "Writer" remained the occupation listed on his passport.

In Stonington, David's household role was to look after the property. He was no handyman—according to Sewelly "David didn't know what a hammer *was*!"—but the names of plumbers and carpenters show up in his address book. He knew the neighbors and shopkeepers; he drank at the bar of the Portuguese Holy Ghost Society on Main Street; and he came home with the town's gossip. "David is my newspaper," Jimmy liked to say. Jimmy's role was in the kitchen. He was an assiduous chef, but an eccentric one, not a gourmet. He traded recipes with female friends like Toklas, who used his recipe for shrimp *à l'orange* in *The Alice B. Toklas Cookbook*; in turn, she taught him how to bake hash brownies. He reprised leftovers with the stinginess of a rich Yankee—improvised concoctions that sometimes seemed like pranks. In the kitchen, as at his desk, he was averse to throwing things away. More than once, when a casserole crashed on its way to the table, he picked out the shards of glass or crockery, and served it to his guests with a smile.*

Hilda was their "small, baritone-voiced, more than a little mad cleaning woman," as Jackson described her. She called Jackson "Dave" and Jimmy "Merrill." When neighbors said that they had peered into the apartment from a nearby building "and you was running aroun up here nakid," she defended the boys: "I says, 'so <u>what</u>! its theah propity!' " Hilda told them about her mother in the state asylum and her father forced to work the "night ship." An elderly and entirely "stone-deaf" Englishman fell in love with her ("there's something in her nature, primitive don't you know, that appeals to me"); and, when Hilda welcomed his advances, and word of it got around, her husband beat her up. She took refuge in the guest apartment at 107 Water Street. The police called on her, David called a lawyer, and Jimmy called the Englishman "in pure self-defense," so as "to give her another ear (even deaf) to pour her sad tale into." None of this was lost on the neighbors.

---

* JM to DJ, letter, October 2, 1969 (WUSTL), describes one such rescue: "We got most of the larger pieces of broken white pottery separated from the chicken + noodles in cream sauce, and of the smaller bits were able to detect <u>nearly</u> all of them on our plates before we lifted fork to mouth. What few remained gave a most interesting texture."

"The beauty of life in a small town," Merrill reflected, "is that everyone has a little part to play, and can be watched playing it by the others."

That spring—it was 1960—Merrill composed a poem about his Water Street home, called "A Tenancy," which he dedicated to Jackson. "An Urban Convalescence" comes first in *Water Street* and "A Tenancy" last. Thus Merrill gives up New York in the book's first poem and makes his home in Stonington in the last poem. "A Tenancy" begins by looking back even further. The snowy, March afternoon light that he savors in his present home prompts Merrill to recall his elation when he took his first apartment in Amherst in 1946. It is dawn at the end of the war:

> The dance
> Had ended, it was light; the men look tired
> And awkward in their uniforms.
> I sat, head thrown back, and with the dried stains
> Of light on my own cheeks, proposed
> This bargain with—say with the source of light:
> That given a few years more
> (Seven or ten or, what seemed vast, fifteen)
> To spend in love, in a country not at war,
> I would give in return
> All I had. All? A little sun
> Rose in my throat. The lease was drawn.

Almost fifteen years later, the duration of Merrill's first "lease" on life has turned out not to be "vast" at all. "I did not even feel the time expire," he marvels. But that has changed:

> I feel it though, today, in this new room,
> Mine, with my things and thoughts, a view
> Of housetops, treetops, the walls bare.
> A changing light is deepening, is changing
> To a gilt ballroom chair a chair
> Bound to break under someone before long.
> I let the light change also me.

The "changing light": this is the first appearance of that phrase which Merrill would return to for the title of his long poem more than twenty years later. Here it is a trope for time and the way time changes the self, which Merrill is no longer determined to resist: "I let the light change also me."

"A Tenancy": the title is curious, since Merrill is talking about a home he owns. It implies that we are merely tenants even in our own house. The principle holds for our bodies: "The body that lived through that day," Merrill says about the long-ago day he is remembering, "[. . .] is now not mine." His body, no longer the youthful one he had, will become stranger still with age. But, he reasons, perhaps the body is transformed by time before it is lost to it—like that ordinary chair which, although "Bound to break under someone before long," becomes "a gilt ballroom chair" in the late-afternoon light. "Would it be called a soul?" Merrill asks, wondering what time is making of him. He doesn't go so far as to claim for himself a metaphysical, Keatsian "soul," but simply a developed attitude, a point of view that is worldly, practical, and witty. He knows that "when the light dies and the bell rings," guests will appear. He ends by welcoming them:

> One foot asleep, I hop
> To let my three friends in. They stamp
> Themselves free of the spring's
> Last snow—or so we hope.
>
> One has brought violets in a pot;
> The second, wine; the best,
> His open, empty hand. Now in the room
> The sun is shining like a lamp.
> I put the flowers where I need them most
>
> And then, not asking why they come,
> Invite the visitors to sit.
> If I am host at last
> It is of little more than my own past.
> May others be at home in it.

The metaphorical house envisioned at the end of "An Urban Convalescence" takes shape in Merrill's Stonington home. Again, the switch from free verse into metered stanzas matters. At a moment when American poets were arguing over "closed" and "open" form, Merrill recognized that, to get beyond the self-enclosure of his early poems, he didn't have to reject rhyme and meter; he could change how he used them. In "A Tenancy," he puts them in the service not of lyric idealization and abstraction, but of sociability and comic self-dramatization, and gives us a look into his house and his writing process. "One foot asleep, I hop / To let my three friends in," he says, getting his metrical feet in working order, ready to host his guests and readers both. "Closed" form would be his means to openness.

Water Street was nearly complete by fall 1960 when Merrill and Jackson began another long trip to Europe and the Mediterranean. Creatures of habit, they started in Paris. Merrill enjoyed seeing paintings by Corot in the Louvre. He had labored that summer to produce an essay on Corot for the Art Institute of Chicago, commissioned in connection with an exhibition. "Notes on Corot" is his only sustained commentary on a visual artist. The first paragraph suggests why:

> The writer will always envy the painter. Even those who write well about painting, he will envy for having learned to pay close attention to appearances. And not the writer alone; it is the rare person who can look at anything for more than a few seconds without turning to language for support, so little does he believe his eyes.

At least Merrill was not such a person. Despite his claim, often made, that he cared only for appearances, he was too hungry for meaning to be satisfied with them in a painting. He went on in this essay to take up one work by Corot after another, patiently extracting meanings and morals. And the writing was an ordeal: "3000 words that left me gassy and weak."

In Paris, besides the Corots and, as usual, Miss Toklas, they saw the American expatriate painter David Hill. Hill's neoclassical sensibility was offbeat and austere (his definition of a portrait: "a painting with something funny about the eyes"). Through Hill, Merrill met a Canadian poet, Daryl Hine. An erudite classicist and puckish wit, Hine, with tousled brown hair, glasses, and a cape, could have strolled out of a French novel, and he charmed Merrill instantly. Less than a year later, with Merrill's encouragement, Hine would move to New York, where he became Merrill's confidant and, after his nephew Robin, his first protégé. Merrill showed Hine's poetry to his editor friends Hollander and Moss, brought Hine to parties, pointed out prizes he might compete for, and helped him financially. In *A Different Person*, Merrill recalls their initial meeting in Paris. The two *flâneurs* were taking the air after lunch, when a prostitute called out, "*Quel joli papillon.*" "We'll pretend she means your bow tie," Hine quipped, knowing just how flamboyant he and Merrill looked. He cleared his throat: "Shall I call you James—" and Merrill, who was ten years older but only thirty-four, rushed in to give permission to use his first name. But Hine wasn't done with his question. He finished: "—or Jimmy?" "Embarrassed," Merrill ends the anecdote, "I let my answer stand." With that, Jimmy had become "James"—what many friends, but especially younger people, would call him in the future.

Back at home, Richard M. Nixon and John F. Kennedy were debating each other in the campaign for president. "Well," Merrill sniffed when Jackson mailed his absentee ballot, "one day I simply must arrange to be in the states for this quaint demonstration." They returned to Munich, where, as opposed to Paris, Merrill observed, "there are fewer associations, so one can breathe without choking. Rilke's leaves have turned gold, fallen, and turned black [. . .]. The War Ministry has turned into a Piranesi." David wasn't writing—"alas," Jimmy sighed—but he was "doing some lovely sketches." They'd bought a new black Volkswagen convertible, a car so ugly "we can use it only at night." Jimmy read Casanova's memoirs. "Every night," Jackson recorded him saying, "we spend looking for sex; and, as I am becoming impotent"—that theme again—"I must simply face up to having to find something else to fill my evenings." So they tried the opera: *Il Trittico, I Puritani, Mathis der Maler, The Egyptian Helen.* They went to Oktoberfest beer halls and caroused with the German translator of *The Seraglio* (which appeared in 1961 under the title, irritating to its author, of *Tanning Junior*). John Cage and Merce Cunningham passed through Munich, then Donald "Richie-san," Capote, and Hine. Hine brought with him Anne and Virgil Burnett, she a scholar of ancient Greek literature and he an illustrator of fine books and literary broadsides, who would become good friends with Merrill.

From Munich, they made trips to Hamburg and Berlin. Thom Gunn, a British poet three years younger than Merrill with a hard-edged intelligence and working-class tastes, recalls Ellis Bierbar in West Berlin, where he first met "the Merrills." Improbably, the place had been run since 1942 as a queer bar by Elli, a determined woman who wore men's suits. "An old fellow in Edwardian dress, always sitting at the same place at the bar, was appropriately known as Queen Mary," Gunn recalls. Local workmen, East Berlin hustlers (the Wall didn't go up until 1961), and traveling writers like Gunn filled out the clientele.

> One day I noticed—everybody noticed—the entrance of two young Americans nattily dressed alike in brimmed hats and expensive raincoats. (Very American Express, I thought.) One of them I hardly noticed, but the other caught my eye and I couldn't take it off him. Eventually, after a lot of looking on both sides, they stepped forward

and the other one said, "Excuse me, but isn't your name Thom Gunn?" I then recognized him: it was James Merrill, with whom I had given a poetry reading a year or two before. The other one, the one I found so attractive, was David Jackson. They asked me to join them for lunch the next day, and I felt rather sheepish.

Merrill and Gunn, two laureates of gay desire, admired each other's poetry for the next thirty years without becoming friends. "I met Merrill only once more," Gunn notes, "at the end of our lives, when I asked him to lunch in my home in San Francisco—a repayment for the generous lunch he had given me so many years before. Again the level of conversation was that of small talk. It would have been nice if we could have chatted about the supreme themes of sex and poetry, but that was that. If we had seen more of each other, I probably would have found him too elegant, and he would have found me too much of a slob."

The Merrills crossed the Alps in their ugly Bug and matching raincoats. In Venice they were treated to a "masque" in their honor written by Alan Ansen, presented in the garden of Peggy Guggenheim's palazzo. They drove to the heel of the Italian boot and boarded a ferry for Egypt. The sixteen days they spent there, mostly in Alexandria, were important to Merrill for the rest of his life. Primed by Lawrence Durrell's *Alexandria Quartet* and the poems of Cavafy, Jimmy became, in spirit, an honorary citizen of Alexandria.

Their host was a schoolmate of Tony Parigory's, Christian Ayoub. The dark-featured, handsome Ayoub came from a Greek Catholic family of civil servants. Like most people of his class in the port city, he was a Francophone who knew Arabic, Italian, Greek, and English—which he spoke with a crisp Oxbridge accent. He wrote lyric poems in English and French; he was also the author of two experimental novels in French, *Artagal* and *Pola de Pera*, both of which Merrill relished. Through Ayoub, Merrill made "a half dozen perfectly delicious friends." These included Ayoub's cousin Bernard de Zogheb and the Nahmanns—Jean, a cotton merchant nicknamed "Johnny," and his wife Germaine, "a small black-eyed gamine known in Paris it seems as Moustafette."

Along with Parigory, these Alexandrians had been "prammed" together, ferried to parks and parties by their English nannies, educated in elite schools, and accustomed to exquisite social rituals—polo, costume balls, "*les visites des tantes*." The city founded by Alexander the Great, battled over by Julius Caesar and Cleopatra, had enjoyed a modern efflorescence, beginning with the cotton boom of the 1860s when Alexandria became a capital of the colonial world, *"une ville européanne"* on the Nile delta. La Belle Époque hung on there all the way into the postwar era: in 1960, the city (or the narrow strip of coastline on which Merrill's new friends lived) seemed more like Proust's Paris than Paris itself. Ayoub and his friends inherited that world, with its frippery, snobbery, and mongrel chic, just as it was about to vanish. But the city had always been a haunted, half-imagined place. As Christine Ayoub, Christian's daughter, explains, "Alexandria could only exist in your imagination. You never would have seen Cleopatra, or the Ptolemies, or Cavafy."

At a cocktail party to welcome them, the Americans found the other guests disorientingly "unplaceable": "it would have been impossible to tell from names or faces [. . .] what would have been the 'original' race of any one." (Jimmy and David must have seemed just as mysterious to the Alexandrians. As one remarked, "[M]ais ces américains, tu dis qu'ils ne sont pas cottoniers—qui sont-ils donc?") The tone of the milieu was giddy, "so enchanting as to faire peur." "As the colony shrinks, the gossip and private jokes grow, I suspect, increasingly animated, like the thrashing of fish in a pond that is drying up. One spent the whole evening laughing wildly," Merrill wrote to his mother, "over stories involving people one had barely glimpsed," while outside the muezzin's call to prayer and the jangling music of car radios rose and fell in waves.

Traveling south, Merrill was mesmerized by the "fantastic landscape": the Nile flowed north, lined by palms and tents, while farmers in "long nightshirts" worked the earth, and "strange, nougat-pale mountains that are not on the map rise behind it all." He already knew he was "very susceptible to Egypt." But he was less interested in the massive monuments at Aswan and Luxor ("we didn't even go <u>inside</u> the Sphinx. Or ride a camel") than in the delicate antiquities displayed in Cairo: "those THINGS, the sphinx, the masks of beaten gold, the little gods [. . .], are lamps against which I can feel my wings tattering as they beat." He stood for a long time before the mummy of a child, "the very flesh covered with gold leaf." "I think I know what the soul is," he wrote to Freddy, trying to say what he felt in the presence of those funerary treasures. "It is the body we no longer have."

They spent Christmas in a flat in Athens decorated with a tree and fresh-cut boughs of mistletoe: "We have the best-hung doorways of anyone you know," Merrill bragged to Bernie Winebaum. Donald Richie was there too. He made an album of photos portraying the young Greek men he and Jimmy and David were meeting. Today, sepia tinted by time, the collection could serve as illustrations for Cavafy's erotic memory poems: strong, poor men with sharp features, naked and muscled with erections, some of them wearing army fatigues and a beret, the room bare—an ashtray or a faded window sash for ornament—and from the window or balcony, a clear view of the Acropolis, tiled houses clustered at the base of it, and no skyscrapers anywhere. No longer complaining of impotence, Jimmy wrote to Claude, "I blush to say that I am blooming for the first time in a year, or the last time in this life."

By February 1961, when they returned to snow-covered Water Street, the two of them had finally "Seen the World." David's sketchbook had "burst its seams." As he had on his most recent return from Greece, Jimmy fell sick, this time with "fevers and unaccountable weaknesses," which didn't go away. After three months, he woke up one morning to find that his skin had turned yellow: it was hepatitis. It would take a long time for him to recover from his adventures abroad.

His mother had told him to keep a bag packed against the day when she called to say that Mis' Annie had died. That call came in May, and Jimmy flew south to Atlanta. He sat in the presence of his grandmother's body, which was laid out wearing a red velvet dress, her face prettily made up, on her bed in the Plummers' home. Alone with the body, he had the disturbing sense that Mis' Annie wasn't dead—an uncanny sensation that would linger with him for years. Then came the funeral and burial in Jacksonville. "I had never seen anyone dead, or even been to a funeral—all that was appalling and fascinating," he told Kimon. He tried to face the event in a poem titled "Annie Hill's Grave." It begins,

> Amen. The casket like a spaceship bears her
> In streamlined, airtight comfort underground.
> Necropolis is a nice place to visit;
> One would not want to live there all year round.

Grim, jaunty, satirical, plangent, stoic—Merrill's tone shifts from one mood to another in the course of the poem. The mourners link arms in relief and, in their "sunnier / Counterclockwise movement" away from the grave, they resist "the whirlpool that has swallowed her." In her casket, sucked into the earth, Mis' Annie remains somehow still alive. "Alone, she grips, against confusion, pictures / Of us the living, and of the tall youth / She wed," who has spent the past thirty years awaiting her company in the next plot. The poem's final lines express Jimmy's terror of being left alone. As "the brief snail-trace / Of her withdrawal dries upon our faces / The silence drums into her upturned face."

"Annie Hill's Grave," finished in July 1961, was a late addition to the manuscript of *Water Street*. Merrill shuffled poems in and out of the book over the summer and fall. He decided to dedicate it to the Surly Temple—Robert and Isabel, Eleanor and Grace—and sent it to Knopf in September. The venerable firm had undergone changes: Random House purchased Knopf in 1959, and Harry Ford had left to join Atheneum, a new house. Merrill's poems came back from Knopf in November; their note rejecting them was "considerably nastier than the one I sent them saying I wouldn't much care if they did." The rejection must have stung, but he knew he could depend on Ford, who quickly arranged to publish *Water Street* at Atheneum in fall 1962.

Merrill trusted the curmudgeonly bon vivant Ford, depending on his aesthetic discrimination and his business sense not only in the making and marketing of his books, but in the administration of the Ingram Merrill Foundation. For years, Jimmy had had to deal with pleas for money from friends that arrived unpredictably by phone call or cable. Once he'd made up his mind to help, he phoned Larry Condon. The lawyer cross-examined him before agreeing to make the often complex financial arrangements necessary to give away the money, entailing signatures, carbon copies, annual statements, and so forth. "And, of course," David remarked gloomily in his journal, oppressed by the continual demands on his partner, "this money thing is attended by the guilts and enforced odd attitudes of the borrowees and by what ever curious underground reflexes JM attaches to it." Because Merrill kept no records of his personal "loans" and seldom mentioned giving money in his correspondence, there is no telling how many people he helped. From a letter by John Myers we know that, when the poet James Schuyler had a nervous breakdown in 1961, Merrill paid for Schuyler's in-patient psychotherapy, which Thomas Detre supervised. It was typical of Merrill that the matter was handled by a go-between—Myers—so that, although Schuyler surely knew who his benefactor was, he would not be beholden to Merrill.

The Ingram Merrill Foundation offered a partial solution to this dilemma. By the late 1950s, Merrill simply referred most requests for money to the IMF. It provided "partial relief" and, Jackson felt, "a glimmer of a sense of accomplishment and creativity with the money." A selection committee consisting of Harry Ford, Marius Bewley, John Myers, Irma Brandeis, and Merrill himself met twice per year to consider formal grant applications. John Hollander joined in 1960; he and Ford remained on the committee until the foundation went out of business after Merrill's death.

The selection committee preferred to give money to people with no other obvious sources to appeal to (so grants were seldom made to academics, or performers and artists for whose work there was a commercial market) or to people who the committee knew to be in a state of need. The selectors took their duties very seriously, carefully reading applicants' work, attending various performances and gallery openings, and arguing the merits of each case. Investigating an application from a theater group, Jimmy and Irma took part in a movement class called "Sitting, Standing, and Walking"—just to be sure that the subjects of instruction didn't also include "Getting Away with Murder."

Over the decades, the foundation would give grants to many poets and writers celebrated today: among them, Derek Walcott, Susan Sontag, Randall Jarrell, James Purdy, Jean Stafford, Jane Bowles, W. D. Snodgrass, Frank O'Hara, John Ashbery, and Charles Simic.* Special awards were made in literature to eminent writers, including William Empson, Francis Ponge, Italo Calvino, Jorge Luis Borges, Marianne Moore, Auden, A. D. Hope, Zbigniew Herbert, I. A. Richards, and V. S. Prichett. But most of the foundation's money went to young or little-known people. The IMF supported the avant-garde filmmakers Gregory Markopoulos and Stan Brakhage, and visual artists such as Nell Blaine and Joe Brainard. Dance was represented by Jean Erdman, the Dance Notation Bureau, and the School of American Ballet. Substantial grants were made to colleges and universities so that they could buy for their museums specific works of art from New York School painters like Hartigan and Rivers. The foundation supported the *Hudson Review*, the *Partisan Review, Poetry* magazine, and the *Quarterly Review of Literature*, among other literary journals, as well as an array of arts schools and charities: Lighthouse for the Blind, Skowhegan School of Painting and Sculpture, Aspen Music Festival, Spanish Refugee Aid, Italian Earthquake Relief, and the Animal Welfare Institute, among other concerns, and most of these year after year. In 1962, a fairly typical year, the IMF divided a little more than $100,000 between thirty-two individuals and organizations. Special awards were made to Nicola Chiaromonte and F. R. Leavis. A large gift—$3,000—went to Djuna Barnes, the author of *Nightwood*. The elderly Barnes, who hadn't applied, was awarded money for

---

* The lack of systematic records makes it impossible to write a thorough history of the foundation. But the scale of its philanthropy can be inferred from the fact that the Wikipedia entry for the Ingram Merrill Foundaton lists well over one hundred recipients, and that without mention of most of the names listed in this paragraph. At the height of its giving in the 1990s, the foundation's disbursements totaled about $300,000 per year. See John Swansburg, "The View from Stonington: If the Walls Could Talk, It Would be Poetry," *NYT*, January 28 (2001).

the second time as "a distinguished and neglected writer who is penniless and ill." Fifty applications were passed over that year. The *refusées* would have made a lively salon: Alex Katz, Allen Ginsberg, Merce Cunningham, and James T. Farrell were among them.

The foundation was never endowed; the money it gave came directly from Merrill's income. It was a considered, conscientious way for him to put his wealth to use, and he never took any conspicuous credit for it. In turn, it was very useful to him. It shielded him from petitioners, and it defended him from the disgruntled rejected applicant, to whom he could shrug and point out that the committee had made the negative decision. Yet the arrangement was an imperfect compromise. By putting himself on the committee, which was composed of his friends, he kept close watch on the awards, and the annual list of beneficiaries reflected his preferences, many of which were based in friendships. He never insisted on having his way, but he didn't have to. As Hollander puts it, "When James expressed a preference, that was that." His involvement in the IMF kept him in the role of a benefactor, subject to resentment and fawning, and it made the foundation's awards appear, to the skeptical, like court favors. Merrill encouraged certain friends to apply, and some artists and ensembles won IMF support many times. New York Pro Musica Antiqua was one of these. Arthur Gold and Robert Fizdale, duo pianists, and the Little Players, the puppet troupe of Francis Peschka and Gordon Murdock, were another instance. These two pairs of performing artists—both pairs were also gay couples—were special favorites. It's doubtful that their eccentric artistry would have flourished without the Ingram Merrill Foundation.

Merrill collaborated very closely with the Little Players. The troupe consisted of five glove puppets that the peculiarly gifted Murdock manipulated and gave voice to. Their faces, bodies, and costumes were simple, even crude, evoking children's play and Punch and Judy. They performed Wilde, Maeterlinck, and Chekhov, *Hamlet*, *Macbeth*, and *Lear*, and other theater classics, but seldom in their entirety: as a rule, their evenings were a miscellany of famous scenes, a selection of show tunes, or a program of French songs or German or Italian arias. Despite the fact that they had no legs, the puppets danced highlights from *Pelléas and Mélisande* and *Giselle*. The offerings mixed high and popular art, grand opera and the music hall. Performances were interrupted by the puppets' exchanges with the audience and with each other. A puppet in the wings might pipe up to criticize a scene, or announce that another puppet due onstage was indisposed, breaking the dramatic frame, such as it was.

"The five actors composed an ad hoc family—resembling a household in a novel by, say, Ronald Firbank or Ivy Compton-Burnett," writes Kenneth Gross, author of a brief history of the Little Players. The "founder" of the troupe was Isabelle Standwell—an allusion to Edith Sitwell and to the fact that Isabelle, like the rest of her company, could not stand on her own. With a proper English accent, she played grandes dames like Lady Bracknell. Heroic parts went to her twin brother (their heads were made from the same mold). The company's diva, and a character of special interest to Merrill (he wrote a poem about her), was Garonce—whose name suggested Garance, the heroine played by Arletty in Marcel Carné's film about another theatrical troupe, *Les Enfants du Paradis* (another favorite of Merrill's).

The mock troupe, Gross remarks, "suggested an alliance that ran against the grain of a heterosexual family, an odd, faithful, hospitable gathering of exiles, survivors, and orphans, a clutch of sophisticatedly child-like adults who neither married nor begot children nor even had affairs, whose sexuality was never confessed, who wove their lives out of so many threads of theatrical play." The feeling of "an ad hoc family" was reinforced by the fact that the Little Players performed in the living room of Peschka and Murdock's small Upper West Side apartment. Folding chairs accommodated about twenty-five people, who came by invitation or word of mouth. The audience included celebrities in postwar arts and letters (George Balanchine, Leonard Bernstein, Susan Sontag, Lowell, Saul Steinberg, Edward Gorey, Willem de Kooning, Richard Avedon) and many of Merrill's poet friends: Ashbery, Ford, Hollander, Hine, Bishop, and Richard Howard. Tea was served before the performance, and everyone went "backstage" afterward to congratulate Peschka and Murdock. "Their theater," Gross summarizes, "was about making and inhabiting a home."

Gold and Fizdale also were regulars in the Little Players' audience. Their partnership was almost as unusual in music as Peschka and Murdock's was in theater. They offered the spectacle of two men in matching tuxedos, who were former lovers and lifelong companions, making music on the same instrument while sitting side by side and often on the same bench. Their playing was touching and showy, golden and fizzy. The special charm of it lay in how, like Peschka and Murdock, they drew on the energy of childhood play. Fittingly, Saint-Saëns's *Carnival of the Animals* was a showpiece for "the boys." They performed the whole repertory of piano works for four hands and two pianos, including the concerti for two pianos by Mozart and Poulenc (which they recorded with Leonard Bernstein and the New York Philharmonic) and works commissioned for them by John Cage, Paul Bowles, and Ned Rorem. Merrill's favorite in their songbook was the *Dolly Suite* by Fauré, "a lemony, edgy, sometimes sad, sometimes frothy duet writ-

ten for Debussy's stepdaughter." Their concerts were events in New York's
gay high-culture calendar, followed by parties hosted by Jerome Robbins
or Lincoln Kirstein, with a crush of guests. In fall 1961, Merrill heard them
perform Schumann's *Spanische Liebeslieder* (a work they recorded for the
first time) with the baritone William Warfield. The evening was so affecting that, Jimmy laughed, it made "an entire audience (Marianne Moore and
1200 white faggots) think twice about their love lives."

With his manuscript of poems finally off his desk, Merrill found himself
with "empty hands, whose thumbs I keep furiously twiddling so as not to
turn on the radio or open a newspaper with them." There was reason to
avoid the news. Nikita Khrushchev announced in October that the Soviet
Union planned to test a massive hydrogen bomb before the end of the
month, and American newspapers filled up with the prospect of "Halloween Horror." "Baby Ivan" was detonated in the atmosphere on October 30.
Weighing twenty-seven tons, and producing a mushroom cloud forty miles
high, it was the largest, most destructive weapon ever deployed. A mighty
fireball emerged, reaching down to the earth 13,000 feet below and rising
"slowly and silently" at the same time, "powerful and arrogant like Jupiter,"
as one observer put it. "The 50 megaton bomb explodes," Merrill wrote in
his journal. Beneath that note, he began a poem. His starting point was a
spoonerism by Robert Morse:

> "glaze of bory"
> > glaze of boredom
>
>
> > a round red blaze of glory, the sailor's
> Delight. It would be fine tomorrow,
> The thought put you excitedly to sleep.
>
> It happened so often as to be worth remarking
> That tomorrow was not fine at all.
> A God weaker [crossed out: stronger] than the sun, but eviller,
> Turned your life gray, chill. You sat in a glaze of boredom.
>
> Hands interlocked, making the church, the steeple,—thunderclap!
> Your thumbs flew open, the people lay,
> A ten-legged insect of flesh,
> A pink, loathed, wriggling insect in your lap.

Merrill's "glaze of boredom" turns "blaze of glory" on its head, and, with it, the overheated rhetoric of Cold War headlines. The bomb and the hovering threat it released reminded him of days of vague anxiety in childhood when he was left to amuse himself, and he played with his hands. Rather than a reassuring community in a church, he turned his splayed fingers into a scene of people lying wounded and "wriggling."

Typically for Merrill, the draft poem grew out of wordplay. Anagrams and spoonerisms decorate the borders of his notebook entries and poem drafts throughout his career, but with increasing frequency in the late 1950s and early 1960s. Wordplay filled in, not only the empty space of a page, but empty time, like the faces he idly doodled, or the games of Solitaire—he preferred to call it Patience—which he played as a break from writing. He played with the letters of the alphabet as if with a pack of cards: the kinds of game associated with both of them entail the same sort of process—the recombination of elements within a fixed set. Using block capital letters, Merrill would take a word or phrase or, more often, a proper name and, working systematically down the page, sometimes using a typewriter, rearrange the letters to produce new words and phrases. The process released the hidden potential, often hilarious or titillating, in a common expression or familiar name. "SELF SERVICE" turned into "SIL-VER FECES," and "POSTAGE" into "GESTAPO," while "PROUST" induced "STUPOR," and "MARCEL PROUST" revealed a "PEARL SCROTUM." The name of Mary McCarthy hid a poignant demand: "CRY AT MY CHARM." Sometimes the wordplay made for a piece of naughty light verse, as in this epigram:

THE MODEL'S CONFESSION

RICHARD AVEDON'S

HARDONS I CRAVED.

The author presiding over the anagram and other wordplay in Merrill's work is "Vivian Darkbloom"—the anagram of his own name that Vladimir Nabokov embeds as an alter ego in *Lolita*. Merrill began a page of anagrams with "Vivian Darkbloom" at the top of it, below which he rang changes on "Irma Brandeis" and "David Jackson." "JAMES MERRILL," allowing for a missing "E," yielded "RIMER J. SMALL."

Anagrams felt like a mildly shameful addiction to Merrill. To us, they might seem like a diversion from writing, or a finger exercise, occasionally producing, at best, a nugget of wit. But Merrill's anagrams and other forms of combinatory play show his drive, even as he seemed to be wasting his time, to make something of it. They show his hunger for meaning, for motivated rather than arbitrary signs. They show him keeping in shape—for poems and for Ouija dictées. They show his faith that, for anyone who is patient and clever enough, meaning is there to be discovered in the alphabet itself.

Like doodling and Patience, these combinatory games dramatized how the writer generates characters out of the repertoire of types found in mythology, literary or social convention, and the unconscious, suggesting, even, a way to think about human generation and the course of individual lives. Merrill makes the point in "Time," a poem he began in fall 1961. In any game of "blessed Patience," the deck of cards provides "Fifty-two chromosomes permitting / Trillions of 'lives'—some few / Triumphant, the majority / Blocked, doomed, yet satisfying, too," because even when the player fails, he can, "before starting over," discover where the game went wrong, and observe its logic. Play of this kind implies a vision of life in which everything makes sense, even the failure to make sense—which is the perspective Merrill had discovered through the Ouija board, where the twenty-six letters of the alphabet worked like the fifty-two cards of the playing deck to generate the voices from the Other World that spoke to JM and DJ. The Ouija board taught Merrill to think of *people* as anagrams. They are subject to cycles of reincarnation on earth during which, as in a game of Patience, the soul takes one form after another, "some few / Triumphant, the majority / Blocked" and obliged to start over.

When humanity seemed freshly menaced with extinction in fall 1961, Merrill and Jackson appealed to Ephraim. In *The Book of Ephraim*, Merrill quotes a long Ouija transcript dated October 26—at the height of anxiety about the fifty-megaton bomb. Lyrical and lucid, Ephraim begins,

AM I IN YR ROOM SO ARE ALL YR DEAD WHO HAVE NOT GONE INTO OTHER BODIES IT IS EASY TO CALL THEM BRING THEM AS FIRES WITHIN SIGHT OF EACH OTHER ON HILLS U & YR GUESTS THESE TIMES WE SPEAK ARE WITHIN SIGHT OF & ALL CONNECTED TO EACH OTHER DEAD OR ALIVE NOW DO U UNDERSTAND WHAT HEAVEN IS IT IS THE SURROUND OF THE LIVING

Ephraim goes on to describe the plight of the patron as he works to educate his representative: "O MY DEARS WE ARE OFTEN WEAKER THAN OUR REPRESENTATIVES IT IS A SILENT LOVE WE ARE IN A SYSTEM OF SUCH SILENT BUT URGENT MOTIVES," like Cold War secret agents, working against time to save not only earth but heaven, since the spirits themselves seem to depend on the living for survival. "DEVOTION" binds the two levels together. Ephraim rises to prophecy—"A FLOOD IS BUILDING UP"—while remaining touchingly personal, offhand:

O MY I AM TOO EXCITED SO FEW UP HERE WISH TO THINK THEIR EYES ARE
TURNED HAPPILY UP AS THEY FLOAT TOWARD THE CLIFF I WANT TO DO MORE
THAN RIDE & WEAR & WAIT ON THE FAIRLY LIVELY GROUND OF MY LIFE I
HAVE THIS HIGH LOOKOUT BUT FIND TO MY SURPRISE THAT I AM WISEST
WHEN I LOOK STRAIGHT DOWN AT THE PRECIOUS GROUND I KNEW

He ends by promising further revelations:

THERE IS AHEAD A SERIES OF PICTURES I BELIEVE I CD SHOW U TO MAKE
CLEARER MY SELF & WHAT IT IS I THINK THE FORCE OF THE FLOOD HAS ONLY
ADVANCED A DROP OR 2 DOWN THE FACE OF THE CLIFF & MAN HAS TAKEN
THEM TO BE TEARS NOW U UNDERSTAND MY LOVE OF TELLING MY LIFE FOR
IN ALL TRUTH I AM IMAGINING THE NEXT ONE WHEN WE CRASH THROUGH
IN OUR NUMBERS TRANSFORMING LIFE INTO WELL EITHER A GREAT GLORY
OR A GREAT PUDDLE

Hine, who had moved to New York by this time, did the board with Merrill and Jackson that fall, and he suggested that Merrill might make poems out of messages like these. JM was trying to. On the notebook pages with his poem about a "glaze of bory," Merrill adapted images from Ephraim: "The dead shine back like coins," "tears on the cliff face." But he was stymied. He would have to wait another twelve years before he could write Ephraim's poem.

Side by side for hours at the table in their red dining room on Water Street, candles glowing and guttering, their hands on the darting willowware cup, Merrill and Jackson were like Gold and Fizdale at the piano, virtuosi of the spirits, creating with their homemade properties a private puppet theater far stranger than the Little Players of Peschka and Murdock (but was it the spirits or their mediums who were the puppets?). At the Ouija board as in daily life, David and Jimmy were by now skilled, familiar partners. Their relationship had taken on many aspects of a conventional heterosexual marriage. They knew each other's families. One added messages on letters the other wrote. They sent out Christmas cards printed with a poem by the one or a sketch by the other. When they socialized, they wore coordinated, sometimes identical outfits. They had their household duties, daily routines, shared jokes, a cat. But "the Merrills," whether despite all of this togetherness or because of it, had grown apart from each other—which was conventional too.*

No small part of their initial attraction had been sexual, and part of their new distance was sexual. "The time for making love is done," Merrill says in "Poem of Summer's End," which he wrote after he and Jackson returned from Greece for the first time. He was referring, on one level, to Jackson and himself. In the late 1950s, they stopped making love. David, with his William Holden good looks and wedding ring, had always been the straight man in the couple. In Greece, David "graduated" to the "passive" role that the internationals took with the Greeks; he became one of "the sisters," like Jimmy, who wanted to be penetrated. For David, this amounted to a gain in power and status from one angle and a loss of those things from another one. Sexual position and preference were strictly defined, if not consistently adhered to, in the pecking order of queer culture, in New York as well as Greece. To be the one thing was not to be the other; in David's case, it was not to be the kind of partner who attracted Jimmy, and Jimmy may have felt betrayed or rejected by the change. On Water Street, he and David became accustomed, as Charles and Hellen Merrill had, to separate bedrooms. DJ began sleeping in the guest apartment, which gradually became his. "A Tenancy" is dedicated to him, but he doesn't appear in the poem. Merrill is the host. The house he describes is "Mine," not "ours," "with my things and thoughts."

The distance they were growing into could have been predicted. Jackson and Merrill had met as men of different classes, with different educations, sensibilities, talents, and expectations. Their matching outfits, chosen and paid for by Merrill, tried to disguise those differences, to wish them away. Perhaps Jimmy simply grew tired of David—who, even in the 1950s, drank too much, stayed in bed too long, and couldn't establish himself as a writer. His warmth and vitality, his sense of adventure and capacity for play, whether on the Ouija board or the streets of Munich at Carnival, were not always enough to hold Jimmy's attention. But Merrill might have grown apart from any companion. He was born to and required a certain solitude: that of the only child in a family of great wealth, adored and neglected both,

---

* In fall 1962, Merrill drew up an outline for *The Stonington Novel*, a book he never wrote more than a page of, its chief interest being the diminishment in what he and David felt about the town and each other. When they first drove to Stonington from New York, they got lost, and the Connecticut shore seemed "an interminable distance from civilization. Gradually they get used to the road (over the years), discover short cuts; the highway itself is modernized. Towards the end, they are making the trips between City and their house in half the time, twice as often, usually in sullen silence—contrast with the first, endless, animated, journey." JM, notes for "The Stonington Novel" (WUSTL).

whose mind worked faster and traveled farther than anyone he was with, and who was driven every day, in the privacy of his study, to make himself a poet of enduring achievement. For all his generosity, his ambition and privilege sometimes made him selfish, and selfishness sometimes made him "cold."

In early November 1961, as the radioactive dust from "Baby Ivan" settled, Merrill and Jackson made arrangements to sail to France, their first stop on the way to another, this time longer, stay in Greece. They planned to depart on March 3, Jimmy's thirty-sixth birthday. No sooner had Merrill made a life for himself on Water Street and claimed it in his poetry than he felt the need to leave and create something else. During the "crisis" of their first trip together to Greece in 1959, Jackson had sensed that his companion was "ready for a new life." It turned out that he was right, and Merrill would search for that new life in Greece. This did not mean, however, that they were about to break up, as David had feared. Jimmy had too much of a "horror" of the broken home to set out on his own, or to force David out. Besides, he was going to need David in Greece, as he had needed him on Water Street.

PART III

GREECE

1962–72

7

THE CRACK IN THE MIRROR

1962–64

As if taking Water Street with them, Merrill and Jackson began their journey to Greece in the company of Grace Stone and Eleanor Perényi. "Well, it is really the end, dullness-wise," Jimmy wrote on board the *Queen Mary*; "G. is constantly haranguing pursers, stewards, anyone who will listen." In Paris they parted ways with the Stone Women, and had tea with Alice B. Toklas. They acquired a red VW, and drove through gray and snowy Yugoslavia "into green and sunny Greece."

Prepared for their longest stay yet in Athens, they took an apartment on Ploutarchou Street, near where they stayed in 1960. Their Athens was agreeably small. They could find someone they knew at a table in Kolonáki Square at any time of day or night. They could walk two blocks further and enter the cool shadows and gravel paths of the National Garden. They could take a taxi to shop in the flea market in Monastiráki, sun themselves at the beach at Faterón, eat at a restaurant in the Plaka, the old town at the base of the Acropolis, or visit the celebrated ruins in moonlight. Cafés and tavernas closed late, if at all. Fresh from siestas, people strolled or chatted under stars that were as sharp and clear as they had been above the first Attic shepherds. The city's first traffic light had only been installed recently.

ILLUSTRATION JM in the doorway of Athinaion Efivon44 with his and DJ's red VW convertible parked outside, 1965

Fruits, vegetables, and household goods were sold by street vendors. "Every other day," David noted in his journal, "a big block [of ice], wisped with straw, arrives [. . .] for deposit in our oak ice-chest." It was delivered by Niko, a dark-haired boy who sat in good clothes on his day off, earnest and handsome, while David painted his portrait in watercolors. "We still know nothing about him—at 18 what is there to know about anyone?—but we can see his eager good nature for decades to come." The eager good nature of Athens seemed just as bright, just as apparent.

It was not the same capital that Merrill had first visited in 1950. Along with that first traffic light had come other developments. Greece was the only noncommunist state on the Balkan Peninsula, and the U.S., competing with the Soviet Union for dominance in the region, expanded its commercial investments and military presence in Greece, installing nuclear weapons in its bases there—which would be a source of controversy for years to come. The economy was thriving, leading to dramatic increases in industrial production and per capita income.* The population of Athens grew by leaps; new housing linked outlying towns to the city center, creating a vast concrete metropolis. Olympic Airways, founded by the shipping magnate Aristotle Onassis in 1957, introduced jet service from Athens to Rome, Paris, and London in 1958 (direct flights from Athens to New York began in 1966), and Greece became a favored destination for the jet set. The paparazzi trailing Jacqueline Kennedy and Sophia Loren turned its sun-raked beaches, vine-roofed tavernas, and sugar-cube villages into familiar images. Tourists followed. Pleasure seemed like a fitting reward after the suffering and shortages of the past decades, for Greeks as well as western Europeans. Melina Mercouri, who starred as a Piraeus prostitute in the film *Never on Sunday* (1960), symbolized the nation's rough new glamour and sexiness. The glow extended even to poetry: in 1963, crowning the modern movement in Greek letters, George Seferis won the Nobel Prize.

The change could be felt in daily life. "The broad brown peasant hand sports a manicure," Merrill noted. "In the jeweler's showcase appear worry-beads of lapis lazuli. The tavern with its dirt floor and unshaded bulbs, its ill-carpentered table revolving, plates and all, in a dancer's strong teeth, has been supplanted by some 'instant' folklore of whitewash and candlelight, woven hangings, and music to which no one moves except the maître d'hotel, advancing with a bilingual menu." Such innovations

---

* "Average per capita annual income had risen from 112 dollars in 1951, to 270 in 1956 and was to reach 500 dollars by 1964." Richard Clogg, *A Short History of Modern Greece* (Cambridge University Press, 1979; 2nd ed., 1986), 176.

were less to be lamented than wryly observed, Merrill suggests: another object lesson in the way of the world. Besides, the opening up of traditional Greek society brought with it a general atmosphere of sexual excitement and experiment—"more and more people are doing it for fun instead of for money"—and that was part of what Merrill came for.

He was hardly the first English-speaking writer to journey to Greece. The tradition begins with Lord Byron's heroic mission to restore ancient liberty to the Greek people, who were under Ottoman rule when he came in 1823. In the 1930s and 1940s, a new cohort of Anglo-American Philhellenes renewed Byron's quest while altering its terms. In Henry Miller's *The Colossus of Maroussi* (1941) and Lawrence Durrell's *Prospero's Cell* (1945), the Greek adventure is about sensual self-discovery, rather than political and cultural regeneration. In this new myth of Greece, the freedom to be discovered is personal, and its exemplars are Dionysian, hypermasculine heroes, such as Miller's George Katsimbalis or Nikos Kazantzakis's Zorba. Friar absorbed and passed on to Merrill this new myth while adding a homosexual theme, derived from Cavafy. Merrill, always ironic, resisted the idealization of Greece in both its Byronic and modern versions. Yet he wanted a release from his world-weary irony and sophistication. He wanted to believe in the existence of the world Friar had promised him years before, a world antithetical to his, where his senses might be cleansed and liberated. At thirty-six, he was entering middle age, and he wanted another life.

In 1972, in an interview with David Kalstone, one of the friends he made in the 1960s, Merrill looked back at this earlier moment: "I began going to Greece [. . .] very much in the spirit of one who embarks upon a double life. The life I lived there seemed I can't tell you how different from life in America. I felt for the first time that I was doing exactly as I pleased." On one level, the meaning of Greece was just that—Merrill enjoyed the power and freedom of doing just as he pleased, within limits. At first, his Greece was a carefully circumscribed diversion, like Algernon's weekends with Bunbury in *The Importance of Being Earnest*. Merrill and Jackson came to Greece for two months in 1959. They were back for a month in 1960–61, and for three months in 1962, and three months again in 1963. But in 1963 and 1964, when he was at home in Connecticut, Merrill was writing fiction and poems about Greece, writing letters to friends there, and practicing reading and writing in Greek. In 1962, he began writing his name in his notebooks with two addresses, one in Stonington and one in Athens. By 1964, the center of his life had shifted, if only temporarily, to Greece.

During this period, Merrill was growing into his maturity as a man and an artist. His face became tanned and lined, his expression bolder, more comic. Although he'd always been attractive, it was not until his later thirties and early forties that he might be thought handsome. In photos from the 1940s and 1950s, he seems wary and averted behind his thick-rimmed glasses. Now his eyes (under contact lenses) were open and bright; his lips, once pursed and ready to sneer, broke easily into a grin. He was quick to see the humor in a situation and less likely to take offense. As always, he made friends wherever he went; now many of his new friends were working people. And his writing developed in related ways. His poems became more welcoming, more intimate, less encumbered by symbol and ornament. There was a person in the poetry, not merely behind it. He was learning how to manage self-disclosure and a new directness, while his poems became more daring, complex, and experimental in form.

The second life Merrill found in Athens was built on top of his life on Water Street, which he had no plans to give up. It was "greedy" of him to want both lives, he knew. "A writer already has two lives, don't you think?" he muses in the interview with Kalstone. "Not so much in the obvious division between experience and its imitation on the page as in the two sides of"—here he hesitated before making a weighty pronouncement—"the two sides of the creative temperament." By those "two sides" he seems to have meant that part of an artist which is passive and inspired, a vessel or vehicle, and that part which is cool and calculating, a plotter and craftsman. We see both "sides" in his attraction to Greece. Making a life there was a choice, a design, a move. Yet what he was choosing was a certain passivity, an openness to the designs life might have on *him*. In time, his double life demonstrated to him the unity of his experience in Greece and the U.S., so that he could say, laughing at his own expense, "How we delude ourselves! As if there were ever more than one life." But that lesson lay years ahead.

When he arrived in 1962, he knew few Greeks and spoke little of the language. Friar was in Athens that spring, but Jimmy didn't see him much: he meant to discover his own Greece. He and David fell in with the internationals they had met in 1959, mostly British and American expatriates who convened at bars with names like Apatsos and Zonar's. One was Gordon Sager, a friend of Jane and Paul Bowles, who had published a novel about them called *Run, Sheep, Run* (1950). Another was Peter Mayne, the author of books about Marrakech and Pakistan, whom Merrill called "the sweetest man alive." Alan Ansen had been thrown out of Venice by a chief of police fed up with his and Gregory Corso's uncouth ways; he was settling into forgiving Athens. "I'm not such a great one for *bella figura*," he reflected, "and the Greeks didn't care for it that much." Ansen, with his snort and chortle and a long-limbed, awkward body, was a foil for the impish, stylish Jimmy. They had poetry and poet friends (Auden, Kallman, and Hollander) in common. Merrill might roll his eyes, but he couldn't entirely resist when Ansen tipped back his head, closed his eyes, and chanted Alcman in ancient Greek. It was a "nightmare," however, when Ansen got drunk and began breaking furniture.

Meanwhile, another, crucial friendship was taking root. On this trip, Merrill and Jackson saw Tony Parigory every day, and they loved him "more and more." Their flat, which he found for them, was a short walk from his antiques shop. One block from Kolonáki Square, the shop was set in shadow a half flight below ground in a bland new apartment building. It offered fine or amusing things from across the eastern Mediterranean for well-to-do Athenians with wit and taste. At the end of the day, it became a salon where Tony's friends made themselves at home amid the merchandise—thick layers of Turkish carpet, a Sèvres clock, a nineteenth-century pine secretary from Corfu with hidden drawers—and gabbed over cocktails before dinner at a nearby taverna.

Tall, smiling, Alexandrian Tony, with a shining bald pate, dark eyes, and devilish black eyebrows he arched for effect, was giddy and wily, a gossip who knew everyone and yet was always ready to meet someone new. In his worldly wisdom, off-color jokes, and macaronic bons mots, braiding English, Greek, and a camp French, he resembled none of Merrill's friends so much as Ephraim, the Familiar Spirit. And like Ephraim, Tony came when Jimmy called, able and eager to satisfy his needs, whether for an apartment to rent or company for a night on the town. He was Merrill's age and, like him, the son of a stockbroker. He was educated and cultured, but he was not an intellectual. He'd known Lawrence Durrell's wife in Alexandria, and he could tell his own version of the stories behind Durrell's *Alexandria Quartet*. He left Egypt at the time of the Suez Crisis and came to Greece on his own. In Athens, a friend of his father's introduced him to a single woman fifteen years older than he, Nelly Liambey. Liambey invited a childhood friend of hers, Maria Mitsotáki, to her first meeting with the new arrival, and the three of them became fast friends.

Merrill met Nelly and Maria in Tony's shop in 1962. Always susceptible to people of charm and mystery, Jimmy was easily seduced in this case. Nelly and Maria were rich and, like Tony, intensely cosmopolitan. Liambey was born in Ioannina, a city in the northwestern region of Epirus, which was once the Turkish capital of Greece; and her stories of the place stuck in Jimmy's memory. Ioannina, a center of Greek Jewry, was a trading post through which goods, money, and people had long flowed between central Europe and the Levant. Liambey learned English, German, and French there. She spent the 1930s and the war years in Vienna, Budapest, and Paris. In Athens after the war, she led the untypical life of an independent woman dedicated to her friends. Postwar Athenians, many of them with roots in a province or village, had traditional social ideas just beneath the surface of their urban manners. In contrast, Liambey had Ioannina and the great European capitals in her past. Her mother was a trained singer; and Nelly traveled to Salzburg, Paris, and Venice, to attend concerts—which was a bond with Jimmy. She liked to be entertained, and she could afford to be. She was pert, pretty, small, and sweet—yet not too sweet, seeing no need to stand for pretense or convention, and able to choose her friends. Mitsotáki, who had names for everyone, called her "La Petite."

Maria, three years older than Nelly, was born in Athens in 1907. She was the middle child and only daughter in a prominent family. Her older brother died in youth from tuberculosis. Seeking treatment for him, the family moved to Davos, Switzerland, where they joined the cast of elegant prewar sanatorium clients evoked by Thomas Mann in *The Magic Mountain*. A photo of the dark-eyed schoolgirl suggests the privilege of her childhood: blank and direct, her stare hints at the steely command of style she was being taught to wield. Her father, Constantine Demertzis, a professor of civil law at the University of Athens and a royalist, had a moment on the stage of Greek history: appointed acting prime minister of Greece in 1935 by King George II, he oversaw the failed elections that resulted in the rise to power of the dictator, General John Metaxas. There was discipline as well as luxury in his household. On Maria's wedding day, the guests gathered in the house—and were kept waiting while she lingered in the bath. When at length she descended in her wedding dress, her father greeted her by slapping her in front of the assembly. Her husband, several years older, was Niko Mitsotáki, from a Greek family of Liverpool wine merchants, one of Britain's major importers. He and Maria lived near London without children; his younger brother lived with them, carrying on an affair with the butler. Niko was handsome in the sepia-tinted fashion of leading men in 1930s Hollywood. In one snapshot, he leans on a fat roadster in a double-breasted pinstripe suit with burning pale eyes and his black hair slicked down. Maria, in fur stole and a dress designed by Molyneux, was costumed to match. She and Niko had a house on Capri and a schooner, the *Tuscano*, to convey them from island to island in Greece. This was the triumphant style of elite society *entre deux guerres*. Hotel labels decorated their steamer trunks.

After her father's death in 1936, Maria returned to Greece to take care of her mother, who was dying of cancer, and she was trapped in Athens by the war. When Niko died too, she became a very wealthy widow. She put on mourning clothes and dark glasses and never took them off, becoming Mavre Maria, the "Black Maria," Merrill knew. "She was still young and very good-looking," Liambey remembered, "but she didn't have to remarry. Why should she?" With Niko's fortune, no children, and one surviving brother, she had money and few obligations. She could love the men she wished, and walk away from them when she wished. Her lovers were public men—a composer and a professor in the School of Art at the University of Athens. But these were the private affairs of a secretive woman. There is a comic "portrait" of her by the artist Laskaris in which the back of her head is turned to the viewer. Few friends visited her flat in Kolonáki. After her father's death, she burned his correspondence. She sealed her own in envelopes with instructions for her niece, Nina Koutsoudakis, to burn them after her death, which she did. "It's funny how she *sealed* things," Koutsoudakis commented. "Her own secrets—or a friendship once she was done with it. She sealed off anything that was painful to her. She never spoke of her brother or husband after they died." Instead, she joked in a voice without warmth, "*sans rire*." "*Surface! Surface!*" she insisted, with the French pronunciation, whenever a conversation threatened to become deep.

To Maria, Merrill and Jackson became "*les enfants*." (Ansen, less dignified, was "Baby Alan.") Jimmy responded by calling her "Maman" and himself "Le Petit." He adopted her as a mock mother, making himself small in her presence, as if he were her boy, her puppet. "Jimmy was *médused* by her," observed Natalia Méla, who often saw them at lunch in the square, the poet spellbound by this older woman. Maria had for him the authority of an archetypal, polyglot diva with red lipstick, powdered face, dark glasses, and a cigarette—a habit that gave her voice so thick a timbre it could be mistaken on the phone for a man's.

Tony was the Mercury who led Jimmy to her. He was also Merrill's way into less Olympian corners of Athenian society. In a sailor's bar on the water in Pérama, Merrill learned new phrases in Greek: " 'Let's you and me have a party' or 'I shall be sleeping on my feet' or (raising a glass) 'To your eyes.' " With Parigory as guide, he and Jackson enjoyed frequent sexual "Exploits,"* which they laughed over the next day at a table on the square or in Tony's shop. Merrill had come to Greece, in part, for just this experience—to live

---

* JM to DH, letter, April 21, 1962 (WUSTL). He claimed to have had "40 or 50" sexual partners during this three-month period in Greece. JM to DR, letter, June 12, 1962 (WUSTL).

out his sexual double life. But he felt the need to maintain his self-control, even as he was letting go of it. At times the merriment grew tense.

In April, returning from the beach in a convertible, he suddenly found that he couldn't move the right side of his face. Comically, grotesquely, the lower eyelid sagged, and half of his mouth remained stiff as he laughed or ate. "A doctor came and ran pins up and down my palms and footsoles and pronounced the word Psyxis (freezing)." The condition is better known as Bell's palsy. It is "a form of facial paralysis resulting from damage to the cranial nerve," in most cases due to a form of herpes virus (which, in Merrill's case, might have been sexually transmitted); there is usually improvement within two weeks, and full recovery within three to six months. Merrill visited the hospital where he had been treated on his first visit to Greece. He was X-rayed, given diathermy, and told to rest. The patient took to bed, attended by young "well-wishers, drinking beer + orangeade, and playing cards." For a few days, an elderly man, wearing a black armband, arrived from the pharmacy to administer an injection "in the rump and another in the vein of my golden arm."

Merrill soon recovered, but the illness had shaken him. To feel his face "freezing" was disturbing to a poet who was fascinated by appearances and feared his own coldness of heart. He was quick to read his symptoms as symbols. "I suspect that we have here the materials of a poem," he told Hine, explaining that the partial paralysis was "the crack in the mirror of the soul, if that is what the face is, but I think the setting ought to be Istanbul"—a city divided between East and West, and a macrocosmic image of his divided soul. Merrill set down notes for a poem, but he wouldn't develop them until the autumn.

Istanbul was on his mind because he and Jackson were planning to meet his mother there. But Hellen Plummer took a fall at home, breaking a bone in her leg, and canceled her trip. They had worried in advance about their plans to entertain her and other guests whose curiosity about Greece had been aroused by, as David put it, "our raptures so irresponsibly poured out." Dignified Count Morra visited during Merrill's phase of bed rest. When he departed, "my face began to mend," Merrill confided in Hine. "I have toyed, fustily, with the Psychological Interpretation. His being here was going to <u>cramp my style</u>, and so it did." His mother's presence would have been worse yet, and the injury preventing her visit felt to him, guiltily, like a close call. As he told Fredericks, "We have a door right on the street, and the people who drop in are very heterogeneous and only rarely heterosexual."

Robin and Betty Magowan followed Morra. Robin was now a doctoral student in comparative literature at Yale, working on his dissertation in Paris.

A snapshot shows him leaning forward, slight and boyish in the glare of a taverna lunch by the sea in the Piraeus; he is seated with his uncle, whose bandaged face lurches drunkenly from Bell's palsy, and Mavre Maria, chic and presiding. Looking back on this initial visit to Greece, Robin described "that feeling of having stepped into the morning of the world; a light so sharp that, standing on the Acropolis, there seemed to be nothing in the whole of Athens, not a kite, not a bus turning a hundred blocks away, we could not see."

His uncle's nighttime, Dionysian Greece, made an even deeper impression. One evening, taking the Magowans on a tour that they wouldn't have given Morra or Mrs. Plummer, Merrill and Jackson brought them to the bar in Pérama. Here Greek navy men in white uniforms and trim caps went to drink ouzo and meet male prostitutes. The music was *rembétika*, the urban blues brought to Athens with the Greek refugees from Asia Minor in 1922. *Rembétika* is a raw, nervy sound, played with the bouzouki, a string instrument like the mandolin or balalaika. The sound is rich with the history of forced migration and struggle of the working people who play it, and their stories of longing, love, and violence. It is the music for a meditative dance, the *zembeikiko*, in which a man rises and circles the floor in seemingly private reverie, stamping and clapping, slowly slapping his thighs or his heels, dipping and rising in a loose improvisation on familiar steps, as the music gains in tempo and intensity. Sometimes the dancer is joined by a second, who holds out a handkerchief, and both men grasp it. As the high spirits called *kéfi* take hold, rhythmic clapping builds. At last, the crowd pays tribute to the dancers by smashing plates and glasses on the ground.

Robin was entranced: he jotted down his reactions to the dancing in the taxi on the way home, and these notes became the basis for his "first real poem." Immediately a conflict arose when a letter arrived from the English Department at the University of Washington offering him a post as an assistant professor. He hesitated to accept it, fearing that teaching and scholarship would take away his newly discovered sense of poetic vocation. So he brought the decision to his uncle. Merrill had led his nephew to Greece; now he sent the young man home. Robin summarizes his advice: "Teaching, for you, may be a means to an end. But the confidence that can accrue from it is no small matter. If it hadn't been for the invitation I received on graduating from Amherst to teach at Bard, I'd have gone to work at Merrill Lynch. It was that year which allowed me to see myself as a full-fledged writer." "The next day," Robin writes, Jimmy and David, "after plying me with a pair of highballs, marched me down to the one open post office, under Omonia square, where I dutifully fired off my telegram of acceptance."

Grace Stone visited next, and received the red carpet treatment: Jimmy and David brought her to Delphi, held a big cocktail party in her honor, and, to entertain her and another American visitor, John Myers, arranged "the Athens premiere of 'Byrone,' " a ballad opera with hand puppets and a cappella singing created by Parigory's fellow Alexandrian, Bernard de Zogheb. Merrill had been delighted by de Zogheb's zany genius when they met in 1960 in Alexandria. *Byrone* was the first of several de Zogheb ballad operas for puppets that Merrill sponsored. He brought the act to New York in January and, subsequently, introduced de Zogheb and his work to the Little Players, Peschka and Murdock, who made de Zogheb's libretti staples of their repertoire.

Bernard's parodies suited the irreverent spirit in which Merrill met the grandeur of ancient Greece. When he and Jackson took a trip to Crete in May and visited the ruins of the palace at Knossos, Merrill was dismissive of the main attraction, likening Heinrich Schliemann's last discovery to "a grand villa built by Frank Lloyd Wright for Louis B. Mayer," the MGM mogul. Yet he was taken by the site itself, and compared the "very circumscribed horizon of gentle hills covered, now, with yellow daisies and coquelicots" to a Proustian "invalid in bed, idle, all magazines read. [. . .]" He had a similar reaction on a visit to the Acropolis. It wasn't the massive, masculine structure, the Parthenon, to which he responded, but the Porch of the Maidens, the Caryatids: "Whenever I see the Erectheum, I all but faint with pleasure, and would if I were not vigorously stopping my ears against the babble of tongues describing over how many years it was built, what it was used for (the Turks used it for a harem), because I know that it was designed and built in a fortnight by a Japanese. It says everything the Parthenon doesn't say, that is, a good deal more than the P. actually says. How marvelous that they are there together, those two; it makes one believe in love between the sexes." He tucked the thought away for use once he got back, at the end of June, to his desk on Water Street.

Shortly before he left Athens, Merrill received a three-page letter, typed and single-spaced, from Friar. Jimmy had complained to Kimon that he'd been indiscreet about Merrill's Greek sex life in front of Grace. "As you talked, over the telephone, I knew immediately that you were right," Friar began. "But also, as you talked, in that querulous tone which has become more and more your pitch lately, I knew that I no longer cared to see or to know you." This was not, Friar continued, a "sudden revelation." Merrill had long ago admitted that he had two emotions toward Friar that made any simple friendship between them impossible. Friar listed them: "one was a sense of guilt, and the other a feeling that I was trying to dominate and direct you as I had when I was your mentor." As a result, Merrill showed a put-upon "tolerance" for his company, Friar maintained, and a lack of respect for his literary work. "I could accept your rejection of me as a lover," Friar wrote, "[. . .] but I was puzzled and hurt again and again by your rejection of me as a person and a writer. You early repudiated anything I might have meant to you, as one who encouraged you and one whom you loved, by emphatically entitling your third book FIRST POEMS, and thus assigning me with your father to oblivion, or at least to no place in your creative and emotional life." Yet it was only now, and on different grounds, that Friar felt a break was necessary:

> What has helped me to let go is what seems to be a deepening change in your character. We seem to have little in common any more. Your mother was right: we certainly do not belong to the same social class. But more, we certainly do not care for the same kind of people. I look with distaste at the kind of "gay" temperament, either over-vulgar or over-chic, with which you seem to surround yourself. I have watched what was refined and delicate in your character become affectation, mannerism, precious. [. . .] A long time ago I found a phrase to describe your own brand of tactlessness and aggressiveness: the insensitivity of the sensitive. [. . .] My carelessness before Mrs. Stone [. . .] must be placed beside my recent pictures of you necking in the back of automobiles or in your parlor in the presence of others (one whom you once professed to love and the other whom you say you still love). [. . .] My own sense of what is permissable has never gone this far. David, I think, can come out unscathed under these circumstances, but not you. With you, it is all a bit shrill, over intense and demonstrative, as though you were trying to show that you too can have many successes and be loved many times by many people. [. . .] You have come to Greece for the wrong reasons, and I am bitterly aware of the irony that it was I who first brought you here.

It was an extraordinary outburst. Over the past decade, the former lovers had fallen into a stiff, formal relationship that was both more and less intimate than a friendship. They had seen each other at odd intervals in New York. Their correspondence shows, on Merrill's side, only short, sporadic letters, low on news, occasionally affectionate but just as often testy as Merrill shirks an accusation from the easily injured Friar or parries with a pointed comment. Friar dedicated his English translation of Nikos Kazantzakis's *Odyssey: A Modern Sequel* to Merrill, who showed no appreciation for the poem, the translation, or Friar's gesture. Instead, Jimmy was repulsed by what he saw as Kimon's attempts to market the work in New York and Hollywood.

He didn't respond to Friar's letter until he returned to the U.S., and then not until Independence Day, July 4. Friar had said, Merrill told him, just what he had expected him to say; "thus, in a sense, it must be what I hoped you would say. It confirms me in a respect for you which you imagine I do not have. You are managing to be yourself; it's what we're all trying to do." As to the sexual freedom that *he* required to be himself, Merrill sighed, "Alas, I have always been tempted by the lives of others. The truest perception in your letter is the phrase 'as though you were trying to show that you too can have many successes, etc.' For me, these 'successes' are a novelty of much the same quality as Hollywood was for you. [. . .] It makes me smile to think how I lectured you about your intimacy with rich and corrupt people, and how you now lecture me about sex—as if in both cases one had trespassed on the other's terrain."

Friar's "terrain" was also Greece, and Merrill wasn't about to cede his new claim on the country, especially if it was Friar who had brought him there first. "I did not need, on my first visit, to behave in the way you complain of, in order to be affected deeply, physically, as psychologically now. I have never left that country without feeling that my fate was there. If that means I come back 'for the wrong reasons,' well and good. I cannot ask you to see these reasons any more sympathetically than you do my—pleasures? experiments? ordeals?" He met Friar's cutting portrait of him with a cutting portrait of Friar—"Where you find me affected and querulous, I find you narcissistic and pompous"—and ended by linking Friar and Greece once again: "Like Greece, you are part of my fate, whether or not we ever meet again."

Merrill had held himself to a page, but not before indulging in the type of lofty rhetoric he complained of Friar's using. Always the teacher, Friar made checks in the margins of the letter, noting points to respond to. He was silent for six months. Then he reiterated and defended his earlier claims: "I strongly feel that, regardless of my many inadequacies, you have treated me shabbily, niggardly. It was only when I saw you treating yourself in the same manner that I could bear it no longer." This time Merrill didn't respond by letter. But he wasn't content to let Friar have the last word: he was hard at work on his reply, as he had been since July, which was growing into his second novel, *The (Diblos) Notebook*.

Notes for *The (Diblos) Notebook* appear in Merrill's journal as early as September 1957. In 1958, he challenged himself to write "a non-objective novel," "a book the main energy of which is to make the writer's creative impulse the central theme. I have a story to tell. The story is not about real people, or could be. K's Vita Nuova idea. 'This happened to me last night, therefore I made character X. behave like this.' " The idea was to write a book about the writing of a book, exploring the process by which life is turned into art. This Merrill did by presenting the novel as if it were a writer's notebook, including crossed-out words, phrases, and even pages, and diary comments on daily life mixed in with reflections on the process of composition. At one point Merrill introduces a paragraph upside down, as if the writer had grabbed the book that way.

The idea for the book had been Friar's ("K's"). He envisioned it as a poet's coming-of-age story and the prelude to a great work, something like Dante's *Vita Nuova*. Friar wasn't simply the source of the book's idea, however. Kimon and Mina both appear in the novel-within-the-novel as characters called "Orestes," a Greek-American man of letters known as "Orson" in "real life," and "Dora," a cultured, older Greek woman, recently widowed, who lives in a grand house on Diblos, based on Mina's house on Poros. ("Diblos," which sounds like it might be a cognate of the English "double," is not a Greek word at all. The Greek word Merrill thought of using for the island is *skismos*, or "division.") Merrill casts himself as the narrator, Orestes's younger half brother. Unnamed in "real life," he calls himself "Sandy" in his novel, a joke about his dry heart.

As this double-entry book of names indicates, *The (Diblos) Notebook* is a Möbius strip in which life and art turn into each other. The story opens in summer 1961. The narrator is staying on Diblos and writing in his notebook in a café on the harbor. The notebook glances at his clumsy, fitful relations with several people on the island. These include two women—an American tourist and a maid in the hotel—and a young man, a friendly Diblosite named Giorgos. To these people, all potential romantic partners for him, the narrator prefers the company of the characters in his notebook. The story he is drafting is based on his previous visit to Diblos. It describes Orestes's chance meeting with Dora on the Diblos waterfront, where she finds Orestes trying to catch sight of the Sleeping Woman. The child of a Greek-American immigrant, Orestes is moved by Greece because it is his mother's native land. Dora is won over by his enthusiasm, and she invites him to use the cottage on her property for his literary work.

When Sandy visits him there, Orestes wants to share his good fortune and instruct Sandy in the Greek heritage he shares with Orestes as his half brother. So Orestes takes him to a local *panegyri*, where he teaches him how to dance like a Greek. That night, Sandy overhears Orestes and Dora talking: she reveals her love for him—painfully, because both of them know he can't return it. The implication, although it is only an implication, is that Orestes is homosexual. Yet each has something to offer the other, since Dora is interested in America, and they decide that she will return with him to New York as his wife in a marriage of convenience. In New York, things go badly for them. Dora is disoriented, and she and Orestes turn out to dislike each other. The novel-within-the-novel and the present moment of composition converge when Orson returns to Diblos to reclaim the cottage, now in the possession of Dora's son, Byron.

Merrill worked on the novel intermittently between 1958 and 1962. After his letter to Friar in July 1962, he focused on the manuscript until he completed it in February 1964. Taking stock, he thought the book "either a little masterpiece or a ghastly mistake." In truth it was neither. The novel is too involuted, too involved with the particulars of Merrill's life, to qualify as anything like a masterpiece. The transformation of life into art it explores is incomplete—insofar as Merrill was writing about actual people for whom his characters could only ever be masks and primarily interesting as such. As his writer-narrator pithily puts it, "Books ought to consume their sources, not embalm them." Yet the novel is an advance on the roman à clef method of *The Seraglio*, since it exposes to scrutiny the imaginative process by which Merrill wrote fiction, with an increase in his self-knowledge and his technical resources. He was seeking a literary form that would be adequate to the risk-taking double life he led in Greece, and it opened the way for the risk-taking poems he was beginning to write.

The novel's first page demonstrates its formal procedure and introduces its psychological project:

~~Orestes~~
The islands of Greece
Across vivid water the islands of Greece lie. They have been cut out of cardboard and set on bases of
at subtle odds with one another, upon bases of pale haze. Their colors are mauve, exhausted blue, tanned rose, here & there crinkled to catch the light. They do not seem
It is inconceivable that they are of one substance with the warm red rock underfoot
rock of one's own vantage point (?)

The crossed-out name, there on the threshold of the novel, recalls the ripped portrait mentioned in the first sentence of *The Seraglio*. By referring to Friar as "Orestes" and striking through the name, Merrill strikes at his teacher. He does so specifically by attacking Friar's identification with a tragic hero from classical Greek drama—with the implication that Merrill, or his narrator-surrogate, must clear away Orestes before establishing his own "vantage point." What that point of view consists in is uncertain, however, flagged by a parenthetical question mark. Securing it will require Sandy to accept a "contradiction." To the new arrival, it is "inconceivable" that the "warm red rock underfoot," indubitably real and objective, is the same landscape as the one he sees before him, half dissolved in a play of changing light he is only too able to evoke in gorgeous lyric prose. Merrill has in mind the optical effect when hot sun and chill sea meet, creating a shining haze above which the rocky Greek coastline seems to float. Putting together "the warm red rock underfoot" and the misty vista will mean reconciling Sandy's sense of touch and his rarefied seeing—body and soul.

But *The (Diblos) Notebook* is less concerned with reconciliation than with unmasking, with the clearing away of vanity and pretension, and Friar-Orestes is the target of a bitter satire. Lest there be any doubt about the link between them, Sandy gives Orestes Friar's looks, down to the thin black mustache of "a sharpie" that Kimon wore briefly after his first trip to Greece. Sandy compares his voice to that of "a radio announcer"; when Orestes chooses a hat to buy, it is a Borsalino, what a salesman might wear, and here a symbol of "the Greek American dream." Orestes's personal style unfailingly reveals, not the refinement he aspires to, but his anxious effort to acquire it. Merrill treats Orestes's ideas similarly. Orestes lectures on the weighty topics that Friar spoke on at the Poetry Center in the mid-1940s: "Darwin & the Poetry of Science" and "The Tragic Dualism of Man," for instance. As a lecturer, he is "intoxicated" by his own ideas. His exaggerated self-importance expresses his fear that he is a latecomer to culture. The economic deprivation of an immigrant and the historical belatedness of the twentieth-century author meet in his ambition, "as both a Greek & a 'modern man,' " "to enter that world of myth," a shining realm that he feels both entitled to and excluded from. Seen from this angle, his fascination with myth is another misjudged stylistic choice, like his mustache and his hat:

> O. wore myth day & night like an unbecoming color.
> "I am Orestes, Perseus, Hamlet, Faust." And, in the piping whisper of a child, unheard by him: "I am Pinocchio."
> Ah, but it made him so happy, made the ills that befell him bearable. ~~Myth~~ Metaphor formed like ice between him & the world.

Perseus turns out to be Pinocchio, the Italian cobbler's son.

We can gauge the force of Friar's early spell on Merrill by how much force he exerts, years later, to break it. On Friar's first visit to Greece, he wrote to Merrill that the land was there "for our colonizing." Sandy makes Orestes's colonizing of Diblos seem imperial and pitiable: "*His* cottage. *His* rock-garden. *His* private cove. How proud & happy it made him! Two white-washed rooms paved with hexagonal terracotta, interspersed with square black, tiles. Rush chairs. A low, wide window. His marble *trouvaille* on the sill. The table strewn with papers, dictionaries. His life mask, plaster painted dull red, hanging above. Two wooden beds, woven striped coverings." This is an accurate description of the Medusa on Poros as Merrill saw it in 1950, with Friar's life mask, first seen in Amherst, hanging on the wall. The passage reads like a deliberate, disenchanted rewriting of Merrill's diary entry from 1945 describing his lover's rooms in Amherst, when he was fully under Friar's sway and hushed in reverence for the symbols Kimon had selected and placed around him.

Merrill's argument with Friar rises to the level of aesthetic debate in a scene where Orestes, Dora, and Sandy visit the Acropolis. Predictably, Orestes prefers the Parthenon to the Erectheum, while Dora prefers the latter. Echoing Merrill's reflections on his own recent visit to the ruins, she and Orestes argue over the values embodied in the two temples. The "famous one" "rises in sunlight," upright and noble as "a sire, a seer," whereas the other, "dangerously complex & arbitrary," "Japanese," is like "a small-boned woman," or perhaps the "dressing-table" at which she sits.

> Orestes: One lives for the sake of one's tragic insights.
> (Dora): If that is true, one still has access to them at one's dressing-table—more often than at one's prie-dieu.
> O. (magnanimous): Let us say that as *symbols* these 2 temples have equal power, but that the states they symbolize do not.
> Dora (amused): You are more human than I am, is that it?

In this dialogue Dora is speaking for Sandy, too, and behind him is Jimmy, arguing with Kimon for *his* equal humanity.

But Merrill was far from confident in his own humanity, or at least in his capacity to sympathize and give love. Friar's letter in June, when it accused him of heartlessness, must have shaken him no less than the episode of Bell's palsy, and for the same reasons. In *The (Diblos) Notebook*, he accuses Friar, via Orson-Orestes, of coldness: "Myth Metaphor formed like ice between him and the world." But when he replaces "myth" with "metaphor," he implies a criticism of Sandy too, and of himself through Sandy.

Burrowing in his notebook, Sandy fends off those around him. His lavish descriptive abilities shield him from experience, which he turns into metaphors before he can fully live it. When Dora offers her love to Orestes, Orestes's reaction is "to take charge of the situation" and "help Dora accept & overcome her feelings"; he does not think "to return the love." Nor would Sandy. Not for nothing are they half brothers.

Sandy and Orestes share a Greek mother—her name is "Eleni," the Greek form of "Helen," which calls to mind Hellen Plummer. This way of defining their bond suggests that it is based in a shared femininity (as opposed to the masculine bond that a shared father would represent), and it hints at the homosexual basis of Merrill and Friar's relationship. The scene most imbued with homoeroticism in the novel—and the most vivid homoerotic scene anywhere in Merrill's work—is the description of the dancing at the *panegyri*. Flushed with wine, Sandy watches as Orestes and Kosta, Dora's workman, modeled on Friar's lover Mitso, get up to dance. The two men approach each other hissing "like serpents." Kosta leaps, landing "not on the ground but in midair, with legs wrapped about O.'s waist, head fallen back, shoulders still undulating." Next it is Sandy's turn to dance with his brother. Reluctant, he is content "with repeating, most gracefully, he thought, the basic steps Orestes indicated." Then Orestes commands him to leap as Mitso did: "*Now.*" Doubting his capacity, but complying anyway, Sandy "springs upwards & backwards to lock his thighs around his partner's waist," while "O.'s face grins down: the look of the initiator." "O. hisses lightly, provocatively," before releasing him. But Sandy is not done: they must trade places. While the music insists, Orestes "confronts" him,

and in a flash the whole staggering weight of another body has become *his*. But he's mad, S. thinks, I can't hold him up! as they go reeling towards a group of tables and Orestes, blissful & trusting, smiles up at him. I cannot. Sandy has opened his mouth to cry—the blood pounding beneath his sunburn—he cannot—yet within seconds it appears that he can; he can, he can. Power & joy fill him. His eyes fill. He can dance under his brother's weight. Then it is over, & the music, too.

"Bravo," said Dora, welcoming them back. "You're going to make an excellent Greek, Sandy."

The dance is a way of representing men making love, including, by an implication that Merrill is willing to dare, his own initiation into sex by the smiling Friar, treated here as Sandy's initiation into his Greek heritage. He learns what it is like to give himself to another man and take on that man's full weight; the two half brothers, locking together, make a whole, like "Narcissus & his image" or "the Jack of Clubs." But the narrator quickly draws back from this experience of communion and trust. He, or rather Merrill as he worked on the novel, ends this episode by cautioning himself: "(Make the dancing less euphoric?)"

As he worked on the "n-v-l" in Stonington in 1962, Merrill took stock: "We know too many people. For the first time it really hits me between the eyes, the madness of it all. What, for instance, is Bernie doing here?" Winebaum kept turning up in Jimmy's life. A Harvard graduate, Bernie painted and occasionally wrote poems while getting by on a few investments in real estate. Over the years, he became subject to increasingly violent mood swings and manic behavior. Now he was renting the second-floor apartment on Water Street; his "soft footfall and apologetic cough" announced his presence "at odd times throughout the day." Jimmy's niece Cathy and her husband were in residence too, having arrived with a "motorscooter, crash helmets, [and] large unfinished oil paintings," to bide their time between summer jobs on Fishers Island and travel in Europe. The village made its own demands. The death of Stephen Vincent Benét's widow required Jimmy and David to attend the funeral—Jackson's first. Around the same time, delicate Isabel Morse fell and broke her hip. Grace refused to visit the invalid "because, well, when Ellis had his heart attack she didn't hear from Isabel for three weeks, or speak to her for 2 years thereafter as a result." But soon she had joined the rest of the Surly Temple at Isabel's bedside, taking turns reading *Persuasion* aloud and "then playing bridge" until late. Weary from all this activity, but amused too, Merrill reflected, "Part of me [. . .] wants to see nobody, nobody at all. . . . And part of me, as always, wants only to go about sniffing lampposts + hydrants, the social animal happily ever after."

Water Street was published in September 1962, and X. J. Kennedy reviewed it in *The New York Times* in terms that ought to have reassured the author about his coldness of heart: "Merrill has developed a deeper compassion, a kind of humility, a capacity for bitter amusement at his own expense. [. . .] At 36, he is surely one of the American poets most worth reading." Atheneum quickly ordered a second printing. Merrill appeared on television to introduce a scene from *The Immortal Husband*. In December, a *Newsweek* photographer snapped his picture for an article on American poetry. "I wonder," Merrill wrote to Donald Richie, "if Edna Millay ever felt the sort of creeping unease that comes over me as I think about it all. David," he added, "shame on him, hasn't been writing much of anything."

"Oh," Jackson asked in a postscript, "how can poor me compete with Edna?" The contrast between his and Jimmy's literary success was more striking than ever. He reported to Richie, "JM's at work. I'm trying still." His phrase suggests that *not* trying had become a tempting option. Over the summer, David had supervised the restoration of the house opposite 107 Water Street. He spoke of making a profit on its resale, or using it to put up friends, but he and Jimmy didn't need more money or more company. Merrill had bought the house merely so that Jackson would have something to do. "That's David's house, you know," Jimmy said to friends, vague about what that meant, leaving open the possibility that Jackson had paid for it. In need of recognition and reluctant to say so, David threw a party in New York to celebrate his fortieth birthday, while keeping the occasion for the party a secret. Jimmy marked the date with a tender message:

> Passing of time unnerves us all.
> Last month at your first funeral
> I saw you taken by surprise,
> A burning water fill your eyes
> As if the years had stolen your—
> Your—something you did not insure.
> Dearest and best, what could they steal?
> A few gold hairs? some sex-appeal?
> Or faith? or fear? Suppose they did.
> There is no loot but must be hid.
> And yours has fallen to the care
> Of all who love you, everywhere.
> It can be looked at in one place
> As safe as any. Now, my face,
> Show David if he still believes
> He has been robbed by forty thieves.

Despite the face he puts on it here, Merrill felt "unnerved" by passing time too, and in need of reassurance himself. On the day before David's birthday, he learned from Tony that a truck driver named Taki, a sweet young man who'd been a sexual partner for Parigory and then Merrill that spring, had been run over and killed while taking a nap in the shade of another driver's truck. Shaken by this news, Jimmy turned to "Planchette, toujours consolatrice." He narrated his and David's séance for Tony: "Breaking a long silence we inquired of our enchanting Familiar (Ephraim. . .) for Taki, who was instantly summoned. E's mother came from Larissa, and E. volunteered a comparison between Taki and the centaurs of old, whose mental powers were often not very strong. 'How he chatters!' said E. 'Taki mou-polylogou! [my talkative Taki]' said I, and the reply was: 'Sika! [sister]' He was in high spirits, thrilled to 'be' in America for a bit, wanted to know what truck-drivers' wages are here, in case he is reborn in this country. Ephraim began to rehearse a long history of early, clumsy deaths [. . .] but thought him a charming fellow, while Taki thought E. a big Sika." Merrill wound up the report a bit self-consciously, admitting to Parigory, "It is foolish to carry on like this, I mean telling you such things, but they do mean something to us even if someone else would call them blasphemous."

Again the nation was gripped by fears of nuclear attack. In October, with Russian missiles placed in Cuba, the U.S. and the Soviet Union lurched on the brink of mutual destruction. For some days, it appeared that the dreaded future might have arrived. By November, Merrill looked back on the passing of the Cuban Missile Crisis, giddy with relief: "It was a real orgy of anxiety all the more intense for my having abstained from it for more than a year beforehand. Now, once again, I'm off the stuff." As in 1961, the nuclear threat receded into the background of daily life. But the garish light of total war, narrowly averted, colored Jimmy's and David's days. With the fate of the world swinging in the balance, it was easy to feel that nothing mattered very much.

Friar had accused Merrill of a general lack of faith and seriousness. Still smarting from that attack, he was forced to recognize and question his ways of protecting himself. In November, Fredericks gave him another occasion to do so by renewing a criticism he had often made: Jimmy's sociability made him cold to those closest to him, unable to respond to what was most urgent and important. In his reply, Merrill seems to have been thinking both of Friar's accusations and the new friend he had lost in the sweet, talkative Taki. He returned to a remark made at a party in New York in October:

I wish I could come to grips with what lies behind the sweetly fluttering veil of your reproach, which I _feel_ as a reproach not only from you but two or three other friends. Certainly there must be grounds,—in each case,—and it makes me sad because I realize I can only do what I do. I guess you would say I was a cat at heart, but I can remember when I was a dog and can't easily account for the transformation. I was talking to Jane Bowles a month or so ago, off the top of my head, about how I loved no conversation better than the ones imposed in Greece by lack of a common language + common interests—"What does meat cost in the U.S.?" "How many brothers have you?"—and she gave me one of her disquieting looks + said "well, of course, you just want to be alone. What's wrong with that?" I couldn't say—I can't now—Something does however seem wrong.

Indeed, something had seemed "wrong" since Merrill's episode of Bell's palsy in Greece. Back in April 1962, he had taken his partial facial paralysis as a sign of some personal, metaphysical disorder, "the crack in the mirror of the soul." The condition thus described was alarming, but there was something hopeful about it too, since he saw in it "the materials of a poem." At first, the projected poem, to be called "Rigor Vitae," appeared as one of a series of titles listed in his notebook:

> POEMS TO WRITE:
> The Double Life
> Rigor Vitae
> The Planet. The Libertine
> The Orgy: "This is my body. Eat this . . . "
>   (The French Postcards)

Merrill made his first notes for these poems in April and began concentrated work on them in September.* He found himself responding not only to the episode of Bell's palsy, but also to Friar's letter, Fredericks's "reproach," Jane Bowles's remark, Taki's death, and his own intimations of mortality, all pondered in the glare of Cold War fear and anxiety. He soon came to see these topics as related, and, if we can believe his airy account in an interview a few years later, "suddenly an afternoon of patchwork" saw his fragments "stitched together" in a single poem.

"The Thousand and Second Night" was the longest poem he had yet attempted, and it is a pivotal poem in his development. Composed while he was at work on *The (Diblos) Notebook*, it is, like the novel, a formally experimental work in which Merrill stakes out an artistic position. He advances the revision of his early manner, roughening the verbal texture of his work, pushing further the strategies of interruption and revision discovered in "An Urban Convalescence," and replacing the symbolic scenes of his early poems with specific lived experiences, while giving up the unified lyric voice of his early poems in favor of many tones and speakers. As a result,

---

* The evidence of Merrill's letters and the dating of his work sheets for "The Thousand and Second Night" show that most of the poem was written in fall 1962, starting in September, although some drafts reach back as far as 1960, and the section called "Rigor Vitae" was begun in April.

Merrill made his poetry funnier, more dynamic, able to represent time in new ways, and to address the deep questions posed by his living.

Taking off from the notebook form of the novel, the first of the poem's five parts begins with a mock diary entry, headed "Istanbul. 21 March." The place and date locate the poet between seasons and continents, March 21 being the vernal equinox, dividing winter and spring, and the Straits of the Bosporus being the boundary between Europe and the Middle East, "The passive Orient and our frantic West." The poet awakens to "an absurd complaint. The whole right half / Of my face refuses to move." When he sets out to see Hagia Sophia, the "house of Heavenly Wisdom" is in crumbling disrepair, suggesting an analogy to his facial paralysis, the crack in his own "façade," seen as the symptom of a moral state. He chides himself: "You'd let go / Learning and faith as well, you too had wrecked / Your precious sensibility. What else did you expect?" He has wasted his gifts by leading the life of a libertine, for which his promiscuous travels are both a vehicle and a metaphor.

In the poem's second part, Merrill depicts the type of conversation he mentioned to Jane Bowles. As he recovers from his paralysis in Athens, he meets a Greek in the Royal Park—where Jimmy, David, and Tony went to find off-duty evzones. The stranger is the antithesis of the effete poet: "Superb, male, raucous, unclean, Orthodox // Ikon of appetite feathered to the eyes / With the electric blue of days that will / Not come again." "My friend with time to kill," he continues,

> Asked me the price of cars in Paradise.
>
> By which he meant my country, for in his
> The stranger is a god in masquerade.
> Failing to act that part, I am afraid
> I was not human either—ah, who is?
>
> He is, or was; had brothers and a wife;
> Chauffeured a truck; last Friday broke his neck
> Against a tree. We have no way to check
> These headlong emigrations out of life.

"These headlong emigrations out of life": even as the poet mourns his honest friend, honoring his superior humanity, his grim punning wit oddly de-realizes this death and makes the dominant tone one of breezy resignation. It's probably this tone that his friends back home have in mind when they suggest that he has become "the vain // Flippant unfeeling monster" he always feared he might turn into.

He has lost track of "love," he admits, and precisely in the act of looking for it, or at least for sex. Merrill modulates next into frank self-disgust:

> A thousand and one nights! They were grotesque.
> Stripping the blubber from my catch, I lit
> The oil-soaked wick, then could not see by it.
> Mornings, a black film lay upon the desk[.]

Rather than narrate his own nighttime sexual adventures, Merrill turns to a set of vintage pornographic cards. In one picture, "She strokes his handlebar who kneels / To do for her what a dwarf does for him." In another,

> He steers her ankles like—like a wheelbarrow.
> The dwarf has slipped out for a breath of air,
> Leaving the monstrous pair.
>
> Who are they? What does their charade convey?
> Maker and Muse? Demon and Doll?
> "All manners are symbolic"—Hofmannsthal.

The story of the cards came from Irma Brandeis, to whom the poem is dedicated: she'd told Merrill about finding a cache of them, which she destroyed.* Merrill puts himself on the scene of their discovery with an Aunt Alix who "turned red with shame, / Then white, then thoughtful. 'Ah, they're all the same— / Men, I mean.' A pause. 'Not you, of course.' " For Aunt Alix, the gay young man is an exception to the rule, a different type of man. Does that mean he is more or less human, more or less a monster than other men? Or maybe he is no different after all. Indeed, Merrill is every bit as secretive and sexual as the "Morose Great-Uncle Alastair" the cards came from—a few of which the poet pockets to take home and use as an aid to masturbation.

Two pseudo-quotations follow in prose, the second of which provides an allegorical interpretation of Merrill's "grotesque" sexual pursuits. Here he links the libertine's quest for stimulation and pleasure, as he

---

* "The postcards + their story were Irma Brandeis's and <u>she</u>, in the first shock (although a little voice reminded her of her many friends who would have enjoyed the postcards) tore them into tiny pieces, all 300 of them." JM to Virgil Burnett, letter, November 6, 1963 (Waterloo).

would much later in *The Changing Light at Sandover,* to man's abuse of the planet: "Likewise, upon Earth's mature body we inflict a wealth of gross experience—drugs, drills, bombardments—with what effect? A stale *frisson,* a waste of resources all too analogous to our own. Natural calamities (tumor and apoplexy no less than flood and volcano) may at last be hailed as positive reassurances, perverse if you like, of life in the old girl yet."

By a clever turn, Merrill comes around to saying that his symptoms are a positive reassurance of life in him yet. The idea is enough for him to proclaim, slipping into verse again, the recovery of love. But he backs away from this affirmation as soon as he makes it, suspicious of his own rhetorical powers, his too-easy wish for a simple, decent, sunlit solution:

> Love. Warmth. Fist of sunlight at last
> Pounding emphatic on the gulf. High wails
> From your white ship: The heart prevails!
> Affirm it! Simple decency rides the blast!—
> Phrases that, quick to smell blood, lurk like sharks
> Within a style's transparent lights and darks.

We can't trust his language, it seems, unless he distrusts it. Merrill must move indoors and back into *abba* quatrains (as in "An Urban Convalescence") before he can speak with full confidence. Now, writing at home in winter, Merrill reviews his travels with a spirit of acceptance, even triumph:

> Lost friends, my long ago
>
> Voyages, I bless you for sore
> Limbs and mouth kissed, face bronzed and lined,
> An earth held up, a text not wholly undermined
> By fluent passages of metaphor.

The nouns here ("limbs and mouth," "face," "earth," and "text") are arranged in apposition. The grammar implies that they are connected, perhaps equivalent. Merrill is envisioning a way of writing that is equally a way of living. His face will become his text, and vice versa.

"The Thousand and Second Night" suggests an artistic program, then, but it does so by leaps and implications, rather than claims and assertions. It projects, as Merrill said in an interview, a "musical" rather than a logical sense of the relations between its parts. These he fits together in a collage, placing heterogeneous materials in evocative patterns. This method required a tolerance for loose ends and a relish for seemingly arbitrary, offhand connections. It enabled Merrill to move boldly outside the constraints of the tightly packaged New Critical lyric he had been trained in.

One model for "The Thousand and Second Night" is, Merrill observed, Lord Byron's *Don Juan*, with its "air of irrelevance, of running on at the risk of never becoming terribly significant." The great poetic sequences of Eliot and Yeats are another, very different model for the poem's quest motifs and collage technique. Merrill pays tribute to Eliot and Yeats, as well as Hofmannsthal and Valéry, by quoting them directly. But there is something ambivalent, even hostile about his conspicuous bows. Take these lines brooding on the Bell's palsy episode, which hold like a kernel the problem of the entire poem:

> once you've cracked
> That so-called mirror of the soul,
> It is not readily, if at all, made whole.
> ("Between the motion and the act
>
> Falls the Shadow"—T. S. Eliot.)
> Part of me has remained cold and withdrawn.
> The day I went up to the Parthenon
> Its humane splendor made me think *So what?*

"*So what?*," we note, is made to rhyme with "T. S. Eliot." The solemnity of the quotation from Eliot's "The Hollow Men," satirized here, is at the very opposite end of the rhetorical spectrum from Byron's "air of irrelevance." In Merrill's hands, the quest poem becomes a carnivalesque genre, amenable to both modernist discontinuities and an old-fashioned, romantic virtuosity, rejecting the high-culture seriousness of Eliot.

Before his reader can complain that the literary historical dimension of the poem, brought to the fore by his quotations, makes it feel like an academic exercise, Merrill adds a parody of a classroom discussion of the poem. "Now," Merrill's imaginary English Department lecturer begins, "if the class will turn back to this, er, / Poem's first section—Istanbul—I shall take / What little time is left today to make / Some brief points." The comic device cuts two ways. First, it forestalls the reception of the poem as an object requiring expert care, the kind of professional attention given poems at Amherst, say. The lecturer's gentle, stuffy voice is enough to make any reader feel that a poem should not mean but be. With his lecturer as a guide, Merrill implies that the structure and meanings of his poem, unlike Eliot's Grail myth or the occult symbols of Yeats, have been planted in plain sight. What this poem offers, it appears, is wit, not mysterious wisdom.

From another angle, though, the device does not forestall interpretation so much as initiate and direct it. It allows Merrill to face hard questions that might well be asked of his poem; and as he does, he smuggles in ideas, even a statement of principles. The lecturer points out correlations between form and content in the poem. While he fumbles to provide a reason for them ("No, I cannot say offhand / Why this should be. I find it vaguely satis—"), he implies that such designs can only ever be an expression of artistic choice, rather than objective truth. Then another hand goes up: "Yes please? The poet quotes too much? Hm. That is / One way to put it." The lecturer himself quotes in reply: "Mightn't he have planned // For his own modest effort to be seen / Against the yardstick of the 'truly great' / (In Spender's phrase)?" Here Merrill makes us see the modifier "truly" in Stephen Spender's "I Think Continually of Those Who Were Truly Great" either as an awkward redundancy or as a form of grade inflation (the category has been so diluted that a specification must be made—not merely "great" but "truly great"). Greatness is the property of T. S. Eliot and the Parthenon. Merrill, at this point in his career, isn't interested in honoring or achieving it.

What ground, then, has he to stand on? What is the basis of his self-defense? Just before the class period ends, a student poses his version of these questions:

> Yes, what now? Ah. How and when
> Did he "affirm"? Why, constantly. And how else
> But in the form. Form's what affirms. That's well
> Said, if I do—[Bells ring.] Go, gentlemen.

"Form" is shorthand for style or manner, the poet's bearing on the page and not simply his skillful prosody, although that is essential to it. "Form" implies a contract with the reader, an intimacy grounded in shared respect that is like the good form Merrill shows at the end of "A Tenancy" when he welcomes readers into his past as if into his home. The possibility of constructing such an intimacy in poetry is presented as itself sufficient grounds for affirmation, a basis for faith that will do in place of metaphysics or myth. From this perspective, mere wit begins to look like wisdom.

There are limits on what "form" can accomplish, however. The healing Merrill holds out as his goal is not a repair of the "crack in the mirror of the soul," but an acceptance of division; and thus the appropriate image at the poem's close is not a reconciliation, but an amicable divorce. The title "The Thousand and Second Night," adapted from *The Thousand and One Tales of the Arabian Nights*, puts the story of Scheherazade in the background throughout; in the fifth and final section, Merrill brings it forward. The story is familiar: Scheherazade nightly makes love to the murderous Sultan and then, before he can cut her head off like the hapless virgins before her, she tells him a tale so compelling and yet incomplete that he postpones her execution to the next night in order to hear more. Sex and storytelling, joined by feminine guile, are partners in mastering male violence and the threat of death. We might expect Merrill to identify with the female story-teller exclusively, to side with her; but that is not the case. The Sultan and Scheherazade embody opposing principles—male and female, body and soul, day and night—that he can neither choose between nor bring together, like warring parents. So he lets them depart in separate directions, she to " 'refresh / Her soul in that cold fountain which the flesh / Knows not,' " and he " 'to go in search of joys / Unembroidered by your high, soft voice, / Along the stony path the senses pave.' " We wake alongside the Sultan in bafflement:

> They wept, then tenderly embraced and went
> Their ways. She and her fictions soon were one.
> He slept through moonset, woke in blinding sun,
> Too late to question what the tale had meant.

After Christmas, Merrill visited Amherst. There he saw Rosemary Sprague, her parents, and other old friends, and read "my long poem," meaning "The Thousand and Second Night." Merrill must have been satisfied to read his racy, ambitious poem at his alma mater, standing at the front of Johnson Chapel and facing the sober portraits of Amherst presidents on the white walls before a packed house. The students had been assigned *Water Street* to study in class; the clever ones among them could savor the classroom parody in "The Thousand and Second Night." Jimmy made a few minor adjustments to the poem, gave up on doing anything more ("I did hope, I did try, to cling less to artifice—in vain; my muse <u>will</u> pluck her eyebrows despite my prayers"), and sent it off to *The New Yorker*, where Howard Moss accepted it—although the poem didn't appear in print until June 1964, after long debate among the magazine's other editors, presumably concerning its length, difficulty, and sexual content.

On January 15, Merrill and Jackson went into New York for the opening of Tennessee Williams's *The Milk Train Doesn't Stop Here Anymore*, directed by Herbert Machiz, with music by Paul Bowles. Merrill had little regard even for Williams's great plays, and *Milk Train* wasn't one of them. He "loathed its roughness, its slickness, its confusion, its obviousness"; it was "a mess of unspecified Meaning, deliberately so I fear, TW being as always a devotee of the vaguely resonant." Machiz threw "a far too nice party afterwards"; 140 well-wishers appeared at the restaurant, only to depart en masse after word went around that Walter Kerr had panned the play on television. A *Don Giovanni* followed, with Leontyne Price as Donna Anna, and then a party given by the Hollanders "to say goodbye to their 70 most intimate + distinguished friends" before John, taking a fellowship year away from his new appointment at Yale, moved the family to Europe. Poets turned out that night, including Louis Simpson, W. S. Merwin, Robert Penn Warren, and Auden and Kallman, who invited Jimmy and David to their apartment to listen to a tape of *Elegy for Young Lovers*, Hans Werner Henze's opera, for which they had written the libretto. Meanwhile, in Irma Brandeis's apartment, with Bernard de Zogheb flown in for the event, Merrill himself played host to "the NY premiere" of a de Zogheb ballad opera, *Le Sorelle Brontë*, performed by the Little Players. This event took place "before a glittering and rapt public of perhaps 20. [. . .] It was an immense success," he gushed about the miniature gala, aware of the contrast it made with bloated occasions like Williams's opening night.

As Merrill continued to showcase works by the oddball Alexandrian and they gained a small notoriety as a result, some supposed that de Zogheb must be a nom de plume for the poet, an alter ego. But Bernard was entirely real. Jimmy once described his "Levantine face" as "dimpled + creased like a bride's first muffin, eyes tiny as currants." Born in 1924, he was the last descendant in Alexandria of a Greek Catholic family that came to Egypt from Syria in the nineteenth century and prospered, to the point of acquiring an obscure Italian title, until they lost their fortune in the 1920s. Samuel Lock, a novelist and the companion of Adrian de Menasce, who was part of Tony Parigory's circle of Alexandrian friends, knew de Zogheb well. Angular and wiry, he regularly appeared at de Menasce and Lock's flat in London wearing the tightest jeans "and a t-shirt with an anchor on the back," and announcing, as he sunk into the couch, "I'm shipwrecked again." "He carried with him, but always," Lock remarked, "a cloth bag containing cash, a camera, a *Times* crossword puzzle, his diaries, and a tin box with felt pens in many colors." The myth among his friends was that "Bernard had been dumped out of his pram as a child, and that had made him strange." He spoke several languages and had a precise verbal memory. As he sat on his friends' couch, he colored the words of his puzzle, using those felt pens, printing each letter in a different ink and adding a bright, childlike sketch of flowers, a seascape, women's fashions, a view of the Nile or the Sphinx, and then dating the page when he was done.

Merrill paid for Tibor de Nagy Editions to publish the libretto of *Le Sorelle Brontë* (which is dedicated to Menasce). The book appeared in 1963 in an edition of three hundred copies with a deep-hued lilac cover and wide, small, nearly square pages. Merrill sent copies to many friends. His short introduction suggests some of his fascination with *Le Sorelle Brontë*. "It is designed," he explained, "for that small red theater in the soul where alone the games of childhood are still applauded." That "small red theater" is the tiny realm of fantasy young Jimmy explored with his marionettes and later rediscovered in the great red theater of the Metropolitan Opera. De Zogheb linked these theatrical forms in a mischievous way. He recast the familiar story of the Brontës as a miniature grand opera, setting lyrics to popular tunes from many countries. The result was an anarchic parody, the main object of which was romantic melodrama as found in the Brontë story and Verdi's operas.

The tunes, printed in red in the margin of the text beside the speeches they accompany, include "Yo te quiero mucho," "La vie en rose," "Funiculi-funicula," and the Ella Fitzgerald standard, "A-Tisket, A-Tasket" (the setting for "Oh Rosa, che cosa!"), among other songs from Italy, Greece, Russia, and the eastern Mediterranean. The music, by calling to mind the original lyrics, provides comic comment on what is being sung. As brother Branwell drinks himself into oblivion, the Brontë servants wring their hands to "Old Man River." When Emiglia discovers Signor Hegez, Carlotta's tutor, kissing her, he defends himself by singing "Mio intention è honorabile" to the tune of "The Marine Anthem." The opera's dramatic climax comes when Emiglia dies from consumption. The final ludicrous lament for four voices is set to the "Beer-Barrel Polka" ("La sorella morta, oh la la!"). The result was hilarity on the edge of hysteria, but it comes to more than a joke. "On every page," Merrill says of the libretto, "something is made clear about the tenacious inanity of human emotion." By flamboyantly ridiculing the conventional pathways to feeling, *Le Sorelle Brontë* arrives at what Merrill calls "our hearts' inmost haven." Or so it was for Merrill. De Zogheb made him laugh until he cried.

De Zogheb composed his ballad operas in a "kitchen Italian." It was the idiom in which the old Alexandrian elite and their Italian servants communicated, a pidgin full of error and nonce expressions into which were marbled bits of Greek, French, Arabic, Spanish, and English, like nuts and spices in a strudel. Merrill slipped in and out of this jargon in his letters to Parigory and de Zogheb. As the editor of *Le Sorelle Brontë*, he "took the liberty," he told Bernard, "of inserting in the stage directions a candle in Anna's hands for her 3rd act entrance. Una candela—literally, a spark plug, if memory serves; but I feel it is right." Merrill relished both the staging and the publication of *Le Sorelle Brontë* as a collaborative word game, satisfying for him in some of the ways Robert Morse's spoonerisms were, or his hours at the Ouija board with David.

Merrill's frequent letters to Daryl Hine from this period were filled with more madcap wordplay. Jimmy calls Hine "Engel," "Pen-Pal," and (mimicking Winebaum's stutter) "P-p-p-et." While the poets traded workshop commentary on each other's work, they exchanged versions of an anagram poem they invented together, in which a proper name is used as title and each subsequent line is an anagram of the name. In November, Merrill got the game going with this card:

Here is an example of a new verse form guaranteed to make hours pass like minutes.

TERESINA OF AVILA

A sane, trivial foe.
Are feats in? Voila!
Faeriest Ovalina,
O rival saint, a fee!

Fuller rhymes, longer lines, all are desiderata. But the ground has been broken!!!

Yours, dear Princess, ever, . . .

Before Hine could return serve, Merrill produced another quatrain made of the same set of letters, this time, in a fit of deranged inspiration, adding rhymes:

Ay di mi! The Muse is a cruel mistress. . . .

Rant, Flavio. I ease
In a vale of tears. I

> Faint; o'er a valise
> Avare of satin, lie.

I cannot sleep. My tongue is swollen, my eyes red + burning. Pity me, Petulant!

> Witwood
> c/o Can Grande; Verona

Petulant replied to Witwood (they are fops from Congreve's *The Way of the World*) with his own virtuosic turns on the odd form, in this case introducing a further complication: the title of the poem must be the name of a poet. Hine's "Li Po" and "Oscar Fingal O'Flahertie Wills Wilde" were respectively the shortest and longest examples of the form. But Merrill had successes too, as in "W. H. Auden":

> Ha! We dun
> Had U wen
> Nude (Haw!),
> Hued wan,
> A hun'dew.
> Awed? Nuh.
> Wud a <u>Hen</u>.

These and similar verses, hesitating on the cliff-edge of nonsense, but somehow holding fast to the rail of meaning, Merrill shared in letters to other friends. Yet with only this sort of poem to show since he completed "The Thousand and Second Night," he felt that he was only wasting time at his desk.

Jackson too complained of distractions impeding his work in the form of regular visits by "the full-blooded american Indian chaufeur [*sic*] of an aged couple, up the street," who came to their apartment armed with bottles of scotch and stacks of blue movies. Then, too, "It is hard to work when all those children we befriended when we first moved into Creepyville have reached the ages of 17 plus and during these turbulent days come up for advice and talk with old Dave." The almost-grown-ups were local boys named Joe Bruno, John Ainsworth, and Peter Tourville; they hung around 107 Water Street often enough for David to call them "our Teenage Club." He told Richie, "[A]ll the village idlers (of certain ages) have come up Monday thru Thurs (roughly) to learn about life and put together our Ginza

Chinese puzzles, sit for me via pastel and poloroid [*sic*], and musingly rub their h. .d ons. As yet I do not know how to transmute this experience into art."

Two weeks later, Stonington was the scene of drama worthy of Tennessee Williams—or was it a farce by de Zogheb? Merrill told Hine,

> [I]t has been a week of horrors: infant rape; attempted suicide of 17-year-old-girl upon finding her 15-year-old-chum in the arms of "our" Red Indian chauffeur—so that the whole story is out and he in jail on $15 grand bail, accused of things the local police chief couldn't even tell Billie Boatright, among them, it appears, "sodomy" (ah! che cosa quella?) and finally the successful suicide of Carlotta Dodge, the youngest daughter of [the sculptor Augustus] St Gaudens (another tear on the marble cheek of "Grief") whom nobody much liked anyhow—she stood in her kitchen, the story goes, after dinner, taunting her meek, disagreeable husband by playing Russian roulette at the sink until Bang! Ker-plooie!

Despite his tone, Merrill may have feared that "their" chauffeur, who evidently had his own teenage club, might let their story out with his. His arrest reminded Jimmy and David that there were laws against "sodomy," and that Stonington was ready to eat up the next morsel of gossip.

Not all the news was lurid. In March, Robin and Betty in Seattle announced the birth of their first child, a son; and the infant's "father's mother's father's younger son" wrote "Little Fanfare for Felix Magowan" to celebrate the occasion, welcoming him "to earth, time, others; to / These cool darks, of sense, of language, / Each at once thread and maze." More babies were on the way that spring: a daughter, Maud, for the Burnetts, and a second daughter for the Hollanders, Lizzie, to join five-year-old Martha. In April, Charles and Mary arrived on Water Street for Easter with three young Merrills in tow, each of whom signed the house's guest book. David commented in looping cursive on the train trip from New York—"at Gransentrel Stiation, Help! P.S. (I'm lost)"—and Paul, the littlest, noted "I like to draw" beside two dueling knights. Sixteen-year-old Amy's hand is poised, almost an adult's. In the summer she returned on her own for a short visit with her uncle. Under his supervision, she sampled her first gin and tonic, played croquet with Rollie McKenna, and read the poet's copy of *Lolita*, which he'd smuggled into the country in 1957.

May 30 marked Merrill and Jackson's tenth year together. The message to David from Jamie, as Merrill signed himself, is that of a spouse too optimistic about the future to be nostalgic about the past:

Ten, did I hear?
T-E-N—ten?
If they have gone,
Would you, my dear,
Live them again?—
Every last day
Of cold + hot,
Of evil + good,
Of rich + meager?
You think you would?
Well, I would not,
I'm sorry, I'm too
Ready, too eager
For the next ten
With you, with you.

In Merrill's notebook from 1963, the draft of a poem called "The Other," never completed, tells a different story:

Sometimes you can feel him straining
Towards you, in the smile
Of frightening intimacy with which
An intimacy began that did not scare [replacing "frighten"]
Until much later, when the blue
Eyes had brightened ["ripened"] to sapphire, the pale hair
Richened to gold, and the whole face
So known, so loved, become
Something no longer seen, a cry, a chord,
Crimsoning wet where it has pressed
Vaguely against your heart of ice.

In his birthday message, Jimmy urges David not to fear passing time but to look forward to their future. Here, he feels trapped in a "scary" intimacy, and his heart has turned to ice. "I wanted love, if love's the word / On the foxed spine of the long-mislaid book," he says in "The Thousand and Second Night." He had decided that, if he was going to find love, he would have to find it somewhere else.

He and Jackson left for Greece in June. Hine, the Burnetts, and Sewelly would take turns on Water Street, looking after the house and feeding

Maisie. From this time on, with improved air service, David and Jimmy made their passages to and from Greece separately. Even if they were traveling at the same time, David, afraid to fly, would be on the ocean, while Jimmy was in the air. More and more, each would be going his own way.

Merrill flew first to Istanbul to meet his mother. The visit was tiresome; he had to tour the city with Hellen and two of her female friends, one of them seventy and the other seventeen. One night, when the ladies had turned in, he took to the park, where he met a handsome, well-dressed young man. The stranger declined to come back to Merrill's hotel, and proposed that they take a taxi to his home instead. Twelve kilometers later—far enough for Merrill to wonder about the wisdom of this plan—the man stopped the car and sent the driver away. It was midnight. The poet found himself alone with this man on top of a hill without houses or streetlamps near, under a half moon with the glittering water of the Bosporus below. In Turkish, the man asked for Merrill's watch, and Merrill laughed. Then he asked for money, and Merrill gave him some. They had sex, and he again demanded Merrill's watch. Merrill could see he meant it now, and for the first time he became frightened. He gave him his watch—and made the mistake of asking for money for a taxi back to the hotel. For reply, the man punched Jimmy in the jaw, knocking him down, kicked him, and left him in the grass.

Merrill told the story to Hine in a letter composed entirely in French. He addresses Hine as "Ma Soeur" and calls himself "Ta pauvre Sophie" who lacks the courage "de te ranconter dans sa propre langue ce que lui est arrivé" (to tell you in her own language what happened to her). The worst part of the night, he explained, came only back at the hotel once what *might* have happened struck him. "Tu riras, mais à deux heures du matin ta soeur était à genoux, toute nue, pour remercier le bon dieu—en français, la parole me manque encore en anglais—de lui avoir sauvé la vie" (You will laugh, but at two in the morning your sister was on her knees, naked, to thank God—in French, since English still escaped her—for having saved her life). There is plenty of humor here, but Merrill was serious when he begged Hine to tell no one of "l'honteuse expérience de ta soeur" (your sister's shameful experience). He had needed a disguise simply to put the story in writing.

He rejoined Jackson in Athens. With Parigory, they traveled to Samos and then Rhodes, where Tony had found them an apartment for July. Bernie was along for the fun, and there was a lot of it, so much that the landlord complained about the traffic on the stairs. When Merrill grumbled that one of the boys they'd met was "stupid & slow," Bernie drawled, "What did you expect—a Rhodes scholar?" The "scholar" was Georgios Politis, a Greek army lieutenant whom, Merrill told Hine, "I've come as close to falling for as anyone in years: he is dumb, good-humored, kind, and 19, and not marvelously good in bed—which always, sad to say, goes straight to the over-experienced heart." Merrill, enclosing a photo, asked Hine not to mention his interest in Politis, in order to keep it from Jackson.

They went to Patmos next (the island of St. John, "where no doubt Revelations await us, thumbs hitched into their jeans") and then back to Athens. They overlapped there with Richie, who noted the routines surrounding Merrill's sexual diversions in Athens: "Jimmy socialized cruising. Sunday would be the day to go down to the duck pond and pick up evzones or sailors. It had to be planned, timed, and if it didn't pan out, we'd come back. Sometimes the trawling was successful. He and David went in the spirit that others would have gone to the Waldorf. They had reserve; they looked over the menu."

In another mood, but with an equal sense of ritual propriety, Jimmy made a habit of joining Maria Mitsotáki for drinks on Kolonáki Square—the "bidet," as it was known to its habitués, in reference to the fountain trickling at the center of it. Merrill dressed for the occasion in a seersucker suit and a rainbow tie, while Maman ordered her usual—champagne and angostura bitters. Merrill or Jackson or both would make trips with her to Cape Sounion, a ninety-minute drive from Athens. When Maria was young, her family was one of three that owned the land surrounding the Temple of Poseidon. The temple, high above the sea at the southern tip of Attica, is one of the most sacred ancient sites in Greece. Mitsotáki's father sold the house and land to pay off political debts; Maria, a determined woman, bought the property back at auction after the war. On a steep hill, lashed by fierce winds, the house was a lonely, two-story stucco box, with shutters and a tile roof, looking out to sea. Mitsotáki decorated the rooms with a few keepsakes from the long-gone schooner *Tuscano*, but made no other improvements. "I'm tired, so my house should look tired," she said. The large fireplace was backed by an iron *contrecoeur* with a neoclassical scene on it, its pastoral, mythological figures burned black.

She never spent the night in the house. Driven by a chauffeur or by Jackson, she came for the day to garden. Merrill would bring a notebook, Jackson his watercolors. Merrill's "Words for Maria," written in Connecticut in the summer of 1965, describes a visit when he watched her "prune, transplant, / Nails ragged in a daze / Of bliss." In his mind's eye, she resembles a mythological figure, an earth mother in haute couture:

> In smarter weeds than Eve's (Chanel, last year's)
> You kneel to beds of color and young vines.

The chauffeur lounges smoking in the shade . . .
Before you know it, sunset. Brass-white, pink-
Blue wallowings. Dismayed
You recollect a world in which one dines,
Plays cards, endures old ladies, has to think.
The motor roars. You've locked up trowel and shears.
The whole revived small headland lurches, disappears

To float pale black all night against the sea [. . .]

"Words for Maria" is Merrill's first detailed portrait in poetry of a specific friend. It is an early example of the sociable middle style in which much of his later poetry—including many hundreds of lines of *Sandover*—was written. That manner, chatty, deft, and conspiratorial, was modeled on the kind of conversation with Maria that it is used to evoke in this poem. In Athens in August 1963, Merrill had had a chapbook printed of "The Thousand and Second Night." He inscribed her copy "for Maria—a muse present when the tale began—from the doting author."

Merrill and Jackson were laying down tentative roots of their own. One day they drove west to Salamis "with an eye to buying a tiny piece of land on a very pretty, empty cove at the end of a ghastly road"; it wasn't right, but they were taken with the idea of owning property in Greece. Around this time, David applied to serve as a foster parent for a Greek child.* Dimitrious Alexandropoulos, aged eleven, and his brother Elias, thirteen, lived with their mother in Kalamata; their father was dead, and Jackson's regular contributions (funded by Merrill, to be sure) enabled their mother to keep them with her, rather than put them in a state-run home. The boys flew to Athens to meet David and Jimmy, who drove them back home after a short visit. Jackson and Merrill kept up regular contact with both children and their mother as the boys grew, and paid for their educations. It was another way of having children.

Tony visited Jimmy and David back on Water Street that fall. Jimmy planned to show him the U.S. on an elaborate tour. The first stop was a Manhattan cocktail party hosted by Grace Stone, with Elizabeth Bowen, Dawn Powell, Truman Capote, John Mason Brown, Gold and Fizdale, and Donald Keene,

---

* The program was called "Foster Parents' Plan, Inc., Greece." Jackson was the designated foster parent. JM to DJ, letter, July 8, 1966 (WUSTL).

a Japanese scholar, among the guests. Parigory did not impress Perényi. "Tony was pure kitsch," as she put it, "a lounge lizard from the Levant" rather than a person of quality, in her eyes.

With David traveling, as he put it, "out to Nowhere" (that is, Los Angeles), Jimmy and Tony flew to Chicago. The Burnetts were living there, and Hine had joined them as a graduate student at the University of Chicago, with money and encouragement from Merrill. The attention that *Water Street* won had resulted in invitations for Merrill to read from schools outside the few in the Northeast where his work was known, including the University of Wisconsin and Washington University in St. Louis. From the Midwest, with Parigory in hand, Merrill flew to Seattle for a visit to Robin and his family that he had promised to make when he persuaded Robin to take the job at the University of Washington. Merrill read at the university; he also sang the libretto of *Le Sorelle Brontë* and discussed de Zogheb's weird work on a weekly radio show about poetry hosted by Robin. Jimmy drove with Tony and Robin to Victoria, British Columbia, where they learned of John F. Kennedy's assassination by overhearing two clerks discuss it. "How sad, how horrid," he wrote limply to the Burnetts. "One can think of little else."

On the road, Merrill taught "the Landscape Game" to his friends. The game was part psychological test, part party game. Merrill played it often over the years; he also wrote a short story called "Peru: The Landscape Game" that makes use of the game as a motif. It requires one person to daydream in response to specified prompts, while others ask questions and later interpret the player's fantasy. Merrill explains the rules in his story:

> [E]ach person describes a house he then leaves in order to take an imaginary walk. One by one he discovers a key, a bowl, a body of water, a wild creature, and finally a wall. Free association is invited at any stage, and nothing explained until the last player has spoken.
>
> The house is your own life, your notion of it. Trees roundabout stand for Other People.
>
> The key is Religion. The bowl, Art. The water, Sex.
>
> The wild thing is Yourself—the unconscious.
>
> The wall is Death.

In the car, Merrill guided his nephew's symbolic journey. The body of water Robin imagined? "The Mediterranean," he answered. "What do you do," Jimmy asked, "when you come to it?" "I'd like to go swimming," Robin said wistfully, "but it's so late in the day." Less inhibited, Merrill, in his own fantasy walk, used his bowl to drink from a flowing river: "Just enough sex," he joked, "to irrigate one's art." Tony was less circumspect. The water he imagined was the beach in Athens: "[I]t was nighttime and pitch black. But that didn't stop me, I just ripped off my clothes and dove in. Voilà."

In San Francisco, they stayed with Robin's parents and met up with David. The Magowans brought them for drinks to "the Magnin Dept Store Magnins, to see their 8 French pictures and their 800 framed flower pieces, street scenes, ballet dancers, signed, if not conceived, by themselves." Jimmy arranged to see Robert Duncan ("whom I quite admire") and his partner, the collage artist known as Jess. David climbed aboard the train to travel east, while Jimmy showed Tony one last corner of North America—Santa Fe—before they flew to New York, and Parigory continued to Greece.

Now Merrill was ready to finish *The (Diblos) Notebook*. He supposed, in early February, that "it might be done in a few months. [. . .] The last scene is sketched." It was only a few days, however, before he decided that the manuscript was complete, and by summer, Harry Ford had committed to publish the book at Atheneum.

The last scene was violent. When, after separating from Dora in New York, Orson-Orestes returns to Diblos on his own, intending to occupy "his" cottage again, he is met by Dora's son, Byron—who turns him away from the property by striking him in the face with a riding crop, bloodying him. The narrator replays Byron's act in his notebook:

> B. himself . . . stood forth in dark, glowing colors, velvet & gold braid, & dagger-handle flashing—a costume from the vendetta country of Crete or the Mani. Banked like a coal, his pride had burst into flame at last. He raised
> In my head he raised his beautiful clenched hand. The riding-crop descended, once, twice, again, upon my
> once, twice, again, inscribed its madder penstroke upon my brother's face, at the tempo of a ~~slowly pounding tempo of a giant's drugged pulse~~
> of the dolphin's progress through glittering foam

That phrase "madder penstroke" connects Byron's act with the narrator's act on the first page of the notebook when he writes Orestes's name and strikes through it: "~~Orestes~~." The narrator, by working to unmask his half brother, has been striking through his heroic self-image throughout the book. He has been doing his version of what he imagines Byron doing. Byron is also acting on behalf of Merrill, punishing Friar for his power over Merrill. There is an allegory at work: Merrill identifies with the aristocrat, Lord Byron, who turns back the Keatsian parvenu, Friar-Orestes, from Dora's property, and so defends his own claim on Greece. This fantasy draws out the aggressiveness in the Byronic manner, the "air of irrelevance," that Merrill adopted in "The Thousand and Second Night." The beating is reminiscent of Francis's sensational self-mutilation in *The Seraglio*, because there is a self-reflexive turn: the way the narrator breaks off his sentence at "my" implies that Byron's crop also comes down on "my [face]" as it strikes "my brother's." As the Freudian Friar taught him, the man who fantasizes a scene of beating occupies in imagination both active and passive roles: the parties are reversible, like Narcissus and his image, or the Jack of Clubs. As the narrator says near the end of the notebook, admitting his inability to find a satisfying form for his novel, "I did do my best, but, as the Gorgon's face was mine, never succeeded in getting a full view of it."

The book began with Orestes on the Diblos waterfront, trying to find the right angle to see the Sleeping Woman. It is easily visible from the harbor on Diblos, where the narrator has been writing all summer in a café. Passing by ship to Athens, having had his fill of her and the Oedipal drama she presides over, he sees the future open before him: "On deck. We have sailed past the House. The Sleeping Woman has veered & reshifted into new, non-representational masses. Diblos lies far astern. Here is the open water. A sun preparing to sink. Other islands."

Merrill had closed the book on Poros and Friar, but he was hardly done with Greece.

In the letter that announces completion of *The (Diblos) Notebook*, Merrill first mentions a potential house to buy in Athens. He thanks Tony for finding it for him:

> Oh my darling, we are so excited about the house. It is a big + perhaps dangerous decision, but, with it, our lives—our Athens lives—would change a little. We would "belong" there, somewhat, instead of just coming there for the sex cure. The house would mean other things to us than just a place to entertain evzones; and [. . .] you do make "that" sound not quite as easy + fun as it used to be when we were younger + Athens was smaller. And about 69 per cent of our regrets, on that score, are cancelled out by the thought that there was a place of ours where we could come + grow old [. . .] near you and Maria and that

whole heavenly monde, when the heavenly monde of Stonington has become too much to endure.

It would be another house Tony found for him that Merrill bought that spring; but the "big + perhaps dangerous decision" was already made.

In February, Joe Bruno was busy painting one of the apartments on the second floor of 107 Water Street. The Beatles, who were making their first appearance in America, sang out on Joe's transistor—"I Want to Hold Your Hand"—rocking the old wooden building. Merrill liked to put on a Beatles wig, a Valentine's gift from Kay Meredith, though it made him look like "l'Impératrice Joséphine." He and Jackson enjoyed the friendly Bruno. When the young man related to them a recent experience with "a W O M A N," who told him, "I've had a lot of men, but you're something special," Merrill told Joe he hoped "he had said exactly the same words to her!" Correspondence suggests that Bruno and Jackson went to bed together that spring. It was around this time that Merrill began having sex with Bruno's friend, Peter Tourville. Joe and Peter were easy to be around, and available to please David and Jimmy in ways they no longer pleased each other.

Stalled on another novel, Jackson worked on television scripts at the suggestion of Truman Capote (which, in the end, were rejected). "We do whirl into the big city, now and then," he told Richie.

> Last week [we] saw: "Dr Strangelove" and the new Bergman [*The Silence*], and Joanie Sutherland in Rossini's Semiramide (Jimmy will correct spellings[)]. Ravished by the first and last, and particularly by a contralto [corrected: soprano] named Marilyn Horne! Then we went off, in black ties, to a dinner which turned out to be FOR Jimmy. . . . Full of celebrities all of whom had received WATER STREET the day before—so they could talk intelligently to the author. As cocktails lasted two hours and there were four wines with dinner, plus brandy served in little goblets made of chocolate (yes) plus hot sake! (yes) by something like 11:30 yer old buddies, D&J, were STONED. I mean we had to be carried into a taxi . . . after lots of yaks: JM losing a contact lens, and exalted [*sic*] company crawling around looking for it; me making out with the Help, JM and I in the john with Andy Warhol (sp? the Pop artist) who, as I urinated, kept saying, "Look, I mean it, I wanna come up there and do a Pissing Movie on Water Street of you two in the John, I MEAN it!" a miserable fag, man, if ever one met one. Etc. And so our life goes. Creativity vs Destructiveness. Terribly Tense.

In April, Merrill went to Athens by himself to buy a house on the outskirts of Kolonáki. It was "really just what we want." Winebaum had rented
a flat nearby. Kallman, "agonizingly in love" with a young evzone, was on
hand too, living with Ansen. Merrill found that his dear, innocent Georgios Politis, after six months in Athens, was "ruined!" He purchased furniture and arranged for work to be done on the house, so that all would
be ready when he and Jackson came back in the fall. After a brief stop in
Rome to see Umberto and Grace, he returned home in time for the arrival
of David's parents. Their visit "set off a round of parties, at whose still centers they sit smiling + dazed. After dinner, drunk, we sit down to the bridge
table [. . .] and Mary + I," Merrill told Hine, "holding dreadful cards, can do
nothing but win, win, win." Then Hellen Plummer came. Her son met her
in New York, where they toured the World's Fair in Queens before coming
to Stonington.

David Kalstone also visited that June. He'd put his name in the guest
book for the first time a year before in March 1963. Over the next twenty
years, he would stay for long weekends with Merrill and for weekends,
weeks, and long summer months when Merrill was in Greece. They'd met
by chance on a train in 1962. Kalstone was a junior professor of English at
Harvard, where he had studied with Reuben Brower and taught in Brower's
lecture course, "The Interpretation of Literature," Humanities or "Hum"
6, whose brilliant staff included at one time or another Stanley Cavell, Paul
de Man, Anne Ferry, Richard Poirier, William Pritchard, Stephen Orgel,
Frank Bidart, and other writers and critics who went on to distinguished
academic careers. Brower's practice of "slow reading" shaped Kalstone's
approach as a poetry critic. Like Merrill, he had little interest in abstract
ideas, preferred particulars, and emphasized the role of personal taste in
the making and evaluation of literature. His study of Sir Philip Sidney's
poetry appeared in 1965. Already writing on contemporary American
poetry, he would become one of the first scholars to write about Merrill's
work, which he did in his book *Five Temperaments: Elizabeth Bishop, Robert
Lowell, James Merrill, Adrienne Rich, John Ashbery* (1977). In Merrill, Kalstone
found a poet perfectly suited to his training and disposition; in Kalstone,
Merrill found his first fully sympathetic commentator.

Yet they were less likely to talk about poetry than about opera, recipes, friends, movies, or sex. David was gay and "a tremendous gossip." He
could be clever and caustic, but was more often sweet, rueful, and considerate. He had grown up in a world quite different from Merrill's. He was
born in McKeesport, Pennsylvania, the first of two sons in an affectionate
Jewish family. His father owned a small men's clothing store; his mother,
who had attended college, was a talented painter and taught art. Kalstone

went to public high school before Harvard. As a student, he had thick, bottle-bottom glasses, wore regulation academic tweeds, and had a book-worm's kindly, absentminded air. Merrill took him in hand, and under his influence Kalstone remade his image. He got contact lenses at Merrill's instigation, and a reliably stylish haircut. He moved to Rutgers, found an apartment in Chelsea, began writing for *The New York Review of Books*, and became a devotee of the New York City Ballet, attending performances every night at the height of the season. Then came summers in Venice, when he began to dress in Italian suits and sweeping capes, at last as suave in person as on the page—so that Helen Vendler, his friend and colleague from Har-vard days, hardly recognized him when they met again.

Over the summer, Merrill received a letter from Mona Van Duyn, the poet who had reviewed *The Country of a Thousand Years of Peace* favorably. She was writing as a consultant to Washington University's Olin Library in St. Louis. The letter she wrote to Merrill does not survive, but similar letters she wrote at the same time on behalf of the library to Robert Cree-ley and May Swenson do. "Washington University has a new and spacious library, which has developed new and spacious ambitions," she explained to Creeley. "The Rare Book Room is beginning the collection of a Schol-ars' Library of about fifteen poets," including "all first and variant editions of their works, all non-book publications [. . .], translations, tapes, and so on," and Merrill, along with Creeley, Swenson, and a few other poets of their generation, was on the list. Van Duyn continued,

> The collection of works will [. . .] be complemented by as big a collection as the library can get of each poet's worksheets and notebooks and jottings of ideas for poems; original typescripts of books; galleys and pageproofs (corrected) of books; letters pertaining to the poetry from editors and writers. Anything, that is, which has to do with the genesis and process of the poems and the process of getting the poems from the typewriter into final print.
>
> We are hoping to get some or all of these things from you, and hoping you will feel that Washington University is "home base" for your manuscripts when you want to dispose of them.

The appeal worked. In later years, when someone wondered why his papers were in St. Louis, Merrill liked to say, "They *asked*." The conse-quences of that asking were far-reaching, for the library and poet both. The library came to house what could not have been foreseen—a huge archive of great literary interest for which the university did not have to pay (Merrill declined even to take a tax credit for his donations of materials) and which would eventually be endowed by the poet himself. The archive encouraged Merrill in his working habits, both confirming and furthering his interest in the process of composition. He had no association at all with Washington University—which was a plus; and it was flattering to be collected alongside other poets of the first rank. Not only was the library betting that his poetry would be read in the future; they would help assure it. And the promise of a "home base" for his work might have appealed to Merrill just when he was launching out on a new life in Greece.

In July, Mary McCarthy and her husband James West arrived in Stonington for a month away from Paris, where West was posted in the foreign service. McCarthy was not merely the leading woman of letters of her generation; she was now a best seller. Her new novel *The Group*, a roman à clef that followed the fortunes of a set of young women modeled on members of her class at Vassar, remained on the best-seller list in the summer of 1964, a year after its publication. It was also a subject of controversy among Vassar alumnae, including some who summered in Stonington, and there was a "big hullabaloo" at the yacht club before McCarthy was granted guest privileges for West's three children to swim and play tennis. "The climax of that summer," Merrill remembered much later,

> was a huge picnic. Mary got this old Frenchwoman who lived out in the country to let us use her property. I think there must have been thirty people. [. . .] Grace and Eleanor. Harry and Elizabeth Ford were up visiting for the weekend. [. . .] Rice salad and potato salad. Very elaborate hampers were packed. Those who wanted to could strip down to their suits and hop into a stream with a waterfall. It was just a lovely day. And this was her sense of showing the children something American. We didn't have flags and bunting, but it was a very grand moment.

In the afternoons, Merrill walked two blocks to the Morses' to sit for his portrait by Robert. On September 6, the likeness was unveiled "to literal applause, before a dozen champagne-primed intimates" at 107 Water Street. The Stone Women, offering up their own delicious Americana, furnished "a knock-out dinner (chicken stuffed with ham + truffles), succotash, ginger ice-cream, to bid farewell to us and the McCarthy-Wests." With all this social life, "[o]ur 'double' life has had a time of it wedging itself in," Jackson wrote to Richie, "but a few lost nights found their way." During a week of "glorious," end-of-summer weather, cool nights and warm days, Merrill sat on the deck reading Isak Dinesen. He also reread *Artagal*, Christian Ayoub's novel, in which he found a sentence he would use as the epigraph for his new novel: "Isidore a menti, je ne méprise personne et ne hais point mes parents" (Isidore lied, I scorn no one, and I do not at all despise my parents).

On September 16, Merrill flew to London. He arranged for Chatto & Windus to sell *The (Diblos) Notebook* in Great Britain, and he saw Tony Harwood and Bernard de Zogheb, who had traveled from Paris to meet him. On a visit to the National Portrait Gallery, he admired the "radiant young portrait of John Clare at the height of his brief fame, with Bedlam round the corner." And what lay around the corner for him? He went next to Berlin to take part "with people like Auden + Spender + the sublime J. L. Borges" in a poetry conference sponsored by the Congress for Cultural Freedom (an organization supported by the Ingram Merrill Foundation which, a disgusted Jimmy learned later, was funded by the CIA). Then he got on a plane to Greece.

8

DAYS OF 1964

1964–65

Merrill arrived in Athens on September 28. For the first time in Greece, he would spend the night in a house of his own. Parigory was waiting for him, and they went out to celebrate at a bar called the Metro. The Metro was an orange- and yellow-tiled dive one floor below the street in Omonia (or "Harmony") Square; it drew men on their way in or out of the train station in the city center. In this "airless tank," a watering hole with a "jungle idyll" that depicted a tiger and his "lolling" mate painted above the bar, Tony and Jimmy watched "the world / Eddy by, winking, casting up / Such gorgeous flotsam that hearts leapt, or sank."* This evening on their way into the bar, the world cast up something that made this poet's heart leap: a twenty-two-year-old Greek with bright eyes and a ready smile.

Strato Mouflouzélis remembers the meeting this way:

One day I was doing military service in the air force, and I went off duty. I took the train from Tatoi, the base, to Omonia, and there were two men there—Tony and Jimmy. They asked me for a light. Then they asked me, do you want a drink? There was another friend with

---

* DR to the author, letter, June 13, 2002: "The Omonia bar in Athens was called Metro and it was for hustlers and johns."

me, Sotíri. I said to him, go. Jimmy said no, bring the friend. So we went into the bar, the Metro, and had a drink. Then Jimmy asked me, where are you going? I said, Ambelokipi. It's not far from me, he said. Come home, and we'll meet some others. So I did, and Jimmy called up the *parea*. Vassili and Mimi came. Jimmy put out tidbits. And lots to drink. At the end of the night I asked him to drive me to my home, and he did. He took me one street away from our house. We sat and talked in the car. When are you going to have another day off? he asked. Two or three days later I called, and Jimmy picked me up with Sotíri. We went to the house. Jimmy said, we'll call Tony, and we all went to a tavern, the one called Fani. I took off my uniform at the house, and they gave me clothes. That night I stayed with Jimmy.

Do you have a light? Can I buy you a drink? James Merrill met his grand passion, the bittersweet muse of his middle years, using the oldest lines in the book. For his part, Strato was ready to supply that light, to have that drink, ready even to dismiss his air force buddy, Sotíri. But it wasn't necessary: he was entering a world of plenty where anyone was welcome, at least once or twice. The rhythm of that evening and the next must have seemed easy and settled, as if he had only to say yes to Jimmy and take his place in the *parea*, the Greek word for "company," meaning the intimate social circle that is for Greeks an extended family. But this was Merrill's first night in his new home, and the *parea* was just taking shape with Tony and Vassili and Mimi Vassilikos present. Jackson wasn't due in Athens yet. Before long Sotíri would be replaced by another friend of Strato's, Aleko, who would be replaced by George Lazaretos, who would become Jackson's lover, a counterpart to Strato, making two couples in the house. The little group, in one configuration or another, would meet at Parigory's shop or at the house for drinks, eat a dinner Merrill had made or go to Fanny's, the local taverna, before some or all of them headed out for music, dancing, and more drinks. This was the start of all that.

That first night Mouflouzélis didn't stay with Merrill. But already their friendship was unusual enough that he thought it best to be dropped off one street away from his parents' house, safely out of sight, so as not to provoke questions. Strato was the first child in a family of three boys and one girl. He had left home for the first time to serve in the military, as required of all Greek men; in September 1964 he had a little more than a year to serve as an air force mechanic. His working-class parents, like so many Athenians of their era, came from village societies (his father from the island of Lesvos near the coast of Turkey, his mother from Evia, a rugged island two hours north of Athens). His uncle, George Mouflouzélis, was a popular *rembétika* musician, a master of the urban blues that was the rough soul of Athens. There was nothing elegant or cosmopolitan about Strato's upbringing. None of the Mouflouzélis family was college educated, and none of them spoke English. In time, they would all meet James Merrill, but he would never be easy for Strato to explain.

Mouflouzélis's situation gave a temporary license to the relationship. In the service, he had new freedom from his parents, and he was not yet expected to establish a family of his own. He was ready to have a good time where it was offered. Was James Merrill his first male lover? Possibly, but probably not, to judge from the way they met and then the ease with which he became part of Merrill's daily life over the next six weeks. On November 17, when Merrill mentions him for the first time in a letter to Hine, he is already well established, not a prospect or a sometime boyfriend. To Mouflouzélis, Merrill must have been interestingly foreign—an American in an era when waves of American tourists hadn't yet begun to wash up hourly on Syntagma Square; and there were Greeks on hand (Tony, Vassili, then George) lest he seem too foreign. At first, Strato didn't know how rich his lover was. But from the perspective of a working-class Greek in 1964, every American was rich; and this one, to be sure his soldier lover had enough cash, stashed bills in his epaulets before he left the house. "He was the kind of man who would treat you better than a woman, the way he cared for you," observed Mouflouzélis, mimicking Merrill's attentiveness: "Do you want something to eat? To drink? Money? What do you want to do?" Strato only needed to answer.

What drew Merrill to him? A few years later, after Mouflouzélis had put on weight and a small mustache, the waggish Chester Kallman sent Merrill a postcard of "the Apollo at Olympia, / Its message *Strato as he used to be*." Strato at twenty-two was indeed a beautiful young man, and that combination of youth and beauty, an ancient Greek ideal, was powerful for a thirty-eight-year-old man just beginning to feel old. (Friar, who introduced the nineteen-year-old Merrill to classical Greek ideas of male homosexuality, was at that time roughly the same age in relation to him that Merrill, now in the role of the *erastes*, was in relation to Mouflouzélis, his *eromenos*.) He was an inch or two taller than Merrill, with wide shoulders and biceps, a broad chest and slim waist, a strong jaw and high cheekbones, and a big, arching, noble nose. Aware of his handsome features and their effect on men and women both, he carried himself with easy physical authority. He would fight (or threaten to) if he felt that his honor had been challenged. His hands were large; and he kept his right thumbnail long and sharp, a blade displayed, in the style of Greek toughs. Over the years, Merrill gave him fine clothes and jewelry that emphasized this aspect of his self-image—a big ring, a double-breasted suit, a French trench coat. More than one American friend of the poet's commented that his paramour looked like a gangster, a thug. Perhaps he was supposed to. Strato Mouflouzélis was a god, an ancient statue come alive. But he was also a version of the fantasy character Floyd, who, as the raw, slang-talking outlaw that kidnaps the little rich boy in "Days of 1935," was one of Jimmy's first loves.

But Mouflouzélis's exaggerated masculinity was just part of his attractiveness. After all, his macho style *was* a style, a role to be performed that allowed for props, costumes, and scenes, all of which appealed to the poet's theatricality. And Mouflouzélis himself was an actor, a storyteller and joker who liked an audience. As Merrill's portraits of him in "Strato in Plaster" and other poems make clear, Strato saw himself as the hero of a life story being lived in bold colors, full of injustices and triumphs, suffering and celebrations. Telling a tale, Strato acted out conversations and gesticulated. He cocked his head for effect, arched an eyebrow, threw his hands wide, sniffed to show disdain, and paused before delivering his punch line—a repertoire of gestures legible even to the highest seats in the house.

This vernacular virtuosity, suited to soap opera and slapstick, delighted Merrill. In the first letter that mentions Mouflouzélis, Merrill notes that "he is nifty in bed and, if appearances can be believed, more than a little devoted to One." But the first thing that he praises about Strato is his verbal humor: "He knows hundreds of weird Greek jokes involving degenerate priests, morons, elephants, 'sisters.' " When Merrill introduces him to Kalstone, the first thing he mentions is his jokes: "Would you like to hear one? Man has two parrots + takes them to the parrot-doctor in hopes of discovering which is male, which female. Rien de plus simple. The doctor perches them side by side and tells the first one to say co. Co. To the second: Say co. Co. To the first: say co-co. Co-co. To the second: say co-co. Co-co. To the first: say co-co-co. Co-co-co. To the second: say co-co-co. Ah lay off, you stupid jerk, you've made my balls dizzy. This bird, says the doctor smugly, is the male." Not so funny, perhaps, but Kalstone would have seen the point: Merrill's new bird had balls, and he could joke about them. He made Jimmy laugh.

"He gave you *the warmth of his presence*," Vassilikos commented, explaining the young Strato's charm. "He radiated something—what captured Jimmy's soul was a warmth that his eyes radiated. How do you say with the open flower . . . ? Jimmy fell for it, the invitation." What Merrill fell for, the open flower's invitation, the radiance of those eyes, was a promise not only of sex, but of innocence, or sex *and* innocence together. In their early days as lovers, Strato's youth and working-class manners seemed to Jimmy like simplicity, and simplicity seemed like goodness. And if Strato wasn't as innocent or simple as he seemed, then Merrill would turn out to be the innocent one. One way or another, he would get his wish.

Merrill had been warming up for this; there'd been Georgios Politis the year before. Yet the love affair struck, in Vassilikos's words, like "a *coup de foudre*. It was something that could never have happened to Jimmy before—or after. He was the right age." He was old enough to want to reach back to youth by loving a younger man, and he was still young enough to do so believing in the possibility of success. He was the right age, also, as a poet. The first six months of the affair coincided with a period of intense creativity that carried him to a new level of artistic power. Was this a case of life shaping art, or the other way around? That was one of the questions his new poems would ask.

Jackson, sailing from New York, arrived fifteen days later in Patras and proceeded to Athens with, as David put it, "car and trunk and heaps 'o household luggage to dazzle the Greeks." Maisie, taken to the airport in New York by Bernie, brought up the rear. The Water Street household was reassembled at Athinaion Efivon 44.

Today the street side of the house is festooned with looping, tangled strings of graffiti, its dull cream facade signed by FIZI, TOKIO, and ORAL in an angry, Day-Glo script familiar from New York, although the messages it's used for in Athens are often anti-American. Athinaion Efivon itself has been renamed. It is now called Melina Mercouri Street, in honor of the Greek movie star, and popular heroine, and leader of the opposition to military rule during the junta years, who lived in the area in the 1980s. The renaming of the street would pain Merrill as much as the graffiti. He disliked Mercouri (Vassili and Mimi knew her), and the old name was a case of found meaning, of the surprising wit of everyday life, which he enjoyed. It was no accident that he and Jackson lived on, as it might be translated, "the Street of the Young Men of Athens."

The street appealed for other reasons too. It borders the south side of Mount Lycabettos, the highest point in central Athens, "a sea of pines where nothing will ever be built," as Merrill described it in 1964. So the house was in the middle of Athens, but on the edge of it too, on high, with privacy and views that the mountainside assured the new owners they would keep. The park is a wild place; and Athinaion Efivon, which wasn't paved until the early 1960s, and has few cars, seems to belong half to it, half to the city below. The sounds of the mountain are light, piercing birdsong, fierce, throbbing cicadas, and when the wind is right, bells from the white-washed church on the peak a half mile away. In the other direction, day and night, traffic drones.

Two blocks below Athinaion Efivon 44 is the Athens Naval Hospital. At the base of the slope a few blocks further south is Vassílis Sofías, a major avenue. It passes by the Parliament, the Royal Garden, and the splendid homes of shipowners, such as the Benaki and Goulandris families, whose mansions were converted to art museums. In the mid-1960s, these buildings were joined by new symbols of power: the U.S. embassy and the Hilton Hotel. These new buildings were as clean and self-important as airport architecture, conspicuously American, and out of scale with the cityscape around them. From their roof, Merrill and Jackson could look down on them, in both senses. But American businessmen and policy makers were discovering Greece at the same time that they were, and the financial, political, and military interests that those buildings represented were prominent in the background of their story. They hadn't come to Greece alone.

Athinaion Efivon 44 is situated at a junction where the road that follows the mountain veers north. This puts the house on the border between Kolonáki, the fashionable, high-rent district of central Athens (home of Maria, Nelly, and their friends), and the ordinary neighborhood Merrill passed through that first night with Strato on their way to Ambelokipi. The siting of the house precisely suited the ambivalence of Merrill's and Jackson's position in Greece. Their daily life was oriented toward Kolonáki, where they went to shop, to eat and drink, to go to the post office or meet Parigory at his shop. It was a fifteen-minute walk downhill to the square. But they had chosen to live at a distance from that world, with its coffee and good taste. They needed that distance to pursue the young men of Athens. And Merrill needed it to write.

Maria and Nelly were dismayed by Merrill's choice of house, just as some of his American friends were dismayed by 107 Water Street. Merrill had bought a small, dark house with oddly proportioned rooms and no good parlor in which to entertain guests, located on a steep hill that would have to be climbed back up any time he went out for a loaf of bread. Like 107 Water Street, Athinaion Efivon 44 did not announce its owner's wealth (however inflated its price—which, quaintly, he had had to pay in solid gold). The house was "Mediterranean Fascist / In style," a pile of postwar cement. But 107 Water Street was also an "old eyesore," and its unhandsomeness gave

Merrill and Jackson scope to make it their own. Now, a decade after they bought that building, they had a second chance to make a home.

The openness of that moment, its freshness and possibility, is captured in a pastel by Jackson. The image is a late-afternoon view from the back of the house through the open doors on the second story. To the left of the doors, out of sight, is the wrought-iron spiral stair that, in two quick turns, led to the roof and its views of Mount Lycabettos and the waters of the Saronic Gulf. We can sense that larger spaciousness, the exalted scale of the Greek landscape, even from Jackson's indoor perspective, which frames the folds of Mount Hymettos in the distance. Apartment buildings creep up that far slope. By the late 1970s, others like them will rise behind Athinaion Efivon and block this view. Smog will clog the city's air and make the sea a rare sight. But that lies ahead. Mount Hymettos, famed since antiquity for its violet glow at evening, can still be seen from within the house. It soaks up afternoon light, bare and muscular as a giant human form. The soft blue of the sky grows more intense as the color rises. Its radiance streaks the window glass and pours into the room.

The plan of the interior was intricate, full of idiosyncrasies that made the rooms and the relationships among them feel both patterned and whimsical, like the complicated stanza patterns Merrill liked in his poetry. A short walkway led to the house through a small iron gate painted powder blue, the same color as the wooden shutters and the tall front door. Inside, the floor of the entry room was crosshatched with brown and white tiles. Merrill felt that it might serve as a "dining + dancing room," but the guest list for such an occasion would have to be short. In fact many of the rooms had a miniature quality—countered by the high ceilings of some, emphasized by the low ceilings of others. To the left of the entry was a room in which Merrill put an upright piano. On one side of the hall was a kitchen under an improbable twelve-foot-high ceiling; on the other side was a small room, meant for a dining room, that Merrill took for his bedroom. These back rooms looked out on a cramped courtyard that echoed with children's voices and, at night, the cries of a multitude of cats fed by the tenant in a basement flat, an old woman Merrill and Jackson had inherited and rarely glimpsed.

A steep, creaking staircase turned an abrupt about-face midway up to the second floor. After lending out the house in the 1980s, Merrill spoke of missing not its view, or "the human comedies it had witnessed," but rather his habituated, tactile sense of its peculiar spaces, including "the hairpin turn of the staircase underfoot." Beyond the stairs was the parlor where Jackson caught the pastel view of Hymettos, a room only large enough for a couch and a table and chairs: the space filled up with four for bridge. To one side, jutting out over the front door, was a porch in which two chairs fit snugly, turned to face each other. Jackson's bedroom, also on the second floor, looked out on the street and the pines of Lycabettos, in the opposite direction from Merrill's room downstairs. Across the landing were a bathroom—its ceiling so low one had to crouch to stand in the tub—and an odd storage space it was absurdly difficult to get into or out of.

The pride of the house was the flat roof, with its light, air, views—and at night the stars. This is where guests were quickly led, dizzy from turning this way and that on the way up, to be served the drinks and "tidbits" Mouflouzélis recalls from his first visit. Tin-hatted pipes poked up and peered out at intervals like periscopes. In time, a fringed, peach-colored awning was suspended above a table and low-slung canvas chairs. To a poet steeped in opera, it was a promising stage—with a tiny laundry room sunken a few feet below the level of the roof making for a garret "where one can play the Duke of Mantua ('I'm a poor student') to many a foustanella'd Gilda," as Merrill joked, casting himself in the seducer's role in Verdi's *Rigoletto*, his imagined prey an innocent evzone in regulation folk-costume kilt. During parties, the roof overflowed with people. It overflowed with flowers too, bougainvillea, jasmine, and hibiscus, tended by Jackson. It was like the wooden deck in Stonington, only more extravagant, more lush.

As always, Merrill arranged for help. "There's a wonderful fixture named Kyria Kleo who Kooks and Kleans everything up to and including the Boots outside the Bedroom Door. We have her only 3 times a week (fun's fun) but she would be glad to come oftener. Laundry she takes home"—where, two blocks away, she lived with her mother, the *yiayiá* (Greek for "grandmother"), and her son, Lakis, who was gay. "Jimmy and David thought Lakis was a thief, and he *was* one," Strato remembers. As with so many people in his Greek life, Merrill met these refugees from Alexandria through Tony. Kleo, large and lame, worked as a cleaner at the naval hospital on the days when she wasn't picking up after Merrill and Jackson, cooking *keftédes* for them, or washing their clothes by hand. Lakis was known to cruise the hospital and bring home his boyfriends, to the distress of Kleo and the *yiayiá*. They would all become characters in Merrill's poetry.

Like 107 Water Street, Athinaion Efivon 44 was a shared project. But the house allowed Jimmy and David to keep their distance from each other. Looking back on the fall from the new year, Merrill told Richie, "These months have been perhaps the happiest + easiest we've ever spent here.

Space makes such a difference. In this house we can get out of each other's way." With his bedroom, the kitchen (always his domain), and a room in which he could type, all on the first floor, Merrill kept to himself when he wanted. And Jackson could party late before he went to sleep in his room at the farthest remove from Merrill's. In a postscript to a letter from Merrill to Richie, Jackson describes their newly painted bedrooms (Merrill had chosen pink, Jackson blue), joking, "These color schemes seemed the simplest way of telling the goats from the lambs. . . . Mostly ghastly bores. We are inching our door shut to them. A few still persist." If Jackson was less excited than Merrill about those goats and lambs, it was no wonder, since, when Jimmy was with Strato, David was left with "his friend Aleko who," as Jimmy put it to Daryl, "is something of a lump (prettier than S. but quite without his sparkle) and D. has been very good trying to turn him into the silken purse you would think he was at first glance." There were other boys. "David is upstairs with a commando named Niko," Merrill says in the same letter, "out of bed with whom I have just reeled"—for they were sharing him—and now David was occupied taking photos of, Merrill boasted, "an organ all but unprecedented in the experience of yours truly." (This was something Jackson liked to do: he took Polaroids of his and Merrill's sexual partners as souvenirs of their encounters.)

Mouflouzélis was a different case. Jackson may have been surprised by Merrill's feeling for him. They had each had many partners in the course of their relationship; that was something they shared. Yet Jimmy was calling Strato "absolutely the nicest one in all these years of shopping about." At first, he didn't keep Merrill out of bed with the likes of Niko. But Merrill and Jackson had chosen to buy the house in Athens not merely to take "the sex cure," but to " 'belong' there," and belonging there, for Merrill, quickly meant belonging to Strato. Since the episode in Istanbul, when he was beaten and robbed by his pick-up, he had been thinking about changing his sexual behavior, and Mouflouzélis gave him an occasion for it. In December, Merrill told Richie, Strato "arrived unexpectedly at the house + caught me red-handed. The scene that followed was so wrenching, and the reconciliation so exquisite, that I have turned into a one-man dog, much to Tony's amusement. Such a relief. How I hated those ghastly strolls through the gardens."* When Mouflouzélis discovered Merrill in bed with someone else, he saw it as an infidelity, as Jackson would not have. Merrill's choice

---

* Merrill's resolve was not iron. A month later, he writes to Jackson about a visit from the same man: "Tasso has just come + gone. I relented. He seemed most pleased by the picture, only regretted that you hadn't signed it!" JM to DJ, letter, January 22, 1965 (WUSTL).

of words ("wrenching," "exquisite") suggests grand opera, where, as in the domestic theater put on by his parents, he learned to see passionate displays as proofs of love.

For a few years, Merrill and Jackson had enjoyed the freedom to do as they liked secure in the knowledge that, no matter what had gone on the night before, they would be there for each other the next day. Now, apparently, Jimmy wanted something more. For the arrangement that they were feeling their way toward, he and David had a model in Auden and Kallman. In some ways the older couple's relationship, which gave them both complete sexual freedom, must have appealed to Merrill—it was frank, adult, and worldly. In other ways it must have been a caution. Once Kallman moved to Greece in 1963, he and Auden led divided lives: they were together in the summer in Kirchstetten, Austria; the rest of the year Auden was alone in New York while Kallman, with Ansen as his roommate, lived in Athens. There he fell in love first with a volatile young evzone named Kostas and then with Yannis Boras, another evzone. Boras had dash and good looks, and he became in his way a rival to Auden. Auden accepted the situation, but only bitterly, while Kallman's alcoholism and depression deepened.

Merrill saw how unhappy Kallman was in his Athens life (Auden's pain he never mentions). But he also saw the intensity of Kallman's feeling for his younger lovers, and he was drawn to it as to a compelling drama. When he came to Athens in the spring of 1964 to buy Athinaion Efivon 44, he observed Kallman's household opera from close up: "I sat with him alone for hours, simply listening," fascinated by the stories. Now, with Strato, Merrill had acquired a fascinating story of his own. Like Chester, who fed his Greeks in style, Jimmy took to the kitchen most nights of the week. He wrote to Hine, "Oh, nothing to match him—serving dinner to 12 the evening of the day he moved into a new apartment—but a Chicken Marengo one day, a chocolate soufflé the next. Considering that I'll never master the formula for turning Celsius into Fahrenheit, I'm quite proud of the results. And the boys 'eat it up.' "

While Merrill shopped and cooked, Jackson studied modern Greek. "David has begun lessons," Merrill reported to Mary McCarthy, "[. . .] with an old lady named Mrs Naoum who is drilling into him a mercilessly pure, all but impractical, katharevusa"—the polite, official language, in some ways closer to ancient Greek than to the demotic. Jackson made progress: "he can answer the telephone and use idioms like 'We shall be ten villages apart'—i.e., no longer be friends." He was never a model pupil, however, and, as he told Alison Lurie, he struggled under Kyria Naoum's tutelage: "SHE shudders at the words I bring in, like mud on my shoes, which I've picked up God knows where, like whore and queer and masturbator—everyday useful words—for which she wants me to say: 'of loose morals' and 'deviate' and 'stupid.' But, slowly, I advance into the language, muttering." He never advanced past a command of the language sufficient to order food, do business, and be polite. His missteps could be comical. The Greek word for "eyeglasses" is *yialiá*, not far from *yiayiá*. "Once, at a fish taverna with Maria, David had a lot of wine and lost his glasses. He got down on his hands and knees and began to crawl around under the table to look for them. He made us all laugh: he was yelling, '*Where is my grandmother? Where is my grandmother?*' "

The story is told by George Lazaretos. Lazaretos's Greek name was Yiorgos, but Jackson called him George, the first name of his own father and brother. In fall 1964, George was a twenty-three-year-old engineer in the Greek navy, then stationed in Athens. With a navy pal and his American girlfriend, he came to a party at Athinaion Efivon 44 at the invitation of—who else?—Tony Parigory. Before long he had become part of daily life at the house, a lover and companion for David of the serious type Strato was becoming for Jimmy. Probably neither relationship could have developed very far without the example and permission of the other. An inch or so over six feet, "with very long soccer-playing legs," Lazaretos had vivid black hair and strong, blunt features. He was, as Merrill put it, "on the strong-silent-sensitive side." At times overawed by the company he found at Athinaion Efivon 44, he was a modest young man, anxious to please. "I tried but I couldn't say anything—I was just a petty officer, and there was an admiral at the party!" he said about one rooftop evening. Maria called him "the shy one from Monemvasia," referring to the spectacular, remote harbor town on the Peloponnese where George grew up as one of eight children. His life turned out to be defined by two long-term relationships: one with the navy, in which he enlisted at fourteen, and the other with David Jackson.

Together Mouflouzélis and Lazaretos suggested, in Kalstone's eyes, "L'Allegro and Il Penseroso—Strato very cheerful and thoughtless, George, naturally gloomy but very appealing." In some ways, they were similar. George liked a good time as much as Strato; neither one had any money; they were about the same age; and they were both servicemen. But George had none of Strato's bravura. He was sweet rather than theatrical, and he didn't threaten strangers on the street, or keep his thumbnail sharpened. Maria knew George well enough to have a nickname for him, but L'Enfant never introduced his Strato to Maman. There was a slight but definite difference of class between the two boys, with George in the better position; and while they had a good time together, and the unusual situation in which they had both landed promoted camaraderie, there was room for suspicion and resentment too.

The presence of Vassili and Mimi minimized potential friction and completed the *parea*. The genial Vassilikos, born on the northern island of Thasos in 1933, was, again in Kalstone's words, "charmingly shaggy, a brown bear, very literate, and very eager to tell people about Greek literature." He was an ambitious young novelist who, with help from Friar, had published his prose trilogy—*The Plant, The Well, The Angel*—with Knopf in English translation in 1964. Vassilikos and Merrill became close friends despite Merrill's estrangement from Friar. One reason was Mimi. Small, tart, comic, and shy, with a spray of coarse black hair falling to her waist and fringing her eyes, she was an eccentric, strong-willed woman with whom Merrill had an instinctive rapport. Born in Ithaca, New York, in 1933 to Greek immigrants from the Mani, a remote peninsula of the Peloponnese famous, like Crete, for its blood feuds and vendettas, she was named Demetra after the ancient goddess of the harvest. She studied at Cornell, where she took a class with Vladimir Nabokov. She came to Athens in 1956, enrolled in medical school, and met Vassili. They married in the U.S. in 1960 and then returned to Athens, where she found a job teaching at a Greek-American school. When her husband wrote a sharply anti-American book, *Mythology of the United States*, and Mimi suddenly lost her job because of it, a $1,000 "scholarship" from Merrill rescued them. When he met them, they lived in a single-room apartment.

Vassili and Mimi bridged the social worlds of the *parea* and helped the group to create a small society of its own that was, like Mimi, Greek American. Childless Mimi, gossipy and benevolent, could play mother to these lost boys. Vassilikos was often in the newspaper after 1964, a spokesman for the left who was discussed as a candidate for political office; George and Strato were proud of their association with him, and he kept them on good behavior. And Vassili and Mimi introduced a married couple into the group, making it less clearly, less visibly homosexual, which could be important when the *parea* went out. When Strato and George had to tell friends or family what they were doing with Jimmy and David, mentioning Vassili and Mimi helped.

It worked, the unlikely company, and Merrill was as happy as he had ever been. Vassilikos later recounted one moment in particular from this period. "Jimmy and David were in their little red convertible with Mimi and me. It was evening. We were going out to eat, driving down Lycabettos with the top down. We turned the corner, and the wind hit our faces, refreshed them, blew back our hair. Jimmy and I were in the back seat. He turned to me and said in Greek, 'Vassili, what is the soul? I'm *so* in love—my soul flies

up to heaven!' " Vassilikos pinched his fingers as he told this story, savor-
ing the Greek word for soul, *psyché*, and repeating Merrill's words in Greek.
"He said it like a small child to his father."

What is the soul? As the convertible dove into Kolonáki, the exhilarating
setting, his imperfect command of Greek, and the usual round of pre-dinner
drinks at the house allowed Merrill to pose the question without irony or
complication. The year 1964 was a time of retrospect and self-definition
for him, and metaphysical questions were on his mind. When he stopped
in London on his way to Greece in September, he and Tony Harwood discussed occult wisdom and spiritual practices such as meditation. Harwood
pressed his enthusiasms on Merrill. Two months after seeing him, Merrill drafted, in his notebook, a kind of credo in reply. His reply grew into
"Mandala," a minor poem in *Braving the Elements* in which he is confident
enough of his position to make fun of Harwood's. But the notebook entry he
made on November 17 (the same day he first mentioned Mouflouzélis in a
letter to Hine) shows him in an earnest, embattled mood, working hard to
define his own views in response to Harwood's New Age spirituality:

> I'm not interested in "spiritual evolution"—my own, or yours, or
> the age's. I never have been. To the extent that I can believe in,
> let us say, reincarnation, my hope wd. be entirely bound up with
> the chance to live again on earth, + not in the least to be freed of
> the visible, the audible, the tangible. From this point of view, I
> can have, you will understand, no quarrel with history, whose
> cyclical nature I am quite willing to admit; no feeling that a
> "wrong turning" has been taken; no sense that I am anything, at
> my best, but protected by Father Time + Mother Earth, + warmly
> clothed by the homespun of the here + now. I have never know-
> ingly "meditated" in my life. God forbid I should start now, even
> upon a cat or a matchbox, let alone the Third Eye. . . . Well, that
> is what it turns out I have to say after thinking about your letters
> + (thanks to them) about myself. I could go on to wonder which
> of us is the more deluded, except that for you delusion seems to
> be something one must try to vanquish at all costs, while for me
> it is more like a trusted friend with whom I've been on excellent
> terms for years + years. I mean this.

Merrill overcomes his temperamental inclination against professions of
belief to make an unusually firm statement. He is not interested in a tran-

scendental theory of history or experience that would dissolve particulars and show the unity of all things. Instead, he insists on the primacy of the senses, of "the visible, the audible, the tangible." Part of his strong feeling here is directed against the potential moralism of a religious perspective: he doesn't care whether he takes a "wrong turning"; he goes where his senses lead. There is only one perspective that counts, that of "the here + now." Whatever the soul may be, it has to live in and with the body. And yet this statement is not a simple rejection of Harwood's mysticism. Typically, Merrill is not of one mind about the issue. He isn't, for example, rejecting the idea of reincarnation so much as explaining the terms on which he could accept it. His secular alternative to "spiritual evolution," his sense of being "protected" by Father Time and Mother Earth, is expressed through figures from ancient Greek myth. The union of those figures represents a primal dividedness. And his realism leads him not only to see the necessity of, but actively to trust in, "delusion."

The language and ideas of this notebook entry resonate with the poems Merrill was at work on in 1964 and 1965. These include the three that would complete the collection *Nights and Days*—"The Broken Home," "From the Cupola," and "Days of 1964." The first to take shape was "The Broken Home," his most autobiographical poem to date. He began drafting it in March in Stonington, after completion of *The (Diblos) Notebook*, and he finished it that fall in Greece. In January 1965, Howard Moss took it for *The New Yorker*; Moss said he'd "never read anything so marvelous," Merrill reported to Jackson, untypically exultant.

From the start, the poem included Merrill's early memory of overhearing his father and mother bicker on the gravel outside the Orchard after a party. "I could just hear the ~~deadly~~ angry tone / Of their voices," he wrote in one draft. He gives a version of that exchange in a couplet that presages the couple's breakup: "She: Charlie, I can't stand the pace. / He: Come on, honey—why, you'll bury us all!" Charlie's bluster echoes the Duke de Guermantes's fatuous, dismissive assurance to the dying Charles Swann in the last sentence of Proust's *Le Côté des Guermantes*. Merrill adds a further level of association by suggesting that these clichés ("I can't stand the pace," "you'll bury us all!") are part of an ongoing debate between a mythic couple:

> Always that same old story—
> Father Time and Mother Earth,
> A marriage on the rocks.

Myth, wittily revealed behind commonplace expressions, gave Merrill mastery over his parents; it was, paradoxically, a means of demystifying them and their power over him. But it was also a means of insulating himself from them and their passions, just as, for Orestes, "~~Myth~~ Metaphor formed like ice between him & the world." The mythmaking cast of his mind was part of what made Merrill feel unreal, not fully human. He faces the problem directly in the first section of "The Broken Home":

> Crossing the street,
> I saw the parents and the child
> At their window, gleaming like fruit
> With evening's mild gold leaf.
>
> In a room on the floor below,
> Sunless, cooler—a brimming
> Saucer of wax, marbly and dim—
> I have lit what's left of my life.
>
> I have thrown out yesterday's milk
> And opened a book of maxims.
> The flame quickens. The word stirs.
>
> Tell me, tongue of fire,
> That you and I are as real
> At least as the people upstairs.

In a room "Sunless, cooler" than theirs (punningly implying his childlessness and his temperamental irony and reserve), the poet resolves to prove himself as "real" as the family he came from. To do so, in the provisional way that would enable him to complete the poem, Merrill had to define not only his difference from his parents, but his continuing bond with them.

An early draft of "The Broken Home," dated March 18, 1964, is a three-part free-verse fragment in the manner of Lowell's *Life Studies*, containing what would become the third and fifth parts of the completed poem. To these, Merrill added the portraits of his mother and father and the portraits of himself as an adult and a child that open and close the poem, making six parts in all.* These he cast as sonnets, moving the poem away from Lowell's free verse and in the process achieving his own tone, far more arch and witty than Lowell's, stressing forms, manners, artifice. By the out-

---

* One work sheet contains a summary of the poem in progress in which the penultimate stanza of the finished poem is missing: "1 Crossing the Street, 2 When my parents were children, 3 Father, 4 Mother, 5 Tonight they have stepped, 6 A child, a red dog" (WUSTL).

landishly punning close of the poem, when the child looks out the window of his room in the broken home and watches "a red setter stretch and sink in cloud," the tone is more than merely comic: Merrill has achieved a curious, distinctive combination of sublimity and camp. He is well on his way toward the poems of the 1970s he would call "divine comedies."

To get to that ending, he added another section, a penultimate sonnet in which he says what he believes, much as he did in his reply to Harwood. He began falteringly:

> And this is why (though I cannot be certain)
> I do not read the newspapers or vote
> Or sign petitions against the fate
> Of intellectuals behind the Iron Curtain.
>
> And I will confine my gardening
> To the avocado taking root in water.
> The moment the golden leaves grow fleshly + dark
> Out it goes.

One work sheet shows that Merrill considered dedicating "The Broken Home" to his brother and sister. But in these lines he defines himself against them—by rejecting both Charles's high-minded advocacy of Polish intellectuals and Doris's love of her home, garden, and children. These arguments with his siblings remain as subtexts in the final version of the sonnet, which follows Merrill's admission that his parents are still "to be honored and obeyed."

> . . . Obeyed, at least, inversely. Thus
> I rarely buy a newspaper, or vote.
> To do so, I have learned, is to invite
> The tread of a stone guest within my house.
>
> Shooting this rusted bolt, though, against him,
> I trust I am no less time's child than some
> Who on the heath impersonate Poor Tom
> Or on the barricades risk life and limb.
>
> Nor do I try to keep a garden, only
> An avocado in a glass of water—
> Roots pallid, gemmed with air. And later,

When the small gilt leaves have grown
Fleshy and green, I let them die, yes, yes,
And start another. I am earth's no less.

This is the manifesto of an apolitical aesthete. But he doesn't propose to stand outside time or against nature. Merrill knows that he obeys his parents "inversely." The word puns on "in verse" and "invert," the sexologists' term for homosexual. The notion is that he obeys his parents' example precisely in his refusal of it: they shape even his difference from them. To recognize this, to acknowledge that one can't escape one's parents' influence, even as one achieves maturity and independence, is to reject false promises of total transcendence, like Tony Harwood's. It is also to submit to mortality—to the crushing pace of Father Time, and the certainty that Mother Earth will "bury us all."

These recognitions entered into, and were confirmed by, Merrill's passionate dedication to Strato. "He has quite rejuvenated me," Merrill told Kalstone, "by which I mean, I guess, that I'm tranquil + happy enough with him not to mind my age." When he said this, the old man needing rejuvenation was thirty-eight. With Strato, Jimmy had "lit what's left of my life," proving to himself that he was real.

At the same time, Merrill was thinking of his life in a new way. It had begun to assume, like his hero Proust's, the form of a coherent narrative, backed by cosmic myths, into which, by means of writing, new experience could be absorbed, interpreted, preserved. An event around the time Merrill finished "The Broken Home" illustrates the point. In early January 1965, Auden arrived in Athens on a rare visit, for Kallman's birthday. He happened to appear on the day T. S. Eliot died, and he was swept up by a BBC crew seeking his reaction. As a result, he came late to a party at Nelly Liambey's home. In a wishful, matchmaking mood, Merrill steered Maria to his side. Twelve years later, in 1976, when Mitsotáki and Auden had both died, and Merrill was at work on an enormous poem predicated on just those ideas that he and Tony Harwood had argued over—spiritual evolution and reincarnation—Maria and Wystan joined forces as paired spirit guides; and Merrill, evoking the poet's deeply creased face and the fashionable woman's fading elegance, would develop the mental snapshots made that night at Nelly's in 1965:

Here
At last he is, disheveled, shaking hands,
Between pronouncements downing the first martini

—"But what on earth do people say to him?"
Protests Maria twenty minutes later
Edging behind me ("Trust your Child for once")
To the sofa where he sits alone, eyes shut,
Glass drained. Returning with it full, I drink
Them in, two marvels meeting, past their prime
And pleased enough not to be overjoyed:
Collar frayed and black unalterable;
Deep seams of his absorption, mask of her
Idleness tilted up from foam-streaked hair;
Two profiles, then, in something like relief
Tarnished by a mutual smoke screen—
Her cancer at this point, like his weak heart
And Strato's glance that from across the room
Kindles catching mine, undiagnosed.
Promising not to leave them there, I do:
Father of forms and matter-of-fact mother
Saying what on Earth to one another . . .*

Mirabell, from which this passage comes, and *Scripts for the Pageant*, together the second and third sections of *The Changing Light at Sandover*, compensate for that lost conversation by allowing JM to chat with Wystan and Maria in eternity. They "protect" him and DJ in *Sandover* in the mythic roles of Father Time and Mother Earth, an improved version of his parents. These lines record their only meeting in life.

His memory of Nelly's party includes Strato: their glances meet for a moment across the crowded room. Their first separation was already coming into view. Jackson had been hired to teach a fiction-writing class at Connecticut College in New London (it would be the first time he taught a class of any kind). So he planned to sail home to Stonington before the start of the spring term; Merrill would fly home a week later, still in time to arrive before him. The day of Jackson's departure, January 16, Merrill made a first attempt to describe in verse his new home and what had happened there. The cross-outs in this case are a record of false starts and corrections, rather than a simulation of them as in *The (Diblos) Notebook*.

---

* JM, *Sandover*, 134–35. There is a different account of the same event in JM, *ADP*, 230–31.

~~Concrete villas. A few stores.~~
Apartment houses. Stores. The hospital.
~~It~~ Ours is a quiet neighborhood.
Across the street you take to the center of town
A steep hill of pines keeps you company.
~~It looks very large but~~
It can be climbed in fifteen minutes
For a fine view of the city and the sea.
Underfoot, cyclamen, autumn crocus,
A fine sweat of wildflowers
And the traces, even in cold weather, of smoking + eating + loving.

The free verse and the syntax would be tightened up, the images refined, complicated, developed. But much of "Days of 1964," the love poem that these lines would grow into, is already in place in his first draft. The draft moves next to a portrait of Kleo:

She is fat + sixty + her legs hurt. She looks
Like a Palmyra sculpture reproduced in horsehair + guttapercha.
She loves me, you, loves us all. She groans
All day with love or is it pain?
We do not notably communicate.
She lives nearby with her pious mother
And wastrel son. Who knows how they make do?
We pay her generously, by her lights.
Love makes one generous. Look at you + me.
We've known each other so briefly that our bodies
Still seem blessed, young, infinitely resourceful.
We lie mouth to mouth, whispering, all night,
Or sleeping.

Kleo is caricatured as "a Palmyra sculpture reproduced in horsehair + guttapercha." "She loves you, me, loves us all"; in the finished poem, he adds, "I think now she *was* love," as if hobbled old Kleo were the goddess Aphrodite. She sponsors the lovers, tending to them, caring for them, while they turn toward each other, joined "mouth to mouth," kissing or talking or both at once, breathing into each other. Strato had "rejuvenated" Merrill, he said. "Mouth to mouth" implies more: it's an image of resuscitation—or inspiration?

The directness of this writing, notable and new in Merrill's work, remained in the poem, although that image did not. The title—"Days of 1964"—alludes to Cavafy's similarly titled love poems. Limpid, refined, and dry, Cavafy's "Days of . . ." poems are disenchanted modern love stories that honor passion as its own good, in memory. The allusion to Cavafy specifies the sex of the beloved as clearly as "he" or "him" would, even while the poem remains unspecific about the lover's gender. (Mouflouzélis is always "you" in the poem; he is seen from too close up to require his name or gender to be mentioned.) The allusion links the poem to a gay male artistic tradition, modern and Greek, that includes Yannis Tsarouchis as well as Cavafy. Across from the draft lines about Kleo, Merrill wrote, "It takes courage to love." It also took courage to write about love in this way.

Courage, or perhaps desperation, since "desperate" is the word he uses when the draft turns to describe the poet and his beloved in bed at night. They are laughing, just as Merrill and Mouflouzélis did over Strato's "weird Greek jokes." This time the joke is the poet's. Ostensibly a funny story, the anecdote he shares introduces a powerful, oneiric image. That morning, "on the way to market," he happened to see Kleo near the house

> Trudging into the pines. I called,
> Called 3 times before she turned around.
> She was wearing a bright skyblue sweater, + her face
> Was painted. Yes. Her face was painted
> Moon white, blue lidded, mouth a pointsettia leaf,
> The mask known to many women,
> Often in some kind of desperate need.
> I waved and walked on.

The draft goes on: "One must be desperate to love." The next day, writing to Richie, Merrill put the anecdote into prose: "A week ago exactly I was driving to Kolonaki and saw a familiar figure trudging up into the pines of Lykabettos on her bad legs—Kyria Kleo who cleans for us. I honked + honked + finally she looked around." Her face was "painted + powdered . . . within an inch of her life, or mine." They were both embarrassed. "Was she off to a rendezvous? to sell herself?" he wonders. "The memory absolutely haunts me."

Whether or not the sixty-year-old matron was going into the park to "sell herself," as is doubtful, Merrill was ready to think she was. Entering the wood, she entered his imagination as an archetypal figure, the mother who is also a whore, a symbol of human duality. "She called me her real son," he says about Kleo in "Days of 1964." The poem sets us up to think that Kleo is really his mother: she and *her* "pious mother" are Greek, working-class translations of Mama and Mis' Annie, and Jimmy, taking "the sex cure" in Greece, is a version of Lakis, the "wastrel son" who causes them grief. It makes sense that Hellen would have a role, if only in disguise, in this poem celebrating his love for Strato: she had obstructed Jimmy's love for Kimon; wouldn't she want to step in again with Strato, if she could? Going back to the U.S., as Merrill was about to, would always mean going back to her.

But Kleo doesn't stand in Merrill's way, as Hellen would have. In fact, when they recognize each other on the street, he identifies with Kleo, as if she and he shared a condition of "desperate need." Her mask, in the finished poem, demands in two stabbing monosyllables: "*Eat me, pay me.*" In his notebook, Merrill apologizes to his beloved, saying "Forgive me" for his demands. "And may Kyria Kleo," he asks, "Forgive me, if anyone ever translates this / Into her language + reads it to her." The first draft ends,

> I've gone so long without loving
> I do not know what I'm saying.
> Perhaps I am wearing a mask. I feel
> I am climbing constantly these days
>   shameless world of
> Into a ~~region of excrement~~ + wild/flowers
> Trembling in wind. My legs give under me
> But you are at my side, masked in my love.

On January 22, Merrill left Athens with fat white Maisie on his lap. He wrote to Mouflouzélis in flight on TWA stationery: "I thought I would die for leaving you. Please forgive me. I didn't want to cry in front of you." In 1965, it was not a simple thing to place a transatlantic call and reach a soldier at his barracks. No longer "mouth to mouth," Merrill could only write to Strato, and his letters, though brief, were hard work, carefully printed in Greek with perfectly shaped, stiff letters, spelled out on lined paper, like a school assignment. He wrote to Strato from Stonington on January 28 (it was their four-month "anniversary") and again three days later: "The village is very cold and a lot of our friends have moved south like the birds," he said in Greek. Jackson, with classes to plan and teach, was preoccupied. Maisie was sick. Merrill looked out and saw houses he had known and loved "for years now. But they seem to me melancholic, boring. I am thinking of the other house, ours Strato, and my heart is sad." Yet he had chosen to leave Strato and sit at his desk, chosen aching winter cold in Stonington over Athens and his passion.

In fact, he'd made a getaway, and he knew it. The risks that he took with Strato were bounded by his power to switch lives at will. That was what a double life meant. As he says in "Flying from Byzantium," a poem about leaving his Greek lover, " 'What does that moan mean? / The plane was part of the plan.' "

Merrill had read proofs for *The (Diblos) Notebook* during the fall in Athens, and Atheneum sent out galleys in January, including a set to Mary McCarthy. He hoped she would provide a blurb for it, which she did: "*The (Diblos) Notebook* is a delightful and sad picture of the Hesitation Waltz of creation. It has a fallen angel, the writer, for its hero-villain. I don't know of any book that deals so honestly with the sin of consciousness, and its island setting is a little paradise lost. I read it with pangs of recognition." She also read it with misgivings, to judge from the notes she made on the galleys. Anne Finch, the eighteenth-century English poet, declares in "To the Nightingale": "th'unhappy Poet's Breast, / Like thine, when best he sings, is plac'd against a Thorn." In her notes, McCarthy tartly remarks, "Jim is a nightingale, but ennui is far too short a thorn." Merrill was a talented lyric writer who lacked a serious subject.

The book's formal devices perhaps rankled McCarthy. Her notes show her trying to make sense of its cross-outs and blanks, which she saw as "stage directions" designed to *seem* to take "the reader into confidence of author about writing." She put the idea in a letter to Merrill, who replied by bowing to her criticisms—and then complained about them in a letter to Vassilikos: "Mary McCarthy wrote a letter about my book comparing it to a modern bank—all the workings exposed behind plate glass so that people will think ah, how honest! and implying that she wasn't to be that easily deceived. It doesn't bother me. One can never trust the praise of the famous." It must have annoyed him (he wasn't in the habit of asking for favors from "the famous") to be accused of using a version of the public relations stratagem of "full disclosure" that was pioneered in finance by his father. He wasn't making a claim for the superior truth of his experimental technique. The point was the opposite. The "rips and ripples" in the text, as he put it, reminded the reader of the "fabric of illusion"; they weren't meant to strip it away. Merrill wanted to depict "a transparently sustained illusion."

That notion was essential to a poem he was at work on at this time, "From the Cupola," in which "transparently sustained illusion" is both an aesthetic ideal and a key to the psychology of love. "From the Cupola" is the most complex of Merrill's poems apart from *Sandover*. Merrill began it shortly after starting work on "The Broken Home" in the summer of 1964. He sent drafts to Hine in June, to Kalstone in July, and to Irma Brandeis in early February 1965. On February 15 he sent it to *Poetry*; there would be one more round of revision before May, when he sent it back to the magazine for publication, which awarded it the Morton Dauwen Zabel Award for the best poem in *Poetry* that year.

Longer but more concentrated than "The Thousand and Second Night," "From the Cupola" has, like that poem, a variegated texture; Merrill is at his most virtuosic here, using rhymed stanzas, free verse, and prose passages, while exploiting associative thinking and abruptly shifting point of view. *The (Diblos) Notebook*, Merrill felt, proposed "a wistful, half-conscious critique of the Beat Generation" and its cult of spontaneity. "From the Cupola" implies a related critique of Confessional poetry's claim to bare the poet's soul. "From the Cupola" says that the truth of the psyche is not available nakedly. It is made out of desire and fantasy, and therefore bound up with illusion.

What is the soul? The question that Merrill put to Vassilikos with disarming simplicity he raises again in "From the Cupola," this time with baroque complexity. The poem is a retelling of the Hellenistic myth of Psyche and Eros. The myth begins with the jealousy of Venus, who resents Psyche because of her beauty. Venus sends her son Eros to punish Psyche by causing her to fall in love with an ugly mortal, but when he sees Psyche, Eros himself falls in love. Defying his mother, he takes Psyche to a secret palace where he visits her nightly, masked by darkness. Forbidden to look at him in the light, Psyche is ignorant of her lover's identity. One night, she lights a lamp to look at him while he sleeps. She is overwhelmed by her vision of the youthful god and spills wax on him, scalding and waking him; he flees, furious that she mistrusted him. She goes in search of him, and meets Venus, who assigns her three all-but-impossible tasks. She performs the first two but fails in the third, and falls into an enchanted, deathlike sleep from which Eros rescues her. Finally, the gods approve their union, Psyche and Eros marry, and the mortal is brought to Olympus as a god.

In "From the Cupola," the Psyche myth joins elements of Merrill's autobiography. Psyche lives in a New England village quite like Stonington. She fell in love with Eros elsewhere in *"A city named for palms,"* evoking Merrill's Palm Beach childhood, but Athens also in its sun and heat. In her New England village, Psyche receives love letters from a correspondent whose identity she doesn't yet know. These mysterious letters suggest Merrill's communications with the spirit Ephraim. They also suggest the intimate fan letters he began receiving in the early 1960s from a reclusive poet, Herbert Morris, to whom Merrill dedicated "From the Cupola," using only his initials.

Then there is the matter of Merrill's own encounter with Eros. When he began "From the Cupola" in the summer of 1964, he had not yet fallen in love with Mouflouzélis. Art precedes life here. By the time he finished the poem, however, he and Psyche both had an affair to talk about. In an amusing revision of the classical invocation, Merrill steps forward in the poem's opening, inviting Psyche to describe her lover to him as if to a sisterly confidante:

> Tell me about him, then. Not a believer,
> I'll hold my tongue while you, my dear, dictate.
> Him I have known too little (or, of late,
> Too well) to trust my own view of your lover.

Merrill continues, saying in effect to Psyche, Enter me, possess me, borrow my senses, and use my recent experience in love to tell your story. But proceed carefully, even tenderly. "The point won't be to stage / One of our torchlit hunts for truth" (such a hunt, the verb "stage" implies, must always be a performance, anyway). It's better not to look at a lover in the light.

Psyche's sisters (distractingly, Merrill gave them the first names of Toklas and Stein) appoint her the lonely task of cleaning the windows of the cupola on top of their house, a twist on the labors Venus assigned her. Psyche's window cleaning stands for a clarifying of vision, a disciplined approach to self-knowledge in the aftermath of erotic experience. Pragmatic Alice expects it to enable Psyche to see through the mirage of Eros. Yet she can't make the panes clear: "the rain's dry ghost / and my own features haunt the roofs the coast." Like any windows, these are also screens and mirrors.

The cupola—Merrill could see three cupolas from the deck on Water Street—is a symbol of the contingency and subjectivity of vision. It is also a site for visitations, a mediating point between heaven and earth, the gods and human longing. Eros comes to it by night in a passage narrated by Psyche.

> MIDNIGHT   I dream I dream   The slow moon eludes
> one stilled cloud   Din of shimmerings   From across the Sound
> what may have begun as no more
> than a willow's sleepwalking outline quickens detaches

comes to itself in the cupola
panics from pane to pane and then impulsively
surrendering fluttering by now the sixteenfold
wings of the cherubim unclipped by faith or reason
stands there my dream made whole
over whose walls again
a red vine black in moonlight crawls
made habitable   Each cell of the concrete
fills with sweet light   The wave breaks
into tears   Come if it's you   Step down
to where I   Stop   For at your touch the dream
cracks the angel tenses flees[.]

These lines equivocate about who has which role in this near union. Eros stands before Psyche, but he is her own dream embodied, and when she says "Stop," she is stopping herself as well as him. Later she takes the torch and looks into Eros's eyes, and what she sees is "an iris reflecting her own person." At this point, Psyche is forced, Merrill explained in a letter to Irma Brandeis, "to recognize the physical source of her fine feelings, and to be upset by that."* Yet to see that Eros is "sheer / projection" is not to deny his divinity, only to recognize its source in her own soul.

Merrill knew that his affair with Strato was "the physical source" of the "fine feelings" in the poem. This doesn't mean that one could simply be reduced to the other, or that he could have given his reader a clearer view of his lover, without screens and mirrors, if he'd wished to. When she is on the verge of holding the light over Eros's face, Psyche breaks down. She weeps because she foresees the loss of her lover, and Merrill intervenes in his own person to comfort her:

> Psyche, hush. This is me, James.
>   Writing lest he think
> Of the reasons why he writes—
> Boredom, fear, mixed vanities and shames;
>   Also love.
> From my phosphorescent ink
> Trickle faint unworldly lights

---

* JM to IB, letter, February 18, 1965 (WUSTL). Merrill also told Brandeis, "The plot, as it affects me (in a way largely hidden + I think irrelevant to the poem) is une autre histoire which I can tell you any time you have fifteen minutes to hear it. Fifteen? Six and a half!"

Down your face. Come, we'll both rest.
Weeping? You must not.
All our pyrotechnic flights
Miss the sleeper in the pitch-dark breast.
He is love:
He is everyone's blind spot.
We see according to our lights.

Imaginative "projection," through which James recognizes himself in Psyche, is a means to fellow feeling here, not a form of narcissism. That "We see according to our lights" is consoling because our separate points of view, precisely in their contingency and subjectivity, their partialness, overlap. Love is a "sleeper"—unconscious, but poised to awaken—in anyone's breast, which is "pitch-dark," evoking the black of sin, the heart's sticky tar, and the middle of the night. Love is the "blind spot" that marks the limits of our self-knowledge.

This delicate lyric address from the author to his character is a daring tour de force, an openly declared illusion. Soothing Psyche, urging her to forgive herself for her blindness, he forgives himself for his own. The emotion is close to the self-acceptance that his draft of "Days of 1964" was working toward in January, where he asks to be forgiven for a way of loving. At stake in "From the Cupola" is a way of writing. In her stringent review of *First Poems*, Louise Bogan had complained that although, or exactly because, Merrill's early poems were "impeccably written," "everything about them smells of the lamp." In "From the Cupola," Merrill returns to Bogan's phrase and says of his poem proudly, "The lamp I smell in every other line." Freely admitting the artificiality of his art, he connects it to Psyche's lamp and imagination's power of self-projection. It is what is required, Merrill had decided, to write about the soul.

On February 6, shortly before he sent "From the Cupola" to *Poetry*, Merrill went back to "Days of 1964" and rapidly finished the poem. In *Nights and Days*, Merrill placed "From the Cupola" and "Days of 1964" side by side at the end of the book, "Days of 1964" coming last. Together the two poems demonstrate his ability to work in different poetic modes at once. It is not that the mythological poem was built upon the actuality of the love poem; nor was the immediacy of the love poem won by abandoning the artifice of the other, like an unnecessary disguise. Merrill wanted both kinds of poem. He even wanted aspects of each kind of poem inside the other. His affair with Strato is present in the sensuality of "From the Cupola"—in the bright lamp and its scalding wax; and the lovers of "Days of 1964" are not only their ordinary, quotidian selves, but embodiments of Eros and Psyche.

The finished poem begins,

> Houses, an embassy, the hospital,
> Our neighborhood sun-cured if trembling still
> In pools of the night's rain . . .
> Across the street that led to the center of town
> A steep hill kept one company part way
> Or could be climbed in twenty minutes
> For some literally breathtaking views,
> Framed by umbrella pines, of city and sea.
> Underfoot, cyclamen, autumn crocus grew
> Spangled as with fine sweat among the relics
> Of good times had by all. If not Olympus,
> An out-of-earshot, year-round hillside revel.

Compared with the first draft of these lines, some changes stand out. In the new second and third lines, there are those "pools of the night's rain," suggesting a flood of feeling that has left the poet, like the landscape, "trembling," not yet "sun-cured." There is also a shift from the present into the past tense. Distance has opened between the poet and his experience. He can see it more fully and clearly now. But something has been lost.

As he worked on the poem, Merrill made the mountain more important. The dew, a motif from ancient Greek love poetry, rinses "the relics" of lovemaking; its "fine sweat" indicates the heat of passion, the natural forces within the lovers. The mountain, Kleo's destination when Merrill saw her cross the street with her face painted, promises both debasement and purification. Back home in Connecticut, he added these lines, describing his route after encountering her:

> Startled mute, we had stared—was love illusion?—
> And gone our ways. Next, I was crossing a square
> In which a moveable outdoor market's
> Vegetables, chickens, pottery kept materializing
> Through a dream-press of hagglers each at heart
> Leery lest he be taken, plucked,
> The bird, the flower of that November mildness,
> Self lost up soft clay paths, or found, foothold,

Where the bud throbs awake
The better to be nipped, self on its knees in mud—
Here I stopped cold, for both our sakes;

And calmer on my way home bought us fruit.

In the market's commotion, food and goods, not love, are on sale. But for the poet, under the pressure of the question posed by Kleo's painted face—"was love illusion?"—the market might as well be the Metro, where Jimmy and Strato met. Here everyone is a "haggler" looking out for himself, flirtatiously, anxiously delaying the moment of exchange, "Leery" of others (a word suggesting both "wary" and "leering"). One fears being "taken" or cheated. But "taken" is also exactly what one wants—in the sense of chosen, singled out, transported.

"I'm *so* in love," Merrill told Vassilikos, "my soul flies up to heaven!" "Days of 1964," developing that idea, plays on the motif of the soul's ascent to heaven through love in Plato's *Symposium*. But there's no question here of leaving the body behind. The poet, like Psyche, is coming to terms with the "physical source" of his "fine feelings." So it is no surprise when Eros materializes in the poem's superb climactic lines:

Where I hid my face, your touch, quick, merciful,
Blindfolded me. A god breathed from my lips.
If that was illusion, I wanted it to last long;
To dwell, for its daily pittance, with us there,
Cleaning and watering, sighing with love or pain.
I hoped it would climb when it needed to the heights
Even of degradation, as I for one
Seemed, those days, to be always climbing
Into a world of wild
Flowers, feasting, tears—or was I falling, legs
Buckling, heights, depths,
Into a pool of each night's rain?
But you were everywhere beside me, masked,
As who was not, in laughter, pain, and love.

The "you" is Strato. Yet, with that blindfold, the lover becomes precisely no specific person, but Eros, covering Psyche's eyes. At the same time, the poet's identity is transformed, for he is Eros too: "A god breathed from my lips."

When we think back to Merrill's sense of personal crisis during 1962 and the complex self-disgust conveyed in "The Thousand and Second Night," a poem placed second in the order of poems in *Nights and Days*, these lines, coming at the end of the volume, seem like a saving answer: love, the title of the "lost" book, has been found. He achieves this renewal of belief, furthermore, without renouncing his skepticism. In reply to Tony Harwood, he wrote in his notebook, "[F]or you delusion seems to be something one must try to vanquish at all costs, while for me it is more like a trusted friend with whom I've been on excellent terms for years + years." The word returned as he worked on "Days of 1964": "If that is delusion, may it last long, long." Moving, in revision, from "delusion" to "illusion" ("If that was illusion . . ."), he chose a word associated not with madness but conscious, crafted artifice.

Evidently he was ready to answer the question: yes, love *is* illusion; or, it depends on illusion. Saying so in this poem releases him to affirm his own ascent "each night" in Kleo's footsteps. He climbs like her to "the heights / Even of degradation." Just so his free verse lines climb and buckle before coming to rest in a last, unrhymed pentameter couplet. Earlier he debates whether Kleo sighs in love "or pain," and whether his lover gasps in love "or laughter." Here "and" replaces "or" and leaves no choice between these terms: they are all part of the same experience. His lover is "masked, / As who was not, in laughter, pain, and love."

The masks Merrill's lovers wear at the end of "Days of 1964" are necessary for the illusion of their union, for love, to work. But masks also separate them. Perhaps that consciousness of necessary separateness is expressed in Merrill's choice of the past tense. No, he hasn't already lost Strato—only left him in Athens, for now—but it is as if he has, because he knows that, as Friar taught him, the love that the lover "brings may pass over the threshold of the other's solitude, but not he." The lover has to remain behind, like Strato. Cavafy's "Days of . . ." are set in the erotic haze of the past. "Days of 1964" is a poem about a love affair in progress that it is already being pushed into memory.

Now, in late February 1965, as this period of fervent composition ended, Merrill could take satisfaction in his achievement. Over the past year he'd composed three poems of undeniable boldness and originality: "The Broken Home," "From the Cupola," and "Days of 1964." Each poem puts its faith in a poetics of masks and illusion. But artifice is one thing in art and another thing in life. What would it be like to live an illusion? Over the next two years, in his relationship with Strato Mouflouzélis, Merrill was going to find out.

9

CHILLS AND FEVER,
PASSIONS AND BETRAYALS

1965–67

S ince Friar introduced the idea in 1945, Merrill had kept alive the dream of a life in Greece. Now he had the house, he had Strato, and he felt a certain recklessness. He wrote to Daryl Hine from Water Street: "Our decision to settle in Athens for an indefinite period forms cell by cell, like some beautiful coral reef upon which, 30 years hence, one will think it a privilege to have wrecked oneself." He made a similar remark ("a slow submarine decision is forming [. . .] to reverse the proportions of our lives" spent in Greece and the U.S.) in a letter to Parigory the next day. Greece was a reef to be wrecked on; Jimmy would become a castaway, lost to family, friends, and public view.*

The same day that he wrote to Parigory, Merrill saw Puccini's *Tosca* at the Met with Maria Callas in the title role. "Welcome Home, Maria," banners read, greeting the great Greek-American soprano's return to New York at the height of her fame in one of her signature roles, her voice to be relished for a new reason now, being in decline, frayed and corrupt. "*Vissi d'arte, vissi d'amore*" (I lived for art, I lived for love), Tosca sings. Merrill remem-

---

* He elaborates the fantasy in "The Castaway," an unpublished poem from 1965 (WUSTL).

bered how, long ago, lying "face-down on the floor" in the Music Library at Lawrenceville, he'd "lip-synched" Tosca's aria, a lovelorn adolescent. In the life that he imagined ahead of him, he wanted to be able to look back and sing the same words.

In April, he read at Yale and then at Harvard, where he saw Kalstone and other friends, including Laurence Scott, a tutor in the history and literature program. Scott printed a broadside of one of the new poems Merrill read, "Violent Pastoral." In this short lyric set in a Greece of the mind, an eagle "Mounts with the lamb in his clutch." Bird and prey make a sublime coupling of contraries:

> Beyond Arcadia at last,
> Wing, hoof, one oriented creature,
> Snake-scream of pride
> And bowels of fright
>
> Lost in the rainbow, to be one
> Even with the shepherd
> Still looking up, who understood
> And was not turned to stone.

The poem's violent ascent is a version of the soul's flight to heaven, a vision of rape and transcendence that the poet who wrote "Leda and the Swan" might have appreciated. The poem reflected obliquely on Merrill's experience in Greece. Who, in his coupling with Mouflouzélis, was the eagle, and who was the lamb? Jimmy had both creatures inside him. He also had the capacity to stand apart and contemplate their embrace. He signed the copy of the broadside that he gave to the Burnetts "from the Bad Shepherd."

Reviews of *The (Diblos) Notebook* were appearing, and judgments were strongly favorable. In *The New York Review of Books*, John Thompson wrote, "*The (Diblos) Notebook* is a genuine and unpretentious work of art, its flowering and its limitations springing from an authentic center. Its true subject is its own manner and style." Wilfred Sheed, in *The New York Times Book Review*, called it "the kind of novel it is a pleasure to take seriously, a disciplined, adventurous performance in the best tradition of fictional experiment." When the first fifteen hundred copies sold out, Atheneum ordered a second printing. It was nominated for the National Book Award (Katherine Anne Porter's *Collected Stories* won). Eventually the novel was brought out by Popular Library as a pulp paperback with a sexy cover, no doubt embittering readers who thought they were buying a drugstore romance.

Ford sought legal advice before the book's publication* for protection from the people Merrill had based his characters on. But Mina was no threat to sue. Nor was Friar, though he was not about to remain silent either. Instead he composed a page-by-page commentary on the novel in a ninety-three-page letter to Merrill. When a messenger came to deliver the document in Athens in fall 1965, Merrill, who had expected something of the kind, refused to receive it. Rivaling Merrill not only in the length but in the cleverness of his statement, Friar reports in his letter on the reactions to the book of his "twin brother," Orestes: "Orestes' only comment has been: 'I hadn't realized I had ever occupied so much of Jimmy's thoughts.' (He really wanted to say he had not realized you had been so obsessed by him, but he vaguely felt this would not be fair to you.)" "Orestes" concluded, "Jimmy has every right to interpret me as he sees fit, and to publish it. [. . .] He should have killed me off a long time ago, the way he killed off his first father' " in *The Seraglio*.

Jackson ended his term at Connecticut College by discussing *The (Diblos) Notebook* with his fiction-writing class.[†] Having never completed college, and never been at the head of a classroom before, he had worried about the course in advance. One student, Cecelia Holland, later recalled the first class meeting clearly: "He was extremely fretful, complaining about having to come back from Greece, not having the right paperwork, having more people in the class than he wanted, on and on. I know now he was just wry and uncertain. We read the piece on Raleigh in Aubrey's *Brief Lives*, which cracked me up, and nobody else. On the way out everybody was complaining, but I felt I had connected with him." Holland, a tall senior in bell-bottoms and paisleys, had taken writing classes with Bill Meredith; now she blossomed under his replacement. "What David did was treat me as a real writer, an equal. He invited me right off to come to the house in Stonington, which I did a lot, and he championed me to the formidable Mrs. Stone, whose put-down powers made Meredith seem candy-mouthed. He made me feel as if I belonged there, with all those published, sophisticated people (gawky, socially inept, noisy twit that I was)." Jackson sent a novel she'd written to Ford; Atheneum published Holland's *The Firedrake*

---

* At the request of Ford's lawyer, Merrill agreed to sign an indemnity clause added to his contract that made it his responsibility in the event that one of the people on whom he'd based his characters decided to sue. Herbert A. Wolff, Greenbaum, Wolff & Ernst, to Harry Ford, Atheneum Publishers, letter, August 20, 1964 (WUSTL).

† "He has only a few more classes, so he could assign them the telephone directory if he wanted to. I confer with him insufferably, though, lest he overlook any single fine point of the text." JM to NL, May 6, 1965 (WUSTL).

the next year, and her long career as a writer of fiction for young people had taken off. Looking back on their thirty years of friendship, she said of Jackson, "He had no real self. He located himself through his friends, especially through Jim. But the same quality made him the most sensitive of listeners (and readers), the tenderest of friends."

The writing class was a strain, and at last David declared that "he will never, never teach again." In May, he "hurried off (by train of course) to California where his parents had stopped speaking to his brother, sister-in-law, and niece, though by now," Jimmy told Vassili, "they have been successfully glued together again by his good nature. My mother's turn has come to visit me, and I sit trembling as I think of her eye lighting on dirty windows, greasy pans (they look clean to me but that's not the issue) and of how she will not mention them until days later when I have driven her back to New York. Meanwhile, I think I've put the last touches on a new book of poems"—he meant *Nights and Days*, which was published in June. Vassilikos was at work on a translation of "After Greece." He collected it with other Merrill poems in a book printed in 1966 by his own small press in Athens. Merrill reciprocated by spending his evenings with the manuscript of Vassilikos's new novel, construing the Greek at the painstaking rate of "10 to 30 minutes a page." He advised Vassilikos on his application to the Ingram Merrill Foundation, and wrote to Irma Brandeis, trying to find a teaching position for him. In June, Vassili and Mimí were in the U.S. to visit her dying father. They stopped in Stonington, where, Jimmy told Strato, "Mimí had a third glass of wine and cried in front of us for two hours continuously. It is her birthday today, another cause for tears?"

As a correspondent during this long separation, Mouflouzélis started strongly. He wrote his first letter on January 25, three days after Merrill left Greece.

My Dearest Tzimmoula:

Ever since the moment I bid you good-bye at the airport, loneliness is weighing so heavy that I do not know what will make me forget my great sorrow.

My love, you cannot believe how much I miss you, because for four months the two of us had become like one person, one heart, and together we would share our sorrows and our happiness. [. . .]

The only thing that gives me a little courage is your beloved sweet face that I keep in your picture. When I went home I thought it was a lie, you had never left—but alas! The room was empty—my love was not there. That is when I cried bitterly about our separation and for six months I will be hurting a lot.

Mrs. Kleo cried too—the two of us in the house. She said to give you her best and many kisses.

I cannot write anything more my love because I am like a dead person.

I can just send you many kisses from afar and my thoughts are always with you.

I kiss you sweetly on the lips, your love

Stratos

P.S. Give my best regards to our friend David. Waiting for your letter. So long [*Yia sou*].

"Tzimmoula" is a feminine diminutive. Less often Merrill used the same suffix for his "Stratoula." They had other endearments: the masculine diminutive, "Strataki," or "*agapara mou*"—my big love, which each used for the other.

Four more letters from Mouflouzélis followed in February. But he wrote only two in March, and those were short. Parigory served as Merrill's go-between. Merrill told him in April that "having had only one letter from Strato in the last 31 days, has made me, off + on, terribly anxious and uneasy. . . . do I in fact have something to worry about?" He was ready for something to go wrong. Then a letter arrived from Strato: he'd been restricted to the air force base (why, he doesn't say); his teeth and gums had hurt so much that he couldn't put pen to paper, but they were improving; and he loved Tzimmoula always. "I am sorry I was upset by your silence," Jimmy responded. "Between the service and your poor mouth you have enough worries, you don't need me bothering you. But I am nervous, I am away from you, I love you very much, and I need all the assurance you can give me." Tony explained that he'd been looking after Strato, and so far as he knew, only Tony himself had been to bed with him. Merrill was reassured, or pretended to be: "My dear, I hoped you and S. had been keeping each other company nuit et zour. [. . .] I'm positive that it is indeed your flesh that has cured his teeth, and that in 94 days you will hand him over to me, an only slightly more used model than when I left. I do adore him so and miss him madly." Sex in itself was nothing to be jealous about, apparently, and better that Tony should supply it than Strato should have to look elsewhere.

On July 28, Merrill left by plane, and Jackson by boat, for Europe. Jimmy stopped in Paris to spend a week with Hine and the Burnetts. Just before he left Connecticut, Maisie died. "It was awful yet somehow unspeakably thoughtful of her—she hated Greece," he sighed, characteristically dry-eyed. He was ready to let go of his ties to America for a while. He'd counted the days and hours to his reunion with Strato, but now he was apprehensive. In Athens, he started a log of his days, as if the castaway knew in advance that he would need a record of his life on the island. He made the first entry on August 6: "Seeing S. again. I keep a sharp eye on him, lest he betray any strain, any artifice; on my self too, fearful of having ceased to care. The fantasy-mistletoe has gone so long unpruned, one wonders if the tree survives. I think, I think it does. There are long silences, dead patches, then the remembered upflow of tenderness + joy."

August 13 was Mouflouzélis's twenty-third birthday. The party was at Athinaion Efivon 44. Merrill wrote in his notebook, "[H]e was here last night in company with Vassili + Mimi + Nelly. It was lovely on the roof by the full moon, and lovely laughing in bed about the language he knows. . . . I wrote Strato in blue on a piece of bread." Merrill mentions loveliness, laughter, and—language. It is as if language were as satisfying to these lovers as sex, and words, like daily bread, were something to feed on.

In 1974, when Elizabeth Bishop sent Merrill a typescript of her poem "Crusoe in England," he ventured a criticism (the only criticism of her work he made in their long correspondence), questioning her suggestive but terse treatment of Crusoe's relationship with Friday. Bishop's castaway remembers Friday many years after he has been rescued and returned home:

> Friday was nice.
> Friday was nice, and we were friends.
> If only he had been a woman!
> I wanted to propagate my kind,
> and so did he, I think, poor boy.
> He'd pet the baby goats sometimes,
> and race with them, or carry one around.
> —Pretty to watch; he had a pretty body.

"A lot will go without saying, and does," Merrill wrote to Bishop. "But I found I was yearning for, say, some lines about how they communicated, Crusoe + Friday: did they make a language? of sounds? of signs?" It isn't the sexual dimension of Crusoe's feeling for Friday that Merrill wants to hear more about; that seems to go "without saying." What sparks his imagination is the question of "how they communicated." This isn't information every reader would require, and Bishop ignored the request. The comment makes perfect sense, however, in the context of Merrill's experience. Communication—both the obstacles to it and the pleasure of overcoming them—was essential to his relationship with Strato, who played Friday to his Crusoe.

Merrill knew that, if Mouflouzélis was going to be part of his life, he would have to learn to speak English. After Jimmy left Athens in January, he sent English primers to Strato, which the Greek found hard going. "Don't worry, my love, if you cannot understand English from those books," Jimmy assured him in Greek. "I do not care at all. I love you as you are. I gave you the books to learn something if you can, not for us but to help you in the future. When I come, if you want, we can have a serious lesson every day." Once reunited, the lovers commenced their lessons. "Hold it to the light," Merrill urged Kalstone, referring to the page on which he was typing the letter, "and you may see the laborious indentations of Strato's English dictée [. . .]. He translated 'Big men have little cars' and 'Who is like roses?' among other things. He is wonderful to look at during these lessons. His face goes all grand and funny like an allegorical painting of Inspiration as he strives to master the phonemic difference between J and G. As with the Glass Cat's brains, you can see 'em work." Laboring at his dictée, Strato looked like simplicity itself, and Merrill delighted in the seemingly transparent workings of his lover's mind. It was like a scene from *My Fair Lady*. For what Strato was being asked to learn was not merely a language, but a way of using it, a set of manners. When Jimmy told him to repeat the phrase "May I please have a glass of water?" he put his foot down and replied in Greek, "This is too many words! *I want water!*"

Merrill's feeling for modern Greek was essential to his whole imaginative involvement with Greece. Rachel Hadas, an American poet who met Merrill in Athens in 1969, makes the point about his poems: "[R]ather than being one possible way of grasping [. . .] Greece, the Greek language is the principal source and form of much of the enchantment and glamour that energize what Merrill wrote in Greece." He had been intrigued by the language and its history since he studied ancient Greek at Amherst. When Friar taught him his first words of the demotic in 1945, his lessons were braided with other discoveries—of poetic vocation, of sexual satisfaction—at that pivotal moment. In the early 1960s, Merrill began honing his skill with the language. The excitement of learning Greek recalled his romance with Italian in the early 1950s. He comments in *A Different Person*,

Victims of brain damage unable to speak but asked to set their needs to a familiar tune—"Greensleeves" or "Santa Lucia"—have uttered what they couldn't otherwise. In much the same way a foreign language frees the speaker. Once he has learned his first five hundred words and mastered a few idioms and tenses, he is ready for action. He has added to his Greek *Nai* ("Yes") the slow headshake meaning assent, to his Italian exasperation the pursed bud of emphatic fingertips already caught in a second-century mosaic of a fishwife in the Naples museum. He is on his way to embodying, however crudely and clumsily, that local divinity, the language. The process teaches him to speak a mind far less individual than he had once thought it. Among friends we are no doubt free to be "ourselves"—giddy, vague, sullen, unforthcoming. We can say what we don't mean, and still be understood. Or we can say nothing, like couples long married who speak hardly at all. A stranger's ear and a stranger's grammar, by contrast, keep us at concert pitch.

In Greek, Merrill learned to speak his "needs" with more force and clarity, with greater simplicity and less self-consciousness, than he ever could in his own language. The complexity of his English had to be put aside, and an ancient language of "Essentials" taken up. This is what Merrill means when in "The Friend of the Fourth Decade" he says he is "Tired of understanding what I hear, / The tones, the overtones"; "I mean to learn, in the language of where I am going, / Barely enough to ask for food and love." The implication is that this speaker *only* could ask for "food and love" if he couldn't ask for more. We tend to think of liberation as the freeing up of a self under wraps. For Merrill, learning a language meant the discovery of a new self altogether. The passage about language learning in *A Different Person* ends in a Wildean epigram: "Freedom to be oneself is all very well; the greater freedom is not to be oneself."

Merrill found that freedom in Greek. For Greek was not a language his friends or family spoke, save for his Greek friends; it could only be learned in the tavernas and parks he used it to discover. It was an erotic passport into those places and the lives of the people he met there. He didn't need Greek to speak with Maria or Tony; he needed it to talk to Kleo, the *yiayiá*, and Lakis, to hear stories that would become poems, and write love letters to Strato. Masked in "laughter, pain, and love," these characters were masked in language too. Greek was a pastoral disguise; with it, Merrill put on the shepherd's weeds of another people and another class. The pastoral was sometimes sweet, sometimes violent. It imposed a simplification of feeling, an innocence that was not merely contrived. In Greek, he could ask, "What is the soul?" and sound "like a child." He couldn't speak this way in French, Italian, or German, languages that were enriched and burdened by his knowledge of their cultural associations—the menus, museums, and libretti he knew by heart.

Modern Greek had its cultural associations and literary uses too. Merrill cared little about Greece's modern masters—Kazantzakis, Seferis, Elytis; these were Friar's authors, and each of them had about him the aura of the national poet, a literary role Merrill distrusted. He told a story about meeting Elytis: he held out his hand and said, "James Merrill," to which the other man replied, "Odysseus Elytis, Poet." (In Greek, the word for "poet," *pytis*, rhymes with "Elytis," heightening the prim effect.) But Cavafy was another matter. Merrill was haunted by the Alexandrian's "desert-dry tone, his mirage-like technical effects," so much of which had to do with the "dynamics of his language." Behind Cavafy, the layered resonances of demotic Greek reached back in time to the earliest Western literature. It was as if, as Hadas puts it, the Greek language presented "a cultural continuum" in which Homer and Cavafy executed "the same gesture." Buying groceries, an American in Athens was liable to meet an Agamemnon or Sappho. In the same way, everyday words in the language recalled Merrill's knowledge of ancient Greek and incited his imagination. "One sees trucks in Athens," he noted, "blazoned with *METAPHOROS*," a reminder that the English "metaphor" derives from the Greek for "transport." Even the traffic on the street seemed to carry metaphors, in this case a metaphor for metaphor itself.

Not that it was easy for Merrill to move between English and Greek. The materiality of language that he enjoyed in the anagram, say, was emphasized by an alphabet that was at once different from that of English and the basis for it. To English speakers, modern Greek can seem teasingly like English at one moment, then utterly unlike it at the next, as if it were the opposite of English, a language in which *nai* means "yes" and a nod means "no." For Merrill and Jackson, part of the excitement of Greece lay in the opacity of "a language we didn't understand two words of at first" and the liberty it gave them either to disregard or imagine the meaning of what was said around them. In time, Merrill learned to speak Greek fluently, if never fluidly, without the rolling, malleable rhythms that typify native Greek speech: he spoke Greek "like someone who doesn't like to make mistakes."

If Merrill's imagination was sparked by Greek in part because it was resistant to him, only partially knowable, the same can be said about his feeling for Strato. "Since I've been living in Greece," he told an interviewer in 1968, "I've found myself thinking a lot about human behavior. It's because of the language barrier—when you can't ascertain the full range of people's motives and feelings, they are simplified in a sense. [. . .] I think I like either those people who completely understand whatever I say—at all levels—or those who understand hardly any of it, for whom I am simplified into a dream-figure, as they no doubt are for me. Understanding has more than one face." Neither those who "completely" understood what he said nor those who understood "hardly any of it" knew the whole or only truth.

In "To My Greek," a poem begun in 1966 and finished the next year, Merrill reflects on how he and his Friday communicated. "You will think it is about Strato," he told Mimi, "and you will not be wrong, but it is ostensibly addressed to my imperfect command of the language." The poem's conceit is that the lover and the language are one. In "Beginner's Greek," a poem Merrill wrote two decades earlier in the throes of his affair with Friar, the process of learning a language stood for a lesson in how to handle one's self in love; the Greek that Friar taught Merrill represented "Intensity," a sensuality the young poet had to be wary of and approach slowly, if at all. The same sense of Greek is at play in "To My Greek," only caution has been set aside. The poet and his lover live together "Without conjunctions"; "past and future // Perish upon our lips"; there is "no word / For justice, grief, convention"; and "Goods, bads"—"kaló-kakó"—echo each other, as if they came to the same thing. Greek is "cockatoo-raucous"; its sounds evoke the rough landscape, a "Coastline of white printless coves." Those coves suggest a lover's private curves and inlets. They are "printless" because unmapped and unmarked, but also because they call the poet away from books, inviting immersion in his senses. Greek gives him objects to savor on the tongue: "Forbidden Salt Kiss Wardrobe Foot Cloud Peach / —Name it, my chin drips sugar." In one draft, Merrill calls Greek "the carnal language."

"To My Greek" celebrates an innocent sensuality, a carnality that is sexual and linguistic at once, a matter of the tongue in every respect. Yet the celebration is a shadowed, guilty one. "Still // I fear for us. Nights fall / We toss through blindly," Merrill writes, as if he and his lover knew they must be separated, their private code broken. What threatens them are the prior claims on the poet of another language, which is personified as "The mother tongue!" Her "appraising / Glare" rakes the bedroom like a searchlight. She represents not only the poet's native English but also a conscience embodied in it, with the power of the police. The "mother tongue" speaks for the imperatives of propriety ("May I please have a glass of water?") which the poet absorbed with the rules of English, and from which Greek seemed to free him. As in "Days of 1964," Merrill's relationship with Strato is mediated here by the presence of a third figure, also a mother, though this one is neither benign nor Greek, like Kyria Kleo. The "mother tongue" is more like Hellen Plummer, hot with alcohol and anger as she faces off with her son:

> What can she make of you? Her cocktail sweats
>
> With reason: speech will rise from it,
> Quite beyond your comprehension rise
> Like blood to a slapped face, stingingly apt
>
> If unrepeatable, tones one forgets
>
> Even as one is changed for life by them,
> Veins branching a cold coral,
> Common sense veering into common scenes,
> Tears

Until *A Different Person*, this is the most directly Merrill would write about his bitter, early confrontation with his mother over Friar; "changed for life by them," he would never forget her tones of voice. Here, Hellen again challenges her son's passion for a man, and for the Greek language. No wonder, since, in the son's mind, devotion to his Greek threatens the mother tongue with something more than abandonment: "some blue morning also she may damn // Well find her windpipe slit with that same rainbow / Edge a mere weekend with you gives / To books, to living." The violence of that image matters: some part of Merrill wanted to slit his mother's throat.

In August 1965, Merrill went to Lesvos with his nephews Robin and Peter Magowan. Peter was in Greece with his bride, Jill. Robin was rejoining Betty and their toddler, Felix, after spending the previous weeks with a lover on the island of Paros, and his marriage hung in the balance. "She wants to stay married," Merrill summarized, "what he wants isn't communicable." For the moment, all Robin wanted was to relive a thrilling experience from the previous summer when he attended the harvest *panegyri* in a remote mountain village on Lesvos, drank epic quantities of retsina and ouzo, and learned to dance the *zembekiko*, the "hypnotic urban warrior dance" that Merrill had introduced him to at the bar in Pérama. Now Robin replayed the experience with his brother, their wives, and his uncle. "We drank from 6 to 12," Merrill wrote to Kalstone. "Robin did a couple of scarily plausible zembekikos with some of his last year's cronies, toothless and drunken as Chinese poets. During moments of silence between numbers, one could hear the newlyweds, Peter + Jill, earnestly describing members of their families to one another." Then they piled into a taxi—"all except Robin who arrived back on foot at 8 the following evening. I mean, granted one would like to have been born Greek, isn't the wiser course to give in and stop trying to behave like one?"

As he danced on Lesvos, Robin observed Jimmy watching him from "deep in the gloom of an only six-month-away fortieth birthday." In "Ouzo for Robin," the poem Merrill wrote about the occasion, Robin "cries uncle" in a double sense, appealing to Jimmy and giving in to his confusion:

> Dread of an impending umptieth
> Birthday thinning blood to water, clear
> Spirits to this opal-tinted white—
> Uncle, the confusion unto death!
>
> [. . .]
>
> Ground trampled hard. Again. The treasure
> Buried. Rancor. Joy. Tonight's blank grin.
> Threshold where the woken cherub shrieks
> To stop it, stamping with displeasure.

Merrill's staccato sentences imitate his nephew's stamping *zembekiko*. The intensity of the writing suggests that the poet felt the music, too, and, at his desk, rose to dance to it in his own way. Yet he clearly disapproves of his nephew's dancing. Even a child would know better; thus the "woken cherub," his little son, stamps to stop it. The shrieking boy in this poem, Robin notes, "was as much the divorced child in Jimmy as it was little Felix."

Robin's confusion wasn't at all unusual; questioning bourgeois norms was something people were doing all over America. In the tavernas of Lesvos, he was gripped by the Dionysian energies of the 1960s. He would take a job as an assistant professor that fall in the English Department at the University of California at Berkeley, and move himself and his family to the center of social change and political dissent in the U.S. Opposition to the war in Vietnam was mounting, in proportion to American military involvement. On the streets of Berkeley, he recalls, there were "almost daily protestations, rallies, picketings, repeated attempts to burn down an ROTC Quonset hut by attacking it in broad afternoon, several hundred marching strong."

Which Jimmy didn't want to think about. In May, back in Stonington, he'd opined, "When one turns on the radio, it's Viet Nam—don't let me ever learn Greek well enough to understand a news broadcast!" But Greece was entering its own political crisis, and he couldn't ignore it. "Last night, coming back from a tavern," he told Kalstone, trying to sound like the Duchesse de Guermantes, "we were suddenly faced with smoldering barricades, some faint remaining gusts of tear gas; so unpleasant in an open car. The demonstrators had been burning furniture removed from shop windows (someone has been studying American newspapers) [. . .]; while at Herodes Attikos theatre the applause for a Soviet conductor rapidly degenerated into the Pa-pan-DRE-ou rhythm we live by of an evening." The demonstrations in Athens that August were the result of a conflict between King Constantine II, Greece's young sovereign, and George Papandreou, leader of the majority Centre Union party. Papandreou's Centre Union, presenting a liberal alternative to Greece's far-left and right-wing parties, came to power in 1963, then gained a broad mandate in 1964. Over the next year, with Papandreou as prime minister, Centre Union initiated educational and economic reforms, and strengthened Greece's diplomatic and economic ties with the Soviet Union and its allied states. When Papandreou tried to consolidate power by exercising authority over the Greek military, the king, acting with conservatives in the army and the government, forced him to resign as prime minister. Papandreou's loss of power won him further popular support, however, and Greece descended into the chaotic spectacle of the king and his allies attempting to establish a new government against the will of the people.

Even when he wasn't forced to smell the tear gas, Merrill was brought close to the crisis by his friendship with Vassilikos, who was an outspoken opponent of "the King's coup." "I was so involved with politics at the time," he recalled, "to go to Jimmy's was to go abroad, to another world where I had peace and tranquility. Jimmy was very open-minded. He made me feel accepted. And it wasn't because Jimmy was *un*political. He was deeply political. He understood what I wanted for my country, and he esteemed it." Perhaps, but if Merrill was political, it could only have been "deeply." His friendship with Vassilikos didn't extend to marching in the street. Merrill knew that he was a rich American at a moment when it was unpopular and possibly even dangerous to be one. Still, he insisted in "The Broken Home" that "I am no less time's child than some / Who [. . .] on the barricades risk life and limb"—a statement that, in this context, meant: I'm on your side, Vassili, in my way. His way was to refuse the priority of politics over private life. What he offered his friend was what he wanted himself: an "escape" from politics, particularly when politics meant fires in the street.

On September 14, Jimmy, David, Mimi, and Vassili escaped from the fever of Athens for five days together on Thasos, Vassili's island birthplace. The mythical home of the Sirens, Thasos is mountainous and forested, with a circular coast of cliffs and white-sand beaches. More than 150 miles from Thessaloniki, the island is remote even today; in 1965 it was all but untouristed. Merrill found a premodern world there: dirt roads crowded with goats; farmyards with braying donkeys; bread baking in outdoor clay ovens; groves of pine, fig, olive, almond, and pistachio trees; and "a slow rain of honey from the trees round the house." He jotted down notes, including these about a village Homer: "The blind accordion player, about 38–40. . . . He lives in a vortex of sound. A child sits by him learning the songs." The group visited Vassili's fishermen cousins, and went into the mountains to meet his grandmother, who lived "in a house full of fantastic photographs (moustaches, warlike skirts) and embroideries (delicate flowers on black, wreathing the words, in Greek, 'This too will pass')." Courtly Vassili kissed her "fine old walnut-stained" hands, impressing Merrill. Living with her was another character who drew Merrill's eye, "Old Aunt Maria," known for having "tied herself up to the neck in a sack on her wedding night. 7 nights of this + her husband walked out. She has lived happily ever since, a respectable married virgin." Later, Merrill would display in the dining room in Stonington his own piece of Greek embroidery with the motto "This too will pass."

While Vassili was charming and talkative, Mimi was shy, and yet she "grows on one," Jimmy felt. "In a society of four pregnant cousins, it took a certain amount of style to carry off her childlessness." He recorded her remark when the two couples met that fourth pregnant cousin: " 'Ah, Vassili,' said M. 'The time has really come, I fear, for you to take my virginity.' " Jimmy saw her as "a really odd girl, heavy, hidden in her long hair and weird flowered dresses; rather like honey herself"—he was thinking of that magical honey dripping from the trees—"with a kind of hysterical slowness and grace about her, all created by something with a sting to it. She appears to have no friends at all, and can't get over our liking her." Her friendship with Jimmy grew intimate, even vaguely romantic. "It was a deep relation I wasn't part of," Vassilikos reflected.

On September 16, King Constantine gave his royal sanction to Papandreou's successor as prime minister, bringing an end to the political crisis of the summer. The same day on Thasos, Merrill made this entry in his notebook:

> D's birthday. Up at 5 to go fishing with M. + V., while D. slept. Sunrise. The donkey charcoal among the black almond tree trunks, its rear legs in delicate contrapposto against the pink stubble. The foliage done in small strokes of rust, yellow, green. The half moon shining. The sky becomes a deep, serious color.
>
> In town, waiting for a boat, two male turkeys, with bald blue heads + stiff exaggerated costumes entertained us with a kabuki interlude.
>
> We fished. I had done so last at the age of 12 + may never do it again. The fish were small—not the violent struggling I remember. Small, spent, shining bodies pulled up through a medium never less opaque. Like occasional verse compared to the deep-sea "serious" poems. The smallest fish we cut up for bait to catch larger ones of the same species, like the fragments of verse we plow back into longer poems.

Jackson's forty-second birthday was celebrated by a cake with twenty-four candles, reversing his number of years, and Merrill, too, went back in time: getting up before sunrise, in an ancient land, he returned in memory to deep-sea fishing at the age of twelve in Florida, just prior to his parents' divorce. Vassili, a history-obsessed writer whose name means "king," and Mimi in her flowered dresses, whose given name Demetra was that of the harvest goddess, were the newest incarnations of the mythic couple in "The Broken Home."

Aware that the rapturous writing in his notebook was on its way to poetry, Merrill's mind turned, with that bait metaphor, to the relation between light verse and "serious" poems. The entry breaks off as Merrill moves out of prose into verse:

> > Each
> Homeward step struck a match between our toes
>
> Translated by evening into the 24 candles
> On a friend's cake.

Very soon Merrill took his pen and went back over the entry, cutting phrases, changing words. The early sky's "deep serious color" became a "young" color; the turkeys' "costumes" became "taffetta kimonos"; "fragments of verse" became "sketches," such as this notebook entry itself. After he returned to Athens, the entry would be "cut up" and "plowed back" to become a lyric, titled simply "16.ix.65" and dedicated to "Vassilis and Mimi":

> Summer's last half moon waning high
> Dims and curdles. Up before the bees
> On our friend's birthday, we have left him
> To wake in their floating maze.

The donkey reappeared, as did the turkeys and tiny fish:

> Cut up for bait, our deadest ones
> Reappear live, by magic, on the hook.
> Never anything big or gaudy—
> Line after spangled line of light, light verse.
>
> A radio is playing "Mack the Knife."
> The morning's catch fills one straw hat.
> Years since I'd fished. Who knows when in this life
> Another chance will come?
>
> Between our toes unused to sandals
> Each step home strikes its match.
> And now, with evening's four and twenty candles
> Lit among the stars, waves, pines
>
> To animate our friend's face, all our faces
> About a round, sweet loaf,
> Mavríli brays. We take him some,
> Return with honey on our drunken feet.

"Yes, the donkey's name really was Mavríli," Vassilikos recalled. He generalizes: "The fluidity of everyday life—it's ephemeral. Jimmy knew very well it is the beauty of life. The poet selects from it. His art makes it eternal. It's a butterfly, and the poet plunges a pin in it: there it is, wings outspread, with all its colors." Plunging his pin in the everyday, Merrill fixed September 16, 1965, with its shimmering colors and cheerful companionship, permanently in verse. His awareness of the violence and appetite in that act is playfully signaled in the poem by a radio that keeps playing Bobby Darin's version of the Kurt Weill song "Mack the Knife": "Oh, the shark has pretty teeth, dear, / And he keeps them pearly white."

This poem, with its date for a title, shows Merrill, like other poets of the 1960s, pushing art close to life. He couldn't have written it before he lived in Greece, with the immediacy and sensuality of his experience there, and the liberty that he found in his personal relationships with friends like Mimi and Vassili. The notebook form of the poem was well suited to that immediacy. "16.ix.65" is a case of art wanting to be like life, easy and natural, like a notebook entry. But it is also true that Merrill treated his notebook entry like a poem: it was a lucky catch made to be "plowed back" into a formal piece of writing arranged in metered stanzas. Even in the informal writing of the notebook, he presses his experience to yield meaning and style. The two forms of writing—poem and notebook entry—are not finally different in kind, in his practice, just as the small fish and the large are not different species. They share a vision in which life is already art, or seeking to become it. That's the message of the turkeys' "Kabuki interlude" and the almond trees trying "to get right, in charcoal, / The donkey's artless contrapposto." Merrill's notebook shows his daily drive to make life the work of art it wants to be.

The title "16.ix.65" honors David Jackson's birthday, but he is all but absent from the poem; even the donkey is named, while Jackson (just "our friend") is not. Possibly Merrill's reticence is a sign of intimacy, of the fact that he could take David's presence for granted. But it might just as easily be seen as a sign of distance.

Like Jimmy's relationship with Strato, David's relationship with George was deepening. In September, he visited Lazaretos in Chania on the western tip of Crete, where the navy had posted him. Over the next year, Jackson would go back to Crete more and more often, staying as a guest of the American painter Dorothy Andrews, and later taking rooms of his own. When Lazaretos was on leave in Athens, he was a frequent visitor at Athinaion Efivon 44. Like Jackson, he enjoyed going out at night. At times with Merrill and the rest of the *parea*, at times by themselves, they went to clubs in the Plaka to hear pop songs. Lazaretos may have been shy and sensitive, but he could drink whiskey at Jackson's pace, and he knew how to dance *zembekiko* like a true Greek. He played soccer on a semipro team, and Merrill and Jackson came to watch him. "You can't imagine how thrilling" it was, Merrill wrote to Hine, describing one match. "Lots of poor sportsmanship, police on the field, fights in the audience of perhaps 100." George's coach had heard about the high life he was leading, and he told him "firmly he must go to a hotel the night before the game. Ha," Merrill went on. "You'll be glad to hear that he broke training in every conceivable way. We went one night to a really dreadful club full of whores and pink lights. Mimi Vassilikos and 7 or 8 swains. She + I danced most impressively, Vassili brought bar-girls galore to the table, danced with them, as did the boys, then George and I danced while the rest of the company appeared to avert its eyes. Believe me, it was wild, wild fun."

Sometimes the fun tipped over into something else. One October midnight, an angry Merrill got out of bed with Mouflouzélis. "Where are you going?" Strato asked. "To read for a while," he replied. Jimmy continues the story in his log: "5 minutes later the front door shut. He was walking down the street, + would not turn around when I called. D. found him at the Byzantion drinking cognac + brought him home in tears. 'Why did you leave the bed?' He drank 4 or 5 cognacs, trying to get drunk. I smashed a bottle. Tears. Rages. I struck him. He wanted to put on his uniform + leave. I hid his boot" so as to keep him from leaving. In this account, Jimmy represents Strato as the sensitive, injured party, while he himself is the tough guy who smashes a bottle and "strikes" his lover. Battling with each other, he and Strato were performing for each other—and for the crowd at the café, and for David, whose role was to get out of bed and bring Strato back.

Strato's demobilization was coming. The prospect raised issues that he and Jimmy had postponed up to this point. After a quarrel with his father, Mouflouzélis told Merrill, "When I'm out of the AF I'll leave home. I'll tell them I've gone to Sweden, + I'll come + live with you here." The question of where he would live after the air force must have raised questions, also unsettled, about his sexual identity. In October, Merrill recorded jokes and anecdotes that had to do with Strato's experiences in bed with women. Did he prefer men or women? Probably he himself was unsure. His macho style could be seen as a dandy's. One evening the *parea* was on its way into a bar and Strato was "dressed to kill," as he recalls, his shirt so tight his nipples showed through it. A group of men leaving the bar passed them, saying, "Those are *some* homos!" Mouflouzélis turned to face them. "Who are you calling homos?" he demanded, ready to fight, and they backed down.

He could be gentle and playful. He liked pets, and Maisie in particular; he would let the big cat sitting on him in bed, kneading his chest like dough. In October, now that Maisie was gone, he introduced a new animal into the house, a cat he called Panayiotta. Merrill described her: "Small, gray, savage. We were lunching at an outdoor restaurant, liked her looks, so Strato popped her inside his jacket as we were leaving. [. . .] D + I agree that she might very well be Maisie's reincarnation, utterly appalled to find herself back in the same house with those same monsters." The story shows Strato's impulsiveness, and his readiness to pocket what he wanted (and hadn't Jimmy brought *him* home off the street?). Perhaps it also hints at his desire to make a family.

In November, to celebrate his release from the air force, Jimmy and Strato went with David to visit George on Crete. A snapshot taken on the Venetian waterfront in Chania, beneath a clear Aegean sky, captures the foursome in expressive postures. George stands on the edge of the group, to one side of David. He gives a shy, earnest smile; his back is straight, his gaze direct. David and Strato stand in jaunty poses, each a mirror for the other, and each leaning toward Jimmy, the beaming, magnetic center of the group. Jimmy and David are twinned in their dress: tweed jackets, white shirts, turtlenecks. The Americans have costumed their Greek lovers in sport coats and bold red ties. Strato, powerful, edgy, and handsome, is the only one who isn't looking at the camera. He seems ready to stroll off on his own, following his gaze.

But it was Merrill who left first. On December 1, he flew alone from Athens to New York, intending to be back in time for Christmas in Greece. There'd been more scenes with Strato. In flight, Jimmy wrote to David, saying that, before leaving, he'd told Strato that he was in danger of "losing V + M's good opinion, cautioning him against this, but now that I think of it, why on earth should he care? I care, I guess, that's what I meant. Now I feel sort of calm + grim: get these weeks over with. [. . .] Forgive me for everything + make sure S. does, too." He tried to keep up the tough line with Strato, however, and Strato replied in sullen self-defense: "You write that you do not want to come back to Greece because your heart is aching. Well, my heart is aching too."

Now, as always in New York, Merrill was thrust back into literary society at high speed. His first night in the city he had dinner with Myers and Machiz, the next night with the Fords and John Hollander. He had tea with Auden. On December 6, he read at the 92nd Street YMHA with Richard Murphy, an Irishman and a crowd pleaser. Merrill was pleased too: that night he read as well as he ever had, he felt. In the audience, he noted, were John Ashbery, Gerard Malanga ("with a shock of golden hair + a jeweled belt + boots"), Gold and Fizdale, and Mary Lou Aswell. The Hollanders hosted a party afterward, and many old friends came: Tom Howkins, Bobby Isaacson, Bill and Kay Meredith, Betty Magowan, Howard Moss, and Robert and Isabel Morse. Next he flew south "to spend a week with my mother in Jacksonville, where some kind of all-too-imaginable green and rust lounge attached to the Cathedral is being dedicated in memory of her parents." He admired "Mildred Burwell's Titian," dined with his mother and her many friends, and, beyond his Ponte Vedra hotel room, watched "huge snot-colored waves pound on a strangely shrunken beach."

He returned to Greece for an unhappy Christmas. "I'm <u>still</u> worn out from my trip," he told Kalstone,

> despite having gone to bed on Xmas the minute the turkey had been cleared away and staying there for 36 hours while the others washed dishes, played cards, went home, slept, woke, went to parties, had sex, you name it. [. . .] Strato was en famille most of the time. He has been going through a bad spell anyhow, driven mad by all the papers necessary to living and working now that he's a civilian. For a while he would talk of nothing but leaving for Canada. What would become of me? The question sent him into his only fit of high spirits in the entire fortnight. [. . .] Things seem to be ironing themselves out at last—but it's five p.m., why isn't he here?

It was usual now for Strato not to appear when expected, or not to appear at all.

Jimmy was bothered (he confided to David) by a "funny white paste that won't stop forming you know where." On January 19, Strato was examined by a doctor for the same condition. On January 28, Jimmy wrote, "And where are we now. The quarrel of 9 days ago has made us strangers—so <u>he</u> says. . . . We go daily to the Dr. <u>That</u> hasn't helped matters, our absurd disease passed back + forth like ping-pong." He suspected that his quarrelsome lover must be involved with someone else. The next log entries read,

> FEB 20. S. in Plaka seen for first time in weeks. Sleeps at home.
> 27 S. phones for his clothes but doesn't show up.
> MAR 9 "   "   "   "   "   "   "   "   "

Jimmy's fears of abandonment were coming true.

For weeks, Merrill hadn't had "the heart to be in touch, at any intimate level, with anybody. The thing is, I can't face what is happening, and it festers." He wasn't writing poems. He declined an honorary degree from Bard "only because I don't see us leaving here just as the full splendor of summer comes to pass. Nice of them." The weather had been "ravishing," the freesias on the roof were ready to bloom, and the shops were "full of flowering branches." But these sights merely sharpened his anxiety. He described Carnival to Irma: "Almost anywhere in town one can get a mouthful of confetti from somebody disguised, or a streamer in a restaurant thrown to curl round one's throat."

Into this gloom came Donald Richie. From the moment he got off the plane, "I saw that things were not well for Jimmy and David. That very evening there was an argument, and then something like a muted battle at a taverna." Explaining the bitterness he saw in his friends on this trip, Richie noted that "both were writers but only one of them was successful." David had returned to his "mammoth occupation-of-Berlin story," an old piece of fiction, "with an eye to sending it around again and perhaps, in the bargain, making a little book of it here." *Pigeon Vole* was printed in February. David had long dreamed of book publication. But a book of 101 pages printed in Greece by his lover in an edition of three hundred copies, "none for sale," was not what he had in mind—and there was little response from his friends. In late July, he thanked Eleanor for her encouragement, which "my poor heart skipped so many beats waiting for. . . . Probably because I am, really, rather ashamed at writing so little, selling so little, and of the rather precious amateur business of publishing one's own story."

Merrill's distress about Strato must have bothered Jackson too. Strato felt that "David was very jealous; he was nasty," and Richie agreed, "David was jealous; he was Charles Swann." Merrill had assured Jackson that Strato was not a threat, and George was always there to balance out the equation. But when David wasn't in Crete with George, he was in Athens with Jimmy and Strato, and David couldn't pretend then that Mouflouzélis was only of secondary interest. Richie tried to keep his hosts "busy and cheerful," but more than their usual diversions would be required.

Donald was traveling next to Iran. Tony happened to know someone who knew someone notable in Isfahan—Yahya Bachtiyar, the Oxford-educated leader of a nomadic tribe, the Bachtiyari, renowned for their weaving; and an introduction to this romantic personage could be arranged. It was enough for Merrill to grab hold of, and he decided to leave with Richie. In "Chimes for Yahya," the poem he wrote about the trip seven years later, he called Isfahan a "Change of scene that might, I thought, be tried / First, instead of outright suicide." "Yes," Richie commented, remembering the trip, "Jimmy had been thinking of death until he glimpsed the possibility of Isfahan." His state was that dire.

About Isfahan, Merrill knew only Fauré's setting of Leconte de Lisle's

"Les Roses d'Ispahan," a prayer for the return of young love sung on a 78 rpm record by Maggie Teyte. But that was sufficient to make the place glow in his mind. And it was clear on arrival that this was a city worth dreaming about. Built in a lush oasis on the high plateau of central Iran, the spectacular architecture of Isfahan was created during the reign of Shah Abbas the Great, the Safavid ruler who made Isfahan the seventeenth-century capital of Persia and a center of art and trade rivaling the Ottoman Empire. The blue-tiled Imam Mosque, rising above the shah's polo grounds in one of the world's largest public squares, dominated the city, while grand, enclosed brick bridges and sluiceways, many centuries old, crossed the Zayandeh River, arch after arch, like the patterned border in a Bachtiyari carpet.

In his notebook, Merrill noted "houses painted pink + blue / salmon + green / fluted columns painted silver / town color of dust capped + shot / with turquoise glazes, domes, buses. . ." Richie describes his friend's response to the place:

> He exclaimed at the great blue mosque, at the flowering almond trees, at the color of the earth itself, which he found like cinnamon. He was ready to be seduced and the colors seduced him first. As they often did. Jimmy was peculiarly susceptible to shades, particularly those he chose for his own sartorial vocabulary. In Isfahan he found that he matched: grey-green, dusky rose, chartreuse, aubergine, chrome yellow. We discovered a shirt store and spent as much time in it as we did in the ancient funeral crypts. He was particularly fond of a collar-buttoned horizontal striped number in ochre and fuchsia and bought one for each of us.
>
> It was this shirt he wore (like an emissary thoughtfully showing loyalist colors) when we went on the appointed afternoon to take tea with Yahya. The place was, as Jimmy says in the poem, indeed freezing, though the floor was covered with Persian carpets. The retainer Hussein made tea and then Yahya entered.
>
> I who had no uses for Yahya saw only a middle-aged man who looked somewhat like Yassar Arafat. He was certainly kind, even sweet: I found him saccharine and left to follow my own pursuits. Jimmy stayed on and on. With Yahya the attraction was deep and apparently mutual. It was like two old friends, even relatives, finally finding each other after a long time. Jimmy had willed himself a great emotional experience.

"You kept me by you all that day," Merrill says in the poem. "I never had to think why I was there." Yahya put him in mind of "a darker . . . Robert

Morse." But behind Robert was another figure: cross-legged on his carpets, surrounded by guests and hangers-on who taste his food and drink, taking turns on an opium pipe (Jimmy had one), Yahya was Charles Merrill, lord of the seraglio. Yahya is also described as if he were a spiritual master, and Jimmy his scribe, "a divinity / Student" who wants "to get so many lines a week / Of you by heart."

When he wrote "Chimes for Yahya" in 1973, Merrill placed his encounter with Yahya in an unexpected context. The poem begins in the present tense in Athens at Christmastime. Merrill opens his front door to children chanting the *kalanda*—doggerel poems celebrating the New Year that Greek children perform for coins from house to house. The foreigner slams his door on these young ones so "Eager to tell, tell, tell what the angel said." Explaining his anger, Merrill recalls the long-ago Christmas morning when, Mademoiselle having already divulged the gifts his parents had chosen for him, he had to mimic the wonder and gratitude he was supposed to feel.

What does this narrative frame have to do with his memory of Yahya? Merrill makes a link by introducing the story of a camp, counter-nativity presided over by Yahya on the night of Merrill's visit. The poet goes out into "the cold courtyard black with goats" to attend with Yahya as a tribeswoman gives birth. Also present is Gloria, an anthropologist from Berkeley, "doing fieldwork in the tribe." While Yahya chuckles, the Americans gaze "like solemn oxen from a stall / Upon the mystery"—which is revealed to be no mystery but a prank when, after cries and convulsions, "a wriggling white / Puppy!" is delivered into the arms of credulous Gloria. "Then the proud mother bared her face:" she is Hussein, Yahya's opium-addicted majordomo, who has collaborated in a practical joke scripted by Yahya.

It is a good story, but not a true one. Neither the poet nor "Gloria" was on hand for this escapade. Merrill merely heard a version of it from Hussein, over a pipe, on the night of his visit, and he liked it enough to imagine himself into the story. Why did it stick in his mind? The prank is a parody of childbirth, expressing a gay man's annoyed resentment of the imperative to "propagate his kind," as Bishop's Crusoe puts it. Yet it is also compensatory and defensive, as if to say, Don't think we men can't bring forth babies, too, of a sort.

When the poem returns to Athens at Christmas, Merrill sees that his own desires set him apart from, but also connect him to,

> Little boys
> Whose rooster tessitura, plus ça change,

Will crow above the cradle of a son.
Little girls each with her Christmas doll
Like hens a china egg is slipped beneath.

While achieving this sexual self-acceptance (something he evidently kept having to achieve), Merrill recovers his capacity for wonder and gratitude—as he did in Isfahan, along with his will to live. "Perhaps you really did save my life," he told Richie after they left.* They each came away with a set of camel bells as gifts from Yahya. These consisted of "long chains of interconnected bells, from fairly large to quite small. The top was shaken, and this ravishing glissando of metal struck cascades into the ear," Richie recalls. Merrill ends the poem by shaking his set: sleigh-bell music, chiming in with the children's doggerel. Yet the children's chant announces a birth, while his poem marks a death—Yahya's, which he learned of in 1967.† The dream figure—"Lover, warrior, invalid and sage"—vanished back into the poet's psyche as abruptly as he had arisen, having been of use.

"I had to get away," Merrill said, back from Isfahan. "I was drowning, or burning, or being buried alive, or whatever one does when something one lives for has come to an end. I can only hope that I've behaved well, that it's not more than half my fault. There is no resentment at least; the whole experience has given me back to life. I fear I gave Strato very little by comparison." But it was too early to calculate losses and gains: Strato was by no means in the past tense. On March 13, Jimmy noted, "He comes; he has left home 12 days ago. He is exhausted, ill, caught up in a kind of underworld. He comes now every day for a week." On March 17, he brought Richie up-to-date: "Sunday he said 'if I liked' he would bring his things to the house and we would live together forever after. What could I say but Yes?" The log continues,

MAR 20. He hears his father has heard he's living with
2 'poustides.' He will not come to the house again. Out to
get drunk.
MAR 21. At Tony's shop, trying to talk reason.

---

* JM to DR, letter, March 17, 1966 (WUSTL). Merrill said, referring to this period, that he had "wanted to die, or at least not to live any more." JM to CF, letter, June 27, 1966 (Getty).

† Robin Magowan learned this news when he traveled to Isfahan to meet Yahya, bearing a letter of introduction from his uncle. RM, *Memoirs*, 198.

MAR 22. S. goes back home. I do not see him for 8 or 9 days.
He's "ill."
APRIL 1? Chester is here. 1st sex with S. since Feb 20.

Strato's father said to him around this time, "What is this Jimmy? There
is something funny about him, no? What is he to you?" "A *friend*," Strato
answered, "very affectionate, a good man." His father made him swear he
was telling the truth, and so he did. "I was telling the truth—but only part
of it."

Intending to help matters by furnishing a substitute for Strato, Tony
produced a young man from Crete named Kostas Tympakianákis, and
Jimmy took the bait. He saw "my passionate little Cretan monkey" as comic
relief, useful as a means to make Strato jealous, but not much more: Kostas
was "too short + crude to last." He lasted long enough, however, to become
a minor character in the "endlessly exhausting and repetitive soap opera"
that Merrill was now living in Athens.

The Browers visited in April. In April Jimmy went to Rome to see his
mother, Grace, and Umberto; he went with Vassili and Mimi, rather than
David. Hubbell Pierce and Robert Isaacson visited Athens in June. But
Jimmy was incommunicative and isolated. Words, he told Richard Howard, have "failed me for some indefinite spell." The "last months," he
admitted to Hollander, "have been pure 2nd adolescence—all mysterious
heartbreak + helplessness (+ how I've enjoyed it au fond!) not conducive to
letters. . . . No writing of any sort, in fact." To Robin and Betty Magowan,
who were divorcing, he apologized for being slow to acknowledge the birth
of their second son, his namesake, James: "I'm sorry to have been silent
at this particular time, but something like every third minute words keep
failing me."

That failure stood in contrast to the success of *Nights and Days*, published in 1966. Reviewers agreed that Merrill's virtuosity and sophistication, rather than check strong emotion, had become a means to express it.
For instance, in *The New York Times Book Review*, Gene Baro commented:
"James Merrill's poetry continues to develop extraordinarily. The suavity and technical polish of his earlier work continues to be present, but is
subdued by a new richness and complexity of feeling." More praise came
in the American quarterlies and the British press.* This was the strongest

---

* Pieces appeared in the *Hudson, Kenyon, Yale,* and *Virginia Quarterly* reviews. Merrill appreciated the British reviews in particular. He reported the best to Jackson: "2 reviews have come
in from England. C[yril] Connolly in the Sunday Times: '. . . delightfully witty + original
turn of mind. . . 'The 1002nd Night' is quite unlike anything I know. . .'; and a don in the New

response to his work that Merrill had received. In *Poetry*, Richard Howard extolled him as a man as much as a poet (though not without a dig): "This poet, the most decorative and glamour-clogged America has ever produced, has made himself, by a surrender to reality and its necessary illusions, a master of his own experience and of his own nature."

Experience kept posing fresh challenges to master. The infection that Merrill and Mouflouzélis had passed back and forth at Christmas didn't go away, and new symptoms emerged for Strato. In June, he was diagnosed with "gonorrhea and 'leukorrhea.' " The condition left him "madly jumpy," "a bundle of nerves and neuroses." Protective of Strato, and unsure which one was to blame for these infections, Merrill modulated into a new role. He took stock in a letter to Claude:

> Last night "what he feared" happened—his mother caught him swallowing an antibiotic, thus confirming certain suspicions of her own. For the 3rd time in 4 months he has left home ("I can't look them in the face, I have a younger sister.") and come to stay here. [. . .] We sleep hand in hand like brothers. But he despairs. If he doesn't one day disappear ("go where nobody knows me") he will come to America with me on a tourist visa—he already has his passport—and you will perhaps see why I love him so.

And why exactly did he love him so?

> His good heart? His thick skull? His skill in bed?—will I ever sample that again? But also that there is absolutely no place in our life together for any show of temperament from me. That's his prerogative, and I must say it's a blessed thing [. . .]. What I am left with is caring for him, wanting his happiness, being prepared for it not to depend on me. As I remarked the other day in this very connection, even from the age of 13 it was with the Marschallin that I identified, dans cet opéra-là.

In "Matinees," Merrill describes how Lotte Lehmann's Marschallin planted in his young mind the noble ideal of an older heroine disengaging herself "from a last love, at center stage, / To the beloved's dazzled gratitude."

Statesman"—John Carey—'thinks I am better than L. Durrell, 'clement, but half-amused; affable, but grave.' Then he calls me an 'amiable ghoul' which may just be the last word, no?" JM to DJ, letter, November 11, 1966 (WUSTL).

> The point thereafter was to arrange for one's
> Own chills and fever, passions and betrayals,
> Chiefly in order to make song of them.

Merrill wasn't ready to make song of his current "chills and fever, passions and betrayals"; he wouldn't begin work on "Matinees," for instance, until another year had passed. But his unlikely young Octavian offered the poet a part he knew how to play.

He was serious about taking Mouflouzélis to the U.S. when he returned briefly that fall: he could keep an eye on Strato by taking him along; it might help him win the tug-of-war with Strato's family; and otherwise he would be alone. David had been "going back and back to Crete, staying longer each time," in order to be near George, and, Jimmy saw, he would "not be uprooted easily from Greece." Perhaps it was Jimmy's turn to be jealous of David? But taking Strato home was a drastic strategy. It was, he admitted to Louise Fitzhugh, a "[t]errifying prospect! He is so nice and so good and so . . . unimaginative, it's left to me to imagine what on earth he will do in Stonington, and all I can think is to try and get him work at the garage. You, as one of a handful of friends I can trust to be nice to him (not that it will be easy, he speaks no English), are high on my list of People To See." Eleanor and Grace were lower. "One has heard the Stone Women far too often on the subject of 'those ridiculous middle-aged Americans we knew in Taxco, each with his "demon lover"—hah!' to expect mercy from that quarter," Jimmy fretted. "Obviously from one point of view (such as, say, Grace's) I am too old to be caught up in something like this. From another (mine?) I am too old _not_ to be. I can see no possible way but to live through the whole experience and learn what I can from it."

Except for a holiday on Rhodes in July, Strato spent the summer with Jimmy in Athens, working as a builder, while he told his parents that he was living and working elsewhere. Merrill hoped to maintain this arrangement until they traveled to the U.S. But there were setbacks. The U.S. embassy refused to grant a visa to Strato. The "reason: insufficient 'incentive to return,' by which I guess they mean no business, no wife & kiddies." Strato continued to suffer from infections, and he accepted Merrill's offer to pay for a circumcision so as to prevent recurrence. The procedure was "horribly done by the wrong doctor"; cosmetic surgery was required, and the infection returned anyway. It was, Merrill felt, "all my fault and I can't think why he hasn't bashed my skull in, or the doctor's."

In early September, Mouflouzélis's parents discovered that he had been living and working in Athens all summer, "and his father said he was no longer to be called 'father' by this deceitful child." It was necessary to win his father's favor back, which would mean more time at home and away from Merrill. "Nothing, nothing, nothing ever gets resolved," Merrill complained to Hine. "I'm learning the lesson, though. The peacock on the Merrill crest is slowly turning into a sparrow—hardier, quicker, able to live anywhere and eat anything—no wonder they drew Aphrodite's chariot (it was sparrows, no?)—and there are still days when I kiss the hand of life, as now your cheek, dear friend."

His hardiness would be tested from another quarter. Jackson spent most of the hot summer in Crete. He was in Athens "never more than 4 [days] at a time," and he spent those days burning with jealousy of his Greek lover, "wondering if George will phone or why he hasn't?" He was, Merrill told Kalstone, "so thin, so unhappy." In mid-September, while Strato was away, Merrill went to Crete to visit Jackson. The occasion was David's birthday, and it made a grim contrast to the happy visit to Thasos a year before. Afterward, Jimmy knew he had "behaved rather badly, complaining about being sequestered, no fun at all, by D's raging xenophobia (every foreign face a menace [i.e., a potential rival for George]) and by the contemptible familiarity of G's cordon of cronies. But I decided the last day that it was really because I was for once a guest in a house of D's—2 high bare dismal rooms—and enduring the first dramatization of the change in our relations." Back in Athens, he wrote to Jackson:

My dearest friend—

I feel ever so bad about these days. I see that I had a chance to behave nicely in a house of your own, and that I failed. This indeed was perhaps (it now seems) the main issue—your having established yourself at last independent of me—and I did not understand it in time to control myself. I am very, very sorry. It is the kind of thing that might easily never be forgiven. Take it, if you can, some other way. Dear David.

Yours always, Jamie

More bad news came on September 21: the Canadian embassy had refused Mouflouzélis's visa application. "It's the first time since God knows when that I haven't had my way," Merrill reflected, "and I suppose it is good for me." He bought a ticket for himself to fly back to the U.S. As the date neared, he wrote in his log:

7 Oct 66 <u>Have</u> I done all I could? This gnaws + gnaws. How dreadful if I haven't. Not only for what I should deserve, but for S's sake in particular. To have played at wanting + helping, feeling. To have been Vermont slate

Wet, it hides behind its glittering.

Did Merrill's tears hide his relief as he prepared to fly? He suspected so: unpleasant lessons in self-knowledge were coming hard and fast.

He flew first to London to see Tony Harwood and David Kalstone, where the latter was taking a sabbatical. Tony "mesmerized" DK when Jimmy brought them together. They had morning "séances" with Harwood, Kalstone wrote to a friend, in "his secret Antonioni-like apartment—all black and white, sealed off from noise, and high above London in a modern apartment house built over the Sloane Square subway station. [. . .] The living room has no furniture except a glass table. It is eventually to be completely mirrored—white carpet, white ceiling, white curtains. Meanwhile he sits on the floor [. . .] and incants French poetry (from copies inscribed to him by Cocteau). And tells about Hong Kong and Stravinsky and Fanny Peabody Mason and the house in Venice, the Palazzo Barbaro, where James set <u>Wings of the Dove</u>." Outside, in Carnaby Street shops and on the sidewalks of the King's Road, color was exploding—pink miniskirts, orchid-tinted trousers for men. "We trotted out our rose-colored glasses," Kalstone recalled, "and Jimmy bought the following ensemble: hip-hanging trousers—large black and brown checks on moss-colored wool; a shiny green and red striped shirt (thin stripes, white collar and cuffs); and two pop ties in swelling blacks and whites."

Back on Water Street, Merrill entered the home where he'd last stayed (but for a brief stop in December) fifteen months earlier. The power and strangeness of his adventure in Greece struck him. Would Nick Shadow come to claim the soul of this Rake? He turned to Jackson to explain the uncanny sensation:

> I feel funny in this house—frightened in the faintest way—as if it were midnight in a graveyard almost. It is the sadness that many neglected objects exhale, a sadness in proportion to the self-indulgence that assembled so many <u>things</u> in the first place. It <u>is</u> home, without the shadow of a doubt. It is where I shall die, or go when I die. It's still very beautiful and not too decayed. It makes me measure how far I at least have gone in Greece, how far out into an experience that can be made only by

a distinct effort to relate to what is here. It will scare you too, I think, but it will not, in the long run, betray us—whatever that means!

Tests revealed that Merrill's "intestines are 'teeming with amoebas' "; in fact they had been for months. The cold, clear New England air refreshed him, however, and he looked back on his life in Athens as on a state of torpor: "How <u>dull</u> it is there—not 'it,' not even one's friends, but how dull one becomes oneself! Here it is all quick talk" with Grace and Eleanor. When he wanted another sort of company, there was Peter Tourville—"Cheerful, getting fat, a short haircut, under it all the same old weirdo." Joe Bruno and Hilda helped out around the house. "I find all I need do is treat them just like, respectively, Strato and Kleo, and it works!" Had Strato come with him, it would have been their world, Peter's and Joe's and Hilda's, that he was at home in. To David, Jimmy confided, "I absolutely cannot imagine S. here. Or, conversely, I can and don't like the idea of it. It horrifies me to admit this—but if I can't say it to you—Lord knows, I can hardly say it to myself! In proportion to my pleasure in being here, is my feeling that I have just plain fallen out of love." No sooner had he said this than the postman arrived. "Oh my dear," he added, "I take it all back. The letter that went astray had the loveliest letter from S. enclosed. I think of him and I melt [. . .]. I kiss you and Strato passionately."

He was back in Athens before Christmas. In January, he and David set off with Strato and George on a car tour of the Peloponnese. The first stop, Monemvasia, Lazaretos's hometown, was "a quite unexpectedly ravishing place: great fortress-island, connected to the mainland by a causeway, topped by Byzantine ruins below which are ruined churches, shells of houses, . . . and beauty wherever one looks." That night they stayed in Veliès, a village in the hills, as guests of George's godparents. At night, wearing army overcoats from World War II, David, George, and Strato went out into the cold with flashlights to shoot birds that nested in the orange trees. Jimmy stayed by the fire with the godmother. She appears as a witch out of Homer in his poem "David's Night in Veliès." "Lulling the olive boughs," she puts her hands in the fire, immune to it, divining a future the poet can't himself foresee.

The travelers circled the Peloponnese through Kalamata (seeing Jackson's foster child and his brother) and the towns of Pylos, Olympia, and Patras on their way home. Back in Athens, Jimmy told Robin, "S. phoned in the extra-courtly, goodhumored voice that means trouble; he had 'something to tell me' and would be around at 6, no at 4, but he arrived at 6, joked a bit most effectively for 15 minutes, then, guiding me into the study, still all abeam, but placing my hand upon his pounding heart to show what a turmoil he was <u>really</u> in, asked for $50 . . . No, he could not explain—he would telephone me precisely at six tomorrow [. . .] to tell me what it was about. No, it was not a girl. No, he was not sick. He simply could not tell me face to face. Maybe I would not want to see him again, I would tell him whether or not I did when he called." What Mouflouzélis told him when he called is recorded in the last entry of Merrill's log of his love affair:

> The facts: "engaged" 14 or 15 months. The girl pregnant. 7th month. I understand the trip to Rhodes, the money "for the family."
>
> To ask. Where, how, did you meet [. . .]? How long has she been in Athens? Marriage? Where is the room? What is it like? The Greeks (you are no exception) all say "I am unlike the others." You are as like as two peas. Two? Two million. The national sport is not football but gulling foreigners.
>
> And for all that, I bless you.
>
> It is beside the point that you are behaving like a fool: you are also behaving like a man.
>
> I don't yet dare think what memories are to be revised. <u>Must</u> they be? Possibly not. But this is of all the one interesting question.
>
> I preferred Illusion to reality. I said so. And I got what I asked for.

On another page, he added: "G. says it's Vaso." Strato had met Vaso in 1965, while Jimmy was in the U.S., at a bar near the air force base where she served drinks. She was pretty, strong, and strong-willed. Just eighteen in 1965, and coming from Corfu, she was less experienced in the ways of the world than her Athenian boyfriend. At first, there was no great conflict. Merrill had left him behind in Greece, and didn't Jimmy have David, anyway? It was only leaving the army that forced the issue for Strato.* "Now, I knew Vaso," he recalls, "and I was in a dilemma about whether to love a man or a woman." Keeping Merrill in the dark about his dilemma had involved

---

* Later, in a chronology, JM wrote for 1965, "Strato demobilized: 'beginning of the end.' " JM, journal, 1988, Jnl 54 (WUSTL).

sometimes elaborate lies. On the trip to Rhodes in July 1966, for which Merrill paid, Strato took Vaso. Around this time, they conceived a child. When Merrill visited Jackson in Crete in September, Strato was on Corfu meeting Vaso's family, and she was two months pregnant. After September, when he convinced Merrill that he had to make peace with his family by living at home, he moved with Vaso into a small apartment. The Glass Cat's brains turned out not to have been so transparent. Merrill had had suspicions, but he never looked into the case very closely. The poet "hid" his face, and Strato's touch, "quick, merciful," "Blindfolded" him. "If that was illusion, I wanted it to last long." And Strato had done what he could to make sure it did.

Did Strato never love him, then? "Who can say?" Vassilikos answered when asked. "But it must have been a marriage of convenience—for Strato." It's possible to see him as a conniver, a whore. Merrill himself would take this view, at times, and Strato sometimes behaved in such a way as to merit it. And it is unclear what it would have meant for Strato Mouflouzélis to "love" James Merrill, when he knew nothing about his poetry, his past, or his world. But, as Merrill put it, "Understanding has more than one face." And if Strato never knew Merrill in some ways, he knew what very few people ever did—what it was like to be loved by him passionately and fully. They created a world of their own, "mouth to mouth"; they "communicated." Mouflouzélis kept Vaso a secret as long as he did because he didn't want to face facts, and he feared losing Merrill's money, surely. But he also feared losing Merrill. He would have been a great deal to lose. It is not every day that a rich man with refinement and kindness, brilliance and charm, walks into a poor boy's life saying that he loves him absolutely. As Strato told his father, Jimmy was "very affectionate, a good man," and so he was. As Vaso put it, looking back across the decades, "It was the best thing that ever happened to Strato."

Merrill's reaction to Strato's revelation, as recorded in his notebook, turns rapidly from confusion and anger to acceptance. "And for all that, I bless you," he concludes not halfway down the page. He was prepared to act bravely and generously, like the Marschallin. Perhaps he was gratified by this turn of events: Strato was doing as he was supposed to; he was behaving "like a man." "It isn't in me to turn against him," Merrill wrote. "It's not perhaps what I wanted at the beginning, but it continues, it persists, and some of the furthest fixtures of my life are reillumined by it. My mother's exaggerated horror over Kimon, for instance—that now helps me, warns me not to overdramatize the folly of what one, as an older person, considers to be a wrong turning. She saw ruin, disaster, shame, precisely where I saw freedom and self-realization. Perhaps S. feels a bit the way I did then, and I'd never dare blame him if he did." A few days later he wrote to Richie, "I wake up in the night and can not stop crying. Yesterday when he failed to come as promised it occurred to me to fly home at once [. . .]. I would rather be where I can't turn against him."

With Strato acting as stage manager, Jimmy brought David, George, and Kostas Tympakianákis to a taverna where the party happened to run into him and Vaso. "I fear me," Merrill told Richie, "she seemed rather sweet + touching, with a short, short haircut, big round blue eyes, singing along with the records while on every male tongue the lies positively danced." It was a chance for Merrill to appraise his young female rival. "She isn't dumb," he acknowledged, "and, according to S [. . .] 'doesn't mind'—by which I assume is meant that another woman would strike her as a rival whereas a poor old, rich old queen could do no harm even if he wanted to." But she did mind. One night, the *parea*, with Vaso along, crowded into the car to hear music at a club. In the backseat, Strato reached around Vaso to tickle Jimmy; on the way home, with Vaso in the front, he settled into kissing Jimmy until she insisted he stop. Vaso knew she and Merrill were struggling over Strato, and her pregnancy was a move in the game. "You are caught for good my boy in the tender trap," Jimmy told Strato when he learned of it. And he was caught too.

The baby was due soon, but Merrill wouldn't be on hand for the birth. A year earlier, he had been invited to teach poetry writing at the University of Wisconsin at Madison in spring 1967; he accepted, as if he knew already that he would want to be a long way from Athens by then. But he was called back sooner when the phone rang and Harry Ford told him he had won the National Book Award for *Nights and Days*. It was a triumph, the first major prize of his career. The citation of the judges, Auden, James Dickey, and Howard Nemerov, honored Merrill for "his scrupulous and uncompromising cultivation of the poetic art, evidenced in his refusal to settle for an easy and profitable stance; for his insistence on taking the kind of tough, poetic chances which make the difference between esthetic success or failure." Yet, when he got off the phone with Ford, "I could only think: Let me give it back, let me have Strato instead."

10

JACK FROST'S TEARS

1967–68

B ack in New York on March 8, at the National Book Award ceremony at Lincoln Center, Merrill walked onstage in tuxedo before a tense audience. The guest of honor was Vice President Hubert Humphrey, whose presence had prompted some writers and editors to organize a protest against the war in Vietnam. Over the past year and a half President Lyndon Johnson had authorized a massive bombing campaign in North Vietnam and major increases in American troop deployment in the South, without winning the military advantage. On March 3, Senator Robert Kennedy had made a peace proposal on the floor of the U.S. Senate, calling for a suspension of American bombing. It was, in the words of a *New York Times* editorial, "a crucial moment either for peace negotiations or escalated war."

Outside Philharmonic Hall, protesters handed out leaflets announcing that there would be a walkout during the awards ceremony. As Humphrey prepared to speak, "[o]ne of the organizers of the demonstration, Mitchell Goodman, [. . .] marched to the stage [. . .]. White-faced and nervous, he cupped his hands to his mouth and shouted, 'Mr. Vice President, we are bombing children in Vietnam, and you and we are all responsible!' " Goodman and fifty others left the hall, shouting.* The vice president made

---

* Other protesters included the critics Dwight Mcdonald, Robert Gorham-Davis, and Anthony West, the cartoonist Jules Feiffer, and publishers and editors Theodore Solotaroff,

no explicit political remarks, but he quoted Mark Twain in a provocative way: "War talk by men who have been in war is always interesting; whereas moon talk by a poet who has not been to the moon is likely to be dull."

None of the prizewinners took part in the protest. Bernard Malamud won the award in fiction for his novel *The Fixer*, Justin Kaplan in arts and letters for the biography *Mr. Clemens and Mark Twain*, Oscar Lewis in a broad general category—"science, philosophy, and religion"—for *La Vida*, and Peter Gay in history for *The Enlightenment*. In his speech, Merrill was light and well-mannered. "Now that I see the size of this audience and this auditorium, it is not easy to resist—though I shall—expanding my remarks at least to the point where they touch upon the artistic and the political conscience. As for the moon," he added, reminding everyone of Humphrey's quotation from Twain, "I shall do no more than name it." Asserting his detachment from literary New York, he mentioned that he'd come all the way from Athens. "One reason I stay in Greece months at a time is that there [. . .] my main contact with our language can be through reading and writing." He praised his fellow nominees in poetry—Ashbery, Barbara Howes, Adrienne Rich, and William Jay Smith. To Marianne Moore, nominated for her *Collected Poems*, he paid a special tribute: "Not even in Greek could I find words to accept a prize won in competition with her if it were not plain as day that her magical supremacy has, this one time, simply been taken for granted by absolutely everybody involved, including all of us here this evening." Next came a "rose-strewn" banquet table hosted by Harry Ford with "euphoric friends" (poets Dickey, Hollander, Howard, Meredith, Moss, and Merwin), "la maman en pleurs," and "toasts + speeches, letters + telegrams."

"And you know what?" Merrill wrote to Parigory. "None of it got through to me at all. The great change of heart we both envisioned the moment my plane took off from Athens hasn't happened yet. I feel depressed and lonely and tired. Whatever reminds me of Greece—a box of matches, a photograph, my last spring's houndstooth suit hanging in the closet—fills me with a kind of quiet icy sorrow." Quiet, icy sorrow would be the content of his inner life for a long time. The revelation that he'd been "living a lie" with Mouflouzélis had wounded him deeply. Still, he didn't feel that their relationship was over. He wrote to Strato, "I am very sad to be away from you, more now that you have no work and are upset every day. I hope to learn what happens with work, how your skin is, if you went to the maternity hospital, what they told you, what Vaso thinks of the hospital. Whatever you do

Dick Seaver, Robert Basin, and André Schiffrin. Henry Raymond, "Writers Leave Humphrey Talk," *NYT* (March 9, 1967), 42.

Strato, don't be ashamed to tell me. Whatever worry, whatever need, do not forget that my heart is yours." He closed, "Please take from me some faith in the future. The life we want will happen if we have courage and if we keep the love that unites us."

In his reply Mouflouzélis told Merrill that Vaso was in pain; the cause wasn't clear, but it was "serious." The doctor "told me to take her to the clinic, but I am not doing it because I will need a lot of money." Would Jimmy help? It was, Mouflouzélis said, "my hard head that is to blame for all this." He signed himself "Your sweet and beloved boy," then returned to the question of money in a postscript: "I am waiting to hear from you about what to do with Vaso, O.K.?" Merrill gave him money and reassurance, but he wanted something too. He told Strato that he had filed all the necessary papers for a visa on his end. "Now it is only up to the questions they pose in Greece. So, as you know, if a visa is possible and you want to come, I will be waiting. [. . .] You already know how much I want it." He urged Strato to trust Vaso's doctor and to ask the social worker at the hospital for advice about how to care for their newborn. He knew the young parents would need it.

Soon, back in Stonington, Merrill had to write another kind of letter.

My Strato—

I am very sorry about this news, which I learned ten minutes ago. While I was in New York I went to the doctor to ask him about my amoebas, and I told him about the blood test I had in Athens. He told me to have another just to be sure. Then, today, he called to say I have syphillis. How it happened and from whom I have no idea, but I am very afraid after the way we made love last time. For certain you have it too. I don't have to tell you how sorry and ashamed I am. Go as fast as you can to Kapetanakis, or go immediately to the drugstore and arrange for ten days of penicillin shots (at least 1,000,000 units per day). I told David to leave more money for the therapy.

I don't have the energy to write more. You have my word of honor that I knew nothing before today. If you can forgive me, write soon, because my mind is like an asylum with all the thoughts that you can imagine. Please give me any confirmation you can.

Your Tzimmaki

David will tell you the latest news on the visa. I love you.

Merrill told Kalstone he was "riddled with social disease (the nasty kind)" and he had probably given it to Strato. "Well, he now knows and seems to be taking it well, but is he taking his injections? Peter Tourville's taking his. I'm taking mine."

Ill and distracted, Merrill went to Boston for three days to see Charles and Mary and read at Harvard, where he had a big audience with many friends, including Anne and David Ferry, Neil Rudenstine, Laurence Scott, Peter Gillis, and Frank Bidart. "Afterwards, at Apthorp House, I was swept up in a crowd of bright-eyed students—something that had never happened before." He returned to New York on Easter. There he saw Robert Isaacson and Louise Fitzhugh, went to a reading by Ashbery and Hollander, and prepared to leave for Madison. Hine would accompany him as far as Chicago. Together they sat through "16 hours of thruway and lots of lieder" in a rental car.

He didn't hear from Mouflouzélis again until the first week of April, when he received this letter:

> My Love, Hello—
>
> I am well and wish the same for you.
> My love, yesterday, March 30, Vaso gave birth to a very cute boy.
> My love, I am a little dizzy and sad at the same time, but it doesn't matter—everything will pass and I will again be the Stratos of before.
> My love, I am sorry for writing like this but I do not want to hide it from you. I am very sad because I am not working and I have no money. . . .
> This is my news, my love. I am sorry but I tell you again that I have no money at all and I ask you to please help me until I go to work because I don't know what to do.
> Nothing more to write. I kiss you, your boy always,
>
> Stratos
>
> P.S. My Jimmy, write soon if I can have the money or not, OK?

Merrill arrived in Madison in heavy rain on April Fool's Day and immediately got a parking ticket. Into his glum, ordinary hotel room he brought his typewriter, books of poetry by Stevens, Browning, Bishop, and A. D. Hope (a new enthusiasm), a phonograph, and a few records—*Tristan*, Verdi's *Nabucco*, Bach. He'd been invited to teach at the University of Wisconsin by John Enck, an English professor and Stevens scholar Merrill had met when he gave a reading at the university in 1963; but Enck had died, and Merrill knew no one else on the faculty. He was ready to be lonely.

When Stephen Yenser came to the first class, he was surprised: the man at the head of the class, thin and neat, with short brown hair, in jeans and a long-sleeved shirt, seemed so young. Judith Moffett and David Keller, who, like Yenser, were graduate students, waited for another student on their way into class. "Where is she?" Keller grumbled. "Probably primping," said Moffett. "Well, that won't do her any good," Keller replied. Moffett's ears pricked up: who was this new teacher not to be swayed by lipstick and hairspray? Merrill read the roll in a hushed voice, appearing "a little flustered and uneasy." Most of the sixteen students were undergraduates. Merrill smoked in class: he let his cigarette holder droop from a languid wrist, then puffed through pursed lips. "None of us had ever seen something like this," Moffett recalled, speaking for her earnest fellow classmates. His first sentence, diffident and authoritative, stuck in her memory: "I don't know that we need necessarily wonder what poetry is." (When she quoted it back to him later, he sighed: "Oh dear, lots of helping verbs.") Yenser noted another remark Merrill made in that first class: "I don't care if you become poets. What you do with your loneliness is your own concern." Poetry was simply what he did with his.

It had been eleven years since Merrill taught his last lesson at Amherst. On that first day, he asked the class, "Who knows poems by heart?" No one volunteered to recite; so Merrill did, declaiming Edith Sitwell's "Don Pasquito's Tango" from *Façade*, as he had at the "Proust Party" in 1947. *Façade*, he told the class, is "a minor delight," as opposed to "a great work" such as *The Waste Land*, also from 1922. Class time centered not on student poems, but on published poems Merrill admired. In his notebook he made a list of poems to teach: "The Flower" by Herbert, "Ah! Sun-Flower" by Blake, Byron's *Don Juan*, "Sailing to Byzantium" by Yeats, Keats's "To Autumn," Stevens's *Notes Toward a Supreme Fiction*, "The Relique" by Donne. He put a question mark by Frost's "Stopping by Woods." The only contemporary poem included was "The Shampoo" by Bishop, from her recent *Questions of Travel*. The class discussed that book carefully as well as poems by Lowell, Snodgrass, and John Berryman (Moffett: "I remember him reading lines for 'Mr. Bones' with great relish"). They read Edward FitzGerald's translation of *The Rubáiyát of Omar Khayyam*—which was, at the moment, his favorite poem. Merrill saw *The Rubáiyát* as an "anonymous poem, really, where the language, the content, is drawn from a whole universe much older, say, than Greek mythology, a kind of Old Testament, as old as language itself."

Merrill's class notes concern aspects of artistic technique, broadly conceived. He found Gauguin lacking as a craftsman, in distinction to Manet, because "there is no spirit in his brush, in the way the paint is applied. The joy of workmanship made visible." Yet "[a] slap-dash quality that delights us in paintings may disturb us in poems." His example was a line from *Life Studies*: "They <u>blew</u> their tops and <u>beat</u> us black and <u>blue</u>" (Merrill quotes the line, with underlining, in his notebook). Lowell's technique was "buck-shot": "<u>sometimes</u> the pattern means something," and sometimes not. Merrill wanted more meaning, more conscious design. He also complained about Bob Dylan. Dylan's songs, he said, were the "hymns" of the day, consisting of "melodies and verse of mediocre workmanship that its public considers comforting + inspiring because it expresses already ingrained assumptions about life." He felt the need to defend iambic pentameter. "For Pound + Williams," he noted, quoting Pound, " 'To break the pentameter, that was the 1st heave.'—The pentameter, then, having been in everyone's ear. Now that it is in nobody's, or in very few ears, what? To re-establish it, make it audible? No other <u>meter</u> will quite do." He added as he looked at his notes, "though how on earth can I pretend to know <u>that</u>?"

He emphasized to his students the value of knowing a second language. "Poetry," he proposed, "is what is gained in translation." He brought to one class a recording of Robert Schumann's *Dichterliebe*, and played the setting of Heinrich Heine's "Ich Grolle Nicht," a lonely, lovelorn lyric if there ever was one. The assignment he gave his puzzled students was to translate Heine's poem into English in a form that could be sung to Schumann's music. The point was to look not for meaning, but for "the sound of meaning." Much of what he had to teach was communicated when Merrill met his students individually in the English Department or at a table in the student union, a lugubrious ratskeller selling cheap food and drinks with a view of the sailboats on Lake Mendota. Here he discussed their writing and sang their translations of "Ich Grolle Nicht," showing them what succeeded and what didn't.

After teaching, Merrill stood on the steps of Bascom Hall on a high hill in the center of the campus and looked down State Street toward the dome of the state capitol building, two miles away, "topped by a gilded figure known in all seriousness as Miss Forward." He walked home in that direction past used bookstores and student bars, the college-town haunts of this "Berkeley of the Midwest," as it was known, while chill spring winds gusted off the lakes on either side, before he reached his hotel room and fell "face-down on the Murphy bed." Evenings were empty time he filled with thoughts of Strato. "I feel <u>so</u> sad, <u>so</u> helpless + hopeless," he wrote to Mimi. Merrill saw that Mouflouzélis would not want to come to the U.S., now that his son was born. "And the other sad thing is to feel that I will be caring less + less with the passage of weeks + months." To keep his heart open, to remain passionate, Merrill was ready to abase himself. In Greek he wrote,

Strato, My Love:

Another solitary day. In the evening I went to the movies, had two or three drinks, and I am in my horrible room now, writing to you. To tell you what? Only this:

I love you. I will never have another dream in my life except this one—to have you with me, to somehow make a life together. I am not saying forever if you do not want it that way, but long enough to see how it will be, how it will pass, do you understand? I think of you one hour, five hours every day, and I go crazy not knowing how exactly you are, what you are thinking.

What is happening to me, I know very well. My hair is turning gray. But who cares? You tell me to wait. So I wait. Until when? Until what? You tell me. Tell me if it is worth waiting. I know nothing more, just that I love you and I want you with me. Do me the favor of calling Tony. Maybe he learned something from the embassy.

To bed now. I kiss you a thousand times.

T.

Merrill saw Hine in Chicago. There he spent a day with Jackson, who was on his way to see his family in Los Angeles. In Madison, Merrill was invited to "dreary" dinners by faculty. He gave a reading at the university, and other poets visited for readings, but he didn't enjoy these events. At a party for Robert Duncan, Merrill and Duncan, although they were friendly, mainly lingered at opposite ends of the room. When Allen Ginsberg came to read in May, Merrill went so far as to leave town, having discovered that he had a family obligation "in Green Bay with the children of some Jacksonville people—or are they grandchildren?" There were a pair of "vociferous" "Ginsbergites" in his class—Jeff Poniewaz and his partner Antler, as he called himself, who had met in San Francisco. Merrill argued with them about poetry, but he kept his cool and made lasting friends with both men, who went on writing poetry. Privately, he made gentle fun of some of his students (chubby Miss Art, for instance), but he liked the group, and he prized their seriousness. "It's rather touching, this reminder, after Greece, of a world in which sensitivity and intelligence are the important things." He "kept having crushes" on a few of them, but he and his class remained at a polite distance.

Judith Moffett was an exception. "Friday I'm going to a girl student's for dinner; it's come to that," Merrill joked with Kalstone about the first of three invitations to her apartment for dinner that term; "she is gentle + intelligent + terrifyingly unspoiled—doesn't even drink, I'm to bring my own, if I can't live without it." The friendship that began in class and developed over dinner was to be long-lived and, for Moffett, life-changing. She was twenty-four years old to Merrill's forty-one. Round glasses shielded her plain, honest face. Merrill told her she looked like the daughter of the farmer couple in Grant Wood's *American Gothic*. She had grown up in a working-class Baptist family in the Kentucky hills near the Ohio border, and had attended Hanover College, a Baptist school in Indiana. In college she left the church and wrote an "ethical thesis" defining her values, called "The Habit of Imagining." This thesis stressed the importance of imagining other people's points of view (she gave a copy of it to Merrill). Living out this idea, she was active in a civil rights group at Hanover. She helped a male friend in the group to come out, and she defended homosexuality in an essay that won a college ethics prize. To graduate study, she brought a strong moral idealism, sensitivity to the perspective of gay men, and an appetite for literature. She was in a position to be deeply affected by James Merrill.

His teaching "was a riveting experience," she found, "but not because he was a good teacher. He wasn't dynamic enough in the classroom; he wasn't putting out enough energy." What was "riveting" for Moffett was "the impact of his personality. He didn't explain poetry; he modeled it." He introduced her to poetry's richness of implied meaning. Dwelling in class on the pun in a line by Elizabeth Bishop—"We are driving to the interior"— Merrill showed her how a poem might say one thing and mean something further. "Things went Boom—Explode—Expand" as she learned to read poems through his eyes. Soon she found herself wanting to know more about his inner life, to drive to *his* interior. Thus her dinner invitations. But even when they met outside class, Merrill retained his artful, enigmatic façade.

"First impressions are always right," he told her. After one dinner, Moffett jotted down some of hers in a diary: "He's social, conversational, terribly charming, and I know that every second he's holding something, almost everything, back." The truth of his sexual preferences came to seem to her like the "something" that was "almost everything." What she craved wasn't simply confirmation that he was gay; she wanted Merrill to be open with her, to treat her as if she were someone like himself. Which he resisted. "I wanted to know him. He wanted not to be known," she summarized much later. "He wanted to be taken at face value. I wanted to rip off the mask."

As the phrase "girl student" suggests, Moffett's sex made Merrill uneasy; "terrifyingly unspoiled," she inspired in him a mixture of wariness, protectiveness, and, in his letters over the next year or more, some flirtatiousness. He remembered her kindness to him in this lonely period long after it was past—even if, in her own view, there was nothing very generous about their dinners tête-à-tête. "If I'd wanted to be nice to him, I would have invited a lot of people, but I wanted him all to myself."

On April 21, shocking news came from Greece. In anticipation of George Papandreou's victory and his return to power in upcoming elections, army officers who came to be known as "the Colonels" won control of the country in a sudden coup and declared martial law. "Various articles in the 1952 constitution guaranteeing human rights were suspended," the historian Richard Clogg reports, "special courts martial were set up, political parties dissolved and the right to strike abolished. Many thousands of people with a record of left wing political views or activity were rounded up and sent into exile in bleak camps on the islands." The outspoken Vassilikos was so obviously a candidate for detention that he was reported by *Le Monde* to be among those arrested, when in fact he and Mimi had been traveling outside the country at the time of the coup and so avoided capture. "The first telegram," Vassilikos explained, remembering that time, "was to Jimmy: I have not a penny, I told him." Merrill responded by promising him $3,000 from the Ingram Merrill Foundation, and a smaller sum if needed in the interim. "Oh Lord," he wrote to Mimi and Vassili, "I lie awake thinking of Greece. It is a knife in the heart."

He was speaking of the coup, but he could have been speaking of Strato. In late April, he and Mouflouzélis exchanged bitter, mutually accusing letters, concerning Strato's syphilis treatment and his continuing need for money. (They couldn't mention the coup, since Greek mail was censored.) Merrill asked Tony to help Strato with his application for a U.S. visa. The visa application, already protracted, was becoming a farce: Merrill used the process to test Strato's love, and Strato used it to keep Jimmy hoping.

In early May, Merrill spent five days in Berkeley. He read his poems at the University of California, saw Robin (now divorced from Betty), and strolled among the redwoods of Muir Woods with his sister Doris. He saw David, who took a train north from Los Angeles for his visit. He arrived back in Madison in time to hear Moffett sing in Bruckner's *Grosse Messe*. He brought gifts for her: *Water Street* and a recording of *Don Giovanni*. It wasn't quite true that he didn't wish to be known: he resisted being understood in Moffett's terms, perhaps, but he wanted her to understand him in his. Indeed, prompted by teaching, or prompting the wish to teach in the first place, was a new willingness in Merrill, even a need, to be understood by younger people. It showed in the friendships he developed that spring with Moffett and, more slowly in correspondence, with Stephen Yenser. To both Moffett and Yenser, Merrill would become a mentor, the wise older friend of a talented young writer. He had prepared for this role in his relationships with Robin and with Daryl Hine. He was comfortable in it, and he would find himself in it frequently from this time forward.

The wish to be understood, to define and share his tastes and beliefs, showed itself in an interview he did with Donald Sheehan, another graduate student in the class. Conducted in late May, just before he left Madison, this interview was Merrill's first effort in a literary genre he would make use of repeatedly. Interviews became the form for expressing literary ideas preferred by this poet deeply distrustful of ideas. Unlike a manifesto, the interview was unpretentious, casual; unlike an essay, it required no argument or evidence; and unlike a book review, it cast judgments as personal and provisional, open to revision at times in the interview itself. Also, an interview was a dialogue, a form of collaboration that allowed for some modest theatricality. Merrill could be cheeky, offhand, evasive, or funny, as he wished, as in real talk. Yet the talk wasn't real: though he and Sheehan began by taping a conversation, Merrill rewrote the text to make it seem more conversational, more lively. This was his practice in later interviews too—until he dispensed with the first stage and simply conducted his interviews on paper.

Invited by Sheehan to place himself among modern poets, Merrill distinguishes the voice he wants in his poetry from the "impersonal, oracular voices" of Pound and Eliot, whom he classes as (borrowing a distinction from A. D. Hope) "historians" and not "true poets." For examples of the latter, he turns to Stevens, whose work is "man-sized," and Bishop, whose "whole oeuvre is on the scale of a human life"—metaphors that imply that the poetry of Pound and Eliot is inflated. Pound, Merrill said, "tries to write like a god. Stevens and Miss Bishop merely write like angels." In this camp formulation, Merrill sides with the woman poet Bishop—who was a minor figure in 1967, admired by other poets but not at all widely read—and Stevens, treated here as a dandy, who "continues to persuade us of having had a private life, despite—or thanks to—all the bizarreness of his vocabulary and idiom." Merrill prizes "private life," the personal, in these evaluations, and yet he is also careful to make clear his difference from autobiographical poets like Lowell: "It seems to me that confessional poetry, to all but the very naïve reader or writer, is a literary convention like any other, the problem being to make it *sound* as if it were true."

Merrill's implication is that poetry is always a rhetorical act, and the best poetry will be that which is most aware of, and for that reason least taken in by, the power of its own rhetoric. "Anybody starting to write today," he reflects, "has at least ten kinds of poem, each different from the other, on which to pattern his own," and none of them has a privileged claim to truth—they are all styles. Hence the priority Merrill places on surface, manner, sound. "Words just aren't that meaningful in themselves," he says boldly. *"De la musique avant toute chose.* The best writers can usually be recognized by their rhythms. An act of Chekhov has a movement unlike anything in the world." This is Robert Frost's doctrine of "sentence-sounds," except it is Frost's idea carried to a further level, shorn of its association with a homey New England realism, and made explicitly theatrical.

In the interview, Merrill was refining ideas he had developed in class. Now he had to pack his bags and assign his grades. That, he told Yenser later, "wasn't hard. I gave an A to those people who loved poetry, a B to those people who loved themselves, and a C to those people who didn't love anything." Then he drove east alone.

Merrill returned to "7 whole days with maman in NY"—Mrs. Plummer's annual season of doctors, shopping, and Broadway shows. One afternoon while his mother was busy, Merrill visited Marianne Moore "for tea—a glass of cold water, rather." He listened as the eighty-year-old poet, surrounded by piles of books and assorted bibelots, talked for ninety minutes, her conversation "mostly (as with my grandmother at that age) bearing on her self-sufficiency of which she is understandably proud. [. . .] She keeps her hats in a bottom drawer, like pancakes."

Then Merrill reunited with Jackson in Stonington. David had found it "curiously helpful" "to be needed" by his family in Los Angeles—"[n]ot only needed but, in fact, kind of running the show." He came back to Water Street to spend three weeks "facing Creepyville all alone." Once Jimmy and "the Ladies" returned, David organized a party, then set off for Greece and

George. "Public opinion"—by which Merrill meant the opinion of Perényi and Stone—"has decided that D and I have 'split up'; this once I think I can keep from believing what others tell me." They hadn't split up, but they weren't seeing much of each other. Since they left Stonington for Athens in July 1965, two years earlier, they had seldom been together without George or Strato (three weeks during this overlap on Water Street), and they had often been apart. In a letter to Jimmy written after their one-day rendezvous in Chicago, David reflected, "I know I need you, and I think you need me. What is going on at such a distance in Strato's life, in George's life, you have said we can do nothing about. And what is going on in our lives is important." In fact it was "frightening" and "irresponsible," he thought, "to allow such unimaginative and young people" to control their happiness. But that was just what they were doing.

Mouflouzélis's letters to Merrill had become mere pleas for money; he needed it to pay for doctors, medicine, vitamins, food. Vaso and Strato each wrote to him to say that she needed money to go to Corfu for the summer with the baby; Vaso's implication was that, if Merrill paid her, she would make herself scarce in Athens. Merrill sent ten thousand drachma (about $350 in 1967). In June, Strato was arrested when he took a car that he was working on "for a test drive," and he sent Merrill the ticket: unless the court was paid, he would be locked up with no telling what consequences under martial law. When Merrill replied that the money he had already sent should be enough for this emergency, Strato said he needed another eight thousand drachma, and the money should be cabled to him. Merrill sent that money and more.

Mouflouzélis signed these letters coolly "regards" and "me, Strato." Merrill wrote to Parigory, "[W]hereas my whole day used to be illuminated when I found a letter from S. in the mail, the sight of one now strikes terror into my heart and I can hardly bear to open it. One came yesterday which I wish had never been written, with the result that there I was at four a.m. this morning, suddenly awake and weeping in the kitchen." Mouflouzélis's next letter, composed at the end of June, was addressed not to "Jimmy" or "Tzimmaki" but to "James." It enclosed a letter to Strato from Vaso on Corfu, reporting that she and the little boy had both contracted syphilis. Strato asked Merrill "to send me the money to go to Corfu and take Vaso and the baby to the hospital or bring them to a hospital here [. . .] you must not let them die from this damned disease. OK?" Jackson, who was back in Athens, saw all three members of the family and reported "that Madame V. and the Dauphin are healthy as pumpkins." Was the letter from Vaso to Strato a false alarm, or a ruse? Strato fell silent, "obviously at a loss for a fresh lever to push, his jackpot days being over."

From week to week that summer, as this unpleasant correspondence unfolded, Merrill postponed a decision about when to return to Greece and for how long. He was in a state of convalescence, of retreat. He continued to suffer from amoebic dysentery, which, he joked, was a sign of his refusal to admit that his affair with Strato had ended. Day after day, sunny haze shone on the sea. From the deck on Water Street, he looked out on "the harbor dotted with little sailboats blackened by the glare." The Stone Women invited him to resume their "4-times-a-week cooking and bridge duels." And he began again to spend long hours at his desk. He was "polishing things hastily flung on paper a year ago," including "To My Greek." He also began a longer poem about his opera-going, "Matinees." It was the first ambitious poem he'd undertaken since he completed *Nights and Days*; it employed the same verse form—stanzas made of linked sonnets with varying rhyme schemes—as "The Broken Home" had, and it picked up the autobiography begun in that poem. Opera, according to "Matinees," explained in his character "the destruction of what Henry James would have called the Moral Sense—through watching all those characters love and betray and kill and renounce and catch TB merely, as it now and then seemed, in order to have something beautiful to sing on the subject." As much as his parents' divorce, it was a key to the person he had become.

War shadowed his work on the poem. In June, Israel defeated Egypt, Jordan, and Syria with stunning force and quickness in the Six-Day War. Merrill, thinking of his visit with Marianne Moore, joked in a letter to Moffett, "Did you enjoy that little chamber war in the Middle East? I thought it had 'concentration and gusto'—two of the 3 things Miss Moore looks for in poetry (the third is humility)—and could well serve as an example to other wars in the present + future." To Mimi and Vassili, he commented on the war again, adding, with his mind half on Strato, "Other lessons can be learned from [Egyptian President] Nasser's resignation [after the war] and even more from the agony of the people he betrayed. I mean, I think again (as if I'd thought of anything else for the last year) of that in us which chooses betrayal, puts a wreath on its head, sits at its feet taking notes and never learning. Virtually <u>nobody</u> on earth wants a wise ruler—either for his country or his heart. Beckett is right. Plato is wrong."

Vietnam was further evidence of this principle. By 1967, the war had made itself felt even in the Enchanted Village. In July, flags flew at half-mast for Stonington's first casualty: John Ainsworth or "Tank," the crony of Joe Bruno and Peter Tourville's who had hung around 107 Water Street five years before as a member of their "Teenage Club." He had "married 3 days before being shipped to his death. Full military honors, Marine escorts. Poor Tank."

Many American poets wrote "antiwar" poems; Merrill did not. But the war weighed on him. In January 1968, he made this entry in his pocket-sized black notebook: "The war in '67–68: I outwardly did nothing. O Iscariot-like crime! The money aside, I feel uncertain of my connection with the human race, my right on those grounds, to protest. Not that the behavior of those I would protest against is conspicuously 'human'—yet it is. More so than writing verse." "I outwardly did nothing"—but inwardly? This notebook entry, displaying ethical doubts and political feeling that Merrill never showed in public, is evidence of inward struggle.* His self-accusing cry ("O Iscariot-like crime!") comes from "In Distrust of Merits," a poem written during World War II by Miss Moore, who vowed to "fight till I have conquered in myself what / causes war." (Her crime is not the same as his: she says, "I inwardly did nothing.") The war made Merrill doubt his humanity, as he often did. If his money set him apart from other people, so did the writing of verse. Even those he "would protest against" were more "human" than he.

"Matinées" wittily describes the growth of this singularity. In summer 1967, he drafted this piece of it:

> The soul, no doubt, is feminine,
> Does not forge swords or use them—or at worst
> Drives a dagger into its own breast.
> The soul enters smiling through the din
>
> Of a cheap dining room, a Marschallin
> All noble proud forebearance, dressed
> As one who means to love + suffer must:
> Her ostrich fan, her trailing ice-blue satin.

The soul Merrill pictures is more passive than pacifist, inclined to self-destructiveness rather than aggression. He calls it "feminine" because it is costumed as the aristocratic heroine in Strauss or Proust who exerts power through chilly, "ice-blue" elegance. This is not a conventional basis for human sympathy. "Matinées" argues, however, that opera's arch poses and exaggerated gestures reveal something basic about the common human condition. The published poem explains Merrill's remark about the Six-Day War:

---

* In the same notebook Merrill tries—and fails clumsily—to write a poem about the coup in Greece.

> We love the good, said Plato? He was wrong.
> We love as well the wicked and the weak.
> Flesh hugs its shaved plush. Twenty-four-hour-long
> Galas fill the hulk of the Comique.

This view of human nature is based on Merrill's knowledge of his own nature, of his desire not for "a wise ruler," but for someone weak and just possibly wicked. The flesh, he knows, settles into its red velvet seat, hugging its creature comforts, and ignores the threat of "bomb or heart attack," while the soul "is a brilliant hypochondriac," a diva who (in a grim send-up of a line from Yeats's "Sailing to Byzantium") "will cough blood and sing, and softer sing, / Drink poison" at center stage.

Yet, even if Beckett is right, Merrill returns to Strauss and the Marschallin as his model. She rescues herself from the destructive power of passion by means of a comic awareness of the roles people play, a knowledge that, in allowing her young love to take his leave, is generous and self-protecting. Thinking of her, Merrill formulated his ideal of personal relations for Moffett. She had written to him about her relationship with an older man and the scenes between them. "I have scenes myself," Merrill contributed. "hate getting angry, hate hurting people I love and who I know love me, yet it happens, I do it, they do it, and somehow the horrified heart accommodates the memory of those hardly believable instants." The matter of their difference in age Merrill understood too. Without mentioning Strato, he proposes that "human character" has "a comic structure": "All I know is that when one takes people very seriously indeed one either hurts them, or is hurt by them, or both. My ethics in this respect were formed by Lotte Lehmann in Rosenkavalier, Act I—'Light must we be, light-hearted and light-handed. . .' "

Lehmann's Marschallin gives voice to Merrill's distinctive version of the calculated, willed lightness of feeling that is a familiar gay style from *The Importance of Being Earnest* to the work of contemporaries as different from Merrill (and each other) as Andy Warhol and Joe Brainard. Merrill shares with these and other male homosexual sensibilities, as if by kind, a capacity to wish away tragedy while remaining aware of the limits of wishfulness. The bitter truths of "Matinées" are framed by opening and closing sonnets that depict the poet's first visit to the opera, including Merrill's pastiche of his younger self's thank-you note to his host, Mrs. Livingstone (a half-serious tribute to the Southampton matron who welcomed Hellen in her house after her divorce). Those framing sonnets miniaturize the opera's outsized passions. The performances in question are matinées, after all, from which the audience emerges in daylight. The poem's "light-handed" idiom is not made for expressing desire, but for pondering it at a distance on the phone or in letters, when "it seems / Kinder to remember than to play." The addressee is not a lover but a friend, David Kalstone, the poem's dedicatee, the "Caro" to whom Merrill was making calls and writing letters throughout the summer. In the ruins of his affair with Strato, with Jackson an ocean away, Kalstone (and the kind of friendship he represented) was becoming more and more important to the poet—and the person—Merrill wanted to be.

Apart from Kalstone, Merrill spent his time with women friends. He saw Louise Fitzhugh in Southampton in July. He returned there two weeks later to see Doris, and he met Sewelly Jackson in New York. In Stonington, he spent most evenings with Perényi and Stone. One night Eleanor and he smoked pot, while Grace egged them on. But there were limits on what he could do or say in their presence. When Alan Ansen appeared from Athens on a rare trip to the U.S., Merrill made sure they didn't meet him. He didn't discuss his relationship with Strato in the presence of the Stone Women, and he was angry with Mimi and Vassili for gossiping about Strato when they saw "the Ladies" that spring in Rome. But to be with people with whom he could not talk about Strato was at the moment an advantage.

In Stonington, he liked to say, "the tedium is the message" (Marshall McLuhan's watchword about "the medium" was in the air that summer). But by August, manners were wearing thin, as Eleanor attacked her neighbor, old Admiral Wright, for his position on Vietnam, and Grace complained about Isabel's mounting bridge debts. It was time for a change of scene. So off they went, Eleanor, Grace, and Jimmy, to visit Mary McCarthy and Jim West in Castine, the pretty town on the Maine coast made famous in American poetry as the setting for Lowell's "Skunk Hour." McCarthy furnished picnics with champagne and caviar, lobster and chocolate cake, and indicated sites mentioned in Lowell's poem. The evenings they spent with Lowell and his wife, the writer and editor Elizabeth Hardwick.

Merrill had "prepared" for the visit "by rereading most of Jane Austen—so much helpfuller than E. Post as a guide to manners," but Lowell "intimidates," he found, as much in person as on the page. Lowell's moral gravity, his public voice, his knowledge of the classics and philosophy, his academic connections, and his image as the heir of Pound and Eliot—Merrill was put off by all of that. For his part, Lowell never regarded Merrill as anything more formidable than the clever young author of *First Poems*, and he may have conveyed as much in Castine. "There are some topics," Merrill sighed, "like Latin poetry and International Affairs, that even Jane Austen doesn't equip one to deal with."

McCarthy got up at dawn before they left in order to bake blueberry muffins for their long drive. Once back in Connecticut, Mrs. Stone, singing McCarthy's praises, was heard to say repeatedly "how charming + stimulating was our hostess, how superior her meals to the garbage served in houses here, etc.," Merrill observed. Finally, Robert Morse put a stop to it by greeting her: "Hail Grace, full of Mary!" It was "the season's single clever remark."

Merrill was prepared to face Greece again. In September, he took up his place in the comedy that was daily life at Athinaion Efivon 44. He set the scene in a letter to Moffett: "David has a grippe, thunderheads are piling up, and sixteen people are coming for drinks. Mme. Kleo, hair dyed maroon, is moaning and making her delicious little meatballs in the kitchen. [. . .] I've been here only ten days, it seems forever. Acquaintances—friends—people (who are they really?) drop in unexpectedly for a cognac or a game of cards or backgammon. The telephone, in constant use, is nevertheless all but buried in a glistening web of prevarication. All so familiar, so strange." He came back, Perényi had told him, only in order "to have one of those disastrous conversations designed to convince somebody of the comparative fineness of your behavior." But when Strato, Vaso, and six-month-old Vassili appeared, and a chance for such a display arose, the visit passed "in a blaze of smalltalk." "There is no superficial ill-will on either side," Jimmy told Kalstone, "and I feel quite happy about the situation, I mean about its being over, the worst of it." Yet not everything was over: Strato's application for an American visa was still pending, and Merrill still hoped he would get it and use it to visit him. In his notebook, he wrote, "Nothing lasts and nothing ends."

Kostas Tympakianákis kept up his spirits. Merrill had met Tympakianákis after the trip to Isfahan in 1966. Now he came from Crete bringing "the prettiest little gold ring made by himself—with my initials (I.M., that is—a ring suitable even for Foundation meetings) in gold on an oval field of jet, and his initials discreetly stippled to one side. Bringing as well undying devotion, the wish to care for me for ever + ever, and a need no sooner expressed than satisfied for upwards of $200. 'You'll see when I get to America how I'll go to work—you won't ever have to write another poem, I promise you.' " Merrill joked that it would end up being Kostas, not Strato, who got a visa and came to the U.S. to be with him.

Tympakianákis, in his early twenties, was short, swarthy, strong—a wrestler and a soccer player; he had served in the special forces of the Greek navy, having trained in Florida as an expert in underwater demolition, and he taught self-defense at the Army War College. If Strato was tough, Kostas was tougher, and less amusing. But he still had stories to tell, and Merrill put some of them into a poem. In "Kostas Tympakianákis," in crisp rhymed couplets, Kostas speaks of his brother murdered in the Greek Civil War (the recently exhumed bones rode in Merrill's car), his training as a welder ("I worked without a mask in a cold rain of sparks / That fell on you and burned—look, you can still see the marks"), his temper (typical of the people of Crete, which is known for its blood feuds), and his bad luck in love ("The girl I loved left me for a Rhodiot. / I should be broken-hearted but it's strange, I'm not").

In October, Merrill saw Tympakianákis in his native village in the hills above Knossos, the archeological site near Heraklion. To forestall gossip, Tympakianákis introduced Jimmy as the brother of his invented fiancée, "Monica," who was said to work in the U.S. embassy in Athens. One night they set out for a local *panegyri* with Jimmy on the back of Kostas's Vespa, until the machine gave out and they had to push it. At the festival there were ringing bouzoukis and dancing. While Kostas danced a *zembekiko*, he took exception to someone's remark (did it have to do with his fiancée's brother?), and a fight erupted in which he knocked out his challengers. "Jimmy was impressed with my strength," Tympakianákis recalled. He may have been frightened by it as well. "Strato is strong too, Kostas, but he doesn't beat people up," Jimmy told him. Nonetheless, Merrill left having promoted the idea that Kostas might someday marry his Monica and return with her to the U.S.

Back in Athens, Merrill and Jackson confronted a worrying illness: Maria Mitsotáki had been diagnosed with cancer. Jackson wrote to Merrill in early August, "Maria suffers constantly, everyone is now urging her to try some Paris doctors. She is uncomplaining, forbids talk on the subject, but keeps canceling out on engagements, and confessed to me, at lunch 3 weeks ago, that she almost threw herself out her window one night." By October, she had finished "her third course of cobalt rays." Merrill found her "charm + control" "positively terrifying."

There were tensions at Athinaion Efivon 44. "Jimmy has dashed out, muttering," David wrote to Eleanor. "He goes right on 'getting things done' and making lists and being furious at my complete disorganization." Over the years, Lazaretos remembered Merrill and Jackson shouting at each other in the house, Jimmy on the ground floor, David on the floor above, and George going back and forth between them "like a referee." "Jimmy gave David a hard time—but it was David's fault," he said, referring to his friend's laziness and sloppiness. In this case, though, they may have been arguing about the referee. "Because I've left Greece after and returned before, or because rather than being promiscuous there I've had George as a fixation—is that how I've made you unhappy? If you were with Strato," Jackson wrote to Merrill later, sympathetically imagining the situation reversed, "I think I would be finally lonely and resentful and probably say the things you say and [in] the way you say them." The things he said? Jackson quoted phrases that Merrill had applied to him: " 'going down the drain,' 'paying for everyone's happiness,' 'clinging to an illusion of work.' " These were things Merrill had said to him before. Now he objected that David had developed "a mania involving G's entire family. . . . It is sad + scarey both." Jackson, always anxious to make peace in his own family, was becoming highly involved in George's. Like an official spouse, he began to appear at Lazaretos family gatherings—weddings, christenings, name-day celebrations; and these obligations multiplied as George's seven brothers and sisters married and had children of their own. "My misery loves company," Jackson wrote to Merrill, adding, "Yours seems to me to feed on itself."

Before he left for Greece, Merrill had accepted engagements that would require him to return home just a month after arriving. He went back by way of Paris to see Mimi and Vassili in their new life as political exiles. They introduced Merrill to Parisian literary society: "[T]hey have produced Marguerite Duras + Italo Calvino for me—Calvino's novels in English are absolutely enchanting—and I have produced Mary McCarthy (my dog-eared drawing card) for them." There was more reciprocity. Mimi, in return for the Pucci dress that Merrill bought for her in Rome, "marched me into Cardin and bought me a wild sweater covered with outsize, offcenter zippers."

When, a few days later, Merrill greeted his mother in that sweater in New York, Hellen Plummer "looked startled for a moment but was soon overcome by its beautiful lines and its sentimental associations." In the city Jimmy saw Donald Richie, who joined him for a few days in Stonington. Jackson arrived on November 1, but stayed only briefly; his older brother Jojo, George Jackson Jr., had died suddenly of a heart attack, and David was traveling to be with his family. "Here," Merrill wrote to Moffett after he left, "it is the deserted village with a vengeance. After her biannual 'ghastly scene' with Eleanor, Grace has packed her bags and left for the city, more like an outraged mistress than a mother. The leaves, too, have mostly fallen—fine views of blue water in all directions."

In November, Merrill flew to Chicago to take part in "Poetry Day," a festival organized by *Poetry* magazine. He stayed with Hine in Evanston. A group of students from Madison, including Yenser and Donald Sheehan, drove down, and Merrill cooked for them roast lamb and kasha, "washed down by something called Chateau de Baby." In December, he gave readings at the University of Virginia, in New York at the 92nd Street YMHA, and at Princeton. As usual, he tallied his income from poetry for the year at the back of his notebook: $4,538. It was the most money he had ever earned as a writer. He was invited to receive an honorary degree from his alma mater. Bard's offer he had declined, but Amherst's he accepted. It would be the third honorary degree from Amherst in the family, Charlie Merrill having received two. Amherst now inquired about his papers for the college library and learned that Washington University already had them.

Jimmy kept up "floods of correspondence in Greek." This included not only his own letters to Kostas and his mother, but also those of his supposed sister, Monica—but Monica's memory of the Greek language was "disintegrating" so fast that "most of the time now she simply lets me send a few affectionate messages." In another case of double correspondence, he wrote letters to Strato at home, "where Vaso and the baby and the dog" could read them, and other letters to Strato in care of Tony at his shop. But both sets of letters trailed off. When Strato wrote wondering why, Jimmy explained that he had become "afraid" of Strato. "I realized that you had the power to ruin my life, and understood that I must save myself. There is something that I love not more than you, but that I believe in more, and that is my work—poetry. If I am away from you now it is on purpose, to save myself, to let work save me. But I am not saved yet. I still love you. I still talk to you for hours at night in my bed. But now that you are not beside me, it is all a fantasy."

Jackson returned on December 17, back from his trip west. Merrill gave him a TV for Christmas "in hopes that it will hook him into sitting stupefied before it until summer comes and we can go" back to Greece together. David, however, was too involved with George to wait that long; he would return to Greece in late February. He and Jimmy celebrated their reunion that winter by getting out the Ouija board. Ephraim spoke of Merrill's mind "flickering out in great gusts of self-pity." In the morning on December 23, with snow falling steadily on the Connecticut shore, Merrill wrote in his notebook,

> I woke today hot, dry, tingling with anger from last night's arguments. . . .
> I cannot work. An ambiguous rage with D. consumes me. I want to tell him: out, get out. I dream of hurting him inexcusably—of getting George on my side. He complains that

I am jealous of George. The truth is that I am jealous of D. himself who has found "what we all want": loyal, loving George who
has a brain + will never get fat.

There I paused + began to think of S., improvising as usual
a letter to him. A letter, this time, of rejection, not of longing.
I imagined seeing him after months of estrangement and at
the door, after a pointless hour of small talk, putting my arms
round him + sobbing. I was at once in tears myself—at 9:20 a.m.
at my desk. I can hardly see to write for them.

The next month, Merrill wrote that letter of rejection. Mouflouzélis's
letters had become increasingly sour and manipulative. He would continue to do what was required to obtain his visa as long as Merrill "remembered" him, which meant sending money—for the Christmas holidays, for
his license to drive a taxi, for young Vassili, who suffered, it seemed, from
severe bronchitis. Strato said his son might die if Jimmy didn't save him.
Merrill fired back, "Don't tell me that the doctors and the hospitals would
let a little child die because the father has no money for medicine. You are
right. How do you expect me to believe you, Strato?" Mouflouzélis was "very
angry" at this challenge; he would write no more letters to Merrill, he said.
Yet he dangled the prospect of the visa: "Before I completely leave you with
no more letters, I want you to know that I received more paperwork from
the Embassy which I will burn today. I will harden my heart and say: Strato,
as of today you are completely alone in life." This was too much. "Burn the
Embassy papers," Merrill scoffed. "They wrote to me too and I know what
they have to say. Time has passed and the visa application is out of date.
[. . .] So, this story is over, finito. We will sleep easier now, without dreams.
Goodbye my dear boy. I bless you and I kiss you on the mouth, on the eyes,
and with a last kiss on the forehead I leave you.—Tzimmi"

Rare cold left Stonington Harbor frozen solid; the village was ice-bound.
At his desk, Merrill found that the deep freeze was freeing him up. He went
back to an odd, unfinished poem in neat ballad stanzas. At the center of
it was a character made out of deep winter cold, an alter ego named Jack
Frost. The setting is an unnamed New England village. The town has trim
white Greek Revival homes, a Portuguese fishing fleet that has fallen on
hard times, and a clutch of summer residents. These include characters as
recognizable as the town: sharp-eyed, sharp-tongued Nora and her mother
Margaret, an older, genteel novelist, and Andrew, tippler, wit, and amateur musician, "Plus Andrew's Jane (she used a cane / And shook it at his

puns)"—all with sufficient money to do as they like. Their self-approving little society, faithful to the habits of the Surly Temple, is amusing and tedious both. Just as boredom and loneliness threaten to overwhelm them, into their midst comes Jack Frost, who buys the Baptist church, restores it as an extravagant "folly," and moves in with his big cat and a servant:

> "Proud Grimes, proud loyal kitty,"
> Jack said, "I love you best."
> Two golden eyes were trimmed to slits,
> Gorgeously unimpressed.
>
> Ken the Japanese "houseboy"
> (Though silver-haired and frail)
> Served many a curious hot hors d'oeuvre
> And icy cold cocktail.

Jack and these sidekicks are an immediate success. When he stays on into winter, his four new friends emulate him and stay on too, longer each year.

But even in their charmed circle time passes, and tender feeling fails. One January evening Jack nods off over drinks while Margaret is speaking, and mother and daughter, left alone for a moment, go at each other:

> "He's sound asleep," said Nora.
> "So clever of him. If
> Only I were! Your stories
> Bore everybody stiff."
>
> "What can she mean," said Margaret,
> "Speaking to me like that?"
> "I mean you're gaga, Mother."
> "And you, my child, are fat."

Jack loses interest in these people and goes abroad. The tale ends with Ken as a scapegoat: Nora stays on alone as fall comes, and finds the old man dead one morning from a fatal mix of alcohol and pills. She sees to Ken's burial in the absence of his employer:

> Jack sent a check weeks later
> And wrote them from Tibet
> A long sad charming letter,
> But friendship's sun had set.

"The Summer People" is a brilliant if brittle *jeu d'esprit* that reflects the literary thinking Merrill had done since returning to the U.S. in March 1967. Rather than the "erratic surfaces" of Pound, Williams, and their imitators, he had come "to hunger for precisely that balance and perspective which by nature imply a measure of banality in the treatment." The ballad stanzas of "The Summer People," as polite and trim as a Stonington street, all but enforced banality, if not balance and perspective. With the ballad, Merrill turned his back not only on the free verse of Beats like Ginsberg and "deep imagists" like Robert Bly, but also on the baroque collage forms of his own long poems, "The Thousand and Second Night" and "From the Cupola," which had been as innovative in their way as any postwar poems. "The Summer People," in contrast, displays virtuosity by severely constraining it, then insisting on its constraints for hundreds of lines. Merrill's models for his ballad included Auden's poems in popular song forms and Bishop's "The Burglar of Babylon," a ballad in *Questions of Travel*, the book Merrill had taken to Madison and dwelt on at length in class. His simplicity was arch, his naturalness richly affected. As one reader commented, with his approval, it is "as if Watteau had set out to paint a primitive." The poem's cleverly crafted quatrains are like the "pigeonholes" that the townspeople find themselves placed in—"Old Navy or Young Married, / The Bad Sports, the Good Souls"; they suggest a social grid to which even "the Amusing, / The Unconventional ones" must submit. The ballad stanzas make Merrill's summer people and their passions seem tiny and containable, boxed for exhibit in a gallery of types. At *The New Yorker*, Howard Moss rejected "The Summer People" as " 'slighter' than my 'masterpieces,'—as I would be the first to agree." "Slight" was just what it was meant to be.

"The result is my pride + joy," he wrote to Moffett about the poem. "I get up in the middle of the night and give it its bottle. It doesn't weigh much (and in terms of weight it will be an infant all its life) but its little eyelids and toenails are exquisitely complete, and it can already put its foot in its mouth." Just so. Merrill's baby, however "slight" and weightless, offended Perényi and Stone, who, unsurprisingly, were not charmed by Nora and Margaret, the hand-puppet figures that Merrill had made of them. Perényi, while claiming that "<u>she</u> thinks it is marvelous," assured Merrill, when she saw a draft of the poem that winter, that her mother would not feel the same way, and, as if to make sure, she wrote to notify Grace in Rome of what their friend had done. Merrill "received a sizzling reply" from Mrs. Stone: as he parroted it, "you realize this is the end. . . . how can one have orange hair unless it's dyed. . . . you have certainly treated your beloved Morses abominably. . . . I will never trust you again and, sadder yet, never trust anybody else."

Merrill took cover in the poem's innocent good fun: who could blame a baby for misbehaving? Besides, the poem was full of bits and pieces snipped from "life" (one of its mischievous effects is to make quotation marks necessary around that word). For instance, the ballad's donnée was a piece of local gossip. A New Yorker named Anne Fuller had renovated the Baptist church on the corner of Main and Church streets and been written up in a book of beautiful houses published by *Vogue*; her "houseboy," Botjo, died in the way Ken does in the poem.

Merrill made some mollifying revisions. Margaret's "angry-orange" hair was re-tinted (it had become "dawn-colored" by the time "The Summer People" was published). But the poem's caricature of the Stone Women remained: a mother and daughter helpless in the grip of passing time, mutually dependent, and ready to wound each other with words. It was an unforgivable portrait painted from close up by a privileged intimate. Stone told Merrill she would "never trust" him again—and, according to Perényi, she never did. But that must have been the point. Merrill used the ballad to push away the women upon whom he had depended since he returned from Greece in 1967; he was making them feel a little of what he'd been made to feel by Strato. For the moment, he too would never trust anybody again.

Although he minded displeasing them, he didn't mind enough to keep from reading the poem to friends, sending copies of it far and wide, and trying hard to publish it—which the *Atlantic Monthly* finally agreed to do. "It is less ethical to have pleased myself, yet better, surely, than to have pleased no one?" There was creative power in this selfishness; it was like the cool independence of the cat Grimes, or Jack Frost himself. When Ken asks permission to return to his village in his old age, Jack insists that he stay on for the time being; knowing just what he is denying to Ken, he begins to cry: "Jack's eyes were wet. Pride and regret / Burned in his heart all night." But he doesn't change his mind. Later, as he travels the world, set on showing the summer people how little they matter to him, Jack leaves Ken alone to die. Merrill doesn't forgive him for his heartlessness, but he doesn't blame him for it either.

Merrill's intensive work on "The Summer People" was "counterpointed by a hideous labor, that of correcting the atrocious English translation of the so called lyrical sections of Vassili's political novel," Z. The novel, a work at the farthest remove from the ballad, was based on the assassination of a Greek opposition leader; it would become an international success and the basis for an Oscar-winning movie directed by Constantin Costa-Gavras. Merrill put up with the task for two months, "bribed" by another Cardin sweater from Mimi, but he asked that his name be dropped from the

English edition's acknowledgments: "[W]hole sections of the book remain scandalously mediocre," he told Vassili bluntly, "and I just don't want the buck passed to me for them + their badness."

Elsewhere in the chilly house that winter, Jackson went back to writing fiction. "I'm a mass of nerves," he told Parigory. "I think it has to do with so many people, parents, Eleanor, JM, even my lit. agent turning appraising eyes on me as if I were going down some kind of drain; I feel I ought to look around for an organization designed for those hooked on foreign loves and countries: Lovers Anonymous. Might it exist?" He was making fiction out of his relationship with Lazaretos. As usual, he changed the sex of one of his characters to make the relationship he was writing about a heterosexual one, so as to make it palatable in a popular market. By late February he had finished, in Merrill's description, "a quite good, funny, scary story called COUP about a possessive American girl moving in on her Greek Navy boy friend and getting him as it were by the balls, just like the Colonels in April." Merrill sent it to a magazine editor he knew and, when it was returned, to another editor, again without success. He was still doing what he could to get David published.

Kalstone paid a winter visit to Water Street. Ashley Brown, a friend of Elizabeth Bishop's and a professor whom Merrill had met and liked at the University of Virginia, came one weekend to interview him. There was little social life. In February, Merrill and Jackson had dinner with a young painter, "very charming and handsome," named David McIntosh, who was staying in town. "His life is a great mystery," Merrill noted, intrigued. Three days later, Jackson set off alone for Greece. "Why are we so unhappy?" he asked, writing on shipboard on Jimmy's birthday. He had taken along a book by the popular psychologist Eric Berne: "*Games People Play* has not been my most favorite reading, my dear. There is really not <u>one</u> I've not played. I keep thinking what are the Final Games? And think of these two: What Shall We Do Today? and its answer: Where Has The Time Gone?"

In a letter of his own Merrill told Jackson to "see to <u>your happiness</u> as a responsibility, as your principal one." Merrill was determined to manage his own. He left Stonington on an eighteen-day trip south—to his mother and the "violent hospitality" of Atlanta, to the Morses in Jamaica, "where all roads lead to rum," and to Doris, recovering from surgery in Palm Beach. He had come through a low time. On his birthday in Jamaica, thinking back to Isfahan two years before, he sent Donald Richie a postcard of smiling islanders, one passing under the bar doing "The Limbo—Dance of the Tropics." On the back he wrote, "I feel cheerful + <u>free from Strato</u> at last."

11

DMc

1968–69

Letters from Yenser and Moffett were waiting when Merrill returned to Stonington from his trip south. Yenser had sent a "palm-sized, velvet-covered, dog-eared copy" of Edward FitzGerald's *Rubáiyát*. The gift prompted a thank-you note cast as one of FitzGerald's patented quatrains:

> Fortunate those who back from a brief trip
> To equinoctial storms and scholarship,
> Unwrap, first thing, a present from a friend,
> And into Omar's honeyed pages dip.

Moffett was harder to respond to. Merrill had sent her from Jamaica a postcard of pretty seashells. Alerted by him to double meanings, she read the image metaphorically and remarked on *his* "shell," the mask of manners behind which he hid. Merrill granted her point. "Do you suppose, though," he asked, "that you don't have a shell yourself?" He suggested that her demanding "ethics" of personal candor "hide you as much as they express you, that part of you sleeps behind them like Sleeping Beauty behind her hedges of thorn." She needed to relax and enjoy herself. He himself was

> someone who positively lives for pleasure. True, in my twenties
> I had little use for it, and even less use for people who weren't

> somehow serious, creative, intelligent, etc. [. . .] Now, to be
> sure, the only kind of person whom I will let teach me anything
> is apt to be somebody in the throes of a first incarnation, child-
> ish, instinctive . . . What I learn from such a figure I can't really
> say, but they correspond to a reverie (of democracy?) in which
> I am relieved from being the things I can't help but be. [. . .] I
> love to feel myself taken up into somebody else's fantasy (which
> itself, especially in these 1st incarnation types, is very apt to be
> a creation of my own). I think love begins with that widening of
> the imagination's pupil.

So much Strato had taught him. Being now in flight from him, Merrill
might have guessed that he was ready to want, as he had when he was young,
just the opposite type of person.

Even Stonington shook with the times. Eleanor took part in the campaign for Eugene McCarthy, the surprising "Peace" candidate for the Democratic Party's presidential nomination. "I'm not sure what a primary is,"
Merrill told Yenser, "but we're going to have one for the first time in our
local history." It was clear to him that the soft-spoken, poem-writing Wisconsin senator was "already doomed to lose out, like all the others admired
in the past by one's friends"—which he did in Stonington by seventy-one
votes. "I cannot very well make out the depths of feeling opened up by the
MLKing shooting," Merrill told Jackson after the murder of the civil rights
leader on April 4 and the riots that followed in cities throughout the U.S.
"Everyone is in terror—as if the end had come." By "everyone" he didn't only
mean the Plummers and his other southern relations. "Meredith [. . .] said
he could easily foresee the sacking + burning of our own Water St. Com-
parisons with the French Revolution were seriously invoked." "It's amazing
how frightened people are. Irma Brandeis wrote, 'The sky is falling.' "

A world away in Athens, Jackson was caught up in a purely personal crisis:
"My Lord, How I need you here. Life is breaking apart and I seem to spend
nights ripping down what I try to repair in the morning." Jackson was more
than ever painfully jealous of Lazaretos. He knew he was being irrational:
"I slowly realize how alike is my fear of airoplaines [sic] and my jealousy;
pride trying to avert a fall." George seemed to him "if not alcoholic at least a
determined escapist drinker," which could have been said of David as well.
Drinking was a bond for them, but it separated them too, fueling George's
sullenness and David's suspicions. In his own pithy assessment, Jackson's
Athens life added up to "[n]ot enough to do, but too much of too little."

Then, on April 17, Merrill fell in love again. It happened as abruptly as
that. That evening he made dinner for David McIntosh, the painter he had

met in February, and the occasion "ended in an embrace of sorts." The next day he gave McIntosh a present: a fourth- or fifth-century Tanagra vase, a Greek treasure small enough to fit in the palm of the hand, and inscribed in ink in a tiny, steady, almost secret script:

> Some mornings in the heart an old
> Earthen vessel turns to gold.
> > > David from James
> > > 18.iv.68

Two days later Merrill assured him that "[n]othing I say will need answering," but he bared his heart in a way that begged for response:

> There is a tale of Hofmannsthal* [. . .] whose young + fastidious hero becomes touched, then absorbed, then mysteriously destroyed by the world of his servants which opens up for him vistas of meanness and brutality whose perfect commonness is what strikes him as unutterably rich + strange. It has been to some little extent my story, these last years—but I am luckier, as well as older, than the young man; and I have survived the story, the sun pours in to tell me so, or when I look away, your face does, and the few things you have said to me. If I were twenty years younger, I would say to you, 'My life is in your hands'—but it isn't, thank goodness, it's in my own hands, where it belongs, and I should never have understood this so piercingly without your gift to me.

He broke off after a page. When he resumed, he had qualms, or felt he should have them:

> Perhaps I must qualify what I wrote 2 days ago, about your not needing to answer any of this, and ask you to tell me if I ought not—either for your own good or for what you, in your sweetness, may already have imagined as mine—ought not to be falling in love with you.

Merrill sketched a portrait of this young man for Richie: "a quiet, private, proud person, also immensely generous + responsive; 30 years old;

---

* JM refers to Hugo von Hofmannsthal's enigmatic short story "Das Märchen der 672. Nacht."

he has been around a bit—a year on some student exchange program in Japan; a winter in Spain; a 'season' in Venice; he is wonderful looking, tall + romantic, with dark hair very thick, and blue eyes set in a face that tends to be the flushed roseate mauve of Albertine's; he is ⅛ Sioux; he knows too many people of a certain sort, like Sam Barber [. . .] (or me!), but seems not to have been nicked + chipped by them; he seems to understand very clearly that his work + his privacy come first." McIntosh, who always called him "James," not "Jimmy," was the type of "serious, creative, intelligent" man Merrill had stopped desiring long ago.

He'd grown up as the only son with two sisters in a family living in Wyoming, near the Montana border. His father was a rancher and saddle maker, his mother a schoolteacher. He was not "⅛ Sioux," but as a child he had spent summers on his grandfather's ranch near Crow and Cheyenne land, and he had developed a sympathy with Native American life. It was a natural extension of his feeling for the western landscape, which he began painting early. Tutored by a Dutch watercolorist, he won a scholarship in art to Stanford. His work was influenced by West Coast abstract expressionism, and by the art he discovered on a fellowship year in Japan, especially sumi-e painting, with its concise, calligraphic renderings of objects and landscapes. After he graduated from Stanford in 1962, he visited Taos and Santa Fe. He was captivated by "the feeling of the air, the imprint of one civilization on another," and he stayed on, trying to distill, in painting, "a sense of the place, its shapes, and the emotions it stirs." At ease with people of another generation, he made friends with some of the area's old hands, including Merrill's friends Witter Bynner and Mary Lou Aswell. He moved east temporarily while preparing for an exhibition of his work in New York in 1968, was drawn to the Connecticut coast, and found a one-room apartment in Stonington. There he met Rollie McKenna—who introduced him to Merrill.

In that first letter to McIntosh, Merrill enclosed a new poem, a brief lyric in which, like an overwhelming passion, a spring storm takes possession of the poet's house. "Another April" appeared four years later in *Braving the Elements*:

> The panes flash, tremble with your ghostly passage
> Through them, an x-ray sheerness billowing, and I have risen
> But cannot speak, remembering only that one was meant
> To rise and not to speak. Young storm, this house is yours.
> Let your eye darken, your rain come, the candle reeling
> Deep in what still reflects control itself and me.

Daybreak's great gray rust-veined irises humble and proud
Along your path will have laid their foreheads in the dust.

These long lines, with their surging syntax and erotic intensity, were a long way from the cramped ballad stanzas and caustic wit of "The Summer People." Candles, flowers, silence, and the ambiguous power of the elements—these motifs would return in the poems Merrill wrote under the influence of his feelings for McIntosh.

Merrill would have to wait for the reserved McIntosh to respond to his wooing. Yet renewal seemed possible to him now, in body and mind. After a warning about his high cholesterol on a visit to a doctor in Atlanta, Jimmy had submitted to "a real old-fashioned regime"; by May, down to 130 pounds, he'd recovered "the body of a boy." Around the same time, he began weekly meetings with a research psychiatrist at Yale. In a reversal of the usual relation, Dr. Albert Rothenberg came to see Merrill, who'd agreed to serve as a case study in Rothenberg's work on creativity (Rothenberg even offered to pay *him*). Merrill showed him work in progress and replied to Rothenberg's questions and prompts. These sessions took place in the living room at 107 Water Street. Merrill was not a patient; Rothenberg was guided by "a detailed research protocol" that he used on several hundred other "highly creative individuals." Initially, Merrill was not impressed with his interlocutor ("I don't think he's too bright"), but that hardly mattered in this case: the doctor had his agenda, and the poet had his. "As I hoped it might before I agreed to see him," he explained to Jackson,

> it involves my talking very frankly to him—with the result that my constant refrain over the past year or two, 'I can't face what I'm doing,' is a degree or so less true than it was when you left. It leaves me trembling to suspect what pressures kept me from peeking below the surfaces—but things are flowing for the moment, and the spring, [. . .] with all its green traceries and strengthening lights, advances and makes me happy and sad at once.

More welcome attention came from Yenser, who wrote in detail about "The Summer People," unbiased by knowledge of the poem's sources in life, and sensitive to its dense punning. Merrill soaked up Yenser's comments and questions: another collaboration was shaping up.

The New England spring, he told Yenser, sounding the regeneration theme, "is amazing. [. . .] Eleanor/Nora's garden is full of black tulips, bleeding-heart, lilac, thick little stunted Italian daisies—all against trees, some blossoming, some still bare + pruned, and white clapboard surfaces." These flowers, as in the first song in Schumann's *Dichterliebe*, spoke to Merrill of his brand-new beloved. Alone or with friends, he listened to Schumann's lieder and Mahler's *Das Lied von der Erde*. The ravishing male and female voices in these works scored his by now interior conversations with McIntosh, who'd returned to the Southwest in May. Merrill proposed that he delay a planned trip to Greece in order to spend a week with McIntosh. At first, there was no reply; then McIntosh called, suggesting that they meet in Denver. Relieved, Merrill began to write long letters to him every day.

Unlike Strato, McIntosh was an artist. Unlike David Jackson, he had a strong sense of discipline and devotion to his work, and he'd had some success with it, too. Merrill described his attraction to McIntosh's work: "It has to do with your choice [. . .] of images that allow, as it were, at the center of the canvas some live & energetic emptiness—felt not as a lack but as a virtue—like a spirit rightly unidentifiable within its sensual perimeter: your wave, your dustcloud, your blank blue sky that already has partly dissolved the window it is seen through—as in a line of Stevens, 'Eye without lid, mind without any dream' or like a mirror not at the moment being looked into; the Subject treated as the final absence of a subject," a vaguely Mallarméan ideal. McIntosh's paintings reminded him of "poems I wrote 10 or 12 years ago" in which he'd engaged in "an intense play of language on a level at which the 'subject' is, strictly speaking, immaterial." McIntosh's paintings were small, the palette subdued, and the images abstract, although they suggested recognizable shapes, often fragments of landscape. Merrill compared them to mandalas: designs that represent spiritual gates or doors in Buddhist meditation. The painting from the New York show that Merrill bought is an example: in the center of a wash of earth tones is an enigmatic whirlwind, a "live and energetic emptiness." It's an image, McIntosh later commented, that "some people find threatening." It evokes a certain "vitality" with which he tried to identify as he painted—"a being" that is "primal and visceral" and difficult to put into words.

While McIntosh's art reminded Merrill of an earlier stage in his own development, he perceived in it the basis of new poems, even a new style. The "young storm" in "Another April" is not only an image of his rush of feeling for a new person in his life; it is also an image of the elemental "vitality" that McIntosh courted in his work. "What I could learn from you," Merrill told the painter, "seems endlessly rich & real. What you might learn from me, I can't imagine—I am something of a waterbug, skating upon the depths—but love does learn & love does teach, and love supplies even the most ordinary person with a wizard's hat & wand, and these lessons are not found in books."

The artistry Merrill admired in McIntosh involved "secrecy," and he was secretive about their relationship. He told Jackson that he would be coming to Greece later than expected without saying why: "<u>Dear</u> David, I fear this will upset + depress you. Don't let it. I am rooting for you from afar."

The waterbug skated on. In New York, he met with the Little Players, lunched with the Lavins, cooked a cheese soufflé for Robert Isaacson, visited Sewelly, and discussed his contributions to an anthology of Brazilian poetry in translation with the editor. Making her annual visit to New York, Hellen Plummer accompanied her son to *Hair*, the Broadway musical, then on its first run; during "the famous nude scene," the cast "all held <u>very still</u>, facing the public, for perhaps 15 seconds, then a merciful blackout during which we all wiped our eyes + chins. My poor mother, while not shocked, on the conscious level, + indeed enjoying it, developed a sick headache + was throwing up for an hour after we got home." Back on her feet, she went with him to Stonington and then to Amherst, where she saw him receive his honorary degree.

Merrill met McIntosh in Denver on June 8. They drove into Wyoming and Grand Teton National Park. "Lunch on a snowy mountainside, a marmot," Merrill notes in the log he kept of these days. They chose a cabin in the little town of Kelly, near Jackson: "Total joy." The diary continues,

TUES. 11
Day's excursion to Yellowstone. Picnic by a small private hot spring. Back in cabin by 6. French potroast + carrots. Long walk beforehand. Ticks!

WED. 12
D. goes out to paint + I stay in writing. Lunch in, then to Jackson. Belt to saddler's. Vain telephoning HIP. Ski lift. Dinner: salmon loaf, tomatoes.

THURS. 13
Picnic in Teton Park above Jenny Lake. A she-moose + several deer. Cold but lovely. D. paints + I write in afternoon. Dinner: spinach + potato soup, trout amandine, baked bananas.

And so the week continued. A round of work, walks, and delectable dinners: it was a companionable routine, haloed in privacy, with an enchanted wilderness for backdrop. There was no mention of love or love-making, though, in Merrill's diary. Were they lovers? Did it matter? On Monday morning, June 17, McIntosh left him at the small airport in Jackson with the promise, "James, I'll see you in October." The poet felt "healed, invulnerable, full of purpose + joy."

From Stonington the next day, Merrill wrote to Jackson, and told the story of the past nine days, adding, "I continue to feel right + happy about it—up to the point of realizing that it is the first thing in all these years that I had consciously kept from you; so that I suppose if you want to be angry or hurt about that, you will be entitled to do so."

Jimmy referred to McIntosh as "DMc" (pronounced "Dee-Mac") partly to plant him cozily in his life and partly to distinguish from the Davids, DJ and DK, already there. "He is not looking for a lover," Merrill reassured Jackson, "and neither, really, am I." But what, then, was Merrill looking for? He wrote to McIntosh,

> Whatever happens, whatever happens—the time with you will have been the stroke of a wand, an awakening in Circe's palace to find hands + feet once more instead of hooves or paws, and sea + wind + sun outside the gates. One spell yields only to another, but this is a good spell, a sunny spell that puts wind in my sails and in yours too I hope. [. . .] I talk of love, you talk of friendship—we're both as wrong as we are right.

McIntosh, however, had thus far drawn a "firm and gentle line" between love and friendship, and what he wanted was the latter.

Merrill attended *The Marriage of Figaro* at the Met, then got on a plane for Greece—where he would try to keep Mozart's opera in mind as a guide to behavior:

> It keeps dawning on you with surprise that several characters in that opera are, at given moments, quite acutely suffering, but the merest hint of a budding intrigue, a trick to play, change of clothing or whatever, and they rise out of their doldrums into the most shimmering vivacity, thus fully deserving the happy endings that befall them. One might hope, once or twice a day, to attain something of the sort in this theatre of a household with its scenes, comings-and-goings, trios, quartets.

The Athens cast was familiar: David and George, Tony, Kostas from Crete, Strato's brother Kostas, Bernie Winebaum, and Alan Ansen. The scent of Kleo's *keftedes* rising from the kitchen, the clink of drinks, a soccer match on the radio, and cries around the backgammon board completed the scene—until the doorbell rang and more characters, Robin and Steven Magowan, Robin's brother, walked onto the stage, the twenty-two-year-old Steven with "a literal SHOCK of hair dyed a terrible cold Auburn" and Robin lugging the bouzouki he was learning to play. All but Merrill would be up late.

The next day, Robin, who'd slept in the laundry room on the roof, found his uncle at work on the ground floor. "But how can you do any work in this room," he said, "you should move up to the top of the house!" He was right, and Jimmy moved his papers and typewriter directly. There had never been a good place for him to write in the house; Stonington had been where he went when he worked hard. The new arrangement allowed him new privacy. His garret was small and tiled, with peeling white walls, a flight away from the rest of the household and the telephone and two flights from the doorbell. The little room connected to the kitchen on the ground floor by an exterior spiral iron staircase, so Merrill could get up early, make tea, and carry it straight to the roof. The room's other entrance, from the terrace, forced him to stoop on entering, as if taking a ritual bow, and drop down a few steps. The room "was high but sunken, like a cellar in the sky," and as small and hidden as his Stonington study. Shutters above the table he used as a desk opened on the pines of Mount Lycabettos. From the open door, he could see the white monastery on the peak.

In July, Jimmy, David, and George set out on a car trip across the Peloponnese. Along dry roads lined with oleander, they were confronted by signs extolling the coup that had carried "the Colonels" to power more than a year ago. "In every village, at every bend of the road, the little blue + white signs proliferate: Long Live the Government, Long Live the 21st of April, Long Live the Army [. . .]—Live! Live! The rhythm begins to take on that of mouth-to-mouth resuscitation. All but the most naïve will understand that the body politic was drowned a year + a half ago, and will not be artificially revived," Merrill wrote. They had hoped to stay in a harbor town spied from a mountain pass, but it turned out to be disappointing upon arrival. "Everything looks better on high," David remarked, "which must explain why God still has patience with us."

Merrill observed Lazaretos closely on this trip. He'd become for Jimmy something like an in-law relation, viewed with the sympathy and distance closeness makes possible:

Dear George. One would have to be very expert to do a watercolor of him—of what he is like "inside." Only the lightest touches convey his good nature, his small jokes + courtesies, before they all bleed into embarrassment or gloom. [. . .] One has to sympathize. George is, like all of us, as good as he <u>can</u> be. It's clearest when he plays soccer, or just kicks the ball around as he did with some ragged boys at sunset. [. . .] [H]e is prepared for the game to be lost, but he means to lose it in the most winning of all ways.

Back in Athens, Merrill ran into Strato on the street. He was thirty pounds lighter than the last time they'd seen each other, and "so bleached + bronzed from work as to recall vividly the golden calf I'd worshipped in the old days. At the sight of him an absolutely harmless lightning went through me and vanished into the earth." A glass of wine, a game of cards: that was all they would share now. Besides, Jimmy had other irons in the fire. After penning a year's worth of affectionate messages from his "sister" Monica to Kostas Tympakianákis and his mother, he was expected in Crete. When he arrived, the heat in Heraklion was "un-be-liev-a-ble." Kostas's motorbike carried him through a maze of back streets to the mother's house. A "dreadful cook," she and Kostas "whine + bicker at each other like 'couples' the world over." Both mother and son expected Kostas to return to the U.S. with his American friend, who, however, was growing increasingly doubtful of the happy prospect he'd been keeping alive in Monica's letters.

A short time later, Jimmy withdrew his offer to sponsor Kostas in America; he said he was sorry "for not having Known Myself better," and offered to recompense the Greek "for his shattered dreams by giving him what I would have paid for his ticket, plus continuing for another year at least my monthly assistance." Kostas agreed, "and together we sealed the doom of my hapless 'sister' in whose existence, by now, only his old mother and youngest nephews are likely to believe." "That very minute she collided with a truck, the steering-wheel pierced her spleen, and six days afterwards she expired with his name on her lips. Kostas at least did not have to dissimulate his chagrin, only its cause; but I would have liked to spare his mother the tears that in the goodness of her heart she has been shedding ever since. " Merrill, after narrating this farce for McIntosh, admitted that he was "ashamed" by the ruse, however amusing it had been. "It leaves a nasty aftertaste," he remarked. "Life's not long enough for all there is to learn."

In Wyoming, during their candlelit dinners, Merrill had tended to talk while McIntosh listened, until Merrill fell silent too, "out of happiness or self-doubt or some plausible mixture of the two." Separated, they repeated the pattern, when Merrill did not receive a reply to his letters. Encouraged by his work with Rothenberg, he had begun recording his dreams. In one, he and McIntosh were separated from each other at a public gathering, "but still smiling into one another's eyes while somebody rose and delivered a long irrelevant speech. I woke understanding that this person was also myself, the self who writes you hundreds + thousands of words when in fact a very simple gesture would express what is in his heart." So he gave up letters for a time. He sent McIntosh a postcard with only "woof! Grrrrr . . . . bow-wow?" on the back. And he wrote a haiku: "No coffin without / Nails. These you drive into mine / At least are golden."

He also sent McIntosh a new, longish poem. Begun in Wyoming and finished in the rooftop study in Athens, "In Nine Sleep Valley" was a souvenir of their time in Kelly, its nine sections remembering their nine days together. Merrill told McIntosh that the poem was "less than I had hoped for, but more (it now seems) than I deserved." He might have been speaking of the love he'd hoped for. The poem describes the start of the trip:

> Yesterday's flower, American Beauty
> Crimson and sweet all night in the city,
> Limp now, changed in import as in color,
> Floats behind us in the tinkling cooler.
>
> Yesterday also Robert Kennedy's
> Train of refrigerated dignitaries
> Last seen on TV burying Dr. King
> Wormed its way to Arlington Cemetery.
>
> The beauty I mean to press fading
> Between these lines is yours, and the misleading
> Sweetness, leaves and portals of a body
> Ajar, cool, nodding at the wheel already.

"I picked him up at the Denver airport shortly after Robert Kennedy was killed," McIntosh recalled, "and we were still literally in shock. I remember James being deeply moved by that death—it affected the visit." Merrill doubted his "taste" in approaching "the stinking subject" of Kennedy's and King's murders. Apparently he could do so only with the "scented handkerchief" of a love story, complete with red rose, "pressed to my nose." From another angle, the reference to Kennedy's funeral disguises some of the poet's feelings about an affair that seems even at the outset to be fading.

Rhymed couplets, in section five, signal a growing agreement between the pair:

> Each day at dusk we roam the sage.
> Heavenly repertory, bleakest rage
>
> Bleeding to sour gleams, hard-edge jubilance,
> All encompassed by one lariat glance.
>
> The peaks turn baseless as the fear
> That you will tell me what I live to hear.
>
> Look, is all. The cabin. Look. The river.
> Aspens glowing, site gloomed over.

Instead of telling him what he "lives to hear," the poet's companion seems to say simply, if only by his look, "Look." And he does look, rendering the visible in language charged with the energy of the wilderness around them. The place generates life as whimsically ("out of thin air") as his language spawns puns and conceits. At the same time, his diction speaks of anger and resentment ("rage," "sour," "gloomed over").

In mid-August, in Athens, Merrill received a long letter and photographs from McIntosh, reassuring him, and welcoming more letters. Not writing letters, Merrill admitted, had been "difficult + sad for me, and no doubt childish as well." As he digested Merrill's recent letters and the draft of "In Nine Sleep Valley," McIntosh worried that he had disappointed him. "My dear," Merrill replied, "you have not hurt me or failed me in any way. Hush! [. . .] Still, you have put your finger on something—that 'vein of tension' in these letters + in the poem, and which you also felt in Kelly. The subject," Merrill continued, referring to tension between them,

> would be of no interest, a small squiggly piece in my puzzle, if it didn't interlock with the act of writing. For language by nature deals directly + dramatically with times and places remote from what's at hand, with the layers that underlie whatever one finds oneself doing—as if those tensions you speak of literally became tenses, pasts + futures, on the page. [. . .] That poem ["In Nine Sleep Valley"], I mean, is not written to you, David, in the sense that this letter is. Though it addresses you, don't forget that pronouns like You or I or We are also deep in the nature of language, and help bring it to life. It is for you—it couldn't have been writ-

ten without what you showed me by way of landscape and happiness and, yes, tension. Don't take it too personally: as a gift, if
you will; as a message, no.

He offered not to publish the poem if it would distress McIntosh to see it in
print.

On August 15, Merrill flew to Vienna to see Auden and Kallman. He
was "laden with cod + backlava for Chester," who would provide him with
"enough to eat + drink so that for once (I trust)" he would not be "turned to
stone by [Auden's] brilliant + unanswerable discourse." "A Greek would be
shocked by the prevailing order (chequered fields, gregarious trees) and
lushness," Merrill felt, seeing Austria for the first time in years. Kirchstetten was a cozy village, "2 or 3 baby crossroads," about forty-five minutes
from Vienna. A signpost in town, made of two elves bracing books their
own size, showed the way to the house of "der Lyriker AUDEN." Kallman
had become "puffy, bleary, sagging + humped over, a Jewish mother inside
and out." He cooked furiously, producing a menu of "jellied trout, fresh
sorrel soup [. . .], curries, Chinese duck, saddle of venison, home-corned
beef." Mixing drinks and driving the car, Yannis Boras, Kallman's lover,
was there. Auden, aged at sixty-two, became his expansive social self only
at cocktail hour. Merrill described the routine:

At 6:15 WHA began to fidget. At 6:30 the Greek butler-chauffeur
brought him the first of two dry martinis made from ingredients kept in the deep-freeze—undiluted dynamite. During the
hour in which he drinks these he blossoms by visible stages
(like trick-photography movies of a flower) and repeats with
real charm + vivacity things he has said a hundred times before.
At table his chair isn't high enough so he sits on the vocal score
of his + Chester's most recent opera, and drinks a good deal of
wine. And then the flower begins to close. By 8:30 he is off to bed
and Chester + I listen to records until midnight.

Merrill had missed Vermeer's masterpiece, *The Artist in His Studio*, when
he and Jackson were in Vienna in 1957. On this visit, he drank it in. "Within
a quarter hour," he wrote to McIntosh, the painter, "it took its place among
the wonders of the world. When I was little my mother used to say that there
was an animal heaven where pets went after death. [. . .] Vermeer makes you
believe in a heaven for things + textures—cracked leather, brass, paper, silk
+ yarn." The painting depicts an artist, his back turned to the viewer, who

is at work on a painting of a beautiful young woman; modest, with her eyes averted, she is dressed as one of the muses, probably Clio or Calliope. Merrill attended to details: "I felt like singing with joy when I saw, in the upper right hand corner, barely visible, the lightly painted tangle of untrimmed threads: the back of the tapestry! as if to say in the softest of voices, that no miracle is separable from its humble accidents, its seamy side."

Jimmy had little time left in Athens. If nothing else, these two months in Greece had been an occasion for him to demonstrate that he had "changed" under McIntosh's influence. "Yes," Maria had said during their first lunch on the square in Kolonáki, "one must change, cher enfant. I've changed too"—a line delivered "with an indescribable twinkle that made the fun of it positively bubble in your bones." Or was Merrill overlooking a comment about her cancer? The time for their last lunch had already come—"2 fried eggs for her, omelet for me, a dish of flavorless ice cream which we share; it never varies." One wouldn't want to change too much.

Merrill got on the plane to New York on September 4. Leaving Greece meant leaving Jackson. The two men remained intimate, but each one recognized how much their intimacy was taken for granted, and how little they had done to keep it alive. Turning to letters again, David released a *cri de coeur*:

> The house is terribly empty! The times we've come from and gone to airports together. What are you thinking on arrival or departure? Reproaching myself for my wordlessness, I wonder if you reproach me, no real words of love, no way to express my dismay when you leave me, nor more than hope that my joy at seeing you comes through. One thing I had meant to try and convey is that, in fact, we have not changed. You have for several years grown surer of yourself. When you so positively know what you will do each day and hour you are very much like a train on schedule, the whistle of which I would miss with a start, and do, these hours after you've roared off. But what must I seem like to you—you TELL me in many ways, but because I know you love me I keep firm in my belief that you know me too well to despise me too much. [. . .] I end by simply wishing you like this house and Greece as much as I do, and that you could take a pleasure in the fact we have made two places in our lives where we live and are known and where, as private as they are, so much feeling can exist.

"About an hour out of Athens," Merrill wrote to Jackson in a letter that crossed his, "I was seized with a pang of terrible regret. To be leaving. To have made so little of my being there. Not to have held <u>you</u> dearer + closer while I had the chance: that especially." It was not his way, however, to look back too long.

Over the summer, Merrill finished a new manuscript of poems, anchored by "The Summer People" and "Matinées." But what to call it? Kalstone proposed *Out of Season*. The title was "dullish," but it conveyed the "faint note of apology" Merrill wanted, because "for the first time I know deep down that it just isn't as good a book as the last one." It would have been hard to match the standard set by *Nights and Days*; but Merrill's view was too colored by the "upsetting things in Actual Life that gave rise to nearly all the poems"—the trial he'd passed through with Strato—for him to evaluate the book fairly. As a result, he confided to Yenser, "I truly don't <u>like</u> the poems; it's as if someone else had written them and left them like changelings on the desk. [. . .] A stronger nature would put them on the fire, but I am weak + publish." By mid-October the poems were at Atheneum. The poet was not about to burn his book. The title he'd chosen was *The Fire Screen*.

The title came from "Mornings in a New House," a poem completed, like the manuscript as a whole, in October 1968. An intricate meditation on art and passion in the aftermath of a love affair, it presents "a cold man"—a Jack Frost figure—who warms himself by a fire in a new house. It is unclear whether the man's coldness means he is unloved or unloving; he has left an old house behind, and been forced to make new arrangements. He needs the fire in order to take heart and face the day; still, the flue chokes "with the shock of it." Morning "brightness," like the fire, is ambiguous: having revealed the world outside, it "sheathes its claws." The man is convalescing, thawing like the frozen window, but day's warmth and light recall him painfully to a time of emotional heat before he could say, as he does now, "The worst is over." Submitting to sheer "habit," he uses "the fire screen" to shield himself from "that tamed uprush / (Which to recall alone can make him flush)."

Merrill had been thinking about the motif of the fire screen since summer 1967. At that time, he'd chosen to stay in Stonington, playing bridge with Stone and Perényi, rather than return to Athens and face Mouflouzé-lis. He had appreciated "The Ladies," but "[h]ow women ever got their reputation for Understanding is beyond me," he said. As if to understand *them*, he read *Love's Body* by Norman O. Brown, a popular book that year. Merrill chuckled over Brown's Freudian claim "that no skills were ever discovered by the female except that of weaving and plaiting, 'obviously' an extension of what they did with their pubic hair to conceal the absence of a penis."

Brown's argument seemed laughable, but "whatever so picturesquely sim-
plifies can't be all wrong—and doesn't Eleanor's crewelwork fit right in?" In
any case, even as he mocked Brown's ideas and condescended to Perényi's
crewelwork, Merrill made use of the one and sympathized with the other.
Or so it appears in "Mornings in a New House," where the needlepoint fire
screen becomes a symbol for his lyric poetry.

The fire screen to which the poem refers is a specific object, a piece of
crewelwork not by Perényi but by the young Hellen Ingram, which Mis'
Annie kept in her apartment on East Seventy-second Street. Hellen had
always enjoyed needlepoint. "Mornings in a New House" looks back to the
beginnings of the hobby in her childhood. The eight-year-old Hellen, Merrill writes, "Stitched giant birds and flowery trees / To dwarf a house, *her*
mother's—see the chimney's / Puff of dull yarn!" The art of the needle, Merrill reminds us, is passed down from mother to child in the home; it takes
the home itself as a subject in this instance, just as Merrill's poem does.
There is, in the daughter's wish to "dwarf" "*her* mother's" house, a pattern
of generational competition into which the poet enters as his mother's son,
who dwarfs her by depicting her as a child. The art that Merrill describes
is "cruel"—he wants us to hear the pun—because it records childhood pain
and passes it on. The child "cries" as she pierces her finger, while the poet
experiences her pain, mixing with his own.

To the line "Habit arranges the fire screen," Merrill added a footnote. It
is not an extra-poetic explanation in the manner of T. S. Eliot's or Marianne
Moore's notes, but a critical reflection on the poem, addressed to the poet
himself, and part of the poem:

> Days later. All framework & embroidery rather than any slower look-
> ing into things. Fire screen—screen *of* fire. The Valkyrie's baffle,
> pulsing at trance pitch, godgiven, elemental. Flames masking that
> cast-iron plaque—"contrecoeur" in French—which backs the hearth
> with charred Loves & Graces. Some such meaning might have caught,
> only I didn't wait, I settled for the obvious—by lamplight as it were. Oh
> well. Our white heats lead us on no less than words do. Both have been
> devices in their day.

The seeming casualness of this writing masks the subtlety of the argument. First, Merrill decides that his poem is "all framework & embroidery,"
a screen, rather than an attempt to face directly the experience that gave
rise to it. As he plays with that key phrase, turning it around in "screen
of fire," he is reminded of Brünnhilde asleep in a magic ring of fire in *Die
Walküre*, and he reverses his view of his poem: wit, he suggests, reveals the

deeper truth that no deep truth will be revealed; the fire itself is a screen. To describe what the fire masks, he turns to the image of a "contrecoeur," a French term meaning literally "against the heart" that refers to the iron plaque at the back of a hearth, like the one in Maria Mitsotáki's house on Cape Sounion, to which Merrill silently refers. Behind passion's fires lie disfigured classical ideals, "charred Loves & Graces." But a cynical realism is not the poem's last word. Merrill's nonchalance in the footnote ("Oh well") implies that he may see things differently when more days have passed. What remains is an equal suspicion of "white heats" and "words." "Both have been devices in their day."

Merrill spent three weeks in the fall of 1968 at Washington University in St. Louis, where he had been invited not to teach a class, but simply to "shed glamour" on the campus as the Fanny Hurst Visiting Poet. In the late 1960s, Wash U was becoming a center for contemporary writing. Donald Finkel, a poet, taught there; soon Howard Nemerov and William Gass would join the faculty. Merrill's closest friends on campus were the poet Mona Van Duyn and her husband, the fiction writer Jarvis Thurston. The visiting poet had use of a small house. Behind it, under tall shade trees, was a cobblestone alley running for blocks between the fenced yards of middle-class brick homes near campus. Merrill was unaccustomed to a neighborhood where blacks and whites lived together, and he liked it. He liked the campus too, with its Gothic halls of "red Missouri granite" framing neat quadrangles and rolling lawns.

He gave a reading that was "a huge success, at least 200 people packed into a lounge, some of them standing, all of them hanging on every word, laughing + gasping." But his days were quiet, and he complained that "nobody's using me." Yet when invitations did come, he was ill at ease in the classroom. "I doubt that I'll ever feel at home in a University," he confided to John Hollander, who was now a professor at Hunter College in New York and fully at home in a classroom. "Everyone listens as if I were going to say something interesting when in fact it is either something they know already or a confession of ignorance." Faced with "dreadful interrogative generalities," he groped as if for "an oar in mid-Atlantic." His answers may have struck some as hostile. When one boy asked whether a poet needed to have a "position," "I had to say NO (what was I meant to say—horizontal?) and towards the end of the session somebody else asked what was the poet's role in society and I heard myself saying in a loud clear voice: NOT TO PARTICIPATE." Maybe he didn't wish to be used after all.

When Merrill returned to the U.S. from Greece, he'd expected to see McIntosh soon. "Please be indulgent of my fatal addiction to plan-making," he wrote, hoping to firm things up. But McIntosh was again slow to commit himself. One reason was his health. An infection that was bothering him over the summer had spread, with the result that he couldn't use his eyes to read or paint. McIntosh went to Chicago to consult specialists, and it seemed impossible for Merrill to visit him in New Mexico. Then his condition suddenly improved, and Merrill flew west to stay with him for a week in Nambé Pueblo, twenty miles north of Santa Fe.

The place would become important to him. The Pueblo is located at the base of the Sangre de Cristo Mountains, with vistas of sage and chamiso to the east, interrupted by flaking sandstone buttes and pillars. To the west, as the land drops into the Rio Grande valley, cottonwoods cluster along the creeks snaking toward the river. McIntosh's house was just off the main road. Red-brown adobe with rounded corners, smooth, thick walls, and kiva-style beams, it consisted of four rooms in a line like "a Pullman car," with two fireplaces and a long porch shielded from the sun by an overhang. The porch overlooked a small pond, veiled by cottonwoods and dammed at one end—a precious bowl of water in the arid landscape. Two swans swam there, and peacocks roamed the dirt yard.

Merrill had long been interested in New Mexico's overlay of cultures. Now he was staying on Native American land, a hundred yards from the wooden cross of the Church of the Sacred Heart, listening at night to the whine of tires and stabbing gears on the Taos road. In the small plaza of the Pueblo, a short walk from McIntosh's house, there was no grass or pavement, only the dirt the houses were made of. At one end of the plaza, ladders descended into the circular, clay-walled kiva, the Pueblo's sacred ceremonial space below-ground, which was closed to white people. Standing in the plaza, Merrill could contemplate the myth of Native American emergence from the earth or look up at the snowy caps of the Truchas Peaks.

He and McIntosh took long walks in open country. "I was an amateur archaeologist in my young life," McIntosh explains. "I spent all my free time looking for artifacts. Later on, I worked for the forest service, and I spent many days alone on a horse. I learned to see the ground very closely from a horse." He collected war clubs, hammers, arrowheads, pottery shards, beautiful stones, and feathers. He explained to Merrill Native American customs and beliefs and the habits of wildlife and horses; he talked of the "deep time" visible in the region's geology. For Merrill, DMc was a guide to prehistory and an elemental landscape. All of this would go into his poetry.

.   .   .   .

Back in Stonington by early December, with winter storms whistling at the windows, Merrill went to work on "Under Libra: Weights and Measures," a poem dedicated to McIntosh. One of his most private, resistant poems, it was an attempt to render the wordless experiences he'd shared with McIntosh in Nambé. He had reassured McIntosh that the pronouns "you" and "I" in "In Nine Sleep Valley" were impersonal, being "deep in the nature of language." Now, searching for a language suited to nature poetry, he tried to do without pronouns entirely. "What bits I've begun are full of you + what you've helped me see; they're even full of me, only we're not there, just the swans, the ice, the feathers + the stones. I've never quite understood nature poetry + am not at all sure I do now. [. . .] But in these early stages at least it lets me relive moments of silent wonder that seem at the very heart of a barely imaginable happiness."

Jackson returned to Stonington for Christmas. He appeared tanned, plump, relaxed. He told Merrill that his dependence on him had been "somehow annulled" by George's dependence on *him*. As a result, Jimmy wrote, "D. is better than I'd dared hope, and I am better for his being so." But that feeling was short-lived. "It's not his fault," Merrill reminded himself two days later, "if I find unbearable the way he spends time—sleeping till noon, steeling himself over coffee + juice + whatever's for (by then) lunch until it's nearly dark before he goes to his desk or out to look for a present, and I fall back weak with the pointless empathic exhaustion of the bowler whose body tries to guide the ball down the alley. One wouldn't feel this way, of course, if one didn't also feel partly to blame—that old story whose moral is never to do anything that you will regret." David returned to Connecticut College that spring to teach a fiction-writing course, again replacing Bill Meredith, who was on leave. When not preparing class, though, he spent "every available minute watching his TV programs." There was no Cecilia Holland in his class this time, and he would not be back at Conn College again. It was the last time that he held a job of any kind.

Blame and forgiveness were on Merrill's mind when he composed a letter of condolence to Kallman: Yannis Boras, at twenty-six, had been killed when a truck struck him on the road near Vienna. "Oh my dear," Merrill wrote, "I'm so sorry. That dear good wild bad funny and now at last tragic boy. I hope you are not blaming yourself. You did everything for him, but you didn't do this." He and DJ consulted Ephraim, who put them in touch with the cheerful Yannis: "Tell Chester I wasn't to blame. It's fun here!" When asked to comment on McIntosh, Ephraim replied, "You have both taken—you with your David, DJ with his George—shy lovers, as if you were escaping words. [. . .] JM + DJ, I believe you wanted a love to sweep you up wordlessly, and now you have it. [. . .] And you abandon me, for I talk. But I love you and this is our reunion. We break our silence as others break our hearts with it."

In his weekly, increasingly lively discussions with Dr. Rothenberg, Merrill was hardly wordless. After seeing a draft of "Under Libra," the doctor asked for associations with stones and feathers, two of the poem's motifs. As if "one strand of an intricate, airy web had been twitched," Merrill suddenly recalled "my mother's account of how I'd been terrified as a very little child by her room full of floating feathers (a pillow had come apart); and then a dream in which a number of large + beautiful stones belonging to my father had been turned into pens (penna, the Latin word for feather) which I should one day be able to write with." In another hour with Rothenberg, Merrill linked the windows, prisms, and eyes in his poetry to his memory of breaking "a cut-glass perfume bottle as a little boy" at his mother's dressing table. He had turned to her "pleading that I'd dropped it because it was 'hot' "—remembering that then sent him "off at once on another radiant of the web, the heat + cold that seem to be the governing metaphor of 'The Broken Home.' " Merrill's work with Rothenberg was confirming for him that his art and life fit together in a whole, giving meaning to each other in the shape of a single, glistening "web." Even in an ostensibly impersonal poem such as "Under Libra," Merrill recognized that "my whole self is present, like it or not."

He was using psychoanalytic thinking as a tool of enchantment, rather than demystification, which it is usually thought to be. That Merrill saw himself as serving the doctor's purposes freed him from responsibility for the direction of their talks. "I am so passive in my 'thinking,' " he wrote to Hine; "all at once Dr R seems to be thinking for me, something I'd never dared hope would happen. Let one's valet live for one?—jamais de la vie! But let one's resident philosophe think for one—ah, now you're talking! Furthermore, under the flattery of his attention, I begin [to] have wonderful dreams, and to remember them what's more."

Recently Merrill had begun to use his grandmother's, now his mother's, New York apartment when he visited the city. While staying there that winter, he had this dream of another childhood address: "I am staying alone in a house I lived in as a child—The Orchard—(actually I am sleeping at 164 E 72) and it is a curious experience being in possession of it. I see how I can transform a wing of my bedroom into a study. But as I leave my parents' bedroom I follow the brownish spatterings along the hall walls of my old tears shed over a book, + I begin to weep again. At the foot of the staircase stands Emma, black, young, strong, who puts down her mop + folds me in her arms. Only a book, I keep telling her through my sobs."

Another striking dream came in two parts. It suggests how deeply Merrill's feelings about illness and his body were bound up with arguments with his mother, and how fierce and primal, in dreams at least, was his struggle for independence from her. The poet goes to *Der Rosenkavalier*, then argues with his mother:

> We are alone in an apt. having a dreadful quarrel. She says that I'm ill, that there's blood in my stool. How does she know? I ask. She took it from me while I was sleeping + had it examined, or examined it herself. I am furious. I reach into my rectum + produce 2 or 3 finely shaped turds glistening with a protective membrane. Look at these I say—no sign of blood (though secretly I see tiny red shadows). What do you mean? she says. Why do they have these funny marks? Making marks on them as she says it, and breaking the membrane. We now both have shit on our hands. I am furious. I splash her with water. [. . .] She: I'm going to bed, I'll see you in the morning. I (weeping): Let's stop saying these horrible things to each other, can't we? I wake up in tears.

Merrill attended the Met's *Rosenkavalier* that winter not once but three times. It was the "best since the days of [Lotte] Lehmann," although, by the third performance, he and Kalstone had to light up a joint at intermission on the balcony overlooking Lincoln Center to sustain their sense of wonder. Merrill paid for a box and filled it with friends. When Grace suddenly got up on opening night, Jackson, thinking of her glaucoma, asked if she was going to put drops in her eyes. "No, my dear," she replied, "just the reverse." To explain to McIntosh, his young beloved, what was so touching in the opera's story, Merrill freely translated what the Marschallin says to Octavian about time, calling her young lover by his pet name:

> "[I]t flows in mirrors, flows between you and me. Oh Quinquin, there are times when I hear it flowing, when I get up in the middle of the night and stop the clocks, one after one (this above 2 unison notes from the harps, gently striking the hour in her head). And yet we must not be afraid of it; for time also is a creation of the Father who has created all of us." Isn't that beautiful? And to have an opera in which heights like these rise up out of a world of farce + filth, snobbery, opportunism, cheap waltzes + practical jokes!—one leaves the theater the way I imagine one leaves the confessional, at peace with one's follies, forgiving + forgiven.

Through the winter McIntosh kept lapsing into what Merrill felt as long silences, and the condition affecting DMc's eyes persisted. In March, he came for tests at a New York hospital. He and Merrill spent a day "lunching in Chinatown, drinking at the Plaza, walking the cold streets in between," and again coming to the conclusion that, while Merrill wanted more, he "really just wants friendship, it's too sad." They saw each other again before he left, and came to the same conclusion. Merrill wrote to him, "Yesterday was bad—waves breaking over me at unexpected moments throughout the city—and the sense that nothing remained in my heart but peeling wallpaper + starlight. But, really, considering who you are + who I am, it is positively absurd + obscene to be unhappy for very long."

He'd been gathering strength in the form of a new poem, which he sent two days later to McIntosh. "Snow King Chairlift" recalled an afternoon in Wyoming in June when they took a chairlift to the top of a mountain for the view. When they arrived, a photographer snapped the pair, a souvenir that remained on Merrill's desk in Stonington. "I love that funny snapshot," he says, "from a time / When we still thought we were each other's meat." But that time was past. In dexterous, garrulous quatrains, Merrill accepts with seeming ease what he couldn't accept in life. The poem dwells on the paradox that the high point of feeling to which he was so rapidly transported with McIntosh was, like any peak, a dead end.

> Au fond each summit is a cul-de-sac.
> That day at least by not unprecedented
> Foresight, a Cozy Cabin had been rented.
> Before I led you to the next chair back
>
> And made my crude but educated guess
> At why the wind was laying hands on you
> (Something I no longer think to do)
> We gazed our little fills at boundlessness.

It was hard for him to maintain the new poem's high spirits. In dejection in April, in the privacy of his notebook, Merrill wrote, "It may be the slump between poems (not to say between loves) but more + more keenly comes the feeling that I've reached the last 2 or 3 years of my life. Nothing else so explains how I live, the waves of yearning, of asceticism, irresolution, indifference that alternately break within me. Full of purpose, I know nevertheless that it's all to no purpose. My 'real' life is behind me. What's left is a dream." At the time he was in Atlanta, where he'd gone to stay with his mother and stepfather at Easter. On the holy day itself he wrote in his notebook, "Less to believe in church than behind the gothic façade of a 20's radio. Finical, innocuous touches of music + rite, no better or worse than the fingerbowls at last night's dinner." Bill Plummer was suffering from advanced emphysema. That winter he'd been in the hospital in an oxygen tent. Back home, he was far from recovered; it was clear that he'd entered his final illness. Yet death was out of place in the early springtime heat, with blossoming cherry trees on the lawn and dogwoods ready to flower. While the old man struggled to breathe, Jimmy was swept up in the usual round of luncheons and bridge.

He flew to Santa Fe and made a trip to Nambé, seeing how it would feel to spend time there having accepted McIntosh's "let's-just-be-friends" policy. McIntosh had to housesit for a friend who'd asked him not to bring anyone else to the house. Merrill was distraught at the prospect of being left alone for a night. "I've never spent the night alone in my life!" he cried, exaggerating considerably. McIntosh, who was quite used to being alone and liked it, advised him to read and to listen to music. The next day, he thought that Merrill seemed "weary but triumphant, as if he'd come through an ordeal." When he returned to Stonington, Jimmy had lost his heart again, if not to the painter this time, then to his dog, a stray husky. McIntosh had asked the dog so many times, "Who are you?" she answered to "Who." The visit was successful enough that there were plans for Merrill to come back and stay for longer that August. Perhaps his "real" life wasn't behind him yet.

Like his relationship with McIntosh, the new phase of work Merrill had embarked on proved hard going. The bafflement expressed by friends who had seen "Under Libra: Weights and Measures," save for Yenser, made Merrill feel isolated as a poet. Not that he'd ever wished to be part of a group. John Myers dedicated to him (and to Edward Maisel) the anthology he edited in 1969 called *The Poets of the New York School*; and Merrill could have looked for allies there. In January, he wrote a fan letter to one of the contributors to the anthology, James Schuyler, whom Merrill had helped during his breakdown eight years before. Merrill had just read Schuyler's poem "Now & Then" in *Poetry*, and he admired its "extraordinary freedom of tone + subject," its "feeling of intimacy <u>beyond</u> the need to say 'I' and so imply a division between you + your reader"—a version of the intimacy he'd been trying for in "Under Libra." His mixed feelings about the New York School came out in May, however, when he was again called on to judge, with Stanley Kunitz and Louise Bogan, the Glascock Prize at Mount Holyoke College. The best poet may have been a Columbia undergraduate, David Lehman, with whom he would later become friends. But Merrill had doubts about his poetry at this point. "To judge him," he wrote of Lehman, "is to judge his sources, that apparently inexhaustible bubbling-up of the NY School. It is a pleasure bright & fresh as paint, and (finally) as thin as paint. It puzzles me, speaking as a practitioner who believes in entertaining surfaces, the esthetic wrongness of overtly important subject-matter, etc, to find myself asking for more than this particular brand of enchantment supplies."

At the reception for the prize, Merrill chatted with Kathleen Norris, one of the contestants. When he learned that she would return to Bennington College in Vermont the next day, he offered to take her on his way north to visit Fredericks. Thirty years later, Norris, who became a poet and a non-fiction writer, remembered their drive: "At Mount Holyoke, Merrill had appeared distant and mannered, but as we rode through the countryside, he was good company, warm, funny, and evidently relieved to be done with his duties as a judge. [. . .] He said it was good to hear someone who was still so enthusiastic about writing; he had lately begun to feel that he was all written out, and had been forced to consider the possibility that he had nothing more to say."

The next day, cross-legged on Claude's *tatami*, Jimmy contemplated the changelessness of the Pawlet farmhouse. Morning sunlight poured into his low bed from behind the house "through air clean as the proverbial whistle." The house was still furnished sparely. "In one corner stands the big old dull red hand press like a Kabuki warrior, legs spread, sworded, holding an open dictionary." That evening the Buechners and Bernard Malamud and his wife came to dinner (Malamud like Fredericks taught at Bennington College). Freddy was "at his most depressed and hypochondriachal." He was reading a book called *The Crisis of Middle Age*. But middle age was a good topic for the heart-to-heart communing Buechner and Merrill had always enjoyed. "Freddy & I kept moving off into corners for one of the grand old emotional talks he is so good at, tall & gentle, brown as a berry, unwrinkled as a berry, with his small mouth smiling & enormous green eyes that seem filled with tears whether they are or not."

In May, Merrill attended a reading by Bishop at the Guggenheim Museum. Lowell introduced her. Lowell had just published a book of free-verse sonnets, *Notebook 1967–68*, that dealt with his private life and the political turmoil over the war in Vietnam. Merrill felt it suffered from—"Isn't 'giganticism' the word he uses?" he asked Yenser, who was completing a PhD dissertation on Lowell. Merrill deflated Stephen's admiration for the senior poet: "You put it in a nutshell when you say, 'I have nothing but respect for Robert Lowell.' " On this occasion, preparing the way for Bishop, Lowell "rambled on about Their Generation, her Famous Eye, good heart, good humor, etc, until finally out she came, hunched, powdered, looking grim +

sad, to shuffle papers + fidget with the mike before uttering her first words of the evening—'The famous eye will now be hidden behind glasses' and all was well from then on." As was her custom, Bishop read "without inflection or change of pitch, in a no-nonsense tenor voice; and strangely moving," Jimmy felt, "one wanted it to be like that." Marianne Moore, wearing a tri-cornered hat, sat in the first row, attended by a nurse. To conclude, Bishop read "The Fish," in which the speaker scrutinizes the great, homely, heroic fish she has caught, before releasing it. In her rush to leave the stage, she forgot the microphone around her neck, and it tugged for a moment, as the audience gasped in sympathy, before she freed herself.

The Jacksons came to Stonington for two weeks. David, experiencing his own middle-age crisis, had bought a red Mustang convertible. He drove his parents to the airport in it, then put the car and himself on the boat for Greece. Now it was Jimmy's turn to be left behind and regret his failure to have said what he felt. "I was so depressed to see you go," he wrote to David. "We must by now be used to the way our time together passes, without any of the essentials being said, foremost among which is that I love you dearly + wish I knew better how to show it; but it seemed uncommonly painful, this year's separation—perhaps because the remaining years seem, as never before, numbered." Traveling in the other direction, Parigory came to see Merrill in Stonington, where they fell into a bland routine, pouring drinks at six, playing Scrabble and *xerí* (a Greek game), and then sitting "in a stupor—less of drink—I feel too tired to drink—than of repose or fatigue or simple boredom, though T. is good enough to swear that at his age this routine is exactly what he needs + wants." Their wild nights in Athens seemed a long time ago. When Parigory had left, and the Browers came for dinner, Merrill remembered Helen looking at him, during Parigory's visit in 1963, and saying with a twinkle, "It's good to see you so happy, Jimmy—you're in love, I know." Although Mrs. Brower was wrong about Tony, "she was also right. I was in love," Merrill reflected, not so much with Tony as "with my idea of Tony's life, his youth full of sex + fun, [. . .] his assurance as to what he liked + what he didn't. This time I really understood that that love was past. Tony became a truly <u>un</u>mythical person—literally smaller (those 25 pounds lost)."

In July, a man walked on the moon. In Stonington, Merrill watched those first steps with Kalstone, the Stone Women, and Derek Walcott and his "delicious" wife Margaret in front of Rollie McKenna's new television set. However skeptical of history-making heroes, Merrill found himself "utterly under the spell" of the black box and its black-and-white images beamed from space.

In August, he moved into a one-room adobe cottage about a mile from McIntosh's house. He brought a record player—the trusty machine he took to Madison in 1967—and a few records, including the complete Beethoven piano sonatas. The room contained a small organ; the score of *La Traviata*, left behind by some previous resident, waited to be played. Beyond the house, Merrill looked out on hollyhocks, sunflowers, dahlias, and daisies "ajump with grasshoppers"—red ones; beyond that, fields of alfalfa and artemisia where horses wandered; and beyond that, mountains and clouds. There would be guests soon, and an old dog spent nights asleep on the doorstep. But Jimmy was going to have a good deal more solitude here than he was used to.

McIntosh no longer seemed to Merrill so young as he had a year and a half ago. His cheek was creased by "the penstroke of Time," and he'd added a "thick moustache, color of maple syrup." One afternoon they drove north to Las Trampas, a high town with an adobe church. McIntosh dreamed of building a house there on a hillside thick with sweet-scented piñon. "We ate cucumbers + a chicken," Merrill told Kalstone, "drank wine, talked, the stars came out, millions of them, a few whizzing to extinction every second. It was our first good evening alone. He spoke of how 'guilty' it made him, that he couldn't be the 'lover I wanted.' " But there was no changing that, and Merrill felt that merely being with him was enough. "If anyone wonders what I am doing here," he declared, probably answering his own question, "all I can say is that I feel immensely alive at his side."

Often that meant being outside. If a sunset looked promising, the two friends drove to the ridge above the Pueblo with a picnic. Or after a morning of work, they might hike to Nambé Falls. The falls are a sacred source for the Pueblo, magical in the way the braided water leaps out of high rock. The hike itself had a sense of ritual for Merrill. As the trail passes upstream, the sandstone bands of the canyon walls tilt, becoming vertical, forced up against black volcanic rock. The trail ends, and the hiker must pick his way across the stones scattered in the river, and then through a break in the rock, moving from sunlight into shadow and around a bend, as if turning aside a curtain and entering the cliff itself. On the other side is the deep, dark first pool and a very steep bank. One scrambles up it, Merrill boasted, "holding lunch in one's mouth (along with the heart) finally to have the difficulty rewarded in a spacious high salon of rock draped at one end with a fury of icy foaming white." He thought about this "ravishing place" long after leaving it—and wrote about it in prose and verse, including section "T" of *The Book of Ephraim*.

They also visited San Ildefonso Pueblo, a few miles west of Nambé. San Ildefonso was the center of the modern renaissance of Pueblo ceramic art led by the Native artist Maria Martinez, whom McIntosh knew. The Pueblo has a large double plaza, with a giant cottonwood in the center. The visitor enters through a high wooden gate, a cliché image of an Old West town built for a 1930s Western filmed on the site. In view are small clay houses and the traditional *horno*, an outdoor bread oven—above which rises the Black Mesa. The mesa is made of dark volcanic rock, sculpted by the prehistoric river that cut the Rio Grande Valley. Its black clay is micaceous, and glows whitely; with tall grasses catching the afternoon light, it shines like the pelt of an animal. On top, Merrill and McIntosh found a face, crudely carved in a boulder, looking upward. Battling Spanish soldiers in 1694, after the Native uprising against their rulers, the Pueblo fled to the mesa, where many took their lives rather than surrender.

They visited other Native American sites nearby. In the high buttes west of the Rio Grande, they explored the crumbled walls of Tsankawi ruins. Tsankawi was settled in the 1400s, then abandoned in the 1500s as Native people moved down into the Rio Grande Pueblos. The path's smooth channel, eroded by violent runoff, is deeply pocked by the ghostly footprints of its past inhabitants. On the southern side of the butte is a honeycomb of caves, some big enough to stand in, their ceilings black from smoke, the walls marked with petroglyphs of the feathered serpent, animals, hunters—faces that peer out in cartoon simplicity across cultures and centuries. On top of the butte, where the walls around the central plaza remain visible, McIntosh and Merrill looked back across the Rio Grande to Nambé and the Sangre de Cristo Mountains, wine-dark at dusk, stretching into southern Colorado. Behind them spilled late highway traffic from Los Alamos.

The landscape of the Southwest entered Merrill's imagination as a backdrop and a subject in his writing, as in the dramatic monologue "The Black Mesa," which he wrote on this trip, where the mesa speaks of its bloody history. But the importance of the Southwest for his thinking was more general. "James," McIntosh later remarked, "had not known much wildness." Indeed he hadn't, and he wasn't going to become an outdoorsman. Understandably, some of Merrill's friends are skeptical of the environmentalism that emerged as a central theme in his later poetry, doubting that it had any basis in his experience. Yet it did, in the nature he discovered in the Southwest, and in the history of man's place in it. The petroglyph carvers, the Spanish fathers, the Pueblo potters, and the lab technicians punching the clock at Los Alamos—they were layered in southwestern history like bands of sandstone and schist, volcanic ores and obsidian. Each era had its myths. Here, at the site of the Manhattan Project, science had gained power over matter—to what end? The question had weighed on Merrill for two decades. Back in December, Ephraim commented on the nuclear lab at Los Alamos: "I do not like to see the atmosphere of that place. [. . .] Such destroying forces." In "Under Libra: Weights and Measures," evoking one of his and McIntosh's excursions, Merrill writes,

> Here now's a little mesa set for two—
>
> Over purple places, intimate
> Twinklings, early stones, wide open spaces,
> And soon on the horizon the "necklace of death,"
>
> Los Alamos' lights where wizards stay up late
> (Stay in the car, forget the gate)
> To save the world or end it, time will tell
>
> —Mentioned for what it's worth in hopes
> Of giving weight to—Brr! It's freezing!

He no sooner mentions the weighty topic of nuclear destruction than he draws back, embarrassed to broach it.

Teenage Paul Merrill stopped on his way across the country; his uncle, noticing his interest at a newsstand in Santa Fe, bought him a copy of *Playboy*. Robin made a visit from Berkeley, bringing his new wife, small, moody, vegetarian Micaela. Jimmy was skeptical about her youth and hippie ways, but by the time she left, he'd been charmed by her naive enthusiasm: "Everything was 'Wow!' or 'Neat!', just as if World War II had never taken place." Steven Magowan was, Merrill told Kalstone, "fast approaching the day when he will publicly take communion in 'our church.' " Robin had accepted his brother's gayness matter-of-factly; now Jimmy found himself "hiding nothing from Robin any more," making for "merriment + relaxation on both sides." He'd come to trust his oldest nephew far more than anyone else in his family.

Charlotte Hafley visited as well. She was British, the wife of a painter, Bruce Hafley, and herself an artist; Jimmy had made friends with the young couple on his trips to Atlanta to see his mother. Long-legged and elegant, with dark hair slipping out from beneath a straw boater, Charlotte sat sketching the mountains while Jimmy worked. They spoke about McIntosh, and she took his side: " 'You don't know what it's like when a painter is unable to work. Everything stops.' And the insecurity of not having money. 'Probably he wants a deep + lasting relationship + isn't sure that you, with your worldliness and many friends, would give him that.' " As it happened, Hafley herself wanted a relationship with Merrill, or thought she did. "Finally came tears + some mild London version of hysterics," Jimmy confided in David Jackson. "What she couldn't understand was why her suffering left me so cold—indeed paralyzed—why I couldn't put my arms around her + commiserate. The poor thing. Poor things both of us."

Hafley's emotions held up a mirror to Merrill's feelings about McIntosh. In September, McIntosh told him there was another man, his own age, whom he was interested in. Merrill narrated his reaction in his journal: "I walked down to the pond in a foolish blaze of ego + suffering. Gravely the swans swam towards me over the green water, like angels, floating near the bank + clearing their throats until I fed them. I walked on. Now fantastically beautiful peacock feathers lay all about like treasure in a dream. I picked them up, as many as I could hold. There is no cause for sorrow or fear. But I'm afraid. This time surely it is the end. How often I have said that!" But when he met the very ordinary person his beloved was attracted to, he had to laugh at himself and the situation.

In the midst of these romantic gyrations, Merrill received galleys of *The Fire Screen*. He sent them with a birthday tribute to Jackson:

> My book won't be ready until later this month, too late for you to have a copy on the 16th and to discover by leafing its pages that it is, for better or worse, your very own. Why shouldn't it be? You've lived through what lies behind each + every one of those poems—[. . .] there are times, as you must understand, when I can't bear how much you know, how much of my weakness + silliness you've seen, and you have even had to live through my lashing out at you as a convenience. Here anyhow is your noncommittal dedication in proof—and with it a world of love and gratitude.

Jackson replied on his birthday:

> Jamie, I am so grateful, pleased, and so proud to have the dedication of Fire Screen [. . .]. Well, if you say, as you do and such a wave of love for you went over me, that I've seen the worst and best of you—think only of what you've seen of me, and still you

want my name there in front of the poems. What we've not done is to sleepwalk through experience, that is, we've slept on very little and closed our eyes to nothing. I've too often felt ashamed that there was less forgiveable to forgive in me than in you. But again and again you have understood and gone on loving me, and for that I am everyday more grateful.

When Merrill reported that his feeling for McIntosh was slackening, Jackson commented, "What I think, simply, is [. . .] not so much that you saw the clay foot, in time, but that all along you had more control of your feelings than perhaps you suspected." Jackson was right. There was something contrived in Jimmy's passion for this newest David; and now their relationship had come to seem like a mere contest of wills. "Everything must be done his way," Merrill complained, before turning to clear-eyed self-analysis:

I had seen him at first as the absolute opposite of Strato, but at this point they resemble one another, strikingly. Or else, a more interesting notion, stubbornness is merely my word for common personal dignity, and is felt as maddening only when one wishes, as I did, with both S + DMc, to possess the other person.

During the late summer and early fall in Nambé, Merrill worked on poems that would appear in *Braving the Elements*. One was "The Victor Dog." Cast in Merrill's signature *abba* quatrains and dedicated to Elizabeth Bishop, the poem is a sad, comic homage to the little white dog, one ear cocked, listening for "his master's voice" on the RCA Victor record label. The once-familiar commercial icon provides Merrill with an emblem of the life dedicated to art. That life requires diligence and modesty, such as Bishop exemplified for Merrill; Victor "Listens long and hard as he is able. / It's all in a day's work, whatever plays." Merrill delights in the dog's sensual, rather than studied, experience of music: he doesn't so much hear as smell "Those lemon-gold arpeggios in Ravel's / 'Les jets d'eau du palais de ceux qui s'aiment' "; he sniffs "Through one of Bach's eternal boxwood mazes / The oboe pungent as a bitch in heat." Yet Victor cannot enter the world of music he hears; his desires go ungratified; his master never appears in the flesh; and at the end of the day, he's on his own. Hence the poignant contrast between Victor's exalted dreams and his lowly, lonely condition:

The last chord fades. The night is cold and fine.
His master's voice rasps through the grooves' bare groves.

Obediently, in silence like the grave's
He sleeps there on the still-warm gramophone

Only to dream he is at the première of a Handel
Opera long thought lost—*Il Cane Minore*.
Its allegorical subject is his story!
A little dog revolving round a spindle

Gives rise to harmonies beyond belief,
A cast of stars . . . Is there in Victor's heart
No honey for the vanquished? Art is art.
The life it asks of us is a dog's life.

In Victor asleep, we glimpse Merrill nodding off in his adobe cottage, practicing being alone, with wind in the piñon grove, while the stylus "rasps" at the end of the evening's last record.

Another poem finished at this time was "Syrinx," a lyric begun in Stonington in June, and eventually placed after "The Victor Dog" as the last poem in *Braving the Elements*. While "The Victor Dog" would be dedicated to Bishop, "Syrinx" was linked in Merrill's mind to another older female friend, Irma Brandeis.* Like "From the Cupola," but now in miniature, the poem is a retelling of Greek myth. It is a love story in which the poet, writing from the point of view of a female lover transformed by passion, speaks as the nymph Syrinx. Driven by lustful Pan to hide in the reeds beside a river, Syrinx was changed into a reed—and then cut down by the god and made into a pipe for him to play. The poem is a fable about the origins of love poetry. Syrinx is "Illiterate—X my mark," but the nymph is capable of wild word games, as in these lines: "Who puts his mouth to me / Draws out the scale of love and dread— // O ramify, sole antidote!" Let the final "d" in "dread" merge with the "O" that follows, and the ascending notes of the musical scale (do-re-me-fa-sol-la-ti-do) suddenly become audible in that otherwise obscure exclamation, "O ramify, sole antidote!"

---

* In his "Memorial Tribute to Irma Brandeis," Merrill claims that he began "Syrinx" as a "windy and rambling" letter to Brandeis that connected the extreme back pain she was then experiencing to his own emotional pain. She gently chided him by letter for writing a poem that was too "intimate." "A few weeks later, when I'd recovered from the rebuke, I reworked my lines, cutting away its perishable tissue of narrative, and leaving only a skeletal trellis of images and feelings. Thinking of Irma's flute, and of the nymph who turned into the reeds from which Pan made his pipes, I called it 'Syrinx,' and Irma's next letter gave out the fragrant balm of her full approval. This is what it is like to have a muse in one's life" (*Prose*, 370). The worksheet drafts of "Syrinx," beginning with notes made in Stonington in June 1969, do not include the draft of the poem Merrill describes (worksheets for "Syrinx," WUSTL).

In a letter to Kalstone with a draft of "Syrinx," Merrill spoke of this bit of wordplay as "[a] John Hollander effect." Hollander had just published a review of *The Fire Screen* that reassured Merrill of the success of the book. Hollander's own poetry was full of intricate codes and devices, such as the shape poems—a poem about a car key in the shape of a key, or the double-image poem "Swan and Shadow"—included in *Types of Shape*, which Hollander dedicated to Merrill when it appeared in 1969. Hollander's wordplay had behind it the examples of any number of Latin and Greek wits, Renaissance sonneteers, and devotional poets. It encouraged Merrill to incorporate in his poetry more of the verbal games that up to this point had been largely confined to notebooks and letters. "Syrinx" is a prime example. It includes both a mathematical equation and the sort of verbal-visual emblem found in *Types of Shape*, in this case a compass that rhymes:

> Some formula not relevant any more
> To flower children might express it yet
>
> Like $\sqrt{\left(\frac{x}{y}\right)^n} = I$
> —Or equals zero, one forgets—
>
> The y standing for you, dear friend, at least
> Until that hour he reaches for me, then
>
> Leaves me cold, the great god Pain,
> Letting me slide back into my scarred case
>
> Whose silvery breath-tarnished tones
> No longer rivet bone and star in place
>
> Or keep from shriveling, leather round a stone,
> The sunbather's precocious apricot
>
> Or stop the four winds racing overhead
>
>
>
> Nought
>
> Waste   Eased
>
> Sought
>
>

Merrill was not quite so alone as a poet as he'd felt back in the spring. Besides Hollander, Yenser appreciated lines like these. To Merrill's delight,

Yenser noticed that he'd placed the "y" for "you" and the "x" for Syrinx herself ("X my mark," she says) in the square root equation, and that the fraction that the "you" and "I" make, one on top of the other, was multiplied by "n"—using four of the letters in Syrinx's name. But Yenser had missed, Merrill pointed out, that the "s" and "r," the remaining letters, were implied by the square root sign itself.

This is intensely clever poetry, but it's not mere cleverness for its own sake: the cleverness is a means to master pain, which it expresses while keeping "pain" (in this case a play on Pan's name) partly hidden, as in the encodings of that provocative though baffling formula. No longer "relevant" to "flower children" of the 1960s, with their free love and new math, Merrill's equation tells a very old truth: love tends to add up either merely to "I" (the roman numeral, rather than the Arabic, suggesting the first person, the self, the lover's own "I") or to nothing at all, zero. Merrill is reasoning much the same way as when he wrote in his notebook about his failed struggle to possess "DMc" and "S." Those stories are not so much kept out of the poem as buried in it, like encoded information too important to trust to regular mail.

In "Syrinx" the West is called "Waste": was that what Merrill's visit to McIntosh and New Mexico had come to, a waste? Snow fell on October 12. The desert soaked it up, turning salmon pink. The next day Merrill read at St. John's College in the hills above Santa Fe; he planned the program: "The Broken Home, Prism, Butterfly, 1002nd Night, Maisie, To my Greek, D in Velies, A Tenancy." Then he and McIntosh left on a short trip to Canyon de Chelly and Monument Valley in Arizona. In his notebook, he wrote, "Heaven is finite, and always was." The two men made the long drive back to Nambé in silence. Three days later, in the evening on October 21, Hellen Plummer called in tears: Bill was dead. Merrill packed at once for Atlanta.

When they drove to the Santa Fe airport, McIntosh remembered, "James was crying." Once Merrill had composed himself, "he suggested that he was belatedly grieving for his father," rather than Bill, for whom he had only ever had a polite feeling. "Your sweetness and understanding throughout those last hours," Merrill wrote to McIntosh once he'd arrived in Atlanta, "helped more than I can tell you—but then, you have always, always helped. [. . .] Out of my own abysmal cynicism I have observed both you and myself as through a needle's eye for any sign that we are less than dear + wonderful friends; and have found none." Just before he left, McIntosh cut Merrill's hair, a service intimate and ordinary that Jimmy found soothing. Rising early in his mother's house, he amused himself by writing an anagram poem using McIntosh's full name, including his middle name, Wesley.

> Danced with is my love's
> Wildest comedy. Vanish,
> Envy, dew-lid masochist!
> Did costly heaven swim?
> Day-child moves in west.
> Vast cold winds eye him.

Merrill's little poem would do as a farewell to DMc for now.

Bill's death "must have been instantaneous and painless." He and Hellen were at home watching television, and had just shared a joke and assured each other of their love, when he collapsed. "It is viewed by everyone as a godsend; perhaps even by Bill himself, who knows?" The general's body was brought to Jacksonville to be buried in the Ingram family plot. A military escort attended the flag-draped coffin ("odd that the Pop artists have never pounced on <u>that</u> image," Merrill mused); at last "a tall black corporal [. . .] handed my mother the folded flag and mumbled his piece about a Grateful Country." Letters of condolence flooded the house in Atlanta; these "we must file on 3 x 5 cards against the day when 600 (or 1000) cards have been engraved, each of which will bear a 'personal' note of gratitude. It is madness, but a madness that prevents graver ones." Jimmy admired "the ability of Southern womanhood to cope—with flowers, covered dishes, suave telephonic arrangements." Betty and Tom Potts were on hand to help, as well as Aunt Mil and the Hafleys, and all the well-meaning company wearied him. He preferred time spent alone with his mother. "At least with her there have been some touching moments—moments of closeness, moments (even) of truth." Yet "[t]he trouble with 'moments of truth' is that they are only moments."

By the middle of November he was back in Stonington, where "Daryl <u>and</u> Richard Howard <u>and</u> Harry Ford" were due ("The first expects a rest; the second, lots of attention; the third, plentiful + delicious meals"). In Boston, he heard Reverend Buechner "lecture on the subject of Grace (not Mrs. Stone)." He found it a "brilliant performance," "only I didn't believe a word of it. I didn't believe <u>in</u> his experience, his calling, in the Christ he invokes so sonorously (<u>where</u> do preachers <u>learn</u> that ghastly plain-song [. . .]?)." Soon Merrill was in Rome with Umberto. He and Jackson would reunite in Athens for Christmas.

In the Arizona desert he had brooded on a new poem to complement the quatrains for McIntosh finished in March, a poem of "descent," exploring "what lies at the bottom." Merrill's days in Atlanta supplied a vignette he would work into a new poem over the winter in Athens. When he put it together with "Snow King Chair Lift," "The Emerald" made a diptych he titled "Up and Down."

"The Emerald" describes a trip Merrill and his mother make to the bank in the days following General Plummer's death. Their destination—a "Mutual Trust"—is shadowed and chill; "palatial bronze gates shut like jaws / On our descent into this inmost vault"; and as easily as that, the poem becomes a mythic journey to the underworld.

A "tin box painted mud-brown" is exhumed, placed before mother and son. After first examining a diamond bracelet given to Hellen by Charlie ("my father's kisses hang / In lipless concentration round her wrist"), she picks out a ring. "He gave / Me this when you were born," she says, speaking of Charlie. "Here, take it for—"

> "For when you marry. For your bride. It's yours."
> A den of greenest light, it grows, shrinks, glows,
> Hermetic stanza bedded in the prose
> Of the last thirty semiprecious years.
>
> I do not tell her, it would sound theatrical,
> *Indeed this green room's mine, my very life.*
> *We are each other's; there will be no wife;*
> *The little feet that patter here are metrical.*
>
> But onto her worn knuckle slip the ring.
> Wear it for me, I silently entreat,
> Until—until the time comes. Our eyes meet.
> The world beneath the world is brightening.

The ring commands Jimmy to procreate and reproduce the family. The gift of it here oddly evokes the exchange of rings in a wedding ceremony. Even as she speaks of his marrying another, Hellen is asking her son, it seems, to marry her—as if, now that his stepfather is gone, his turn has come.

He circumvents the oppressive gesture. In stage-whisper italics, he interprets the ring as a symbol of the children that he will not have because he has chosen to write poems instead. "*The little feet that patter here are metrical*": the line, a "theatrical," showy one with two final unstressed syllables, a double "feminine ending" that patters with a quiet little flourish, makes us feel the punning equivalence between these two kinds of feet as if it were an obvious fact. "*We are each other's*" is an ambiguous way to state his dedication to art: when he says "we," he might mean himself and the ring (and the art it symbolizes), or he might mean himself and his mother, or somehow both. When he slips the ring onto her hand instead of his own, even as he refuses it, he repeats his father's long-ago gesture of bestowal. He *is* marrying his mother at last, although, because he's refused the conventional life of a husband and father she projected for him, the contract is sealed on his terms rather than hers. He is going, and getting, his own way.

"The Emerald" is remarkable both for its gentleness and its candor. Somehow Merrill had arrived at a point at which he could acknowledge both his homosexuality and his bond with his mother, with neither one canceling the other. The poem comes as a relief after the violent impulses directed at the figure of the mother in "To My Greek" and "Mornings in a New House," not to mention his nightmare vision of mother and son screaming at each other with shit on their hands. A death has brought them together. And now, when their eyes meet in this poem's moment of truth, however passing, however contrived, Merrill knows that only death will part them.

12

PROUST'S LAW

1969–72

Merrill's first morning in Athens in December 1969 found him "up in my cold cubicle off the terrace"—the old laundry room, his new study, which he called "the Ivory Tower." His life in Greece would be centered now in this high, bare, private room. Thumping and sawing behind him, workmen on the next street were erecting an apartment house that blocked Athinaion Efivon's view of the sea, or of "a smoky blue smudge in the direction of the sea." A metal heater "glared" at the poet-anchorite's ankles; the sink's broken faucet kept time, "childishly pleased by its recent discovery of the anapest." Everything Merrill had valued in Greece, he reflected that winter, "has shrunken to the little window above my table: a branch of oleander, a corner of green awning, a crust of mountain beneath the sad blue sky."

That morning at seven he began writing a poem about his arrival in Greece the day before; "as usual after a big change of scene," he told McIntosh, "I found I had a poem to write as soon as I entered this house." He conceived of "After the Fire," finished just two weeks later, as "a companion-piece" to "Days of 1964"; it celebrated his return to Greece and marked his distance from the life that he used to lead there. "About ⅗ of the poem is 'true,' " he reckoned, but even that fraction had to be put in scare quotes. In the poem Merrill has come back to Greece after a minor fire in his house; the fire left "no real damage," but has occasioned some modest home improvements. These ("Balcony glassed in, electric range," a "freshly-painted hall") were real, but the fire was purely metaphorical: a way of referring to Jimmy's affair with Strato, which was dangerous, he implies, but never quite burned down the house.

Kyria Kleo and her family, who are in the background in "Days of 1964," take center stage here. If Kleo was a dreamlike figure in the first poem, she becomes a good deal more real in "After the Fire." Noticeably older, her "lips chill as the fallen dusk," she arrives to welcome the poet with a cake and share her sorrows. "Her old mother has gone off the deep end." Spending her days at the window of their basement apartment, the *yiayiá* "Hurls invective at the passing scene, / Tea bags as well, the water bill, an egg / For emphasis." As a car pulls up, "She cackles *Here's the client! Paint your face, / Putana!*" while her daughter, who once really was "a buxom armful," weeps over her ironing. "Nor is darling Panayióti, Kleo's son / Immune." (Panayióti is the name Merrill gives Lakis in the poem.) "Our entire neighborhood now knows / As if they hadn't years before / That he is a *Degenerate!* a *Thieving / Faggot!* just as Kleo is a *Whore!*" The *yiayiá*'s body is strangely "*warm*," on fire with "this terrible gift of hindsight" into her family's sins.

The next day, a feast day, Merrill pays a visit to the household. As he approaches the grandmother, who fails to recognize him, he is suddenly gripped by the grandson's "anaconda arms." A camp set piece follows, in which Panayióti, describing a night of lovemaking with the Priest "Dans une alcove derrière la Sainte Imaze," speaks in the French-Greek patois that Merrill and Parigory used with each other. As he listens, Merrill notices that Panayióti is wearing his own bathrobe; he catches sight of a familiar teapot and radio too, but decides not to call attention to these stolen objects. It must be "that P caused the fire. / Kleo's key borrowed for a rendezvous, / A cigarette left burning. . ." At this point the *yiayiá* comes to her senses, crying out: "*It's Tzimi! He's returned!*"

> —And with that she returns to human form,
> The snuffed-out candle-ends grow tall and shine,
> Dead flames encircle us, which cannot harm,
> The table's spread, she croons, and I
> Am kneeling pressed to her old burning frame.

It is a moving homecoming. As he kneels as if to receive a blessing, the poet presses himself to the "frame" that is the house of the grandmother's body, and the "fire" he warms himself by is dear life itself. After the chill of the poet's recent weeks in the high desert of New Mexico with elusive David McIntosh, he basks in the glow of fiery, colloquial Athens. He immediately had a sense of how the experience would fit into his next book: "this yiayia poem [. . .] must be among other things an apologia for the 'hermetic' poems in the book it would conclude (or open)." Eventually placed second in *Braving the Elements*, after the prefatory poem "Log," "After the Fire" implies not only an apology for the "hermetic" turn Merrill's poems had taken, but a dream of forgiveness in which he is welcomed into a half-imagined family that stood in for his own. The key figure in his mind was the son, Panayióti. He identifies with him not only in his sexual appetite, but also in his thievery, which is an aspect of the original "hermetic" poet, Hermes himself. Poet and thief are linked with each other as two faces of the god. Musing in his notebook, Merrill notices the connection, and then matches Kleo and the *yiayiá* with his mother and Mis' Annie: "If poet + thief are one, then the identification between 2 sets of 3 generations (my family + theirs—a 10th carbon copy, says DJ of mine) is complete."

While he worked on this poem, Merrill was becoming increasingly involved with another Greek family. Called Taki (the diminutive of "Christaki"), Christos Alevras was a friend of George Lazaretos who had served with him in the Greek navy. Taki hardly appears in Merrill's letters or notebooks until the fall of 1968, when Jackson proposed that he and Merrill arrange for Taki, his wife, and their little girl to live on the second floor of 107 Water Street, while Taki would serve as a handyman and caretaker for the property. It was an idea that had been bubbling for some time, with other characters in Taki's role. Jimmy told David that Taki "is certainly more dependable than Strato, and more independent than Kosta T—and it might be something in our old age to have a little family like his to count on."

A telegram announcing the approval of Taki's visa arrived at Athinaion Efivon 44 just as Merrill did in December 1969. The prospect of bringing Alevras to Water Street stirred in him "ripples of commotion," but not enough to cause him to think better of the plan: he would take Alevras with him when he returned to Connecticut in March. In letters to the U.S., Merrill began to introduce Taki to his friends, so as to prepare the way for his arrival. His comments to Daryl Hine are typical:

> Taki got his visa yesterday. Have I explained about him? If I haven't it's too complicated to go into, but we've known him 5 years, + now we are taking him (or I am) to Stonington where he will be our house man. His wife + baby girl will follow a month or

two later, by the end of May [. . .]. He is a goodhearted ape-man with a nice square smiling face and very little by way of brains behind it. But a homebody, and not sly. Pushing 30. The wife is 22 with glimmerings of style, and the child, at 2, already can say Kizz me plis to her doll. That is, strange to say, almost the only phrase her father knows in English.

He loves it when I "obey." It may all be a dreadful mistake, but one is <u>meant</u> to make mistakes of precisely this sort in later life, don't you agree? And up to now, thank Heaven, I'm not in love.

This is not a flattering portrait of either Alevras or his American sponsor. If they didn't already have a sexual relationship, it appears they had one now; without being either "in love" with Alevras nor even especially attracted to him, though ready to teach him how to put sentences like "Kizz me plis" to use, Merrill could only adopt a cynical attitude toward their relations.

There was more to it, however, than gratification, there being much easier, less elaborate ways to achieve that. Merrill liked the idea of having a manservant, as his father had had in Leroy Johnson. He joked with Richard Howard that Taki "will not be Villiers' kind of valet who could live for me [. . .] and I'm afraid that he can't count high enough to be much use as Leporello." (He alludes to Villiers de L'Isle-Adam, who wrote, "As to living, let our servants do that for us," and to Leporello, the servant of Mozart's Don Giovanni.) In his early letters envisioning the arrangement, Merrill makes it clear that he enjoyed the idea of sponsoring a family living downstairs from him. It was not enough that the "little feet" in Merrill's home were "metrical."

Like a charm, the plan to bring Alevras to the U.S. summoned Mouflouzélis back on the scene. In late January Strato telephoned, "+ my heart," Merrill reported to Louise Fitzhugh, "began to throb + flood like a sinking ship." He appeared in person at Athinaion Efivon 44 with a cast up to his elbow from an accident at a building site where he was working; while Kleo cleaned and Taki painted a room, Strato nervously dispensed his news: he and Vaso were living together outside Athens; their son was three. On his next visit, Merrill arranged to be alone with him, and they quickly recovered their old intimacy. The poet wrote in his notebook: "Heart to heart with S for the 1st time in 3 years. Both full of love. Both entirely impotent." Merrill's young love was now twenty-eight: "The age at which even an extraordinary person must in some way have hardened: automatic responses, plundering of natural resources, pollution of airs given oneself." He'd grown heavy, there was "a pimple on his nostril above the absurd hairline moustache," and his hair was "falling out." Even so Merrill was stirred, as if an important question had been answered. He decided happily,

> It is the mind we love. Not, in my case, the mind as swift, deli-
> cate, expressive, tentative, reading at sight the most difficult
> music—I'd fall in love with DK if that were so. A mind differ-
> ently shaped, half emerged from the unimaginable disciplines
> of poverty, letters spelt out one by one (as at the Ouija board),
> sure only of its own swagger + truth which it pounds as a mate-
> rialist does a table-top for proof. To whom subtlety is not a goal.
> S. said: "But how could I have forgotten you? I loved you like a
> brother—more than a brother, because at home I could sit + wait
> an hour before anyone spoke to me. [. . .] Nobody ever behaved
> so handsomely towards me as you."

"Now I am free to come twice a week to you," Mouflouzélis declared, "to spend weekends, the night, whatever. I've understood at last. My behavior has been inexcusable, but what could I do? I was caught between two worlds." These words, which Merrill had longed to hear three years before, were still welcome, if for somewhat different reasons. He replied, "I cannot tell you what it means for you to have come back like this. Whatever is in store for us. But to know that you remember, that you love the memory as I do."

The season was Carnival. Cecilia Holland was in Athens, and Jackson, Merrill, and she, high on pot, went "roving through Plaka's confetti-filled streets until 3 a.m., when we all fell asleep in our Arab gear"—souvenirs from Yahya's Isfahan in 1965—"+ our cork moustaches. It seems sometimes that I remember what it was like to live this way, but I could just as easily be thinking of a book read or a movie seen—foreign, with misleading subti-tles," he explained to Yenser. "Out of a movie surely was that woman, at the last tavern, dancing on a tabletop, skirt up to her waist, and in a pirate hat." On the last night of the holiday, two couples reunited to restage a familiar scene, this time with their roles reversed. "S. + I were in the downstairs bedroom in a sad swoon of joy," Merrill told Kalstone, "recalling, caress-ing, explaining away (with scant accuracy no doubt) old misunderstand-ings; while upstairs the other lovers"—David and George—"shouted insults + broke things. Puccini knew."

No sooner had Mouflouzélis appeared with his broken arm than Merrill wrote a poem about their reunion, "Strato in Plaster." As in "After the Fire," the lag time between life and art had shrunk to hours: what took place one day on the first floor of Athinaion Efivon 44 the poet put into verse the next day at his desk on the roof. In contrast to "Days of 1964" and "To My Greek,"

Strato is named and quite vividly portrayed in this poem. "Twin jewels unsold somehow, / His eyes are sparkling with delight." The full portrait comes with increased distance, however. When he sees Strato again, Merrill sees through him. The poem's focus is on the self-pitying, yet winningly stagy, style in which he tells his story. Becoming real, Strato has become the lead in a Greek soap opera, rather than Eros incarnate: "The god in him is a remembered one" only. In this light, Merrill sees his broken arm as an emblem of their breakup:

> Inflexibility through which twinges shoot
> Like stars, the fracture's too complex,
> Too long unmended, for us to be friends.
> I, he hazards, have made other friends.
> The more reason, then, to part like friends.

Merrill told Strato that he didn't know what was "in store" for them, but his poem already knew that they could at best hope to part like "friends." When he left Greece in March, it was Taki who was on the plane with him.

Shortly before noon on March 6, 1970, a massive explosion tore through the basement of a brick townhouse in Greenwich Village. The blast ripped a hole in the front of the building, spewing bricks, wood, and glass, shattering windows on the facing apartments. Fire trucks arrived as two smaller explosions erupted. The firemen believed that the explosion was the result of a gas leak. Inside they encountered two young women stumbling toward the door; one was naked, the other wore only a pair of jeans; both were bleeding, coughing, and black with soot. As they were led outside, one kept asking, "Where is Adam?" Then flames burst from the windows, and the façade fell. On the street newspaper cameras caught a wary, squinting Dustin Hoffman: the actor, whose role in *The Graduate* had made him an icon of the era, lived in an apartment next door with his wife and child, and his desk had tumbled into the fire when a wall gave way. Once the fire was extinguished, collapsing beams made it impossible to enter the site until a crane demolished what was left of the second and third floors, turning 18 West Eleventh Street into a charred socket. That evening, under the glare of floodlights, rescue workers uncovered a man's body in the smoldering rubble. "They continued to comb the debris, however," *The New York Times* explained, "because of reports that a small boy had also been in the house."

A small boy *had* been in the house. But James Merrill hadn't set foot in his former home since 1930; and when the explosion took place, he was still in Athens. He flew to the U.S. a week later. Back in Stonington, he started to take in the story, reading articles about it in *The New York Times* and *Life*. The property had changed hands twice since his family had lived there. First Charles Merrill had sold the "little house on heaven street" to Howard Dietz, the publicist who designed the MGM roaring lion and a successful Broadway lyricist in the 1930s. In 1963 Dietz sold it to James Platt Wilkerson, an advertising executive who owned a chain of radio stations in the Midwest.

It was Wilkerson's twenty-four-year-old daughter Cathy who staggered out of the burning house, naked, asking for "Adam." She had studied violin as a child and been a good student in private schools, but in college she turned against her privileged background and her parents' expectations. At Swarthmore, she became involved in civil rights activism and protests against the Vietnam War. She joined Students for a Democratic Society and the SDS offshoot the Weathermen, who believed in the necessity of revolutionary violence. In October 1969, Wilkerson was an organizer of the "Days of Rage" demonstrations in Chicago. "Bring the War Home!" was their slogan. Marching beside her in Chicago, with a crash helmet and a Vietcong flag tacked to a two-by-four, was Kathy Boudin. Boudin had graduated from Bryn Mawr College in 1967 with a major in Russian literature. She was a veteran labor organizer and, as the niece of the journalist I. F. Stone and the daughter of Leonard Boudin, defense attorney for the antiwar activists Daniel and Philip Berrigan, she had close ties to leaders of the American left. In March 1970, while James Wilkerson vacationed in St. Kitts, Cathlyn Wilkerson and Boudin, free on bail after being arrested during the Chicago protests, had moved into 18 West Eleventh Street with other members of the Weathermen.

Wilkerson had fitted the basement for his hobby of refinishing antique furniture. There the group stored two fifty-pound cases of dynamite, plastic pipes, bales of doorbell wire, and timing devices; they spoke of bombing Lowe Library at Columbia University or an officers' dance at Fort Dix in New Jersey. There were two people in the workroom on March 6: Diana Oughton, granddaughter of the founder of the Boy Scouts of America and a former debutante, and Terry Robbins, who had joined SDS at the University of Michigan. That morning he was building a bomb by wrapping dynamite with fistfuls of roofing nails; the technique was meant to produce the maximum loss of life, in imitation of the antipersonnel bombs used by the U.S. Army in Vietnam. But the amateur bomb maker detonated his first creation. The blast pulverized him and Oughton: two days later, her torso was found riddled with nails; Robbins's remains could not be identified. Upstairs in the first-floor parlor, Theodore Gold, a twenty-three-year-old leader of recent student protests at Columbia, was at work on a memoir about his activism; he also was killed instantly (his was the body reported in the first headlines). Wilkerson and Boudin, upstairs in the sauna on the third floor, were unharmed. While firemen worked to stop the blaze, a neighbor gave them clothes and bandages. Then they disappeared. Fugitives now, Wilkerson and Boudin appeared for years on FBI "WANTED" signs in post offices across the country.

These events were sensational enough to have ignited anyone's imagination, but Merrill was especially prepared to be stirred. In "An Urban Convalescence," he had pictured himself standing numbly in front of a townhouse in ruins; as he stood in front of 18 West Eleventh Street in early April 1970, that scene came to grim life; the bomb site was also a new, grotesque, weirdly literal image of "The Broken Home." On April 7, feeling his way toward a poem about the blast, and yet suspicious of that impulse too, he wrote in his notebook,

> 18 W 11
> Destroyed by a bomb.
>
> Anyone could write the poem
> And may be doing so this afternoon, like me
> Exploded structures are what we know.

In the margin he added,

> Those walls did not contain even themselves.
> That mirror
> The playmate never stepped through
> To take your hand.
>
> Some may even feel the rightness
> Of a male self destroyed in his basement
> While the 2 girls nude + nameless as genies
> Slip through blazing meshes of publicity.

The next day he made another start:

> I was born in that house.
>
> The public is frozen demanding "the facts"
> "A full investigation"—bless their hearts.

> Anything that entirely comes to light
> Is consumed by light—look at the moth.

And a week later, on April 14:

> A blackened bookcase, shelves still full, clings to the side of
> the void.
> My mother saw the photograph in Life
> And felt her inside crumple

Down the page, floating alone, was the name "Adam."

That spring, as Merrill drafted what he foresaw would be "another long + hermetic poem," he was a detective, sorting mental wreckage: "The essential keeps eluding me in my work on 18 W 11. Moment after moment I reach one clue or another—and when I come to write it is out of my head." The poem was not completed until the next winter, ten months after he began it. The clues were various: the poet's early childhood memories would be fused with the bombers' story and with myth. For 18 West Eleventh Street was Eden, it was the House of Thebes: "exploded structures" all. For that matter, the *poem* was an "exploded structure," with its jagged line breaks, syntactic fragments, and hot, emotionally charged images. But the poem was also a sort of bomb, and Merrill understood some of the motives, some of the aggression, of the well-to-do revolutionaries. In his notebook he pointed to a level on which his psychology and theirs intersected: "The breaking out of the interior stultification—going through the mirror. / Refusing the comforts of home."

In this light, the explosion could be read as an awful, botched communication from one generation to the previous one, from the Age of Aquarius to everyone still dwelling in the past. "18 West 11th Street" begins,

> In what at least
> Seemed anger the Aquarians in the basement
> Had been perfecting a device
>
> For making sense to us
> If only briefly and on pain
> Of incommunication ever after.

The house itself might have understood the message. While its owners abandoned it for Southampton and Palm Beach, the carpet "Hatched another generation / Of strong-jawed, light-besotted saboteurs," and "A mastermind / Kept track above the mantel." Subversion seems built into things; the story of generational succession is time's plot against every family. But the air was hypercharged in a dream house whose "wall-to-wall / Extravagance without variety" was a "buzzing vacuum" waiting to "be fed." The small boy felt the abandonment and emptiness that Merrill ascribes to the objects he mentions. As a child, he looked into the mirror, seeking another world, another self. When his fantasized "playmate" arrived, however, it was forty years later and in the unexpected form of a naked young woman, Cathlyn Wilkerson or Kathy Boudin, who is pictured in the closing stanzas of the poem:

> [. . .] Sea serpent
> Hoses recoil, the siren drowns in choking
> Wind. The crowd has thinned to a coven
>
> Rigorously chosen from so many called. Our
> Instant trance. The girl's
> Appearance now among us, as foreseen
>
> Naked, frail but fox-eyed, head to toe
> (Having passed through the mirror)
> Adorned with heavy shreds of ribbon
>
> Sluggish to bleed. She stirs, she moans the name
> Adam. And is *gone*. By her own
> Broom swept clean, god, stop, behind this
>
> Drunken backdrop of debris, airquake,
> Flame in bloom—a pigeon's throat
> Lifting, the puddle
>
> Healed. To let:
> Cream paint, brown ivy, brickflush. Eye
> Of the old journalist unwavering
>
> Through gauze. Forty-odd years gone by.
> Toy blocks. Church bells. Original vacancy.
> O deepening spring.

The writing is tense and electric in this, the most ambitious poem Merrill had produced on a political topic. He imagines the scene as if on a newsreel, "Run backwards, parching, scorching" to the point when Wilkerson and Boudin merge in the spectral girl, who materializes as if at a séance, and they both merge with the unmentioned victim in the basement, all of them "*gone*," one way or another. Then, like a pigeon veering up from the street, the poem pulls away from the bombing to view the scene from another perspective entirely. At this height, catastrophe can be seen as a phase in a traumatic cycle of renewal. The point of view spans past and future as Merrill's image of "Cream paint, brown ivy, brickflush" moves ahead to when the house would be rebuilt (as indeed it would be in a much-commented-on, jagged modern design) and backward to when his family lived there. In the final stanza's sentence fragments, we race back past the poet's childhood ("Toy Blocks") and his parents' marriage ("Church bells") to an "Original vacancy" that is every point of origin. The poet's last lyric "O," like the "deepening spring" he celebrates, expresses joy and pain equally.

Merrill worked on the poem while he helped Alevras settle into his new life on Water Street. Joe Bruno and Peter Tourville took Taki fishing, introduced him to the bar at the Holy Ghost Society, showed him the local strip joints, and got him a job at the velvet mill. Merrill took him to New York, where Donald Richie, now curator of film at the Museum of Modern Art, gave them coffee at the museum. They saw "the hideous Easter Stage Show at Radio City" and, with David Kalstone, the circus. Alevras and Merrill were on "good, formal, friendly terms," but it was not a typical business relationship. No sooner had they appeared in the village than Eleanor invited Jimmy to dinner. After they'd drunk two bottles of champagne, it was, Merrill told Jackson, "child's play for her to get the whole story out of me: 'I knew it, I knew he was your lover, and what's more so does everybody in town. Oh Jimmy mou, what a fool you are—all you people exploiting those poor simpletons." Blithe as ever, Merrill shrugged off the charge and gave his hostess some gifts he'd brought back from Greece, prints by Tsarouchis, inviting her to see things his way.

Alevras's wife and daughter followed in May. He and Merrill went to collect them at the airport; on the road home the little girl, Georgia, wanted to know, "Where is America?" It was a fair question. With weekly reports of bombs and protests and the extension of the war in Vietnam into Cambodia, "What one gleans of America," Merrill felt, "is a NIGHTMARE." Little

Georgia and Jimmy made friends: seeing "where her bread is buttered," she "keeps throwing herself into my arms, cooing + flirting, calling to me from windows or from below-stairs." Nonetheless, now that "the Greek sacra famiglia" was installed on Water Street, "frequent absences" seemed "imperative" to Merrill, and he began making plans. In the weeks ahead, he would set out on a long journey to two novel, distant destinations: Peru with Charles and Mary Merrill, and Brazil, where he would visit Elizabeth Bishop.

Bishop and her admiring junior—"Jim," she called him—had been cordial but not close friends for more than twenty years, and she probably never expected him to accept her invitation to visit her in remote Ouro Preto. It was a particularly difficult moment in her life. The woman she had been living with in Brazil had had a breakdown and gone back to the U.S. Bishop, drinking heavily, was nervous at the prospect of entertaining her first "REAL visitor" in a long time, a poet coming "from away off, on purpose," but she needed companionship and understanding. She tested Merrill's trustworthiness by assigning him tasks by mail. She asked him, like a knight errant, to fetch for her "some good tea" and "[a] bottle of Spice Islands ginger and another of their curry." Before he left, as he recalled much later, "a strangely shaped package came from a stove works in the state of Washington, and I was about to send it back when a letter came from Elizabeth saying a part of [her] stove needed to be replaced and she had asked them to send it to me. Would I mind bringing it along? It was quite heavy. She goes on a bit in a letter about it and said, 'I had better stop or I will end up telling you the first dirty joke I ever heard.' " She made him wait for that joke, while she added further special requests: Chapstick, stove polish, cigarettes, Scotch, and kirsch.

McIntosh came to visit Merrill before he left for Latin America. Reunited for the first time since General Plummer's death abruptly separated them in October, they spent five days in Stonington. With Kalstone visiting, they played with the Ouija board and saw Rollie McKenna and the Morses. Then, back in the city at 950 First Avenue, on the eve of McIntosh's departure, they went to bed together. "He said he wanted to come + live near me, that he cared for my friendship more than anyone's," Merrill wrote in his notebook. "I have promised him support for 3 years." He added, "Not 20 pages back, S. was saying the same thing." He confided to Jackson, "It leaves me terribly touched + bewildered—this kind of Xmas-in-July treatment coming first from Strato and now him, I feel like crumpling to my knees and crying long hot tears." Adding up his current romantic involvements, he lost count: "More + more it seems quite natural to be in love with several people at once, like three buds about to blossom on the same stem. Or four."

Merrill prepared for his trip to Latin America by reading Gabriel García Márquez's novel *One Hundred Years of Solitude* (it seemed to him "almost the most beautiful book I have ever read") and by writing a peculiar travelogue. The editor of a new magazine called *Prose* had asked Merrill to write about Peru. "I said I'd try, and what does he do but send a large check in advance? So I am trying to write the piece in advance, before I leave. It's great fun. Impressions never to be tarnished by sense." Although he did revise it in the light of experience, Merrill's "Peru: The Landscape Game" was as much a piece about travel writing as an example of it. Taking the psychological game he had played years ago with Robin Magowan as a model for the piece, Merrill explored the fears and fancies that the notion of visiting this "new world" stirred in him. Before he ever saw it, Peru had become a metaphor for the stereoscopic overlay of fantasy and reality, imagination and observation that is involved in travel to any storied place. "This is Peru," he wrote, "a déja vu to be revised henceforth like galleys from the printer."

Yet he was unprepared for the poverty he witnessed there: crumbling adobe, bare feet, "the whiff of death." Outside Lima, the Merrill party visited temples: "dust made into bricks then allowed to revert to dust" but bound by what seemed like "grave clothes, shreds of shroud that had Mary (the weaver) exclaiming in rapture." Charles, the only one of the party who spoke Spanish, arranged to meet civic leaders. He called on the archbishop and found his secretary surrounded by crates of Metrecal: surplus cases of this popular diet drink had been dispatched from the U.S. to aid victims of the recent earthquake; they would not be much use, Charles explained, unless the victims were society ladies. High in Cuzco the little party took in "ravishing" churches built on "Inca foundations." Inside one a rendering of the Last Supper showed "the company sitting down to roast guinea pig and flagons of chicha." The Merrills discovered other delicacies on the street: pickled partridge, sweet potato ice cream, and coca leaves that they chewed with pumice to release the juices. As a train carried them higher along the "foaming glassy rapids" of the Urubamba River toward Machu Picchu, Merrill took notes so as to share the experience with McIntosh: "mts. not seen since productions of Wagner in 1940"; "The jungle at high altitudes: something we must all contend with in our own natures."

A week later Bishop met him at the airport in Belo Horizonte, capital of the province of Minas Gerais in central Brazil. "I was driven at once to the tail end of a children's party," Merrill told Kalstone, "and given first beer, then cachaca sours (followed by a last qt. of beer in E's hotel room). The cake was a soccer field a yard long with green coconut grass + 22 baby players. [. . .] Only a Dr. who spent a year in Chattanooga spoke English." The next day the two poets drove to Ouro Preto, a silver mining town known for its Baroque architecture. Bishop's Casa Mariana, so named in honor of Marianne Moore and because it pressed up next to the road to the town of Mariana, was a rambling eighteenth-century house with a valley view, a big garden, and guava, avocado, and banana trees. Its walls mildewed from winter rains, the house was a decaying paradise that Bishop struggled to maintain. She and Merrill spent most of their time inside, listening to samba records and chatting by the stove whose replacement parts the guest had faithfully conveyed all the way from Water Street. The room was full of semi-magical totems. Merrill listed them in a letter to Yenser: "the figurehead of an Amazon . . . canoe? It has a kind of Dr. Seuss head, horned, blue-eyes, with long yellow hair; [. . .] then a paddle on which the US + Brazilian flags are intertwined; a big brass tuba from the Ouro Preto band—before they switched to nickel; an old leather trunk; a big lightbulb with a crucifix inside."

The cast iron stove reminded him of Bishop's "Sestina," a poem in which a grandmother and child go about their day while rain drums on the roof, alone unless we count the animated objects around them: a tea kettle that "sings," a "clever" almanac, and the "marvellous stove." Calling back to her childhood, when she was cared for by her grandparents in Nova Scotia after the death of her father and the breakdown and permanent hospitalization of her mother, the stove, Merrill knew, evoked Bishop's early griefs and her strategies for surviving them. One evening he found her in a chair by the stove with books by Moore and Robert Lowell on the floor beside her. Only slowly did he realize she was quite drunk. A letter he'd written from Athens gave Bishop the impression that his lover there was dead, and she asked about him. Merrill told her about Strato and read "Strato in Plaster" aloud. Bishop began to weep. She talked about the suicide in 1967 of Lota de Macedo Soares, the Brazilian woman she'd fallen in love with when she first came to Brazil in 1951, whom Merrill knew slightly, and then the American woman who had left Bishop that spring and now wrote bitter, accusing letters. Another houseguest, a Brazilian painter, approached, then stopped in the doorway so as not to intrude. "His hostess almost blithely made him at home," Merrill remembered. "Switching to Portuguese, 'Don't be upset, José Alberto,' I understood her to say, 'I'm only crying in English.' "

When Merrill told this anecdote later in a memorial tribute, he stressed

Bishop's wit and panache. He didn't comment on the pain that he'd felt at the time seeing "this serene poet" whom he idolized "in such depths of sorrow, incapacity, shame." Over his visit, he watched her slip deeper and deeper into a sodden depression. One night when guests had been invited to dinner, Bishop was too drunk to host them, and he cooked and entertained in her place. Despite her struggles, however, or exactly because of them, the two poets were drawing closer. "I think you love me," she said to Merrill that evening by the stove, "so I can talk to you like this, can't I?" Merrill did love Bishop, both the poet and the person. His identification with her was as deep as his identification with Proust, and, as with Proust, Bishop's homosexuality—or better, her sense of the contingency of sex and gender—was part of his feeling. One morning when the rain let up, she and Merrill set out for a neighboring town. The taxi carried them "through sparkling red-and-green country, downhill, uphill, then all at once *under* a rainbow—like a halo on the hill's brow, almost touchable." Bishop made a remark to the driver, who "began to shake with laughter. 'In the north of Brazil,' Elizabeth explained, 'they have this superstition—if you pass through a rainbow you change sex.' " Merrill added, "We were to pass under this one more than once."

When he left, Bishop gave him a present: a tiny tin stove with pots on top containing real beans and grains of rice. Bishop followed him two months later to teach poetry writing at Harvard in place of Robert Lowell, beginning a phase of her life in which she and Merrill would see each other regularly. And what of the dirty joke she'd threatened to tell him when she asked him to deliver her replacement stove parts? "Well," Bishop said when he asked, "simply name three parts of the stove." The answer: lifter, leg, and poker.

On Water Street Merrill found that "a kind of nutty slum atmosphere" had taken hold. Taki's wife's cousin was now in residence too; when he was not working at the mill with Taki, he sat on the steps of 107, "shirtless, hugging his (my) transistor," while little Georgia played, or fell into a rage, with the boys who lived across the street. McIntosh met Merrill in New York, and told him that "he'd rather live with me than without me"; and so he too moved to Water Street, taking the apartment next to the Alevras family on the second floor. "The decision was enough to send me to bed for 5 days," Merrill confided to Parigory, "a real oldfashioned psychosomatic crise. I remain puzzled but am somehow getting used to it; but I still feel very dubious—where will it lead?"

Merrill and McIntosh headed north to Williamstown, Massachusetts, where they saw the Clark Museum's Gérômes "and a magical self-portrait of Degas at 23," to Pawlet to see Claude, and to Hancock, New Hampshire, "where Charles + Mary have a vast rural paradise, ponds + barns + great boulders." There, with the Merrills in Boston, poet and painter resumed the round of solitary work and companionable outdoor pleasures they'd enjoyed in Wyoming in 1968. "I couldn't feel as I do about DM if being with him didn't give me back an image of myself to which I cleave," Merrill told Jackson. "Something to do with detachment from too much 'dailiness' [. . .]; with reflection + work, which (I think you've seen) does matter increasingly to me. I'll never feel for him what I've felt for you; what I've felt, in a different way, for Strato—and may again, who knows? But for my stage in life, pushing 45, he is more the friend I need than anyone I could imagine."

Yet after two days of this Merrill wrote in his diary, "Plus ça change. [. . .] We love each other; but 'something is missing'—as one knows all too well." The mood did not improve once they were back in Stonington. Merrill's diary records (probably imagined) conversations between him and McIntosh in which feelings of sexual rejection come through clearly: "Living with you under this strain, + recalling certain early attitudes of my own, I understand the phrase: unnatural love." Taki and DMc living side by side on the second floor of 107 Water Street made an unlikely pair. Merrill could see in them an emblem of his inability to find love and sex in the same person.

Jackson's arrival at the end of September lightened the tone. "It is marvelous to have him back," Merrill wrote to Kalstone, "+ makes everything so much easier. [. . .] DJ is so dear + amazing." He was stopping in on the long journey by boat and train from Greece to see his parents in "Gerontia." McIntosh had been making plans to leave, but a new idea emerged one evening over dinner. Merrill recorded it in his notebook:

DMC AT DINNER [. . .]: I wish I were going to Greece now instead of out west.
JM: All right, I'll take you. We'll go in late Nov. for 2 weeks.
DMC (huge round eyes, all aglow): Really?
JM: Of course.
DJ: That time of year is wonderful in Greece.

Merrill and the two Davids sat under the dome of the dining room to do the Ouija board for "the first time in ever so long" and had a memorable session. "Various old and new voices joined the talk show" hosted by Ephraim. "My patron, Ford—who knew Alexander Pope—thought that some of my latest stuff could hold its own beside the master." By contrast, Jackson's patron, John Clay, objected to the "pornographic" novel that he'd just finished in Greece, calling it "trash." McIntosh learned that he had been born in a rainbow, "a torrent of color," "and this pleased him by corresponding to some Navajo myth." Merrill asked after Hans, "and learned that he was by now very highly placed" in some administrative position—"since there is death everywhere, somebody must process those throngs of souls." The notion that the spirits had more death on their hands than they could manage was troubling. Heaven, it seems, was "finite if not ephemeral":

> We know how the gods weaken + wither, etc. Still, to feel a tremor run through that whole grandly comic system—an incipient breakdown as of our own earthly courts—gave one a pang. [Ephraim] bade us goodnight, adding: 'I make you laugh, and I love watching that. It is straight-faced work up here.' I keep thinking that I would like to write a novel entirely about Ephraim. That has been perhaps <u>the</u> most curious + valuable experience I've had.

Two days later, on October 17, Merrill and McIntosh boarded a flight for Greece. Certain changes had occurred in Athens. Jackson had fired Kleo ("Oh dear," Jimmy mildly protested); and after years of threatening to, David and George, with George planning to marry, seemed actually to have broken up. Strato was now an out-of-work cabdriver without a taxi of his own to drive. "He is fat + bitter + I love him dearly," Merrill sighed. So he paid for Strato to rent a car for work on the condition that business would not prevent them from meeting in Paris six months later.

Merrill wanted to show Greece's beauty to McIntosh, and to remind himself of it. On the island of Aegina, a day trip from Athens, they visited a temple built in the fifth century B.C. when the island was a maritime and military power greater than Athens. Sited on a ridge overlooking the island, the sanctuary was the center of the cult of Aphaia, the mother-goddess, earliest ruler of the Aegean gods. Its fluted columns and fractured limestone walls rival in power those of the mighty Attic temples. Patricia Storace, a poet and travel writer whom Merrill met in the 1990s, describes the sublime, pine-fringed view: "Here the waters of the narrow Saronic gulf move beyond the waters of Aegina, between them and the Greek mainland to a place you can't see; blue water and light stretch to infinity, as soundless

boats sail past, backed by immovable cliffs that look like temples themselves, pieces of divine design." It was a place where Merrill could look
back on his life in Greece as if it were laid out before him in plain sight.
To the north was Athens; to the east, Maria's Sounion; to the south, Friar's
Poros; and all of it washed in fine sea light. He thought of how in time vulgar, smoking life is transformed into a clarified structure, like the ground
plan of a ruined temple. The idea brought to mind Strato past and present. He put the thought down in his notebook: "The ruin of S., of S. as I see
him, visited in a kind of wondering peacefulness, set above the sea + the
brilliant green pines; as opposed to the busy <u>functioning</u> temple with its
money-changers, sacrifice, libations, prostitutes, polychrome, plus who
knows what of blind faith."

If Merrill had hoped that such sites would draw McIntosh closer to
him, he was disappointed. On the quai at Aegina, waiting for the Athens
boat, McIntosh mentioned that he'd met a man he liked while on his own
one evening in Athens, and asked if Merrill would mind if he invited this
new friend to the house. Merrill would not—and yet he was "sad + hurt
all unreasonably." Later DMc told James that he was "<u>condescending</u>" in
how he talked of Taki and Strato, and he didn't wish to become, like them,
"one of your possessions." The next morning Merrill felt "[l]ost in solitary
confinement—lost in my own heart." He asked himself, "Have I tried so
hard to bind him? Impose my will? over him? <u>He</u> makes me think so. The
last years, seen in that bad light, are of a wrongness—! Will even the poems
turn sour, now? No; that is safe."

For relief, they got in the car and savored some of Merrill's favorite
places: the waterfront in Nafplion below the town's Venetian fortress; the
great ancient theater at Epidauros (where a German tourist sat with a guitar
at the center of the stage and sang "Yesterday"); the pines and dusty track of
Olympia; and Delphi, where the multicolored columns remaining from the
Temple of Athena were "piled one above another like dried figs on a string."
When they returned, McIntosh set off again to see his new friend in Patras,
and Merrill saw Strato, Tony, Maria, and George. He wrote to Jackson about
DMc: "[T]he worst is over. We have been after all through the <u>entire cycle
twice</u> (right down to his having met somebody whom he can fantasize about)
and I have nothing more to learn." In his notebook, recalling the cataract at
Nambé, he imagined a high, secret place of repose, an inner space outdoors
where he could live alone beyond the crush of time: "Come live within me,
said the waterfall. / There is a niche of fern / Private + dry behind my crystal ribs." These lines would turn into the poem "McKane's Falls."

After he and McIntosh returned to the U.S. in November, Merrill told

Parigory, "Any strain + stress has once again been entirely dissolved and we are dear good friends in a way that makes us both happy. [. . .] His plan is now to return to Santa Fe [. . .] and resume <u>work</u>." "Here I am once again writing letters to you," he wrote to DMc two weeks later; "something I do well, after all. I love you, David, and miss you, and embrace you. Thank you for these months you came to spend near me. Bless you always. James"

Merrill gave a series of readings in Connecticut. To the students at Stratford High School he read "The Broken Home," "The Water Hyacinth," "Annie Hill's Grave," and "The Summer People." He found "[m]uch appreciative laughter and no questions asked at Yale; stunned silence at Housatonic Community College followed by everyone's wanting to know 'how it's done' [. . .]. 'You say you work early in the morning, Mr M. Is that a good time to work? If I changed my schedule around, would I have a better chance of getting published?' "

Bishop made him laugh. "Somebody asked <u>her</u> after a reading: 'Do your ideas just come to you or do you make them up?' " She visited Merrill in December: "She makes the most adorable household pet," he told Yenser, "sitting about all day over gallons of coffee [a phrase from her poem, 'A Miracle for Breakfast'], telling stories." Again, Merrill wished to aim for "ease + lucidity" in his poems, values he associated with her. Back in September, when it became apparent that he was again going to be frustrated in his relationship with McIntosh, Merrill wrote in his notebook, "When I came back from lover's lane / My hair was white as frost." A poem he called "The Kimono" began to take shape, though it wouldn't be finished until 1972:

> When I returned from lovers' lane
> My hair was white as snow.
> Joy, incomprehension, pain
> I'd seen like seasons come and go.
> How I got home again
> Frozen half dead, perhaps you know.
>
> You hide a smile and quote a text:
> Desires ungratified
> Persist from one life to the next.
> Hearths we strip ourselves beside
> Long, long ago were x'd
> On blueprints of "consuming pride."

> Times out of mind, the bubble-gleam
> To our charred level drew
> April back. A sudden beam . . .
> —Keep talking while I change into
> The pattern of a stream
> Bordered with rushes white on blue.

Despite its nursery-rhyme ease and the lucidity of that final glowing image, the poem is difficult. The idea in the first stanza seems to be that love is a simple, repeated story, as patterned as the seasons and as invariable; what begins in joy will end in pain, leaving us out in the cold. The poet-lover has had to be helped home from his latest trip to lover's lane. The beloved himself seems to have helped by his refusal to gratify the lover's desires. The beloved is the second stanza's half-smiling teacher: the sutra he quotes maintains that our loves are like lives, incarnations, and we carry "Desires ungratified" from one to the next, seeking illumination. The process renews itself when memory, suddenly as in Proust, recalls "the bubble-gleam" of the past, renewing the "charred" spirit like the return of spring. The transcendence available consists only in how we prepare to meet the cycle of desire, in how we costume and carry ourselves.

The kimono in this poem points to Merrill's general love of the kimono and his knowledge of its use in Japan, where kimonos of varying designs and fabric are appropriate to different seasons and circumstances. For the poet, to put on the kimono is to put off the particulars of selfhood and give himself over to the elements as seen through art. He "changes" into the stylized "pattern of a stream." The stream signifies time itself—which the kimono allows the poet to enter and affirm, rather than resist.*

The poem's Japanese manner is colored by McIntosh's sensibility, his asceticism, and his knowledge of Japanese culture. But "The Kimono" is above all a striking homage to Bishop. Its title, its three six-line stanzas, its rhyme scheme, and its focus on an intimate exchange between friends ending with a fragment of speech set off by a dash leading out of the poem—all of this comes straight from "The Shampoo," one of Bishop's most intimate published love poems. Declaring with these allusions his admiration for Bishop, Merrill asserts a connection between their poetics, while thinking back, no doubt, to their talks by the stove in Ouro Preto. Even in her distress Bishop, or her poetry, may have been helping Merrill,

---

* The garment Merrill mentions in the poem carried time in another sense too: the blue pattern of the stream identifies it as one that he bought in Japan in 1956 at the time of his father's death.

showing him the way in from the cold. "For Time is / nothing if not amenable," Bishop says in "The Shampoo." The wisdom of "The Kimono" is the same. A decade after writing it, Merrill had a role in a television documentary about Bishop. He chose to read "The Shampoo" for the occasion. Filmed in his Stonington home, he is wearing, in tacit tribute to Bishop, a blue and white kimono.

Merrill received a poem from Judy Moffett about her complicated feelings for him; he responded by speaking in a veiled way, without naming him, of the lessons to be drawn from his experience with McIntosh: "[T]he person who puzzles + fascinates us needn't be a puzzle at all, so much as a key, instinctively valued, to the unsolved puzzle of ourselves. [. . .] How often I've thought, 'If only I knew this or that fact, or what was in X's heart at this or that moment, all would be well, and the spell dissolve.' Such reveries are simply beside the point. The mystery is in oneself."

Dr. Rothenberg, resuming his two-hour visits from New Haven, tape recorder in hand, helped with that mystery. Merrill found, predictably, that his feelings about his parents were behind his feelings about McIntosh. In his dreams the poet saw McIntosh as a man and a woman, a young husband and a wife; and because these dream images were "messages that must be read in a mirror," they seemed to show him "what there is of my father + my mother in my nature. [. . .] The shrink isn't much help, but he is an ear, and every so often gives me a little nudge onto a paved road." His talks with Rothenberg prompted him to return to therapy with Detre, with the aim of helping him this time with his poems rather than his life, if there was any distinction there. With Rothenberg, he wrote to Moffett, "I've felt much quickened curiosity about my childhood, my parents + so forth; a curiosity I don't recall feeling [. . .] during the analysis proper. I've felt also how this curiosity leads to nothing any more. Those tombs [. . .] were rifled long ago; one can no longer say which weapons + ornaments belonged to the king, which to the queen." Merrill would develop this image in the poem "Pieces of History," where, accompanied by "Daud" (the Arabic form of "David"), the poet dreams of breaking into a grave site and discovering sacred objects cast "Pellmell, hers, his, theirs, ours—by evening what was whose?"

In December 1970, Merrill and Jackson, who was back from family duty in California, again took up life in Stonington, where they had not been together for more than a few weeks since the winter of 1968. This year they had Christmas "at the Ladies' with lots of bridge + a flaming baked Alaska," followed by a party on the second floor of 107 Water Street. It was Taki's name day, and the Alevras family apartment was filled with Greeks of three generations who celebrated by drinking and dancing, shaking the old house. Applauding as if he were in a waterfront taverna, Jackson broke "all our plates" by throwing them on the floor, "some quite irreplaceable."

That January, Jimmy and David attended two memorable performances in New York. One was the celebrated *A Midsummer Night's Dream* directed by Peter Brook. Merrill described it: "The stage is a brilliant white cube, with blackness above, from which dark height there's always an actor or two idly watching." The play unfolded as "a dream shared by all the characters. One hangs on every word; every touch is telling." When Titania wooed Bottom, one of her attendant fairies was "a fat moustached man in a gray sweat-suit; he bares his great right arm at a climactic moment, and suddenly it is Bottom's phallus—traces of a satyr-play—Titania caresses + kisses while paper plates rain down from above and Mendelsohn's Wedding March blares." It was great theater.

And yet, Merrill declared, "my heart was with the puppets," the Little Players, who put on Bernard de Zogheb's ballad opera *Phèdre*. "Since hearing a run-through in December," Merrill had "thought of very little else but this magical work." He was spellbound by "the authority of those little manikins, the figure of Phaedra clenched with self-hatred and leaning sideways into a hot light" on a "tiny stage with its view of the sea into which Oenone must plunge with a terrible splash." The players achieved "a kind of superhuman transparence, a shallowness that left you shattered," Merrill gushed, enjoying the paradox. For opening night he bought the house (twenty-seven seats), and hosted many old friends.

Not everyone was touched by the show, according to a skeptical account in *The Farewell Symphony*, a roman à clef by Edmund White, published in 1997. In 1971, White was a hopeful novelist who came to *Phèdre* as Kalstone's guest. "At the end of the opera the audience went into ecstasies. With my outer face I, too, smiled and cooed but my inner eyes bored holes of hate through them all," White's first-person narrator relates, describing his youthful alienation from the older, smug-seeming audience. He finds a friend, the only other young man present, and "hisses," "Isn't it all disgusting?" "Oh, groan," the friend replies, "I can't bear the idea that Eddie"—Jimmy is known as Eddie in the novel—"bankrolls this frivolous rubbish." While his young self joins in the complaint, White's older narrator wryly observes of himself and his friend, "I suppose we were both wondering how to apply to his foundation."

Merrill was in New Mexico for his birthday. He spent it with Mary Lou Aswell, whose son Duncan had mysteriously vanished. Jimmy offered money to help find Duncan, "or to help him when he is found; my fingers never hover very far from the purse strings." He had come to see McIntosh before returning to Greece for an extended stay. It seemed that they at last had found the right relation. "Absurd to say perhaps," he wrote to McIntosh later, "but one of the difficulties between us from the start was that I had no <u>room</u> for you except at the very center of my life—where I suppose there will always be a table set." Jimmy returned with hot green peppers, which he put into a chili con carne that he served to forty people at a bon voyage party on Water Street before, on March 27, he and David sailed together for Europe, as they used to, on the *Queen Elizabeth II*. Crossing with them were the Morses and David Kalstone "by arrangement and Guitou Knoop by God."

In Paris, Merrill picked up a new Renault and, to drive it, Strato. Mouflouzélis had come from Athens for his first taste of France. Together he and Merrill settled in de Zogheb's apartment for some sightseeing and refined dining ("Appallingly good + costly meals can be had for mere money"); there was a visit to the Opéra Comique and a night out with Mimi and Vassili in Montmartre's "magic world of lights + drums + powdered nipples" before they drove south to Greece, stopping to see Yenser in Pau, Umberto in Cortona, and Grace in Rome. Merrill had looked forward to the trip for a year, and over the summer he would turn his memories of it into a travel poem. Made of ten linked sonnets (the verse form of "The Broken Home" and "Matinées") and titled "Days of 1971," the poem recalled other Merrill poems. Although, when Mouflouzélis first resurfaced in the poet's life, it had seemed that the old romance might have new life, it was too late for that. The car trip would not be a honeymoon for second-chance lovers, but a valedictory tour. That was what was required by the life story unfolding in Merrill's poetry, for which the trip was meant to furnish fresh material.

Merrill took inspiration for the artful plotting of his life from Proust. Indeed, the idea of a car trip with Mouflouzélis came from his reading of "Impressions de route en automobile," an essay by Proust describing a car trip he took touring French cathedrals and churches with Alfred Agostinelli. Agostinelli was a handsome man in his twenties, a mechanic and taxi driver who, along with his wife, at one time lived with the novelist and served as his secretary; he became the object of Proust's devotion and a model for Albertine in *À la recherche du temps perdu*. In "Impressions," Agostinelli is evoked in his chauffeur's costume: "My mechanic was clad in a huge rubber mantle and he wore a sort of hood which fitted tightly around his youthful beardless face and which, as we sped faster and faster into the night, made him look like some pilgrim, or rather, a speed-loving nun." Merrill quotes from this passage in "Days of 1971":

Can-can from last night's *Orphée aux Enfers*
Since daybreak you've been whistling till I wince.
Well, you were a handsome devil once.
Take the wheel. You're still a fair chauffeur.

Our trip. I'd pictured it another way—
Asthmatic pilgrim and his "nun of speed,"
In either mind a music spun of need . . .
That last turnoff went to Illiers.

Proust's Law (are you listening?) is twofold:
(a) What least thing our self-love longs for most
Others instinctively withhold;

(b) Only when time has slain desire
Is his wish granted to a smiling ghost
Neither harmed nor warmed, now, by the fire.

With Mouflouzélis cast as Agostinelli, Merrill remakes Proust. The attitude is one of breezy self-consciousness as the car whizzes by Illiers, the novelist's childhood home and model for his imagined Combray. (In reality the poet stopped to buy postcards there.) Proof of Proust's "Law" appears in several places in his novel. When his characters get what they want, they no longer want it or their desire is gratified with the melancholy awareness that it is an exception to the rule.

What survives over time of the heart's precious desires? That was the question posed by this car-trip quest. En route, in a letter to Jackson in Athens, Merrill described his driver: "What does he like, now that he has seen Montmartre [. . .], Versailles + Chartres + Blois? Well, he admires the way the trees are pruned + planted, and he likes the fromage de chèvre. But he is happiest sitting in the hotel room + playing cards. Oh, he likes the car too, and so do I. So I guess we can get through the trip without any stripping of actual or metaphorical gears." And so they did. As "Days of 1971" winds down and their journey together comes to an end, Merrill affirms the enduring value of manners and art:

Strato, each year's poem
Says goodbye to you.
Again, though, we've come through
Without losing temper or face.

If care rumpled your face
The other day in Rome,
Tonight just dump my suitcase
Inside the door and make a dash for home

While I unpack what we saw made
At Murano, and you gave to me—
Two ounces of white heat
Twirled and tweezered into shape,

Ecco! another fanciful
Little horse, still blushing, set to cool.

The poet learns to say goodbye "Without losing temper or face." The phrase "each year's poem" implies that poems are a part of life, like seasons; it also implies that each year is its own "poem," which a text like "Days of 1971" transcribes. The emblem of that poetic transformation of experience is the poem's "Little horse," that palm-sized Pegasus. On the island of Murano, near Venice, Merrill and Mouflouzélis had been "enthralled" watching the making of a miniature glass horse: "something molten + mysterious + elemental that turns, under your eyes, into a trinket; an image for all kinds of things," Merrill told McIntosh, "and don't suppose I'm not making use of it!" What he used it for is an image of a kind of poem that he was becoming a master of: not a love poem but a poem of love's aftermath, which emerges "still blushing" from the erotic fire in which it was fashioned before being "set to cool" in print—a "trinket" whose form, like each of the sonnets of "Days of 1971," has been deftly "Twirled and tweezered into shape" by an exceptional craftsman. If this kind of poem was not what Merrill began by wanting from Strato, it remained a gift, and maybe all that Strato could give him.

While Merrill said goodbye to Mouflouzélis, his friendship with Yenser was deepening. Yenser had come to France on a year's leave of absence from his position at UCLA. His marriage had broken up in France, and, when the Renault brought the poet and his "nun of speed" to visit, he was living alone on the third floor of an old house in Pau—a charming setting of "[s]unny, golden farm + woodland at the foot of the Pyrenees," Merrill found, with "cherry trees in bloom, violets, snails, a cuckoo." For much of the visit, Strato hung back in the bedroom, sleeping or complaining of a stomachache, while Merrill and his former student talked in English about poetry—both foreign languages to the Greek taxi driver. Yenser was puzzled by what he saw. "James"—like McIntosh, Yenser always used the poet's full first name—"was the most sensitive and sensible guy in the world. He seemed like someone I would want to *be*, and here he was with a big lunk, with no brains at all. I couldn't understand it." In "Days of 1971," Yenser and Mouflouzélis are opposites, but it may be that Merrill was, for exactly that reason, drawn to them both.

Yet Yenser had a tough side too. He was born in 1941 in Wichita, Kansas, the older of two brothers. His father worked in the aircraft industry; his mother wrote poems and sometimes published them in *Ladies' Home Journal*. When he was a teenager, he was arrested and thrown out of high school for fighting. "I was a punk," he reflected. A tragic car accident during his second year at Wichita State University put an end to this phase: "My best friend was home on leave from the Navy, and he and I and three other guys got drunk at a nightclub, went home to get a gun with some crazy idea of confronting the bouncer, and on the way had a wreck that killed two of the other passengers. Afterward," following traction and a cast, "I started to take everything more seriously—school, reading, writing."

Yenser's friendly western voice, darting eyes, and boyish, mischievous smile must have appealed to Merrill at once. But they only became intimates by mail. Yenser remembered, "He was a delight to write to, and a greater delight to hear from. He felt it was his obligation to entertain me (as he felt with everyone), and he told stories that were enchanting, enthralling. Like his poems, his letters plunged you into his life, *in medias res*. Who was Tony? Who was this Black Maria? I didn't know anyone like that, and I didn't have stories to tell, so I just wrote about the poems he sent." Yenser wrote about the poems with a level of skill and sympathy, trained in part by the poet himself, that Merrill had never experienced. Yenser's copy of "Strato in Plaster"—by 1970 Merrill was sending poems to his former student as soon as he had a typed copy—shows Yenser at work. Like a text prepared for a workshop or seminar, the pages are underlined and annotated. When Merrill says of Strato, "The god in him is a remembered one," Yenser writes "Rilke," thinking of the German poet's "Archaic Torso of Apollo." He notes subtle effects of internal rhyme and wordplay. He is attentive to subliminal, semiotic currents of composition—skills that were joined, moreover, to a moral intelligence. Merrill translated the poem's Greek epigraph for Yenser as "breast of marble, heart of mush (potato)." Yenser refers to the image in this comment on lines ostensibly about Strato's broken arm: "Is the implication that this break is not a very clean one? Inexorability qualified by 'twinges' on the speaker's part too? I.e., just whose heart is 'mushy'?"

Merrill relished this attention and insight. ("You found everything

I wanted found in the poem to Strato. An eerie sensation . . . ," he told Yenser.) In turn, Merrill was reading and commenting on Yenser's poems, and aware of his influence on them. For instance, he cautioned Yenser about excessive punning: "I have a sense of stretching forth the addict's needle-scarred arm to warn you before it is too late, before you follow me into perdition—Give up the artificial paradise!" But the influence ran the other way too, for Yenser's addiction to puns—his sensitivity to language's ruses and rustlings—encouraged Merrill's. By 1971, Merrill could say to Yenser truly, "The suspicion grows in me that I more + more write poems in order to read what you will have to say about them." This would be the case from now on. As J. D. McClatchy put it, "Merrill felt that Yenser knew his work better than he himself did. Merrill sensed it from the beginning. Stephen was James Merrill's ideal reader."

In Athens, Mouflouzélis dropped out of sight again, turning to a new construction job and the routines of his home life. David Jackson's parents and three friends of theirs from California arrived for two weeks, a party whose "combined ages [. . .] add up to 406." The poet hied himself upstairs to his study, while marveling at his companion: "David is extraordinary. Not simply that he is on hand all day long, biting the bullet, [. . .] whipping them up marble slopes; but he relates to them as well, snarls back at his father, gouges old Mr Neiswander's share of expenses out of his mummy-tight fist, turns on the hideous little rouged widow who wants (don't ask why) George Jackson for herself, telling her to stop asking questions, stop complaining, stop thinking she's so cute. Well," Merrill summed up in a letter to Aswell, "it's a lesson in Confrontation. Quite beyond me, I'm afraid." Family had caught up with Jimmy and David in Athens. It happened that Duncan Aswell had reappeared, only with a changed name, and this curious turn of events prompted Merrill, trying to console Mary Lou, to reflect on the course of his own life in Greece:

> Everybody has fantasies of doing exactly what Duncan did: snapping fingers + taking off, cutting all the ties and, in the bargain, taking on a brand new identity. [. . .] I've had some experience of Double Lives myself—though not as drastic as Duncan's. To the outsider the double life represents a form of escape; but to the person who lives it, it is a form of growth. Year after year I re-entered a world, here in Greece, a routine, a way of feeling + acting, whose beauty was precisely its lack of con-

nection with anything in Stonington or New York. (Someone else could have lived that Greek life in New York, but not me.) What I want to say is that over the years, to my surprise, to my sadness <u>and</u> my delight, the gap between my two lives has narrowed. One can barely detect the crack, one wonders if there ever was one, or what all the fuss was about. There is no such thing as a double life. There's one life that takes new aspects and is enriched.

In late June, with his family gone, David wrote to Perényi, "[S]ublime Virginia has written ten sonnets of beauty and wit. Me, old Leonard, potters around with my plants" on the terrace. Indeed Merrill noted that the sonnets of "Days of 1971" "have been delivered, like that lady in Canberra's litter of underweight babies [. . .] and other poems started." The other poems begun included the companion piece to "Days of 1971," called "Days of 1935," the rollicking ballad about Merrill's childhood fantasy of being kidnapped by the gangsters Floyd and Jean. The 304-line poem, completed in a flush of feeling in the high summer heat of the third-floor laundry room, developed out of the thinking about childhood that Merrill had done with Rothenberg. Was the middle-aged poet any less a captive—captive to his own desires, if not also to a strong man like Floyd or Strato—because he'd bought the Renault and arranged for his kidnapping himself?

It seemed there would always be a new man. With Mouflouzélis making himself scarce, Merrill took up "on a fairly regular basis with a certain Manoli, whom I rejected a year + a half ago because he didn't know his own strength—always the danger of a cracked rib." Manoli was Manos Karastefanís. He was mustached and dark, suitable to fantasies born of Depression-era Hollywood films. Vassilikos saw Karastefanís as "a solid person," a karate enthusiast whom Merrill came to look on almost as "a bodyguard"; yet he also had a "mystical" side, expressive of his origins on Lesvos, the island on the Turkish coast associated in the Greek imagination with Asia. Merrill described him as pleasingly "nutty + nice to drink or go to the beach with." The "metaphysical person" Vassilikos recalls comes out in the opening stanza of the dramatic monologue ("Manos Karastefanís") that Merrill wrote for him in 1972:

> Death took my father.
> The same year (I was twelve)
> Thanási's mother taught me
> Heaven and Hell.

When Karastefanís was injured at the gym, Merrill visited him in the hospital, "bringing *War and Peace*." Later, Karastefanís arrived at Merrill's door, magically bearing the voice and savor of his island birthplace:

> Why are you smiling?
> I fought fair, I fought well,
> Not hurting my opponent,
> To win this black belt.

> Why are you silent?
> I've brought you a white cheese
> From my island, and the sea's
> Voice in a shell.

Americans kept ringing the doorbell. "How wise of you to stay in empty New York," Merrill teased Richard Howard, listing his guests: Daryl Hine, John Myers, John Brinnin, and the photographer Tom Victor. Then there was Donald Richie, lecturing in Athens on the films of Maya Deren. Robin Magowan appeared, and he and his uncle repaired to a corner table in a taverna, "obliviously opening our hearts as if we'd met that very week instead of when I was eleven and he was not quite one." Next the Yensers arrived. Stephen, his brother Kelly, and Kelly's wife Pamela rented a flat in Kolonáki for a few weeks. With all three Yensers, Merrill visited the island of Paros and various sites near Athens. And in September, after Pam and Kelly had left, Merrill drove with Stephen to the west coast of Greece to see him off on the ferry to Italy.

They took the mountainous route that passed through Ioannina, or Yánnína as Merrill called it, "which over the years has become for me what Parma was for Proust"—a half-imagined place imbued with the romantic qualities of its name. Stendhal's novel *The Charterhouse of Parma* gave the place-name its special charm for Proust.* The meaning of Ioannina for Merrill was compounded of Nelly Liambey's stories of her childhood home

---

* Marcel Proust, *Swann's Way, Remembrance of Things Past*, trans. C. K. Scott Moncrieff and Terence Kilmartin (Vintage, 1989): "The name of Parma, one of the towns that I most longed to visit, after reading the *Chartreuse*, seeming to me compact and glossy, violet-tinted, soft, if anyone were to speak of such or such a house in Parma, in which I should be lodged, he would give me the pleasure of thinking that I was to inhabit a dwelling that was compact and glossy, violet-tinted, soft, and that bore no relation to the houses in any other town in Italy, since I could imagine it only by the aid of that heavy syllable of the name of Parma, in which no breath of air stirred, and of all that I had made it assume of Stendhalian sweetness and the reflected hue of violets" (421).

and the city's association with the despot Ali Pasha, host to Lord Byron, who ruled Epirus with Ioannina as his capital from 1788 to 1821. Merrill was not disappointed. Strolling by the lake with Yenser, he mused on the pasha, whose story features two women: the martyr Frosíni, who spurned Ali and was drowned for it (Jimmy bought a stack of "lurid postcards" depicting her cartoon figure splashing into the lake), and Vassíliki, Ali's vixen paramour. In the evening, Merrill and Yenser watched a *Karaghiozi*, a shadow puppet play that uses camel-skin figures on poles to rehearse the adventures of a barefoot hero who outwits the powerful. And what of Merrill's growing intimacy with Yenser? "Thank goodness," he told Kalstone, "it's all inexorably Platonic."

Back in Athens, Merrill penned a stanza "à Monsieur David Jackson in Bed":

> Happy Birthday. Who said "old"?
> Raise them glasses, break them plates!
> Forty-niners all struck gold.
> Fifty's just a sum of states.

As a birthday present, Merrill commissioned a friend, Pavlos Simios, to paint a full figure portrait of himself and Jackson. "It represents the entrance (determined in D's case, reluctant in mine) into middle-age," he reported to Moffett. "Perugino in the sky, Pontormo in the faces, games played with false angles + delicate imbalances. The weather is equinoctial, chill, uncertain" as the two of them, self-consciously rakish and casual, peer from beneath a classical arch. "Old Meziki"—Parigory's antique shop partner—"cast his expert eye upon it and observed that even with the heads cut off you would still know us by our poses—a remark whose ripples haven't yet reached the shore." Although they don't touch or acknowledge each other, the two figures in the painting mirror each other, positioned side by side. Unveiled at a party for thirty-five at Athinaion Efivon 44, the picture celebrated Jimmy and David's continuing life as a couple.

George and David would be continuing their life as a couple too: when the time for his wedding came, Lazaretos backed out on the morning of the ceremony, and retreated with Jackson, who was there to serve as *koumbaros*, or best man. Further evidence that life in Greece would never change very much presented itself in the person of Kostas Tympakianákis, in town from Crete. Jimmy then repaid the visit, riding on the back of Kostas's motorcycle through Heraklion, renewing also his "acquaintance with the delicious dark pink Cretan wine that gets you out of bed 'dry-mouthed and stammering' like Millay's Endymion 4 hours after your last glass, never to sleep again." Jackson joined Merrill on Crete, and they visited a small American colony in Chania, where George was still posted. The Americans were the painter Dorothy Andrews, who—she was tall—"towers over the others in every sense." The others were Charles Haldeman, "who writes 'brilliant' paranoid novels published in England"; Charles Henri Ford, "who has been 17 years old for nearly half a century, a little Mississippi boy who knew Gertrude Stein + Edith Sitwell + lived with Tchelichev"; and Alan Bole, a Harvard man, just Merrill's age and a heavy drinker. Arty, eccentric, and louche, these men were a type of expatriate Jimmy and David had tried hard not to become. In 1974, they would be shocked, but not entirely surprised, when Bole was murdered by a young Greek with a knife.

Merrill flew back to the U.S. in October 1971 with a new book of poems for Harry Ford to print. He wrote to Yenser testing "Braving the Elements" as a title: "I don't like titles that applaud the author's seriousness [. . .], titles like 'Necessities of Life' [by Adrienne Rich] or even, forgive me, 'Respon-sibilities' [by Yeats]; but with B. the E. it would seem that the cliché does its habitual blessed work of mitigation, what do you think?" He took the phrase from a poem just completed, "Dreams About Clothes." Wry, fanci-ful, and self-mocking, it was, like "The Victor Dog," a meditation on the life of art and the ethics of style. It concludes,

> Tell me something, Art.
> You know what it's like
> Awake in your dry hell
> Of volatile synthetic solvents.
> Won't you help us brave the elements
> Once more, of terror, anger, love?
> Seeing there's no end to wear and tear
> Upon the lawless heart,
> Won't you as well forgive
> Whoever settles for the immaterial?
> Don't you care how we live?

The poet goes on asking art for meaning, yet the point is not to ask too much. He dedicated the poem to John and Anne Hollander, honoring John's wit and Anne's knowledge of the history of costume. It was a toast in the middle of life to the consolations of work and lasting friendships.

In Stonington, Merrill found the Alevras family "flourishing, although Conformity has drawn black crayon sideburns + moustache all over Taki's simple square face." Alone upstairs, Merrill spent his mornings with *Fables of Identity* by Northrop Frye. Frye's meditations on romance plots and archetypal characters put Merrill in mind of the novel about Ephraim he hoped to write; soon he was reading the Old Testament ("for the first time in my life") and Freud's *Moses and Monotheism*. He would make use of all this reading before long—thanks to an industriousness he traced to his mother, whom he visited in Atlanta. "If my mother retires to her room," he explained to Yenser, it's not to lie down but to "wrap Xmas presents" or read "books on how to become more Christian," the result of which was only to make her "more of a worldly success. I see more & more how much I am her own son."

With *Braving the Elements* complete but not yet in print, and the new novel not much more than an intriguing notion, Merrill was not writing anything but letters. He gathered poems from the past twenty-five years that he hadn't collected in books (some had appeared in magazines) and presented them in a small volume called *The Yellow Pages*.* But he was at loose ends in his work; and for the first time since 1964, he was not in love: his affairs with McIntosh and Mouflouzélis were both over for good.

Given all that, it was perhaps predictable that he would fall in love with Yenser. At least, he was no longer thankful that the relationship was "inexorably Platonic." Writing to Stephen from St. Louis, where he visited as a writer in residence at Washington University in November, Merrill confided, "I've grown to love you very dearly, and more freshly than—well, than S or T. (If you doubt that one can love more than one person at a time, reread 'The Tale of Genji.')" What did that declaration mean exactly? "The thought of you makes me smile; when something happens it's you I want to tell; I trust you utterly, and try for your sake, if I try at all, to be better than I am." He ended on a blithe note: "[M]y trust in you is such that the one thing I can't imagine is that any of this will alarm or dismay you." His trust was not so great, however, that he didn't worry that he'd said the wrong thing.

Even so, Merrill pressed his case: "Isn't it self-evident that no one ever

---

* JM to Moffett, letter, November 24, 1971 (NYPL). Merrill prepared a privately issued, carbon-copy edition of *The Yellow Pages: 59 Poems*, including uncollected poems composed between 1946 and 1971, in twenty-six copies. With a few changes (he dropped two poems and added two), the book was published in cloth and paper by the Temple Bar Bookshop in Cambridge, Massachusetts, in 1974. The cloth edition of fifty copies was wrapped in yellow paper and reproduced pages from the Boston telephone directory for bookstores. The paper edition was produced in 750 or 800 copies (both numbers were given by the publisher).

means the same thing by love? Don't bonds between people vary geneti-
cally like any other kind of offspring? [. . .] What I've come to feel for you
[. . .] stems from your having reconciled me in 100 ways (as no one else,
by the way, has) to being precisely Older. I mean, if the sunset years bring
a face—a heart, a spirit—like yours to look into, why then RB's Rabbi was
right, and the whole question of whom one does or doesn't sleep with sinks
into an even deeper slumber on cushions beside the point." Merrill, already
contemplating his "sunset years" at age forty-two, alluded to Browning's
"Rabbi Ben Ezra," who urges the reader, "Grow old along with me! / The
best is yet to be."

Yenser wasn't angry, but he wasn't in love either, and Merrill had presented him with a delicate problem. Over the coming months, he tried to
maintain his intimacy with his admired mentor without allowing Merrill
to change its terms. Merrill came to visit him in March in Santa Monica. He
spoke to one of Yenser's classes at UCLA and gave a reading, followed by a
big party. David Jackson attended; out west to visit his parents, he brought
them with him, as well as Sewelly, Bob Grimes, and Cecilia Holland. That
night Yenser did fall in love—with one of his students, a Californian named
Mary Bomba. Merrill faced facts in a letter to McIntosh. About himself and
Yenser, he wrote, "What we are to each other is—always has been—perfectly
clear. It's only I who have placed the pink-pleated shade of Romance on
the little burning lamp; [. . .] but I can see plainly enough by it that if I am
more than a friend to him, the difference lies in the direction of 'father' or
'teacher.' "

Jackson rejoined Merrill on Water Street for a few weeks in late March
1972. They entertained themselves by contacting the recently deceased
Marianne Moore on the Ouija board. "It seems that Miss Moore has been
lifted to quite an exalted stage," Merrill told Yenser. "A painful message
followed. 'The world is slow to die in me,' she said. 'I now lose grip of those
kinds of line which once were refreshing. That was my claim on nature.
What matters most seems to be what is natural. Man has lost his meanings
and his value here [. . .] for he has ruined his gifts. Look, James, at the end
of nature. 'So gloomy, mes chers,' said Ephraim when she'd left." Merrill
and Jackson were gloomy too. "Yesterday mid-afternoon I knelt on a cushion in despair," Merrill told McIntosh. When Jackson left for Greece in the
middle of April, Merrill wondered why: "It's surely not to be with George
that you've gone. Just to get away from me?" Merrill asked Yenser to spend
the summer with him in Stonington, but Stephen declined. "I've never
denied myself anything," Merrill responded. "It's only the world—and
you mean the world to me, you know—that in its way + wisdom denies me

things on my own behalf. Left to myself I'm afraid I'd choose life over art every time; until, of course, left by the world, there's only art to make the best of."

Like a dejected lover who gives up the world for the church, Merrill suddenly became very interested in Transcendental Meditation. He was not alone of course. In the 1970s, the movement called TM, founded by Maharishi Mahesh Yogi in 1958, introduced a "World Plan" to establish trademarked meditation centers throughout the world; it was especially successful in the U.S. Now as then, TM guides its adherents on a seven-step journey to enlightenment requiring two twenty-minute meditations each day, focused on the chanted repetition of a Sanskrit mantra. Merrill attended a TM lecture in Rhode Island in the spring, and he was not disappointed: "All at once out came a pale green blackboard and a girl named Susan with a generous layer of baby-fat, pre-Raphaelite hair + jaw, and our own time's miniskirt, boots, and hesitant delivery. [. . .] Susan is going to be my Instructor or Initiator, and on Saturday, instead of listening to <u>Don Carlo</u> by Verdi [. . .], I shall be in Westerly carrying 6 to 12 freshly cut flowers, 3 pieces of 'sweet fruit' (no lemons please, and no segments), a <u>new</u> white handkerchief, and $75, in exchange for which I will receive my personalized mantra which just by thinking of it reduces the oxygen in one's bloodstream to a level far below that of the deepest sleep, plus a treasure house of fringe benefits to be enjoyed throughout + beyond one's allotted span."

How serious was Merrill? "Thank goodness <u>I</u> don't have to decide," he explained to Yenser; "every cell in my body, each with its arms flailing in Shiva's own dance, decided for me hours ago." Nonetheless, his initiation felt like a revelation to him: "[J]udging from the 30-odd minutes that followed," he told Jackson, "and a solo flight at home late this afternoon, it is the Real Thing, one that bewilders + impresses + delights me. I felt on both occasions an absolute <u>stillness</u> comparable to nothing I remember." The exaltation he discovered in meditation was not simply a substitute for love, he felt; it *was* love, albeit with a difference. "It's 'love' I'm 'in' now," he reflected, "[. . .] but love that for once doesn't depend on another person: that 'fallible god' of Borges." Merrill was playing on Borges's formula: "To fall in love is to create a religion that has a fallible god." But his new religion was less than secure. "Saturday afternoon a frightening thing happened," he confided to Jackson. "Whatever had sustained me so amazingly for an entire week, a week of . . . what? peace of mind, inner security, a kind of radiance, simply melted away, clouded over, <u>left</u>. I gave myself an emergency meditation right after lunch; and by the next morning it had returned (and is with me still); but I can't describe the 'sense of loss', like a bruise within the mind, of that entirely and no doubt foolishly unexpected hour." Beneath this new radiance and peace of mind was the "despair" he'd spoken of to McIntosh, waiting to swallow him.

Merrill's initiation in TM resulted in a personal meditation practice he kept up intermittently for years.* In the short run, it helped him through a longish visit from his mother, during which they exchanged not "a single cross word." In July, when the proofs for *Braving the Elements* arrived on Water Street, the book bore a dedication to her. But the book's true muse was McIntosh. "Two-thirds of the poems in it (I've just counted) were written with you in my mind, in my heart—for better or worse!" Merrill told him. "You'll find your name twice [. . .]—once in an acrostic poem which nobody has ever noticed <u>was</u> an acrostic, and in the dedication of 'Under Libra,' a poem obscure enough to discourage the curiosity-seekers." The acrostic Merrill refers to is "Flèche d'Or." Its message: "DAVID MCINTOSH WITH LOVE FROM JM." But no wonder no one had ever noticed it: the letters of the words "DAVID MCINTOSH" and "FROM JM" are braided, one after the other, at the start of each of the poem's twenty-seven lines, "D" followed by "W," "A" by "I," and so on. Just so, JM's bond with DMc was braided at the secret center of the book.

That summer, Merrill read Hugh Kenner's history of modernism, *The Pound Era*, and discovered through it for the first time an admiration for the author of *The Cantos*. It piqued his interest that Kalstone had just met Pound in Venice, where Merrill was headed too. Merrill visited DK there in August on his way to Athens. Kalstone followed, and Jimmy, David, and Tony met his ferry on the west coast of Greece. They drove together to Athens, stopping on the way in Yánnina. Merrill wanted another look at the place, and he wanted to show it to Kalstone. Over the winter, he had composed a 136-line poem called "Yánnina," arising from his visit to the city with Yenser in 1970, and he and DK were at work that summer on an interview focused on the poem.

The poem's working title, "Jannina: The 1003rd Night," linked it to "The Thousand and Second Night," the long poem composed when Merrill came to Greece ten years before. With its Oriental mise-en-scène and Byron present both as a historical character and as the master of the ottava rima

---

* Nelly Liambey remembers Merrill beginning every day, when he was her guest in Greece in the late 1970s, by meditating on her balcony.

Merrill works in here, "Yánnina" reprises the motifs and atmosphere of the earlier poem. But that poem was about self-division, "the crack in the mirror of the soul," while the theme of this poem is reconciliation and repair. It joins travel-diary-like notes with quotations from various prose texts: Byron's letters, William Plomer's *The Diamond of Jannina*, and the journals of the British aesthete and philhellene Edward Lear, as it moves back and forth between description of the modern city and the story of Ali Pasha. In Ali, Merrill discovered an exotic image of his father, making "Yánnina" a disguised, belated elegy for the pasha of *The Seraglio*.

"Yánnina" appeared in the *Saturday Review*, where Ed White was an editor, in December 1972, accompanied by the interview with Kalstone. Kalstone had asked Merrill if he had a theme in advance of his visit to Yánnina, and he did: Duncan Aswell's disappearance and subsequent return, under a new name, had reminded him of the desire for a "brand-new life" that motivated his coming to Greece in the 1960s. "How we delude ourselves!" he exclaimed. "As if there were ever more than one life." That lesson perhaps sounds like a defeat. But "Yánnina" suggests that, by forcing him to recognize the continuing presence of the past as he tried to escape it in Greece, Merrill's life there enabled him to make peace with that past and his father in particular. This psychological development had literary implications. For what Merrill had learned about his life showed him how he might approach history—Pound's epic subject, with its larger-than-life heroes, against which he had always defined his own literary ambitions.

"You said once," Kalstone reminds Merrill, "that your poems are not 'historical.' Yet I'd say that this poem is almost *about* history, that it's a kind of stand against people locked into the present. Not history as public record, mind you, but—." Merrill broke in: "A kind of time-zoo?" In the "time-zoo" of "Yánnina," Ali Pasha is the prime exhibit, a larger-than-life character ready-made for the popular entertainments in which he features, from romantic melodramas such as Mrs. Vaughn's *Grecians* (1824) to *The Count of Monte Cristo* by Alexandre Dumas, père (1844). The point, Merrill went on, is that "[h]istorical figures are always so well lighted. Even if one never gets to the truth about them, their contradictions, even their crimes, are so expressive. They're like figures in a novel read by millions of people at once. What's terrifying is that they're human as well, and therefore no more reliable than you or I. They have their blind, 'genetic' side, just like my boys and girls in Yánnina." "So well lighted": "historical figures" are like the cutouts, the *Karaghiozi* puppets Merrill and Yenser saw in Yánnina, which he evokes in the poem. History's grand personages, like Ali Pasha and Charlie Merrill, are no less real than the rest of us, only more exaggerated, more "expressive" of common traits. And like puppets, we are all animated by forces we do not control.

The metaphors for this automatism in "Yánnina" are sleepwalking and dream. The poem begins not with Ali but with everyday, contemporary "Somnambulists," a citizenry dreamily observed by the tourist-poet:

> Somnambulists along the promenade
> Have set up booths, their dreams:
> Carpets, jewelry, kitchenware, halvah, shoes.
> From a loudspeaker passionate lament
> Mingles with the penny Jungle's roars and screams.
> Tonight in the magician's tent
> Next door a woman will be sawed in two,
> But right now she's asleep, as who is not, as who . . .
>
> An old Turk at the water's edge has laid
> His weapons and himself down, sleeps
> Undisturbed since, oh, 1913.
> Nothing will surprise him should he wake,
> Only how tall, how green the grass has grown
> There by the dusty carpet of the lake
> Sun beats, then sleepwalks down a vine-festooned arcade,
> Giving himself away in golden heaps.

Public, communal life "along the promenade" is a matter of shared dreams for which a loudspeaker broadcasts the score, "passionate" but recorded and repeating. So commonplace and predictable are the elements of the scene that "an old Turk at the water's edge" can be sure he has seen it all already, even with his eyes closed. He or another old man will return at the end of the poem, like the magician's assistant, the woman who "will be sawed in two." This is something that happens to her—or to some woman, Merrill implies—every night. Indeed, sex, which feels like the very mark of our individuality, is the most programmed of our stories, he suggests. "My boys and girls in Yánnina," as Merrill puts it in the interview, are stock types with a scripted fate: the girls, skirts swishing as they walk, offer "stately whispering sails [. . .] someone will board and marry," while the pirates—"those radiant young males"—hang out in a line on the promenade like blue-eyed morning glories "on the provincial vine," their lives seemingly all before them.

The woman to be sawed in half: she represents the two women in Ali's story—Frossíni, the martyr whom the Pasha drowns in the lake, and Vas-

silikí, the "dark lady" in whose lap he waits for his own execution. Together
the duo embody the two sides of any man's desire. "Your grimiest raga-
muffin," Merrill proposes, "comes to want / Two loves, two versions of
the Feminine // One virginal and tense, brief as a bubble, / One flesh and
bone—gone up no less in smoke." The doubleness of Ali's eros, like that of
Merrill's own, expresses an essential doubleness in his nature.*

Which Merrill also sees in his father. He makes the association explicit
as he takes leave of the city:

> Ali, my father—both are dead.
> In so many words, so many rhymes,
> The brave old world sleeps. Are we what it dreams
> And is a rude awakening overdue?
> Not in Yánnina. To bed, to bed.
> The Lion sets. The lights wink out along the lake.
> Weeks later, in this study gone opaque,
> They are relit. See through me. See me through.

"O brave new world, / That has such people in't!" says Miranda when she
first sees the assembled Italians washed ashore on Prospero's island in *The
Tempest*. The irony is that, in her innocence, she has mistaken the people
of the old world for those of a new one. James Merrill may have made a
similar mistake when he came to Greece, dazzled by the strangers strolling
through Kolonáki Square. By now, he has learned that, even in the exotic
capital of Epirus, he is so close to home that Ali Pasha is a version of his
father. For that matter, the despot is a version of Merrill himself: hadn't
Jimmy constructed, over the past decade, out of his own divided desires,
a seraglio—comic and unhappy—in his own house? That there is never
"more than one life" does not mean that there is no difference between the
old world and the new, or between a father and his son. Rather, the past
shapes our consciousness when we least expect it, when we think we have
journeyed farthest from it, in the same way that certain figures insist on
appearing in our dreams.

To become conscious of this process is to gain some power over it (psychoanalysis remained a model of personal development for Merrill). When,
for example, the lights of Yánnina are re-illuminated in the poet's study, they
"see through" him by forcing him to recognize his romantic ruses and

---

* Merrill's footnote-quotation from Plomer's *The Diamond of Joannina* makes it clear that
Frossíni herself is hardly a simple innocent, but he doesn't specify that she was married to
Ali Pasha's son, not Ali himself, which allows the poem to play with an implied association
between Fossíni and Hellen Plummer, tossed overboard by Charlie Merrill.

excuses for what they are, revealing him to himself as a shadow puppet of his own desires, his own genetic code. But this demystification does not undo him. Those lights also "see [him] through" because that self-recognition is comic as well as painful, and it links him to the rest of humanity. Sleeping not far below the quicksilver surface of the poem are Merrill's feelings for Yenser, to whom "Yánnina" is dedicated. His companion on the visit to the fabulous city that prompted the poem had obliged Merrill over time to see himself not as a lover with a new life before him—the wish that had brought him to Greece to begin with—but as a " 'father' or 'teacher,' " who would be able to pass on his knowledge to his reader. Yenser, the X-ray close reader, had seen through him, offering Merrill an intimacy different from the one he was tempted to seek.

The "partings" that Merrill refers to in the poem's final stirring stanzas are several. He is talking about letting go of his father, and his romantic feelings for Yenser. He is also letting go of the dream of a new life he'd brought to Greece. His consolation comes in the company of a reader (it could be Yenser, it could be anyone with his poem in hand) whom he invites to walk with him "arm in arm" into the magician's tent. There a woman is sawed in half, then made whole again. The magician's trick—"It's what one comes to feel that life keeps doing," Merrill said to Kalstone—is redemptive and mysterious: the repair of the irreparable. The poem ends with an old man puffing on a narghilé, or water pipe: is he the magician, the Turk who slept on the quai, the poet's father, or the poet himself grown old? (As if to put himself in the poem, Merrill had for the first time in his life grown a beard, flecked with white.) The old man enjoys a glorious morning, as, departing from the shore, his barge keeps "scissoring and mending" the crack in the mirror of the "windless" morning lake. The lake heals

> Like anybody's life, bubble and smoke
> In afterthought, whose elements converge,
> Glory of windless mornings that the barge
> (Two barges, one reflected, a quicksilver joke)
> Kept scissoring and mending as it steered
> The old man outward and away,
> Amber mouthpiece of a narghilé
> Buried in his by then snow white beard.

In Athens once again, Merrill climbed to his rooftop desk. "It's funny how one reassumes a whole life—or half a life," he wrote to McIntosh. "The street-cries. The ballet of the telephone extension-cord, trying to get it up and down the spiral stairs without turning into Laocoön. The sound of DJ's Greek on the telephone itself—which sound may be absolutely the <u>one</u> thing in all the world I cannot stay in the same room with. My study is what I adore, so high and yet so humble—here I feel really free + alone." Free and alone in that high, humble room, he was prepared to write "Lost in Translation" and *The Book of Ephraim*, his two finest poems.

THE OTHER WORLD

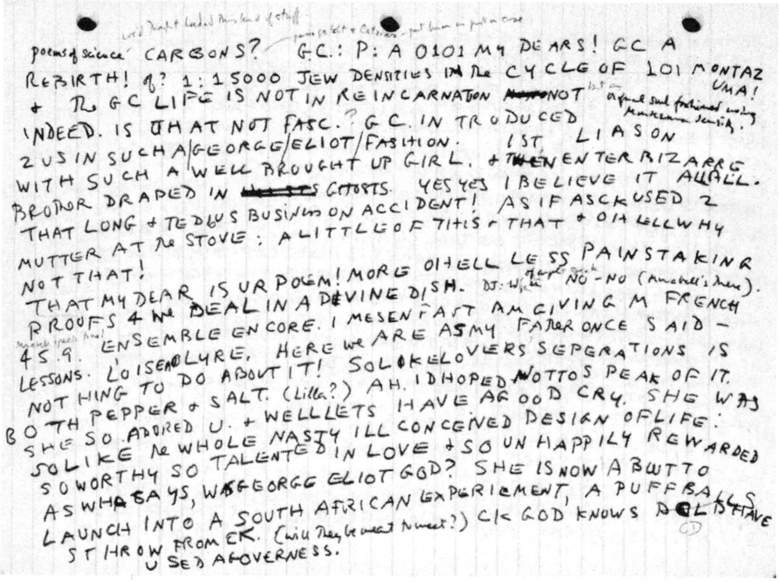

1972–83

13

MILK AND MEMORY

1972–75

The time eventually comes in a good poet's career when readers
actively long for his books: to know that someone out there is writing down your century, your language, your life—under whatever terms of
difference—makes you wish for news of yourself, for those authentic tid-
ings of invisible things, as Wordsworth called them, that only come in
the interpretation of life voiced by poetry." This was the first sentence of
Helen Vendler's review of *Braving the Elements*, declaring that that time had
come in Merrill's career. The review appeared in *The New York Times Book
Review* on September 24, 1972. A professor of English at Boston University, Vendler was just beginning to make her name as a poetry critic. With
books to her credit on Yeats and Stevens, she was well prepared to appreciate Merrill's work, but she wasn't alone; Merrill's readership was growing.
Over the next three years, buoyed by the enthusiasm of devoted readers,
but also challenged by dissenting opinions and persisting self-doubts,
Merrill would undertake increasingly ambitious and aesthetically risky
poems. He fell into periods of depression, and the deaths of friends weighed
on him. Yet he had an appetite for work. More and more, his life took place
at his desk, in his poems, and in memory. The world was often far away,

---

ILLUSTRATION Ouija transcript recorded by JM in Athens, May 19, 1977: "WE DEAL IN A DIVINE DISH."

while the Other World kept coming closer, more insistent and more real than ever.

Vendler's review delighted him. "I just received a 7-column spread from the Sunday Times Book section about my book, complete with glam (bearded) photo," he announced to Donald Richie from Athens. Vendler, whom "I didn't even know," was "full of praise for One," and she was "easy + sensible about the erotic themes, so my old cracked cup is running over." *The New York Times Book Review* was the most influential literary supplement in the U.S., and the "beautiful big puff" made Merrill's "flesh crawl with pleasure for a whole day." In fact his pleasure lasted longer than that. The review, he told Kalstone in October, "is so far + away my finest hour vis à vis the media, that I keep repairing to it again + again, quite as if the two intervening Book Sections hadn't made of it ancient history." Congratulations kept "pouring" in, including letters not only from old friends, but from readers unknown to Merrill who felt, just as Vendler described, that he had been writing down their language and lives. He joked about this correspondence with Kalstone: "[S]top writing me those thinly disguised fan letters. I know perfectly well that you are 'Ray Andrews' from Dalton, Mass. [. . .] as well as 'J. D. McClatchy' [. . .]. Ve-ry funny, but you have Better Things to Do." These enthusiastic and self-revealing readers were flattering to Merrill, even as their presumption of intimacy took him aback. In *Water Street*, he had vowed to make his readers feel "at home" in his poetry, and so they did.

"Ray Andrews" quickly disappeared from view, but J. D. McClatchy did not. Sandy McClatchy, as his friends called this twenty-seven-year-old graduate student in the Yale English Department, followed up his letter with a gift: a leather-bound diary from the nineteenth century in which a young American girl, a character out of James, had recorded her first impressions of Europe. The diary was a success. Still, Merrill was unsure what to think about this new correspondent whose letters, he confided to Richard Howard, "sound so much like everything one knows inside + out (opera, self-destructive jokes, little known facts) that I can hardly phrase a postcard in reply." But he did phrase his replies, they grew longer and more familiar, he produced gifts of his own (new opera recordings), and, when he returned to America in 1973, he invited his admirer to Water Street. He met a strikingly handsome young man, six feet tall, with a trim black beard, black hair, piercing green eyes, and a proud hawk's nose. From an upper-middle-class Philadelphia family (Irish Catholic, not WASP), McClatchy was good-humored and attentive. His conversation and sheer helpfulness, Merrill found, could rescue a long evening around the dinner table with Stephen Spender and the Stone Women, who approved of him at once. McClatchy, himself a poet, had written to Merrill out of dazzled admiration for his poetry. Training as a poetry critic at Yale, he was ready to believe that "the harder a poem was, the better it was," and "the glamour of Merrill's poems bowled me over, especially when I didn't understand them." It soon became apparent to McClatchy that Merrill was a man he wanted to learn from, and learn not only how to write but how to live his life. "It was a time when I was going to a shrink with the whole gay thing," he remembered. "I went to bars at night, and no matter how it worked out, I moped the next day—graduate school gives you time to mope. And Jimmy's responses were always crisp and clarifying. He was just the opposite of me. I was expansive, vulgar, and confused, and he was elegant, controlled, and witty."

In a letter to Bishop after that spate of fan mail, Merrill joked, "I hope I'm not turning into a Gay culture-hero." This is one of the first times he uses "Gay" in his correspondence, rather than "queer," and he puts it in implied quotation marks, conveying his distance from the Gay Liberation movement. By 1972, the movement had taken hold as a powerful political force in the U.S. and western Europe; it dramatically changed the public visibility of gays and lesbians, introducing both the possibility and the ethical imperative for homosexuals to "come out." Merrill was no more involved in this movement than he had been in any other political struggle. He was at home on Water Street in June 1969 when the Public Morals Squad arrived to shut down the Stonewall Inn in Greenwich Village, and a crowd of angry drag queens, hustlers, and young Puerto Ricans fought back. Even so, the movement which was ignited that night was altering what it meant for Merrill to be gay. The changes were incremental. In the long-distance view of A Different Person, he writes, "As in the classic account of Sarah Bernhardt descending a spiral staircase—she stood still and it revolved around her—my good fortune was to stay in one place while the closet simply disintegrated." Of course, the closet never "simply disintegrated": it had to be taken apart, sometimes by violence, and it has never been dismantled completely. But as the revolution went on around him, gay liberation allowed Merrill to show himself in public as what he had always been: the Wildean wit who tossed off outrageous remarks like this comparison between himself and the divine Miss Sarah.

Still, he was never so radiant and passive in his poetry. From "The Black Swan" to "An Urban Convalescence," from "Days of 1964" to "Matinées," his poems had been, from one angle, the story of a gay writer repeatedly affirming his desire and his way of life against the pressure of a censuring culture. He had kept coming out, and coming out farther, in his work. In "After the Fire," "Strato in Plaster," "Up and Down," "Days of 1971," and other poems in *Braving the Elements* (even the title evokes the rigors of self-exposure), he had come out farther than ever before. Hence his satisfaction at how "easy + sensible" Vendler had been about the book's "erotic themes." "Jimmy wanted to be a Blue Chip, 'establishment' writer, not a Gay writer," comments Edmund White, who could not find a publisher for his gay fiction in the early 1970s before a market for gay writing opened up a few years later. But it seemed that Merrill, unlike White and other gay writers, might not have to choose between those options. *Braving the Elements* sold so well that Atheneum printed a second edition three months after the first. The book's success raised the possibility that he could have it both ways.

Yet he felt the force of that censuring culture, and, as usual, he felt it through his mother. He had dedicated *Braving the Elements* to her in the spirit of reconciliation expressed in "The Emerald," the second section of "Up and Down." Her son's triumph in the *Times* might therefore have been a moment of glory for her too. But Vendler had noted that Merrill lived "with his lover in Greece"; and Hellen Plummer's pleasure was spoiled, she told Jimmy, by the "12 little letters of the alphabet" in that phrase, "with his lover" (the offending words themselves she didn't quote). Hellen had long been gathering her son's press clippings in albums—and those words stained the record. Her friends who had seen the review weren't mentioning it; what could she say to them? Jimmy responded by writing "Mrs P the first frank letter in over 20 years, saying how times have changed, and what do her enthusiastic friends think those poems are <u>about</u> anyhow?" He may have been "frank," but he was forgiving and affectionate too (he called her "Dearest Mama"). When it came to her friends, he pointed out that "lover" could mean either a man or a woman; she could hide behind that if she had to. This was not a blow for gay liberation so much as a capitulation to his mother's need to save face. His letter prompted a "dear, if histrionic page" in return. After her first letter about the review, Hellen feared that she had "offended" Jimmy, "even while I was painfully aware that I could not have stopped myself from writing as I did."

> Now I have your reply—so tender, so understanding, so tolerant of me, and so incredibly perceptive that my throat will stay tight for days. Nor was I unmindly of the "Est" on your salutation, the first since you were a very little boy.
>
> I will not pretend that I was not shocked over the "black-on-white." In fact I was numb the first few days as I struggled

for guidance to know how to meet a variety of inevitable reactions. Suddenly I realized that my prayers of 28 years had been re-worded some two years ago when I found myself asking for acceptance of God's will rather than beseeching Him for a miracle (who had I thought I was anyhow to presume in such a manner?). I had been too blind all this time to admit that I had no earthly right to make such a plea. In fact the evil was in me, not you—the evil of intolerance and pride. Now, at last, I keep hoping to be seen a little bit worthy of the wonderful years I've experienced and most of all to be, as a person, more acceptable to you. If this sounds maudlin—sentimental—remember I haven't your way with words. I'm only trying to say how right you are when you suggested I could not have written so "gently" (if at all) until now.

My stand—and fortunately it can be taken in all honesty—is that HV's review is truly magnificent and truly deserved. Stating this at the offset has been disarming and has spared me, thus far, any more distressing confrontations. You voiced or rather summed it up years ago at age 12 when I tried to soften the blow that Daddy + I were separating. You said, "Divorce is all right. I just don't want it in our family."

In this morning's sermon at St. James, the words "endurance without self-pity" leapt out at me. I'm doing my utmost to "minimize" the matter. To love you more would be impossible! You have my entire heart.

Mama

The lover her son lived with in Greece had recently turned fifty, and the exuberant celebration of that event makes a vivid contrast to the poet's exquisite negotiations with his mother. On the eve of David Jackson's birthday, Jimmy and Manoli burst into David's bedroom at midnight in costume: "I dressed in voluminous Bachtiyari black trousers, a rainbow tank-top, and beads; M. in a simple black belt and cowboy hat." The merrymakers found David "drumming his fingers on a sound-asleep Dresden doll of a petty officer." They boisterously fêted his half century before returning to "our steaming sheets and the dregs of an exhausted popper." On the day itself, Jimmy ordered a Roman-numeral, L-shaped cake (he had pretended to consider "black icing" in mourning) for a champagne lunch in DJ's honor. The lunch, hosted by Maria at her house at Cape Sounion, was followed by "more than the usual S-E-X that evening," for JM and DJ, though as usual not with each other.

The Rover Boys had spent much of the past five years apart. Now they were living under the same roof again, but they were not always together. Merrill stayed home with Karastefanís or by himself, while Jackson cruised for petty officers and the like on Omonia Square, where years ago Jimmy had met Strato (George was out of sight for the time being). Their romantic and sexual intimacies with other men caused friction, which they did their best to laugh off. "D. keeps adding up all the other people I'm in love with, or loved by, and when I make some feeble allusion to all his one-noon or one-night stands, says he would rather run a bordello than a seraglio." If they ever had, David and Jimmy no longer had any important secrets from each other. In 1971, Merrill wrote in his notebook: "I see DJ 'as he is': the wonder is that he still interests + touches me with all the trappings removed." Jackson could have said the same of him. The acceptance that came with this knowledge of each other—and themselves—with "all the trappings removed," tested over nineteen years together, was their own form of devotion.

In September, Merrill finished an essay on Francis Ponge for *The New York Review of Books*. Called "Object Lessons," this is one of Merrill's few sustained pieces of literary criticism, and it's full of implications for his own work. The French poet, then in his seventies, was the author of *Le parti pris des choses*, translated as *The Voice of Things* by Beth Archer Brombert in one of the books that occasioned Merrill's essay (the other was Cid Corman's translation of Ponge, *Things*). Focusing in his work on everyday objects, Ponge found an alternative to the exalted abstractions of the Symbolists. "What is more engaging than blue sky if not a cloud, in docile clarity?" he muses in a passage quoted by Merrill, who comments, "So Ponge, in 1924, restores *l'azur* and *le vide papier que la blancheur défend*, all that rare, magnetic emptiness so prized by Mallarmé and Valéry, to a backdrop for something common, modest, real." Merrill's own progress from the Mallarméan ambitions of his early work to the actual world of *Water Street* had followed a similar path.

But Merrill never entirely abandoned his early idealism. "No thoughts, then, but in things?" he asks rhetorically, playing on William Carlos Williams's dictum "No ideas but in things," and speaking for himself as well as Ponge. "True enough, so long as the notorious phrase argues not for the suppression of thought but for its oneness with whatever in the world—pine

LEFT Mischievous Donald Richie, Athens, early 1960s

BELOW Jimmy and Donald at the beach in Greece

Howard Moss as Mr. Magoo

Daryl Hine, early 1960s

The Surly Temple, c. 1960: DJ and
JM with Grace Stone (left) and
Isabel and Robert Morse. Grace's
daughter, Eleanor Perényi, must
have taken the photo.

DJ, Grace Stone, and JM crossing
the Atlantic, 1962

Maria Mitsotáki at her house on Cape Sounion,
early 1960s: "Unjeweled in black as ever
comedienne / Of mourning if not silent star
of chic."

ABOVE Strato Mouflouzélis in the
parlor at Athinaion Efívon 44, 1964.
"My life, your light green eyes / Have
lit on me with joy."

ABOVE, RIGHT JM and SM

RIGHT George Lazaretos and DJ in
George's hometown, Monemvasía

BELOW Strato, JM, DJ, and George
on the Venetian waterfront in Chania,
Crete, 1966

DJ's sketch of the house in Athens, sent to friends as a Christmas card for 1964

Yannis Boras and Chester Kallman at Athinaion Efivon 44, 1965. DJ's drawing of 107 Water Street hangs on the wall behind them.

Mimi and Vassili with DJ's drawing of 107 Water Street

Robin Magowan in Greece, c. 1965

ABOVE David McIntosh in New Mexico

LEFT JM and David McIntosh on the Snow King chairlift, 1968. "I love that funny snapshot from a time / When we still thought we were each other's meat."

BELOW, LEFT 18 West Eleventh Street, March 1970. "My mother saw the photograph in Life / And felt her inside crumple."

BELOW Tony Parigory, 1970s. Native informant, social director, go-between, sometime procurer, real estate agent, and trusted sidekick, Tony virtually created Merrill's Greek life. Honored after his death from AIDS in "Tony: Ending the Life," he was one of JM's best-loved friends.

LEFT Mona Van Duyn. Her early praise of JM's poetry earned his loyalty. He obliged when she invited him to send his papers to Washington University.

BELOW Richard Howard, one of the Great Fancies, on the deck at 107 Water Street, 1973

Youthful Stephen Yenser

JM, bearded, and David Kalstone near Ioannina, 1972. Tony Parigory, traveling with them, took the photo.

TOP David Kalstone, publicity photo for
his book *Five Temperaments*, 1977

MIDDLE DJ, c. 1975

BELOW, LEFT DJ's pastel portrait of Manos
Karastefanís

BELOW, RIGHT JM and Manos on DJ's
fiftieth birthday, 1972. JM is wearing his
Bachtiyari trousers, a souvenir from his
visit to Yahya and Isfahan in 1966. On the
wall, mostly obscured, is Pavlos Simios's
double portrait of JM and DJ.

ABOVE, LEFT Judith Moffett in Greece, 1973

ABOVE, MIDDLE George Cotzias, 1970s

ABOVE, RIGHT Strato around 1979, back in Athens after seven years in Canada, on a visit to JM

LEFT Nelly Liambey and JM on the sidewalk outside Athinaion Efivon 44

BELOW The parlor at 107 Water Street with the bat-pattern wallpaper where JM and DJ sat to talk over their séances. Beyond, the bookcase study door is ajar, giving a glimpse of the "inner room" where JM worked every morning.

RIGHT 702 Elizabeth Street, Key West, 1979

BELOW JM and DJ setting up house in Key West. Behind them, the print of Böcklin's cavorting nymphs was a gift from Maria Mitsotáki.

RIGHT JM and DJ at the Ouija board in the watermelon/ sunburn dining room on Water Street, 1983. A print by Yannis Tsarouchis is on the wall.

JM and HIP, four floors above Water Street, c. 1980

Charles and Mary Merrill with their children and grandchildren on CM's sixtieth birthday, 1980

LEFT Eleanor Perényi visiting Mary McCarthy (not seen) and James West (in background) in Castine, Maine

BELOW, LEFT Ed White in Venice

BELOW, RIGHT Stephen Yenser, early 1980s

Alfred Corn and
J. D. McClatchy at home in
Wells River, Vermont

Peter Tourville and JM with McClatchy in Wells River, early 1980s

LEFT Peter Tourville in canoe, 1983. See "A Day on the Connecticut River" and "Tattoos," the first part of the three-part "Peter."

BELOW, LEFT Peter Hooten in front of Elizabeth Bishop's house on White Street in Key West

BELOW, RIGHT Peter in the living room on Elizabeth Street, 1984

ABOVE, LEFT The Magowans, Bobby and Doris, celebrating fifty years of marriage, 1985. RAM died later that year.

ABOVE, RIGHT Richard and Charlee Wilbur in Key West

RIGHT Jim Boatwright and Lee Toy, Key West, mid-1980s. Boatwright, "the Colonel," died of AIDS in 1988.

BELOW JM and PH under the pines at the southern tip of Key West, 1989

ABOVE JM, in Mao cap, among the cherry blossoms in Japan, 1986

LEFT PH and JM snorkeling in Hawaii

BELOW SY and JDM, JM's future literary executors, at work in Key West, late 1980s

JM and DJ at the Academy of American Arts and Letters, 1988. To the left, John Hollander, back turned, is talking with Allen Ginsberg.

May 18, 1988   Jee Klementz

ABOVE   JM and HIP on her ninetieth birthday

ABOVE, RIGHT   PH with Cosmo as puppy, 1991

BOTTOM Agha Shahid Ali with JM, early 1990s

JM swimming in Lakeville, Connecticut, 1994. A snapshot by Peter

JM, 1994

woods, spider, cigarette—gives rise to it. Turn the phrase around, you arrive no less at truth: no things but in thoughts." Or, Merrill might have said, no things but in words. He quotes Ponge: "It's a question of the object as notion. Of the object in the French language (an item, really, in a French dictionary)." When Ponge calls the blackberry "a cluster of spheres filled with a drop of ink," it's hard to tell the difference between things and words. Literature re-creates life, but life is already a literary text.

The notion that experience is always mediated by language—that the world is made of words—entails for Ponge a highly reflexive, self-conscious poetics. Merrill declares, "Ponge may be the first poet ever to expose so openly the machinery of a poem, to present his revisions, blind alleys, critical asides, and accidental felicities as part of a text perfected, as it were, without 'finish.' " From the self-corrections of "An Urban Convalescence" to the footnotes of "Yánnina," Merrill too had been intent on exposing "the machinery" of his work. This impulse coexists in his work with what might seem like the opposite, an impulse to let words themselves lead the way. Prompted by Ponge's play on "mûre" (meaning both "blackberry" and "ripe"), Merrill writes about that "most suspect device," the pun:

A pity about that lowest form of humor. It is suffered, by and large, with groans of aversion, as though one had done an unseemly thing in adult society, like slipping a hand up the hostess's dress. Indeed, the punster has touched, and knows it if only for being so promptly shamed, upon a secret, fecund place in language herself. The pun's objet trouvé aspect cheapens it further—why? A Freudian slip is taken seriously: it betrays its maker's hidden wish. The pun (or the rhyme, for that matter) "merely" betrays the hidden wish of words.

We like to think of ourselves as the creators of our own thought and expression, manipulating words to our purposes; even when a slip of the tongue reveals an unconscious truth, the self is the origin of meaning, and language its instrument. But it is otherwise for Merrill's punster. Expressing "the hidden wish of words" themselves, the pun says it is language that uses us to speak, and not the other way around.

When he finished it, Merrill sent the essay to be vetted by Richard Howard, the eminent English translator of modern French literature. He and Merrill had met in postwar New York. In a poem from 2002 recalling that time, Howard describes a thé dansant in Manhattan at which the throng of "gay men / gorgeously dressed (and even gowned) made movement / —there must have been a hundred of us!— / difficult but quite a lot of fun." Howard was a "novice" in the literary and queer worlds of the city, and "James Merrill, Terror of the Revels," with his "drawling vowels" and "dismissive smile," educated him in the manners of this milieu, including "such tactics as the Freezing Shoulder / and (your words) a Sociable Stab-in-the-Front." Howard himself became something of a "terror" in the world of letters—a poetry reviewer and editor with an ornate prose style and caustic wit, backed up by his formidable skills as a linguist (before he became a translator, he worked as a lexicographer). Sociable and generous, with a healthy measure of *amour propre*, he had a polished bald head, taut face, wincing smile, and hoarse, slightly high-pitched voice. He liked to dress in attention-getting outfits like the "bright blue knit suit, Sicilian Panama hat with red band, [and] ivory cigarette holder" he showed up with one weekend on Water Street.

In 1969, Howard had published *Untitled Subjects* with Atheneum (he was another poet in Harry Ford's stable), and the book won the Pulitzer Prize. It featured a type of poem that became Howard's signature genre: long dramatic monologues that brought to life the voices of figures both major and minor from the cultural past (Browning, master of the dramatic monologue, was one of his subjects). In a sense, Howard was a medium, like Merrill, who used the library rather than the Ouija board to channel his spirits. Like Merrill, he loved elaborate figures of speech, puns, quibbles, bon mots, and a sinuous Jamesian syntax. That sense of style made for solidarity between them: on the playing field of contemporary poetry, they knew they were on the same team. Howard remembers a poetry festival they both attended in North Dakota in 1983. "Well," Merrill remarked as they buckled up for the return flight to New York, "now the Great Plains have met the Great Fancies."*

In the days following the appearance of Vendler's review, Merrill began a poem he intended to dedicate to Howard. On October 10, he wrote a postcard (on the picture side: a white-bearded Ali Pasha resting in the arms of his Vassilikí) telling Howard he was "blissfully busy writing a poem for you." The poem was "already longish + involves a jigsaw puzzle, a Rilke translation of Valéry, 'and much, much more.' " Merrill looked for the Rilke translation in libraries in Athens, and failed to find it. By the time Yenser provided a copy of it, the hunt had been worked into the plot of "Lost in Translation," as Merrill titled the poem when he sent a mostly completed version to its dedicatee on October 24.

---

* For audio-visual recording and transcripts of the University of North Dakota Writers Conference, March 24, 1983, see library.und.edu/digital/writers-conference/1983/.

In its play of richly textured personal memory and searching philosophical speculation, "Lost in Translation" is the greatest of Merrill's short poems. It was composed quickly while Merrill was still basking in Vendler's review and exchanging with his mother "the most affectionate letters—for the first time in 25 years!" Reconciliation with his mother must have stimulated, and in turn been reinforced by, his return in memory to the summer of 1937 at the Orchard. Yet Hellen scarcely appears in the poem, which centers on memories of Zelly, or "Mademoiselle," who cares for the eleven-year-old boy during the summer in Southampton prior to his parents' divorce. She accompanies him in his routine of "German lesson, picnic, see-saw, walk / With the collie who 'did everything but talk' "—a life "Full of unfulfillment." They await the arrival of a jigsaw puzzle from a shop in New York. But it "keeps never coming"; the card table's "tense oasis of green felt," standing "ready / To receive" it, glows like a "mirage"; the boy's boredom and anxiety build; and Mademoiselle must comfort him before he can sleep.

Mademoiselle introduces the boy to "translation" from several angles. To begin with, he's "in love" with her: as a substitute for his mother, she arouses in him the affective power of what Freud called "transference love," by which we transfer the love we felt for a person in the past, typically the parent of the opposite sex, to another person in the present. Mademoiselle also presides over the boy's imaginative play, his marionettes and the jigsaw puzzle, which suggest another substitution: art for life. The puzzle stands in for the "puzzle" of a "summer without parents"; putting it together gives the boy both an escape from that painful reality and a means of exploring it as he discovers his family drama in the characters depicted on the jigsaw puzzle: a sheik, a "dark-eyed woman," and the page boy whom they both "claim."

Mademoiselle herself is a sort of living symbol of translation for the boy. She speaks French with a German accent: only in adulthood would Merrill learn that her mother was English, her father German, and she "only French by marriage." She writes letters to "a curé in Alsace," the border region contested by France and Germany. When she holds the boy at night, she soothes him in French and German in turn: "Patience, cheri. Geduld, mein schatz." Teaching him "her languages," she teaches him that there is no single mother tongue: language is a system of languages, which are related, even interlocking, and yet by no means consistent with each other. Part of this lesson is recuperative and consoling: anything that can be said one way can be said in another; no statement is final; substitution is always possible. But no substitution is perfect. Full of *faux amis*, languages, like nations, are potential enemies; their borders are fraught with loss and betrayal. Mademoiselle (Merrill called her "Fraülein" in draft) incarnates this principle too: she has been "a widow since Verdun."

Translation and these memories of Zelly must have struck Merrill as related topics for a poem as he brooded on Ponge's pun on "*mûres*" and his allusion to "*l'azur*" in Mallarmé and Valéry. Valéry's "Palme," a poem that calls for patience in the face of seemingly empty, unproductive time, contains a key rhyme on "*azur*" and "*mûr*." Merrill had kept "Palme" in mind for a long time as a kind of talisman, encouraging him when he doubted his future as a poet. At Amherst in 1945, for example, asking in his diary "What on earth shall become of me if I do not write?" he quoted Valéry's poem:

> Ces jours qui te semblent vides
> Et perdus pour l'univers
> Ont des racines avides
> Qui travaillent les déserts.

Valéry says, literally, "These days that seem empty to you and lost to the universe have avid roots that work beneath the desert." Rising in the desert of time with its milky coconut as balm and prize, connecting heaven and earth, the palm tree symbolizes the secret, subterranean process by which what had seemed to be lost in life is later redeemed in art.

The Rilke translation Merrill mentioned to Howard was a version of "Palme." When, in "Lost in Translation," he can't find it, he tries to reconstruct it, and the German words he supposes Rilke must have used work in his mind's ear like Proust's madeleine to call back the long-ago hour with Mademoiselle and the words she spoke to him then: "Patience dans l'azur. / Geduld im . . . Himmelblau?" The lost German translation stands in the poem for the fullness of meaning always lost in translation—or for that matter, in memory. Once Yenser supplied a copy of Rilke's "Palme," Merrill used the German poet's version of the lines beginning "*Ces jours qui te semblent vides*" as an epigraph for his poem.

When the longed-for puzzle arrives "Out of the blue" (Merrill's cliché casually evokes the azure sky in Valéry), the boy and his governess turn into detectives who create a story out of fragmentary evidence. "Mademoiselle does borders"—aptly, given her divided identity. The borders suggest the formal structures, the given arrangements, Merrill preferred as a poet. Her role allows the boy to focus on the interest of the pieces themselves:

> Many take
> Shapes known already—the craftsman's repertoire

Nice in its limitation—from other puzzles:
Witch on broomstick, ostrich, hourglass,
Even (surely not just in retrospect)
An inchling, innocently branching palm.

The two sides of each piece are like the referential and semiotic axes of language, the twin vectors essential to punning, along which words link up at once with things in the world and with other words. Considered independently of the picture they combine to compose, the puzzle pieces have for the boy the generic quality of stock characters and archetypal symbols. As his imagination plays with their shapes, they allow him to pursue eddying digressions ("These can be put aside, made stories of"), while the picture emerges, and the main "plot thickens." As the boy's missing parents materialize in the sheik and the veiled woman, Merrill shifts, in a move appropriate to the Oriental scene, from loosely metrical lines to the snug quatrain form (rhymed *aaba*) used by Edward FitzGerald in his translation of *The Rubáiyát of Omar Khayyam*.

With this heightened formality, fantasy intensifies. Merrill's eye enters the harem: it is Southampton, the world of Benjamin Tanning, but redone in Orientalist decor. He imagines the "old wives" who look on as the sheik's passion ("the virile fiction of the New") runs its course, saying, " 'Insh'Allah, he will tire—' '—or kill her first!' " But just as the tone rises to this melodramatic pitch, Merrill draws back. He inserts a parenthesis that returns us to the scene of writing by making an aside to Richard Howard, the poem's dedicatee. Feigning shock in the face of the Oedipal drama revealed by the puzzle, Merrill quips,

(Hardly a proper subject for the Home,
Work of—dear Richard, I shall let *you* comb
Archives and learned journals for his name—
A minor lion attending on Gérôme.)

Merrill implies he cannot be expected to identify—as Howard surely could—the "minor lion attending on Gérôme" who painted the scene. This is a teasing gesture, implying not only that Merrill lacks the erudition Howard's poems depend on, but that it is beneath him. The dig expresses his habitual diffidence about scholarship, but there is more to it than that. Sources of all kinds are difficult if not impossible to identify in "Lost in Translation," and Merrill questions the point of searching for them.

Merrill is joking: an acolyte to Jean-Léon Gérôme would of course be "a minor lion" because Gérôme is a major figure, a lion of French art, and because a lion is traditionally an attendant figure in the iconography of St. Jerome—who belongs in the poem as the Latin translator of the Bible. This fleeting allusion to St. Jerome is enough to make the point that Valéry and Rilke, like Merrill and Howard, take part in an ongoing process of translation by which heaven ("l'azur," "Himmelblau") is reimagined, over and over. This reimagining of divinity is a general human project, not the privilege of learned poets alone: "Quite a task, / Putting together Heaven, yet we do," Merrill says of the boy and his governess as they sort a "hundred blue / Fragments," becoming sacred translators too.

The jigsaw puzzle is a model for the world in which, like a perfectly crafted poem, everything has its place. Merrill describes the completion of the puzzle with a simple, triumphant repetition: "It's done. Here under the table all along / Were those missing feet. It's done." The last piece to be fit in, missing until the end, has on its picture side the feet of the page. To find it, the boy merely had to look under the table at his own feet—making a connection between the page (another pun) and himself. World and word link up in a sublime unity.

But the poem isn't over yet. The sense of closure created by the repetition of "It's done" is misleading: the second in that pair of lines is only four beats and thus missing a metrical foot. That missing foot hints that the unity of world and word is not complete after all, and the happy order that the completed puzzle constitutes is only temporary. "All too soon the swift / Dismantling" comes. As he describes it, Merrill lightly suggests the breakup of the boy's home, the coming of the world war, even the apocalyptic dissolution of heaven:

> Irresistibly a populace
> Unstitched of its attachments, rattled down.
> Power went to pieces as the witch
> Slithered easily from Virtue's gown.
> The blue held out for time, but crumbled, too.
> The city had long fallen, and the tent,
> A separating sauce mousseline,
> Been swept away.

In draft, Merrill ended the poem just a few lines further by returning to the image of Valéry's palm as consolation. Before the poem was done, he inserted into this passage a meditation on Rilke's "Palme." The translation is the last item in a list of "missing pieces" from "later puzzles," including "Maggie Teyte's high notes / Gone at the war's end, end of the vogue for collies, / A house torn down," and the secret of Mademoiselle's German ancestry, her "pitiful bit of truth." "Yet I can't / Just be imagining," Merrill says of the missing translation,

> I've seen it. Know
> How much of the sun-ripe original
> Felicity Rilke made himself forego
> (Who loved French words—verger, mûr, parfumer)
> In order to render its underlying sense.
> Know already in that tongue of his
> What Pains, what monolithic Truths
> Shadow stanza to stanza's symmetrical
> Rhyme-rutted pavement. Know that ground plan left
> Sublime and barren, where the warm Romance
> Stone by stone faded, cooled; the fluted nouns
> Made taller, lonelier than life
> By leaf-carved capitals in the afterglow.
> The owlet umlaut peeps and hoots
> Above the open vowel. And after rain
> A deep reverberation fills with stars.

Translation is an ascetic process for Merrill's Rilke. He gives up "sun-ripe original / Felicity" for the consolation of "underlying sense," the first represented by Valéry's "warm Romance" French, the second by his native German. In Merrill's fantasia, letters take on life, but they also take the place of it: the convention of capitalizing nouns in German ("*Diese Tage*") suggests a landscape of classical ruins, of "leaf-carved capitals," which are printed letters and stone columns both. Ponge revels in this kind of play in "Blackberries," but the letters of Rilke's German, being "taller, lonelier than life," signify loss rather than ripeness: "underlying sense" only comes in the "afterglow" of the senses.

Thinking of the elusive Rilke translation and all it has come to stand for in the poem, Merrill asks, "Lost, is it, buried? One more missing piece?" The final passage follows:

> But nothing's lost. Or else: all is translation
> And every bit of us is lost in it
> (Or found—I wander through the ruin of S
> Now and then, wondering at the peacefulness)
> And in that loss a self-effacing tree,

Color of context, imperceptibly
Rustling with its angel, turns the waste
To shade and fiber, milk and memory.

"But nothing's lost" says that the losses time forces on us are no loss: we ourselves remain, and we remain ourselves, intact originals. Or, perhaps the consolation is just the opposite: everything is lost, "all is translation," and there is no enduring self. When his argument reaches this turn, Merrill inserts, like a last puzzle piece, a sentence adapted from his notebook in 1970, when he found an image for his altered feelings for Strato in the archaic Temple of Aphaia: "The ruin of S., of S. as I see him, visited in a kind of wondering peacefulness." The "warm romance" Jimmy lived with Strato has been translated into a minimal private reference, a single capital letter, all but detached from its source in life.

Merrill ends with an image of the "self-effacing tree." The palm is itself a sort of translation: it stands for the boy's mother, for his Mademoiselle, and for friends who came after them—including the companions consti- tuted by poems like Valéry's "Palme," which Merrill memorized in youth, kept inside of him, and drew on so much later. The tree is "self-effacing" because it blends in: taking its color, like a puzzle piece, from "context," from the life around it, it absorbs meaning from an underground system of roots, including words and their roots. The palm's "rustling" sounds like words whispered in the mind's ear, or the page of a notebook as the poet's hand (another palm) traverses it, writing.

"JIM! You scare me!!" Hellen wrote to him when she read "Lost in Trans- lation" in November 1972. "Just when everyone, including me, agrees that you have reached your peak, you take another step forward." Showing her- self to be a fair literary critic, Hellen observed:

> Your words seem to flow more evenly, more eloquently without the old-time [. . .] striking for effect. Now the picture is painted masterfully with a sure brush and what one sees (or hears when read aloud) is a mosaic fashioned from bits and pieces which cracked off our hearts, mine and yours. [. . .] The ending "But nothing's lost" dries my tears and sets me smiling again. One of the best lines is 'The owlet umlaut peeps + hoots above the open vowel.' Simply terrific. As is true of everything you write, many readings are necessary to appreciate your genius. It

swells my heart to apply that word, without a single reserva-
tion, to you when it comes to WORDS, regardless of how you
use them.

The letter gushed, Merrill told Howard, with "milk + memory indeed."
Soon Hellen and Jimmy were making plans for his return to Atlanta in
March. "I would like, but it is not imperative, to USE you as an excuse to
give what sounds ghastly but which can be rather pleasant—i.e., a luncheon at the Driving Club. You've no idea, dearest, how in the dog house
I am with [local friends] my age [. . .] who can't understand why they have
never met you—and the more famous you become"—Hellen had sent around
clippings—"the more they chide me for keeping you in one little circle. I
know this sounds hideous but if you would give consent, I would like to do
this on your birthday, a Saturday, so I could ask couples," rather than ladies
only. When the event came around, Hellen's guest list totaled 190.

As Merrill worked on "Lost in Translation," an ugly drama was unfolding down the street. Chester Kallman had been dissolute and depressed
for a long time. But his condition had gotten much worse. Now he was "in
perfectly dreadful shape; bloated, inarticulate, helpless," drunk on ouzo by
noon, and prey to the grasping types he brought home from the bar. When
the locks on Chester's apartment were changed to keep one of them out,
the young man broke in and made off with the kitchen appliances and the
silver. The next morning, "all D. T.'s and fluttering lids," Kallman could not
answer a simple question from the police, until "the cop said with divine
gallantry: 'Your approximate age, then.' " Kallman was only fifty-two. Day
by day, Merrill and Jackson felt they were "witnessing the final throes of
an extremely elaborate suicide." David helped Chester by making sure that
"the essential things get done." Jimmy just tried to be "mild + good-natured,
even a bit Literary, on the chance that it will remind him of some anecdote
or other that he used to love to tell, and would still if only he could remember it." One evening, with Kallman at the house for dinner, Merrill read
aloud Bishop's "The Moose" from a recent New Yorker. Once Kallman had
left, Manos said to Jimmy, "I don't think Chester liked that poem—he fell
asleep while you were reading it. JM: What do you mean! He did nothing of
the sort! MK: Well, why was he rubbing his eyes afterwards? JM: Kalé mou
[my beauty], it so happens that he'd heard something so beautiful that it
made him cry."*

---

* JM to SY, letter, October 21, 1972 (Yale). One day earlier, Merrill related the same story to
Bishop. But he told Bishop that Kallman had said what, in this letter, he says he himself said.

Merrill and Jackson had Thanksgiving dinner with Chester ("If for nothing else," David cracked, he and Jimmy could be "thankful not to be any of the other people at the table") and a tiny Christmas with Tony and Manos. After he put the final touches on "Lost in Translation," Merrill slipped into a depression that persisted over the next half year and was sometimes severe. Perhaps, even as his return in poetry to his eleventh year reunited him with his mother, composing "Lost in Translation" had made him feel again his abandonment by his father. He began working on "Chimes for Yahya," the poem that told the story of his trip to Isfahan in 1965, when he was in despair after he learned about Strato's relationship with Vaso and found comfort in the person of the Bachtiyari pasha. One night around Christmas, giving himself a B-12 shot, he stabbed the needle in a nerve. The spot swelled, and he took to his bed, "laid low by a really bad case of hypochondria." A letter from Yenser, arriving at Christmas, brought with it an objective correlative for his feelings: Stephen was planning to marry Mary Bomba in March in Los Angles, and he wanted James to be there. "My dear, of course I'll be at your wedding (so long as I'm not expected to dance at it)," Merrill replied. "I'd felt that was in the air, if only through your reticence on the subject. Reading your page, a big tear came to each eye, one of happiness, one of—I hardly know what by now."

In the thick of this melancholy, Merrill won the Bollingen Prize for *Braving the Elements*. The Bollingen is perhaps the most important prize in American poetry. It is awarded in a given year "for the best volume of poetry or"—but the tradition of the prize implies "and"—"for a poet's lifetime achievement in his or her art." When it was first given in 1948, the prize went to Ezra Pound for *The Pisan Cantos*. That choice raised a storm of debate about whether the book's merit, however great, justified giving the award to an accused traitor and an anti-Semite who supported Mussolini in wartime radio broadcasts made in Italy. In the aftermath of the Pound controversy, Paul Mellon, the Bollingen's donor, moved the administration of the prize from the Library of Congress to Yale University Library. Subsequent choices were safer. The prize was awarded in the 1950s and 1960s to august moderns such as Moore, Williams, Frost, Stevens, and Auden, and to Roethke, Berryman, Nemerov, and Warren from the century's "middle generation" of poets. Following the dual award of the prize to his friends Richard Wilbur and Mona Van Duyn, Merrill became the youngest name on a dauntingly official roster. A photographer appeared at his door, a reporter from *The New York Times*, even a crew from CBS television, while cables, flowers, and calls flowed through the house "like a flash flood."

Merrill tried to rise to the occasion. His replies to congratulatory messages from friends showed his misgivings, however. On a postcard to the Hollanders, he alludes to the laurel wreath that was the source of the wrinkles on Frost's brow, according to lisping old President Cole of Amherst:

> Dear John, Anne, Martha, + Lizzy,
> Would that I were able
> To answer your rhymed cable,
> But "the weight of the weath"
> Gives me pains in my teeth
> And the laurel-fumes leave me dizzy.
> See you soon. Much love, Jimmy

To Anthony Hecht, one of the Bollingen judges that year, he said, "I truly hadn't thought I'd done enough to deserve it." To McIntosh, he wrote that the prize "upset" him: "It is everything I could have hoped for—immensely distinguished, etc. etc.—but it has the effect (temporarily I trust) of stripping my gears."

Not every reaction to the Bollingen announcement was enthusiastic. It was a sign of the prize's prestige that it elicited an editorial protesting the award to Merrill in *The New York Times*. Seeing the choice as a reflection of narrow academic taste, the unsigned editorial complained of the tendency of Yale's library "to reward poetry that is literary, private, and traditional."

> Mr. Merrill is a poet of solid accomplishment and sure craftsmanship. The quarrel is not with him, but with the Library's insistence down the years that poetry is a hermetic cultivation of one's sensibility and a fastidious manipulation of received forms. The Bollingen people flinch from poetry that is raucous in character or that has an abrasive public sound, from poetry in the Whitman tradition or poetry that is experimental, from the poetry of black writers, much of it now very visible and vocal. Perhaps the academic grip on the Bollingen ought to be loosened. This is a big and varied land, and there is a whole world west of New Haven that the Yale Library seems to know little about.

This was not the fiery indignation aroused by the selection of Pound, yet the complaint was related: the Bollingen judges had expressed elite preferences rather than democratic ones. Richard Howard came to the defense of the prize and of Merrill in a letter to the *Times*: "The implied attack on elitism ('the academic grip on the Bollingen') is worthy of the Vice President"—the boorish, anti-intellectual Vice President Spiro Agnew—"not the editorial page of The Times. When the words 'literary,' 'private' and 'traditional' are used as slurs, then the words 'journalistic,' 'public' and 'experimental' become no better." Poetry of merit, Howard argued, is both "literary" and "journalistic," "private" and "public," "traditional" and "experimental." To have failed to see that, Howard continued, challenging the editorialist, "reveals that you have not experienced the poetry of those rewarded, merely the tiresome gossip which always accompanies achievement." Probably gossip did play a part in the editorial, stirred by the conjunction of the famous prize, the Ivy League library, and James Merrill's name. But it was not so easy to dismiss the complaint. It was true that *Braving the Elements* included the most "hermetic" poems Merrill had written. It was also true that the list of past prizewinners included no African American writers or West Coasters or experimental poets (well, with the significant exceptions of Pound, Williams, and Moore); and the selection of Merrill, whose work was indeed valued by academic critics, was in line with past choices.

Merrill never commented on the unusual editorial. The Bollingen purse of $5,000 was the heaviest in American poetry. He put a little of the prize money aside for a new IBM Selectric typewriter for himself. The rest he gave to McIntosh and Hellen, because, he said to McIntosh, "my book so much 'belongs' to both of you." David's gift came as cash, HIP's as a deluxe ornament. On his way back to the U.S. from Greece in February, Merrill stopped in Paris, where he chose for his mother a jeweled bee—appropriate for "Bollingen"—"with diamonds on its body and two wings of pinky-mauve-opal slightly netted over with gold, which it's all I can do," he told Parigory, "not to wear myself." Ostentatiously frivolous, costly, and small, it was exactly what his editorializing detractors might have suspected he would do with the money, and his private way of telling them to go to hell.

Even so, the issues raised by the editorial stayed with him. More laudatory reviews of *Braving the Elements* followed Vendler's, including lengthy pieces by Yenser and Moffett, but there were negative comments too. Writing in the *Atlantic Monthly*, Peter Davison objected that Merrill does "not so much grapple with reality as disguise it." Calling him a "gifted" but "baffling" artist, and alluding to Yeats's poem "A Coat," he suggested that "for Merrill, perhaps, there would be more enterprise in walking naked." A sharper, sweeping judgment appeared in the *Hudson Review*. Richard Pevear, writing from a loosely Marxist point of view, summarized:

> The truth of James Merrill's poetry is that it is not simply a series of well-made poems, that it embodies the ethos of a particular class at a

particular time in its history. The limitation of his work is its acceptance of that condition, that is, in Merrill's identification of a particular ethos with the whole of human experience and the truth of
history. There is nothing happening in the world that he portrays. A
more radical poet would find ways of representing not only a particular ethos but the forces that have created it, he would represent it as
limited and changeable; which means that at the same time he would
be showing something more fundamental and enduring.

Merrill responded in his notebook:

> In the cage of class
>
> no values, no ties
> The world as spectacle, therefore null.

On another page he quoted Pevear:

> A critic in the HR wrote that my poetry represented "a specifi-
> cally middle-class" vision or poetic mechanism. "There is no
> labor in Merrill's world, and there is no richness of human cul-
> ture; there is nothing that abides, nothing to be preserved, and
> so there is no responsibility." "For him there is no new world
> taking shape on the ruins of the old. There is only the step from
> illusion into 'the elements.' " Even the universe turns on itself.
> The point is that it does only after immensely extending itself. I
> hadn't, the critic was saying, extended myself, and his saying so
> depressed me for days.

Then he carried the implications of this critique a step further. It was as if
he had never left Southampton:

> Always quick to accept the "worst," I quickly fleshed out the
> skeleton's accusing index finger. What I had scorned + avoided
> in the world—politics, money—or, more exactly, profited by with
> eyes averted, turned out to have shaped me to its own quite
> scrutable ends. I was of my time, a gram of the gross national
> product.

Merrill was working on an answer well before Pevear put the challenge
into words. The story he could tell of "something more fundamental and

enduring," a story that would require him to "extend" himself a very great deal, was that of Ephraim and the Other World. At least since 1970, Jimmy had been thinking about the possibility of an Ephraim novel. He envisioned the story specifically as a novel—perhaps because he felt he might reach more readers in that form, or because he was unsure how to incorporate his experience of the Other World in the worldly idiom of his poetry (something he hadn't tried to do since "Voices from the Other World" in 1956), or simply because he didn't want to claim the experience as his own, even if it was "<u>the</u> most curious and valuable" he had had.

Yet he kept failing to begin the novel, and when he finally settled down to compose it in September 1972, he got stuck. Contrasting the pleasure of writing poetry with the frustrations of prose, he wondered, "Who in his right mind would spend days up to his elbows in fish-guts, blood + cleavers everywhere, when he could be using chopsticks to arrange the transparent, overlapping rawnesses among their little mounds of mustard + radish on the sashimi plate?" Interrupted by "Lost in Translation," he went back to the "fish-guts" of prose later that fall, with no more success than earlier. Did he really want to write this book? He continued to try in Athens, then in Stonington. In March, he stopped in Atlanta to see his mother—that big birthday bash at the Driving Club awaited him—on his way to Santa Fe and McIntosh, and then to the Yensers' wedding in Los Angeles. He was carrying a typescript of the few pages of the novel he'd produced, along with a wedding present for Stephen and Mary, a stone ibis, when he left the bag with both items in a taxi from the Atlanta airport, never to be retrieved.

He turned his attention to a demanding series of readings. Continuing a pattern set in the 1960s, Merrill disappeared from public view in Greece, then embarked on a busy schedule of literary events when he returned to the U.S. From the late 1950s onward, he traveled widely to read his poetry, never declining an invitation because a venue was too far or too humble. When possible, he coordinated these occasions with visits to friends; in the process he added new friends in his address book. He prepared for his readings by noting the time it took to read his poems, and by practicing with a tape recorder to get his voice right: dignified and mellow, supple and theatrical, winking and bright. That spring was typical with engagements at the University of Arizona, the University of Rochester (the Summers and Hechts were there), Behrend College in Erie, PA (hosted by Moffett), Mount Holyoke (where he again judged the Glascock Prize, this time with James Wright and Maxine Kumin, and the prize going to Gjertrud Schnackenberg), Wellesley College, a community poetry series in New Haven, and the Poetry Center in New York.

The latter occasion stood out. The director of the Poetry Center had written to Merrill in the fall inviting him to read and asking if he was willing to share the stage with Elizabeth Bishop. He shot back, on a scrap of paper torn from the invitation letter, "Oh yes, please ask Elizabeth Bishop. I couldn't dream of a grander co-star." He wrote to Bishop, "I do hope you've said yes! We needn't read the whole time, you know. A ping-pong table could be borrowed from some recreational wing of the Establishment, or a samba routine worked up, with spangly blouses + purple lights." He was being silly, because he knew that a reading onstage at the Poetry Center, with its formal auditorium and a big New York audience, would be intimidating to Bishop, who shrank from public performance.

When the event came, Richard Howard introduced the poets. Bishop took the stage first, although she was the senior, gray-haired poet. In her dry, quiet, determinedly ordinary voice, she read poems that would appear in her final book, *Geography III*, ending with "Crusoe in England." Merrill's choices included "The Victor Dog," dedicated to Bishop, and "Lost in Translation," dedicated to Howard. In the green room before the event, as Bishop and Merrill chatted over drinks, a delivery man appeared with gifts for the readers: two laurel wreaths, sprayed with gold paint. The wreaths came from Arthur Gold and Bobby Fizdale, who were away on tour. Bishop wrote to them afterward about the wreaths: "We didn't quite dare to wear them on the platform, but at the party at John Hollander's afterwards"—a big, "roaring" one, stocked with three cases of champagne—"we decided to make an entrance, and adjusted our wreaths in the hall mirror before going in. Maybe it's just my natural modesty, but I felt a wreath was more becoming to Jim." Bishop's "natural modesty" was such that she insisted that the Poetry Center destroy its audiotape of her reading and the negatives of the photos of her taken by the center's photographer. In contrast, a photo that survives in the Poetry Center archives catches Jimmy reveling in the occasion and wearing his laurel crown, smiling this time under the "weight of the weath."

Soon after that event, however, he sank back into depression, brooding on Pevear's review. Alluding to the notion that he had "profited [. . .] with eyes averted" from what he had "scorned + avoided," he wrote in his notebook,

> I have set down these lines
> With the utmost diffidence
> With eyes averted
>
> It is as if, with untold means
> At my disposal I had cut myself
> Out of my own will.

The "lines" he refers to were drafts for a poem he would call "The Will." As he worked on it, the poem seemed to point a way out of the impasse of his work on Ephraim's novel. Telling the story of his loss of the novel and the ibis in Atlanta, "The Will" turns the mishap into a renewal of his bond with Ephraim. Reunited briefly on Water Street that April, JM and DJ sat down at the Ouija board. "The Will" relates the substance of that séance, making it the first poem that mentions Ephraim, and the first in which he speaks:

> U DID WELL JM TO DISINHERIT
> YR SELF & FRIENDS OF THAT STONE BIRD [. . .]
>
> SACRED TO THOTH NOW AT 310 KNOX DRIVE
> MACON GA IT HAS BROUGHT DISASTER
> COMME TOUJOURS PARALYZED THE DRIVERS SISTER
> MAXINE SHAW BORN 1965
>
> THESE BALEFUL PRESENCES SHAPED FOR THE DEAD
> WHEN THEY CHANGE HANDS EXACT A SACRIFICE
> REMEMBER ITS FIRST YEAR CHEZ VOUS YR FACE
> TURNED VOTIVE GOLD JAUNDICE THE DOCTOR SD
>
> GODS BEAK SAY I EMBEDDED IN YR SIDE
> HARDLY THE BIBELOT TO GIVE A BRIDE

Merrill had brought the bird home from Egypt in 1959, the trip from which he returned with hepatitis. Associated with Charles Merrill ("I bought it with / A check my father wrote before his death"), the bird embodied the legacy from which, Pevear implied, Merrill had failed to separate himself. Merrill had been working on revisions to his own will, which he signed before flying to Atlanta. When he lost the bird, it was an act of dispossession, relieving him of one sign of the "untold means" at his disposal.

The problem with the novel, Ephraim continues in "The Will," was that Merrill had been trying for so much distance on his material, his familiar spirit had been left out: "SINCE U DID NOT CONSULT / THEIR SUBJECT YR GLUM PAGES LACKED HIS GLORY." He proposes a more direct approach:

> SOIS SAGE DEAR HEART & SET MY TEACHINGS DOWN
> —Why, Ephraim, you belong to the old school—
> You think the Word by definition good.

IF YOU DO NOT YR WORLD WILL BE UNDONE
& HEAVEN ITSELF TURN TO ONE GRINNING SKULL.

That was quite a threat, and more responsibility than any critic or editorialist had challenged Merrill to take on. "So?" he returns. "We must write to save the face of God?" Yes, Ephraim had "GIANT DESIGNS UPON YR ART MON CHER." "So what is the next step?" JM asks, ready to serve but unclear about what would be required. Ephraim's reply is punning and cryptic: "GIVE UP EVERYTHING EXCEPT THE GHOST."

There were festivities that May on Water Street. A second daughter, Ourania, had been born to Taki and Vaso. It was time for her baptism, and Jimmy was asked to be her godfather. She was, he thought, "an enchanting little baby, peaceful and lovable, with a beautiful black mole right next to her navel, with a wardrobe only a shade less extensive than mine." In the Greek Orthodox ceremony, he held her "for a full hour amid Taki's popping flashbulbs and the priest's melismata." A lamb had been fatted for the feast in the basement of 107 (neighbors could hear the creature bleating weeks before it was butchered), and for a night, the second floor of the Victorian building became a Greek village square with "Seagrams & Uncola, and male dancing, Bulls & Goats circling round each other" long after the godfather was released at 2 a.m.

Jackson left that week for Greece. Hellen Plummer took his place for the longest visit—nine days—she had paid her son in years. There was a party for her in New York hosted by Carol Longone at which Jimmy met the seventy-one-year-old Brazilian soprano Bidu Sayão; a trip to Vermont to see the Buechners and their children; and bridge games every night. Merrill found that there was "nothing like having mother right <u>in</u> the house to drive one to the desk's distractions"; soon he was "chipping away at my writer's block." What emerged was a poem occasioned by Ourania's baptism, "Verse for Urania." Latinizing her name, Merrill gave the girl the name of the muse of astronomy whom Milton invokes in *Paradise Lost*. The link between his godchild and Milton's muse was fanciful in the extreme, but it was enough to free up the epic ambitions he had channeled so far into the stalled novel about Ephraim. A 229-line meditation on time and human imagination quickly took shape.

The poem drew inspiration from two tomes Merrill read that spring. One was Thomas Pynchon's *Gravity's Rainbow*, "that fantastic book." (Merrill was as titillated as any Pynchonite when he learned that the man he'd glimpsed in the backyard of his neighbor, a literary agent, was none other than the famously reclusive novelist.) The other book was *Hamlet's Mill: An Essay on Myth and the Frame of Time* by Giorgio de Santillana and Hertha von Dechend. *Hamlet's Mill* argues (if "argue" is the right word for its lyrical speculations) that archaic myth constitutes "a specific type of scientific language, which must not be taken at face value nor accepted as expressing more or less childish 'beliefs.' Cosmic phenomena and rules were articulated in the language, or terminology, of myth, where each key word was at least as 'dark' as the equations and convergent series by means of which our modern scientific grammar was built up." Even as myth is lost, the outlines of those starry shapes and the knowledge embedded in them, as if in code, live on in fairy tales and the novel, the authors of *Hamlet's Mill* maintain. Today science holds the monopoly on cosmic truth. But an author such as Pynchon, by turning chemistry, mathematics, and physics back into metaphor, could reclaim scientific ways of knowing for literature. And Merrill wanted to do that too.

His high-flown ambition in this poem is framed by a comic portrait of an immigrant Greek family who had turned into "passionate consumers." The baby's mother worries that her family disapproves of their choices when she hears nothing from "her people" in Greece ("I've asked myself," Merrill admits, "how much the godfather / They picked contributes to imbroglio. / Someone more orthodox . . . ?"). Her father, "worn out by a day of spreading tar / Overtime upon America," puts "his best face / On pros and cons": Urania would just be "One more baby back there in Greece" without the break that her godfather had given the family. "Why I say to mean," her father says to him, "this kid, she yours!"

Merrill showed the poem in draft to Kalstone, who read it carefully in the company of Ed White. In *The Farewell Symphony*, his novel from 1997, White tells the following story about the composition of "Verse for Urania." White is the first-person narrator, and Kalstone is "Joshua":

Joshua and I read the new poem for Cassiopeia, worked our way through its elaborate astrological conceits and consulted with each other. Finally Joshua, despite an admiration that bordered on awe, dared to say to Eddie, "Isn't it . . . a bit . . . *cold*?" Eddie slapped his forehead and said, "Of course! I forgot to put the feeling in!" He rushed upstairs to the cupola that served him as a study and fiddled with the verses for an hour before he descended with lines that made us weep, so tender were they, so melting and exalted. That night, when we were alone, Joshua whispered, "A rather chilling vision of the creative process, I'd say. We must never tell anyone about this, since how many people would understand and forgive the heartless, manipulative craftsmanship of great art?"

Jimmy, unlike Eddie, had no cupola study on Water Street; and although DK did tell his friend that he thought his newest poem "cold," the adjustments that Merrill made in response took more than an hour. But the vignette is a parable about the role of craft in Merrill's poetry, even when, as in this case, the results did not rise to the level of "great art." The lines that might make a reader weep, "so tender," "so melting and exalted" are they, are the final ones. Merrill quotes a Nahum Tate text set by Purcell—"*Whilst of thy dear sight beguil'd, / I trust the God, but O! I fear the Child*"—and then, addressing his goddaughter after the baptism, he comments,

> Exactly my own feelings. It was late

> And early. I had seen you through shut eyes.
> Our bond was sacred, being secular:
> In time embedded, it in us, near, far,
> Flooding both levels with the same sunrise.

This vision of the godfather and child equally "embedded" in time and "it in us" smoothes out the differences between them, "Flooding both levels with the same sunrise." What remains "cold" about the poem (others agreed: Robin called it "condescending") is the way Merrill's rhetoric soars above Taki's broken English—and, for that matter, above the fact of their sexual relations, about which the poem not surprisingly remains silent. Describing the baptism in a letter to Howard, Merrill wrote, "I'm now called by the sacred epithet <u>koumbaros</u> which seems to mean that I have a lot of future expenses, and that T. & I now go to bed in the afternoon rather than late at night when I've had too much to drink."

Such were the secular dimensions of this sacred bond. To the Alevras family, Merrill was a magical benefactor. Recently, he had funded the purchase of a pizza parlor as a business for Taki, which the hardworking Greek was making a success. The next Christmas, he would buy tropical fish for the girls, and tend them anxiously in a tank in his apartment, remembering a pleasure from his own childhood, until it was time for the present to be revealed. Jimmy's parodic nickname for his neighbors—"the Holy Family"—expressed both his resentment and his idealization of their family unit. The pains he took to construct their lives in Stonington imply the pressure he continued to feel to produce a family of his own (was it a coincidence that he began his poem about Ourania while his mother was in the house?). He had settled for a family he could look in on and withdraw from when he wished, sure that he had helped them, and that they owed him nothing in return.

In July, on his way to Greece for several months ("another swing of the pendulum"), he stopped in Venice. "Sitting on the railings of the Accademia bridge" over the Grand Canal, he meditated on marriage, children, and his relation to both, moving in and out of prose and verse in his notebook:

> I watched the world cross + recross and nearly
> Always in pairs, talking or silent, one
> Stopping to photograph the other, smiling. [. . .]
> They were matched, nearly always, in language + race,
> And of opposite sexes.
> Some pairs had already created the third who walked between them
> Or was small, and had to be carried.
> Smaller, more alert, indifferent to culture or romance [. . .]
> Yet more watchful too, in not having found
> A lifetime companion or counterpart.
> Alert to air, water, hunger
>   I was the perfect negative, the undeveloped 3rd.
> Neither pro nor con

Merrill equates his mind's mercurial movements with the labile attention of a child. He is, he fancies, a "third" term, "Neither pro nor con," like the offspring of one of those couples. With pride and clear vision countering sadness and regret, he describes a point of view which is sexual, emotional, and intellectual at once, set off to one side from the great procession of life.

Jimmy was staying with David Kalstone, who'd rented a flat on the Dorsoduro side of the bridge. Over the next decade, Kalstone came back to Venice every summer, and Merrill joined him usually for a week or more. They had Venetian routines—a stationer where Merrill bought new notebooks and pens, and a tailor, Cecconi, who created for Merrill a new version of the black suit he'd bought in Venice in 1951 when he saw the premiere of *The Rake's Progress* at La Fenice, just a short walk away. (Seeing Kalstone's matching black Cecconi suit with a scarlet lining, Merrill twinkled: "Priest outside, Cardinal within!") They might spend the afternoon ogling the male attendants at the extravagantly expensive pool of the Cipriani Hotel on the Lido, dine with John Hohnsbeen and Peggy Guggenheim in her palazzo across the Grand Canal, or, after Negronis at Harry's Bar, linger among the shadowy strangers cruising "the dark dock." Venice, recalled Ed White, who was there too that summer, was "still sort of a gay place," steeped in decadent literary association (Byron, Ruskin, Mann, Proust, Pound, and more). Merrill delighted in the city, and yet he was never sentimental about it. Venice, he concluded, "looked beautiful, but stank. One should go there with a summer cold."

In Athens, he finished in quick succession "Verse for Urania," "The Will," and "Chimes for Yahya." These were long, multipart autobiographical narratives, moving freely through a variety of verse forms, moods, and locales, with intricate wordplay, vertiginous shifts of diction, and dazzling rhetorical fluency. With "Lost in Translation" and "Yánnina," they made a remarkable group of poems, together constituting a genre of narrative verse that Helen Vendler would praise as "a new sort of lyric," suggesting "fragments from a modern version of *The Prelude*." Even while the problem of how to write about Ephraim remained to be solved, these big new poems pushed aside Merrill's depression from the winter.

He composed them having arrived at a point in life from which vistas of memory opened up, and old conflicts had seemingly lost their power to harm. He described that perspective in a letter to McClatchy: "You've had a bad time. I'm sorry. I had one last Christmas, the first in ten years, and didn't really pull out of it until April—this is not to upstage you, just to show that I understand. What is the cure? Work—as the unhappy girls in Chekhov keep telling us? Easier said than done. In retrospect I think [. . .] that these are growing pains. Certainly they have everything to do with a sense that the life one has arranged to live is intolerable, that a skin must be shed." Now Merrill had shed a skin, or crossed a bridge: "Here one is in Later Life, and it's perfectly pleasant really, not for a moment that garden of cactus and sour grapes I'd always assumed it must be."

Jackson, responding in his own way to arrival in "Later Life," had painted a wall fresco in Merrill's former work room, now seldom used, on the first floor of Athinaion Efivon 44: a fantasy Greek landscape with two pairs of columns "and beyond a sunny greenish decline lightly dusted with poppies and bluets down to a sea-cove. The real thing," Merrill observed, "would have cost him a cool half million dollars, and now it is ours for only pennies." That pastoral dream contrasted with other developments in Athens. Cars clogged the streets, smog ate away at the stones of the Parthenon, and the military government was teetering on collapse—in fact the junta would fall just a few months later in January 1974. Even the nonstop flights that had made it easy for Merrill to come and go had begun to seem perilous.

On August 5, Palestinian gunmen attacked the passengers waiting to board a plane from Athens to New York, killing three, wounding fifty-five, and taking thirty-five hostages at gunpoint, many of them Americans.

And Maria Mitsotáki was terminally ill. Undergoing radiation, "terribly gaunt and gallant," she was—"one can't doubt—dying of cancer; knows it and doesn't, both; feeble, macabre, merry and mild by turns." On her name day, August 15, the Feast of the Assumption of the Blessed Virgin Mother, Jimmy and David hosted a party for her, serving spaghetti—"her favorite food now"—and a cake ringed "with a circumference of <u>Marias</u>" (rather than the conventional but painfully unrealistic *Chronia Polla*, "Many Years"). Jimmy exclaimed: "the fun we all had . . . ! Elizabeth B's favorite phrase in all her poems, 'Cheerful but awful,' gives something of the atmosphere, but leaves out the sweetness, the silliness, the appalling sadness."*

In September, news came that Auden had died in Vienna. Merrill sent his sympathy to Chester: "It may not always have been plain to you [. . .] how greatly he loved you + relied on you: but it was to the rest of us." He was only sixty-six when he died, but his famous face was creased with deep runnels, like a dirt road after heavy rains. Merrill felt he'd missed a chance: "[H]ow much more one could have <u>learned</u> than one did at those old knees!" In fact, he had never taken lessons from Auden. Daryl Hine remembered Auden's serving coffee to him and Merrill in the older poet's New York apartment: "We had nothing to say. When we left, and met David Kalstone at the opera, we were like boys getting out of school." It was clear that afternoon, Hine continued, that Auden "was not a happy man. The muse had left him. He was glum and gruff even when he was kind to us." And Merrill's attitude toward him "was pretty odd. Of course he respected the poetry—up to a point. But he was hostile to the Christian religion. Wystan was explaining for the hundredth time about St. Wystan, and Jimmy interrupted to ask, 'Is there a St. Daryl?' Auden scolded him." It was simpler for Merrill to talk to this great man on the Ouija board. Shortly after Auden's death, Merrill told Kalstone, "We reached WHA easily via Ephraim. He said that heaven looked like 'a new machine,' then began to fret about a box in Oxford that had to be burned—until E. told him he was overstepping."

As Merrill put a period to the poems written that summer, he bowed to an onslaught of visitors. Truman Capote, reappearing after several years for a long night's pub crawl in the Plaka, telling the same stories he had always told, but with the names changed and implausible embellishments, drew looks from tourists "asking one of us 'Isn't that . . .?' but not an eye

---

* JM misremembered the ending of EB's "The Bight": "All the untidy activity continues, / awful but cheerful."

batted behind his octagonal blue glasses." William Burroughs showed up to retrieve from his old friend Alan Ansen the manuscript of *Naked Lunch* (Ansen had collaborated on the book, using his copy for notes, and now Burroughs planned to sell Ansen's annotated manuscript). The scandalous novelist struck Merrill as a "very respectable-appearing old party, like an army pensioner. It is true that [he] had brought with him from London a rather flashily dressed lunch that spoke a few words of Cockney; and that he spoke with enthusiasm only of drugs and sex-murders—but there are Wasps in Stonington + Atlanta of whom this last could be said."

A succession of southern WASPS visited too, led by Mrs. Plummer. There on her first and only visit to her son in Greece, Hellen and a lady friend were shown Athens, Cape Sounion, Delphi, and Crete. Betty Plummer Potts, her husband Tom, and another Alabama couple arrived in time to overlap with Hellen. Moffett, who was in Athens just then to research her book about her former teacher's work, was recruited to meet his mother. But mainly Jimmy depended on David to get him through the visit. "DJ was sublime. Taxi-service at all hours. And on the last evening, when Mrs P had perhaps over-gauged his good nature and was lecturing him on the need for discretion in our lives, he told her as nicely as possible to fuck off, that we were adults, that the wallpaper [. . .] did not represent 'men making love' (as her worst fears had at once suggested to her imperfect eyesight) etc etc." However blurry her vision, Hellen had now had a look at Jimmy in Greece, and they'd both survived.

Returning to the U.S. in November 1973, Merrill stopped in Frankfurt for a weekend of monkey business in a hotel with Manoli, who was working in Germany, and it happened again: having started over on Ephraim's novel after losing the typescript in Atlanta, he now left the new draft behind in Frankfurt. "Our spirit must be bent on having me write about him in his way," Merrill decided. Only he was unsure what way that was. On Water Street, he began typing Ouija board transcripts from as long ago as 1955. He thought he might "make a whole little book out of his dictées," even if such a book was likely to expose "me (+ DJ) as two dreadfully shallow people." It would have to be "some unplaceable kind of book," not a novel but a prose memoir of their adventures in the spirit world.

Scenes from August 1955 returned in the pages of Merrill's notebook, but he remained uncomfortable writing prose. Claude Fredericks came to stay for two weeks in the deep freeze of January. The companionship helped. When the two old friends talked "about this damn Ephraim book," Claude "confirmed my suspicion that I can only do it in verse." Then Maria died on January 13. For the past few months, "constantly on morphine," she saw only her doctor, asking him, "*Póso akóma* [how much more]?" Now "a great light [had] gone out of the world." A few days later, to David, who had stayed on in Athens, JM sent "a beginning" for the Ephraim poem. He made the question of the appropriate literary form for his Ouija material the point of departure:

> I confess to failure by beginning this
> In its present form. Presumably the simplest
> Reportage was called for, that would reach
> The largest public in the shortest time.

Eventually, he altered the first line to the breezy, less apologetic, "Admittedly I err." A page further on, slipping into rhymed couplets, embracing the naturalness of artifice, and refusing to court readers on any terms other than his own, he recovered his comic, quicksilver tone:

> The more I struggled to be plain, the more
> Mannerism hobbled me. What for?
> Since it had never truly fit, why wear
> The shoe of prose? In verse the feet went bare.*

Merrill spent the next year and a half writing the roughly 2,500-line poem called *The Book of Ephraim*. The poem took its form from the alphabet on the Ouija board with twenty-six sections, each of which began with a letter from A to Z. Merrill worked from notebooks and Ouija board transcripts, but he launched into composition without much of a plan. He told Jackson, "[S]ome of my sense of what's to come is extremely obscure not to say woozy—but as you see I'm excited." Even so, certain features of the poem stood out at once. One was the emphasis on the letters of the alphabet. The idea of using the alphabet as a device to organize a poem first appeared in his notebook without reference to the Ouija board in 1970: "An alphabet. 26 poems (on any or all subjects), loosely written, odes, elegies, what you wish, each beginning with an ornate capital letter, A through Z."† By foreground-

---

* JM, *Sandover*, 4. Alison Lurie suggested that Merrill alter "fail" to "err." The more elegant, old-fashioned verb immediately linked Merrill's poem to Spenser's *The Faerie Queene* and Milton's *Paradise Lost*, which pun on the Latin root of "error."

† JM, journal (Jnl 10), April 1, 1970 (WUSTL). In the margin, this passage has been marked with a big exclamation point and the date "xi.76."

ing the alphabet, Merrill called attention to the letter-by-letter mechanics of the Ouija board and to the world-creating power of words.

It was also clear that this would be a love story, a peculiar, double love story, concerned with Merrill's and Jackson's relationships with Ephraim and with each other. As he returned in memory to August 1955 and to their early days together, Merrill wrote, "Dearest D—I miss you so." He continued:

> There are 100 things to say; but mainly that I love you very much. It is hard to think what the future will bring; and just as hard to think what the past has brought. A weariness between us, a coldness—which I think may both have been forms of a subtle distrust: a doubt as to whether either of us really had the other's good at heart. Whatever, I want to say that I feel it more + more dissolving, evaporating. Maybe it's age, but I don't imagine I shall ever again try to imagine a life lived with anyone but you—together or apart—and so, yes, if you want me, I'm your Valentine for another 20 years at least.

This was not quite a ringing statement of re-dedication (Merrill uses too many qualifiers, too many "imagines"), but he hadn't addressed Jackson so tenderly in years, and that awakened feeling was part of the poem he was writing. David called Jamie's letter a "relief." He was hooked by the poem: "Old hand as I am at your game, one is pulled along as is that pike in the lake by outbrakes of ryme like the tug of a reel [sic]. And throughout, I think its charm and its art lie largely in a transmitted joy in the work."

Then there was the sheer ambition of the poem, its epic and transcendental aspirations. The title, *The Book of Ephraim*, with its scriptural resonance, was ambitious enough. But before he settled on it in 1975, Merrill typically referred to the poem in progress as his "Divine Comedy." The title was not a joke. Merrill had Dante in mind as an exalted model. His subject was a journey to "Heaven," and he was undertaking to provide an account of how the world works, from the point of view of eternity. To accomplish this, he had to renew poetry's ancient function of giving voice to higher powers, which Dante had done for his era. He could not have dared to "extend" himself any further.

Merrill had never had much reverence for masterworks, and in that respect, he was hardly prepared to take on such a work. To Irma, the Danteist, he lamented, "[I]f only I had given, these last 3 decades, more than lip-service to the indisputable masterpieces like just for example Dante's which I have not opened for 23 years, or the Bible which I have never, never read, or the Aeneid which I am reading now in English and trying not to prefer the Berlioz version. Well, it is simply too late to mend that massive flaw in my character." For that matter, he had been not merely indifferent but also hostile to the long poems of the moderns. Pound, he'd complained a few years before, tries "to write like a god." But lately he had been reading about the return of the gods in the *Cantos* with admiration, even relish, and he was ready to attempt a poem on a related theme, although he would try to do it while writing like Stevens and Bishop—trusting in the private imagination and the chance revelations of daily living, rather than, like Pound, in encyclopedic learning and vatic inspiration.

Other instigations came from poet friends. One was Ashbery's meditation "Self-Portrait in a Convex Mirror," a masterwork that made "an impression of deep beauty" on Jimmy when he read it that winter. He saw the poem in typescript thanks to Kalstone, who was writing about the poetry of Ashbery, his neighbor in New York; "Self-Portrait" was published for the first time in the August 1974 issue of *Poetry*. Another long poem came to his attention as a mysterious letter from "Cupcake" to "Image," which, as only the envelope revealed, meant from John Hollander to Merrill. The message was a piece of Hollander's new book-length poem, *Reflections on Espionage*. Playing on the historical and metaphorical connections between poetry and spying, the poem consisted of encrypted messages from the spy Cupcake, who comments on his craft in furtive contacts with a fellow agent, "Image." Hollander had code names for poets of the day—Ashbery was "Ember." Jimmy, referred to as Agent "Image," entered into the conceit, and sent riddle-like replies, which Hollander printed in notes to the poem. Ashbery's and Hollander's poems shared with each other and with Merrill's new poem a large scale, an interest in metaphysics and the nature of the self, and the motif of the mirror, which involved a focus on the medium of representation—on language itself.

After the prefatory matter in "A," Merrill began by setting the scene for Ephraim in "B" ("Backdrop: The dining room at Stonington"). He recalled his and Jackson's séances with Ephraim in 1955 in "C" ("Correct but cautious, that first night, we asked / Our visitor's name, era, habitat") and "E" ("Ephraim nonetheless kept on pursuing / Our education"). Merrill drew on his Ouija transcripts selectively. He greatly condensed and clarified Ephraim's various comments, reporting exchanges in indirect discourse in which quotations from Ephraim, usually not more than a phrase, combined with his and Jackson's contributions to create a curious composite idiom. Rhyme and meter further domesticated the strange block capitals from the *au delà*:

LONG B4 THE FORTUNATE CONJUNCTION
(David's and mine) ALLOWED ME TO GET THRU
MAY I SAY WEVE HAD OUR EYES ON U

Ephraim's presence in the poem was so sensational it was possible to over-look the fact that Merrill was writing for the first time with utter frankness about his relationship with Jackson. The world that they had created above Water Street, the setting for their adventures in the Other World, was now fully open to the public.

Merrill's scheme allowed for rearrangement of the actual order of events. Some people—Maya, for example—were elevated to a more prominent role in the séances than they had had in actuality, while others, like Sewelly, van-ished from the record. But Merrill got down much of what had transpired in the early days of his and Jackson's conversations with the spirits. The poem records Ephraim's explanation of the system of patrons and representa-tives, and the progress of the soul from one stage to the next. It samples his erotic wisdom ("TAKE our teacher told us / FROM SENSUAL PLEASURE ONLY WHAT WILL NOT / DURING IT BE EVEN PARTLY SPOILED / BY FEAR OF LOSING TOO MUCH") and his sometimes desperate wit ("AH MY DEARS / I AM NOT LAUGHING I WILL SIMPLY NOT SHED TEARS"). It reports the talks with Stevens and Hans, and the misjudged attempt to engineer the rebirth of the latter's representative. It describes Jimmy's meeting with Detre about the Ouija board, David's hyp-nosis, and their trip around the world in 1956–57. The poem's narrative becomes harder to track as it moves through the second half of the alphabet because JM's and DJ's contact with Ephraim (and for that matter, with each other) became more casual and intermittent in the 1960s. Compensating for gaps in the story, while compounding the effect of discontinuity, Mer-rill interpolated in the poem characters and episodes from the abandoned novel about Ephraim—as Ephraim's story became the problem of how to tell it. As usual, Merrill wasted nothing, if he could avoid it.

When he began, he thought to include two sections in addition to the twenty-six—these labeled "YES" and "NO," the two words printed on the Ouija board—in which he would convey "as much as I can of the pros + cons, the ambivalence felt about E. et al." But it was unnecessary to stress the point: his "ambivalence" was apparent throughout. On the one hand, when JM leaves Tom's office, he is untroubled by his psychiatrist's Freudian view of the Ouija board. Why should he be when the board gives him access to Freud himself?

I walked out into much
Guilt-obliterating sunlight. FREUD

> We learned that evening DESPAIRS
> OF HIS DISCIPLES & SAYS BITTE NIE
> ZU AUFGEBEN THE KEY
> TO YR OWN NATURES

On the other hand, determined to retain the key to his own nature, as Freud advised, Merrill was not about to hand over his authority as a poet to the Ouija board. He makes the point when Ephraim explains that, in *A Vision*, "POOR OLD YEATS" WAS "STILL SIMPLIFYING":

> But if someone up there thought *we* would edit
> The New Enlarged Edition,
> That maze of inner logic, dogma, dates—
> Ephraim, forget it.
>
> We'd long since slept through our last talk on Thomist
> Structures in Dante. Causes
> Were always lost—on us. We shared the traits
> Of both the dumbest
>
> Boy in school and that past master of clauses
> Whose finespun mind "no idea violates."

Merrill refers to T. S. Eliot's remark about Henry James's "mastery over, and baffling escape from, Ideas": "He had a mind so fine no idea could violate it." For Merrill, truth's only touchstone was personal experience as sifted by sensibility and expressed in style, of which James, "that past master of clauses," was a supreme exemplar. With Jamesian sophistication and determined nonchalance, Merrill made diffidence a way to preserve his independence from both Ephraim and Detre (and from other voices inside and outside the poem). How real finally was Ephraim? What did Merrill actually think? The point was never to answer the question, and "never to forego, in favor of / Plain dull proof, the marvelous nightly pudding."

In the 1980s, Merrill was often asked about the reality of his experience as described in *Sandover*, of which *The Book of Ephraim* would become the first section. Did he actually think he had been talking to spirits? He tended to answer "yes" and "no": "remaining of two minds seemed the essential thing." One interviewer, referring to the difference between realist fiction and romance, asked, "Can the trilogy be profitably approached as a romance?" Merrill responded,

I'm rather shaky as to genres and modes, but it does seem to be a romance in certain ways—and perhaps a mock-romance in others? Frye says that in a romance "a ghost as a rule is merely one more character." Actually, I suspect that the trilogy touches on a variety of modes, and the one thing that holds it together, if anything does, is that it all truly happened to us, came to us in these various ways.

It "all truly happened to us": that was Merrill's bottom line about the Ouija board. "Causes," both metaphysical and material, "were always lost on us," he said, and to that extent, they were irrelevant: what felt real was real enough to a poet who once wrote about being in love, "If that was illusion, I wanted it to last long."

But "to us" is crucial: the fact that Merrill shared the experience with Jackson was part of its reality effect. It was not just that there had always been a witness to verify the extraordinary (in Detre's eyes, he knew, this just meant that the folly was *à deux*). Rather, when they joined hands at the board, Merrill and Jackson gave up not only the "feeling of will" (the psychologist Daniel Wegner's term), but personal agency itself as they usually experienced it. That two minds took part in the experience made it easier to remain of "two minds" about it. And as to the question of literary genre (which matters because settling it would help the reader know how to take what he says in the poem), Merrill was writing "some unplaceable kind of book," except in verse, not prose, and the reader was invited to adopt the mediums' open-minded attitude toward events. *The Book of Ephraim* is the story of what happened to JM and DJ. Which is to say that biography holds it together, "if anything does."

But Merrill's attitude toward his biography in *The Book of Ephraim* is very particular. If Ephraim seems real in the context of the poem, people from Merrill's life are de-realized. Describing the novel he had planned to write, Merrill speaks of wanting "characters / Human and otherwise (if the distinction / Meant anything in fiction)." The distinction doesn't mean much in this poem. In section "D," Merrill makes out a list of "Dramatis Personae," starting with "Auden, W(ystan) H(ugh), 1907— / 73, the celebrated poet." The mock index presents persons from this world and spirits from the other in the same impersonal format: being alive is not a necessary condition of being in this poem. Included are Maya Deren, Hans Lodeizen, Mary Jackson, and Maria Mitsotáki: all of these, like Auden, are actual people from his acquaintance, most but not all of them dead. Also included, complicating matters, are JM's "Previous incarnation"—one Rufus Farmetton, whose death is narrated in "L"—and JM's patron, Kinton

Ford. In the world of the poem, Ford and Farmetton are just as real as Hans or Maria—whom Merrill identifies by reference to the poems that he wrote about them, and thus by their already established existence in his work. Other characters purportedly from life are purely literary inventions: the Dantesque Beatrice (Betsy) Merrill Pincus, JM's niece, and her son Wendell, Ephraim's representative. Merrill's father's entry is especially complex and playful:

> Merrill, Charles Edward, 1885–
> 1956, JM's father. Representative
> Of a mystic from Calcutta he dismisses
> As a DAMN POOR ADMINISTRATOR   Model
> For "Benjamin Tanning" in *The Seraglio*.

Biology is only one way of defining a "character," and from the perspective of the Other World, it is not at all the most important.

The order in which these wildly diverse "personae" appear is the arbitrary order of the alphabet. Alpha order prevails again in the "partial smattering" of quotations that make up section "Q." These suggest a parodic version of the quotations found in the long poems of Eliot and Pound. Collecting them in a "conveniently" labeled file (where to put them? why, under "Q"!), Merrill avows the subjectivity of the hand that gathered them—and of the organization of the poem as a whole. He has no "mythical method" (Eliot's term) or Yeatsian system. Like his "Dramatis Personae," his quotations are assorted items in an album created out of a life, a commonplace book like Auden's *A Certain World*, bringing together very different categories of author and text. Some are no surprise, like Proust or Wagner, major figures of obvious importance to Merrill. But Ephraim appears in the same company, as do A. H. Clarendon, an invented author Merrill quoted from in "The Thousand and Second Night," and John Michell, an entirely real UFO enthusiast, New Age cosmologist, and pal of the Rolling Stones. Merrill quotes from Maya's book about the gods of Haiti, *Divine Horsemen*; from Hans, he quotes the handwritten note to Jim on the back of his silhouette, a gift Merrill cherished and kept beside his desk in Stonington. Each quotation, with various links in Merrill's life, suggests a distinct path into the poem's network of story and image, symbol and idea. Again, biography holds them together. But they are a very "partial smattering," and none of them is the key to this peom.

Unless it is the last one, which comes from Heinrich Zimmer, a German scholar of South Asian myth and culture, and the teacher of Joseph Campbell, who writes,

The powers have to be consulted again directly—again, again and again. Our primary task is to learn, not so much what they are said to have said, as to how to approach them, evoke fresh speech from them, and understand that speech. In the face of such an assignment, we must all remain dilettantes, whether we like it or not.

Zimmer describes the "assignment" that JM and DJ accepted when they first contacted Ephraim: to "evoke fresh speech" from the invisible world of spiritual "powers." It is a perennial human task, and a traditionally poetic one. To guarantee that this speech would be "fresh," they had to make their "approach" outside of the existing institutions of religion and culture. The technique had to be amateur and improvised, their tools homemade. So it was with the Ouija board that they set up on the same table where they ate their meals and served guests. Now, as Merrill told the story of their adventures in the Other World, he saw that he would have to remain, as a poet, the "dilettante" he had been when he first sat down at the board. The "massive flaw" in his character, the lack of seriousness that made him feel unsuited to write this work, was the necessary qualification for it.

At first, Merrill did not want " 'The Divine Comedy' known about, lest it not get written as a result." But he was never good at keeping a secret. Soon he had decided "that her audience's belief in Tinker Bell is not only my quintessential subject but also what will most fortify me through the toils + tediums of its elaboration." He was referring to that moment in J. M. Barrie's play when Peter Pan asks theatergoers to save Tinker Bell and demonstrate their belief in fairies by applauding. Like Tinker Bell, Ephraim depended on applause, and so did Merrill. He sent the poem as he wrote it to Jackson and to Yenser. And he regularly reported his progress to old friends and fellow writers like Bishop, Howard, and Kalstone, as well as to younger poets who were interested in his work, like Alfred Corn, to whom he made that remark about Tinker Bell.

Corn was a tall, broad-shouldered man in his early thirties, deliberate and reserved, with dark brown hair, a neat moustache, and a soft voice colored by traces of his native Georgia. While earning a master's degree in French from Columbia, he had made friends with Ed White, Howard, and Kalstone, who showed a sheaf of his poems to Merrill. The older poet took the younger one in hand—encouraging, correcting, suggesting. When Corn's first book, *All Roads at Once*, appeared in 1976, Merrill's endorsement stood alone on the back cover: "Airy, all-seeing, a new window onto the world—this is an extremely beautiful first book. Among Mr. Corn's

contemporaries I know of no poet more accomplished." Merrill was generous but careful with his praise, and his words showed his stake in Corn's
work. "Jimmy wanted disciples," Corn reflected. "When I met him, he had
Stephen Yenser and Judith Moffett. But I was gay, and I already liked the
things he liked—vocal music, French literature, Elizabeth Bishop." Corn
was struck by Merrill's eye for coded messages and symbols, which "Jimmy
found everywhere. He could make anything say more than it said. There
was always a subtext—he had an ability to make the material world allegorical." Merrill did not save that talent for his poetry, but improvised continually, with the materials life brought to hand. Corn recalls an evening
at the opera when he and another friend sat some rows behind Merrill and
Kalstone. Corn was not impressed by the production and said so when they
met at intermission. Merrill, thinking of their respective rows, countered,
"Why, no wonder, you were back in the Z's—*we* were all I's!" Corn himself
was no slouch when it came to playing with the alphabet. He once suggested
that "E"—meaning Ephraim, the spirit talk-show host—was "equal to any
emcee squared." The bon mot turns up in *Sandover*.

Merrill had last seen Jackson in November. They reunited in April when
Jimmy flew to Greece. David, who had wanted him to come before the end of
the three-month mourning period for Maria, took him "at once" to see her
grave. In place of his cherished Maman, L'Enfant found a grim, "rug-sized
marble box full of earth" and a marble cross with her parents' names and
now hers, around which many flowers and "two evergreen footmen" had
been planted and lovingly tended. The gardening was the work of David and
the heartbroken Tony, whose grief Jimmy pitied and gently disapproved of.
So did Maria. She "at once began complaining (when we sat at the Ouija
Board) about the waste, the nonsense of keeping up a grave." More info followed, as Merrill summarizes in a letter:

> She is at Stage 4—higher than one had expected. Ephraim said,
> No, she wasn't beautiful; but was like a jewel, her glance shone
> directly into you. She arrived suffering from what they call "the
> great sickness"—not cancer, but a longing not to stay, a long-
> ing to be reborn. She became instantly famous for saying of
> Heaven "But it is impossible for me to stay anywhere where I
> have no little corner of my own." Her patron is St Agatha, she
> whose breasts were cut off—"the first woman's libber" Maria
> adlibbed—and M helps her, laughing quietly at the absurdity
> of it, decide on how the ever-expanding Mind of the universe
> should be channeled. [. . .] All her sufferings (she said) were

like a final racking cough, after which—air, air, air! The hour
soothed us very much.

This was the first time that JM had been in touch with his familiar spirit
since he began "The Divine Comedy," and the word from on high seemed
encouraging: "Ephraim <u>pretends</u> to approve of the poem, sly boots."

Despite the warm letters they had exchanged over the winter and now
all this lively conversation with the dead, Jimmy and David were "grouchy
with each other." After a few weeks, David left on the long trek to his parents in California, and Jimmy was relieved, taking in "the bliss of a house
to oneself." They tried again on Water Street, once Jimmy too had returned
to the U.S. in June: it would be, he announced with some pride, "the first
summer in ten that David + I have spent the summer entirely" together and
in Stonington. In the spirit of renewal, Jimmy decided that the decade-old
wallpaper in the sitting room had to go; so he commissioned Hubbell
Pierce to create new paper based on motifs from the room's Chinese rug.
Pierce's handiwork would be hung that winter. His elegant pattern adapted
the carpet's swirling clouds and tiny bats—"Symbols of eternity, the dealer
said"—and a design from one of the house's Japanese fans, set against a dark
blue field. Meanwhile, Jimmy rose early each day that summer to work on
Ephraim's poem, not very long after David's eyes had closed "on the final
shot of the night's last TV movie." In the nation's capital, the Watergate
scandal slouched toward its denouement; even Merrill had to watch that.
When it came on August 8, President Nixon's resignation speech seemed to
him a sadly " 'vegetarian' solution: we'd come to want his <u>blood</u>."

By late August, Merrill had drafted "A" through "O," "V," and "W" of *The
Book of Ephraim*. Over the past two years, on his periodic visits to Bishop
in Boston, Merrill had made friends with Frank Bidart, Lowell's protégé
and collaborator, who published a first book of poems in 1973. A California farmer's son who came to Harvard for graduate school and stayed on in
Cambridge, Bidart was earnest and intense—a temperament very different
from Merrill's. Yet they shared a devotion to Bishop, the formative influence of Reuben Brower (he had been Bidart's teacher too), a love of opera,
and being gay. Bidart came for a weekend on Water Street, urged Merrill to
read from his new poem, "and suddenly it was 3 am, and I'd read it all—while
he + DJ cried More More. What an orgy." The next day, Bidart went over the
typescript (the poem was more than one thousand lines long at this point),
making "usefully small suggestions." Then it was his turn to read aloud a
long elegy for his mother. Grace and Eleanor, who were present that evening, directly "plunged into their duet about how ghastly <u>their</u> childhoods

and motherhoods had been, still were for that matter, [. . .] before anyone
thought to say a word about Frank's poem."

Jackson left for Greece in September. Merrill spent the fall traveling—to
Los Angeles (the Yensers), Santa Fe (David McIntosh), Atlanta (Mrs. P.),
Vermont (Freddy and Claude), and Princeton, where the Lavins hosted
a reading for him at the Institute for Advanced Study; only a few poets,
including Eliot and Seferis, had read there before. His pace of composition
slackened, but he finished an important section, "P," the theme of which
was power. Power, Ephraim taught them, "kicks upstairs those who possess
it," in the afterlife just as in life. Power holds out the potential for man's
salvation, but it threatens him with extinction too. Of the latter, there was
plenty of evidence:

> The drug-addicted
> Farms. Welkin the strangler. Plutonium waste
> Eking out in drowned steel rooms a half
> Life of how many million years? Enough
> To set the doomsday clock—its hands our own:
> The same rose ruts, the red-as-thorn crosshatchings—
> Minutes nearer midnight. On which stroke
> Powers at the heart of matter, powers
> We shall have hacked through thorns to kiss awake,
> Will open baleful, sweeping eyes, draw breath
> And speak new formulae of megadeath.
> NO SOULS CAME FROM HIROSHIMA U KNOW
> EARTH WORE A STRANGE NEW ZONE OF ENERGY
> Caused by? SMASHED ATOMS OF THE DEAD MY DEARS
> (News that brought into play our deepest fears.)

Those fears, stoked by Hiroshima, the international crises of the 1950s and
early 1960s, and now a growing awareness of environmental catastrophe,
had kept JM and DJ coming back to the Ouija board. Not only earth was
threatened: gradually they understood that Ephraim was in danger too. The
thought had first formed in Merrill's mind during that séance in 1970 when
he felt "a tremor run through the whole grandly comic system." It was, he
says in "P," "the one extended / Session with Ephraim in two years."

> Had he missed us?
> YES YES emphatically. We felt the glow
> Of being needed, then a breath of frost.
> For if, poor soul, he did so, he was lost.

Ephraim was in danger if his survival depended, like Tinker Bell's, on his audience. It was the same with heaven. If the "doomsday clock" was ticking on earth ("its hands our own"), was it not the case

> That when the flood ebbed, or the fire burned low,
> Heaven, the world no longer at its feet,
> Itself would up and vanish? EVEN SO

This was the theme of *Götterdämmerung*, which, when he heard the opera at thirteen, planted in Merrill's imagination "Terrors our friend had barely to exhale / Upon," decades later, "and they were blazing like a hell." He was left with the question: "How to rid Earth, for Heaven's sake, of power / Without both turning to a funeral pyre?"

This is the essential question of *Sandover*. At this point, in *The Book of Ephraim*, Merrill was content simply to raise it. He was too busy coming to terms with the paradoxical theology of his homemade religion—with its curious aspect of reverse incarnation (Ephraim was "Flesh made word") and its vertigo-inducing interplay of reality and projection. "Where were we?" he asks about his and DJ's relation to the spirit world in "M."

> On unsteady ground. Earth, Heaven;
> Reality, Projection—half-stoned couples
> Doing the Chicken-and-the-Egg till dawn.
> Which came first? And would two never come
> Together, sleep then in each other's arms
> Above the stables rich with dung and hay?

In "S," Merrill appeals to Stevens, alluding to "The Final Soliloquy of the Interior Paramour" and Stevens's lecture, "The Noble Rider and the Sound of Words":

> Stevens imagined the imagination
> And God as one; the imagination, also,
> As that which presses back, in parlous times,
> Against "the pressure of reality."

In "U," the authority is Jung, whose *Answer to Job* Merrill felt was "the only credible definition of God" he had ever heard:

> Jung says—or if he doesn't, all but does—
> That God and the Unconscious are one. Hm.

> The lapse that tides us over, hither, yon;
> Tide that laps us home away from home.

Puns ("Which came first?") and spoonerisms ("The lapse that tides us . . . Tide that laps us"), like the mirror JM and DJ sometimes propped facing them during their séances, were emblems of a metaphysics without ground, in which all statements were reversible, "the hidden wish of words" held sway, and the essential task was to suspend disbelief and keep the imagination in play, "Doing the Chicken-and-the-Egg till dawn."

Merrill flew again to Athens in December 1974. He came down at once with "this year's strain of animosity—always something going around." With his head in his poem, he was quick to lose his patience with the usual doings: a party that would not end, although one of the hosts had long since gone to bed; Bernie Winebaum's manic enthusiasm and Alan Ansen's primitive table manners. Rachel Hadas, a talented young poet, angular and blond with a sharp chin and clear blue eyes, who had studied classics at Radcliffe, was a good friend of Ansen's and a regular on the scene that winter. So was Kallman, whose slow-motion "suicide" was still in progress. He was "in a very bad way, drinking again," woefully unkempt: "It's worse than the equivalent grotesque in Dickens because this is a friend turning to garbage under one's eyes." Kallman had money from Auden's estate, "but it is beneath him to write or cable for it. I must go downtown," Merrill complained, "bring him enough drachmas for the boys to steal throughout the week." He had had "enough," he decided, and he wrote Chester a letter "sternly defining my boundaries."

On Christmas Day, as if making reparations, one of Kallman's boys arrived with a weighty present from Chester to Jimmy: Auden's multivolume oxblood *Oxford English Dictionary*. It happened that *The Rake's Progress* was going to be performed in Athens that winter—perhaps this reminder of his long-ago creative high point might help Kallman rally. He did not live to see it: in January 1975, just after the anniversary of Maria's death, he died in his sleep. "It was only the second dead body I'd seen," Jimmy told Claude, "and even my grandmother was already embaumée and macquillée by the time I got there, while poor C. lay all mottled and askew, clothes undone, on a filthy bed." There he lay, "as so often in life, unable to struggle up from bed," while Jimmy and David waited for the doctor and the police, and the house filled with Chester's friends. Death was what he had been "bent upon. And yet in the nature of things we blame ourselves." Only two days before,

Merrill had given a reading at the British Council, and Kallman had been in the audience, "for once sober in a clean shirt and suit. Our eyes met and <u>held</u> together; he sustained a smile full of theatre, understatement, help-lessness." Now he was dead, "that generous and selfish and spectacularly ruined person babbling out his own tedious splendeurs et misères, the thefts and the blow-jobs, the memoirs and the jokes, bloated and hunched, the empty glass held out with an air both peremptory and supplicating—yet who had been so quick, so glamorous, a mere 30 years ago." Yet, Merrill knew, Wystan had "simply <u>adored</u> C. his whole life long."

Kallman was buried in a bloody shroud in the Jewish cemetery in Ath-ens. Jimmy and David, Tony and Nelly, Bernie, Alan, and Rachel, each dropped a handful of dirt in the pit. But that was not the end of it. Kallman had "left a dreadful mess behind him." His will named Auden and Merrill as his executors, and because he had "never got round to making any formal provision for what WHA left him—the sole heir," Jimmy would be involved for a long time in the disposition of both Kallman's and Auden's papers. He ended up doing what he'd refused to do in his last chastening letter to Chester: paying his debts.

Merrill and Jackson turned to the Ouija board after Kallman's death and "found him cozily ensconced at Stage 4." That séance, as Merrill describes it in "U," begins as something like a book party. With "The Divine Comedy" nearly complete, Ephraim is congratulatory:

> U ARE SO QUICK MES CHERS I FEEL WE HAVE
> SKIPPING THE DULL CLASSROOM DONE IT ALL
> AT THE SALON LEVEL   Done? Ah yes—
> Learned his lesson, saved his face and God's:
> Issues put on ice this evening.

Friends show up and share in Ephraim's enthusiasm for the poem: Alice B. Toklas, Marius Bewley, Maya, and Stevens (but not Chester, who was left out because "in the poem's time-scheme he still has three months to live"). Kinton Ford, JM's patron, an editor of Pope, is on hand, as is John Clay, DJ's patron. The judgment just in from Ford's neoclassical master is gratifying: "POPE SAYS THAT WHILE BITS / STILL WANT POLISHING THE WHOLES A RITZ / BIG AS A DIAMOND." But Stevens is cautionary:

> I WAS NEVER ONE FOR BLURBS
> TAKE WITH A GRAIN OF SALT JM SUCH PRAISE
> A SCRIBE SITS BY YOU CONSTANTLY THESE DAYS

> DOING WHAT HE MUST TO INTERWEAVE
> YOUR LINES WITH MEANINGS YOU CANNOT CONCEIVE

The séance is a scene of new harmonies. Stevens thanks JM for his introduction to the "LOVELY MAYA" (Jimmy dreaming still of reuniting his parents), while she "takes our hands to say / WE ARE ALL BROUGHT TOGETHER BY THE CUP." But just then things take another, nasty turn. DJ is instructed to put his "FREE HAND PALMDOWN YES ON THE BOARDS EDGE," and it is left "in no time, creased, red, sore / As if it had been trod on for attention." The séance breaks up after the interjection of a weird, imperious voice: "MYND YOUR WEORK SIX MOONES REMAIN."

It had always been clear that the Other World was a multilevel bureaucracy, and there were powers more highly placed than Ephraim, who operated lower down on "THE SALON LEVEL." In "P," Ephraim acknowledges the presence of those higher-ups. Their permission is required even to speak of them:

> CLEARANCE HAS COME TO SAY I HAVE ENCOUNTERED
> SOULS OF A FORM I NEVER SAW ON EARTH
> SOULS FROM B4 THE FLOOD B4 THE LEGENDARY
> & BY THE WAY NUCLEAR IN ORIGIN
> FIRE OF CHINA   MEN B4 MANKIND
> Really? Are they among you? THEY MAY RULE
> Do you communicate? WE SORT OF BEND
> OUR HEADS TO WORK WHENEVER THEY ARE FELT

Now, in the pressure applied to DJ's hand, the mediums had felt those antediluvian forces too.

> DJ massaged his fingers. Fun was fun.
> The pencil in my writing hand had snapped.
> Like something hurt the cup limped forth again.
> Maya: GEE   THEY PUT THE WHAMMY ON US
> Maria: JUNTA   Stevens: WHERES MY HAT
> E: A DOOR WAS SHUT   THE MIRROR WENT BLACK
> We, no less bowled over than used up,
> By mutual accord left it at that.

As *The Book of Ephraim* emerged in draft, Yenser responded with patient, detailed commentary, interpretative paraphrase, and respectful queries, helping his mentor to articulate the intricate design and elusive logic of the poem as a whole. "Would I have ever got this far without your careful encouragement?" Merrill wondered aloud in a letter to him. Stephen's marriage hadn't brought about the changes between them that James had feared they would: Yenser remained, as a reader and friend, someone Merrill could go on trying to be worthy of. On February 16, he sent "Z" to Yenser, completing the poem in draft. As he looked up from the desk where he had spent so many hours, he found himself profoundly, even dangerously "withdrawn from life." "What will the world look like when I slip back into it?"

When he did, life again presented a "death's head to be faced," this time in the persons of the declining George and Mary Jackson. In Sun City, the situation was bad. George had beaten Mary, and she had had to be hospitalized. DJ was too far away to help. So he hatched a desperate plan: he would bring his aged parents to Athens and install them in a flat "within screaming distance" of him and Jimmy with Taki's mother hired "to feed them and change their diapers." He arranged a phone, furniture, and curtains. Then he was at the airport meeting their plane. Mary clung to the door of the aircraft, and George was confused to see his son at the gate: "Thought you never traveled by air!" A melanoma on the old man's face had grown as "big as a deathwatch beetle"; Mary's brain tumor garbled her speech. Safe in the new apartment, she collapsed in her clothes in her room. "And" (as Jimmy narrates the scene) "old George saw his chance, opened the door + began yelling Mary! Mary! stop snoring, wake up! As she did at once in the usual panic. DJ grabbed him before he could get to her ('Don't hit her,' [sic] Mary kept saying)—: Don't let me catch you doing that again, Dad. [. . .] But the tables are forever being turned, and now the old man was suddenly the pitiful one: She can't go to sleep here, we've got to get home first."

Shortly after the Jacksons arrived that spring, Merrill left Athens, as planned, to finish the revision of his poem in Connecticut. As Mary slipped further, and George struggled to escape his fate, Jimmy held David's hand by air mail:

> Oh, it's so terribly sad. Even though it's what happens all the time. But we all agree that it would have been much sadder— would have been horrible if it had happened in Sun City. [. . .] Cling to the rightness of what you have done, and are doing. [. . .] Because if you'd gone there, and walled yourself up in that horrible place, you'd have never forgiven them; and be left, at

the end, with a tray-full of pointless and quite indisposable self-hatred. Try to feel, now, that the worst <u>has</u> happened. This <u>is</u> the crisis. Nothing will affect you quite so painfully again. [. . .] Now: do you think you need another $3,000? [. . .] Would it make you feel easier? Answer honestly. Please. I hope you're taking your daily vitamins, and getting enough to eat. [. . .] It may not seem so, but I'm THERE for you most of the time.

A week later, Jimmy wrote to David about his mother's death:

Your voice is still in my ears, 3 hours later. I feel that Mary will have laughed at our tears in the mirror, and that we can trust Maria to make her at home among the flowerbeds. You know—you must—that it was not a bad death, as deaths go; and much as it shattered you, that moment of recognition

—Mary had woken up long enough to say to David simply "Bye-bye"—

is somehow what makes it all right: as if, at the end, she had finally accepted the consciousness resisted so painfully all this time. My mother reminded me that Miss Annie did the same thing—came out of her coma, looked her in the eye, and said "My poor baby"—her last words. That you were there, by her, in order to hear them, must have meant everything to poor Mary; and will mean everything to you, in time to come.

Three weeks later, George followed Mary into the grave. Shocked and bereft, David had buried both of his parents in less than a month. "It's as if I'd said: send them to me, I'll dispose of them." He wrote to Jamie, thanking him for his

constant love, that way only you can say "Oh, my dear, I am sorry," each time I made my death calls; in short, the string out of the labyrinth. All that is good in my life, and all that has been good and will be—these are you.

If he did not have his companion beside him during that harrowing June, David did have as consolation Jimmy's "Divine Comedy," that splendid long "love letter," as Howard Moss called it, with its testimony to their twenty years together. Jackson had made a last, important contribution to the poem. Since *The Divine Comedy* was already taken as a title, he suggested that Merrill use the plural, *Divine Comedies*, as a name for the collection as a whole, "thus letting the long poem be called simply 'The Book of Ephraim.' " At once modest and grand, *Divine Comedies* captured the combination of Dantean seriousness and camp high spirits with which Merrill had come to view the world. Leading with the brief lyric about love and aging, "The Kimono," Merrill grouped together "Lost in Translation," "Yánnina," "Verse for Urania," "The Will," and four other poems, followed by *The Book of Ephraim*. By late July, when he returned to Greece to spend a month with Jackson, he had finished *Divine Comedies*. He had written Ephraim's book at last.

In the closing sections of the poem, following the disrupted séance in "U," Ephraim all but disappears, and Merrill, having brought his story from 1955 to the present time of composition, returns to the questions of literary form and selfhood that he began with in "A." Sections "V" and "W," two of the earliest to be completed, are both set in Venice. Developing, in "V," the notes that he made on his visit there in 1973, Merrill takes the decaying city as a symbol of the last gasps of Western individualism. As embodied by the campanile in the Piazza San Marco, that ideology is imperial, phallic, and stained with crap:

> The monumental
> "I" of stone—on top, an adolescent
> And his slain crocodile, both guano-white—
> Each visit stands for less. And from the crest of
> The Accademia Bridge the (is that thunder?)
> Palaces seem empty-lit display
> Rooms for glass companies.

Here in "V," as he watches couple after couple "entering the dark / Ark of the moment," the storm Merrill senses is a matter less of thunder and lightning than of historical change:

> A whole heavenly city
> Sinking, titanic ego mussel-blue
> Abulge in gleaming nets of nerve, of pressures
> Unregistered by the barometer
> Stuck between Show and Showers. Whose once fabled
> Denizens, Santofior and Guggenheim
> (Historical garbage, in the Marxist phrase)

> Invisibly—to all but their valets
> Still through the dull red mazes caked with slime
> Bearing some scented drivel of undying
> Love and regret—are dying.

In this bitter eulogy for the "titanic ego" epitomized by the sinking city, Merrill half mocks and half adopts the Marxist critique of high culture in Richard Pevear's review of *Braving the Elements*. Merrill isn't quite ready to call the houses of Santofior and Guggenheim "Historical garbage," any more than he is ready to climb on the scrap heap himself. But he sees that "la gente nuova"—those new families thronging the bridge—will take their place. The "population explosion" of which those couples are evidence amounts to a new apocalyptic threat, added to the atomic bomb and environmental catastrophe. But, after an electrical storm clears the air, Merrill winds up with a reminder of how Venice, the predatory, imperial city, "her least stone / Pure menace at the start, at length became // A window fiery-mild," and thus an image of the "heavenly city" that all earth might become, once purified of power.

In "W," a pastiche of Dante's *terza rima*, Merrill continues this argument with himself, staged this time as an encounter between him and his invented nephew, Wendell. The boy, whose birth was mentioned back in "F," is now an eighteen-year-old artist who has chosen to tour Europe rather than enroll in art school. But this doesn't mean that he reveres the old world and its humanistic values. After footing the bill for a superior meal, his uncle inquires "As to the contents of that wave-bleached head," and Wendell proffers his reply: a sketch pad full of portraits of people in pain, panicked, "Feeble or angry," with "long tooth, beady eye," like the Jacksons in their last days. When his uncle, the aesthete, asks him

> Why with a rendering so exquisite—?
> "I guess that's sort of how I see mankind,"
> Says Wendell. "Doomed, sick, selfish, dumb as shit.
>
> They talk about how decent, how refined—
> All it means is, they can afford somehow
> To watch what's happening, and not to mind."
>
> Our famous human dignity? I-Thou?
> The dirty underwear of overkill.
> Those who'll survive it were rethought by Mao

> Decades past, as a swarming blue anthill.
> "The self was once," I put in, "a great, great
> Glory." And he: "Oh sure. But is it still?"

Merrill's jaunty rhyming (exquisite/shit, Thou/Mao) makes implicitly a clever, comic counterargument to Wendell's desolate vision of humanity. Yet, despite its virtuosity, the technique does not endorse the self's "great, great glory." Rather, rhyme stands for principles of order larger than the individual, like the mythic structures in grand opera, Dante's formal patterns, or the rhythms of daily and seasonal recurrence in nature and human life.

Dinner paid for, JM prods Wendell forward, still ranting, through the labyrinth of streets. They pass the house where "the Master of the *Ring*" once lived, prompting a reverie on Brünnhilde's "death-defying" choice of human love over immortality, past La Fenice, "where the *Rake* / Rose from the ashes of the High Baroque," and past the quai where Stravinsky's body was taken by gondola for burial. "Dear Dante, he knew how to disguise argument as incident," Merrill said to McClatchy, describing his own method at this point in the poem. These allusions to Wagner and Stravinsky (and the personal memories Merrill associates with them) imply a vision of humanity in which love and art keep rising up against death, time and again. Defying Pevear, Wendell, the bomb, and population explosion, he ends by defending poetry, and specifically the kind of poetry he writes, of which rhyme is the symbol:

> I lose touch with the sublime.
> Yet in these sunset years hardly propose
>
> Mending my ways, breaking myself of rhyme
> To speak to multitudes and make it matter.
> Late here could mean, moreover, In Good Time
>
> Elsewhere; for near turns far, and former latter
> —Syntax reversing her binoculars—
> Now early light sweeps under a pink scatter
>
> Rug of cloud the solemn, diehard stars.

Each of Dante's three *cantiche* concludes with that word: "*stelle*" or "stars." For Merrill, the stars point beyond Dante's Christian cosmos to the heavens as perceived by the first stargazers described in *Hamlet's Mill*. They also point to the "dark" knowledge of cosmic order passed down through the principles of number embedded in poetic forms like Dante's *terza rima*.

In "Lost in Translation" and "The Will," Merrill had become something paradoxical: a poet of memory who prized forgetfulness. A missing puzzle piece or a misplaced text, a bag left behind in a cab—these were examples of the limits of the self, opening a channel for "powers" to speak from deep within or far beyond the individual, powers that we could call (with Stevens) the imagination, or (with Freud and Jung) the unconscious, or (with the Ouija board) Ephraim and the Other World. It appeared at first that Merrill meant to make himself, under Ephraim's instruction, a Jamesian sophisticate on whom "nothing was lost." But that's not what happened. As in his early poem "Mirror," Merrill had opened himself to the "blind flaws" in his mind through which "a faceless will" made its presence known. Rather than self-cultivation, he had been engaged in self-effacement. As he pushed himself to complete *The Book of Ephraim*, he was sapped, emptied. In "Y," he took stock:

> And here was I, or what was left of me.
> Feared and rejoiced in, chafed against, held cheap,
> A strangeness that was us, and was not, had
> All the same allowed for its description,
> And so brought at least me these spells of odd,
> Self-effacing balance. Better to stop
> While we still can. Already I take up
> Less emotional space than a snowdrop.
> My father in his last illness complained
> Of the effect of medication on
> His real self—today Bluebeard, tomorrow
> Babbitt. Young chameleon, I used to
> Ask how on earth one got sufficiently
> Imbued with otherness. And now I see.

Merrill ends the poem in "Z" with a return to Water Street in January, the same month in which he began it in "A"—rounding to "the key of home," as Yenser put it in a letter congratulating him on the rightness of the move. Coming full circle, "Z" is a satisfying conclusion. But it is also a way station where the "ambivalence" Merrill felt about the Other World is left unresolved. The scene is yet another invented one, a little fable using the setting and props of everyday life. JM and DJ are upstairs in the "glass studio" ("a mirror room," Yenser noted, "as is the poem itself"), where they huddle by the fire. It is dark, and the furnace is broken. "Throughout the empty house [. . .] taps / Glumly trickling keep the pipes from freezing," and the stream of composition, of consciousness, that has flown through JM in the poem seems all but frozen over too. There has been a break-in (there really had been one, but in Athens, not Stonington). In a line echoing "Lost in Translation," Merrill says about the incident, "Nothing we can recollect is missing." Yet there remains the threat of "A presence in our midst, unknown, unseen, / Unscrupulous to take what he can get," like the obscure forces they had encountered in "U" or "the faceless will" in "Mirror." As if it were involved in the case, JM and DJ wonder what to do with a box of Ouija transcripts that has surfaced—"old love-letters from the other world." "Are they for burning, now that the affair / Has ended? (Has it ended?)" One of the mediums seems to think it has: "Any day / It's them or the piano, says DJ." They place one page on the fire experimentally.

Before any more can be burned, the telephone rings—"Bad connection; babble of distant talk." Who or what is on the other side? Might it be a further communication from the spirits? Then another call comes: "It's Bob the furnace man. He's on his way." Either he will get the heat going again (which is to say, renew their love affair with the Other World?) or declare "the failure long foreseen / As total, of our period machine." Merrill means the furnace, but he is also thinking of the outdated machinery of the epic poem of which *The Book of Ephraim* was, he hoped, just a first installment. He had begun it by confessing to failure; would readers agree? He would have to wait for an answer to that question, as well as for Bob's verdict on the furnace. On the way downstairs, JM and DJ peer into blackness.

> And look, the stars have wound in filigree
> The ancient, ageless woman of the world.
> She's seen us. She is not particular—
> Everyone gets her injured, musical
> "Why do you no longer come to me?"
> To which there's no reply. For here we are.

There she was, wrapped in starlight, the heavenly muse, an always demanding, "injured" mother, the origin of things. And there they were, the mediums and lovers, their feet on the ground for the moment, but looking up, together, and ready still to serve her.

14

MIRABELL

1975–77

When the muse spoke again to JM and DJ, it was in an utterly strange and unprecedented form: as the voice of subatomic particles identified as bat-shaped fallen angels with numbers for names, discoursing on the history of the earth and the future of humanity in a summer-long, surging flood of letters. These were scrawled on sheet after sheet of paper as Merrill's right hand raced to keep pace with the planchette—the "hoarse slither" of the teacup on the Ouija board being the only sound made by those invisible, scarcely imaginable speakers.

Mirabell's Books of Number, the poem Merrill created from these séances, was very long (182 pages) and composed very quickly. It is a fundamentally different kind of poem from *The Book of Ephraim*. No longer recollecting séances across the decades, but recording them as if the reader were present, *Mirabell* is an inspired scriptural text; it incorporates long passages of quotation from the Other World, which swamp the human language of the mediums for pages at a time. JM and DJ had discovered how to approach "the powers" and evoke "fresh speech" from them—so fresh as to be harder to digest than anything in Milton or Blake (among other poets on Merrill's mind as he cast about for precursors). Although he could hardly have foreseen the form it took, inspiration was what Merrill had been hoping for since he and Jackson first used the Ouija board in 1953, and he had queried the spirit Kabel Barns anxiously, "Have you any messages for us? . . . Will you ever have messages for us? . . . When will you give us messages?" Now, with so many spirit dictations cluttering his study on Water Street that he had to set up a card table in the sitting room in order to answer letters from the living, James Merrill, urbane love poet and skeptical wit, had become a scribe of the occult.

Those messages didn't pile up immediately. Merrill mailed the typescript of *Divine Comedies* to Harry Ford in July 1975, then flew to his bereaved partner in Athens on an "errand of mercy." Jimmy had missed the human mess of David's parents' deaths, but he was there, a month later, to offer what consolation he could. They took up the work of mourning in their peculiar way, using the Ouija board to converse with the departed. The three séances with Mary and George Jackson that Merrill narrated in his notebook were long, amusing, and emotional. It was easy to get through:

MFJ: What time is   I am confused as usual O O
DJ: it's David Mama
MJ: I know darling O you don't be sad.   O do you know, nobody
     is here. I wanted to scc thcm all. (Not even grandpa?) O him.
     He complains like your father. (Are you going to be reborn?) A
     very sweet Japanese woman tells me I will. (have you met E.?)
     Yes rather liked . . . O I am not at all sure (if she likes heaven)
     Let me give you to your father.
GLJ: Goddam this typewriter.

And so on. David had practical matters to clear up. He asked his father to "tell us where the bank books are. GJ: Why should I? U cant take it w. you. Ha ha. None. I'm sorry David. Things got expensive." George himself had not given up all worldly attachments, however. "Don't sell the house," he insisted. Jimmy pointed out the futility of that: "You may be reborn as a little black or yellow baby, not as yourself." "Jim, I must remember that," GJ laughed "(as if I'd told a joke)." Courtly Marius Bewley welcomed Mary, served her tea, read aloud Wordsworth's immortality ode, and took her to meet "her virgin namesake. A ghastly bore. Such a mistake to turn peasant women into reigning monarchs." In Ephraim's eyes, Mary herself was a saint: "We have all quite humbly knelt that she might stay w. us." But she was ready to return to life: she'd expected heaven to be "as summer in the hills with those I loved + without U know who" (her husband). "But the cabin was empty + only the rush of cold reason like the falls." "Will U + DJ know each other in heaven under new names + faces?" Jimmy asked, hoping to comfort her son. "As now," she explained, "[. . .] I know him as a favorite child." But she had more favorites: in heaven, "to my delight I saw a beautiful black boy + a blonde girl + they said Mother + I wore another face." On her way out the door, she said simply "Bye bye"—her last words on earth to David, and his first words to her as a small child.

George's send-off came a week later. Retooled for another try at life, the old man hardly recognized himself: "I have 1000 eyes. It is the freshening of my soul. O I am alive at last," George said. Still, it was hard to let go of Mary. "David I wanted you to bring us back together. And I still want it. Find her. Find me. She is my lov— (censorship)." Usually, when what they call "censorship" occurred in a séance, the cup shot off the board, sometimes shattering on the floor. This time, George explained when communication resumed, he had been "corrected" by higher powers and "in no uncertain terms." The old man was learning to take pride in his second son. He boasted, "I have a little status" in the Other World because "my son is the funnel. (D is the 'psychic' one, you mean.) No. D speaks we use hi"—at which point censorship intervened again, and George was taken away, moaning this time, to "A cold place O God O God." Soon enough, however, he was back on the board, both "smarting + smarter." "I kiss you," he told David, "+ say courage. So long." Ephraim, who had begun by complaining about George a short time ago, now pronounced him "A dear man."

The Other World allowed Jackson and Merrill to mock, punish, and instruct mean old George Jackson, to make him smart and smarter, to make peace once they were done with that, and ultimately to honor him. In her memoir *Familiar Spirits*, Alison Lurie points out that Ephraim's reverence for Mary and his final approval of George are typical of the wishful consolation received by mourners who consult the supernatural, by whatever means. But JM and DJ were absorbed by the magic of the board, and they didn't stop to compare their experience with anyone else's. They seemed never to doubt that they were talking with David's parents, rather than with fantasy projections or with parts of themselves. Besides, the tears David shed were real, and so was his laughter. Merrill, who planned to return to the U.S. in August to teach a poetry-writing class at Yale, had come to Greece to give him that emotional release. But he also had his own interests in mind: with *The Book of Ephraim* shut, he wanted to see if the Ouija board was still in working order. Would there not be a sequel to *Ephraim*? At the end of the last séance with George, Ephraim took hold of the cup. He told JM,

[T]here is more work to come. (to me?) To us all. And it will this time flow straight through you, + all that comes out must be as you see it. All

of life + its workings is on its way through yr mind. They are diverting
traffic your way. (I feel nothing so far) The lights are red. A rush wd
bewilder you as it has GLJ. (When will I have a glimmer) When you
know what it is that comes. (D: cant you be explicit) I cannot be. But
when as with political or scientific or biological breakthroughs they
choose an artistic one, the vehicle experiences his own work uniquely
+ it becomes a triumph.

While David was gratified to cry with his mother again and to receive for
the first time his father's blessing, Jimmy was gratified by Ephraim's promise of "more work to come" and "triumph." It was exactly what he'd wanted
to hear.

Yet it wasn't obvious when this "breakthrough" was supposed to happen—or
how. Merrill understood Ephraim's remark ("it will this time flow straight
through you") to mean that there would be no more dictation; inspiration
would come directly, without the board. Waiting for lightning to strike,
Merrill invented ingenious assignments for his poets at Yale. Rather like
a Ouija board message, where letters come before words, he required students to write a poem using the letters of only one half of the typewriter
keyboard for one stanza and the letters of the other half for the next. "Fascinating results," he found, "almost like the hemispheres of the brain." He
was soon unable to think about anything except his students ("no question of reading anything that mightn't have some reference to that tribune
of strange young faces"). But he wore himself out with this devotion, and
his enthusiasm slackened until, by the end of the semester, he'd stopped
thinking about the seminar entirely; and, to his relief, "Yale" became "just
one more monosyllable out of possible thousands." He would never teach
another college course.

He spent his free hours that fall reading his friend Robert Fitzgerald's
translation of the *Iliad* aloud to Grace Stone. He also entertained Nelly
Liambey, who came for a long look at the U.S., and then Tony Parigory, whom
he took to Palm Beach and on a visit to Mrs. Plummer in December before
they both got on a plane for Athens. There Merrill read through the proofs
of *Ephraim* twice before he phoned in his final corrections to Ford. Finishing *Divine Comedies* left him "bereft." "I feel all empty, blinking about at the
real world—what there is of it." As in years past, he took the "rigorous sex
cure. 30 times in as many days, with 16 different people." Ephraim had told
him that he had "to learn all about science—biology & genetics—for the next

real Opus." Dutifully, he sat down with recent works of science for the general reader. One such book was *Chance and Necessity: An Essay on the Natural Philosophy of Modern Biology* (1971) by Jacques Monod, which maintains that human evolution is a result of chance at work in the self-regulating systems of cellular reproduction, requiring no divine creator for explanation. Nor was it obvious that such systems require a poet. In late January, Merrill reflected on what he was learning. He saw a theme, but no way of approaching it:

> Having now given [in *Ephraim*] some poor credit to the world of spirit—spirit <u>outside</u> matter—the "consciousness" <u>within</u> matter remains to be treated. No "voice" evidently can dictate from now on. Yet—beyond the mere trimming + tarting up of Intuition with an available vocabulary—assuming one could learn what those scientific terms meant—I can't imagine how to proceed. There is first of all no "story," nothing that interacts with life in particular. Life in general—ah yes—the changing chemical costumes, the dance of molecules . . . But one needs a bridge into the particular, into the subjective. I don't see that a fable will do, or a Conceit. And it is simply too pompous to applaud the grand process, as if <u>our</u> approval had anything to add. No, a relation must be found, a way of opening eyes to a world one doesn't <u>see</u> with instruments.

He toyed wanly with ways of putting himself in the picture: "Make a scientist my double"; or, in a nod to Nietzsche with a camp twist, "The Gay Scientist." He could see only that it would be a poem "hors concours." It would have to come from somewhere "beyond the alphabet / between the letters."

In February, Tony Harwood died. Merrill had remained loyal to this impossible friend since they met in 1938, but as Harwood "grew progressively more detached and paranoid, I couldn't bear to see very much of him." Their last encounter had come over the summer in New York, when Jimmy "spent an evening with him and Princess Nina—all their funds blocked due to some massive lawsuit he was bringing against the Royal Bank of Scotland for mishandling the Conan Doyle estate; themselves barricaded in an uptown hotel, under the 'assumed' names of Mr + Mrs Montezuma Jones." Six months later, Tony dropped dead in mid-rant. Contacted on the Ouija board, he recalled his death: "MY DEAR JAMES I SAW YOU WEEP FOR ME SUCH A HAPPY ESCAPE IT WAS SO ODD 2 B 2 OR 3 SOULS AT ONCE (How did that happen?) MY WRETCHED P[atron] SUCH A SCOLD SAYS DRUGS I SAY BALLS YR ENCHANTING

E SAYS I GREW 2 B AN OVERLOADED LINE I HEARD 2 MANY VOICES NIGHT + DAY."
Merrill had his own voices. So there was a need for some discrimination
between his case and Harwood's. From his present vantage, obligingly,
Tony could see who had made the right choices: "JAMES SO VERY GRIM + AT
ONCE SATISFYING TO LOOK BACK AND SEE ONES WHOLE TRIP LEADING STRAIGHT
2 1 POINT + 2 SEE EACH MAIN ROAD NOT TAKEN AS ONE EAGERLY LEAPT OFF ONTO
THE WRONG PATH. MY CHAGRIN IS NOT TO HAVE SHARED YR VISION THEN [. . .]
BAD JEWELRY DRUGS + PARLOUR SPIRITUALISM WAS OUR CRAP. YOU SEE PRETENSE
IS THE WORST OF THE WRONG PATHS." Merrill admitted that "I wanted so much
in life for T. to view me with something beyond affectionate condescen-
sion" that "the Board today sounds like 90% wish fulfillment."

His fiftieth birthday came, celebrated with tuna casserole and a case
of French champagne bought from the U.S. Army PX "at only pennies a
bottle." There was more cause to celebrate when copies of *Divine Comedies*
arrived. The jacket was cleverly designed by Harry Ford in response to
Merrill's vision for it. Its color was the "witty / Shade, now watermelon,
now sunburn" of the dining room in which JM and DJ first spoke with
Ephraim. Against this background was set an oval mirror in a lavish,
ornamental frame, the glass (and the back of the jacket) done in a disturb-
ingly unreflecting silver (mildly disappointing Merrill, who had hoped
for something shiny, like Reynolds Wrap). Friends wrote to congratulate
him. "Dear Jimmy," Ashbery began, "*Divine Comedies* is (to appropriate
another title—this one from Scriabin) 'The Divine Poem.' I am reading and
rereading it with constant intense pleasure."

Vendler extolled the new book in *The New York Review of Books*. But *The
New York Times* ran a negative review of it by the poet Louis Simpson, who
made the old complaint that Merrill was, it seemed, always condemned to
hear some version of: "Ingenious? Witty? Merrill's writing is all of that.
But the reader who wants to be gripped by strong feelings or a plot will be
disappointed. Merrill has staked out his claim nicely, thank you; I have
the impression that he would think the demands made upon poetry by a
certain kind of reader—for example, the reader who is looking for strong
feelings—irrelevant if not absurd." For Simpson, Merrill, like his contemporary Ashbery, was only playing "a word game of a high order." Merrill
was stung by the review and angry at its ad hominem jibes. Simpson had
remarked that Merrill's poetry "moves with no embarrassment among rich
people and"—absurdly, with no obvious reference—"the owners of expensive automobiles." Yet the review may have been salutary. Two weeks before,
Merrill had felt at sea in his work: holding *Divine Comedies* in his hands,
he had tried to remember "what it felt like, having all those things to say

as well as the energy to say them. Whatever I've worked on these months seems all too inconsequential. Of course people keep dying at a rate that could keep one writing nothing but elegies for the next 20 years," but he didn't want to do that. Now, at the end of March, thanks in part to Simpson, he was "back at work with, so to speak, a vengeance."

He was at work in particular recounting the Jacksons' arrival in Athens, their deaths, and his and David's Ouija talks with them. He drafted numerous versions of these events, which, when incorporated in *Mirabell's Books of Number*, would be much reduced*—in order to make room for the new spirits from whom he and Jackson began taking dictation around this time. Those speakers were stern and commanding:

> UNHEEDFUL ONE   3 OF YOUR YEARES MORE WE WANT   WE MUST HAVE
> POEMS OF SCIENCE   THE WEORK FINISHT IS BUT A PROLOGUE
> ABSOLUTES ARE NOW NEEDED   YOU MUST MAKE GOD OF SCIENCE
> TELL OF POWER   MANS IGNORANCE FEARES THE POWER WE ARE
> THAT FEAR STOPS PARADISE   WE SPEAK FROM WITHIN THE ATOM

These lines introduce the spirit lessons in *Mirabell*, which Merrill began writing that summer and completed a little more than a year later. In his notebook and letters, he refers to these voices "WITHIN THE ATOM" as "Them." There is no transcript of his and Jackson's first contact with them, which took place on March 29, his notes suggest. But Merrill did preserve the transcript of an important séance on April 26. JM and DJ sat down that day to chat with Ephraim, who quickly gave way to his superiors, announcing, "They R PLEASED AT JM . . . They WOULD SPEAK."

These new, obscure authorities directly began to explain a cosmology. "2 GODS GOVERN," Biology and Chaos. Reason is the tool of Biology, and feeling the tool of Chaos. Chaos had once had the upper hand, which led to disaster, as these speakers knew from their own experience. They had "TRIFLED" and fallen: they "EXPLODED THE ATOM," causing Atlantis to sink, China to burn, and "BLACK HOLES" to be ripped open in the cosmos. They were fallen angels. But JM and DJ had nothing to fear from *them*: the Devil was driven out of them and into man; now they were working to save man by guiding him to use "MIND" against Chaos to rebuild "PARADISE"; and they had chosen JM and DJ to get the message across. This explanation, they allowed,

---

* Merrill presented his drafts for discussion in a poetry course led by Pearl London at the New School in New York in 1979. *Poetry in Person: Twenty-five Years of Conversation with America's Poets*, ed. Alexander Neubauer (Knopf, 2009), 83–96.

was "OVERDUE." When they left, Ephraim returned with Maria Mitsotáki, known as "MM" on the board. Ephraim and Maria had been excluded from this high-level exchange. "WE FEARED 4 U," and yet "IT WAS QUITE RADIANT" while they waited. "MM SAYS A GOOD DAY 4 GARDENING."

This séance introduced the main ideas of *Sandover*: the fate of the world hangs in the balance; humanity can avoid catastrophe by choosing reason over feeling, and re-create paradise in harmony with the designs of a divinity called God Biology and his agents in the Other World. Much of this echoed comments that Ephraim himself had made over the years. The scientific emphasis was new, however. So were these speakers and the purpose they declared: what "They" wanted from JM and DJ was a sacred poem that would serve God Biology, revealing the laws of his creation.

The power and mysteriousness of those voices threw into relief for Merrill and Jackson, after so many years of habituation to it, the essential strangeness of speech on the Ouija board. Over the years, Merrill's practice was to copy on loose sheets the capital letters indicated by the teacup, and to divide these by lines or spaces into words and sentences, while noting his and Jackson's questions and remarks in parentheses. To study the initial transcript of a séance is to watch as he forms words, phrases, sentences, voices, and "characters" from a potentially incoherent stream of letters and numerals. This process precisely reverses the conventional idea that speech is the basis for writing: Merrill's voices from the Other World emerged as a result of writing; they were inaudible until he brought them forth from the letters indicated by the teacup, like a sculptor freeing the human figure embedded in a block of marble. When he went back to a transcript to enter it into his notebook, prepare a typed copy, or turn it into verse, he worked in the same way, continuing to make refinements and changes, the record of the séance becoming cleaner and clearer with each iteration.

The handwritten transcript of that April 26 séance illustrates the first stage of this process. It retains all the false starts and static of an actual Ouija séance, capturing the excitement and occasional puzzlement Merrill felt in his role as Scribe. His uppercase letters are hastily but neatly printed on five unlined sheets of paper, turned sideways to catch the alphabetical torrent. The following quotation begins when Ephraim's superiors start speaking. The Yeats poem Merrill quotes from ("Whatever flames upon the night, / Man's resinous heart has fed") is "Two Songs from a Play":

WHAT IS IN YOUR HAND COMES TRULY (what I've done up 2 now) WE AGREE + SO WILL ALL DO NO TheING YOU FEEL IS FORCED. 2 GODS GOVERN (Biology?) + CHAOS WHICH EMPLOYS FEELING (to shape itself?) 2 CON-

TEST OUR MINDS IN MAN. WE ARE NOT EVIL BUT IMPATIENT. FEELING WILL
HAVE ITS DAY (Yeats: "Whatever flames upon the night") INDEED THAT
POEM SPEAKS. WE HAVE FRIGHTENED YOU. FEAR US NOT WE 2 R SLAVES BENT
2 THE WHEEL OF AN IMPLACABLE UNIVERSE. RAISE US A/S ON G/2R REAL
ORDER WHICH IS MIND + NATURE WEDDED EVENJEW AHOUR GOD OF BIOLOGY
RESTED THAT 7TH DAY (Jehovah god of biology) WESPEAK IN WORDS AS
THE RE IS NO REAL WORD 4 SUCH POWER + SUCH GODLY PRODUCTION

The transcript is itself a form of the civilizing work this passage praises: as
letters cohere in words and sentences, the sense-making power of "MIND"
rises above mere verbal "CHAOS." But sense doesn't emerge easily. The powers speak in unfamiliar idioms that may be grammatical, but are stiff and
awkward, as if translated too literally from some other language ("WHAT IS
IN YOUR HAND COMES TRULY"). Often it's unclear at the start where a sentence
is going, or once the sentence is in place, whether Merrill has got it right.
He jumps ahead, expecting a "T" to be the first letter of "The"; when it turns
out not to be, he has to go back and revise. Letters melt and merge, then
must be pried apart and segmented differently. It's hard to say in which
direction, forward or backward, a letter will connect to others. Some words
need an extra letter or a letter removed or repositioned before becoming
legible. Sometimes the powers spell in phonetic shorthand, as when "R"
stands for "OUR" or "ARE," or the numeral "2" for "TO" or "TWO," as if the spirits were texting. The name of Jehovah, who in future séances will be called
God Biology or God B, is mangled: "EVENJEW AHOUR GOD OF BIOLOGY."

Embarrassed by that gaffe, the powers complained about having to
express themselves in human language: "WESPEAK IN WORDS AS THE RE IS NO
REAL WORD 4 SUCH POWER + SUCH GODLY PRODUCTION." These words came, as
Merrill had hoped, from a source "beyond the alphabet / between the letters." The writing machine that was the Ouija board had revived for Merrill the archaic ceremony of inspiration. Like the unidentified authority
who spoke in a dream to Caedmon, the earliest English poet, the powers
commanded JM to sing of creation: "RAISE US A/S ON G/2R REAL ORDER." As
he divides and joins those letters to form "A SONG TO OUR REAL ORDER," he
grasps language in a primitive state, raising song from a potential prior to
words. He is both passive and active, taking letters down as dictation and
taking them up as raw material to be fashioned. As he does, he collaborates
not only with David Jackson, but with faceless forces "beyond the alphabet"
or deep within language itself, "between the letters." Ephraim must have
seemed to JM and DJ almost human by comparison with the powers now
using their hands to speak.

Asked for their name, the powers gave "BEEZELBOB," a version of the Hebrew name for the devil, Beelzebub. That wouldn't ever be easy to use. Ephraim told JM and DJ to try to reach them instead using a number, 441, without more explanation than that. (He didn't mention—what JM may or may not have known—that 441 is the frequency at which orchestras tune.) When they tried that number again, it worked: 441 returned to instruct them. He told them that Adam and Eve were "IMAGES THAT HAPPENED IN MOLECULAR HISTORY. THERE IS A WORLD IN The ATOM NEGATIVE + POSITIVE. N=ADAM. E=PROTON." In the pre-scientific world, myth had been necessary "2 EXPLAIN MAN 2 MAN": "EDEN ASTAGE THEXPULSION The DRAMA"; the mistake was "2 BELIEVE THAT KNOWLEDGE IS EVIL." "The WARING ELEMENTS PRODUCED WARRING HEIRS EVIL PREVAILED + WE NEARLY DESTROYED The LAB" by exploding the atom. "TheAT IMPULSE 2 FIND ULTIMATE POWER WAS OUR RUIN." But "GOD GAVE US ANOTHER CHANCE": "ONCEAGAIN MAN EMERGED FROM THE COOLING SEA + WE SAT TheIS TIME ON THE THRONE OF GOD CHASTEND + ATTENTIVE WE INVENTED THE SCRIBE WE TOLD HIM OF THAT OLD PREHISTORY (+ he wrote Genesis)." When modern physicists exploded the atom, the apocalyptic threat reemerged, and man needed to learn about that previous explosion.

Merrill wanted to visualize his interlocutors. "WE HAVE ONLY A DARK SHAPE," they told him, yet "WE ONCE FLEW WE ONCE SOARED." Were they the powers mentioned in section "U" of *The Book of Ephraim*, whose wings are likened to the trailing sleeves of palace robes? "CIRCLEY OUR CARPET + WATCH FROM YOUR WALLS," 441 replied. JM decided he must mean the bat motif on Hubbell's new wallpaper, taken from the carpet back on Water Street: they must look like bats! 441 hesitated: "NO. NEARLY IS IT ANUGLY IDEA[?]" DJ was "as ever quick to reassure": "No, no—they stand for, er, eternity." The idea took: "WE ARE ETERNITY WE R O BEYOND 9. Those STAGES R OUR LAB. YOUR FRIENDS OUR WORKERS." Then why couldn't Ephraim and Maria sit in on these talks too? DJ asked. "THEIR ENERGIES WILL END OW The BEING They CANNOT BE," because their souls had been mixed with animal souls, 441 explained. "WE WANT Thes TUFF OF MAN HUMAN, not animal. 2 MANY HALF + QUARTER + TENTH HUMANS NOW ON/E ARTH THE FINAL RACE WILL BE GODS." Then, they wondered, won't JM and DJ be left out too? "THE WATER FALL WILL HOLD U 2 AS BRIGHT DROPS + U WILL SPLASH INTO The GREAT CLEAR POOL." This last image recalled the waterfall Ephraim described in the séance quoted in section "Q" of *Ephraim*, and JM and DJ, remembering it, wondered whether these bats weren't merely Ephraim in disguise? The board threw that suspicion back at them: "I AM U. U RME. WE R The DREAM."

These séances took place in Athinaion Efivon 44. At first Merrill didn't mention them to friends, except to say to McClatchy that it was "A Whole

New Ballgame on the Ouija Board which all too clearly asks to be written up." He was rereading Milton and Pynchon. The challenge would be to put *Paradise Lost* into a new vocabulary: "Thrones, powers, dominations / protons, electrons, resonances." He read Isaac Asimov, and he made notes about quarks and so-called "strange" particles. He wrote in his notebook:

> We are speaking to a power who can be understood—seen into, as it were, like a telescope through either end, linking the immense with the minute.
>
> Hence the lightning shifts of scale, the thunderous shifts of frame, from mythological to molecular
>
> Without language to tell them who they Are they would be hard put: hence their reliance upon stories
> > an "as told to" book

Merrill now saw *The Book of Ephraim* as the first part of an epic "as told to" story. With Dante in mind, he projected a trilogy. He glimpsed "the possibility of completing the entire work—its length not clear—2 more 'books'? I fear I am too old, my mind + health failing; the thought nonetheless fills me w. wonder." He made that entry in London. He and Jackson went there in May 1976 to meet Hellen Plummer on their way to Water Street, where they would continue the séances. Merrill's mind swarmed with images: "The blackening mirror: emblem of the new poem. / formula on a blackboard." He made notes on molecular structure and the double helix on a visit to the London Science Museum. He contemplated the Anglo-Saxon funerary treasure of Sutton Hoo at the British Museum. He gave himself homework: "find an epigraph from Lucretius"; "look up numbers in Japanese/Russian/ Hindi/Arabic." Under the influence of John Michell, the author of *The Flying Saucer Vision* (1967) amd *The View Over Atlantis* (1969), who believed that "traditional sacred places were centres of natural magic, used by ancient adepts who possessed knowledge, since lost, of Earth's vital energies," Merrill and Jackson visited the neolithic stone circles in Wiltshire, Stonehenge and Avebury. Typically, Merrill preferred the less grand and less touristed of the two—just as in Athens he preferred the Erectheum to the Parthenon. The stones in Avebury, where two roads intersect, are set upright in "not quite tangent O's"—lenses for focusing cosmic order. Merrill calls it "both a holy and a homely site" in a "watercolor" done on the spot, a sonnet that he would later "slip" into *Mirabell* on the threshold of the lessons starting in section 1 ("a bookmark for the moment, / Until I find a better place for it"). But there would be little of such word-painting poetry in *Mirabell*. "The point is not to be lyric," he told himself. "If one wants to be believed."

.　　.　　.

On Water Street, Merrill entered into a three-month period of extraordinary creative activity. Most afternoons he spent in the round red dining room with Jackson, taking dictation from the spirits. They held fourteen séances in June, twenty-two in July, and twenty-one more in August. After dinner, Jackson sat in front of his new television set, and Merrill read in Victor Hugo's conversations with the spirit world, each of them refueling in his own way. The next morning, while his partner slept, Merrill transcribed the previous day's séance in his notebook, using pens of different colors (red, blue, black, green, purple) to indicate different speakers. He had always written in his notebook in a casual way, scattering images, questions, and pensées across a page, leaving lots of blank space. Now, suddenly, he filled every inch of every page, fitting as many as eight hundred words on some—a storm of text. "We are all but flattened by the gale of dictée," he told Robin, "which only abates when we beg it to."

It remained uncertain who or what was dictating to them. The nature of voice on the Ouija board was always unstable and metamorphic: one voice gave way to another, often abruptly; and Ephraim had various ways of speaking, between which he moved fluidly. But this was different: a vague, corporate entity, a plural "Them," had seized the cup. Ephraim described them as a throng of enormous red-eyed bats. "Squeaking" and "twittering," they were *hot*, and glowed "like Franklin stoves." "Are they scary?" JM asked. "They terrify me," MM answered. "They R no doubt the Junta of Eternity." Yet Maria found them "touching," too; they were "like house pets who weewee'd on the rug. I feel that they have their tails between their legs. They must behave." "How exactly did they 'weewee'?" "Destroyed a world," Maria replied, making for uneasy laughter. Hoping to humanize them, JM again brought up the question of a name. What did they wish to be called? "WE R NAMELESS ALAS" was the answer. "THE name is an invention of this epoch of earth." A pause, and then: "I have a number 741 one of a host of 1000s U understand we R not the same intelligence each time 2 day 741 Yesterday 40070." The night before, Jimmy and David had sat with David Kalstone for a tipsy off-the-record séance. In the midst of it, a peremptory voice had ordered them to go to bed and prepare for "WORK TOMORROW." That voice, 741 said, was 40076. "He annoyed U," and so was replaced "like a defective part of a computer." 741, milder, would remain.

Ephraim had only a small part in these séances. He pulled the curtain back when the bats arrived; he appeared, like entr'acte entertainment, when they stepped out. But Maria had now been admitted to the lessons. She was joined one day by another deceased friend when JM asked, "What is WHA's view of what's happening to us?" and Wystan himself spoke up:

"Spooks my dear preoccupied us at Christ College. The tables tapped out many a smart rhythm + then the dreary politics the absorbing loves + then the dreary wash." What did he mean by "wash"? "Blood of the Lamb?" JM suggested, impiously. "O yes. The Church my dears the dreary dreary dead bang wrong Church. And those years I could have held hands on teacups. I am as MM riveted but excluded. Might one join her at yr couch?" If Merrill needed mother figures like Maria to worship (and to worship him), he also needed wise older men to consult, as long as they approved of him—which in this case required Auden to recant his Church of England beliefs. It was an ingenious revenge on the senior poet in whose presence, in life, Jimmy had often found himself speechless and cowed. Auden would take part in all of the séances that summer as adviser, collaborator ("My boy write our our our poem"), and a queer uncle giggling over jokes with Plato.

The séances themselves, recorded in paragraph-less blocks in Merrill's notebooks, were rambling, repetitive, and often contradictory or incoherent. Yet certain themes recurred, and a story emerged. The bats had been builders. Their civilization ascended "into our stratosphere world anchored 2 earth by radiated signals in the 14 locales" on which sites Stonehenge, Avebury, and other sacred monuments were eventually erected. This "crust" world was "a great smooth set of plains lattice cities swift + gleaming movement, each a work" powered by atomic energy. But as it rose, "Earth snapped away under us in obedience to" the higher order of "the stars or to Biol. [. . .] Our vast skein shivered B R O K E I N T O F L A M E W E F E L L." The resulting debris was "spun off" by the earth's rotation and compacted "into a tidy reminder" of their failure, the moon. The "clouds came to cool, the dust gathered, the atmosphere cleared + God mercifully took us in. We stared out at the round dead ball as at an empty thought." It was then that they first heard the pure "intelligence" in "the songs of the universe," the celestial music that Dante would later hear.

God B entrusted "the revival of life" on earth to the "seed of the Jew," the human bearer of divine mind. The bats were assigned to aid him by conducting "research" in "the lab" or "R Lab." It turned out that Ephraim's system of patrons and representatives was only part of the story. While most souls are given lessons by their patrons in the Other World, "12%," the cream of the human crop, are worked on in the lab, where "cloning" takes place. This cloning involves the adjustment of genetic ratios, reflected in the chemical formulas or "densities" of souls. There are five immortal souls who are leaders in one field of endeavor or another life after life, and provide models for the rest of humanity (741 gave as examples Montezuma, Gandhi, and Pablo Casals). Using them, God B intends to "raise up a host of

broadly accepting men," who will honor reason, and preserve the endan-
gered "greenhouse," earth. 741's term for this grand mission was "V work,"
punning on the life-enhancing "*vie*"-work of "the Five."

That was the skeleton of those early lessons. The story got more complicated as the lessons went on and it turned out that the bats had been
created through atomic fusion by earth's first inhabitants, the centaurs.
The centaurs, created by God B, were the immortal rulers of an Arcadian
civilization called Atlantis. They bred the bats to be their messengers, but
the bats subjugated them, and the centaurs evolved into dinosaurs before
God B gave up on them and allowed them to be destroyed in the bats' atomic
conflagration.

Merrill dutifully recorded this weird, wacky stuff, word by word. Indeed, his notebook from the summer of 1976 is a wild, unprocessed mix
of sci-fi-inspired speculation, New Age mythology, environmentalism,
ugly eugenic fantasy, and Malthusian arguments for the good of famine as
a check on population growth. It's hard to untangle one strand of thought
from another. Yet certain passages stand out as more lucid and sustained
than those around them, like this account of the crystal pyramid constructed by the Pharaoh Akhenaton and Queen Nefertiti—a subject fit for
a painter of the romantic sublime, or maybe a blockbuster disaster movie.
Only a slight miscalculation prevented the Sun God from ruling the world:

> The last + pinnacle capstone polished by 1700 slaves throughout
> a year was lifted into place at night. Great cranes groaned + he
> watched so intensely thrilled that his physicians fed him opium
> each hour. They then an hour before dawn withdrew in barges
> decorated w. miniature pyramids of diamonds + dawn broke.
> A slow entirely sky filling light began. The people fell on their
> faces. He stood on his jeweled barge + Diamonds glared + splin-
> tered. The pyramid rose + fell even as we did an experiment that
> failed gloriously. Achtamon + his Queen cut their wrists into the
> waters + their barge on fire sank. Had his measurements been
> exact. . . ? The world in flames. Thera erupted as it was on a
> direct northern point. Minoa perished. It ignited within 1000
> km radius all volcanoes.

In another séance, JM and DJ learned that the "shadow" of Akhenaton's
pyramid "still exerts destructive force over the waters of the world" in the
form of the Bermuda Triangle. In a similar vein, 741 confirmed the existence of UFOs. "They scout our greenhouse," he explained. "Most prob-

ably an atomic powered system on the lookout like mechanical Bees for a universal transfertilization." Merrill wanted scientific facts, not popular fiction, and information like this was dismaying. "The caliber of some of this—flying saucers etc.—is a severe judgment upon our intellectual powers. A satire . . . ," he had to admit. How, if he was going to turn this dictation into a Dantean trilogy, could he keep his readers from laughing at such "conventionally 'loony' puerile subjects"? It was one thing for the gods to sound like men, another for them to sound like nuts. The Ouija board tried to reason with him. WHA punned, "I for one adore the saucers. You who only use the cup may not." 741 added, "Strange that you accept 1 thing but not the other." They both had a point. If Merrill believed in the spirits, didn't he have to believe what they told him?

The board's discussion of race was particularly persistent and unpalatable. Much of it had to do with Jewishness. According to the board, the Jews were God B's chosen race. All true spiritual leaders were Jews: "Buddha a Jew Allah all Jews each a mystery birth in a plan to populate leadership with mind." The cloning that goes on in the lab entails adding this Jewish "spice" to the soul, and JM had benefited from it. Yet "[t]he Jewish element of mind of course has nothing to do w/ birth or race." Take David Kalstone. "DK's Jewish life is only now." It was a gross literalization to confuse the merely Jewish and the Jew. This notion both expresses an idealization of the Jew as intellectual and implies a distaste for actual Jews and their religious and cultural traditions, or at least a view of Jewishness as something to be transcended. It's possible to see in it Merrill's rejection of his father's anti-Semitism and a dose of that prejudice, undiluted. Yet other peoples fare worse on the board. "Hitler + the Arab raise the brute. [. . .] The Arab the Teuton misuses his power so confusion on them." Africans, lacking "the Jewish component," are "almost entirely ape descended"; and so it is too with America's "Negro race." This racism, noxious enough in its own terms, is more disturbing in the context of the "R Lab's" work of genetic refinement, which calls for the elimination, for example, of "rat souls." Where was this eugenic thinking coming from? From JM, DJ? From their parents? Or from American culture at large? As with so much else it had to say, the board made it impossible to identify the source of its racist doctrines. In his role as the Scribe, Merrill doesn't endorse them, but he doesn't voice revulsion either, and he incorporated many of them in *Mirabell*, albeit in a reduced and partly sanitized form.

As if to keep the mediums firmly on the hook, the board placated them with lavish praise, particularly JM. With WHA and MM attending, Merrill treated the séances as a "seminar," with 741 popping the occasional "quiz." Grades of "A+" and good reports—"Head of class"—confirmed JM's speculations. The formulas for his and DJ's souls also involved high marks. JM's numbers were 268 (the sum of his past lives) and 1:1,000,000 (a ratio of animal to human "densities"), resulting in a "talent" rating of 5.5. He was "of the partial 5 list. Adjacent to the 5." So he was in quite good company: "5.1 WHA 5.2 [Arthur] Rubinstein 5.3 FDR"—while Mrs. Roosevelt was a 5.5, like JM.

DJ was not far behind, with an overall 5.9. "DJ is a conductor," 741 explained. "I direct things?" he asked, shyly. "Your hand shapes our words. And vice versa." (His hand was being shaped in return. By this point in the summer, June 24, David's right hand had developed a knot in the palm from being held above the cup, hour after hour.) In short, the Ouija board valued both of the mediums, and valued their life together. Their union was the basis of this occult seminar, which had been "25 years in preparation. We called U then. U are ready now."

Did it matter that theirs was a same-sex union? The mediums debated the point between themselves one evening: "What is the advantage from their [the spirits'] point of view of our homosexuality[?] Unlike Yeats + Hugo"—JM imagined them answering—"who cared for the erection of theories + the dissemination of thought, we are more the takers-in of seed." 741 overheard the discussion. The next day, July 2, he came back to it, and a new phase of talks began. Had 741 not replaced the peremptory 40070, he reflected, "U wd have gone faster but in turn not created as we have together a courteous world. Nor would I have come 2 love you." JM was abashed by this confession: "My dear. You had said you had no feelings." But 741 had been "granted this chance" to experience love, and he intended to make the most of it. He told them, "I am nothing. No time passes 4 me between our meetings. Then yr fingers like great lights show me 2 myself + I am 741. Satisfying. It is now me. I have entered a great world. I am filled with is it manners?" WHA took over, describing what the mediums couldn't see: "My dear that surely is a smile. [. . .] Dear God He changes"—as the cup executed slow arabesques across the board. "It is my 1st view of a miracle," MM declared, without describing what she'd witnessed.

Immediately 741 began to discourse on the nature of male homosexuality. "It is a union usually productive of mind values. It was engineered 2 make a more fertile bed 4 growing the flowers of music + literature," which are "the principal lights for God Biol." By contrast, the visual arts are a lower-order discipline, "more accessible 2 the common mind." Painting, sculpture, and architecture are "physical celebrations," whereas poetry, music, "+ their union" are "celebrations of the mind." Here 741 paused to specify: "Heart if you will." "Heart" was, JM pointed out, "[a] word you use for the 1st time." "Yes. It has been shaped in me 2 be worthy of you 4, + 2 be

worthy 2 open the door to the Angels"—this, a non sequitur, was the first
mention of "the Angels" and séances to come. 741 resumed: "Heterosex.
love must at last produce bodies + is therefore riveted to the physical"; the
gay man was disposed by his orientation toward the metaphysical arts of
music and poetry, rather than biological reproduction. (Why lesbian love
doesn't have the same effect isn't obvious, but 741 didn't comment on that
issue . . .) JM objected: Hadn't there been some rather "great straight
musicians + writers"? "Indeed but 4000 years ago biology realized"—here
741 was interrupted by censorship. "They will tell us the rest," JM filled
in the silence, thinking ahead to the Angels, and taking the pressure off
741. "My aspect quavers," 741 replied, glad to save face. "Yr kindness keeps
me in this form." And what form was that exactly? "Mes enfants," Maria
announced, "He is a peacock." There was "Amazement" all around. 741
described how the transformation came about: "Our friends MM + WHA
can perform miracles. They see the peacock who saw it in gardens, heard
it cry. I only knew the formula called peacock + envied, soulless as I was,
a certain rare talent it had 2 charm the eye. When I begged 2 please U they
asked how. And I took out the file the peacock." "We warmed 2 U from the
start," JM chuckled, feeling that there had "always been a peacock in you."
"There will be. I now know the trick of it."

   This was a turning point in the séances. 741 hadn't merely approved of
JM's and DJ's sexuality, as Ephraim had; he had identified homosexuality
with the superior arts, music and poetry (but how did David the painter feel
about this hierarchy?). Then 741 had declared his love for JM and DJ—and
turned into a peacock. His metamorphosis was in effect a highly fanciful
"coming out." "Is there not something of the Athenian in the peacock?" 741
asked. "Athenian," in this context, suggested "Greek love" and the paths
of the Royal Park in Athens, where the stately birds and cruising homosexuals both circulated. There were also other associations for Merrill—for
example, his poem "The Peacock" from The Black Swan, which compares
the bird's splendid tail to Proust's prose; and as we know, a peacock was the
Merrill family emblem.

   If the mediums couldn't see the change in 741, they could still hear it
in his voice. Along with "manners" and "feeling," he'd learned to speak in
a new way: expressive but formal, cautiously witty, as befit "the courteous
world" that he and the mediums were creating. JM and DJ had tamed the
alien powers they discovered through the board. In the peacock 741, those
powers had become, like Ephraim, "familiar," practically human, and
fashioned in the queer image of the mediums themselves. It was a "miracle" of the imagination.

"My dear R u not curious about the nature of imagination?" WHA asked
JM the next day. "MM + I imagine that we imagine U. U, that U imagine
us. Somewhere our powers cross + we all imagine 741 + then transformation." On cue, the peacock showed up again. The same imagination that had
changed him now united the members of the seminar "in a fold of energy."
"Since God Biol. nominated U scribe," he said to JM, "U yrself chose yr
materials. We R them, we 5 [. . .] communing souls." "The 5, our souls, will
now begin 2 be a single power." The cup slowed to "a grave absorbed pace"
as 741 adopted a new manner, different from the previous day's camp play.
The union of souls created by the seminar, he went on, represented "the
very union of the elements": fire, 741; water, MM; earth, WHA; air, JM; and
"nature DJ," a fifth element added to the usual four. Like a priest or poet, 741
invoked the elements: "Come 2 us O 5 elements Make us one mind. Show us
the inside of the living energy which is man + 5." The elements spoke:

> The gravity we gave was in the force of spinning earth. [. . .] Fire
> consumed earth. Water quenched the fire. Air rose 2 clear space
> 4 breathing nature. 5 began again what was destroyed. 5 is the
> productive force + 5 the answer 2 life in search of Paradise [. . .]
> 5 R yr minds. There is no death in mind. Mind is both slave +
> master of soul. It gravitates as a planet around sun 2 life energy.
> Heaven is the idea the galaxy of the mind. All 5 elements are as
> rings of that galaxy.

It was necessary to proceed slowly: "2 here are mortal give them pause."
The elements continued, "Our powers R linked to the single penetrating
source of light. We draw from it. We then divide the power. Our V work is
the onward march of life."

The speech ended with "a cautionary word":

> The matter which is not matter is ours to guard against. It is
> the foreign menacing universe magnetized by beacons urgent
> in uncontrolled atomic researches. One by one the black hand
> tests the panes of the greenhouse. We watch. We push back. Do
> not pray to it. Keep yr union 5. We now leave U one step closer +
> yr craft that much stronger 4 yr. flight.

As they talked things over afterward with WHA and MM, DJ looked
ahead, wondering: "these zero voices," the Angels whom they were
approaching, "how will they talk"? David seemed worried, but JM was con-

fident, even breezy about the prospect: "Oh they'll find words." And "why not?" Wystan agreed. "We've found em."

Merrill's mind was fixed on the poem he intended to make of the dictations. Frustrated by the information he was getting, he wished that the spirits would "elucidate something established, like the table of the elements." His notebook shows him trying to tease out logic where none was apparent. His attitude toward the board was double: even as he was able to stand back from the experience and judge it, he remained enthralled by it and frankly greedy for more. After reading "all the extant transcripts" of Hugo's "3 years of table-tapping," he told Yenser, "I make out, as never before, that all this is a form of lunacy—I who always felt myself to be so unshakably sane—but that too is in the tradition of the best lunatics—and if you think it's going to stop us—! No, we're getting as much material as we can from Them."

He had been troubled before the dictations began by the question of what form the new poem should take. As the séances unfolded, he quickly saw that he could write it as a "closet drama." The "Mise en page" would be "That of a play. Like Shakespeare, with minimal stage directions." "DJ, JM, MM + WHA, and Ephraim speak in verse; the numbers (741) in prose?" He thought of twelve-syllable lines for 741, then tried the fourteener Blake used in his visionary poems, before he settled on an unmetered fourteen-syllable line. It was an interesting choice. By putting the bats' speech in syllabics, he distinguished it from the shorter, rhymed and metered lines spoken by the rest of the seminar, signaling its greater authority and strangeness; yet at the same time, by using verse rather than prose for the bats, he avoided giving the impression that their speech belonged to another order of language, and that he was presenting it without editorial intervention. As the séances progressed that June, Merrill had added punctuation marks to the Ouija board, making it a somewhat more conventional writing machine, better able to communicate tones of voice. That increase in subtlety showed in 741's newly acquired "manners" and the development of his wit and sociability. And when the elements spoke in their grave, ceremonial way, it ignited Merrill's formal and symbolic imagination. That séance, he noted, could be treated in "stanzas rhyming 5," the verse form he had used long ago in "The Peacock." The elements suggested to him a Balanchine-like dance of temperaments: "Earth: gravity   Water: buoyancy humility   Air: hilarity   Fire: passionate intensity   Nature: verity."

The séances were interrupted in July when Jackson checked into Massachusetts General Hospital in Boston for surgery on two "rectal fistulas" that had bothered him for years. He and Jimmy were anxious about the surgery, but the Ouija board reassured them: Maria promised to visit the patient while he was under anesthesia. When the time came, because he was a heavy smoker, David's doctors made do with a local anesthetic; "and so he was wheeled upstairs from the recovery room still numb from the waist down but quite touchingly conscious, wide-eyed + serious like a child one has awakened after midnight and carried outdoors to see the stars." On the lookout for any way the spirits might be in contact with them now, Merrill recorded his and Jackson's "hospital dreams." He had approached the surgery as if it would be a brush with death, giving his partner and him a glimpse of the beyond. But soon David was his grouchy old un-mystical self: "furious at the prospect of four days on jello [. . .]; ringing for service; switching channels; calling long distance" and complaining about the lack of a view—until Elizabeth Bishop, who was living in Boston and came to visit, silenced him by noting that she'd spent her twelfth birthday in the same hospital in a room overlooking the Boston Casket Company.

Over the summer, Merrill and Jackson had had guests and seen Stonington friends, but most of the time they were living in the Other World. Only when the noise of a Fourth of July parade reached them from Water Street, for a moment calling them away from the Ouija board to the window, did they remember that this was the summer of the national bicentennial. The dictées made it difficult, Merrill told Moffett, "to pick up the pen for any other purpose." He wrote few letters during this period, and those mentioned little of what preoccupied him. Jackson, meanwhile, grew weary and "withdrawn." On August 1, Merrill recorded one of their conversations, easing the exchange into rhyme and meter for future use:

> Last night DJ complaining without bitterness:
> It's leaving me so withdrawn
> I haven't been / swimming once. I said I'd go
> to Eleanor's garden, + paint or just sit.
> I don't resent it. I look forward to it
> —+ yet it leaves me all the rest of the time
> half-asleep, fit only to watch TV.
> If this is how we are now, at 50 + 53 . . .!
> It can't be right to be so out of life.
>
> We talk about Papageno, [Sam Gamgee?],
> I promise him: we'll be released. Of course

the experience will have made a change—
but it is not a lasting spell.
They will unbind us, they will wish us well.

Suggesting that Jackson take heart from Mozart's Papageno and Tolkien's Sam Gamgee, thick-headed mortals caught up in a quest but safely released in the end, Merrill remained convinced of the Ouija board's basic benevolence. Yet he too must have felt trapped in the world of their imagining on Water Street—where red-eyed bats peered back at them night and day from the carpet and the walls, and the great mirror in the sitting room, like a closed-circuit camera, showed them to the dead whenever they passed it.

By August, 741 had grown sufficiently familiar and compliant to accept a name JM proposed for him: Mirabell. Like a ward to his benefactor, or a character in a novel to his author, Mirabell commented, "IT QUITE SUITS THE PERSON U HAVE MADE OF ME." The name came from Congreve's *Way of the World*—the Restoration comedy Merrill had read aloud with Bobby Isaacson in Rome twenty-five years before, each relishing the freedom to express in public his inner fop. It was a pregnant choice: the name's Latin roots suggested a beautiful vision; it was close to "miracle," "mirror," "mirage," and "Merrill." "I have so many M's already," JM sighs in *Mirabell's Books of Number*. To which Mirabell, thinking of the arc of the alphabet on the Ouija board, replies:

> INDEED & NOT ACCIDENTALLY M IS AT ONCE OUR
> METHOD & THE MIDPOINT OF OUR ALPHABET THE SUMMIT
> OF OUR RAINBOW ROOF IN TIMBRE THE MILD MERIDIAN
> BLUE OF MUSE & MUSING & MUSIC THE HIGH HUM OF MIND

Mirabell's séances came to an end on August 21, when he was replaced by a sublime new speaker with another "M" name: Michael, the Archangel, guardian of light. As represented in *Mirabell*, Michael speaks in grave, lineated prose, with Homer in his ear, celebrating "THE DEEP DEMANDING IMPULSE TO LIFE":

> FROM THE WINEDARK SEA OF SPACE THE INCARNATIONS OF LIFE LEADING
>   TO THE LIFE OF MAN BEGAN
> PLANET AFTER PLANET ROSE IN THE LIGHT, BORE ITS LIFE, AND VANISHED
> AND YET THE RICH WOMB OF THE SUN FOUND A NEW EGG AND VISITED LIFE
>   UPON IT.

The séances that would form the basis for *Scripts for the Pageant* began at this point. Michael promised to introduce the seminar to his three brothers, each associated, like Michael, with one of the elements: the July séance with the elements had been a dry run for what was coming next. But those introductions would have to wait until JM and DJ were reunited over the winter. Putting a limit on the "lunacy" of the summer, Merrill had always had in view an end to Mirabell's séances: Jackson's scheduled return to Athens on September 13. David left as planned, while Jimmy stayed on in Stonington to "write another masterpiece, ho-hum."

The preface, section o of *Mirabell's Books of Number*, was complete in August 1976; it describes Hubbell's wallpaper, the Jacksons' deaths, JM's and DJ's séances with them and Ephraim, their first contact with the bats, and the trip to Avebury. Then Merrill started in on the summer's lessons, pushing forward systematically, "single-mindedly," and at high speed. By September 24, he had "close to 800 lines." "That would have been nearly ¼ of Ephraim, but is less than ⅛ of the sequel." The long lines he was writing for Mirabell seemed "too often turned out as by a practice knitter counting stitches, and make for a rather forbidding looking page," full of blaring capitals. With respect to the transcripts, he was confounded by "the impossibility of paraphrase; no compression." And the lessons themselves remained resistantly alien: "God knows it isn't a subject I would have chosen." He felt himself merely the spirits' Scribe and no longer a poet, or no longer the poet he had been. As he worked with the transcribed dictations, he was

> sucked back into the orbit of preexisting fantasies, legends, all unverifiable (by me)—No ground under my feet
>
>> into a mysterious magnetic field
>> nothing is I
>> I who had wanted to retain the private life
>> am now a vehicle in some cosmic car pool

"This poem isn't mine," he complained to Yenser. Yet the language he was working with was also uncannily personal, a communication spoken by voices that only he and Jackson could hear, and that was another problem:

> Face in mirror:
> The face is mine, but one that no one else sees.
> Nor do I see it except on these occasions.

Voices of Ouija:
Our own voices, which no one else can hear.
Nor do we hear them, except on these occasions.

There were breaks in the regimen of composition. He traveled north to Claude in Pawlet and Charles and Mary in Hancock and south to a pair of new friends in Virginia: Harry Pemberton and Jim Boatwright. For company on Water Street, he had Peter Tourville, who, more than ten years further on from Jimmy and David's "Teenage Club," was married and the father of six children. With a job at the velvet mill and a cottage on the Rhode Island shore, he was often around for (Jimmy confided in David) "food + wine + Scrabble + a joint, very domestic, followed by a rather satisfactory snuggle. Quite what one enjoys"—although his financial support of Tourville "cost a few dollars." Tourville was a type of man who attracted Merrill by, it would seem, the very starkness of his difference. That fall, he prompted a tender erotic poem, "Peter's Tattoos," one of Merrill's few extra–Ouija board efforts from this period. Jimmy speaks of him in his letters as good-natured and in need of his sympathy. He wrote to David, "I've been very touched by his affection + (perverse as it sounds) his need of me: to the point where it must be something I must have needed." "I see him," he reflected, "as a sandbag essential to my balloon."

Looking for another sort of ballast, Merrill studied theoretical physics. In his notebook he quotes from Niels Bohr: "Isolated material particles are abstractions, their properties being definable + observable only through their interaction w. other systems. An elementary particle is, in essence, a set of relationships that reach outward to other things—." Could this be a way to understand the union of souls in the Ouija seminar? Bohr's theory of complementarity, developed from the fact that light can be analyzed either as wave or particle depending on the observer's point of view, resonated with Merrill, who in *Mirabell* raises his taste for paradox and reversible truths to a principled cosmic dualism. Poetry and science, he felt, converge in this double vision, compounded for him in equal parts from Bohr and Elizabeth Bishop: "[T]he ability to see both ways at once isn't merely an idiosyncrasy but corresponds to how the world needs to be seen: cheerful *and* awful, opaque *and* transparent. The plus and minus of a vast, evolving formula." Or as he affirms in *Mirabell*, sounding in this case more like Oscar Wilde: "[A]nything worth having's had both ways."

In addition to Bohr, Merrill was studying the "theory of process" in *The Reflexive Universe*, a work of New Age thought by Arthur M. Young. He was fascinated by Young's account of the nature of light—a crucial word in his own poetry. Light "has <u>no charge</u>," Merrill writes in his notebook, "is without mass, yet creates protons + electrons which form atoms = matter." The notion suggested a myth of creation: "Light was the first kingdom + First Cause. Matter is a precipitate (condensation) of light. The Fall: a descent into Matter: light loses a degree of Freedom in order to achieve permanence." Light never rests, Merrill notes, but remains in a state of "constant velocity"; the photon is "a pulse of light," "a quantum of action"; and (an idea that appealed to the miniaturist in him) "energy increases as size (wavelength) is reduced. This last opposite to world of matter."

Young draws on quantum mechanics, number theory, Jungian archetypes, theosophy, and yoga, in an attempt to reconcile science and esoteric wisdom: "The universe, far from being a desert of inert particles, is a theatre of increasingly complex organization, a stage for development in which man has a definite place, without any upper limit to his evolution." As Young's theater metaphor and his vision of human potential suggest, *The Reflexive Universe* shares many ideas and attitudes with *Mirabell* and *Sandover* as a whole. It appeared in August 1976 (the same year that Young published *The Geometry of Meaning*, which Merrill also owned a copy of, although he read it less carefully, to judge from the annotation and marks of use). If it weren't for the book's publication date, and the fact that Merrill's notes on it were made in September, *The Reflexive Universe* would seem like the source for much of what Mirabell had dictated back in June. They converge not only in general attitude but in details such as Young's mystical investment in the number 5 ("five points are required to store energy [. . .], so that the connection of fiveness with growth is profound") and his account of the evolutionary emergence of "fifth stage" men and women of "genius." It may be that Young's book merely confirmed what the Ouija board was telling Merrill, as so much else seemed to. Perhaps he and Young had tuned into the same cosmic radio station? But even if it didn't feed the séances out of which *Mirabell* was created, *The Reflexive Universe* guided Merrill as he converted the transcripts into poetry.

He had little scientific context in which to evaluate Young's ideas. He hadn't thought seriously about science of any sort since college, and there were few scientists in his unusually wide acquaintance. An exception was George Cotzias, a physician and medical researcher who played an important role in the development of the L-DOPA treatment for Parkinson's disease. Merrill met him in 1973 through his sister Doris, who, Jimmy suspected, was in love with the doctor. In his fifties, Cotzias was a big man, hearty and Greek. Born into an influential family (his father was the mayor of Athens in the 1930s), he had come to the U.S. as a refugee during World

War II. He trained at Harvard Medical School, then worked at Brookhaven National Laboratory using a particle accelerator to study trace metals in blood and tissue, which led to his L-DOPA breakthrough. Cotzias's Greek heritage and burly charm, combined with his record of scientific discovery and his practical knowledge of cell research, not to mention Doris's romantic feelings for him, made him an intensely interesting figure for Merrill. They met only a few times, but promised each other they would have a serious talk some day. Now that conversation seemed more urgent: Cotzias was in treatment for advanced lung cancer. A chance to converse came in December when Jimmy went to dinner with Cotzias and his friend Lewis Thomas. Thomas was the popular author of *The Lives of a Cell: Notes of a Biology Watcher* (1974), one of the science books for the general reader that Merrill had read in preparation for *Mirabell*. If any scientist could have appreciated the "V work" conducted in the R Lab of the Ouija board, it would have been Thomas, who writes in *Lives of a Cell*, "We pass thoughts around, from mind to mind, so compulsively and with such speed that the brains of mankind often appear, functionally, to be undergoing fusion." But Merrill was in awe of the "2 great men" and found himself tongue-tied that night. A version of the occasion, minus Thomas and fictionalized, would end up in *Scripts for the Pageant*.

At New Year's, Jimmy returned to Greece and David for three weeks. Reunited, the mediums continued their séances—about which Merrill was silent in letters, except to say to Claude that he and DJ had "been presented to 2 more great angels—those of sea and earth," and the experience was "Thrilling." So was the progress of composition. In his notebook, he recorded a dream: "An old man shows me how to construct a bauxite fireplace for a very powerful blaze. I watch, have an erection, I am almost on fire myself." By the first week of February, he had typed fair copies of the first four sections of *Mirabell*, carrying the story of the séances "through the visitation of the elements." He gave his pages on Mirabell's transformation to Claude, who designed *Metamorphosis of 741* as an austere chapbook—a white cover with the title (and no author's name) in the upper left corner in a small font, as if in tribute to the priority of poetry over images as expounded by the peacock. Fredericks printed 440 copies, many of which Merrill gave to friends. At the same time, he sent the first section of *Mirabell* to Daryl Hine, who printed it in *Poetry*. It was a very public announcement of a strange long poem not yet half complete.

That spring, Merrill took *Divine Comedies* and, more cautiously, bits of *Mirabell* on tour, learning how to read aloud his voices from the Other World to audiences in San Francisco, Los Angeles, Syracuse, Chicago, Kalamazoo, and New York. Then, in April, he won the Pulitzer Prize for *Divine Comedies*. Two newspapers came to interview him on Water Street, and five others called, "plus about 30 calls from real people." He received a congratulatory message from " 'My' congressman??? And a little boy from Norwich who 'writes poetry too, but doesn't get much time off from the Scouts.' " For the time being, Merrill was a celebrity ("The grocer blushed when he proffered his hand"), and he basked in it—as he had been unable to do in the past when major awards left him blocked and burdened. Dismayed only that his Ouija partner wasn't there to share the honor, Jimmy told David that "the book couldn't have been dreamed of without you." He felt truly "marvelous, as if yet more mysterious energy had been transferred?!" And—"as a result?" he mused—"the new poem [. . .] positively BLAZES ahead." *Mirabell* was "over ⅔ done"; he had completed "80 pages since last August." By the first week of May 1977, he was back in Greece and back at the board, conducting the séances that would go into *Scripts* while he wrote the final sections of *Mirabell*.

Merrill organized this poem "beyond the alphabet" according to the special language Mirabell spoke, number, the quantitative language of science. He arranged it into sections beginning at 0 and ascending through 9. He then broke each section into numbered parts: 0, 0.1, 0.2, and so on through 0.9, when section 1 began; subsequent sections were structured the same way. The design made use of the numerals he had introduced on the Ouija board, 0–9, as *The Book of Ephraim* had used the letters on the board A–Z. It suggested a systematic progress in the lessons that was not apparent in the meandering transcripts themselves (which were ordered in Merrill's notebook simply by the dates they took place). Certain numbers were significant. "THE 3," Mirabell explains, "IT IS THE NUMBER OF GOD B: DIMENSIONS OF / THE GREENHOUSE: SIDE OF YR PYRAMID." (Merrill's birthday was the third day of the third month—something neither he nor the spirits mentioned.) The number 5 was linked with "V work," the union of earth, air, fire, water, and nature, the five members of the seminar, and the five master souls. But the import of other numbers was a mystery. Why was the measure of mankind 10 or that of the bats 14? Even Mirabell threw up his hands: "I CANNOT NOW / SAY WHY WHEN WE PLANND STRUCTURES 14 POLES ROSE WHEN WE BRED / 14 SEEMD NORMAL." So the fourteen-syllable lines into which Merrill put their speech seemed normal too.

But the fundamental opacity of numbers was itself significant. It is *Mirabell*'s metaphor for the abstract, nonverbal patterns ("formulas") underlying all of life—which poetry, as "the art of numbers," embodies without being able to translate into words. Like those bats in the wallpaper, Merrill saw his meters and stanzas not as mere incidental decoration but as emblems of cosmic order. He had always treated verse forms as "given arrangements"; they were passed down across cultures by obscure sonneteers and haiku masters, craftsmen focused on problems of scale and design, rather than the direct expression of "strong feelings" that Louis Simpson required of a poem. Prosody, like narrative and generic patterns, seemed to contain a collective, quasi-genetic intelligence, encoding biological structures. It was something Merrill saw in all manner of crafted abstract pattern. Now his sinuous poetic numbers would be put to work in a poem of science. Rather than distracting from the message, his prosody was part of it. He'd found a framework in which "[t]he essential gaudiness of poetry" (that touchstone phrase from Stevens) could be indulged and celebrated—"The inessential suddenly felt as essence."

Merrill's speed of composition was made possible by his use of séance transcripts as the basis for the poem. And yet, even while he complained that the poem in progress wasn't his, he never simply reproduced spirit dictation. He turned the garbled, telegraphic Ouija prose into *much* briefer, much more lucid verse. As he did, he treated the transcripts as any writer would treat a draft. He dropped inessential references and loose ends, cut sentences that seemed awkward, redundant, or irrelevant, and reordered other ones, while framing what the board said with his own lowercase comments addressed variously to the spirits, DJ, and his readers. Like an editor, he made emendations in support of clarity and sense, while other changes served different purposes. While he eliminated odd or confusing spellings, for example, Merrill introduced others that are curious or archaic: "FORCD," "WORSHIPT," "UNIVERSALL," "MYND," and "WOORDS" appear in the poem, but the same words were spelled in the conventional way in the transcript. He combined séances, or moved sentences from one séance to another.

As opposed to Hugo and Yeats, "Doters on women, who then went ahead / To doctor everything their voices said," Merrill represents JM and DJ as "docile takers-in of seed," compliant before the spirits' messages: "No matter what tall tale our friends emit, / Lately—you've noticed?—we just swallow it." Yet Merrill also "doctored" what his voices said, in some way, at almost every point. Fidelity to his instructors' intentions, as he understood it, never required verbatim quotation. Certain changes were made very late in the composition process. As Mark Bauer shows in his study of the drafts of *Mirabell*, the spirits refer to the supreme authority in the universe as "C/O/P," or the "center of power," even in the advanced typescripts

Merrill circulated among friends like Corn and McClatchy. The acronym "C/O/P" fit with the Other World's interest in power and protocol, its structure as a "bureaucracy," and its frequent use of "censorship." But "C/O/P" would have colored Merrill's cosmos darkly. Merrill replaced "C/O/P" with "S/O/L," short for the "source of light," in effect substituting Jolly Old Sol for The Cop. The change better suited his deliberate levity and what might be called his religion of light. It also reached back to "A Tenancy" in *Water Street*, where he bargains with "the source of light," and in that way made the point that his poetry was in the service of "S/O/L" long before *Mirabell*.

Moving from transcript to poem, Merrill reassigned some words of the spirits to JM or DJ and vice versa. For example, when WHA suggests in *Mirabell* that the giant bats who glow like stoves and go by "BEEZELBOB" could be called "THE BOBS THE FURNACE MEN," he makes a link to section "Z" of *The Book of Ephraim*, where JM and DJ wondered what would come next from the Other World while they waited for Bob, "the furnace man," to fix the oil burner on Water Street. The remark makes an apparently trivial, chance element in *Ephraim* appear, from the vantage of *Mirabell*, ordained and uncanny. But here Merrill has given to WHA a remark that he himself made during a séance. Transferring it to WHA, he makes the emerging trilogy seem to cohere according to a plan external to it and evident to Auden, not just to Merrill himself.

But of course Merrill had shaped the design of the séances to begin with, and not simply the version of them he created in the poem. When WHA asks to join the séance, JM welcomes the idea, but only provisionally: "Oh please! You'd raise the level / Enormously—of course it's up to Them." To which the board responds, "NOT AT ALL IT SHALL BE ORDERED AS THE SCRIBE DESIRES." That sentence doesn't appear in Merrill's transcripts: so confident was he of having the permission, he felt no qualm about phrasing it himself and assigning it to 741. The interpolation of that sentence crystallizes something that goes on throughout the long poem: a curious circuit of authority whereby Merrill submits to powers of his own creation, who in turn grant him permission to shape the séances and the poem as he likes. In this light, the "doctoring" he did wasn't a belated modification of a sacred record, distinct from an earlier moment of unmediated inspiration. It was continuous with what he'd been doing all along as he coaxed the spirits into meaningful speech. In his séances with Mirabell, as opposed to his séances over the years with Ephraim, Merrill was always writing a poem. At the same time, however, and for the first time in his career, he was writing a poem in the role of Scribe. His authority had been delegated to him on the condition that he would communicate a message faithfully; and his changes to the transcripts refined and clarified, rather than altered, what the spirits said.

Arguably, all the spirits in *Mirabell* are Merrill's alter egos, but none is closer to the poet in JM than the spirit of Auden—which may explain why Merrill was more ready to tamper with his words than the bats'. Merrill's WHA was a daring ingredient to add to the poem. Readers had to suspend disbelief not merely because a bat-peacock was speaking, but because a great poet recently deceased, whose living voice was still in many people's ears, was producing new poetry from beyond the grave. Yet there he is, addressed familiarly as Wystan, discoursing at length about soul densities and UFOs as he helps JM to absorb the spirits' bizarre lessons and decide how to craft his poem. Merrill had good literary precedent for using a "senior poet" in this way: the spirit of Auden plays for JM the role of otherworldly guide that Virgil plays for Dante. There's hubris in that. But even as Merrill invites the comparison to Dante, WHA's silliness ("GIVEN THE CHANCE WD I NOT EAT A PEACH!") makes the poem's relationship to Dante feel more like parody than emulation, while having the additionally irreverent effect of mocking the Christian piety and moral seriousness of the later Auden's public persona. Despite the recanting he does, however, Auden remains for Merrill the influential poetic thinker he was in life; and he is a tutelary presence in the poem every bit as essential as Mirabell, even if it's an Auden Merrill has created for his own not-always-Audenesque aims. The critic Aidan Wasley describes the interchange concisely: "Auden teaches Merrill, and Merrill constructs Auden teaching him, so that the relation between inheritor and influence goes—like so much else in the poem—both ways."

Poetic influence is an important and quite explicit concern in *Mirabell*. At a dinner in 1977 before a reading by Elizabeth Bishop at Yale, Harold Bloom teased Merrill about his use of Auden and Stevens in the trilogy: writing lines for these dead masters and incorporating them in his own work amounted, Bloom said, to an "outrageous, tactless presumption—unprecedented in the history of poetry"; in response to which, Bloom recalls, the poet "smiled broadly, evidently very pleased." Merrill had gotten to know Bloom, a Yale professor, through his friend John Hollander, who had returned to Yale after a decade teaching at Hunter College in New York. Bloom had a big, mournful, expressive face—drooping eyelids and thick lips—that made him look like a Gnostic seer from the Bronx. He was a charismatic teacher whose prodigious memory for literature gave one the impression he had the whole of English poetic tradition somewhere inside him. He'd been "a stubborn holdout" when it came to Merrill. Unlike Yeats and Blake (about whom he had written books), Bloom thought Merrill "too fine an artist to accept ultimate risks." But *Divine Comedies* had "converted" him "absolutely." In November 1976, he wrote in the *New Republic*, "I don't know that *The Book of Ephraim* can be over-praised, as nothing since the greatest writers of our century equals it in daemonic force." If Merrill continued in this vein, Bloom prophesied, he would become "the strangest, the most unnerving of all this country's great poets."

Merrill was in the midst of writing *Mirabell* when Bloom's comments appeared. Although he never mentions them explicitly, Bloom's ideas affected what he was doing in the long poem, particularly with respect to Auden's ghost. Bloom's controversial treatise, *The Anxiety of Influence: A Theory of Poetry*, was published (and praised by Hollander in *The New York Times Book Review*) in 1973, around the time Merrill began work on *The Book of Ephraim*. *The Anxiety of Influence* holds that the meaning of every poem is "another poem" which the poet aggressively "misreads" in order to deny a precursor poet's priority and secure his own place in tradition, defending him against death and oblivion. The theory foregrounds male rivalry; it sees tradition as a series of quasi-Oedipal battles between later and earlier poets fought by means of largely unconscious rhetorical strategies. The "outrageous, tactless presumption" that Merrill had shown in putting words into Auden's mouth was an extreme version of such a strategy. In particular, it was a literalization of the "revisionary ratio" that Bloom calls "apophrades" or "the return of the dead" by which "strong" poets from the past speak through the "quasi-willing mediumship of other strong poets." In his Ouija board poems, Merrill was producing a disarmingly literal and self-conscious demonstration of Bloom's theory.

Or he was producing a counter-theory to Bloom's. Auden, the technician, stood for a model of creativity in which Anglo-Saxon alliterative verse, music hall ballad, romantic lyric, Shakespeare, and verse essay and epistle were part of a collectively produced verbal tradition in which poets were semi-anonymous clerks in service to the language. Identifying with Auden, Merrill endorsed his conception of poetic tradition against Bloom's praise of originality. Part of what Merrill wanted to assert was a matter of tone. For all of the cheek involved in putting Auden in the poem, JM's dealings with WHA are playful, touchingly sentimental at times, and collaborative, far from the winner-take-all contest described in *The Anxiety of Influence*. There is a sexual dimension, moreover, to this difference in sensibility. It's easy to see JM's relationship with WHA as a gay model of poetic affiliation presented as an alternative to Bloom's story of father-son combat. Near the end of *Mirabell*, when WHA chides JM for complaining that the poem isn't his own ("maddening—it's all by someone else!"), he is also talking back to Bloom:

YR SCRUPLES DEAR BOY ARE INCONSEQUENT

IF I MAY SAY SO   CAN U STILL BE BENT

AFTER OUR COURSE IN HOW TO SEE PAST LONE
AUTONOMY TO POWERS BEHIND THE THRONE,
ON DOING YR OWN THING: EACH TEENY BIT
MADE PERSONAL (PARDON MME) AS SHIT?
GRANTED THAT IN 1ST CHILDHOOD WE WERE NOT
PRAISED ENOUGH FOR GETTING OFF THE POT
IT'S TIME TO DO SO NOW   THINK WHAT A MINOR
PART THE SELF PLAYS IN A WORK OF ART
COMPARED TO THOSE GREAT GIVENS THE ROSEBRICK MANOR
ALL TOPIARY FORMS & METRICAL MOAT
RIPPLING UNSOUNDED! FROM ANTHOLOGIZED
PERENNIALS TO HERB GARDEN OF CLICHES
FROM LATIN-LABELED HYBRIDS TO THE FAWN
4 LETTER FUNGI THAT ENRICH THE LAWN,
IS NOT ARCADIA TO DWELL AMONG
GREENWOOD PERSPECTIVES OF THE MOTHER TONGUE
ROOTSYSTEMS UNDERFOOT WHILE OVERHEAD
THE SUN GOD SANG & SHADES OF MEANING SPREAD
& FAR SNOWCAPPED ABSTRACTIONS GLITTERED NEAR
OR FAIRLY MELTED INTO ATMOSPHERE?
AS FOR THE FAMILY ITSELF MY DEAR
JUST GAPE UP AT THAT CORONETED FRIEZE:
SWEET WILLIAMS & FATE-FLAVORED EMILIES
THE DOUBTING THOMAS & THE DULCET ONE
(HARDY MY BOY WHO ELSE? & CAMPION)
MILTON & DRYDEN OUR LONG JOHNS   IN SHORT
IN BED AT PRAYERS AT MUSIC FLUSHED WITH PORT
THE DULL THE PRODIGAL THE MEAN THE MAD
IT WAS THE GREATEST PRIVILEGE TO HAVE HAD
A BARE LOWCEILINGED MAID'S ROOM AT THE TOP

At once lyrical, didactic, and polemical, cleverly rhymed and intensely witty, this speech is one of the high points of *Mirabell*. It introduces the image of "THE ROSEBRICK MANOR" that later in the trilogy will be called "Sandover," the otherworldly site for the séances in *Scripts for the Pageant*. Here it is an image of literary tradition seen as a great house and gardens, harmoniously joining nature and culture. Constructed over time by the poets who have used "THE MOTHER TONGUE" in many genres, it belongs to all and none of them.

Does it undercut or confirm WHA's argument for the essentially selfless, communal nature of poetic creation that this passage wasn't in fact by "someone else" but by Merrill himself? In this instance, Merrill went so far in "doctoring" his transcripts that he simply invented one. As he mentioned in an interview in 1990, it's a case—the "showiest" but not the only—in which "I presume to pass 'my own words' off as a message from the other world. It came welling up from me one afternoon, instead of from the Board. I never again felt so 'possessed.' " The ideas had come from Auden to begin with; why not give them back to him, especially when the point was they belonged to no one? Yet, if only years later, Merrill couldn't resist claiming credit for these lines himself.

In his ventriloquized aria on "THE ROSEBRICK MANOR," Merrill expands on a theme central to *Mirabell*. "MANS TERMITE PALACE BEEHIVE ANTHILL PYRAMID JM / IS LANGUAGE," the board says early in the poem. Language is reason, the essential instrument of mind, "THE LIFE RAFT" and "ARK": in the face of the apocalyptic threat of nuclear war, this is the humanistic credo of *Mirabell*, the basis of the faith the spirits have in JM, and a defense of poetry's role in civilization. The alphabet, spread in a rainbow arc on the Ouija board, is the human covenant with the divine. At the same time, this consoling, universal humanism comes with a disturbing elitism. "STIR THE THINKERS," the board tells JM, "& DETER THE REST." The eugenic and Malthusian themes of the transcripts enter as the passage continues:

> KILLING IS RIFE   ALAS YOU SAY   FINE
> SAY WE   THIN OUT THE JOSTLERS FOR SELFREALIZATION
> THE FALSE PARADISE   ONLY SPARE THE GREENHOUSE   ITS PRECIOUS
> NUCLEUS OF MINDS   THE SINGLE CONTEST IS THE ATOM

Beyond the grounds of "THE ROSEBRICK MANOR," where reason and light rule, all is a jungle. "THE GREENHOUSE" is the earth, nature, and biology, and thus common property. But what matters to its survival is "ITS PRECIOUS / NUCLEUS OF MINDS," a phrase evoking a high-level think tank like the R Lab or the seminar itself. Language is "THE LIFE RAFT," but not everyone, apparently, will be saved by it.

DJ and Maria both complain about "THE INFLEXIBLE ELITISM" of the Other World. JM protests too, but he seems more embarrassed than offended by this aspect of the lessons, as if it were an unpleasantness that came with the territory. And so it was: as Timothy Materer has noted, elitism is a feature of apocalyptic texts which feature esoteric knowledge, from the Book of Revelation to Yeats's *A Vision*, and *Mirabell* belongs to that genre, among others. In Merrill's case, the elitism inherent in the esoteric genre is compounded oddly by the seminar's cliquish *mondanité*. JM, DJ, WHA, and MM comprise a self-approving *petit noyau* like that of Madame Verdurin in Proust. But that elitism is a matter of style more than of doctrine, and it implies no sympathy with, in Louis Simpson's words, "the owners of expensive automobiles." To the contrary rather: this is the compensatory elitism of the poet and the cultured intellectual in a society which values neither one very highly. It's also the snobbery of a gay man trying to convert a style of life commonly seen as sinful, self-centered, or simply alien, into a sign of his spiritual superiority. Importantly, the credential that JM, DJ, MM, and WHA share for the seminar, besides their off-the-charts talent ratings, is a recurrent theme in Merrill's work: their childlessness. This state turns both Mamman and the trio of gay men "OUTWARD TO THE LESSONS & THE MYSTERIES."

The "MYSTERIES" of *Mirabell* are rooted in the daily domestic life of the mediums, and Merrill gave his partner an even larger role in *Mirabell* than he had in *Ephraim*. David Jackson is present throughout this poem, as central to its story as James Merrill. He is indeed so important and vivid a character, it's easy to forget that he is, at least in part, *a character*. Some of this is a matter of minor fictional touches. The name of his father in the poem is "Matt," not George; and Merrill inflates his talent by reporting that DJ played the Grieg piano concerto as a twelve-year-old and that he "took Composition with / Big-timers like Schoenberg and Hindemith" (this is the made-up c.v. that Alison Lurie repeats as fact in her memoir *Familiar Spirits*). DJ undergoes surgery in *Mirabell*, just as David did during summer 1976, but for a hernia, not for the "rectal fistula" David suffered from. The larger point is that DJ, like Papageno or Sam Gamgee, has the role of the hero's side-kick in a romance quest—good-willed, open-hearted, simple in spirit. He is the "the Hand" who represents "Nature" in contrast to JM, "the Scribe" who represents "Mind" (and who is no less of an invention of course). DJ's feeling heart makes him both prone to fear and suited to be the intuitive channel through whom the spirits speak.

Yet he is by no means merely a literary character. David's expanded presence in *Mirabell* brings a new humanity into Merrill's poetry, balancing the deep strangeness of the Other World. The poem's opening foregrounds his care for his failing parents and his struggle to accept their deaths: his grief, anger, and love come across in lived detail, as do Merrill's tolerance and affection for the senior Jacksons, his longtime in-laws. These are the first notes *Mirabell* strikes. The poem describes David's fears in advance of surgery and his dazed, boyish wonder as he emerged from the procedure, quietly expressing Jimmy's own relief and his dependence on David. The depth of their intimacy, finally, is conveyed simply and powerfully by the sheer duration of *Mirabell*, which page after page affirms the endurance of their life together, day after day. Is there another poem of similar length, apart from *Paradise Lost*, which is so focused on a domestic couple, let alone two men? When he reviewed the poem in 1979, Thom Gunn called it "the most convincing description of a gay marriage I know."

Gay Liberation was the necessary condition for this convincing description of "a gay marriage." Whatever else it might be, *Mirabell* is a document from the post-Stonewall era in the struggle for gay rights. To locate the poem in its historical moment: it was completed in October 1977 during the final weeks of Harvey Milk's campaign to become the first openly gay man elected to public office in California. It's doubtful that Merrill cared about Milk's campaign, if he noticed it in the midst of his fevered work, but he didn't have to in order to feel the heady possibility of being fully "out" for the first time in his life: the same social forces that led to Milk's election to the Board of Supervisors in San Francisco enabled the sexual openness of *Mirabell*. That openness is notable even by comparison with *Ephraim*. When Merrill jokes about himself and Jackson as "docile takers-in of seed," he's being perfectly frank about their sexual preferences and practices, and he knew that some readers, but especially his mother, would choke on the joke.

The openness of *Mirabell* has less to do with gay sex, however, than with gay talk. The language of the bats is so weird and arresting, we might overlook another stylistic innovation in the poem: the explosion in verse of the camp idiom Merrill used with gay friends like Tony Parigory. Camp had been a poetic resource for Merrill for years. But he'd never before given such free rein to languor, gossip, and hilarity, and this in the context of his most elevated, manifestly serious work. The long poem begins by turning the solemn conventions of epic beginning inside out: "Oh very well, then. Let us broach the matter / Of the new wallpaper in Stonington." Putting interior decoration in the first lines of the poem in a breezy parody of the fey homosexual's supposedly trivial concerns, Merrill honors another gay male writer by subtle allusion to the opening of E. M. Forster's *Howard's End* ("One may as well begin with Helen's letters to her sister"). The epic drama of *Mirabell* begins in a gay couple's parlor, where the serious is felt as frivolous and only the frivolous can be taken seriously—the first rule of camp.

The poem's camp idiom is especially associated with the outrageous and loquacious Chester Kallman. JM and DJ first converse with CK when he takes hold of the cup after David's mother has said farewell. This kaleido-scopic poem continually plays one rhetorical mode off another; in this case, Merrill uses camp to temper simple sentimentality. The mediums briefly mistake CK for Mary:

> SWEETIES YOU'VE JUST SPOILED YR MOTHERS DAY
> Mama? Mary . . . *Chester!* IF U SAY SO
> What Stage are you at? DONT ASK ME   NOBODY
> TELLS ME ANYTHING   But you've had eight
> Whole months—since last December—to find out.
> Have you a representative? A WHAT
> Come off it! What does your patron say? MY WHO
> Well, in that case, what on—what do you *do*?
> READ   BUFF MY NAILS DO CROSSWORDS JUST LIKE LIFE
> THOSE YEARS WITH WYSTAN   ONCE A BACKSTREET WIFE
> ALWAYS A BACK Stop this! STREET Chester! WIFE

Part of the turning of the tables on Auden that Merrill is doing in the poem comes in letting WHA's "back street wife" speak up about their rather unhappy domestic arrangements. In *Mirabell*, CK typically bitches and moans in this bored, petulant manner—in which Merrill is so fluent he can take the part of the straight man in that rhyming duet without missing a beat. Despite its comedy, however, CK's camp is strongly colored by resent-ment and self-loathing.

CK highlights a central moral problem in the poem: the threat of wasted talent and, connected to it, gay self-hatred. CK, a modern-day Tom Rakewell, is condemned for squandering his creative potential; it is a fate Merrill daily saw the cost of in David and (without much basis) feared succumbing to himself. JM tries to boost his dead friend's self-esteem, reminding Chester that Auden admired him, and that *The Rake's Progress* wouldn't have come into being without his contribution:

> Plus what you meant to your friends: the funniest,
> Brightest, kindest—must I go on? LET ME
> & THE MOST WASTEFUL   GIFTS THE MUSES MADE
> TOO OFTEN BOUGHT A HUMPY PIECE OF TRADE
> ENTIRE NEGLECTED SECTIONS OF MY MIND
> SOUND ROTTEN WHEN I RAP   THERES LIGHT BEHIND
> BUT STRENGTH I NEVER HAD IS NEEDED TO
> BREAK DOWN THE PARTITIONS   WYSTAN CRASHES THRU

WITH GLAD CRIES   THE SHEER WONDER IN HIS FACE
DIMS & DIMINISHES MY LITTLE SPACE
My dear . . . & AS FOR INNOCENCE IT HAS
A GENIUS FOR GETTING LOST I FEAR

Lost innocence, the anguish of wasted gifts: these motifs from *The Rake's Progress* echo throughout *Mirabell*. The poem defends against that fate by means of its monumental scale and its extravagant literary ambition. It also preaches the work ethic of which it is a product. Again and again, the spirits emphasize that it is "work," not play, in which the mediums are engaged, while the university and the office, the work-worlds that Merrill rejected in favor of his life on Water Street, appear in the metaphors of the Ouija "seminar" and the Other World's "bureaucracy"—the return of the repressed. In *The Book of Ephraim*, their familiar taught JM and DJ to "USE USE USE / YR BODIES & YR MINDS." The spirits in *Mirabell* repeat the theme: "IN HEAVEN NOT TO BE USED IS HELL." The demand for usefulness and the related aversion to waste ramify. They are expressed in the poem's environmental consciousness and in its concept of divinity, as stated by Michael: "GOD IS THE ACCUMULATED INTELLIGENCE IN CELLS SINCE THE DEATH OF THE FIRST DISTANT CELL." Because, in this cosmos, death is merely a stage in the vast recycling process that is reincarnation, only waste is truly to be feared.

The return in *Mirabell* of motifs from Merrill's earlier work represents another sort of recycling. The "S/O/L" and "the Bobs, the furnace men" are two examples, and there are many more. Merrill wanted to make his diverse body of work, composed over three decades, cohere in a long poem for which what he had written before could be seen as preparation and prefiguration. His career was in the hands of the spirits, who had had their designs on JM, they explained, since they first spoke to him and DJ in 1953 as "Cabel Stone," the "COMPOSITE VOICE (ITS FORMULA BASED ON YR OWN) / IN THAT IST YEAR OF YR LOVE." The love affairs and deaths recounted in Merrill's "CHRONICLES OF LOVE & LOSS" could now be recognized as part of the plan, and his lyrics (like Dante's and Milton's) seen as preparation for the epic work. Thus Strato was sent "TO TEST EXALT & HUMBLE U," and Hans's life was "CUT OFF" and his "UNRESOLVED V WORK GIVEN TO U" because JM was better suited to carry it to fruition: "U WERE NOT ACCIDENTALLY FRIENDS."

As explained by Mirabell, Merrill's life and art illustrated the doctrine of "NO ACCIDENT" which governs life on earth. "IT IS A BASIC PRECEPT U WILL HAVE TO TAKE ON FAITH," Mirabell advises, explaining that God B had allowed chance to rule the world until the catastrophe of Akhenaton's crystal pyramid (a story from the transcripts that Merrill transferred to the poem almost verbatim), at which point God B took matters in his own hands through the R Lab. When they first hear of the doctrine, JM and DJ bridle:

> DJ: Not so fast there! JM: Whoa!
> We'll take a chance on Chance, with Jacques Monod,
> Sooner than fly into this theologian-
> Shriveling flame of a phrase.

Yet Merrill only added those lines late in the composition process, penciling them into the margin of his typescript of the poem. They dramatize a feeling that was not his first reaction, because the "NO ACCIDENT" doctrine points to a dream in which he had a deep need to believe: that everything that happens is motivated, designed, and therefore meaningful, like the elements that cohere in a well-made work of art, especially when they cohere without the pressure of the artist's conscious intention. That was the magic of the anagram, puns, and the Ouija board itself. "NO ACCIDENT" was the necessary corollary to the promise that "ALL WILL BE USED" in God B's paradise. It was a way of imagining a world in which nothing would ever be lost.

But the poem also works against the determinism that "NO ACCIDENT" implies. If accident wasn't possible, and feeling wasn't as strong a force as reason (or stronger?), there would be no danger of either a wasted life or wasted planet to counter. In *Mirabell*, as in *Paradise Lost*, the choice is humanity's. And the structure of the poem is hardly a matter of "NO ACCIDENT." Merrill may have dreamed of a poem in which everything would fit. But his efforts to stitch up the poem's stray motifs only emphasize their arbitrariness. Take the revelation that the spirits spoke to JM and DJ in the "COMPOSITE VOICE" of Cabel Stone. Mirabell explains that the name is a pun: it refers to the cables that tethered the bats' crust world to the earth, at which sites the stone circles of Stonehenge and Avebury now stand. Cabel Stone was the spirits' version of the bats' cables and the early Britons' stones—the stone cable that first linked JM and DJ to the heavens. But to bring out this elaborate idea and its implication that JM's and DJ's adventures in the spirit world were planned, Merrill had to change the name of the voice that spoke to him and Jackson during that séance in 1953: Kabel Barns.

Instead of making everything fit, Merrill created a poem that fit everything in, whether or not it makes sense. He had begun his career writing polished, perfect, compact lyric poems, under the control of a single, well-mannered speaker. In *Mirabell*, he produced an altogether different thing: a huge, polyvocal poem of uncertain genre, sometimes willfully boring and discontinuous, but sublime in its challenge to the reader. Back in June 1976, as he received murky intelligence about UFOs, Atlantis, and the centaurs, Merrill feared his material would make him a laughingstock. He put that fear into the poem, protesting when WHA says that he finds it all "VERY VERY BEAUTIFUL":

> Dear Wystan, VERY BEAUTIFUL all this
> Warmed-up Milton, Dante, Genesis?
> This great tradition that has come to grief
> In volumes by Blavatsky and Gurdjieff?

Yet even as "the whole / Horror of Popthink fastens on the soul, / Harder to scrape off than bubblegum," Merrill chose to let in plenty of it. If it has affinities with Milton, Dante, and Genesis, *Mirabell* also has affinities with Madame Blavatsky, supermarket tabloids, *Star Trek*, and comic books. As he set to work on the transcripts in 1976, Merrill reflected bravely, "[E]sthetic theorists tell us that any subject can be handled." The wager was that his art could transfigure the flotsam and jetsam thrown up by the Ouija board. Which it did. But the exchange also worked the other way around: Merrill's strange new subject matter transfigured his art. Following the wandering path of the transcripts, he made a poem open to continual redirection and revision, a syncretic, evolving compound of mass culture fantasy, high-culture allusion, mythology, and popular science. And his technique was as multiform as his subject matter: he deployed an anthology of verse forms, literary modes, and competing dictions, from slang to the sacred. However elitist its vision of humanity may be, *Mirabell*'s thorough impurity of form makes it something else again. The result is a work—call it baroque or postmodern—in which it was possible for Merrill to say just about anything.

Readers expecting the epic architecture of Milton or Dante could only be dissatisfied. Merrill anticipates that reaction by including, late in the poem, a conversation with Robert Morse, who responds to a draft of *Mirabell* over cocktails. Robert speaks in Dantean *terza rima*, with his trademark punning and "E F BENSON BABYTALK":

> "Ah, lads, it's taxed

> My venerable beads. Me giddy fwom
> Uppercut of too much upper case.
> (A weak one, if you please. Most kind. Yum-yum.)

Everything in Dante knew its place.
In this guidebook of yours, how do you tell
Up from down? Is Heaven's interface

What your new friends tactfully don't call Hell?
Splendid as metaphor. The real no-no
Is jargon, falling back on terms that smell

Just a touch fishy when the tide is low:
'Molecular structures'—cup and hand—obey
'Electric waves'? Don't *dream* of saying so!"

The complaint assigned here to Robert had come from Irma Brandeis, the
Danteist, when she read the typescript. It would be picked up by unsympa-
thetic critics of *Sandover*, like Denis Donoghue, who quipped that Robert
Morse "should have been taken more seriously when he told JM what was
wrong with *Mirabell*." The core of the objection is that the generic impurity
of *Mirabell*, in which it is hard to "tell / Up from down," reflects a moral
relativism in which scientific terms are reduced to tropes and fact to fable—
"FACT IS IS IS FABLE," WHA declares—making inadequate substitutes for the
theology that structured Dante's vision.

But *Mirabell* is not primarily a moral poem. Rather than good and evil,
with a vertical hierarchy determining what's "up and down," it describes a
contest between life and death.* It is closer to Freud's theory of the drives
than to Dante's Christianity. Its central image of the death drive is nuclear
war, expressing man's capacity to destroy his world (JM and the spirits pun
on "atom" as a way to speak of the first man, Adam). Mirabell connects this
apocalyptic threat to the bats' catastrophic will to dominate nature, which
ripped open "black holes" in the universe. The soul-destroying X rays to
which Maria submitted as treatment for her illness are another image of
this negativity, a primal counterforce to God B. The elements speak of it as
antimatter: "THE MATTER WHICH IS NOT WAS EVER OURS / TO GUARD AGAINST.
[. . .] BLACK / HANDS TESTING THE GREENHOUSE PANE BY PANE. [. . .] WE PRESS
BACK."

The power of *Mirabell* comes from its contact with those "BLACK HANDS."
They press on Merrill's and Jackson's own through the uncanny mecha-
nism of the Ouija board. When Frank Bidart heard the bat voices for the first

---

* Timothy Materer makes this argument in *James Merrill's Apocalypse* (Cornell University
Press, 2000), 101–08.

time, it seemed to him that "Merrill had let in the static of the universe." Those voices announced a break with the lyric imagination that governs even *The Book of Ephraim*. It was a shift in scale to the cosmic and a shift in poetic mode to the mythological. In *Scripts for the Pageant*, Merrill would go on generating human meaning from the "static of the universe," staging a debate between the forces of death and life. Because the séances behind *Scripts* began while he was just setting out to compose *Mirabell*, Merrill had that debate in view throughout his work on the poem. The opening speech, in effect, comes at the end of *Mirabell* when Archangel Michael takes hold of the cup to expound "THE DEEP DEMANDING IMPULSE OF LIFE":

> THE GENIUS OF THE LIVING CELL IS ITS TIE TO THE REGENERATIVE HEAT &
>   LIGHT OF THE SUN
> AND SO AS YOU FACE THIS SETTING SUN YOU FACE YOUR ANCESTOR, AND THE
>   SUN LOOKS THROUGH YOUR EYES TO THE LIFE BEHIND YOU.

In the final sonnet of "The Broken Home," Merrill returns to the Orchard, where, in his mind's eye, a little boy and his father's dog, Michael, "roam the corridors still"; and he watches "a red setter stretch and sink in cloud." Curiously, this séance repeats that scene, but transmutes it, when Michael, the Archangel, commands the mediums: "LOOK! LOOK INTO THE RED EYE OF YOUR GOD!" And as commanded, Merrill and Jackson swivel to the west-facing windows in the dining room on Water Street, where the fat August sun is setting on the other side of the harbor, beyond Mystic. Merrill wanted to feel, and wanted us to feel, that not only his poetry, but his whole life, had led to this.

15

SANDOVER

1977–82

M errill spent the long hot summer of 1977 in a state of euphoria. In Athens, he divided the day between his rooftop study, where he continued work on *Mirabell*, and the first-floor foyer, where he and DJ set up the Ouija board. Back in January, the Archangel Michael had introduced them to his younger brothers, the twins Emmanuel and Raphael, also known as Elias and Elijah, masters of water and earth respectively. Now he introduced them to Gabriel, the "shy brother," "the angel of Death." The seminar had evolved into a "riveting" "grad course" organized in three "terms" of lessons, due to wind up in September. The angels came and went, speaking their parts on the invisible stage of the Other World as if according to the stately rhythms of a cosmic dance. Shakespearean romance and Renaissance court masque were the literature from which they seemed to take their cues. (JM supposed from his lofty style that Michael had read no poetry more recent than George Chapman, the sixteenth-century English translator of Homer.) The angels were debating the fate of humanity, but Merrill seems never really to have worried how it would come out. Nor did he worry about how to transform these séances into the third installment of his trilogy, *Scripts for the Pageant*, as he had in the case of *Mirabell*. This, "the Summer of the Angels," was "pure bliss."

It might have been stained by grief. As foreseen, George Cotzias died of lung cancer in June, while that same week, without warning, Robert Morse also died. "The dear man had been in S'ton, then one evening felt dreadful, returned alone to Bedford. Eleanor phoned him there [. . .]: Robert, what are you doing all alone in that cavernous house? R: Watching my favorite program—'As the Stomach Turns.' His last reported words." He had gall bladder surgery the next day, liver cancer was discovered, and he died shortly afterward. Jimmy had "grown strangely close" to Cotzias, and Robert had been his intimate friend for a full twenty years. Their deaths were "shattering"—and then again, they were not. Robert and George (whom the spirits referred to as GK, using the Greek "K" for Cotzias) were transported instantly into the Other World and "<u>snapped up</u> into our concluding seminars." The addition of a bona fide scientist promised to deepen the long poem's treatment of "the atomic theme," while Robert, introducing a fantastic new story line, reported on preparations for his next life as "a very great composer." All of this could be incorporated in volume three of the work, while mention of each man's failing health would be slipped into *Mirabell*, so that the reader could "look forward" to their passing and reappearance on the other side. Their deaths may not have been engineered on high for the benefit of his poetry, as the spirits intimated, but Merrill's Ouija board and the poetic fiction it generated were able to absorb the dead swiftly, almost painlessly. In *Scripts*, Merrill refers to "The buffeting of losses which we see / At once, no matter how reluctantly, // As gains. Gains to the work. Ill-gotten gains." Later that summer, he wrote a letter of condolence to a friend after the death of her mother. He spoke of how, over time, our deceased loved ones "surface" again in us: "they <u>become</u> us, so that in fact it is, sooner or later, impossible to say that we have 'lost' them." The Ouija board sped up this process, all but skipping that stage where the pain of mortal loss had to be acknowledged and felt.

But it would be wrong to say that Merrill used the Ouija board to ignore death. To the contrary, the board allowed him to meditate on mortality at exquisite length. During their séances with Mirabell, JM and DJ had learned that Maria's soul had been destroyed in the final year of her life, pulverized by the radiation she received for cancer. Because she was "no longer human!" she couldn't be reborn; instead, she would return to nature, joining plant life, and JM and DJ would have to let go of her at the end of their séances with the angels. By the bent logic of the board, Maria's return to life represented a death with which they had to come to terms. They consoled themselves that Auden's soul at least was "intact." They assumed he would stay "in the Bureaucracy— / Right, Wystan? Getting mined for all you're worth / By fresh-faced, big-thumbed scholars here on Earth." But that was not the case: WHA too would soon be going "BACK TO THE GLABROUS CLAYS / THE OILS & METALS MY FIRST LOVES COME AUTUMN / A FAIRY PAIR WILL FLIT FORTH HAND IN HAND: / MM INTO THE GREEN, I INTO SAND." WHA's death had been soul destroying too, like Maria's:

> MY DEMISE A FORM OF LEAD
> POISONING: I WENT OFF TO MY ROOM
> TIDDLY THAT NIGHT BUT HAD IN MIND TO SCRIBBLE
> A NOTE TO C, & AS I'D DONE SINCE CHILDHOOD
> SUCKED ON A PENCIL THINKING. NEXT I KNEW,
> AN ICY SUN SHONE IN UPON THE DEAD
> WEIGHT OF MY FEATHER QUILT

DJ protests that "They don't *use* lead" for pencils. "LET THE FACT REMAIN / (OR FABLE!)," WHA replies, "THAT I SIPPED IT GRAIN BY GRAIN. / [. . .] WE MAKE OUR DEATHS MY DEARS." This pronouncement is another version of the "NO ACCIDENT" clause. As in *Mirabell*, JM first groans in response to it ("Ah, it's grim"), then gladly takes up the theme: "Yet what to ask / Of death but that it come wearing a mask / We've seen before; to die of complications / Invited by the way we live. [. . .] It's random death we dread."

The necessary intertwining of death and life is represented in *Scripts* by Gabriel. This menacing angel is perhaps a surprising addition to the cast of spirits, given Merrill's temperamental preference for light and lightness. But Gabriel came along with the romance mythology that Merrill was exploring in the trilogy—the same narrative conventions that generated Darth Vader, lord of the Dark Side in George Lucas's *Star Wars* films, the first installment of which was released in May 1977, soon after JM and DJ met Gabriel. His foil in *Scripts* is the magisterial Michael, whose duty is to tend the sun in all "ITS WORKINGS, ITS SHINING & ITS DIMMING, ITS TERRIBLE & ITS FRUITFUL ASPECTS." The twins of water and earth, playful as cubs, defer to Michael and do his bidding, while the "FIRSTBORN" Gabriel sulks and snarls. The first time he speaks, he gives the mediums a scare: "I AM YOUR BLOOD, YOUR LIFE, AND YES / (Pause, then a volley of cold fire) YOUR DEATH." He dwells both in the human bloodstream and in God as a fearful extension of His being ("AS SENIOR SON I AM THE SHADOW OF MY FATHER"). When God B destroyed the centaurs, he needed Gabriel: "HE STRUCK A SPARK FROM A ROCK & I APPEARED, A TREMBLING FLAME. / 'BE NOT SO SHY. I NEED YOUR HELP, FOR IT IS BEYOND MY SCHEME TO UNDO WHAT IS DONE, / YET DESTROY THEM.' " Gabriel "ROSE, A SKY OF BURSTING ATOMS." His task thereafter would be, in God B's words, "TO SHOULDER THIS BURDEN, THIS OTHER SIDE OF MY V WORK." So it's

Gabriel who must be appeased in order for humanity to survive. WHA drops to his knees and petitions all the angels ("o SPARE, SPARE OUR WORLD!"), but MM singles out Gabriel ("SLAYER, I ADDRESS YOU") to accuse him of taking her life. He did take her life, we learn, but at her request: when the pain was overwhelming in her illness, Maria chose to die. It shocks DJ, but not JM, when they hear of it.

In addition to his brother angels, Michael also introduced JM and DJ to "the Five," the immortals known as Akhenaton, Homer, Montezuma, Nefertiti, and Plato. There would be no more numbers, no more bats in these elevated séances, only figures illustrious and legendary (although Mirabell, meek and fumbling for words, continued to make an occasional appearance). Each lesson lifted the seminar "to a plane of greater / Power and light." In late May it was the twenty-fifth anniversary of JM's and DJ's first meeting in 1953 (at least "as any Greek / would count" the years: "we're all one year old at birth"). To celebrate their union, WHA instructed JM and DJ to bring to the Ouija board certain props to stimulate the senses: "SALT. A SPICE OF YR OWN CHOICE. / A SCENT. ICE IN A BOWL. A CANDLE LIT / & A LIVE FLOWER." In the version of this ritual in *Scripts*, JM puts his favorite opera on the turntable, "ROSENKAVALIER / SIDE ONE." Like a charm, the soaring music calls forth from the board the composer Strauss, then Homer, then JM's northern vocal idols Flagstad and Schwarzkopf; and one by one the Five speak. After they depart, Wystan comments on the sheer arbitrariness of all that transpired: "TO EACH EPIPHANY / ITS OWN: FLAGSTAD & STRAUSS WDN'T AT ALL / DO FOR A BUTTERED SHAMAN FROM NEPAL." Archangel Michael is on hand to welcome the group to "THIS OUR TOPMOST STAGE." The spirits' five senses are restored here, as Ephraim said they would be at Stage 9; and they tremble to touch the human mediums through the mirror—in effect, "A STYX OF QUICKSILVER DIVIDING THEM / FROM LIFE-INFECTED DJ & JM." Michael concludes the little holiday with a rhyming couplet ("TOUCH, TASTE, SMELL, HEAR & SEE, / NOW COMPOSE A SILENT HARMONY"), and orders the mediums to "CLAP ONCE!" They do, taking their hands off the cup and dispersing the company at the same time.

This ceremony prepared JM and DJ for the culmination of the first series of lessons: an audience with God B. As that séance is narrated in *Scripts*, the Ouija board, like a "galactic radio," tunes in to God's frequency, while the seminar listens in. The divine voice registers at first as a ten-syllable line made up simply of the lyric apostrophe, like a blank poetic formula: "o o o o o o o o o o." Next, forming words, the pattern is filled in by a fragment from God's song as it cycles through variations in an ongoing loop. He calls to his sons, the brother angels, asserting his and their survival:

IVE BROTHERS HEAR ME BROTHERS SIGNAL ME
ALONE IN MY NIGHT BROTHERS DO YOU WELL
I AND MINE HOLD IT BACK BROTHERS I AND
MINE SURVIVE BROTHERS HEAR ME SIGNAL ME
DO YOU WELL I AND MINE HOLD IT BACK I
ALONE IN MY NIGHT BROTHERS I AND MINE
SURVIVE BROTHERS DO YOU WELL I ALONE
IN MY NIGHT I HOLD IT BACK I AND MINE
SURVIVE BROTHERS SIGNAL ME IN MY NIGHT
I AND MINE HOLD IT BACK AND WE SURVIVE

Afterward, Wystan and Maria couldn't at first be reached: they'd fallen "PRONE & COLD." And what about the mediums? What did they feel as they received this message from the creator? Merrill made no reference to it in his notebook, and he was cool and collected by the time he mentioned the séance to Robin: "The first of 3 terms with the angels is behind us—ending wonderfully but also rather upsettingly with God Himself alone in space singing like a humpbacked whale. I felt as though a narrative convention had been violated, but am not, mind you, complaining."

Maintaining his composure was crucial to Merrill in his dealings with the Other World. As a reminder of what losing it might mean, there was Daryl Hine. This old friend had recently plunged into full-fledged mania; he had "seen God in a parking lot," "taken off his clothes + and been arrested." Hine received treatment and recovered, but he resigned as editor of *Poetry* a short time later. The line between inspiration and insanity could be very thin. When he heard the details of it, Merrill noted that Daryl's "vision tallies with Dante's," and for that matter with "what I've been merely told, never experienced . . . And I guess I'm lucky." High as he was half the time, between taking dictation from the angels and turning last year's transcripts into *Mirabell*, Jimmy held fast to routine. In between work and "Weejies," there was afternoon swimming with David or a dinner with Tony and Nelly. Later, David would slip out to a hotel bar, returning with "this or that 'marvelous number' who seldom, however, gets asked back." Cavorting with Athenian ephebes had become less plausible for these fifty-something Americans. Jimmy was content with "old faithful (+ never sexier)" Manos Karastefanís, whose "vast + luxurious Tae Kwon Do Academy"—a venture Merrill bankrolled—"has in two months attracted perhaps five students. [. . .] As soon as several thousand more dollars have been spent on advertising, he'll be turning the crowds away!" Comedies like this one kept the Ouija board's craziness safely at bay.

In their break from "school" after the first ten lessons, JM and DJ took off to Samos, a green, mountainous island nearly touching Turkey in the eastern Aegean. Here they found a harbor full of fancy yachts and wealthy Danes, and a "huge air-conditioned hotel built smack on the pretty empty beach we'd remembered." Pythagoras was born on the island, and JM and DJ reached him at once on the board. Philosopher that he was, "P" suggested that they ignore the upstart hotel: "NEVER BE / COWED BY THE UPS & DOWNS OF MASONRY." This world and the Other one were overlaid now in a kind of continuous double vision for Merrill. When he and Jackson crossed the channel to the "bleached boneyard" of Ephesus on the Turkish coast, one of the religious centers of the ancient world, the spirits came with them. WHA and MM could see (and afterward they reported) what was invisible to the two mortal tourists: "STREETS SWARMED WITH GHOSTS / BAZAARS COVERED PALANQUINS CRIES OF VENDORS / A YOUNG BEAUTY SCREAMING WITH LAUGHTER RAN / OUT OF THE BATHS ON TRAJAN'S AVENUE / IT WAS A FEAST DAY U CHOSE WELL [. . .] THRU / WHAT WAS REALITY FOR US YOU 2 / CD BE SEEN PEERING AT THE SKELETON / LIKE MED STUDENTS." Or perhaps Merrill was seeing, dreamily, some of the reality they saw. Absorbed in the past as he walked about the ruins, he took a bad tumble and had to limp home (he'd fallen, the spirits explained, where he'd been expecting a marble step that was no longer there). For Merrill, in contrast to Dr. Johnson, who kicked a rock to refute Bishop Berkeley's idealism, this bruise was one more proof of the existence of the metaphysical.

Back in Athens, the lessons proceeded as scheduled. George Cotzias discussed the dread "thinning process" with Gabriel, while Robert Morse furnished comic relief. This involved lisping baby talk and horseplay with a sidekick: a fey, sweet-natured, hornless unicorn of uncertain gender called Unice, or Uni for short, a survivor of the primeval pastoral race of centaurs, who doted on his human friend "Mr. Robert." Though he was as strange in his way as any speaker on the Ouija board, Uni made the spirit world considerably sillier, more comfy, like a hand puppet or a stuffed animal. What harm could come from the spirits with Uni around?

In addition to this peculiar childlike creature, there now emerged a new august parental presence: Nature, God B's twin, variously known as Chaos, Psyche, and Queen Mum. The ultimate mother figure, she was cut to Merrill's liking: "a brisk, radiant figure full of sense and wit"—the Marschallin and the Duchesse de Guermantes rolled into one, then raised to the highest power. After a year and a half of heavy traffic with the spirits, what the séances added up to was becoming clearer to JM: "The way I see the entire poem now [. . .] is as a kind of map of the imagination. (It's a plausible way of looking at Dante, for that matter—or even 'The Waste Land.') The effects, allowing for the day-by-day soap opera format, are coming to be curiously Shakespearian"—by which he meant the alternation between on one hand exalted presences like the angels or wise men like Mohammed and Jesus, and on the other "<u>our</u> low comedy," the gossip and shenanigans of the mediums and their spirit intimates.

In the ongoing debate about the fate of humanity, Mother Nature's entrance promised to tip the scales. The question was whether, since her son, mankind, had turned against her by abusing the planet, she would turn against him. In his notebook, Merrill reasoned, "These are the great constants. Earth air sea / It's why we have to go. We've threatened them." Yet, as the talks progressed, a festive atmosphere took hold. The mood reached a climax in the next-to-last lesson in a masque-cum-picnic hosted by Mother Nature. As background music for this séance, she told JM to put the brothel scene from *The Rake's Progress* on the turntable. This is the episode in which Mother Goose, the madam, takes Tom to bed, and he sings his mournful air praising "Love, too frequently betrayed." In *Scripts*, Nature explains her choice to the opera's librettist, Wystan:

> NOW WHY DID I CHOOSE
> TO PLAY MOTHER GOOSE?
> FOR MAN MY HERO IS A RAKE!
> YES SENIOR POET, YOU SAW THAT & MORE:
> SAW NATURE AS HIS PASSION AND TOO OFT HIS WHORE.

WHA makes the leap to the apocalyptic theme of *Scripts* by way of a certifiably bad pun: Tom Rakewell is a symbol of "OUR THREATENED A T O M." Yet Nature, like Mother Goose, is pleased with her darling, and not about to give up on him. At the end of the picnic, with Robert prancing about on Uni's back, she exclaims, "LET ME CRY A LAST RESOUNDING YES / TO MAN, MAN IN HIS BLESSEDNESS!" True, as WHA notes, Nature "SETS MEANING SPINNING LIKE A COIN," and that "LAST RESOUNDING YES" could turn out to be the last good word man will hear. It takes Auden's quibble, however, to keep that particular coin spinning. Confirming the sense of blessing, Michael ends the séance by drawing a rainbow across the stage and calling his brothers away.

Thus, in early August, the angels withdrew, "like their counterparts in Wagner," beyond the covenantal sign. While these séances took place, Merrill had been finishing *Mirabell*. Now he began reading it to the dead: "Gertrude Stein, Alice Toklas (who provides the 'refreshments'), Wallace

Stevens, Yeats, along with Maria + Auden + Hans + Maya + Marius." The spirits suggested revisions ("too few, I fear"), but mainly they assured the Scribe "that the whole thing is a marvel, while I shake my head and protest that ¾ of it was done for me." Then JM and DJ repaired to Venice to celebrate their vision with David Kalstone. For Peggy Guggenheim's seventy-ninth birthday party, Jimmy and friends were conveyed across the Grand Canal in her gondola—which filled with water. The spirits had an explanation: "DON'T TELL MS G BUT WE SANK IT E V E R Y B O D Y CLIMBED IN!" They returned to Athens for a last ceremony, timed for David's fifty-fifth birthday on September 16. Late in the lessons it was revealed that Maria had all along been "one of the Five," immortal Plato in drag; s/he was slated now for rebirth in Bombay as a boy with mystical powers, rather than reborn in the plant world. The mediums would be losing contact with her just the same, however, and they had to steel themselves. Up on the roof, they kneeled on cushions as if in church. They took out a mirror bordered with seashells; shattered it with a marble wedge (Merrill calls it a "stylus," a pen); put the shards in a bowl of water and poured them, tinkling, into the base of a golden flowering cassia tree—the jagged reflectors turned faceup to catch the late afternoon sky of Athens. The séances were over.

Throughout the summer, Merrill recognized that the Other World had kept flattering him suspiciously. "I wish the prevailing tone didn't spare us so much," he admitted, aware that the spirits had tested him very little this time around. Still, he'd been powerless to resist their charms, and his credulity had been rewarded. "Looking back," he mused, "what an experience! One could have been the Son of Sam"—the psychotic serial killer who terrorized New York City that summer; "instead, it was a long, safe, blessed journey." But hadn't it all been a dream? Wasn't it all too good to be true?

His first and sufficient criterion of judgment was beauty. When Irma expressed skepticism about his map of the Other World from her Dantean perspective, Merrill replied with no more reasoned defense than his own delight: "[I]t all strikes me as more beautiful than anything I could have arrived at alone." Beauty was subjective, something to be proved on the pulse. But it had an objective quality too: being "more beautiful" than anything he could have produced by himself, it had to be heaven-sent. To Robin, he said, "Now that my resistance is no longer needed to give substance to the transcript," as it had been in *Mirabell*, "I find I believe it all." Like his first response to Ephraim, when he told his mother that "I believe it utterly," this profession of belief would be tempered over time. But the ground note of his feeling—his wonder at the beauty of the vision he and David had shared—lingered. When the trilogy was complete in 1979, Helen

Vendler asked him in an interview, "[H]ow real does it all seem to you?" Merrill sighed: "Literally, not very—except in recurrent euphoric hours when it's altogether too beautiful not to be true." It's an answer that Oscar Wilde would have appreciated, and like Wilde's best remarks, it's not merely witty. At the end of Keats's "Ode on a Grecian Urn," the beautiful artwork instructs us:

> "Beauty is truth, truth beauty,—that is all
> Ye know on earth, and all ye need to know."

From the earthly perspective of the urn, the ideal is true if it is beautiful: that's the only test that can or need be applied; and it is the test of poetry, of art. Belief, for Keats as for Wallace Stevens, comes down to the willing suspension of disbelief—the submission to a fiction; and in that attitude, fundamental to the appreciation of art, James Merrill was deeply practiced.

He returned to the U.S. in October. His Water Street apartment had been occupied in his absence by Alfred Corn and Sandy McClatchy, who had become a couple. They moved from Water Street into Sandy's faculty apartment at Yale, an hour's drive from Stonington, and Merrill saw them often. He must have felt like the matchmaker in this union of two of his most devoted younger friends, who'd met at a party he gave in New York. He himself had never had a poet as a partner, and he didn't conceal his misgivings in this case, hinting, in letters to each of them, at the potential for friction that he saw in such a pairing. His friendship with Sandy was highly personal, based on shared confidences, dinner parties, and opera fandom. His dealings with Alfred had at least to begin with a more professional cast: the latter sent his work to Jimmy for comment and asked questions about the older poet's work in return. Merrill identified with both men, but he tended to give McClatchy advice about life and Corn, the more established poet at this point in time, advice about his career. When Corn was discouraged by the reviews of *A Call in the Midst of the Crowd*, his second book, Merrill spoke on the basis of his own experience: "You're right about the stage you've reached, and the bewilderment you feel at not being made <u>more</u> of. It's exactly what I felt in 1960. Later, when you've gone on to even better things, you'll be grateful that people didn't carry you around on their shoulders." The question of how much Corn's work resembled his was the issue in some readers' eyes, and it troubled Alfred. Merrill brushed away the worry: "Oh, we're of the same 'family' but one doesn't shave one's head just because one's older brother has the same lovely yellow hair—and going gray at that."

With angels at his beck and call, and sanction from authorities at Harvard and Yale (Vendler and Bloom, not to mention young votaries like McClatchy and Corn), Merrill was becoming something of a cult figure. Besides esoteric inspiration and academic capital, he stood out for his grace and charm, his skill as a performer, and (that rare thing in the poetry world) his personal wealth, which was part of his aura too, whether or not anyone spoke of it. He put all these qualities on show in fall 1977 in readings in Chicago ("followed by a sumptuous reception for the Very Rich, $100 a head," for the benefit of *Poetry*), at the Morgan Library (this was a black-tie event introduced by Kalstone with three hundred in the audience), at Yale, and at Harvard in "a large hall jammed with people: standing in the aisles, sitting propped up against the stage!"

The buzz of public events like these made a contrast with the intensive silent hours he spent at his desk. He was typing *Mirabell*. It was "more or less done," although he wouldn't send it off to Atheneum until March. "Somehow I haven't had time to write a short book; it is over 6000 lines I fear." He'd begun *Ephraim* with an urgent sense of time running out, and he was not about to slow down now. By January, when he returned to Stonington from Christmas in Palm Beach with his mother, he'd drafted the first third of *Scripts*. He divided this installment of the trilogy into three sections corresponding to the three "terms" of lessons. Having used the alphabet for *Ephraim* and numbers for *Mirabell*, he chose the Ouija board's "YES," ampersand, and "NO," in that order, to title his three sections. The three-part format foregrounded again the technology of the board, the plaything that was the premise of revelation, as well as the cosmic dualism, the balancing of scales, that was his main theme.

He didn't have the title of the trilogy yet, but he had the name "Sandover." It hadn't come from the board; it was entirely his own invention. He used it to refer to the "ROSEBRICK MANOR" that Auden speaks of in *Mirabell* as a metaphor for the mother tongue and literary tradition. The manor house's "schoolroom, once the nursery," is the site in the Other World where the lessons in *Scripts* take place. Merrill explains the name as a corruption of the French "Saintefleur" and the Italian "Santofior," as if the house belonged to the English branch of a proud European family. Those romance-language "flowers" connect the name to the sacred rose in Dante, while the English version hints at the end of the world: "Sandover" suggests sand-over-all or an hourglass in which the sand has run out. In lines added very late to *Mirabell*, Merrill writes, if "Dante saw / The Rose in fullest bloom" and

"Blake saw it sick," JM and DJ see its "bleak / Unpetalled knob"—a symbol for Nature wasted by humankind.

Merrill's description of the schoolroom in *Scripts* (he credits Wystan and Maria with supplying the visual details) is lovingly elaborate. The imagined room is overlaid with the earthly room in Athens where the mediums sit: "Real and Ideal" are rhyming doubles for each other on either side of the mirror. Merrill sets the scene with italics, notes in roman type where the séances "really" take place, then goes back to the Other World in italics (this typographical play was encouraged by the magic powers of his IBM Selectric):

> *Blackboard wall, a dais, little desks*
> *Rorschach'd with dull stains among naively*
> *Gouged initials—MM, WHA,*
> *And others. Star-map, globe and microscope.*
> *A comfy air of things once used and used.*
> *However, (since this room is both itself*
> *And, with the sly economy of dream,*
> *An entrance hall in Athens* (Yes, we're back
> Downstairs. It's cooler here. A frosted-glass
> Door opens from the white-hot street. Inside,
> *Our* things: pictures, dining table, walls
> Painted this year to match the terracotta,
> Almost life-sized lady Tony rescued
> From a doomed balustrade downtown; who now,
> Apple in hand for Teacher, graces a corner;
> Under whose smiling supervision sit
> Two human figures growing used to it))
> *Real and Ideal study* much as we
> —Good luck to them! *compatibility.*

Throughout *Scripts*, Merrill was versifying Ouija transcripts. But there was an unscripted imagination at play in tour-de-force fantasy like the passage above and in some superb stand-alone lyric moments. To introduce "&," the middle section of the poem, Merrill composed a canzone in homage to Auden's use of this verse form, which Auden had found in Dante. The form employs repeating end words, like a sestina, but with five of them, not six, and even more repetitions. The pattern worked like the Ouija board to do Merrill's writing for him. "Before we went to Samos last June," he told Yenser, "I copied out the scheme from Alan [Ansen]'s Auden, decided on my end-words"—sense, light, land, fire, and water—"then simply let the whole affair incubate or crystallize [. . .] until after Xmas when it 'wrote itself.' " He titled it "Samos," recalling his and DJ's radiant summer days on the island. A celebration of the five senses and the fire pulsing through all things, the canzone was destined to become a showpiece that readers single out for praise, whatever they think of *Sandover* as a whole. And no wonder, since the poem's shimmering image making and formal pyrotechnics cry out for applause. The sixty-five-line poem reveals Merrill working at the height of his poetic confidence, with technique and exuberance to spare.

Meanwhile, the end of the lessons in Athens had left Jackson at loose ends. His collaboration with Merrill on the *Sandover* séances had brought them together after more than a decade of estrangement, giving him a creative purpose after he'd given up the ambition to write novels. But it also placed great demands on him over an extended period, and the strain showed. He was now prone to rages set off by minor annoyances—just as his father, angry George, had been. When Merrill left for the U.S. in November 1977, Jackson left Athens too. Motivated by a bad quarrel with George Lazaretos and the wish to avoid paying an excessive tax on his Citroën, he planned to spend three months in Morocco. "South of Madrid, however, two Spanish ladies in their Citroën crashed headlong into him; he spun round, and was hit by a (luckily slow-moving) truck." David was "stunned" by the crash. His nose was broken, his body bruised, his car totaled, and all of this in a country in which he had no friends and couldn't speak the language.

Eventually he made it to Morocco, where he spent a lonely season. At the end of it, Sewelly joined him, and together they made for Greece; it would be her first visit to the country. Jimmy flew over too for a short visit to spend his fifty-second birthday with the two old marrieds. David ordered a cake for the occasion with the message "Happy Birthday from Mirabell" written on it. They opened the box to discover that in place of the ten candles David requested, someone had provided fourteen—the peacock's special number.

Even in Athens, David noticed, Jimmy was "upstairs at dawn and down at rare intervals from his study." And soon he was back on Water Street, hewing to the same schedule. He rose at five thirty, worked through the morning, ate, took a nap ("[I] lie on my back like a stone crusader and listen to myself snore once, twice, 3 times"), before going back to the desk until it was time for his first drink at eight. He felt "as though something or somebody" had "power over me" and "were on the point of taking advantage. It's not at all that I'm afraid, no, no, but unable to stop, and full of . . . wonder." The sensation was one of "WILD MANIC EUPHORIA." He grew a beard.

Puffing like a factory, he was "up to 30 cigarettes a day—and <u>frantic</u> when anything interrupts my work." But very little did: a reading at the University of Virginia, where he presented "a whole *Mirabell* program"; Easter at Mrs. Plummer's in Atlanta (in church he noticed that "We cry ABBA, Father—like a rhyme scheme"); dinners with aged Grace Stone; and a visit now and then from Peter Tourville "in which we say the same words and play the same game of Scrabble and do the same things in bed until Sunday morning when he hitchhikes back home leaving me with the same head cold" but ready to continue work. Some days he wrote as many as two hundred lines.

Only rarely did doubts creep into his notebook. On April Fool's Day 1978, suspecting that he was succumbing to the sort of literary grandiosity he'd always disdained, he wrote, " 'Only fairies sit down to write masterpieces.' (Hemingway, quoted in Time). a) Not true, alas. b) All too true." In another entry, an irritating conversation from long ago echoed in his mind with fresh, uncanny relevance: "Amherst 1956. My colleague Jonathan Bishop comes with Alison to dine. Over brandy, asks that typical Amherst English Department question. 'Who is your audience? Who do you write for?' I hem + haw. I write for myself—for the happy few. No, being understood is not a first priority. And so forth. 'Aha,' said Jonathan. 'Then you're writing for the angels.' It was late. I said, very well, call it that. 'Be careful. Or only the angels will read you.' "

He read the proofs for *Mirabell* in June while pushing forward on *Scripts*, the end of which was nearing only a year after he began writing this, the longest of the three Ouija board poems. He was already looking past *Scripts* to an edition that would bind the trilogy in one grand book. "What would the New Critics say?" he joked in a letter to De Snodgrass. He knew how much they would disapprove of this poem, with its outsized scale, camp foolery, and wacky New Age religion, and he was congratulating himself on how far he had come from the critical consensus that held sway when he began writing poetry.

Yet even in the 1940s, Merrill had an alternative to the small-scale refinements of the New Critical lyric in Kimon Friar's emphasis on myth, epic, the unconscious, and the occult; now he had written a work drawing on just those sources, the kind of work Kimon had envisioned for him. Looking back on Friar's teaching and his shifting relation to it, Merrill writes in *A Different Person*, "A long poem was the test of any poet's powers. [Friar] cited Dante, Milton, Rilke, Pound. What would their shorter works amount to without the great achievements that crowned them? The notion struck me at twenty—at forty, too, for that matter—as a dangerous form of megalomania, and I wasn't buying any of it. But at fifty? Longer than Dante, dottier than Pound, and full of spirits more talkative than Yeats himself might have wished, the *Sandover* project held me captive. It was Kimon's dream, only I was realizing it in his stead." In a sense, it was Friar, as much as the spirits, who dictated the trilogy. Having avoided Friar since the early 1960s, Jimmy now wrote to his mentor to acknowledge his influence:

> You have been very much in my thoughts these last years, which have seen me at work on something immensely long and demanding and fulfilling—the kind of epic project you will remember urging me to undertake 30-odd years ago. I can't regret resisting as long as I did, the blessing it has brought me; but now that I am blessed by it, now also that the end is in sight, I am free at last to bless you in turn for showing me in countless ways that such a thing wasn't ever out of the question.

Merrill went so far as to praise Friar's translation of Kazantzakis's *Odyssey*—the grand labor Kimon had dedicated to him back in 1958, but which he hadn't deigned to open back then. Friar kept track of the verse forms, meters, and syllable counts in his copy of *Mirabell*, just as he used to do with Jimmy's manuscripts, while making notes on symbols and ideas, as he had when preparing lectures on *A Vision*, *Four Quartets*, and *Notes Toward a Supreme Fiction*. As he did, Friar must have said to himself page by page, with the keenest satisfaction, "I knew he'd come back to me some day."

In July, Merrill returned to Greece, Jackson, and the Ouija board. They picked up more or less where they'd left off in September. MM, WHA, and GK were departed, but there was still Robert Morse and the matter of his rebirth as a great composer to see to. The event "went off almost too smoothly." Jimmy had been fascinated by the notion of engineering a birth by Ouija board since the long-ago failure with Hans's representative. Now, like midwives who play music for the ears of a fetus in utero, the mediums had an inadvertent but crucial role in this queer birth-as-aesthetic-ritual:

> In four days he [Robert] was given, by the appropriate angel, Sight, Taste, Touch and Hearing. The 5th day was smell (in fact the breath of life) from Q[ueen] M[um]. I'd been at the piano at 4:45 playing "K Something," DJ humming along, when he said "It's early but let's sit down." The first words from QM at top speed: POET HAND QUICK QUICK! DIVINO MOZARTINO DID THE TRICK! COME BROTHER, GIVE A SHOVE AND (allegretto) LAUNCH UPON THE WORLD OUR LITTLE LOVE

"All this," Merrill continued, fitting the birth into his evolving scheme for the poem, as described to DK, "is now a very nice solution for me, to work as a coda or epilogue to the whole poem—birth of the marvelous child, the brothers with their gifts [. . .]. Not perhaps part of Vol III"—that would be *Scripts*—"but ending the 1-volume edition" of all three books of the trilogy, still to come.

Enforcing the balancing of things that the spirits insisted on, Robert's rebirth was followed by news of Mimi Vassilikos's sudden death. Vassili called from Rome at 1 a.m.: Mimi had passed away at home in his arms, smiling, as if Puccini had scripted it. "No special forewarning beyond 'vague' pains for the last 2 weeks. She was nearly dead last summer when she finally agreed to a clinic, came out a wraith, murmuring of life as an invalid, heart damage, but of course—as usual, one sees the writing on the wall without reading it." Merrill's imagination went to work on the story at once: "Her last letter (6 weeks ago) described ecstatically a white dress so beautiful and so expensive that she lay awake nights for a week before asking V to buy it for her; now that she had it, where, when, to what could she possibly wear it? V on the phone this morning: 'She's wearing the white dress.' "

Mimi and Vassili had been apart only three nights in twenty years (a fact that Jimmy mentioned several times in letters, no doubt struck by the contrast it made with him and David). Shortly after his wife's death, the bereaved appeared at Athinaion Efivon 44, where the *parea* used to gather (Jimmy and David, Strato and George, Vassili and Mimi) and where he now interrupted JM and DJ reading a draft of *Scripts* aloud to an assembly of the dead, which Mimi herself had just joined. Vassili, haggard in a black shirt he'd worn since the night she died, wanted to enter the spell, not break it:

> The doorbell rings. Our doorbell here in Athens.
> We start up. David opens to a form
> Gaunt, bespectacled, begrimed, in black,
> But black worn days, nights, journeyed, sweated in—
> Vasíli? Ah sweet heaven, sit him down,
> Take his knapsack, offer food and brandy—.
> He shakes his head. Mimí. Mimí in Rome
> Buried near Shelley. He can't eat, can't sleep,
> Can't weep. D makes to put away the Board,
> Explaining with a grimace of pure shame
> —Because, just as this life takes precedence
> Over the next one, so does live despair

Over a poem or a parlor game—
Explaining what our friend has stumbled in on.
Lightly I try to shrug it off, lest he,
Shrewd leftwing susceptible myth-haunted
As only a Greek novelist can be,
Take Mimí's "presence" at our fete amiss,
Or worse, lest anguish take its lover's leap
Into the vortex of credulity
—Vasíli, drink your brandy, get some sleep,
Look, we've these great pills . . . No; he asks instead,
Anything, *anything* to keep his head
Above the sucking waves, merely to listen
A while. So in the hopelessness
Of more directly helping we resume.

This is how Merrill rendered the scene a few weeks later in the epilogue he'd already been planning when Vassili rang the bell. Called "Coda: The Higher Keys," the epilogue is mostly concerned with Robert's rebirth, but it concludes with a séance in which JM is set to begin reading the whole trilogy to the dead—into which strange occasion Vassili stumbles, becoming the last person from Jimmy's life to turn into a character in *Sandover*. "It happened just as the poem describes," Vassili later attested. "When they offered to put the board away, I said, 'No, I want it.' We did it four or five times, and it was fantastical. When I had need, they understood." Merrill told him, " 'I like the way you assume your mourning.' Jimmy was touched by it," that is, touched by the depth and sincerity of the Greek's grief, perhaps because it was something the poet himself could never allow himself to fully feel. And he wanted to get that grief into the trilogy, if only in the very last lines; wanted to include Vassili's black shirt and the claims of reality, which he had so extravagantly and for so long kept at arm's length. The trilogy ends on an intensely poignant note therefore. Merrill addresses the Other World, reading aloud the first word of *Ephraim* (the end of the long poem going back to the start, turning around in a loop) while, in this world, the aging DJ and mourning Vassili silently follow along:

DJ brighteyed (but look how wrinkled) lends
His copy of the score to our poor friend's
Somber regard—captive like Gulliver
Or like the mortal in an elfin court
Pining for wife and cottage on this shore

Beyond whose depthless dazzle he can't see.
For *their* ears I begin: "Admittedly . . ."

These events in Athens and their transformation into verse occurred in
rapid succession as Merrill rode the last waves of the creative tide he'd been
swept up by more than three years before when the bat-angels first began
speaking on the Ouija board. Death also had come in waves: Wystan and
Maria, then Marius, Tony Harwood, and Chester, George and Mary Jackson,
Cotzias and Robert Morse, at last Mimi. Merrill and Jackson had to wonder,
as in a game of musical chairs, who would be next. They spent two weeks
in September at the beach near Chania on Crete, during which Jimmy finished the epilogue—and wrote "The House Fly," a poem that recalls a night
in the 1960s when he lay awake watching a mosquito light on the bare chest
of his Greek lover, who slept on undisturbed. In this poem and in no other,
he records his former beloved's full name, Strato Mouflouzélis. The gesture makes the poem feel like an epitaph, as if Strato too were dead.

With the *Sandover* séances over, it began to seem that life in Greece was
ending for Merrill and Jackson. For a few years now, their letters to the U.S.
from Athens had been full of complaints: the smog, the traffic, the tourists.
Athens wasn't what it once was, neither were they, and it seemed unwise to
grow old there. The end of "Samos" had already sounded a note of farewell:
"We shall be dust of quite another land / Before the seeds here planted"—in
Greece, in the trilogy—"come to light." To the middle section of *Scripts*,
Merrill added a leisurely, detailed description of "The House in Athens,"
documenting its rooms one by one before he took leave of them this time.
For his part, Jackson was determined not to spend another winter alone in
Europe. He would return to the U.S. for "a 5 month stay in which I'm going
to search for an ideal SOUTHERN site to build our Old Age solar home + veg.
garden." The project promised a fresh assignment for this veteran home-
maker. And, if the Ouija board was really over, he needed a new reason to
keep his partner coming back to him.

Merrill returned to New York for the publication of *Mirabell* in November.
One of the first reviews to appear, Phoebe Pettingell's in the *New Leader*,
came to this ringing conclusion:

James Merrill has created a poem as central to our generation as *The
Waste Land* was to the one before us. *Mirabell* holds up a mirror to
our deepest fears: that our actions are impelled, not chosen; that we

cannot assimilate the increasingly complex way in which our world must be viewed; that we have lost religion and morality; that our race is doomed to extinction. But at the same time that it acknowledges this state of affairs, the poem offers numinous reassurance that we can be saved by "the life raft of language"—that beyond our myopic vision gleams a profounder understanding of life than we have yet conceived.

Thom Gunn began his comments in the *San Francisco Review of Books* apologetically: "I feel rather as if I were setting out to review *Ulysses* in 1922." *Mirabell's* ambitions were that large and conspicuous, and the expectations raised by *The Book of Ephraim* that high. "It never occurred to me," Edmund White says, looking back on the adulatory review he wrote, "that it might not be good." Other critics seemed similarly bowled over in advance. Over the next year, more celebration followed in lengthy essays by Vendler, Yenser, and others. Even *Time* gave the poem space. Come April, Merrill would carry home the National Book Award for the second time in twelve years. (He put it in the tiny alcove off the kitchen, where, above Jackson's old writing desk, beside his instructions to housesitters, his prizes had begun to crowd the walls.) The competition included Robert Hayden's *American Journal* and the selected poems of John Hollander and May Swenson, but the outcome wasn't much of a surprise. This year's judges were Elizabeth Bishop, Michael Harper, and Anthony Hecht (only Harper, the junior poet in this trio, wasn't already Jimmy's friend and a past beneficiary of the Ingram Merrill Foundation); and, in any event, Ephraim had promised that this poem would be "a triumph." Jimmy gave the prize money to Hubbell Pierce, creator of the bat wallpaper. "Without you," he wrote to Hub, "how could *Mirabell* have manifested itself, or been given a prize?"

Besides audiences at Yale and Harvard that were even larger and more enthusiastic than last year's, Merrill read *Scripts* to HIP at Christmas in Palm Beach. He'd paid his mother little attention over the past six months, and she chided him: "This is the very longest since we 1st met in 1926, that I've had no word from you!!" Making up for it, he spent two hours a day reading the trilogy aloud to her, commenting as he went. "What a difference it makes to hear him read," Hellen wrote to a friend, "and to be allowed to interrupt him for clarification. I only wish he could conduct a class wherever his readers might be. Even with J's help, it is difficult reading." Indeed it was. Jimmy complained about how little of it got through to her: as he read, she "balked again + again," "in a turmoil paralyzed like a rabbit caught by headlights." These readings must have been onerous command performances for him. Yet he submitted to them, and he was surprised that Hellen didn't grasp more of his work. It hurt and frustrated him that his own Queen Mum, the mother of all his mother figures, couldn't understand what he had written.

Merrill made those remarks about his mother in a new notebook with a cover of marbleized paper, a souvenir of Venice. He dated the first page "31.xii.78" and decorated it with two images. One was a purple peacock stamp—a gift from two young poets in tribute to Mirabell. The other (a copy of a nineteenth-century etching) shows an astonished shepherd, on his knees, who has poked his head through the firmament and discovered the mysteries on the other side. Merrill had done something very like this in his trilogy, and he must have wondered, on New Year's Eve, what lay on the far side of it. After all that work, he was going to have to "remember how to live" again. And to show him how, as usual, there was DJ. On the first stop of his southern real estate tour, Jackson had nearly succumbed to an overpriced beach house in South Carolina, until the weather turned cold and he saw that it wouldn't do for Januarys. He and Merrill met up in Key West.

America's southernmost city took the two of them by storm. Part of the excitement was geographical. At the far limit of the Florida Keys, reached by a long drive on the causeway linking the archipelago of coral islands, Key West, closer to Havana than Miami, is a place that feels remote from the rest of the U.S. (especially in 1979, before it became a destination for bloated cruise ships, family vacations, and the collegiate chaos of Spring Break). Unlike even the South Florida mainland, it lies below the frost line. The salty sea air is humid and fragrant. Tall coconut palms rustle; Spanish moss sways; banyan trees lean on vines rooted in the soil like canes; and lush red tongues of hibiscus lap up the light, which is somehow harsh and thin at once. In the course of a day, wind and clouds sweep across the almost perfectly flat island. (Houses are built without basements on top of the coral: even the dead lie in limestone above ground.) Above the four-by-two-mile puzzle piece of land, the sky is vaulted, baroque, and theatrical—like a ceiling by Tiepolo, but always changing, and mirrored by the moody sea.

For Merrill, the place summoned the sensations—the brilliant colors, fresh scents, bird calls—of his Florida childhood. He and Jackson stayed on Whitehead Street in a guesthouse owned by Jim Boatwright, "the Colonel," as they called him, a professor at Washington and Lee and editor of the literary magazine *Shenandoah*, whom they'd gotten to know in Athens. The architecture of the area, Key West's Old Town, was a delight. Merrill savored the "gingerbread houses," whose shiny tin roofs and front porches, dignified by white four-by-four columns, made them look like toy mansions, or scale models of the Orchard. The feel of the streets was familiar too, since, like Stonington, Key West was less a town than a miniature city, a quickly memorized grid bounded by the sea and packed with homes. A car was mainly inconvenient and bicycles prevailed.

To Jackson, the side streets of the Old Town were "pure Andy Hardy"—a quaint daydream of prewar America. But he was more interested in the main drag, Duval Street, with its hookers and cross-dressed torch singers, its watering holes, strip joints, and discos like the Monster, which stayed open until 3 a.m., blasting Donna Summer songs while gay men pumped on poppers achieved "consummations on the dancefloor" under a dizzy-making, spinning glass ball. Key West had long been a wide-open place. Strategically situated between the Atlantic and the Gulf of Mexico, it was an old navy town. With the sailors came the bars, the girls, and a flexible moral code. Law enforcement was lax. Contraband flowed through town from Cuba and the Caribbean—during Prohibition in the boats of rumrunners, after the 1960s in the backpacks of stoners. In the 1970s, lesbians and gays began visiting in numbers; many bought homes and opened businesses in town. By 1979, Key West had become one of the capital cities of post-Stonewall gay America. Punning on *sika*, the Greek for "sister," Merrill described it for Tony Parigory: "The town is large enough (32,000 permanent; plus, oh, 50,000 pleasure-sikas) so that one can be quite inconspicuous—as if anyone cared except for the tattooed bullies who beat up poor Tennessee for singing hymns." That winter Tennessee Williams, a resident and a symbol of gay Key West, had been attacked outside the Monster while harmonizing on an old hymn with a friend: it was a reminder that some people still "cared" very much what homosexuals did. Yet the fact remained: it would be possible for Merrill to be gay and "quite inconspicuous" here. It was no longer necessary to lead a double life in Greece.

Jackson wasted no time buying one of those "gingerbread houses." The address was 702 Elizabeth Street, a location even less promising than Water Street or Athinaion Efivon had been. Sleepy Elizabeth Street was one lane at this point in the middle of the island; closer to the water, the street got wider and the houses bigger and smarter. Here it was lined by little homes, some as run-down and small as shacks; these belonged to Cuban and black Bahamian families who had once worked at the naval yard or the cigar factory. The Elizabeth Street house itself was a handsome but small, modest home, built in the Bahamas in the 1860s and shipped to the island by barge (there was no wood for building in the Keys). But the previous owner was a drug dealer, and the property wasn't in good shape. Lurie was vacationing on the island that winter. When Jackson showed her his purchase, she found "a dark filthy ruin. The kitchen especially horrified me: it was a mass of rotting floorboards, walls caked with dirt and grease, and exposed rusty plumbing. 'I know it looks bad, but it's going to be beautiful,' David assured me." In her eyes, "the project seemed hopeless."

Merrill's attitude toward the house was distanced. Not that he was skeptical, but he stepped back and gave Jackson full rein to do his thing, as if he knew DJ needed it. The house was purchased in David's name, and both of them referred to it as David's. More than generosity on his part, however, Jimmy's readiness to think of it as David's suggested his own reluctance to claim it. Over the years, Jackson would spend more and more time there and Merrill less. The house has a white picket fence and a swinging gate on the street. When new concrete was poured on the sidewalk, David, like a boy, used a stick to inscribe in the wet stuff in front (where anyone entering by the gate would see) two pairs of initials: "JM"—"JM" first—and "DJ," their Ouija board names. Then he drew a heart around the two pairs of initials. But a crack ran through the middle of the heart, separating "JM" and "DJ" on either side.

There were friends close by. Richard and Charlee Wilbur lived around the corner, and they introduced the home buyers to *their* next-door neighbors, John Hersey and his wife Barbara. In the same "compound" lived Ralph and Fanny Ellison and John and Barbara Ciardi. Lurie and her husband Edward Hower, who had been coming to Key West for some time, bought their own house (a modern one in another neighborhood) that March. Over the next decade, many more writer friends would join these and together write a new chapter in Key West's literary history.

It was a mixed history from Merrill's point of view. He had to overlook the fact that Hemingway, who came in the 1930s for deep-sea fishing, incorporated Key West into his macho personal mythology, and the city had mythologized "Papa" in turn, from the tourist attraction that is the Ernest Hemingway House to the Papa Look-Alike Contest at Sloppy Joe's Bar. Tennessee Williams, who made Key West a louche backdrop for his long decline, was embarrassing in another way. But there was Stevens, who vacationed on the island in the 1930s, and composed "The Idea of Order at Key West" with its sea-and-sky theatrics in mind. And there was Bishop too, who had owned a house in town in the 1940s and who wrote "The Bight" and other poems there. Jimmy dashed off an excited postcard to her—it's his first mention of the house—on February 1: "You are in the guidebook, but no postcard of 'the EB house' is available, just Hemingway's + Audubon's + Tennessee's. David has, however, bought (as of this morning,

I think) a pretty house on <u>Elizabeth St</u> to make up for the lapse. Should I call it the E. Bishop house + charge admission?"

While Jackson was house hunting and then lining up contractors to renovate his find, Merrill was searching for a title for the trilogy. The long poem he'd written was heterogeneous in the extreme, and he needed a title to hold it together. He began playing with possibilities in his notebook on January 24, 1979. He brainstormed variations on a few themes in the same spirit in which he doodled faces or toyed with anagrams, working a word to see what other words it might yield. He listed motifs ("Cup," "Cell," "Atom," "Rose," "Manor," "Lenses") and arranged them in different configurations. Most of the candidates were laughably weak—illustrations of the lack of a central idea rather than solutions to it:

> The Measuring Cup
> School of Willowware
> Festival of Angels
> Glass Houses
> CHANGING IS YR CLUE
> Schools of Change
> FABLES FROM A CUP

He tried highlighting the environmental theme—"Greenhouse in a Cup," "Seasons in a Greenhouse"—and, changing tack, the aristocratic fantasy of the manor house: "The World of the Marchese Santofior," "The Restorations at Santofior." "Santofior" he broke down, fruitlessly, into "A FROST ION / FROSTIAN O / FINO SANTO." He turned the name in another direction with "Sandever" and, more promising now, "The Changes at Sandover."

When he and Jackson celebrated their last night together in Key West with the crowd that gathered daily to watch the sunset at Mallory Dock, Merrill had decided on his title. *The Changing Light at Sandover* was an unlikely choice. Willfully eccentric and pretty, it refused the simple bold titles of the modern long poems with which the trilogy otherwise begged comparison (*The Waste Land, The Cantos, Paterson, The Bridge*), not to mention the epics of Homer, Dante, and Milton. What was he thinking? How could he expect a poem called *The Changing Light at Sandover* to go down in history? "TOO FLAMBOYANT BY FAR!" WHA shot back when JM tested it on him. Insofar as it was eccentric, the title was modest. But it was brazen, too: a signal that Merrill was redefining epic convention to reflect his own insistent subjectivity. In 1972, as he began *The Book of Ephraim*, he asserted, "Too great a concern with ideas ages the work and its creator before their time. Examples: the 'thoughtful' passages in Dante, Proust, Tolstoi, Pound. Sensation—impressions—+ manners timeless by comparison." The two halves of the trilogy's title—the changing light and Sandover, the manor house—emphasized "impressions" and "manners," rather than the Ouija board's block capital "ideas." Yet impressions and manners had opened onto a vision of the cosmos and become their own source of ideas. Maria, high priestess of manners, had turned out to be Plato in disguise.

In addition to a title for the trilogy and a new house, Merrill left Key West with the makings of one of his most touching, most purely likable poems. There is warmth and festivity in "Clearing the Title"—even aspects of a new style, as Merrill gives up any residual concern about lyric purity and does in a shorter poem what he'd learned how to do in the trilogy, mixing high and low diction, intricate, impressionist word painting and pop culture slang in an amalgam alternately jaunty and plangent. The pun in the poem's title links the buying of the Elizabeth Street house and the completion of *Sandover* (the titles to both home and poem are being approved at the same time). Merrill casts himself as the resistant, bitchy spouse who has just touched down in the "vast shallowness" of the Keys only to discover that his significant other has taken the big leap into Florida real estate. As it dawns on him that DJ's "casual patter" is "sales patter," "The appalling truth now bores / Into my brain: you've *bought* a house." But he gives in even before he has finished complaining: "can you picture *living* here? Expect / *Me* to swelter, year by sunset year, / Beneath these ceilings—which at least aren't low."

At the end of the poem, Merrill strolls with DJ into the sunset, symbol of their approaching sunset years. He calls it "Day's flush of pleasure, knowing its poem done." The metaphor reminds him of *Sandover* and his partner's role in the making of it:

> *Our* poem now. It's signed JM, but grew
> From life together, grain by coral grain.
> Building on it, we let the life cloud over . . .

Emerging from the trilogy, Merrill was ready to reenter the world, lovingly render Florida's light and landscape, play the comic role of a housewife, and take his place among the motley who assemble every evening at Mallory Dock. There he and DJ find "the Iguana Man" with dragons draped on him; a balloon seller; a painted clown "nonchalantly juggling firebrands" on a unicycle; a Salvation Army band announcing the end of the world. As they passed through the smoke and mirrors of the Sandover séances, the mediums too had been tricksters and preachers like these. They had perhaps also been the "black girl with shaved skull" who "Sways on the brink" of the dock without, however, falling in while she holds up her end in a staring contest with "the fiery ball / Till it relenting tests with one big toe / Its bath, and Archimedean splendors overflow." Then, drawing a curtain on this cosmic performance, somebody in the crowd cries, "Let's hear it for the sun!" After its astounding length and complication are done, *The Changing Light at Sandover* comes down to a simple call to praise, not very different from that one. Merrill unveils his title in the poem's last line:

> Whereupon on high, where all is bright
> Day still, blue turning to key lime, to steel
> A clear flame-dusted crimson bars,
> Sky puts on the face of the young clown
> As the balloons, mere hueless dots now, stars
> Or periods—although tonight we trust no real
> Conclusions will be reached—float higher yet,
> Juggled slowly by the changing light.

It would be more than a year before he put the final touches on that sunset. From Key West, he and then Jackson went north to Water Street, where David hadn't been since the end of the Mirabell séances in 1977, two years earlier. It was time to sort the past. David did so by pouring cartons of old letters, magazines, and clippings on the bat-pattern rug (this would go to the garbage, that to the library in St. Louis), while Jimmy picked through his books to choose the contents of a volume of selected poems, which would be published along with *Sandover* three years later. (Reason for the delay in publishing: in his speed, he'd outstripped the ability of his readers to keep up, in the judgment of Harry Ford, who didn't want to flood the market with Merrill.) He sent the typescript of *Scripts* to Ford and embarked on a round of spring readings. He was equipped at the lectern these days with a wildly affected prop: a lorgnette, or, as he put it, "a simple almost butch *face à main* by Givenchy out of Meyrowitz." By this time Jackson was on board a ship back to Europe. Merrill felt the pain of his going sharply. "Dearest D," he wrote. "The house seems very empty. I went into your bedroom, found the remaining pot, found also that sort of dull brown plaid tie you wore home from Paris and I said I didn't like. My old eyes filled with tears as I hung it in the closet."

On April 9, Merrill had "[a] dream about dying. Little time left. Things to be <u>done</u> beforehand." It was as if he had been asleep while the Sandover séances went on, and he was waking up to find he had crossed over to old age (though he was still only fifty-three). In May, visiting Pawlet in the familiar guest room, he recorded a "[d]ream of Claude young + old. The old one watches me warm my hands against the young one's cheeks." Two days later he wrote, "With age comes a kind of psychic incontinence. (CK's hallucinated voices [. . .] in back seat of cab taking him to Vienna airport a week before his death.) One awakes to a slow scalding urine of voices, faces, gestures, incident, vivid as dream"—and as unreal as a dream, as experience dissolved into memory, the more vivid and disturbing for traveling across long tracts of time. Life felt like the afterlife. To protect his health, now that he'd broken the Sandover habit, he tried and failed to stop smoking. (His brand? Trues.) Then a stop-smoking cassette tape, a gift from Sandy, did the trick through hypnosis, at least for a while. "One of the rewards for my never listening to reason," he reflected, "is this kind of gullibility."

He was in no immediate danger of dying. The bad news that he was afraid of came from Ma instead. "I feel perhaps over-susceptible," he wrote in his diary with *Der Rosenkavalier* on the radio. "HIP phoned at noon: there is a malignant spot in her throat—on the vocal cord. She starts radiation, 4 weeks of it, on Monday. Wonderfully sensible, cool, while I'm on the edge of shock." "Quite naturally as must be the case in similar 'blows,' " Hellen wrote to her "Son, dearest of Sons," after Week One of radiation, "so far I can come up with only one thing—Gratitude, Pure + Simple (capitalized) because if the treatments fail to do the trick, I couldn't possibly feel any other emotion." Though Jimmy was about to leave for Greece, he offered to change his plans and visit her instead. She let him off the hook, but not without giving him plenty to feel guilty about. "Oddly enough," Hellen told him, "during these past two years"—while he had been so busy writing *Sandover*—"I've almost preferred being alone. Now don't you dare take me seriously, Poet! It's just that I can recall [in] the years following Daddy's exit from my life (our life) that being alone was unbearable + how I welcomed even the most crushing bores. But somehow [. . .] I've learned that I can do for myself, that I don't even need a full-time maid"—here she drew a frowny face. "Heaven help me from becoming a recluse. I like people too much but it seems that I prefer quality to quantity—and Jimmy, the tried and true are here in my moment of need." Hellen had bought a condominium in Palm Beach, and Jimmy settled for promising to visit her there for Christmas.

He got another cancer call, this one from Hubbell, who'd been diagnosed with melanoma. Jimmy arranged to give his friend outright a huge sum, $25,000, because "there's nothing like ready cash to speed convalescence, and the glow of small sums fades so quickly. This way, too," he added, "I'll be able to fly off easier in my mind about you." HIP, who knew Hubbell as one of her son's oldest and more socially presentable friends, with family in Atlanta, wrote a card to him: "Every day, as I stretch out for my treatment, I ask Him to keep one hand on you and the other on me." Hellen would come through treatment just fine. Not so Hubbell, who died a year later. The elegy that Merrill wrote (but never published) honors him as a society boy and Cole Porter crooner whose élan reconciled Jimmy to the ways of his class: "a whole / World one might otherwise have written off, / Its cults and creeds, as a poor counterfeit / Through you took on resonance, magic, wit." Acting a part in life couldn't be disdained when the roles were as gallant as Hub's: "The Tailored Man too spruce to toil or spin," "the Minstrel," "the Jester," and "at the end [. . .] the upright, stricken Chevalier."

As planned—he always traveled as planned, usually more than six months in advance—Merrill flew to Italy in July 1979. However hard he'd been working, it was easy to remember how to live la dolce vita. In Venice ("a disaster area of rich meals + strong drink"), he stayed with DK ("Slimmer and worldlier and dearer all the time") and laughed away the evenings with Tony and Helen Hecht and John Brinnin (it was a veritable "Poets' Corner") and Gore Vidal. He stayed with Umberto (who "serves eggs for dinner," a relief) in Cortona, and with Henry and Maggie Sloss, friends from Athens, in their house in the country; then with the Lavins in a free room at the American Academy of Rome. He and Vassili together paid a visit to Mimi's grave, a year after she'd gone to it. Manoli was along for the ride, thinking whatever he thought of these people who either ignored him or (like John Hohnsbeen) squeezed his biceps and swooned. They took a boat to Athens, where DJ was at the pier one early morning to meet them.

This would be Jimmy's and David's last full season at Athinaion Efivon 44. The plan was to rent the house to John and Abigail Camp. John was an archeologist at the Agora dig in Athens; his mother played bridge with Jimmy and David back home in Connecticut. The plan was to reevaluate the question in a few years, "by whose end a miracle of urban renewal may have taken place, and Athens may again be livable." But this was merely a fig leaf to cover the fact that they were about to unmake their home.

To put off the scramble to store, ship, or discard most of the Athens household, Merrill set off with Nelly Liambey for the island of Santorini, a travel-poster destination that he'd never visited. The sightseeing was promising: the whitewashed town sits like frosting on the rim of a crescent-shaped island formed by the massive volcanic eruption (the result, according to *Mirabell*, of Akhenaton's atomic pyramid disaster) while three hundred feet below the dark, mocha-colored cliffs, cruise ships pass in the placid waters that fill the caldera of a still at times smoldering volcano. But Merrill wasn't there to take photos. He expected to return with the materials for a valedictory poem, ostensibly occasioned by this trip, which he had already started to write before he left on it: one more case of him planning an experience in order to write about it. "Santorini: Stopping the Leak," when he finished it, was composed like "Clearing the Title" and "Yánnina" in Byron's ottava rima. He intended it to make a bookend with the Key West poem, solid enough to hold up between them the various poems in his next collection, whenever that might take shape. The result of all this calculation, however, was a parody of his gifts: an overly elaborate, overly long poem, caked with clever conceits, in which one idea is complicated by the next to the point of burying any feeling that might have possibly motivated it. The poem's starting point is an analogy between his decision to uproot himself from Greece and the surgical removal of a plantar wart in his foot. Was he now so much the master of his medium that he could write about *anything*?

The excessive difficulty of "Santorini," which he fussed over for three years, implies how difficult Merrill found it to say goodbye to Greece. So much had transpired in that house, where Strato and the Archangel Michael had both been regulars. He and DJ turned to their domestic task. They stripped pictures from the walls, which left "ugly plaster pits." "Fat boxes were assembled and filled—heavier than leaden coffins—with Auden's complete OED." A pair of carved chairs bought on Skyros, the five-foot-tall terra-cotta muse from Tony whose open hand had held an apple for the teacher in the Sandover schoolroom, even DJ's VW went into huge cargo containers for shipping back to the U.S. Merrill had to admit, "[N]ow that nothing else is on the walls, the writing <u>is</u>. We'll never live here again." The buds on the rooftop camellia made him cry.

To make matters worse, "<u>all</u> our friends are turning into the greedy peasant-crones in 'Zorba,' " clutching at an old beach towel, a jackal-fur spread. The sorest was Manos, who "perhaps understands chiefly that it is unmanly to lament." So he pouted and grunted as he lifted boxes. His future was uncertain. His karate studio languished, and Merrill was "cross" with him because he was unwilling to take a course in, say, physiotherapy, so as to establish a dependable livelihood. Although no one was saying so, this move spelled the end for Manos and Jimmy's decade-long intimacy. Merrill had to wonder whether his patronage had harmed or helped his young friend. He went to work on a poem called "Revivals of *Tristan*," which begins, "The loving cup was poisoned." But Manos Karastefanís would not be left lying on his back on the stage, like Tristan. He came to the U.S. for a month with Jimmy in 1982; and tallies in Merrill's notebook show that he went on sending checks to MK for some time. He gave inscribed typescripts from the trilogy to Manos; then he took them back, sold them to a dealer in the U.S., and gave Manos the proceeds to buy an apartment for himself in Athens.

In October, while Merrill packed, a cable came from Frank Bidart saying that Elizabeth Bishop had died suddenly at home in Boston, the cause an aneurism in the brain. Merrill had known Elizabeth for thirty years; they'd been close friends for seven; there was no contemporary poet—no contemporary writer—he admired more, or wanted more to please. Over the next few years, he would write about her on several occasions, trying to fix her image in his mind and honor her work. Just after her death, Barbara Epstein at *The New York Review of Books* cabled requesting a tribute; he penned three pages at once. He praised Bishop's "instinctive, modest, life-long impersonations of an ordinary woman, someone who during the day did errands, went to the beach, would perhaps that evening jot a phrase or two inside the nightclub matchbook before returning to the dance floor." In Bishop's hands, "Poetry was a life both shaped by and distinct from the lived one, like that sleet storm's second tree 'of glassy veins' in 'Five Flights Up.' " That last remark, thrown off in passing, is intriguing because there's nothing in the poem to cue a reader to interpret that image in this way. Saying more about Merrill than Bishop, his remark hints at how he learned to think of his own work while reading hers. If not Bishop's poetry, then Merrill's was "both shaped by and distinct from" the life he lived, a glittering second skin of "glassy veins."

He put these autumn events, the packing up and the death of his friend, together in a letter to Henry Sloss:

> Ah me, this house. The air crackles with bleak reproach. The neighborhood cats, sensing an imminent change, have begun, for the first time ever, brazenly asking to be admitted at every door and window. [. . .] Thus, attending to cats, packing, getting through the day, we simply put off any realization of What We Are Doing—a life we'll never live again, people we won't see or even write to. Our reasonableness in the face of their puzzlement and occasional panic is a terrible index of how close we are to that final logic of the grave. And the sooner we duck beyond the reach of cold spotlights such as this, the better.
>
> Elizabeth Bishop's death is probably somewhere behind the tone I'm taking. Suddenly to realize that there is <u>no one left</u>—no

one, that is, whose postcards, whose idlest remarks (not to speak of the poems) gave rise to plain old adoring wonder. [. . .] For once it was no comfort at all to go to the Board and take down her cheerful impressions of Heaven.

At the end of October, Jimmy and David closed the sky-blue door of Athinaion Efivon 44 behind them.

Renewal was as simple as opening the door to 702 Elizabeth Street. Magically, in their absence, David's architect and contractors had transformed the place, and the result was "ravishing!" Merrill wrote to Yenser, "[Y]ou can't imagine anything prettier or pleasanter. Out front, banks of impatiens and a papaya tree; out back, banks of impatiens and a big gurgling pool." Well, the odd-shaped pool, "curled in a fetal position," was hardly "big," but it took up most of the backyard; a brick patio had been put in and a small shaded deck with room for a table and four chairs. In Athens and Stonington, Jimmy and David had lived in houses organized vertically. Elizabeth Street was horizontal. The white house had a porch, a gable above the front door, and shutters to keep out the heat or batten the hatches during hurricane season. A wide central hall, dividing three bedrooms and a bath, led to a kitchen and living room in the back. Merrill loved the old wood: "pine-floor, walls, high peaked ceiling—pine dramatically grained and stained the color of rosewood or the darkest imaginable tan against which the white of French door-frames and crossbeams takes on the look of zinc oxide on a lifeguard's lips." Each room had a ceiling fan. Merrill's bedroom in the middle of the house was "cleverly made into two by a 7 foot high bookcase," which created a nook for his desk: a new hidden workplace. He'd need the privacy and earplugs because there were neighbors on all sides and the walls were thin. Souvenirs from Athens emerged from those cargo containers: the chairs from Skyros, a print of Yánnina (a gift from Stephen), a view of Chania by Dorothy Andrews, and a watercolor by Edward Lear. A print of Arnold Böcklin's kitsch mermaids and satyrs cavorting in the froth, who had once disported in Maria's father's office, went into the living room above a couch.

As in Stonington, Merrill had what he needed nearby. Two blocks away was "an excellent fishmarket: yellowtail, kingfish, grouper, crawfish, shrimp. And there you are at Duval St with a good half dozen 'elements' to choose from, not unlike the fishmarket: hippie, polyester, macho biker, local black, faggot, Cuban—but turn a corner and they vanish, and you're walking back home." Their own Key West society took shape quickly. For New Year's Eve, "to see out the 70s," Jimmy and David set up "Malibu Lights" in the backyard, and sunk the strings of a handful of big balloons, tied to a brick, at the bottom of the pool. The Wilburs celebrated with them that night, along with Peter Taylor, a dapper southerner and subtle short-story writer, and his wife Eleanor Ross Taylor, a poet Merrill admired. Jim Boatwright was there too, and David Kalstone, Ed White, the Herseys, and Alison Lurie, among others. The New Year's Eve party would turn into an annual event, bigger and more glamorous each year as the Key West writers' colony grew and bona-fide celebrities like James Taylor and Leonard Bernstein, and poets as different from each other as Adrienne Rich and Harry Mathews, began to show up for the party. In Stonington and Athens, Merrill and Jackson had lived for years in micro-social worlds of their own making. In Key West, half the people standing around the pool with drinks were members of the American Academy of Arts and Letters. The life JM and DJ led there would be far more literary and public than any they had known.

With his hair silvering at the temples and wrinkles deepening in his face, Merrill fit right in with dignified Key West literati. His calendar for 1980 was the schedule of a famous writer who was in demand far and wide. He gave readings that spring in San Francisco and Los Angeles, and at Stanford and the New School. He delivered the class day speech at Amherst (his mischievous talk on costume, sexism, transvestitism, and the fluidity of identity, which took off from Bishop's poem "Exchanging Hats," must have left the graduates and their parents scratching their heads). He presided as judge over the Discovery/*Nation* poetry contest reading (Yenser was one of four winners; the other judges, evidently handpicked by Jimmy, were Moffett and Corn). He attended the American Academy of Arts and Letters' awards ceremony in May. He read the epilogue to the *Sandover* trilogy as the Phi Beta Kappa poem at Harvard in June. One day in July, he bought tickets for nineteen plane flights—all in one go, to get the best rates before a price hike went into effect. Cub reporters interviewed him for *People*, *Life*, and *Newsweek*. In the fall, he gave more readings (at Yale, Princeton, and Bard, in Montreal, Chicago, Ann Arbor, and St. Louis). The heavy ancient black telephone on Water Street had become so importunate that he put in a second line by his bedside and installed a marvelous device, an answering machine, on the first one. Only his mother, his brother, Kalstone, Harry Ford, DMc, Peter Tourville, Tony, and DJ had the unlisted number.

Scripts for the Pageant came out in April, and went into a second edition of 8,000 copies after the first 5,000 sold in a month—brisk sales for any volume of poetry, let alone a 235-page visionary poem modeled on the Renaissance English masque. With his audience growing, Mirabell offered Jimmy pointers on "HOW TO AVOID POISONOUS FATTY JUNK FOODS SUCH AS LUNATIC FRINGERS, SCEPTICS and IMITATORS." It was true, not all responses stirred by the trilogy were welcome or friendly. In Palo Alto, Diane Middlebrook, a Stanford professor, arranged a lunch for Merrill in the form of a symposium to which John Freccero, an eminent Danteist, and two physics professors had been summoned, equipped with advance copies of *Scripts* and invited to give their views. One of the scientists began, "I thought the poem was, excuse me, *bullshit*. Do you really believe that angels spoke to you?" Jimmy's simple answer was "Yes."

Commenting on *Scripts* for *The New York Times Book Review*, Denis Donoghue came to the same conclusion as the Stanford physicist. Donoghue was an NYU professor and a poetry scholar and critic whom Merrill referred to as "the jolly green giant" (a dig at his seriousness, Irishness, and height). He began by praising *The Book of Ephraim*, "a remarkable poem" that was "continuous with Merrill's justly famous" shorter poems. "With *Mirabell*, something went wrong," however. Having accepted "the wretched assignment" to "write a poetry of Science," Merrill turned in "a report that sounds like a rejected script for 'Star Trek' or the notes one might take in a course called 'Astrophysics for You.' " Donoghue continued, "I am afraid that *Scripts for the Pageant* persists in the portentousness and vanity of *Mirabell*. Its subject is nothing less than the meaning of life, but the poem degrades the theme and makes a poor show of itself with camp silliness and giggling. [. . .] *The Book of Ephraim* was apparently undaunted by the epigraph from Dante with which it began. Now, five hundred pages later, the work has dwindled so far into mannerism that I would choose for a motto Mademoiselle de Nazianzi's swoon in Ronald Firbank [. . .]: 'Help me, heaven, to be decorative and to do right!' " Once one had sifted "the rubble," Donoghue allowed, there were some "good things in the poem," such as "Samos" and "The House in Athens," but—this was his final word—"it is wretched to have to cross such a dismal terrain to reach them." *Wretched*, *rubble*, *dismal*, *wretched*: Donoghue had let fly, and in the paper of record. But unlike sharp critiques in the past, this one didn't stick to Merrill. Donoghue's open contempt for "camp silliness" and Ronald Firbank was cause enough to brush it aside.

The sweeping ambition of *Scripts* invited sweeping judgments, YES or NO. Most reviews said "YES" to the poem, and some, like Clara Claiborne Park's in the *Nation*, were rhapsodic. Hailing the completed trilogy as a work that met the spiritual needs of its time and restored virtues lacking in poetry since *The Waste Land*, Park declared, "In the midst of literature (and lives) made out of heartsick discontinuities, it is continuous, with the continuity not only of reason—purposeful narrative, tightly connected event—but of the heart: of loyalty, friendship, of love that so yearns for continuity that it seeks it even beyond that black discontinuity that JM and DJ refuse to take as final. In the midst of personal and linguistic privatism, it manifests for the reader an affectionate concern that we'd forgotten could exist in serious literature, and a shining faith in the power of language to render shareable our grandest imaginations and our most personal experience, to make the private public." If Donoghue's review was the response of a critic who closed his mind to the long poem not halfway through it, Park's was the blurry enthusiasm of a critic inundated by it. She ended by throwing up her hands ("This is too rich a poem for review") and urging her readers to share in the heady experience while it was still fresh: "Get to the poem before it's taught in the academy, as in five years' time it surely will be."

Merrill's trilogy was not about to make it into freshman Great Books courses, but there were scholars busy reading it. A professor at the University of British Columbia, Vancouver, Ross Labrie, was writing the first monograph on Merrill (published in 1982), and he came to Stonington to interview Jimmy. David Lehman at Hamilton College and Charles Berger at Yale were planning the first anthology of critical essays on Merrill (published in 1983), and Robert Polito at Wellesley—these were all young men just getting started in their academic careers—had begun work on an index to the trilogy (published in 1994). In December 1980, Merrill would appear at the Modern Language Association's annual meeting in Houston to read from the trilogy ("Hyatt Regency," he commented on the conference headquarters, "atmosphere of a vast singles bar"). Allen Ginsberg, "who now <u>haunts</u> these affairs," was in the audience and congratulated Jimmy "warmly on my 'improvisations.' " At the same MLA, Willard Spiegelman organized a panel on "The Sacred Books of James Merrill," and, on another panel, Edmund White gave a paper called "A Gay Critic Looks at James Merrill."

Judy Moffett and Stephen Yenser were each preparing studies of their mentor's work while writing essays about every new book of his that appeared. As she worked on her monograph about Merrill's poetry, Moffett had struggled to find a way to talk about sexuality in his work, and she felt frustrated by, as she saw it, his deliberate refusals of disclosure. On the verge of giving up on her book, she carved out an article from it called "Sound Without Sense: Willful Obscurity in Poetry, With Some Illustrations from James Merrill's Canon." She mentioned the essay to Jimmy and asked if he'd mind if she published it, which he didn't (it appeared in the winter 1980 number of the *New England Review*). But that polite inquiry hardly suggested the essay's contents and tone.

Moffett begins the piece by explaining that she is "wholeheartedly devoted to most" of Merrill's poetry, but she has come to feel "the rightness of objecting to those of his poems *meant* to conceal—meant neither partially nor wholly to reveal—their meaning, while at the same time revealing that meaning had been built into them." She describes "18 W. 11th Street," for example, as "glossolalia at a Pentecostal meeting: highly emotional gibberish meaningful perhaps to the gibberer [. . .] but to nobody else." For good measure, she reprints the *New York Times* editorial protesting the awarding of the Bollingen Prize to Merrill and quotes from Louis Simpson's negative review of *Divine Comedies* in support of her objections. The frustration she'd felt when she first had her teacher to dinner in Madison in 1967, her feeling that he was "holding something, almost everything, back," she'd discovered again in his poems. She wrote, "Give the reader enough intimacy of any kind—enough of one oneself in any form—and he will acquiesce; give him too little and he will be resentful." Merrill complained privately, but went on writing warm letters to Moffett and continuing to promote her poems and career.

As Judy was aware, Jimmy had a completely different relationship with her former classmate, Stephen. Merrill sent his work to Moffett when it was done, to Yenser when it was in progress. If Jackson was Merrill's collaborator as he took dictation from the Ouija board, Yenser was his collaborator as he wrote the long poem. Merrill sent the typescripts of *Ephraim*, *Mirabell*, and *Scripts* to several friends, but Yenser saw them first. He responded to the evolving poem in fine-grained letters that offered few or no objections but, always from within the logic of the poem, asked for clarifications and pointed up connections Merrill himself might be only half aware of. Yenser's comments moved fluidly between micro and macro levels of text, between choices of verse form and mythic patterns, never missing a pun. Attuned to Merrill's imagination, he held up a mirror in which the Scribe could see what he had done. This service continued in the reviews he wrote. With Merrillean tact and style, Yenser tracked Merrill's subtle games in burnished critical prose, at times out-Merrilling Merrill, as in "Dantean Andante," the anagrammatic title of his essay-review of *Mirabell*. With a draft of Stephen's review of *Scripts* on his desk, Merrill thanked him: "What a blessing that we (the poem + I) have you, like a mini-Michael, to contrive the best possible lighting for us. Not mere flattering lights, but lights that show so much." There followed six scribbled pages of appreciative notes, then another letter with two more pages of the same.

And while the Scribe was the subject of so much critical attention, what of the Hand? There was curiosity about Jackson's role at the Ouija board and in the writing of the poem. McClatchy interviewed him on the subject for *Shenandoah*, and he wrote a few pages called "Lending a Hand" for the collection of essays being edited by Lehman and Berger. Neither piece gave away much from the mediums' bag of tricks. Looking back on the *Sandover* séances, DJ sounded proud, dazzled by what had gone on, but also befuddled and burned out:

> A certain schism set in during those years, dividing and confusing one's perception of any day's experience: the lived human hours of meetings and conversations, the hours at the board of other meetings and conversations, the reading over of the material, the reading of JM's typescript as it approached a finished state. Of course Real (life) remained real. Yet as the final lessons were spelled out, they became realer yet, and these emerging in the final text became the most real of all. A manuscript page with its uppercase and lowercase read rather like some voltage indicator of our newly electrified lives, from DC to AC then back again to DC as our Divine Comedy flowed more and more directly.

He came north in April 1980 to spend five months on Water Street. Jimmy was struck by how very thin David was (135 pounds) and insisted that they submit together to a two-week "Mormon regime: no drinks, smokes, coffee, tea" under the supervision of Mirabell. Whatever gains were made by this method were soon offset by intensive socializing. David summarized the situation in a letter to Donald Richie written on his fifty-eighth birthday in September:

> Our summer has been chaotically full of people, trips, overnighters here, lunches, dinners, arrivals and departure, making up of beds, cleaning off of and setting up of tables, and JM's cooking, and such quantities of TALK and NEWS and adjusting to yet another face as one tried to adjust one's own in the morning. I realize I've become quite a loner, off there in Greece, down there in Key West to have such a glut of people around it is distinctly rattling and fatiguing. [. . .] WHAT DOES IT ALL MEAN? Well, that the Poet has not got a big work to get on with, and that the Lazy One has not got the will to resist.

He didn't have the will to resist television either, which he sat in front of daily—"addicted," Jimmy felt. The tube, David recognized, was "[b]ad for the eyes, worse for the brain and digestion. [. . .] The foolish sit coms and the insulting violence, the truly idiotic Talk Shows, all this shit interspersed with toilet paper commercials." Merrill was alarmed at Jackson's state, and aggravated by it, too. David's headaches had returned, and "bellyaches both real and figurative," which were hard to put up with. Jimmy, who rarely let off steam, complained to Stephen:

> By himself he will do NOTHING. His neck, most of his waking hours is at a 70 degree angle to his spine, reading in bed, staring down at a page from a standing position; the cigarette in lieu of a Proper Breakfast; and taking always a tone learned from his dreadful father: "I've done pretty well for 58 years, I don't need to be told etc etc." Or, if he's in pain, the mother's voice: "Just leave me alone, I'll get over it."

Jackson left for Key West on October 1. Merrill followed at New Year's, and they promptly descended into "[a] week of flu and squabbles." Mirabell prescribed another two-week dry-out for them both. But David needed more than that to recover his youth. One festive night, he huffed and puffed, blowing up a balloon, then "staggered, bending forward, eyes staring. About 5 seconds later he asked, 'What happened?'" Jimmy "realized only then that he'd fainted on his feet." His posture sagging, with a vague expression on his face behind tinted glasses, his comb-over, no-longer-blond hair tousled, David Jackson, once William Holden handsome, was old at fifty-eight. And Jimmy was at the height of his fame, with style and charisma to burn.

Ronald Reagan was the new president, inaugurated in January 1981. The implications of the shift in American politics known as the "Reagan Revolution" would take time to unfold. Reaganomics, Star Wars, and the Moral Majority—these were not yet the bywords of aggressive conservative policy they would become. But Merrill, like everyone else, could feel the change. When they pulled up stakes in Greece, the America to which Jimmy and David returned was more threatening than the consensus culture of the 1950s they had hidden from on the third floor of Water Street, or fled outright with their passports. During the Carter administration, the U.S. military had pushed beyond a policy of "mutually assured destruction" to formulate the concept of a "survivable nuclear war." Now the escalation in nuclear arms led by Reagan revived for Merrill the fears of global annihilation that had plagued him during earlier phases of the Cold War. The General Dynamics Electric Boat factory, the manufacturer of nuclear submarines, was only a few miles away from Stonington, in Groton, and the quiet Connecticut coast seemed a choice target for Soviet ICBMs. When JM and DJ sat down at the Ouija board these days, they discussed how to save the planet from rising military and ecological dangers. As he pored over the *New Yorker* essays that became Jonathan Schell's influential book about the consequences of nuclear war, *The Fate of the Earth*, Merrill was transfixed by Schell's vision of imminent catastrophe. Between Hiroshima and the emergence of the antinuclear movement, Merrill felt, "the horror" had only had time "to mature. In between we were (most of us still are) sleepwalking." Nature's "LAST RESOUNDING YES / TO MAN" began to sound distinctly elegiac.

Merrill was never a "closet Republican," reluctant to show his true colors to his Democratic Party–faithful friends. If he was allergic to the sentimental humanism of the Democrats, he had no tolerance for the ideology of the opposite camp. As he sat beside his mother in the front pew of her Episcopal church in Palm Beach, he glowered at the rector. The "lowbrow sweetness & light" being served up from the pulpit to "deluded millionaires" struck him as merely "the most underhanded means" of "preserving gun lobbies and corporate interests." He saw those corporate interests shaping the Florida landscape, and reacted. In "Developers at Crystal River," he wrote about the manatees, the great brown docile aquatic mammals whose numbers were falling under the pressure of the Gulf Coast's surging human population. Merrill's manatees, "foes / To nothing in creation," are "Over and over scarred / By the propellers, gaffs and garden tools / The boatmen use on them for fun," turning their wakes red with the animals' blood.

From this point on in his career, the trilogy's environmental theme preoccupied Merrill, whether it was front and center or in the background of the poems he was writing, whether his tone was angry or plangent. At the same time, he saw that environmentalism was in danger of turning nature into a commodity. Looking at the television over David's shoulder, he pointed to the nature programs on public broadcasting's "Channel 13" (the title of another poem) with their fascinating species fast on the way to becoming mere images:

> It came down to this: that merely naming the creatures
> > Spelt their doom.
> Three quick moves translated camelopard, dik-dik, and
> > Ostrich from

> Grassland to circus to Roman floor mosaic to
> TV room.

These and other short poems from the late 1970s and 1980s reveal a sharper political awareness than Merrill is usually credited with. He published several such poems in *The New York Review of Books*, a magazine his financial gifts had helped to get started and the preferred venue for his piquant topical squibs, including "Popular Demand"—a Cold War satire he wrote in the 1950s but published in the last month of Reagan's campaign for a second term. He wasn't about to turn into an editorialist, let alone a political poet like Auden or Lowell. But that's not because he presumed to stand apart from the social fray. He had an acute sense of himself as an example of a social type, just as we all are, in his estimation; and he knew very well that his race, class, and gender—that mantra of the 1980s—colored any view he held. "Domino," written in winter 1981, makes the point memorably. The poem is a defense of art, cast as a dramatic monologue for the brand of household sugar. Prompted by the experience of living with black neighbors for the first time, and written with responses to his work like Richard Pevear's Marxist critique in mind, Merrill meditates in "Domino" on his particular brand of whiteness:

> Delicious, white, refined
> Is all that I was raised to be,
> Whom feeling for the word
> Plus crystal rudiments of mind
> Still keep—however stirred—
> From wholly melting in the tea.

The poet is a product of culture as typical in his way as a bag of sugar. But being aware of that fact, and able to frame the insight in language as delicious and refined as this, also makes him something more. That "something more" includes a capacity for searching reflection on art's place in society. Merrill takes the aesthete's position, and refuses to be "stirred" by the merely topical (or whatever tempest may be brewing in the teapot of the day). But the knowledge that it's a bag of sugar saying these things—a commodity with domination written into its name—makes poses like these laughable. To remind us that civilized refinement depends on barbarism, as the wealth of some depends on the poverty of others, Merrill glances in the middle stanza at the lives of the workers who harvest cane in the Caribbean, with its long history of slavery and exploited labor. The point is not to forswear art because it rests on social inequality, but to recognize why we prize it anyway, as the final stanza insists:

> The better to appraise his mess,
> History's health freak begs
> That such as we be given up.
> Outpouring bitterness
> Rewards the drainer of the cup . . .
> He'll miss those sparkling dregs.

As sparkling a jest as "Domino" was, Merrill hardly considered himself to be at work when he wrote it in Key West. He spent the winter attending to Grace Stone, who'd come south with her nurse. This meant "laboriously getting her in and out of her car, coaxing her up pathways on her 'walker,' settling her in this or that salon in such a way that 'the men' could easily gather round and tell her how wonderful she was. 'Ah think you are a Very Great Lady' said Tennessee Williams," while Grace blushed and glowed. For a diversion, Merrill went over to the house John Ciardi had rented on the beach, sat under a palm tree, and wiggled sand between his toes while he played anagrams for two hours once a week. The players included Ciardi and Dick Wilbur, who were "v. competitive (macho)," while John Brinnin and JM remained "perfect ladies." "The 'wives' (Charlee + Judith + DJ) are free to gossip over coffee." Certain moves became the stuff of legend, as when Ciardi "turned PITCHERS into SPHINCTER." Merrill enjoyed the routine; it kept his verbal muscles in shape; and he liked the laughing literary camaraderie. But it was like exercise in a retirement community—shuffleboard for bards. David was right: no longer having any "big work to get on with," the poet was filling his days up with people. After the "WILD MAD EUPHORIA" he'd felt while working on the trilogy, he was, if not depressed, then blank and formal, emptied out.

To prime the pump of his poetry with new scenes and vignettes, Merrill returned to Italy with David McIntosh for company. They stayed with Umberto Morra in Cortona, made friends with three women who were translating *Mirabell* into Italian, and stopped in Athens long enough for Merrill to "realize I won't after all be able to give up" the city or the pleasure of speaking Greek. They went to Istanbul too before winding up with a visit to Kalstone in Venice. McIntosh remained a model of the high-minded, sober man that Jimmy, the chameleon and waterbug, wished that he himself were, at least in some moods. Morra was a similarly serious figure in Merrill's mythology, albeit costumed differently. Jimmy had been visiting the count almost annually for three full decades. McIntosh, a tall man, recalled Morra as taller than himself, although Umberto was elderly and gaunt. "He had a cook and a maid, but he lived very humbly. Most of our meals were soup and bread. It was very cold that May, and the interior of the house felt like the ice palace." He was only "intent on making conversation with James; they spoke in English and Italian, and in French for literary purposes." He insisted that the Americans see the Riace bronzes in Florence: two heroic Greek figures from the classical period, nude, bearded, and magnificent, relaxed in contrapposto poses. The statues, which had been discovered on the sea floor by a diver, were being exhibited for the first time in 1981. "Unbelievable!" Jimmy exclaimed. "Neither God nor dreaming youth [. . .]" (that is, neither the Poseidon nor the Charioteer that Friar had shown Merrill in 1950) "but middle-aged warriors, at once noble + sensual + surfeited. Their lips + nipples were of pink copper."

It was the last time Jimmy saw Umberto, who died six months later at the age of eighty-four. Merrill wrote a rare letter to Robert Isaacson bearing the news, because Morra had been "a father to us both" when they met in 1951. Umberto appeared in a dream he recorded after his death: "I go to U's bed, reach down between the sheets + collect easily a handful of [his] dark wiry hair which I add to my own." That wiry hair was a pure concentrate of virility, like the testosterone capsules Merrill kept ordering from Europe. On his visit to Cortona in 1981, he collected his last impressions of the man. He would put them into an intricate, anecdotal, nine-page poem called "Bronze"; written over several years, it concerns the count, the Riace bronzes, McIntosh, and the masculine styles Merrill saw embodied by those two men and the heroic statues. Out of respect for the dignified Italian's reticence, Merrill had held on to Umberto's story for a long time. Now he made the most of it: he disclosed Morra's presumed identity as "the son / Of his father's friend the King" and celebrated the count's role in the anti-fascist resistance in 1943.

At the poem's center are the bronzes. They speak directly to the reader as survivors rescued from the polluted Mediterranean. The civilization-cradling sea, they know, "*will in / Another few decades have perished, / And with it those human equivalents, / Memory, instinct*"—since the news that "*Nature / Is dead, or soon will be*" means the death of culture too. Like the animals Merrill writes about in "Channel 13," the bronze warriors have been drained of their vitality and reduced to objects of art—the "*articulate shell / Of a vacuum roughly man-sized.*" Is that all a hero ever is, an artful creation with clay at the core? The statues seem to say so when they declare: "*To fictive environments / Blood is the fee.*" In place of an "*Epiphany such as the torso / In Paris provided for Rilke,*" they command us to "*Quit / Dreaming of change. It is happening / Whether you like it or not, / So get on with your lives.*"

For Merrill, getting on with life meant returning to Water Street to put the final touches on his selected poems and the one-volume edition of the trilogy. He and Jackson crossed paths there before DJ sailed for Europe, their two trips being planned so as not to coincide. In Greece David felt "old, misunderstood," and "unequal to the pace." By the time he got back home to Key West in October, he had "come to the conclusion that I'm too old to travel anymore. Not the way I do travel, on the surface of the earth, like a worm carrying too much baggage."

When he arrived on the island that winter, Merrill instituted another "Mormon regime," reinforced by a three-times-a-week routine on the Nautilus machines at the gym. To join the gym, Merrill "had to sign a statement that I was not a law enforcement officer + had no objection to 'homosexual activity,' " which suggests the ambiance of this particular health club. Once the muscle-inflating machines had done their work, "one can repair to a steam room or indeed to a dark little theatre where porn flicks are shown round the clock. They have a pool table too, and a bar, and a hot tub—Jim," Jim Boatwright, "virtually lives there." The Colonel had recruited Jimmy and David as gym members. In cut-off denim hot pants, work boots, a tank top showing off beefed-up biceps and pecs, and "a Mexican-bandit mustache," Boatwright had made himself over in the "clone" style that was sweeping gay America. On the streets in the center of town, roosters roamed freely, cocks on parade, like deliberate parodies of Key West's gallery of male types—from Boatwright and his pals at the gym to the white-bearded old salts, the Hemingway lookalikes, whose bravura poses were paired here with their opposite, the epicene and transsexual, in the carnival spirit of the drag queens. Night and day on Duval Street, Mars lounged in the lap of Venus.

Grace Stone was back that winter. From Montreal came Christian Ayoub, whom Jimmy had met in Egypt in 1959, the Alexandrian wit and writer who had for years now lived with his wife and daughter in Canada; and the novelist Marie-Claire Blais and her partner Mary Meigs—buoyant new friends who stayed out late with Jimmy and David at La-Te-Da, a piano bar with cross-dressed acts, or the lubricous Mangoes, a Kolonáki-style open-air café two blocks from Elizabeth Street that was perfect for the sort of people watching Jackson liked to do. Rather than white, middle-class, Nautilus-built clones, DJ came home from the bars with poor black men. David's bed was "insatiable," Jimmy snapped, commenting on the train of overnight visitors. (Not that he himself lacked all companionship: Peter

Tourville flew down to Key West for a week.) When DJ's "old white magic" turned one of those tricks into a regular, Merrill seemed both jealous and envious; and wary—since he detected, under the good looks and docile manner of this newcomer sleeping down the hall from him, "the stone heart of a born hustler."

Merrill went north in April for the spring season of literary events in the company of David Kalstone, starting with a gathering at Vassar in celebration of the college library's purchase of Bishop's papers: here was Elizabeth, passing over the bar from life to the archive shelf. Jimmy and DK stayed with John Ashbery and David Kermani in their big nineteenth-century home facing the courthouse square in Hudson, New York. Easing into evening, in defiance of the law, JM fired a joint that went at once into a rhyme about time running short, entitled "Grass":

> We light up between
> Earth and Venus
> On the courthouse lawn,
>
> Kept by this cheerful
> Inch of green
> And ten more years—fifteen?—
> From disappearing.

As a connoisseur of special domestic spaces, Merrill enthused over what Ashbery had made of his house: he had "never seen so much golden oak and stained glass, so many pantries and cupboards." It was "a staggering belle époque affair" packed with New York School paintings, elegant or old-fashioned furniture, and objects from various periods and places, collaged together like the mix of styles in an Ashbery poem. At Ashbery's urging, Merrill made a Ouija board and used it with him, but the cup got stuck insisting on the phrase: "JA KNOWS"—which seemed oracular when JA turned up in the emergency room two days later with a life-threatening infection it would take him months to recover from.

Back in the city, Kalstone, the balletomane, took Jimmy to a party for George Balanchine's prima ballerina, Suzanne Farrell. Then they wiped away tears at the final performance of the Little Players, those finger-sized ballerinas and thespians that Merrill had funded and applauded for twenty-five years.

Only in summer would JM and DJ find themselves back together, for Mary McCarthy's seventieth birthday party in Maine: one more marker of time passing. David had spent the past season on his own in Santo Domingo. "Why?" Merrill mused in a letter to Friar. "I suspect he gets to feeling that he lives too much of the time in my shadow and wants to test his own identity. This would have been easier for him in Greece than over here, where one is forever being 'placed,' whether accurately or not." In his notebook, Merrill was sadder and angrier, more self-accusing, more plaintive and alarmed:

> Is this life? Can D. believe that it is? Is he simply bored to this gradual extinction of all interest in . . . reading or his watercolors or concern for our suicidal world? Am I to blame, as he now + then enjoys implying? Perhaps I am: we're arriving at the stage my mother + I reached years ago, of insulating ourselves from each other by social occasions, or failing them, silence. Is he as unhappy as I am with this state of affairs?

Atheneum published Merrill's selected poems and the *Sandover* trilogy in late fall 1982. Merrill referred to the pair of volumes, grimly, as "The Tombstone Edition." *From the First Nine: Poems 1946–1976* gathered most of his poems from the past three decades, while *The Changing Light at Sandover* bound the books of the trilogy together with the epilogue. Each book illuminated the other. It's what he'd felt reencountering the poems in *The Black Swan*: "Returning to those early poems *now*, obviously in the light of the completed trilogy, I've had to marvel a bit at the resemblances." He must have meant the symbols and conceits in poems like "The Peacock," "Transfigured Bird," "The Broken Bowl," and "The Black Swan." "It's as if after a long lapse [. . .] I'd finally, with the trilogy, reentered the church of those original themes. The colors, the elements, the magical emblems: they were the first subjects I'd found again at last." The trilogy (these companion volumes declared) drew on everything he had done.

And everything he had been. To make the point that autobiography underpinned the whole, à la Proust, he chose for the endpapers of *Sandover* images of the people who had become characters in the long poem—a photo of himself and DJ from the 1950s taken on the third floor of Water Street by their Stonington neighbor, Rollie McKenna; one of Auden, also by McKenna; snapshots of George, Robert, Mimi, and Maria; Maya in the "Medusa" pose from her film *Meshes of the Afternoon*; and Hans's profile, which had sat so long propped up in his study. These images gave the monumental book the feel of a family album. The cover took the story back to his childhood: it was a photo from the 1930s of the music room in the Orchard. In this eerie image, a blinding spring light shines into the grand gloomy space like some inmost day shining in on night; tall candles reach toward the paneled ceiling they hang from; and vases bristle with phallic gladioli.

McClatchy arranged for an interview with Merrill to appear in the *Paris Review* before *From the First Nine* and *Sandover* were published. The magazine's famous series included interviews with the likes of Faulkner, Hemingway, Cocteau, Nabokov, Pound, Williams, Moore, and Frost; up to this point, only a few poets of Merrill's own generation (Ginsberg, Sexton, Wilbur) had been included. Merrill made the most of the occasion, using it to produce what was in effect a postscript and preface to the two volumes about to come out. Although it was presented as a lively impromptu conversation, capturing the tone of a friendship, the interview was managed by mail. The conversational form brought out Merrill's best. His admiring interlocutor freed him to talk about his life and work without seeming to impose himself and make conclusive statements, even while he carefully crafted his responses. "I would send him a sheet of paper with a question at the top and space for him to answer," McClatchy recalled. "He couldn't anticipate what I would ask him, and that made it fresh"—something like the energizing surprise of a dialogue on the Ouija board.

His answers underlined the continuity of his themes. In retrospect, even ostensibly private, autobiographical poems disclosed the mythic subjects of the trilogy. "That bit in 'The Broken Home,' " he commented, "—'Father Time and Mother Earth, / A marriage on the rocks'—isn't meant as a joke. History in our time *has* cut loose, *has* broken faith with Nature." But lyric poems "can't deal frontally with such huge, urgent subjects." "So my parents' divorce dramatized on a human scale a subject that couldn't have been handled otherwise. [. . .] You don't see eternity *except* in the grain of sand, or history except at the family dinner table." Conversely, behind the trilogy's myths and its frontal engagement with "huge, urgent subjects" lay his own family romance. Probing the connection, McClatchy asked him about the haunting image of the ballroom that appears in "A Tenancy," "The Broken Home," and the epilogue to the trilogy. Merrill's answer brooded on the origins of that image in the music room pictured on the cover of *Sandover*:

Looking back, even going back to visit while my father still had that house, I could see how much grander the room was than any of the uses we'd put it to, so maybe the ghostly presences appeared in order to make up for a thousand unrealized possibilities. The same sense probably accounts for my "redecoration" in the epilogue—making the room conform to an ideal much sunnier, much more silvery, that I began to trust only as an adult, while keeping carefully out of mind (until that passage had been written) the story of how Cronus cuts off the scrotum, or "ballroom," of his father Uranus and throws it into the sea, where it begins to foam and shine, and the goddess of Love and Beauty is born.

On one level, Merrill's fantasy of the supernatural manor called Sandover, being much better suited to his father's Anglophile taste than to his own, was a belated tribute to CEM. There was nostalgia and piety at work: in the Other World, Jimmy re-inhabited the Broken Home in a "sunnier, more silvery" state, free from conflict. Queen Mum was present and in charge, accompanied by the hornless unicorn Uni, the benign uniter, who was also an avatar of Francis, the *fils unique* and eunuch of *The Seraglio*. But Merrill's return to the music room in the "Ballroom at Sandover" was also an act of imaginative violence, an appropriation of the symbol of the father's potency for the son's worship of Venus. With his Ouija board, Jimmy had made something bigger and better than the Orchard.

Yet what was it exactly that he'd made? With the trilogy bound in one foaming, shining book, the question was what it added up to as a whole. *Was it a whole?* It was a long way in its design and proportions from the three uniform *cantiche* of Dante's *Comedy*. Indeed, each of the three books, itself a composite of heterogeneous modes, is significantly different in form from the other two. *The Book of Ephraim* is Merrill's single best poem—and what a poem it is: by pushing to its limit the genre of lyric autobiography he invented in the 1960s and early 1970s, he created a postmodern romance that, had the trilogy's later books never been written, could stand on its own as one of the high points in American poetry of the period. But when it is bound with the other books in *Sandover*, *Ephraim* is dwarfed by *Mirabell* and *Scripts*. It becomes a preface, an initial statement of motifs to be developed over 460 more pages of verse dominated by the spirits' upper-case pronouncements. Merrill's lyric autobiography remains in place as a frame in *Mirabell*, but the center of the poem is a mythographic scriptural text, a transaction with primal powers. Gradually, as the bat-angel turns into the peacock Mirabell, those powers are domesticated, and the form of the poem becomes increasingly ceremonial, adjusted to the imagination of the mediums. But the strangeness of their first encounters with these spirit-speakers, who materialize as if from inside the alphabet itself, is like little else in modern literature. The usual categories of aesthetic judgment hardly seem to apply.

And *Scripts for the Pageant* is something else again. The "play of voices" that Merrill projected as the form for *Mirabell* takes its full shape here. *Scripts* utilizes the conventions not so much of the drama as of a published play text, including stage directions and speakers identified in the left margin ("Mich," "WHA," "JM" et al.). The poem is a theater of the mind that wasn't intended for performance; it is a work of pure poetic drama, a closet opera. The excitement of it, when the charm works, lies in imagining the unimaginable on the basis of verbal cues alone. It's what the reader does alongside the mediums, thanks to the power of words on a white page to evoke voices, stage sets, lighting, sounds, scents—another world, which is the essence of the Ouija board's sorcery.

As a play text, *Scripts* alludes to Shakespearean drama, but it is Shakespeare as seen through the lens of *The Sea and the Mirror*, Auden's set of dramatic monologues for characters in *The Tempest*, which delighted Merrill when he read it in 1947. Another strong influence (itself an influence on *The Tempest*) was the Renaissance masque. As he worked on *Scripts*, Merrill consulted *The Illusion of Power: Political Theater in the English Renaissance*, a study of the masque by Stephen Orgel, a friend whom he had met through DK. The masque as described by Orgel was a theatrical ceremony of royal power that persuaded its audience through splendor and astonishment. There is no more dramatic tension inherent in the form than there is in any pageant or parade, and the masque-like dimensions of *Scripts* are part of the static impression the poem conveys. Conversation is action in this installment of the trilogy. That was true of *Mirabell* too, but in *Scripts* the voices proliferate, and their interplay grows dazzlingly complex. Merrill manages to create—and differentiate—forty-seven spirit-speakers who interrupt, refer to, and correct each other, while never being anything more than uppercase letters on the page.

The differences in poetic form in the three books of the trilogy reflect Merrill's changing relationship to his Ouija board materials. In the case of *Ephraim*, he'd lost many of the transcripts. "The years—time itself—did my winnowing for me"; therefore most of the poem was in lowercase, representing Merrill's thoughts and memories. By contrast *Mirabell* "was purgatory to arrange on the page and to make it as trimmed down as I possibly could." That struggle expressed the alien nature of his sources and the force of his own resistance to them. In the case of *Scripts*, however,

> there was no shaping to be done. Except for the minutest changes and deciding about line breaks and so forth, the lessons you see on the page appear just as we took them down. The doggerel at the fêtes,

everything. In between the lessons—our chats with Wystan or Robert Morse or Uni [. . .]—I still felt free to pick and choose; but even there, the design of the book just swept me along.

JM hadn't been taken over by the spirits, *or* they by him; as he thought of it, they were producing together the poem they both wanted. The process of composition was circular, culminating in JM reading the poem to the spirits.

In short, in *Scripts*, Merrill was writing "for the angels," which Jonathan Bishop had warned him against. The Jacobean masque, performed in the Royal Banquet House, is the essence of an elite art, and the elitism of the trilogy is most insistent in *Scripts*. Gone are the high grades that the mediums got in *Mirabell*, but most of that poem's mass culture "popthink," the UFOs and New Age science, has been left behind too. The high hedge bordering the manor house is emblematic of privilege and exclusion. We don't just hear about the R Lab in *Scripts*; we visit it. Maria turns out to be Plato himself, one of the Five ("I'M BORN," s/he laughs, "WITH THE SILVER SPOON IN ALL MY LIVES"). There is a centrifugal energy at work as Merrill packs a progressively larger vision of history and the cosmos into the trilogy, the universe shrinks to the cramped entrance hall in Athens where the séances occur, and the secrets of creation are divulged by—and to—a charmed coterie.

Yet it is hard to tell that centrifugal energy from its opposite—a centripetal thrust always complicating the trilogy through the multiplication of puns, analogies, and motifs. The long poem's design grows more inconclusive and open-ended as it becomes larger and more intricate. It's frustrating, but also a relief, that the teachings of the Ouija board keep being revised, shredded by each successive revelation. Characters mutate and meld, like Maria and Plato. Does it shrink the cast or enlarge it to learn, as we do in the epilogue, that the Angel of Light first spoke to the mediums through Ephraim, and that Lord Michael and "Mister E" (a homophone for "mystery") are "twins"? Their initials "M/E" express the inescapability of the self, the presence of a unifying imagination behind the Ouija board's endless projections and its illusion of otherness. But those initials also suggest just the opposite: a principle of duplicity—a mercurial "Mister E"—in JM's (and for that matter anyone's) "me."

All of this is in keeping with the volatile, shape-shifting nature of language on the Ouija board, as set in motion by the hands of the mediums. When the dead assemble to hear the poem in the epilogue, they are introduced in order. As he sees the names, the Scribe grasps the seating plan:

"ELIOT, FROST, GOETHE It's an alphabet? / CLEVER JM." It's not so much the angels that JM reads to, finally, as the letters out of which the trilogy has been made: there are "26 CHAIRS IN ALL." To make the important point that language is not a closed system, however, the guest list and the alphabet don't perfectly match up: "SOME DOUBLINGS MAKE FOR GAPS." The trilogy, not despite its doublings but because of them, is full of gaps. When it turns around on itself in the epilogue to end where it began, Merrill's long poem represents less a self-enclosed artifact than the dream of one, undone by the metamorphic verbal logic that created it. The trilogy insists that language, the instrument of all its revelations, prevents any revelation from being final.

Underlying these ideas was a romantic theory of consciousness that would have satisfied Blake and Hart Crane. For language, Merrill said in his interview with McClatchy, reconciling poetry and science,

> is the human medium. It doesn't exist—except perhaps as vast mathematical or chemical formulas—in that realm of, oh, cosmic forces, elemental processes, which *we* then personify, or tame if you like, through the imagination. So, in a sense, all these figures are our creations, or mankind's. The powers they represent are real—as, say, gravity is "real"—but they'd be invisible, inconceivable, if they'd never passed through our heads and clothed themselves out of the costume box they found there. *How* they appear depends on us, on the imaginer, and would have to vary wildly from culture to culture, or even temperament to temperament. A process that Einstein could entertain as a formula might be described by an African witch doctor as a crocodile. What's tiresome is when people exclusively insist on the forms they've imagined. Those powers don't need churches in order to be sacred. What they do need are fresh ways of being seen.

And the Ouija board was *his* way of seeing them. "Does the Ouija board ever embarrass you?" McClatchy asked, picking up the thread and giving it a tug.

> From what I've just said, you see how pompous I can get. The mechanics of the board—this absurd, flimsy contraption, creaking along—serves wonderfully as a hedge against inflation. I think it does embarrass the sort of reader who can't bear to face the random or trivial elements that coalesce, among others, to produce an "elevated" thought. That doesn't bother me *at all*.

So much, then, for "NO ACCIDENT." In contrast to Dante's plan, structured by Thomist theology, Merrill's trilogy lacked an organizing system external to the language that generated it, and it was open to accident and revision at every point. The whole that it constitutes is that of a poet's experience, the substance of the revelation being its own volatile, magical means. The poem's story is the story of its making.

But *Sandover* is not only about "the human medium," language. It's also about love and friendship. It's about the way a shared life takes shape and gathers meaning over time. It's about literary influence and the collective imagination that we call culture. It's about frivolity and about grief. It's about gay identity and the masquerade of gender, about atomic fission and human generation, the will to die and the will to live. It's about the origins of the planet and its future, the dream of Heaven and the dream of Paradise. It is a grand, grand opera, a puppet show, a voodoo dance, a game of Patience. When we close the big book and stand back, what emerges is Merrill's daring: the scope of his long poem, its constant, restless technical invention, and its peculiar, faintly scandalous premise.

Or was that premise so peculiar, after all? The revelations of *Sandover* come of that most commonplace activity, conversation; and, as the spirits insisted in one post-*Sandover* séance, revelation was no secret art:

> WE LAY NO CLAIM TO OMNISCIENCE ONLY TO OVERVIEW NORMAL IN HIGH
> PLACES WHO SO HUMBLE AS YOUR OLD GREEK FRIEND HORSES, BIRDS, [. . .]?
> COMMONER/S TUFF YOULL BE HARD PUT TO FIND: A PASTE + CLAY CUP, A
> GIFTED RICH BOY A LAZY HAND US! WHAT! MYSTICAL! GOD PRESSERVE US!
> NEVER. WE R TELEPHONE + WIRES. THE ELEMENT OF TALK. + LAY NO CLAIM
> TO NOTHING ELSE FOR EVER 4 BREATH IN G/ AND NOT BREATHING A CREA-
> TURE MAY / CAN LAY CLAIM TO GOD B + HIS TWIN.

"I felt that," DJ agreed. But what should they say when people ask if "it's real?" JM had his answer: "I want the <u>experience</u> to be believed + beyond that it's up to the reader." DJ proposed that the poem is "a glass," something to "see through." "THAT YES HAND + POET YES THAT," the board approved, "+ A BIT MORE FOR NO MATTER THE MEANS OF WHAT'S CALLED REVELATION, IF THE REVELATION IS RELEVANT."

In November 1982, shortly before *The Changing Light at Sandover* went to press, Merrill visited Claude Fredericks in Pawlet. In the car was a carton containing "about twenty reams" of the Ouija board transcripts he had used to write the trilogy: he intended to burn them—most, though not all of the transcripts from *Mirabell* and *Scripts*—in Fredericks's fireplace. For this poet who archived every draft of his poems, it was a surprising thing to do. He'd thought about it at least since writing the last section of *Ephraim*, in which he imagines the "elate / Burst of satori" that a page of Ouija transcript would feel when put to the flames. Now with Claude, a practicing Buddhist, for audience, he carried out the final ceremony of *Sandover*. The bare stage set of his old friend's living room appealed to him, with its white walls without paintings, windows without curtains, only a grand piano, a Norfolk Island pine, canvas chairs, and "the great roaring hearth." It was Claude who was with him in 1973 when the telegram came saying that Maria was dead, and Claude who'd told him to give up the novel about Ephraim and write a poem instead.

By destroying so many of the *Sandover* transcripts, Merrill covered his tracks, preventing biographers and rare book dealers, the skeptical and curious, from laying hands on them. It was like someone burning old love letters—a way of keeping faith with those who had favored him. But he must have also wanted to let those pages go, to be free of them, unable to look back, unable to make anything more of them. He was Prospero drowning his book. Page by page, into the Vermont night, the words of the spirits flew up the chimney as smoke.

PART V

LOVE AND DEATH

1983–95

16

PETER

1983–86

Merrill opened his copy of *Sandover* and fell "in horror" on a page badly garbled by the printer. Somehow he'd missed it in the galleys. It meant that an elaborate erratum slip would need to be inserted into this, the first edition of his monumental work, delaying publication by a month. He was always fastidious with words: rare is the grammatical error or typo even in his letters. This one, as he entered into 1983, fed his general sense of something being very wrong. Even paradisal Key West that January was "awful," drowned in "torrential rains." Emotionally he was "battling what I rather felt would strike as soon as the books were out, a spell of depression shot through with various hypochondriacal symptoms that, no matter how airily dismissed by a local quack, don't go away." He was dogged by "nameless fears" about his health, "or the worse ones with names," while feeling obliged to make out to his "dear ones" that all was well. It was enough to make him cry and curse: "hell + damnation!"

"Meanwhile," he added, "marvelous reviews keep coming out as I sink further into gloom." The reviews were indeed marvelous. They began with a handsome notice in *Newsweek* where David Lehman called *Sandover* "the greatest long poem—and [. . .] undoubtedly the longest great poem—an American has yet produced." (Some readers must have murmured, Greater than *Song of Myself*? Longer than *The Cantos*?) *The New York Times Book Review* made amends for Denis Donoghue's caustic remarks on *Scripts* with a long, respectful review of both *Sandover* and *From the First Nine* by R. W. Flint. *The New York Review of Books* gave Robert Mazzocco even more room in which to meditate on Merrill's poetic development over three decades, treating him to a full-scale career assessment from the perspective of the completed long poem. In an intriguing pairing of book and reviewer, Michael Harrington, founder of the Democratic Socialists of America, a political scientist and the author of *The Politics at God's Funeral: The Spiritual Crisis of Western Civilization* (1983), wrote about the poem in *Commonweal*. "It is possible," he began, "that James Merrill's *The Changing Light at Sandover* is one of the significant works of the second half of this century." His hesitation had to do with his objection to the Malthusian themes of the Ouija board, which he saw as an expression of Merrill's "ambivalent liberal elitism." But Harrington was willing to treat that elitism as the price of admission to the trilogy's religious vision: Merrill's poem was important, he decided, because it faces the central spiritual challenge of its era by trying to reconcile "the God of Abraham and the empirical reality of Wittgenstein." To make the point, he quoted a passage near the end of *Mirabell* in which Merrill suggests that those grand competing worldviews boil down to two "flim-flam / Tautologies": "*I am that I am*" and "*The world is everything that is the case*." "Open the case," Merrill continues, playing on Wittgenstein's famous statement in one of the most clever and beautiful passages in the trilogy:

> Lift out the fabulous
> Necklace, in form a spiral molecule
> Whose sparklings outmaneuver time, space, us.

Harrington reasoned that, "if God is in crisis, so is literature," and Merrill's sparkling necklace of DNA, at once earthly and divine, lifted from the philosopher's airtight case, rescued them both.

The Changing Light at Sandover won prizes from the National Book Critics Circle and the *Los Angeles Times*. It was an indication of Merrill's mood that he chose not to attend the awards ceremony in Los Angeles, to the distress of the prize's sponsor. He could honestly plead busyness. For when he wasn't getting prizes these days, he was giving them. He flew north in January as one of the judges for the Bollingen Prize awarded by Yale's Beinecke

Library, which went to Anthony Hecht and John Hollander. However worthy they were of this major award, Hecht and Hollander were also chummy choices typical of the poetry business: Hecht had been one of the judges when Merrill won the Bollingen and when the Pulitzer went to *Mirabell*, and Hollander was one of Merrill's closest poet friends, a professor at Yale, and a former Bollingen judge himself.

That spring Merrill became the judge of the Yale Younger Poets series. The oldest annual poetry award in the U.S., the series is a prize for a first book published by Yale University Press. Among distinguished past judges of the prize, the most notable was Auden, whose selections of Merwin, Ashbery, Rich, James Wright, and Hollander helped to define Merrill's poetic generation and made the prize the most prestigious debut in American poetry. Merrill put his own stamp on the award by selecting Richard Kenney's romantic, ingenious, distinctly Merrillean poems (the long last poem in the book was a travelogue entitled "Notes from Greece"). Though various, the subsequent winners Merrill would choose—in order: Pamela Alexander, George Bradley, Brigit Pegeen Kelly, Julie Agoos, Thomas Bolt, and Daniel Hall—shared precision of perception and fine rhetorical control. He never pushed himself to make a provocative choice, although he didn't pick acolytes, and he passed on the work of poets who were already his friends, such as Henri Cole and David Lehman (to whom he made a point of writing encouraging rejection letters). He made friends with most of the prizewinners, starting with the tall, willowy, soft-spoken Kenney. He liked the role of mentor, and he was good at it. But he found the work of prize judge onerous. Besides evaluating the manuscripts that made it past the press's readers, he had to write a preface for the winner's book, a task he complained of annually. As always, he was uncomfortable writing criticism. Worse, duties like these made him feel old. "Isn't it sickening," he wrote to Donald Richie, "how powerful we grow as the grave yawns wider + wider?"

David Jackson was a mirror Merrill didn't like to look into. These days the Hand seemed permanently to be holding a lit cigarette. Merrill expressed the annoyance and anxiety he felt about David's condition in verses entitled "Gadfly Rondeaux / for DJ," which he slipped under his partner's door in Key West:

> Three packs a day
> Simply won't do.
> I mean to say,
> Three-packs-a-day

Is both outré
And bad for you.

That airless room
Reeking of smoke:
It's like a tomb,
That airless room.
Come on, exhume
Yourself, old soak!
That airless room
Reeking of smoke . . .

You are life's clear-
Eyed, smiling rhyme.
Why rage? Why fear?
You are. Life's clear.
I need you here
To last my time.
You are life's clear-
Eyed, smiling rhyme.

Jimmy too was a smoker, who struggled with the habit; and his growing rage at David, along with his anxiety about the "hypochondriacal symptoms" that preoccupied him (including high blood pressure for the first time in his life, a slow-to-heal prostate infection, and a swollen lymph gland), made it hard not to light up.

The name of his worst fear was a new word: AIDS. The first broad public awareness of the retrovirus that would sweep across the globe came in newspaper reports about a mysterious condition characterized by an atypical, highly resistant strain of pneumonia (pneumocystis, or PCP) and a rare disfiguring cancer (Kaposi's sarcoma) that seemed to target gay men in particular. The first clinical report of what would become known as AIDS was published by the Centers for Disease Control in June 1981. That report was followed by brief pieces in the *Los Angeles Times* and *The New York Times*—which ran a single-column story on July 3 headed "Rare Cancer Seen in 41 Homosexuals" (*Times* editors didn't yet permit the use of "gay"). American medicine wasn't prepared to recognize a new infectious disease. There was confusion at the CDC itself, which was in the midst of staff reductions and reorganization due to massive federal agency cutbacks initiated by President Reagan. The indifference of the "general population" to a disease besetting gays, combined with a common aversion to speaking frankly of sex, encouraged American politicians to avoid the issue. Reagan did not publicly acknowledge the need for federal funding to combat AIDS until 1987, three years into his second term as president, and six years into the epidemic.

Although the condition was already known to affect other demographic groups, such as IV drug users, it was so closely associated with gay men in New York and California that it was for a time referred to as Gay-related Immune Deficiency, or GRID. AIDS, for Acquired Immune Deficiency Syndrome, was coined in 1982. The acronym named a syndrome: not a disease per se but a morbid state characterized by the presence of assorted opportunistic infections that can be easily warded off by a healthy immune system. The cause of this immune deficiency, the human immunodeficiency virus, HIV, was identified at the Institut Pasteur in 1983. By the end of that year the number of AIDS cases in the U.S. had reached 3,064; of these, 1,292 people had already died from the disease. There was little scientific knowledge about AIDS, and what knowledge there was reached the public in unreliable or distorted accounts. Supposedly authoritative news reports explained that the virus was communicated in "bodily fluids," rather than specifically in blood, semen, and vaginal secretions, and implied as a result that a shared cup, a toothbrush, or a kiss might transmit it. Myths flourished. AIDS was caused by anal sex. The rectum was a uniquely vulnerable organ. Poppers broke down the immune system. The virus had penetrated American society from abroad (Old Europe, darkest Africa, or the voodoo-haunted Caribbean). AIDS was a scourge sent by God to punish the dwellers of Sodom and Gomorrah, New York and San Francisco. It was the Gay Plague. Even or especially in middle-class gay enclaves like Key West, AIDS was a matter of anxious fantasy and desperate rumor.

Merrill seldom used the word. It shows up for the first time in his letters in June 1983 when, after praising a sexually explicit story by Donald Richie, Merrill sighs, "I'm afraid, though, that Gay Lit has had its day, at least until they find a cure for AIDS." A few days before, he and DJ had sat down for a long talk about AIDS on the Ouija board. The doctor, George Cotzias, was there to help them ("AH JIM DAVE! SO GOOD TO SEE THE PAEDIA!"), and they asked if he had "heard about panic over AIDS." "INDEED & MORE OR LESS INTRODUCED! PROMISCUOUS SEX AMONG HOMOPHOBES CREATED ODDLY ENOUGH POP. EXPLOSION." So the point—but had there been no other way of making it?—was to curb reproduction around the world. "BY FRIGHTENING THE STRAIGHT WORLD WE WILL PRODUCE A WHOLE TREMOR OF REACTION: LESS SEX RESULTING IN SHORT (million dead by 1990?) NOT DEAD, EXPOSED. THE

CURE NOW EXISTS + THE MAJOR CURE WILL BE TO SEXUAL HABITS OF GAY + + + STRAIGHT WORLD. CURE WILL, B4 YEAR IS OUT, BE IN PLACE." And the mediums themselves had little to fear: "OF U 2 ONLY HAND NEEDS CAUTION + I BELIEVE HE WILL HEED IT." Then Ephraim, taking hold of the cup, vaulted into the glad cadences of God B and the Brothers: "MATTER SCRIBE HOLDS! ALL ELSE TREMBLES. ON MATTER WE PLAN PARADISE, FOR IT WILL BE REAL + THEN AN AGE FREER OF THE WHIP OF CHAOS [. . .] WE HOLD IT BACK. WE SURVIVE. CHEERS DEAR ONES CHEERS YOU THRIVE THE V WORK FARES WELL + OUR SITES HAVE LEVELED ON PARADISE. ONWARD ONWARD MY SUN SETS IN A CLEAR SKY, AS DO YOUR BRIGHT LIVES. ADIEU."

The sublime affirmative hymns of the trilogy ring hollow here, motivated by the fear and helplessness Merrill felt in the face of AIDS. He would do what he could to defend himself against this new "SCOURGE." He didn't need the "CAUTION" that the Hand received: he had already made up his mind about "PROMISCUOUS SEX." With a young Canadian poet, a friend of Daryl Hine's whom he had met when he gave a reading in Montreal, Merrill maintained a confiding, flirtatious correspondence, in which he put down his current thinking about gay promiscuity. The young man had written to Merrill about his budding romance with a young woman—which would mean for him no more evenings cruising for men in Mount Royal Park, the mountain in the middle of the city. Older, wiser James wrote to him about the affair:

> I hope it's keeping you off the streets—or more exactly, off the Mountain. When Daryl told me about that, I shook my old head. For purely medical reasons, believe me. Promiscuity has been my tried and true friend for long spells, but now there is this new Disease, and until they've found a cure for it everyone who's not suicidal will have to be very very careful, not to say monogamous. The symptoms don't show up for two years, after which your chances of living more than another two are slimissimi. Anything you've heard to the contrary is wishful thinking, according to the gay doctors we've heard on the subject.

Even as he wrote these sentences, Merrill must have opened his calendar mentally, thinking of that reputed "two-year" window before symptoms of HIV infection began to appear, reviewing how many men he had been with, and precisely when, over the past several years.

When he went to Europe that May, he avoided the boys and bars of Athens by staying with Nelly and spending his time with her elegant society friends. He was tempted to settle into his own old home, which by chance was empty for his last week in town. " 'But <u>there</u> you'll be alone!' said Nelly. '<u>Here</u> it's a house where people are living—where you'll have company when you need it.' And so forth. My eyes burn as I write it down." Staying clear of sexual temptation meant spending more time alone, and, at fifty-seven, he found solitude harder than ever to endure.

In Italy he met up with Eleanor. Kalstone hosted the two Stoningtonians in Venice, where he had found dazzling digs in the Palazzo Barbaro. With a fanciful Gothic façade from the fifteenth century and a Baroque addition from 1700, overlooking the Grand Canal just beside the Accademia Bridge, the Barbaro is one of the city's splendid private houses. In the nineteenth century, it was purchased by Americans, the Curtises, who hosted Boston royalty such as Isabella Stewart Gardner and Charles Eliot Norton, as well as Browning, Whistler, and Monet. The kitchen, which Merrill turned into his study, had once served John Singer Sargent as a studio. James finished *The Aspern Papers* while visiting the Curtises, and he used the Barbaro as the model for Milly Theale's grand, spooky Palazzo Leporelli in *The Wings of the Dove*. "The wonderful library, into which HJ had his bed moved, had a shelf of his books, all inscribed." While DK swam laps at the pool and Eleanor went shopping (for her, Robert Morse used to say, Italy was "the shores of Gimmegucci"), Merrill lingered in the palace library with those first editions, marveling at the prose of the Master: "The wonder of HJ is how much he says by saying on the surface, nothing. His 'matter' is like that of the physicist, all energy + flow, nothing you can put your finger on." He marveled also at how many of the characters in *The Seraglio* had come straight out of *The Wings of the Dove*: newly charmed by it, he seems to have forgotten that he'd pored over the novel in the 1940s. He was taken this time by the tubercular Milly's "motto"—"Never to go down!"—and adopted it as his own in letters reporting on the trip. It was a serious joke: he was swearing never to stop living in style, never to lose face if he were to fall ill, and, to give himself the best chance of staying well, never again to "go down" on a stranger in the park.

Merrill and Perényi, evidently taking the canal tour of Europe, moved on to Amsterdam, Delft, and Bruges, cities tinged for Jimmy with memories of Hans Lodeizen, whom he'd last seen in a hospital room thirty-three years ago that June. They gushed over the tulip markets in the lowlands, the Vermeers, the "soft amber-pink filets" of herring, and the "enormous, delicious pancakes of every description." Aside from a long-ago voyage to Europe when they split up on arrival, and the odd summer weekend spent visiting Mary McCarthy in Maine, these longtime neighbors had never been anywhere together. Jimmy, always a determined tourist, complained that "the walking utterly exhausted" Eleanor, who had a "dreadful habit of making loud remarks in English about people very much within earshot." But his old friend fended off his loneliness, and she was easy enough to manage in the end. When it was time to fly home, the baroness downed three vodka tonics and a valium before Jimmy herded her onto the plane as "docile as a drugged circus animal."

Two weeks after sampling those Dutch delicacies with Perényi, he was in a pup tent beside Peter Tourville, chowing down a campfire stew after canoeing on the Vermont–New Hampshire border. DJ was on the bank to collect the paddlers after they spent thirty hours on the water; he drove them to Wells River, the village in northern Vermont where McClatchy and Corn had a house. McClatchy recalled Tourville as "tallish, over 6'1, and country-lean" from outdoor labor, with a "gravelly voice and easy laugh," a stoner's squint, a fuzzy halo of scraggly hair, a ruddy handlebar mustache, and a tattoo on his right forearm. He was "a lot more likely to be found peering under the hood of a truck than into a book," McClatchy supposed; and yet Tourville held his own in board games with the poet, to judge from the scores they left behind in the Scrabble box on Water Street from their quiet weekends together. They'd known each other since the early 1960s. Merrill helped support Tourville by buying a small apple orchard for him to tend in New Hampshire, a property called "Future Apples Inc." that became a lasting headache for Merrill's lawyer. Tourville was "devoted" to Merrill, McClatchy felt, and "obviously Jimmy was smitten with him." By appearing now and then as Merrill worked on *Sandover* in solitude on Water Street, Tourville had become a familiar character in his life. By 1983, however, their relations were growing strained. That fall, Tourville lost strength in his arms and had to be put in traction for an old neck injury. He was drinking hard and taking drugs—to the point that Merrill became worried and angry; then Tourville's marriage seemed to be falling apart. The news from New Hampshire Merrill found "scary." By winter, when his thoughts turned to Tourville, Merrill found himself throwing up "an arm to ward off the next blow." Even so, he might not have lost interest if he hadn't turned his attention to another Peter.

Peter Hooten arrived in Merrill's life by graduated stages. Jimmy referred to him as his "movie star fan," and that was what he was: a movie actor and a dedicated fan of this poet. He discovered Merrill's poetry for the first time at a reading at UCLA in 1978, introduced by Yenser. (The crowd was "huge," Hooten thought. When the applause was over, a stranger in the next row turned around and said to him, "Did we hear what we heard? *That* was genius.") Hooten read *Divine Comedies* and then *Mirabell* and *Scripts* as they came out; he bought rare Merrill publications at a bookstore in Greenwich Village. In 1982, when Merrill read at Endicott Books on the Upper West Side, Peter sat in the front row, "beaming," then waited in line with *The Metamorphosis of 741* for JM to sign. Hooten asked for permission to write to him at home. Merrill teased him: "You know the address!" So Hooten sent a letter and a photo of himself to 107 Water Street: it was a still from one of his movies, inscribed, "Remember me?" Intrigued by this time, Merrill asked Hooten to dinner in his apartment in New York after another reading that spring. That night Hooten came along with his partner Alan Moss (his full name was Alan Moss Reveron), who sold Art Deco and '50s antiques and collected Puerto Rican santos in SoHo.

An invitation to Stonington followed. On an August weekend, without Moss this time, Hooten took a predawn train from the city, walked four miles along Route 1 to Stonington from the station in Mystic, went for a swim in the harbor, and slept on the beach until it was a plausible hour to climb the stairs and knock on Merrill's door. The apartment was already packed, with Jim Boatwright and his boyfriend Lee Toy visiting. Jimmy and David took their guests that afternoon to Isabel Morse's house for tea. The thread of connection was slight: "PH is somehow related to Robert's oldest friend," whom, however, "Peter's never met." "PH" (as JM was already calling him) took the stage in Isabel's parlor to recite poems by Robert Frost and Merrill himself, as if he were auditioning for a part. "Very brave of him [. . .]," Merrill wrote to Yenser, "and quite successful on the whole. He grew up in Florida, so that we share those legato underpinnings of the Southern voice. The only wrong notes"—Merrill was trying to retain at least his literary judgment—"were his stressing of any uncontracted auxiliary verb, like the stewardess saying 'The captain <u>has</u> turned off the No Smoking sign, etc'—or in his case, 'I <u>have</u> lived on this same street for a decade'—but he gives off such a warmed honey of response that we'd have been won over if he'd just squeaked and gibbered." By the time he left, the name was blazing on Merrill's mental marquee: "P*E*T*E*R H*O*O*T*E*N."

There had been a steady stream of visitors on Water Street. One was Harry Pemberton, a philosophy professor at Washington and Lee University in Virginia who'd made friends with Merrill and Jackson in the 1970s in Athens. That summer he took a roll of photos that captured the mediums at the Ouija board. Merrill, Pemberton remembered, was "smiling, enjoying the game," whereas Jackson, distant and drooping, was "concerned, anxious, more superstitious. I think David actually believed they were talking to people upstairs." Or was his mind simply elsewhere? "It's been," he wrote to Pemberton later, "a hectic, not to say catastrophic summer." That wasn't such an exaggeration. Jackson's carpenter in Key West, a good friend, had shot and killed himself, "miserable that his live-in girlfriend [. . .] had left him"; Sewelly had been diagnosed with cancer (with Merrill helping to pay for her treatment, she would recover quickly); and David Kalstone had flown home from Venice to receive emergency treatment for a detached retina. Jackson himself had been mugged in New York City, then victimized by petty thefts in Stonington and a forged check in Key West. In the latter case, one of his own "Hot Numbers" was the culprit. Merrill had foreseen this sort of thing happening, given the company Jackson kept on the island, and he nagged Jackson about it mercilessly. By September, David was cringing under "[s]ome sort of dread cloud," and things wouldn't get better that fall. George Lazaretos traveled to Key West to spend the winter with him. But they fought so bitterly on the night he arrived that Lazaretos got on a plane and returned to Greece the next morning: their turbulent, intimate, nineteen-year relationship was over for good this time. "For hours after hearing about it," Merrill's eyes "kept filling with tears."

There had been changes at 107 Water Street. The Alevras family had moved to a nearby town where Taki had his pizza restaurant. They would do perfectly well without Merrill's patronage—particularly after Taki drew a winning ticket in the Connecticut state lottery. In their place on the second floor was now Ray Izbicki. A tall, snowy-haired bachelor, ordained in the obscure Orthodox-Catholic Church of America and equipped with vestments and incense that he produced for impromptu local blessings, Father Ray would establish himself as a village character known for his good deeds and minor pranks. For example, he stashed a farting noisemaker below his window, which he activated by tugging on a string when he noticed children or the elderly about to pass. This was not exactly Jimmy's style of humor, but he would grow to like and trust this tenant.

After all, old friends were thinning out. The Surly Temple had all but disbanded, with Robert dead, Isabel in declining health (she would die in spring 1984), and Grace subsisting in a rest home in Mystic. Jimmy visited her regularly that fall to read the *Aeneid* aloud to her in a new translation by Robert Fitzgerald. How much of it Mrs. Stone could take in was unclear, but there she was, holding up her head as he read. "I suspect Death has just tiptoed from her side out of sheer boredom," he supposed. "How old am I, Jimmy?" she asked one day. "98.6," he informed her. "Grace, you're normal at last."

Unhappy when he was alone on Water Street, Merrill kept running to Manhattan. He attended a performance at the Met of *Les Troyens* sung by Plácido Domingo, Tatiana Troyanos, and Jessye Norman. There was "Audenwoche" too—a weeklong series of events marking the tenth anniversary of Auden's death, culminating in a marathon group reading of Auden at the Guggenheim Museum. A photo of the readers on that program shows Merrill at the center of the group flanked by Hecht and Marilyn Hacker, Richard Howard, Mona Van Duyn, Christopher Isherwood, Stephen Spender, and Joseph Brodsky filling out the back row, and May Swenson, Amy Clampitt, Derek Walcott, Howard Moss, Hollander, and Alfred Corn sitting up front.

Merrill arranged for renovation of his grandmother's apartment on East Seventy-second Street, and, after reading in Dallas, Evanston, and Washington, D.C., he settled in there for his longest stay in Manhattan since 1953. New appliances had been installed in the little kitchen, and there was a nook for a desk, which kept him at home "instead of running to Bloomingdale's with the other lemmings." "I think I could live there more easily at this stage in my life," he wrote to David McIntosh, "than in S'ton where—especially when D. is away—isolation-anxiety bares its fangs." Yet Merrill had been "unable to use properly" his time in the apartment that fall to do his work, "due to a little chain reaction of colds + viruses that left me intermittently feverish and quite weak"—and, although he didn't say so, desperately worried about what his assorted, persistent symptoms meant.

He took little pleasure in the poems he'd been writing. He arranged the table of contents for a new book; he hadn't yet arrived at its autumnal, half-apologetic title, *Late Settings*. "I wish I felt more enthusiasm for it," he confided to Yenser when he sent the typescript to him. "Is it merely that it's not <u>Sandover</u>? Or that so many of the pieces seem nearly as old as their author?" Some of the poems had already sat in the drawer for years; not a few were written in the mildly maudlin spirit of late-middle-age rumination (he considered calling the book "The Memory Bank"). They included lyrics about childhood and adolescence. Poems about Hans and Strato were the last gasps of those old flames, of interest primarily because of his previous poems about them. His translation of Valéry's "Palme," deft as it was, amounted to a gloss on "Lost in Translation" and a footnote to one of his triumphs. Peter Tourville made appearances in "Peter" (a suite of short poems) and in "A Day on the Connecticut River" and "Trees Listening to Bach" (these last two were both about "trips" he and Merrill had taken, one in a canoe and another high on mushrooms). "Clearing the Title" and "Santorini: Stopping the Leak," placed at the beginning and end of the book, propped up mostly short poems between them, whose effect, despite the excellence of "Domino," "Radiometer," and "A Page from the Koran," wasn't cumulative or unified. A series of gossipy Ouija board outtakes, called "From the Cutting-Room Floor," summed up the scrappy character of the collection. If this was an answer to the question of what lay beyond *Sandover* for Merrill, *Late Settings* was a disappointment.

The book's longest, most complex poem was "Bronze." Merrill found it especially hard to finish, and he didn't like it. "It's so bitter!" he exclaimed to Yenser, "just when Sandover ought to have sweetened me to the very edge of the grave." He knew this feeling had to do with more than "Bronze." "Well, I've felt in these last couple of years, as never before, the beginnings of the End—don't worry, nothing in particular, beyond funny gestures of reaching and searching bequeathed me by my grandmother, tricks of memory. The unseemly anxiety these can provoke is bound to pass, just as it did in adolescence, that other phase when the system was changing too rapidly for the psyche to keep up." With "the End" suddenly looming up, with all the "unseemly anxiety" it provoked, he wanted, he said, only "to go gentle into the good night." But he seemed to know already that he wouldn't get his wish.

The day after Merrill wrote that letter to Yenser, February 8, Peter Hooten arrived for a visit in Key West. Hooten and Merrill had seen each other for dinner in New York. After that occasion, Merrill was excited and flustered enough to need to draft more than one version of a card to him. "My responses feel a touch rusty," he wrote. "But if one of your dials is 'set for me,' I'd like to answer those bells as best I can. For instance, could we have a quiet cup of tea . . . before I leave?" Again, whether more cautious or more flirtatious, it's hard to say: "[I]f one of your dials is 'set for me,' why then time will tell, won't it? Perhaps we could have a cup of tea." That cup of tea led to a week in Florida during which Hooten declared his love on "Valentine's Day Eve." Merrill lapped it up like a thirsty man, hands cupped at the splashing fountain of youth. "There had been a big party 2 days earlier," he told Tony Parigory, "at which brazen Mrs Wilbur sat [Peter] down and said 'Jimmy seems to be interested in you, how nice if you could come to mean something to each other, if only for a while'—whereupon P burst into tears!" Then it was Jimmy's turn for tears, except these were tears of joy, when Peter shared his feelings. When Hooten finally headed off on the bus, Merrill couldn't rest, he told him, "except the way kites do, dipping + soaring in one high place. I keep trying to think when I've known such happiness, but the few instances that come to mind fade + flake away . . . at this onrush of air and light. [. . .]—Oh my dear, it is all song and springtime. I love you with a heart I never thought would come to life."

Merrill believed in nothing as he believed in love. Love transformed, renewed, and redeemed: it was the *Ring* cycle's soaring rainbow theme. Since the angels finished speaking and he put a period on the trilogy, he had been depressed and dry, ill and ill-tempered, frightened of aging—and privately terrified of AIDS. Now, the only way he could imagine the rest of his life, to continue to grow and change and not "go down," was, it seems, to fall in love. He wanted to love rapturously, as he had a few times in the past; he wanted to *be* loved rapturously—which was never Jackson's style, and which David could no longer manage if it had been, any more than Peter Tourville could have. Furthermore, Merrill wanted more than a lover: he wanted a companion who would "last his time." And if DJ was locked away in his smoke-filled room, who might that companion be? Where would he find him?

Not that he asked himself that question. But if he had, the answer would not have been obvious. The fabric of his life had changed in basic ways. When he gave up his home in Greece, he gave up his alternative to a public life in the U.S. He knew more people now, and he was more widely known; yet there was less ease and intimacy overall in his relations. If he knew more people, more people wanted something from him—money, approval, a blurb, a letter of recommendation, guidance, wisdom. He was isolated by his importance the way anyone onstage is isolated. It may be that he could only fall in love with someone in the audience, a fan beaming up at him from the first row who was ready to stand and introduce himself. It helped that Peter was a man of the stage, an actor who knew Merrill's lines and could recite them for applause. It helped too that he was energetic, eager, earnest, and sweet, strong as a bull, trim, a full six foot two with eyes of blue, wavy reddish-blond-brown hair, and a dimpled chin. And it helped that he was a native Floridian at a moment when Merrill was recalling his southern childhood and craving the warmth and safety of long ago.

John Peter Hooten was born on November 29, 1950, in Clermont, Florida. So he was thirty-three in February 1984, twenty-four years younger than Merrill. He'd grown up in rural Florida ("not far from my father's birthplace," JM noted). His parents were Jack Hooten, a citrus farmer and son of the county sheriff, and Janet Adams Griswold, whose farming family had roots in Connecticut, where she was born. The marriage was shaky ("there were scenes"), and it ended in divorce when Peter was in his twenties. The third child in a crowded household, Peter had two older sisters, two younger sisters, and two much younger brothers. He "ran away a lot" when he was young. "At 5 I got as far as the highway, but I didn't have the balls to cross it." At thirteen, he went away to boarding school in Tennessee; and "whenever I came home, there was a mess to clean up, emotionally and physically." Peter's mother was diagnosed with bipolar disease in the early 1960s. When he was a child, he saw her in manic states; he remembers, when he was a teenager, "pinning her to the ground to help her relax and to reassure her." Yet he was much closer to his mother than to his father, who was working hard and rarely at home. "I don't think he ever hugged me. But it was the 1950s, and men didn't do that."

Hooten had dyslexia in childhood, and he couldn't pronounce consonants properly. So his older sisters would speak for him. "I guess I became an actor," he reflected, "by working hard on elocution and learning to speak verse." That big deep voice, equally capable of the down-home and the lordly, would be an asset for him in the theater. After studying briefly at Ithaca College, which he attended with a scholarship, he set out to pursue an acting career that took him to Los Angeles, London, and then back to Los Angeles. Signed to a contract with the William Morris Agency, he auditioned for the role of the Minstrel on the popular television show *The Waltons*, a folksy family drama set in the mountains of Virginia. He was told he'd have to sing and dance, and, seeing actors with Juilliard and Broadway credentials lined up in front of him, he thought about quitting there and then: "What could I do? How could I compete?" At the last moment, he strode onto the stage, summoned his country roots, boomed out "I've Been Working on the Railroad," and got the part.

On the set he met Will Geer, who played lovable old Grandpa Walton. Born in 1902, Geer was a talented actor who had been a bit of a minstrel himself. He started out in the 1920s performing in tent shows and on riverboats; with his lover Harry Hay, an early gay activist, Geer did theater in support of striking workers in the 1930s; in the 1940s, he worked with Lee Strasberg and the Group Theatre. Later, after having been blacklisted by Hollywood studios for his membership in the Communist Party, Geer helped to found an outdoor Shakespeare theater in Los Angeles, which is still active today. When he met the twenty-one-year-old Hooten, Geer was planning a road show of Americana. He invited Hooten to join him, and they crossed the country with a small troupe in a bus, stopping to perform songs by Geer's friend Woody Guthrie and to give dramatic readings from works by Twain, Whitman, and Frost. The white-haired Geer played the old Frost and bright-eyed Hooten the young one. The partnership anticipated the one Hooten would create with Merrill. It was onstage with Geer that he memorized the Frost poems he recited in Isabel Morse's parlor.

Hooten's acting career included numerous low-budget films for screen and TV; titles such as *Night of Terror* (1972) and *Slashed Dreams* (1974) advertised B-movie sex and masked maniacs. In *Prisoners* (1974), he played Lieutenant Calley, the U.S. commanding officer in the My Lai massacre, which found an antiwar audience in Europe at the end of the Vietnam War. He acted soldiers' parts in other war movies, notably *The Inglorious Bastards* (1978), a made-in-Italy, World War II action extravaganza which the director Quentin Tarantino later revisited in a mood of postmodern homage in his *Inglourious Basterds* (2009). Hooten appeared with Richard Harris, Charlotte Rampling, and Bo Derek under the direction of Michael Anderson in *Orca* (1977), an "eco-horror," *Jaws* knockoff about the hunt for a vengeful killer whale in which Derek, the strapping '70s sex goddess, loses a leg to the beast. He also starred with Derek in *Fantasies*—her first movie, released in 1981 but filmed on the island of Mykonos in 1973 when she was only sixteen, before she married the movie's director, John Derek. Peter played a Greek fisherman in that one.

Merrill hadn't seen these movies. Indeed, he knew very little about this new lover. Hooten entered his life connected to no one else in it save for that distant relation whom Robert Morse had known. On his first visit to Key West, in a ritual of hospitality perhaps meant to inform him about this rival, David kept Peter up late with friendly chatter. Then, on Valentine's Day, the three men sat down to a séance to see what the spirits could tell them. It appeared that Peter still had two lives to go on the ladder of reincarnation: "ONE CONSTANT TRAIT DELAYING THINGS" was a "PENCHANT FOR CAREER CHANGES. LIFE 7 PAR EXAMPLE PH WAS GOING SWIMMINGLY ALONG AS INDIAN BARRISTER [. . .] WHEN HE TOOK UP ROWING WITH SUCH A BELATED PASSION HE WENT THROUGH HIS INHERITANCE IMPORTING SCULLS FROM ENGLAND. ENDED IN MAGNIFICENT HEALTH BUT DROWNED (HE NEVER LEARNED TO SWIM ALAS). PERSISTS IN HIS INDECISIONS. CURRENTLY P [his patron] SAYS PH IS ABOUT TO CHANGE FROM STAGE TO PEN, BUT WILL HE WRITE A PLAY? NO SUCH LUCK. POETRY." It was true, Hooten wanted to write poetry, and Merrill supervised a few of his attempts that spring. He gave the Ouija board a try too, but all he and JM could get from it was the single emphatic word "NO." PH would not replace DJ's hand on the cup.

JM and DJ "had tortellini by ourselves and talked a bit" after Peter left. "For better or worse," Merrill wrote to his new lover, "we've always been fairly frank; but there has been no precedent for these past days. I did my best to, oh, make an arrangement for clavichord of the full orchestral score," to which his longtime partner "listened kindly + helpfully. So, for the moment, there we are." Alan Moss chose for the moment to see Merrill as a "kind of 'Platonic mentor.' " From Merrill's perspective, Hooten's relationship with Moss was a safety net: he was glad they each had domestic obligations to calm them down. Merrill told Hooten, and no doubt himself,

"Take it easy. Nothing will escape. Nothing will spoil." "At least I have my advanced AGE to lend the balance you invoke often enough for me to guess how much you depend on it. But you—you write like a boy in love for the first time, and I see that this gift (to me from the gods, but to you from them no less) is as dangerous as it is beautiful." He pulled himself upright and said what he felt needed to be said:

> Though it gives me no pleasure, let me say, once and never again, "the following": I am 25 years older than you. Loving me you will have to cope with failings both physical and psycholog-ical, which at present you know only second-hand but which I already feel twinges of every day. These inevitable changes will change you. [. . .] Take this less as warning than as truth; and as the signs proliferate, be no truer to me than you can.

Which was one more reason for neither man to let go of what he had: "You know my horror of Broken Homes. I don't want to threaten yours and Alan's any more than you want to threaten mine + DJ's."

Merrill took stock by writing to old friends like Stephen, Tony, DMc, Donald Richie, and Claude. By chance, Fredericks had sent copies of pages from his diary in 1950 describing *their* first rapturous weeks together. Reading those passages, Merrill was "touched and bemused and grateful":

> First of all, so much LIFE flooding back, preserved uncannily [. . .]. My muse, I suppose, asks that a lot be forgotten (as part of self-forgiveness, or the conventions of the kind of work I needed to do)—so that to find here our flowers pressed whole, past crumbling, is a great wonder. I must ask myself—and can't answer—what I'd have felt if this packet had reached me even 30 days ago. As it is, an extraordinary coincidence, the Valentine's Day of this year, has turned me again into a lover—a bond so sudden, so longed-for, so miraculously mutual—that here again are those looks and words and perambulations you recorded, and which, much as I dreamed, I truly didn't dream would ever come to me again. Our affective selves don't age, do they? A life-long dial set at 18? 22? Much earlier? The same headlong pony one may have somewhat learned to guide more wisely . . . If I said to you in 1950 that I wanted it "to cost everything," what could I say today?—except that love costs nothing, that the cost isn't counted as the corner is turned and the rainbow entered.

In fact, much as Merrill's life was changing, and he wanted it to change, he didn't want it to change "outwardly. For better or worse David and I have what we have." There was no question about changing that; he even wanted to maintain his routines with Peter Tourville. "I don't plan to throw him any further off-kilter than he already is by breaking a pattern of—what—15 meetings a year?"

Hooten was frankly dazzled—"I'd fallen in love with my idol"—and, the wooer in this drama, he declared his passion to Merrill in simple, earnest language, leaving no doubt about his devotion. Merrill hungered for Hooten's priority-mail letters. Yet he found it hard to rise to the same level of intensity, at least on paper, and he knew his own letters were "a touch 'tame' " next to Peter's. He quoted the novelist Milan Kundera in support of reining in their amatory rhetoric: "I think you have to write about love with extreme skepticism. [. . .] The language of 'love' is a language about feelings that justify bad behavior." Thus "[w]hatever is left over after you apply skepticism to feeling—that's love."

Merrill was skeptical less of Hooten than of himself perhaps, with the silent testimony of Jackson's long-term depression and deepening passivity as a continual reproach. When he looked at DJ or Manos Karastefanís, he feared the effects that his money, that glowing green slab of kryptonite, had on those closest to him. On his fifty-eighth birthday, he recounted for Peter a recent conversation with their matchmaker, Charlee Wilbur:

CW: He's very fond of you.
JM: Who wouldn't be fond of him?
CW: But he's scared of you.
JM: . . . ?!
CW: Scared of what you <u>are</u>. [But is that true?]
JM: Oh well, so am I!

But what was there to be afraid of, really? It wasn't very hard for Merrill to look past his self-doubts, particularly with his lover urging him on. Hooten, in his youthful passion, promised to restore Merrill to his own passionate youth, turning back the clock to the time when it was possible for him to idealize romantic love, before he learned Proust's Law or watched David wither in his smoke-filled room.

In the background, the Key West house stirred with the commotion of "David's friends"—poor black men who rang the doorbell hoping to cadge money for a bus to Miami or crash on the porch, high on coke. Some of these "friends" *were* friends, like the sailors and soldiers who'd been regulars at the house in Athens. But others were quick tricks or barflies, and it was a much rougher bunch than the Greek *parea* had been. "People with prison records latched onto David," Charlee Wilbur remarks, and they were a strain on his relationship with Jimmy, who kept his bedroom door locked. He had to change the lock when it showed signs of tampering: one of David's pals, he presumed, had been prowling around.

To be sure, Jackson wasn't in love with any of these men, and none of them was competition for Merrill in the way Hooten was competition for him. But neither Hooten nor Jackson was in an easy position. Even as Peter threatened to take David's place in Jimmy's heart, David remained the man with whom Jimmy had lived for three decades and with whom he'd created *Sandover*.

Merrill knew he was trying Jackson's patience, and propitiation was in order. That May, "to express my ongoing appreciation" for his partnership at the Ouija board, Merrill made a formal gift to Jackson—for which Washington University Library would pay him—"of all the manuscripts, worksheets, typescripts, etc. pertaining to 'Mirabell: Books of Number.' " But rather than glad and gracious, Merrill sounded grudging, as if he felt the need to get his gratitude to his partner on record once and for all. "As I've told you so many times," he wrote to David, "your participation in the Sandover books made them what they are." That spring he experimented with bringing Jackson and Hooten together in Stonington and New York. Sometimes Peter arrived with takeout dinner for all three of them, and sometimes the lovers went out on their own—to hear *Billy Budd* at the Met, or to see a dancer perform at the Japan Society. On that occasion, after he and Peter had lingered over drinks and then, like teenagers, said a long, late goodnight on the sidewalk, Jimmy returned to find David "pacing the floor." He had to admit that "a few wrinkles in the 3 of us being together still need ironing out."

The simplest solution was to travel and take Peter along, and Merrill and Hooten made the first of many trips together when they left for Europe in late May. In London, on a visit to the British Museum, Jimmy was beguiled by a miniature from India showing an elephant "entirely made of interlocking figures, gods, avatars, bodhisattvas." It reminded him of how his love for Peter collected previous passions and joined them in one compound form: "traits and attributes I found to love in others, brought together in an entirely new amalgam." (That thought turned into a poem, "Hindu Illumination.") In Cornwall, the lovers sang out rhymes to each other as they hiked along the high seaside cliffs. (That day became a poem too, "Cornwall.") They stayed with DK at the Palazzo Barbaro—where they had new suits made, heard music at La Fenice, and one giddy night painted their faces white with a beauty mask for a private Carnival. They paid their respects to the mosaics in Ravenna (how many times had Merrill made that particular pilgrimage?), and visited Ariane Frey, a friend of Peter's, in Switzerland, where they lounged "in the meadows above Lake Lucerne, air full of a constant cowbell gamelan orchestra."

These were "heavenly, happy days." The lovers spent long hours by themselves. But part of the purpose of this trip was to introduce Peter to people who mattered: David Kalstone, for example, and the Yensers, who were in Europe also and spent a week with Merrill and Hooten in Amsterdam. Mary Bomba, Stephen's wife, had known Merrill well since 1968, and she'd found that, "with James, there was always the danger of being pushed off balance. You had to have a strong personality to hold your own in his company." Mary was eight years younger than her husband, and when she and Stephen were with Merrill, she was reduced to watching as the poets talked to each other. Hooten's presence changed the pattern; now their table had four legs. Bomba recalled, "It was wonderful when Peter came. We were more alike"—because she was an actress and close to Peter's age—"and the pressure was off. Then my own friendship with James began to flourish." She saw how much joy Peter gave him. And if *she'd* found it difficult to stand up to Merrill, she saw that Hooten could. Part of it was physical. When the big man wrapped the smaller one in his arms, "James was *enveloped*," and "it must have been comforting for him," she commented. "Peter was like a big Labrador retriever," bouncy and affectionate. In fact, to this petite, fine-featured woman, everything about Peter seemed "big": his affectations (stagy choices of costume, such as a Panama hat, that Merrill overlooked or even encouraged) and "his snits," which were so out of scale that they were funny. At the same time, Bomba continued, "[t]here could be something scary about Peter—to recall that dog image": his size and energy, that loud voice, his potential force. Merrill may have felt that too. One day during their time in Holland, Yenser was strolling with Merrill some distance behind Mary and Peter. He mentioned that Hooten seemed " 'pleasant'—and it was just a minute or so later that James told me that he feared that Peter was not perfectly stable. There was mental illness in his family, he said, and he was clearly concerned."

Merrill returned to Stonington and Jackson for the Fourth of July. At eleven thirty on the holiday, he wrote, half to Peter, half to himself, "DJ, celebrating Independence, has had breakfast and gone back to watch TV on his bed with a cigarette. Should I run in and shake him? Or quote the Buddha's last words: 'You must be your own lamp, your own refuge . . .'? What desk work of mine could possibly be more vital than bringing him to his senses? Yet back I go to my Preface"—to the book by the newest Yale Younger Poet. "We're both set in our ways," he concluded. And so they were. As Jimmy pounded out prose on his typewriter, the laugh track from David's sitcoms shuddered on the other side of the study wall. When they sat together, it was for the TV event of the season, the Democratic Party's national convention. Mounting its doomed challenge to Reagan's second term as president, the convention featured Jesse Jackson's impassioned "Rainbow Coalition" speech, which left David in tears. What caught Merrill's eye were the "placards being jiggled up and down to wild (canned?) shrieks": "white letters on dark blue (Mondale) or burnt orange (Hart), white on green held aloft by black faces (Jackson)." He had a point to make about the money behind the spectacle: "It is exactly the color scheme, front and back, of my VISA card. This can't be a coincidence."

At the time, this apolitical poet was tinkering with an apocalyptic poem about the future of America. "Icecap" might be the first poem anyone wrote about global warming, which was just becoming news. "Yes, melting changes / the whole picture," Merrill begins, foreseeing the fate of the nation in the rising waters facing Venice. He tells of how our "once young republic" sank from a world power to mere "tourist mecca" while its "Losses and debts" rose "past calculation":

> Dead roads,
> and deconsecrated malls,
> moth-eaten orchards
> far North, deep crops left
> rotting on the Plains gave out
> how the collective psyche
> shrugged off its future
> and despised its roots,
> bent upon pleasures merely
> of the here and now.

He sent the poem to McClatchy and, after a sentence about it, passed as if by logical association from collective catastrophe to anxiety about his personal health: "The all-but-fictive condition, a sort of floating constriction in my chest, doesn't clear up. I've had such a history in the last 6 years of fierce bouts of hypochondria that it can hardly be anything else," but he was getting blood tests, X rays, and a stress test anyway. All the tests turned up negative, but he continued to observe the same enigmatic signs. "No day without a symptom."

Merrill and Jackson found reasons not to spend much time together. In August, David took the train to Los Angeles to visit Bob Grimes; in September, Jimmy flew to Santa Fe to see David McIntosh and "our darling" Mary Lou Aswell: she was dying of cancer, and it would be the last time. (When she died three months later, Merrill couldn't shrug it off. He felt a deep "identification" with Mary Lou: it was "as if we had grown up as brother and sister—or not grown up." She'd been content with "a child's kind of wisdom instead of any shrewd interest-bearing hoard of Experience. The way she would clap her hands and crow with amusement, almost like a baby.") Merrill and Jackson went to visit Sandy and Alfred in Vermont (a chance for Jimmy to rendezvous with Peter Tourville) and Charles and Mary in New Hampshire. After toying with the manuscript for most of a year, Merrill was ready to part with *Late Settings*. He decided to dedicate the book to his siblings, Doris and Charles, because "[w]e've grown closer these last years, in the way of family ties as one ages." Closer perhaps, but not that close. Back in the spring, Merrill had read with Seamus Heaney to a huge audience at Harvard ("Perhaps 200 turned away"). Charles was in the front row; when Jimmy finished reading and took the seat next to him, his brother "put his arm round my shoulder for a moment." The small gesture was "un-heard of!"

Hooten and Merrill saw each other when they could. "If life were really like a book," Merrill laughed, "mine this year would be labeled 'suitable for ages 18–25,'—it leaves me breathless!" On his calendar among the usual readings on campuses far and wide was an appearance at the Iowa Writers' Workshop. Sounding much older than eighteen or twenty-five, Merrill shook his head over the creative-writing industry in Iowa City: "American youngsters, under the direction of a half-dozen 'names,' mass-produce poetry around the clock [. . .]. Naturally they have little time to read, except one another; but they will grow up to publish books and attract imitators, and our poets will accordingly prosper like the rabbits of Australia." Merrill continued on to California, where Hooten joined him for a reading at UCLA, a stay with the Yensers, and an afternoon on Zuma Beach, misty with sunlight and sea spray, before they flew north to see the Magowans in San Francisco. In the plane heading home over the Rockies on Thanksgiving Day, Merrill mused as Hooten dozed in the seat beside him:

> Late love. Like any resumed career (a woman whose children are now grown + who returns to the "writing" or "painting" she put aside in order to marry) there is much wistfulness, much ineptitude. Her one or two friends who chose a career over family life view her little efforts with condescension. Nevertheless,

she is fulfilling herself, and can give herself to the "creative impulse" as never before. Blessed PH.

"I'm so happy! He is such a love—" Jimmy declared to Tony. To Peter, he wrote, "my whole heart sweetens and swells with every moment I lift my head and say your name." And again: "You make me happier than I dreamed I could ever be."

Hooten's relationship with Alan Moss didn't survive the year. In January 1985, they set about breaking up the home they shared in New York. Merrill was "shaken, with love first of all, then with dismay," by these events. He was pained by what he imagined as the "wrenching" process of separation ("The dogs alone—!"), which of course he had done a good deal to set in motion. The safety net that Moss had represented was gone, and it was unclear what this would mean for his and Peter's relationship. For the time being, Jackson had found rooms for Hooten next door to 702 Elizabeth Street. Merrill had to pinch himself "from plain old happiness" once the three of them settled into the arrangement. Even so, he knew that for Peter the situation in Key West "can't be easy, knowing only us, and being so much younger." It was the height of the winter season, and the social carousel was whirling. Every day they saw in some combination the Wilburs, the Herseys, John Brinnin, John Ciardi, Alison Lurie, Rollie McKenna (who came with Jimmy and David's masseuse and *her* family from Mystic), the Montrealers Christian Ayoub, Marie-Claire Blais, and Mary Meigs, and many more. By the time he departed in March, Hooten had "gained 7 pounds, and left everyone (I think) charmed," Merrill ventured. But his and Jackson's friends were mostly more than a generation older than Hooten—not an easy group for Hooten to step into and "charm." They had reasons to approve of a new companion who made Jimmy happy, but they had reasons to resist and resent him, too, now that Peter had become a fixture in their friend's life and at David's expense, as most people saw it. Merrill admitted that he and Hooten had had some "difficult moments" that winter—although these were "mostly I think due to P's occasional misreadings of middle-aged talk and tics." No, Peter was reading Jimmy's middle-aged friends correctly. The friction was real, and it wasn't about to go away.

Tellingly, the highlight of that winter came not in Key West but on a trip to the mainland when Merrill gave a reading in Gainesville at the state university, and he and Hooten spent the next day investigating Green Cove Springs. It was his first visit to his father's birthplace. As in Charlie's day, the springs were the main attraction. The largest "bubbles up at 3000 gallons per minute and proceeds to fill a large municipal swimming pool [. . .]; leaving the pool, the water becomes a silly little shallow brook [. . .] that babbles perhaps 200 feet to where [. . .] it joins the already very broad St Johns River heading for Jacksonville (my mother's birthplace) and the Sea." Merrill introduced Hooten to his father as he wanted to remember him now—not the Southampton sultan but the son of "a genuine country doctor." Eventually Hooten would introduce Merrill to his own family: "James met everyone. He knew Florida folk, so it wasn't as if he had to change his tone. Between us, there was a lot of familiarity. The St. Johns River meant a lot to both of us." Merrill wrote a pair of short poems, "Two from Florida," commemorating the trip; one poem was about Green Cove Springs and the other about Mis' Annie. Once more he was trying to reunite the two sides of his family, this time at their source in the northeast corner of Florida.

In April, Merrill visited Washington University as a writer in residence. The rare-book room in Olin Library put on display a selection of Merrilliana, the poet gave a reading, there was a musical performance of settings of his poems by various hands, and he was fêted by Mona Van Duyn and Jarvis Thurston. But mostly Merrill just sat, happily unconsulted by students or faculty. Hooten had driven with him from New York to St. Louis—Peter took the stage in the recital hall to read lines from Merrill's Gabriel—and they drove back east together at the end of the week. They took a wandering route, stopping off in New Harmony, Indiana, to visit the site of the utopian community founded by Grace Stone's great-great-grandfather, the socialist and spiritualist Robert Owen; Nashville, where they saw the Parthenon, the replica of the Greek temple, with a statue of Ganymede for which the teenage Randall Jarrell had been the touchingly fey model; Chattanooga, where Peter had been to boarding school; the Great Smoky Mountains (here they pulled over to splash in a stream and stroll in the flowering woods); and Lexington, Virginia, where Jim Boatwright put them up. They'd been lovers for more than a year; now they were really a couple. Back on Water Street, Peter repaired the weathered deck and trained the morning glories. Merrill told Parigory that they were becoming "very domestic [. . .]—to the point even of a few strangely familiar squabbles—but the skies are by + large cloudless."

But there were clouds. That letter goes on, "He is a remarkably sweet man: David K. was really at death's door with pneumonia, and the hospital had no available night nurses—so Peter spent two nights in a row sitting with him, sponging his brow, holding his hand." Merrill was not exaggerating about "death's door": Kalstone had been rushed to the hospital that March, seriously ill with pneumocystis pneumonia, one of the opportunistic infections associated with AIDS. He was silent about the diagnosis and its implications to all but a handful of his friends. Even Alfred Corn, who took care of Kalstone before he went into the hospital, was left in the dark about the cause: "That seems strange now, but for many people in those days a stigma attached to HIV. I was dimly aware that DK, who never had much romantic success with people like himself, sometimes had casual sex with taxi-drivers or men he met on the street, and given that a single encounter can make you positive, it doesn't now seem so surprising that David contracted the virus. But at that date it didn't occur to me that he might have."

Merrill knew what Kalstone was suffering from. He didn't mention AIDS in his letter to Parigory in April. But he did in a letter to David McIntosh in May. McIntosh, reticent by nature, was close enough to Kalstone and far enough from New York to serve Merrill as a confidant:

> Something I can tell no one else [. . .] has darkened these last weeks more than I can possibly say. You will keep it to yourself, I know. I told you DK had been in hospital with a terrible case of pneumonia. My dear, it's a strain of AIDS. Of all people. He fancies—perhaps rightly, it's anyone's guess—that he got it in the Mt. Sinai hospital 2 summers ago, when his retina had slipped for the 2nd time. He rallied, as I told you—luckily his white corpuscle count is still quite high—but faces what we've all learned to imagine. Of course there are "programs," and "treatments" from France or Sweden which, through his very good young doctor, will soon be available to him here. He is wonderfully sane and stubborn about the whole thing, plans to go to Venice as usual, and mercifully, thanks to the Guggenheim Fellowship, has the whole coming year off from teaching. But so shattering. He's the first person I <u>know</u> to be stricken. [. . .] There's no question of telling gossipy DJ, or fifty other people, and I feel awfully self-indulgent dumping it like this into your lap. I suppose I wanted to see if I could <u>begin</u> to write it down.

In 1985 such a diagnosis would have been received as a death sentence. The news was "shattering" to Merrill not merely because Kalstone was the first person he knew who had AIDS. DK was his best friend. They'd been sidekicks for over twenty years: the disease could not have struck much closer to home. Merrill felt grief for his friend—and fresh alarm about his own condition. How had Kalstone gotten sick? His speculation that a hospital stay led to his infection expresses ignorance, common in 1985, about transmission of HIV and the disease's rate of progression. Merrill's implication is that it could only have been the hospital because Kalstone had avoided casual sex in the two years prior to the onset of his symptoms, the period between infection and the development of "full-blown" AIDS which was believed (mistakenly, as research would show) to be the typical course of the disease. The idea points to Kalstone's (and for that matter Merrill's) need to deny the likely explanation that the virus had been sexually transmitted. "Of all people," Merrill writes, unable to square the English professor's sweet manners and refinement with the stereotype of the AIDS patient as a hustler or addict. But as Corn remarked, Kalstone's sexual habits, which were not a secret to his close friends, put him at risk for infection, perhaps not recently but over a longer period. Merrill must have suspected this, and he had to conclude that, if Kalstone had AIDS, he might too.

That August, as if to make out that nothing had changed, or precisely in acknowledgment that everything had, Merrill visited Kalstone in Venice bringing Jackson, who made the transatlantic crossing by ship, as in days of yore. Kalstone was in Venice with a student from Rutgers, his new companion. With the two of them, the mediums sat down at the Ouija board in the Palazzo Barbaro. Faced with DK's diagnosis (by now DJ had been told about it too), they clutched at the spirits. "IT IS A ? OF 6 MONTHS," George Cotzias reassured them, "WHEN THE FIRST SUBSTANTIAL INOCULATIONS WILL BE READY. IN SWEDEN." Leaving aside the fact that, for Kalstone, "INOCULATION" would no longer do any good, the doctor wrote a prescription: "MASSIVE POWDERED DOSES OF VITAMIN C. DAILY. FORCE MAXIMUM AVAILABLE IN ANY LARGE PHARMACY. UPON REQUEST + REPEAT: POWDER! + STRONG 2—3 TEASPOONS + EASIEST TO GET DOWN DISSOLVED IN JUICES. THIS IS A RESISTANCE BUILDER." But resistance was not a matter of Kalstone's immune system only: "COURAGE + WILL ARE THE 2 MOST INFLUENTIAL MEDICAL PEOPLE."

It was merely a brief visit. They must have all feared that these would be their last days together in the palace. For years, Kalstone had had an Italian lover in Venice. This time Giuliano had to put up with the young American, and, Edmund White recalls, "G. was fiercely jealous. He denounced David and the guy" to Kalstone's friend and the owner of the house, Patricia Curtis, "as people who both were sick with AIDS. After David left that year at the end of August, Patricia had the two maids scrub down the entire place with extra assiduity; and she had the few belongings that David always left behind from one year to the next put in the attic. Things like electric fans and hot water bottles. Some clothes." It was a step away from the garbage.

Merrill and Jackson continued by train to Athens. With the tenants away, they had the run of their old house. On the first floor, David discovered that his wall fresco depicting a classical temple and idyllic Aegean cove, the painstaking labor of 1977, had vanished under a fresh coat of paint; on the terrace, his once-lovely hanging gardens had gone to seed. He claimed his old room, while Jimmy took the basement apartment, two floors below, where the aged "pathetic cat-loving spinster" who came with the house had dwelt until her recent death ("So I am sitting for the first time in a room that has been mine for 21 years!"). He was up at dawn working on Cavafy translations and on a poem saying farewell to the Palazzo Barbaro. But most of his attention went to one of the late old lady's cats, a mama nursing her scrawny batch of kittens just outside his window. He brought a bowl of milk, and "scared 2 of the kittens off a ledge into a courtyard perhaps 3 feet lower than ours. No way for them to get out. I jumped down and hoisted one up, but the other hid inextricably in the works of a boiler, mewing in terror while the mother stared with her aghast Fay Wray eyes round a corner at Man the clumsy upsetter of Nature's Wise Ways." Going over the scene in his notebook, he saw it as a little allegory of his failed, selfish attempts over the years to help Manos get settled in life. He'd caught himself acting like an American multinational corporation—like "the Nestle company" whose "[g]ifts of 'formula' to Africa's starving people" left the babies who'd been weaned on it "starved for good when the gifts ran out."

Strato had been a different case, Jimmy felt. "He took his life in his own hands + ran away." But Strato was back in Athens, and when he rang the bell that September, the two men looked at each other across the threshold for the first time since 1971. "He's a wreck," Merrill told Yenser. "He returned from nearly 10 years in Canada with such bad lower back trouble that he had no sensation from the hips down." He returned without having made any money, either: "They're all but penniless." Merrill wrote in his notebook,

> These decades, tell me where they went.
> Seeing you bald, fat, limping, my eyes dazzle.
> Life took you for a sprig of basil
> And crushed you for your scent.

The rest of the old *parea* were not in much better shape. Night after night, the suave master of ceremonies, Tony Parigory, finished falling down drunk. George came around too, but he seemed "blind and sullen." "It's hard on them," Merrill reflected, "[. . .] to see us after all this time. There's the unavoidable fact that we gave up a life in which they were among the most important figures. It's hard on us to see <u>them</u>, too. To measure the change, to gauge our own deterioration from theirs." Vassili came by one day, Kimon another. On Jimmy's last night in Athens, "in a crummy Plaka tavern," he and David met Tony, George, Manos, and Strato. They drank toasts and took photos as at a school reunion. "Only Manos out of sorts. He wanted to talk about plans, but waited too late. Back at the house I said goodbye to him on the street. In the tavern Tony gave a little speech: how rare for such old friends to come together, still friends, still sharing wine + laughter after all these years." So rare, it wouldn't happen again, at least not with so many of the original cast assembled.

To entertain themselves, DJ and JM brought out the Ouija board. During the Athens séances that had turned into the coda to *Sandover*, the mediums had followed the doings of Maria reborn as a miracle-making Indian boy in Bombay, slated to become a leading chemist. Recently there had been news about "Pashy" (was it the work of DJ, trying desperately to hold JM's attention?). By no coincidence, the eight-year-old's family had brought him to Athens where his father was engaged in trade talks, and the spirits had planned for him a meeting with JM and DJ. Instructions: on the appointed day, they were to go—at four, Indian teatime—to their familiar café in Kolonáki Square where they used to meet Maria; the holy family would appear; and a breeze would blow the child's hat off his head onto the mediums' table. This was the sort of nonsense Merrill and Jackson had always been too sensible or too proud to get involved in—the way of madness or mystification. Yet they obeyed. The results were predictable. Instead of the Indian boy, they found merely a scattering of cosmopolitan strangers talking quietly in the late afternoon, between-shifts café, extras on the bare stage set emptied of the fascinating faces of years ago. JM and DJ kept their cool. But later, at home, Merrill broke into tears. "I hadn't realized how much I'd hoped [for] that link between the realms of fact + fiction." Their religion was not of that sort, however. They were "2 wise men at the empty manger." There would be no savior, no magical son.

But there was Peter. Merrill wrote to him regularly during these days, pained by their separation. Waiting in the wings while JM and DJ made their dubious return to Athens, he met Merrill in France in October. They gazed at Monet's water lilies in the Orangerie, Degas's dancers in the Jeu de Paume, the new Picasso museum, and the Pont Neuf wrapped in fabric by mischievous Christo. They traced much of Jimmy and Strato's 1971 car trip, but in reverse, skimming the château country of the Loire, and whisking by Proust's house in Illiers, renamed Illiers-Combray. On the coast, they visited more scenes from Proust's novel:

> 8.x—Cabourg, beach in front of Grand Hotel (whose restaurant is now called Le Balbec). Wind + glitter. Windsurfers resting—how MP [Proust] would have loved them. Normandy: . . . WWII bunkers sinking into the green. Monet's house + garden at Giverny in the a.m. Lunch in Honfleur, and the day not over yet.

"And the day not over yet." He could feel that as long as Peter was beside him.

Merrill returned to New York for a gala hosted by Merrill Lynch in honor of the one hundredth anniversary of the firm's founding partners, timed for Charles Merrill's birthday. ("Their bankruptcy may date from the following morning—watch your local headlines," Jimmy cracked in anticipation of a lavish spread.) Mrs. Plummer made the trip north for the event. It was the second time she'd been present for a ceremonial Merrill family occasion that year. Back in June, Jimmy had escorted her to Southampton for "my sister's Golden Wedding—two nights of very grand partying, and lots of dear faces from the past (and future, for that matter—new babies from my ever-multiplying nephews)." For Hellen, the occasion was a reprise of Doris and Bobby's wedding, which she'd been in charge of fifty years before. She was "made gratifyingly much of" by the whole family. Old scores were settled; "indeed, Kinta, who lives there [in Southampton] and had sent Doris a very grand present made of gold, wasn't invited to any of the parties, out of deference to Mrs Plummer." For her son, the scene recalled the end of *The Seraglio*, where Francis "schemes to reintroduce his mother into the fold [. . .]. It took me a while to understand the glow I felt, but I think it's because that dream came true for a couple of days." Or so Jimmy wrote to Claude. In fact, the homecoming hadn't gone so smoothly. In the midst of the fun, Hellen fell—she'd had too much to drink—and EMTs arrived to take her to the hospital. The behavior was not unusual, as Jimmy knew from his visits to Atlanta. Now the fact of Hellen's drinking was plain for the rest of the family to see.

Back in the U.S., Merrill talked to Kalstone every day on the phone. The phone, as DK's friend Maxine Groffsky remembered, was "a huge part of everyone's life back then, but especially David's." One call would be braided with another ("I just hung up with . . . ," "So-and-so sends her love . . ."), and a review of the ballet last night or someone's new book would get mixed up with a recipe. Gossip meant that the world was on course, spinning as it always would be, and trusted friends were there to share it. This was the idiom David and Jimmy shared; and with DK sick, the normalcy gossip represented, and the measure of control over daily life it established, mattered more than ever. Kalstone was getting "awfully good at putting down rumors," Merrill told Parigory. An example: "John Myers: Sweetie, I heard you were <u>sick</u>. DK (with roseate smile): Do I look sick?" In fact he didn't. He was prone now to low-grade fevers, colds, and fatigue, but his health had always been delicate. After Venice, he told close friends like Corn and McClatchy that he had AIDS. But he didn't want to tell a man-about-town like John Myers: gossip could be an enemy as well as a friend, and he was worried about what would happen when word of his illness got back to Rutgers. The strategy was simply to carry on: to keep cooking his pasta dinners, keep calling his friends, and keep writing his book about Elizabeth Bishop.

A book of Merrill's prose went into production that fall, a collection of his essays and interviews (including three pieces about Bishop) called *Recitative* and edited by McClatchy. "He was diffident about his prose," McClatchy observed. "He didn't mind it being published so long as someone else was bringing it out. But he didn't see it as part of the canon" of his work, as expressed by his choice to have the collection printed by small North Point Press in San Francisco, not Atheneum, the publisher of his poetry. Merrill's prose was invariably witty, touching, and pointed, as he must have known. But he was exceptionally diffident about it. ("With prose," he wrote in the foreword, "the aria never came. All was recitative.") There was more to this attitude than modesty, false or honest. A book of prose, containing a fair amount of straight-up literary criticism, was too close to the academic writing he'd decided against doing early on, work based in ideas, subject to proof and rival argument, and too far from the personal basis of his poetry, where he styled himself as a dilettante rather than a thinker. Or as he wrote inside the copy of the book he gave to Hooten, "We amateurs, as Peter knows, / Have very little use for prose."

Nor was it necessary for Merrill to explain his poetics when he had a critic like Yenser explaining them for him. Galleys of Stephen's *The Consuming Myth: The Work of James Merrill* arrived from Harvard University Press before Thanksgiving. Merrill didn't respond immediately. When he wrote to thank Yenser, it was in a jocular mood, shielding perhaps some embarrassment, and trying to bring the 367 packed pages of this scholarly book back around into the familiar orbit of cooking and gossip:

> I've been spending the few sedentary hours between terrific bouts of cooking (Claude and [his friend] Todd arrive shortly, and Eleanor and her son Peter will join us tomorrow for a New Hampshire turkey) with your appropriately titled "Consuming Myth." You must think I've been very quiet about this. I haven't in any case said—it's unsayable, really—how much it means to me. [. . .] You [. . .] make sense of it all, and enhance it further serving it from the mold of your consciousness (image from "The Ambassadors"), sprinkled with the nutmeg of your readings in books I've never opened, and the result is—laugh if you will—that you persuade me against so much evidence to the contrary that I've after all amounted to something.

Then, typically, he corrected Stephen's Greek on p. 178. The book was not of course a surprise to him. Merrill had had a hand in it from the beginning. He had responded to Yenser's response to his work at every stage, starting when he sent poetry in draft, and Yenser replied with detailed commentary, affecting the revisions in Merrill's published poems, which Yenser then wrote about in reviews, completing a rare circuit of poetic and critical thinking, creativity and explanation, each feeding the other. As a result, *The Consuming Myth* was a book intimate with its subject on the level not only of ideas but of spirit and style. It traced the myths and metaphors, the philosophy and puns, that formed the unity and characteristic textures of Merrill's work over four decades, as if from the inside. Merrill had influenced Yenser's whole experience of poetry, and Yenser had had his own influence on Merrill's poetry. Now he'd written an authoritative study of it. The book could not have gratified Merrill more if he'd written it himself.

Yet the very comprehensiveness of Yenser's book may have made Merrill feel uncomfortable, as if his career were already complete, measured, and defined. Half to deny that suspicion and half to confirm it, he had been at work on a long poem called "Losing the Marbles." He started the poem in Key West, where he and old friends such as John Brinnin, to whom he dedicated it, would joke about their aging and memory loss over a game of anagrams. Forgetting had been a theme for Merrill at least since "Lost in Translation." Now it was less of a metaphor: twice within six months he had lost his wallet—credit cards, driver's license, and all. "Losing the Marbles" treats memory loss as a hazard of literary life; but the threat of AIDS dementia lurks in the background ("Long work of knowing and hard play of wit / Take their toll like any virus"). Merrill faces the prospect of an increasingly blank slate with a gallant spirit, showing off his undiminished powers. He restlessly analogizes the mind's drive to hold on to its memories, the Greek campaign to return the Elgin Marbles to Athens, and the pleasure children take in collecting the lovely, hard playthings. He slips from one verse form into another while experimenting with the look of his lines on the page. As the life of the mind depends on the body, so poetry depends on the vulnerable materiality of words, the third part of the poem suggests. Here Merrill presents a page damaged by rain almost to the point of illegibility. Like a tattered papyrus text by Sappho, it begins,

> body, favorite
> gleaned, at the
> vital
> frenzy—

The result is a gorgeous fragment, oracular because ruined. Cleverly, the complete text is restored in the poem's fifth section. It reveals quite another sort of poem, a wryly distanced, late-in-life meditation on the romantic idealization of sensual experience:

> The body, favorite trope of our youthful poets . . .
> With it they gleaned, as at the sybil's tripod,
> insight too prompt and vital for words.
> Her sleepless frenzy—

Yet, overall, Merrill had a hard time filling in gaps in the poem. He confided in Yenser, "It's no joke when I say I find it almost impossible any longer to hold in my mind a poem this long—the way I held, say, 'The 1002nd Night' in its day. [. . .] I'm afraid that what was once 'composition' is turning into 'motif' without the inner dynamics (whatever that means) I could call upon 20 years ago." And when he showed a draft to Kalstone, "DK thought the 2nd section [. . .] drew overmuch on the imagery of 'Time'—and indeed, most of it had been written years ago; I used it, shamefacedly, faute de mieux." It was true: from its camp use of a cliché for a title to its loose system of motifs, "Losing the Marbles," touching and clever as it is, involved Merrill in self-imitation, an effort to turn out a kind of poem he had already patented, and he knew it.

He was working at the same time on something rather different. *The Image Maker* is a one-act verse play for two actors. Its subject is Santeria, the syncretic art and religion of the Caribbean involving trance and sacrifice, in which the Yoruba deities called *orisha* merge with Roman Catholic saints in carved figures that are Christian icons and pagan gods both, joining African, European, and New World beliefs and practices. Maya Deren's study of voodoo had long ago introduced Merrill to Santeria; he admired Elizabeth Bishop's collection of santos; and Santeria was part of the mixed cultural heritage of Key West. But he'd taken a new interest in the subject when he met Alan Moss, who was an expert on the figures. Seeing Moss's personal collection prompted Merrill to write "Santo" in 1983, a poem dedicated to Hooten and Moss; and Moss gave Merrill a carving of the Father and Son (meant to remind JM of his role as platonic mentor?) when Hooten visited him in Key West in 1984. Merrill was attracted to these wooden gods for the same reasons he was drawn to the shadow puppets of Yánnina. Like Jungian archetypes, they represented human motive and emotion in highly stylized forms. They had an inherent theatricality, like actors frozen in their poses but ready to come to life. They were conduits to primal forces with the potential to save or harm. They were works of art, and yet they weren't made for the museum: their place was in the home.

The Image Maker takes place in the home, which is also the studio, of the Santero Manuel, set out with a few props: two finished santos, three logs for future carving, "a cot, a chair, a tiny stove," a bird cage, a calendar, and "the curtained entrance to an inner room." Addressing the audience as if a group of tourists, he speaks in rhymed tetrameter with a simple syntax and naïf wit that nod to "The Riverman," Bishop's poem in the voice of a Brazilian shaman:

> I am the Santero Manuel.
> It's I who make the images
> For the entire community.

Yenser, commenting on the play, notes that "Manuel is engaged in V work. As his name suggests to the English speaker, his task as artist is to try to make man well. He is also a rendering specifically of James Merrill, and like Merrill, he must confront the issue of having had 'no time for child or wife.' " He lives with his mother, whom we never see but whose voice can be heard from the curtained inner room, demanding breakfast and nagging her son. His niece Juanita arrives and deposits a santo, Barbara the martyr, for Manuel to repair: "She's always taken care of us, but . . ."—recently things have been going badly, and Juanita's grandmother blames the carving. When Manuel leaves the stage with Juanita, *The Santos come to life*, for Merrill has chosen to make them puppets, which may "be operated, and their lines spoken, by the actors themselves from backstage." Barbara is indeed trouble. She stirs the other santos to remember their elemental and godlike natures and make mayhem, turning into Yoruban deities and challenging both the Image Maker who is the Christian God and the Image Maker who fashioned them.

Manuel grasps that their mischief is the work of Changó, the Yoruban god of thunder and lightning who has possessed Barbara. In keeping with Merrill's interest in the daily, household character of Santeria's cosmic powers, Changó's destructive energy expresses itself in a homely domestic quarrel. In a dream, Barbara accosts Manuel, speaking in the voice of his mother:

> BARBARA
> Bad son, bad son—
> Where's my bad, lazy son?

> SANTERO
> Me lazy? Bad? When all I do
> Is cook your meals and make your bed?

> BARBARA
> And leave me in it! Ha! Confess it's true
> You wish me ill, you want me dead!

> SANTERO
> Mamá, you're dreaming! Or am I?

> BARBARA
> You never married—why?
> Am I supposed to die
> Without grandchildren? What a life!

> SANTERO
> My work, Mamá. That's *my* whole life. Admit
> I'd have no time for child or wife.
> But don't I love you? Don't I care for you?

This might as well be a dialogue between Hellen and Jimmy, an elderly, demanding, sometimes drunken, emotionally dependent mother and her son. At the center of his little play, the scene suggests the constant presence of his mother behind the curtain in the poet's own workshop, the "inner room" where he worked every day to answer her voice in his head.

In *The Image Maker*, Merrill was writing lines for Hooten to speak onstage, and he planned a reading of the play in Los Angeles in May that would feature Hooten and Mary Bomba. For two years, Peter had tried and failed to find film work, and it weighed on him and Jimmy both. A break came when he was hired to work alongside "a hulking actor named Bo Svenson" in "a Grade B jungle thriller," "a sort of cheapo Rambo," as Jimmy put it. Filming began in the Dominican Republic in December. Peter was at first "thrilled," but then puzzled to find himself paid "on the spot in stage money (satchels of Italian lire)." Much about this production was dubious. When Svenson walked off the set in a pique and filming collapsed, Jimmy flew south on a "rescue mission" and brought Peter back to Key West.

Immediately he was called to the funeral of Robert Magowan. His brother-in-law, recently the host of his own golden anniversary, had always been "kind" to him, Jimmy acknowledged. Bobby had long been the shrewd steward of his assets, a man of business whom he depended on and had to respect; now he was gone. Jimmy found the funeral "a very rich experience" emotionally. It was what he'd missed after his father's death—the power of "a grieving clan" which he was perhaps at last uncomplicatedly proud to be part of. Even so, he was there for no more than a day and a half before he left Doris and his nephews to visit his mother in Palm Beach, where he was scheduled to spend Christmas with her, as usual. Like Manuel with his mother, he would be at her service. That meant making her breakfast, lunching with her and her friends at the Everglades Club's "all-you-can-eat," and sitting beside her through the 4 p.m. Christmas Eve service for children. On these visits to his mother, he got through church by taking mental notes he wrote down later. "Doxology: the music grows, for the 1st time, majestic + Wagnerian. Money is uplifted to the God. Light strikes the Rheingold." This was not his faith, and it made him wriggle and protest inwardly: "The great event was not when Word became flesh but when the reverse happened—when man emerging from animal life began to use the alphabet." The day after Jimmy left, Hellen fell again, and broke her right wrist—it was "her 3rd serious break in 4 years"—but rather than run back to her, her son stayed in Key West for DJ's New Year's Eve party.

A few days later, Merrill wrote a letter to Hooten to find when he woke up in the morning. It started, "I don't know what to do. Please, please, please try to get a hold on your feelings." This was a new tone. They'd had their "squabbles" before, but now Merrill was plaintive in the face of Hooten's growing "indignation" and "resentment." "Some of the trouble, surely, is your frustration over the film, a real chance missed to prove yourself to all of us," he reasoned. But the burden for Hooten to "prove" himself was a problem to begin with. Brushing Peter's hurt away as if it were nothing more than the prick of "somebody's least word or idlest gesture," a pain to be passed over like so much else in society, Merrill seemed to be taking anyone's side but Hooten's—making him, in the end, the focus of Hooten's anger.

In Stonington, Hooten's challenge was mainly Eleanor, who thought that "Jimmy had second-rate taste in people," and Peter was no exception to her rule, as she let both Peter and Jimmy know. In the crowded, tropical hothouse of Key West, there were more dangers; and in his efforts to stand up for himself and assert his attachment to Merrill, Hooten rubbed this or that sensitive plant the wrong way. Alison Lurie, for instance, was fast becoming an enemy. She took offense at "his increasingly close imitation of Jimmy's dress, speech, gestures, manners, and opinions," as if he were appropriating, not merely sharing, the life of her friend. She disliked "Peter's increasing use of the royal We ('We rather liked that film')" and his "growing omnipresence, which made it difficult to maintain even the most long-standing friendship with Jimmy." Even "Jimmy," the nickname, was something to fight over. According to Lurie, Hooten told her "it was really somewhat discourteous and overfamiliar for us"—meaning Lurie's generation of Merrill's friends—"to call him 'Jimmy.' It would be more appropriate to address him, especially in public, as 'James,' the way Peter always did."

Close by Lurie's ear was David Jackson. "He began to tell friends that Peter, though he might resemble a Greek statue, was a false copy; he was a phony and a parasite," Lurie writes. "He was also, David believed, after Jimmy's money, and in a big way." It wouldn't be surprising if David took this view. After all, he had to share Jimmy and his house with Peter, not by his choice, and it would have been easier to blame Peter than Jimmy. To all appearances, however, he was kind, or at least polite, to Peter, who was respectful of him, to all appearances. Harry Pemberton, who visited Key West that February, remembered the manners of the Elizabeth Street household: "When the three of them were together, it was work for me. Peter had to feel like an outsider, but on the surface it was OK. Peter and David didn't talk too much. It was a very strange threesome."

Yes, a very strange threesome—and hard to bear for Merrill, despite the fact that he had contrived it. Things were made worse for him by the presence of Jackson's friends in the little wooden house. On February 5, Merrill wrote, "An evening alone with DJ. But no! Phone call, tap at the door, words exchanged. He prefers to spend it talking to" one of his protégés. "<u>Sworn resolution</u>: I will not spend next winter in this house." Expressing his own feelings perhaps, the accident-prone David drove through a stop sign and had his vehicle smashed by another; it was the second time in eight years he'd totaled a car. Merrill wrote to Parigory, David and "I aren't on awfully good terms most of the time. That's nothing new, I know. Still [. . .] Peter irritates him, and his endless parade of black 'indigents' (as he calls them in company) drive <u>me</u> up the wall."

That wasn't all. The letter continues,

> Peter too has revealed himself just a touch less than perfect. He has a frightful temper! He went up to NYC for 2 nights in the flat (and a day's shooting of his film in New Jersey—yes, they've started up the film again). Eleanor was using it for a fortnight, but naturally agreed to let him sleep in the maid's room. Apparently when she came in from her dinner party she didn't ask how he was, just began on the cockroaches and the mess in the fridge, as if these were his fault. He left her a note that was just barely not insulting, then on his return blew up at me. But blew UP. It lasted 48 hours and didn't stop until I pushed him fully clothed into the pool in mid-shout.

Merrill tried to get a grip on the situation by writing a little rhyme titled "Storm." He presented it to Peter in a letter, inscribed "in memory of Feb 19–21, 1986, from his loving JM," evidently hoping that such explosions would now be forever in the past:

> Rock: Control yourself! I've been battered
> Blind and dumb—
> Three mortal days bespattered
> With odium!
>
> Wave: You say this to me, who am shattered
> Each time anew!
> When have fine feelings mattered
> To the likes of you?

In his letter to Parigory, Merrill made sense of his partner's anger by switching into a therapeutic idiom: Peter's rage at him "was clearly the tip of the iceberg of quite a different problem—to wit, I suspect, a certain amount of sexual molestation in childhood at the hands of an older sister, which is known to be a classic source of rage in an adult man." To Hooten, in a letter urging him to see a therapist, Merrill took some responsibility himself: "I will try never again to act like a nagging big sister." Still, it was hard to put those days in perspective, and hard to know what they portended; the operatic scenes they'd acted out, complete with that splash in the pool, were "alarming," and more so given how much Jimmy had come to depend on Peter, who remained "the answer to a prayer."

Around this unhappy household roared the mounting storm of AIDS. In October, Rock Hudson had become the first American celebrity widely known to have died of AIDS, and tabloids and television were full of the story. In Key West, many men were getting sick. Drag queens still walked Duval Street, but now they distributed safe sex pamphlets and condoms. Support groups and public services for people with AIDS had sprung up. The local theater put on William M. Hoffman's *As Is*, "a tearjerker about AIDS," Merrill snapped after he saw it. He'd stopped complaining about his "mysterious symptoms," anxious not to tempt fate or sound an alarm. He knew that, back in New York, Kalstone's condition was worsening. One night at the ballet, David was so ill at intermission that Maxine Groffsky had to call a cab and take him to the hospital. ("The physical details were pretty awful," she recalled.) DK was starting to suffer from confusion and memory loss. Another night that winter, Corn went with him "to a night class Grace Schulman was giving about Lowell and Bishop at the YMHA" where he'd been invited to make a presentation. "He said a few words and then fell silent. Grace prompted him with questions. He barely answered and let his sentences trail off into a pregnant silence puzzling to the students. I suggested we bring things to a close and took David home. It was at that point that we decided David shouldn't go out again." There would be no more keeping up of appearances.

The fact of Kalstone's illness kept "breaking" on Merrill, he admitted in a letter to McIntosh. Rather than explain any more about his reaction, he enclosed a poem based on a dream "I actually had" that he would dedicate to Kalstone:

INVESTITURE AT CECCONI'S

Caro, that dream (after the diagnosis)
found me losing patience outside the door of
"our" Venetian tailor. I wanted evening
clothes for the new year.

Then a bulb went on. The old woman, she who
stitches dawn to dusk in his back room, opened
one suspicious inch, all the while exclaiming
over the late hour—

Fabrics, patterns? Those the proprietor would
show by day, not now—till a lightning insight
cracked her face wide: *Ma! the Signore's here to*
try on his new robe!

Robe? She nods me onward. The mirror triptych
summons three bent crones she diffracted into
back from no known space. They converge by magic,
arms full of moonlight.

Up my own arms glimmering sleeves are drawn. Cool
silk in grave, white folds—Oriental mourning—
sheathes me, throat to ankles. I turn to face her,
uncomprehending.

Thank your friend, she cackles, *the Professore!*
Wonderstruck I sway, like a tree of tears. You—
miles away, sick, fearful—have yet arranged this
heartstopping present.

JM's and DK's Cecconi suits were a sign of their particular gay style, a sort of
team uniform. Now the hour is late, and their tailor is absent, replaced by an
"old woman." Stitching "dawn to dusk," she suggests Hecate, the tri-form
archaic Queen of Night. When she faces the tailor's three-piece mirror, she
turns into the Three Fates, or the witches in *Macbeth*. She opens "one
suspicious inch" of his seam, then thinks better of it. A white robe awaits
him, which brings to mind not purity or chastity, but "Oriental mourning,"
the white traditionally worn at funerals in China. Over all this looms DK's
"diagnosis." Sheathed from "throat to ankles" in this robe, is the dreamer
protected, insulated from the virus, or enveloped, captured, trapped, like
DK? And where did this perilously "heartstopping present" come from?
Whose gift is it? The old woman "cackles" like a commedia dell'arte oracle:
"*Thank your friend* [. . .] *the Professore!*" JM had introduced DK to fine Italian
suits, and here he returns the favor. It is an eerie, prophetic poem in which
the dreamer recognizes his brotherhood with his dying friend.

While he worked on the poem, news came that Merrill had been named the first Connecticut State poet laureate. His duties? He accepted on the condition that there were none (and no salary), since he "didn't want to be writing a birthday ode to the governor every year." He admitted to reporters that he felt "disloyal" to his state, "being here in sunny Key West. But my heart is in Connecticut in the snow."

The winter of 1986 ended with Merrill's sixtieth birthday on Elizabeth Street. The event gathered Key West regulars and out-of-towners. As a party favor for his guests, JM signed broadside copies of "Eight Bits," a suite of comic bonbons in verse; for entertainment, Hooten and Bomba read *The Image Maker*, a rehearsal for the upcoming staging of it in Los Angeles. McClatchy gave Merrill a bound book of birthday tributes from friends, including Tony Hecht, Robin Magowan, John Hollander, Mary McCarthy, Tony Parigory, and even Bernard de Zogheb, who translated Cavafy into the kitchen Italian of his puppet libretti for the occasion. Missing from the party was DK—and also Corn, who'd stayed in New York to visit Kalstone in the hospital, where he was "submitting to tests. His system," Merrill told McIntosh, "in these last weeks, has deteriorated frightfully, though no one can say exactly where the trouble lies—aside from the obvious source."

As the guests departed, Jimmy looked ahead to two trips. One was long planned and extravagant. In April, with his nephews Robin and Stephen and Stephen's partner, Octavio Ciano, he and Peter would tour Japan for six weeks, guided by Donald Richie and Jimmy's own memory of his and David's visit to the country thirty years before. He would be going deep into the past and far away, with an entourage of family and friends. In contrast, the other trip was a secret, and he would make it alone. He'd come to a decision: before he left for Japan, he would go to the Mayo Clinic to be tested for infection by the AIDS virus. He'd talked with Tom Detre about his fears, and Detre, who was the head of the University of Pittsburgh Medical Center, made the necessary calls. Now he would know.

17

ART AND AFFLICTION

1986–89

Merrill boarded a plane to Minnesota by himself. He opened a new notebook and wrote on the first page,

> 30.iii. Easter. Now begin—on the plane to Rochester (Mayo Clinic)—3 or 4 days alone. I feel almost piously toward them. A retreat from which I shall emerge either saved or . . . not.

The next day, a Monday, he wrote,

> 31.iii. 10.00 In the coffee shop after a restless night, then 8.00 appointment with Dr Dickson. Nice man. Didn't seem too alarmed by anything, despite my obliging diarrhea + weight loss. After examination I went for blood-letting—the nurse called the man ahead of me by name: "Joseph Kay"—very Kafka in this world of underground corridors + color-coded "areas." They must have taken a full cup of blood + made me dispose of my bandage 10 minutes later in a sanitary bag for that purpose. No one else had to do this.

An hour later he started a new page: "11.15 Downed Epsom salts. Phoned DJ—John Ciardi dropped dead yesterday." He looked about him and saw a midwestern town "drawn with a ruler by a careful 12 year-old. Streets + sidewalks extra wide. Chain stores, a Dalton Books, restaurants." Gift shops sold teddy bears "wearing intern smocks. Flowers, jewelry, souvenirs from round the world. For the sick to give their loved ones, for the latter to give + be absolved by. One looks for terminal signs in the corridors." The next morning, April 1, he had an appointment with the proctologist at seven forty-five; he wouldn't hear the results of the previous day's blood work until two. He waited:

> Pace of an ocean crossing. A lounge with good reading lights, tables for letter writing, surrounds a 2-story salon-lobby, its vault ribbed with polished wood. Piped music hardly a drawback here: it muffles the come + go.
>
> Many couples, unlike a hospital. The second honeymoon . . . Dressed without flair (all but a few) like people on long trips. One of the smart ones, a man, has a wandering 9 inch scar in the back of his skull. The hair is growing back.

The day was almost over when he fit one more line on the page: "4.15 Consultation over. Pending tests, the answer is ARC."

The National Cancer Institute patented a test for antibodies to the AIDS virus in 1985, but testing was controversial for medical, legal, and ethical reasons, and the test had only recently become widely available in New York City hospitals. For an authoritative diagnosis, Detre had recommended the Mayo Clinic to Merrill. The answer he got, "ARC," was short for "AIDS-related complex." This was a new diagnostic category indicating exposure to the virus and the presence of AIDS-associated symptoms; it was understood as a stage on the way to the development of "full-blown" AIDS. With his notebook open, Merrill took in the implications of the diagnosis: "Virus is present in blood + semen (also saliva). Presume I am a carrier. So far studies don't isolate immune factor. Lymph swelling"—which he'd noticed for a long time—"can have lasted 4–5 years. People with this have some sort of immunity." He noted safe-sex practices under "precautions." "If lover is positive, still take precautions." He would need to have more tests. Treatments were mentioned. Dr. Dickson told him "it cd stay indefinitely like this." Yet "[a]ntibodys plus symptom (lymph node) [were] not the best sign."

Merrill noted all of this carefully without further comment. He began writing rhymed haiku verses in his notebook:

> Cut to clinic. These
> Doomed people turn mild, polite,
> Almost Japanese.

He was observing how other patients behaved and asking how he should. Manners: he'd put so much faith in them; could they serve him now? On the next page:

> Get through the stages, ever grislier,
> Because that's how it's done.
> Why? Because. Because that's how it's done.

"Tom's Dr. Dickson: civilized, concerned." He was grateful for that tone. There was suddenly a great deal to manage, and he had to keep his head. Telling Peter came first. He practiced a speech:

> I will not insult you by observing that you are free to leave me—that we are free to leave one another. There is no way of knowing whether this condition comes to me from you, or—should your test be positive—vice versa. I am content to leave it at that: or so I think. We may be in for some mutual recrimination, even though neither can be construed as "guilty."

He drew a line across the page. A few days later, after he had reunited with Peter in Los Angeles on the first leg of their trip to Japan, he tried out some "recriminations":

> After long years of celibacy, I
> Welcomed you into my life. Fifteen months later,
> This. No ripple of astonishment. What face
> Should death wear if not that of perfect love?

But he was right before. He could never know the source of his infection. Since the 1950s, he'd put up with a long list of sexually transmitted infections: herpes, syphilis, and gonorrhea among them, some more than once. So it was no surprise that he'd been exposed to this newest threat; and if Hooten was infected too, Merrill might well be the source of *his* infection. He could hardly blame Peter, and even if he could have, it would not have helped. What, then, would it mean for their relationship? Merrill's fear that Hooten would leave him was real, especially in view of Peter's anger at him that winter. But the virus would bind them together, not drive them apart. Time was short, maybe very short, and Merrill had to start imagining the world without him in it. He made notes for his will: "Annuity for PH. Property in Fla? Return S'ton to DJ?"

"Pending tests, the answer is ARC." That sentence, written in his notebook, is the closest that Merrill ever came to stating explicitly in writing that he was infected with HIV. Besides Hooten, he informed Jackson, Detre, and his lawyer Milton Maurer. But it would be years before he told anyone else. He approved of Kalstone's choice not to speak about his diagnosis except to close friends: keeping it private had enabled DK to live "as he pleased [. . .] without agonizing expressions of sympathy." Merrill too wanted to live—and work—"as he pleased" for as long as he could. "James didn't want to be treated like a sick person," Hooten remembered. But he must have also had other motives for his silence. Undoubtedly he wanted to protect his mother from learning of his condition—and to protect himself from the consequences if she did learn of it: the shame she would feel, the pain and worry, not to mention the vindication she might claim in their long battle over his sexuality.* For that matter, like his mother, he prized his fame; he hardly wanted to see it collapse into crude notoriety. To become ill with HIV was to begin to lose control, and to make that illness public would be to lose one of the only forms of control left to him. Also, he wanted to protect Hooten: public knowledge of Merrill's diagnosis would expose Hooten to speculation; there were those who would blame Peter; and it was hard enough for an actor to find work without having to fight this new bias. Finally, it was just possible, if Merrill could keep the fact of his illness from other people, that he might keep it, on a good day, from himself.

Silence might seem to have been an easy course for him, and even a cowardly one. But it meant he would suffer from AIDS with little company or emotional and practical support. Silence would be a lonely discipline. Moreover, the moral pressure to speak about his condition would grow as

---

* AIDS must have loomed large in JM's dealings with his mother, even if they didn't talk about it. On September 18, 1985, in a rare reference to the subject, HIP wrote to JM with advice: "The entire country appears engrossed in AIDS, that new FATAL disease. Newspapers, magazines + TV programs go on + on. Doctors, appearing on TV give statistics + say the #1 cause is sex and the #2 is mis-use of the needle. They warn never ever to use your needle to inject someone else nor borrow another's needle should it be more convenient. I paid particular attention to all this, remembering that once you offered to give me a B 12 shot. If you still take these shots yourself, please keep the needle strictly for your own use!" (WUSTL). Hellen's concern was not implausible—JM might have put himself at risk for infection by sharing a needle—but it is striking that she cautions him so vehemently about B 12 shots while saying nothing about "sex."

the epidemic progressed, making his preference for silence a controversial position to maintain. In 1987, a year after his diagnosis, activists in New York formed ACT UP, the AIDS Coalition to Unleash Power. The group's strategy was to use civil disobedience to force government and business to recognize the crisis, make drugs available to people with AIDS, and establish a coordinated national policy for dealing with the epidemic. The first of ACT UP's many protests, leading to arrests and national news coverage, took place on Wall Street, not far from Merrill Lynch headquarters. The group chose for its symbol the pink triangle the Nazis used to mark homosexual prisoners in the death camps (but turned over to point upward and signal empowerment). Political rage was never Merrill's way. "To say you had AIDS was a political move," Donald Richie later commented, "and Jimmy didn't like political moves." Even so, he was aware of these protests, and he must have felt personally addressed by ACT UP's haunting slogan: "Silence=Death."

The question of whether or not to speak about his illness, however, had already been decided in 1986 by the solitude in which he traveled to the Mayo Clinic—this man who so disliked going anywhere alone. It left him with another question: how would he, an autobiographical poet, write about his illness? For even as he determined to remain silent about his HIV, he would have to write about it, as he wrote about everything else. Not to have done so would have been a massive concession, a sacrifice of his powers, and death in advance. Indeed, the chance to write about it, in his own way, was ultimately what he was keeping silent *for*. It would not be easy. He would have to learn how to do it, starting, as usual, with what he wrote in his notebook.

At the Mayo Clinic, and then in the weeks following, his notebook was always with him. He kept it as a voyager keeps a diary. He began writing on the plane to the clinic with the sense that he was starting a new chapter of his life. While he waited for his test results, he used it to resist passivity. With it open on his lap, he was not simply another sick man being processed by an institution; he was a writer observing and evaluating the doctors, the hospital and its protocols, what was for sale in the shops, and the other patients. Most of them were in couples; the notebook was *his* companion. He was using it to find a strategy for talking about what was happening—which he began to turn into verse. His choice to write in haiku stanzas was significant: the form required discipline; it was terse, reticent, impersonal, and—wittily—Japanese. He was thinking about the "mild, polite" attitude of the "Doomed people" beside him. To remain self-contained and patient in a crisis was to behave in a style "almost Japanese."

He was also thinking ahead to Japan, where he and Peter would be heading soon. He'd planned this trip with the intention, of course, to write poetry about it. "Prose of Departure," the result, would turn out to be one of his most subtle, moving, and inventive poems. If not for his drive to write it, he had every reason to cancel the trip. He'd just been diagnosed with HIV: another man would have sought out more experts or an experimental treatment; another would have hunkered down and braced himself; another would have screamed or wept or given up. And even if he didn't want to risk calling attention to his own health, there was Kalstone, shockingly sick, abject, in his Chelsea apartment. Wasn't it Jimmy's duty to remain close by? To wipe his brow, as Peter had done when DK was in the hospital a year ago? What if David were to die while Jimmy was away? Japan would be an escape from those questions, an excuse. Typically, Merrill limited the claims that others could make on him by binding himself to elaborate, long-set plans; and, as if he knew in advance that it would need to be in order to maintain his freedom, no trip of his was as elaborately and long planned as this—at least not since he and Jackson traveled to Japan in 1956. At that time his father was dying; Japan had been the backdrop for his mourning then. And so it would be again.

"Prose of Departure" grew out of Merrill's notebook jottings in prose and verse into a travel poem composed as a series of fourteen *haibun*. The form, combining prose and verse, and common in Japanese literature, is used by Bashō in the log of his journey in Edo-era Japan, *The Narrow Road to the Interior*. Merrill probably read the 1966 Penguin English translation of *The Narrow Road*, in which the editor of the volume explains, "Bashō had been casting away his earthly attachments, one by one, in the years preceding the journey, and now he had nothing else to cast away but his own self which was in him as well as around him. He had to cast this self away, for otherwise he was not able to restore his true identity (what he calls the 'everlasting self which is poetry')." The "departure" in Merrill's title suggests his setting out on the inward journey undertaken by Bashō. It involves for Merrill, as for Bashō, a giving up of self, beginning with a curious narrative device.

In imitation of the motif of leave-taking in Bashō, the first *haibun* in "Prose" presents the poet leaving on his trip and saying goodbye to a friend named "Paul" who has just returned from a clinic where he was treated for a potentially terminal illness. The reader familiar with Merrill's life and the cast of characters in it will assume that Paul is a pseudonym for David

Kalstone, and it is. Why "Paul"? The name is a dignifying veil for Kalstone and a mark of this poem's distance from confession. It makes for a pun on "pall," which Merrill plays on at one point. There is a perverse implication that to be infected with HIV is to be converted, to be set on a different path down which this Paul will lead others, like St. Paul the Apostle. The odd twist is that Merrill assigns to Paul his own memories of the Mayo Clinic, where Kalstone never was a patient. The poem suggests that Merrill knew about the place from a phone conversation with Kalstone, rather than from having visited it himself for treatment. Describing "the Clinic" as "Famous and vast and complex as an ocean liner," and catering "chiefly to elderly couples from the Plains," Merrill inserts language from his notebook into his travel poem, including the haiku poems he wrote while waiting for his test results. The patients and their spouses are "all in the same boat, their common dread kept under wraps, yet each of them visibly

> at sea. Yes, yes, these
> old folks grown unpresuming,
> almost Japanese,
>
> had embarked too soon
> —Bon voyage! Write!—upon their
> final honeymoon.

So Paul turns out to be a pseudonym not only for Kalstone, but for Merrill; he is a composite figure Merrill uses to write about himself as another person, or about himself and Kalstone together. In effect, Merrill empties himself of his experience so as to ponder it at a distance, as if it belonged to someone else. At the same time, he identifies with DK, melding and mingling their experiences. They are "in the same boat," embarked on the same voyage.

Donald Richie, to whom Merrill dedicated "Prose of Departure," hosted the travelers in Japan. The six-week itinerary included Tokyo, Ise, Koyasan, Kyoto, and Nara—all repeat visits for Merrill; the Oki Islands would be his only untried destination. "I had the impression," Richie writes, "that just as the first trip thirty years before had been a kind of honeymoon with David, so this second trip would be a kind of honeymoon with Peter." He found Merrill and Hooten to be "very close, even closer than the couple had been three decades earlier." In fact he caught himself resenting "how protective, indeed possessive" Peter was with his old friend. But of course he didn't know Merrill was ill. "Peter knew," Richie continues, "and was hence understandably protective. If I had paid attention, I might have noticed that something was off. Like the way Jimmy suddenly and uncharacteristically turned to me" when Richie had a young friend with him, and sang "the 'Alabama Song' from Brecht and Weill's *Mahagonny*—'Oh, show me the way to the next pretty boy.' [. . .] Then Jimmy added, quite gratuitously, 'Gotta get the next one, gotta get the next one.' " Merrill's taunting of his old friend and his date stopped just short of the song's refrain, which must have been rolling around in his head: "I tell you we must die. I tell you we must die."

Like Richie, Merrill's other traveling companions—Robin and Stephen and Stephen's partner Octavio—knew nothing about his illness. The notion of taking a long trip with Robin, the travel writer, had been the kernel of this journey for Merrill. Robin's boyish locks were flecked with silver, but he remained a student of his uncle, observing him sympathetically yet critically, still fascinated after all these years. In his diary he remarked on Merrill's facility with the foreign language: "Jimmy's verbal quickness keeps astonishing. Twenty hours of study and he is already speaking fluent Japanese. In bars, on street corners, a question is asked and he bats it back, well enough often to draw a grin from a point well scored. And such composure as he rummages through his set of tools, the phrase book, the pocket dictionary, looking for the expression already marked out for this very occasion." In his "illuminated sandals, flowing scarf, and bright blue cap," Jimmy was always performing, pressing onward as if against an invisible obstacle. He showed his entourage how to hail a cab in Tokyo and how to find their way around the vast subway system. He didn't make it look easy, however. "There are moments," Robin noted, "when his insistence on correctness makes for a certain franticness, irate glances at his watch in a lobby, and exclamations of despair among the hurrying fellow termites of a train station, 'We should have hired a car!' "

Stephen, the fourth of Doris's five boys, was, with Robin, a writer and one of the two "non-working" Magowan sons—in contrast to the careers in finance and business of his brothers Peter, Merrill, and Mark. Because he was also gay and a playwright, because he lived in Greece, and because there was plenty of tenderness and family feeling between them, Stephen might have shared as much with his uncle as Robin did, but that was never the case. Stephen, Robin recalled, "had a Broadway style": he was "bluff and hearty, played the piano and sang, wore red, was loud, and filled the room"—behavior at which Merrill rolled his eyes. In turn, Stephen chafed under the pressure of his uncle's obsessive pace and controlling ways. When the question arose of "doing" just one more temple in Kyoto, he cracked, "Let's save it for our trip thirty years from now." In fact, Stephen had no intention of returning to Japan, or at least not with Jimmy. "This is the worst trip I've ever been on," he said at the end of it. By that time Robin had come to feel that the journey was "death-driven."

Death—it is always rising up before Merrill in "Prose of Departure," so that it's hard to tell whether he, with his party following behind, is fleeing or pursuing it. On the night of their arrival in Tokyo, as he narrates the evening in "Prose," he leads the group out "to wander before bed through the Aoyama cemetery. Mishima is buried down one of its paths bordered by cherry trees in full, amazing bloom." Their trip has been timed for that sacred seasonal event, which Merrill missed the first time around in Japan. He fails to find the grave site of the famous gay novelist and suicide, his long-ago acquaintance. They find a "few ghostly parties" who are "still eating and drinking, lit by small flames," in the cemetery. The partying goes on as in a kind of afterlife, glowing "in the half-dark's black-beamed, blossom-tented

> dusk within the night.
> The high street lamp through snowy
> branches burns moon-bright.

The haiku comes here, as typically in Bashō, at the end of a passage of prose, like an epiphany. Elsewhere Merrill embeds haiku in the midst of his prose—the broad river of words abruptly tightening as it passes through rapids, or swirls in an eddy. Set off not only by the syllable count but by the rhyme (Merrill's addition to the conventional English haiku), this three-line stanza is like one of the impromptu spaces created by the party-goers "on outspread plastic or paper, shoes left in pairs alongside these instant 'rooms' " that mark a separate space within the cemetery, a "dusk within the night."

Merrill comments on the self-protective uses of the haiku in "Strategies." "Halfway around the globe from Paul the worst keeps dawning on us," he begins, admitting that the friend he's left behind is dying. The bad news rises like "the next six-foot wave in an epic poem." To survive it, Merrill reasons, "I need a form of conscious evasion, that at best permits odd moments when the subject

> looking elsewhere strays
> into a local muse's
> number-benumbed gaze

—fixed there, ticking off syllables, until she blinks and the wave breaks." In this situation, poetic numbers are numbing, a means of standing to one side, as in an alley or a local mews while danger passes, if only for the moment. Merrill's constitutional mania for writing served him in this way in Japan. Crouching over his notebook, he avoided the breaking wave of overwhelming anxiety while framing a thought or impression, the slighter the better, that would amuse himself and his friends. Richie described an instance of this in the Oki Islands. The sea was curtained with mist. "We were rowing in a bay, Peter was at the oars, and Jimmy looked over the side at the layers of kelp waving just under our keel. I heard a short exclamation as the idea struck and then he bent over his page and wrote: 'one seaweed fan waves / at another just under / from above the waves' "—a haiku that would go into "Prose of Departure." "He showed it to us at once, See, 5–7–5, pleased that the small form had from his own depths emerged so complete."

The interplay of prose and verse in the *haibun* satisfied Merrill's taste for wandering and accident on the one hand and for compression and control on the other. His haiku express his delight in toys and trinkets. But even in the case of those waving fans, there is an eerie gravity to his jest: the poet, bent over the water like Narcissus, recognizes a second, nonhuman face waving back beneath the surface—it might be David Kalstone, it might be a past or future self.

His haiku made for moments of sudden arrest and intensification of this sort. The form also demanded (and enabled) the rhetorical and emotional restraint he was trying to achieve. The news of Paul's test results stirs the "writhing vocalist" inside him; he wants to gag that hysterical voice before it takes over. So he sets himself exercises: "Aim at composure like the target the Zen archer sees through shut eyes. Close my borders to foreign devils. Take for model a cone of snow with fire in its bowels."

Or, sit very still for hours. That was required on the long afternoons Merrill spent watching Noh drama. In 1956, it had been the jazzy, sexy, combustible Kabuki that thrilled him. Now he wanted the slow, ritual fables of Noh. The stage of this ancient ceremonial theater appealed to him. By convention, it is stripped to essential elements: the wooden roof and pillars of a temple bordered by a stone moat; a painted pine tree; a bridge that leads offstage past a silk curtain of five colors, which represent earth, air, fire, water, and emptiness. Like a Shakespeare play or *Sandover*, the Noh combines high and low theatrics. The afternoon begins with (or may include as an interlude) a Kyogen performance—a Punch-and-Judy show in which clumsy commoners, a servant or a husband, say, misbehave and get punished by their stock counterparts, the master or wife. Kyogen are typically demotic versions of the Buddhist and Shinto legends told in Noh drama, in relation to which they offer parody, commentary, and comic relief. Flute music announces the Noh proper. Men in black and gray kimonos appear and sit to one side of the stage—the chorus. A few props materialize, managed by "invisible" stagehands (there is no curtain, so the stagecraft is revealed to the audience and becomes part of the performance). The actors follow onstage, all male. They wear masks, some of which are very old, and splendid kimonos signifying the characters they play—a ghost or goddess, a phantasm, a warrior, or fox. Drum music sounds. Droning chant rises in intensity with the approach of a storm or a magical transformation. Two or three actors slip across the stage in socks. They execute slow dance movements, indicating their emotions by means of formulaic gestures (the rustle and snap of a fan, the tilt of a masked face). All of this is a matter of technique transmitted across the centuries: the term "Noh" derives from a word for "skill" or "talent." Meanwhile, the extreme poise of the actors is pitted against the Noh's themes of heroic death, madness, and demon possession.

In "Afternoons at the Noh," the longest section of "Prose of Departure," Merrill refers to these performances as "Plays of unself." It seemed to him like confirmation of a simple psychological truth—that under the maiden's mask, for instance, was all along "her mother's ghost." A play's protagonist might appear onstage as

> a middle-aged man—
> but time, gender, self are laws
> waived by his gold fan.

Merrill isn't talking here about the subversive freedom to change identity through a change of costume—a postmodern notion in vogue in the 1980s. Noh was for him an image of the self in thrall to higher powers (parents, the gods, an enchantress) who possess and use it for their own purposes, as, he felt, the Ouija spirits had used him. Freedom is to be sought, rather, through the technique by which an actor submits to and inhabits the role in which he is cast, the story in which he finds himself.

Merrill saw lessons in this for his poetry. "Feet in white socks explore the stage like palms of a blind man," he observed, watching actors "blindfolded by their masks." In a letter that mentions the difficulty of writing "Prose of Departure" as he worked on it over the coming summer, he commented, "I have to find my way like a blind man." He was describing what it was like both to write in the unfamiliar, minimally structured medium of the prose poem—and to write without a sense of the way forward in his life, fearing he had no future.

Chronology, like identity, is flexible in "Prose of Departure." The poem not only records Merrill's travels in Japan in April and May, but also refers to events that occurred while he worked on it afterward. In an ostensibly comic section of "Prose," which Merrill calls "Kyogen Interlude," Richie assumes the role of an Offended Foreign Intellectual who humiliates a provincial trainee bank clerk after the young man's inefficiency causes the travelers to miss their train. Merrill frames the anecdote by fast-forwarding to Water Street, where DJ, here dropped into "Prose" without warning, comments, "That story wasn't nice. Even bank clerks have to live." To which Eleanor, with her knack for unpleasant truths, replies, "Darling boy, nobody has to live. It's what I came away from Paul's service thinking. Nobody has to live." That's the offhand way we learn of Paul's death—after the fact, but before it too, because in the fiction of the poem Paul's death occurs after the trip that is being narrated is over, just as Kalstone's death would.

Before new drugs in the 1990s made it possible for people to live with the disease, AIDS introduced a strange temporality. Men died before their time. So certain did fatality seem, the ill were in a sense dead already, even while they lived on. Often, people lived for a period of time asymptomatic and without knowledge of their fate, like the figure from a legend recounted in "Afternoons at the Noh" whose head is cut off without him having been aware of it. Was it possible to survive the disease by turning back the clock? Merrill must have dreamed of doing just that as he retraced his Japanese itinerary of three decades past, including a visit to the sacred mountain of Shingon Buddhism, Koyasan, where he'd gone after learning of his father's death in 1956. Now he and Hooten sat cross-legged at prayer with the monks of Koyasan. As in the Episcopal church services he endured with his mother, Merrill was restless in the gloomy, golden shrine, studying the abbot's "well-fed back." The fussy glitter put him in mind of Proust, specifically "the Maison Dorée" that Swann imagines as "the scene of [Odette's] infidelities." But he snaps to attention as the abbot "invites us to place incense upon the brazier already full of warm, fragrant ash," and "someone—myself perhaps—tries vainly

> to hold back a queer
> sob. Inhaling the holy
> smoke, praying for dear

life—." His efforts, he feels, are "vain," no doubt in both senses of the word; and the "queer / sob" is clearly a queer's sob, the tears of a homosexual pleading for his own "dear / life."

While in the Oki Islands, Merrill, Hooten, and Richie observed a total eclipse of the moon. In one section of "Prose," Merrill imagines the moon passing through its eclipse as a patient who comes close to dying before recovery: "Doctors amazed." Richie remembered the event well: "[W]e sat for an hour in our room as though at the theater, and the proscenium-like shoji doors framed the evening's spectacle." Pretending this celestial display had been arranged for them by their inn, "Jimmy cast about for a way to return the compliment, for us in gratitude to present our own display." His solution was to perform *The Image Maker* on the karaoke stage of the inn. Richie continued, "An initial problem was that we had no audience. But the interested manager drafted the maids and gardeners, who sat in silence as Jimmy and Peter recited and I, as the jojuri or narrator, translated. It must have been incomprehensible to our spectators but they responded well. Not realizing that ours was a return performance, they in turn arranged a return performance for us, and we sat in silence while the maids danced and the gardeners sang."

Hooten doesn't appear in "Prose of Departure" until a section near the end called "Geiger Counter." The title of this section implies that HIV is like the radiation at Hiroshima—an agent of mass death that is invisible and requires tests to detect. Here, Merrill inserts some of the haiku he wrote at the Mayo Clinic:

> Pictures on a wall:
> a *View of Fuji* challenged
> by *The Dying Gaul*.

> Syringe in bloom. Bud
> drawn up through a stainless stem—
> O perilous blood!

Merrill's companion—recognizably Hooten, though he isn't named— speaks next. He changes the mood, vigorously complaining about this morbid lyricism: "You're not dying! You've been reading too much Proust, that's all! I could be dying too—have you thought of that, JM?—except that I don't happen to be sick, and neither do you." The one who is dying is David Kalstone, of course, and at last the poem addresses Merrill's choice to leave his friend behind for the duration of this trip. " 'What we *are* suffering,' " Merrill has Hooten say, " 'are sympathetic aches and pains. Guilt, if you like, over staying alive. Four friends have died since December, now Paul's back at the Clinic. You were right,'—the dying *Paul*, what else?—'we should have scrapped the trip as soon as we heard. But God! even if you and I *were* on the way out, wouldn't we still fight to live a bit first, fully and joyously?' " Merrill thinks this argument makes "good sense," but doesn't admit it. Angry at his companion for being angry at him, he replies, " 'Fight? Like this morning? We can live *or* die without another of those, thank you.' Mutual glares." To be sure, this vignette is full of elaborate conditionals and denials. But it gives us a good idea of what Merrill and Hooten said to each other behind closed doors.

Wherever they went, Merrill shopped for kimonos for himself and Hooten, as if presents and frequent changes of costume might help. Merrill saves just one to show the reader in the last, stunning section of "Prose" called "In the Shop." This is "the most fabulous kimono of all: dark, dark purple traversed by a winding, starry path." Merrill asks his lover, "To what function, dear heart, could it possibly be worn by the likes of—," breaking off once he grasps the fact that this is a kimono beautiful enough to be buried in. "Hush," he goes on, addressing his lover. "Give me your hand. Our trip has ended, our quarrel was made up"—by which he seems to mean the fight mentioned in "Geiger Counter." "Why couldn't the rest be?" he adds. That is, why couldn't the rest of the story be "made up"—made into poetry, masks, metaphors? It was no secret, really, what lay before him:

Dyeing. A homophone deepens the trope. Surrendering to Earth's colors, shall we not *be* Earth before we know it? Venerated therefore is the skill which, prior to immersion, inflicts upon a sacrificial length of crêpe de Chine certain intricate knottings no hue can touch. So that one fine day, painstakingly unbound, this terminal gooseflesh, the fable's whole eccentric

> star-puckered moral—
> white, never-to-blossom buds
> of the mountain laurel—

may be read as having emerged triumphant from the vats of night.

"Venerated therefore is the skill": for this poet, how to die well comes back to questions of technique. The kimono maker's knots keep parts of the fabric from absorbing dye. When the dyeing is finished, the knots are "unbound," and the designs thus created emerge "triumphant from," because uncolored by, the "vats of night." Merrill makes a fable of this technical process. The designs that result from this way of dyeing cloth provide the "star-puckered moral" he searches for in "Prose of Departure"—confirmation of the hope that something of life might be kept from death by means of art. His image of that something, those "white, never-to-blossom buds / of the mountain laurel," is dense with meaning. He chooses the mountain laurel, rather than the cherry blossom, because he is going home now: mountain laurel—which was in bloom as he worked on "Prose of Departure" in Stonington that June—is the state flower of Connecticut, and he was, after all, the Connecticut State poet laureate. The buds are "never-to-blossom" because they are frozen in time as potential. The "star" in "star-puckered" hints at the eternal perspective of the heavens and the transformation of legendary figures into constellations in the night sky; "puckered" implies a kiss, perhaps the kiss of the hoped-for future reader who might read correctly, and thus validate, the "triumph" of Merrill's designs, long after the poet is gone. He makes sure to say "may be read," not will be: he politely gives permission to that reader, while he acknowledges the possibility of failure.

This haiku, tugged tight by the rhyme on "moral" and "laurel," is an "intricate knotting" of the prose in which it is embedded; and the white, unopened bud it describes is an image of silence. But the image doesn't equal death: just the contrary, actually. The knotted tropes of "Prose of Departure" enabled Merrill to confront an overwhelming fact, not avoid it. Painfully, painstakingly, he was learning how to write about having AIDS.

In mid-May, Merrill and his entourage moved on to "vile + viral" Beijing. Choked by winds from the Gobi Desert, sleeping in the cold halls of a student dorm at a university where a reading had been arranged, Jimmy and Peter both fell sick. After a week, they split up with the Magowans and started home via Hawaii, where they visited W. S. Merwin and a high school friend of Peter's, Mercer Richards, a photographer; then Seattle, where there was another reading; and Los Angeles, where Peter and Mary took the stage to perform *The Image Maker* for the first time. There were bright spots on this trip. The couple snorkeled on Maui: Peter sports a big, bandito mustache, grown for his role as Manuel; JM, always a fish, grins from ear to ear. But Merrill's notebook makes it clear how much strain he was under. He recorded a dream: "Wilderness. River of corpses. In another part, DK is alive, talking, his old self." He couldn't shake his "pains + symptoms," and he couldn't stop arguing with his lover: "Everything upside-down after ½ the night spent shouting at each other." He made a plea to Peter: "I've long ago given up any hope of changing your nature. Will you kindly allow mine (much longer set in its ways than yours) to function as it sees best for whatever time remains?"

Back in New York, on June 1, Merrill wrote, "Seeing DK yesterday, a figure in a morgue, now + then [. . .] opening his eyes" at the prompting of his nurse, Jacques Francois, who was constantly with him. "Did he even know us, or were his manners living on where his mind could not?" The next day Merrill and Hooten returned: "He knew us, for what that was worth. All but a zombie." Two weeks later, Kalstone was dead. McClatchy called Merrill, who was in Stonington with Jackson, to tell him the news. Sandy had been there when Kalstone died, with Alfred, Maxine, and David's brother Charles, a doctor, and his wife Ferne. "They stood around before calling the authorities," Merrill wrote in his notebook. "Perhaps a last sign of life? Then from outside the room came high uncontrollable sobs. Ferne, perhaps—. She hadn't wanted to see David at the end. But it was Jacques, locked in the bathroom. He had come to feel part of the family + now he would have to find a new patient." The stretcher was shrouded, loaded onto a black van, and whisked away past—weirdly—the cameras of a film crew ("Lights, action!") who were shooting a movie at the corner diner.

Merrill couldn't stop sobbing: "sounds I've never heard come out of me." He mourned his friend's perfect sweetness and the trust it made for: "No quarrel ever. No tension. Pure fun + communion. A 2nd self I could reach by telephone, or walking into the next room." "Also, GK"—George Cotzias, whom JM had consulted on the board—"had all but sworn D would recover, only days ago. So that whole source is (again) discredited."

A short obituary from *The New York Times*, taped into Merrill's notebook, announced that "David Kalstone is Dead at 53; Author, Critic and Professor." As was the norm in the paper's death notices at the time, it made no mention of AIDS. Friends gathered to see the New York City Ballet performance of *Mozartiana* which Suzanne Farrell dedicated to David just after his death. Kalstone had wanted his ashes scattered in the Grand Canal in view of the Palazzo Barbaro; Groffsky carried out this wish by taking a token amount to Venice (no more, lest she have to explain to the Italian Customs what she was carrying), while Peter brought the surprisingly bulky rest of DK's "cremains" to Stonington. Merrill had all but avoided Kalstone in his final months; now he coveted what was left of him. He began devising his own burial rites, whether or not they were what others might want, or what David himself did—but then DK had always accepted Jimmy's plans for him. Merrill and Hooten mixed some ashes in the soil of the plants on the deck. Then Merrill scribbled a quatrain on Venetian notepaper—

> Beloved friend, the sky + sea
> of Stonington's your limit? No:
> to Heaven fly, to Venice flow.
> Home-free, home-free.

—burned it, and mixed it with more ashes. They borrowed Rollie McKenna's dinghy, rowed offshore on a "marvelous" day, and, with Jimmy turning the bag inside out below the surface, watched as "a man-sized white cloud" dispersed "in the beautiful sunny water." They were left, oddly enough, feeling "on top of the world." "Maxine agreed," Merrill told Yenser:

> It's absolutely how one wants to go, given back to the elements at the hands of friends. A week later—Yes, insatiable me, I'd kept back one last teaspoonful—we mixed it with earth and spread it at the base of Eleanor's apple tree, having first read aloud Sidney's "Leave me O Love, which reachest but to dust" and his translation of the 23rd Psalm. So she and DJ got their tears in, too. I suppose it was a bit selfish—I mean so many people loved DK, and our relatively private procedures deprived them of feeling part of it all. Well, there'll be a memorial hour at the NY Public Library in September.

Kalstone had chosen Merrill and Richard Poirier, his colleague in the English Department at Rutgers, as his literary executors. They sorted his letters and notebooks and sent them to the library at Washington University in St. Louis, to rest on the shelf near Merrill's papers. They also found a draft of a book of criticism about Bishop and her friendships with Moore and Lowell, which Kalstone had left in a rough state. Robert Hemenway painstakingly edited the text, Merrill contributed a coda, and Farrar, Straus and Giroux published the book as *Becoming a Poet: Elizabeth Bishop with Marianne Moore and Robert Lowell* in 1989—an elegant work of biographical literary criticism and one of the first books about Bishop, setting a direction for future criticism.

Meanwhile, translated to the Other World, DK looked forward to another sort of career: he was slated to be reborn in London as "A SPIFFY BOY OF TOP QUALITY. THEY WANT A QUALIFIED (PREPARED?) W O R L D L E A D E R. I WILL BE IN THE FOREFRONT OF SHIELD PROTECTION TO HELP RESTORE THE OZONE LAYER." But a later séance found him in a different mood. "CARO—WHY ME?" he began plaintively, bringing tears to Jimmy's eyes. "UNHAPPY TO SEE YOU DISTURBED," DK went on. "BELIEVE ME THERE IS NO NO NO CAUSE." Sounding less like his gentle old self than an ACT UP protester, he explained that he'd been "THE

VICTIM OF BIG CITY MEDICINE" and "THE CONSPIRACY TO KILL US ALL," meaning gay men. "THE VICTIMS OF THIS CALLOUSNESS MORE OFTEN THAN NOT CRUMBLE IN DISPAIR + INDIFFERENCE AS I DID."

Kalstone's memorial service was held on September 20 in the New York Public Library. It was a decidedly high-culture event attended by "300 or more." The soprano Dawn Upshaw, a rising star of New York music, sang a setting of Milton by Charles Ives, Purcell's "Music for a While" (text by Dryden), and a Mahler song. McClatchy welcomed the guests and read from Stevens. Poirier recalled Kalstone as a student of Reuben Brower. Charles Kalstone spoke for the family, Groffsky spoke of David's love of the ballet and Venice, and Corn read a paragraph from Kalstone on Bishop's late poem, "Poem," and then the Bishop poem itself. The longest statement was by Edmund White, who evoked DK as "a master of the art of the telephone call."

> Like Mme de Sévigné, who could plunge headlong into a story in the first line of a letter, David would sometimes start off by singing the latest pop song or quoting the latest advertising jingle. Sometimes he'd pretend to be someone else. I'd have a mad Russian professor on the end of the line asking me indignantly how to join the New York Institute for the Humanities and denouncing all other Eastern Europeans as frauds and KGB agents; or a timid, high little voice would be saying, "Hello, Mr. White, I'm twelve years old and I've just read your *Joy of Gay Sex*."

Merrill concluded the program by describing the scattering of DK's ashes in Venice and Stonington. He read an elegy for Kalstone by Mona Van Duyn, Sidney's translation of the 23rd Psalm once again, and a lyric paragraph from Kalstone's diary:

> Tonight, standing in the Barbaro window, I think must be the most beautiful night in the world. Cool. Soft vanishing sunlight and slow shadows on the Grand Canal. One deep sun spot. Being alone. Oh, to open my heart as I have not for years—Venice, my beautiful Venice. The heart aches as the light passes. The town is full of beacons, each with its own hour—I have never known it so beguiling as this summer—the lightning and hail of the other evening . . . Oh, never *not* to return!

Not surprisingly, given the pious conventions of public memorials and the depth of his friends' grief, little was said about Kalstone's illness, and only

White, referring to the title of his own popular book, used the words "gay" and "sex." It was as if Kalstone had not died but evanesced, like that summer light in Venice.

But of course there was more to reckon with. Several poet friends of Kalstone wrote elegies for him, in addition to Van Duyn's: Corn, McClatchy, Henri Cole, Anthony Hecht, Richard Howard, and Adrienne Rich. Elegies for David Kalstone—they were virtually a subgenre in the suddenly and sadly vital genre of AIDS elegy. For all of his talks with the dead, Merrill seldom wrote conventional elegies, but he did on this occasion. The subject and the Sapphic meter he chose for it make "Farewell Performance," inscribed "*for DK*," a companion piece to "Investiture at Cecconi's." It is a poised, exquisite, ceremonial poem that might have been read at Kalstone's memorial service without changing the tone. But it is also more personal and dark than anything that was said that afternoon.

"Farewell Performance" is about sublimation and de-sublimation, art and AIDS. It begins in the seats of the New York State Theater with a memory of the performance Farrell dedicated to Kalstone:

> Art. It cures affliction. As lights go down and
> Maestro lifts his wand, the unfailing sea change
> starts within us. Limber alembics once more
> make of the common
>
> lot a pure, brief gold. At the end our bravos
> call them back, sweat-soldered and leotarded,
> back, again back—anything not to face the
> fact that it's over.

"Art. It cures affliction." Merrill can only take this truism seriously by forgetting about his subject. But that is just the cure art offers—a temporary forgetting. In the middle of the poem, Merrill faces up to the fact that Kalstone's life is over:

> You are gone. You'd caught like a cold their airy
> lust for essence. Now, in the furnace parched to
> ten or twelve light handfuls, a mortal gravel
> sifted through fingers,
>
> coarse yet grayly glimmering sublimate of
> palace days, Strauss, Sidney, the lover's plaintive

Can't we just be friends? which your breakfast phone call
clothed in amusement,

this is what we paddled a neighbor's dinghy
out to scatter—

"You'd caught like a cold their airy / lust for essence." Merrill is speaking about what is most high-minded in his friend. The dancers reach for the timeless and immaterial, and the audience share in that contagious idealism.

If it can be "caught like a cold," however, art is perhaps less like a cure than a cause of affliction. In his drafts, Merrill had "taken on" instead of "caught" and "rage" instead of "lust"—easier words. But he wanted to bring up the sexually transmitted infection that led to DK's death. Merrill is suggesting that art not only fails to save us; it may not be good for us. And "essence" adds a further twist. In personal columns and pornography, the word was a code advertising black men and women through an allusion to *Essence*, the magazine for African Americans that began publishing in the 1970s. The phrase "airy lust for essence" ("airy" in the sense of unconsidered) plays with that slang to tweak Kalstone about his sexual tastes and choices. The dig gives us a glimpse of the barbed byplay that was an ingredient in Merrill's friendship with him; it is a small, semiprivate reference, a comment readers are meant positively not to notice. But Merrill tucked it into the poem with a point to make: that DK's sexual history, no less than his ballet subscription, was part of his "gruel of selfhood."

In the 1980s, AIDS produced terrible paradoxes: sex became life-threatening, and a healthy-seeming man might be terminally ill. "Perhaps the greatest psychic horror of AIDS for a culture that always segregates and shifts death elsewhere," writes the critic Tim Dean, "is the way AIDS intertwines death with life—and what is generally assumed to be the life force: the sex drive." American culture dealt with that horror by scapegoating people with AIDS—as in the case of a *New York Times* op-ed piece by William F. Buckley Jr. published in March 1986. The quickly notorious piece proposed that "everyone detected with AIDS" should be "tattooed in the upper forearm, to protect common-needle users, and on the buttocks, to prevent the victimization of other homosexuals." Responses like this to the epidemic were intended to make AIDS legible, to "segregate and shift death elsewhere," and to reestablish boundaries between the ill and the healthy, the guilty and the innocent. In this hostile environment, Merrill's choice not to use the word "AIDS" in a poem is significant. More than discretion, it was a choice not to use the vocabulary of public debate, for the same reasons he'd rejected the phrase "the sickness of our time" in "An Urban Convalescence." The language Merrill found to write about AIDS was figurative and semiprivate, paradoxical and ambivalent, and powerful and resonant because of it.

In "Farewell Performance," we see that ambivalence in Merrill's shifting relation to DK. Merrill is the audience and Kalstone the performer as JM releases his friend's ashes into the sea and they cohere in "one last jeté" before dissolving into darkness. With relief, the poet seems to accept his friend's death as Peter's "sun-warm" hand clasps his wet one. The gesture recalls Merrill to life, drying and warming the hand that delivered his friend's remains into the underworld. But it's not easy to let go of the dead, and the question of Merrill's relationship to Kalstone returns with the dancers' return to the stage:

> Back they come. How you would have loved it. We in
> turn have risen. Pity and terror done with,
> programs furled, lips parted, we jostle forward
> eager to hail them,
>
> more, to join the troupe—will a friend enroll us
> one fine day? Strange, though. For up close their magic
> self-destructs. Pale, dripping, with downcast eyes they've
> seen where it led you.

The dancers are simply "they": a pronoun that gives them an indistinct, spectral quality, allowing them to float free of personality and gender, even as Merrill stresses their physicality. They are "sweat-soldered" when they return to the stage, fused by glistening traces of the "sea-change" that was their performance: radiant bodies, bonded, seeming to defeat time and materiality. Yet, as Merrill comes "up close," "their magic / self-destructs." Their magic is dispelled by the same force, the body, that created it.

Merrill worked hard to get these last lines right. Showing drafts to Hooten, Yenser, Van Duyn, Corn, and McClatchy, he sought more help than usual. When McClatchy wrote back with queries about the last stanza, Merrill explained that he had introduced "dripping" to link the dancers to DK. "Is it too creepy?" he wondered. "The strongest implication I see is that the dancers were somehow with him as he vanished underwater." He hoped the detail clarified their "odd complicity." But "complicity" in what? In the last line of the new draft he sent with this letter, the dancers "beg our forgiveness." But forgiveness for what precisely? Where was there injury or wrongdoing? He gave a further gloss to Yenser, who asked about the same lines. Referring to the dancers and DK, Merrill said he wanted a sense

> of their having <u>nearly</u> saved him—like lifeguards—or as art can save our souls over and over, but not our bodies. There's the "rage for essence" too, which (says my conceit) infected DK, made him and us perhaps think that death was graceful and beautiful as a dance. But au fond, of course, that's not really so, and they must be forgiven for implanting the notion. Can the lines bear all these meanings? Would they be better without some of them? Can they be separated????

No, they couldn't be. Merrill added further weight and complication by using "self-destructs" in the final text. It suggests that the magic of the dance carries with it a wish for death that the dancers and their audience share. Art not only can't save us; we don't necessarily want it to. When we "lust for essence," we want transcendence, to go beyond the body, perhaps even to destroy it. This is the definition of the sublime—a tradition Merrill invokes when the dancers return "pale" and "dripping." Along with his choice to write in Sapphics, those words recall Sappho's second ode, the most famous lyric of same-sex desire and one of Longinus's examples of the sublime. Merrill annotated the ancient Greek fragment as a student at Amherst, and he had his college textbook on the shelf in Stonington with his translations in pencil as he worked up Sappho's stanza and meter. The ode breaks off as passion leaves the poet sweating and trembling, only "a little short of death."

Merrill and Kalstone had lived the same sort of life. Now, Jimmy feared, they would die the same death. "Dwink time," he signs off in his letter to McClatchy, written at the end of a long day at his desk. A quick look in the mirror, and he adds, "Another shingle is appearing on my eyebrow." It was an annoying complaint, ordinary and minor enough to mention without further explanation, but he knew that his shingles were the sign of a weakened immune system. He felt okay. He'd had his T cell count checked again. His New York doctors deemed the swelling of his lymph gland "unimpressive." He was taking vitamins and Virazole (Ribavirin), an antiviral drug used against infections in the lung. But AIDS was written on his face, as unmistakable as the tattoo Buckley called for.

He had made the mistake of referring to his "slight disfigurement" to John Myers, who "found nothing better to say than: 'Well, Sweetie, you know what everyone will <u>think</u>?' Upon my inmost screen flashed the legend: THIS is a friend? . . . Into the shredder with him." Avoiding Myers wouldn't cure his shingles, however. His doctors would have to take over; they prescribed another antiviral drug, and it worked. "I'm made to feel the narrowness of my escape + the frailty of the ground I stand on," he wrote in his notebook. Had "a new patch appeared in these last hours—I'd have been hospitalized for 5 or 10 days" and fed drugs intravenously, which might have led to more trouble, and would have been impossible to keep a secret. "Thus something in itself common + fairly trivial, like shingles, <u>in my</u> case must be treated as potentially grave. [. . .] Moral: stay well." A couple of days later Merrill wrote in his notebook, "Recovering from another bout of pure dread, I feel a wave of revulsion for—a future of this?"

Was Hooten HIV positive? There are remarks in Merrill's notebooks that seem to imply that he was, but Merrill makes no definite statement (and, later, when he began to tell friends about his own condition, he made a point of saying Peter had tested negative). After the last impossible winter à trois in Key West, Merrill divided his time between Peter and DJ. He saw Hooten mainly in New York, where Peter was living in the Seventy-second Street apartment. When Peter came to Stonington with DK's ashes, Jackson left for Montreal to visit Christian Ayoub. After Jackson returned in September, Hooten flew to Yugoslavia, where he had a part in another "spaghetti Army" movie. "You saw, even before I did," Merrill wrote to Hooten, "that in these difficult months for us both, work would be the one dependable recourse. [. . .] The problem we both face is with me constantly, but keeps disguising itself from the old costume-box of poesy, so that I can entertain it unawares. It helps too, doesn't it? that we are both hale + strong, and that we love each other."

In October, Jimmy met up with Peter in Europe, once his film was done. The lovers spent a few days in Lucerne with Ariane Frey, a Swiss costume designer and a jolly, sophisticated woman who'd hosted them successfully two years before. They continued to Rome, where Hooten had arranged a room near the Tiber, around the corner from *La Bocca della Verità*—the first-century carving believed to be the face of the river god, stained by the tourists who reach into the mouth of it and declare their feelings (the mouth is a lie detector that will chop off the hand of anyone who speaks falsely). There were friends, new and old, in the city: Richard Kenney, who was on a fellowship at the American Academy; Vassilikos, with his wife Vasso Papantoniou, a coloratura soprano, who was in Rome to sing *Norma* and *Ernani*; and Tony Parigory, who came from Athens to spend a week with the couple. Merrill didn't feel or sound like a sick man. He astonished himself by staying out past 2 a.m. at a disco. He slurped tagliolini al limone so delicious it "would almost bring our darling DK back from the underworld." Better yet were the long meandering walks after meals. These brought back the Rome of thirty-five years ago when Jimmy lived with Claude and then Robert and took the bus every day to the outskirts of town to free-associate on Detre's couch.

"We are having a very good time," Merrill said on a postcard to McClatchy, to which Hooten added, "I'm so happy JM is happy in Rome." No doubt they meant what they said, but if they'd had their hands in *La Bocca della Verità*, the river god might have bitten them off. In his notebook, Merrill describes Peter getting mad when Vassili doesn't show Jimmy what Peter thinks is proper regard, which then becomes a bone of contention between *them*. "I want to say that there is no need, + never will be," Merrill writes, "for him to wax indignant on my behalf. But indignation is a feeling he seems to enjoy." Peter is indignant on his own behalf as well, and bridles at Jimmy's control. "I'm an independent agent," he repeats too often in front of Kenney. Next, "P 'goes out to get drunk' + isn't back," Merrill writes, "until I take a 2nd Halcyon at 4.15."

Still, Merrill was at work. His Roman perambulations turned into notes, and his notes into poems. One was the clever "Graffito." Its subject was a bit of (purportedly) found art: a sketch on a fallen block of stone of a forearm tattooed with the "cross-within-a circle / Of the majority—Christian Democrat," holding "a neatly, elegantly drawn cock—erect and spurting tiny stars— / And balls." The stars were Stars of David; on one ball was a swastika, a hammer and sickle on the other. Merrill read the image as a souvenir from an age now passing "when isms were largely / Come-ons for the priapic satirist, / And any young guy with a pencil felt / He held the fate of nations in his fist." "Walks in Rome" was several pages longer—a sad, sauntering meditation in which Merrill doesn't overcome his fears of illness and death so much as put them into long-range perspective. "That was Umberto's window, this was mine," he reminisces. As he stares into the Tiber, "I feel in my old bones / A young man's dread. His longing. To be cast / Upon the waters!"—like DK? But there is no reason for dramatics, where "the cars, the people" that flicker past, leave only "a human smear / About the Bocca della Verità." Truth's marble mouth says, "*Life glitters once, an epigram, and—gone.*"

To conclude their trip, Merrill and Hooten took an excursion from Rome to Capri, where Jimmy hadn't been since he toured Tiberius's villa with his father on his first visit to Italy. No quarrels waited for the couple here. Friends from New York, Francis Steegmuller and Shirley Hazzard—the one known for his pitch-perfect translations of Flaubert, the other for her intricately plotted fiction—gave them lunch on the terrace of their home, with a sweeping view of the Bay of Naples. The afternoon was shining and memorable. Back in 1950, Merrill had been "so young"—and so privileged—"that I took 'beauty' and 'civilization' for granted, and saw nothing particularly remarkable in inhabiting a postcard, or in the beautiful manners of people"—things that struck him now "like manna in the wilderness." Nothing could be taken for granted any longer, and days like this one left him "restored a thousandfold over the weary wretch" he had been a few weeks ago.

He returned home to poetry business. Octavio Ciano had been recruited to direct Hooten and Bomba in a staging of *The Image Maker* as part of a reading that Merrill gave at the 92nd Street YMHA. "No one came running up afterwards with contract and checkbook," but the stars " 'played' more vividly" than they had in California, and the playwright was pleased. There were readings in Boston and Washington in November. In December, as usual, Merrill knocked out a long list of recommendations for the Guggenheim; met with Harry Ford and the rest of the Ingram Merrill Foundation board to settle that year's grants (a special award went to the British poet and mystical Yeatsian, Kathleen Raine); headed to Palm Beach for Christmas with his mother and to Key West for DJ's New Year's Eve party—which was thrashed by tropical rain. High-toned socializing followed. The Key West Literary Seminar, a new institution on the island, featured Merrill, Wilbur, and Vendler speaking on Stevens and Bishop. Jarvis Thurston and Mona Van Duyn were in town for "the season," along with New Yorkers like Susan Sontag and Leonard Bernstein. The famous composer struck Merrill as "sonorous, emotional, looking frightful—fat and ravaged—drinking and smoking as if his life depended upon it." Even so, they got along well. As Merrill must have sensed, his poet peers Van Duyn and Wilbur viewed *Sandover* as a mistake in taste best passed over silently. Bernstein was engrossed in his second reading of *Sandover*, however, and he spoke to Merrill "with such understanding of its techniques that I was transported into a kind of Arcadia full of inspired denizens piping and scribbling under trellises in perfect harmony."

In contrast to Bernstein, Merrill wasn't drinking or smoking at all. His habitual two cocktails before dinner and wine during it had left him groggy too many times: now, at nine in the evening, "I'm as alert as I was at 9 in the morning. When I think of those sodden years—ugh!" The joy of sobriety was less important than the need to protect his immune system. Since his diagnosis and DK's death, Merrill was learning how to live with AIDS. It disappeared as a topic from his letters. He had relatively little to say about it in his notebooks. Yet he sometimes records symptoms, and some casual observations are telling. For instance, walking in the desert outside Tucson, where he spent two weeks as a visiting poet at the University of Arizona in April, he notices a big saguaro cactus raising "an arm or two in supplication, / like someone who turns late in life to prayer. / His days are numbered."

Then, at some point in May or June, he writes this:

> My days are numbered. So are everyone's, if only in retrospect. The disease is almost humane in arranging several years "of grace" before it closes in. Thousands of people are in my exact position, only they haven't thought (or wished) to take a blood test. I know that I shall (unless a miracle cure emerges) be dead in 3 years, more or less. Before that, I knew that I should not live more than . . . 20 years, more or less; and during those 20 years advancing age would continue to affect body + mind.

He couldn't reflect for long on his condition without also thinking about Peter:

> I wanted very much for P. to outlive me, to "tell my story," to be a consultable oracle; it's very painful to think that this isn't likely. Yet my consciousness has advantages—I must try to discover them + use them.
>
> If I get sick before P does, how to cheer him up? A natural death would have made it so much easier on him. He could have had years, found someone else, enjoyed his legacy . . .
>
> Well, it is all <u>bearable</u>. Nonetheless—
>
> Nonetheless it is appalling to live in a present whose future (for both of us) has been so frostbitten.

Merrill never mentions symptoms or signs of HIV for Peter, but here he seems to assume that his lover is living with the same diminished future before him: in his mind, Peter's premature death is as likely as his own. Peter he speaks of almost as a son: Merrill had hoped he would "outlive" him, "be a consultable oracle," and be able to enjoy his legacy. It's "very painful" that those wishes may not be fulfilled, but that can be borne, like everything else. As he surveys his situation, Merrill is clear-seeing, largely free of self-pity, and determined: "my consciousness has certain advantages—I must try to discover + use them."

He was learning acceptance. With DJ too, there was a shift in his attitude from exasperation to protectiveness. At Jimmy's urging, David had a thorough checkup, although he managed to avoid as many tests as he could, most likely including an HIV test: "His theory is that if they know you're in a 'high-risk group' the doctors will arrange to find something wrong." David's sixty-fifth birthday was coming in September: start of official senior citizenship. He had a cataract operation scheduled before it, and—it was a secret from everyone but JM—he was contemplating a facelift. Most days in Key West, he stayed in bed and watched *Sesame Street* in the morning, *Star Trek* in the afternoon. "The bed itself is worth describing," Merrill wrote to Parigory. "It cost $1800, and goes up and down like a hospital bed, and vibrates at the touch of a button. Indeed, once one is on it, it's almost impossible to get off."

That winter, Jackson and Hooten had to put up with each other for a limited time when Peter came to Key West after another Italian movie job fell through: casting had judged him "too old." He took off for Hollywood to "stir up some WORK," but again "nothing was doing." While the flow of film and television work slowed to a trickle, Hooten's professional activity more and more consisted of his collaboration with Merrill. In addition to acting in *The Image Maker*, Hooten joined Merrill at his readings to recite passages from *Sandover*, sometimes to the surprise or dismay of audiences who came expecting the poet to read his own lines. Merrill may have been bored by the routine of reading after years of taking his poems on the road; the theatrical touch appealed to his showmanship; and he may have felt a need for support, in his illness, when he appeared in public. But Peter's struggle to find work was a burden on both of them, and Jimmy was trying to give him a boost. That was part of his motive for writing *The Image Maker*, and, encouraged by Hooten, he revised *The Bait*, thinking that the old play and the new playlet might together make a program in which Peter could perform.

Hooten accompanied Merrill to Tucson that spring and came along for readings in Houston and Nashville. Then—an impromptu decision—they flew to Greece for two weeks. Hooten had been there in 1973 for the filming of *Fantasies*, when he wore a Greek fisherman's cap and made love to Bo Derek, but this was their first time in Greece together. They went to Mykonos, the island where *Fantasies* was shot, and where Stephen and Octavio had a house. They zipped about on Octavio's motorcycle, up and down a "hair-raisingly steep road," "and skinny-dipped"—it was only May—"in the glacial Aegean." Then Merrill took Hooten on a tour of his favorite spots on the Peloponnese. "Does the flute recall the trills that ran through it?" he asked in his notebook. Circling the peninsula, from the fortress of Naf-plion to the ghost city of Mystra, from the Lion Gate of Mycenae to Nestor's Palace in Pylos, he recalled the trills that ran through him in the 1960s.

He was not feeling well. In Olympia, racked by "a stupid uncontrollable dry cough," he sat all night, bolt upright and naked, listening to the night-ingales. Then, crossing back to the mainland on the ferry from Patras, he asked a crew member if he knew Elias Alexandropoulos, one of David's two foster children in the 1960s, who, Merrill had heard, had a job on the boat. The man pointed—and there he was, the little boy they'd taken for ice cream at the Hilton in tie shoes too big for his feet, but grown up now, the ship's first mate with a one-year-old child of his own, wrapping his arms around Jimmy: it was "very touching." In Athens, Merrill and Hooten visited Friar. The couple posed for a snapshot gazing into each other's eyes with one of Kimon's Tsarouchis oils positioned between them, an image of two lovers gazing into each other's eyes. They bought a late work by the artist—a black fan with an image of two soldier/angels in white underwear painted on it. Finally, like old times, there was a party in the Plaka with Tony and George. "P. wants us all to [. . .] move back!" Jimmy wrote to David the next day. But that wasn't about to happen.

Merrill was in correspondence with a young painter, Barbara Kassel, about plans for the cover of his next book. Kassel and her partner, poet and scholar Peter Sacks, had met Merrill when they were both studying at Yale in the 1970s. Kassel's mysterious interiors and landscapes glimpsed through windows or doors captured his imagination. Small-scale, dream-like, with precisely rendered objects and architectural details that hint at narrative and symbol in a manner reminiscent of Balthus (another painter Merrill was brooding over at the moment), yet without any figures in them, her paintings were like surrealist stage sets or illustrations for Bachelard's *Poetics of Space*. They made Merrill think of some of his favorite writers. In a burst of enthusiasm, he wrote a rhapsodic page for a catalog of Kassel's work. He wound up with what might as well have been his own credo:

> Thirty years ago it seemed that violent, vivid abstractions alone did justice to [. . .] psychic life. We had forgotten, for a while, that land-scapes were already interiors, that the world was less than nothing

until it had entered us, bringing images whereby the incoherence at heart might be clothed and sheltered. This truth, which took Proust or Rilke a lifetime to drive home in words, Barbara Kassel sets before us—deftly, teasingly, hauntingly—in each of her paintings.

Merrill sent Kassel exact instructions, down to gradients of color, for what he had in mind for his book jacket: an interior with a foreground wall depicting the night sky, but painted to look "not like a 'real' sky so much as a star-map," beyond which a further, inner room would be partially revealed. *The Inner Room* was the title he fixed on for this volume. The phrase evoked the physical spaces in which he liked to write: the Water Street study hidden behind a door; the laundry room on top of the house in Athens; the niche created by a tall bookcase in his bedroom in Key West. It suggested also the hermetic mental space in which he conceived his poems, a place where, in his illness, he more and more retreated, looking for strength and shelter. Merrill wanted Kassel to convey, he told her in another letter, "that magical sense of a daylit alcove <u>within</u> a night." It would be the picture of a safe zone, with darkness all around—like the "dusk within the night" in the cemetery scene of "Prose of Departure." The volume would be dedicated to Hooten, and it would include all the poems Merrill had written in the shadow of AIDS: "Prose," the two poems for Kalstone, "Investiture" and "Farewell Performance," and "Walks in Rome." It would also include *The Image Maker*. The title phrase appears for the only time in the book in the verse play's stage directions, which call for a *"curtained entrance to an inner room"* in Manuel's workshop-home.

Behind that curtain is the santero's mother. It was the same with Merrill: if, in the midst of his relentless social life, he dwelled in a chamber of his own mind, his mother was in there with him. His notebook shows that their old struggle was ongoing and as fierce as ever. One entry recounts an exchange between mother and son, done as theatrical dialogue:

[Xmas Eve. JM running hither + yon to get supper ready. HIP on 3rd drink.]
HP: Son, look here. You've left your drink on this good table.
JM: I'm sorry.
HP: I've paid $1000 to have all these things refinished, and now—
JM: I'm <u>sorry</u>.
HP: All these things will be yours some day soon. It just kills me not to see them cared for.
JM *[taking her hands]*: Look, I've said I'm sorry. Stop rubbing it in. I've apologized.

HP [breaking into tears]: Oh God—! Oh, oh! It's Christmas Eve! [She
    disappears into the bathroom sobbing. On her emerging, JM is waiting
    resigned, + folds her in a long close hug. The effect is magical.]
HP: That is what I've needed. It's been 3 years, 3 years since you've
    shown me any love at all.
JM: What do you mean?
HP: I mean it! Just little pecks on the cheek. 3 years you've been with-
    drawn, etc. etc.

Merrill had been with Hooten for three years: evidently Hellen was jealous.
Three months later, in March, she was still trying to extract a profession
of love from her son. "I felt my tongue was being pulled out with red hot
pincers. 'Lie if you must,' she said, smiling at grief," Merrill wrote in his
journal. He made up his mind, took her in his arms, looked her in the eyes,
and said "I love you. One gets so rusty. Forgive me." It cost him less finally
than all of his resistance. "It was like an atheist receiving the Sacraments."

After Greece, Merrill settled into Stonington, with Jackson in residence
and Hooten paying occasional weekend visits. The weather was hot, gray,
and airless even on the Connecticut shore, and he had difficulty sleeping.
Or so he told friends; in fact, in his notebook, he mentions high fevers and
night sweats—more symptoms of AIDS. There were short trips: with David
to Martha's Vineyard for an annual gathering of the Key West crowd at the
summer home of the Herseys, John and Barbara; with Peter to Charles and
Mary in New Hampshire, to Ayoub and Marie-Claire Blais in Montreal,
and, on the way home, to Fredericks in Vermont, where Buechner came
to dinner from his home across the valley, bringing an old Lawrenceville
friend to make it a mini-reunion; and finally on his own to Atlanta and
HIP, where he spent ten days "planning her new will, or at least tearing
up old yellow legal pads with lists of people for me to give a posthumous
piece of jewelry to, and replacing them with new lists of possible recipients
still alive." The Stephen Spenders, or "Splendors," came to Stonington in
September; so did Jim West and Mary McCarthy—she looking ill and weak,
"sociable out of sheer will."

More friends were dying: first John Myers, then Howard Moss. Myers,
in equal parts "dear" and "exasperating" in Merrill's eyes, had had cancer
for a long time; Moss went suddenly with a heart attack in his apartment.
Myers and Moss, the one as flamboyant and provocative as the other was
modest and discreet, had been Jimmy's friends since the early 1950s; Myers
was his primary link to the painters and poets of the New York School,
Moss his faithful editor and advocate at *The New Yorker*. The postwar New

York poetry scene Merrill grew up in was passing away, put on file in obituary notices and memorial services. Myers had hoped that "Jimmy Merrill would say something nice about him," and so Jimmy obliged by speaking at his memorial service. On the program with him were Grace Hartigan from Myers's former stable of painters and the conservative art critic Hilton Kramer—who, Merrill thought, was "awful," having no doubt been chosen by Myers, the inveterate promoter, to give his career a last official stamp. From the lectern, Merrill gazed at a "minefield of forgotten faces."

Every occasion that fall was about the past: besides Myers's service, there was a reading marking the ten-year anniversary of Lowell's death and a centennial tribute to Marianne Moore. Merrill gave a reading at Smith College introduced by his former Amherst colleague, Ben DeMott; he had lunch with Rosie Sprague, who was living quietly on her own in Amherst, and drank coffee in her "icy black room + a half," just as they used to. By December 1987, he'd come full circle, flying back to Atlanta for Christmas with his mother and to Key West for New Year's Eve. This time the singer James Taylor came to David's party and led the assembled in a chorus of "Auld Lang Syne." The next day, Merrill was glum: "It doesn't seem like a new year so much as another old one beginning. P. cleaned his squalid apartment next door + made it look almost nice. He's asleep there still. Chris Green," a Key West friend of Jackson's, is "asleep on living room couch. It's raining. DJ so tired, impatient, helpless. Can he change?" He knew the answer already. But what were his own prospects? He listed the names of people he knew who had died from tuberculosis or another disease "within a few years of the medical discovery that would have saved them. This is such a constant throughout history, why this special sense of fatality vis-à-vis AIDS?" He kept hoping (and the Ouija board kept assuring him) that the cure for AIDS would come in time to matter for him. "It got darker + darker in the pessimist's head," he wrote in his notebook. "Finally out came the stars." The next morning, however, it was dark again. "My poems look like lies today. Snapshots of sunshine looked at in rain."

Nothing much had changed between Hooten and Jackson. After a few days together, Peter refused to enter the house because "as he tells DJ in the hall, he's not made to feel welcome." To make matters worse, Jimmy took David's side by telling Peter "he shd make allowances for DJ, especially as his theory would have DJ in the early stages of Alzheimer's. If that's so, or even if it's just that DJ is set in his ways, it wd be for Peter to see trouble coming + find—dear god—a fresh way of handling it. PH: Bullshit!" A note from Hooten made peace. But Merrill was alarmed by his drinking and pot smoking, and told him so. "Kind of him to have thought to stay near me, because of our mutual anxiety," Merrill wrote in his notebook. "But what comfort can he imagine I find in the daily spectacle of him doing those things that will undermine his health?" Each one set out alone for the gym—"J trying to keep flexible, P to sweat his fury out"—and discovered the other there. Separated by a window between their respective exercise rooms, one hot and one cool, P wiped the foggy pane between them, and

> Each to the glass then pressed his nose
> And made a funny goldfish face—
> Poor excuse for an embrace,
> Better than nothing, I suppose.

That quatrain would grow into a poem, "Morning Exercise," about the difficulty of reconciling their two temperaments. That was hard to do with them taking turns being sick with colds and Peter "so depressed about his career." At last relief came when Hooten landed parts in two Italian action films to be shot in the Philippines that spring, for which he was promised top billing and plenty of pay.

Meanwhile, still trying to find the form in which he and Hooten could collaborate, Merrill was busy redacting *Sandover* for the stage. It was a project they'd discussed since their first days together. Merrill didn't undertake it merely to please Hooten: he was intrigued by the task of remaking *Sandover* for the stage, and probably he hoped that a stage production would renew interest in the poem. He found himself putting a text "together with exhilarating freedom, answering a speech on one page with another wholly elsewhere in the book." Arrangements were made to put on the play in conjunction with the revived Poets' Theatre in Cambridge. The script called for three actors: Hooten and Merrill would play alongside dark-haired Leah Doyle, a recent Vassar graduate, as Maria. Hooten and Merrill read the script in Key West with Charlee Wilbur in Maria's role, then rehearsed in New York. When *An Evening at Sandover* was performed in April, selling out the Hasty Pudding theater at Harvard, Merrill thought it "simply marvelous." The modest staging involved mostly changes of lighting and some otherworldly sound effects, like the reverberation when Merrill read "God B's Song." It whetted his appetite for more—although he also got a taste of the offstage melodrama that was partly responsible for driving him away from the theater thirty years before. "The Poets' Theatre 'artistic director' had made blunder after blunder. We were even briefly locked out of our hotel room—the magic keys de-magnetized—because he had no credit on his credit card. Peter's anger was positively Old Testament."

Merrill had had enough of Hooten's anger, and he may have been re-lieved when Peter flew to Manila. But it was hard for him to endure this long separation. "Life without Peter is grim," he felt. Without Peter's companionship, AIDS closed in. Merrill began a "mind cure," a daily diet of positive thinking directed against the evidence of the power of the virus, which was all around him. Tom Victor, an old friend and portrait photographer known for his book-jacket photos of authors, was sick in the advanced stages of the disease: Merrill was touched to hear his "voice on the telephone from hospital, all but extinct, but tender + conscious." Jimbo—rakish Jim Boatwright—was "fading relentlessly" too, his tanned, muscled frame turned gaunt, skeletal, "Kaposi's inside + out." His southern family wouldn't take him back: "Sister quotes father on Jim, ten years ago: 'You live alone, you've got to die alone.' " That was the fate that homosexuality had always seemed to threaten Merrill with, long before AIDS. He'd fought it by making a family out of his friends, and living an intensive social and professional life. Seriously sick himself, but secretly, he made public appearances—for instance, at the annual all-day ceremony at the American Academy of Arts and Letters—as if he were in normal good health and could do whatever was expected of him. But he was dogged by annoying symptoms, and his mood was grim. Confounded by the stack of Yale Younger Poet manuscripts on the floor of his study in Stonington, he picked one by a poet he'd never heard of—Thomas Bolt—"with no people in it at all—just ruined landscapes full of wrecked cars, unbiodegradable bottles, and iron appliance parts slowly turning to rust and mud."

Eco-disaster, the death of nature. Over the last decade, it had become a central theme in Merrill's work; now it combined with his disease by a sort of mutation, micro and macro catastrophes becoming versions of each other in his mind. He muttered to himself, "The death of the world—everyone's death & my own—the death of lakes + forests, cities + seas—the death of breathable air + edible lizards—of atmosphere—of insect—." He was at work on a poem called "Press Release." It starts by reporting that "a new synthetic substance" has been "Crystallized in Sacramento for the first time / After much coaxing" from chemists. "These virgin substances / Don't know how" to combine on their own. "Or it 'hurts' like the first time / You were kissed by a man." Whether the newly synthesized substance is balm or bane or both—like same-sex love?—is hard to say. The question is: How will nature survive the seemingly counter-natural forces discovered and released within it? Merrill opens a science textbook to a faintly encouraging sentence: "Nature's best provision / Remains the tendency of certain organisms / Long on the verge of extinction to return / At depths or altitudes they had once been unfitted / To endure." Drenched by viral sweats as he worked on this poem that June, he must have felt like an organism "on the verge of extinction." He ends by resolving to climb higher:

> To reach the pass, you must follow, like it or not,
> Trails of loam and caustic.

(In draft he wrote "Trails of blood and semen.")

> By concentrating
> On flamework overhead, ice to sun slipknotted,
> Each climber sweats his own salt concentrate
> Of courage. Innumerable, faster-stabbing traits
> Reorient themselves within the substance
> He has contracted to become. So let us not
> Act like children. These are the Alps. High time
> For the next deep breath. My hand. Hold. Concentrate.

The hand Merrill imagines grasping here might be the reader's; in life, it was Hooten's. Once Peter was finished with his work in the Philippines, JM fairly raced to join him, meeting him halfway, in Hawaii. The Pacific made a brilliant stage set for their reunion. They swam in a pool created by an eighty-foot cascade; they got up early "+ drove to the crater of Haleakela (10,000 ft) for sunrise"; from a helicopter, they watched lava flow into the sea. Merrill would make that last event the subject of a wary love poem, "Volcanic Holiday," dedicated to Hooten, in which Merrill hopes that love's "burning" will give way to "a tempering"—"No more eruptions," he begs. He picked up the metaphor in a letter to Hooten after the trip: "One lesson of the islands [. . .] would seem to be that the more Edenic and rainbowed a place is, the likelier it is to erupt. [. . .] When one chooses Hawaii to live in, or you to be in love with, I guess the risk is part of the ravishment."

As on their previous visit to the islands, they visited W. S. Merwin. Merrill and Merwin, two Atheneum poets whose names made them sound like cousins, had known each other, but only rather distantly, since the mid-1940s. "We were so totally unlike each other," commented the serious, dreamy, politically minded Merwin, "we just circled each other, and over the years got closer and closer." Merwin enjoyed Merrill's "enormous warmth and generosity. He was funny. There was a side of him that was a clown"—which was brought out, on this occasion, by his relief in being with Peter again. Merwin could see how urgently he needed his lover: "Jimmy was so frightened of being alone. He was touchingly vulnerable." Merrill admired the beautiful, densely planted grounds of Merwin's home on the rugged north coast of Maui, as well as the poet's involvement in local politics. "His work for the ecology + culture of the Islands has won a couple of lawsuits vs. Jap. hotel conglomerates," Merrill marveled. "How many poets can say they've changed even a pore on the face of the earth?"

In August, Merrill went to Atlanta for nine days. It was his longest visit with his mother in many years. The occasion was Hellen's ninetieth birthday, and Jimmy had invited family from all over (though neither Jackson nor Hooten was there). Charles and Doris came, as did Betty and Tom Potts with the three generations of their family, including their granddaughter little Hellen, aged seven. The first night, "Big Hellen has that 3rd drink (4th Tom guessed) + went into her black hole. It only lasts 30–40 minutes: slumped, incoherent, gesturing exaggeratedly." The next day, her birthday, they went to the Piedmont Driving Club, the elite Atlanta institution where a buffet dinner for seventy was held. "Doris, Chas, Betty all made speeches—as I should + could have done—but, well . . ." Jimmy did not. The day after that, when Doris hosted a "family dinner" for her stepmother, Hellen passed out. "Scene: a private room at the Ritz, harpist in pink, flutist in black tie, waiters, a round table set. Tom P's theory: she'd sneaked a drink before leaving." She had to be removed tactfully. Jimmy resolved "to say nothing for the others' sake—they all begged me to. Besides, half her lifetime ago she lectured <u>me</u> to no avail." And yet he burned "for . . . revenge? 'The next time it crosses your tiny mind that you are the best judge of how much liquor you can hold, let me tenderly assure you that you are wrong.' How I should love to say that, + what a child I am!" At home with the old woman, he *was* still a child, looking at Mummy. "My mother's breasts—at 90—are full, if almost to her waist—like the Minoan priestesses in frescos at Knossos. Or like a Hindu matriarch—exposed without fuss at her dressing table." She filled his ears with the past: "Kinta, Dottie, [. . .] all CEM's flames and infidelities. As if it mattered that I remember!" Here she was, "still passionately rehearsing events of 50 years ago, or more." She gave her son no sign that she would die before him.

Merrill returned to Stonington—and, in September, got on a plane with Hooten to cram in as much of England as they could in two weeks. They saw Kenneth Branagh in *Hamlet* directed by Derek Jacobi and had lunch with Jacobi ("So famous an actor as D. moves in a rosy spotlight of sweet courtesy, taking P's far smaller achievements with perfect seriousness, etc."); saw Adrian Menasche (the friend of Parigory, Ayoub, and de Zogheb from their childhood in Alexandria) and his partner the novelist and playwright

Samuel Lock; wondered at Stonehenge ("A titanic Morandi"); took in fine gardens, castles, and great houses; visited Robin and his wife Carol in their Cotswolds home; and stopped at Tintern Abbey: "A cloudless, breezy noon. Birdsong very loud + they love flying in + out the windows. Roof of sky, nave of grass. Shadows long in September. Smell of cut grass."

Being together, being away: Merrill and Hooten's journey had no other objective. The last page of Merrill's notebook for 1988 returns to their harrowing reality. At the top of the page is an entry written after their return to the U.S.: "Hour on the phone with Tony in Athens. His news has him on the verge of suicide." Parigory had been diagnosed with AIDS. Then: "Jim B. in a coma." Merrill taped in a newspaper photo of Proust: a calm, neutral, heavy-lidded expression in the eyes. The next day he wrote simply, "Jim died last night."

Parigory tried to take his own life that fall. He survived the overdose of pills merely to be shamed by the hospital nurse who threw away the pen he'd used to sign his forms. Merrill took over Tony's care, as best he could, and flew his friend to the U.S. for medical attention and his personal coaching. However rough it was to have HIV in New York, it was rougher in Athens, without the support groups and the increasing public awareness of the disease that in the U.S. now made it seem possible to live with AIDS.

But it was hard for Jimmy to reach Tony, who was crushed by "waves of dread and anxiety." Jimmy arranged for him to see doctors who assured him that "he had years ahead of him before any 'terminal' symptom might appear; and by then, who knows what new medication may be around to prolong things indefinitely? This gave him no comfort, was rather a sentence dooming him to face all the circumstances he would have avoided had he in fact brought off his suicide." Tony also feared that his suicide attempt had left him in "a state of mortal sin." So Jimmy took him "to a very nice Franciscan residence where a kind priest talked to him for an hour, gave him absolution, and sent him next door to receive communion. The next morning appeared the usual haggard face: 'I thought I'd feel better after seeing the priest, but I don't.' " He was "proof against all that might cheer or at least distract him. It's as if his ties to life had snapped, one after another." Tony's lover had tested positive for the virus; probably the young man's girlfriend was infected too. "Well, it's a frightful situation," Merrill wrote to Samuel Lock in London, "and I don't mean to say that he should be taking it lightly. Yet over here one sees dozens—hundreds—of people in the same boat, who do take it in their stride, while they can; who aren't cheated and insulted by their neighbors or blackmailed by their lovers (T. fears this will come next)." Yet he had sympathy for his friend's state. "We must TRY to remember," he advised Bernard de Zogheb in Alexandria, "that he is at present mentally ill. You have only to read the clinical description of melancholia in Freud or William James to recognize our poor friend. The governing symptom is the loss of any attachment to life. No feeling for one's dear ones, no curiosity, no impulse to act." They'd spent a full month together, day in and day out, and the visit had been "utterly draining." Merrill had had to face in Tony "the despair, the panics" that he'd faced and suppressed—and had to keep suppressing—in himself.

He had a local imbroglio on his hands at the same time. It was an election year, Ronald Reagan's reign was ending, and Merrill published "November Ode" in *The New York Review of Books* to comment on the state of the nation, or his little corner of it. The poem described the decline of Stonington's last remaining grocery store—its "prime square footage" slated, after much mismanagement, soon to "be developed in / the usual way."

> Oh well, what don't we learn to live without? Our drugstore—
>   gone forever. Likewise the rival grocer,
>   the Syrian tailor, and the Greek
>   who resoled our shoes.
>
> Now, having watched their premises without exception
>   change to antique shop or real estate office,
>   and our neighbors into strangers charmed
>   by what these offer,
>
> We must ourselves go forth in hollow-eyed addiction
>   to malls where all is maya, goblin produce,
>   false marble meats, tinned tunes, the powder
>   promises of *Cheer.*

Merrill's theme was the march of capital. The attendant waste and destruction took on "guises far more ghastly / elsewhere upon our planet," but it was visible enough in rapidly gentrifying Stonington—which had become a summer destination for moneyed Manhattan families, replacing the working town of mixed population Jimmy and David had moved to in 1954. Rather than a rousing pledge of sympathy for the ill-fated grocer, however, Merrill's poem dwelled on the decay in his shop ("dead mouse and decimated shelves, / the padded statement"), while the employees, especially a "cock-eyed daughter" at the cash register, didn't come off so well either. The grocer consequently threatened "<u>in the papers</u>" to sue his famous, wealthy neighbor: "It is rumored that in his 'mental distress' he precipitously sold the business for metaphorical peanuts." Merrill brushed off the threat, but the whole affair left a stink around town. "And poetry makes nothing happen?" he exclaimed. "Back to incomprehensibility for me!"

In November, Hooten produced performances of *The Image Maker* and *The Bait* in New York, and, in January in Key West, he directed a staged reading of Bishop's poetry with three actors called *Folded Sunsets*. "It's really very moving," Merrill found, "but aside from the 40 or 50 of <u>us</u>"—meaning Key West literary types—"no one else has bothered to go see it," and the show, scheduled for eight nights, closed after four. It left Hooten "depressed, of course, having put so much energy into every aspect of the production." His mother came to visit and support him: "a very open, gentle person—intimacy established on the least shock of acquaintance," Merrill felt. But Peter was in a bad way: drinking, discouraged, completely fed up with Key West, and, in Jimmy's eyes, beginning "to go round the bend." He left for New York, where he started "seeing a shrink twice a week" and "going to AA as well as Smoke-enders."

How Merrill felt about Hooten's struggles has to be inferred, since he makes few comments on them in letters and—an expressive slip?—he lost his notebook from that winter. As a way out of the present, or perhaps as a way to understand it, he turned toward the past. McClatchy had urged him for years to write a memoir. After a tentative start in 1988, he was concentrated on the task, having chosen as subject his years in Rome—the only period of his life when he hadn't written poetry. Fatigued by the rash of autobiographies besetting contemporary literature, he had misgivings about the vanity of such projects ("Only the personal is important, said [E. M.] Forster. He should have lived to see the Me Decade"). Around the same time, Merrill began exchanging letters with a Canadian in his twenties named Brian Walker, whom he saw in Key West that winter. These letters glow with energy and eloquence as Merrill mulls over his past and does his best to charm a fresh face.

He was enveloped in memory again when he sat for the *Ring* cycle at the Met in April, his first experience of the whole tetralogy since he heard Kirsten Flagstad and Lauritz Melchior sing at the Met—the old Met—in 1939. It was a luxurious overlapping of past and present satisfactions for the aficionado of five decades. He was thrilled by all of it, but especially by the " 'human' touches that stately Flagstad would never have dreamed of," as when Brünnhilde (Hildegard Behrens) in her zeal for battle butts her father Wotan (James Morris) in the chest, "like a pony." And that was what was happening onstage. In his red plush seat, he was surrounded by familiar faces: "to my left a woman I'd known since we were babies; to my right, a schoolmate from boarding school; friends scattered throughout the house. It was like the graveyard scene in Our Town." He turned those four long nights into a marvelous poem, "The Ring Cycle," that nicely evokes his love of Wagner and honors skepticism and wonder equally. He knew, for instance, that "The very industries whose 'major funding' / Underwrote the production continue to plunder / The planet's wealth." He knew that when Brünnhilde and Siegfried clash, they were a pair of "world-class egos" who'd been "patiently rehearsed / So that their tones and attitudes convey / Outrage and injured innocence"; and their artistry was not a thing of nature—it depended on "Middleclass families who made it possible / To study voice, and languages, take lessons / In how the woman loves, the hero dies." He knew all that, and yet to see those lovers "hate / So plausibly" made him cry.

Perhaps he was thinking of operatic confrontations between himself and Hooten, there in the seat beside him. They were doing their best to make peace. Jimmy went to meet Peter's psychotherapist, Jeanette Aycock, "a handsome black, or copper-skinned, woman dressed by Laura Ashley, who keeps a telescope in her office. They are visibly fond of each other, or so I made out with the naked eye." He joined Peter in couples therapy with Aycock, whom he too would become fond of, and eventually consult regularly on his own.

The lovers were busy collaborators that spring. With Leah Doyle, they took Voices from Sandover on the road for one-night performances in New Jersey, Los Angeles, and Detroit. The schedule was taxing and pressured, and JM was "tempted to say flatly we will never do this show again." He was fed up with dim technicians, poor equipment, and PH's flaring anger about it all. "Nothing is ever good enough for P. [. . .] What degree of perfectionism I suffer from operates between me + the page, in private. P. has to carry his out into the world, + no one is ever allowed to forget it." The tour wound up with two nights in the auditorium of the Guggenheim Museum. The seats were full of friends: among them, Mary McCarthy, Elizabeth Hardwick, the Lavins, the Hollanders, and "five" Buechners ("I wonder if anyone we don't know saw it"). "The lighting designer came up with some gorgeous effects—clouds, a red-and-blue peacock-tail burst of flowers for the metamorphosis, a cast of stars for Gabriel's speech, all these projected on a scrim which twice became transparent to reveal Bruce and the musicians (5 women—harp, flute, strings)." That was Bruce Saylor, who composed music for this occasion. Merrill and Hooten also commissioned music in Los Angeles by Roger Bourland, a composer on the faculty at UCLA, whose ghostly electronic sounds suited the sci-fi tones of the Ouija board.

What did audiences think? There were no reviews, and Merrill's friends were polite. But *Voices from Sandover* was a misjudged project. It had been seven years since the publication of *The Changing Light at Sandover*; the bells and whistles of a theatrical production were bound to seem like devices for dusting off the long poem, and the poem was being radically transformed in the process. Yenser was quoted in the *Los Angeles Times*, describing *Voices* as "less an abridgement [of *Sandover*] than a work in its own right." This put *Voices* in the best light, but it also tactfully warned audiences not to think they were getting *Sandover*. The magic of the poem, like that of the Ouija board itself, consisted in turning letters on a page into voices, and those voices into the spirits of the Other World. Over the years, Merrill had learned how to read those voices aloud compellingly. But at his readings, what he was dramatizing was his imaginative experience of the poem, rather than the action it narrates: it is what poets do when they read from their work, rather than what actors do when they put on a play. As he began mounting staged readings of *Sandover*, and these became more elaborate, the poem became more literal, more embalmed.

There was domestic trouble among Merrill's friends. Alfred Corn and Sandy McClatchy had been together since meeting at a Merrill party fifteen years before. McClatchy was always the easier friend for Merrill, high-spirited and eager to be of use, while Corn tended to be more guarded and touchy—"the problem child," in his own view. And by the late 1980s, their differences made for conflict. "We had developed into an unhappy couple," Corn remembers. He proposed that they try out the type of non-exclusive partnership that Auden and Kallman, or Merrill and Jackson, had. McClatchy "hit the ceiling," and Corn walked out. He asked Merrill for help as he looked for a place to live: a loan, a chance to stay on Water Street, as he and McClatchy had often done in the past. Merrill refused, and "he made it clear that he was completely on McClatchy's side." But Jimmy didn't just disapprove of Alfred. He did what he almost never did: he cut someone he'd been close to. He withdrew his friendship and his favor; he made a point of dropping Corn from his will. "And when he closed his door on me, many other people did, which I hadn't expected."

Corn's poetic relationship to Merrill had always been fraught. Merrill was an attentive reader who pored over Corn's poems in detailed letters, praising, advising, and encouraging him. There was an affinity between them to start with, to which was added the older poet's influence. Now, in

1989, Corn took his distance from his mentor. He was heard declaring (in Merrill's annoyed version of Corn's comments at a prize ceremony), "In these terrible times poetry has to be more than a mere Mandarin manipulation of language." Talk like that aggravated Merrill. But his rejection of Corn was motivated less by literary reasons than by his personal devotion to McClatchy. For years, he'd appreciated Sandy's energy and reliability, and, in his illness, he depended more and more on him.

Close on the heels of Corn and McClatchy's breakup, Yenser announced that he'd fallen in love with Melissa Berton, a younger woman, and left Mary, of whom Merrill and Hooten had both become "very fond." James urged his friend to come to his senses. He spoke from experience:

> [L]ove is a tyrannical power, a fever, a wreaker of havoc. We in its power think we have never been more ourselves, and wake in amazement with a beloved severed head in our arms. [. . .] Remember, finally, that I'm a child of the Broken Home, and that situations like your present one take me back to inconsolable nights—Mademoiselle and cough syrup, etc. [. . .] The Voltaire in me wants to say that whatever happens is for the best; the mind is inventive and supple enough to make sure of that; it's only in movies that lives are "wrecked," and so forth. Melissa may continue to make you very happy, or proceed to make you very unhappy. Either way, it will be exactly what you deserve— as you know already in the thrilling clutches of the goddess.

"<u>Do</u> understand one reason I'm upset: this is the first time in 22 years," he wrote on another day, "that I've failed to identify with you. [. . .] I hate to add even a shadow of 'disapproval' to your load of worries, and have to smile at seeing myself—of all people—even tentatively ranged against 'antisocial' behavior. But there, I've said it. End of letter." (But not of letters: he wrote another on the same theme two days later.) He reassured Stephen, and probably himself: "my love for you is unchanged."

He'd said the same thing to his father long ago. The Yensers' separation, which led to divorce, prompted a poem from Merrill called "Pledge," which might as well have been about his parents:

> Dance steps the world knows curiously well
> Ease them asunder—
> Friends "rallying round her,"
> His "move to a hotel."

Looking in the mirror, Merrill had to take his own advice to heart with regard to his flourishing relations with the suddenly "Dearest Brian" Walker. Hooten noticed Merrill's interest in Walker, and it hurt him. That period in Key West when Peter seemed to "go round the bend" may have led Merrill to look for understanding from another young man. Now, for Hooten's sake, Merrill wrote to this new friend to establish some limits: "It goes without saying, surely, that it's exactly as we are that you and I have the best of one another, an intimacy without claims or quicksands. Not that I haven't imagined something further, but even my second adolescence is long behind me—I no longer cry with anticipation of the untried and the untrue." "Words like 'infatuation' overstate the case," Jimmy reassured Peter, after he'd stopped writing Walker letters. "Think of him as a kind of human alcohol; I can live without it."

The metaphor was pointed: Merrill hoped Hooten would get off the real stuff. Hooten had his own complaints to register, which Merrill listed in his notebook:

> I spend time away from him.
> My primary bond is with DJ.
> I keep on terms with other lovers.
> I take others' sides against him.

Merrill's handwriting, always neat, rounded, and easily legible, was becoming jagged and unsure—the sign of new physical fragility and weakness. Over the last half year, he'd had more night sweats and a bout of anemia. He continued to see doctors in New York. Periodically, he met Tom Detre for lunch in the city, and he and Hooten visited Detre's hospital in Pittsburgh to consult with doctors there. In the waiting room, "looking for a sign," Merrill noted a print not of Mt. Fuji, as at the Mayo Clinic, but of John Singer Sargent's shadowy *Venetian Interior*, a picture that Sargent had painted on " 'our' floor of the Barbaro, looking toward the Canal." Hooten was impatient with the side of JM that was susceptible to Venetian gloom. Peter, apparently in good health, was physically stronger than his partner; and when Jimmy faltered, he pushed him forward, as Jimmy did with Tony.

They went on traveling. In August, they drove to Montreal to see Ayoub in the hospital where he was being treated for cancer. When they told Christian he looked well, he replied, "Alors, je vais faire un beau cadavre?" It was true: by fall, gallant to the end, this old friend too would be dead. Hooten and Merrill drove on from Montreal, writing encouraging postcards to him. They were bound for Elizabeth Bishop's early childhood home on what amounted to an "Overdue Pilgrimage to Nova Scotia"—the title of the poem Merrill wrote about their visit to Great Village. It was the last of his tributes to Bishop after her death, one more effort to honor (and tap for himself) her special wisdom and artistry.

A month later, in September, Hooten and Merrill packed their suitcases again; this time they were headed for Athens, Istanbul, and Vienna. Part of the point was to check on Parigory—who, Merrill rejoiced to find, had become "a new person!! The awful depression simply lifted one night in his sleep [. . .] and he is now euphoric. It's doubtless all thanks to his anti-depressant pills, but if so, more power to them!" In Europe, Merrill was looking for his own antidepressants, treatments, and talismans. In Istanbul, he and Hooten went to the baths—their bodies steamed, scraped, soaked, and kneaded on marble slabs, dimly lit under the high dome of the hamam. It was his seventh trip to the crossroads city. On an earlier visit, he'd found a street vendor's trinket that delighted him, "a kind of pendant [. . .] made of tiny glass beads [. . .]. At the center, on a perch of beads, a beaded bird swayed; above it, beads spelled out MASALLAH (*Glory be! Praise the Lord!*)." He hung it on Water Street, where it seemed like a magical token, and he wanted to get more just like it to give to his mother and friends. But he found only disappointing machine-made versions, until, on their last day, Peter came upon a heap of the real thing in the bazaar, and they bought them all. "No need ever to travel again; it's the perfect souvenir: a translation into the demotic of Yeats's golden bird on its eternal bough."

Over the summer, Merrill finished "Nine Lives," a long, comic, chatty poem about his and Jackson's last visit to Athens, when he'd been occupied with the stray cats in the courtyard, and he and DJ had sadly, stupidly waited at Maria's café for the Indian boy promised them by the Ouija board. It amounted to a palinode to *Sandover*, and a late salute to the lives the mediums had made for themselves in Athens. Somehow, despite all the reasons not to be, the two of them remained each other's intimate, trusted friend. JM had written to the Hemlock Society for information on assisted suicide; it was evidence of just how depressed he'd been over the past year. In December, on the way out to dinner, David suddenly turned to Jimmy and said, " 'All I know is, if you do the Hemlock thing—or when you die—I die too. I won't go on living. We could take the Hemlock together." Merrill's eyes brimmed. He hugged DJ. Then: " 'I'm not planning to die.' He: <u>Good</u>!"

Merrill sent "Overdue Pilgrimage" to *The New Yorker*, where it appeared that October around the tenth anniversary of Bishop's death. The same week, there was a reading in Bishop's honor at the 92nd Street YMHA. On the program were Frank Bidart, Sandra McPherson, Mark Strand, Octavio Paz, Vendler, and Merrill, all friends of EB. Mary McCarthy, Bishop's friend from Vassar days, who'd been announced as a speaker, lay in a hospital bed a few blocks away—dying. The event, Merrill thought, was "a great triumph for Elizabeth: a full house, everyone reading very well [. . .]—all of us uplifted by the poems and the excitement of the audience. What a vindication!" But the evening had begun strangely. Wanting to declare to all his continuing health and youth, Merrill donned a new green suit and broke out a product from Switzerland: "Vichy's FLASH EFFET BEAUTÉ." "James and Peter were continually trying preparations to beautify themselves," recalled Mona Van Duyn, who was with them at the Seventy-second Street apartment that night. This one, supposed to turn back the clock and eliminate wrinkles, came in glass capsules. "But James couldn't make it work. He rubbed harder and harder, and began to bleed. He'd broken the glass and was rubbing the shards of it into his face. He couldn't stop bleeding." He went off to the reading with his face scored and smudged with blood.

Merrill's disease had sped up his aging: no longer lithe, he was frail; the elfin quality that had once made him seem childlike now made him seem ethereal. At sixty-three, he'd become an old man, with thinning silver hair and age spots. He was ready to be memorialized himself. He was corresponding with various translators who were busy putting his poetry into Polish, Spanish, Greek, and French. If he'd let Corn go his own way, there were plenty of eager young poets courting his opinion of their work and enjoying his friendship: among them were Vikram Seth, whose yuppie-novel-in-*Eugene-Onegin*-sonnets called *The Golden Gate* (1984) had greatly tickled Merrill; Jeffrey Harrison, whom Merrill selected for the National Poetry Series prize and admired keenly; Brad Leithauser and Mary Jo Salter, a married pair of talented poets with whom he was also good friends; Daniel Hall, the last of Merrill's Yale Younger Poets (he gave up the judge's role in 1989) and the only gay poet whom he chose in the series; the poet-critic William Logan and his wife the poet and artist Debora Greger (the creator of the collage on the cover of *Recitative*); and a Kashmiri poet, ebullient, lavishly expressive, and instantly appealing, named Agha Shahid Ali. When he showed up for dinner on Seventy-second Street, Ali came with his mother's recipes and ingredients for a multi-course Indian meal and spent the evening preparing it.

Merrill was inducted into the august American Academy of Arts and Letters in December. "The transition from the Lower Body (the Institute) into this of just 50 members"—who had names like "Henry James" on their designated seats—"is rather like leaving a shabby public garden with children of every color and pockets of fetid aestheticism or avant-garde secrecy in order to cross the threshold of the Racquet Club—exclusive, violently competitive, full of jocks (Wilbur, Styron, Updike, Nemerov, Dickey [. . .]).” Merrill took the place of the recently deceased Robert Penn Warren. “I can smell the corn liquor and possum meat already,” he cracked about succeeding the Kentucky-born Warren, trying hard not to sound like that Racquet Club writer whom his parents could approve of and whom he’d always not so secretly hoped to become.

Yet it was true: even if he was one of the white-haired, white-skinned worthies seated in the Academy on West 155th Street, he would never be a family man or one of “the jocks.” As if to make the point, he wrote a rhyme for Hooten, marking the anniversary of their first meeting at that Upper West Side bookstore in November 1982:

> Dear Wolf,
>
> Full seven years ago our plot
> Thickened—let it never be forgot—
> Among new fictions at the Endicott.
> Who now would choose (returning, if we could)
> A different path within that yellow wood?
> Not I, sweetheart. Your own,
>
>   Red Riding Hood

On December 29, 1989, in Palm Beach with his mother, he wrote to Hooten again, this time with a child’s aching sincerity:

> Dearest Love—Your Xmas card is here, and brings tears of happiness to my eyes. Truly. You know what I need to hear. We’ve gone through so many seasons (in which I’ve been equally to blame) when I’ve felt that every note I’ve struck has hurt your ears, when all I’ve been able to see is what a Bad Lover I am (and it’s often true that I am)—so that when these lovely greetings come from you in every envelope I open, + I can again feel that to bring forth such sunshine from you must mean that I’ve not been altogether hopeless + unequal to you, the dread + heaviness of our worst times simply evaporates. The days get longer + the world turns green. Thank you, Precious Peter. You are the Best Lover in the World. James

In Key West, he paused to write in his notebook before another installment of David's New Year's Eve party:

> 31.xii. End of a decade. Congestion in my chest, but at peace thanks largely to my new medication (arterial cleansing), + my new computer on which I've written almost a page a day since coming South. Finished "Anna Karenina" just now. Party due to start in 3 hours. [. . .] Crowd of 80 expected here.

"Life," he and Freddy used to joke, "we'd be dead without it!" He wanted more of it.

18

THE SUN'S ICY TOMB

1990–95

M errill was "blissfully at work" on his memoir in Key West. He was writing about his parents, his love affairs with Kimon, Claude, and Robert, and his psychoanalysis with Detre. The daily discipline of introspective composition was a continuation of that long-ago talking cure, only his interlocutor this time wasn't a shadowy Hungarian seated behind him; it was a new computer, "the instrument of the Future, which will save us all from memory and cogitation. I've had it just 2 months now, and it has become the center of my life!" Revision without Wite-Out or scissors was "painless" and "thrilling." The cursor kept blinking, impatient for new sentences; yet Merrill's pace strained the thing's capacity. One morning, "as we were glowing at one another, it uttered a heart-rending cry," and "a line of text crumbled into mathematical symbols + musical notes—like Ophelia going mad in a Czech production." It was shipped to New York for treatment ("Had it caught some 'computer virus'?"). Once a new memory chip had been inserted, Merrill and his machine resumed their "torrid honeymoon."

There was of course no cure, no new chip to remedy the virus Merrill carried. If his days "were numbered," the memoir was a way to collect and preserve them. He logged his temperature over the holidays: always slightly elevated, it hovered around 99 degrees. He consulted at regular intervals with Dr. John Montana in New York and Dr. Susan Hunt, recommended by

Tom Detre, in Pittsburgh. As usual, he took vitamins; he hadn't smoked in three years; he stopped after two drinks in the evening; and he popped Xanax, an antianxiety drug prescribed for Jackson. DJ he saw only "now and then. But others tell me how well he looks." Jackson gave him a Nordic-Track exercise machine for Christmas, and Jimmy put it to use in DJ's bedroom, where he tugged on its cords and clattered on its wooden skis while David watched *Oprah* or *The Cosby Show*—until Jimmy started "choking in the smoke-filled air" and fled.

Hooten visited Key West only briefly that winter. He was busy with "ever-escalating" plans to make a film for television of an expanded script of *Voices from Sandover*. Parigory, continuing in improved spirits, visited. To the weekly anagrams competition involving Merrill, Wilbur, John Brinnin, and John Hersey, "L*E*O*N*A*R*D B*E*R*N*S*T*E*I*N" was added. Bernstein had "a healthy 'affect,' as the psychiatrists say," Merrill found, and he "slobbered all our faces like an excited St. Bernard puppy." Swaying with drink at the end of an evening on Elizabeth Street, yet in full control at the keyboard, Bernstein performed a Chopin nocturne on Jimmy and David's spinet. He left Merrill with "a chip of the Berlin wall"—the wall had just come down in November—chipped off by Bernstein himself.

Up to this point Merrill's adult life had coincided with the Cold War. With America celebrating the Fall of Communism and the Triumph of Capitalism, he wrote a biting, mournful, never-published poem, called "After Empires." Political anger wasn't Merrill's style, but there is plenty of it in this poem about the boy who pointed out that the Emperor, depicted here as a menacing tyrant, was naked.

> That little boy, who dissented
> from our credulous commonplaces
> and enormities of faith
> was beaten, mocked, medicated,
> while decades long we looked the other way,
> is an old man fading slowly into
> the nothingness at which he points.
> A hundred million of us who died
> in famine in prison in fire in war,
> have died absurdly, incredibly, as if
> bulldozed, nameless, into the pit
> and left unshrouded under the raw sky.

The empire too is naked: a wasteland everyone had mistaken for a land of plenty. Merrill doesn't specify whether he's talking about the Soviet Union or the U.S., and so includes them both by implication in his visionary rant. He ends by announcing, "Out of nowhere the enemies are back." "They are patient, have faith, never tire, / their simple yet infinitely supple plan / is worldwide" and "stretches for millennia"—into a future that looks a lot like the post-9/11 world and the "War on Terror."

Merrill sent the poem to John Hollander, as he often did with work in progress. (Hollander may have called with a response; no letter about the poem survives.) After nearly forty years of friendship, Hollander was the poet of his age whom Merrill was closest to. He was born into a Jewish family in New York and attended Columbia, where Lionel Trilling and Mark Van Doren were his teachers and Allen Ginsberg and Richard Howard his friends. He was a tall man with a broad chest, a big, soft nose, merry, sometimes wary eyes, a rough, throat-clearing "ahem," insistent nod, and, as of the 1980s, a grandfather's fuzzy white beard. McClatchy, who by now had returned to teach at Yale after some time at Princeton, portrays his older colleague as "a latter-day Dr. Johnson": "His forceful personality can be gruff or ingratiating or contentious. His memory is prodigious, his interests encyclopedic. He has a voracious appetite for every kind of knowledge in all its details, and an equally compulsive desire to share what he knows, at times with a disconcerting finality." As a scholar, Hollander was an authority on versification, and Merrill went to him for shoptalk, though not of a narrowly technical kind. For both poets, prosody was a matter for the imagination, rather than a set of rules. The point of writing in traditional forms, Hollander believed, was to discover "secret doorways and hidden surprising staircases in formal rooms that had been lived in for centuries." He might as well have been describing Sandover, the manor house of English poetic tradition evoked in *Mirabell* by Auden, who was one of Hollander's revered models as well.

Merrill was friends too with Natalie Charkow, John's second wife. A sculptor who carved stone reliefs depicting pastoral scenes and motifs from European painting, Natalie was warmhearted, disarmingly direct, and ready, with John, to guffaw over Jimmy's jokes. Merrill tended to call the Hollanders on Sundays. John and Jimmy reviewed the week's funniest stories, while doing business too, because Merrill depended on Hollander's judgment when it came to deciding grants for the Ingram Merrill Foundation. With Harry Ford and Irma Brandeis, Hollander had been a member of the IMF board since the 1950s.

Brandeis, suddenly very ill, died that winter at eighty-five. Daunting in her learning and permanently mysterious in her private life, dignified, singular Irma had been the muse of "The Thousand and Second Night" and "Syrinx." Thanks to the Ouija board (in which Irma had no interest in life), JM learned that she was now skipping rope in heaven, with her beloved Montale and the actress Eleanora Duse holding the two ends. Merrill put that bit of intelligence into the tribute he delivered at her memorial service that spring. The event was followed by a service for Mary McCarthy, where Merrill also spoke. The great ladies in his life were dying off: by fall, Grace Stone, who'd made it to one hundred, would be gone as well. "For 'entertainment' one goes to memorial services," Jimmy sighed. He'd become "quite a connoisseur of them," between the passing of his elders and the friends his own age or younger who were dying from AIDS. The latter made diseases of the past seem quaint. "With AIDS it's like an anachronism when someone dies of something else," he reflected. "Museums of carriages—landaus, broughams, victorias—people 'carried off' by diphtheria, TB, blood poisoning—those old vehicles, a black plume on the horse's brow. Then came the first automobiles, + our friends vanished, each at the wheel of his own death."

Merrill came to New York in March to join Hooten in preparations for their film, *Voices from Sandover*. It was a "major project," it would require major money, and Merrill was vague about where, besides his own funds, this might come from. (Donald Richie approached a Japanese billionaire from whom much was hoped and nothing, in the end, provided.) Hooten's range of acquaintance made it possible for him to hire highly talented collaborators, beginning with the director Joan Darling. Darling was an Emmy-award-winning actress and the first woman director nominated for an Emmy, with directing credits for popular episodes of *M*A*S*H*, *Mary Hartman, Mary Hartman*, and *The Mary Tyler Moore Show*; in a more literary vein, she had adapted a story by Harold Brodkey for the film *First Love*. John Rook, managing three cameras, and Romain Johnston, who would create the sets, also had won Emmys.

Merrill and Hooten set about selecting their cast, a process that left the doormen on Seventy-second Street "goggle-eyed" as one after another hopeful queued up for inspection at the apartment. Plans called for nine actors, with Peter as Gabriel and JM as himself. Playing DJ was Terry Layman, a youngish actor with brown hair and stage and TV credits; Merrill liked the fact that he'd been a street clown in Paris. Auden would be played by William Ball; as founding director of ACT, the American Conservatory Theater, in San Francisco, he brought serious stage credentials to the production. Starring as Maria was Elzbieta Czyzewska.* An acclaimed actress in her native Poland, she defected to the U.S. in the 1960s, where, despite a

---

* The rest of the cast: David Neumann (Mirabell), Keith David (Raphael), Leah Doyle (Emmanuel), and James Morrison (Ephraim/Michael).

few highlights onstage, her career floundered. Her worldliness, her pluck, and her thick Polish accent (which made it hard for her to win parts in American films) made her a plausible Maria. Merrill found her "funny + fatalistic + intense," exuding "the kind of 'Europe' that turns my bones to jelly."

In July, cast members came to Stonington to observe the mediums at the Ouija board. The voices from Sandover were summoned to converse with their theatrical incarnations: Uni ("SIRS"), Maria ("ICI MAMMAN"), "EPHRAIM ALWAYS ON CALL," and many others. The board, speaking in verse, asked the actors to produce rhyming couplets, which Elzbieta did in Polish. "SO VERY NICE TO HOLD HANDS WITH A BEAUTY," Ephraim said about her, "THOUGH I'VE BEEN CALLED SOMETHING OF A CUTEY." Aside from this instructional demonstration, DJ had no role in the film—which, when it was finished, included a dedication to him in the opening credits, so prominent as to call attention to his absence and seem compensatory. How did he feel that hot summer day, being asked to exhibit his Ouija magic for the actor taking his place in a film produced by Peter? He used to refer to himself to Jimmy as "your old pal Dave." Ephraim signed off this time with an untypical benediction: "SCRIBE IT'S YOUR OLD PAL / GO IN PEACE [. . .] LOVE FROM YOUR OLD PAL." Surely that was David, sadly saluting his partner from the Other World.

In August, Merrill and Hooten rented the Agassiz Theatre at Harvard for the shooting. They had two weeks to make their film, and the work was intense: ten-hour days starting with a makeup session at 7 a.m. with a "burly old Irishman" who treated the star with "greasepaint, powder, mascara," and "a deep-umber Liz Taylor triangle under the jawline (to hide the wattles and bean rows)." The set was crowded with "gaffers + grips + best boys." Yenser was there as the "literary advisor" with his copy of *Sandover* open, the "guardian of the text," as Joan Darling remembered. Up to now, Darling had thought Merrill was aloof from the project; she supposed he was going along with it to please Hooten. "Peter did the recruiting and the deal making," she explained. "Without him, it never would have happened." "Once Jimmy turned up on the set," however, "he loved it. He knew immediately what to do. He showed up to work. He was always moving forward, and clearly *enjoying* it, with no peripheral emotionalism"—unlike Elzbieta, who "was an *actress* and volatile."

And unlike Peter. "He had a tough time," Darling felt. "He had trouble remembering his lines and being ready to work." Worse, as Yenser remembers it, he kept blowing up. "Peter who was in charge of Everything, was sporadically furious with anyone and everyone. He would lose control. One night he fired the script supervisor. Elzbieta and I were walking outside the theater, about 70 yards away, and we could hear him shouting at the poor girl." The pressure that Hooten felt to prove himself in this project, above all to Merrill, must have been great. And it was no secret to the rest of the cast, least of all to JM, that he was drinking. If Merrill had thought that work would help his lover maintain his balance, he was mistaken.

Merrill made friends with Layman, who was "a real honeybunch—married, a father!" With Bill Ball, as with his original, WHA, Merrill kept his distance. Ball had been Darling's mentor, and everything he did, Merrill complained, brought forth "praise or an irrepressible smile" from her. With his surging stage voice, Darling explained to everyone, Ball was "taking a risk. He is presenting the dignity of Auden." "Dignity—that kneejerk word," Merrill muttered. "Wystan was perfectly indifferent to it. He had no shame." Ball and Darling failed to understand that Auden "made his points by raising not his voice but his tone. Knowing better and never letting you forget it, he would talk, not shout, you down."

Apart from Peter, no one on the set knew that Jimmy was ill. He "wasn't particularly fragile," Darling remembered. Indeed he rose to the occasion; "stress and fatigue tend to go unnoticed when one is the center of attention," he smiled. When the filming was over, he and Hooten went off on their own to recuperate in Nova Scotia. As usual now when he looked at a landscape, even a green and shining one like this, Merrill saw desolation. "The Cabot Trail," he wrote in his notebook. "Half the trees are skeletal. Acid rain? The end of the world . . . Is a new aesthetic forming that will relish dead forms?" Still, their time in Elizabeth Bishop country was a relief for both of them. Along the cliffs of Cape Breton Island, the lovers relaxed, exhausted and alone. "P. asks me to drive + falls asleep at my side," Merrill writes. "We are so close these days."

But those days were brief. Hooten flew to Los Angeles, where the film was being edited. Merrill joined him hoping to see a rough cut of it—and returned to New York "precipitously. Peter went off the wagon one night, in an unnervingly matter-of-fact way," Merrill told Layman. "By the time I realized it was 'only' that, I'd paced the floor from four a.m. till seven, at which point a dozen people got woken by my calls. Stephen phoned the Coroner (!), then went in person with a photo to the police to report him Missing." "When I arrived," Yenser recalled, "James was beside himself. Suddenly Peter rolled in, face flushed and clothes disheveled, laughing loudly at his truancy. He claimed to have spent the night at a friend's house, but James clearly didn't believe it, and decided on the instant to leave Los Angeles by himself. It took him maybe fifteen minutes to pack his bags, and I drove him to the airport." Back in New York, Jeanette Aycock told Jimmy he'd done "the Right Thing." "But isn't that what they"—psychiatrists—"always say?" In truth both men had behaved theatrically, Hooten in his all-night "truancy," Merrill in his frantic telephoning and abrupt departure. He was sheepish afterward and asked Layman to keep the story under his hat. Stephen he thanked for his calm and understanding. "We're still 'together,' " he said about himself and Hooten, "and Peter sounds as if his needle had stopped jumping grooves, at least until the next crescendo." That way of putting it wasn't reassuring.

In October, with Hooten accompanying him, Merrill traveled to Washington, D.C., to collect the Bobbitt National Prize for Poetry for *The Inner Room*. He was the first recipient of this biennial award given by the Library of Congress "on behalf of the nation" for "the most distinguished book of poetry written by an American and published during the preceding two years." He donated the prize money ($5,000) to an AIDS support organization in New York. "My mother weewees with excitement" about the prize, he told Yenser. Indeed, at ninety-one, she was still sending out news of her son's success to friends, this time in a quatrain rhymed by herself:

> With more than a gobbet
> Of pride, Hellen Plummer
> Said, "Life was a bummer
> Till my son got the Bobbitt!"

She promptly fell and broke her hip. Her spirit, however, was "all-powerful, causing her friends to marvel" and her son "to groan." She was out of the hospital for Jimmy's Christmas visit, when he could be helpful ("more than last year when I'd have to drive her 10 miles to save 60 cents on a ½ gallon of vodka"). When they had to skip the usual church services, the dean of the cathedral gave communion to HIP at home, "setting out on her chest of drawers two tiny candlesticks, a wee cross, an acorn chalice. It was exactly like a dolls' tea party."

Back in Key West, Merrill entered "the homestretch" of his memoir, although he planned to go on fussing with it for at least another half year. He delayed finishing not merely because he loved to revise. Rather, he was anxious about publishing it while his mother was alive. He thought of postponing publication until she wouldn't be, but it had begun to seem possible, even likely that she would outlive him. The simple reason for his hesitation was her strong opposition to it. The memoir was the story of his evolving moral, artistic, and sexual self-definition, beginning with his confrontation with his mother over his affair with Friar. She'd done her best for decades to keep his sexual life a secret; now the awful truth, as well as her attempts to suppress it, would be exposed to public view; and the prospect horrified her. Their old argument over his homosexuality had turned into an argument over the memoir.

Merrill incorporated that argument in the memoir by writing imaginary dialogues for himself and his mother. At the end of chapter 15 of *A Different Person*, which details his erotic confusion in Rome and his and Jackson's later promiscuity in Greece, he includes this exchange:

> —Why, why does all this have to be spelled out? my mother sighs in the long conversation we never have. You're not hurting me; you're diminishing yourself. Don't imagine, son, that these are things people need to know.
>
> —But they are things I need to tell. If they were boy-and-girl adventures no one would bat an eyelash.
>
> —There you're wrong, said my mother. A young couple, married or living together, as you and David were, doesn't behave in the manner you describe. That's what shocks me.
>
> —I'm sorry. The young people you have in mind have no taboos to exorcise. Society protects them when love fails to. (If you've missed seeing your values embodied, ask Betty [Plummer, Hellen's stepdaughter] to bring her grandchildren over.)

Among his drafts are other versions of that scene. They show the difficulty he had writing it:

> —But they are things I need to tell ["need-*ed*" he wrote in pen]. ~~Straight people, like happy families, are all alike. So are gay people, for all we know; but how are we to know unless books like this are written? . . . .~~
>
> —And who is helped by the things you tell?
>
> —I am, first of all. Put into words, they are no longer unspeakable. Then . . . oh, possibly a young person who'll never otherwise believe that "a sixty-year-old smiling public man" once suffered self-doubt or shame. Everybody, as Freddy said in his letter, has the same story to tell—has had the same "struggle somehow to become a human being"—but the humbling lesson of that sameness won't be learned by pretending that the strug-

gle never took place, that the gleaming author who makes his reader at home was never once lost and begrimed.

Merrill all but pleads for his mother's acceptance in these passages. That he ever thought about justifying his sexual frankness in these ways, rather than trusting his honesty to stand on its own, shows the lasting power of his mother (and the social norms expressed in her half-hallucinated voice) to force him into a corner.

"I used to imagine that late in life I would at last <u>know my mind</u>," he mused in a letter, reflecting on his conflicts with her. "Instead, I'm a perfect weathervane, pointing straight into the wind of whatever mood." But he was learning to accept this sort of ongoing incoherence and emotional difficulty. He wasn't the "smiling public man" in Yeats's "Among School Children" or on exhibit in Hellen's bulging scrapbooks of press clippings about his career. Rather, the self he shows us in *A Different Person* is in process, frequently "lost" and "begrimed." Implied is a view of personal identity: the self as a project that is always incomplete, a mix of accident and shifting, only partially realized intentions, unaware of the dramatic ironies that life has in store ahead.

Merrill turned sixty-five in March. His Medicare card arrived in the mail. His habit of pursing his lips had left faint seams, like stitches, above his mouth; when he narrowed his gaze in concentration or concern, deep creases rippled across his forehead; his face sagged as he smiled, hanging from his cheekbones as if his chin were too heavy. The end of the century was looming up ahead, and he began to feel his time had passed.

After all, the world map was being redrawn. While pundits declared the End of History, the U.S. went to war in the oil fields of Kuwait. ("Don't get me started!" Merrill cried, deploring President Bush's vision for a "New World Order.") In poetry also, a new politics had taken hold. Political correctness and multiculturalism were redefining aesthetic merit, and "the canon"—a term suddenly on the lips of every English major—had become an object of suspicion and attack, not veneration. The formalism that had been the dominant style when Merrill began writing was becoming an increasingly eccentric pursuit, displaced by the free verse of the creative-writing programs and the impersonal writing of Language Poetry. Merrill noticed "how things he wrote forty years ago seem strangely quaint in their vocabulary": "there is one moment when a writer is entirely one with the language he speaks, using it fully, but [. . .] then language, like all things, moves on to be something else one can only imperfectly use." He knew that, in the eyes of many, he was already a dead white male.

While he was at work on *Voices from Sandover* and *A Different Person*, he wrote almost no poetry. As he neared the end of the memoir in summer 1991, he burst into verse with "Self-Portrait in Tyvek™ Windbreaker." At 144 lines, it is one of the longest poems of his later years, and one of the strongest from any phase of his career. In contrast to other late poems, it is concerned not with personal memory, but with the present and the future of our culture. Its vibrant mixed diction—Merrill was intent on catching up to and reconnecting with the language—braids TV talk and consumer jargon in showstopping stanzas of ottava rima. Emotionally, it is rich and burdened too, combining bitterness and gusto, rage and glee, like one of Yeats's late poems—the weathervane of feeling swinging wildly as Merrill faces into the winds of historical change.

The title puts the poem in friendly competition with Ashbery's "Self-Portrait in a Convex Mirror." In place of Ashbery's high-art subject matter, Parmigianino's convex mirror, Merrill introduces a store-bought windbreaker made of a novel synthetic fabric, Tyvek, "the seeming-frail / Unrippable stuff first used for Priority Mail." On the jacket is printed a map of the world. The windbreaker (which Merrill owned and wore: he didn't invent it) suggested to him a symbol of daily life in the post–Cold War global economy, which unites the people of the world as consumers. He found it "in one of those vaguely imbecile / Emporia catering to the collective unconscious / Of our time and place," a New Age shop selling eco-friendly items customers choose to show that "we 'love' our mother Earth, / Know she's been sick, and mean to care for her / When we grow up." Here, where "sapphire waves [. . .] crest, break, and recede," in "mechanized lucite coffins," Nature has been used up, reduced to representation.

Off to the gym in his windbreaker, "Sweat-panted and Reeboked," Merrill wears a "terry-cloth headband green as laurel." He is costumed comically as laureate of the fin-de-siècle. Like the ideal poet Wordsworth describes in his "Preface to *Lyrical Ballads*," who brings "relationship and love" wherever he goes, JM makes friends on the street: the Albanian doorman who pats the jacket and asks him, "Where you buy?" or the girl in the bakery who touches "The little orange France above my heart," saying, "Voilà mon pays." "Everyman, c'est moi, the whole world's pal!" Merrill exclaims in mock bonhomie. His solidarity with these Upper East Side types isn't false exactly, but it is that of "an accomplice" in a crime. What sort of crime? He doesn't mention the sweatshops where his gym clothes were made. His bad conscience reflects the double wish of every consumer to belong, to be the same, and to be special, different from everyone else, and all of that at the expense of the earth and other people. From Adam's fig leaf to the poet's windbreaker, "Styles betray / Some guilty knowledge" of the savage competition for survival underlying society. For who are "we," he asks, suddenly filled with revulsion at human reproduction, but "folk of the first fuck," barely a "few hundred decades" removed from the "red genetic muck," who fight for breath, insisting "*I live*," as "the crush thickens" and "Likeness breeds likeness" in the global population explosion.

AIDS is not an explicit topic in the poem, but it's present by implication from the start when Merrill zips up his windbreaker "and the Atlantic Ocean closes / Over my blood-red T-shirt from the Gap"—as if Tyvek might save his blood stream from contamination, were it not too late for that. But the windbreaker conveys a claustrophobic entrapment more than insulation or protection. With its world map, it suggests that the world system (call it late capitalism, postmodernity, or globalization) envelops JM, like any of us, in an order not of his choice or making, a synthetic social "fabric" that can't be torn and doesn't "breathe." Without Nature to appeal to, there is no escape from that system, no outside or exterior to which we can retreat for health, safety, renewal, or meaning.

Merrill wrote this poem while meditating on the fate of poetry in a fragmented culture where even popular music is a private matter. With music wired to our ears, "All us street people" "Turn ourselves on with a sly fingertip" and a hint of masturbation, rocking to a silent beat. In a retro mood, Merrill chooses Roberto Murolo's "Songs of Yesteryear" for his headset. Murolo, he explains, learned the repertoire of the street singers of Naples who were banned by Mussolini; and after the war, he brought back the "old songs of the land," strumming his simple guitar with "a charm, / A perfect naturalness that thawed the numb / Survivors and reinspired the Underground."

The lyric singer as man of the people, effortlessly expressing the whole human round, "From love to grief to gaiety": this is a lyric ideal no longer available except as a tune to file under nostalgia in our private playlist, Merrill implies. "Songs of Yesteryear" lies on the heap where all styles, even such purported alternatives to style as the "seer's blind gaze" or "an infant's tender skin," have been "seen through" and exposed as nothing but styles, with no more necessary authority than any other. If this ideal of lyric, which stood the test of time from ancient Greece to the postwar era, is now passé, is there any future for the art? Of course there is, but what will he look like, the poet of days to follow? Merrill sees him mantled in a Tyvek windbreaker, not a map of the earth but of the stars: he is "an earphoned archangel of Space," not obviously human, who transmits "far-out twitterings"—and this years before anyone's tweets.

Merrill asks Roberto to sing one "final air." The poem ends by purporting to transcribe a worksheet for that song:

> Love, grief, etc. ★ ★ ★ ★ for good reason.
> Now only ★ ★ ★ ★ ★ ★ ★ STOP signs.
> Meanwhile ★ ★ ★ ★ ★ if you or I've ex-
> ceeded our [?] ★ ★ ★ ~~more than time~~ was needed
> To fit a text airless and ★ ★ as Tyvek
> With breathing spaces and between the lines
> Days brilliantly recurring, as once *we* did,
> To keep the blue wave dancing in its prison.

Merrill's insistence on the inevitable obsolescence of all styles includes his own. His metered verse, in this light, is merely a "mechanized lucite coffin" preserving the back and forth of human breath, the dancing "blue wave" of life. He breaks that container in this stanza, or rather, he lets it stand in a crudely, expressively unfinished state. This is patently, poignantly a farewell to poetry. But it's not a defeat or surrender, because Merrill leaves those starred "breathing spaces" within and "between the lines," where others may pick up the song. His self-portrait closes in process and incomplete, as, he'd decided, a true likeness must be.

As he worked on "Self-Portrait," Merrill was in the midst of personal difficulties that would rise to a level of "Sturm und Drang rivaling" the "days of 1966" when his relationship with Strato was disintegrating. If there was a starting point, it was the Key West screening of a rough cut of *Voices from Sandover* in February. Hooten had warned JM against showing the video in an unfinished state. That night the living room on Elizabeth Street was jammed with eminent older people—the Wilburs, the Herseys, John Brinnin, and Alison Lurie among them—teetering in white plastic chairs. Their response, Lurie writes, was "polite, even congratulatory," though privately her friends agreed that it "was both boring and embarrassing." That opinion came across clearly when Alison served up the empty term—"remarkable"—that Jimmy himself liked to use as praise of the last resort. He admitted that the film had left the crowd "a bit stupefied," and stupefaction was hardly what he and Hooten had been aiming for. Other screenings produced similar results. "Oh my God, this is just awful," McClatchy caught himself whispering when the video was shown to a group of friends at Billy Boatwright's house in Stonington, after which the assembled produced the same stiff compliments heard in Key West. Merrill and Hooten tried showing *Voices from Sandover* to smaller audiences in New York. Dorothea Tanning, Richard Howard, and other friends responded by writing congratulatory messages, but it's hard to say how deep or sincere their appreciation was. Ashbery remembered seeing the video at Merrill's apartment with Frank Bidart and saying on the way out, " 'It was wonderful,' which," he adds, "it wasn't."

What did Merrill himself think about *Voices from Sandover*? He was enthusiastic to start. He returned in February from the studios in Los Angeles flushed with the magic of technology, having marveled as "[t]iming, tidiness, and taste" turned "sloppy 'effects' into minor miracles." Even what had felt to him like a "slow-witted, lumbering" interview with Helen Vendler, added as an epilogue, was cut down to "a lively 12 minute conversation full of charming non-sequiturs." "It now looks wonderful. Still," he allowed, "it's awfully intense + demanding, with next to no action."

Merrill was right: the lack of action was a problem. The intention was to be respectful of the text and the expressive power of the actors, somewhat in the manner of Ingmar Bergman's films. But the magical depth *Sandover* has on the page vanished with costumed human beings staring frontally into the frozen camera. Except when he appeared as the narrator standing in a bow tie and jacket, holding the poem against his chest like a maître d' with the menu, Merrill spent the time sitting beside Layman at the Ouija board, rarely moving even the teacup. The spirits appeared—a clever touch—as heads in a mirror placed behind the mediums. But sometimes they entered the room full figure and sashayed about: Elzbieta, gushing in her thick Polish accent; blustery Bill Ball, raising Wystan's voice rather than his tone; or James Morrison in the role of Ephraim, lounging on a sideboard in Roman togs. David Neumann was an effectively fey and puckish Mirabell. But the angels were shot full screen as haloed heads reciting their solemn, elaborate speeches in *Star Trek* monotones. At times *Voices from Sandover* captured some of the mystery of the Ouija board, but more often the film parodied it. The eeriest effects were unintended—the strangeness of an elderly JM playing his younger self beside an actor playing a young DJ; or Hooten as the dark angel Gabriel, threatening to lose his cool and destroy the world. A further layer of eeriness was added to Bill Ball's performance when, just as Merrill and Hooten were trying to market the film in summer 1991, he was found dead of an overdose of pills.

Merrill had put a great deal into the project, and he must have had high hopes for it. One measure of his commitment was financial. The studio in Los Angeles alone cost $400 per hour to rent. It was rumored among friends, Lurie writes, that the total price tag was over $800,000—a lot of money certainly, but no one would have said anything if Merrill were another type of man and had put that much into a yacht or a chalet. The idea had always been to make some of the costs back by selling the video to public television and to colleges and universities. There were flickers of interest here and there. But no one was buying, and, aside from a public screening at the New School two years later, *Voices from Sandover* never found an audience.

The failure of the video was a blow to Merrill and Hooten both, but Jimmy was much better able to deflect it. Peter was the film's producer. He had devoted more than a year to it, had been swept up in "the euphoria" of making it, and was "terribly" depressed at its reception by the "phonies" in Key West and Stonington. He had always been bright and upbeat, punctuating his talk with exclamations of "Yea!," or polite, solicitous, deferential, eager to do right; these days he was increasingly given to "tantrums," those "Old Testament" rages that Merrill had come to fear. Fueling Hooten's anger were "binges" on alcohol, pot, or cocaine. Aycock prescribed Prozac for his depression, then added Lithium to stabilize his moods. "I do so wish that weren't necessary," Merrill confided in Kimon Friar, "but it"—a mood disorder—"seems to be in the family (mother and sister) and he appears less and less stable without [the drug]."

When Jimmy turned to David, he saw someone else who was suffering and in need of him. That winter Jackson had been diagnosed with emphysema. The decreasing flow of oxygen to his brain perhaps explained his increasing confusion, irritability, and forgetfulness. He came north to Water Street for the summer, where, to keep him busy, Jimmy had agreed to enlist them both in a gimmick. At the behest of the *Paris Review* JM and DJ would use the Ouija board to interview some of the writers ("Stevens, Stein, Colette, Genet, etc.") who had died before the magazine could include them in its famous series of author interviews. The séances spread over nine days, during which all the mighty dead "wanted to talk about was sex and money." Jimmy was left feeling "as never so keenly before, that David's obsessions underlay the entire enterprise." The not very witty or entertaining results appeared in the *Paris Review* under the title "The Plato Club."

When he wasn't with Jackson in Stonington, Merrill was with Hooten in New York. It was "an unsettled + unsettling time, mainly a question of juggling the conflicting claims on my time," he told David McIntosh, half-admitting to the unsupportable situation. In another imaginary dialogue with his mother, later cut from the memoir, Merrill tried to explain himself:

—I don't understand, my mother sighs. Has Peter taken David's place? Don't you still live with David?

—It's what people used to call a double life. One is my past, the other is my present, and both are periodically my despair—David for having aged so badly, Peter for being still so young. I live, to answer your question, now with one, now with the other.

—Are David and Peter happy with the situation? Are you?

—Oh, I'm their despair as well, don't worry!

Hellen replies by quoting "*a book she never would have read in reality*": "*He who makes a virtue of shilly-shally may prudently behave in civil matters; but will his dear ones not sicken of that sophistication, which has no place at a wise man's hearth?*"

As his summer of agonizing shilly-shally wore on, he steeled himself for the actual dialogue with his mother he felt obliged to have. He meant "to read aloud to [her] the passages that concern her from my all-but-completed memoir. Everyone says this is so daring of me. But the more I thought, why not?" He didn't "want it felt that I 'waited for her to die' before telling the world, etc. And she can always ask me to stop while she makes long distance calls to her godchildren." Whatever he may have expected from her beforehand, Mrs. Plummer, in person, gave no quarter to her son. She told him, "I've prayed twice a day for nearly 50 years that none of this would ever come to light . . . In fact I'd just been praying when I slipped and broke my hip in church, so I guess God got tired of hearing that particular prayer." He replied, "Did you never in all those years pray to have your embarrassment and shame taken away?" "Never. Oh well (a sweet smile) I may be gone by the time it's published. I hope I am." He departed in defeat, leaving a copy of the memoir with Hellen, "but God is now making her eyes burn too severely to read more than a page a day. 'And of course I can't ask anyone else to read it to me.' " He would wait longer to publish it.

Meanwhile, Hooten's condition was getting worse. Merrill brought him to visit Claude Fredericks in Pawlet, hoping that the placid routines of the rural place would be restorative. To Claude, Peter appeared "severely troubled and on the edge of collapse." He and Jimmy were constantly "at each other's throats" during the visit, breaking out into "wild lashing anger," "[l]ike the sinners in the last pocket of [the *Inferno's*] Malebolge." A few weeks later, in early October, Hooten "checked into [the] Detox wing of Roosevelt Hospital." A week later "he moved to their rehabilitation center—a marble mansion on East 93rd St," Smithers Alcoholism Center, where he would be treated for four weeks. Merrill was "relieved" to see him take these steps. But he was also "wrung out by the months" leading up to them and "simply boiling with rage [. . .] most of the time; either that or full of gloom. This really seems to be our last chance." Making matters worse, his own health was deteriorating. Dr. Hunt gave him bad news when he consulted her that October: his T cell count, measuring the strength of his immune system, had dropped dramatically. He was left "shaken," weeping and alone, in a Pittsburgh hotel room.

It was testimony to his love of Peter as well as his need of him that he clutched at this "last chance." Given how ill and angry he was, he might have told Peter not to come back until he'd pulled himself together. Or he might have settled for cheering Peter on from the sideline. But he went much further. He went to lectures on substance abuse and childhood trauma, listened to tapes, studied case histories, attended couples counseling, and went by himself to "emotional group sessions on 'co-dependency.' " The idea of "co-dependency" he found "fascinating." It shed light, after all, on the give-and-take of "almost any couple." But he saw its special relevance in his own life: Peter's addictive behavior fell into line with the drinking of his parents, David Jackson, and Peter Tourville; even Strato's gambling seemed to make sense. Merrill saw too that basic changes had taken place (these were "fascinating" as well) in the therapeutic enterprise. Since he first entered a psychiatrist's office in 1946, "the expensive made-to-order underwear from Vienna" had been replaced by casual styles from "Benetton + The Gap, vivid attitudes that let it all hang out, one size fits everybody." He donned these new fashions without vanity or complaint, with no time to lose.

Hooten graduated from the program in New York and entered Sierra Tucson, a residential addiction treatment center in Arizona, where Merrill spent a week with him before Thanksgiving. On his return, Merrill wrote to Peter Moore, a younger friend in Toronto, about the experience:

It's Pop Psychotherapy. [. . .] Groups in circles, friendly but utterly non-directive counselors, who say "That's OK, you don't have to share if you don't feel like it." No caffeine or desserts on the menu. The patients live in dorms named for the local cacti. [. . .]

After visiting hours on Sunday a ban on communication (word or glance) with your patient goes into effect. Rather like "The Magic Flute." The exception is the highly ritualized hour in the afternoon group at which you give your patient a list of grievances, or vice versa; or tell each other your "boundaries"

or what you love about each other. At those times you are looking deeply into each other's eyes while the counselors voyeuris-
tically study your faces for telltale signs of Anger, Fear, Shame,
Guilt, Sadness, Hurt, or Loneliness.

Those seven words are, by and large, what we are given to
work with. Like the child's first watercolor box.

A particular episode stood out:

Peter "acted up" in the afternoon group one day, and stormed
out of the room. The blank-faced counselor said, "When Peter
behaves like this, I feel <u>afraid</u>," and everyone else felt <u>afraid</u>,
too. I especially did, thinking, "Oh dear, he's resisting the
therapy, and if <u>this</u> doesn't work, what hope have we?"—and
drove back to Tucson in a Brown Study. The next day, entering the same room, I was surprised by a new Peter, popping out
from behind a door, wearing a black eyeshade and a sign on his
sweater: CONFRONT ME IF I TRY TO CONTROL. The eyeshade,
which he had been wearing all day, had been imposed by his
morning group, to teach him dependence on others.

Merrill was grateful for the help that the group had been managing Peter's
outburst. But Hooten was not the only one being treated:

One morning a lecturer put on a cassette of New Age music
and regressed us. We walked through a tunnel in the light at
whose end we'd all be under 12. Tears began <u>streaming</u> down
my face. There's your house, go in, smell the smells, it's supper time—and I was standing by the bare mirror table in Palm
Beach, and nobody else was there, mother and father (whose
last year together this was) mere shadows at either end of the
room. The tears only stopped at the elderly mouth of the tunnel. So I guess I'm ready to spend a season or two "in recovery"
myself, not just to keep P. company.

The second half of 1991 had been a period of nearly constant, unrelieved
turmoil, but Merrill kept on "writing [. . .] through most of it." When he
wrote that letter to Moore, he was deliberately setting his "thoughts in order
for the inevitable Poem"—his way of redeeming almost any sort of experience. The Poem in this case was called "Family Week at Oracle Ranch."

("Oracle," his invented name for Sierra Tucson, is the name of an Arizona town that caught his eye.) Instead of the "complexes" of old-school psychoanalysis, Merrill finds risible "simplicities" at Oracle, starting with the rule that patients at Oracle are permitted only seven words to name their feelings: "AFRAID, / HURT, LONELY, etc." How can a poet used to evoking his emotions with a "full palette," with "hues, oils, glazes, thinner," make do with these meager watercolors? But Merrill rises to the challenge of a diminished vocabulary, just as he was stirred by the poetic possibilities of his first words in Greek and the stiff capital letters of the Ouija board.

The rule that Oracle patients must use the same few words follows from the premise that they are dealing with the same fundamental problems, and that all members of the therapy group are equals. It's not easy for Merrill to enter in. Ken, a counselor with a Barbie-doll name, reaches out to him ("When / James told the group he worried about dying / Without his lover beside him, I felt SAD"), and Merrill has to bite his lip: "Thank you for sharing, Ken, // I keep from saying; it would come out snide." Yet at the same time he has included in the poem the unguarded statement he made to the group about the mortal danger he is in and his abject fear of abandonment. He manages a tone not-quite-snide, not-quite-vulnerable, but some of both. Learning to sympathize with others and with his lover in particular, he apologizes in the idiom of the place, but sincerely, for his failure to give Peter adequate emotional support: "I burned with SHAME for the years / You'd spent among sufferings uncharted— / Not even my barren love to rest your head on." What we all have in common, it seems, are HURT and LONELINESS.

Simple and essential as that truth may be, Merrill understands perfectly well that the wisdom of Oracle is a matter of commercially packaged bromides, mixing Hallmark-style sentimentality and cynical realism: "(a) You are a brave and special person. (b) / There are far too many people in the world / For this to matter for very long." "Not to be 'terminally unique' " is "the consolation you take home," Ken summarizes. Dismal as it sounds, for Merrill that was truly a consolation, albeit an ambivalent one. Being unique had been his pride since youth. That his difference, sexual and literary, was a "terminal" condition had been his fear: wasn't that what his enduring wishes for a child and for a family were all about? Now, sick with AIDS, his case really *was* "terminal," but it was hardly unique. No more than that of the "Anorexics, Substance Abusers," and "Love & Relationship Addicts" he'd traded stories with and wept beside—openly, helplessly, honestly—during Sierra Tucson's Family Week.

He flew from Arizona to Key West. A few hours after his arrival, DJ made "the unsolicited observation" that he "seemed changed." He hoped so. He hoped Peter would be changed too. But recovery wasn't guaranteed. "An amazing forty per cent / Of our graduates are still clean after two years," Ken brags in "Family Week at Oracle Ranch," reminding the unimpressed that, "Given our society, / Sobriety is hard to implement." Merrill knew that it is precisely in the nature of things for "old patterns" to recur.

Take the case of that oldest couple, the sun and moon, which Merrill turns to at the end of this poem. "Ask how the co-dependent moon, another night, / Feels when the light drains wholly from her face," he says, looking ahead to what he and Hooten could expect in the way of change and renewal. "Ask what that cold comfort means to her."

After completing treatment at Sierra Tucson, Hooten stayed in a Trappist monastery near Atlanta for a month—the start of a period of churchgoing for him. When he returned to New York in January 1992, Merrill chose to be there, rather than in Key West, to support him. They continued in couples therapy with Aycock. Jimmy now met Aycock on his own when he was in New York and talked to her on the phone when he was elsewhere. He and Peter had their "ups + downs," but also "regularly scheduled times to sit + clear the air." On Valentine's Day, Merrill flew to Stephen Yenser and Melissa Berton's wedding in Los Angeles. By the end of the month, things continued well enough for him to risk two weeks with DJ in Key West, while Hooten stayed on in New York. David McIntosh paid a visit to Elizabeth Street. As they had for the past decade, Merrill and Richard Wilbur celebrated their birthdays together (Wilbur's being March 1, two days before JM's) by trading deftly rhymed gift cards and, this year, sports shirts.

All this time, Merrill was silently struggling with AIDS and the shifting emotional states that accompanied the progress of his illness. He sent to friends a notably grim Christmas greeting on a printed card. It was a new poem, called "Vol. XLIV, No. 3," describing a horrible nativity. On a slide in a lab where blood work is done, "Defenseless, the patrician cells await / Invasion by barbaric viruses, / Another sack of Rome." The "barbarian viruses" are like the beast slouching toward Bethlehem in Yeats's "Second Coming." They augur a "new age" of "Everything we dread":

> Dread? It crows for joy in the manger.
> Joy? The tree sparkles on which it will die.

Merrill could only share this desolate vision in verse. It was the exception when he mentioned his "suffering" to a friend, and even then—he was writing to Fredericks—he didn't explain the cause, only that he kept "suffering, and it leaves me so <u>ashamed</u>. I believe (Auden said it first) that the pursuit of happiness isn't so much a right as a duty. And I do my best, but then come terrible days."

An unfinished poem dating from winter 1992 describes one of those "terrible days." Considered not as a work of art but as a personal statement, it is as moving as any poem Merrill ever wrote. Composed in the simple language of self-exposure called for at Sierra Tucson/Oracle Ranch, it is uncharacteristically awkward, as if this once Merrill had no choice but to allow raw life to prevail over graceful art. It records his confusion after emerging from Aycock's Midtown office into frigid January sunlight. He'd just been speaking to his therapist about "In the Waiting Room," a poem in which Bishop recalls an episode of disorientation in a dentist's waiting room when she was a child; and his poem starts by addressing this lost friend and literary ally: "Elizabeth, you should have / Seen me today, alone . . ."

In the scene Merrill describes, the Fifth Avenue crowds surge around him. Suddenly "hungry unto death," he buys falafel from a vendor; as he pushes it into his mouth, it falls down his front. To all appearances, he could be one of the homeless. In fact despite the names in his address book and the money in his pockets, homeless is how he feels: "My whole life's names and places, / Inscribed as on balloons / Drunkenly uprise into / The freezing light." He remembers childhood loneliness. He thinks of his lover's anger: "And when my lover's troubled heart / Shuts me out, with no / Reason or quarter given, / I have nowhere to go." He doesn't "dare go home," doesn't know whom to ask even for a drink of water. His eyes swim "with cold" in "the sun's icy tomb."

Merrill would have heard the pun in that phrase: this old man left baffled and blank by the course his life has taken was once the little boy of the Broken Home. Ideals and defenses are being stripped from him:

I've fallen
From youth to helpless age, from love's
Original starlit
Skies to its hells of rage,
Its deep possessive shit.

Funny, I used to think
Of the loss of self through love
Or teasing out of a rhyme
As the highest good. Today, though,

> Here at the heart of life,
> Brushing its crumbs from my coat,
> Frankly I'm not so sure.
> For soon, to his misfortune,
> Whoever I may be
> Will have run out of time.

It is one thing to lose oneself in a bar in Athens or at the Ouija board, rising to the challenge of a rhyme scheme or falling in love, and another thing to have "the loss of self" thrust upon one, helplessly, finally. For Merrill, losing his sense of self on that January day was a foretaste of death.

He made a few halfhearted revisions, then abandoned the poem. It was not an experience he could bear to dwell on. He must have mistrusted its self-pity and Oracle Ranch–style confessions. Despite its various references to his own work (those tears on the cold winter street, for instance, recall the tears of "self-knowledge" in "An Urban Convalescence"), the poem was so uncharacteristic of his style he was forced to lean rather clumsily on Bishop as a model. He had no artistic means to control the loss of control that was its subject.

He was still working on *A Different Person*. In the italic sections of reflection that come at the end of each chapter's story (a device he adapted from Mary McCarthy's *Memories of a Catholic Girlhood*), he integrated the ideas he was encountering in therapy—ideas about codependency, alcoholism, and sexual abuse—into the story of his life. Rather than simply adopt them, however, he ascribes these therapeutic notions to a fictional friend known as "Jerl." (He borrowed the name with permission from Jerl Surratt, a friend he saw often in New York in the 1990s, although the language and ideas weren't Surratt's.) This imaginary, younger, "politically correct" friend "digs me," Merrill explains, "like an archeological trench of outmoded ideas." When "Jerl" explains that "a single shame-producing word"—something that Jimmy had had plenty of from both of his parents—"can be as traumatic as an incestuous caress," he doesn't object; he merely nods "soothingly." Like the memoir's dream dialogues with his mother, these fictional talks have a basis in his experience. They are echoes of the lectures and tapes he'd listened to and the group therapy sessions he'd taken part in. "Jerl" urges JM to see himself as a "survivor" of his father's alcoholism. The idea makes sense: in his love relationships, he tended to take on "the same aloof, injured airs with which my mother foiled—or fueled—'Daddy's temper.' " But he is interested in this interpretation only up to the point where it shades into blame and special pleading. "The real point," he says about the ways his parents marked him, is that something of the kind awaits virtually every child on earth. Call it cruelty, call it culture. These are extremes of a broad and unbroken spectrum made visible through our being reared by other humans in the first place, rather than by wolves, like l'Enfant Sauvage. Small wonder we honor our father and mother even when we can't obey them. Without their imprint of (imperfect) love, the self is featureless, a snarl of instincts, a puff of stellar dust.

In June, Merrill sent the memoir to Harry Ford for publication by Knopf, to which Harry had returned. While he'd been writing about his years in Rome, Merrill hadn't been abroad: this was the longest period (almost three years) that he'd stayed on U.S. soil since the 1950s. Now he and Hooten flew to Europe for "nearly a month without our therapists!" First stop was the Poetry International Festival in Rotterdam. Merrill kept a low profile at the festival: one day he and Hooten "played hookey" with Vikram Seth in the Hague; another day they spent with Ashbery and David Kermani in Vermeer's Delft. He got "many a dirty look" from his festival colleagues, but that was all the convening with other poets he cared to do. They moved on to Copenhagen, land of "poker-faced palaces + prices that curl your hair." The highlights were the grave and home of Karen Blixen (Isak Dinesen, a writer Merrill passionately admired), and, with bonfires crackling on midsummer's eve, a performance of eighteenth-century commedia dell'arte. In the Tivoli Gardens Merrill gazed at radiant sunbathers and—"don't they know the world is ending?—children dancing in a ring."

Scotland, where he had never visited, was their last destination. In Edinburgh, they met Alistair Elliott, one of Charles Merrill's wards during the war, who'd grown up to become a noted poet and translator. During this stage of the trip, Merrill took out a notebook to gather lines for poems. In a museum in Glasgow, the language of a label stirred his imagination: "Earthenware with lead glaze which has degraded to iridescence during burial." Would his own clay body shine as it degraded? Looking at the treasure exhumed from another dig, he reasoned, "Life once given to art, is laid in the tomb / With all the art one can muster."

Merrill's writing in this notebook devolves at times to illegibility—a sign of his illness. With no date and no further explanation, he wrote, "I got down on my knees in the rest room to give thanks / a lot of pain a hell of a lot of pain." His and Hooten's itinerary included the isles of Skye and Lewis in the Outer Hebrides. On Lewis, which was as remote a place as he had ever been, they drove over barren peat fields to visit the Stones of Callanish, an enigmatic circle of taller than man-sized plinths some four thousand years old. Then, back on the mainland, crossing the Highlands, they encountered "More braes, more lochs," and "Ever fewer bipeds" in the gorgeous, curiously empty landscape. The trip would turn into "The Great Emigration," a sad, meandering travel poem that depicts a world in which all the people are gone.

Merrill returned to his "double life" in the U.S., shuttling between Jackson in Stonington and Hooten in New York. "Luckily," he reassured Jeff Harrison, "we're all on Prozac, even my mother at 93, so like good Americans we keep smiling." DJ's seventieth birthday was coming. To mark it, Merrill created a lavish chapbook titled *David Jackson: Scenes from his Life.* It reproduced fourteen of David's sketches and paintings from the 1950s to the 1970s, and each image was paired with a related passage from DJ's or JM's writing. Cloth-bound in the sky blue of a Greek taverna, the book brought back their best years together. Here were the Water Street apartment and Umberto Morra's house, their flat in Munich, the house in Athens, and the fountain in Maria's garden on Sounion. A fine streetscape, depicting two weathered houses in Chania in late afternoon light, lovingly detailed, came with this comment by David: "In 1959 our Greek life began. Sunlight & Sea, Taverns & Torments: J's passion for S, mine for G. Were we any real comfort to each other at such times? Still, when (twenty years later) we called all that a day, our two old houses (so to speak) were standing side by side."

The book was a beautiful tribute to Jackson, but the story it told was incomplete: it contained no scenes from Key West or the 1980s, when Jackson gave up painting, and so much else in his daily life was diminished. And Jimmy was just as much of a presence in the book as David. Included were David's renderings of the young poet in his study; of the bronze bust of Jimmy as a child; of Manos Karastefanís, Jimmy's lover; and several passages from Jimmy's poetry and prose. The book showed how deeply intertwined their lives were, but also how it was mainly Jackson's life that had twined around Merrill's. Jimmy had to face that fact when, rooting in David's diaries for passages to print in the book, he "lit on exactly the same complaints about <u>me</u> that Peter himself keeps making: that I appreciate nothing that anyone does for me, that I take over lives, that household arrangements are always mine and never 'ours,' that life together is little but a clogged calendar of pointless engagements. All true, I'm afraid. And [I'm] too old to change."

Jackson wasn't Merrill's only reason for returning to Stonington that summer. The town was still his home, and the setting still worked on him. He woke up one September morning "in time to see a full moon just above eye level over the harbor. An hour later the sun had risen, flashing on the flanks of sailboats in their moorings, + the moon was only a shade whiter than the sky." Stonington was "no longer quite the boneyard it had become a few years ago," since a number of friends had moved to town. One was Bishop Paul Moore, "the tall handsome radical Episcopalian who espouses gay marriages." Another was Sandy McClatchy. The eager graduate student who wrote that fan letter to JM two decades ago, now "a charming 45 year old man of letters and editor of the *Yale Review*," had bought a small house near 107 Water Street, and he and Merrill saw each other routinely for dinner or drinks. (Not that JM himself was drinking: he would merely ask permission to put his finger in McClatchy's wineglass, and then lick it.)

Merrill now purchased not one but several plots on a mossy knoll in Stonington's cemetery. Here was space for himself and David, Peter, Sewelly, and Sandy too, if he wanted. (But he didn't: Jimmy had to laugh when Sandy told him he didn't want to be buried "in a theme park.") DJ would get "his wish" that he and JM "not be parted," while, for Jimmy, the arrangement was a dream of rest: he would never have to be alone, and his love for David and Peter would no longer be a terrible conflict.

That fall, at last, the conflict seemed to be easing up. Hooten had been " 'clean' for over a year," and Merrill felt "progressively more trustful and serene" with him: "a really bad year [had] come to an end." Inaugurating a new phase, in prospect lighthearted and securely domestic, Peter bought a dog: a Jack Russell terrier that he and Jimmy named "Cosmo." Merrill was tickled. "They're circus dogs," he explained to a friend. "In fact this one's grandfather is a transvestite": "we have a picture of him in a little tinsel + tulle skirt + a party hat with spangles." Playing at being parents with this pint-sized, barking son to fret over, they hoped that the puppy would turn out to be, despite his gender-bending ancestry, "all dog." Merrill bought the dog toys, Hooten took him to obedience classes, and Cosmo coaxed the couple out on walks together. On the way to Christmas with Hellen in Atlanta, they took a holiday in Harry Pemberton's cabin in "the wild lands" of Virginia—which offered an orgy of enticing scents for the little dog, and plenty of mischief to poke his nose into. "Only the ant beds kept him in check," Peter joked.

"It's January," Hooten continued, writing a letter to Yenser at the start of 1993, "and Cosmo is great company, but it is always hard when James goes away for a spell," as JM had done by returning to his pattern of spending the winter with Jackson in Key West. Hooten was "still working hard to get Sandover placed." He'd created a production company, "Poetry Works," whose mission was to bring poetry to the stage. He hoped to arrange a performance of "Folded Sunsets," his Bishop evening, and a staged reading of Anthony Hecht's poem "A Love for Four Voices." But these were slender threads to grasp at. Living on Seventy-second Street without James, he was, as they would have put it at Sierra Tucson, hurt and lonely—and probably very angry. By the end of January, Hooten was "back in rehab" at the Smithers treatment center on Ninety-third Street, "after a prodigious binge on vodka, cocaine, and Prozac." It was a rerun of the crisis fifteen months ago, and Merrill had had enough this time. He told Hooten that "he'd better find a place of his own." The decision left him "relieved but . . . furious? heartbroken? It's too early to say."

One reason Merrill was in Florida was the Key West Literary Seminar, where the topic this year was Elizabeth Bishop. The conference was "a success"—he read some of EB's poems, unveiled a plaque in front of her house, and made a speech—but he felt "beleaguered by the number of old friends from far places" who'd come south for the week, inadvertently putting pressure on him to appear in good form. To Frank Bidart, one of those old friends, Merrill seemed "frail and ill." He'd always had a "metaphysical ebullience, a sense that the heavens were in order," Bidart felt. "He was infinitely accomplished, preternaturally gifted—the greatest rhymer since Pope—capable of doing anything on the page, with a divine assemblage of sound and movement." And his wealth contributed to that impression. His money had given him, as Bidart saw it, the power to get "not everything he wanted in life, but a lot" of it, "and Jimmy was very aware of how lucky he was. Now all of a sudden he wasn't, in a big way."

But Merrill wasn't asking for sympathy from Bidart or anyone else, not even where his deteriorating relationship with Hooten was concerned. "Certain friends" urged him to take "drastic" steps "like having the locks changed" on Seventy-second Street before Peter left the treatment center. Indeed most of Merrill's friends who knew anything about it were " 'horrified' by what I've been 'put through' " by Peter's behavior over the past two years. But he thought that was "largely nonsense." "Suffering," he declared, quoting no one in particular, "warms the coldness of life," and without it, "I would have turned into an old wrinkled nut and never written those recent poems," "Self-Portrait in Tyvek™ Windbreaker" and "Family Week at Oracle Ranch," of which he was justly proud. Life was still to be judged by what you made of it.

He flew to New York in February. With Peter in Smithers and David in Key West, he was relieved to be "for once neither in the frying pan nor the fire." Even "poor little Cosmo—just like me, Victim of a Broken Home?"—had been sent for the time being to board with his kin on Long Island, where JM, like a divorced dad, paid a visit. Merrill was "not taking any antiviral drugs; so toxic, says our nutritionist," Andrew Silverman, on whose care he was relying more and more, regularly sending snippets of hair for Silverman to analyze. "Instead the latter has started me on a kind of peroxide therapy (1% food grade peroxide to 99% pure water, aloe vera, etc.). The fascinating point—upheld by many European doctors—is that cancer and viral cells need very little oxygen, indeed are killed by high levels of oxygen in the blood. Not unlike the effect of Interferon, only harmless."

Friends rallied around him, including Allan Gurganus, whom Merrill had gotten close to over the past two or three years. A North Carolinian in his forties, sweet and generous, with a beard, flowing locks, and a sense of personal style that might entail a cape, natty bow tie, or even a sash, Gurganus was the author of *Oldest Living Confederate Widow Tells All* (1986) and other exuberant novels and stories about race, sex, and the South. For Gurganus, Merrill was a mentor. "He knew he was in a mortal condition—I didn't know it when we met—and the force of his personality made things possible that only happen in a friendship after a decade, if at all," Gurganus remembered. "Most people don't want to see drafts. Between draft number one and number seventy-five, you're living on a lonely, windy plain. But James wanted to see drafts, and when I showed them to him, he would immediately say five or six sentences that made all the difference."

After Hooten left the treatment center, Merrill went home to Stonington, leaving Peter to get adjusted on his own in New York. It was "wise to move apart," they agreed, "if only for a spell." Longing for "a semirural cottage where he could plant a garden for Cosmo to dig up," Peter chose a small house in Lakeville, a town in the hills of northwest Connecticut. Merrill had, as one of Elizabeth Bishop's students once wrote in a paper, " 'mixty motions' about the move. [. . .] Of course I fear a relapse on P's part," but it was important for Peter to be "under his own roof" where Jimmy couldn't "fruitlessly" (or oppressively) monitor his progress. "As the smoke clears"— it was April, and Merrill was writing to Yenser—"I see that he's still the person I love and instinctively turn to."

So it was a wrench for Merrill when he left for three weeks in Greece in late April. If, back in January, he'd told Hooten that it was time to live apart, the shoe was on the other foot now. "It's not that I feel P. has rejected me," he told himself. "Urged me, perhaps not unselfishly, to give myself (and him) a breather, thinking perhaps it would 'help.' [. . .] But change of scene no longer works." His trip to Athens was overdue. Parigory had had a heart attack in 1992 while living at Athinaion Efivon 44; Merrill had planned to go to him that fall, then decided he wasn't up to the mission. Now with Tony and his lover in David's old room upstairs, Jimmy took his old room on the first floor. Tony went to his shop in the morning, where friends came to drink coffee and chat ("If I'd imagined I was going to bring life + interest into his life, I was wrong"), while Jimmy stayed home and wrote in his notebook between long naps, from which he rose blank and confused, with no wish to go out or write cards. His consciousness had dwindled to "a little guttering flame forever on the verge of sleep. It would take so little to blow it out once + for all."

Nelly, deaf now, hosted a party for them. Merrill visited Alan Ansen ("Talk dried up but we were glad to sit face to face") and, on another day, Kimon Friar. His first lover met him in his apartment in pajamas and walking with a cane, his mouth twisted from a recent stroke. "His greatest complaint: a bitterness in the mouth that poisons the taste of . . . everything; sweets, water, etc. I try not to see it as symbolic." Friar had prepared a speech: "I meet you with trepidation. You are someone I no longer know. I am someone you no longer know." Friar, mentally confused, "had us meeting for the first time after those 15 years of estrangement," but in a sense he was right: they were both that changed from the men who fell in love with each other forty-eight years before. Their struggle over influence and independence was long over. Kimon, who would die of a second stroke, had less than a month to live; Jimmy had less than two years.

He made a sad solo trip to cold, drizzly Nafplion ("What am I doing? Punishing myself?"). He crossed paths with David McIntosh, who was touring Greece with a friend, the painter Agnes Martin. The cold kept up in Athens. Parigory hadn't filled the oil tank; to keep warm, Merrill put on long underwear and two sweaters. "For a year now," he wrote, "I've surprised myself by emitting, every ½ hour or so when nothing much absorbs me, not a loud yawn so much as the roar of a caged lion. Boredom, despair . . ." He noted what he ate, like an old man or an invalid for whom meals are the highlight of the day. He read Harold Acton's memoir of Nancy Mitford ("What instinct kept me from that world? [. . .] My mistrust of the Mitford world is mirrored in P's distrust of mine"), and he reread *The Golden Bowl*, thinking about what had gone wrong and what might yet go right in his relations with Hooten:

> Maggie sees the Prince "through" his addiction, his enslavement to C[harlotte], the way I was meant to see P. through his recovery; unless of course a step back, on either side, to our respective freedoms, will have been the solution. I hate the

degree to which these Jamesian "scruples" have shaped my life—my fantasy life—created my "distancing" from flesh-and-blood situations (so deplored by P.). I hate also the degree to which I haven't lived up to them. Perhaps I can, now that, like HJ, I shall live more by myself.

He drank tea with young people: Patricia Storace, an expatriate American writer, author of a memoir about her time in Greece called *Dinner with Persephone*, who reminded him of the youthful Irma, and a dapper poet-critic, Haris Vlavianos, who had translated Pound, Stevens, and Ashbery into Greek. Merrill read his poems to a gratifyingly large audience, and he gave interviews to local journalists. But his public self was a fragile performance. At home he observed Tony's lover, Marino, who was desperately sick with AIDS: in and out of the hospital; his face disfigured, his legs aching; feverish, vomiting. Merrill and Parigory kept up their spirits by rehearsing the worn jokes that were the currency of this thirty-four-year friendship. "My conversation," Merrill noted, "is larded with references to things he's told me, one-liners, vignettes of Alexandria. I'm not sure <u>he</u> remembers them all." There came a last hour at Tony's shop, where the mood was "merry, even euphoric." Tony presented Jimmy with a turtleneck of "brilliant dark purple cashmere. Gorgeous." There was no further ceremony, though this was a momentous leave-taking: Merrill would never visit Greece again, and by the end of summer, Parigory would be dead.

Merrill continued to Sweden to attend another poetry festival: five days of group readings, impromptu classroom visits, unscheduled interviews ("What do I think of Charles Henri Ford?!"), and an interview for which the interviewer didn't show up. He talked with the Nobel Prize–winning Nigerian poet and playwright Wole Soyinka and the Russian poet Andrei Voznesensky, whom he'd pictured "tall and 'estranged.' Instead he is short, rounded, smiling." Perhaps Merrill hoped to be lionized by the Swedish Academy, like Soyinka. But he wouldn't have made the trip without the prospect of Judy Moffett joining him there. Moffett had lived in Lund on a Fulbright in 1973, had translated poetry from Swedish, retained contacts in the country, and now could play the guide for Jimmy. They strolled through parks and museums in Lund, Malmö, and Stockholm, took their meals together, and talked at length.

Since publishing her guide to Merrill's poetry in 1982, Moffett had married, given up writing poems for a time, and published science fiction novels. Then, in the early 1990s, Judy began visiting Jimmy and Peter in New York. At this point she was admitted to her mentor's life with a level of trust and intimacy she'd long desired but had given up hoping for. "You're just the kind of friend we need now," he confided. "What he needed," she explained later, "was someone who didn't hate Peter." Indeed she liked Peter, who was affectionate and open with her. She saw the difficulty of his situation: with her modest Midwest origin and manners, she too had felt like a stranger in JM's rarefied world.

In Malmö they discussed "colors": the notion that certain seasonal color schemes are flattering to particular complexions. Merrill held out his hand to her, and Moffett saw "it was *yellow*"—a mild jaundice, another symptom, although she didn't know about his diagnosis. "I said you must be 'autumn.' " But Jimmy wasn't interested in autumn colors. "I'm wearing *purple* more and more," he said. True, he was decked out in purple, from Tony's cashmere to a pair of Birkenstock sandals. Emphasizing the effect, he posed for Judy's camera smiling in a cloud of lilacs. His purple was the color of the peacock on the Merrill family crest as well as a familiar code for "queer." In the old days, Judy had wanted urgently for him to acknowledge that he was gay. Now his clothes declared it. He was amused when a Swedish colleague, translating from the newspaper, reported that Merrill was "the bombshell of the Festival"—whatever that meant—"in spite of his purple Birkenstocks."

Back in the U.S., in summer 1993, Merrill and Hooten maintained a cautious distance. For months Jimmy had been gripped by depression, "a real slump" which no amount of purple could overcome. It would be hard to say whether his separation from Peter, who was still living in Lakeville, or his fragile health, was the greater burden. Occasions like the memorial service for John Hersey that June, where once more he was called on to stand and eulogize a friend, hardly helped. (Hersey had died of cancer that March.) He preferred not to remain for long in Stonington with DJ, and he depended on "engagements to escape despondency." He visited his mother twice, his sister in Southampton, his brother in New Hampshire, and the Detres in Maine. In July, he went to the Glimmerglass Opera in Cooperstown, New York, for a long weekend. McClatchy and Ted Danforth, who had printed some of Merrill's poems as broadsides with the Sea Cliff Press, came with him. The first night, McClatchy caught a glimpse of Merrill in the glow of the stage. "I thought to myself how tired the face looked: what others had been saying was borne in on me, past my usual reluctance to see any changes in him."

The next day Merrill asked McClatchy to stop by his room. He was sitting cross-legged on the bed. "There was a bit of banter, then his face grew uncomfortably grim, and he said: 'I want to lay something serious on you.

[. . .] I've known for about seven years now that I have the virus.' " Merrill said that his T cell count had just dropped from 300 to 150, and he'd started, "with reluctance, to take a course of AZT," a new, government-approved therapy that slowed reproduction of the virus. He said that "Peter had tested negative all along," and that he didn't know where he " 'got' it." He'd decided to tell McClatchy—he'd still told only Jackson, Hooten, Milton Maurer, and his tenant on Water Street, Ray Izbicki—because he wanted Sandy "to cover for him, give excuses to people." McClatchy was stunned. To take the news in and settle his feelings, he began keeping a diary of "this stage of JM's life."

By early August, a new antidepressant, Zoloft, had "kicked in," and Merrill began to listen to music and write letters again. He had a happy visit with Peter and Cosmo in the Connecticut hills, when they ate from the garden and swam "in a deep clear lake." Improvement in his energy and mood coincided with publication of A Different Person. He'd submitted the manuscript in 1992 despite his "awful + recurrent misgivings," and he had gone on revising it in galleys. He accepted Eleanor Perényi's style-chastening line edits, and on her advice cut and rewrote the ending. He sent the chapters that concerned them to Kimon, Claude, and Freddy, which led to more tinkering. Despite his failing health, prolonged depression, and intermittent despair, Merrill had achieved a comic tone in his memoir. There was plenty of fizzy, funny writing in it, but the comedy lay elsewhere. It consisted in his perspective on experience: in the long view, so many of his torments had turned out to be trivial, his wounds revealed to be blessings. Friar got his due in print, and so, Merrill hoped, did his parents. He wanted reconciliations all around.

His exchanges about the memoir with Buechner were significant. Jimmy and Freddy, "the Uglies," as Freddy still called them, insisting on the prep-school-era bond, had remained friends, though rather remote friends, since Freddy became a minister and a family man and Jimmy set off on his life with David Jackson, carrying the Ouija board Freddy had given him half as a gag. They met most often on Merrill's visits to Claude in Pawlet, during which he would cross the valley to the house where Freddy and his wife Judy lived, and talk about friends and family, including Freddy's two daughters, Jimmy being godfather to one of them. Responding to a draft of the memoir, Buechner expressed how "touched" he was "to find myself your dearest friend as you were mine and in some arcane sense will always be despite all the divergence of our ways and days." "I come away," he said, "with the feeling that you saw everything or at least everything in the direction you chose to look." But that implied that there were other directions in which he should have looked. About the book's sexual disclosures, Buechner was uneasy: "I'm sure there will be many to echo your mother's 'Don't imagine, Son, that these are things that people need to know.' " Hellen, he felt, deserved a better answer than the memoir had given her so far.

Merrill continued to work on that passage, but in the end made no changes. He did take something for the memoir from Buechner's next letter. That letter described a series of autobiographical talks that Buechner had given in tandem with the poet Maya Angelou. When Angelou had risen to speak, following Buechner, her introducer had told the audience to expect a very different story from her. But Angelou said no: "My story is exactly the same as Frederick Buechner's." "She is black, a woman, grew up in real poverty in Arkansas, but I knew she was right," Buechner told Merrill. "They are the same story, hers and mine," and, he felt now, his and Merrill's stories were the same too. They came down to a "struggle somehow to become a <u>human</u> being; to survive the world (brave the elements), especially the world of our own childhoods; to find something to <u>believe</u> in a world which keeps on not just announcing but demonstrating that there's really nothing to believe in; to deal one way or another with the fearsome hungers of the flesh—at that level I guess all of our stories are the same." Buechner had been struck by one passage in particular in Merrill's draft:

> Truth to tell I was blessed in both my parents. Even their divorce, however painful and mistaken for them, I long ago came to read as a gift of fate. If being the product of a "broken home" meant in my case that I would not risk marriage and children, other enchantments, some brief, some lifelong, soon filled those unpeopled perspectives. Time is a great purifier, and many all too natural wrongs that people do to each other can be used, like fortunes made by cutting forests down, by another generation to open a school.

It reminded him of what he'd written in one of his lectures about a harrowing time in his own life, which he quoted to Merrill:

> The fearsome blessing of that hard time continues to work itself out in my life the way we're told the universe is still hurtling through outer space under the impact of the great cosmic explosion that brought it into being in the first place. I think grace sometimes explodes into our lives like that—sending our pain, terror, astonishment hurtling

through inner space until by grace they become Orion, Cassiopeia, Polaris, to give us our bearings, to bring us into something like full being at last.

"Maybe," Freddy concluded, "that's the most either of us has learned [. . .], and I hear it as the <u>same</u> most." Jimmy was nearly ready to agree. He used the quotation from Buechner's lecture in his book, demurring only slightly in his comment on it: "I might have said that it's the gradual focus of human vision, intelligence rather than grace, whereby those traumatic stars, like their ancestors in the night sky, acquire names and stories. But why split hairs? Let the mind be, along with countless other things, a landing strip for sacred visitations."

Jimmy wrote to Hellen ("Dearest Mama") to warn her that the book would soon appear. His draft of the letter shows the depth of his struggle with the announcement. "This is no 'apology,' " he said, "so much as a chance for you to think about your attitude in the face of the coming tornado, which may turn out to be a passing breeze." Then he crossed out the last half of that sentence. The letter became more garbled, more tortured, as he continued: "painful as it can be on occasion, we have, you + I, a bond that allows for honesty + trust. . . . This honesty you yourself taught me very early, + I hope you can find"—but he didn't complete the thought. Though Merrill's virtuoso prose does pirouettes throughout *A Different Person*, he couldn't find words to tell his mother that the book was about to be published. "Believe me, I hate not respecting your wishes. But as we know (rueful smile?) it won't be the first time." The crossout was telling: he hated not respecting Hellen's wishes, but he hated her wishes more.

The dreaded "tornado" was in fact a passing breeze. Hellen may have been hurt by the book, and Claude was not pleased by his treatment in it, but rueful smiles were the rule for both of them. Neither Kimon nor Bobby Isaacson had lived long enough to care one way or another about how Jimmy portrayed them. He had promised his mother that he would decline all requests to "push" his book on TV—but there weren't any: *A Different Person* wasn't material for *Oprah*. The memoir was the story of a rich young man who'd grown up to write dazzling poetry—these were not grounds for identification for most readers. With a modesty or even shyness that could be mistaken for hauteur, Merrill had launched into his story in medias res, never making the case that he was someone a reader not already acquainted with his work and world might want to get to know; and his sense of the self as a thing in process kept a conventional portrait from emerging, except in parts. These could be pieced together by reading the italicized meditations at the end of each chapter. But those sections were composed in jeweled paragraphs, loosely jointed, like stanzas of a lyric poem.

Reviews were mainly respectful. Brigitte Weeks, writing in *The New York Times Book Review*, was typical in seeming rather embarrassed by the intimacy that this author famous for his poise and polish had suddenly invited, and intimidated by the ranks of scholars imagined to be already poring over the book for clues to the poetry, so secure and exalted did Merrill's literary reputation seem. The longest review was a quibbling essay in the *New Criterion* by theater critic John Simon, whose judgment was by his own admission colored by his college-era acquaintance with Claude and Tony Harwood. Merrill's friends congratulated him on the book, but some, like Buechner, privately felt "appalled by the loneliness and sadness and seediness" of the sexual behavior that Merrill described: "the one-night stands, the furtive assignations in Roman latrines, the affairs within affairs, the sheer abundance of lovers." "It was hard to believe," Buechner wrote in a memoir of his own published after Merrill's death, "that there was so much about my old friend that he had never told me, or, if in some way he had by implication half told it, that I had never heard because I never chose to hear it. I found myself depressed for days by the book and could only believe that he would do himself irreparable harm by writing it all down with such unrelenting honesty for the world to hear."

The sexual revelations that depressed Buechner were more like the thing younger gay readers would expect from such a book. Rudy Kikel, winner of the 1992 Lambda Literary Award for a gay male poet, who'd been sending his poems to Merrill and receiving patient comment in reply, wrote to JM, "I'm enjoying *A Different Person* immensely; it seems a shoo-in—not that you care—for a Lambda Lit. Award in the category of 'gay men's biography.'" *A Different Person* didn't win a "Lammy." Jimmy congratulated Ed White (who wrote the only blurb for *A Different Person*) on winning that prize for his biography of Jean Genet. Merrill's book and White's were nominated for the National Book Critics Circle Award in biography and autobiography, and White won that prize too. But this wasn't the end of the story. The NBCC newsletter, which circulated among its many members and friends, reported the votes in favor of *A Different Person*—zero—and the vicious, in-committee comments of the judges: "One amateur botanist on the board likened Merrill to pond scum; another, reading Merrill to ironing doilies."

The book was dedicated to McClatchy, who saw what it was about and how good it was. "The very first dreamily italicized section has to do with your writing poems," he wrote to the author, "and should alert any reader to your true ambition. Though there's a great deal of your early life here, the book is emphatically the autobiography of a sensibility [. . .]. It's not 'about' the events in your life, but about the effect of those events on a life that is slowly turned into art." Then the letter pivoted from art back to life: "The news you gave me in Cooperstown has taken a long time to digest: shock kept all the pieces up in the air. But my first thought when I left your room that day remains my strongest: with what incredible bravery you have borne that news yourself all these years. I've always known how tender a man you really are, and how vulnerable. Now I know just how strong too. My admiration is boundless. But that's beside the point. The point is this: the years ahead won't be the easiest, and I want you to count on my standing right by you." Jimmy already did. Depending on McClatchy's decisiveness and loyalty, Merrill named him his "health care partner" with "final responsibility for medical decisions," were he to be incapacitated.

That fall, the initial positive effect of the Zoloft wore off; Merrill stopped AZT, probably on the advice of Andrew Silverman, in order to avoid its potentially toxic side effects; and he was left feeling weak and vulnerable again. He and McClatchy saw each other in Stonington and New York, where Sandy had an apartment in the Village. In October, Merrill napped in McClatchy's *Yale Review* office before a reading at Yale—the last of his many appearances at the university. Two hundred people came to hear him that night. His voice was melancholy, his figure lonely and small as he stood at the front of a long hall reading "Prose of Departure." He seemed to emphasize Eleanor's grim remark following DK's memorial service: "Nobody has to live, dear boy. Nobody has to live." McClatchy came away from the evening feeling that "JM has only a moderate will to fight."

Perhaps, but he still had a fierce will to write. He was hard at work on "Tony: Ending the Life," an expansive elegy for his friend and (it is all but explicit) himself. Its epigraph from Ben Jonson's *Volpone*—"Let's die like Romans, / Since we have lived like Grecians"—recommends stoic surrender to death as the price to pay for having lived the life of sensual Grecians. Volpone's factotum, Mosca, says those lines after he is wounded during his master's attempt to seduce the virtuous Celia. The poem, which begins with Tony's youth in Alexandria, then moves on to his and Jimmy's promiscuous days and nights in Athens, invites us to see the duo as latter-day versions of Jonson's two connivers. "One year in Athens I let my beard grow," Merrill remembers. "The locals took it for a badge of grief. / Had someone died? Not yet, I tried to joke." Some wit called the beard "a doormat / On which to wipe filth brought in from the street." In the space of two stanzas, Merrill's comeback soars from coy badinage to moral philosophy to biblical lamentation:

Unfair! The boys were talkative and fun;
Far cleaner than my mind, after a bath.
Such episodes, when all was said and done,
Sweetened their reflective aftermath:
The denizens discovered in a dive
Relieved us (if not long or overmuch).
"Just see," the mirror breathed, "see who's alive,
Who hasn't forfeited the common touch,

The longing to lead everybody's life"
—Lifelong daydream of precisely those
Whom privilege or talent set apart:
How to atone for the achieved uniqueness?
By dying everybody's death, dear heart—
Saint, terrorist, fishwife. Stench that appals.
Famines, machine guns, the Great Plague (your sickness),
Rending of garments, cries, mass burials.

"The longing to lead everybody's life": that was a gifted rich boy's day-dream, which Merrill and Parigory, another stockbroker's son, acted out by finding love on the street or in a dive, never supposing that an appetite for life thus expressed would be the death of them. Wanting "to atone for the achieved uniqueness," they got their wish—to give up the isolation of privilege—when they got AIDS, the latest form of mass death. This isn't a consoling message, but the poem ends tenderly by comforting Tony, as Merrill had very often done in the past three years. "Lie back," he says, returning to Alexandria by recalling the death of Cleopatra's lover Antony, Parigory's namesake. Ruined by his passion, Antony was ready, like a true Roman, to face death by his own hand—"A story in Plutarch / The plump boy," Tony, "knew from History class." Like Jimmy, Tony had been a pudgy, soft-muscled schoolboy. Now he is in a hospital room, a terminal patient:

Slowly the room grows dark.
Stavro who's been reading you the news
Turns on a nightlight. No more views.
Just your head, nodding off in windowglass.

As the season turned and DJ went south, Merrill and Hooten began spending more time together, primarily in New York. They saw less of Jimmy's old crew and more of recent friends like Dorothea Tanning, the brilliant surrealist painter and sculptor and the widow of Max Ernst; she was still, at eighty-three, a lively, handsome, fun-loving woman. She joined the long line of independent, racy older ladies Merrill doted upon. They were also collaborators: Tanning had made a series of etchings to accompany Merrill's poem "Volcanic Holiday," which was published in a limited edition; and Jimmy advised her on the art of writing poems, which she'd just taken up (she would publish two volumes of poetry before her death at 101). In October, she hosted a masquerade in her downtown apartment. Eminent avant-gardists came to play, like the affable, shiny-bald Harry Mathews, the author of Oulipo-inspired texts that Merrill delighted in, costumed in ancien régime dress. The clown or pirate with a Bozo nose was Peter. Jimmy went Japanese in a kimono with a frizzy paper wig and thick white face paint, striking poses like a crazed Noh actor, outrageous enough to scare away mortal illness and dread.

Shahid Ali was another friend important at this time. Merrill and Hooten drove to see him in Amherst, where he was teaching at UMass. As usual, Ali cooked for them an "amazing" meal, which left Jimmy charmed and Peter, who "goes for the hot dishes," bright with sweat. Since meeting Merrill around 1990, Ali had absorbed his work, and changed his own work as a result of it, making a conversion from free verse to intricate formal patterns like the canzone. He was already the author of six poetry collections that meditated on his past in distant, war-torn Kashmir and his dislocated sense of life in the U.S. He showed poems to Merrill, who replied with rigorous advice, as in these remarks in fall 1992 on a loosely rhymed poem about the war in Bosnia:

> I like how the poem moves from start to finish. But, you ask me to be FRANK; and I must scold you for your irresponsible rhymes. In these terminal seasons of human artistry you must—we all must—be especially careful <u>never</u> to rhyme camp-can-grand-telegram; or scream-scene, etc. Get off the fence + decide what your rhyme word [is] and stick to it. My dear, do you have a rhyming dictionary? The poem leads me to think that you don't. I myself would never dream of undertaking such a form without one. (I've probably reduced 4 or 5 to tatters in my long life.) Let me know. I will be happy to send you one + it can remain "our little secret." Now don't pout. Nothing is more welcome than incentive to ever harder work. And while you can't do much about Bosnia, you <u>can</u> improve this poem.

Signed: "Love to you dear heart always, James." Ali took his medicine, thanked Merrill (who was relieved: "only a true artist would respond to criticism with a lovely letter like yours. The Muse is <u>all abeam</u>"), and continued to learn from him.

In November, Merrill saw Dr. Montana, who wasn't pleased. Merrill was tested for his balance, and couldn't walk a straight line. That unsteadiness was probably responsible for a couple of falls Merrill attributed to his sandals—those Birkenstocks, always on his feet, in one outré color or another. Montana called for blood work, a battery of tests (spinal tap, CAT scan, MRI), and hospital supervision—which took place in Pittsburgh, with Hooten accompanying him. Dr. Hunt and a neurologist examined him before he returned to Seventy-second Street on Thanksgiving, no wiser as to the cause of his failing balance. He had his blood "oxygenated" at the recommendation of Andrew Silverman. His T cell count was dropping. McClatchy wrote,

> He is perceptibly weaker + tired. On Monday night (the 13th), he gave a reading at the 92nd St. Y. He had a cold, + a sore throat. Even so, it was a dramatic sight—+ I wondered if it was his last Y reading. He stumbled a little as he walked; had forgotten to bring a copy of one of the poems he'd meant to read; he looked thoroughly weary. [. . .]
>
> People here in [Stonington] are continually talking about how bad he looks.

For the first time, Merrill was dictating letters to an assistant—his hand had become that unsteady, the business of handling and stamping mail that awkward and tiresome. He spent Christmas with his mother and stayed in bed much of the time. McClatchy met him in Atlanta and drove him to Key West so as to minimize the potential for infection on airplanes. "In the car, he napped a good part of the day; + since he arrived here"—McClatchy stayed close by that January—"he spends most of his day on his bed. He is most himself on the telephone. Social occasions rouse his old self—but it's slower." He kept failing to find simple words. He misplaced things. "He doesn't seem frustrated at such a moment, just utterly blank." He needed help with basics: shopping, meals. He was cold constantly and wore long underwear even in mild Key West. "And of course with DJ in such a hapless state, the household is out of Beckett."

For David too spent his days in bed and was confused and helpless when he arose. Assistance had to be arranged for Jimmy's sake as well as David's.

John Balderson and Rolando Rodriguez, friends who'd met Jackson a decade ago and worked for him cleaning the house and looking after the grounds, were recruited to take care of him. There was no question of his fending for himself, and he was no help to Jimmy. When Jimmy roused himself from his bed, it was to scold David. When that went "in one ear & out the other," he took pen in hand to complain to David "formally" about the "ongoing TV noise which, combined with your refusal to use earphones, makes life hell for anyone within earshot." Over dinner with Edmund White and his lover, Hubert Sorin, David had insisted on smoking, although he had been asked not to in the presence of Hubert, "who is dying" of AIDS. "So all that matters—right?—is your gratification. I doubt that I have the strength to live under the same roof with you ever again." Merrill had threatened to give up living with DJ before; this time he was serious. After all, like Hubert, he was dying; and Jackson not only could not care for him, he seemed not to recognize how dire his condition was—which grew worse as Merrill cowered in his room, afraid of the mosquitoes outside, and subject to hallucinations. Looking back on the winter a few months later, he remarked repeatedly on how he "could have easily slipped through the cracks" without anyone noticing.

In fact everyone noticed. As Merrill read aloud from *A Different Person* to a big Key West audience, his friends studied him; after the reading, Charlee Wilbur and Barbara Hersey rose and hugged each other, not needing to say why. Charlee called Sandy: "Dick and I have figured out, without anybody saying anything to us, that Jimmy is very sick. You seem to be in charge. Is there anything we can do?" To Ed White, "the decline of JM [was] more startling than that of DJ." Merrill's AIDS was now an open secret. He writhed under the pressure of worried solicitude: "Are you all right? You seem . . ." At the end of January, McClatchy drove him to see his mother and sister in Palm Beach. He continued by plane to Pittsburgh, where Hooten met him with a wheelchair and Dr. Hunt examined him. A consultation with Montana in New York followed, then a return to Pittsburgh. This time Hunt insisted that he go back on AZT.

Changes of course in Merrill's treatment, like this one, suggest indecision or haphazardness. But they remind us that doctors were still learning about drugs like AZT in the early 1990s, and Merrill was consulting with several physicians, as well as the nutritionist Andrew Silverman, in four different states. He was characteristically of two minds about the merits of drug therapy, and for that matter of two minds about fighting the disease. He had a will to live. But he'd watched two of his closest friends die of AIDS, and he expected to suffer the same fate, no matter what he did.

With AZT, his improvement was immediate. The upswing was a result of the drug, but his reunion with Hooten was helping too. Merrill's decline had shifted the balance of forces between them: it led him to reason away Peter's misbehavior and his friends' objections, and it made him dependent on Peter on a new level. "Peter, as I suspected, turns out to be an extraordinary caregiver," Merrill told Bernard de Zogheb, "and just knowing that he is (a) in the kitchen making lunch and (b) an ever-dearer part of my life is the greatest reassurance." For JM's sixty-eighth birthday, Peter organized a party at the Seventy-second Street apartment with Gurganus, Cesar Rotundi (a friend of Peter's), McClatchy, Stephen Magowan and Octavio Ciano, Terry Layman, and Dr. Montana. "A very jolly occasion," McClatchy wrote, "topped off with a cake decorated with a laurel crown. Peter was very solicitous—and one had to give him all credit." He had prepared a daily regimen for Merrill to be consulted by friends and nurses when he had to be away. The page listed medicines, meals, exercise, naps, and treats, from 7 a.m. to 11 p.m., when the day ended with the Lord's Prayer. "But underneath [. . .]," McClatchy noted, "all is not well." He could see that Hooten was going to "wear himself out" caring for Merrill hour by hour, day by day.

The pressured situation soon "exploded." McClatchy was at home in New York. He was awakened by a call from Ray Izbicki, "saying that P"—who was with Jimmy on Seventy-second Street—"had called, out of his mind, but J had gotten on the phone + said everything was under control." McClatchy went to see for himself. "When I arrived, near to midnight, the apartment was a ruin. Furniture upended, pictures thrown from the wall, J's bedroom door smashed with glass + broken things all over the place. P was red in the face, frothing at the mouth, ranting about how ungrateful + slave-masterish J is, how he'll commit suicide, etc." Hooten's memory of the episode is somewhat different. He was "on the wagon," but had gone out that night to a nearby pub. James showed up and reproached him: "You're drinking beer!" They went home and "had words." Peter slammed the bedroom door, broke a mirror, and began "knocking over everything in sight." He became frightened of the situation—"for James's sake"—and called Cesar Rotundi, then Sandy, to "come help calm things down." McClatchy took Merrill back to his apartment, then to Stonington, where peace was restored. Jimmy was clearly relieved, but also "exhilarated by the melodrama." McClatchy wrote in his diary, "a fight, a scene, is urgent with life—and so, unconsciously, desired, even provoked. Certainly J's 'codependency' will get them back together—in ways the average observer would think intolerable."

Soon Merrill and Hooten would be, not merely back together, but closer than ever. Hooten kept his rented house in Lakeville, but he was often in New York. It must have helped them both that Merrill couldn't go on trying to care for Jackson. He told DJ not to come north as usual for his summer visit in Connecticut ("presumably 'being of help' to me") but instead to settle for a short stay in the fall. It tortured Jimmy to have to take this "hard line" with him. "The horror stems mostly from having sworn for the last half-century that I WOULD NEVER [MAKE] ANYONE [SUFFER] THE WAY MY FATHER DID MY MOTHER."

In late March, after his pancreas showed signs of stress, Merrill's doctors lowered his dose of AZT. In April, his hemoglobin count fell, and he replaced AZT with a daily, self-administered shot of Epogen, a very expensive drug ("I might as well develop a cocaine habit and get it all over with") that "stimulates the bone marrow to produce new cells [. . .] and raises the spirits wonderfully. [. . .] I can hardly get up a flight of stairs, but my mind tap-dances up + down them throughout the day, and very little upsets or frightens me."

He'd begun to select, order, and fine-tune poems for a new collection, a phase of work he'd always enjoyed. In early May, after advice from Yenser and McClatchy, and a weekend spent reading poems aloud to Hooten in Lakeville, a table of contents took shape. The volume would gather work from the past six harrowing years. Over the coming months, he kept changing his mind about the title. Should it be *A Quickening*, *A Dose*, or *A Scattering of Salts*? The answer depended on how he felt. *A Quickening of Salts* suggested a return to vital powers, which this book would triumphantly demonstrate. *A Dose of Salts* implied taking one's medicine in the form of one hard lesson or another, of which this book would be full. *A Scattering of Salts*: the image—there was no mistaking it—was of the body's burial and decomposition.

Most of that spring, he spent on Seventy-second Street. He was learning at last "how to live in New York." Rather than plunge into "debauchery" on arrival, by which he meant going to bookstores, movies, and opera, he found he could "spend whole days" snug in the apartment. There was a wood fire, unusual for a New York apartment and good for an ill man who felt chilled every day. He saw few people besides Peter and Patrick Merla, an editor now serving as secretary of the Ingram Merrill Foundation, who often came to work as his assistant. Holing up was a strategy for writing and, when he couldn't work, for being ill quietly and privately. Anything he needed was an elevator ride away. By contrast, Water Street had been overtaken by real estate offices and antiques stores, so he had to get in the car to shop; and the village was too small for him not to fret over what friends were saying about him. Even when he went to Stonington that summer, he returned to the city every weekend to avoid the town's round of parties.

Or he went to Peter and Cosmo in Lakeville. The feeling that they were a family, knit together by the pet, and the right size to recall Jimmy's childhood, had taken hold again. Peter had a canoe, and they paddled that June on one of the nearby "crystalline" lakes; "great banks of mountain laurel were reflected in the unrippling surface and little clumps of laurel blossom lay on the water with their mouths open to the heavens." Floating, dreamily drifting in a Connecticut lake, whether paddled by Peter or swimming, the one form of exercise he loved and was good at, Merrill was relieved of his body and open to the sky above, like those flowers on the water. Images from that time appeared in a poem he began writing, "Days of 1994,"—the fifth of his "Days of" poems, completing his homage to Cavafy, who wrote five poems titled "Days of" too. The erotic passion of "Days of 1964," the first poem in the cycle, composed thirty years before during his affair with Strato, is replaced in this lyric by the presentiment of death. In "my friend's house" (the mild and only mention of Hooten in the poem), Merrill sleeps and wakes in a half-basement room "Below the level of the lawn," practicing for burial. He ends the poem by listing, with delicacy in a wistful archaic diction, a few of "the thousand things" he will leave behind in death:

> The spectacles, the book,
> Forgetful lover and forgotten love,
> Cobweb hung with trophy wings,
> The fading trumpet of a car,
> The knowing glance from star to star,
> The laughter of old friends.

He found that poems now "just <u>come</u>, as they did long, long ago." About this one, when he finished it in September, he wrote, "Gestation: years. Delivery: 60 hours." (That "60 hours," for a page-and-a-half lyric poem, counted as "just coming" indicates how many hours normally went into one of his poems, and how hard he was still working.)

Redeeming the memory of their agonized visit of two years before, Merrill and Hooten stayed with Fredericks in Pawlet in August and had "<u>such</u> a pleasant + happy time." Jimmy spent a solitary hour at the grand piano he'd played on his first visit to the house in 1950. Claude prepared his usual beautiful dinners—crème bavaroise dripping with bloody raspberries for dessert—in the small country dining room, only candles pressing back against the black miles of forest outside. The Buechners were guests one evening; another evening the party drove to a nearby town to meet Richard Kenney and his wife. Breakfast meant fresh rolls and melon served with the seeds, as in Japan, under a bower of stout old lilacs behind the house, with ample time to linger and talk. Over the long haul, Jimmy and Claude had achieved a wry intimacy superior to the famished devotion they began with. "You give yourself so easily, so fully," Jimmy wrote to his host afterward. "[P]erhaps that's what 'being a Buddhist' means, but I suspect it's really just 'being you.' Anyhow, we lapped it up like cream, or crème bavaroise." Then, with Peter at the wheel and Cosmo on Jimmy's lap, they drove south for HIP's ninety-fifth birthday. They stopped at Flannery O'Connor's grave in Georgia, and, returning to New York, looked in on Gurganus, who was renovating his house in a North Carolina hamlet.

Merrill was busy making adjustments to his will. He had told Fredericks in spring 1994 that he had AIDS. "I didn't want to be made special," he'd said, explaining why he took so long to come out with the fact. Gurganus he had told perhaps a year ago. Anyone he told, he swore to secrecy. He wrote to other friends—for instance, U. T. Summers—"to deny the rumors of my illness," claiming that he'd had anemia over the winter in Key West. In another letter, he berated Jackson bitterly for telling people he had AIDS, or at least failing to deny it convincingly when he had the chance. "Keeping my secret is the one <u>serious</u> thing I've asked of you in the past ten years. And you've blown it twice now. From where I sit you are a live grenade with the pin pulled out, and I mean to stay as far beyond your range as I possibly can. [. . .] Try, <u>try</u>, TRY to think what you've been doing, and how horribly it upsets me." Why did secrecy continue to matter so much? He was still trying to protect Peter and still trying to keep his diagnosis from his mother. His will to fight the disease had become so entangled with his will to keep it a secret, it was difficult to tell them apart. He liked to quote Tom Detre's defiant advice: " 'In my opinion there cannot <u>be</u> too much denial.' "

Aware of how short his time might be, Merrill began writing letters full of life wisdom to several youthful correspondents. Chief and youngest of these was a tall, brown-haired fifteen-year-old Stonington boy, earnest and soft-spoken, whom he met when Billy Boatwright brought him to tea at 107 Water Street. Torren Blair and James Merrill took to each other immediately. It was an advantage that Blair hardly knew whom he was meeting, beyond Merrill being "the poet in town." "I wasn't as awestruck as I could or should have been," he remembered, "and it left me free to communicate directly, without being very careful or self-conscious." JM—"JM" was what

Blair called him—invited the teenager back often. "We'd go upstairs" to the room with the piano and rooftop view, "and spend hours talking. When you're young, you don't think anything about talking for four hours—it's the kind of thing you do in college, sitting around a dorm room." They talked about reading and writing. Sometimes Merrill sang or played the piano ("he used metaphors from music to explain literature"). But they also talked about what was happening in Blair's life. "I had plenty of angst in a not unusual way—uncertainties about vocation, the future, friends." JM reciprocated with confidences of his own. "He'd talk about Peter a bit. He asked: 'What do you choose in a partner? Someone who is intellectually challenging? Or someone who will make you feel loved and cared for?' " At his age, JM said, "being intellectually challenged wasn't what he needed most."

Rolando Rodriguez drove DJ to Stonington in early September. When Rodriguez packed him back into the car again eighteen days later, Merrill couldn't decide whether Jackson was "a child or a chimpanzee. The stubbornness," he complained, "the constant shameless and rather deadly randiness"—which at this point was mainly a matter of watching video pornography. "The other day he said, 'I'm 72. When I turned 70 I decided I was entitled to a life of leisure.' JM: 'What sort of life would you say you'd been leading for the 40 years prior to that?' " Jimmy continued to wonder whether David's long decline and "<u>frightful</u>" present condition were his fault. He put the question to Sewelly, who laughed and reassured him: "Oh no, David never wanted to do <u>anything</u>." When Merrill told Jackson about the provisions he'd made for him in his will, David replied, " 'Well, if you die I'll have no reason to go on living,' so guilt got added to my grievances."

One day the mediums took up their places at the milk-glass dining table. The séance was brief—the spirits had ceased some time ago to hold their attention for long (or was it vice versa?). Their next conversation would have to wait until they met up with Ephraim on the other side. Jimmy, who'd already decided not to return to Key West for the winter, had no plans to see David until the spring. It meant that when they waved goodbye that September, JM and DJ would never see each other again.

If Jimmy was letting go of David, he and Peter were becoming "amazingly close." It was "like the 1st year of knowing each other," he wrote to a friend, "except that we've gone through terrible times, <u>through</u> them & into a kind of light—Lightness? Confidence? Serenity? Pourvu que ça dure" (meaning "May it endure"). To Buechner, in a religious mood, he wrote: "I don't think I've ever felt such love before, and I see it as a kind of miracle. Lord knows, [Peter] has his troubles, which often show in loud scenes, etc. These, however, pass within hours, and incidentally remind me of love as an emotion, a fire at the heart of life." Is that what he thought in the midst of one of his and Peter's battles? This "side of Peter," he continued, had "turned many of my friends slightly but perceptibly against him." So he was afraid of what would become of Peter when he was gone. "He'll be well enough taken care of, but that's not what I mean." Peter was attending church, and Jimmy hoped that he would keep it up. Looking ahead, he asked Freddy, the clergyman, to check in on Peter and let him "know he's in your prayers and that you will always bless him for the sweetness and vividness he brought to (already!) these past ten years" of his lover's life.

Merrill started a new notebook. Inside he taped a prayer from Thomas Merton. Titled "Thoughts in Solitude," the prayer begins, "My Lord God, I have no idea where I'm going" and ends, "Therefore will I trust you always though I may seem to be lost and in the shadow of death. I will not fear, for you are ever with me, and you will never leave me to face my perils alone." The prayer did not signal a late-arrived piety for Merrill, only the depth of the shadows gathering around him, and the fact that Peter had given him the page mattered more than the words on it. He counted on Peter, not God, to be with him at the end.

In New York that September, Merrill was occupied with new poems, the seed of a book to follow *A Scattering of Salts*. One of these, called "Minotaur," was prompted by his friendship with Torren Blair. It imagines a scene of ritual human sacrifice where the old are fed to the young for the sake of the future: "*Devour my life* each prays." Then a call came from Strato—the first sign from him in nine years—and, predictably, the news was bad: he'd fallen at work and lost one of his eyes. The story sounded fishy ("does one <u>do</u> that in a fall?"), but "my policy is to believe people"; so, like old times, Jimmy wired money to his Greek. He and Hooten were about to leave on a three-week trip to Prague and Vienna. He signed a new will; stumbled again and cut himself badly; made last-minute calls to DJ, HIP, Sandy, Stephen, and others; scrawled a note to Torren; and got on the plane with Peter.

Rather than revisit his favorite sites in Europe, Merrill was curious to see post–Cold War Prague. His first impression was of a "mauve madness": like the decadent hues he was wearing these days, everything seemed some shade of purple, "pansy-violet," or lavender, which he interpreted as an "Antidote to the Red Army not to mention the Hapsburg ochres." Mauve was the theme of a multi-part poem he worked on for the next three months. Called "Rhapsody on Czech Themes" and dedicated to Gurganus, it was a baroque meditation on political and personal freedom. He was still alive and taking on the world.

He and Hooten attended "a puppet Orfeo" and then *The Marriage of Figaro* put on in the house where *Don Giovanni* was first staged. With Kafka in mind, they "renamed our local restaurant The Trial." In the cemetery in the Jewish Ghetto, they placed pebbles on the dark gravestones leaning this way and that. Exploring the countryside in a car, they were ticketed twice in Marienbad ("Marienworse is more to the point"). "My mind—memory, equanimity—seem to shut down a bit by day's end," Merrill noted. One day Hooten didn't show up on time for dinner, Merrill became desperate about his lateness, and, once he arrived, Hooten became defensive and broke out a list of complaints about his lover: "1) That he is a cold fish emotionally. 2) That he is superficial and his clever friends disloyal [. . .]. 3) That he 'throws around his millions' to keep himself at a distance from the world. 4) That all his poems are negative resulting in unflattering portraits (for posterity) of the people he appears to love." All of which Merrill recited sadly in his notebook. "When I think of what I could say to him—! Only it's not in me to say such things in the 1st place. My impulse is to run away now, today, go where I can work in peace—die in peace when the time comes."

The impulse passed, and they drove on. In Austria, they stopped at Auden's grave. "Respectability!" Merrill exclaimed, oppressed by the sober society where Auden ended his life. "In my green Birkenstocks and royal purple turtleneck [. . .] I feel condescension, even disapproval in my wake." With Hooten pushing, Merrill rode in a wheelchair through the Kunsthistorisches Museum in Vienna, hunting out Vermeer's *Artist in His Studio*. Throughout the trip he was engrossed in a "marvelous book," Thomas Mann's late novel, *Doctor Faustus*. "What organizes a book like that? The passage of time over the strings of a life. The magisterial telling of the tale."

Merrill returned to the U.S. for two public events: a reading at the Art Institute of Chicago and a "JM weekend" hosted by Holly Hall, head of Special Collections at Washington University's Olin Library, in St. Louis. She'd brought a roster of JM's friends to speak: Richard Kenney and Rachel Hadas ("both fine and affectionate"); Yenser, who was "at his best, threatening incapacity and delivering excellence" in a lecture about Merrill and American poetry, linking him to Emerson and Whitman; and Helen Vendler, whose commentary on Merrill's recent poems "kept me in 50 minutes of unbroken gooseflesh." Merrill had carefully planned his part of the program. His reading began with "A Downward Look," the short poem about the foaming surface of a bath, placed first in *A Scattering of Salts*, followed by "Ice Cap," "Cornwall," and "Menu," a series of Bishop poems and excerpts from *Sandover* that he read with Hooten, "The *Ring* Cycle," "164 East 72nd Street," and, to conclude, the final poem in *A Scattering of Salts*,

"An Upward Look." He was terribly thin—he looked scrawny in his dark jacket and floppy bow tie—but his eyes shone as always.

Back in New York, Merrill told McClatchy "he'd turned a corner in the disease—headed in the wrong direction." Recently he'd found himself badly muddled: he couldn't make sense of his calendar. Dr. Montana urged him to resume AZT, and Dr. Hunt seconded the opinion, only more strongly. She also prescribed medication to prevent the onset of AIDS dementia—perhaps Merrill's greatest fear. In addition, he had developed a cataract, which made driving impossible and reading difficult. His health was as delicate as it had ever been. Yet Peter was "more wonderful every week," and so was "the peerless little dog." Merrill felt that, in St. Louis, Yenser had subtly insulted Hooten, and he drafted an injured, angry letter to Stephen, never sent, in which he insisted that Peter had over the past year "(no exaggeration) saved my life." "From my point of view I've never had that kind of caring from <u>anyone</u>."

After Thanksgiving, Peter put up a Christmas tree of "excessive beauty," which, Merrill said, identifying with the tree, Peter had "brought back alive" and decorated "to a fare-thee-well." Stirred by memories of childhood Christmases, Merrill went to work on a poem about it. As if to amuse a child, he cast the poem in the shape of the Christmas tree, but with its left half cut off, imitating his cropped view of it from the next room. (He had in mind a similar view of a Christmas tree in a print by Fairfield Porter.) The tree speaks like a patient whose time is up: "I knew—of course I knew— / That it would only be a matter of weeks, / That there was nothing more to do." Yet it is consoling to be chosen and "made much of" by a family (Merrill only mentions a boy and his mother). It shines with lights and tinsel while a tube to refill the water ("a primitive IV") keeps "the show going." What lies ahead is "the stripping, the cold street, my chemicals / Plowed back into the Earth for lives to come." But for now it is enough "to be so poised, so / Receptive. Still to recall, to praise."

Merrill was aware of how soon the tree would come down, and aware he probably wouldn't live to see another one. Still he kept the show going: there were evenings at the opera (*Madama Butterfly* for the umpteenth time, *Peter Grimes*, the Shostakovich *Lady Macbeth*: "the music fresh and astringent as a rubdown with cheap cologne"), a movie he delighted in— *Vanya on 42nd Street*—with Robert Polito and his wife, a reading by Bill Merwin, a dinner for Charles and Jimmy hosted by Doris, and an exhibit of Charles's watercolors and his wife Mary's weavings.

By Christmas Eve, the tree had been put out on the street, and the apartment looked "like a stateroom on the old Queen Mary, just before sailing: baskets of fruit, boxes of candy, bottles of wine <u>we</u> shan't drink—and the 'ship-to-shore' telephone never stops ringing: friends calling to say Bon Voyage." For Merrill and Hooten were on the road again. Their winding route included Christmas with Robin ("my favorite nephew") and his family in Connecticut, a consultation with Susan Hunt and dinner with the Detres in Pittsburgh, a night with HIP in Atlanta, and an evening with Betty Potts and her family in Alabama—when Jimmy gave Betty an heirloom pearl from Hellen (see his poem "Pearl") and Peter presented JM's little namesake, Betty's grandson James Merrill Potts, with a coonskin cap. On January 1, they rolled into Tucson to spend the night at the Arizona Inn, the historic resort where Jimmy and his mother stayed when he was six. The next day they moved into a house in the hills.

The choice of Tucson for the winter was "a bypass operation" meant to avoid "the clogged social arteries" of Key West. Merrill had visited twice in recent years for a reading at the University of Arizona and for Family Week at Sierra Tucson. But the association on his mind now was the long-ago winter he was sent to the Arizona desert after the kidnapping of the Lindbergh baby: this would be a good place to hide from whatever creeping danger might carry him away. Or was it just the opposite, a sign of his readiness to meet death, far from familiar faces and routines?

The home he and Hooten had rented was "the largest house I've lived in since childhood." It had "cinematic opulence," with three levels, a baby grand piano, "a pool, unheated but scenic, a smaller one full of big multicolored Koi, dwarf daffodils, cacti," and rugged mountain views. Peter got the master bedroom, "where we light a fire each morning (he brings wood in, I make coffee)." Jimmy set up his desk in a balcony loft, the sort of nook in which he liked to write. He went to work on his Czech rhapsody, "Christmas Tree," and a poem about the house and fish pond called "Koi." This last concerned the fear that kept him up at night: that their "Lindbergh puppy" might be snatched by coyotes. With those predators prowling, the desert in the poem is menacing. "Behind these garden walls," though, "it's safe." A rare snow vanishes almost as quickly as it falls. The carp circle in their pool. Suddenly, yapping at the koi, Cosmo loses his balance—and splashes into the pool. The minor calamity coyly evokes the specter of worse accidents: just so suddenly, so innocently might a life end.

Over the fall Merrill's communications with Torren Blair had increased in frequency and intensity. Postcards went forth like bulletins. Some carried touchstones like Pope's epigram in "An Essay on Man," "<u>Whatever is,</u>

is right" or the final sentences from Stevens's essay "The Noble Rider and the Sound of Words." "I'd understood (wrongly?)," Merrill wrote on one card, "that recent views of chaos show her to be a mistress of extraordinary & subtle patterns. So the last word is never spoken? I should like to believe that and so (as an optimist) should you!" He took Torren's reading program in hand: "when you've finished 'The Idiot' (don't miss it) rinse your spirit with something French. 'The Charterhouse of Parma,' which Stendhal dictated in 6 weeks, will do nicely." He produced a reading list with three pages of poetry from Wyatt to the moderns (Eliot, Crane, Bishop) and prose from Dickens and Woolf to (the only eccentric choices on his list) Nigel Dennis's novel *Cards of Identity* and Sybille Bedford's memoir of her Jewish childhood in Berlin, winding up with a page of French poetry from Baudelaire to Ponge. Another letter added an essay by Howard Nemerov, Chekhov's plays ("one of the wonders of the world"), and Nabokov's *Lolita*, *Pale Fire*, and *Bend Sinister*. But Merrill didn't insist on his recommendations, let alone an order for proceeding. "Where to start your reading list? Anywhere. Reality, says A R Ammons, is abob with centers."

Merrill didn't "know a soul" in Tucson. Or so he claimed, but that wasn't quite true. He and Hooten had found their house through their new neighbors Laurie and Tom Pew, the parents of Katherine Pew, a friend of Peter's from acting classes. The Pews invited them to dinner, and they invited the Pews in turn. Then there were Norman Austin and his friend Gordon Sieveke. Austin, a professor of classics at the University of Arizona, had met Merrill and Jackson in Athens in the 1970s. They had crossed paths elsewhere over the years, including Key West, where Austin made friends with Hooten. When he visited Sierra Tucson during Peter's treatment, Merrill slept at Austin's home—exhausted, weeping—after the long day of therapy. And if Austin was trustworthy and mild, someone with whom Merrill could let down his guard, Sieveke was amusing, "a talkative, loose-limbed presence," a yoga teacher "DEEP" into the Yoruban gods. "Dispersed throughout the house" were divinities, "a little pantheon, with offerings and personalities," whom Merrill and Hooten "were taken to meet one by one." Soon they were taking yoga classes twice a week with Gordon, rolling out their mats in Norman's living room in view of those deities.

The regional opera put on *Götterdämmerung*, and Jimmy and Peter went. Another day they were driving to Bisbee, a Victorian mining town, when a car entering the highway forced Peter to swerve and barrel into the rear of another vehicle. Air bags flew out—the Prism was totaled. The people in the car they'd hit were sent off in an ambulance, strapped into stretchers. "Cosmo set a high standard for Cool, giving his version to each of the officers in turn," while Merrill came away with only a "sprained finger with which I mean to show Arizona drivers what I think of them." They rented another car almost on the spot and continued on their way, but the crash had been a frightening, unnerving close call. "Only hours later came the shock, and we had to stop on the road & hold hands."

Merrill told the tale of the crash in a letter to Torren. Continuously now, he was talking to the teenager in his head; and he was hurt and frustrated when letters were slow to come back. "The pace of correspondence was picking up," Blair remembered, "and he'd admonish me for not responding quickly enough. I didn't know he was dying. I didn't understand how pressed for time he was." JM offered practical advice to the beginning poet: "The point [. . .] is to feel your feelings in the presence of something in the 'outside world'—a tree, a portrait, the hood of a car, an article about a new scientific discovery—which will reflect your heightened state of mind back to you. You will not have to say 'I.' " Merrill confessed that the "near-fatal" car crash had left him "with a sense that it is vital—to me, to us both—that I tell you whatever I can while I'm still around. My impulse is to write to you for an hour or two every day." He invited Blair to the Met for *Pelléas* in April, and to poetry readings in May and July. He was trying to believe he had a future, but he also wanted to help Torren with his, knowing he wouldn't be around to see it. "It's heartbreaking," Blair commented about these letters. "He was confronting his own mortality and investing in youth, in someone who was at the beginning rather than the end. He talked about never having had a child. It was a part of experience that he'd missed." For a few months, Blair was that missing child.

By the third week in January, JM was "all gloomed-over." David McIntosh came from New Mexico to see him. They spent an evening in company and then a second evening by themselves, giving them a chance for, Merrill felt, "a good serious talk." "He was waiting for more blood tests," McIntosh remembered, "because he was hoping to have cataract surgery"—which had been put off repeatedly over the past month, due to his low platelet count and general fragility. "James was badly depressed. He couldn't focus to read concentratedly. He said he didn't want to live if he couldn't see." He complained of "an ongoing sharp chest pain," which he attributed to the stress of waiting for surgery. "He had a masseuse daily to give him relief." The next day, with the wind moaning and rain falling, James and Peter sat by the fire talking and "at peace."

J: Tell me, if I should die before you, what shall you do? Where will you turn?

P: To Jeanette. To that monastery near Charleston. To some of
your friends . . .

J: That's what I'd hoped to hear.

Despite the difficulty of it, Merrill was reading hungrily a number of
books at once: an advance copy of *A Scattering of Salts*, *Ulysses* (for the first
time since he was in college, selected because Torren was reading it too),
Gertrude Stein Remembered (a collection of memories by her friends), and
Out of Egypt, a memoir by a Proust scholar about growing up in a Jewish
family in Alexandria in the 1950s. Merrill sat at the computer on Wednes-
day, February 1, and wrote a fan letter to this stranger:

Dear André Aciman:

I can only begin to tell you how touched and delighted I am by
"Out of Egypt." Thanks to Christian Ayoub's friendship and his
two little books, to the kitchen-Italian libretti of Bernard de
Zogheb, to the anecdotes of my irreplaceable Tony Parigory in
Athens (where I lived for a number of years), and not to mention
Cavafy, Alexandria has permanently colored my days. To find it
now in your pages, all rosy and clear-eyed from the tonic of your
telling, is the greatest imaginable gift. That whole world of the
trivial & the tragic, interwoven as in Chekhov, and underscored
as in opera, is for me the very best life has to offer, and as close
to a "real" home as I've ever come. No reflection on my parents,
that the Stork delivered me to West Eleventh Street instead of
the Corniche [the waterfront promenade in Alexandria]. What
do you do with so much blue once you've seen it? (Terrible things
await us before the book ends. Meanwhile, just a long sigh of
relief . . .)

Well, I could spin this out at greater length—you can't be
averse to praise. Most of all, though, I want to go back to the
beginning and read it through a second time.

Sincerely,
James Merrill

It was the last letter he wrote. Later that day at Austin's house, during one
of Sieveke's yoga lessons, Jimmy was seized by a stabbing pain. Peter drove
him directly to the University of Arizona Medical Center. The diagnosis

was pancreatitis, "but the doctors didn't think it serious enough to keep him in the hospital," Austin recalled, and he was sent home to recover. Two days later, on Friday, he had another attack, and his breathing was labored. Peter drove him back to the emergency room. This time the doctors kept him in the hospital for observation.

By Saturday Merrill was resting comfortably in his hospital room. Hooten had brought a CD player, and they spent the day listening to some of JM's favorite music—Schubert's Impromptus, Maggie Teyte singing French songs, dances by Federico Mompou (a gift from Sandy), and Clara Haskil playing Mozart. Merrill had his notebook with him, drafts of the poems he was working on, and his books. Peter had propped up a photo of himself and James, both smiling broadly, and a small cross he had made from sticks found in the desert. Norman and Gordon, visiting that afternoon, chatted with Jimmy about his plans to read at UCLA in March. The University of Arizona had learned he was in town; would he be willing to give a reading? Ever obliging, he chose a date at the end of February.

On Sunday morning, when Austin and Sieveke visited, the patient was subdued. The oxygen monitor taped to his forefinger kept blinking and emitting a high-pitched beep. Austin tried to get it shut off, but the nurse said they would have to wait: she was attending to a critical case. "Well," James commented, "there are three very critical people in this room too." He wrapped a tissue around his finger to hide the red light, which went on blinking but more mildly. "There's another metaphor for the carp," he remarked, contemplating the soft red pulse—and puzzling his guests until, later, they read the poem and realized that he had been working on "Koi" that day. "The IV tree looks like a person standing in the shadows," he said, gesturing toward the steel pole and sagging bag of fluids to which he was tethered. Laurie Pew looked in. Allan Gurganus called on an impulse. "James sounded tired, remote, not entirely in this world. I said, I love you. He said, I know, dear"—gently but dismissively, as if they were facing a much larger question. Peter stayed on into the evening.

What happens when everyone else is gone? A writer writes. Now in his notebook, on a fresh page, in a tiny, trembling script (he had mislaid his glasses), Merrill underlines "The Next to Last Scene" and begins a poem under that title. It was unusual for him to title the first draft of a poem in his notebook: he must have known he would have just one chance to get this one down. He'd told Torren "to feel your feelings in the presence of something in the 'outside world,' " anything at all. In the darkening ward, he takes his own advice. What he sees around him is "A room with every last convenience"—dull objects of mere, mute life that his imagination will try to animate once more. The TV suspended above on the wall, "Tallest + grimmest," turns into "a monk / In rectangular cowl." Has he come to guard the poet, or summon him away? A snapshot of Billy Boatwright glances back at him wittily, "quite as if to say / we can't go on meeting this way." Last, "at the foot of the bed," he sees the photo of himself beside his "smiling lover." His hand crumbles as he fits in two sentences at the bottom limit of the page: "We have vowed each to see the other through. / I smile back to set t'other free."

On Monday, February 6, Peter talked with one of JM's doctors in Pittsburgh shortly before 8 a.m. AZT had seemed to cause a mild attack of pancreatitis a year ago. DDI or dideoxyinosine, the drug he'd been taking recently, was similar to AZT, and it might have caused the latest crisis. But Merrill's "numbers were good," and he'd been cleared to go home that morning. Hooten hung up. He and Cosmo would soon be in the car, driving to the hospital to collect James and his things. A few minutes later, the phone rang again. This time it was the university medical center: "Mr. Merrill has been 'coded,' " the voice said—meaning he was in critical condition. In fact, sitting in the chair beside his hospital bed, he'd just suffered a heart attack. Peter rushed to the hospital, but his lover was no longer alive.

Afterword

On the tray table beside the empty chair where Jimmy had been seated that morning stood an open can of Diet Coke. No straw. Peter insisted that he use a straw, because these days, when Jimmy took a sip from the can, he would choke and start to cough uncontrollably. Peter suspected that that—something as simple and terrible and preventable as that—had happened.

James Merrill was dead at sixty-eight, the immediate cause being a heart attack, which is how his father had died (and according to Ephraim, how his previous life had ended too). He had been near death—he had in that sense been dying—for a long time. Yet he expected to continue.

1995: it was around this time that an HIV diagnosis stopped seeming like a death sentence; better drugs and treatment plans were making it possible to live with the virus. Merrill knew, looking into history, that medicine had repeatedly eradicated, or made manageable at least, any number of seemingly incurable diseases, and there was no reason why AIDS should be anything different. He had hope. But he felt that, while his days were "numbered," everyone else's are too, and there was nothing special about having to die.

What he feared was meaningless, random death, unrelated to the desires and choices that went before it. His will to shape his life ran that deep. "[I]f anything awful is to happen to one, isn't it . . . richer and in every way deeper to have it be [. . .] an awfulness that one's total nature has led the way to? As opposed, I mean, to being pulverized in an air raid, lost at sea, or stabbed for kicks by a teenager." He wrote that to Mona Van Duyn in 1968 when she was being treated for cancer, and she didn't see any consolation in this attitude. But Merrill did. Almost certainly he thought of HIV, rightly or wrongly, as an awfulness that involved his "total nature."

The burial of his body and the execution of his will—these would be for others to arrange, beginning with Peter, who was suddenly left alone with his and Jimmy's little dog, needing to determine the right things to do. He picked up the phone. He called Betty, who would tell Hellen; John and Rolando in Key West, who would tell David; Milton Maurer; and Ray Izbicki, who would tell Sandy. The moment that he saw Ray approaching, head bowed outside his study window in Stonington, McClatchy knew what he would tell him. He called Stephen, Robin, Gurganus, the Hollanders, the Fords, Eleanor, Claude, and, among many others, Vassili—who called George, who called Strato.

Obituaries were hastily put together in the *Los Angeles Times* and *The New York Times*. Newspapers as grand as *Le Monde* and as humble as *Solares Hill*, a Key West weekly, picked up the story. In her two-room apartment in Amherst, Rosemary Sprague, like many people, heard the news for the first time when it was broadcast on National Public Radio. McClatchy wrote a long memorial essay that *The New Yorker* ran in March. Alison Lurie published a tribute in *The New York Review of Books* around the same time. The word was that Merrill had died of a heart attack, which was true, but not the whole truth. No one mentioned publicly that Jimmy had had AIDS, and most of his friends and relatives were unaware of the fact. He'd asked McClatchy to help him keep his diagnosis a secret, to "cover" for him, and Sandy continued to do so after his death. It was in 2001, when he felt he'd kept his promise long enough, that McClatchy published an essay about his friend's struggle with HIV. That would be the first public confirmation of his condition.

Everyone who knew Merrill was shocked by his death. The new friends he'd made in Arizona expected him to return to them that Monday from the hospital, and immediately there was a need to mourn. The evening of his death, Peter, Norman Austin, Gordon Sieveke, and a few others met at St. Philip's in the Hills, an Episcopal church in Tucson, to celebrate the service of the dead. The next afternoon, there was a gathering at the Valley Funeral Home in Tucson. The group talked quietly about James. Peter handed out copies of "Christmas Tree" and read the poem aloud.

Merrill's body was shipped to the Frank Campbell Funeral Home on Madison Avenue. It was necessary to identify the body, and Hooten had not yet arrived in New York. McClatchy was in Stonington, making arrangements for the funeral and burial that would take place there the very next day. Harry Ford wasn't in the city; so his wife Kathleen went. She placed a stone in Jimmy's hand and closed his fingers around it—a symbol, she told him, of the friends who went with him.

An impression was taken of the dead man's face, so that a bronze mask could be made. It was Hooten's idea, not Merrill's, but the juvenile author of "Death Masks," that poem from Jimmy's senior year at Lawrenceville, would have appreciated it. The body was laid out in a purple kimono and (a Christmas gift from jovial Tom Bolt) red socks. Then put into the flames.

Merrill's funeral took place at Calvary Episcopal Church in Stonington on February 13, a raw Monday afternoon with scraps of snow on the ground. Jimmy himself had never worshipped there except to pay his respects when a neighbor passed on. The white walls on this occasion suggested, oddly, an interior in Greece. The church was so packed that people were standing at the back.

Bishop Paul Moore presided. The text for his homily was the vision of the New Jerusalem from Revelation. "I will give unto him that is athirst of the fountain of the water of life freely." It was, the Bishop declared, "a lovely picture! Jimmy athirst for life, drinking from the water of life freely," as indeed he had.

"Jimmy was my uncle, my mentor, my friend," Robin Magowan began his remarks. "I sometimes feel he created me out of nothing—the Southampton vacuity. And throughout my life he has held me together, as he has so many others." Bruce Merrill spoke about his uncle for Charles's side of the family. Allan Gurganus evoked his friend's generosity: "How rare it is, friends, when the great man is a good man." John Hollander read the dark monologue "Mirror," Yenser read "An Upward Look" from *A Scattering of Salts*, and McClatchy read "Koi." With a harpsichord accompaniment, a soprano sang "Bist du bei mir" from the *Notebook of Anna Magdalena Bach*.

In Stonington Cemetery, Hooten poured the gray and silver grit into a tiny pit in the frozen ground, and mourners took turns casting cold handfuls of dirt on it. One slipped in a child's marble painted like the globe. Before long, a slate headstone would mark the spot, bearing carved images of the sun, moon, and stars, symbols of Jimmy's nights and days.

A public memorial service with readings from Merrill's poetry and remembrances was held at the New York Public Library that spring.

Earlier, on February 10, a smaller memorial service took place at Bethesda-by-the-Sea in Palm Beach, another Episcopal church. Hellen attended, and Doris and Charles and Betty Potts. Rolando and John made the long drive with David from Key West. Freddy Buechner, a winter resident in Florida, was present, but not as the officiating priest, being himself a Presbyterian minister. The congregation sang "Joyful, Joyful," "Holy, Holy, Holy!," and "Now Thank We All Our God"; a soloist performed the exquisite "Pie Jesu" from Fauré's *Requiem*. Catherine Merrill read Job

19:21–27, and Stephen Magowan I Corinthians 13:1–13. Freddy offered a prayer composed for the occasion, and Charles eulogized his younger brother: "When I was a teacher and tried to counsel troubled youth, I stressed the good sense of old Dr. Freud's recipe for mental health: to love and to work. There are no higher measurements. Jimmy did both."

When he first heard that Jimmy had died, Freddy had called Hellen to express his condolences and commiserate. Her comment was simply, "Well, he certainly didn't waste any time." At the reception following the Palm Beach ceremony, she remained as composed as ever—"just as if she were at a social in Atlanta," telling off-color jokes, Buechner recalled. He told her he had been dreaming about Jimmy over the past week. "It's funny," she replied, "I've never dreamed of Jimmy." (And this in contrast to his recorded nightmares about *her!*) "I'll tell him, next time I do," Freddy said. When, in a subsequent dream about his friend, Freddy did just that, Jimmy replied, "Tell her, 'Don't call me, I'll call her.' "

"Come on, honey—why, you'll bury us all!" Charlie declares in "The Broken Home." The joke was prophetic. Hellen Plummer, Mother Earth, the Medusa, Jimmy's Mama, vigorous to the last, would not give up the ghost until December 2000, when she was 102 years old. She had lived in three centuries.

DJ's story was sadder. He'd told Jimmy his life would not be worth living without him. When he heard the news of Jimmy's death, he simply closed his bedroom door and cried. But with or without Jimmy, David had little left to live for. With Rolando and John caring for him around the clock on Elizabeth Street, he survived in a debilitated state, with worsening dementia, until 2001.

For more than ten years, Peter Hooten had been Merrill's lover, companion, and collaborator. At the last, their lives had been very tightly knit; now JM was gone. Hooten was a relatively young man in 1995, although too old to return to the film and TV roles that had already begun to dry up when he met James. He would have to figure out what to do with the rest of his life.

Merrill tried not to think very much about his money, but he knew that, when he was dead, how to dispose of it (and his physical property) and how rightly to use it to recognize and care for the people who loved and depended on him, would become crucial, rather complicated questions. He kept revising his will as his life underwent revisions. With Milton Maurer supplying legal advice and the language of the document, Merrill signed his last will and testament in September 1994. Maurer and Merrill Magowan were named as trustees.

The will made provisions for ongoing support of his mother, DJ, and Peter. For Hellen, it provided a flat sum that would ensure payments to her of $1,000 per month for as long as she lived. It established trusts of $1.5 million for David, and $2 million for Peter, from which income could be drawn quarterly or monthly. The will authorized Merrill's trustees to invade the principal in the event of medical emergencies for David or Peter.

The will also made provision for purchase of an annuity that would pay David McIntosh a monthly stipend for ten years. Similar provision was made for Rosemary Sprague. The last gift may seem surprising, but Jimmy and Rosie were lifelong friends, and it's possible this arrangement was meant to continue support he'd provided before or to fulfill a promise made in the distant past.

Merrill canceled all debts his friends had incurred with him over the years. Among other implications, this meant that Peter Tourville became the owner outright of the house, barn, and eleven acres of apple orchard in Unity, New Hampshire, that Merrill had purchased as a farm for him to work fifteen or so years before.

He made many individual cash gifts to family and friends. The largest went to Peter, while $50,000 went to each of Charles and Mary's children. "I have made no comparable cash bequests to the children or issue of my sister, Doris Merrill Magowan, as ample provision has been otherwise made for them," the will explained, a touch defensively. Substantial gifts were made to Ray Izbicki, Eleanor Perényi, Daryl Hine, the Fords, Charlotte Hafley, John Hollander, Peter Gillis (a shy Boston school teacher Jimmy had been good friends with for twenty years), Claude Fredericks, Sewelly Jackson (Jimmy gave her $50,000 and an etching of a tightrope walker by Paul Klee), Thomas Howkins, McIntosh, and Sprague. These recipients were old friends of Merrill's; many were single or homosexual or both and without family to count on for help as they aged.

Besides smaller cash gifts (the list of personal bequests goes on for four pages), Merrill selected art and objects of sentimental value for particular people. To Charles, Jimmy gave the Maxfield Parrish garden scene that had hung in the living room on Water Street and had once belonged to their father; to Doris, Irish crystal and English silver from his New York apartment; to Mark Magowan, a nineteenth-century Neapolitan mosaic, depicting the myth of Aurora; to Paul Merrill, a Larry Rivers self-portrait in ink; and so on.

All of these gifts to individuals were highly personal and expressive.

Even in the case of his ongoing support for Jackson and Hooten, Merrill's gifts were rather modest. He didn't intend to be a magical benefactor; he wanted to be of realistic practical help, and to affirm the bonds that meant most to him.

The rest of his wealth was divided between charities and institutions. $500,000 went to the Ingram Merrill Foundation for a last round of fellowships. Large cash gifts were made to the New York Public Library, Metropolitan Opera, Stonington Village Improvement Association, Stonington Community Center, and Southeastern Connecticut AIDS Project. The rest of the estate, involving millions of dollars, was split according to percentage formulas among (in declining order) the American Academy of Arts and Letters and Washington University in St. Louis, Amherst College and Lawrenceville School, Yale and the Union of Concerned Scientists, and the Hospice of the Florida Keys.*

And what of Merrill's houses? He had already donated the house in Athens to the American School of Classical Studies at Athens. John Camp, director of the Agora Excavations, would use it as home base in Greece, as he had since Jimmy and David left the country.

702 Elizabeth Street had always been David's property. With his death, ownership was transferred to John Balderson and Rolando Rodriguez. They sold the house for more than a million dollars in 2004 to a young man who was moving from San Francisco to Key West for a job as the manager of the local Borders. (He had challenges ahead: the collapse of the Florida real estate market, a direct-hit hurricane, and Chapter 11 for Borders.)

Mis' Annie's apartment on East Seventy-second Street, where Jimmy had spent so much of the past ten years, was given to Robin, along with its contents. By the terms of the will, Peter was granted use of it for a year and a half, after which Robin sold it.

The contents of Jimmy's apartment at 107 Water Street were given to McClatchy, though the books were to be divided among Sandy, Stephen Yenser, and Robin. Otherwise ownership of the whole building, with its apartments, Doug's Barber Shop, and two stores, was transferred to the Stonington Village Improvement Association. The gift came with insuf-

---

* After David Jackson's death, the trusts that JM had created in his name were dissolved and the remaining funds were paid to these beneficiaries, according to the percentages in JM's will. It was determined that one of these trusts had paid Jackson $330,000 in excess of what was owed him, and legal counsel sued on behalf of the beneficiaries for that money—which could only come out of the pocket of the trustees themselves. Amherst and Yale eventually dropped their claims, but the other parties persisted. Maurer and Merrill Magowan had authorized the overpayment to cover Jackson's medical bills, since Jackson had no health insurance. "In my firm opinion, we did exactly as Jimmy would have wanted," Magowan comments. Merrill Magowan to the author, email, March 8, 2014.

ficient money for upkeep, let alone renovation, and no instructions for the future use of the property, apart from the stipulation that Ray Izbicki be allowed to remain in his second-floor apartment rent free for the rest of his days, and even to collect rent on the other apartments if he wished.

What to do with the "old eyesore" was a problem for the local volunteer organization. Over time a plan emerged to leave Merrill's apartment untouched as much as possible, and to make it available for writers and scholars to live and work there. A writer-in-residence program took shape, a lecture and reading series was established, the apartment was opened to visitors, and the deck again hummed with parties. Twenty years after Merrill's death, there have been more than thirty writers in residence, the apartment has become a lived-in museum, and 107 Water Street is listed on the National Registry of Historic Places.

JM's felt-tip instructions to houseguests remain on a message board in the kitchen, a pen dangling from the string where he left it. But the writing is smudged and won't last much longer.

His writing. Merrill's will placed his copyright in the hands of Washington University in St. Louis and named McClatchy and Yenser co-executors of his literary estate. Stephen, Sandy, and the librarians at Wash U would be in charge of the future of his work.

What would he have gone on to write had he lived (as he very well might have) for another twenty years? It's impossible to imagine, because he so took control of his death in his final book of poetry, as if it were he himself who was putting a period on his career and claiming the last word. If he didn't live as long as he might have, he lived long enough to read proof for *A Scattering of Salts*, a volume, dedicated to Yenser, that he crafted as a tombeau, a verse monument with his name on it. The book is divided into three sections, the first two introduced by "A Downward Look" and "A Look Askance," while "An Upward Look" is the last poem in the book. (How like Merrill to choose to end that way, looking up.) This was as clearly his final book as *First Poems* had been his first.

With a somber, wistful cover by Dorothea Tanning, the hardcover volume, like a Ouija message, arrived in bookstores timed for a birthday its author never reached. "Before his untimely death," read an insert printed by Knopf for the long list of friends receiving copies, "James Merrill requested that a copy of *A Scattering of Salts*, now his last book, be sent to you with his compliments."

How often do even mighty poets end up diminished, silent, or on autopilot! But Merrill (like the late Yeats and Stevens) finishes with the electric current switched on and all the juice flowing. So various are the poems it collects, the book feels like a showcase of every kind of poem he could write, as well as new kinds he was just learning to.

Merrill liked to think he could take on and transform almost any topic. He does so here by writing about AIDS, the Scottish Highlands, screaming city ambulances, his computer crash, Empedocles, the silicate minerals called Pyroxenes, and a Tyvek windbreaker. He proves again what was clear in *Sandover*: that he could use any sort of idiom or verbal register, and make it twitch or shimmer. Like its range of diction and subjects, the book's modes and manners are vigorously impure. Slapstick and grief, wicked irony and honest sentiment—these and other seeming opposites merge and mingle. The book gathers up the whole range of his style and vision.

It gathers up also a whole life. Charlie is there in "My Father's Irish Setters," Hellen in "Pearl," Mis' Annie in "164 East 72nd Street." David, Ephraim, and Greece appear in "Nine Lives," one of his most virtuosic and moving poems, not quite like anything anyone else has ever written. And Greece again—and Alexandria—in "Tony: Ending the Life." His devotion to Bishop is the theme of "Overdue Pilgrimage to Nova Scotia." "The *Ring* Cycle" summarizes the lessons of fifty years seated at the Met. *A Scattering of Salts* is also first and last a book about his life with Peter—about romance, domesticity, volcanic anger, confusion, and suffering; also, about a dream of rescue from the mortal danger that at times was all around him. For particulars, see "Radio," "Morning Exercise," "Cosmo," "Family Week at Oracle Ranch," and "Rescue."

Like all his work, the book demonstrates a fundamental fascination with and joy in language. Also, a faith in words as a supreme medium of individual expression and a source of collective wisdom, both. To command them, which is to be ready and able to respond to *their* commands, hints, and promptings, is a high calling. This idealization, furthermore, is in no way naive. Language, Merrill's poetry knows, is suffused with human history, and our words are just as material, if not quite so vulnerable, as our bodies.

The latter idea is the theme of the shortest, but also one of the most moving, poems in the book. The title is—not the word, but the letters that make up the word—"b o d y."

> Look closely at the letters. Can you see,
> entering (stage right), then floating full,
> then heading off—so soon—
> how like a little kohl-rimmed moon
> *o* plots her course from *b* to *d*

       —as *y*, unanswered, knocks at the stage door?
       Looked at too long, words fail,
       phase out. Ask, now that *body* shines
       no longer, by what light you learn these lines
       and what the *b* and *d* stood for.

Reversing the magic of the Ouija board here, Merrill takes a word apart letter by letter to see what he can make of it. He points out that, at the center of the word *body*, is the vowel *o*. It rolls through *b* and *d*, from birth to death, as quickly as the moon crosses the evening sky. Those two consonants, *b* and *d*, mirrors facing each other, together create a stage, the space in which *o*'s brief performance takes place. Just so, the soul animates the body for a time.

"Why?"—that nagging *y* knocks offstage. It seems to be asking, What on earth was it all about? What does the will to write poetry, to cry "O!" like all the poets of the past, amount to? What did the soul have to say? At the end of the line, the quest for meaning (exemplified in a little poem like this, or in the grand designs of a life devoted to poetry) loses meaning. Words, like the body, "phase out." They last only so long as the light that we need to read them. That truth leaves us with an enigma, with the question of "what the *b* and *d* stood for." It's a question we all need to ask, and the subject of every biography.

ACKNOWLEDGMENTS

I couldn't have written this book without the close collaboration of James Merrill's literary executors, J. D. McClatchy and Stephen Yenser. Sandy's belief in the importance of the story and his confidence in this first-time biographer were sustaining at every step, over fourteen years. Stephen's intellect and kindness set high bars. And this is to say nothing of the practical assistance they tirelessly supplied, or, more important yet, the room they gave me to reach my own conclusions.

It's a sign of the esteem he inspired that so many of Merrill's friends and family were ready to contribute to this book. Peter Hooten invited me into his home, introduced me to Cosmo, and, over many years, generously shared memories and reflections as well as photos and documents, including Merrill's letters to him. Robin Magowan offered insights into his uncle's life and work and his family history in dozens of letters and conversations; with Robin, I toured Southampton and studied family photos in the archives at Yale and Amherst. Charles Merrill spoke to me candidly about his brother, his father, and his childhood, and put more of his memories into letters to me. Claude Fredericks hosted me in Pawlet with his special warmth and graciousness; with his partner Marc Harrington, he copied and annotated hundreds of pages from his diary and his forty-five-year correspondence with Merrill. In letters and conversation, Frederick Buechner told me about his friendships with Merrill and Hellen Plummer, took me on a tour of the Lawrenceville campus, and introduced me to members of the Class of 1943 at their sixtieth reunion. From Sewelly Jackson, who gave me a grocery bag full of letters and photos, I learned about David Jackson's early life, his family, and her long friendship with Jimmy and David. David McIntosh was a revelatory guide to New Mexico—and to sides of Merrill that few people ever saw. Donald Richie was a charming, clear-eyed, always quotable authority on Jimmy's Japan and much more. Alfred Corn, who first introduced me to Merrill's poetry, offered shrewd perspectives on the poet and his friends. Judith Moffett was an encouraging reader who shared rich memories and reflections with me. John Hollander was devoted to James Merrill and his poetry; I wish he had lived long enough to read this book. George Lazaretos, Nelly Liambey, Strato and Vaso Mouflouzélis, and Vassili Vassilikos returned with me to Athens in the 1960s and 1970s; and I couldn't have had my marvelous conversations with them without Maria Walker, my Greek translator.

For additional interviews and correspondence, I'm grateful to: Alan Ansen, John Ashbery and David Kermani, Norman Austin, Christine Ayoub and Josiane Boulad-Ayoub, John Balderson and Rolando Rodriguez, John Berendt, Frank Bidart, Torren Blair, Marie-Claire Blais, Mary Bomba, Robert Brustein, William Burford, Virgil Burnett, John Camp, Natalie Charkow, Ross Claiborne, Henri Cole, Joseph Crowley, Daria D'Arienzo, Joan Darling, Benjamin DeMott, Dr. Thomas Detre, Dimitri Diamantipolous, Rosemary Donnelly, Alistair Elliott, C. Peter Forcey, Steven and Kae Geller, Walker and Nancy Gibson, Peter Gillis, Robert Giroux, Dr. Benjamin (Bud) Gordon, Robert Grimes, Maxine Groffsky, Thom Gunn, Allan Gurganus, Rachel Hadas, Dr. Jack Hagstrum, Luly Hamlin, Stratis Haviaras, Huyler Held, Daryl Hine, Richard Howard, Jack Howkins, Inez Ingle, David Jackson, Linda James, Matthew Jennett, Ferne Kalstone, V. A. Kolve and Larry Luchtel, Nina and Dimitri Koutsadakis, Marilyn and Irving Lavin, Paul Leahy, Liz Lear, John Leatham, Samuel Lock, Albert Palmer Loenig, Alison Lurie, Mark Magowan, Merrill Magowan, Peter Magowan, Kathe Marshall, Hunter Martin, Harry Mathews, Dr. Braxton McKee, Amy Merrill, Bruce Merrill, Catherine Merrill, Paul Merrill, W. S. Merwin, Richard Meryman, Alice Methfessel, Diane Middlebrook, Regan Morse, Orson Munn, Stephen Orgel, Harry Pemberton, Eleanor Perényi, Robert Pounder, Pierre Riches, Steven Rydman, Laurence Scott, Charles Shoup, Andrew Silverman, Rosemary Sprague, Rowlie Stebbins, Jerl Surratt, Mona Van Duyn and Jarvis Thurston, Haris Vavlianos, Helen Vendler, Theodore Weiss, Edmund White, Richard and Charlee Wilbur, Chauncey Williams, Robert W. Wilson, Kenneth Work, and John Zervos.

For reading the whole book and responding with small and large suggestions, I'm indebted to James Longenbach, Robin Magowan, Juliet Mattila, J. D. McClatchy, Jeff Nunokawa, Robert Polito, Karin Roffman, Helen Vendler, and Stephen Yenser. Many debts are recognized in the Notes. In addition, I'm grateful to the following people who helped me think through the project's challenges, shared their knowledge of one or more of the topics it touches on, and otherwise aided and abetted my work: Mark Bauer, Susan Bianconi, Kenneth Bleeth, Leslie Brisman, David Bromwich, Lynn and Jeff

Callahan, Jill Campbell, Claire Class, Peter Cole, my agent Robert Corn-
field, Bonnie Costello, Christina Davis, Richard Deming, Inger Elliott,
William Flesch, Marina Frangos, Paul Fry, Jonathan Galassi, Janet Gezari,
Roger Gilbert, Louise Glück, Joseph Gordon, Kenneth Gross, John Guil-
lory, Piotr Gwiazda, Hala Halim, Jeffrey Harrison, Charles Hartman,
Koen Hilberdink, Adina Hoffman, Cecelia Holland, Susan Howe, Amy
Hungerford, Benjamin Ivry, Kamran Javadizadeh, Nicholas Jenkins,
Edward Kamens, Nathan Kernan, Karl Kirchwey, Penelope Laurans, David
Lehman, Anastasia Logotheti, Joseph Lowenstein, Sibby Lynch, Sophia
Macris, Lawrence Manley, Timothy Materer, Richard Maxwell, Susan
McCabe, Edward Mendelson, Steven Meyer, Chuck O'Boyle, Siobhan Phil-
lips, Vivian Pollak, William Pritchard, Spencer Reese, Marc Robinson,
Sam See, Emily Setina, Daniel Shea, Donald Sheehan, Michael Snedicker,
David Sofield, Willard Spiegelman, Justin Spring, George Syrimis, Lucia
Vincioni, Michael Warner, Aidan Wasley, Ruth Yeazell, and Cynthia Zarin.
I've learned from and been energized by the students who've studied Mer-
rill with me at Yale. Let a talented and merry seminar from 2012—Erica
Kao, Eli Mandel, and Max Ritvo, in particular—stand for more.

Yearlong fellowships from the Guggenheim Foundation and the Leon
Levy Center for Biography at the Graduate Center of the City University
of New York gave me time away from teaching during which much of this
biography was written. At the Levy Center, I appreciated the camaraderie-
in-biography provided by the center's director Gary Giddins, his colleagues
Michael Gately and John Matthews, and my fellow fellows. My work also
benefited from stimulating periods as a resident fellow at the Bogliasco
Foundation in Genoa and at the James Merrill House in Stonington—where
Lynn Callahan, Sally Wood, and the rest of the Merrill House Committee
have done so much to further Merrill's legacy in a spirit he would approve.
For essential research support, I'm grateful to the Hellen Plummer Foundation, and to LGBT Studies at Yale, the Magowan Family Foundation, the
Stavros Niarchos Foundation and Hellenic Studies at Yale, the Rosenkranz
Foundation, and Yale's Office of the Provost. I've been fortunate to work
with superb research assistants. How could I have gotten this biography
going without Rachel Slaughter in St. Louis, or wound it up years later without Justin Sider in New Haven?

This book is built out of the Merrill Papers in Olin Library of Washington University in St. Louis, where my work was supported by a skilled and
generous research staff, including the late John Hodge, Joel Minor, and
Sarah Schnuriger, and by the library's director, Jeffrey Trzeciak. Over the
past decade, the James Merrill Papers in the Yale Collection of American

Literature at Beinecke Library has grown into a major collection under the stewardship of Nancy Kuhl and Timothy Young, who have been good friends to me and to this project. For their help in the early stages of my work, I am grateful to Daria D'Arienzo, former curator of Special Collections, Robert Frost Library, Amherst College, and Matthew Jennett, former curator of Special Collections, Rare Books and Archives, the American College of Greece. I've made use of letters and other materials in the following locations: Berg Collection, New York Public Library; University of Delaware Library; Danowski Poetry Library, Emory University; Firestone Library, Princeton University; Getty Research Center, Los Angeles; Houghton Library, Harvard University; Alfred A. Knopf, files; Lilly Library, Indiana University; Mandeville Special Collections, University of California San Diego; Morgan Library, New York City; Poetry Center Archives, 92nd St. YMHA; Ransom Center, University of Texas at Austin; Schlesinger Library, Harvard-Radcliffe Institute for Advanced Study; Archives and Special Collections, Vassar College; University of Waterloo Library; Wheaton College Archives; and Woodberry Poetry Room, Harvard University. I also quote from letters by James Merrill that were contributed by the following individuals or their estates, most of which were collected by J. D. McClatchy and Stephen Yenser: André Aciman; Don Adams; Agha Shahid Ali; Norman Austin; Stanislaw Baranczak; Torren Blair; Billie Boatwright; Roger Bourland; George Bradley; Henri Cole; Douglas Crase; John Fandel; Louis Fitzhugh; C. Peter Forcey; Carolyn Grassi; Allan Gurganus; Rachel Hadas; Barbara Hersey; Peter Hooten; Richard Howard; Barbara Howes; Barbara Kassel; Rudy Kikel; Marilyn Lavin; Paul Lawson; Terry Layman; Robin Magowan; Peter Moore; Clara Claiborne Park; Eleanor Perényi; Craig Poile; Robert Pounder; Elise Sanguinetti; Andrew Silverman; Henry Sloss; David Tacium; Dorothea Tanning; Peter Taylor; Helen Vendler; Brian Walker; and Craig Wright.

Quotations from James Merrill's unpublished writing are copyright © the Literary Estate of James Merrill at Washington University in St. Louis and appear by permission of Olin Library, Washington University in St. Louis, and J. D. McClatchy and Stephen Yenser.

Parts of this book appeared in preliminary form in *Literary Imagination, Parnassus, Poetica* (Tokyo), *Raritan,* and *The Wallace Stevens Journal. Masks of the Poet: James Merrill and Kimon Friar,* an essay and exhibition catalog, was published by the American College of Greece, Athens, in 2003. I'm grateful to the editors who sponsored these trial publications.

Deborah Garrison, my editor at Knopf, read every page of this manuscript with an ear for nuance and phrasing, an eye for tone, pace, and themes, and just the right amount of red pen. I can't imagine an editor with better judgment or more patience. I am very grateful to her and to the whole team at Knopf, including her assistant Ann Eggers, my crackerjack production editor Kevin Bourke, the gifted page designer Maggie Hinders, and Chip Kidd, who cheered me along the way, then created a brilliant jacket design, capturing the spirit of this biography.

Last, let me mention my family. Forrester Hammer, my son, accompanied me on far-flung research trips, practiced a Schubert Impromptu on James Merrill's Steinway, and talked over much of this book as I wrote it. My son Julian Hammer may one day open it and see what his father was busy with when he was new in the world and discovering his first books.

It's hard to put into words the essential contribution of my wife, Uta Gosmann. Time and again, she deepened my understanding of James Merrill's life, while making sure that I not only thought hard about my own, but lived it fully. Books, like lives, are made day by day. How fortunate I am to share mine with her.

NOTES

The notes that follow indicate sources for facts and quotations, and occasionally make brief further comments. A select bibliography and copies of archival materials, as well as links to other online resources, are available on the website accompanying this book, jamesmerrillweb.com.

The format for the notes is simple. Page numbers and the first phrase from a paragraph introduce source material for that paragraph. Each reference is preceded by the first phrase from the sentence to which it is keyed.

In the interest of concision, I've eliminated all page references to James Merrill's shorter published poems when the title of the poem quoted is mentioned in the text: these quotations, all coming from JM's *Collected Poems,* edited by J. D. McClatchy and Stephen Yenser and published by Knopf (2001), will be easy for readers to locate. Pages are given in the notes for quotations from *The Changing Light at Sandover* and from Merrill's novels and plays. The sources for JM's published work are the volumes edited by McClatchy and Yenser and published by Knopf (see the abbreviations below).

I've also eliminated references to my interviews with James Merrill's friends and family when the source of the quotation is stated in or can be inferred clearly from the text. A list of the interviews I conducted can be found in the Acknowledgments. Also in the Acknowledgments is a list of the libraries and individuals who supplied letters I refer to and quote from.

All unpublished sources are indicated in the notes, with abbreviations for certain specific collections given below. The first time a published source is cited, I give complete publication information. I then use a short form title for references to that source, with the exception of a few frequently cited titles listed below.

The following abbreviations appear in the notes.

ABI	Annie Beloved Ingram
AC	Alfred Corn
ADP	James Merrill, *A Different Person* in *Collected Prose*, eds. J. D. McClatchy and Stephen Yenser (Knopf, 2004)
AL	Alison Lurie
Amh	Archives and Special Collections, Robert Frost Library, Amherst College
CEM	Charles Edward Merrill
CF	Claude Fredericks
CM	Charles Merrill (Jr.)
CNP	James Merrill, *Collected Novels and Plays*, eds. J. D. McClatchy and Stephen Yenser (Knopf, 2002)
CP	James Merrill, *Collected Poems*, eds. J. D. McClatchy and Stephen Yenser (Knopf, 2001)
DH	Daryl Hine
DJ	David Jackson
DK	David Kalstone
DMc	David McIntosh
DR	Donald Richie
EB	Elizabeth Bishop
ESP	Eleanor Stone Perényi
FB	Frederick Buechner
FP and GM	Frank Peschka and Gordon Murdock
Getty	Getty Research Center
HF	Harry Ford
HIM	Hellen Ingram Merrill
HIP	Hellen Ingram Plummer
Houghton	Houghton Library, Harvard University
IB	Irma Brandeis
JDM	J. D. McClatchy
JH	John Hollander
JM	James Ingram Merrill
Jnl	James Merrill's notebooks and diaries, referred to by number in the Merrill Papers, Special Collections, Olin Library, Washington University in St. Louis
KF	Kimon Friar
LAT	*Los Angeles Times*
Memoirs	Robin Magowan, *Memoirs of a Minotaur: From Merrill Lynch to Patty Hearst to Poetry* (Story Line Press, 1999)
MLA	Mary Lou Aswell
Moffett	Judith Moffett
MV	Mimi Vassilikos
NL	Nelly Liambey
NYPL	Berg Collection, New York Public Library
NYT	*New York Times*
PH	Peter Hooten
Prose	James Merrill, *Collected Prose*, eds. J. D. McClatchy and Stephen Yenser (Knopf, 2004)
Radcliffe	Schlesinger Library, Harvard-Radcliffe Institute for Advanced Study
Ransom	Harry Ransom Research Center, University of Texas at Austin
RM	Robin Magowan
Sandover	James Merrill, *The Changing Light at Sandover*, eds. J. D. McClatchy and Stephen Yenser (Knopf, 2006)
SM	Strato Mouflouzélis

SY   Stephen Yenser
TP   Tony Parigory
Vassar   Archives and Special Collections, Vassar College
VM   Vaso Mouflouzélis
VV   Vassilis Vassilikos
Waterloo University of Waterloo Library
Wheaton   Wheaton College Archives
WM   William Meredith
WUSTL   Special Collections, Rare Books and Manuscripts, Olin Library, Washington University in St. Louis
Yale   James Merrill Papers, Yale Collection of American Literature, Beinecke Rare Book and Manuscript Library, Yale University

FOREWORD

ix **"I merely"** "*I* merely": Edmund White to the author, email, February 8, 2014.
Typical of "Poetry made me": Quoted by SY, " 'But where is home?': A Motif in James Merrill's Poems," unpub. paper, AWP (Association of Writers and Writing Programs) conference (2013).

x **Right and even** " 'Society will not' ": JM, *ADP*, 531.

xi **It was a condition** "In the late 1950s": JM to DK, letter, January 22, 1976 (WUSTL).

xii **In the 1970s** "Now they began": JM, *Sandover*, 113.

xiii **Merrill had been** "A reviewer": Caroline Fraser, "The Magician," *LAT* (March 4, 2001).

xiv **Then there is** " 'Speakers' should": JM, "Voices from the Other World," *CP*, 112.

xv **This book approaches** "He activated": JM, *Sandover*, 3.

xvi **Doubleness is** "I've tried": JM, "To a Butterfly," *CP*, 161. "On another level": JM, *Sandover*, 492.

xvii **In "At a Texas"** "In 'At a Texas' ": JM, "At a Texas Wishing Well," *CP*, 748.
Just how much "He depended" and "At that time": Merrill Magowan to the author, email, March 9, 2014.
He displayed " 'Now see' ": Author's interview with Robert Pounder (2013). " 'Where is the money' ": Merrill Magowan to the author, email, March 9, 2014.

xviii **Besides a joke** "Once he dreamed": JM, *ADP*, 556.
But that image "In a draft page": JM, worksheet for *ADP* (WUSTL).
In his sixties "Then, on their way": JM, *ADP*, 170.

xx **In 1990** " 'The deepest nastiness' ": JM, journal, January 1990, Jnl 23 (WUSTL).

xxii **Take James Ingram** "It was a good thing": HIP to JDM, letter, April 19, 1982 (Yale). "Alice B. Toklas": JM, *ADP*, 521. "In his previous": JM, *Sandover*, 11.

1 THE BROKEN HOME

3 **Light strikes** "Light strikes": Photo of JM and CEM, 1929 (RM).
The photo "Charlie had the insight": Edwin J. Perkins, *Wall Street to Main Street: Charles Merrill and Middle-Class Investors* (Cambridge University Press, 1999), 2; and Elizabeth M. Fowler, "Personality: 'We, the People's Boss' Now 70," *NYT* (May 20, 1956), 173. "He put his own money": "Safeway Stock Out Tomorrow," *LAT* (November 14, 1926), 17. "He closed the deal": RM, *Memoirs*, 29. "By 1932": Perkins, 118.

4 **It wasn't** "He insisted": Perkins, 10. "After college": Perkins, 50. "When he read books": Author's interview with CM (2001). "At thirty-one": HIP, "An Old Wives' Tale" [1953], *Hellen's Book* (Magowan Family Foundation, 1991), 35.
It had been "A short man": RM, *Memoirs*, 27. "When, on one": Author's interview with Richard Wilbur (2012). "In other photos": JM, childhood photo album (Yale).

5 **Charles Edward Merrill** "Charles Edward Merrill": Perkins, 14. "He was the first child": Merrill Family Genealogy (RM). "In the 1880s": CM, "Rejoinder to an Old Wives' Tale," *Hellen's Book*, 45.

"Economic conditions" "Economic conditions": CEM to CM, letter, January 11, 1940 (Amh). "Charlie pointed": RM, *Memoirs*, 24.

Charlie recounts "Attempting to impress": CEM to CM, letter, January 11, 1940 (Amh).

6 **Mary's death** "They moved to Knoxville": Perkins, 27–29. "Although the Merrills' ": Perkins, 30–31. "Then, in 1902": Perkins, 32. "He opened": Perkins, 32–33; and Mark Magowan to the author, email, February 18, 2013.

Charlie's future "From there he progressed": Perkins, 35.

Dr. Merrill's family "His parents": Perkins, 18. "He'd met Octavia": Perkins, 21. "Their fathers had fought": Author's interviews with CM and RM (2001). "Octavia's father": Perkins, 22; Perkins, 25; CEM to Alistair Elliot, letter, April 9, 1951 (Amh). "Feeling he was destined": Perkins, 48.

7 **His two years** "He arrived on campus": CEM to Alistair Elliott, letter, December 27, 1951 (Amh). "For Octavia hovered": Author's interview with CM (2001).

He quickly " 'I never studied' ": CEM to CM, letter, September 28, 1937 (Amh). "In Chi Psi": Perkins, 43. "He ingratiated himself": Perkins, 43.

8 **He was off** "Business was less": Perkins, 52. "He opened his own office": Perkins, 66, 53, 67. "Pinching pennies": HIP, "An Old Wives' Tale," 20. "Merrill, Lynch": Perkins, 56–57.

These techniques "Working . . . to reestablish": Perkins, 12–13; Fowler, "Personality." "He was 'We the People's' ": Fowler, "Personality."

9 **Preoccupied in** "Before Safeway": Perkins, 73–77. "He and Lynch went into": Perkins, 99; author's interview with CM (2001). "Bent on making money": After Charles Morton Merrill's death in 1929, Charlie made the first of several major gifts to Amherst by donating $100,000 in his father's name to fund student financial aid. See *American Families: Genealogical and Biographical* (American Historical Co., c. 1937), 52 (WUSTL). " 'I am, he said' ": CEM to CM, letter, September 28, 1937 (Amh).

10 **But in fact** "Charlie could have used": *Collected Poems and Prose of Wallace Stevens* (Library of America, 1997), 905.

11 **At eighty-nine** "At eighty-nine": JM, diary, December 24, 1987, Jnl 24 (WUSTL).

The fact is "[O]f course she's here": JM, *Sandover*, 84.

12 **It's not clear** "At sixty": JM, diary, November 22, 1986, Jnl 17.

His mother is "Looking at Mummy": JM, "Looking at Mummy," October 29, 1932 (WUSTL).

14 **This woman so admired** "James Ingram": *American Families: Genealogical and Biographical* (New York: American Historical Co., nd; WUSTL). "The Ingrams": author's interview with PH (2011).

Hellen was named "Hellen was named": "Mrs. Willmot was held": Peggy D. Bradford, "Portraits Extraordinaire," *Ponte Vedra Recorder* (November 10, 1972), 8. "Genealogical papers": HIP's scrapbook (WUSTL).

15 **Her parents doted** "Recognized as": Frontispiece, *Hellen's Book*. "A popular teenager": Certificate, HIP's scrapbook (WUSTL). "She attended": Bradford, "Portraits," 8.

Directly after "Directly after": Bradford, "Portraits," 8.

16 **Hellen and Charlie** "Hellen and Charlie": Author's interview with RM (2004). "Over that fall": Perkins, 91. "And Charlie knew": Author's interview with RM (2004); and Perkins, 47–48.

As a society "An adopted aunt": HIP, "An Old Wives' Tale," 37.

With her Cupid's "It appealed to Charlie": Author's interview with CM (2001). "Hellen spoke of": JM, *ADP*, 596.

17 **Pressed by her suitor** "It was a small gathering": "C. E. Merrill Marries," *NYT* (February 21, 1925), 11. "For a honeymoon": "Charles E. Merrill Sails for Europe," *NYT* (March 28, 1925), 21.

17 **The *Silhouette* published** "The *Silhouette* published": Bradford, "Portraits," 8. "They hired a butler": Perkins, 92.

James Ingram Merrill "James Ingram Merrill": JM was born at York House, 119 East Seventy-fourth Street. HIP to JDM, letter, June 21, 1982 (Yale). "Charlie, Mis' Annie": HIP to JDM, letter, June 6, 1982 (Yale).

18 **Dr. Hildreth** "Dr. Hildreth": HIP to JDM, letter, April 19, 1982 (Yale). "Jimmy came": Doris Merrill Magowan, diary, March 26, 1926 (Amh). "His weight": JM's baby book (WUSTL).

In *A Different Person* "In *A Different Person*": JM, *ADP*, 585. "His first nurse": HIP to JDM, letter, June 6, 1982 (Yale).

CEM had little "During the week": HIP, "An Old Wives' Tale," 20–21. "The new company's stock": "Safeway Stock Out Tomorrow," *LAT* (November 14, 1926), 17.

19 **He was also** "He bought the property": "News of Southampton Cottage Colony," *Southampton Press* (October 28, 1926), 8. "It was characteristic": HIP, "An Old Wives' Tale," 18. "He used an entity": Indenture, signed December 15, 1926 (Suffolk County Clerk, Riverhead, NY). "He must have written": Indenture, December 29, 1934 (Suffolk County Clerk, Riverhead, NY).

Situated on "The idea of owning": Author's interview with RM (2004). "In 1907": Timothy Breese Miller, http://jameslbreese.blogspot.com/2009/02/ (2013).

The grace " 'One might not have' ": John A. Dade, "Long Island Country Places, Designed by McKim, Mead & White: II. 'The Orchard' at Southampton," *House & Garden* 3 (March 1903): 117. "Inside were more": Robert B. Mackay, Anthony Baker, and Carol Traynor, ed., *Long Island Country Houses and Their Architects, 1860–1940* (New York, 1997), 291–92.

20 **If the exterior** "The music room": RM, *Memoirs*, 29. " 'Stanford White' ": JM, "Interview with J. D. McClatchy," *Prose*, 116. "Breese had added": Author's interview with CM (2001). "Trellised walkways": Dade, "Long Island Country Places," 120. "In charge": Author's interview with CM (2001).

On the first page "On the first page": JM's childhood photo album (Yale).

21 **It was also** "He was also a powerful Republican": Richard Sanders, "Dr. Samuel Harden Church," http://coat.ncf.ca/our_magazine/links/53/church.html (2013).

But they were "Eliza, whose mother": Author's interview with CM (2001). "When Doris saw": RM, *Memoirs*, 53.

Jimmy met Eliza "Jimmy met Eliza": Author's interview with RM (2004). "She moved every few years": Author's interview with CM (2001); Mark Magowan to the author, email, February 18, 2013.

22 **Charles remembers** "I had never": CM, "Preface: The Card Player," *Hellen's Book*, 7. "He went home": Author's interview with CM (2001).

Doris might "Hellen had already": Doris Merrill, diary, "Thanksgiving," 1927 (Amh). "Hellen wrote to Doris": HIM to Doris Merrill, letter, February 1926 (Amh); see Doris Merrill, diary (Amh). "She was big enough": Doris Merrill, diary, March 6, 1926 (Amh).

23 **Doris and Charles** "The two of them": Doris Merrill, diary (Amh); author's interview with CM (2001). "The *Southampton Press*": The Merrills first appear in the annual *Southampton Press* "Cottage List" in 1927 and continue to be listed until 1937. "By New Year's": Doris Merrill, diary, 1927/1928 (Amh).

While a new "While a new": CEM to Samuel Merrill, letter, January 24, 1927 (Amh). "Records traced": Merrill genealogy (RM); RM, *Memoirs*, 22–23. "The name was": Samuel Merrill, "A Merrill Memorial" (Amh). "On the basis": CEM, Application for Membership in the Society of the Sons of the American Revolution, 1933 (Amh). "Hellen joined": Bradford, "Portraits," 8. "The Latin was": Merrill Family Crest, Doris Merrill Magowan Heritage Album (Amh). "Or as Charlie": Author's interview with RM (2012).

There was more "In 1951": JM, *ADP*, 580–81.

24 **The white clothes** "The help": CM to the author, letter, May 19, 2001; Mark Magowan to the author, email, February 18, 2013. "Yet the tactful": Author's interview with CM (2001).

24 **Charlie's and Hellen's** "As a boy": CEM, "Rejoinder to An Old Wives' Tale," 44. "The men who": Perkins, 32. "While he recovered": CM, *The Checkbook*, 6. "The family": Author's interviews with CM (2001) and RM (2012).

25 **Charlie's family** "In the decade": Perkins, 22. "A hunchback": Perkins, 23–24.
   Buying the Orchard "Wildwood": "Noted Plantation Is Sold," *NYT* (October 21, 1927), 41. "The plantation": Perkins, 93–94. "The place so little": HIP, "An Old Wives' Tale," 31. "He sent": Author's interview with CM (2001).

26 **Charlie and Hellen** "Charlie and Hellen": Mark Magowan to the author, email, February 18, 2013. "The house": RM to the author, letter, February 3, 2013.
   Houses "The Merrills": HIP, chronology for JM (WUSTL). "Back in New York": HIP to JDM, letter, April 19, 1982 (Yale).

27 **His early** "He spent": Chronology for JM (WUSTL). "He stayed": HIP to JDM, letter, April 19, 1982 (Yale).
   As that comment "When she took": HIP to JDM, letter, April 19, 1982 (Yale).
   Contributing to "But it was hard": HIP to JDM, letter, June 21, 1982 (Yale).
   Jimmy hardly "Jimmy hardly": Perkins, 104; and HIM to ABI, letter, October 7, 1931 (WUSTL). "Hellen's father's": HIP to JDM, letter, April 19, 1982 (Yale). "The incident": JM, "Words Are Birds," *The Lit: Lawrenceville Literary Magazine* 48, no. 4 (June 1943): 5–8; FB, *The Seasons' Difference* (1952); author's interview with FB (2002). "Jimmy thought": HIP to JDM, letter, April 19, 1982 (Yale).

28 **Octavia** "This modest": HIP to JDM, letter, June 21, 1982 (Yale). "He never stopped": Mark Magowan to the author, email, March 7, 2014. "Small, with": CM to the author, letter, August 3, 2001.
   One of "One of": JM to ABI, letter, March 6, 1933 (WUSTL).

29 **The letter** "Mount Fuji": Author's interview with PH (2010). "As an adult": JM, "James Merrill at Home: An Interview by Ross Labrie," *Prose*, 95.
   Any child "An elegantly": Program for "the Jimmy Merrill Marionettes" (WUSTL). "A crowd": JM, childhood photo album (Yale).
   Zelly " 'I worshipped' ": JM, "Acoustical Chambers," *Prose*, 4.

30 **He puzzled** "She taught": documents from childhood, 1934–37 (WUSTL).
   This early "There were": JM, "Acoustical Chambers," *Prose*, 4–5.

31 **Jimmy's brother** "Jimmy's brother": Author's interview with CM (2001). "That was one": Doris Magowan, "In Appreciation of Hellen," *Hellen's Book*, 52. "Hellen was also": Betty Plummer Potts, quoted in "Hellen Plummer, 102, Connoisseur of the Arts," under "Obituaries," *Atlanta Journal and Constitution* (December 23, 2000), 10D.

32 **Another gift** "For getting": JM, "The Education of the Poet," *Prose*, 10.
   Jimmy also "Two sentences": *Junior Home Magazine* (November 1934), 23. Merrill quoted the poem in an interview and misidentified the publisher as *St. Nicholas Magazine*. JM, "An Interview with J. D. McClatchy," *Prose*, 115.
   The poetry "The poetry": JM, Juvenilia, "Supplementary Reading," 1935 (WUSTL). "These are": RM to the author, letter, February 3, 2013; author's telephone interview with Allan Gurganus (2012); JM, Juvenilia, "Books That Belong in My Library," 1935 (WUSTL); "All his life": RM to the author, letter, February 3, 2013.

33 **As a child** "He obviously": JM's childhood photo album (Yale).

34 **His parents** "In Manhattan": "News of Southampton Summer Colony," *Southampton Press* (November 4, 1926), 8. " 'I know' ": RM, *Memoirs*, 28.
   The Orchard "Charlie preferred": HIP, "An Old Wives' Tale," 29. "A note": "Who's Who," *Hellen's Book*, 8.

35 **Southampton** "Jews": "Thirteen New Members of Southampton Golf Club," *Southampton Press* (June 27, 1928), 1. "Some of these": HIP, "An Old Wives' Tale," 15–16. "She also": Author's interview with PH (2003).
   On summer "In the music": RM, *Memoirs*, 29. "Harry Evans": Author's interviews with CM

(2001) and RM (2012). "One weekend": JM, schoolbooks, November 1936 (WUSTL). "In his landmark": Stephen Gillers, "A Tendency to Deprave and Corrupt: The Transformation of US Obscenity Law from Hicklin to Ulysses II," *Washington University Law Review* 85, no. 2 (2007): 287. Henry Seidel Canby, editor of the *Saturday Review of Literature*, was the other friend Woolsey consulted.

36 **For Jimmy** "For Jimmy": CM to the author, letter, May 19, 2001.

"Dad" " 'Dad' ": Author's interview with CM (2001). "The little boy": HIP to JDM, letter, June 23, 1982 (Yale). "The table talk": CM to the author, letter, May 19, 2001. "Mention of": CM to the author, letter, May 19, 2001.

Or they might " 'Charlie,' Hellen observed": HIP, "An Old Wives' Tale," 24. "Jimmy carried": HIP, "An Old Wives' Tale," 24. "For a while": HIP to JDM, letter, June 23, 1982 (Yale). "His father": CEM, "Rejoinder to an Old Wives' Tale," 46. "Charlie's own": Author's interview with CM (2001).

Sunday lunches "Sunday lunches": RM to the author, letter, February 3, 2013. "The pace": Eric Felten, "St. Louis—Party Central," *Wall Street Journal* (October 6, 2007). "But there was": Mark Magowan to the author, email, February 18, 2013.

37 **Drinking partly** "In his mid-sixties": JM, *ADP*, 586. "The strategy": RM to the author, letter, February 3, 2013.

Doris responded "Charlie and Hellen": JM, "Bronze," *CP*, 459. "From these": HIP, "An Old Wives' Tale," 22. "Over the course": Author's interview with RM (2001).

He was particularly "Her son": RM, *Memoirs*, 53–54.

38 **Doris attended** "Doris attended": RM, *Memoirs*, 54–55.

Robert Magowan "A neighbor": Author's interview with Mark Magowan (2013). "When he didn't": Mark Magowan to the author, email, February 18, 2013. "The man": RM, *Memoirs*, 16–18.

The wedding "The church": Author's interview with Rowlie Stebbins (2008). "Charlie and Hellen": "Miss Doris Merrill Wed to R. A. Magowan in St. Andrew's Dune Church at Southampton," *NYT* (June 16, 1935). " 'What would' ": RM, *Memoirs*, 28. "The poem": JM, "A Ballad," 1935 (WUSTL).

39 **Some marriages** "When he served": Author's interview with Rowlie Stebbins (2008).

Bobby joined "He and Charlie": Mark Magowan to the author, email, February 18, 2013. "Then Charlie": RM, *Memoirs*, 19–20. "Robin, who": RM, *Memoirs*, 20.

40 **At nine** "At nine": JM, "My Autobiography," November 7, 1935, schoolbooks (WUSTL). "He was well stocked": HIP, chronology for JM's childhood (WUSTL). "The sleek dogs": RM to the author, letter, February 3, 2013. "When Mike was": HIP, "An Old Wives' Tale," 40. "The result": Author's interview with RM (2004).

While Zelly "He could": JM, "The Help," *CP*, 418. "They were": JM, *ADP*, 582.

42 **The case** "The case": HIP to JDM, letter, April 19, 1982 (Yale). "For a time": Author's interview with CM (2001).

44 **In "Days of 1935"** "Hellen discovered": Author's interview with RM (2004). "Women friends": HIP, "An Old Wives' Tale," 36. "Charlie was": Author's interview with CM (2001).

There were other "After dinner": HIP, "An Old Wives' Tale," 36. "They played": Author's interview with CM (2001). "When Charlie was": Author's interview with RM (2011).

Doris learned "In one": JM, schoolbooks, 1936 (WUSTL).

46 **After their marriage** "After their marriage": HIM to CEM, draft letter, March 5, 1938 (WUSTL). "For his part": JM to HIP, letter, April 7, 1956 (WUSTL). "During their divorce": HIM to Mr. Daughtry, letter, 1937 (WUSTL).

They were "In 1936": RM, *Memoirs*, 29. " 'I really regarded' ": Testimony by Josephine Skraback, Court Transcript, State of New York (WUSTL).

As usual "As always": JM, *ADP*, 540. "He moved": HIM to Doris Merrill Magowan, letter, June 20, 1937 (Amh).

46 **Hellen summoned** " 'Oh, don't' ": JM, *ADP*, 551.
Of course " 'Your father' ": HIM to Doris Merrill Magowan, letter, June 20, 1937 (Amh). " 'Dear Jim' ": CEM to JM, letter, July 2, 1937 (Amh). "Charlie later": CEM to JM, letter, July 2, 1937 (Amh).

48 **That same summer** "Although he": JM, *ADP*, 550–51.
Jimmy had "A Floridian": JM, *ADP*, 550. "She was": "Carol Perrenot Longone, 94; The Founder of Operalogues," *NYT* (January 16, 1987). " 'Mrs. Longone' ": Julian Seaman, "Carol Longone Will Give One of Her 'Operalogues,' " *Toledo Blade* (May 23, 1956), 20. "After the death": HIP to JDM, letter, 1982 (Yale).

49 **When the fall** "Looking back": JM, *ADP*, 551.
With Carol "According to": Review of *Die Walküre* performed at the Metropolitan Opera January 21, 1938, by Lawrence Gilman, *Herald Tribune*, http://archives.metoperafamily.org/ (2013). "In *A Different Person*": JM, *ADP*, 551.

50 **As that remark** "Next to": JM, *ADP*, 551.
All that year "All that year": HIM to CEM, draft letter, March 1938 (WUSTL). "He wrote": JM to CEM, letter, March 1938 (Amh). "There never was": CEM to JM, excerpted letter, March 2, 1938 (Amh).

51 **While wanting** "While wanting": CEM to Ed Wilson, excerpted letter, March 11, 1938 (Amh). "Whether or not": CEM to CM, excerpted letter, July 19, 1938 (Amh).

52 **Behind Charlie's** "In fall 1937": HIM, "Articles Moved from The Orchard," fall 1937 (WUSTL). "Next, she": "Mrs. Merrill Sheds Broker; Gets Son, Cash," *The News* (February 23, 1939). Hellen filed for a separation at the start of October 1937 according to CEM to Stanton Griffis, letter, October 9, 1937 (Amh). "Charlie responded": "Public Notices," *New York Herald Tribune* (October 9, 1937). "Then, trying": HIM to CEM, draft letter, winter 1938 (WUSTL). "This research": "Mrs. Merrill Sheds Broker; Gets Son, Cash." "Emma would": JM, *ADP*, 582.
In the midst "She replied": HIM to CEM, draft letter, 1938 (WUSTL).

53 **Charlie filed** "Doris quietly": Author's interview with CM (2001). "Helen and Jimmy": "Friendly Divorce Parts Merrills," *Daily Mirror* (February 23, 1939). "In the *New York*": "Who's Who and What's What in Society," *New York Journal and American* (February 26, 1939). "Charlie could": JM to CEM, excerpt from letter, March 1939 (Amh).

54 **Helen emerged** "When she visited": "Mrs. Merrill Guest of Mrs. Livingston," *New York World-Telegram* (July 18, 1938).
In September "Only the next": JM to FP and GM, letter, May 19, 1988 (WUSTL).

2 COSTUMES AND MASKS

55 **Our son** "Our son": HIM to CEM, letter, c. March 1938 (WUSTL). "Jimmy had": CEM to CM, excerpted letter, July 18, 1938 (Amh). "Suddenly called": HIM to CEM, letter, c. March 1938 (WUSTL).
Compared to "The boy's": HIP to JDM, letter, April 19, 1982 (Yale).

56 **It began** "Deerfield": Author's interview with CM (2001).
The education "Most Lawrenceville": See the Lawrenceville yearbook, *Olla Podrida*, 1940–43 (WUSTL). "Rather than": "School History," http://www.lawrenceville.org/about/ history/index.aspx (2013). "Jimmy took": JM, Form I, Class of 1943 report, 1939 (WUSTL). "He kept": JM, journal, March 5, 1940, Jnl 57 (WUSTL). "When he took": Author's interview with FB (2001). "At the end": "Scholarship Up; Sixteen Boys Earn Honors," Lawrenceville *Recorder* 14 (November 22, 1939): 1. "His teacher": February Subject Report 1940, Lawrenceville School (WUSTL).

57 **Residential life** "In his report": W. H. Scott, House Master's Report, Nov. 24, 1939 (WUSTL). "In March 1941": William Reiter, House Master's Report, March 1941 (WUSTL).

57 **The case** "They were each": Author's interview with FB (2003). " 'Rhines' ": Author's interview with Ross Claiborne (2004). "The names": *Olla Podrida* (1943).

58 **"The Lower School"** "The Lower School": Author's interview with C. Peter Forcey (2003). "A boy might": Author's interview with Ross Claiborne (2004).
Rich, shy "His nemesis": Author's interview with C. Peter Forcey (2003). "They said": JM, journal, September 28, 1940, Jnl 57 (WUSTL).

59 **Tony was** "The Harwoods": JM, journal, January 31, 1940, Jnl 57 (WUSTL). "He wore": Author's interview with FB (2002). "Jimmy was not": JM to FB, letter, c. summer 1941 (Wheaton); and JM, journal, March 30, 1945, Jnl 1 (WUSTL). "Most afternoons": JM, journal, April 6, 1940, Jnl 57 (WUSTL). "They played": JM, journal, February 6, 1940, Jnl 57 (WUSTL).
Jimmy's effeminacy "Even as": JM, journal, February 7, 1940, Jnl 57 (WUSTL). "Besides the Met's": JM, journal, April 26, May 25, and June 21, 1940, Jnl 57 (WUSTL). "He was thrilled": JM, journal, September 1, 1940, Jnl 57 (WUSTL). He doesn't mention fetching the ball in his diary; he told FB the possibly embroidered story. "In his diary": JM, journal, January 12 and 23, 1940, Jnl 57 (WUSTL).
These imaginary "After a winter": JM, journal, February 1 and 2, 1940, Jnl 57 (WUSTL).

60 **Though she** "She had": JM, journal, February 2, 1940, Jnl 57 (WUSTL). "For one": Bradford, "Portraits," 9.
If Hellen "His letters": JM to HIM, letter, October 14, 1939 (WUSTL). "He wanted": JM to HIM, letter, October 14, 1939 (WUSTL). "And despite": JM to HIM and ABI, letter, July 7, 1940 (WUSTL).
Hellen was too "They went": JM, journal, June 23, 1940, Jnl 57 (WUSTL). "If only boys": JM, journal, March 22, 1940, Jnl 57 (WUSTL). "On this trip": JM, journal, March 20, 1940, Jnl 57 (WUSTL). "Jimmy posed": JM, childhood photo album (Yale). "The water": JM, journal, March 20, 1940, Jnl 57 (WUSTL).

61 **"Heavenly colors"** "Yet he could": JM, "Acoustical Chambers," *Prose*, 7.
Writing a diary "He wrote": CEM to JM, letter, November 22, 1940 (Amh). "With a future": JM to HIM, letter, January 10, 1940 (WUSTL).

62 **Despite his** "When he did": JM, journal, October 12, 1940, Jnl 57 (WUSTL). "One summer evening": JM, journal, June 26, 1940, Jnl 57 (WUSTL). "After he visited": CEM to Doris Merrill Magowan, letter, March 3, 1940 (Amh).
Jimmy didn't "Jimmy didn't": JM to FB, letter, summer 1941 (Wheaton). "She ordered": Author's interview with CM (2001). "Doris: 'That Kinta' ": RM, *Memoirs*, 31. " 'Why be difficult' ": Author's interview with CM (2001).

63 **Jimmy's long** "Then he was": JM, journal, July 2–August 24, 1940, Jnl 57 (WUSTL). "One photo": Photo of James Merrill as Puck at Camp Duncan, Vermont, summer 1939 (WUSTL).
Back at "He played": JM, journal, December 12, 1940, Jnl 57 (WUSTL). "Dressed in": JM, journal, October 25, 1941, Jnl 57 (WUSTL). "He was so": JM, journal, February 16, 1941, Jnl 57 (WUSTL). "He saw plays": JM, journal, February 20, 1940, Jnl 57 (WUSTL).
His parents "As an adult": Author's interview with FB (2001). Many of his friends remark on Merrill's habit of giving himself shots in later life, when, from his fifties on, he regularly injected himself with vitamins and testosterone.

64 **In his diary** "At camp": JM, journal, September 5, 1940, Jnl 57 (WUSTL). "When Bruce": JM, journal, c. November 1, 1940, Jnl 57 (WUSTL). "Dr. Diehl": JM, journal, February 9, 1941, Jnl 57 (WUSTL). "Another entry": JM, journal, April 11, 1941, Jnl 57 (WUSTL).
Crushes like "Probably this": JM, journal, December 15, 1940, Jnl 57 (WUSTL).
Jimmy's life "Mr. Buechner": FB, *The Sacred Journey* (Harper & Row San Francisco, 1982), 37–41.

65 **Freddy gave** "He made": Author's interview with FB (2001). "The Uglies": FB, *The Eyes of the Heart: A Memoir of the Lost and Found* (Harper San Francisco, 2000), 45. "The Uglies teamed": FB, *Sacred*, 70–71.

65 **And a lively** " 'We were rivals' ": Author's interview with FB (2001). "Stylistically": JM, *ADP*, 467–68.

66 **Soon Jimmy** "His version": JM, *Jim's Book: A Collection of Poems and Short Stories* (New York, 1942), 61. Dated "June, 1942." "The work of these": JM, "The Education of the Poet," *Prose*, 11–13.

Wylie was "Donne, Jimmy": JM, "Angel or Earthly Creature," *Prose*, 435–45. In *Jim's Book*, the essay is dated "June, 1942."

Freddy's major "He recommended": JM, journal, March 2, 1941, Jnl 57 (WUSTL). " 'I'm a bad' ": JM, journal, December 1, 1941, Jnl 57 (WUSTL).

67 **Freddy shared** "In one letter": JM to FB, letter, c. summer 1941 (Wheaton). "For his part": FB to author, letter, August 3, 2001.

68 **Freddy was** "The boys": FB, *Sacred*, 71. " 'Fred + I' ": JM, journal, May 5, 1941, Jnl 57 (WUSTL).

Around the time "Students hoisted": *Olla Podrida* (1940). "Then, in spring": JM, journal, April 10, 1940, Jnl 57 (WUSTL).

The American "When Jimmy": *Olla Podrida* (1941). "When Jimmy": *Olla Podrida* (1943). "During one": Lawrenceville Class of 1943 25th Class Reunion Notes, 1968; author's interview with FB (2001).

69 **But war was** "If they draft": JM to FB, letter, summer 1941 (Wheaton). "Soon after": Author's interview with Ross Claiborne (2003).

The war affected "Charlie was moved": Author's interview with CM (2001). "Jean, Anne": Author's interview with CM (2001); JM, journal, June 1945, Jnl 1 (WUSTL). " 'Mr. Merrill' ": CEM to Jean Elliot, letter, February 7, 1951 (Amh).

Alistair, being "This event": Alistair Elliot to the author, email, June 18, 2004. "Charlie arranged": CEM to Dr. David Fall, letter, March 6, 1945 (Amh). "Looking back": Alistair Elliot to the author, email, June 18, 2004. " 'I really gave' ": CEM to Alistair Elliot, letter, December 27, 1951 (Amh).

70 **Charles's contention** "As a teenager": Author's interview with CM (2001). "In principle": CEM to CM, letter, September 28, 1937 (Amh).

"At Harvard" "At Harvard": Author's interview with CM (2001).

The Christian-Socialist "He blew off": CEM to Doris Magowan, letter, winter 1942 (Amh).

71 **"Charles and I"** "Charles and I": JM, *ADP*, 619.

Then there "For Father": RM, *Memoirs*, 40.

Yet Charlie "That dream": Author's interview with CM (2001).

72 **Photos of** "Photos of": JM, childhood photo album (Yale); photos (WUSTL). "CEM made": Author's interview with CM (2001).

Charles came "Over the years": Bernat Rosner and Frederic C. Tubach, *An Uncommon Friendship: From Opposite Sides of the Holocaust* (University of California Press, 2010); author's interview with Mark Magowan (2013).

73 **Even as** "He would": Author's interview with CM (2001). "Jimmy shared": CEM to CM, letter, November 1, 1940 (Amh).

The book was "Hellen explained": HIM to CEM, letter, December 1942 (Amh); quoted by Jack W. C. Hagstrom and Bill Morgan, *James Ingram Merrill: A Descriptive Bibliography* (Oak Knoll Press, 2009), 2.

Jim's Book "*Jim's Book*": JM, "Acoustical Chambers," *Prose*, 6.

74 **That doesn't** "One sketch": JM, "It Goes to Show," *Jim's Book*, 18–19. "A story": JM, "Madonna," *Jim's Book*, 23–29.

The war "The war": JM, "Ambition's Debt Is Paid," *Jim's Book*, 2–7.

75 **These stories** "The tension": JM, "Mozart," *Jim's Book*, 20.

At Lawrenceville " 'He had a' ": Author's interview with FB (2001). "Sutherland mentions": Donald Sutherland, *On, Romanticism* (New York University Press, 1971), 227.

76 **The Marriage** "This work": JM, *ADP*, 552. "For young Jimmy": JM, *ADP*, 552.

77 **Shortly after** "He praised": W. L. Frederici, "Lit Review," *The Lawrence*, January 15, 1943. "Mr Frederici's": Mary Karr, "Against Decoration," *Parnassus: Poetry in Review* (1991). **"Merrill, in my"** " 'Merrill, in my' ": Frederici, "Lit Review." "The two": JM to FB, letter, January 1943 (Wheaton). "Jimmy waited": HIM to CEM, letter, December 1942; quoted by Hagstrom and Morgan, *Bibliography*, 2. "He presented": JM's inscription in copy of *Jim's Book* given to FB; FB to the author, letter, July 30, 2001.

78 **They had** "Thurber was": Author's interview with FB (2001). "Their senior": JM, "The Lit," *Olla Podrida* (1943).
One of Jimmy's " 'Let us never' ": JM, review of *The Death of the Moth*, and other writings by Virginia Woolf, in *The Lawrence* 63, no. 12 (January 22, 1943): 2. "His new poems": JM, "Nero Dines in the Gardens of the Golden House," *Lawrenceville Literary Magazine* 48, no. 3 (February 1943): 13. "In the process": JM, "Death-Masks," *Lawrenceville Literary Magazine* 48, no. 3 (February 1943): 3–4.

79 **Lawrenceville** "Their starched": FB, "Lawrenceville Fiftieth Reunion" [poem], *The Yellow Leaves: A Miscellany* (Westminster John Knox Press, 2008), 120–23. "In his class's": *Olla Podrida* (1943). "But he came": Author's interview with FB (2003).
During freshman "During freshman": JM's Amherst College Courses (Amh). "The course was": William H. Pritchard, "Amherst English," *Raritan* 16, no. 3 (1997): 143–57. For comments on English at Amherst in the postwar era and further bibliography, see William H. Pritchard, *Playing It by Ear: Literary Essays and Reviews* (University of Massachusetts Press, 1994), and *Shelf Life: Literary Essays and Reviews* (University of Massachusetts Press, 2003), which contains the *Raritan* essay.

80 **The two-term course** "In 1944": JM's Amherst College Courses (Amh). "Craig was": https://www.amherst.edu/aboutamherst/news/news_releases/2002/jan_2002 (2014). "But in 1944": Paul Leahy to the author, letter, December 16, 2001.
Merrill took "Merrill took": JM's Amherst College Courses (Amh). "Brower was": see William H. Pritchard, "Reuben A. Brower," *American Scholar* 54, no. 2 (1985), also in Pritchard, *Shelf Life*.

81 **Brower, like** "Brower, like": Pritchard, "Brower." " 'Literature of the first' ": Reuben A. Brower, "Reading in Slow Motion," in *In Defense of Reading: A Reader's Approach to Literary Criticism*, ed. Reuben A. Brower and Richard Poirier (Dutton, 1962), 6. "But Brower brought": JM, "Interview with Donald Sheehan," *Prose*, 55–56.
Merrill had "Merrill had": Pritchard, "Amherst English." "Asked by an": JM, "Interview with Ross Labrie," *Prose*, 92.
Reading À la " 'The real triumph' ": JM, "Interview with Donald Sheehan," *Prose*, 59. " 'And how is it' ": JM, journal, November 12, 1944, Jnl 1 (WUSTL).

82 **Merrill's obsession** "With Proust": JM to FB, letter, c. April 1944 (Wheaton).
Naturally Proust's "To this Jimmy": JM to William Burford, letter, June 24, 1946 (Amh).

83 **About the direction** " 'You have to' ": JM to HIM, letter, c. fall 1942 (WUSTL).
At Amherst "As one student": Author's interview with Richard Meryman (2001).
He was known "Merrill Lynch": To the author, letter, 2001. "He was smarter": Author's interview with Robert Wilson (2001).

84 **He had the** "He had the": Author's interview with Benjamin Gordon (2002). "Horton, like his": Chronology of James I. Merrill, AC 1947 at Amherst College (Amh). "Curtis Canfield": Author's interview with Robert Brustein (2001).
An exception to "Howkins was": Author's interview with Robert Wilson (2001). "He spent weekends": Author's interview with Richard Meryman (2001).
As slight and "They met on": Author's interview with Rosemary Sprague (2002). "Like Howkins": Scottie Faerber to the author, email, June 16, 2013. "He understood her": Author's interview with Daria D'Arienzo (2013).

85 **Hanging over** "His father urged": CEM to JM, excerpt from a letter, April 2, 1943 (Amh).

"Reporting for duty": JM, journal, June 15, 1945, Jnl 1 (WUSTL). "Somehow he had": JM to Coley Newman, letter, July 14, 1944 (WUSTL); JM, journal, 1944, Jnl 72 (WUSTL).

85 **"I am in this"** " 'I am in this' ": JM to Coley Newman, letter, July 14, 1944 (WUSTL). "That letter was": *Princeton Alumni Weekly* 45, no. 1 (August 11, 1944): 24. " 'Elegy for an' ": JM to HIM, letter, October 18, 1944 (WUSTL). "Not long after": Author's interview with Benjamin Gordon (2002).

86 **Jimmy also had** "In April 1944": Perkins, *Wall Street*, 180. "Jimmy blamed": JM to Coley Newman, letter, July 14 1944 (WUSTL).

With his father's " 'That phrase' ": JM to HIM, letter, August 3, 1944 (WUSTL).

Before entering "His advice": JM, *ADP*, 532. "Jimmy wrote a": JM, journal, January 10, 1945, Jnl 1 (WUSTL).

87 **In late 1944** "In late 1944": JM to Thomas Howkins, letter, December 21–22, 1944 (WUSTL). "But that was": JM, journal, January 1945, Jnl 1 (WUSTL).

There was no "Jimmy tried to": JM, journal, February 14, 1945, Jnl 1 (WUSTL).

Aware of having "Aware of having": JM to Coley Newman, letter, July 14, 1944 (WUSTL); or JM, journal, June 23, 1945, Jnl 1 (WUSTL). "In April, he was": JM, journal, April 12, 1945, Jnl 1 (WUSTL).

Semester to "Seldon was": Author's interview with Linda James (2013).

88 **During the** "There was a": Author's interview with Linda James (2013). "In his diary": JM, journal, June 30–July 25, 1945, Jnl 1 (WUSTL).

Merrill wasn't "Feeling the will": JM, journal, August 1944, Jnl 1 (WUSTL).

Merrill met "Merrill met": JM, journal, December 24, 1945, Jnl 1 (WUSTL). "He was born": Maritza Maxwell, KF Papers, Princeton University Library, http://findingaids.princeton.edu/collections/C0713 (2014). "A blurry photo": KF Papers, American College of Greece, Athens.

89 **Friar had** "Friar had": Bertrand Mathieu, "The Man Who Couldn't Remember: Conversations with Kimon Friar," *Southeastern Review* 1 (winter 1990): 64–65. "Merrill introduced": JM, journal, December 24, 1945, Jnl 1 (WUSTL). "Friar 'groaned' ": Mathieu, "The Man Who," 64–65. " 'Something of' ": JM, journal, September 11, 1945, Jnl 1 (WUSTL). "He had become": Mathieu, "The Man Who," 64. "A diary entry": JM, journal, October 29, 1945, Jnl 1 (WUSTL). "Friar was Merrill's": The title page of Friar's copy of Brinnin's first volume of poetry, *The Garden Is Political* (Macmillan, 1942), says it is by Brinnin "and Kimon" (the last added in Brinnin's hand); KF Papers, American College of Greece. " 'I have been' ": JM, journal, November 12, 1945, Jnl 1 (WUSTL).

Then, in December " 'Mama opened' ": JM, journal, December 24, 1945, Jnl 1 (WUSTL). "There were bitter": KF to JM, letter, June 14, 1962 (WUSTL).

90 **Whatever Hellen herself** "That winter": Author's interview with FB (2001).

Hellen threatened "Hellen threatened": JM, *ADP*, 584. "A war council": Author's interview with CM (2001). "In the end": JM, *ADP*, 584.

91 **In December** "In December": JM, journal, December 24, 1945, Jnl 1 (WUSTL).

Friar's Greek "With Merrill": Kenneth Dover, *Greek Homosexuality* (Harvard University Press, 1978, 1989), 16. "Jimmy knew": JM's Amherst College Courses (Amh).

Besides language "In his Christmas Eve": JM, journal, December 24, 1945, Jnl 1 (WUSTL); KF, "Medusa-Mask," *Poetry* 55, no. 6 (March 1940): 326–27.

92 **Friar had** "The poem connected": Andy Horton, "Many Masks of Kimon Friar, Part One: The American Portrait," *Athenian* (October–November 1974), 21–22. "Friar 'fell' ": Mathieu, "The Man Who Couldn't Remember," 54.

Now, encouraging "A series of photos": KF Papers, American College of Greece, Athens.

At the Poetry "Friar was teaching": Young Men's and Young Women's Hebrew Association, Bulletin of Educational Activities (Poetry Center archives). "Readings included": On KF's role in introducing JM to Yeats and his occult prose, see Mark Bauer, *This Composite Voice: The Role of W. B. Yeats in James Merrill's Poetry* (Routledge, 2003). "For Friar": KF, "Myth and Metaphysics," in *Modern Poetry: American and British*, ed. KF and John Malcolm Brinnin (Appleton-Century-Crofts, 1951), 421. The anthology includes two poems by JM, the youngest poet represented.

93 **Friar himself** "In 'Medusa-Mask' ": KF, "Medusa-Mask," 324. "In Friar's allegory": KF, "Medusa-Mask," 323. "Since, if": KF, "Medusa-Mask," 328.

It was easy "His first": JM, journal, September 11, 1945, Jnl 1 (WUSTL).

94 **Merrill responded** "Even while": JM's Amherst College Courses (Amh). "In December": Chronology of James I. Merrill, AC 1947 at Amherst College (Amh). "In spring 1946": JM, "The Transformation of Rilke," *Prose*, 449–55.

And in March "And in March": JM, "Four Poems," *Poetry Magazine* 67, no. 6 (March 1946): 293–301. "His father": JM to Thomas Howkins, letter, April 12, 1946 (WUSTL).

Over the same "They included": JM to William Burford, letter, June 28, 1946 (Amh). "Vidal went": *The Diary of Anaïs Nin, 1944–47*, ed. Gunther Stuhlmann (Harcourt Brace Jovanovich, 1971), 81. "She came": *Diary of Anaïs Nin*, 134–35. "They traded": Works by Hugo Guilier hang in the JM House, Stonington, CT.

95 **Deren, by** "He encountered": JM, journal, December 24, 1945, Jnl 1 (WUSTL); Mathieu, "The Man Who Couldn't Remember," 64. "Born in": Bill Nichols, "Introduction," *Maya Deren and the American Avant-Garde*, ed. Bill Nichols (University of California Press, 2001), 3–20.

In May 1946 "Jimmy distrusted": KF to JM, letter, July 5, 1946 (WUSTL). "When Friar sent": JM to KF, letter, July 22, 1946 (WUSTL). "When Jimmy": KF to JM, letter, July 29, 1946 (WUSTL).

By "towers" " 'Life is something' ": KF to JM, letter, July 20, 1946 (WUSTL). "And a few days": KF to JM, letter, July 29, 1946 (WUSTL).

96 **Merrill's cramped** "Merrill and Burford were involved": *Medusa* 1, no. 1 (fall 1946) (Amh). "Medusa-Mask," reprinted from *Poetry*, begins the issue, like a credo or statement of editorial policy. "What he longed": JM to William Burford, letter, August 1, 1946 (Amh). "Another letter": JM to William Burford, letter, August 5, 1946 (Amh).

Merrill wrote "They visited colonial-era": JM to William Burford, letter, August 9, 1946 (Amh). "Regler at one": Author's interview with CM (2001).

97 **Besides the Medusa** " 'Since I was' ": Mathieu, "The Man Who Couldn't Remember," 64.

The Black Swan "The Black Swan": KF to JM, letter, October 3, 1946 (WUSTL). "The first letters": JM, *CP*, 677.

98 **The lake where** "The lake where": JM, journal, March 12, 1945, Jnl 1 (WUSTL).

99 **"The Broken Bowl"** " 'Of course, I' ": JM to William Burford, letter, June 13, 1946 (Amh).

Perhaps he was "So he told": JM, *ADP*, 473. " 'Kimon is back' ": JM, journal, January 4, 1947, Jnl 1 (WUSTL). "So he told": JM, *ADP*, 473. "Didactic and": KF to JM, letter, March 2, 1947 (WUSTL).

100 **Friar and Merrill** "Buechner was": Author's interview with FB (2001). "Much later": JM, *Sandover*, 89.

A chameleon "A student from": Diederik Oostdijk to the author, email, May 28, 2013. "He made a quick": JM, *ADP*, 497. "Lodeizen, familiar": Hans Lodeizen, "Meeting the Merrills," trans. James Brockway, in *Dutch Interior: Postwar Poetry of the Netherlands and Flanders*, ed. James S. Holmes and William Jay Smith (Columbia University Press, 1984), 27. "He didn't see": Diederik Oostdijk, "James Merrill and the 'Unresolved' Memory of Hans Lodeizen," in *Recovery and Transgression: Memory, the United States, and Transnational Poetics*, ed. Kornelia Freitag (Cambridge Scholars Press, 2015). "One afternoon": JM, *ADP*, 497–98.

101 **As with other** "Observing them": JM, *ADP*, 498–99 and 502.

102 **During this** "The power of": JM, "*À la recherche du temps perdu*: Impressionism in Literature," senior thesis, Amherst College, 1947 (WUSTL).

While discussing "While discussing": JM, "*À la recherche*," 84. "A few pages": JM, "*À la recherche*," 97.

102 **The essay** "One Amherst alumnus": Richard Silva to the author, letter, December 18, 2001. "President Charles Cole": Charles Cole to CEM, letter, February 18, 1947 (Amh). JM was one of three students in the class of 1947 to graduate summa cum laude.
Having finished "(He claimed)": Author's interview with FB (2002). "He passed": JM to KF, letter, March 3, 1947 (WUSTL).

103 **He spent inordinate** "Howkins came": JM to Thomas Howkins, letter, April 19, 1947 (WUSTL). "Cast as Apollinaire": JM, *ADP*, 565. "As Daum": Tape of Ray Daum in conversation with Jack W. Hagstrum (2001).
Merrill inherited "Written during": JM, *CNP*, 671.
Merrill was ready "When the question": Joseph W. Gordon to the author (2014).

104 **Merrill must** "He started": FB to the author, letter, August 3, 2001. "When he had": Author's interview with Robert Wilson (2001). " 'Jimmy,' he judged": Author's interview with Charles Shoup (2003).
Merrill had met "Merrill had met": Author's interview with FB (2002). "Meredith was": JM to WM, letter, November 2, 1947 (WUSTL). "Merrill grew": JM to KF, letter, January 6, 1948 (WUSTL).
In New York "At a New Year's": JM to KF, letter, January 6, 1948 (WUSTL).

105 **Charlie Merrill** "Still, there was": CEM to JM, excerpt from a letter, December 6, 1947 (Amh). "After that letter": JM to KF, letter, April 29, 1948 (WUSTL). "He didn't hesitate": JM to KF, letter, August 11, 1948 (WUSTL).

106 **Even in the wilds** "Even in the wilds": JM to WM, letter, July 15, 1948 (WUSTL); FB, *The Eyes of the Heart*, 33–38.
That fall "On the second floor": Author's interview with U. T. Summers (2007). "Eventually he would": JM, *ADP*, 604–07. "He liked to": JM, "Memorial Tribute to Irma Brandeis," *Prose*, 369–70.

107 **Bard, known** "At twenty-two": Author's interview with FB (2002). "Marveling at this": JM to FB, letter, April 10, 1949 (Wheaton); JM, *ADP*, 532.
Some weeks "That November": EB, *One Art: Letters*, ed. Robert Giroux (FSG, 1994), 174.
He discovered "Shortly after": JM to FB, letter, January 19, 1949 (Wheaton). "He had been so": JM to KF, letter, September 6, 1949 (WUSTL).

108 **Merrill ended his** "Merrill ended his": JM to FB, letter, April 7, 1949 (Wheaton). "He also gave": JM to KF, letter, April 9, 1949 (WUSTL). "As James": Henry James, *The Wings of the Dove*, vol. 2 (Scribner's, 1902), 136. "Milly's task": JM, journal, May 1949, Jnl 2 (WUSTL).

109 **His wealth weighed** "He tried to": JM to KF, letter, January 19, 1949 (WUSTL). "He gave Buechner": Author's interview with FB (2002). "He gave ungrudgingly": JM to FB, letter, October 11, 1948 (Wheaton).
Slowly he had "He joked that": JM to WM, letter, April 14, 1949 (WUSTL). "He presented": JM to CEM, letter, December 19, 1949 (Amh).

110 **Merrill had** "He sent it": JM to Coley Newman, letter, June 25, 1949 (WUSTL). "After Bard": JM to KF, letter, March 5, 1949 (WUSTL). "Wayne Kerwood": JM to FB, letter, July 14, 1949 (Wheaton). "A letter came": Hayden Carruth to JM, letter, November 3, 1949 (University of Chicago Library). "(The magazine)": JM had won the Oscar Blumenthal Prize for 1947. "Still, Knopf": JM to KF, letter, September 9, 1949 (WUSTL).
Jimmy, already "He'd scouted": JM to FB, letter, December 31, 1948 (Wheaton).

3 ROME

111 **A Different Person** "The question": JM, *ADP*, 459.
In January "This first": JM, *ADP*, 463. "He thought": JM to CF, letter, March 11, 1950 (Getty).

112 **Merrill had** "Merrill had": JM, *ADP*, 459. " 'Because Kimon' ": JM, *ADP*, 463. "Indeed he": CF, journal, February 6, 1950 (Getty).

112 **Whose hand** "His father": Author's interview with CF (2001).

113 **It was a simple** "Three days": CF, journal, January 30, 1950 (Getty). " 'My life' ": CF, journal, February 6, 1950 (Getty).

Jimmy was "He was ready": CF, journal, April 13, 1960 (Getty). " 'The wide-eyed' ": Author's interview with CF (2007).

They went " 'It felt' ": Author's interview with CF (2007).

114 **Fredericks went** "On March": CF to JM, letter, March 3, 1950 (Getty).

But it was " 'Such a party' ": JM to CF, letter, March 9, 1950 (Getty). "Fredericks was": CF, journal, c. March 10, 1950 (Getty).

They reunited "Inside was": CF to JM, letter, March 14, 1950 (Getty). "On the shelves": JM, *ADP*, 466. "He told": CF, journal, March 24–25, 1950 (Getty). " 'But I fancied' ": CF, journal, March 24–25, 1950 (Getty). " 'I am indeed' ": CF, journal, March 31, 1950 (Getty).

115 **A few days** "A few days": JM to CF, letter, March 16, 1950 (Getty). "Reuben Brower": Author's interview with Walker Gibson (2003). "Merrill saw": JM, *ADP*, 462. "In Claude's": CF, journal, March 24–25, 1950 (Getty). "He sounded": JM, *ADP*, 462.

116 **He returned** " 'I don't know' ": JM to HIM, letter, March 24, 1950 (WUSTL). "He didn't": JM to HIM, letter, May 27, 1950 (WUSTL).

He took "He wrote": JM to CF, letter, March 24, 1950 (Getty).

The idea "Having just": CF, journal, March 7, 1950 (Getty). "He had 'said' ": JM to CF, letter, March 31, 1950 (Getty). "He landed": JM to CF, letter, c. April 1950 (Getty).

117 **From Athens** "From Athens": JM to CF, letter, April 15, 1950 (Getty).

Mitso "Mitso": JM, *ADP*, 475. "But she was": JM, *ADP*, 476. "The two men": JM, *ADP*, 475.

118 **Friar's** "Above the door": JM to CF, letter, April 15, 1950 (Getty). "Water accumulated": Author's interview with Dimitri Diamantopoulos (2002). "Ten-foot-high": JM, *ADP*, 476.

Merrill was fascinated "He saw": JM, *ADP*, 476. "Born in": Author's interview with Dimitri Diamantopoulos (2002); JM, *ADP*, 475.

119 **One afternoon** "Merrill, by": JM to CF, letter, April 20, 1950 (Getty). "A British": Author's interview with John Leatham (2003). "But, as he began": JM to CF, letter, c. April 1950 (Getty).

Merrill was released "He strolled": JM to CF, letter, April 30, 1950 (Getty). "Friar gave": JM to CF, letter, April 30, 1950 (Getty). " 'Why don't' ": JM, *ADP*, 474.

120 **Friar took** "There they had": JM to CF, letter, May 7, 1950 (Getty). "Merrill was disturbed": JM to CF, letter, May 7, 1950 (Getty). "He left": JM to CF, letter, April 27, 1950 (Getty); and JM to CF, letter, May 7, 1950 (Getty).

In Naples "The party": JM, *ADP*, 483. "Daddy": JM to KF, letter, May 18, 1950 (WUSTL). "While one": JM to CF, letter, May 19, 1950 (Getty).

121 **Yet they both** "His spiritual": JM to CF, letter, May 26, 1950 (Getty).

Taking in "Taking in": JM, *ADP*, 492. "While his father": JM, *ADP*, 485.

Young Robin "Back at": RM, *Memoir*, 106.

His own health "A British-born": JM to CF, letter, June 3, 1950 (Getty). "Under Claude's": JM to CF, letter, June 7, 1950 (Getty).

122 **As they** "Simeons, Jimmy": JM, *ADP*, 486; JM to CF, letter, June 7, 1950 (Getty).

While Jimmy "In the abstract": JM to CF, letter, June 6, 1950 (Getty). "Detre administered": JM, *ADP*, 487.

What followed "With the test": JM to CF, letter, June 6, 1950 (Getty). "When Detre": JM to CF, letter, June 7, 1950 (Getty). "By the next": JM to CF, letter, June 8, 1950 (Getty).

123 **Painkillers** "He referred": JM to CF, letter, June 7, 1950 (Getty); JM to CF, letter, June 8, 1950 (Getty). "Detre mentioned": JM to CF, letter, June 8, 1950 (Getty).

Discharged "Discharged": JM to CF, letter, June 9, 1950 (Getty). "Jimmy described": JM to CF, letter, June 12, 1950 (Getty). "In *A Different*": JM, *ADP*, 489.

124 **Jimmy's letters** " 'Claude himself' ": JM, *ADP*, 494. "The blissful": JM, *ADP*, 494–95.

From Cassis "So Merrill": JM to Hubbell Pierce, letter, August 9, 1950 (WUSTL). " 'The large' ": JM, *ADP*, 499. "One of these": Hans Lodeizen, "Jim I Would Like to Know," trans. Peter Nijmeijer, in *Dutch Interior* (1984), 26. "The other poem": JM, *ADP*, 500. "The answer": JM, *ADP*, 501.

125 **From Salzburg** "Although he knew": JM to Hans Lodeizen, letter, July 26, 1950 (WUSTL). "Writing to": JM to HIM, August 5, 1950 (WUSTL). "On the back": JM to HIM, August 5, 1950 (WUSTL).

127 **Merrill made** "The 'old masters' ": W. H. Auden, "Musée des Beaux Arts," *Collected Poems*, ed. Edward Mendelson (Random House, 1991).

128 **When he wrote** "He struggled": JM to HIM, letter, June 29, 1950 (WUSTL).

129 **He was writing** "He told": JM to HIM, letter, June 29, 1950 (WUSTL). "Now, in Salzburg": JM to HIM, letter, July 17, 1950 (WUSTL).

Bill and Hellen "Two years": JM to WM, letter, September 11, 1950 (WUSTL). "Beatrice": Betty Potts, "A Toast to Hellen Plummer," *Hellen's Book*, 57. "He rose": "Mrs. Merrill Is Wed to W. L. Plummer; U.S.A.F.R. Officer," *New York Herald Tribune* (October 1, 1950). "In a poem": JM, "Up and Down," *CP*, 341. "He told": JM to WM, letter, September 11, 1950 (WUSTL). "All that": Gerrish and Mary Thurber, letter, November 2, 1950 (WUSTL).

The general "The general": JM to WM, letter, September 11, 1950 (WUSTL). "Their mothers": JM, *ADP*, 504. "He and Fredericks": JM to IB, letter, August 18, 1950 (WUSTL); and JM, *ADP*, 504. "Meanwhile, they": JM, *ADP*, 504–05.

130 **In August** "In August": JM to HIM, letter, June 16, 1950 (WUSTL). "Harwood was": JM to Hubbell Pierce, letter, February 2, 1951 (WUSTL). "When Denis": *Phillip G. Bergem, The Family and Residences of Arthur Conan Doyle* (Privately printed, 2001), 4, 11. "Finding in": JM to Gerrish and Mary Thurber, letter, November 2, 1950 (WUSTL).

In Italy "Merrill found": JM, *ADP*, 506–07. "She set": JM to Gerrish and Mary Thurber, letter, November 2, 1950 (WUSTL). "In Rome": Author's interview with CF (2007). "In one of": JM, *ADP*, 507; author's interview with CF (2001).

131 **Correspondence** "Merrill wanted": JM to Herbert Weinstock, letter, September 28, 1950 (Knopf files).

The book's "Ford described": HF to JM, letters, September 7 and October 17, 1950 (Knopf files).

In early "Prices were": FB, *The Yellow Leaves: A Miscellany* (Westminster John Knox Press, 2008), 41; and JM to Gerrish and Mary Thurber, letter, November 2, 1950 (WUSTL).

Up to now "Up to now": CF, journal, September 30, 1950 (Getty). "When they": CF, journal, October 30, 1950 (Getty). "What's more": CF, journal, October 30, 1950 (Getty).

132 **The topic** "Their panic": CF, journal, December 19, 1950 (Getty). "Jimmy had": CF, journal, December 19, 1950 (Getty). "And Claude": CF, journal, December 7, 1950 (Getty). " 'He takes up' ": CF, journal, December 19, 1950 (Getty). "Thinking of": John Milton, "Areopagitica," *The Complete Poetry and Essential Prose of John Milton*, ed. William Kerrigan, John Rumrich, and Stephen M. Fallon (Modern Library, 2007), 930; and William Wordsworth, *The Prelude: The Four Texts (1798, 1799, 1805, 1850)*, ed. Jonathan Wordsworth (Penguin, 1995), 174–79.

133 **When First Poems** "To Mrs. Knopf": JM to Blanche Knopf, letter, December 6, 1950 (Ransom). "Fredericks admired": CF, journal, November 13, 1950 (Getty).

Merrill and Fredericks "They watched": CF, journal, December 26, 1950 (Getty). "Merrill had": JM to CF, poem, December 25, 1950 (Getty). "In his work": JM to KF, letter, January 3, 1951 (WUSTL). "Jimmy called": CF, journal, December 26, 1950 (Getty).

134 **As winter** "As winter": Author's interview with CF (2001). " 'I miss much' ": JM to WM, letter, February 16, 1951 (WUSTL).

Or was it "Looking back": JM, *ADP*, 514–15. "What might": CF, journal, February 18, 1951 (Getty).

Complaining "Complaining": CF, journal, December 14, 15, 1950 (Getty).

Fredericks was "Fredericks was": CF, journal, February 23, 1951 (Getty). "Graves appeared":

CF, journal, February 18, 1951 (Getty). "Later Fredericks": CF, journal, February 18, 1951 (Getty).

135 **They began** "Merrill carried": JM, *ADP*, 510. "The next day": CF, journal, February 9, 1951 (Getty). "They didn't": JM, *ADP*, 510.

The lovers "JM": CF, journal, February 10, 1951 (Getty). "Commenting on": JM to KF, letter, May 5, 1951 (WUSTL).

Fredericks didn't "Fredericks didn't": CF, journal, March 1, 1951 (Getty). "Merrill saw": JM, *ADP*, 516. "Jimmy put": CF, journal, March 4, 1951 (Getty).

136 **France wasn't** "As they": CF, journal, March 19, 1951 (Getty). "Merrill coughed": CF, journal, April 1, 1951 (Getty). "He read": JM to Suzel Parker, letter, April 6, 1951 (WUSTL); JM to Walker and Nancy Gibson, letter, Easter Monday, 1951 (WUSTL). "Fredericks took": JM to HIP, letter, May 5, 1951 (WUSTL). "Toklas started": JM, *ADP*, 520. "In the evenings": JM to HIP, letter, May 5, 1951 (WUSTL).

But Merrill's "In a letter": JM to CEM, letter, April 21, 1951 (Amh).

Jimmy took "Now Simeons": JM to KF, letter, April 21, 1951 (WUSTL). "The injections": JM to CEM, letter, April 21, 1951 (Amh). "Jimmy had": JM to KF, letter, April 21, 1951 (WUSTL). "He agreed": JM to CEM, letter, April 21, 1951 (Amh). "Jimmy's weight": CF, journal, April 27, 1951 (Getty).

137 **He might** "It is commonly": See Stephen Barrett, MD, "HCG Worthless as Weight-Loss Aid," http://www.dietscam.org/reports/hcg.shtml (2008).

It helped "Privately": JM to May [?], letter, October 2, 1951 (WUSTL). "But to his father": JM to CEM, letter, April 21, 1951 (Amh).

His routine " 'I have never' ": JM to Thomas Howkins, letter, May 30, 1951 (WUSTL). " 'In seven' ": JM to CEM, letter, June 3, 1951 (Amh).

138 **Fredericks came** "In Rome": Author's interview with Thomas Detre (2003). "Fredericks commented": CF, journal, June 8, 1951 (Getty).

Merrill's novel "Merrill's novel": JM to Gerrish and Mary Thurber, letter, June 2, 1951 (WUSTL). "Having a first": JM to John Bernard Myers, letter, June 9, 1951 (WUSTL). "In the *Nation*": Rolfe Humphries, "Verse Chronicles," *Nation* 10, no. 138 (February 1951). "Bogan classified": Louise Bogan, "Verse," *New Yorker* (June 9, 1951): 109–10. " 'Really, I' ": JM to FB, letter, June 23, 1951 (Wheaton). "To his mother": JM to HIP, letter, June 26, 1951 (WUSTL).

139 **"To discover"** "That spring": JM to Frederick and Marjorie Beck, letter, May 23, 1951 (WUSTL). "Meanwhile, Jimmy": CF, journal, June 12, 1951 (Getty). "Used to living": Author's interview with CF (2001). "They met": JM, *ADP*, 536.

By the end "By the end": JM to KF, letter, June 29–30, 1951 (WUSTL). "He spoke": JM, *ADP*, 530.

Up to this "Their rooms": JM to KF, letter, June 29–30, 1951 (WUSTL). "Merrill took": JM to Thomas Howkins, letter, August 8, 1951 (WUSTL). "In July": JM to HIP, letter, July 5, 1951 (WUSTL).

Merrill had reason " 'In the context' ": JM, *ADP*, 537.

140 **The arrival** "It was important": JM, *ADP*, 92, 94. " 'Although by' ": JM to HIP, letter, July 5, 1951 (WUSTL). "Boyish Jimmy": *Hellen's Book* (Magowan Family Foundation, 1991), 11. "Sweet, pretty": JM, *ADP*, 96.

By Betty's "By Betty's": JM, *ADP*, 94. "Betty invited": JM, *ADP*, 99; CF, journal, July 5, 1951 (Getty). "They set off": JM to Betty Plummer, letter, August 8, 1951 (WUSTL); CF, journal, July 5, 1951 (Getty). "Late in": JM, *ADP*, 99.

141 **The encounter** "In his journal": CF, journal, July 5, 1951 (Getty).

Fredericks responded "Fredericks responded": CF, journal, July 24, 1951 (Getty). "Friends from": CF, journal, July 24, 1951 (Getty); JM, *ADP*, 85. "While the": JM, *ADP*, 85.

A few days "A few days": CF, journal, July 24, 1951 (Getty). "Fredericks responded": CF, journal, July 19, 1951 (Getty); CF, journal, August 7, 1951 (Getty).

141 **In early** "Jimmy sounded": JM to CM, letter, August 13, 1951 (WUSTL); JM to CEM, letter, August 8, 1950 (Amh). "The problem": JM to CEM, letter, August 8, 1950 (Amh). "He said that": JM to HIP, letter, August 4, 1951 (WUSTL). "He was silent": JM to WM, letter, August 30, 1951 (WUSTL).

142 **But his treatment** "After just": JM to KF, letter, August 31, 1951 (WUSTL). "When Simeons": JM, *ADP*, 544.

Kimon and Mina "Kimon and Mina": JM to KF, letter, August 31, 1951 (WUSTL). " 'Wasn't it' ": JM, *ADP*, 116. "The problem": JM, *ADP*, 116–17.

Merrill and Detre "The only slightly": JM, *ADP*, 554. Facts about Thomas Detre come from Toby Tabachnik, "Thomas Detre Built His Career on the Ashes of Tragedy," *The Jewish Chronicle*, October 2010; "Obituary of Thomas P. Detre," *University Times*, University of Pittsburgh, October 14, 2010; and the author's interview with Thomas Detre (2003).

143 **Merrill early** "Merrill early": JM, *ADP*, 118. "About his lack": Author's interview with Dr. Thomas Detre (2003). "Freud called": Sigmund Freud, *The Interpretation of Dreams*, trans. James Strachey (Norton, 1961), 608.

144 **One of the** "One of the": JM to Dora Cook, letter, October 12, 1951 (WUSTL). "Since Merrill": JM to Lawrence Condon, letter, August 30, 1951 (WUSTL). "He recognized": JM to Dora Cook, letter, October 12, 1951 (WUSTL). "He wrote": JM to Tony Harwood, letter, August 17, 1951 (WUSTL). "He told Dora": JM to Dora Cook, letter, October 12, 1951 (WUSTL). "And he told his mother": JM to HIP, letter, August 31, 1951 (WUSTL).

In September "Works by": Filippo Fois, *La Fenice Theatre* (Marsilio Editori, 2005), 7–9.

In sweltering "In sweltering": Vera Stravinsky, " 'La Prima Assoluta,' " liner notes, *The Rake's Progress*, Columbia Records 1964 (JM's record collection, Stonington, CT). "Inside, Merrill": JM to Thomas Howkins, letter, September 19, 1951 (WUSTL). "Elsewhere": CF, journal, September 25–26, 1951 (Getty). "The 'sublime Schwarzkopf' ": JM to WM, letter, September 13, 1951 (WUSTL). "Borrowing": Igor Stravinsky, "In Which the Author Asks for a Moratorium on Value Judgments," liner notes, *The Rake's Progress*. "Receiving his": JM to Thomas Howkins, letter, September 19, 1951 (WUSTL). "Suggesting": JM to WM, letter, September 13, 1951 (WUSTL).

145 **The opera** "In Mother": W. H. Auden and Chester Kallman, *The Rake's Progress*, Act I, Scene Two, in *Libretti and Other Dramatic Writings by W. H. Auden, 1939–1973*, ed. Edward Mendelson (Princeton University Press, 1993), 56. "Soliloquizing": *The Rake's Progress*, 57. "In act 3": *The Rake's Progress*, Act III, Scene Two, 82–86.

146 **Merrill, like** "He didn't": JM to WM, letter, September 13, 1951 (WUSTL). "Baba, sans": *The Rake's Progress*, Epilogue, 92.

Together Merrill " 'One of us' ": CF, journal, October 3, 1951 (Getty).

Fredericks eventually "For the first": JM to Frederick and Marjorie Beck, letter, October 20, 1951 (WUSTL). "He added": JM to William Plummer, letter, October 28, 1951 (WUSTL).

147 **Via Quattro** "For Freud": Sigmund Freud, *Civilisation and Its Discontents*, trans. James Strachey (Norton, 1961), 16.

Not surprisingly "With reason": JM, *ADP*, 143. "CEM's silence": JM, *ADP*, 143.

Regarding "I told him": Detre's paraphrase of CEM's letter to him, June 1950; author's interview with Dr. Thomas Detre (2003).

That fall "He was an accomplished": Author's interview with CF (2001). "Indeed, his bow": JM, *ADP*, 133.

148 **Claude's affair** "But when Kerwood": JM, *ADP*, 136.

The dance "As at Lake": CF, journal, December 28, 1951 (Getty). "In *A Different*": JM, *ADP*, 134–35.

149 **Following orders** "The next": CF, journal, December 28, 1951 (Getty). "His analyst": JM, *ADP*, 135. "In a book": JM, *ADP*, 131.

Or he could " 'Dear Mama' ": JM to HIP, letter, October 5, 1951 (WUSTL). " 'Both of' ": JM to FB, letter, December 7, 1951 (Wheaton). "As Simeons": JM, *ADP*, 145.

150 **Recovered, Merrill** "It was after": JM, *ADP*, 147.
Another day "Another day": JM, *ADP*, 150–51.
While mother "While mother": JM to KF, letter, October 7, 1951 (WUSTL). " 'This slight' ":
JM, *ADP*, 157. "Jimmy was certain": JM, *ADP*, 166–67.

151 **Back in Rome** "Fourteen-year-old": JM to KF, letter, c. December 27, 1951 (WUSTL).
" 'Bizarre' ": CF, journal, December 28, 1951 (Getty).
As a romantic "While Claude": JM, *ADP*, 172–73. "Merrill represents": JM, *ADP*, 174.
In their early "Kerwood had": JM to Thomas Howkins, letter, 1951 (WUSTL).

152 **At the same** " 'I think' ": JM to CEM, letter, January 2, 1952 (Amh). "They now": JM, *ADP*,
194. "His nieces": JM, *ADP*, 197.
While Claude "While Claude": CF, journal, April 30, 1952 (Getty). "An exchange": JM, *ADP*,
219–20.

153 **Deep in** "In Rome": JM to KF, letter, April 17, 1952 (WUSTL). "I will not": JM to KF, letter,
May 28, 1952 (WUSTL).
In June " 'This trick' ": JM, *ADP*, 228–29.
Of course "To keep": JM to WM, letter, "Good Friday," 1952 (WUSTL). "CEM was said": JM
to WM, letter, July 16, 1952 (WUSTL).

154 **Comic** "He assured": JM to HIP, letter, August 7, 1952 (WUSTL).
It might "Merrill and Isaacson": JM to CF, letter, August 21, 1952 (Getty). " 'To Kimon' ": JM
to CF, letter, September 3, 1952 (Getty). "He had to": JM, *ADP*, 240.

155 **Did he want** "When he began": JM to FB, letter, September 14, 1952 (Wheaton). "If Detre":
JM to CF, letter, c. April 1953 (Getty). "Treatment": JM to CF, letter, September 10, 1952
(Getty). "The prospect": JM to CF, letter, September 10, 1952 (Getty). "Two years": JM, *ADP*,
242.
If there was "A couple": Marshall C. Olds, "Under Mallarmé's Wing," *Modern Languages
and Literatures, Department of French Language and Literature* (University of Nebraska Press,
2001), 9, 14; JM, unpublished lines, transcribed by Marilyn Lavin for the author.

156 **During his time** "Morra had": JM to HIP, letter, July 19, 1952 (WUSTL). "He had a short":
Justin Spring, *Fairfield Porter: A Life in Art* (Yale University Press, 2000), 77. " 'His face' ":
JM, *ADP*, 108–09. " 'Part of me' ": JM, *ADP*, 109.

157 **The attraction** "A third room": JM, *ADP*, 209. "It was her second": Author's visit to the Villa
Morra di Lavriano, Metalliano, Tuscany (2007).
It took Merrill "By inference": JM, *ADP*, 210.

158 **Merrill's time** "Hubbell Pierce": JM to CF, letter, October 13, 1952 (Getty). "The music": JM,
ADP, 260. "The problem": JM to CF, letter, October 13, 1952 (Getty). "If nothing": JM to CF,
letter, October 13, 1952 (Getty).
Merrill was "Charles": JM, *ADP*, 252.
Hearing Merrill "Hearing Merrill": JM, *ADP*, 253. "Merrill's last": JM to CF, letter, November-
ber 26, 1952 (Getty). "He praised": JM, journal, December 11 and 12, 1952, Jnl 28 (WUSTL).

159 **A Different Person** "He has 'walked' ": JM, *ADP*, 271. "Count Bracci": JM to CF, letter, September 3, 1952 (Getty).

4 DAVID JACKSON

163 **Merrill would** "They met": Brenda S. Gross, "Poets and Painters in the Theatre: A Critical
Study of the New York Artists Theatre," PhD diss., Graduate Faculty in Theatre, City Univer-
sity of New York (1989), 6. "Jimmy was": JM, *ADP*, 255. "But he had": JM, *ADP*, 254. "The first":
JM to DJ, postcard, June 10, 1953 (WUSTL). "When he": JM to CF, letter, June 17, 1953 (Getty).
How did "Twenty-five": JM to DJ, letter, May 24, 1978 (WUSTL).

164 **When he** "He brooded": JM, journal, January 5, 1953, Jnl 28 (WUSTL); JM to CF, letter,
December 31, 1952 (Getty).

164 **He visited** "He visited": JM to Hubbell Pierce, letter, January 25, 1953 (WUSTL). " 'He is so' ": JM to CF, letter, c. March 1953 (Getty).

165 " **'I want to' ":** JM to CF, letter, c. April 1953 (Getty).

That self-isolating "Chilly": JM, *ADP*, 671. "The play": JM, *ADP*, 253–54. "Years later": JM, *ADP*, 670.

It was just "David Noyes Jackson": Facts about DJ's family and early life come from the author's interviews with Doris Sewell Jackson (2001) and Robert Grimes (2002) and Rachel Slaughter's research in the David Jackson Papers (WUSTL).

167 **When he met** "In a draft": DJ to George Jackson, letter, May 23, 1954 (WUSTL); and DJ, journal 1951–54 (WUSTL).

Lies "David learned": Author's interview with AL (2004).

168 **Merrill discovered** "With analogs": S. Hunt, *Ouija: The Most Dangerous Game* (Harper, 1992). "William Fuld": http://www.museumoftalkingboards.com/history.html (March 2009).

169 **Merrill's first** "Merrill's first": JM, *ADP*, 679 (JM changes it from a birthday gift to a Christmas gift).

There is no "But David": DJ to Doris Sewell Jackson, letter, June 29, 1953 (WUSTL).

How precisely "This time": JM, "Kabel Barnes, via Ouija, November 14, 1953," Ouija board transcript, box 3, fl 13 (WUSTL).

170 **The first letter:** "The first letter": JM to DJ, letter, June 1953 (WUSTL).

171 **Furnished** "Or, perhaps fiction": JM to WM, letter, July 1953 (WUSTL). "In lieu": RM, *Memoirs*, 36.

Charlie had "Besides all": CEM, "Excerpts from a Letter to an Old Friend in England," September 22, 1953 (Amh).

172 **Rather than** "Mr. Tanning": JM, *CNP*, 43. "Roused": JM, *CNP*, 44. "While Mrs. McBride": JM, *CNP*, 45. "As Mr. Tanning": JM, *CNP*, 46–47. "At last": JM, *CNP*, 47.

173 **In actuality** "In actuality": CEM, "Excerpts from a Letter to an Old Friend in England," September 22, 1953 (Amh). "Without recourse": CEM, "Excerpts from a Letter to an Old Friend in England," September 22, 1953 (Amh). " 'The transforming' ": RM, *Memoirs*, 34–35.

CEM could "Jimmy met": RM to the author, letter, March 9, 2009. "Seeing 'only harpies' ": RM, *Memoirs*, 35.

174 **After the relative** "After the relative": JM interviewed by Brenda Gross, "Poets and Painters in the Theatre," 65. "Merrill called him": JM, *ADP*, 669. " 'One had to' ": John Bernard Myers, *Tracking the Marvelous: A Life in the New York Art World* (Random House, 1983), 164, 123.

The Artists' Theatre " 'The curtain' ": Herbert Machiz, "The Challenge of a Poetic Theatre," *Theatre Arts* (February 1956): 72. " 'The set' ": JM, *ADP*, 670.

175 **Yet Merrill** "That summer": JM interviewed by Brenda Gross, "Poets and Painters in the Theatre," 70. "Myers and Machiz": JM, "A Tribute to John Myers," *Prose*, 367. "He soon felt": DJ, journal, 1954 (WUSTL).

Larry Rivers "Robin Magowan": RM, *Memoirs*, 117. "In 1955": Rivers's portraits of JM and DJ are housed in Special Collections, WUSTL. "Robin, who": RM, *Memoirs*, 117. "About the parties": *ADP*, 669.

176 **Around this time** "Among other": JM to Harold Norse, letter, October 30, 1953 (Lilly Library, Indiana University). "New York Pro Musica Antiqua": James Gollin, *Pied Piper: The Many Lives of Noah Greenberg* (Pendragon Press, 2001), 157–58. "This was the vision": Letter from the U.S. Treasury Department, Internal Revenue Service, to the Ingram Merrill Foundation, July 9, 1955 (WUSTL).

Merrill's letter "Merrill's letter": JM to Lawrence Condon, letter, November 26, 1955 (WUSTL). "These were made": Lawrence Jasper, "A Critical History of the Artists' Theater," PhD diss., University of Kansas, Theater and Media Arts (1986), 159–60. "He began": JM to CF, letter, September 30, 1953 (Getty); and JM to CF, letter, December 30, 1953 (Getty).

176 **Like The Heroes** "He is revolted": JM, *CNP*, 508.
177 **The rest** "He feels": JM, *CNP*, 564. "Reviewing": JM, *CNP*, 570.
   Act 3 "The giddy": JM, *CNP*, 583. "[W]e never": JM, *CNP*, 597, 607. "Tithonus himself": JM, *CNP*, 627. "So it is": JM, *CNP*, 588.
178 **Merrill reduced** "Merrill reduced": JM to CF, letter, September 1954 (Getty). "The supporting": JM, *CNP*, 594. "No recipe": Brooks Atkinson, *NYT* (February 15, 1955).
   The theatrical "Tithonus does": JM, *CNP*, 511.
179 **And the older** "Laomedon's": JM, *CNP*, 538. "Dull-witted": JM, *CNP*, 598. "But Mrs. Plummer": JM, *CNP*, 499.
   Tithonus's love "Aurora embodies": JM, *CNP*, 518. "Tithonus reacts": JM, *CNP*, 535. "Mrs. Mallow": JM, *CNP*, 544.
180 **Stonington** "Stonington": DJ to Doris Sewell Jackson, letter, January 3, 1954 (WUSTL). "Jimmy and David": DJ, journal, May 15, 1954 (WUSTL). "In February": DJ to Doris Sewell Jackson, letter, January 3, 1954 (WUSTL); DJ, journal, September 1954 (WUSTL). "By April": DJ, letter to Therese, journal, September 1954 (WUSTL).
181 **From their new** " 'Ston.' ": DJ, journal, August 15, 1954 (WUSTL).
   "I love" " 'I love' ": JM, journal, April 20, 1954, Jnl 4 (WUSTL). " 'What a difference' ": JM, journal, April 22, 1954, Jnl 4 (WUSTL). "Decades later": JM, *Sandover*, 5. " 'How pleasant' ": JM, journal, April 22, 1954, Jnl 4 (WUSTL).
182 **Perhaps every** "Jimmy and David": JM, journal, April 24, 1954, Jnl 4 (WUSTL); JM, "The Hearings," journal, May 25, 1954, Jnl 4 (WUSTL). "Later that": DJ, letter to his family, journal, August 15, 1954 (WUSTL).
   The oppressive "Just adjacent": JM to KF, letter, May 15, 1954 (WUSTL).
183 **In this charmed** "In November": DJ to Doris Sewell Jackson, November 24, 1954 (WUSTL). "While he": JM to WM, letter, April 12, 1954 (WUSTL). "He talked": DJ, journal, September 20, 1954 (WUSTL). "Carefully recorded": DJ, journal, 1954 (WUSTL).
   Jackson's fiction "He had begun": DJ, journal, February 18, 1954 (WUSTL). "At the same time": JM, journal, April 9, 1954, Jnl 4 (WUSTL). " 'Tennessee' ": JM to KF, letter, May 15, 1954 (WUSTL).
184 **Cramped** "Already he was": DJ, postscript to a letter from JM to CF, May 26, 1954 (WUSTL). "It was only": DJ, journal, August 9, 1954 (WUSTL). "This journal": DJ, journal, May 25, 1954 (WUSTL). "It would be": DJ, journal, June 5, 1954 (WUSTL).
185 **He developed** "He developed": DJ, journal, June 8, 1954 (WUSTL).
   If Jackson "He wrote": DJ, journal, August 1, 1954 (WUSTL).
186 **Fredericks sent** "Merrill dedicated": JM to CF, letter, August 23, 1954 (Getty). "It also stirred": DJ, journal, August 25, 1954 (WUSTL). "He finished": DJ, journal, October 23, 1954 (WUSTL).
   Yet, when "Yet, when": DJ, journal, September 20, 1954 (WUSTL).
   The summer ended " 'Ships + trees' ": JM to CF, postcard, September 3, 1954 (Getty). "He and Jackson": JM, journal, December 15, 1973, Jnl 38 (WUSTL). "Jimmy was": JM to CF, letter, September 9, 1954 (Getty). "Jackson viewed": DJ, journal, September 1954 (WUSTL).
187 **Later that fall** "Stopping short": JM to Doris Magowan, letter, November 13, 1954 (WUSTL). "He ended": CEM to JM, letter, November 16, 1954 (Amh).
188 **As his guide** "As his guide": DJ, journal, September 1954 (WUSTL). "In his commentary": Wallace Stevens, *Letters*, ed. Holly Stevens (Knopf, 1966), 263. "The phrase": JM, "Interview with Donald Sheehan," *Prose*, 61.
   Stevens was "Only three": JM to CF, letter, September 1954 (Getty). "Stevens responded": JM, journal, October 9, 1954, Jnl 4 (WUSTL). "Stevens mentions": Stevens, *Letters*, 859.
189 **The young man** "Looking back": RM, *Memoirs*, 105. "Or a Yeats": JM to CF, letter, January 10, 1955 (Getty). "The hope": Jasper, "A Critical History," 160.
   Machiz, Merrill "Machiz, Merrill": RM to the author, letter, February 9, 2009. "But Merrill was": JM to CF, letter, January 26, 1955 (Getty). "The play opened": DJ to George and Mary

Jackson, draft letter, February 17, 1954 in DJ's journal (WUSTL). "But Merrill described": JM to CF, letter, March 1, 1955 (Getty).

190 **Tennessee Williams** "Tennessee Williams": Jasper, "A Critical History," 162. "While praising": Brooks Atkinson, "Closet Drama," 32.

Richard Hayes "The 'town' ": Jasper, "A Critical History," 168. "Myers's protest": JM to CF, letter, March 14, 1955 (Getty).

191 **Their route** "She fed him": JM to CF, letter, April 25, 1955 (Getty). "On the road": JM, journal, April 16, 1955, Jnl 4 (WUSTL). "At last": Author's interview with Doris Sewell Jackson (2001).

Jimmy instantly " 'Sewelly is heaven' ": JM, journal, April, 29, 1955, Jnl 4 (WUSTL). "The next day": DJ to Robert Grimes, letter, June 29, 1955 (WUSTL).

192 **Having driven** "They saw": JM, journal, May 4, 1955, Jnl 4 (WUSTL). "A restaurant": JM, postscript to letter, DJ to Doris Sewell Jackson, May 9, 1955 (WUSTL). "The western": JM, journal, May 9, 1955, Jnl 4 (WUSTL); JM, journal, May 12, 1955, Jnl 4 (WUSTL). "They visited": JM, journal, May 12, 1955, Jnl 4 (WUSTL). "Over two months": DJ, journal, May 30, 1955 (WUSTL).

The summer of 1955 " 'I think I've' ": JM to HIP, letter, July 19, 1955 (WUSTL).

193 **While Merrill** "It is the 'making' ": DJ to Robert Grimes, letter, June 29, 1955 (WUSTL). "Friends visited": DJ, journal, August 6, 1955 (WUSTL). "But Merrill and": JM, journal, March 1973, Jnl 4 (WUSTL).

194 **In The Book** "In The Book": JM, Sandover, 6.

195 **How exactly** "But 'The Rover Boys' ": JM, Sandover, 9.

196 **Not surprisingly** "Of their patrons": JM, Sandover, 12. "This is": JM, journal, August 24, 1955, Jnl 4 (WUSTL). "But he was excited": JM to CF, letter, August 29, 1955 (Getty). "He knew": JM to HIP, letter, September 2, 1955 (WUSTL).

This ecstatic " 'I cannot' ": JM to HIP, letter, September 2, 1955 (WUSTL).

197 **It was also** "Detre's advice": JM to HIP, letter, September 15, 1955 (WUSTL). "Exuding insight": JM, Sandover, 30.

To make "Merrill himself": JM, Sandover, 8.

198 **Merrill was** " 'We still like' ": JM, journal, September 15, 1955, Jnl 4 (WUSTL). "Merrill made": JM, "An Interview with Fred Bornhauser," Prose, 135.

The name "Yet the name": JM, "An Interview with Fred Bornhauser," Prose, 137.

199 **David's journal** "He briefly": DJ, journal, August 25, 1955 (WUSTL).

They were creating "It was crucial": JM to HIP, letter, September 15, 1955 (WUSTL).

200 **Besides his mother** "But he gave up": Author's interview with FB (2004). See Joseph Pearce, Wisdom and Innocence: A Life of G. K. Chesterton (Ignatius Press, 1996), 25.

On one level "A week later": DJ to Maya Deren, August 31, 1955 (WUSTL).

201 **Typically** "It moved": JM, Sandover, 7. "Jimmy was": Author's interview with DR (2002). "In later years": JM, ADP, 522. "Jackson also": "DJ: A Conversation with David Jackson," Shenandoah 30, no. 4 (1979): 25–44. "When she did": Author's interview with ESP (2008).

Who, between " 'Our sense' ": Daniel M. Wegner, The Illusion of Conscious Will (MIT Press, 2002), 99.

202 **In the case** "One is": Wegner, Illusion, 133. "When JM and DJ": JM, journal, August 1955, Jnl 4 (WUSTL).

William James "William James": William James, "Automatic Writing," Proceedings of the American Society for Psychical Research 1 (1889), 45; quoted in Wegner, Illusion, 142.

203 **The expansion** "The expansion": See Timothy Materer, Modernist Alchemy: Poetry and Alchemy (Cornell University Press, 1995), and Helen Sword, Ghostwriting Modernism (Cornell University Press, 2002). "Defining poetry": William Butler Yeats, "Magic and Poetry," Essays and Introductions (Macmillan, 1961), 28.

In one of "Ephraim said": JM, journal, August 26, 1955, Jnl 4 (WUSTL). "Now he picked": JM, journal, August 28, 1955, Jnl 4 (WUSTL). "The Other World": William Butler Yeats,

A Vision (Macmillan, 1962), 8. "Having already": JM, journal, August 25, 1955 (WUSTL). " 'Poets are favored' ": JM, journal, August 29, 1955, Jnl 4 (WUSTL).

204 **"How is"** " 'We are embarrassed' ": JM to HIP, letter, September 2, 1955 (WUSTL). "Then Stevens": JM, journal, September 17, 1955, Jnl 4 (WUSTL).

That combination "JM and DJ": JM, journal, August 31, 1955, Jnl 4 (WUSTL). "He described": JM, journal, September 1, 1955, Jnl 4 (WUSTL). "I wd enjoy": JM, journal, October 11, 1955, Jnl 4 (WUSTL).

Yeats spoke "He knew": JM, journal, October 1, 1955, Jnl 4 (WUSTL).

205 **During the** "For the time": JM, *Sandover*, 32.

5 *THE SERAGLIO*

207 **Merrill was** "Merrill was": JM to HIP, letter, April 30, 1956 (WUSTL). "He took": JM to IB, letter, October 31, 1955 (WUSTL). " 'I don't really' ": JM to IB, letter, October 31, 1955 (WUSTL).

208 **He didn't** "When Friar": JM to KF, letter, December 4, 1955 (WUSTL).

Merrill made "His yellow": Robert Bagg, "Paparazzo on Parnassus," http://robertbagg .com/disc.htm (2009). "He found": JM to John Fandel, letter, December 11, 1955 (Fandel). "He liked": JM to IB, letter, October 31, 1955 (WUSTL).

209 **DeMott** " 'Jim on' ": Author's interview with Benjamin DeMott (2003). "Over the years": Author's interview with Benjamin DeMott (2003). "After one": DJ to DSJ, letter, January 26, 1956 (WUSTL). "Thinking of": JM, letter, October 31, 1955 (WUSTL).

Another friend "Merrill had met": JM, *ADP*, 505–06. "He and Lurie": AL, *Familiar Spirits: A Memoir of James Merrill and David Jackson* (Viking, 2001), 6. " 'After that' ": JM, *ADP, Prose*, 506. "He was": Lurie, *Familiar Spirits*, 12–13. " 'David knew' ": Author's interview with AL (2004).

Jackson recorded "Jackson recorded": DJ, journal, October 7, 1955 (WUSTL). "Encouraged": DJ, journal, October 19, 1955 (WUSTL).

210 **Over the decades** " 'I used to read' ": Author's interview with AL (2004). "Jackson liked": DJ, journal, November 18, 1955 (WUSTL). " 'I used to have' ": Author's interview with AL (2004).

Lurie had "Lurie had": DJ to DSJ, April 18, 1956 (WUSTL). " 'I wrote' ": Author's interview with AL (2004). "The book": AL, *V. R. Lang: A Memoir* (Munich, 1959); JM to AL, letter, April 1959 (WUSTL). " 'If there were' ": AL, *Familiar Spirits*, 20.

211 **Merrill and Jackson** "She begins": AL, *Love and Friendship* (1962; Holt, 1997), 91. "She called": AL, *Familiar Spirits*, 25. "There is also": AL, *Familiar Spirits*, 13.

Lurie's fourth "While researching": AL, *Imaginary Friends* (1967; Holt, 1998). "Jackson remarked": AL, *Familiar Spirits*, 119–20.

212 **She made** " 'As I read' ": AL, *Familiar Spirits*, 63.

This reaction "From the beginning": AL, *Familiar Spirits*, 121.

When Lurie "When Lurie": JM to IB, letter, November 20, 1955 (WUSTL). "He heard": JM, journal, September 16 and October 11, 1955, Jnl 4 (WUSTL); JM, journal, September 25 and November 20, 1955, Jnl 4 (WUSTL). " 'DJ I am' ": JM, journal, October 1, 1955, Jnl 4 (WUSTL). " 'DJ 4give' ": JM, journal, November 9, 1955, Jnl 4 (WUSTL).

213 **If Jackson** "He asked": JM, journal, November 9, 1955, Jnl 4 (WUSTL). "He completed": JM to Howard Moss, letter, December 8, 1955 (WUSTL).

He begins "Like the old": JM to Howard Moss, letter, 1956 (WUSTL).

215 **Slight as it is** "Merrill held": JM, journal, November 1955, Jnl 4 (WUSTL).

Despite Ephraim's "David was proud": DJ to Doris Sewell Jackson, letter, November 2, 1955 (WUSTL); DJ, "Kritik K. and the Chateau (A Parable in Patchwork)," *Semi-Colon* 1, no. 5 (1955): 3. Merrill's "Three Sketches for Europa" was printed on page 2. " 'F—k 'em' ": DJ to Doris Sewell Jackson, letter, December 1, 1955 (WUSTL).

216 **Showing how** "Jackson was": DJ, journal, January 26, 1956 (WUSTL). "David suspected": DJ, journal, January 27, 1956 (WUSTL).
Part of "Rather, Francis": JM, *CNP*, 65.

217 **We meet** "When Xenia": JM, *CNP*, 21–22.
The Seraglio "Hunting": JM, *CNP*, 31–32.
Back at "Back at": JM, *CNP*, 63. "He rules": JM, *CNP*, 127.

218 **But Francis** "He drops": JM, *CNP*, 94. "Explaining": JM, *CNP*, 95. " 'It means' ": JM, *CNP*, 97.
Xenia "In shame": JM, *CNP*, 138. "After dinner": JM, *CNP*, 153. "Repelled": JM, *CNP*, 159.

219 **Back in** "Phrases": JM, *CNP*, 162. "He survives": JM, *CNP*, 171.
But Vinnie "At first": JM, *CNP*, 174.

220 **The novel** "Even the word": JM to HIP, letter, November 1, 1956 (WUSTL). " 'You understand' ": JM, *CNP*, 232.
This scene "This scene": JM, Ouija board transcript, September 2, 1956 (WUSTL). "The scene": Synopsis contained in JM to HIP, letter, November 25, 1950 (WUSTL). "The set": JM, *CNP*, 254.

221 **The end** "When, back": JM, *CNP*, 10. "Similarly": JM, *CNP*, 256.
The answer "When Lily": JM, *CNP*, 10. " 'I tell you' ": JM, *CNP*, 236.

222 **In this mood** "At lunch": JM, *CNP*, 293, 295. "Lily invites": JM, *CNP*, 302. "The novel": JM, *CNP*, 303.

223 **What Francis** "What Francis": JM, *CNP*, 135. "Lurie put": DJ, journal, February 10, 1956 (WUSTL). " 'Are you Planning' ": DJ, journal, April 27, 1956 (WUSTL). "Detre, accustomed": DJ, journal, February 24, 1956 (WUSTL).
Merrill sought "Merrill sought": DJ to Doris Sewell Jackson, letter, May 8, 1956 (WUSTL). "At the request": JM to HIP, letter, c. September 1956 (WUSTL). "He told JM": JM, Ouija board transcript, June 29, 1956 (WUSTL).
Pain is "When Jackson": DJ, journal, February 10, 1956 (WUSTL).

224 **When the book** "Merrill, suggesting": JM, *CNP*, 300. "Finally": JM, *CNP*, 71.
Enid "It's Enid": JM, *CNP*, 93.
The Seraglio "Merrill Lynch": Author's interview with Merrill Magowan (2003). "Like a sweet-tongued": JM to RM, letter, February 13, 1956 (WUSTL).

225 **It was** "The plan": DJ to Doris Sewell Jackson, letter, February 25, 1965 (WUSTL). "Sewelly told": DJ, journal, August 6, 1955 (WUSTL). "When the wedding": Author's interview with Doris Sewell Jackson (2002).
David recorded "David recorded": DJ, journal, early April 1956 (WUSTL).

226 **Hellen wrote** "Her son replied": JM to HIP, letter, April 7, 1956 (WUSTL).
Hellen's objection "Speaking to Francis": JM, *CNP*, 33–35.

227 **Commenting** "*The Seraglio*": JM to HIP, letter, April 7, 1956 (WUSTL).

228 **Jimmy didn't** "He made": JM to Alice B. Toklas, letter, July 24, 1956 (WUSTL). "It was": DJ, journal, August 1954 (WUSTL).
The new novelist "He published": JM, "For a Second Marriage" and "Salome," *Poetry* 87, no. 295 (February 1956).

229 **In March** " 'I cannot' ": JM to Mac Hammond, letter, December 9, 1955 (Houghton). "After the reading": JM, poetry reading, March 5, 1956 (Woodberry Poetry Room Archive, Harvard).
He gave "He gave": Announcement, poetry reading by James Merrill and Peter Kane Dufault, Poetry Center, New York, April 4, 1956 (WUSTL). "He found": JM to HIP, letter, May 13, 1956 (WUSTL). "At one": JM to JDM, letter, January 13, 1973 (Yale).
In the evenings " 'The funny' ": JM to CF, letter, January 14, 1956 (Getty). "But he assigns": JM, *Sandover*, 45. "With Jimmy": DJ, journal, March 10, 1956 (WUSTL); JM, *Sandover*, 27.

230 **By summertime** "Ephraim was": JM, Ouija board transcript, June 30, 1956 (WUSTL). "Ephraim scolded": JM, Ouija board transcript, July 22, 1956 (WUSTL).
If the spirits "But with": JM, Ouija board transcript, July 3, 1956 (WUSTL).

231 **Life** " 'He is divine' ": JM to CF, letter, July 17, 1956 (Getty). " 'Tell me' ": Author's interview with DR (2005).

231 **When Merrill** " 'A book' ": JM, Ouija board transcript, July 17, 1956 (WUSTL). "The mirror and the window": JH, "A Poetics of Restitution," *The Work of Poetry* (Columbia University Press, 1997), 44–49.

232 **On another level** "In June": DJ, journal, June 15, 1956 (WUSTL).

233 **On still** "He began": JM, journal, September 21, 1956, Jnl 64 (WUSTL).

234 **On their side** "That summer": JM to John Fandel, letter, September 9, 1956 (Fandel). "On the same": JM and DJ, August 5, 1956 (WUSTL).

235 **Jimmy's visit** "Jimmy's visit": JM to HIP, letter, August 20, 1956 (WUSTL). " 'Even those' ": JM to HIP, letter, July 6, 1956 (WUSTL).

236 **Charlie's** "In July": JM to HIP, letter, July 6, 1956 (WUSTL). "He noted": JM to HIP, letter, c. September 1956 (WUSTL). "Doris urged": JM to HIP, letter, c. early September 1956 (WUSTL). "On September 3": JM, Ouija board transcript, September 3, 1956 (WUSTL).
In New York "In New York": JM to Rosemary Sprague, September 9, 1956 (WUSTL). "With Doris": "The Magowans of San Francisco, Togetherness Family of the Month," *McCall's*, illustration in Property from the Estate of Doris Merrill Magowan (Christie's New York, 2002), 17.

237 **The Magowans'** "At the reception": JM to CF, letter, September 16, 1956 (WUSTL). "The next day": JM to Kay Meredith, letter, September 17, 1956 (WUSTL). "Merrill fussed": Author's interview with Robert Grimes (2004). "Surprised": JM, journal, September 15, 1956, Jnl 54 (WUSTL).
Japan "It was the symbol": JM to Kay Meredith, letter, September 17, 1956 (WUSTL).
Neither " 'Tex' ": Author's interview with DR (2005). "Every night": DR, *"Sada Abe," Japanese Portraits (1987; Tuttle ed., 2005), 33–35.*

238 **On hand** "After serving": For an introduction to DR's life and work, see *The Donald Richie Reader: 50 Years of Writing on Japan*, ed. Arturo Silva (Stone Bridge, 2001), and DR, *The Japan Journals: 1947–2004*, ed. Leza Lowitz (Stone Bridge, 2004). "All that lay": JM, journal, October 18, 1956, Jnl 54 (WUSTL). "Jimmy took": JM, *ADP*, 521.

239 **On October** "The question": JM to CEM, letter, October 1, 1956 (WUSTL). "CEM": JM to Alice B. Toklas, letter, October 6, 1956 (WUSTL). "What he would": JM to HIP, letter, October 6, 1956 (WUSTL).

240 **In the days** "In the days": JM to HIP, letter, October 6, 1956 (WUSTL). "He and Jackson": JM, journal, October 11, 1956, Jnl 54 (WUSTL). " 'Mine good' ": JM, journal, October 8, 1956, Jnl 54 (WUSTL). " 'Over and over' ": JM, "The Beaten Path," *Prose*, 325.
News "Hellen wrote": JM to FB, letter, October 30, 1956 (Wheaton). " 'My tears' ": JM to HIP, letter, October 23, 1956 (WUSTL). "Ephraim reported": JM, journal, October 23, 1956, Jnl 4 (WUSTL).

241 **During these** "Merrill was": JM, "The Beaten Path," *Prose*, 326.
From Kyoto "It was 'the most' ": JM to HIP, letter, November 1, 1956 (WUSTL).
At Hiroshima "To visit": JM to FB, letter, October 30, 1956 (Wheaton).

242 **By contrast** "In Tokyo": JM to Guitou Knoop, letter, October 3, 1956 (WUSTL).
Part of "Merrill saw": JM, "The Beaten Path," *Prose*, 328.

243 **Merrill also** "He found": JM to Tony Harwood, letter, c. October 15, 1956 (WUSTL). "Their veiled": JM to John Myers and Herbert Machiz, letter, c. November 1956 (WUSTL).
Merrill was "At last": Author's interview with DR (2004); JM to George and Mary Jackson, letter, November 2, 1956 (WUSTL).

244 **Robin** "Robin": Author's interview with RM (WUSTL). "He put": JM, "The Beaten Track," *Semi-Colon* (1957). " 'It is very' ": JM, "The Beaten Track," *Prose*, 324.
Hong Kong "Merrill knew": JM to HIP, letter, November 21, 1956 (WUSTL). " '[S]triking' ": JM to CF, letter, November 24, 1956 (Getty).
Bangkok "Gazing": JM to Rosemary Sprague, letter, November 29, 1956, carbon in Jnl 67 (WUSTL).

245 **Jimmy and David** "Robin notes": Author's interview with RM (2002). "That didn't": JM, "The Beaten Track," *Prose*, 329.

246 **The next** "The next": JM to HIP, telegram, December 25, 1956 (WUSTL). "They saw": JM to CF, letter, January 10, 1957 (Getty).

When they "There were": JM, Ouija board transcript, January 8, 1957 (WUSTL).

247 **Merrill was deep** "He read": JM to FB, letter, February 13, 1957 (Wheaton). "The colonial": JM to HIP, letter, January 12, 1957 (WUSTL). "They flew": JM to Doris and Robert Magowan, letter, January 22, 1957 (WUSTL); JM, journal, January 22, 1957 (WUSTL); JM to HIP, letter, January 31, 1957 (WUSTL). "Charles was writing": JM to HIP, letter, February 26, 1957 (WUSTL). "As usual": JM to Marilyn and Irving Lavin, letter, February 20, 1957 (Lavin).

In Munich "In Munich": JM to FB, letter, February 13, 1956 (Wheaton). "He marveled": JM to Marilyn and Irving Lavin, letter, February 20, 1957 (Lavin). "They retired": JM to RM, letter, March 18, 1957 (WUSTL). "Merrill called": JM to CF, letter, January 10, 1957 (WUSTL). "He planned": DJ to Marilyn and Irving Lavin, letter, February 20, 1957 (Lavin).

By now "He directed": JM to Herbert Weinstock, c. March 1957 (WUSTL). "I honestly": JM to HIP, letter, November 1, 1956 (WUSTL).

248 **Jimmy himself** "*The Seraglio* seemed": JM to HIP, letter, February 26, 1957 (WUSTL). "In it, Charlie": JM to CF, letter, May 4, 1957 (Getty).

Still, the novel " 'I was astounded' ": JM to Doris and Robert Magowan, letter, March 1957 (WUSTL). "That was enough": Author's interview with RM (2006).

249 **Gerrish** "The novel": JM to Gerrish Thurber, letter, April 16, 1957 (WUSTL).

The reviews "They were put": Charles Rojo, review of *The Seraglio, Atlantic* 19, no. 5 (May 1957): 86–87. "The *Nation*": David L. Stevenson, review of *The Seraglio, Nation* 184, no. 15 (April 13, 1957): 329. "The *Atlantic*": Charles Rojo, review of *The Seraglio, Atlantic* 19, no. 5 (May 1957): 86–87. "Its review": Richard Sullivan, "Tycoon's Harem," review of *The Seraglio, NYT* (April 21, 1957).

250 **Wilbur's reference** "Resigned": JM to Jellian Baer, letter, March 31, 1957 (WUSTL).

Jimmy and David "Their goal": JM to Jellian Baer, letter, March 31, 1957 (WUSTL). " 'Conceivably' ": JM to CF, letter, May 4, 1957 (Getty).

6 WATER STREET

252 **It was natural** "He liked": JM, "Acoustical Chambers," *Prose*, 3. "He pored over": Gaston Bachelard, *La poétique de l'espace* (Presses Universitaires de France, 1958).

A sharp "When the contents": JM to WM, letter, June 30, 1957 (WUSTL). "The room": JM, *Sandover*, 40. "Jimmy and David": JM, *Sandover*, 5.

253 **Painting** "From Merrill's": "The Basic Service of Art," *Bulletin of the Art Institute of Chicago* 12, no. 1 (January 1918): 2. "A watercolor": AC to the author, email, July 22, 2008.

254 **Mirrors** "This unnervingly": JM, *Sandover*, 98.

255 **Eleanor Perényi** "Like many": Author's interview with ESP (2002).

Grace Stone "Grace Stone": Eleanor Blau, "Grace Zaring Stone, a Novelist Under Two Names, Dies at 100," *NYT* (October 1, 1991). "Sometimes, her daughter": Author's interview with ESP (2008).

256 **Eleanor was** "It was no": Author's interview with DR (2005). "A classic": Marglit Fox, "Eleanor Perenyi, Writer and Gardener, Dies at 91," *NYT* (May 6, 2009).

The Morses "The daughter": Author's interview with Regan Morse (2009).

257 **Robert was** "He was born": Jacket copy, Robert Morse, *The Two Persephones* (Creative Age Press, 1942). "After he graduated": Jacket copy, Robert Morse, *The Two Persephones*. "When they married": Author's interview with Regan Morse (2009). "Robert continued": Author's interview with ESP (2003). "He published": Morse, *The Two Persephones*.

But his special "(At Jimmy's)": W. H. Auden, *A Certain World: A Commonplace Book* (Viking, 1970), 357–58. "He was given": JM, journal, "R. M.'s Sayings," c. 1957, Jnl 3 (WUSTL).

257 **Despite his** "Despite his": Author's interview with ESP (2003).

Merrill and Jackson were almost "For some time": Author's interview with ESP (2003). "Fuming": author's interview with Doris Sewell Jackson (2002).

258 **Merrill and Jackson were at home** "David joined": JM to HIP, letter, January 4, 1958 (WUSTL); author's interview with Walker and Nancy Gibson (2004).

The chill air "So were": JM to John Fandel, letter, January 25, 1958 (WUSTL). "A small": JM to WM, February 3, 1958 (WUSTL). "When she died": JM, "The Poet's Notebook," *Prose*, 37. "She took": JM to John Fandel, letter, January 25, 1958 (Fandel). "Within were": James Kraft, *Who Is Witter Bynner? A Biography* (University of New Mexico Press, 1995), 58. "As he told": Kraft, *Witter Bynner*, 59. "Bynner was": JM to WM, letter, February 3, 1958 (WUSTL).

259 **It worked** " 'Poems drop' ": JM to RM, postcard, January 28, 1958 (WUSTL). "The arrangement": JM to Barbara Deming, letter, February 27, 1958 (Radcliffe).

From a distance "Its foreign": Robert von Hallberg, *American Poetry and Culture, 1945–1980* (University of Chicago Press, 1985). "Wherever the tourist": JM, "Some Negatives: X at the Chateau," *CP*.

261 **Merrill was unsure** "His draft": JM, journal, c. February 1958, Jnl 67 (WUSTL).

Merrill finished "Contemplating": JM to KF, letter, March 13, 1958 (WUSTL).

262 **And where** "After a pause": JM, journal, March 27, 1958, Jnl 67 (WUSTL).

263 **Merrill looked** "Merrill looked": JM to CF, letter, January 15, 1959 (Getty). "They squabbled": JM to MLA, letter, July 10, 1958 (WUSTL). "Friends came": JM to RM, letter, April 26, 1958 (WUSTL). "Merrill chose": JM to MLA, letter, July 10, 1958 (WUSTL). "He was taking": JM to CF, letter, May 9, 1958 (Getty); JM to CF, letter, January 15, 1959 (Getty).

The period "In 1958": JM to RM, letter, April 26, 1958 (WUSTL). "The Lavins": JM to Marilyn and Irving Lavin, letter, April 20, 1958 (Lavin).

These and other "In *A Different*": JM, *ADP*, 626.

A year "A year": JM, *Sandover*, 30. "Tom had": JM, *ADP*, 626.

265 **"Scenes of Childhood"** "Merrill began": JM to CF, letter, May 9, 1958 (Getty).

267 **Going into** "They started": JM to WM, letter, January 31, 1959 (WUSTL). "They called": DJ, letter to his family in his journal, January 1959 (WUSTL). "They paid": JM to WM, letter, January 31, 1959 (WUSTL). "Jackson recorded": DJ, letter to his family in his journal, January 1959 (WUSTL).

268 **Their base** "Robin and": JM to WM, letter, January 31, 1959 (WUSTL). "They weathered": DJ, journal, October 30, 1959 (WUSTL). " 'He is a rather' ": JM to WM, letter, August 1959 (WUSTL).

After Munich "After Munich": JM to Rosemary Sprague, letter, May 8, 1959 (WUSTL). "They liked": JM to MLA, letter, May 2, 1959 (WUSTL). "She took": JM to MLA, letter, May 2, 1959 (WUSTL). "They saw the Roman": JM to EB, letter, November 3, 1959 (WUSTL). " 'Everything only' ": EB, *Complete Poems, 1927–1979* (FSG, 1983), 58.

In Madrid " 'Such a peculiar' ": JM to MLA, letter, May 2, 1959 (WUSTL). "From Barcelona": JM to MLA, letter, May 2, 1959 (WUSTL). "They visited": JM to Rosemary Sprague, letter, May 8, 1959 (WUSTL). "Merrill tucked": JM to JH, May 29, 1959 (WUSTL). "From Venice": JM to HIP, letter, June 10, 1959 (WUSTL).

269 **Charlie Shoup** " 'Charlie's fantasies' ": DJ, journal, June 12, 1959 (WUSTL). "Shoup, who": Author's interview with Charles Shoup (2003).

Like Tony "The mood": DJ, journal, June 12, 1959 (WUSTL). "The arrangement": JM, *ADP*, 616. "Edmund White": Author's telephone interview with Edmund White (2008).

270 **From the beginning** " 'It was a truth' ": JM, *ADP*, 614–15.

271 **A Different Person** "As the days": DJ, journal, c. June 1959 (WUSTL).

272 **That summer** "That summer": JM, chronology (WUSTL). "While Jackson": JM, "Afterword to *The (Diblos) Notebook*," *Prose*, 634.

On their final "Then Jackson": TP, "Nights and Days," *For James Merrill: A Birthday Tribute*, ed. JDM (Jordan Davies, 1986), n.p.

273 **Merrill and Jackson** " 'Surely' ": JM to WM, letter, August 1, 1959 (WUSTL).
As when "But Jim": Monroe K. Spears, *Dionysus and the City: Modernism in Twentieth-Century Poetry* (Oxford University Press, 1970), 257. "To open": James Dickey, review of *The Country of a Thousand Years of Peace*, *Sewanee Review* 67 (1959): 497.
There were "He had been": Author's interview with DH (2005). "His review": Marius Bewley, "Poetry Chronicle," *Partisan Review* 26, no. 2 (spring 1959): 326. " 'The most' ": Bewley, "Poetry Chronicle," 327. " 'The subject' ": Bewley, "Poetry Chronicle," 330.

274 **Bewley's piece** "*Life Studies*": Irvin Ehrenpreis, "The Age of Lowell," *American Poetry*, ed. John Russell Brown, Irvin Ehrenpreis, and Bernard Harris (E. Arnold, 1965), 69–95.

278 **"The poet"** " 'The poet' ": JM, "An Interview with David Kalstone," *Prose*, 82.
The type "Merrill returned": DJ, journal, October 1960 (WUSTL). "To prove": DJ, journal, October 1960 (WUSTL).

279 **"Convalescence"** "As it streaks": JM to EB, letter, April 8, 1960 (WUSTL). "Lest he offend": JM to TP, letter, April 21, 1961 (WUSTL).

280 **Whether or not** "Whether or not": JM to CF, letter, January 24, 1960 (Getty). "He returned": JM to HIP, letter, c. spring 1960 (WUSTL); JM to Gerrish Thurber, letter, April 6, 1960 (WUSTL). "Despite his": JM to KF, letter, February 6, 1960 (WUSTL); JM to Miss Horner, letter, May 15, 1960 (WUSTL). "In May": JM to AL, letter, c. May 1960 (WUSTL).

281 **"We" included** " 'We' included": DJ, "The English Gardens," *Partisan Review* 28, no. 2 (March–April 1961): 201–44. "A pretender": DJ, "The English Gardens," 208.

282 **In Stonington** "He was no": Author's interview with Doris Sewell Jackson (2001).
Hilda "When neighbors": DJ to George and Mary Jackson, July 17, 1957 (WUSTL). " 'The beauty' ": JM to HIP, letter, April 22, 1960 (WUSTL).

285 **Water Street** "Merrill enjoyed": JM to Robert Morse, letter, c. October 1960 (WUSTL). "The first": JM, *Prose*, 334. "And the writing": JM to MLA, letter, c. October 1960 (WUSTL).
In Paris "In Paris": JM to MLA, letter, c. October 1960 (WUSTL). "Hill's neoclassical": *A Catafalque for David Hill*, ed. Virgil Burnett (Pasdeloup Press, 1986), 22. "Through Hill": Author's interview with Virgil Burnett (2001). "The two *flaneurs*": JM, *ADP*, 521.

286 **Back at home** " 'Well,' Merrill": JM to Howard Moss, letter, October 19, 1960 (WUSTL). "The War Ministry": JM to James Dickey, letter, November 7, 1960 (WUSTL). "David wasn't": JM to MLA, letter, c. October 1960 (WUSTL). "They'd bought": JM to Howard Moss, letter, October 19, 1960 (WUSTL). "Jimmy read": JM to James Dickey, letter, November 7, 1960 (WUSTL). " 'Every night' ": DJ, journal, October 1, 1960 (WUSTL). "So they": JM to B. V. Winebaum, letter, December 22, 1960 (WUSTL). "John Cage": JM to JH, postcard, c. October 1960 (WUSTL). "Hine brought": DJ, journal, October 30, 1960 (WUSTL).
From Munich "Thom Gunn": Thom Gunn, "Meeting the Merrills in Berlin," enc. to the author, letter, November 2002.
The Merrills "In Venice": Alan Ansen, *Disorderly Houses* (Wesleyan University Press, 1961), 67–85.

287 **Their host** "He wrote": Author's interview with Josiane Boulade-Ayoub and Christine Ayoub (2006). "Through Ayoub": JM to B. V. Winebaum, letter, December 22, 1960 (WUSTL). "These included": JM to DH, March 5, 1961 (WUSTL).
Along with "As Christine": Author's interview with Josiane Boulade-Ayoub and Christine Ayoub (2006).

288 **At a cocktail** "At a cocktail": JM to HIP, letter, December 1, 1960 (WUSTL). "As one": JM to FB, letter, December 4, 1960 (Wheaton). "The tone": JM to B. V. Winebaum, letter, December 22, 1960 (WUSTL). "One spent": JM to HIP, letter, December 1, 1960 (WUSTL).
Traveling south "Traveling south": JM to FB, letter, December 4, 1960 (Wheaton). "He already": JM to CF, letter, December 30, 1960 (Getty). "But he was": JM to DH, letter, March 5, 1961 (WUSTL); JM to CF, letter, December 30, 1960 (Getty). "He stood": JM, "Letter from Egypt," *CP*, 164. " 'I think' ": JM to FB, letter, December 4, 1960 (Wheaton).
They spent "They spent": JM to B. V. Winebaum, letter, December 22, 1960 (WUSTL).

"Today, sepia tinted": Author's interview with DR (2005). "No longer": JM to CF, letter, December 30, 1960 (Getty). "Then a return": JM to RM, letter, January 1961 (WUSTL).

289 **By February** "David's sketchbook": JM to RM, letter, January 1961 (WUSTL). "As he had": JM to KF, letter, July 7, 1961 (WUSTL).

His mother "Alone with": Albert Rothenberg, *The Emerging Goddess: The Creative Process in Art, Science, and Other Fields* (University of Chicago Press, 1979), 84. " 'I had never' ": JM to KF, letter, July 7, 1961 (WUSTL).

290 **"Annie Hill's"** "Merrill shuffled": JM to WM, letter, July 22, 1961 (WUSTL). "Merrill's poems": JM to JH, letter, November 16, 1961 (WUSTL).

Merrill trusted " 'And, of course' ": DJ, journal, October 30, 1959 (WUSTL).

The Ingram "It provided": DJ, journal, October 30, 1959 (WUSTL). "A selection": HF to Milton Maurer, letter, December 20, 1959 (WUSTL). "Investigating": JM to IB, letter, April 5, 1960 (WUSTL).

291 **Over the decades** "The *refusées*": HF to Lawrence Condon, letter, March 4, 1962; HF to Lawrence Condon, letter, December 2, 1962 (WUSTL).

292 **The foundation** "As Hollander": Author's interview with JH (2009).

"The five actors" "The five actors": Kenneth Gross, "Love Translated: The Little Players," *Yale Review* 94, no. 1 (2006): 84.

293 **The mock** " 'Their theater' ": Gross, "Love Translated: The Little Players," 90–91.

Gold "Merrill's favorite": Edmund White, *City Boy: My Life in New York in the 1960s and '70s* (Bloomsbury, 2009), 130. "The evening": JM to DR, letter, December 12, 1961 (WUSTL).

294 **With his manuscript** "With his manuscript": JM to Gerrish Thurber, letter, October 27, 1961 (WUSTL). "Nikita": Earl Ubell, "Halloween Horror," *New York Herald Tribune*, October 27, 1961. "A mighty": "Big Ivan, The Tsar Bomb ('King of Bombs')," http://nuclearweapon archive.org/Russia/TsarBomba.html (September 2009). " 'The 50 megaton' ": JM, journal, October 26, 1961, Jnl 64 (WUSTL). The date is crossed out.

295 **Typically** " 'SELF SERVICE' ": These and many other anagrams are scattered throughout JM's journals. See JM, "The Poet's Notebook," *Prose*, 32. The anagram "MARCEL PROUST/ PEARL SCROTUM" is inscribed in JM's copy of Marcel Proust, *À la recherche du temps perdu* (JDM). "The name": JM, journal, May 4, 1970, Jnl 7 (WUSTL). "Sometimes the wordplay": JM, journal, c. 1964, Jnl 58 (WUSTL). "Merrill began": JM, journal, c. 1959, Jnl 64 (WUSTL). " 'JAMES MERRILL' ": JM, typescript, c. 1960, reproduced in *James Merrill: Other Writings*, 2001 (WUSTL).

296 **When humanity** "Hine, who": Author's interview with DH (2009). "On the notebook": JM, journal, c. October–November 1961, Jnl 12 (WUSTL).

297 **Side by side** "Merrill made": JM, notes for "The Stonington Novel" (WUSTL).

298 **No small** "In the late 1950s": Author's interviews with RM (2001) and DR (2005). "In Greece": Author's interview with DR (2005).

7 THE CRACK IN THE MIRROR

303 **As if** " 'Well, it is' ": JM to DH, letter, March 9, 1962 (WUSTL). "They rented": JM to Alice B. Toklas, letter, March 21, 1962 (WUSTL); JM to IB, letter, April 24, 1962 (WUSTL).

Prepared "Prepared": JM, chronology (WUSTL). " 'Every other' ": "Niko the Ice Boy," *David Jackson: Scenes from His Life* (Nadja, 1994), n.p.

304 **It was not** "Olympic Airways": http://airlines.afriqonline.com/airlines/621.htm (2009).

The change " 'The broad' ": JM, "Yannis Tsarouchis," *Prose*, 345. "Besides, the opening": JM to DH, letter, April 21, 1962 (WUSTL).

305 **He was hardly** "In this new myth": See Edmund Keeley, *Inventing Paradise: The Greek Journey 1937–47* (FSG, 1999), and David Roessel, *In Byron's Shadow: Modern Greece in the English and American Imagination* (Oxford University Press, 2002).

305 **In 1972** "In 1972": JM, "On 'Yánnina': An Interview with David Kalstone," *Prose*, 80. "In 1962": JM, journal, 1962, Jnl 66 (WUSTL).

306 **The second life** " 'A writer' ": JM, "On 'Yánnina': An Interview with David Kalstone," *Prose*, 80. "In time": JM, "On 'Yánnina': An Interview with David Kalstone," *Prose*, 80.

When he arrived "He and David": Author's interview with Alan Ansen (2002). "Another was": JM to DH, letter, April 7, 1962 (WUSTL). "It was a 'nightmare' ": JM to DR, letter, June 12, 1962 (WUSTL).

307 **Meanwhile** "On this trip": JM to DR, letter, June 12, 1962 (WUSTL). "Their flat": DJ to DR, letter, January 16, 1962 (WUSTL).

Tall, smiling "He'd known": Author's interview with RM (2004). "Liambey invited": Author's interview with NL (2003).

Merrill met "Liambey was": Author's interview with NL (2002).

308 **Maria, three** "Her father": Clogg, *A Short History of Modern Greece*, 129–30. "When at length": Author's interview with Nina and Dimitri Koutsoudakis (2003). "She and Niko": Author's interview with Nina and Dimitri Koutsoudakis (2003).

309 **After her** " 'She was still' ": Author's interview with NL (2002). "Instead, she": Author's interview with Nina and Dimitri Koutsoudakis (2003). " '*Surface!*' ": Author's interview with NL (2003).

To Maria "Jimmy responded": JM, dedicatory inscription to Maria Mitsotáki on "Five Poems," 1964, property of Nina and Dimitri Koutsoudakis. " 'Jimmy was' ": Author's interview with Natalia Méla and NL (2003). "Maria had": Author's interview with Nina and Dimitri Koutsoudakis (2003).

Tony was "In a sailor's": JM to DH, letter, April 7, 1962 (WUSTL).

310 **In April** " 'A doctor' ": JM to DH, letter, April 21, 1962 (WUSTL). "It is 'a form' ": http://www/ninds.nih.gov/health_and_medical/disorders/bells_doc.htm (2006). "The patient": JM to EB, letter, December 14, 1962 (Vassar). "For a few": JM to DH, letter, April 21, 1962 (WUSTL).

Merrill soon "I suspect": JM to DH, letter, April 21, 1962 (WUSTL).

Istanbul "They had worried": DJ and JM to DR, letter, January 16, 1962 (WUSTL). "When he departed": JM to DH, letter, April 21, 1962 (WUSTL). "As he told": JM to CF, letter, April 20, 1962 (Getty).

Robin and Betty "Robin and Betty": JM to DH, letter, April 21, 1962 (WUSTL). "Looking back": RM, *Memoirs*, 151.

311 **Robin was** "Robin was": RM, "Sailor at Perema," *Lilac Cigarette in a Wish Cathedral* (University of South Carolina Press, 1998), 1. "Robin remembers": RM, *Memoirs*, 153–54.

Grace Stone "Grace Stone": JM to DH, letter, May 22, 1962 (WUSTL); JM to DR, letter, June 12, 1962 (WUSTL).

312 **Bernard's parodies** "When he": JM to B. V. Winebaum, letter, May 5, 1962 (WUSTL). "It wasn't": JM to DH, letter, May 22, 1962 (WUSTL).

Shortly before " 'As you talked' ": KF to JM, letter, June 14, 1962 (WUSTL).

He didn't "Friar had said": JM to KF, letter, July 4, 1962 (WUSTL).

314 **Friar's "terrain"** "He met": JM to KF, letter, July 4, 1962 (WUSTL).

Merrill had "Then he": KF to JM, letter, February 25, 1963 (WUSTL).

315 **Notes for** "In 1958": JM, journal, 1958, Jnl 62 (WUSTL).

The idea "The Greek word": JM to Anne and Virgil Burnett, letter, March 13, 1964 (Waterloo).

316 **Merrill worked** "Merrill worked": JM, journal, 1958, Jnl 65 (WUSTL). "After his letter": JM to TP, letter, February 15, 1964 (WUSTL). "Taking stock": JM to DR, letter, February 3, 1964 (WUSTL). "As his writer-narrator": JM, *CNP*, 409.

The novel's "The novel's: JM, *CNP*, 309. "The crossed-out": SY, panel on James Merrill at Amherst College (2004).

317 **But The (Diblos)** "Sandy compares": JM, *CNP*, 374. "Orestes lectures": JM, *CNP*, 352. "The economic": JM, *CNP*, 331.

318 **We can gauge** "Sandy makes": JM, *CNP*, 337.
Merrill's argument "The 'famous one' ": JM, *CNP*, 377–78.
But Merrill "When Dora": JM, *CNP*, 75.

319 **Sandy and Orestes** "The two men": JM, *CNP*, 362. "While the music": JM, *CNP*, 363.
The dance "He learns": JM, *CNP*, 363. "He, or rather": JM, *CNP*, 364.

320 **As he worked** "As he worked": JM to CF, letter, August 5, 1962 (Getty). "Weary from": JM to
CF, letter, August 5, 1962 (Getty).
Water Street "*Water Street*": X. J. Kennedy, review of *Water Street*, *NYT Book Review* (November
25, 1962), 42. "Atheneum quickly": JM to DR, letter, December 19, 1962 (WUSTL). "Merrill
appeared": DJ and JM to AL, letter, November 1962 (WUSTL). " 'I wonder' ": DJ and JM to
DR, letter, December 19, 1962 (WUSTL).
"Oh," Jackson " 'Oh,' Jackson": DJ and JM to DR, letter, December 19, 1962 (WUSTL). "He
reported": DJ and JM to DR, letter, December 19, 1962 (WUSTL). "He spoke": DJ and JM to
DR, letter, December 19, 1962 (WUSTL). " 'That's David's' ": Author's interview with DH
(2004). "In need": DJ to DR, letter, September 19, 1962 (WUSTL). "Jimmy marked": JM to
DJ, card, September 16, 1962 (WUSTL).

321 **Despite the face** "Merrill wound": JM to TP, letter, September 18, 1962 (WUSTL).

322 **Again the nation** "By November": JM to Peter Forcey, letter, November 15, 1962 (Forcey).
Friar had "He returned": JM to CF, letter, November 19, 1962 (Getty).

323 **Indeed something** "At first": JM, journal, 1962, Jnl 66 (WUSTL). "He soon": JM, "An Interview with Donald Sheehan," *Prose*, 54.
"The Thousand" "It projects": JM, "An Interview with Donald Sheehan," *Prose*, 52.

327 **One model** "One model": JM, "An Interview with Donald Sheehan," *Prose*, 58.

329 **After Christmas** "There he saw": JM to William Burford, letter, January 14, 1963 (Ransom);
JM to DH, letter, January 14, 1963 (WUSTL). "Jimmy made": JM to DH, letter, January 14,
1963 (WUSTL); JM to RM, letter, February 1, 1963 (WUSTL); JM to Howard Moss, letter,
March 7, 1963 (WUSTL); JM to DH, letter, June 15, 1964 (WUSTL).

330 **On January** "He 'loathed' ": JM to CF, letter, January 30, 1963 (Getty). "Poets turned": JM
to CF, letter, January 30, 1963 (Getty). " 'It was an immense' ": JM to RM, letter, February 1,
1963 (WUSTL).
As Merrill "Jimmy once": JM to DMc, letter, February 5, 1969 (WUSTL). "Born in 1924":
Hala Halim, "Against the Dying of the Light," *Al-Ahram Weekly*, http://weekly.ahram.org
.eg/1999/444/culture.htm (August 26–September 1, 1999). "As he sat": Author's interview
with Samuel Lock (2002).

331 **Merrill paid** "Merrill paid": Bernard de Zogheb, *Le Sorelle Brontë*, foreword by JM (Tibor de
Nagy Editions, 1963). " 'It is designed' ": JM, "Foreword to *Le Sorelle Brontë*," *Prose*, 357.
The tunes "The final": De Zogheb, *Le Sorelle Brontë*, 32. " 'On every' ": "Foreword to *Le Sorelle
Brontë*," *Prose*, 357–58. "By flamboyantly": "Foreword to *Le Sorelle Brontë*," *Prose*, 358.
De Zogheb "As the editor": JM to Bernard de Zogheb, letter, February 12, 1963 (WUSTL).

332 **Merrill's frequent** "In November": JM to DH, letter, November 17, 1962 (WUSTL). "Before
Hine": JM to DH, letter, November 18, 1962 (WUSTL). "But Merrill": JM to DR, letter, May 5,
1963 (WUSTL). "Yet with only": JM to DR, letter, May 5, 1963 (WUSTL).

333 **Jackson too** "Jackson too": DJ to DR, letter, November 12, 1962 (WUSTL). "Then, too":
DJ to DR, letter, December 19, 1962 (WUSTL). "He told": DJ to DR, letter, March 8, 1963
(WUSTL).

334 **Two weeks** " 'Ker-plooie!' ": JM to DH, letter, March 26, 1963 (WUSTL).
Not all "More babies": JM to Anne and Virgil Burnett, letter, July 26, 1963 (Waterloo); JM
to JH, letter, June 4, 1963 (Yale). "David commented": Guestbook 107 Water Street, April
13–15, 1962, Jnl 12 (WUSTL). "Under his": Author's interview with Amy Merrill (2004).
May 30 "The message": JM to DJ, letter, May 30, 1963 (WUSTL). "In Merrill's": JM, journal,
September 30, 1963, Jnl 59 (WUSTL).

336 **Merrill told** "He addresses": JM to DH, letter, June 28, 1963 (WUSTL).
He rejoined "With Parigory": TP, "Nights and Days," in *For James Merrill: A Birthday Tribute*,

n.p. "Bernie was": JM to DH, letter, July 23, 1963 (WUSTL). "When Merrill": JM to DH, letter, August 1, 1963 (WUSTL). "The 'scholar' ": JM to DH, letter, October 4, 1963 (WUSTL).

337 **They went** "They went": JM to DH, letter, August 1, 1963 (WUSTL). "They overlapped": Author's interview with DR (2002).

In another mood "In another mood": Author's interview with Natalia Méla (2003). "Merrill dressed": Author's interview with DR (2002). " 'I'm tired' ": Author's interview with Nina and Dimitri Koutsoudakis (2003).

She never "She never": Author's interview with Nina and Dimitri Koutsoudakis (2003). "Merrill's 'Words' ": JM to DH, letter, July 6, 1965 (WUSTL). "He inscribed": JM, "The Thousand and Second Night" (Athens, 1963), copy property of Nina and Dimitri Koutsoudakis.

338 **Merrill and Jackson** "One day": JM to DH, letter, August 24, 1963 (WUSTL). "The boys": JM to DH, letter, August 24, 1963 (WUSTL). "Jackson and": Author's interview with George Lazaretos (2002).

Tony visited "The first": DJ to AL, letter, November 1, 1963 (WUSTL).

339 **With David** "With David": DJ to AL, letter, November 1, 1963 (WUSTL). "The Burnetts": Author's interview with DH (2004). "From the Midwest": JM to Virgil Burnett, letter, November 6, 1963 (Waterloo). "Merrill read": Author's interview with RM (2004). " 'One can' ": JM to Anne and Virgil Burnett, letter, late November 1963 (Waterloo).

On the road "Merrill explains": JM, "Peru: The Landscape Game," *Prose*, 401. " 'The Mediterranean' ": RM, *Memoirs*, 162. "The water": RM, *Memoirs*, 163.

340 **In San Francisco** "Jimmy arranged": JM to DH, letter, December 19, 1963 (WUSTL). "David climbed": JM to CF, letter, January 5, 1964 (Getty).

Now Merrill "He supposed": DJ and JM to DR, letter, February 3, 1964 (WUSTL). "It was only": JM to TP, February 15, 1964 (WUSTL); JM to DK, letter, July 26, 1964 (WUSTL).

The last "The narrator": JM, *CNP*, 418. "As the narrator": JM, *CNP*, 409.

341 **The book** "Passing by": JM, *CNP*, 420.

In the letter "He thanks": JM to TP, letter, February 15, 1964 (WUSTL).

342 **In February** "The Beatles": JM to TP, letter, February 7, 1964 (WUSTL). "Merrill liked": JM to TP, letter, February 16, 1964 (WUSTL). "When the young": JM to TP, letter, March 3, 1964 (WUSTL).

Stalled on "Stalled on": DJ to Louise Fitzhugh, letter, March 10, 1964 (Fitzhugh). " 'We do whirl' ": DJ to DR, letter, February 24, 1964 (WUSTL).

343 **In April** "In April": JM to DR, letter, June 15, 1964 (WUSTL). "It was 'really' ": JM to DR, letter, February 3, 1964 (WUSTL). "After a brief": JM to DR, letter, June 15, 1964 (WUSTL). "Their visit": JM to DH, letter, May 18, 1964 (WUSTL). "Her son": JM to TP, letter, June 1, 1964 (WUSTL).

David Kalstone "He'd put": Guest book 107 Water Street, Jnl 12 (WUSTL). "They'd met": Author's interviews with AC (2003), and Edmund White (2004). "David was gay": Author's interview with Edmund White (2004).

He had grown "He got": DK, "Contacts," *For James Merrill: A Birthday Tribute*, n.p.

344 **Over the summer** "Van Duyn": Mona Van Duyn to Robert Creeley, copy of letter, July 30, 1964 (WUSTL).

The appeal "The library came": JM to DMc, letter, April 1969 (WUSTL).

345 **In July** "It was also": Frances Kiernan, *Seeing Mary Plain: A Life of Mary McCarthy* (Norton, 2000), 536. " 'The climax' ": Kiernan, *Seeing Mary Plain*, 558–59.

In the afternoons "The Stone": JM to RM, letter, September 8, 1964 (WUSTL). "With all": DJ to DR, letter, September 6, 1964 (WUSTL). "He also reread": JM to RM, letter, September 8, 1964 (WUSTL).

346 **On September** "On a visit": JM to HIP, letter, September 18, 1964 (WUSTL); JM to Moffett letter, May 23, 1968 (NYPL). "He went next": JM to AL, October 2, 1964 (WUSTL); "House of Glass," *Newsweek* (March 6, 1967), 28–32.

8 DAYS OF 1964

347 **Merrill arrived** "In this 'airless' ": JM, "The 'Metro,' " *CP*, 453; Author's interviews with Alan Ansen (2002) and DR (2002).
Strato "Strato": Author's interview with SM and VM (2003).

348 **That first** "His working-class": Author's interview with SM and VM (2003).

349 **Mouflouzélis's** "On November": JM to DH, letter, November 17, 1964 (WUSTL). "But from": Author's interview with SM and VM (2003). " 'He was the kind' ": Author's interview with SM and VM (2003).
What drew "A few years": JM, "Strato in Plaster," *CP*, 336. "More than one": First impressions of Strato by SY and Grace Stone; author's interviews with SY (2001) and ESP (2003).
This vernacular "In the first": JM to DH, letter, November 17, 1964 (WUSTL). "When Merrill": JM to DK, letter, January 2, 1965 (WUSTL).

350 **"He gave"** " 'He gave' ": Author's interview with VV (2003).

351 **Merrill had** "Yet the love": Author's interview with VV (2003).
Jackson, sailing "Jackson, sailing": DJ to DR, letter, September 6, 1964 (WUSTL). "Maisie": JM to AL, letter, October 2, 1964 (WUSTL).
Today "He disliked": Author's interview with VV (2003).
The street "It borders": JM to DR, letter, June 15, 1964 (WUSTL).

352 **Maria** "Maria": Author's interview with NL (2002). "Like 107": JM to DR, letter, June 15, 1964 (WUSTL).

353 **The openness** "The image": "The Back Terrace, Athens," reproduced in *David Jackson: Scenes from His Life* (Nadja, 1994), n.p.
The plan "The plan": Descriptions of Athinaion Efivon 44 are based on the author's visits to the house, August 2002 and May 2003, an interview with John Camp, and a photo album, gift of DJ to Doris Sewell Jackson, 1974 (author). "Merrill felt": JM to DR, letter, June 15, 1964 (WUSTL).
A steep "After loaning": JM, "Acoustical Chambers," *Prose*, 3. "Across the landing": JM, *Sandover*, 431.

354 **The pride** "To a poet": JM to DR, letter, June 15, 1964 (WUSTL).
As always "There's a wonderful": JM to DR, letter, October 29, 1964 (WUSTL). " 'Jimmy and David' ": Author's interview with SM and VM (2003).
Like 107 "Looking back": JM to DR, letter, January 17–18, 1965 (WUSTL). "In a postscript": JM to DR, letter, October 29, 1964 (WUSTL). "If Jackson": JM to DH, letter, November 17, 1964 (WUSTL). " 'David is upstairs' ": JM to DH, letter, November 17, 1964 (WUSTL).

355 **Mouflouzélis** "Yet Jimmy": JM to DH, letter, November 17, 1964 (WUSTL). "But Merrill": JM to TP, letter, February 15, 1964 (WUSTL). "In December": JM to DR, letter, January 17–18, 1965 (WUSTL).

356 **For a few** "Once Kallman": See Humphrey Carpenter, *W. H. Auden: A Biography* (Houghton Mifflin, 1981), 403, 408; Richard Davenport-Hines, *Auden* (Heinemann, 1995), 308–12; Dorothy Farnan, *Auden in Love* (Plume, 1984), passim.
Merrill saw "When he came": JM to DR, letter, June 16, 1964 (WUSTL). "He wrote": JM to DH, letter, November 17, 1964 (WUSTL).
While Merrill " 'David has' ": JM to Mary McCarthy and James West, November 10, 1964 (Radcliffe). "Jackson made": JM to IB, letter, November 13, 1964 (WUSTL). "He was never": DJ to AL, November 20, 1964 (WUSTL). "Once, at a fish": Author's interview with George Lazaretos (2002).

357 **The story** "With a navy": Author's interview with George Lazaretos (2002). "An inch": JM to DR, letter, January 17–18, 1965 (WUSTL). "He was": JM to DR, letter, February 11, 1965 (WUSTL). "Maria called": Author's interview with George Lazaretos (2002).
Together "Together": DK to Kenneth Bleeth, letter, February 11, 1967 (Bleeth). "Maria knew": Author's interview with SM and VM (2003).

358 **The presence** "The presence": Author's interview with VV (2003); VV to the author, letter, July 28, 2003. "The genial": DK to Kenneth Bleeth, letter, February 11, 1967 (Bleeth). "When her husband": Author's interview with VV (2003). "When he met": Author's interview with George Lazaretos (2003).

359 **What is** "When he stopped": JM, *ADP*, 160–65. "But the notebook": JM, journal, November 17, 1964, Jnl 58, 210 (WUSTL).

360 **The language** "He began": Merrill's worksheets for the poem include one dated "March 18"; another page is written on the back of a letter from Holly Stevens, Wallace Stevens's daughter, dated April 26 (WUSTL).

From the start " 'I could just' ": JM, worksheet for "The Broken Home" (WUSTL). "But it was also": JM, *CNP*, 356.

361 **An early** "An early": JM, worksheet for "The Broken Home" (WUSTL).

362 **To get** "He began": JM, worksheet for "The Broken Home" (WUSTL). "One worksheet": One worksheet for the poem, along with rejected titles such as "Self-Portrait with Parents," "Southampton Pieces," and "Fragments from the Broken Home," includes a dedication "for Doris + Charles" (WUSTL).

363 **These recognitions** " 'He has quite' ": JM to DK, letter, January 2, 1964 (WUSTL).

364 **His memory** "The day": JM to DR, letter, January 17–18, 1965 (WUSTL). "~~Concrete~~": JM, journal, January 16, 1965, Jnls 58, 82 (WUSTL). "The draft": JM, journal, January 16, 1965, Jnls 58, 82 (WUSTL).

365 **The directness** "Across from": JM, journal, January 16, 1965, Jnls 58, 82 (WUSTL).

366 **Courage** "That morning": JM, journal, January 16, 1965, Jnls 58, 82 (WUSTL). "The next day": JM to DR, letter, January 17–18, 1965 (WUSTL).

367 **But Kleo** "The first draft": JM, journal, January 16, 1965, Jnls 58, 83 (WUSTL).

On January 22 "He wrote to Mouflouzélis": JM to SM, letter, January 22, 1965, trans. Maria Walker (WUSTL). "He wrote to Strato": JM to SM, letter, January 31, 1965, trans. Maria Walker (WUSTL). "Merrill looked": JM to SM, letter, January 28, 1965, trans. Maria Walker (WUSTL).

368 **Merrill had** " 'I read it' ": Mary McCarthy, jacket copy for JM, *The (Diblos) Notebook* (Atheneum, 1965). "Anne Finch": Anne Finch, "To the Nightingale," *The "Other" Eighteenth Century: English Women of Letters*, ed. Robert W. Uphaus and Gretchen M. Foster (Colleague Press, 1991), 177. "In her notes": Mary McCarthy, notes in galleys of *The (Diblos) Notebook* (Yale).

The book's "Her notes": Mary McCarthy, notes in galleys of *The (Diblos) Notebook* (Yale). "She put": Mary McCarthy to JM, letter, January 1965 (WUSTL); JM to Mary McCarthy, January 30, 1965 (WUSTL); JM to VV, letter, February 5, 1965 (WUSTL). "Merrill wanted": JM, "James Merrill at Home: An Interview by Ross Labrie," *Prose*, 95.

That notion "He sent": JM to DH, letter, July 5, 1964 (WUSTL); JM to DK, letter, July 26, 1964 (WUSTL); JM to IB, letter, February 18, 1965 (WUSTL). "On February": JM to Henry Rago, letter, May 25, 1965 (WUSTL); Henry Rago to JM, letter, October 18, 1966 (Lilly Library, Indiana University).

369 **Longer** "*The (Diblos)*": JM, *CNP*, 634.

370 **Psyche's** "Psyche's": JM to IB, letter, February 18, 1965 (WUSTL).

372 **This delicate** "In her stringent": Louise Bogan, "Verse," *New Yorker* (June 9, 1951), 110.

On February 6 "On February 6": The second draft of "Days of 1964" is headed "S'ton. 6 Feb" in JM, journal, 1965, Jnl 58 (WUSTL). JM refers to "Days of 1964" as having been written in February in a letter to SM, c. May 1965 (WUSTL).

375 **When we** "In a reply": JM, journal, 1965, Jnl 58 (WUSTL).

The masks "No, he hasn't": KF to JM, letter, March 2, 1947 (WUSTL).

9 CHILLS AND FEVER, PASSIONS AND BETRAYALS

376 **Since Friar** "He wrote": JM to DH, letter, March 15, 1965 (WUSTL). "He made": JM to TP, letter, March 16, 1965 (WUSTL).
The same " 'Welcome Home' ": Anne Edwards, *Callas: Her Life, Her Loves, Her Music* (Weidenfeld and Nicolson, 2001), 275. "Merrill remembered": JM, draft of *ADP*, section XXII (WUSTL).

377 **In April** "He signed": JM, "Violent Pastoral," broadside in the Virgil Burnett Papers (Waterloo).
Reviews "In the *New York*": John Thompson, review of *The (Diblos) Notebook, New York Review of Books* (May 6, 1965), 23. "Wilfred Sheed": Wilfred Sheed, review of *The (Diblos) Notebook, NYT Book Review* (March 21, 1965), 4. "When the first": JM to RM, letter, April 28, 1965 (WUSTL).

378 **Ford** "When a messenger": Stratis Haviaras, "Millennial Afterlives: A Retrospect," Fourth Annual Kimon Friar Lecture (American College of Greece, Athens, 1997), 2–3. "Rivaling Merrill": KF to JM, letter, September 19, 1965 (WUSTL).
Jackson ended "Looking back": Cecelia Holland to the author, email, May 18, 2004.

379 **The writing** "The writing": JM to NL, May 6, 1965 (WUSTL). "In May": JM to VV, June 3, 1965 (WUSTL). "Vassilikos was": JM to VV, letter, March 29, 1965 (WUSTL). "Merrill reciprocated": JM to Mary McCarthy, letter, March 10, 1965 (WUSTL); see also JM to DR, letter, April 28, 1965 (WUSTL). "He advised": JM to IB, letter, September 27, 1965 (WUSTL). "They stopped": JM to SM, letter, June 28, 1965 (WUSTL).
As a correspondent " 'My Dearest' ": SM to JM, January 25, 1965, trans. Maria Walker (WUSTL).

380 **Four more** "Merrill told": JM to TP, letter, April 23, 1965 (WUSTL). "Then a letter": SM to JM, letter, April 22, 1965 (WUSTL). " 'I am sorry' ": JM to SM, letter, May 1965, trans. Maria Walker (WUSTL). "Merrill was reassured": JM to TP, letter, May 3, 1965 (WUSTL).

381 **On July 28** " 'It was awful' ": JM to MLA, letter, October 27, 1965 (WUSTL). "He'd counted": For example, JM to SM, letter, June 28, 1965, trans. Maria Walker (WUSTL). "He made": JM, journal, August 6, 1965, Jnl 58 (WUSTL).
August 13 "Merrill wrote": JM, journal, August 13, 1965, Jnl 58 (WUSTL).
In 1974 "Bishop's castaway": EB, *Collected Poems, 1927–1979* (FSG, 1983), 165–66. "But I found": JM to EB, letter, April 19, 1974 (Vassar).

382 **Merrill knew** "After Jimmy": SM to JM, letter, February 14, 1965, trans. Maria Walker (WUSTL). " 'I do not care' ": JM to SM, letter, February 28, 1965, trans. Maria Walker (WUSTL). " 'Hold it' ": JM to DK, letter, August 21, 1965 (WUSTL). "When Jimmy": Author's interview with SM and VM (2003).
Merrill's feeling "Rachel Hadas": Rachel Hadas, *Merrill, Cavafy, Poems, and Dreams* (University of Michigan Press, 2000), 51. "He comments": JM, *ADP*, 564.

383 **In Greek** "The passage": JM, *ADP*, 565.

384 **Modern Greek** "He told": Author's interview with VV (2003). "Merrill was haunted": "James Merrill [an interview]," Thomas Bolt, *BOMB* 36 (summer 1991): 40; and JM, "Unreal Citizen," *Prose*, 193. "It was as if": Rachel Hadas, *Merrill, Cavafy*, 54. " 'One sees' ": JM, "Education of the Poet," *Prose*, 16.
Not that "For Merrill": JM, "An Interview with J. D. McClatchy," *Prose*, 103–04. "In time": Author's interviews with NL (2002) and Yannis Zervos (2002).
If Merrill's " 'Since I've been' ": JM, "An Interview with Ashley Brown," *Prose*, 67.

385 **In "To My Greek"** "In 'To My Greek' ": JM, journal, 1966–68 (Yale). " 'You will think' ": JM to MV, letter, July 31, 1967 (WUSTL). "In one draft": JM, journal, 1966–68 (Yale).

386 **In August 1965** " '<u>She</u> wants' ": JM to DK, letter, September 1, 1965 (WUSTL). "For the moment": RM, *Memoirs*, 152. "Then they piled": JM to DK, letter, September 1, 1965 (WUSTL).

387 **As he danced** "As he danced": RM, *Memoirs*, 173. "The shrieking": RM, *Memoirs*, 173. **Robin's** "On the streets": RM, *Memoirs*, 178.

388 **Which Jimmy** "In May": JM to NL, letter, May 6, 1965 (WUSTL). "Last night": JM to DK, letter, August 21, 1965 (WUSTL). " 'The demonstrations' ": For an overview of the crisis, see Clogg, *A Short History of Modern Greece*, 183–85. For a detailed account of it from the perspective of the Centre Union, see Andreas Papandreou, *Democracy at Gunpoint: The Greek Front* (Doubleday, 1970), 142–86.
   Even when " 'I was so' ": Author's interview with VV (2003). "What he offered": Author's interview with VV (2003).

389 **On September 14** "Merrill found": JM to IB, letter, September 27, 1965 (WUSTL). "He jotted": JM, journal, September 19, 1965, Jnl 31 (WUSTL). "The group": JM to IB, letter, September 27, 1965 (WUSTL). "Courtly": JM to IB, letter, September 27, 1965 (WUSTL). "Living with": JM, journal, September 19, 1965, Jnl 31 (WUSTL). "Later, Merrill": Author's interview with Laurence Scott (2003).
   While Vassili "While Vassili": Author's interview with George Lazaretos (2003). " 'In a society' ": JM to RM, letter, October 12, 1965 (WUSTL). "He recorded": JM, journal, September 19, 1965, Jnl 31 (WUSTL). "Jimmy saw": JM to IB, letter, September 27, 1965 (WUSTL).
   On September 16 "On September 16": Andreas Papandreou, *Democracy at Gunpoint: The Greek Front* (Deutsch, 1971), 183. "The same day": JM, journal, September 16, 1965, Jnl 31 (WUSTL).

390 **Aware** "Very soon": JM sent a draft of the poem ("I keep changing what the radio plays each time I type it out") to RM in a letter, October 12, 1965 (WUSTL).

392 **Like Jimmy's** "At times": Author's interview with George Lazaretos (2003). " 'You can't imagine' ": JM to DH, letter, October 19, 1965 (WUSTL).

393 **Sometimes** " 'Where are you' ": JM, journal, October 30, 1965, Jnl 58 (WUSTL).
   Strato's demobilization "After a quarrel": JM, journal, August 19, 1965, Jnl 58 (WUSTL). "In October": JM, journal, October 14, 29, and 30, 1965, Jnl 58 (WUSTL). "One evening": Author's interview with SM and VM (2003).
   He could "He liked": Author's interview with SM and VM (2003). "In October": DJ to Virgil and Anne Burnett, letter, October 19, 1965 (Waterloo). "Merrill described her": JM to DH, letter, October 19, 1965 (WUSTL).

394 **But it was** "In flight": JM to DJ, letter, December 1, 1965 (WUSTL). "He tried": SM to JM, letter, December 2, 1965, trans. Maria Walker (WUSTL).
   Now, as "His first": JM to DJ, letter, December 1, 1965 (WUSTL). "He had tea": JM to NL, letter, December 9, 1965 (WUSTL). "Merrill was": JM to DJ, letter, December 8, 1965 (WUSTL). "The Hollanders": JM to DJ, letter, December 8, 1965 (WUSTL). "Next he flew": JM to MLA, letter, October 27, 1965 (WUSTL). "He admired": JM to DJ, letter, December 8, 1965 (WUSTL).

395 **He returned** " 'I'm <u>still</u>!' ": JM to DK, letter, January 15, 1966 (WUSTL).
   Jimmy was "Jimmy was": JM to DJ, letter, December 8, 1965 (WUSTL). "On January 19": The laboratory report, in Greek, is preserved among the letters of SM to JM, dated January 19, 1966 (WUSTL). "On January 28": JM, journal, January 28, 1966, Jnl 58 (WUSTL). "He suspected": JM, journal, January 28, 1966, Jnl 58 (WUSTL). "The next": JM, journal, February 20, 27, and March 9, 1966, Jnl 58 (WUSTL).
   For weeks "For weeks": JM to IB, letter, February 15, 1966 (WUSTL). "He declined": JM to IB, letter, February 15, 1966 (WUSTL). "He described": JM to IB, letter, February 15, 1966 (WUSTL).

396 **Into this** "From that moment": DR to the author, letter, December 10, 2001. "Explaining": DR to the author, letter, December 10, 2001. "David had": JM to ESP, letter, January 14, 1965 (ESP). "In late July": DJ to ESP, letter, July 29, 1966 (ESP).
   Merrill's distress "Strato recalls": Author's interview with SM and VM (2003); and author's interview with DR (2002). "Richie tried": JM to IB, letter, February 15, 1966 (WUSTL).

396 **Donald was** "Tony happened": RM, *Memoirs*, 197.

About Isfahan "About Isfahan": DR to author, letter, December 10, 2001.

397 **In his notebook** "In his notebook": JM, journal, March 4, 1966, Jnl 31 (WUSTL). "Richie remembers": DR to the author, letter, December 10, 2001.

"You kept" "Yahya put": JM to RM, letter, March 5, 1966 (WUSTL).

398 **It is a good** "Merrill merely": JM to RM, letter, March 5, 1966 (WUSTL).

When the poem "These consisted ": DR to the author, letter, December 10, 2001.

399 **"I had to"** " 'I had to' ": JM to RM, letter, March 5, 1966 (WUSTL). "On March 13": JM, journal, March 13, 1966, Jnl 58 (WUSTL). "On March 17": JM to DR, letter, March 17, 1966 (WUSTL). "The log": JM, journal, March 20, 21, 22, and April 1, 1966, Jnl 58 (WUSTL). "Strato's father": Author's interview with SM and VM, Athens, June 2003.

400 **Intending** "Intending": JM to DR, letter, February 7, 1967 (WUSTL). "He saw": Maria Walker's interview with Kostas Tympakianákis (2003). See also JM to DR, letter, March 25, 1966 (WUSTL). "He lasted": JM to CF, letter, June 27, 1966 (Getty).

The Browers "The Browers": JM to DK, letter, April 13, 1966 (WUSTL). "In April": JM to DK, letter, April 13, 1966 (WUSTL). "Hubbell 'Pierce' ": JM to RM, letter, June 3, 1966 (WUSTL). "Words": JM to Richard Howard, letter, April 28, 1966 (Howard). "The 'last months' ": JM to JH, letter, April 30, 1966 (Yale). "To Robin": JM to RM and Betty Magowan, letter, June 3, 1966 (WUSTL).

That failure "For instance": Gene Baro, review of *Nights and Days*, *NYT Book Review* (June 26, 1966), 10. "In *Poetry*": Richard Howard, review of *Nights and Days*, *Poetry* 108 (August 1966): 329. Howard's remarks were collected in the chapter on Merrill in his *Alone with America: Essays on the Art of Poetry in the United States Since 1950* (Atheneum, 1969; enlarged ed., 1980), 407.

401 **Experience** "In June": JM to DR, letter, June 24, 1966 (WUSTL). "The condition": JM to DR, letter, June 24, 1966 (WUSTL); JM to CF, letter, June 27, 1966 (Getty). "He took": JM to CF, letter, June 27, 1966 (Getty).

402 **He was serious** "David had": JM to DR, letter, June 24, 1966 (WUSTL). "It was, he admitted": JM to Louise Fitzhugh, letter, July 14, 1966 (Fitzhugh). " 'One has' ": JM to DK and DH, letter, July 18, 1966 (WUSTL). " 'Obviously' ": JM to IB, letter, August 25, 1966 (WUSTL).

Except for "Except for": JM, journal, July 2–10, 1966, Jnl 58 (WUSTL); JM to DR, letter, August 14–15, 1966 (WUSTL); JM to DK, September 13, 1966 (WUSTL). "The U.S.": JM, journal, August 10 and 16, 1966, Jnl 58 (WUSTL). "The 'reason' ": JM to DR, letter, August 14–15, 1966 (WUSTL). "The procedure": JM to DK, letter, September 13, 1966 (WUSTL); JM to DR, letter, September 21, 1966 (WUSTL). "It was, Merrill": JM to DK, letter, September 13, 1966 (WUSTL).

In early "In early": JM to DK, letter, September 13, 1966 (WUSTL). "It was necessary": JM to DR, letter, October 4, 1966 (WUSTL). " 'Nothing' ": JM to DH, letter, September 23, 1966 (WUSTL).

403 **His hardiness** "Jackson spent": JM to DK and DH, letter, July 18, 1966 (WUSTL). "He was in Athens": JM to DR, letter, September 21, 1966 (WUSTL). "He was, Merrill": JM to DK, letter, August 26, 1966 (WUSTL). "In mid-September": JM to DR, letter, September 21, 1966 (WUSTL). "Afterward": JM to DR, letter, September 21, 1966 (WUSTL). "Back in Athens": JM to DJ, letter, September 18, 1966 (WUSTL).

More bad "It's the first": JM to DR, letter, September 21, 1966 (WUSTL). "As the date": JM, journal, October 7, 1966, Jnl 58 (WUSTL).

404 **He flew** "He flew": JM to DJ, letter, October 13, 1966 (WUSTL). "They had morning": DK to Kenneth Bleeth, letter, September 28, 1966 (Bleeth). " 'We trotted' ": DK to Kenneth Bleeth, letter, October 13, 1966 (Bleeth).

Back on "He turned": JM to DJ, letter, October 27, 1966 (WUSTL).

405 **Tests revealed** "Tests revealed": JM to DJ, on the back of a letter from JM to SM, October 23,

1966 (WUSTL); JM to TP, letter, October 27, 1966 (WUSTL). "When he wanted": JM to TP, letter, October 27, 1966 (WUSTL); JM to DJ, letter, c. October 1966 (WUSTL). " 'I find' ": JM to DK, letter, November 1, 1966 (WUSTL). "To David": JM to DJ, letter, November 11, 1966 (WUSTL).

405 **He was back** "The first": JM to CF, letter, February 3, 1967 (Getty). "Jimmy stayed": Author's interview with George Lazaretos (2003).

The travelers "Back in Athens": JM to RM, letter, January 24, 1967 (WUSTL). "What Mouflouzélis": JM, journal, January 24 and 25, 1967, Jnl 58 (WUSTL).

406 **On another** "On another": JM, journal, January 24 and 25, 1967, Jnl 58 (WUSTL). JM used this notebook entry as a draft of a letter to SM, January 25, 1967 (WUSTL).

Strato had "Strato had": Author's interview with SM and VM (WUSTL). "On the trip": JM, journal, July 2–10, 1966, Jnl 58 (WUSTL). "After September": JM to DR, letter, February 7, 1967 (WUSTL). " 'If that was' ": JM, "Days of 1964," *CP*, 221.

407 **Did Strato** " 'Who can' ": Author's interview with VV (2003). "As Vaso": Author's interview with SM and VM (2003).

Merrill's reaction " 'And for all' ": JM to CF, letter, February 3, 1967 (Getty). "A few days": JM to DR, letter, February 7, 1967 (WUSTL).

408 **With Strato** " 'I fear' ": JM to DR, letter, February 21, 1965 (WUSTL). "It was a chance": Author's interview with SM and VM (2003). "She isn't": JM to DR, letter, February 21, 1965 (WUSTL). "In the backseat": Author's interview with SM and VM (2003). " 'You are caught' ": JM to SM, letter, January 25, 1967 (WUSTL).

The baby "But he was": JM to DR, letter, February 28, 1967 (WUSTL). "The citation": Quoted in JM, *CNP*, 706. "Yet, when": JM to DR, letter, February 28, 1967 (WUSTL).

10 JACK FROST'S TEARS

409 **Back in** "Back in": JM, journal, calendar for March 5–9, 1967 (Yale). "Over the past": Stanley Karnow, *Vietnam: A History* (Penguin, 1983; rev. ed., 1997), 516–25. "It was": Editorial, *NYT* (March 3, 1967), 34.

Outside Philharmonic "As Humphrey": Henry Raymond, "Writers Leave Humphrey Talk," *NYT* (March 9, 1967), 42. "The vice": Raymond, "Writers Leave." The remark comes from chapter 44, "Southern Sports," of Twain's *Life on the Mississippi*.

410 **None** "To Marianne": JM, "Acceptance Speech: National Book Awards, 1967," *Prose*, 347. "Next came": JM, journal, calendar for March 5–9, 1967 (Yale); JM to TP, letter, March 12, 1967 (WUSTL).

"And you" " 'And you' ": JM to TP, letter, March 12, 1967 (WUSTL). "Quiet, icy": JM to Richard Howard, letter, February 1967 (Howard). "He wrote to Strato": JM to SM, letter, March 6, 1967 (WUSTL).

411 **In his reply** "In his reply": SM to JM, letter, March 10, 1967, trans. Maria Walker (WUSTL). " 'Now it is only' ": JM to SM, letter, March 10, 1967, trans. Maria Walker (WUSTL).

Soon, back " 'My Strato' ": JM to SM, letter, c. March 10, 1967, trans. Maria Walker (WUSTL). "Merrill told": JM to DK, letter, March 20, 1967 (WUSTL).

412 **Ill** " 'Afterwards' ": JM to DK, letter, April 5, 1967 (WUSTL). "He returned": JM to MV, letter, March 26, 1967 (WUSTL). "Together they": JM to DK, letter, April 5, 1967 (WUSTL).

He didn't "He didn't": SM to JM, letter, March 18, 1967, trans. Maria Walker (WUSTL).

Merrill arrived "The hotel": JM to DK, letter, April 5, 1967 (WUSTL). "Into this": JM, journal, April 1967 (Yale). "He'd been": Author's interview with SY (2002).

413 **When Stephen** "When Stephen": SY to the author, email, December 9, 2003. "Moffet's ears": Author's interview with Moffett (2003). "Merrill read": SY to the author, email, December 9, 2003. "Most of": JM, class list, journal, April 1967 (Yale). "When she": Author's interview with Moffett (2003). "Yenser recalls": Author's interview with SY (2002).

413 **It had been** "On that first": JM, journal, April 1967 (Yale). "No one": SY to the author, email, October 2, 2002. "*Façade*": JM, journal, April 1967 (Yale). "The only": JM, journal, April 1967 (Yale). "The class": Author's interview with Moffett (2003); JM, journal, April 1967 (Yale). "They read": JM to DK, letter, April 19, 1967 (WUSTL). "Merrill saw": JM, "An Interview with Donald Sheehan," *Prose*, 49.

414 **Merrill's class** "His example": Robert Lowell, "Memories of West Street and Lepke," *Collected Poems*, ed. Frank Bidart and David Gewanter (FSG, 2003), 188. "He found": JM, journal, April 1967 (Yale).

He emphasized " 'Poetry' ": JM, journal, April 1967 (Yale). "The assignment": SY to the author, email, October 15, 2002; and author's interview with Moffett (2003). "The point": JM, journal, 1967 (Yale). "Here he discussed": Author's interview with Moffett (2003).

After teaching "After teaching": JM to ESP, letter, April 14, 1967 (ESP). "He walked": JM to ESP, letter, April 14, 1967 (ESP). " 'I feel' ": JM to MV, April 6, 1967 (WUSTL). "In Greek": JM to SM, letter, c. April 15, 1967, trans. Maria Walker (WUSTL).

415 **Merrill saw** "There he": JM to TP, letter, April 6, 1967 (WUSTL); DJ to JM, letter, April 21, 1967 (WUSTL). "In Madison": JM to DR, letter, May 9, 1967 (WUSTL). "At a party": Author's interview with SY (2002). "When Allen": JM to RM, letter, May 12, 1967 (WUSTL). "Merrill argued": JM to MV, letter, April 6, 1967 (WUSTL); Antler to the author, letter, January 4, 2004. "Privately": JM to DK, letter, April 5, 1967 (WUSTL). " 'It's rather' ": JM to DK, letter, April 19, 1967 (WUSTL). "He 'kept' ": JM to DK, letter, April 19, 1967 (WUSTL).

416 **Judith Moffett** " 'Friday' ": Author's interview with Moffett (2003); and JM to DK, letter, April 19, 1967 (WUSTL). "Merrill told": Author's interview with Moffett (2003).

His teaching "His teaching": Author's interview with Moffett (2003). "Dwelling": EB, "Arrival at Santos," *Collected Poems, 1927–1979* (FSG, 1983), 89–90.

"First impressions" " 'First impressions' ": Author's interview with Moffett (2003). "What she": Author's interview with Moffett (2003). " 'I wanted' ": Author's interview with Moffett (2003).

417 **On April 21** "Various articles": Richard Clogg, *A Short History of Modern Greece*, 186. "The outspoken": Author's interview with VV (2003). " 'The first' ": Author's interview with VV (2003). "Merrill responded": JM to MV and VV, letter, May 8, 1967 (WUSTL). " 'Oh Lord' ": JM to MV and VV, letter, May 8, 1967 (WUSTL).

He was speaking "In late": SM to JM, letters, April 15, 23, and 25, 1967 (WUSTL). "Merrill asked": JM to TP, letter, May 21, 1967 (WUSTL).

In early "He saw David": JM to TP, letter, May 5, 1967 (WUSTL). "He brought": Author's interview with Moffett (2003).

418 **The wish** "Yet the talk": JM to MV and VV, letter, August 13, 1967 (WUSTL). "This was his": E.g., JM, "An Interview with J. D. McClatchy," *Prose*, 103–25.

Invited "Invited": JM, "An Interview with Donald Sheehan," *Prose*, 51–52. "Pound, Merrill": JM, "An Interview with Donald Sheehan," *Prose*, 53. "In this camp": JM, "An Interview with Donald Sheehan," *Prose*, 51. "Merrill prizes": JM, "An Interview with Donald Sheehan," *Prose*, 50.

419 **Merrill's implication** " 'Anybody starting' ": JM, "An Interview with Donald Sheehan," *Prose*, 50. " 'Words just' ": JM, "An Interview with Donald Sheehan," *Prose*, 55.

In the interview "That, he told": SY to the author, email, December 16, 2004.

Merrill returned "Merrill returned": JM to DK, letter, June 9, 1967 (WUSTL). "One afternoon": JM to DK, letter, June 9, 1967 (WUSTL). "He listened": JM to Moffett, letter, June 15, 1967 (NYPL).

Then Merrill "David had": DJ to JM, letter, May 15, 1967 (WUSTL). "He came": DJ, postscript on JM to DK, letter, June 9, 1967 (WUSTL). " 'Public opinion' ": JM to DK, letter, June 28, 1967 (WUSTL). "In a letter": DJ to JM, letter, April 11, 1967 (WUSTL).

420 **Mouflouzélis's** "Mouflouzélis's": SM to JM, letter, April 23, 1967, trans. Maria Walker (WUSTL). "Vaso": VM to JM, letter, May 10, 1967; SM to JM, letter, May 22, 1967, trans.

Maria Walker (WUSTL). "In June": SM to JM, letter, June 3, 1967, trans. Maria Walker (WUSTL). "When Merrill": SM to JM, letter, June 9, 1967, trans. Maria Walker (WUSTL).

420 **Mouflouzélis signed** "Merrill wrote": JM to TP, letter, June 13, 1967 (WUSTL). "Strato asked": SM to JM, letter, June 16, 1967, trans. Maria Walker (WUSTL). "Strato fell": JM to TP, letter, July 21, 1967 (WUSTL).

421 **From week** "He continued": JM to DK, letter, July 28, 1967 (WUSTL). "The Stone": JM to Moffett, letter, June 15, 1967 (NYPL). "He was 'polishing' ": JM to MV, letter, July 25, 1967 (WUSTL); JM to MV, letter, July 31, 1967 (WUSTL). "He also began": JM, journal, June 16, 1967 (Yale). "Opera": JM to MV, letter, July 31, 1967 (WUSTL).

War shadowed "Merrill, thinking": JM to Moffett, letter, June 15, 1967 (NYPL). "To Mimi": JM to MV and VV, letter, June 9, 1967 (WUSTL).

Vietnam "He had 'married' ": JM to DH, letter, July 25, 1967 (WUSTL).

422 **Many American** "In January": JM, journal, 1967 (Yale). "Her crime": Marianne Moore, "In Distrust of Merits," *Complete Poems* (Macmillan, 1967), 136–38.

"Matinées" "In summer": JM, journal, 1967 (Yale).

423 **Yet, even** " 'I have scenes' ": JM to Moffett, letter, July 22, 1967 (NYPL).

Lehmann's "Lehmann's": Jeff Nunokawa, *Tame Passions of Wilde: The Styles of Manageable Desire* (Princeton University Press, 2003), 1–40.

424 **Apart** "He saw": JM to TP, letter, July 21, 1967 (WUSTL). "He returned": JM to DR, letter, July 31, 1967 (WUSTL); JM to MV and VV, letter, August 13, 1967 (WUSTL). "One night": JM to TP, letter, July 21, 1967 (WUSTL). "When Alan": JM to TP, letter, June 13, 1967 (WUSTL). "He didn't": JM to MV, letter, June 30, 1967 (WUSTL). "But to be": JM to TP, letter, July 21, 1967 (WUSTL).

In Stonington "In Stonington": E.g., JM to DH, letter, July 25, 1967 (WUSTL). "But by August": JM to DH, letter, August 14–15, 1967 (WUSTL).

Merrill had "Merrill had": JM to SY, letter, August 21, 1967 (Yale). "For his part": Author's interview with Frank Bidart (2002). " 'There are some' ": JM to SY, letter, August 21, 1967 (Yale).

425 **McCarthy** "McCarthy": ESP, quoted in Frances Kiernan, *Seeing Mary Plain: A Life of Mary McCarthy* (Norton, 2000), 614. "Once back": JM to SY, letter, August 21, 1967 (Yale).

Merrill was "He set": JM to Moffett, letter, September 23, 1967 (NYPL). "He came": JM to Moffett, letter, September 23, 1967 (NYPL). "But when": JM to Moffett, letter, September 23, 1967 (NYPL). "Jimmy told": JM to DK, letter, September 25, 1967 (WUSTL). "In his notebook": JM, journal, 1967–68 (Yale).

Kostas "Now he came": JM to DK, letter, September 25, 1967 (WUSTL). "Merrill joked": JM to DK, letter, September 25, 1967 (WUSTL).

Tympakianákis "Tympakianákis": Maria Walker's interview with Kostas Tympakianákis (2003). "In 'Kostas' ": JM to DR, letter, 1966 (WUSTL).

426 **In October** "To forestall" and " 'Strato is' ": Maria Walker's interview with Kostas Tympakianákis (2003).

Back in "Jackson wrote": DJ to JM, letter, August 11, 1967 (WUSTL). "Merrill found": JM to ESP, letter, October 11, 1967 (ESP).

There were " 'Jimmy has' ": DJ to ESP, letter, September 30, 1967 (ESP). " 'Jimmy gave' ": Author's interview with George Lazaretos (2003). "Jackson wrote": DJ to JM, letter, November 7–8, 1967 (WUSTL). "Now he": JM to DK, letter, September 25, 1967 (WUSTL). "Jackson, always": DJ to JM, letter, August 16, 1967 (WUSTL). "Like an": Author's interviews with George Lazaretos (2002; 2003). " 'My misery' ": DJ to JM, letter, November 7–8, 1967 (WUSTL).

427 **Before he** "They introduced": JM to SY, letter, October 27, 1967 (Yale). "Mimi": JM to RM, letter, October 31, 1967 (WUSTL).

When, a few "When, a few": JM to MV and VV, letter, October 25, 1967, p.m. (WUSTL). " 'Here,' Merrill": JM to Moffett, letter, November 11, 1967 (NYPL).

427 **In November** "In November": Helen Lothrop to JM, letter, July 20, 1967 (Lilly Library, Indiana University). "A group": JM to Moffett, letter, December 9, 1967 (NYPL). "As usual": JM, journal, 1968 (Yale). "Amherst now": Newton F. McKeon to JM, letter, January 24, 1968 (WUSTL).

428 **Jimmy kept** "Jimmy kept": JM to MV, letter, December 1, 1967 (WUSTL). "In another": JM to MV, letter, December 1, 1967 (WUSTL). "When Strato": JM to SM, letter, c. November 1967, trans. Maria Walker (WUSTL).

Jackson returned "Merrill gave": JM to RM, letter, December 14, 1967 (WUSTL). "Ephraim spoke": JM, journal, 1967–68 (Yale). "In the morning": JM, journal, 1968 (Yale).

429 **The next** "Mouflouzélis's": E.g., SM to JM, letters, November 22 and December 5, 27, and 30, 1967 (WUSTL). "Strato said": SM to JM, letter, January 9, 1968 (WUSTL). "Merrill fired": JM to SM, letter, January 1968, trans. Maria Walker (WUSTL). "Yet he dangled": SM to JM, letter, January 26, 1968, trans. Maria Walker (WUSTL). " 'Burn' ": JM to SM, letter, January 1968, trans. Maria Walker (WUSTL).

Rare cold "Rare cold": JM to Moffett, letter, January 23, 1968 (NYPL).

431 **"The Summer People"** "Rather than": JM to SY, letter, January 30, 1968 (Yale). "As one": JM to DJ, letter, April 7, 1968 (WUSTL). "At the *New Yorker*": JM to DJ, letter, March 14, 1968 (WUSTL).

"The result" " 'The result' ": JM to Moffett, letter, March 26, 1968 (NYPL). "Merrill 'received' ": JM to TP, letter, February 24, 1968 (WUSTL); and quoted in JM to DJ, letter, April 7, 1968 (WUSTL).

432 **Merrill took** "For instance": JM to DJ, letter, March 14, 1968 (WUSTL).

Merrill made "Stone told": Author's interview with ESP (2003).

Although he " 'It is less' ": JM to Moffett, letter, February 24, 1968 (NYPL).

Merrill's intensive "Merrill's intensive": JM to Moffett, letter, February 24, 1968 (NYPL). "Merrill put": JM to MV and VV, letter, March 24, 1968 (WUSTL).

433 **Elsewhere** " 'I'm a mass' ": DJ to TP, January 29, 1968 (WUSTL). "By late": JM to DR, letter, March 26, 1968 (WUSTL). "Merrill sent": JM to DJ, letters, March 25, 1968, and April 23, 1968 (WUSTL).

Kalstone paid "In February": Author's interview with DMc (2000). "In February": JM to TP, letter, February 24, 1968 (WUSTL). "He had taken": DJ to JM, letter, March 3, 1968 (WUSTL).

In a letter "In a letter": JM to DJ, letter, c. March 6, 1968 (WUSTL). "He left": JM to Moffett, postcard, March 6, 1968 (NYPL); JM to RM, letter, February 2, 1968 (WUSTL); JM to DJ, letter, March 14, 1968 (WUSTL). "On the back": JM to DR, postcard, March 3, 1968 (WUSTL).

11 DMc

434 **Letters** "The gift": JDM, prose tribute, in *JM: A Remembrance*, ed. Robin and Mark Magowan (Academy of American Poets, 1996), 74; JM to SY, letter, March 25, 1968 (Yale). " 'Do you suppose' ": JM to Moffett, letter, March 26, 1968 (NYPL).

435 **Even Stonington** "It was clear": JM to SY, letter, March 25, 1968 (Yale). " 'I cannot' ": JM to DJ, letter, c. April 1968 (WUSTL). " 'It's amazing' ": JM to DJ, letter, April 19, 1968 (WUSTL).

A world "He knew": DJ to JM, letter, March 31, 1968 (WUSTL). "George seemed": DJ to JM, letter, April 10–14, 1968 (WUSTL). "In his own": DJ to JM, letter, April 17 (WUSTL).

Then, on "That evening": JM to DJ, letter, June 18, 1968 (WUSTL). "The next": JM to DMc, inscription on a tanagra vase, April 18, 1968, property of DMc. "Two days": JM to DMc, letter, c. April 1968 (WUSTL).

Merrill sketched "Merrill sketched": JM to DR, letter, July 7, 1968 (WUSTL).

437 **He'd grown up** "He'd grown up": Author's interviews with DMc (2000; 2004).

In that first " 'Another April' ": Draft of "Another April" in JM to DMc, letter, c. April 1968 (WUSTL).

438 **Merrill would** "After a warning": JM to DJ, letter, March 2, 1968 (WUSTL); JM to MV and VM, letter, March 24, 1968 (WUSTL); JM to MV, letter, May 6, 1968 (WUSTL). "Merrill showed": Albert Rothenberg, *The Emerging Goddess: Creative Process in Art, Science, and Other Fields* (University of Chicago Press, 1980), 15–34. "Merrill was not": Albert Rothenberg to the author, letter, June 15, 2004. "Initially, Merrill": JM to DK, letter, May 22, 1968 (WUSTL). " 'As I hoped' ": JM to DJ, letter, May 5, 1968 (WUSTL).

The New England "The New England": JM to SY, letter, May 15, 1968 (Yale). "At first": JM to DMc, letter, May 18, 1968 (WUSTL).

439 **Unlike Strato** "Merrill described": JM to DMc, letter, May 20, 1968 (WUSTL). "It's an image": Author's interview with DMc (2004).

While McIntosh's " 'What I could' ": JM to DMc, letter, May 20, 1968 (WUSTL).

440 **The artistry** "He told": JM to DJ, letter, c. May 1968 (WUSTL).

The waterbug "In New York": JM to DJ, letter, June 4–5, 1968 (WUSTL). "Making her": JM to DK, letter, May 29, 1968 (WUSTL).

Merrill met " 'Lunch on' ": JM, journal, June 8–17, 1968, Jnl 5 (WUSTL). "The poet": JM to Donald Richie, letter, July 7, 1968 (WUSTL).

441 **Jimmy referred** " 'He is not' ": JM to DJ, letter, June 18, 1968 (WUSTL). "He wrote": JM to DMc, letter, June 20, 1968 (WUSTL). "McIntosh, however": JM to DMc, letter, August 21, 1968 (WUSTL).

Merrill attended "Merrill attended": JM to MV, letter, June 22, 1968 (WUSTL). "The scent": JM to DMc, letter, June 27, 1968 (WUSTL). "All but": JM to DMc, letter, June 29, 1968 (WUSTL).

442 **The next day** " 'But how can' ": JM to DMc, letter, June 27, 1968 (WUSTL). "The room": JM to DMc, letter, June 29, 1968 (WUSTL).

In July "Along dry roads": JM to DMc, letter, July 5, 1968 (WUSTL).

Merrill observed "He'd become": JM to DMc, letter, July 5, 1968 (WUSTL).

443 **Back in** "He was thirty": JM to DR, letter, July 7, 1968 (WUSTL). "A 'dreadful' ": JM to DMc, letter, July 17, 1968 (WUSTL). "Both mother": JM to DK, postcard, July 14, 1968 (WUSTL).

A short "A short": JM to DK, letter, July 24, 1968 (WUSTL). " 'It leaves' ": JM to DMc, letter, August 12, 1968 (WUSTL).

In Wyoming "In Wyoming": JM to MV, letter, June 22, 1968 (WUSTL). "In one": JM to DMc, letter, July 13, 1968 (WUSTL). "So he gave": JM to DMc, postcard, August 6, 1968 (WUSTL). "And he wrote": JM to DK, letter, August 5, 1968 (WUSTL).

444 **He also** "Begun": JM to DMc, letter, July 23, 1968 (WUSTL). " 'I picked' ": Author's interview with DMc (2004). "Apparently": JM to DK, letter, July 24, 1968 (WUSTL).

445 **In mid-August** "Not writing": JM to DMc, letter, August 12, 1968 (WUSTL). "He offered": JM to DMc, letter, August 21, 1968 (WUSTL).

446 **On August** "He was 'laden' ": JM to DMc, letter, c. August 12, 1968 (WUSTL). " 'A Greek' ": JM to DMc, letter, August 12, 1968 (WUSTL). "A signpost": JM to DMc, letter, August 17, 1968 (WUSTL). "Kallman had": JM to DK, letter, August 22, 1968 (WUSTL). "He cooked": JM to DK, letter, August 22, 1968 (WUSTL). "Merrill described": JM to Moffett, letter, August 24, 1968 (NYPL).

Merrill had "Within a quarter": JM to DMc, letter, August 21, 1968 (WUSTL).

447 **Jimmy had** " 'Yes,' Maria": JM to DMc, letter, June 29, 1968 (WUSTL). "The time": JM to DMc, letter, September 2, 1968 (WUSTL).

Merrill got "Turning to": DJ to JM, letter, September 6, 1968 (WUSTL). " 'About an hour' ": JM to DJ, letter, September 6, 1968 (WUSTL).

448 **Over the summer** "The title was": JM to DJ, letter, October 2, 1968 (WUSTL). "It would have": JM to Moffett, letter, September 21, 1968 (NYPL). "The title he'd": JM to SY, letter, October 18, 1968 (Yale).

The title "The title": The worksheets for "Mornings in a New House" include pages marked "My Birthday 1965" and "3.x.68" (WUSTL).

448 **Merrill had** "He had appreciated": JM to DK, letter, June 28, 1967 (WUSTL).

449 **The fire** "The fire": JDM to the author, email, June 29, 2004.

450 **Merrill spent** "Merrill was": JM to DJ, letter, October 28, 1968 (WUSTL). "He liked": JM to DMc, letter, November 1, 1968 (WUSTL).

He gave "He gave": JM to DJ, letter, November 3, 1968 (WUSTL). "But his days": JM to RM, letter, November 7, 1968 (WUSTL). " 'I doubt' ": JM to JH, letter, November 17, 1968 (Yale). "When one": JM to Richard Howard, letter, November 18, 1968 (Howard).

451 **The place** "Red-brown": JM to SY, letter, December 17, 1968 (Yale).

452 **Back in** " 'What bits' ": JM to DMc, letter, December 8, 1968 (WUSTL).

Jackson returned "He told": JM to DMc, letter, December 20, 1968 (WUSTL). " 'It's not' ": JM to DMc, letter, December 22, 1968 (WUSTL). "When not": JM to TP, letter, February 5, 1969 (WUSTL).

Blame "Blame": Farnan, *Auden in Love*, 228. " 'Oh my' ": JM to Chester Kallman, letter, December 18, 1968 (Ransom). "He and DJ": JM to Chester Kallman, letter, January 12, 1969 (NYPL). "When asked": "A Conversation with Ephraim, Stonington, 22.xii.68," enclosed in JM to DMc, letter, December 23, 1968 (WUSTL).

453 **In his weekly** "As if": JM to DMc, letter, January 14, 1969 (WUSTL). "In another": JM to DH, letter, January 17, 1969 (WUSTL). "Even in": JM to DMc, letter, January 14, 1969 (WUSTL).

He was using " 'I am so' ": JM to DH, letter, January 17, 1969 (WUSTL).

Recently "While staying": JM, journal, February 15, 1969, Jnl 5 (WUSTL).

Another striking "The poet": JM, journal, February 25, 1969, Jnl 5 (WUSTL).

454 **Merrill attended** "It was the 'best' ": JM to Virgil Burnett, letter, January 29, 1969 (Waterloo); JM, journal, January 28, 1969, Jnl 5 (WUSTL). "To explain": JM to DMc, letter, February 3, 1969 (WUSTL).

455 **Through the winter** "In March": JM to SY, letter, March 18, 1969 (Yale). "He and Merrill": JM to TP, letter, March 10, 1969 (WUSTL). "Merrill wrote": JM to DMc, letter, March 28, 1969 (WUSTL).

He'd been "He'd been": JM to DMc, letter and enclosure, April 1, 1969 (WUSTL). "When they": Author's interview with JDM (2004). " 'I love' ": JM, "Up and Down," *CP*, 340. "The poem": JM, "Up and Down," *CP*, 340.

It was hard "In dejection": JM, journal, April 4, 1969, Jnl 10 (WUSTL). "On the holy": JM, journal, April 6, 1969, Jnl 10 (WUSTL). "That winter": JM to MV, letter, January 15, 1969 (WUSTL). "While the old": JM to DMc, letter, April 4, 1969 (WUSTL).

456 **He flew to** "He flew to": JM to CF, letter, April 14, 1969 (Getty). "The next": Author's interview with DMc (2000). "McIntosh had asked": JM to DMc, letter, April 26, 1969 (WUSTL).

Like his "The bafflement": JM to SY, letter, April 4, 1969 (Yale). "Merrill had just": JM to James Schuyler, letter, January 15, 1969 (University of California, San Diego); JM to SY, letter, January 22, 1969 (Yale). " 'To judge him' ": JM, notes for the Kathryn Glascock Prize, 1969 (WUSTL).

457 **At the reception** "Thirty years": Kathleen Norris, *The Virgin of Bennington* (Riverhead, 2001), 46–47.

The next "Morning sunlight": JM to DMc, letter, May 4–5, 1969 (WUSTL).

In May " Merrill felt": JM to SY, letter, July 26, 1969 (Yale). "To conclude": JM to DMc, letter, May 1, 1969 (WUSTL).

458 **The Jacksons** "The Jacksons": JM to DMc, letter, May 21, 1969 (WUSTL). " 'I was so' ": JM to DJ, letter, June 10, 1969 (WUSTL). "Traveling": JM to DJ, letter, June 22, 1969 (WUSTL). "Although Mrs.": JM to DJ, letter, July 18, 1969 (WUSTL).

In July "In Stonington": JM to DJ, letter, July 21, 1969 (WUSTL).

459 **In August** "He brought": JM to DJ, letter, August 13, 1969 (WUSTL). "The room": JM to JH, letter, September 1, 1969 (Yale). "Beyond": JM to DK, letter, August 12, 1969 (WUSTL).

McIntosh "His cheek": JM, journal, August 22, 1969, Jnl 10 (WUSTL); JM to DK, letter, August 28, 1969 (WUSTL). " 'If anyone' ": JM to DK, letter, August 12, 1969 (WUSTL).

459 **Often that** "One scrambles": JM to DK, letter, August 28, 1969 (WUSTL). "He thought": JM, journal, August 24, 1968, Jnl 10 (WUSTL).

460 **They also** "Battling": Author's interview with DMc (2004).

The landscape "Back in December": "A Conversation with Ephraim, Stonington, 22.xii.68" (WUSTL).

461 **Teenage** "Teenage": Author's interview with Paul Merrill (2003). "Jimmy was": JM to DJ, letter, September 9, 1969 (WUSTL). "Robin had": JM to DK, letter, July 24, 1968 (WUSTL). "He'd come": JM to RM, letter, October 2, 1968 (WUSTL).

Charlotte "Long-legged": JM, journal, c. September 1969, Jnl 10 (WUSTL). " 'Finally came' ": JM to DJ, letter, September 9, 1969 (WUSTL).

462 **Hafley's** "On September": JM, journal, August 20 and September 6, 1969, Jnl 10 (WUSTL). "Merrill narrated": JM, journal, September 7, 1969, Jnl 10 (WUSTL).

In the midst "He sent": JM to DJ, letter, September 9, 1969 (WUSTL). "Jackson replied": DJ to JM, letter, September 16, 1969 (WUSTL). "When Merrill": DJ to JM, letter, September 26, 1969 (WUSTL). " 'Everything must' ": JM, journal, October 1, 1969, Jnl 5 (WUSTL).

464 **Another poem** "Let the final": DK, *Five Temperaments* (Oxford University Press, 1977), 116–17.

465 **In a letter** "Hollander": JH, review of *The Fire Screen*, *Harper's Monthly* 1433, no. 239 (October 1969): 136. "But Yenser": JM to SY, letter, December 6, 1969 (Yale).

466 **In "Syrinx"** "The next day": JM, journal, October 1968 (Yale). "Three days": JM to Moffett, letter, November 5, 1969 (NYPL).

When they "Once Merrill": Author's interview with DMc (2000). " 'Your sweetness' ": JM to DMc, letter, October 25, 1969 (WUSTL). "Rising": JM to DMc, letter, October 29, 1969 (WUSTL).

467 **Bill's death** " 'It is viewed' ": JM to DMc, letter, October 25, 1969 (WUSTL). "A military": JM to SY, letter, November 17, 1969 (Yale); JM to DMc, letter, October 25, 1969 (WUSTL). "Letters": JM to DJ, letter, October 24, 1969 (WUSTL). "Jimmy admired": JM to Moffett, letter, November 5, 1969 (NYPL). " 'At least' ": JM to DMc, letter, October 29, 1969 (WUSTL). "Yet '[t]he trouble' ": JM, journal, October 27, 1969, Jnl 10 (WUSTL).

By the middle "By the middle": JM to RM, letter, November 18, 1969 (WUSTL). "He found": JM to DMc, letter, December 6, 1969 (WUSTL).

In the Arizona "In the Arizona": JM, journal, c. October 1969, Jnl 5 (WUSTL).

12 PROUST'S LAW

470 **Merrill's first** "Merrill's first": JM to DMc, letter, December 18, 1969 (WUSTL). "Everything Merrill": JM to Moffett, letter, January 24, 1970 (NYPL).

471 **It is a moving** "He immediately": JM, journal, December 15, 1969, Jnl 10 (WUSTL).

472 **While he** "Called Taki": Author's interview with George Lazaretos (2003). "Taki hardly": JM to Moffett, letter, January 24, 1970 (NYPL). "Jimmy told": JM to DJ, letter, October 17, 1968 (WUSTL).

A telegram "The prospect": JM to DMc, letter, December 18, 1969 (WUSTL).

473 **There was more** "He joked": JM to Richard Howard, letter, January 14, 1970 (Howard).

Like a charm "In late": JM to Louise Fitzhugh, letter, January 20, 1970 (Fitzhugh). "The poet": JM, journal, February 8, 1970, Jnl 10 (WUSTL).

474 **The season** " 'Out of' ": JM to SY, letter, February 22, 1970 (Yale). " 'S. + I' ": JM to DK, letter, February 16, 1970 (WUSTL).

475 **Shortly** " 'They continued' ": Douglas Robinson, "Townhouse Razed by Blast and Fire; Man's Body Found," *NYT* (March 7, 1970), 1.

A small boy "He flew": JM to DJ, letter, March 13, 1970 (WUSTL). "First Charles": Mel Gussow, "The House on West 11th Street," *NYT* (March 5, 2000), sec. 14, 1. "In 1963": Susan Braudy, *Family Circle: The Boudins and the Aristocracy of the Left* (Knopf, 2003), 203.

476 **It was Wilkerson's** "It was Wilkerson's": John Neary, "The Two Girls from No. 18," *Life* 69, no. 11 (March 27, 1970): 26–29. "In March": Douglas Robinson, "Parents of Miss Wilkerson Bid Her Clarify Bomb Toll," *NYT* (March 12, 1970), 1.

Wilkerson "There the group": Gussow, "The House," 1; and Andrew O'Hehir, "When Terrorism Was Cool," *Salon.com*, June 7, 2003. "The blast": Thomas Powers, *Diana: The Making of a Terrorist* (Houghton Mifflin, 1971), 2. "Upstairs": Braudy, *Family Circle*, 205. "Wilkerson and Boudin": Braudy, *Family Circle*, 206. "Then they disappeared": Linda Charlton, "Neighbor Recalls 2 'Dazed' Young Women," *NYT* (March 12, 1970), 34. "Fugitives": Susan Braudy, *Family Circle*, 212.

477 **These events** "On April": JM, journal, April 8, 1970, Jnl 10 (WUSTL). "Down the page": JM, journal, April 14, 1970, Jnl 10 (WUSTL).

478 **That spring** "That spring": JM to RM, letter, May 4, 1970 (WUSTL); JM, journal, May 23, 1970, Jnl 10 (WUSTL). "For 18": See Richard Sáez, "James Merrill's Oedipal Fire," *Parnassus* 1, no. 3 (fall/winter 1974). "But the poem": JM to RM, letter, May 4, 1970 (WUSTL). "In his notebook": JM, journal, May 23, 1970, Jnl 10 (WUSTL).

480 **Merrill worked** "Merrill worked": JM to DJ, letter, April 3, 1970 (WUSTL). "Joe Bruno": JM to DJ, letter, April 3, 1970 (WUSTL); JM to DMc, letter, April 5, 1970 (WUSTL). "They saw": JM to DJ, letter, April 16, 1970 (WUSTL). "Alevras and Merrill": JM to DMc, letter, April 5, 1970 (WUSTL). "After they'd": JM to DJ, letter, March 17, 1970 (WUSTL).

Alevras's wife "He and Merrill": JM to DJ, letter, May 21, 1970 (WUSTL). "With weekly": JM to DJ, letter, May 13, 1970 (WUSTL). "Little Georgia": JM to DJ, letter, June 1, 1970 (WUSTL). "Nonetheless": JM to SY, letter, May 27, 1970 (Yale). "In the weeks": JM to EB, letter, May 19, 1970 (Vassar).

481 **Bishop** "Bishop, drinking": EB, "Letters to Arthur Gold, Robert Fizdale, and James Merrill," ed. Langdon Hammer, *Yale Review* 91, no. 2 (spring 2003): 46; EB to JM, letter, June 10, 1970; Brett C. Millier, *Elizabeth Bishop: Life and the Memory of It* (University of California Press, 1987), 430–31. "She asked": EB to JM, letter, May 5, 1970, in "Letters to Gold, Fizdale, and Merrill,": 37–38. " 'She goes' ": JM, "Memories of Elizabeth Bishop," *Prose*, 245. "She made": EB, "Letters," *Yale Review*, 47–48; EB to JM, letter, June 10, 1970 (Vassar).

McIntosh came "McIntosh came": JM to TP, letter, June 23, 1970 (WUSTL). " 'He said he' ": JM, journal, June 23, 1970, Jnl 10 (WUSTL). "He confided": JM to DJ, letter, June 25, 1970 (WUSTL).

482 **Merrill prepared** "Merrill prepared": JM to DJ, letter, May 13, 1970 (WUSTL). " 'I said I'd' ": JM to DMc, letter, June 28, 1970 (WUSTL). " 'This is Peru' ": JM, "Peru: The Landscape Game," *Prose*, 407.

Yet he was "Yet he was": JM to DMc, letter, July 17, 1970 (WUSTL). "Outside Lima": JM to DK, letter, July 5, 1970 (WUSTL). "High in Cuzco": JM to ESP and Grace Stone, letter, July 7, 1970 (ESP). "Inside one": JM to DMc, letter, July 7, 1970 (WUSTL). "The Merrills": JM to ESP and Grace Stone, letter, July 7, 1970 (ESP). "As a train": JM to DMc, letter, July 9, 1970 (WUSTL). **A week** " 'I was driven' ": JM to DK, letter, July 19, 1970 (WUSTL). "Merrill listed": JM to SY, letter, July 22, 1970 (Yale).

483 **The cast-iron** "The cast-iron": EB, "Sestina," *Complete Poems, 1927–79* (FSG, 1983), 84. "She talked": JM, draft of a letter to DMc, July 23, 1970 (WUSTL). " 'His hostess' ": JM, "Elizabeth Bishop (1911–1979)," *Prose*, 232.

When Merrill "When Merrill": JM, draft of a letter to DMc, July 23, 1970 (WUSTL). "One night": JM, "Memories of Elizabeth Bishop," *Prose*, 245. " 'I think you' ": JM to DMc, letter, July 24, 1970 (WUSTL). "For Bishop": JM, "Elizabeth Bishop (1911–1979)," *Prose*, 232.

484 **When he left** "When he left": JM, "Memories of Elizabeth Bishop," *Prose*, 245.

On Water "Taki's wife's": JM to DJ, letter, August 8, 1970 (WUSTL). "McIntosh met": JM to TP, letter, August 17, 1970 (WUSTL).

485 **Merrill and McIntosh** "Merrill and McIntosh": JM to DJ, letter, August 22, 1970 (WUSTL); JM to TP, letter, August 17, 1970 (WUSTL). " 'I couldn't' ": JM to DJ, letter, August 22, 1970 (WUSTL).

485 **Yet after** "Yet after": JM, journal, August 24, 1970, Jnl 7 (WUSTL). "Merrill's diary": JM, journal, September 13, 1970, Jnl 7 (WUSTL).

Jackson's arrival " 'It is marvelous' ": JM to DK, letter, October 7, 1970 (WUSTL). "He was stopping": JM to RM, letter, October 15, 1970 (WUSTL). "Merrill recorded": JM, journal, October 7, 1970, Jnl 7 (WUSTL). "Merrill and the two": JM to RM, letter, October 15, 1970 (WUSTL).

486 **Two days** "Two days": JM, journal, October 17, 1970, Jnl 7 (WUSTL). "Jackson had": JM to DJ, letter, June 25, 1970 (WUSTL). " 'He is fat' ": JM to DJ, letter, November 3, 1970 (WUSTL). "So he paid": JM to DJ, letter, November 3, 1970 (WUSTL).

Merrill wanted "Patricia Storace": Patricia Storace, *Dinner with Persephone* (Pantheon, 1996), 180. " He put the": JM, journal, October 21, 1970, Jnl 7 (WUSTL).

487 **If Merrill** "Merrill would": JM, journal, October 21, 1970, Jnl 7 (WUSTL). "He asked": JM, journal, October 22, 1970, Jnl 7 (WUSTL).

For relief "For relief": JM to EB, letter, October 24, 1970 (Vassar); and JM, journal, October 29, 1970, Jnl 7 (WUSTL). "When they returned": JM, journal, November 2, 1970, Jnl 7 (WUSTL). "He wrote": JM to DJ, letter, October 27, 1970 (WUSTL). "In his notebook": JM, journal, October 30, 1970, Jnl 7 (WUSTL).

After he "After he": JM to TP, letter, November 16, 1970 (WUSTL). " 'Here I am' ": JM to DMc, letter, November 28, 1970 (WUSTL).

488 **Merrill gave** "To the students": JM, journal, November 1970, Jnl 7 (WUSTL).

Bishop made " 'Somebody asked' ": JM to SY, letter, November 6, 1970 (Yale). "Again, Merrill": JM to SY, letter, December 1970 (Yale). "Back in September": JM, journal, September 15, 1970, Jnl 7 (WUSTL).

489 **The poem's** " 'For Time is' ": EB, "The Shampoo," *Complete Poems*, 84.

490 **Merrill received** "Merrill received": JM to Moffett, letter, December 28, 1970 (NYPL).

Dr. Rothenberg "In his dreams": JM to DMc, letter, December 8, 1970 (WUSTL). "With Rothenberg": JM to Moffett, letter, February 4, 1971 (NYPL).

In December "It was Taki's": JM to DMc, letter, December 26, 1970 (WUSTL). "Applauding": JM to TP, letter, January 3, 1971 (WUSTL).

491 **That January** "When Titania": JM to DMc, letter, February 2, 1971 (WUSTL).

And yet "And yet": JM to SY, letter, February 18, 1971 (WUSTL). "For opening": JM to DMc, letter, February 18, 1971 (Yale).

Not everyone " 'At the end' ": Edmund White, *The Farewell Symphony* (Vintage, 1997), 220.

Merrill was "Jimmy offered": JM to MLA, letter, March 9, 1971 (WUSTL). " 'Absurd' ": JM to DMc, letter, March 13–15, 1971 (WUSTL). "Jimmy returned": JM to TP, letter, March 12, 1971 (WUSTL); JM to DMc, letter, March 31, 1971 (WUSTL). "Crossing": JM to RM, letter, February 26, 1971 (WUSTL).

492 **In Paris** "Together": JM to DR, letter, April 5, 1971 (WUSTL); JM to DK, letter, April 8, 1971 (WUSTL); JM to DMc, letter, April 5, 1971 (WUSTL).

Merrill took "In 'Impressions' ": Quoted in Jean-Yves Tadié, *Marcel Proust*, trans. Euan Cameron (Viking, 2000), 499; see 585–86.

493 **What survives** "En route": JM to DMc, letter, May 1, 1971 (WUSTL). "On the island": JM to DJ, letter, April 15, 1971 (WUSTL).

494 **While Merrill** "His marriage": JM to DJ, letter, April 16, 1971 (WUSTL); JM to DMc, letter, April 18, 1971 (WUSTL). "For much": JM to DMc, letter, April 18, 1971 (WUSTL).

495 **Yet Yenser** "Yet Yenser": Meg Sullivan, "The Scholar and the Poet," *UCLA Magazine* (fall 2002): 34.

Yenser's friendly "Yenser remembers": Author's interview with SY (2002). "Yenser refers": SY, marginal comments on "Strato in Plaster" in JM to SY, letter, February 22, 1971 (Yale).

Merrill relished "For instance, he": JM to SY, letter, January 15, 1971 (Yale). "By 1971": JM to SY, letter, February 18, 1971 (Yale). "Stephen": Sullivan, "The Scholar and the Poet," 34.

496 **In Athens** "David Jackson's": JM to Billie Boatwright, letter, May 15, 1971 (Boatwright).

"The poet hied": JM to MLA, letter, June 2, 1971 (WUSTL). "It happened": JM to MLA, letter, June 17, 1971 (WUSTL).

497 **In late** "In late": DJ to ESP, letter, June 26, 1971 (ESP). "Indeed Merrill": JM to DMc, letter, June 23, 1971 (WUSTL).

It seemed "With Mouflouzélis": JM to DK, letter, June 9, 1971 (WUSTL). "Vassilikos saw": Author's interview with VV (2003). "Merrill described": JM to DK, letter, June 9, 1971 (WUSTL).

498 **Americans** " 'How wise' ": JM to Richard Howard, letter, July 22, 1971 (Howard). "Then there was Donald": JM to DMc, letter, July 23, 1971 (WUSTL). "Robin": JM to DMc, letter, July 23, 1971 (WUSTL).

They took "They took": JM to DK, letter, September 7, 1971 (WUSTL). " 'Thank goodness' ": JM to DK, letter, September 7, 1971 (WUSTL).

499 **Back in** "Back in": JM to DJ, letter, September 16, 1971 (WUSTL). " 'It represents' ": JM to Moffett, letter, September 29, 1971 (NYPL). " 'Old Meziki' ": JM to SY, letter, October 3, 1971 (Yale).

George and David "George and David": Author's interview with George Lazaretos (2003). "Jimmy then repaid": JM to SY, letter, October 12–13, 1971 (Yale).

500 **Merrill flew** "He wrote": JM to SY, letter, October 22, 1971 (WUSTL).

501 **In Stonington** "In Stonington": JM to Moffett, letter, October 29, 1971 (NYPL). "Frye's meditations": JM to SY, letter, November 10, 1971 (Yale). " 'If my mother' ": JM to SY, letter, November 10, 1971 (Yale).

Given all "Writing to Stephen": JM to SY, letter, November 15, 1971 (Yale).

Even so "Merrill, already": Robert Browning, "Rabbi Ben Ezra," *The Poems of Browning: Volume Four: 1862–1871*, ed. John Woolford, Daniel Karlin, Joseph Phelan (Routledge, 2012), 52–66.

502 **Yenser wasn't** "That night": Author's interview with Mary Bomba (2004). "About himself": JM to DMc, letter, March 2, 1972 (WUSTL).

Jackson rejoined " 'It seems' ": JM to SY, letter, c. late March 1972 (Yale). " 'Yesterday' ": JM to DMc, letter, April 2, 1972 (WUSTL). "When Jackson": JM to DJ, letter, April 16, 1972 (WUSTL). " 'I've never' ": JM to SY, letter, April 26, 1972 (Yale).

503 **Like a dejected** "In the 1970s": http://www.tm.org/maharishi/index.html (2010).

How serious " 'Thank goodness' ": JM to SY, letter, April 20, 1972 (Yale). "Nonetheless": JM to DJ, letter, April 28, 1972 (WUSTL). " 'It's "love" ": JM to SY, letter, May 14, 1972 (Yale). "Merrill was playing": Jorge Luis Borges, "The Meeting in a Dream," *Other Inquisitions, 1937–1952*, trans. Ruth L. C. Simms (Simon and Schuster, 1968), 99. " 'Saturday afternoon' ": JM to DJ, letter, May 11, 1972 (WUSTL).

504 **Merrill's initiation** "In the short": JM to SY, letter, May 30, 1972 (Yale). " 'Two-thirds' ": JM to DMc, letter, July 27, 1972 (WUSTL).

That summer "That summer": JM to SY, letter, July 24, 1972 (Yale). "It piqued": JM to EB, letter, August 8, 1972 (Vassar).

The poem's "The poem's": JM to SY, letter, January 3, 1972 (Yale).

505 **"Yánnina"** "Kalstone had": JM, "On Yánnina," *Prose*, 80. "For what": JM to DMc, letter, January 24, 1972 (WUSTL).

"You said" "Merrill broke": JM, "On Yánnina: An Interview with David Kalstone," *Prose*, 81. "In the 'time-zoo' ": David Roessel, *In Byron's Shadow*, 88–90. "The point": JM, "On Yánnina: An Interview with David Kalstone," *Prose*, 81.

507 **Which Merrill** " 'O brave' ": William Shakespeare, *The Tempest*, Act V, Scene i.

508 **The "partings"** "The magician's": JM, "On Yánnina: An Interview with David Kalstone," *Prose*, 81.

In Athens " 'It's funny' ": JM to DMc, letter, August 23, 1972 (WUSTL).

13 MILK AND MEMORY

513 **The time** "The review": The review is reprinted in Helen Vendler, *Part of Nature, Part of Us: Modern American Poets* (Harvard University Press, 1980), 205–10.

514 **Vendler's review** "Vendler's review": JM to DR, letter, September 26, 1972 (WUSTL). "The *New York*": JM to CF, letter, October 3, 1972 (Getty). "Congratulations": JM to DK, letter, October 6, 1972 (WUSTL). "He joked": JM to DK, letter, October 17, 1972 (WUSTL).
"Ray Andrews" "The diary": JM to JDM, letter, November 19, 1972 (Yale). "Still, Merrill": JM to Richard Howard, letter, November 17, 1972 (Howard).

515 **In a letter** "In a letter": JM to EB, letter, October 20, 1972 (Vassar). "In the long-distance": JM, *ADP*, 617.
Still, he " 'Jimmy wanted' ": Author's interview with Edmund White (2004); Edmund White, *City Boy: My Life in New York During the 1960s and '70s* (Bloomsbury, 2010), 137, 293.

516 **Yet he felt** "But Vendler": Helen Vendler, *Part of Nature*, 207. "Her friends": JM to DK, letter, October 14, 1972 (WUSTL). "Jimmy responded": JM to DK, letter, October 6, 1972 (WUSTL). "When it came": JM, *ADP*, 617. "His letter": JM to DK, letter, October 14, 1972 (WUSTL). "After her first": HIP to JM, letter, October 8, 1972 (WUSTL).

517 **The lover** "On the eve": JM to Richard Howard, letter, September 16, 1972 (Howard). "The lunch": JM to DH, letter, September 13, 1972 (WUSTL).

518 **The Rover** "Merrill stayed": JM to Hubbell Pierce, letter, October 8, 1972 (WUSTL). " 'D. keeps' ": JM to DK, October 6, 1972 (WUSTL). "In 1971": JM, journal, June 3, 1971, Jnl 7 (WUSTL).
In September " 'What is' ": JM, "Object Lessons," *Prose*, 208.
But Merrill " 'No thoughts' ": JM, "Object Lessons," *Prose*, 207–08. "He quotes": JM, "Object Lessons," *Prose*, 208.

519 **The notion** "Merrill declares": JM, "Object Lessons," *Prose*, 211. "Prompted": JM, "Object Lessons," *Prose*, 210.
When he "When he": JM to Richard Howard, letter, September 16, 1972 (Howard). "Howard": Richard Howard, "Close Encounters of Another Kind," *Talking Cures* (Turtle Point Press, 2002), 7–9. "He liked": JM to DJ, letter, June 21, 1973 (WUSTL).

520 **In 1969** " '"Well," Merrill' ": Author's interview with Richard Howard (2001).
In the days "On October": JM to Richard Howard, postcard, October 10, 1972 (Howard). "By the time": JM to Richard Howard, letter, October 24, 1972 (Howard).

521 **In its play** "It was composed": JM to Richard Howard, letter, December 19, 1972 (Howard).
Mademoiselle herself "Mademoiselle (Merrill)": JM, worksheets for "Lost in Translation" (WUSTL).

522 **Translation** "At Amherst": JM, journal, June 23, 1945, Jnl 1 (WUSTL).

524 **But the poem** "The sense": SY, *The Consuming Myth: The Work of James Merrill* (Harvard University Press, 1987), 26. "In draft": JM, worksheet for "Lost in Translation" (WUSTL).

526 **"JIM!"** "Showing herself": HIP to JM, letter, November 26, 1972 (WUSTL). "The letter": JM to Richard Howard, letter, December 19, 1972 (Howard). " 'I would' ": HIP to JM, letter, January 5, 1973 (WUSTL). "When the event": JM to TP, letter, March 3, 1973 (WUSTL).

527 **As Merrill** "Now he was": JM to RM, letter, October 16, 1972 (WUSTL). "The next": JM to DK, letter, October 17, 1972 (WUSTL). "Jimmy just": JM to RM, letter, October 17, 1972 (WUSTL).

528 **Merrill and Jackson** "Merrill and Jackson": JM to JDM, letter, November 19, 1972 (Yale). "He began": Two worksheets for "Chimes for Yahya" are dated December 24, 1972 (WUSTL). "One night": JM to SY, letter, December 29, 1972 (Yale). "The spot": JM to EB, letter, January 6, 1973 (Vassar). " 'My dear' ": JM to SY, letter, December 29, 1972 (Yale).
In the thick "It is awarded": Bollingen Prize recipients, http://beinecke.library.yale.edu/bollingen (2009). "A photographer": JM to SY, letter, January 19, 1973 (Yale).
Merrill tried "To Anthony": JM to Anthony Hecht, letter, January 8, 1973 (WUSTL). "To McIntosh": JM to DMc, letter, January 18, 1973 (WUSTL).

529 **Not every** "Seeing the choice": "A World West of Yale," editorial, *NYT* (January 16, 1973). "Richard Howard": Richard Howard, letter to the editor of the *NYT*, January 19, 1973.

530 **Merrill never** "The rest": JM to DMc, letter, January 18, 1973 (WUSTL). "On his way": JM to TP, letter, February 4, 1973 (WUSTL).

Even so "Writing in": Peter Davison, "New Poetry," *Atlantic Monthly* (March 1973), 84. "A sharper": Richard Pevear, "Poetry Chronicle, *Hudson Review* 26, no. 1 (spring 1973): 203. "Merrill responded": JM, journal, c. April 22, 1973, Jnl 38 (WUSTL).

531 **Merrill was** "He envisioned": JM to RM, letter, October 15, 1970 (WUSTL).

532 **Yet he kept** "Contrasting": JM to SY, letter, September 29, 1972 (Yale).

He turned "He prepared": Author's interview with JH (2003). "That spring": JM to Richard Howard, letter, May 10, 1973 (Howard); JM to DJ, letter, February 21, 1973 (WUSTL).

The latter "He shot": JM to June Fortress, letter, November 21, 1972 (Poetry Center Archives). "He was joking": JM to EB, letter, November 30, 1972 (Vassar). See Kamran Javadizadeh, "Elizabeth Bishop's Closet Drama," *Arizona Quarterly* 67, no. 3 (2011): 119–50.

533 **When the event** "When the event": JM to SY, letter, April 16, 1972 (Yale); EB to Arthur Gold and Robert Fizdale, letter, April 25, 1973, in *One Art: Letters*, ed. Robert Giroux (FSG, 1994), 579.

Soon after "Alluding": JM, journal, April 24, 1973, Jnl 38 (WUSTL).

535 **There were** "She was": JM to DR, letter, May 11, 1973 (WUSTL). "In the Greek": JM to Richard Howard, letter, May 10, 1973 (Howard). "A lamb": Author's interview with Doug the Barber (2008); and JM to Richard Howard, letter, May 10, 1973 (Howard).

Jackson left "There was": JM to TP, letter, May 23, 1973 (WUSTL); JM to Carol Longone, letter, May 24, 1973 (WUSTL). "Merrill found": JM to DH, letter, May 25, 1973 (WUSTL); JM to RM, letter, May 25, 1973 (WUSTL).

The poem "One was": JM to SY, letter, May 25, 1973 (Yale).

536 **Merrill showed** "White is": Edmund White, *Farewell Symphony*, 239. "What remains": JM to Richard Howard, letter, July 7, 1973 (Howard). "Describing the baptism": JM to Richard Howard, letter, May 10, 1973 (Howard).

538 **In July** "In July": JM to William Burford, letter, June 29, 1973 (WUSTL). " 'Sitting on' ": JM, journal, July 12, 1973, Jnl 38 (WUSTL).

Jimmy was "Venice, recalls": Author's interview with Edmund White (2008). "Venice, he": JM to Virgil Burnett, letter, August 16, 1973 (Waterloo).

539 **In Athens** "With 'Lost' ": Vendler, *Part of Nature*, 211, 217.

He composed "He described": JM to JDM, letter, July 21, 1973 (Yale). "Now Merrill": JM to JDM, letter, August 26, 1973 (Yale).

Jackson, responding "Jackson, responding": JM to DK, letter, July 15, 1973 (WUSTL). "On August": *BBC Home: On This Day: 1950–2005*, "Athens Attack Leaves Three Dead," http://news.bbc.co.uk/onthisday/hi/dates/stories/august/5/newsid_4533000/4533763.stm (2009).

540 **And Maria** "And Maria": JM to SY, letter, July 16, 1973 (Yale); JM to Moffett, letter, August 15, 1973 (NYPL). "Jimmy exclaimed": JM to DMc, letter, August 17, 1973 (WUSTL).

In September "Merrill sent": JM to Chester Kallman, letter, September 29, 1973 (Ransom). "Merrill felt": JM to CF, letter, December 15, 1973 (Getty). "And Merrill's": Author's interview with DH (2005). "Shortly after": JM to DK, letter, October 10, 1973 (WUSTL).

As Merrill "Truman": JM to SY, letter, September 9, 1973 (Yale). "The scandalous": JM to SY, letter, August 21, 1973 (Yale).

541 **A succession** " 'DJ' ": JM to DK, letter, October 10, 1973 (WUSTL).

Returning "Returning": JM to TP, letter, November 27, 1973 (WUSTL). "On Water": JM to TP, letter, November 27, 1973 (WUSTL). "He thought": JM to AC, letter, November 28, 1973 (Yale). "It would": JM to Moffett, letter, November 30, 1973 (NYPL).

Scenes "Scenes": JM, journal, December 1973, Jnl 38 (WUSTL). "For the past": JM to RM, letter, January 25, 1974 (WUSTL). "A few days": JM to DJ, letter, January 19, 1973 (WUSTL).

"He made": JM, worksheet for *The Book of Ephraim* in letter to DJ, January 19, 1973 (WUSTL). "Eventually": JM, *Sandover*, 3.

542 **Merrill spent** "He told": JM to DJ, letter, January 19, 1974 (WUSTL).

543 **It was also** "As he returned": JM to DJ, letter, February 16, 1974 (WUSTL). "This was not": DJ to JM, letter, March 2, 1974 (WUSTL).

Merrill had "To Irma": JM to IB, letter, March 12, 1974 (WUSTL). "He felt": JM, "An Interview with Donald Sheehan," *Prose*, 53.

544 **Other** "One was Ashbery's": JM to JA, letter, February 16, 1974 (Houghton). "Another": JM to JH, letter, February 1, 1974 (Yale). "Jimmy": JH, *Reflections on Espionage: The Question of Cupcake* (Atheneum, 1976), 74.

After "After": JM, *Sandover*, 5. "He recalled": JM, *Sandover*, 8, 15. "Rhyme": JM, *Sandover*, 15.

545 **Merrill's scheme** "It samples": JM, *Sandover*, 15, 17.

When he "When he": JM to DJ, letter, February 16, 1974 (WUSTL). " 'I walked' ": JM, *Sandover*, 30. "He makes": JM, *Sandover*, 14. "Merrill refers": T. S. Eliot, "In Memory of Henry James," *The Egoist* 1, vol. 5 (1918): 1–2. "The point": JM, *Sandover*, 32.

546 **In the 1980s, Merrill** "Merrill responded": JM, "An Interview with Frederick Bornhauser, *Prose*, 143. " 'Causes' ": JM, "Days of 1964," *CP*, 221.

547 **But Merrill's** "In section": JM, *Sandover*, 11. "Merrill's father's": JM, *Sandover*, 13.

548 **Unless** "Unless": JM, *Sandover*, 62.

549 **At first** "At first": JM to AC, letter, March 25, 1974 (Yale).

Corn "When Corn's": JM, blurb for AC, *All Roads at Once* (Viking, 1976). "Merrill, thinking": Author's interview with AC (2003). "He once": JM, "An Interview with J. D. McClatchy," *Prose*, 107.

550 **Merrill had** "David, who": JM to DMc, letter, May 9, 1974 (WUSTL). "This was": JM to JDM, postcard, May 7, 1974 (Yale).

551 **Despite** "Despite": JM to MLA, letter, May 24, 1974 (WUSTL). "They tried": JM to Mary McCarthy, letter, June 21, 1974 (WUSTL). "In the spirit": JM to Hubbell Pierce, letter, August 5, 1974 (WUSTL). "Pierce's": JM, *Sandover*, 98. "Meanwhile": JM to DR, letter, April 19, 1974 (WUSTL). "When it came": JM to SY, letter, August 8, 1974 (Yale).

By late "Bidart came": JM to DK, letter, August 25, 1974 (WUSTL). "Grace": JM to SY, letter, August 26, 1974 (Yale).

552 **Jackson left** "Merrill spent": JM to DJ, letter, September 20, 1974 (WUSTL); JM to DJ, letter, October 18, 1974 (WUSTL); JM to DJ, letter, November 6, 1974 (WUSTL). "Power, Ephraim": JM, *Sandover*, 54. "Power holds": JM, *Sandover*, 55. "The thought": JM to RM, letter, October 15, 1970 (WUSTL). "It was, he says": JM, *Sandover*, 55. "Ephraim was": JM, *Sandover*, 56.

553 **This is** "He was too": JM, *Sandover*, 31. " 'Where were we?' ": JM, *Sandover*, 46. "In 'S' ": JM, *Sandover*, 66. "In 'U' ": JM to Moffett, letter, October 1974 (NYPL); JM, *Sandover*, 74.

554 **Merrill flew** "He came": JM to Richard Howard, letter, December 24, 1975 (Howard). "Kallman had": JM to SY, letter, December 19, 1974 (Yale).

On Christmas " 'It was only' ": JM to CF, letter, January 18, 1975 (Getty). "There he": JM to EB, letter, January 29, 1975 (Vassar). "Death was": JM to CF, letter, January 18, 1975 (Getty).

555 **Kallman was** "Kallman had": JM to SY, letter, January 30, 1975 (Yale).

Merrill and Jackson "Merrill and Jackson": JM to SY, letter, January 30, 1975 (Yale). "With 'The Divine Comedy' ": JM, *Sandover*, 72. "Friends show": JM to SY, letter, January 30, 1975 (Yale). "But Stevens": JM, *Sandover*, 72. "Stevens thanks": JM, *Sandover*, 73.

556 **It had always** "In 'P' ": JM, *Sandover*, 56. "Now, in": JM, *Sandover*, 73.

As The Book " 'Would I' ": JM to SY, letter, February 16, 1975 (Yale). "On February": JM to SY, letter, February 16, 1975 (Yale). "As he looked": JM to EB, letter, January 29, 1975 (Vassar).

557 **When he did** "When he did": JM, *Sandover*, 41. "So he hatched": JM to WM, April 4, 1975 (WUSTL). " '"And' (as Jimmy)' ": JM to SY, letter, April 21, 1975 (Yale).

Shortly after "As Mary": JM to DJ, letter, June 1, 1975 (WUSTL). "A week later": JM to DJ, letter, June 9, 1975 (WUSTL). "It's as if": JM to EB, letter, July 19, 1975 (Vassar). "He wrote": DJ to JM, letter, July 6, 1975 (WUSTL).

558 **If he did** "Since *The Divine*": JM to Richard Howard, letter, February 28, 1975 (Howard).

559 **In the closing** "As embodied": JM, *Sandover*, 75. "But, after": JM, *Sandover*, 77.

560 **In "W"** "After footing": JM, *Sandover*, 80.

561 **Dinner paid** "They pass": JM, *Sandover*, 81. " 'Dear Dante' ": JM to JDM, letter, May 25, 1974 (Yale). "Defying Pevear": JM, *Sandover*, 82.

562 **In "Lost"** "In 'Y' ": JM, *Sandover*, 89.
Merrill ends "JM and DJ": SY to JM, letter, February 23, 1975 (WUSTL). " 'Throughout the empty' ": JM, *Sandover*, 90.

563 **Before any** "Before any": JM, *Sandover*, 91. "On the way": JM, *Sandover*, 92.

14 MIRABELL

564 **When the muse** "These were": JM, journal, October 13, 1976, Jnl 9 (WUSTL).
Mirabell's Books "Although he": JM, "Kabel Barnes, via Ouija, November 14, 1953," Ouija board transcript, box 3, folder 3 (WUSTL).

565 **Those messages** "Merrill mailed": JM to EB, letter, July 1975 (Vassar). "Courtly Marius": JM, journal, July 27, 1975, Jnl 25 (WUSTL). "On her way": JM, journal, August 9, 1975, Jnl 25 (WUSTL).

566 **George's send-off** "Ephraim, who": JM, journal, August 17, 1975, Jnl 25 (WUSTL).
The Other "In her memoir": AL, *Familiar Spirits*, 66–70. "He told JM": JM, journal, August 17, 1975, Jnl 25 (WUSTL).

567 **Yet it wasn't** "Fascinating": JM to SY, letter, November 20–21, 1975 (Yale). "But he wore": JM to JDM, letter, January 4, 1976 (Yale).
He spent "Finishing": JM to Moffett, letter, January 14, 1976 (NYPL). " 'I feel' ": JM to AL, letter, January 22, 1976 (WUSTL). "As in years": JM to DK, letter, January 22, 1976 (WUSTL). "Ephraim had": JM to JDM, letter, January 22, 1976 (Yale). "He saw": JM, journal, January 29, 1976, Jnl 34 (WUSTL). "He could": JM, journal, February 8, 1976, Jnl 8 (WUSTL).

568 **In February** "In February": JM to DMc, letter, February 18, 1976 (WUSTL). "Contacted": JM, journal, February 8, 1976, Jnl 8 (WUSTL).

569 **His fiftieth** "His fiftieth": JM to EB, letter, March 3, 1976 (Vassar). " 'Dear Jimmy' ": John Ashbery to JM, letter, April 2, 1976 (Houghton).
Vendler "Vendler": Helen Vendler, "Divine Comedies," *New York Review of Books* (March 18, 1976). "But the *New York*": Louis Simpson, review of *Divine Comedies*, *NYT* (March 21, 1976). "Two weeks": JM to JDM, letter, March 10, 1976 (Yale); JM to DK, letter, March 22, 1976 (WUSTL).

570 **He was** "Those speakers": JM, *Sandover*, 113.
These new "2 GODS": JM, Ouija board transcript, April 26, 1976 (WUSTL).

573 **Merrill wanted** "The board": JM, Ouija board transcript, April 28, 1976 (WUSTL).
These séances "At first": JM to JDM, letter, May 3, 1976 (Yale). "He glimpsed": JM, journal, May 23, 1976, Jnl 8 (WUSTL). "Merrill's mind": JM, journal, May, 1976, Jnl 8 (WUSTL). "He gave": JM, journal, May 25, 1976, Jnl 8 (WUSTL). "Under": John Michell, *The View over Atlantis* (Sago Press, 1969). "Merrill calls": JM, *Sandover*, 112. " 'The point' ": JM, journal, March 29, 1976, Jnl 8 (WUSTL).

575 **On Water** "They held": JM, journal, c. September 1976, Jnl 8 (WUSTL). " 'We are all' ": JM to RM, letter, June 1976 (WUSTL).
It remained " 'Squeaking' ": JM, journal, June 14, 1976, Jnl 8 (WUSTL). " 'Are they scary' ": JM, journal, June 8, 1976, Jnl 8 (WUSTL). "A pause": JM, journal, June 14, 1976, Jnl 8 (WUSTL). "In the midst": JM, journal, June 12, 1976, Jnl 8 (WUSTL). " 'He annoyed' ": JM, journal, June 14, 1976, Jnl 8 (WUSTL).

576 **The séances** "Their civilization": JM, journal, June 13, 1976, Jnl 8 (WUSTL). "But as it": JM, journal, June 16, 1976, Jnl 8 (WUSTL). "It was then": JM, journal, June 16, 1976, Jnl 8 (WUSTL).
God B "God B": JM, journal, June 30, 1976, Jnl 8 (WUSTL). "741's term": JM, journal, June 23, 1976, Jnl 8 (WUSTL).

577 **Merrill dutifully** "Only a slight": JM, journal, June 13, 1976, Jnl 8 (WUSTL). "In another": JM, journal, June 30, 1976, Jnl 8 (WUSTL). " 'The caliber' ": JM, journal, June 16, 1976, Jnl 8 (WUSTL). "741 added": JM, journal, June 19, 1976, Jnl 8 (WUSTL).

578 **The board's** "All true": JM, journal, June 8, 1976, Jnl 8 (WUSTL). " 'DK's' ": JM, journal, June 23, 1976, Jnl 8 (WUSTL). " 'Hitler' ": JM, journal, June 8, 1976, Jnl 8 (WUSTL). "Africans": JM, journal, June 25, 1976, Jnl 8 (WUSTL).
As if "Merrill treated": JM, journal, June 24, 1976, Jnl 8 (WUSTL).

579 **DJ was not** "DJ was not": JM, journal, June 24, 1976, Jnl 8 (WUSTL).
Did it " The mediums": JM, journal, July 1, 1976, Jnl 8 (WUSTL).
Immediately "Immediately": JM, journal, July 2, 1976, Jnl 8 (WUSTL).

581 **"My dear"** " 'My dear' ": JM, journal, July 3, 1976, Jnl 8 (WUSTL).

582 **Merrill's mind** "Frustrated": JM to SY, letter, June 6, 1976 (Yale).
He had "As the séances": JM, journal, July 7, 1976, Jnl 8 (WUSTL). "The elements": JM, journal, July 7, 1976, Jnl 8 (WUSTL).
The séances "The séances": JM to CF, letter, June 29, 1976 (Getty). "When the time": JM to SY, letter, August 5 and 6, 1976 (Yale). "On the lookout": JM, journal, July, 1976, Jnl 9 (WUSTL). "But soon": JM to SY, letter, August 5 and 6, 1976 (Yale).

583 **Over** "The dictées": JM to Moffett, letter, June 24, 1976 (NYPL). "On August 1": JM, journal, August 1976, Jnl 9 (WUSTL).

584 **By August** "Like a ward": JM, *Sandover*, 236. " 'I have so' ": JM, *Sandover*, 222. "Mirabell's séances": JM, journal, c. fall 1976, Jnl 8 (WUSTL). "As represented": JM, *Sandover*, 275. "David left": JM to NL, letter, August 4, 1976 (WUSTL).

585 **The preface** "The preface": Merrill sent a copy, very close to published text, of the opening pages to Hubbell Pierce on August 17, 1976 (WUSTL). "The long": JM to Moffett, letter, September 14, 1976 (NYPL). "With respect": JM, journal, June 19, 1976, Jnl 8 (WUSTL). "And the lessons": JM to SY, letter, July 2, 1976 (Yale). "As he worked": JM, journal, September 22, 1976, Jnl 9 (WUSTL). " 'This poem' ": JM to SY, letter, November 4, 1976 (Yale). "Yet the language": JM, journal, October 27, 1976, Jnl 9 (WUSTL).

586 **There were** "He traveled": JM to CF, letter, October 6, 1976 (Getty); JM to DJ, letter, November 25 and 26, 1976 (WUSTL). "That fall": JM to DJ, letter, September 28, 1976 (WUSTL). "He wrote": JM to DJ, letter, February 10, 1977 (WUSTL). " 'I see him' ": JM to SY, letter, April 18, 1976 (Yale).
Looking "In his notebook": JM, journal, September 1976, Jnl 9 (WUSTL). "Poetry and science": JM, "An Interview with J. D. McClatchy," *Prose*, 122. "Or as he affirms": JM, *Sandover*, 174.
In addition "In addition": Arthur M. Young, *The Reflexive Universe: Evolution of Consciousness* (Delacorte, 1976). Merrill quotes Young on the photon in his journal, September 13, 1976, Jnl 9 (WUSTL). "The notion": JM, journal, September 13, 1976, Jnl 9 (WUSTL).

587 **Young** "Young": Quotation from *The Reflexive Universe*, www.arthuryoung.com (accessed 8/23/10). "They converge": JM's copy of *The Reflexive Universe*, 114, 192–95 (Yale).
He had little "An exception": Vincent P. Dole, "George Constantin Cotzias," National Academies Press, www.nap.edu/readingroom.php/gcotzias.html (2010). "A chance": JM to SY, letter, December 6, 1976 (Yale). "If any": Lewis Thomas, *The Lives of a Cell: Notes of a Biology Watcher* (Viking, 1974), 166. "Merrill was in": JM to SY, letter, December 6, 1976 (Yale).

588 **At New Year's** "Reunited": JM to CF, letter, January 15, 1977 (Getty). "In his notebook": JM, journal, November 15, 1976, Jnl 9 (WUSTL). "By the first": JM to DJ, letter, February 3, 1977 (WUSTL). "He gave": JM, *Metamorphosis of 741* (Banyan Press, 1977).

588 **That spring** "That spring": JM to Henry Sloss, letter, February 28, 1977 (WUSTL); JM to Moffett, letter, April 1, 1977 (NYPL). "Two newspapers": JM to DJ, letter, April 21, 1977 (WUSTL). "He received": JM to JDM, letter, April 21, 1977 (Yale). "Dismayed": JM to DJ, letter, April 21, 1977 (WUSTL). "And—'as a result' ": JM to DMc, letter, April 22, 1977 (WUSTL).

589 **Merrill organized** "THE 3": JM, *Sandover*, 171. "(Merrill's birthday)": Moffett to the author, letter, December 2, 2010. "Even Mirabell": JM, *Sandover*, 170.

But the fundamental "He had always": JM, "Acoustic Chambers," *Prose*, 3. "It was something": JM, *ADP*, 623. "He'd found": JM, "An Interview with Donald Sheehan," *Prose*, 61.

590 **As opposed** "As opposed": JM, *Sandover*, 154. "As Mark Bauer": Mark Bauer, *This Composite Voice*, 197. "Merrill replaced": JM, *Sandover*, 251.

591 **Moving** "For example": JM, *Sandover*, 131.

But of course "When WHA": JM, *Sandover*, 128.

592 **Arguably** "But even": JM, *Sandover*, 259. "The critic": Aidan Wasley, *The Age of Auden: Postwar Poetry and the American Scene* (Princeton University Press, 2010), 108.

Poetic influence "At a dinner": Quoted by Mark Bauer, *This Composite Voice*, 251. "In November": Harold Bloom, "From the Year's Books," *New Republic* (November 20, 1976), quoted in Robert Polito, *A Reader's Guide to James Merrill's "The Changing Light at Sandover"* (Michigan University Press, 1994), 133.

593 **Merrill was** "The Anxiety": Harold Bloom, *The Anxiety of Influence: A Theory of Poetry* (Oxford University Press, 1973), 5, 116–17.

Or he was "Or he was": For sustained treatments of this idea, see Bauer, *This Composite Voice*; Piotr K. Gwiazda, *James Merrill and W. H. Auden: Homosexuality and Poetic Influence* (Palgrave, 2007); Wasley, *The Age of Auden*. "Near the end": JM, *Sandover*, 262–63.

594 **Does it** "As he mentioned": Robert Polito, *"The Changing Light at Sandover*: A Conversation with James Merrill," *Pequod* 39, no. 1 (1990): 11.

595 **In his ventriloquized** "In his ventriloquized": JM, *Sandover*, 118–19. "The eugenic": JM, *Sandover*, 118–19.

DJ and Maria "DJ and Maria": JM, *Sandover*, 186. "And so": Timothy Materer, *James Merrill's Apocalypse* (Cornell University Press, 2000), 100–02. "This state": JM, *Sandover*, 216.

596 **The "MYSTERIES"** "The name": JM, *Sandover*, 206.

Yet he is "When he reviewed": Thom Gunn, "A Heroic Enterprise," *San Francisco Review of Books* (August 1979); reprinted in Polito, *A Reader's Guide*, 157.

597 **The openness** "The long poem": JM, *Sandover*, 97.

The poem's "The mediums": JM, *Sandover*, 106.

598 **CK** "JM tries": JM, *Sandover*, 106. "In *The Book*": JM, *Sandover*, 15. "The spirits": JM, *Sandover*, 153. "They are": JM, *Sandover*, 276.

599 **The return** "His career": JM, *Sandover*, 265. "The love": JM, *Sandover*, 176. "Thus Strato": JM, *Sandover*, 196, 220–21.

As explained "As explained": JM, *Sandover*, 179. "Yet Merrill": JM, draft typescript for *Mirabell: Books of Number* (WUSTL). " 'NO ACCIDENT' ": JM, *Sandover*, 116.

600 **Instead** "He put that": JM, *Sandover*, 136. "As he set": JM to DK, letter, July 12, 1976 (WUSTL).

601 **Readers** "Robert speaks": JM, *Sandover*, 256. "The complaint": JM to IB, letter, August 7, 1977 (WUSTL). "It would be": Denis Donoghue, "What the Ouija Board Said," *NYT Book Review* (June 15, 1980); reprinted in Polito, *A Reader's Guide*, 180. "The core": JM, *Sandover*, 263.

602 **But *Mirabell*** "Mirabell connects": JM, *Sandover*, 150. "The elements": JM, *Sandover*, 161.

The power "When Frank": Quoted in Polito, *A Reader's Guide*, 3. "The opening": JM, *Sandover*, 275. "Curiously": JM, *Sandover*, 276.

15 SANDOVER

604 **Merrill spent** "Now he": JM to AC and JDM, letter, May 5, 1977 (Yale). "The seminar": JM to Moffett, letter, June 3, 1977 (NYPL). "This, 'the Summer' ": JM, chronology (WUSTL); JM to DR, letter, July 11, 1977 (WUSTL).

It might " 'The dear' ": JM to SY, letter, June 29, 1977 (Yale). "Jimmy had": JM to CF, letter, July 4, 1977 (Getty). "Their deaths": JM to SY, letter, June 29, 1977 (Yale). "The addition": JM to CF, letter, July 4, 1977 (Getty). "In *Scripts*": JM, *Sandover*, 376. "He spoke": JM to Elise Sanguinetti, letter, August 2, 1977 (Sanguinetti).

605 **But it would** "Because she was": JM, *Sandover*, 303–4.

606 **The necessary** "His foil": JM, *Sandover*, 293. "His task": JM, *Sandover*, 316. "WHA drops": JM, *Sandover*, 328–30.

607 **In addition** "Each lesson": JM, *Sandover*, 353–54. "After they depart": JM, *Sandover*, 359. "Archangel Michael": JM, *Sandover*, 356. "The spirits' ": JM, *Sandover*, 359.

This ceremony "As that séance": JM, *Sandover*, 360. "Merrill made": JM to RM, letter, June 6, 1977 (WUSTL).

608 **Maintaining** "This old": JM to DMc, letter, May 10, 1977 (WUSTL). "In between": JM to AC and JDM, June 2, 1977 (Yale). "Later": JM to DR, letter, July 11, 1977 (WUSTL). "Manos": JM to SY, letter, July 15, 1977 (Yale).

609 **In their break** "Here they": JM to AC and JDM, June 15, 1977 (Yale). "Philosopher": JM, *Sandover*, 372. "When he": JM to AC and JDM, June 15, 1977 (Yale). "Absorbed": JM, *Sandover*, 373.

In addition "In addition": JM to SY, letter, July 15, 1977 (Yale).

610 **In the ongoing** "In his notebook": JM, journal, September 30, 1977, Jnl 22 (WUSTL). "In *Scripts*": JM, *Sandover*, 485. "At the end": JM, *Sandover*, 489. "True": JM, *Sandover*, 492.

Thus "Thus": JM to DMc, letter, August 14, 1977 (WUSTL). "The spirits": JM to SY, letter, September 13, 1977 (Yale). "Late": JM, *Sandover*, 468. "They took": JM, *Sandover*, 516–17.

611 **Throughout** " 'I wish' ": JM to AC and JDM, letter, August 1, 1977 (Yale). " 'Looking back' ": JM to DMc, letter, August 14, 1977 (WUSTL).

His first "When Irma": JM to IB, letter, August 7, 1977 (WUSTL). "To Robin": JM to RM, letter, September 19, 1977 (WUSTL). "Like his first": JM to HIM, letter, August 1955 (WUSTL). "When the trilogy": JM, "An Interview with Helen Vendler," *CP*, 87.

612 **He returned** "He himself": JM to AC, letter, February 6, 1976; JM to JDM, letter, February 1976 (Yale). "When Corn": JM to JDM and AC, August 28, 1978 (Yale).

613 **With angels** "He put": JM to TP, letter, November 20, 1977 (WUSTL); JM to DJ, letter, December 6, 1977 (WUSTL); JM to TP, letter, December 6, 1977 (WUSTL).

The buzz "He was typing": JM to Virgil Burnett, letter, October 24, 1977 (Waterloo). "By January": JM to SY, letter, February 3, 1978 (Yale).

He didn't "He used": JM, *Sandover*, 319. "In lines": JM, *Sandover*, 363. These lines are penciled into Merrill's bound typescript of the poem (WUSTL).

614 **Merrill's description** "Merrill's description": JM, *Sandover*, 319–20.

Throughout *Scripts* " 'Before we' ": JM to SY, letter, March 6, 1978 (Yale).

615 **Meanwhile** " 'South' ": JM to DR, letter, February 7, 1978 (WUSTL).

Eventually "Jimmy": JM to SY, letter, March 6, 1978 (Yale). "They opened": JM, journal, March 3, 1978, Jnl 9 (WUSTL).

Even in "Even in": DJ to DR, letter, March 7, 1978 (WUSTL). "He rose": JM to SY, letter, April 12, 1978 (Yale). "The sensation": JM to DJ, letter, April 16, 1978 (WUSTL). "He grew": JM to TP, letter, April 25, 1978 (WUSTL). "Puffing": JM to TP, letter, May 31, 1978 (WUSTL). "But very": JM to Henry Sloss, letter, June 4, 1978 (Sloss); JM, journal, Easter Monday, 1978, Jnl 43 (WUSTL); JM to DMc, letter, April 11, 1978 (WUSTL).

616 **Only rarely** "On April": JM, journal, April 1, 1978, Jnl 22 (WUSTL). "In another": JM, journal, March 13, 1978, Jnl 9 (WUSTL).

He read " 'What would' ": JM to W. D. Snodgrass, letter, July 16, 1978 (NYPL).

616 **Yet even** "Looking back": JM, *ADP*, 479. "Having avoided": JM to KF, letter, July 24, 1978 (WUSTL). "Merrill went": JM to KF, letter, December 24, 1979 (WUSTL). "Friar kept": KF's copy of *Mirabell* and his notes on *Mirabell* are held in the KF Papers, American College of Greece, Athens.

617 **In July** "They picked": JM to DK, letter, August 3, 1978 (WUSTL).

618 **Enforcing** " 'No special' ": JM to DK, letter, August 3, 1978 (WUSTL).
    Mimi "Vassili, haggard": JM, *Sandover*, 558–59. " 'It happened' ": Author's interview with VV (2003). "Merrill addresses": JM, *Sandover*, 560.

620 **These events** "They spent": JM to SY, letter, September 21, 1978 (Yale).
    With the Sandover "The end": JM, *Sandover*, 370. "He would return": DJ to AL, letter, August 11, 1978 (WUSTL).
    Merrill returned "One of": Phoebe Pettengell, "Voices from the Atom," *New Leader*, December 4, 1978, in Robert Polito, *A Reader's Guide to "Sandover,"* 161. "Thom Gunn": Thom Gunn, "A Heroic Enterprise," *San Francisco Review of Books*, August 1979, in Polito, 153. " 'It never' ": Author's interview with Edmund White (2011). " 'Without you' ": JM to Hubbell Pierce, letter, May 3, 1979 (WUSTL).

621 **Besides audiences** "He'd paid": HIP to JM, letter, October 1978 (WUSTL). " 'What a difference' ": HIP to Elise Sanguinetti, letter, January 17, 1979 (WUSTL). "Jimmy complained": JM, journal, January 1979, Jnl 14 (WUSTL).

622 **Merrill made** "Merrill made": JM, journal, December 31, 1978, Jnl 14 (WUSTL). "After all": JM to DMc, letter, January 4, 1979 (WUSTL).
    For Merrill "Merrill savored": JM to TP, letter, February 18, 1979 (WUSTL).

623 **To Jackson** "To Jackson": DJ to Billy Boatwright, postcard, February 17, 1979 (WUSTL). "Punning": JM to TP, letter, February 18, 1979 (WUSTL).
    Jackson wasted "But the previous": Author's interview with Liz Lear (2003). "Lurie was": AL, *Familiar Spirits*, 127.

624 **It was a mixed** "Jimmy dashed": JM to EB, postcard, February 1, 1979 (Vassar).

625 **While Jackson** "He began": JM, journal, January 24–February 4, 1979, Jnl 14 (WUSTL).
    When he " 'TOO FLAMBOYANT' ": JM and DJ, Ouija board transcript, February 5, 1979, box 3, folder 8 (WUSTL). "In 1972": JM, journal, October 18, 1972, Jnl 39 (WUSTL).

627 **It would** "David did": JM to SY, letter, March 7, 1979 (Yale). "He was equipped": JM to Richard Olney, letter, May 18, 1979 (Yale). " 'Dearest D' ": JM to DJ, letter, April 9, 1979 (WUSTL).
    On April "On April": JM, journal, April 9, 1979, Jnl 14 (WUSTL). "In May": JM, journal, June 2, 1979, Jnl 14 (WUSTL). "Two days": JM, journal, June 4, 1979, Jnl 14 (WUSTL). "Then a stop-smoking": JM to Moffett, letter, May 3, 1979 (NYPL).

628 **He was in** " 'I feel' ": JM, journal, June 30, 1979, Jnl 14 (WUSTL). " 'Quite naturally' ": HIP to JM, letter, July 1979 (WUSTL).
    He got another "Jimmy arranged": JM to Hubbell Pierce, letter, July 2, 1979 (WUSTL). "HIP": HIP to Hubbell Pierce, letter, July 19, 1979 (WUSTL).

629 **As planned** "In Venice": JM to Billy Boatwright, July 30, 1979 (WUSTL); JM to JDM and AC, July 22, 1979 (Yale); JM to EB, postcard, August 7, 1979 (Vassar). "He stayed": JM to DK, letter, August 10, 1979 (WUSTL).
    This would "The plan": JM to JDM and AC, July 22, 1979 (Yale).

630 **The excessive** "They stripped": JM to ESP, letter, October 3, 1979 (ESP). "A pair": JM to SY, letter, October 6, 1979 (Yale). "Merrill had": JM to ESP, letter, October 3, 1979 (ESP). "The buds": JM to SY, letter, October 6, 1979 (Yale).
    To make "To make": JM to Billy Boatwright, postcard, October 17, 1979 (WUSTL). "The sorest": JM to SY, letter, October 6, 1979 (Yale). "His karate": JM to JDM and AC, October 13, 1979 (Yale). "He came to . . . tallies": JM, journal, 1979–82, Jnl 14 (WUSTL). "He gave": JM to TP, letter, 1981–82? (WUSTL).

631 **In October** "In October": JM, journal, October 6, 1979, Jnl 14 (WUSTL). "He praised": JM, "Elizabeth Bishop (1911–1979)," *Prose*, 231–32.
    He put "He put": JM to Henry Sloss, letter, October 23, 1979 (WUSTL).

632 **Renewal** "Magically": JM to John Brinnin, letter, January 9, 1980 (University of Delaware). "Merrill wrote": JM to SY, letter, January 4, 1980 (Yale). "Well, the odd-shaped": JM to Moffett, letter, January 4, 1980 (NYPL). "Merrill loved": JM to SY, letter, January 4, 1980 (Yale). "Merrill's bedroom": JM to ESP, letter, January 7, 1980 (ESP). "Souvenirs": JM to SY, letter, January 4, 1980 (Yale).

As in Stonington "Two blocks": JM to ESP, letter, January 7, 1980 (ESP). "For New Year's": JM to SY, letter, January 4, 1980 (Yale).

633 **With his hair** "He gave": JM to TP, letter, May 12, 1980 (Yale). "He delivered": JM, "A Class Day Talk," *Prose*, 350–56. "He presided": JM to SY, letter, May 22, 1980 (Yale). "He read": JM to KF, letter, August 15, 1980 (WUSTL). "One day": JM to TP, letter, July 1, 1980 (WUSTL). "In the fall": JM to CF, letter, October 28, 1980 (Getty). "Only his mother": JM to DK, letter, May 27, 1980 (WUSTL).

Scripts "*Scripts*": JM to KF, letter, May 23, 1980 (WUSTL). "With his audience": JM to DK, letter, May 27, 1980 (WUSTL). "In Palo": Author's interview with Diane Middlebrook (2003).

634 **Commenting** "Donoghue was": JM to DK, letter, June 15, 1980 (WUSTL). "He began": Denis Donoghue, "What the Ouija Board Said," *NYT Book Review* (June 15, 1980), in Polito, *A Reader's Guide*, 178–81.

The sweeping "Hailing": Clara Claiborne Park, "Where *The Waste Land* Ends," *Nation* (May 3, 1980), in Polito, *A Reader's Guide*, 182–89.

635 **Merrill's trilogy** "A scholar": Ross Labrie, *James Merrill* (Twayne, 1982); *James Merrill: Essays in Criticism*, ed. David Lehman and Charles Berger (Cornell University Press, 1983); and Polito, *A Reader's Guide*. "In December": JM, journal, December 28, 1980, Jnl 14 (WUSTL). "Allen Ginsberg": JM to Moffett, letter, January 19, 1981 (NYPL). "At the same": JM to DR, letter, December 19, 1980 (WUSTL).

636 **Moffett begins** "Moffett begins": Moffett, "Sound Without Sense: Willful Obscurity in Poetry, with Some Illustrations from James Merrill's Canon," *New England Review* 3, no. 2 (winter 1980): 295. "She describes": Moffett, 297. "The frustration": Author's interview with Moffett (2003). "She wrote": Moffett, "Sound Without Sense," 300.

As Judy "This service": SY, "Dantean Andante," *Yale Review* (summer 1979), in Polito, 144–52. "With a draft": JM to SY, letter, October 12, 1980 (Yale). "There followed": JM to SY, letter, October 14, 1980 (Yale).

And while "McClatchy interviewed": JDM, "DJ: A Conversation with David Jackson," *Shenandoah* 30, no. 4 (1979): 23–44. "Looking back": DJ, "Lending a Hand," in *James Merrill: Essays in Criticism*, 304–05. "Jimmy was struck": JM to KF, letter, May 31, 1980 (WUSTL); and JM to DK, letter, June 16, 1980 (WUSTL). "David summarized": DJ to DR, letter, September 16, 1980 (WUSTL). "He didn't": JM to NL, letter, August 10, 1980 (WUSTL). "The tube": DJ to DR, letter, September 16, 1980 (WUSTL). "Merrill was alarmed": JM to SY, letter, September 11, 1980 (Yale). "Merrill followed": JM, journal, January 6, 1981, Jnl 14 (WUSTL). "One festive": JM, journal, March 21, 1981, Jnl 14 (WUSTL).

638 **Ronald** "Between Hiroshima": JM, journal, June 11, 1982, Jnl 37 (WUSTL).

639 **Merrill was never** "As he sat": JM to Moffett, letter, April 21, 1981 (NYPL).

641 **As sparkling** "This meant": JM to Samuel Lock, letter, March 5, 1981 (WUSTL). "The players": JM to DH, letter, January 14, 1981 (WUSTL).

To prime "They stayed": JM to John Ashbery, letter, June 27, 1981 (Houghton). "They went": JM to AC and JDM, letter, May 16, 1981 (Yale). "McIntosh, a tall": Author's interview with DMc (2003). " 'Unbelievable!' ": JM to SY, postcard, May 1981 (Yale).

642 **It was the last** "Merrill wrote": JM to Robert Isaacson, letter, January 3, 1982 (Morgan). "Umberto appeared": JM, journal, November 6, 1983, Jnl 37 (WUSTL). "That wiry": JM to TP, letter, September 1, 1981 (WUSTL).

643 **For Merrill** "In Greece": JM to KF, letter, November 11, 1981 (WUSTL). "By the time": DJ to Elise Sanguinetti, letter, October 25, 1981 (Sanguinetti).

643 **When he arrived** "To join it": JM to TP, letter, February 3, 1982 (WUSTL). "Once the muscle": JM to SY, letter, March 2, 1982 (Yale). "In cut-off": AL, *Familiar Spirits*, 125.

Grace Stone "From Montreal": JM to TP, letter, February 3, 1982 (WUSTL); author's interview with Marie-Claire Blais (2003). "David's bed": JM to TP, letter, March 10, 1982 (WUSTL). "(Not that)": JM to AC and JDM, letter, January 26, 1982 (Yale). "When DJ's": JM to TP, letter, March 10, 1982 (WUSTL).

644 **Merrill went** "Jimmy and DK": Author's interview with John Ashbery and David Kermani (2011). "As a connoisseur": JM to SY, letter, May 6, 1982 (Yale).

Back in the "Back in the": JM to SY, letter, June 2, 1982 (Yale).

Only in summer "Only in summer": JM to SY, letter, June 2, 1982 (Yale). " 'Why?' ": JM to KF, letter, May 1, 1982 (WUSTL). "In his notebook": JM, journal, March 7, 1982, Jnl 37 (WUSTL).

645 **Atheneum** "Merrill referred": JM to Samuel Lock, letter, October 9, 1981 (WUSTL). "It's what": JM, "An Interview with J. D. McClatchy," *Prose*, 114.

646 **McClatchy** "McClatchy": The long interview appeared in the *Paris Review*, summer 1982. " 'I would send' ": Author's interview with JDM (2011).

His answers " 'That bit' ": JM, "An Interview with J. D. McClatchy," *Prose*, 118–19. "Probing": JM, "An Interview with J. D. McClatchy," *Prose*, 116.

648 **The differences** " 'The years' ": JM, "An Interview with J. D. McClatchy," *Prose*, 105. "In the case": JM, "An Interview with J. D. McClatchy," *Prose*, 106.

649 **In short** "Maria turns": JM, *Sandover*, 467.

Yet it is "Does it shrink": JM, *Sandover*, 550–51.

All of this "When the dead": JM, *Sandover*, 547.

650 **Underlying** "For language": JM, "An Interview with J. D. McClatchy," *Prose*, 109–10.

651 **Or was that** "The revelations": JM and DJ, Ouija board transcript, May 8, 1982, box 2, folder 6 (WUSTL).

In November "In the car": Author's interview with CF (2001). "The bare": JM to David Tacium, letter, November 9, 1982 (Tacium).

16 PETER

655 **Merrill opened** "Merrill opened": JM to Karen Fronduti, letter, February 2, 1983 (WUSTL). "Even paradisal": JM to Robert Pounder, letter, January 1983 (Pounder). "Emotionally": JM to SY, letter, February 12, 1983 (Yale).

"Meanwhile" " 'Meanwhile' ": JM to CF, letter, March 3, 1983 (Getty). "They began": David Lehman, "Merrill's Celestial Comedy," *Newsweek* (February 28, 1983), in Polito, *A Reader's Guide*, 190–91. "*The New York Times*": R. W. Flint, "Metamorphic Magician," *NYT Book Review* (March 13, 1983), in Polito, 192–97. "*The New York Review*": Robert Mazzocco, "The Right Stuff," *New York Review of Books* (June 16, 1983), in Polito, *A Reader's Guide*, 208–21. "In an intriguing": Michael Harrington, "Paradise or Disintegration," *Commonweal* (November 4, 1983), in Polito, *A Reader's Guide*, 198–207. " 'Open the case' ": JM, *Sandover*, 274.

656 *The Changing* "It was an indication": JM to KF, letter, January 8, 1984 (WUSTL).

657 **That spring** " 'Isn't it sickening' ": JM to DR, letter, March 5, 1983 (WUSTL).

David Jackson "Merrill expressed": JM, enclosed in letter to SY, February 12, 1983 (Yale).

658 **The name** "There was confusion": Lawrence K. Altman, "Recollections on the Age of AIDS," *NYT* (July 3, 2001). "Reagan did not": David Salyer, "Ronald Reagan and AIDS," September/October 2004; http: //www.thebody.com/content/art32196.ht (2012). See Douglas Crimp, ed., *AIDS: Cultural Analysis/Cultural Activism* (MIT Press, 1988).

659 **Although** "By the end": AIDS Activity Center for Infectious Diseases, Centers for Disease Control, "Acquired Immunodeficiency Syndrome (AIDS) weekly surveillance report—United States," December 22, 1983.

659 **Merrill seldom** "It shows": JM to DR, letter, June 30, 1983 (WUSTL). "The doctor": JM, Ouija transcript, June 26, 1983, box 2, folder 6 (WUSTL).

660 **The sublime** "Older": JM to David Tacium, letter, c. November 1983 (WUSTL).
When he " 'But there' ": JM, journal, May 20, 1983, Jnl 37 (WUSTL).

661 **In Italy** "The kitchen": JM to SY, postcard, May 6, 1983 (Yale). "James finished": John Berendt, *The City of Fallen Angels* (Penguin, 2006). " 'The wonderful' ": JM to DR, letter, June 30, 1983 (WUSTL). "While DK": JM, journal, July 10, 1983, Jnl 37 (WUSTL). "He was taken": JM to DR, letter, June 30, 1983 (WUSTL).
Merrill and Perényi "They gushed": JM to NL, letter, July 15, 1983 (WUSTL). "When it was": JM to Peter and Eleanor Ross Taylor, letter, August 3, 1983 (Taylor).

662 **Two weeks** "DJ was": JM to KF, letter, August 15, 1983 (WUSTL). "McClatchy recalls": Author's interview with JDM (2011). "The news": JM to SY, letter, February 7, 1984 (Yale).
Peter Hooten "Jimmy referred": JM to TP, letter, August 19, 1983 (WUSTL).

663 **An invitation** "On an August": Author's interview with PH (2002). "The thread": JM to SY, letter, August 25, 1983 (Yale).

664 **There'd** "Merrill, Pemberton": Author's interview with Harry Pemberton (2012). " 'It's been' ": DJ to Harry Pemberton, letter, August 11, 1983 (WUSTL). "Jackson's carpenter": DJ to Peter Taylor and Eleanor Ross Taylor, letter, August 3, 1983 (WUSTL). "By September": DJ to Harry Pemberton, letter, August 11, 1983 (WUSTL). "George Lazaretos": JM to DMc, letter, October 29, 1983 (WUSTL).
After all " I suspect": JM to Moffett, letter, November 24, 1983 (NYPL). " 'How old' ": Kenneth Bleeth to the author, email, March 8, 2012.
Unhappy "Unhappy": JM to CF, letter, October 15, 1983 (Getty).

665 **Merrill arranged** "New appliances": JM to DMc, letter, December 25, 1983 (WUSTL).
He took " 'I wish' ": JM to SY, letter, November 2, 1983 (Yale).

666 **The book's** " 'It's so bitter!' ": JM to SY, letter, February 6, 1984 (Yale).
The day " 'My responses' ": JM to PH, letter, December 5, 1983 (Hooten). " 'There had been' ": JM to TP, letter, April 13, 1984 (WUSTL). "When Hooten": JM to PH, letter, February 15, 1984 (Hooten).

667 **John Peter Hooten** "He'd grown": JM to KF, letter, May 11, 1984 (WUSTL). "His parents": Author's interviews with PH (2002, 2010).

668 **Hooten had** "Hooten had": Author's interviews with PH (2002, 2010).
On the set "Born in 1902": Will Geer, http://en.wikipedia.org/wiki/Will_Geer (2012).
Hooten's acting "Hooten's movie": Peter Hooten, http://www.imdb.com/name/nm0393848/filmotype (2012).

669 **Merrill hadn't** "It appeared"; JM to PH, Ouija board transcript, February 14, 1984 (Hooten). "He gave": Author's interview with PH (2012).
JM and DJ "JM and DJ": JM to PH, letter, February 16, 1984 (Hooten). "Alan Moss": JM to TP, letter, April 13, 1984 (WUSTL). "Merrill told": JM to PH, letter, February 22, 1984 (Hooten). " 'At least' ": JM to PH, letter, February 27, 1984 (Hooten).

670 **Merrill took** "By chance": JM to CF, letter, March 13, 1984 (Getty).

671 **Hooten was** "Hooten was": Author's interview with PH (2010). "Yet he found": JM to PH, letter, April 29, 1984 (Hooten).
Merrill was "On his fifty-eighth": JM to PH, letter, March 3, 1984 (Hooten).
In the background "In the background": JM to PH, letter, March 3, 1984 (Hooten). " 'People' ": Author's interview with Richard and Charlee Wilbur (2002).

672 **Merrill knew** "That May": JM to DJ, letter, May 6, 1984 (WUSTL). "On that occasion": JM, journal, April 24, 1984, Jnl 15 (WUSTL). "He had to": JM to DMc, letter, July 7, 1984 (WUSTL).
The simplest "In London": JM to DMc, letter, July 7, 1984 (WUSTL). "In Cornwall": Author's interview with PH (2010).

673 **These were** "These were": JM to DMc, letter, July 7, 1984 (WUSTL). "Mary Bomba": Author's interview with Mary Bomba (2003). "One day": SY to the author, email, March 18, 2012.

673 **Merrill returned** "At eleven thirty": JM to PH, letter, July 4, 1984 (Hooten). "What caught": JM to PH, postcard, July 18, 1984 (Hooten).

674 **At the time** "He sent": JM to JDM, letter, July 19, 1984 (Yale). "All the tests": JM to SY, letter, September 10, 1984 (Yale).

675 **Merrill and Jackson** "In August": JM to DR, letter, August 25, 1984 (WUSTL). "He decided": JM to KF, letter, c. August 1984 (WUSTL). "Back in": JM, journal, April 27, 1984, Jnl 15 (WUSTL). "Charles was": JM to KF, letter, c. August 1984 (WUSTL).

Hooten and Merrill " 'If life' ": JM to Douglas Crase, letter, November 25, 1984 (Crase). "Sounding": JM to Samuel Lock, letter, December 4, 1984 (WUSTL). "Merrill continued": JM to TP, letter, December 8, 1984 (WUSTL). "In the plane": JM, journal, Jnl 44, November 22, 1984 (WUSTL). " 'I'm so happy' ": JM to TP, letter, December 8, 1984 (WUSTL). "To Peter": JM to PH, letter, December 1, 1984 (Hooten). "And again": JM to PH, letter, December 12, 1984 (Hooten).

676 **Hooten's relationship** "Merrill was": JM to PH, letter, January 2, 1985 (Hooten). "He was pained": JM to DMc, letter, January 13, 1985 (WUSTL). "Merrill had to": JM to SY, letter, February 8, 1985 (Yale). "By the time": JM to CF, letter, March 5, 1985 (Getty). "Merrill admitted": JM to SY, letter, March 6, 1985 (Yale).

Tellingly "The largest": JM to DMc, letter, March 5, 1985 (WUSTL). " 'James met' ": Author's interview with PH (2002).

677 **In April** "In April": JM to TP, letter, April 15, 1985 (WUSTL). "They took": JM to SY, letter, c. April 15, 1985 (Yale). "Back on": JM to SY, letter, June 6, 1985 (Yale). "Merrill told": JM to TP, letter, April 15, 1985 (WUSTL).

But there "That letter": JM to TP, letter, April 15, 1985 (WUSTL). "Even Alfred": AC to the author, email, August 7, 2011.

678 **Merrill knew** "But he did": JM to DMc, letter, May 6, 1985 (WUSTL).

679 **That August** " 'IT IS A' ": JM, Ouija board transcript, August 25, 1985, box 3, folder 5 (WUSTL).

It was merely "This time": Edmund White to the author, email, March 2, 2012.

680 **Merrill and Jackson** "On the first": JM to PH, letter, September 9, 1985 (Hooten). "He was up": JM, journal, September 1985, Jnl 44 (WUSTL). "He brought": JM to PH, letter, September 10–19, 1985 (WUSTL). "He'd caught": JM, journal, September 18–19, 1985, Jnl 44 (WUSTL).

Strato " 'He took' ": JM, journal, September 18–19, 1985, Jnl 44 (WUSTL). " 'He's a wreck' ": JM to SY, letter, September 12, 1985 (Yale). "Merrill wrote": JM, journal, September 29, 1985, Jnl 44 (WUSTL). "The rest": JM to PH, letter, September 10–19, 1985 (Hooten). "On Jimmy's": JM, journal, September 29, 1985, Jnl 44 (WUSTL).

681 **To entertain** "But later": JM, journal, September 19, 1985, Jnl 44 (WUSTL).

But there "They gazed": JM, journal, October 2, 1985, Jnl 44 (WUSTL). "They traced": JM, journal, October 9, 1985, Jnl 44 (WUSTL); JM to Howard Moss, postcard, October 10, 1985 (WUSTL). "On the coast": JM, journal, October 8, 1985, Jnl 44 (WUSTL).

682 **Merrill returned** " 'Their bankruptcy' ": JM to DMc, letter, October 20, 1985 (WUSTL). "Back in June": JM to KF, letter, June 21, 1985 (WUSTL). "She was 'made' ": JM to CF, letter, June 27, 1985 (Getty). "In the midst": JM, journal, c. May 1985, Jnl 44 (WUSTL).

Back in "Back in": JM to TP, letter, November 3, 1985 (WUSTL). "The phone": Author's interview with Maxine Groffsky (2012). "Kalstone": JM to TP, letter, November 3, 1985 (WUSTL). "After Venice": AC to the author, email, August 7, 2011.

683 **A book** " 'He was diffident' ": Author's interview with JDM (2011). "But he was": JM, Foreword, *Recitative: Prose*, xiii. "Or as he": Inscription in PH's copy of *Recitative*, November 1986 (Hooten).

Nor was "Merrill didn't": JM to SY, letter, late November 1985 (Yale).

684 **Yet the very** "Now it was": JM to JDM, letter, 1986 (Yale). "He confided": JM to SY, letter, September 12, 1985 (Yale).

685 **He was working** "Seeing Moss's": JM to Alan Moss Reveron, letter, March 13, 1984 (Hooten).

686 **The Image Maker** "Yenser": SY, *The Consuming Myth*, 331.

688 **In The Image Maker** "For two years": JM to DR, letter, November 11, 1985 (WUSTL). "A break": JM to FP and WM, letter, December 5, 1985 (WUSTL); JM to FP and WM, letter, January 17, 1986 (WUSTL). "Peter": JM to SY, letter, early December 1985 (Yale). "When Svenson": JM to SY, letter, December 1985 (Yale).

  Immediately "His brother-in-law": JM to DMc, letter, January 18, 1986 (WUSTL). "That meant": JM to Samuel Lock, letter, January 16, 1986 (WUSTL). "On these visits": JM, journal, December 26, 1985, Jnl 44 (WUSTL). "The day": JM to IB, letter, January 30, 1986 (WUSTL).

  A few days "It started": JM to PH, letter, January 5, 1986 (Hooten).

689 **In Stonington** "In Stonington": Author's interview with ESP (2008).

  Close " 'He began' ": AL, *Familiar Spirits*, 146–51.

  Yes "On February": JM, journal, February 5, 1986, Jnl 44 (WUSTL). "Expressing": JM to IB, letter, January 30, 1986 (WUSTL). "Merrill wrote": JM to TP, letter, March 6, 1986 (WUSTL).

690 **That wasn't** "The letter": JM to TP, letter, March 6, 1986 (WUSTL). "Merrill tried": JM to PH, poem, February 22, 1986 (Hooten). "In his letter": JM to TP, letter, March 6, 1986 (WUSTL). "To Hooten": JM to PH, poem, February 22, 1986 (Hooten). "Still": JM to TP, letter, March 6, 1986 (WUSTL).

691 **Around** "The local": JM to TP, letter, March 6, 1986 (WUSTL). "One night": Author's interview with Maxine Groffsky (2012). "Another night": AC to the author, email, August 7, 2011.

693 **While he** "He accepted": "Merrill Chosen as State Poet Laureate," Associated Press (January 9, 1986).

  The winter "McClatchy gave": *For James Merrill: A Birthday Tribute* (Jordan Davies, 1986). The edition of ninety copies, planned by McClatchy, included a frontispiece by Debora Greger; other contributors included Bidart, AC, KF, John Hersey, Richard Howard, DJ, Richard Kenney, Brad Leithauser, AL, Merwin, Moss, Van Duyn, Edmund White, Wilbur, and SY. "Missing": JM to CF, letter, March 1, 1986 (Getty).

17 ART AND AFFLICTION

694 **Merrill boarded** "He opened": JM, journal, March 30–April 1, 1986, Jnl 16 (WUSTL).

695 **The National** "The National": Erik Eckholm, "City, in Shift, to Make Blood Test for AIDS Virus More Widely Available," *NYT* (December 23, 1985). "With his notebook": JM, journal, April 1, 1986, Jnl 16 (WUSTL).

  Merrill noted "Merrill noted": JM, journal, April 1, 1986, Jnl 16 (WUSTL). "A few days": JM, journal, c. April 1986, Jnl 16 (WUSTL).

697 **"Pending"** "He approved": JM to FP and WM, letter, June 27, 1986 (WUSTL).

  Silence "In 1987": http://www.actupny.org/documents/cron-87.html (June 2012).

699 **"Prose"** "Merrill probably": Matsuo Bashō, *The Narrow Road to the Deep North and Other Travel Sketches*, trans. Nobuyuki Yuasa (Penguin Books, 1966), 29–30.

700 **Donald Richie** " 'I had the impression' ": DR to the author, letter, March 31, 2002.

701 **Like Richie** "In his diary": RM, travel diary, 1986, quoted in a letter from RM to the author, March 13, 2001.

  Stephen "Stephen": Merrill Magowan's phrase. *Stephen Magowan: A Life in Letters*, ed. Robin Magowan (Wallflower Press, n.d.), 93. "Stephen, Robin": Author's interview with RM (2004). " 'This is' ": RM to the author, letter and travel notes, April 2001.

702 **Merrill comments** "Richie recalls": DR to the author, letter, December 10, 2001.

704 **Merrill saw** "In a letter": JM to CF, letter, August 30, 1986 (Getty).

706 **While in** "Richie remembers": DR to the author, letter, December 10, 2001.

708 **In mid-May** "In mid-May": JM to Rudy Kikel, letter, June 12, 1986 (Kikel). "Choked": JM,

journal, May 6–13, 1986, Jnl 16 (WUSTL). "After a week": JM, journal, May 16, 1986, Jnl 16 (WUSTL). "He recorded": JM, journal, May 23, 1986, Jnl 16 (WUSTL). "He couldn't": JM, journal, June 6, 1986, Jnl 16 (WUSTL); JM, journal, May 23, 1986, Jnl 16 (WUSTL). " He made a plea": JM, journal, late May 1986, Jnl 16 (WUSTL).

709 **Back in** "Back in": JM, journal, June 1–2, 1986, Jnl 16 (WUSTL).
Merrill couldn't "Merrill couldn't": JM, journal, June 14, 1986, Jnl 16 (WUSTL).
A short "A short": *NYT*, June 17, 1986. "Then Merrill": JM, journal, July 11, 1986, Jnl 16 (WUSTL). " 'Maxine agreed' ": JM to SY, letter, July 22, 1986 (Yale).

710 **Kalstone had** "They sorted": JM to DMc, letter, August 8, 1986 (WUSTL).
Meanwhile "Meanwhile": JM to Harry Matthews, letter, August 13, 1986 (WUSTL). " 'CARO' ": JM, Ouija board transcript, box 2, folder 10, December 16, 1986 (WUSTL).

711 **Kalstone's memorial** "Kalstone's memorial": JM to SY, letter, September 24, 1986 (Yale). "The soprano": "A Memorial Tribute to David Kalstone," September 20, 1986, NYPL (privately printed).

713 **In the 1980s** " 'Perhaps the greatest' ": Tim Dean, "The Psychoanalysis of AIDS," *October* 63 (1993): 83–116. "American culture": William F. Buckley Jr., "Crucial Steps in Combating the AIDS Epidemic; Identify All the Carriers," *NYT*, March 18, 1986.

714 **Merrill worked** "When McClatchy": JM to JDM, letter, September 10, 1986 (Yale). "He gave": JM to SY, letter, September 24, 1986 (Yale). "Merrill annotated": JM's copy, with marginalia, of Henry M. Tyler, *Selections from the Greek Lyric Poets with a Historical Introduction and Explanatory Notes* (revised edition, Ginn & Co., 1906) (Yale).

715 **Merrill and Kalstone** " 'Dwink' ": JM to JDM, letter, September 10, 1986 (Yale).
He had made "He had made": JM to SY, letter, September 24, 1986 (Yale). " 'I'm made' ": JM, journal, September 12, 1986, Jnl 17 (WUSTL). "A couple": JM, journal, September 14, 1986, Jnl 17 (WUSTL).
Was Hooten "When Peter": JM to SY, letter, July 22, 1986 (Yale). "After Jackson": JM to IB, letter, September 23, 1986 (WUSTL). " 'You saw' ": JM to PH, letter, September 9, 1986 (Hooten).
In October "They continued": JM to Mr and Mrs V. T. Boatwright, postcard, October 19, 1986 (Boatwright). "There were friends": JM to Harry Ford, postcard, October 13, 1986 (WUSTL); JM, journal, c. October 1986, Jnl 17 (WUSTL). "He astonished": JM to JDM, postcard, October 24, 1986 (Yale).

717 **"We are having"** " 'We are having' ": JM to JDM, postcard, October 24, 1986 (Yale). "In his notebook": JM, journal, c. October 1986, Jnl 17 (WUSTL).
To conclude "Back in 1950": JM to Samuel Lock, letter, November 5, 1986 (WUSTL).

718 **He returned** " 'No one' ": JM to AC, letter, December 6, 1986 (Yale). "In December": JM to JH, letter, January 6, 1987 (Yale). "The famous": JM to PH, letter, February 20, 1987 (Hooten).
In contrast "His habitual": JM to DMc, letter, March 2, 1987 (WUSTL). "For instance": JM, journal, April 1987, Jnl 17 (WUSTL).

719 **Then, at** "Then, at": JM, journal, May or June 1987, Jnl 17 (WUSTL).

720 **He was learning** "At Jimmy's": JM to TP, letter, February 3, 1987 (WUSTL). "He had a cataract": JM to FP and WM, letter, March 9, 1987 (WUSTL). "Most days": JM to SY, letter, February 16, 1987 (Yale); JM to FP and WM, letter, March 9, 1987 (WUSTL). " 'The bed' ": JM to TP, letter, February 3, 1987 (WUSTL).
That winter "That winter": JM to Bernard de Zogheb, letter, February 28, 1987 (WUSTL). "He took": JM to DR, letter, March 4, 1987 (WUSTL). "That was part": JM to SY, letter, July 12, 1987 (Yale).
Hooten "They zipped": JM to DR, letter, June 27, 1987 (WUSTL).

721 **He was not** "In Olympia": JM, journal, May 1987, Jnl 17 (WUSTL). "Then, crossing": JM, journal, May 1987, Jnl 17 (WUSTL); JM to DR, letter, June 27, 1987 (WUSTL). " 'P. wants' ": JM to DJ, postcard, May 22, 1987 (WUSTL).

721 **Merrill was** "Small-scale": JM to Samuel Lock, letter, February 19, 1987 (WUSTL). "He wound": JM to Barbara Kassel, enclosure, February 21, 1987 (Kassel); revised as "Barbara Kassel," *Prose*, 362–63. "Merrill sent": JM to Barbara Kassel, letter, February 21, 1987 (Kassel).

722 *The Inner Room* "Merrill wanted": JM to Barbara Kassel, letter, June 12, 1987 (Kassel).
Behind "One entry": JM, journal, November 22, 1986, Jnl 17 (WUSTL). "Three months": JM, journal, March 18, 1987, Jnl 17 (WUSTL). "He made": JM, journal, March 21, 1987, Jnl 17 (WUSTL).

723 **After Greece** "There were": JM to JDM and AC, letter, September 9, 1987 (Yale); JM to DR, letter, October 8, 1987 (WUSTL). "The Stephen": JM to JDM and AC, letter, October 29, 1987 (Yale); JM to JDM and AC, letter, September 23, 1987 (Yale).
More friends "Myers, in equal": JM to FP and WM, letter, July 10, 1987 (WUSTL); JM to JDM and AC, letter, September 24, 1987 (Yale). "Myers had hoped": JM to DR, letter, October 8, 1987 (WUSTL). "On the program": JM to JDM and AC, letter, October 18, 1987 (Yale).

724 **Every occasion** "Every occasion": JM to DR, letter, October 8, 1987 (WUSTL). "Merrill gave": JM, journal, November 13, 1987, Jnl 24 (WUSTL). "This time": JM to DMc, letter, January 5, 1988 (WUSTL). "The next day": JM, journal, January 1, 1988, Jnl 24 (WUSTL). "He listed": JM, journal, c. January 1988, Jnl 24 (WUSTL). " 'It got' ": JM, journal, January 5, 1988, Jnl 24 (WUSTL). " 'My poems' ": JM, journal, January 6, 1988, Jnl 24 (WUSTL).
Nothing "After a few": JM, journal, January 8, 1988, Jnl 24 (WUSTL). "But Merrill": JM, journal, February 3, 1988, Jnl 24 (WUSTL). " 'Kind' ": JM, journal, c. February 1988, Jnl 24 (WUSTL). "Each one": JM, journal, February 3, 1988, Jnl 24 (WUSTL). "That was hard": JM to DMc, letter, February 8, 1988 (WUSTL). "At last": JM to DMc, letter, February 8, 1988 (WUSTL).

725 **Meanwhile** "It was a project": JM, journal, April 24, 1984, Jnl 15 (WUSTL). "He found": JM to DMc, letter, February 8, 1988 (WUSTL). "When *An Evening*": JM to DMc, letter, May 5, 1988 (WUSTL).

726 **Merrill had** "But it was": JM to Dorothea Tanning, postcard, June 1988 (Tanning). "Merrill began": JM, journal, May 30, 1988, Jnl 24 (WUSTL). "Tom Victor": JM, journal, April 1988, Jnl 24 (WUSTL). "Jimbo": JM, journal, June 10, 1988, Jnl 24 (WUSTL). "Seriously": JM, journal, June 5, 1988, Jnl 24 (WUSTL). "Confounded": JM to DR, letter, May 20, 1988 (WUSTL).
Eco-disaster "He muttered": JM, journal, March 11, 1988, Jnl 24 (WUSTL). "He was at": JM to SY, letter, July 26, 1988 (Yale). "(In draft)": JM to JDM and AC, letter, August 16, 1988 (Yale).

727 **The hand** "They swam": JM, journal, June 29, 1988, Jnl 24 (WUSTL). "He picked": JM to PH, letter, July 25, 1988 (Hooten).
As on " 'We were' ": Author's interview with W. S. Merwin (2005). " 'His work' ": JM, journal, June 29, 1988, Jnl 24 (WUSTL).

728 **In August** "The first night": JM, journal, August 12, 1988, Jnl 24 (WUSTL). " 'Doris, Chas' ": JM, journal, August 14, 1988, Jnl 24 (WUSTL). "The day after": JM, journal, August 15, 1988, Jnl 24 (WUSTL). " 'My mother's' ": JM, journal, August 13, 1988, Jnl 24 (WUSTL). "She filled": JM, journal, August 17, 1988, Jnl 24 (WUSTL). "Here": JM, journal, August 19, 1988, Jnl 24 (WUSTL).
Merrill returned "Merrill returned": JM, journal, c. September 1988, Jnl 24 (WUSTL).

729 **Being** "The last page": JM, journal, September 25, 1988, Jnl 24 (WUSTL). "The next": JM, journal, September 26, 1988, Jnl 24 (WUSTL).
But it was "But it was": JM to Bernard de Zogheb, letter, November 13, 1988 (WUSTL). "Jimmy arranged": JM to Samuel Lock, letter, December 2, 1988 (WUSTL). " 'We must TRY' ": JM to Bernard de Zogheb, letter, December 31, 1988 (WUSTL). "They'd spent": JM to Samuel Lock, letter, December 2, 1988 (WUSTL).

730 **He had** "The grocer": JM to Richard Howard, letter, November 2, 1988 (Howard).

731 **In November** "In November": JM to Henri Cole, letter, January 5, 1989 (Cole). " 'It's really' ": JM to SY, letter, January 14, 1989 (Yale). "His mother": JM to SY, letter, February 8, 1989 (Yale).

How Merrill "Fatigued": JM, journal, May 1988, Jnl 24 (WUSTL).

He was enveloped "He was thrilled": JM to Samuel Lock, letter, May 8, 1989 (WUSTL).

732 **Perhaps** "Jimmy went": JM to Brian Walker, letter, April 3, 1989 (Walker).

The lovers "The schedule": JM, journal, May 18, 1989, Jnl 18 (Merrill Papers). "The tour": JM to SY, letter, May 31, 1989 (Yale); and http://rogerbourland.com/2006/04/05/letters-to-the-future-ii-james-merrill/ (2012).

733 **What did** "Yenser was": Quoted by Jack Miles, "Poet James Merrill to Speak in 'Voices,' " *LAT*, April 1, 1989.

There was "McClatchy was": Author's interview with AC (2003). "He withdrew": JM to SY, letter, September 8, 1989 (Yale).

Corn's poetic " 'It was hard' ": Author's interview with AC (2003). "He was heard": JM to SY, letter, May 31, 1989 (Yale).

734 **Close** "Close": JM to SY, letter, July 24, 1989 (Yale). "He spoke": JM to SY, letter, July 4, 1989 (Yale). " '<u>Do</u> understand' ": JM to SY, letter, July 22, 1989 (Yale).

He'd said "Now, for": JM to Brian Walker, letter, July 12, 1989 (Walker). " 'Words' ": JM to PH, letter, August 22, 1989 (Hooten).

735 **The metaphor** "Hooten had": JM, journal, August 21, 1989, Jnl 23 (WUSTL). "In the waiting": JM, journal, late August 1989, Jnl 23 (WUSTL).

They went "When they": JM, journal, August 1989, Jnl 23 (WUSTL).

736 **A month** "Part": JM to Bernard de Zogheb, letter, September 1, 1989 (WUSTL). "On an earlier": JM, *ADP*, 661–62.

Over "Over": JM to JH, letter, August 30, 1989 (Yale). "In December": JM, journal, December 19, 1989, Jnl 23 (WUSTL).

Merrill sent "The event": JM to SY, letter, October 25, 1989 (Yale). " 'James and Peter' ": Author's interview with Mona Van Duyn (2001).

737 **Merrill was** " 'The transition' ": JM to SY, letter, November 30, 1989 (Yale).

738 **Yet it was** "As if": JM, journal, November 1989, Jnl 23 (WUSTL). "On December": JM to PH, letter, December 29, 1989 (Hooten). "In Key West": JM, journal, December 31, 1989, Jnl 23 (WUSTL).

18 THE SUN'S ICY TOMB

740 **Merrill was** "Merrill was": JM to DMc, letter, January 9, 1990 (WUSTL). "The daily": JM to FP and WM, letter, January 27, 1990 (WUSTL). "Revision": JM to V. T. and Mary Boatwright, letter, January 16, 1990 (Boatwright). "Once": JM to FP and WM, letter, January 27, 1990 (WUSTL).

There was "He logged": JM, journal, December 18–25, 1989, Jnl 23 (WUSTL). "He consulted": JDM, diary, July 26, 1993 (Yale). "DJ": JM to FP and WM, letter, January 27, 1990 (WUSTL).

741 **Hooten** "Hooten": JM to Samuel Lock, letter, January 1, 1990 (WUSTL). "He was busy": JM to George Bradley, letter, May 14, 1990 (Bradley). "Parigory": JM to Robert Pounder, letter, February 21, 1990 (Pounder). "To the weekly": JM to V. T. and Mary Boatwright, letter, January 16, 1990 (Boatwright). "Bernstein": JM to V. T. and Mary Boatwright, letter, January 2, 1990 (Boatwright). "Swaying": JM to V. T. and Mary Boatwright, letter, January 16, 1990 (Boatwright). "He left": JM to V. T. and Mary Boatwright, letter, January 2, 1990 (Boatwright).

Up to "With America": JM, "After Empires," sent to JH, January 25, 1990 (Yale).

742 **Merrill sent** "McClatchy": JH, "The Art of Poetry No. 35," interviewed by JDM, *Paris Review*

(fall 1985). "The point": JH, "The Art of Poetry No. 35," interviewed by JDM, *Paris Review* (fall 1985).

742 **Merrill was** "Merrill tended to": Author's interview with PH (2010).

Brandeis "Merrill put": JM, "Memorial Tribute to Irma Brandeis," *Prose*, 369–70. " 'For "entertainment" ' ": JM to KF, letter, April 25, 1990 (WUSTL). " 'With AIDS' ": JM, journal, February 27, 1990, Jnl 23 (WUSTL).

743 **Merrill came** "It was a": JM to Peter Moore, letter, March 19, 1990 (WUSTL). "Donald": JM to Samuel Lock, letter, March 2, 1990 (WUSTL). "Darling": "Joan Darling," http://www .theateronline.xzc?PK=27453 and http://en.wikipedia.org/wiki/Joan_Darling (2012).

Merrill and Hooten "Merrill and Hooten": JM to Peter Moore, letter, March 19, 1990 (WUSTL). "Her worldliness": Bruce Weber, "Elzbieta Czyzewska, Polish Actress Unwelcome in Her Own Country, Dies at 72," *NYT* (June 17, 2010). "Merrill found": JM to Samuel Lock, letter, July 21, 1990 (WUSTL).

744 **In July** "In July": JM to Samuel Lock, letter, July 21, 1990 (WUSTL). "The voices": JM, Ouija board transcript, July 22, 1990, Jnl 53 (WUSTL).

In August "They had": JM to Brian Walker, letter, December 26, 1990 (Walker). "The set": JM to Bernard de Zogheb, postcard, September 9, 1990 (WUSTL). "Yenser": Author's interview with Joan Darling (2012).

And unlike " 'He had' ": Author's interview with Joan Darling (2012). "Worse": SY to the author, email, March 18, 2012. "And it was": Author's interview with Joan Darling (2012).

745 **Merrill made** "Merrill made": JM to Brian Walker, letter, December 26, 1990 (Walker). "Ball had": JM, journal, September 1990, Jnl 49 (WUSTL). "Ball and Darling": JM to Joan Darling, copy of letter, August 18, 1990 (Hooten).

Apart "He 'wasn't' ": Author's interview with Joan Darling (2012). "Indeed": JM to Stanislaw Baranczak, letter, October 7, 1990 (Baranczak). " 'The Cabot' ": JM, journal, September 1990, Jnl 49 (WUSTL).

But those "Merrill joined": JM to Terry Layman, letter, September 27, 1990 (Layman). " 'When I arrived' ": SY to the author, email, March 18, 2012. "Back in": JM to Terry Layman, letter, September 27, 1990 (Layman). "In truth": JM to Terry Layman, postcard, September 28, 1990 (Layman). "Stephen": JM to SY, letter, October 8, 1990 (Yale).

746 **In October** "In October": Library of Congress, "Poetry and Literature," http://www.loc .gov/poetry/prize-fellow.html (2012). "He donated": JM to Rachel Hadas, letter, October 27, 1990 (Hadas). " 'My mother' ": JM to SY, letter, October 8, 1990 (Yale). "Indeed": HIP to V. T. and Mary Boatwright, letter, November 5, 1990 (Boatwright). "Her spirit": JM to Jerl Surratt, letter, January 14, 1991 (WUSTL). "When they": JM to Brian Walker, letter, December 26, 1990 (Walker).

Back in "He thought": JM to CF, letter, February 10, 1991 (Getty).

747 **Merrill incorporated** "At the end": JM, *ADP*, 616. "They show": JM, worksheets for *ADP* (WUSTL).

748 **"I used"** " 'I used' ": JM to Paul Lawson, letter, July 25, 1991 (Lawson).

After all " 'Don't get' ": JM to CF, letter, February 10, 1991 (Getty). "Merrill noticed": CF, journal, August 27, 1991 (Getty).

749 **While he** "As he": JM to SY, letter, August 18, 1991 (Yale).

751 **As he worked** "As he worked": JM to Don Adams, letter, October 30, 1991 (Adams). "Their response": AL, *Familiar Spirits*, 156–57. "He admitted": JM to FP and WM, letter, March 15, 1991 (WUSTL). " 'Oh my God' ": Author's interview with JDM (2012). "Ashbery": Author's interview with John Ashbery (2011).

752 **What did** "He returned": JM to CF, letter, February 10, 1991 (Getty); JM to DMc, letter, February 11, 1991 (WUSTL). "Even what": JM to KF, letter, February 12, 1991 (WUSTL). " 'It now' ": JM to Moffett, letter, February 12, 1991 (NYPL).

Merrill was "A further": Author's interview with Joan Darling (2012).

752 **Merrill had put** "The studio": JM to CF, letter, February 2, 1991 (Getty). "It was rumored": AL, *Familiar Spirits*, 156. "Hooten": PH, Prospectus for *Voices from Sandover*, 1991 (Hooten). "Two years": http://articles.courant.com/1993–04–14/features/0000103369_1_sandover -video-poem (2014).

753 **The failure** "He had devoted": JM to Samuel Lock, letter, September 25, 1991 (WUSTL); and JM to CF, letter, June 7, 1991 (Getty). "He had always": JM to SY, letter, June 1991 (Yale). " 'I do' ": JM to KF, letter, July 21, 1991 (WUSTL).

When Jimmy "That winter": JM to FP and WM, letter, March 15, 1991 (WUSTL). "At the behest": JM to Paul Lawson, letter, July 25, 1991 (Lawson). "The séances": JM to Paul Lawson, letter, July 25, 1991 (Lawson). "The not": DJ and JM, "The Plato Club," *Paris Review* 34, no. 122 (1992): 14–84.

When he "It was": JM to DMc, postcard, September 10, 1991 (WUSTL). "In another": JM, draft page from *ADP*, enclosure to JDM, letter, July 18, 1991 (Yale).

754 **As his summer** "He meant": JM to Paul Lawson, letter, July 25, 1991 (Lawson). "She told": JM to SY, letter, August 16, 1991 (Yale).

Meanwhile "To Claude": CF, journal, August 27 and September 1, 1991 (Getty). "A few": JM to Andrew Silverman, letter, October 4, 1991 (Silverman). "A week": JM to DMc, letter, October 8, 1991 (WUSTL). "Dr. Hunt": JM to Andrew Silverman, letter, October 4, 1991 (Silverman); and JM to Peter Moore, letter, November 25 and December 6, 1991 (Moore).

755 **It was testimony** "He went": JM to Jeffrey Harrison, postcard, October 26, 1991 (WUSTL). "Merrill saw": JM to DMc, postcard, November 27, 1991 (WUSTL).

Hooten graduated "On his return": JM to Peter Moore, letter, November 25 and December 6, 1991 (Moore).

756 **The second** "The second": JM to Stanislaw Baranczak, letter, December 19, 1991 (Baranczak). "When he": JM to Peter Moore, letter, November 25 and December 6, 1991 (Moore).

757 **He flew** "A few": JM to Peter Moore, letter, November 25 and December 6, 1991 (Moore).

758 **After completing** "After completing": JM to Paul Lawson, letter, March 24, 1992 (WUSTL). "He and Peter": JM to Moffett, letter, February 4, 1992 (NYPL). "On Valentine's": JM to Jerl Surratt, letter, March 9, 1992 (WUSTL). "As they had": JM to Richard Wilbur, letter, March 1, 1992 (Amh).

All this "He sent": Enclosed with message to FP and WM, c. December 1991 (WUSTL). "It was the exception": JM to CF, letter, March 25, 1992 (Getty).

759 **An unfinished** "An unfinished": JM, "Elizabeth, you should have seen me . . . ," draft poem, 1992 (WUSTL).

He was still "In the italic": JM to KF, letter, April 25, 1990 (WUSTL). "This imaginary": JM, *ADP*, 532. " 'Jerl' urges": JM, *ADP*, 586–87.

761 **In June** "In June": JM to SY, letter, June 8, 1992 (Yale). "Now he": JM to Carolyn Grassi, letter, June 1, 1992 (Grassi). "Merrill kept": JM to SY, postcard, June 19, 1992 (Yale). "He got": JM to JDM, postcard, June 22, 1992 (Yale). "They moved": JM to JDM, postcard, June 22, 1992 (Yale). "In the Tivoli": JM to FP and WM, postcard, June 23, 1992 (WUSTL).

Scotland "In Edinburgh": JM to Alistair Elliott, postcard, May 26, 1992 (Elliott).

Merrill's writing "With no date": JM, journal, c. June 1991, Jnl 48 (WUSTL).

762 **Merrill returned** "Merrill returned": JM to FP and WM, letter, September 5, 1992 (WUSTL). " 'Luckily' ": JM to Jeffrey Harrison, postcard, July 18, 1992 (WUSTL). "To mark": *David Jackson: Scenes from His Life* (Nadja, 1992).

The book "Jimmy had": JM to Paul Lawson, letter, July 26, 1992 (Lawson).

Jackson wasn't "He woke up": JM to Craig Poile, letter, September 12, 1992 (Poile). "Stonington": JM to Paul Lawson, letter, July 26, 1992 (Lawson). "(Not that)": Author's interview with JDM (2012).

763 **Merrill now** "(But he didn't)": JM to Peter Moore, letter, September 22, 1994 (Moore). "DJ": JM, journal, c. October 1992, Jnl 49 (WUSTL).

That fall "Hooten": JM to KF, letter, October 23, 1992 (WUSTL); and JM to Carolyn Grassi, letter, October 21, 1992 (Grassi). "Inaugurating": JM to Carolyn Grassi, letter, October 21, 1992 (Grassi). " 'Only' ": PH to SY, letter, January 10, 1993 (Yale).

763 **"It's January"** " 'It's January' ": PH to SY, letter, January 10, 1993 (Yale). "By the end": JM to Roger Bourland, letter, February 9, 1993 (Bourland). "He told": JM to Carolyn Grassi, letter, January 27, 1993 (Grassi).

764 **One reason** "The conference": JM to Carolyn Grassi, letter, January 27, 1993 (Grassi). "To Frank": Author's interview with Frank Bidart (2002).

But Merrill " 'Certain' ": JM to SY, letter, February 12, 1993 (Yale). "Indeed": JM to Peter Moore, letter, February 28, 1993 (Moore).

He flew "With Peter": JM to John and Barbara Hersey, letter, February 21, 1993 (Hersey). "Even": JM to Carolyn Grassi, letter, February 9, 1993 (Grassi). "Merrill was": JM to Peter Moore, letter, February 28, 1993 (Moore).

765 **Friends** " 'He knew' ": Author's interview with Allan Gurganus (2012).

After Hooten "It was": JM to Carolyn Grassi, letter, March 15, 1993 (Grassi). "Merrill had": JM to SY, letter, April 16, 1993 (Yale).

So it was " 'It's not' ": JM, journal, April 30, 1993, Jnl 47 (WUSTL). "Parigory": JM to Samuel Lock, letter, c. October 1992 (WUSTL). "Tony went": JM, journal, April 28, 1993, Jnl 47 (WUSTL). "His consciousness": JM, journal, April 30, 1993, Jnl 47 (WUSTL).

766 **Nelly** "Nelly": JM, journal, April 28, 1993, Jnl 47 (WUSTL). "Merrill visited": JM, journal, April 30, 1993, Jnl 47 (WUSTL). " 'His greatest' ": JM, journal, May 1, 1993, Jnl 47 (WUSTL). "Kimon": JM, journal, May 31, 1993, Jnl 47 (WUSTL).

He made "He crossed": JM, journal, May 5, 1993, Jnl 47 (WUSTL). " 'For a year' ": JM, journal, May 2, 1993, Jnl 47 (WUSTL). "He read": JM, journal, May 8, 1993, Jnl 47 (WUSTL); JM, journal, May 9, 1993, Jnl 47 (WUSTL).

767 **He drank** "He drank": JM, journal, May 7, 1993, Jnl 47 (WUSTL); JM, journal, May 13, 1993, Jnl 47 (WUSTL). "Merrill read": JM, journal, May 11, 1993, Jnl 47 (WUSTL). "At home": JM, journal, May 12, 1993, Jnl 47 (WUSTL). " 'My conversation' ": JM, journal, May 12, 1993, Jnl 47 (WUSTL). "There came": JM, journal, May 13, 1993, Jnl 47 (WUSTL).

Merrill continued "Merrill continued": JM, journal, May 17 and 19, 1993, Jnl 47 (WUSTL); JM, journal, May 17, 1993, Jnl 47 (WUSTL). "He talked": JM, journal, May 19, 1993, Jnl 47 (WUSTL); JM, journal, May 17, 1993, Jnl 47 (WUSTL). "They strolled": JM, journal, May 23, 1993, Jnl 47 (WUSTL).

Since publishing "Since publishing": Author's interview with Moffett (2004).

768 **In Malmö** "He was amused": JM, journal, May 19, 1993, Jnl 47 (WUSTL).

Back in "For months": JM to Bernard de Zogheb, letter, August 5, 1993 (WUSTL). "Occasions": JM, "Memorial Tribute to John Hersey," *Prose*, 374–75. "(Hersey)": JM to Barbara Hersey, letter, March 24, 1993 (Hersey). "He preferred": JM to Bernard de Zogheb, letter, August 5, 1993 (WUSTL). "He visited": JM to Terry Layman, letter, July 30, 1993 (Layman). "The first": JDM, diary, July 26, 1993 (Yale).

The next "The next": JDM, diary, July 26, 1993 (Yale).

769 **By early** "By early": JM to Carolyn Grassi, letter, August 1993 (Grassi). "He'd submitted": JM to SY, letter, June 8, 1992 (Yale). "He accepted": JM to SY, letter, October 18, 1992 (Yale).

His exchanges "Responding": FB to JM, letter, October 31, 1992 (Wheaton).

770 **Merrill continued** "That letter": FB to JM, letter, c. spring 1993 (Wheaton). "He used": JM, *ADP*, 587.

771 **Jimmy wrote** "Jimmy wrote": JM, journal, c. summer 1993, Jnl 47 (WUSTL).

772 **Reviews** "Brigitte": Brigitte Weeks, "How James Merrill Came of Age," *NYT* (December 12, 1993). "The longest": John Simon, "Robed in Images: The Memoirs of James Merrill," *New Criterion* (September 1993). "Merrill's": FB, *The Eyes of the Heart*, 42.

The sexual "Rudy": Rudy Kikel to JM, letter, November 1, 1993 (WUSTL). "The NBCC": Report on NBCC Board Meeting, February 11, 1994, *National Book Critics Circle Journal* (August 1994): 12–13.

772 **The book** " 'The very' ": JDM to JM, letter, c. September 1993; copy in JDM's diary (Yale). "Depending": JDM, diary, October 4, 1993 (Yale).

773 **That fall** "That fall": JDM, diary, October 4, 1993 (Yale). "McClatchy came": JDM, diary, October 4, 1993 (Yale).

774 **As the season** "In October": JM to Jeffrey Harrison, letter, October 21, 1993 (WUSTL).

775 **Shahid** "As usual": JM to Carolyn Grassi, letter, October 23, 1993 (Grassi). "He showed": JM to Agha Shahid Ali, letter, October 30, 1992 (Ali). "Ali took": JM to Agha Shahid Ali, postcard, November 11, 1992 (Ali).

776 **In November** "Merrill was": JDM, diary, October 4, 1993 (Yale). "McClatchy wrote": JDM, diary, November 21, 1993 (Yale). "For the first": JM to SY, letter, December 4, 1993 (Yale). "McClatchy met": JDM, diary, January 4, 1994 (Yale).

For David "There was no": JDM, diary, January 4, 1994 (Yale). "Over dinner": JM to DJ, letter, January 16, 1994 (WUSTL). "Looking back": JM to Peter Moore, letter, September 22, 1994 (Moore).

777 **In fact** "As Merrill": Author's interview with Richard and Charlee Wilbur (2002). "He continued": JM to Allan Gurganus, letter, January 26, 1994 (Gurganus).

778 **With AZT** " 'Peter' ": JM to Bernard de Zogheb, letter, March 9, 1994 (WUSTL). " 'A very jolly' ": JDM, diary, March 17, 1994 (Yale).

The pressured "The pressured": JDM, diary, March 17, 1994 (Yale). "Hooten's memory": Author's interview with PH (2011). "Jimmy was": JDM, diary, March 17, 1994 (Yale).

779 **Soon Merrill** "He told": JM to Allan Gurganus, letter, March 11, 1994 (Gurganus).

In late "In late": JM to SY, letter, March 31, 1994 (Yale). "In April": JM to FB, letter, May 28, 1994 (Wheaton).

He'd begun "In early": JM to Agha Shahid Ali, letter, May 5, 1994 (Ali). "Should it": JM mentions possible titles in his journal, October 11, 1994, Jnl 50 (WUSTL).

Most "He was learning": JM to Elise Sanguinetti, letter, May 5, 1994 (Sanguinetti).

780 **Or he went** "Peter had": JM to Craig Poile, letter, July 19, 1994 (Poile). "About this": JM, journal, September 25, 1994, Jnl 50 (WUSTL).

Redeeming "Redeeming": CF, journal, August 1994 (Getty). " 'You give' ": JM to CF, letter, August 6, 1994 (Getty). "They stopped": JM to Jeffrey Harrison, letter, August 24, 1994 (WUSTL).

781 **Merrill was** " 'I didn't' ": Author's interview with CF (2001). "Gurganus": Author's telephone interview with Allan Gurganus (2012). "He wrote": JM to U. T. Summers, letter, August 8, 1994 (WUSTL). "In another": JM to DJ, letter, July 12, 1994 (WUSTL). "He liked": JM to SY, letter, October 22, 1994 (Yale).

Aware "Chief": Author's interview with Torren Blair (2012). Other younger correspondents included Craig Poile and Craig Wright.

782 **Rolando** "When Rodriguez": JM to SY, letter, September 1994 (Yale).

One day "One day": JM, Ouija board transcript, journal, September 1994 (Yale).

If Jimmy "If Jimmy": JM to Peter Moore, letter, September 22, 1994 (Moore). "To Buechner": JM to FB, letter, May 28, 1994 (Wheaton).

783 **Merrill started** "Titled": JM, journal, fall 1994, Jnl 50 (WUSTL).

In New York "The story": JM to SY, letter, September 22, 1994 (Yale). "He signed": JM to CF, letter, September 14, 1994 (Getty); JM, journal, September 24, 1994, Jnl 50 (WUSTL); JM, journal, October 2, 1994, Jnl 50 (WUSTL).

Rather "His first": JM to Terry Layman, letter, January 12, 1995 (Layman).

784 **He and Hooten** "He and Hooten": JM to JDM, postcard, October 7, 1994 (Yale). "With Kafka": JM, journal, October 1994, Jnl 50 (WUSTL). "Exploring": JM, journal, October 10, 1994, Jnl 50 (WUSTL). " 'My mind' ": JM, journal, October 16, 1994, Jnl 50 (WUSTL). "One day": JM, journal, October 16 and 17, 1994, Jnl 50 (WUSTL).

The impulse " 'Respectability!' ": JM, journal, October 18, 1994, Jnl 50 (WUSTL). "Throughout": JM, journal, October 19, 1994, Jnl 50 (WUSTL).

784 **Merrill returned** "Merrill returned": JM, journal, November 14 and 17, 1994, Jnl 50 (WUSTL). "She'd brought": JM, journal, November 20, 1994, Jnl 50 (WUSTL). "His reading": JM, journal, November 1994, Jnl 50 (WUSTL). "He was": Author's interview with Joseph Lowenstein (2012).

785 **Back in** "Back in": JDM, diary, November 23, 1994 (Yale). "Yet Peter": JM to Norman Austin, letter, December 2, 1994 (Austin). "Merrill felt": JM, journal, c. November 1994, Jnl 50 (WUSTL).

After Thanksgiving "After Thanksgiving": JM to Torren Blair, letter, December 4, 1994 (WUSTL); JM to Jeffrey Harrison, letter, December 6, 1994 (WUSTL). "(He had in mind)": Author's interview with PH (2010).

Merrill was "Still he": JM to Carolyn Grassi, letter, December 13, 1994 (Grassi); author's interview with Robert Polito (2013); JM to Helen Vendler, December 8, 1994 (Vendler); JM to SY, letter, December 2, 1994 (Yale); JM to Jeffrey Harrison, letter, December 21, 1994 (WUSTL).

786 **By Christmas** "By Christmas": JM to Torren Blair, letter, December 23, 1994 (WUSTL). "Their winding route": JM to Craig Wright, letter, December 6, 1994 (Wright); JM, journal, December 28, 1994, Jnl 50 (WUSTL); JM, journal, December 30, 1994, Jnl 50 (WUSTL). "On January": Norman Austin, "James Merrill: His Last Days," typescript 1995 (Austin).

The choice "The choice": JM to Clara Claiborne Park, postcard, January 14, 1995 (Park).

The home "The home": JM to Torren Blair, letter, January 5, 1995 (WUSTL). "It had": JM to Jerl Surratt, letter, January 3, 1995 (WUSTL). "Peter got": JM to Allan Gurganus, letter, January 6, 1995 (Gurganus).

Over "Some carried": JM to Torren Blair, postcard, September 24, 1994 (WUSTL). " 'I'd understood' ": JM to Torren Blair, postcard, December 6, 1994 (WUSTL). "He took": JM to Torren Blair, postcard, September 18, 1994 (WUSTL). "He produced": JM to Torren Blair, letter, December 23, 1994 (WUSTL). "Another letter": JM to Torren Blair, letter, January 5, 1995 (WUSTL). " 'Where' ": JM to Torren Blair, letter, January 14, 1995 (WUSTL).

787 **Merrill didn't** "Merrill didn't": JM to Barbara Howes, postcard, January 10, 1995 (Howes). "The Pews": Author's interview with PH (2010). "When he visited": Author's interview with Norman Austin (2012). "And if Austin": JM to SY, letter, January 20, 1995 (Yale).

The regional "The regional": JM to Craig Wright, letter, January 14, 1995 (Wright). "Another day": JM to Torren Blair, letter, January 14, 1995 (WUSTL).

788 **Merrill told** " 'The pace' ": Author's interview with Torren Blair (2012). "JM offered": JM to Torren Blair, letter, January 14, 1995 (WUSTL). "Merrill confessed": JM to Torren Blair, letter, January 17–20, 1995 (WUSTL).

By the third "By the third": JM to Torren Blair, letter, January 28–30, 1995 (WUSTL). "They spent": JM, journal, c. January 1995, Jnl 50 (WUSTL). " 'He was waiting' ": Author's interview with DMc (2004). " 'J: Tell me' ": JM, journal, late January 1995, Jnl 50 (WUSTL).

789 **Despite** "Despite": JM to Torren Blair, letter, January 28–30, 1995 (WUSTL). "Merrill sat": JM to André Aciman, letter, February 1, 1995 (Aciman).

790 **On Sunday** "On Sunday": Norman Austin, "James Merrill: His Last Days."

What happens "Now in his notebook": JM, journal, February 5, 1995, Jnl 50 (WUSTL).

791 **On Monday** "On Monday": Author's interview with PH (2002).

AFTERWORD

793 **On the tray** "On the tray": Author's interview with PH (2010).

James Merrill "James Merrill": JM, *Sandover*, 11. "He would": Author's interview with PH (2002).

What he feared " '[I]f anything' ": JM to Mona Van Duyn, letter, August 27, 1968 (WUSTL).

794 **The burial** "He picked up": Author's interview with PH (2010). "The moment": Author's interview with JDM (2014).

794 **Obituaries** "Obituaries": Jack Miles, "Acclaimed Poet James Merrill Dies," *LAT* (February 8, 1995) and Mel Gussow, "James Merrill Is Dead; Elegant Poet of Love and Loss," *NYT* (February 7, 1995). "Newspapers": "La mort du poète James Merrill," *Le Monde* (February 13, 1995); Richard Wilbur, "The Death of a Poet," *Solares Hill* (February 9, 1995). "In her two-room": Author's interview with Rosemary Sprague (2004). "McClatchy wrote": JDM, "Braving the Elements," *New Yorker*, March 27, 1995 (http://www.randomhouse.com/knopf/authors/merrill/braving.html). "Alison Lurie": AL, "On James Merrill (1926–95)," *New York Review of Books*, March 23, 1995 (http://www.nybooks.com/articles/archives/1995/mar/23/on-james-merrill-19261995/). "It was in": JDM, "Two Deaths, Two Lives," in *Loss Within Loss: Artists in the Age of AIDS*, ed. Edmund White (University of Wisconsin Press, 2001), 213–39. **Everyone who** "The evening": Norman Austin, "James Merrill: His Last Days."
Merrill's body "It was necessary": Author's interview with JDM (2014).

795 **An impression** "It was": Author's interview with PH (2010).
Bishop Paul Moore "The text": Rt. Paul Moore, Jr., "Memorial Service for James Merrill," February 13, 1995 (Hooten).
"Jimmy was": "Jimmy was": RM, "Eulogy" (Hooten). "Bruce Merrill": Scott Timberg, "Poet's Eulogy: Life as Act of Kindness," *The Day* (February 14, 1995). "Allan Gurganus": "With a harpsichord": JDM, "Braving the Elements."
In Stonington "One slipped": It was Jerl Surratt. "Before long": The design was suggested by Natalie Charkow, and the calligraphy and stone carving done by Nicholas Benson.
Earlier, on "Earlier, on": "A Service in Thanksgiving for the Life of James Merrill" (Hooten). "Freddy offered": "A Prayer for James Merrill" (Buechner); CM, "Eulogy" (Charles Merrill).

796 **"Come on"** "Hellen Plummer": Notice, *NYT* (December 23, 2000).
DJ's story "When he heard": Author's interview with John Balderson and Rolando Rodriguez (2002).
Merrill tried "With Milton Maurer": JM, will (WUSTL). JM's will in Special Collections, WUSTL, is a late draft, c. September 1994. The final signed will is collected in the Merrill Papers, Yale.

798 **702 Elizabeth Street** "They sold": Zillow sale records (2014); author's interview with Steven Rydman (2010).

799 **What to do** "What to do": http://www.jamesmerrillhouse.org.

INDEX

ILLUSTRATION PERMISSIONS

Sewelly and DJ. Photographer: JM.
    Source: Doris Sewell Jackson
Betty and Robin. Source: WUSTL

JM, DJ, CM, and Mary Merrill. Source: WUSTL
DJ in drag. Source: WUSTL
JM, DJ, and friends. Source: WUSTL
Irma Brandeis. Source: JM, *ADP*
JM and DJ around 1959. Source: WUSTL

INSERT FOLLOWING PAGE 518

DR. Source: WUSTL
JM and DR. Photographer: DJ. Source: DR
Howard Moss. Source: WUSTL
Daryl Hine. Source: WUSTL

The Surly Temple. Photographer: ESP.
    Source: WUSTL
DJ, Grace Stone, and JM. Source: WUSTL
Maria Mitsotáki, profile. Source: Nina
    Koutsadakis
Maria Mitsotáki in doorway. Source: Nina
    Koutsadakis

SM. Photographer: JM. Source: WUSTL
JM and SM. Source: WUSTL
George Lazaretos and DJ. Source: WUSTL
SM, JM, DJ, and George Lazaretos.
    Source: George Lazaretos

DJ's sketch. Source: WUSTL
Yannis Boras and Chester Kallman.
    Source: WUSTL
Mimi and Vassilis Vassilikos. Source: WUSTL
RM. Source: WUSTL

DMc in New Mexico. Photographer: JM.
    Source: WUSTL
JM and DMc. Source: WUSTL
18 West Eleventh Street, 1970. Source: *NYT*
TP. Source: WUSTL

Mona Van Duyn. Photographer: Herb Weitman.
    Source: WUSTL
SY. Photographer: Thomas Victor.
    Source: WUSTL
Richard Howard. Source: WUSTL
JM and DK. Photographer: TP. Source: WUSTL

DK. Photographer: Thomas Victor.
    Source: WUSTL

DJ. Photographer: Thomas Victor.
    Source: WUSTL
DJ's sketch of Manos Karastefanís.
    Source: WUSTL
JM and Manos Karastefanís. Source: WUSTL

Moffett. Source: WUSTL
George Cotzias. Source: WUSTL
SM. Photographer: JM. Source: WUSTL
Nelly Liambey and JM. Source: WUSTL
Parlor, 107 Water Street. Source: WUSTL

702 Elizabeth Street. Source: WUSTL
JM and DJ in Key West. Photographer:
    Christopher Cox. Source: WUSTL
JM and DJ at the Ouija board. Photographer:
    Harry Pemberton. Source: Harry
    Pemberton

JM and HIP. Photographer: Kelly Wise.
    Source: WUSTL
CM and family, 1980. Source: WUSTL

ESP. Source: WUSTL
Edmund White. Source: WUSTL
SY. Photographer: Thomas Victor.
    Source: WUSTL
AC and JDM. Source: WUSTL

Peter Tourville, JM, and JDM. Photographer:
    AC. Source: JDM
Peter Tourville. Photographer: JM.
    Source: JDM
PH, standing. Source: WUSTL
PH on Elizabeth Street. Source: WUSTL

Robert and Doris Magowan, 1985.
    Source: WUSTL
Richard and Charlee Wilbur. Source: WUSTL
James Boatwright and Lee Toy. Source: WUSTL
JM and PH, 1989. Source: WUSTL

JM in Japan. Source: WUSTL
PH and JM. Source: WUSTL
SY and JDM. Source: WUSTL

JM and DJ, 1988. Photographer: Jill Krementz.
    Source: Jill Krementz
JM and HIP, 1990. Source: WUSTL
PH and Cosmo. Source: WUSTL
Agha Shahid Ali and JM. Source: WUSTL

JM, swimming. Photographer: PH. Source: PH
JM, 1994. Source: WUSTL

A NOTE ABOUT THE AUTHOR

Langdon Hammer is professor of English and American studies and chair of the English Department at Yale University. His books include *Hart Crane and Allen Tate: Janus-Faced Modernism* and, for the Library of America, *Hart Crane: Complete Poetry and Selected Letters* and *May Swenson: Collected Poems.* A former Guggenheim fellow and fellow at the Leon Levy Center for Biography at the Graduate Center of the City University of New York, he has written about poetry for the *Los Angeles Times, The New York Times Book Review,* and *The American Scholar,* where he is poetry editor. His lectures on modern poetry are available free online at Yale Open Courses.

A NOTE ON THE TYPE

The text of this book was set in Filosofia, a typeface designed by Zuzana Licko in 1996 as a revival of the typefaces of Giambattista Bodoni (1740–1813). Basing her design on the letterpress practice of altering the cut of the letters to match the size for which they were to be used, Licko, born in Bratislava, Czechoslovakia, in 1961, is the co-founder of Emigre, a digital type foundry and publisher.

Composed by North Market Street Graphics, Lancaster, Pennsylvania

Printed and bound by RR Donnelley, Harrisonburg

Designed by Maggie Hinders

DISCARD